Computerization
· and ·
Controversy

2nd edition

Value Conflicts and Social Choices

Computerization
· and ·
Controversy

2nd edition

Value Conflicts and Social Choices

Edited by

Rob Kling

Center for Social Informatics
Indiana University

Morgan
Kaufmann

AN IMPRINT OF ACADEMIC PRESS
A Harcourt Science and Technology Company

San Diego San Francisco New York
Boston London Sydney Tokyo

1991 | 1996

ACADEMIC PRESS
A Harcourt Science and Technology Company
525 B Street, Suite 1900, San Diego, CA 92101-4495, USA
http://www.academicpress.com

Academic Press
Harcourt Place, 32 Jamestown Road, London NW1 7BY, United Kingdom

Morgan Kaufmann Publishers
340 Pine Street, Sixth Floor, San Francisco, CA 94104-3205
http://www.mkp.com

Library of Congress Catalog Number: 95-15420
International Standard Book Number: 0-12-415040-3

Printed in the United States of America
00 01 02 03 04 MM 9 8 7 6 5 4

· Contents ·

P · A · R · T · I
Heads Up! Mental Models for Traveling through the Computer World

v

P • A • R • T • II
The Dreams of Technological Utopianism

P • A • R • T • III
The Economic, Cultural, and Organizational Dimensions of Computerization

Contents

P • A • R • T • IV
Computerization and the Transformation of Work

P • A • R • T • V
Social Relationships in Electronic Forums

P • A • R • T • VII
System Safety and Social Vulnerability

P • A • R • T • VIII
Ethical Perspectives and Professional Responsibilities
for Information and Computer Science Professionals

· Preface ·
to the Second Edition

Public interest in information technologies was stimulated by the availability of relatively inexpensive personal computers in the 1980s. During that decade most professionals in North America began using desktop computers in their work, and North America's middle class began to buy microcomputers for use at home. Many personal computing enthusiasts argued that these technologies would empower lower-level workers and could improve many aspects of social life in North America. A smaller group argued that new technology alone would be unlikely to improve the basic character of worklife or community life.

These debates about the likely social roles of information technologies were scattered through scholarly journals in diverse fields and in mass magazines aimed at several distinct primary audiences. Many students, professionals, managers, scholars, and laymen were hungry for honest, probing discussions of the opportunities and problems of computerization. Charles Dunlop and I edited and wrote the first edition of this book, published in 1991, to help people understand many of the key debates and to have pointers to some of the best systematic studies.

Since 1992, there has been a new burst of public interest and investment in information technologies. It was stimulated by a combination of the promotion of an advanced National Information Infrastructure ("information superhighways") by U.S. Vice President Al Gore and the opening of access to the Internet to people who are not affiliated with special institutions such as universities, government agencies, and industrial research laboratories. Public interest was also fueled by the efforts of telephone companies, cable TV companies, and media companies to seize new markets by promising new services and by trying to form high-profile multi-billion dollar alliances with other firms. All of this talk about "the promise of the new" gave journalists reams of material for thousands of often enthusiastic stories. These stories also helped to heighten public awareness of new possibilities in work, organization, and community life that could be fostered by networked computer systems and on-line information services. As in the 1980s, the debates about information technologies and social life are scattered through diverse journals and magazines so that few readers will readily find the key materials without a substantial search.

This critical anthology introduces some of the major social controversies surrounding the computerization of society and highlights some of the key value conflicts and social choices such computerization entails. A primary purpose in bringing the various articles together is to help readers recognize the social processes that drive and shape computerization—and to help them understand the resulting paradoxes and ironies. This approach differs from the typical efforts of authors to provide one authoritative, highly integrated account. My own viewpoint is reflected in the choice of issues to emphasize and articles that examine them. I wrote a lead article for each part of the book that provides an integrated overview and places each article in context within the debates. These lead articles also identify the ways that specific other selections that appear within other parts of the book also contribute to the debates at hand.

This edition of *Computerization and Controversy* differs from the first edition by including a larger number of articles, as well as many articles that focus on current issues and contexts as they appear in the mid-1990s. While most of the articles from the first edition are still important today, many readers will find the second edition more accessible because the newer articles speak more directly to and focus on technologies that they use.

This quest for articles that focus primarily on technologies that readers work with is a mixed blessing. Many readers will find articles accessible when they discuss the technologies and contexts that they know best. But many information and computer professionals evaluate the appropriateness of a book or article to the extent that it addresses the concrete family of technologies or industrial settings of their immediate interest.

In this approach, professionals who are interested in a topic such as artificial intelligence focus on materials that explicitly examine artificial intelligence; those who are interested in computer applications in medical care focus on studies of health care computing. I believe that such assessments are often too narrow, because many key social aspects of computerization that arise with one technological family or industry have important parallels with other technological families or social settings. Professionals who value this kind of professional provincialism are also likely to underestimate the relevance of studies that are more than a few years old. Unfortunately, they can sacrifice access to a usable professional past by focusing on their excitement about newer technologies which have a smaller body of studies about them to draw upon.

In organizing *Computerization and Controversy*, I have taken a cosmopolitan approach in helping readers understand the ways that key debates crosscut specific technologies and industries. This collection examines controversies that are pertinent to many kinds of computer technologies and social settings, such as the following:

- How appropriate are technologically utopian and anti-utopian scenarios for understanding the future?
- Does computerization demonstrably improve the productivity of organizations?
- Should computer systems be designed to empower workers?
- How do computer system designers often ignore the complexity of women's work?
- How can computerized system designs incorporate social principles?
- Does electronic mail facilitate the formation of new communities, or does it undermine intimate interaction?
- Is computerization likely to reduce privacy and personal freedom?
- What risks arise from computerized systems in health care?
- How concerned are industrial-application computer science researchers about the social consequences of the technologies they develop?

This second edition includes seventy-eight articles that examine the social aspects of computerization from varying perspectives. Some articles are paired to present a head-on debate. Many represent important viewpoints not often found in the conventional literature. The authors include scholars and professionals in computer science, information systems, management, journalism, psychology, law, library science, and sociology. Each of the book's eight parts is introduced with a lead article that frames the major controversies, locates the selections within the debates, and points to other relevant literature. These lead articles share little with the lead articles of the first edition. I have restructured and rewritten each lead article to effectively integrate key ideas from the new articles and to build upon recent scholarly and professional studies. The result is basically a new book rather than a revised book.

Rob Kling
Irvine, California
October 1995

· Preface ·
to the First Edition

Computer systems comprise one of the most distinctive and complex technologies of the late 20th century. In a short span of time, these systems have become ubiquitous. Many of our transactions with organizations are mediated by computer systems, as is reflected in bills, payments, and record-keeping. Commercial jets and advanced weapons systems depend upon sophisticated, computerized navigation systems. Interactive computer systems have become standard equipment in many professions, from the sciences to journalism, and are increasingly appearing in schools at all levels. The meteoric spread of computerization has spawned a large industry that is beginning to rival the automobile industry in importance.

Typically, discussions of rapidly improving computer equipment (and its rapid adoption in organizations and professions) are accompanied by excitement and by high hopes for social and economic improvement. Moreover, the public discussion about computers, as reflected in professional journals and popular media, is generally upbeat. To be sure, there are occasional observations about "computer screwups" that lead to massive billing errors,[1] a blackout of telephone services,[2] or the short-term tragedy of a hapless person who learns when she applies for Social Security that her records show her to be deceased (Kiger, 1987). But situations like these are usually treated as idiosyncratic: amusing for bystanders, they will soon be fixed for those who have been harmed or inconvenienced.

We have produced this book because we see the world of computerization in radically different terms. We see computer systems not only as

---

[1] In the fall of 1989, for example, 41,000 Parisians received letters accusing them of various crimes (murder, prostitution, drug-dealing, etc.) and demanding the payment of a small fine. The addressees should have received letters reminding them of unpaid traffic tickets, but apparently the codes for traffic offenses got mixed up with the codes used for other illegal activities. Officials issued 41,000 letters of apology. (*RISKS-FORUM Digest*, 9 (22); also, *The Guardian*, September 6, 1989.)

[2] A major telephone blackout occurred on January 15, 1990, when a software flaw in AT&T's long-distance switching system caused serious degradation of the company's long-distance service for approximately nine hours. For a popular media account of this event, see the *Newsweek* article, "Can We Trust Our Software" (January 29, 1990, pp. 70–73); more technical discussion may be found in *RISKS-FORUM Digest*, 9 (63, 64, 66, 67).

powerful technology, but also as a powerful factor in social change. Various groups advance visions of computerization in many settings, from workplaces to the networking of nationwide financial operations. Their visions are designed to serve particular interests and sometimes to restructure parts of society (albeit not always in ways that are anticipated). Since computerization usually requires that social practices be altered (and may even facilitate altering them), it is a subtle but important catalyst for social transformation. While there has been far too much hype about the "computer revolution," it is important to understand how computer systems are becoming a pervasive element of organizations and how they affect the way in which people deal with those organizations. Furthermore, many of the opportunities and dilemmas of computerization are systematically connected, even though the key issues are often separated in writings that emphasize either hope or doom.

In our General Introduction, we will explore various ways in which the spread of the automobile in the United States provides a provocative analogy for understanding computerization. Cars have transformed urban America, enabling us to be a much more mobile nation and to live in larger lifescapes. At the same time, cars congest our cities, dirty our air, kill thousands of people annually, and consume immense amounts of space, fuel and money. To understand the role of automobiles in altering society, we must examine whole transportation systems not just individual components like this year's hottest high-performance car. While some of the problems engendered by the automobile can be reduced by technological improvements, many others cannot be reduced without a substantial reorganization of cities, suburbs, and the lifestyles of millions of people. Cars and computers are both devices that have been parts of large-scale social changes. Their advantages and disadvantages often show up only in social contexts (the high-performance car can't drive fast or far in a large city with dirt roads and no gas stations; a car may be an advantage in New York's suburbs but a liability in downtown Manhattan). With cars so firmly entrenched in our social fabric, many of the associated social choices are now limited. But in the case of computers and the organizational systems built around them, important social options are *still* open.

We have found that many students, professionals, managers, and laypersons are hungry for honest, probing discussions of the opportunities and problems of computerization. This book introduces some of the major social controversies about the computerization of society. It also highlights some of the key value conflicts and social choices about computerization. It aims at helping readers to recognize some of the social processes that drive and shape computerization and to identify some of its paradoxes and ironies.[3]

---

[3] One simple irony of the microcomputing industry is that IBM, which has been accused of monopoly practices in the mainframe business, has spawned a dynamic industry of firms that

Many books and articles about computerization focus on emerging or future technologies, such as computers that recognize speech, rely on writing tablets rather than keyboards, or pack the power of a Mac II or '486 PC into a pocket-sized notebook (Moravec, 1988). Other writings focus on social practices that depend upon major advances in computing—e.g., a cashless society or one in which children get expert instruction at home through exceptionally high-quality educational software. During the 1990s we expect to see an endless stream of publications that emphasize the potential of 21st-century computer technologies to alter our social worlds. We share a concern with the quality of life, and our interest in novel technologies reaches well past the year 2000. But we expect that most of these books and articles are likely to characterize computerization and social change inaccurately.

For two main reasons, we focus primarily on the present and near future. First, many people do not understand how and why individuals and organizations computerize today. Since computerization involves a great deal of human behavior, future speculations are useless if they cannot account for contemporary behavior except in technological terms (e.g., by claiming that most people won't feel comfortable with computerized systems until they interact with spoken language). This important point is easily obscured by the steady march of technological innovation. For example, an IBM PC clone with a 80286 processor, or an Apple Macintosh II, computes as fast as a large room-sized IBM mainframe of the late 1960s. Today's microcomputers are much cheaper, can fit on a desk, and are used by millions of people for activities that were very rarely carried out on computers in the late 1960s (e.g., text processing, spreadsheets, and computer-assisted graphic design). Widely available desktop computing was a future scenario of the 1970s. Yet, impressive though these technological facts are, they do not provide an immediate route to accurate social analysis. Many visionaries have argued that broad access to desktop computing will empower workers, make organizations more flexible, and make work less deadening for many employees in routine jobs. Other visionaries see the extensive computerization of work as an occasion for imposing rigid assembly-line disciplines in offices—disempowering workers, fragmenting jobs, reducing skill levels, and increasing the number of deadening jobs.

---

make IBM clones and compatible equipment. It is arguable that microcomputers spread rapidly in the 1980s because of the price drops and technological improvements fostered by this competitive environment. In contrast, the Apple Computer Corporation, which positions itself as the "computer company for the rest of us," has a monopoly on the architecture of its microcomputers. Apple has blocked the development and marketing of Mac clones. Another example is the way in which laser printers have become major fixtures in the development of the "paperless office." Deeper ironies come from the way that computers are often portrayed as an instrument of rationality but can be the focus of nonrational management and problematic social practices.

These are important yet *conflicting* predictions that are worth understanding. Nevertheless, we would be dismissing many important insights about how information technologies are shaped by their adopters and how they do (and do not) change social practices if we assumed that computerization would not really effect important changes until even more advanced (21st-century) technologies were widely available.

Our second reason for focusing on computerization in the present and near future is that people and organizations *today* are making social choices about how to organize with computerized systems—systems that can alter social life as powerfully as automobiles had altered social life by the 1950s. Our analogy between computers and automobiles will suggest that major social choices are made when a technology, even one that is relatively crude in its early phases, is widely deployed. For example, the legal regulations supporting debit cards give consumers much less protection in cases of theft, loss, or error than do the corresponding regulations for credit cards or checks. Computerization presents many important social choices to be made now, and some of them will restrict our social options in the 21st century.

Because of constraints on length, we have not addressed all the topics that we would like to have covered in this book.[4] To economize on space, we have incorporated some themes, especially those of gender and systems design, into sections with other major themes (e.g., work), instead of providing them with their own special sections. And since many of our topics are interrelated, we have often discussed articles from one section in our introductions to other sections. In our various introductory essays, we have also discussed many books and articles beyond those which we have collected here, our aim being to help link key ideas to a larger literature about the social issues of computerization.

Some of our topics have large literatures; others have small literatures. For example, there are many studies of computerization in the contexts of work, future educational opportunities, and privacy, but there are relatively few studies of the health effects of computing, the risks to the public from unreliable computer systems, or the current roles of instructional

---

[4] For example, we have omitted a section on computerization in the military and war, because the topic is well covered in the book edited by Bellin and Chapman (1987). In order to allow adequate space for other topics, we have excised a section on computers in schooling and another on ways in which computer-based systems alter organizational decisions. For simplicity, our book is focused on the United States. Many of the major controversies are also salient in other industrialized countries, although their legal systems, social traditions, and industrial structures alter the details of key social choices. We have virtually ignored controversies of computerization that are pertinent to developing countries (e.g., dependency on complex technologies and first-world suppliers; social stratification and urban-rural economies). And we have not discussed the ways in which computer modeling of complex social phenomena (e.g., population change or economic systems) can have a drastic impact on social policy choices.

computing systems in schools. Moreover, the literatures are diffuse. Key articles are published in the professional journals of computer scientists, philosophers, sociologists, political scientists, educators, lawyers, and managers, as well as in popular magazines.

We have collected articles from diverse sources that might not be readily accessible in many libraries. In addition, we have included several articles that were written especially for this book. While our selections are eclectic, the majority of our articles emphasize social science approaches to understanding computerization, rather than approaches anchored in future studies, technological forecasting, or fiction.[5] We see computerization as comprising a set of social phenomena, and we believe that the social sciences offer a uniquely important vantage point from which to understand them.

We have tried to select readings that would be intelligible to people without an advanced background in any specific academic discipline, although our introductory essays have often drawn upon, and interpreted, more sophisticated and technical studies. (We have also provided references to such studies for readers who want to pursue specific topics in greater depth.) Our introductions provide definitions of terms that may be unfamiliar but whose meaning is presupposed in a selection. We recommend that you read the footnotes—in both our introductions and our selected articles—because they often contain important supplementary ideas.

In choosing our articles, our aim has been to help articulate different sides of key debates and to stimulate further inquiry. Only a small fraction of authors carefully identify major alternative positions in the controversies about which they take sides. We could have saved ourselves a great deal of labor by "letting the articles speak for themselves." Instead, we have attempted to make the key controversies much more accessible through integrative introductions to each section and through leads to related books and articles. Since the literature on computerization is large and widely scattered, we hope that our suggestions for further reading will help readers find useful lines of inquiry and to discover authors and publications that might otherwise have passed unnoticed.

Each of this book's major sections contains an introduction designed to help frame the debates about a topic. We explain how the section's articles relate to the larger literature about computerization and to each other. We also try briefly to create a social context that amplifies the meanings of the selections. At various points, we comment critically on some of the selec-

---

[5] Short-stories, plays, and novels can, of course, play an important role in helping us understand the ways in which new technologies can alter social life. For example, George Orwell's novel *1984* helped many people understand how a politically repressive regime could use information technologies to retain power. And it put terms like "Big Brother" and "newspeak" into everyday language. But we have attempted to focus the central debates by staying within a single genre.

tions, in order to help readers better understand the key assumptions. We have endeavored to be fair but not bland.

We bring our own point of view to these issues, through both our selection of readings and the content of our introductory essays. We are neither indifferent nor always neutral. We like using certain computer-based systems for our own work, especially for writing, organizing records, and communicating via electronic mail. But we also see that computing has inherent social and political dimensions. Organizing themes, such as individual choice, efficiency, productivity, convenience, and aesthetic preference are inadequate for understanding the opportunities, limitations, and potential social problems of computerization, just as they fail to provide adequate illumination of the role of cars in urban America. Since computing requires resources for its acquisition, development, maintenance, and effective use, it has social implications not just in its consequences, but at every stage (Kling and Scacchi, 1982). The cost and complexity of advanced computing systems tends to give special advantage to already powerful groups in shaping their use and in turning them to further advancement of group interests. However, we do not believe that intentions—whether those of individuals, designers, or managers—are good predictors of large-scale social activity. Collective action, including computerization, develops with some non-obvious types of logic.

This is our view, but other analysts see computerization in different terms. Accordingly, the readings presented here include some positions we support and others with which we strongly differ. Above all, we believe that debates about the *social* issues surrounding computerization have not received due attention. Professionals and managers of all kinds, including computer specialists, often take sides through their actions without adequately comprehending the debates and supporting argumentation. We hope that this book will promote a deeper understanding of computerization's key social dimensions and provide a basis for thoughtful and responsible social choices.

References

Bellin, David, and Gary Chapman (eds.) (1987). *Computers in Battle: Will They Work?* Boston: Harcourt, Brace, Jovanovich, Boston, Mass.

Kiger, Patrick J. (1987). "Woman Buried by Bills as Social Security Declares Her Dead," *Orange County Register.* (November 17), pp. 15.

Kling, Rob, and Walt Scacchi (1982). "The Web of Computing: Computer Technology as Social Organization," *Advances in Computers,* Vol. 21. Academic Press, New York, pp. 1–90.

Moravec, Hans (1988). *Mind Children: The Future of Robot and Human Intelligence.* Harvard University Press, Cambridge, Mass.

· Acknowledgments ·

This book has been a collective project that was possible because many friends helped in numerous pivotal ways. It was born because Chuck Dunlop proposed it in 1988 to Sari Kalin, then an editor at Academic Press. Their enthusiasm and dedication helped give birth to the first edition that was published in 1991. Unfortunately Chuck Dunlop was unable to participate in creating this second edition. The second edition has blossomed through the support and enthusiasm of Charles Arthur of Academic Press.

Many people helped me to develop the ideas in my lead articles for each section of this book and to identify useful articles. Mitzi Lewison discussed diverse aspects of the book during the year that I compiled, edited, and authored it. Several people read all of the lead articles and gave me frank comments, including Mitzi Lewison, Beth Meinhard, and Perry Lin.

Many other people reviewed one or more of the lead articles or suggested new materials for the book, including Mark Ackerman, Phil Agre, Claude Banville, Jacques Berleur, Niels Bjorn-Anderson, Hank Bromley, Lisa Covi, Frank Connolly, Bo Dahlbom, Andy Clement, Chuck Dunlop, Margaret Elliott, Elizabeth Finsolt, Beth Givens, Jonathan Grudin, Rebecca Grinter, Suzanne Iacono, Tom Jewett, JinHee Kwak, Susan Landau, Roberta Lamb, Maurice Landry, Edward Mabry, Peter G. Neumann, Mark Poster, and Barbara Simons. These people have congested schedules, but responded promptly and enthusiastically to my requests for frank comments. Their suggestions have markedly improved the book. Many of the authors whose works I include were generously willing to update or condense already published materials to fit this book. In addition, Al Teich and Dianne Martin invited me to workshops on legal and ethical issues in computing which helped deepen my analyses in the lead articles for each section.

My work on this project was facilitated by a special environment at the University of California, Irvine, that supports social studies of computerization, especially, in the Department of Information and Computer Science, the Graduate School of Management, and the Center for Research on Information Technology and Organizations (CRITO). Our research and instructional programs placed me in continuing conversations with Mark Ackerman, Jonathan P. Allen, Yannis Bakos, Lisa Covi, Margaret Elliott,

Jonathan Grudin, Vijay Gurbaxani, John King, Ken Kraemer, Roberta Lamb, Mark Poster, and John Tillquist as well as a stream of visiting scholars who influenced this book in numerous subtle ways.

Carolyn Cheung did a heroic job in managing the blizzard of files that developed into this book with databases and paper files. Partial funding was provided by NSF Grant SRB-9321375 for research about ethical issues and value conflicts in the design of computerized systems that appear in my lead articles for Sections IV and VIII.

P·A·R·T·I

Heads Up!
Mental Models for
Traveling through the
Computer World

P·A·R·T · I

Heads-Up versus Heads-In Views of Computer Systems

Rob Kling

In the 1950s the public fear and fascination with computer systems focused on huge, room-sized machines, which some journalists called "giant brains." Today's hand-held computers pack more computational power than these "giant brains" in a three-pound package. The minimum size of usable keyboards and batteries, rather than the power of computer chips, seem to be the limiting factors in the miniaturization of general-purpose digital computers.

Computing technologies have been dramatically transformed in fifty years. More seriously, the landscape of the computing world has also been transformed. Today, more powerful computers attract much less attention than the expansion of computer-communication networks, like the Internet, which carry more and more stuff—data, gossip, news, opinions, analyses, and propaganda—to tens of millions of people worldwide.

In today's argot, computer networks can connect us all to "a vast world of information." We only have to login and look at the immense opportunities through our video screens. I call this a "heads-in" view of computerization because it emphasizes what we can see through our video windows. In contrast, this book offers you a "heads-up" view of computerization—one that examines the social choices of whether and how to computerize an activity, and the relationships between computerized activity and other parts of our social worlds.

Part I starts with six short articles that can help you better understand specific debates about computerization that are the primary topic of this book. "A Reader's Guide" orients you to the book. "Social Controversies about Computerization" identifies many key controversies, and discusses the structure of the debates about them. "Computers as Tools and Social Systems" examines the limitation of key metaphor—a tool view—that shapes many people's conceptions of computerized systems. Many computerized systems have become more than tools; they are environments that people work in, institutions that people sometimes find hard to change, and so on. "The Seductive Equation of Technological Progress with Social Progress" examines some limits of this conventional point of view. "Learning about the Possible Futures of Computerization from the Present and the Past" argues that we have much to learn about future uses and consequences of computerization by carefully examining past and present experiences. Finally, "Information and Computer Scientists as Moral Philosophers and Social Analysts" develops a controversial and expansive view of these professions.

P·A·R·T · I

B

A Reader's Guide to
Computerization and Controversy

Rob Kling

This book introduces some of the major social controversies about the computerization of society. It also highlights some of the key value conflicts and social choices about computerization. It aims to help readers recognize some of the social processes that drive and shape computerization, and to identify many of the paradoxes and ironies of computerization.[1]

For two main reasons, I focus primarily on the present and near future. First, many people do not understand how and why individuals and organizations computerize today, and what the consequences are for various people, including their managers, other workers, and their clients. Since computerization involves a great deal of human behavior, future speculation is useless if the assumptions that they make about human and organizational behavior cannot effectively account for contemporary behavior. Unfortunately, many projections about the social consequences of computerization are based on overly rationalized views of organizations and markets and relatively romantic views of technology and human behavior. For example, many people think the most important repercussions of computer use will happen in a not-so-distant future time when pocket-sized devices understand spoken language, and people can exchange documents and videos with anyone anytime anywhere via high-speed wireless communications. Technologists and business forecasters enjoy speculating about future life with technologies like these.

But the world views underlying many previous forecasts have often been fundamentally wrong. In *Futurehype*, Max Dublin notes that popular futurists,[2] John Naisbitt and Alvin Toffler, act more as cheerleaders for trends that they would like to see develop rather than as careful analysts of social change. Technologists and professionals confuse their roles as advocates and analysts. For example, for twenty-five years we have heard predictions that some new technology (whether drill and practice, LOGO programming, or multimedia simulations) will revolutionize schooling in North America. I believe that we should read analysts like Stephen Hodas (in Part III) who asks how teachers and schools structure the use of instructional technologies in order to avoid reorganizing the relations of social power between students, teachers, and administrators, before wholeheartedly embracing new technological "cure-alls."

Similarly, many visionaries argue that broad access to desktop computing will empower workers, make organizations more flexible, and make routine jobs less deadening for employees. Other analysts see the extensive computerization of work as an occasion for imposing rigid assembly-line disciplines in offices—disempowering workers, fragmenting jobs, reducing skill levels, and increasing the number of deadening jobs. These are important yet *conflicting* predictions that are worth understanding. Nevertheless, we would be dismissing many important insights about how information technologies are shaped by their adopters, and how they do (and do not) change social practices, if we assumed that computerization "would not really effect important changes" until even more advanced (twenty-first century) technologies were widely available. The articles in this book by Bullen and Bennett; Suchman; Clement; Markus; Orlikowski; Dahlbom and Mathiassen; and Attewell give us important and subtle insights about how managers, professionals, and workers juggle work practices, computing capabilities, organizational routines, gender roles, and power relationships when they computerize. We have a lot to learn from these empirically oriented analysts who examine the social possibilities afforded by new technologies with a keen eye on the ways that organizations also make social choices that powerfully shape the resulting effects. They deepen our understanding of technology and social change from North America's multi-trillion-dollar investment in computer-based

---

[1] One simple irony of the microcomputing industry is the way that visions of "paperless offices" have been developed. Deeper ironies come from the way that computing is often portrayed as an instrument of rationality, but can be the focus of nonrational management and problematic social practices.

[2] A futurist is a professional who studies future social possibilities, in part, by extrapolating trends in demographics, economic structures, technological developments, family behavior, and so on. Like weather forecasters, they may prefer to see warm winters and pleasantly cool summers. Most of us would prefer that their forecasts have some element of objectivity, so that we can best prepare for the most probable weather, or social futures in the case of futurists.

systems that would be lost (or, actually relearned again and again at a high price by those who overemphasize the future without learning from the past.)

The second reason for focusing on computerization in the present and near future is that people and organizations *today* are making social choices about how to organize with computerized systems—systems that can alter social life as powerfully as automobiles altered social life in the 1950s. The analogy between computers and automobiles suggests that major social choices are made when a technology is widely deployed, even one that is relatively crude in its early phases.[3] For example, it is not widely known that the legal regulations supporting debit cards give consumers much less protection in cases of theft, loss, or error, than do the corresponding regulations for credit cards or checks. Computerization presents many important social choices to be made now, and, depending on how they are made, can either enrich people's lives or diminish their hopes.

Which Controversies?

Identifying key controversies about computerization serves as one major organizing theme for *Computerization and Controversy*. This primary criterion led me to select articles that effectively represented different viewpoints, rather than articles that met some other dominant criterion, such as illustrating classic articles (i.e., Pylyshyn and Bannon, 1989), the most recent research (i.e., Huff and Finholt, 1994), the most recent discussion of key issues, or those that take a specific position about computerization. These other approaches have produced some excellent books. But they best serve different audiences and different purposes.

This book examines current controversies of computerization that are vivid today and are likely to be of concern through the year 2000 (and perhaps beyond). I included research studies that report about how organizations actually computerize and how people work and live with computer systems in concrete settings. The research studies have special impacts on professional and political debates about the nature and directions of computerization in highly developed countries. In many cases I have included articles written by diverse professionals and journalists to illustrate some of the alternative viewpoints that energize these debates. However, publishing pragmatics (and readers' pocketbooks, muscles, and patience) limit the size of the book and the number of selections.

I used a few tacit criteria to select controversies to include in this book:

---

[3] See Chapter I–D, "Computers as Tools and Social Systems: The Car–Computer Analogy."

1. Professional Importance: I selected controversies that professionals would find meaningful in their work lives and private lives. I avoided controversies, such as those over research methods and appropriate theories, which primarily interest scholars.

2. Empirical Anchors: I selected topics that could be illuminated by understanding how people live and work with computerized systems. I avoided controversies, such as copyright for electronic texts, that are primarily anchored in legal disputes about the nature of property rights, and so on.

3. Organizational/Professional Focus: I selected topics that are pertinent to the work of information and computer professionals, diverse technical specialists, and managers (as well as to scholars who study these topics). I have ignored the growing role of computerization in popular culture, through films, games, new media, the arts, and entertainment in the broadest sense, because a serious examination of these topics would require a wholly different book. I also believe that organizations, from IBM and Microsoft to movie studies and publishing houses, are major players in the computerization of society, and yet they are often treated as incidental (see "The Centrality of Organizations in the Computerization of Society" in Part III). This book examines computerization in organizations, communities, work groups, and other identifiable medium and small-scale social forms whose behavior participants can sometimes influence. This inclusion of the medium and small-scale organization of social life is an important alternative to the impoverished duality that pits individuals against a monolithic society.

4. Available Materials: I selected topics about which I could find articles that go beyond the obvious.

This book concentrates on computer controversies that are most visible in North America, and western Europe, and virtually ignores controversies of computerization pertinent to less-developed countries (e.g., dependency on complex technologies and first-world suppliers; social stratification and urban–rural economies).[4]

Which Articles?

Certain topics, such as computerization and work or privacy issues, are popular subjects of study, while others, such as health effects or

---

[4] For a study of computerization in Africa, see, for example, Jules-Rosette (1990). For an anthology about computerization in western Europe, see Berleur, Clement, Sizer, and White-house (1991).

democratization, remain relatively unexamined, which results in either the paucity of information available or a veritable embarrassment of riches, depending on the popularity of the topic. It is often difficult to find studies that articulately represent diverse sides of key debates. For example, it is much easier to find articles that defend people's privacy from the encroachments of computerized record systems than it is to find bold defenses for decreasing privacy protection to further other values, such as private profit or police protection. Even so, most observers agree that computerization has decreased people's privacy in the last thirty years.[5] Similarly, the articles about gender issues in computing examine (and find) important gender differences regarding who does what work, how much they are paid, and so on. But I have not found articles that argue that gender discrimination in computing is relatively minor or unimportant, or perhaps argue that there should be more gender discrimination!

Computerization and Controversy contains articles from major newspapers, general scientific magazines, professional and scholarly computer science journals, business magazines, and books written for information professionals and managers. I have selected articles from varied sources that, as a collection, are not likely to be readily accessible in most libraries. Some of the articles appear in print for the first time because they were previously published in electronic-only journals or they were written especially for this book. In addition, some of the authors kindly edited previously published materials for this volume, by updating them, by making them more concise, or by adding explanations that would make them accessible to a wider variety of readers. I tried to select scholarly articles that would be relevant to diverse readers.

While these articles are eclectic, many of them emphasize social science approaches to understanding computerization, rather than approaches anchored in future studies, technological forecasting, or fiction. I have attempted to focus the central debates by working with materials that appear to be nonfiction. I have been frustrated and fascinated by the ways that many scholars, professionals, and students sometimes have trouble seeing the fictional elements of allegedly nonfictional materials. I hope this book helps readers appreciate how many seemingly factual narratives of computerization in social life are crafted to eliminate contradictory or ironic situations that would make the narrative less plausible.

I have selected readings that are intelligible to people without an advanced background in any specific academic discipline. Each section begins with a lead article that draws upon and interprets more sophisticated and technical studies. (I have also provided references to such studies for readers who want to pursue specific topics in greater depth.) These lead

---

[5] See the articles in Part VI for diverse viewpoints as well as Part V's lead article, "Social Relations in Electronic Forums: Hangouts, Salons, Workplaces, and Communities."

articles provide definitions of terms that may be unfamiliar, whose meaning may have been presumed in some selections.

In choosing articles, I have tried to help articulate different sides of key debates, and to stimulate further inquiry. Only a small fraction of authors carefully identify major alternative positions within the controversies in which they take sides. I have attempted to make the key controversies much more accessible through integrative introductions to each section and through links to related books and articles.

I believe that understanding the social repercussions of any technological system requires that we be able to see it from the perspectives of the people who are likely to use it and live with it, or even, in part, live within it. It takes some empathy to appreciate their perceptions; it takes courage to unflinchingly acknowledge the pains as well as the pleasures that new technologies bring to people's lives. I hope that this book will help you better understand computerization's key social dimensions, and stimulate your social and moral imagination.

References

Berleur, Jacques, Andrew Clement, Richard Sizer, and Diane Whitehouse (eds.) (1991). *The Information Society: Evolving Landscapes.* Springer Verlag,

Huff, Chuck, and Thomas Finholt (eds.) (1994). *Social Issues in Computing: Putting Computing in Its Place.* McGraw-Hill, New York.

Jules-Rosette, Bennetta (1990). *Terminal Signs: Computers and Social Change in Africa.* Mouton de Gruyter, New York.

Pylyshyn, Zenon, and Liam Bannon (eds.) (1989). *Perspectives on the Computer Revolution.* Ablex, Norwood, NJ.

Recommended Bibliography

Bellin, David, and Gary Chapman (eds.) (1987). *Computers in Battle: Will They Work?* Harcourt, Brace, Jovanovich, Boston.

Clement, Andrew (1994). "Considering Privacy in the Development of Multi-media Communications." *Computer Supported Cooperative Work,* 2:67–88. (Reprinted in Part VIII.)

Dublin, Max (1989). *Futurehype: The Tyranny of Prophesy.* Viking: New York.

Kiger, Patrick J. (1987). "Woman Buried by Bills as Social Security Declares Her Dead." *Orange County Register,* (November 27):1,5.

Marx, Gary (1990). "The Case of the Omniscient Organization." *Harvard Business Review,* (March–April):4–12. (Reprinted in Part IV.)

Peek, Robin M., Lois Lunin, Gregory Newby, and Gerald Miller (eds.) (in press). *Academia and Electronic Publishing: Confronting the Year 2000.* MIT Press, Cambridge, MA.

P·A·R·T·I

C

Social Controversies about Computerization

Rob Kling

Digital computer systems are among the most intriguing and heralded technologies of the late twentieth century. Interest in computer networks had steadily grown in academia and businesses through the 1980s. Today, the public face of computerization is rapidly expanding to support new kinds of services and social relationships. In late 1993 and early 1994, United States Vice-President Al Gore popularized the concept of an "information superhighway" that would connect everybody to a cornucopia of information services and products, including videos, music, vast libraries of books and reports, and interactive communications. Gore's vision of a seamless information superhighway as an open road into an information-rich frontier where all could travel caught many people's imagination. The Internet, which had previously been an arcane set of services monopolized by university professors, graduate students, and researchers in high-tech firms became an idiom of upper-middle-class conversation. Journalists began listing Internet addresses as part of their bylines. Major newspapers began describing gopher sites and World Wide Web servers as places to obtain additional information. Even men and women who weren't quite sure what "the Internet" meant became a bit anxious that they might be left out of a new necessity for effective participation in North American society. Computerization has become a mass-market phenomenon, along with videos, microwave ovens, and automobiles.

Even without the media hype, there would be much to write about the social aspects of computerization. Computer-based technologies have amplified the abilities of people and organizations in amazing ways. Scientists can model complex phenomena and gather and analyze data on a scale they would have found almost unimaginable fifty years ago. Organizations have developed computerized record systems to track a myriad of details about people (their clients and employees), money (revenue, assets, and payments), things (inventory of all kinds), and relationships between them. Almost anybody who routinely writes books, articles, or reports is likely to use a microcomputer of some kind or at least have their manuscripts typed into one. In addition, computer systems are one of the few technologies where the power and flexibility of the devices increase, while the costs decrease by an order of magnitude every decade.

But computerization is also the source of problems that get relatively little exposure in the popular press and professional magazines. Some of the problems are pragmatic: the dilemmas of dealing with imperfect computer systems that foul up bills, lose key data, or that are just harder to work with than they should be. While these problems may seem to be minor irritants, they foreshadow social problems of much greater significance.

Consider the economic role of computer-based systems. Because much of what we encounter in the press identifies computer-based systems with cost savings, efficiency, and productivity, these consequences of computerization seem almost natural (or, if not natural, still worth acquiring). Certain writers argue that computer-based systems are central to developing a dynamic economy that is competitive internationally—in short, absolutely essential for economic health and well-being. Yet others criticize this view, wondering why organizations that have invested substantial amounts of money in computer systems have not experienced big payoffs.[1] Moreover, some analysts believe that the economic success of computer-based systems can lead to large-scale unemployment in certain industries, with serious consequences for people who do not have (and might not readily obtain) computing skills.

The economic role of computerization is not the only area of controversy. There are some important debates about many issues, including:

Worklife. Is computerization likely to improve or degrade the quality of jobs for managers, professionals, and clerks? How do different approaches to designing computer systems and their social environments alter the character and quality of jobs? Can computer and telecommunications systems improve the flexibility of work by enabling employed people to work at home part or full time?

Class Divisions in Society. Are there plausible ways of structuring extensions to our National Information Infrastructure that will more effectively

---

[1] See the articles by Martin Baily, Paul Attewell, and John King in Part III, as well as my lead article, "The Centrality of Organizations in the Computerization of Society."

enable more people to participate in the mainstream of society? To what extent do electronic publications and digital libraries enhance or diminish the tendency of our society to foster an underclass of functionally illiterate and disenfranchised people?—information-related tasks require new skills, and using computerized services requires expertise in negotiating with complex organizational procedures when things go wrong.

Human Safety and Critical Computer Systems. How safe are people who rely on computer systems such as those that help manage air traffic control or calculate radiation treatment plans for cancer patients? Should computer systems designers who work on such systems be licensed, much like the professional engineers who design bridges and elevators in skyscrapers?[2]

Democratization. To what extent do computer and telecommunication systems offer new opportunities to strengthen democracy through on-line access to the records and reports of government agencies?[3] To what extent does computerization undermine democratic processes in work and public life because the costs and expertise of large computerization projects may lead to centralized control and domination by groups who can control the selection of equipment and expertise?[4]

Employment. How does computerization alter the structure of labor markets and occupations? What kinds of understanding of computer systems are really critical for people who wish to develop different kinds of careers? Do the skill mixes for computer-oriented work help create an underclass with fewer jobs and more barriers for improving their situations? Is computerization creating a "hollow economy" with fewer jobs overall?

Education. To what extent can interesting computer-based programs give students the intellectual and motivational advantages of one-on-one tutoring in a way that is economically affordable? Will access to the Internet transform K–12 schools into more effective learning places? And what drawbacks might there be in the widespread introduction of computers into the curriculum?

Gender Biases. Why are women more likely to be found feeding data into computer systems, while men are more likely to be in the position of specifying the requirements for, and designing, computer-based systems? Is there any special reason why professional positions held largely by women (i.e., librarians and K–12 educators) are more likely to be elimi-

---

[2] See Part VII, and especially Jonathan Jacky's article, "Safety-Critical Computing: Hazards, Practices, Standards, and Regulation."

[3] See Van Tassel (1994).

[4] For a discussion of the ways that computer networks might support democratization, see my lead article for Part V, "Social Relations in Electronic Forums: Hangouts, Salons, Workplaces, and Communities."

nated by the introduction of electronic approaches to information management and education, while men are more likely to be in the professional positions of specifying the requirements for, and designing, computer-based electronic publishing systems?[5]

Military Security. To what extent do swift high-tech weapons and complex computerized command and control systems amplify the risk of accidental nuclear war by shortening the response time for people to decide whether a perceived attack is real?[6] To what extent does the public overestimate the ease and safety of electronic warfare?[7]

Health.[8] To what extent do computer systems pose health hazards through low-level radiation, noise, and repetitive strain injuries? To what extent do computer-related jobs have special health hazards when they require people to work intensively at keyboards for long time periods? Is eyestrain or crippling muscular injuries a necessary occupational hazard for people (programmers and professionals, as well as clerks) who spend long hours at terminals?[9] If there are serious health problems associated with computer equipment or computer-related jobs, should there be tough regulation of equipment or workplaces to enhance people's health and well-being?

Computer Literacy. Must all effectively educated citizens have any special knowledge of computer systems? If so, what kinds of insights and skills are most critical, those that are akin to computer programming or those that are akin to understanding how organizational information systems function?

Privacy and Encryption. To what extent do powerful encryption algorithms provide people with exceptional privacy in protecting their communications? Should the public, including career criminals and potential

---

[5] See footnote 2 of Steven Hodas's paper in Part III for a related discussion of gender issues in instructional computing. The topic of gender differences arouses strong emotions. After Barbara Kantrowitz (1994) and her colleagues at *Newsweek* produced a story that identified gender differences in using computers, they were roundly criticized in an electronic conference on the Whole Earth Lectronic Link, the WELL. See Katz (1994). For an intriguing study of gender differences in electronic discussion groups, see Susan Herring's article in Part V, Chapter C.

[6] See, for example, Bellin and Chapman (1987), although the collection is primarily critical of the risks of high-tech warfare.

[7] See, for example, Aksoy and Robins (1992) pp. 207–209.

[8] There are over 50,000,000 video display terminals (VDTs) in the United States (including those on microcomputers). There is a major debate about the extent to which unusual clusters of miscarriages in groups that work with VDTs are a by-product of very low level electrical and magnetic fields that they often radiate. For a partisan, but comprehensive, account of the debate and the evidence, see Brodeur (1989).

[9] See the articles and debates about repetitive strain injuries in Part VII.

terrorists, be able to communicate in ways that make it impossible for police agencies to monitor?[10]

Scholarship. How easily can electronic publishing give scholars more rapid access to wider audiences? Does it help scholars if readers can access a wider variety of materials that are more up-to-date? Can the quality of information be adequately maintained as academic publications make the transition to electronic formats? To what extent are electronic libraries and electronic publications most usable by faculty and students with funds to buy services and/or adjunct computer equipment? Is electronic publishing likely to modify the criteria for academic career advancement and its tie to publication in paper-based journals?

These controversial issues have not yet been resolved, and they change their focus over time. In the 1960s, many of the debates about computerization were framed in terms of large isolated computer systems, while today they focus on computer networks (cyberspace). Even so, key values often remain important although the social and technical terrain changes. For example, the tension between allowing people maximal privacy and enabling sufficient police access to personal records and documents to ensure public safety was relevant to the design of a giant "National Databank" as well as to recent debates about data encryption (see Part VI). Specialists sometimes disagree about how to characterize key problems and how best to find solutions. The way they are framed often reflects groups' conflicting social or economic interests. This book includes different points of view to enable you to read and understand different approaches to the same set of issues.

References

Aksoy, Asu, and Kevin Robins (1992). "Exterminating Angels: Morality, Violence and Technology in the Gulf War," in Hamid Mowlana, George Gerbner, and Herbert I. Schiller (eds.), *Triumph of the Image: The Media's War in the Persian Gulf—A Global Perspective.* Westview Press, Boulder.
Bellin, David, and Gary Chapman (eds.) (1987). *Computers in Battle: Will They Work?* Harcourt Brace, Boston.
Brodeur, Paul (1989). "Annals of Radiation, The Hazards of Electromagnetic Fields: Part III, Video Display Terminals." *The New Yorker,* (June 26):39–68.
Herring, Susan C. (1994). "Gender and Democracy In Computer-mediated Communication." *Electronic Journal of Communication/REC,* 3(2). (Reprinted in Part V.)

---

[10] For a comprehensive report, see Landau *et al.* (1994) and the debates in Part VI of this book.

Kantrowitz, Barbara (1994). "Men, Women & Computers: Gender Differences in Using Computers." *Newsweek*, 123(20)(May 16):48–54.

Katz, Jon (1994). "Hackers 1, Media Elite 0:" Reaction to May 16, 1994, *Newsweek* article on computers. *New York*, 27(22)(May 30):16–17.

Landau, Susan, Stephen Kent, Clint Brooks, Scott Charney, Dorothy Denning, Whitfield Diffie, Anthony Lauck, Doug Miller, Peter Neumann, and David Sobel (1994). "Crypto Policy Perspectives." *Communications of the ACM*, 37(8) (August):115–121.

Van Tassel, Joan (1994). "Yakety-Yak, Do Talk Back: PEN, the Nation's First Publicly Funded Electronic Network, Makes a Difference in Santa Monica." *Wired*, 2.01 (January):78–80. (Reprinted in Part V.)

Recommended Bibliography

Arterton, F. Christopher (1987). *Teledemocracy: Can Technology Protect Democracy?* Sage, Newbury Park, CA.

Bjerknes, Gro, Pelle Ehn, and Morten Kyng (eds.) (1987). *Computers and Democracy: A Scandinavian Challenge.* Aldershot, Hants., England; Brookfield, Vt.

Computer Professionals for Social Responsibility (1993). "Serving the Community: A Public-interest Vision of the National Information Infrastructure." [URL: gopher://gopher.cpsr.org:70/00/cpsr/nii_policy]

Danziger, James, William Dutton, Rob Kling, and Kenneth Kraemer (1982). *Computers and Politics: High Technology in American Local Governments.* Columbia University Press, New York.

Dunlop, Charles, and Rob Kling (1991). *Computerization and Controversy: Value Conflicts and Social Choices.* Academic Press, San Diego.

Sackman, Harold (1971). *Mass Information Utilities and Social Excellence.* Auerbach, Princeton.

Sterling, Theodor (1986). "Democracy in an Information Society." *The Information Society*, 4(1/2):9–48.

The White House (1993). "The National Information Infrastructure: Agenda for Action." (September 15). [URL: gopher://gopher.tamu.edu:70/11/.data/politics/1993/nii/agenda.dir]

P·A·R·T · I

D

Computers as Tools and Social Systems: The Car–Computer Analogy

Rob Kling

It is common to refer to computer systems as "tools" or even "mind tools." In some cases, such as using a PC as a word processor, this concept seems to fit nicely—it's a kind of advanced electronic typewriter. In other cases, such as using "the Internet" or even automated teller machines, computers are components of a much larger collection of technologies and organizations (including their rules for allowing access, limits on usage, security procedures, pricing, practices for upgrading systems, practices for training diverse staff and people who own the systems, and so on). In these cases, and many more, computers are components in complex institutional systems. We can learn something important about the social aspects of computerization by contrasting computers with another popular technology: cars.

Computer systems seem to offer exciting opportunities, in economic payoffs to business firms, in making many social practices more convenient, and in reducing the tedium in many jobs. At first glance, the problems of computerization can seem small or nonexistent. Sometimes, the magnitude of the problems is still becoming apparent (and public), as in the case of risks from computer systems on which people's lives depend. In contrast, other technologies, such as highly polluting pesticides and materials such as asbestos, are perhaps more *obviously* problematic.

The current situation with computing has important similarities to that of motorized transportation in the early twentieth century. The recent catchy term, information superhighway, links computers and cars as technologies of freedom. But a careful examination of the social effects of cars should encourage us to be cautious rather than euphoric about them and computers.[1]

Privately driven cars are the primary means of motorized personal transportation in the United States today. But even though the benefits of individual cars to wealthier individuals seeking flexible transportation or social status were easily visible from the earliest days of motor cars, larger-scale effects of individual car ownership were more difficult to discern. And today, automobiles still offer people in suburban and rural areas immense convenience in traveling to work and shopping, as well as a means for social relations and leisure.

When motor cars first became popular in the early twentieth century, they were viewed as a clean technology. Larger cities had annoying pollution problems from another primary transportation technology, horses. On rainy days, large pools of horse manure would form on busy street corners, and walking was somewhat hazardous for pedestrians. By the 1960s, we began to view cars as a major polluting technology, since smog visibly dirtied the air of major cities.

Since there were few cars in the early 1920s, it was difficult to predict what impacts the automobile would have simply by studying the uses to which automobiles were put, or by examining the major forms of social organization. If one had wanted to think ahead about what benefits cars would have, and what social dilemmas certain styles of social organization around cars could produce, one would have had to be unusually prescient in the early part of the twentieth century. There simply were not enough cars and a social system sufficiently saturated with them to foresee the major effects with any clarity. But an analyst who thought that automobiles were simply fun to drive, portending nothing ominous regardless of the scale on which they were to be used, would have been mistaken.

In fact, as smog became more visible in major cities, the automobile industry worked hard to argue that there was no link between cars and smog.[2] (The tobacco industry's continuing denial of the reported links between smoking and lung cancer provides an obvious parallel.) By the time that major effects became visible, substantial investments often were already made—investments that would be difficult to alter, even when troubles were clear. By the time the smog had become intense enough to render the mountains surrounding Los Angeles invisible on most days,

---

[1] Richard Sclove and Jeffrey Scheur (Part V, Chapter M) deepen this analysis by examining the politics and social effects of interstate highway development.

[2] See Krier and Ursin (1977). Other more local interest groups also played key roles in the development of road systems within cities. See, for example, Lupo, Colcord, and Fowler (1971).

people had already become dependent not just on the car, but on forms of social life built around cars: nuclear families dwelling in suburban tracts with little public transportation, and living ten to thirty miles from work, friends, shops, and other posts of daily life.[3] In addition, metropolitan regions devote huge resources to motorized transport through the building and renovation of highways, roads, parking lots, garages, and the support of traffic police and traffic courts.[4] It is now almost impossible to restructure these social elements in which the automobile has become a central element.

Smog began developing in major cities around 1940, some forty years after the automobile was developed in the United States. A new form of metropolitan organization in which the urban core was dwarfed by bedroom suburbs developed on a large scale well after World War II. These suburbs, which many urban critics decried as bland, lifeless places, were extremely attractive to young families seeking affordable housing and open spaces relatively free of crime and congestion. (One person's utopia can be another's nightmare.)

Each year between four and five hundred people die in traffic accidents nationwide on each major holiday weekend in the United States. And auto crashes, which resulted in over 43,000 deaths in 1991, are the largest single cause of accidental death in the United States. The signs of car accidents are often highly visible, and ambulance sirens signify human pain and suffering. Even so, the auto industry often fought the addition of safety features for cars.[5]

Treating cars as "transportation tools," as in the fifties jingle, "see the USA in a Chevrolet" doesn't help us understand the opportunities, problems, or dependence associated with cars. Car use is also a habitual way of life in North American suburban and rural regions, as well as most cities. It is institutionalized, taken for granted and hard to alter on a social scale, even when there are big incentives to do so. Policies to reduce urban

---

[3] The first suburbs, which developed in the late nineteenth and early twentieth centuries, were spawned by rail transportation. The automobile and low-interest mortgages played a more powerful role in the development of suburbs *after* World War II.

[4] According to one estimate, about 40 percent of the developed land in the city of Los Angeles is devoted to transportation facilities for cars, trucks, and buses.

[5] See Ralph Nader's (1972) classic that stimulated more aggressive auto safety regulations that were often fought by auto companies. Nader was outraged that certain cars, such as the visually seductive Chevrolet Corvair, were extremely unstable, so much so that they could tip over in normal use. But the movement for enhanced auto safety went on to press for seat belts in the 1980s and air bags in the 1990s. Death rates from automobile accidents declined by about 35% in the United States between 1970 and 1991. Nader's book stimulated a grass roots political movement to better regulate the design practices of consumer goods industries in the United States.

congestion and smog through mass transit and car pools have had modest success at best. Unfortunately, many transportation planners and urban planners have designed major residential and commercial areas in ways that undermine alternatives to cars, such as pedestrian walkways and bicycle lanes (Kling, Olin, and Poster, 1995). Car dependence has had massive side effects besides the production of smog. Oil politics has played a major role in the United States' dealings with Middle Eastern countries, including the 1991 "war in the gulf" against Iraq. Efforts to obtain additional domestic oil have led to environmentally hazardous oil spills from offshore rigs on the California coast. And the distribution systems have sometimes failed when tankers have grounded or collided at sea (e.g., the well-known Exxon Valdez disaster for which Exxon was fined five billion dollars in 1994).

The automobile analogy also helps us appreciate the way in which the links between a better technology and improvements in social life are often ambiguous. The analogy between cars (or actually motorized transportation systems) and computers (or actually computer-communications systems) is suggestive rather than literal. Both of these technologies include highly visible components that many people see as "technologies of freedom" and as highly controllable. However, after thousands of miles of highways and roads are built, and after communities are organized to emphasize high-speed travel, it is hard to quickly reorganize the resulting metropolitan structures to encourage less car dependence (Newman and Kenworthy, 1989).

In fact, cars are part of a complex social–political–technical system for obtaining fuel, regulating car design and drivers, providing insurance, policing roads, and designing cities and suburbs. And with the elaboration and extension of major computer networks for offices, homes, schools, and other organizations, computers are becoming part of similarly large-scale social systems.

Technologies such as computing do not "impact" social life like a meteor hitting the planet Earth. Rather, people and organizations adopt constellations of technologies and configure them to fit ongoing social patterns. Even when the fit is imperfect, people and organizations often alter their practices to accommodate the advantages and limitations of new technologies. Moreover, one can wander widely through major cities with immense computerized businesses and government agencies and still not see signs of computing, whether helpful or harmful. Computer systems and their consequences are not readily visible outside of the workplaces or homes that use them. As a consequence (and like the automobile in its early days), computing can appear to be a clean and safe technology.

Many social observers and computer scientists have been fascinated by the potential potency of computerization to alter social life profoundly. But an overwhelming fraction of the talk and writing about computer systems avoids examining likely problems of computerization efforts.[6] Part of what is required to examine such issues is a willingness to examine computer systems as part of a larger social–technical system, not just as a component.[7] We must also forthrightly examine social behavior as integral to the design of computer systems that support virtual offices, electronic access to information from government agencies, digital libraries, electronic funds transfer systems, and other such systems. The social behavior, technical options, and institutions that are relevant in each of these kinds of systems will differ in important details. Even though there are many uncertainties, these topics are subject to systematic empirical and theoretical inquiry. This book includes several interesting examples and references to many others in the emerging body of systematic research about computerization.

These socially oriented studies of computerization have yet to be enthusiastically embraced by the information and computer science academic communities and public agencies that fund research about computerization. It remains to be seen whether the computer and information industries will be any more progressive than the "smokestack industries," such as the auto industry, in forthrightly supporting systematic social inquiry. Some critics argue that "the logic of capitalism" prevents industrial and commercial firms from routinely encouraging open and honest research about the social aspects of computerization that might not always support the largest sales of their goods and services. These critics can certainly make a strong case for the tobacco and automobile industries; what would it take for the information and computer industries to behave more responsibly?

References

Clement, Andrew (1994). "Considering Privacy in the Development of Multi-media Communications." *Computer Supported Cooperative Work,* 2:67–88. (Reprinted in Part VIII.)

Kling, Rob, Spencer Olin, and Mark Poster (1995). "Beyond the Edge: The Dynamism of Postsuburban Regions," in *Postsuburban California: The Transformation of Orange County Since World War II.* University of California Press, Berkeley.

Krier, James, and Edmund Ursin (1977). *Pollution & Policy: A Case Essay on California and Federal Experience with Motor Vehicle Air Pollution 1940–1975.* University of California Press, Berkeley.

---

[6] As an interesting and extreme example, see Clement (1994), which examines how industrial computer scientists are reluctant to systematically discuss "the dark side" of their inventions.

[7] The new Lamborghini Diablo is engineered so that it can be driven at 200 mph. That is a great capability which cannot be legally realized in the United States. And increasing the speed limits to 200 mph will do little to free up the commuter-hour gridlock that characterizes most metropolitan areas.

Lupo, Alan, Frank Colcord, and Edmund P. Fowler (1971). *Rites of Way; the Politics of Transportation in Boston and the U.S. City*. Little, Brown, Boston.

Nader, Ralph (1972). *Unsafe at Any Speed: The Designed-in Dangers of the American Automobile* (expanded edition). Grossman, New York.

Newman, P. W. G., and J. R. Kenworthy (1989). *Cities and Automobile Dependence: An International Sourcebook*. Aldershot, Hants., England; Brookfield, Vt.

P·A·R·T · I

E

The Seductive Equation of Technological Progress with Social Progress

Rob Kling

Computing is often seen as a "seductive technology" or, more accurately, the centerpiece of seductive visions and dreams. The seduction comes from the hope that vast possibilities for information handling and "enhanced intelligence" can be readily accessible at relatively low cost and little effort. Some of the technological advances of computer systems are quite obvious. In each decade, the power of digital computing hardware increases about tenfold for any given price and physical size. Advances in the power and quality of software have also been steady, but much less dramatic. However, transforming these technological advances into social advances has not been straightforward. This book examines many of the resulting dilemmas.

I am often enchanted by graceful high-performance technologies. I like driving (if not maintaining!) spirited, refined cars. I appreciate fast computers with powerful software and bright, colorful displays. I have benefitted from computer systems with word processors and spell checkers to support my writing. I use databases and automated library search systems to track books and articles, and I communicate with colleagues and students daily via electronic mail. But I also realize that the exercise of my personal preferences for high-performance technologies—raised to a social scale—poses a variety of important social questions.[1]

Some technologists suggest that new computer technologies will address key social problems. Falling prices for computer hardware, the next versions of the PowerPC chip, the next generation of Windows, and a band of smart programmers will solve most of them. The remainder will be solved by faster processors for PCs and supercomputers, gigabit-speed international networks, better environments for programming languages, higher-performance database languages, virtual reality, and some artificial intelligence!

While I am obviously caricaturing this position, I am not fundamentally misstating a view held by many technologists and futurists, and popularized by some journalists. Few writers make these claims explicit; rather, they make them implicitly by focusing attention on new (or "revolutionary") technologies while ignoring key aspects of the social environments in which they are used.

For example, some educators argue that schools could best improve their educational programs by investing heavily in computer-assisted instruction or by connecting to an information superhighway without asking what kinds of equipment most schools can afford to buy, maintain, and train their teachers to use effectively. Transportation experts insist that urban congestion can be reduced through the development and widespread use of smart cars; they place much less emphasis on training smarter drivers.

Many scenarios of "life in the year 2000" assume that social progress will come primarily through technological progress. For example, in 1990, *The Los Angeles Times* published a story about "Life in the Year 1999," which focused on a day in the life of a professional couple who live in a "smart house," one filled with many computerized convenience and security devices. However useful these devices may be, they increase the cost of housing. And they increase the complexity of daily life when the equipment malfunctions or requires special adjustment. During the last decade, the housing market in Los Angeles became among the most expensive in the country. Many working people today cannot afford a house, even a "stupid house." And there are tens of thousands of homeless people in this region alone. I am struck by the way in which the news media casually promote images of a technologically rich future while ignoring the way in which these technologies can add cost, complexity, and new dependencies to daily life. The glossy images also ignore key social choices about *how to computerize* and the ways in which different forms of computerization advance different values.[2]

---

[1] Many people and organizations desiring "high-performance" technologies often have trouble acquiring them because of their cost. And those who are able to appropriate more powerful technologies are likely to widen the gap between themselves and those who lack them.

[2] Kling (1983) examines the character of value conflicts stimulated by computerization. Also see the discussion of value conflicts in the lead article to Part VI, "Information Technologies and the Shifting Balance between Privacy and Social Control."

Many forms of computerization are advanced within an overall framework of industrialization. Our industrial civilization has created the conditions for increasing our general health, physical comfort, and safety. But it has come at the cost of immense environmental pollution in many regions of the country. We have reached a point at which increasing use of energy and industrial products can lead to more smog, more acid rain, more rapid depletion of the ozone layer, more rapid warming of the planet, and so on. Some solutions can also rely on computer technologies. For example, having people telecommute to work may be more environmentally sound than packing the urban freeways with more commuters driving "smarter" cars on their daily trek from home to work. Unfortunately, it is hard to find balanced accounts that carefully examine the social character of different packages of social and technological alternatives and the values which they each support.

Computerization often symbolizes modernism and rationality. Advocates talk about advanced technologies in ways that mix the giddy excitement of adventure with the liberating lure of new possibilities that have few associated problems. For example, it is easy for a national politician to say that "every school, library, and medical clinic in the country" will be connected to high-speed data networks. It is less easy to find funds for appropriate (and rapidly obsolescent) computer equipment, staff training, and support services when school and library budgets are already stressed and these services are often poor. It is harder still to imagine why schooling would change when classrooms are wired if pedagogies and teachers don't also change to inspire inquiry and debate rather than to emphasize rote learning and quiet compliance (Hodas, 1993).

Talk about new technologies offers a canvas in which to reshape social relationships to better fit the speakers' imaginations. The presence of advanced technologies often serves as a sign that the computer-using person or organization is worthy of admiration and trust. It is usually easier for casual observers to spot the presence of advanced computer equipment than to understand how the equipment actually alters people's abilities to carry out their day-to-day activities.[3] Yet, social revolutions are based on changes in ways of life, not just changes in equipment or in adding connections to expansive computer nets. Some of the articles in this book examine the reality that organizations that hope to make "radical changes" from computerization can't just acquire technologies and expect important changes to follow; they have to plan key changes in their practices simultaneously (Part III, Chapter D; Morton, Orlikowski, 1993). Even so, there are important social and ethical questions about the extent to which radical changes in organizations are a form of social progress if they lead many

---

[3] For an interesting case study of the way an organization exploited the image of efficient administration through computerization, see Kling (1978).

people to have worse jobs (Marx, 1990; Clement, 1994), or even no jobs at all in an economy that has few good jobs. It is important for advocates and participants in computerization projects to have some clear ideas of which social practices deserve to be labeled as "progress," whether or not they are enabled with computer systems.

References

Clement, Andrew (1994). "Computing at Work: Empowering Action by 'Low-level Users'." *Communications of the ACM*, (37)1(January):52–65. (Reprinted in Part IV.)

Hodas, Steven (1993). "Technology Refusal and The Organizational Culture of Schools." *Education Policy Analysis Archives*, 1.10 (September). (Reprinted in Part III.)

Kling, Rob (1978). "Automated Welfare Client-tracking and Service Integration: The Political Economy of Computing." *Communications of the ACM*, 21(6)(June, 1978):484–493.

Kling, Rob (1983). "Value Conflicts in the Deployment of Computing Applications: Cases in Developed and Developing Countries." *Telecommunications Policy*, 7(1) (March):12–34. [Reprinted in Charles Dunlop and Rob Kling (eds.) (1991). *Computerization and Controversy: Value Conflicts and Social Choices*. Academic Press, San Diego.]

Marx, Gary (1990). "The Case of the Omniscient Organization." *Harvard Business Review*, (March–April):4–12. (Reprinted in Part IV.)

Morton, Michael S. Scott (ed.) (1991). *The Corporation of the 1990s: Information Technology and Organizational Transformation*. Oxford University Press, New York.

Orlikowski, Wanda J. (1993). "Learning from Notes: Organizational Issues in Groupware Implementation." *Information Society*, 9(3) (Jul–Sep):237–250. (Reprinted in Part III.)

P·A·R·T · I

F

Learning about the Possible Futures of Computerization from the Present and the Past

Rob Kling

The computing world is future oriented. In the computing world, the past is often regarded as a repository of dusty memories of obsolete clunky technologies. In this view, people's past experiences with computerization are primarily an opportunity for nostalgia or simply a point of reference against which the improved present and a magnificent future can be put in perspective. In the extreme forms of this, sometimes advanced by people who work at technological research frontiers, new technologies will transform our worlds so profoundly that there is no meaningful way to anticipate the key changes. The best that one can do is simply ride the wave of technological innovation and enjoy the trip.[1]

Some of the articles in this book show us how we can learn about how organizations shape the use of new technologies. In Part V, linguist Susan Herring writes about the way men and women in academia communicate and share expertise and opinions on special bulletin board systems (Internet LISTSERVs). Many of the people who write about electronic forums expect that electronic links and nifty software will enable people who work in different locations to share their expertise, just like professors. Part III contains MIT professor Wanda Orlikowski's study of the use of Lotus's Notes file sharing and e-mail system in a major consulting firm. While Notes seemed to offer the possibility for consultants in different offices to share their expertise, she found that many consultants were reluctant to learn Notes or to use it. The big problem was not some aspect of Notes' design that could be refined in a niftier version of the software. It stemmed from many of the consultants' beliefs that the company's reward system would punish them for spending a lot of their time learning new software and sharing their expertise about ways to solve business problems!

These articles (and others in the research literature) suggest that the reward systems in organizations can play a major role in the ways people use (or ignore) new information technologies. Technological capabilities may be unused (or turned to different uses) when they are not congruent with local reward systems and cultures. These reward systems and cultures are part of what we call "social context." Many good research studies show that social contexts play powerful roles in shaping the use of information technologies (Kling, 1980; Kling and Jewett, 1994).

But you don't have to be a researcher and study special technologies and organizations to learn from your own experiences of computerization. I will use a personal example to illustrate this point.

I like using fast and colorful computer-based systems for my own work, especially for writing, organizing records, searching library archives, and communicating via electronic mail. Computing has inherent social and political dimensions. If I write this book while using a big monitor in my study at home, I am less accessible to colleagues and students on campus. If I work in my campus office, the stream of discussions with colleagues and students interrupts a flow of thinking and writing. How to organize a socially connected and yet productive work life does not have one simple answer, even with phone, voice mail, e-mail, and fax machines added to the mix of technological support systems. Some days, I prefer to work at home and use a big monitor that I purchased with my own money. I live fifteen minutes from my campus offices and, as a professor, I have a lot of control over where I work, and even when I work (I'm writing this sentence at 11:45 P.M.).

The contrast between my wife's work and mine is instructive. She directs the development of instructional programs to help children learn to read and write (and want to read and write). She works for a high-tech organization whose offices are sixty to ninety minutes from our home, depending on the density of Southern California's (sometimes grueling) urban freeway traffic. She has a new computer that is functionally comparable to mine, and a nicer (color) printer. She is also connected to the Internet. Her job requires a lot of writing, and she would like to work at home several days a week. In practice she rarely works at home. In fact, she has much less control over where (and when) she works than I do. She has several assistants who require significant frequent consultation and supervision

---

[1] See, for example, the end of Hillis's (1992) article. Computer scientist Danny Hillis pioneered the development of massively parallel computers. See my critique of his position in King, Scherson, and Allen (1992).

when they develop graphic materials. These collaborations work best when she sees them and their work, rather than when working by fax and phone. But most seriously, the upper managers of this organization believe in "face work" — that professionals should be at their desks or available for impromptu meetings much of the working day.[2] This is another, more personal, illustration of the ways the context of computer interaction can shape its use and social life.

Organizational behavior and cultural beliefs often shape the routine use of information technologies, and we can learn a lot about the ways that advanced technologies might be used from contemporary experience. Many information and computing professionals view a study that is based on "old technologies" as dated. Although new technologies often allow different opportunities for managing information, we can learn a lot about the interaction of technology and social life from studies that were conducted in the 1970s and 1980s, as well as the 1990s.

Organizing themes such as "individual choice," "efficiency," "productivity," "convenience," and "aesthetic preferences" are inadequate for understanding the opportunities, limitations, and potential social problems of computerization, just as they fail to provide adequate illumination of the role of cars in urban America. Since computing requires resources to acquire, develop, maintain, and use effectively, it has social implications at every stage, not just in its consequences (Kling and Scacchi, 1982). The cost and complexity of advanced computing systems tend to give special advantage to already powerful groups in shaping their use, and in turning them to the further advancement of group interests.

However, the intentions of individuals, designers, or managers have not been good predictors of the effects of large-scale social activity. Collective action, including computerization, develops with some nonobvious logics. I have found the ways that organizations computerize to be particularly fascinating and sometimes remarkably puzzling. The behavior of organizations is central to the large-scale social dramas of computerization. Organizations develop computer technologies, shape public perceptions (especially the popular news media), and are social locations where people work with computer systems and use them to support various business/government services.

We can learn a great deal from fine-grained examination of how people live and work with the computerized systems that are in use today. Today, in North America, Australia, and western Europe alone, about one hundred million people use computerized systems of some kind routinely in their work. And several hundred million people are routine participants in the use of computerized systems for financial transactions, organizational

---

[2] See my discussion of face work, telecommuting, and virtual offices in the lead article to Part IV.

records systems, and so on. Some of my colleagues like to emphasize life in a future society where everyone may carry a dozen "smart cards," and talk to computerized gadgets that open doors, cook dinner, and carry out other routine work. Exciting (or demoralizing) as some of their visions may be, I believe that they often go askew insofar as they ignore important durable features of social life. These durable features, such as people's desire for human contact, or concerns about control in workplaces, are often salient when we examine the use of computer technologies in both existing and emerging workplaces. Consequently, I have loaded this book with articles that offer sharp insights for thinking about our future choices by learning from pivotal experiences of the recent past and the present.

One of the remarkable features of literature about computerization is the peculiar provincialism of many academics and professionals who write about the social aspects of particular families of technologies. There are discrete literatures that are defined by the kind of institution or industry the technology is used in (i.e., health care, commercial enterprises, libraries, manufacturing) or by the technological form (i.e., networking, artificial intelligence, documentary databases). There could be a fertile mingling of theories and concepts for understanding computerization in social life by working across these technological and social domains. To help support that kind of intellectual commerce, I have included in this book articles that examine different kinds of computer technologies in different institutional settings.[3]

A loss of historical perspective also impoverishes many important discussions of computerization. For example, the discussions of advanced National Information Infrastructure (NII, aka "information superhighway") in the United States often treat future NII developments as seamless and based on the convergence of cable television, telephones, and computer networks. Some analysts even refer to a future NII ("the NII") as an integrated entity with which a person could have a single and hopefully simple interface. This country has had an NII for well over one hundred years, and at various stages we added information services based on pony express (mail), telegraph, telephones, radio communications (including emergency services and broadcast), and television. Over the years, we have dropped some of these information services (such as pony express), while others remain, but perhaps less prominently than at the peak of their social significance. Virtually every discussion we have seen or heard in the information and computer science communities about an advanced NII emphasizes wired services like computer networking, and excludes radio broadcast, which serves as an important carrier of emergency services and car-based entertainment. Most discussions of "universal access" to an

---

[3] For examples of conceptualizing across technological families and institutional settings, see Kling (1980, 1987, 1992) and Kling and Jewett (1994).

advanced NII also seem to presume that people would use a simple interface (perhaps no more complex than a nifty combination of voice mail, a VCR, an AM/FM radio, e-mail, World Wide Web browser, and a file manager!). While it is likely that some services may run on common physical cables, I believe that it is implausible for the broad spectrum of diverse information services to be neatly integrated into a simple, seamless, cost-effective capability. The meanings of "universal access" to an advanced NII differ, depending on if one believes Gore's convergence vision, or believes that key services will continue to be segmented or integrated in specialized bundles with relatively complex or costly interfaces.

To bring such historical dimensions to this book, I have included brief relevant histories in my lead articles in the sections on work and privacy and social control. I also selected some articles, such as those by Steve Hodas, John King, and Richard Sclove and Jeffrey Scheur, because they add an important historical dimension to understanding computerization in social life.

Other analysts see computerization in different terms than I do. Consequently, among the authors of the articles that I selected, some develop positions that I support, and others develop positions from which I strongly differ. Above all, I believe many scholars, professionals, and students are not adequately aware of the debates about the *social* issues surrounding computerization. Professionals and managers of all kinds, including computer specialists, often take sides through their actions, without understanding the key assumptions and limitations of their positions. I have learned, and I have seen other scholars, professionals, and students learn, about computerization by truly engaging and deliberating different points of view. One of the important skills for any professional in a design discipline, whether it is architecture, urban planning, information systems, or computer science, is to learn how to see their artifacts from multiple points of view, and especially from the perspectives of the diverse men and women that may use them. Remarkably, the education of many information and computer scientists is often organized around themes, such as "the right way" and "the optimal way," that minimize the relevance of other participants' points of view.

References

Hillis, W. D. (1992). "What is Massively Parallel Computing and Why is it Important?" *Daedalus,* 121(1)(Winter 1992):1–16. Reprinted in *The New Era of Computing,* W. Daniel Hillis and James Bailey (eds.). MIT Press.

Kling, Rob (1980). "Social Analyses of Computing: Theoretical Perspectives in Recent Empirical Research." *Computing Surveys,* 12(1):61–110.

Kling, Rob (1987). "Defining the Boundaries of Computing Across Complex Organizations" in Richard Boland and Rudy Hirschheim (eds.), *Critical Issues in Information Systems.* John Wiley, London.

Kling, Rob (1992). "Behind the Terminal: The Critical Role of Computing Infrastructure In Effective Information Systems' Development and Use," in William Cotterman and James Senn (eds.), *Challenges and Strategies for Research in Systems Development*, pp. 153–201. John Wiley, New York.

Kling, Rob, and Tom Jewett (1994). "The Social Design of Worklife With Computers and Networks: An Open Natural Systems Perspective," in Marshall C. Yovits (ed.), *Advances in Computers*, Vol. 39. Academic Press, San Diego.

Kling, Rob, and Walt Scacchi (1982). "The Web of Computing: Computer Technology as Social Organization." *Advances in Computers*, Vol. 21, pp. 1–90. Academic Press, New York.

Kling, Rob, Isaac Scherson, and John Allen (1992). "Massively Parallel Computing and Information Capitalism," in W. Daniel Hillis and James Bailey (eds.), *A New Era of Computing*. The MIT Press, Cambridge, MA.

P·A·R·T·I

Information and Computer Scientists as Moral Philosophers and Social Analysts

Rob Kling

Computer Science Skills Involve More Than Developing and Integrating Hardware and Software

Information and computer specialists, as well as management consultants, often propose computerized systems that, they argue, will help people and organizations in new ways. These planners often unconsciously engage in oversimplified romantic speculation, even when they prefer to be "hard headed," "factual," and "only technical." Utopian inquiry and its anti-utopian opposite (which are examined in Part II) can be useful ways of exploring future possibilities. Much of the problem with utopian thinking comes when people fail to realize how fanciful some of their assumptions about human behavior and social change are. Visionaries tend to focus primarily on desirable changes and assume that what *should* happen *must* happen after a particular technology is introduced.[1] Their assumptions often go well beyond technology as it is traditionally conceived, embodying views of human–machine interaction, human motivation, and the behavior of social groups. Thus, a critical investigation into visionary viewpoints requires skills that lie beyond hardware and algorithm design.

Paul Goodman argued that technologists, including computer specialists, are primarily social activists who act, in practice, as moral philosophers:

> Whether or not it draws on new scientific research, technology is a branch of moral philosophy, not of science. It aims at prudent goods for the commonweal and to provide efficient means for those goods. . . . As a moral philosopher, a technician should be able to criticize the programs given to him to implement. As a professional in a community of learned professionals, a technologist must have a different kind of training. . . . He should know something of the social sciences, law, the fine arts, and medicine, as well as relevant natural sciences. (Goodman, 1970)[2]

This is a remarkable position, since few information and computer professionals have systematically studied philosophy or the social sciences. One commonplace view of computer science and engineering is reflected in a report by the ACM[3] Task Force on the Core of Computer Science:

> Computer Science and Engineering is the systematic study of algorithmic processes—their theory, analysis, design, efficiency, implementation and application—that describe and transform information. The fundamental question underlying all of computing is, What can be (efficiently) automated? . . . The roots of computing extend deeply into mathematics and engineering. Mathematics imparts analysis to the field; engineering imparts design. (Denning *et al.*, 1989)

How different this view is from Goodman's! It makes Goodman sound somewhat utopian in his desire that computer specialists be independent professionals who will exert a critical influence on the shape of the products they are asked to produce. In the traditional view, technologists are often asked to refine the means they use to implement a product, but not to question the ends they serve. Ian Reinecke goes even further in that direction, suggesting that technical communities are impervious to serious critical analyses:

> Those who know most about technology are in many cases the worst equipped to appreciate its implications for the lives of ordinary people. Consumed by technical and corporate objectives that become ends in themselves, they fail to see that their work may very often be contrary to the interests of their fellow citizens. So frenetic is the pace of change that the few querulous voices raised from their own ranks are swept aside. Where the voices are more insistent, they are branded as renegades, as unstable people whose work has somehow unhinged them. (Reinecke, 1984, p. 243)

---

[1] Or, alternatively, that what should *not* happen will not happen. See the articles in Part II for examples of both kinds of thinking.

[2] Excerpted from Teich (1990) pp. 235–236. Goodman's view has immediate implications for computer science curricula, implications that are still not adequately recognized at many universities.

[3] The Association for Computing Machinery, with over 82,000 members, is the major professional organization for information and computer scientists in the United States.

I do not share Reinecke's wholesale condemnation of technical professionals. Part VIII will examine some key ethical issues of computing, and the way that technical professionals have articulated different positions in the controversies. Moreover, some of the better computer science journals, such as *Communications of the ACM*, publish articles that examine the social aspects of computerization from different vantage points. But Reinecke's criticism is most apt for technologists who remain somewhat selfconsciously indifferent to the social complexities of computerization, except to acknowledge the importance of their own special interests. Further, relatively few of the practicing technologists whom I have met in some of the nations' top industrial and service firms read broadly about the social aspects of computerization. Sadly, a substantial fraction of computer specialists focus their professional reading on technical handbooks, such as the manuals for specific equipment, and on occasional articles in the computer trade press.

Skills in the Social Analysis of Computing

The dominant paradigms in academic computer science do not help technical professionals comprehend the social complexities of computerization, since they focus on computability, rather than usability. For example, the ACM Task Force on the Core of Computer Science, quoted above, claims that all the analyses of computer science are mathematical. I find this view much too narrow-minded to be helpful, and in fact it does not withstand much scrutiny. The lines of inquiry where it might hold are those where mathematics can impart all the necessary analysis. But there are whole subfields of computer science, such as artificial intelligence, computer–human interaction, social impacts studies, and parts of software, where mathematics cannot impart all the necessary analysis. The social sciences provide a complementary theoretical base for studies of computing that examine or make assumptions about human behavior.

In the classic Turing machine model of computability, there is no significant difference between a modest microcomputer like an Apple Macintosh PowerPC and a supercomputer like a Cray Y-MP. Of course, these two machines differ substantially in their computational speed and memory. But the Mac PowerPC, with software designed to match its graphical interface, is a much more usable computer for many small-scale tasks such as writing memos and papers, graphing datasets of five hundred data points, and so on. Unfortunately, the computability paradigm doesn't help us understand a Mac's relative advantage over a Cray for tasks where the ease of a person's interacting with software, rather than sheer CPU speed or file size, is the critical issue.

This contrast between Macs and Crays is a small-scale, machine-centered example. More significant examples can be found whenever one is trying to ask questions like: What should be computerized for these particular people? How should computerization proceed? Who should control system specifications, data, and so on? These are "usability" questions on a social scale. Paradigms that focus on the nature of social interaction provide much better insights for designing computer systems in support of group work than does the computability paradigm (Dahlbom and Mathiassen, 1993; Ehn, 1989; Winograd, 1988; Kling, 1993; see Kling and Allen, Part III, Chapter M).[4]

Mathematical analyses help us learn about the properties of computer systems abstracted from any particular use, such as the potential efficiency of an algorithm or the extent to which computers can completely solve certain problems in principle (e.g., the question of undecidability). As long as a computer scientist doesn't make claims about the value of any kind of computer use, mathematical analyses might be adequate. But the advances in computer interface design that led to the Mac, and graphical user interfaces more generally, rested on *psychological* insights, rather than mathematical insights. Similarly, advances in programming languages, software development tools, and database systems have come, in part, through analyses of what makes technologies easier for people and organizations to use. Although some of these technologies have a mathematical base, their fundamental justifications have been psychological and social. Claims about how groups of people should use computers are *social* and *value-laden* claims.

For example, suppose a computer scientist argues that organizations should computerize by developing networks of high-performance workstations, with one on every employee's desk. This claim embodies key assumptions about good organizational strategies, and implicitly rules out alternatives, such as having a large central computer connected to employees' terminals, with a few microcomputers also available for those who prefer to use micro-oriented software. These two alternative architectures for organizational computing raise important social and political questions: Who will get access to what kinds of information and software? What skill levels will be required to use the systems? How much money should be spent on each worker's computing support? How should resources and status be divided within the organization? Who should control different aspects of computerization projects? and so on. The question here is one of *social and political* organization, in addition to *computer* organization. Since engineers and computer scientists often make claims in these arenas, Paul Goodman argued that ". . . technology is a branch of moral philosophy,

---

[4] See the discussion in Part IV about the social dimensions of systems designs, along with the supporting readings. The computer science programs at a few universities, such as the University of California, Irvine and the Arhus University in Denmark, attempt to integrate serious social analysis into more traditional "technical" computer science.

not of science. It aims at prudent goods for the commonweal. . . ." Many computer scientists are keenly interested in having advanced computer-based systems widely *used*, not just studied as mathematical objects. These hopes and related claims rest on social analyses and theories of social behavior.[5]

Mathematical frames of reference lead analysts to focus on behavior that can be formalized on "optimal arrangements." Social analyses usually help analysts identify the ways that different participants in a computerization project may have different preferences for the way that computing technologies are woven into social arrangements. Participants are most likely to have different preferences when computerization projects are socially complex and when a project cuts across key social boundaries, identified by characteristics such as roles, occupational identity, reward structures, culture, or ethnicity. I do not see social analysis as a panacea. But it helps identify the kinds of opportunities and dilemmas participants will actually experience and respond to in their daily lives.

The education of hundreds of thousands of computer science students has been shaped by the computability perspective. These students typically leave academic computer science programs with some skills in the design and programming of software systems. They take courses in data structures and algorithms, in which they learn to appreciate and carry out mathematical analyses of computer performance. But too often they leave the university essentially ignorant of the ways in which social analyses of computer systems provide comparably important insights into the roles and effectiveness of computing in the world. I believe that many segments of the computing community would understand computerization much better, and be able to play more responsible professional roles, by adopting a more fundamentally social view of computerization.

Social analysis is an integral part of the information and computer sciences, and is a critical skill for professionals in these fields.[6] They are often computerizing parts of their own organizations, as well as making claims about the social aspects of computerization for others. They should do so insightfully and with a sensitivity to the ways that many people's lives are actually influenced by computerization strategies. Social analyses of computerization examine situations analytically, to understand what kinds of assumptions are made about social relationships between key participants, along with the support arrangement for appropriate technologies, the range of technological options, and how these may restructure social life.

---

[5] See my article with Jonathan P. Allen, "Can Computer Science Solve Organizational Problems?" in Part III for a more extended argument.

[6] See Kling and Allen, Part III for a more developed argument.

In a larger perspective, the information and computer sciences, as disciplines, should be able to comment meaningfully about computerization and policy issues in the social order. Computer specialists and professionals also have a special responsibility to share their insights with their employers, clients, and the public in a prosocial way. A computer science of the twenty-first century will be strong in areas that rest on the social foundations of computerization as well as in areas that rest on the mathematical and engineering foundations.

I hope that important technologies such as computing can be sufficiently well understood by many social groups early on, so that important decisions about whether, when, and how to utilize computer-based systems will be more socially benign than would otherwise be the case. This book provides an opportunity for readers to learn more about the nuances of computerization. Through it, I hope to expand the range of legitimate discourse about the social choices of computerization.

Computerization and Social Visions

Often, managers and technical professionals develop computerization projects with relatively simple themes, to enhance the operational efficiency of some organizational practice, to provide a new service, or sometimes simply "to modernize" by using current technologies. Even when the social visions of practitioners are relatively skimpy, computerization projects have important social dimensions, as we will see in the various parts of this book. However, computerization in industrial countries has also been the subject of a large body of popular and professional writing— what computer systems are good for and the character of their problems, which most professionals have been exposed to. This exposure often influences implicit assumptions about computerization. To illustrate key viewpoints of people who write about advanced computing technologies, this book examines some assumptions that shape many visions of computerization in Part II.

References

Dahlbom, Bo, and Lars Mathiassen (1993). *Computers in Context: The Philosophy and Practice of Systems Design*. Blackwell, London.

Denning, Peter J. *et al.* (1989). "Computing as a Discipline," *CACM*, 31(1) (January):9–23.

Ehn, Pelle (1989). "The Art and Science of Designing Computer Artifacts." *Scandinavian Journal of Information Systems*, 1(August):21–42. [Reprinted in Charles Dunlop and Rob Kling (eds.) (1991). *Computerization and Controversy: Value Conflicts and Social Choices*. Academic Press, San Diego.]

Goodman, Paul (1970). *The New Reformation: Notes of a Neolithic Conservative*. Random House, New York.

Kling, Rob (1993). "Organizational Analysis in Computer Science." *The Information Society*, 9(2) (March–May):71–87.

Reinecke, Ian (1984). *Electronic Illusions: A Skeptic's View of Our High Tech Future.* Penguin, New York.

Teich, Albert (ed.) (1990). *Technology and the Future*, 5th ed. St. Martin's Press, New York.

Winograd, Terry (1987–88). "A Language/action Perspective on the Design of Cooperative Work." *Human–Computer Interaction*, 3(1):3–30. (Reprinted in *Computer-Supported Cooperative Work: A Book of Readings*, Irene Grief (ed.). 1988, pp. 623–653. Morgan-Kaufmann, San Mateo, California.

P·A·R·T · II

The Dreams of Technological Utopianism

Hopes and Horrors: Technological Utopianism and Anti-Utopianism in Narratives of Computerization

Rob Kling

Stories about Computerization

This book examines social controversies about computerization and ways to computerize that can be more socially beneficial or harmful. Many key questions that people raise about computerization, in their households, communities, workplaces, and so on, refer to possible future events. For example, university librarians may wonder how they should create a computerized "virtual reference desk" for their clients and shift their spending away from paper-based materials. Managers in a software company may wonder how they can best supervise their staffs and foster teamwork if their team members all work in their separate homes in a large urban area. A young man and woman may wonder whether they can send each other romantic letters via electronic mail and ensure the privacy of their communications. In industrialized societies, millions of professionals and computer specialists ask questions like these every day.

Good answers to questions like these are not always obvious. And thinking through workable answers (and social practices based upon them) can involve a complex web of assumptions about people's rights, the responsibilities of professionals to their clients, how people behave, the capabilities of specific technologies, and the nature of ethical behavior. These answers are usually based on a story, however incomplete, about "the future." The time scale of future behavior may be two months away or ten years away.

This chapter helps you better understand the unstated but critical social assumptions underlying stories about computerization and changes in social life. Every year thousands of articles and dozens of books comment on the meaning of new computer technologies for people, organizations, and society. Much of the literature about computing describes emerging technologies and the ways they expand the limits of the possible. Faster, tinier computers can make it easier for people to find information from their homes and hotel rooms, as well as their offices or laboratories. Larger memories can make more data accessible. Richer display devices, which show lively video, colorful pictures, and text can make interacting with computers a reality for more people. Emerging higher-speed networks can connect thousands of systems, providing communication links only dreamed of a decade ago. The remarkable improvement in the capabilities of computing equipment from one decade to the next excites researchers, developers, and entrepreneurs, as well as the battalions of journalists who document these events in newspapers and magazines. Yet, although we are frequently told that we are in the midst of a momentous "computer revolution," people who use the term rarely tell us precisely what it means.[1]

Accounts of the powerful information-processing capabilities of computer systems are usually central to many stories of computerization and social change. *Authors write about these changes in technology and social life with different analytical and rhetorical strategies* (Kling and Iacono, 1988; Kling and Iacono, 1990; Kling, 1994). Some authors enchant us with images of new technologies that offer exciting possibilities of manipulating large amounts of information rapidly with little effort, to enhance control, to create insights, to search for information, and to facilitate cooperative work between people. Terms like "virtual," "smart," and "intelligent" are often sprinkled through these accounts and help give them a buoyant image. Much less frequently, authors examine a darker social vision when any likely form of computerization will amplify human misery—people sacrificing their freedom to businesses and government agencies, people becoming dependent on complex technologies that they don't comprehend, and sometimes the image of inadvertent global thermonuclear war.

---

[1] The term "computer revolution" is often used more as a moral slogan than as an analytical term. It should mean more than a significant change in the nature and cost of computer technologies. But people who are interested in seeing more computer systems in use refer to this time as a "computer revolution" to help advance their cause. See Kling and Iacono (1990).

Both the optimistic and the pessimistic stories of computerization are often crafted with the conventions of utopian and anti-utopian writing. The utopian and anti-utopian genres of social analysis are about 500 years old, and predate the social sciences by about 350 years. Authors who write within these genres examine certain kinds of social possibilities, and usually extrapolate beyond contemporary technologies and social relationships. Utopian tales are devised to stimulate hope in future possibilities as well as actions to devise a self-fulfilling prophesy. In contrast, anti-utopian tales are devised to stimulate anger at horrible possibilities and actions to avoid disaster.

Although utopian visions often serve important roles in giving people a positive sense of direction, they can mislead when their architects exaggerate the likelihood of easy and desirable social changes. We are particularly interested in what can be learned, and how we can be misled, by a particular brand of utopian thought, *technological utopianism*. This line of analysis places the use of some specific technology, computers, nuclear energy, or low-energy, low-impact technologies, as the central enabling element of a utopian vision.[2] Sometimes people will casually refer to exotic technologies, like pocket computers that understand spoken language, as "utopian gadgets." Technological utopianism does not refer to a set of technologies. It refers to analyses in which the use of specific technologies plays a key role in shaping a utopian social vision, in which their use easily makes life enchanting and liberating for nearly everyone. In contrast, *technological anti-utopianism* examines how certain broad families of technology facilitate a social order that is relentlessly harsh, destructive, and miserable.

This part includes articles by Weiland, Stewart, and Kelly, which illustrate technological utopianism, and articles by Birkerts and Winner, which illustrate technological anti-utopianism. Technological utopianism is particularly influential in North America and often influences writing about new technologies.

Authors craft utopian and anti-utopian writings within a set of conventions that limit what they say. Even though these writings describe possible future events and social forms, their conventions prevent the authors from discussing important social relationships that are also likely. These utopian and anti-utopian writings about computerization form a *genre* of discourse. A genre refers to any body of work that is shaped by a set of conventions. The works that we readily identify as romantic comedies, impressionist paintings, horror films, newspaper editorials, and popular movie reviews

---

[2] See Segal's (1986) article for a description of technological utopianism in the period between 1880 and 1930. The technologies of technological utopians can change from one era to another. But the assumption that a society that adopts the proper technologies will be harmonious and prosperous remains constant.

are constructed with a set of conventions that make them readily intelligible and accessible. Authors and artists who work wholly within the conventions of a genre also limit the kinds of themes that they can effectively examine. Authors of romantic comedies usually don't explore boredom between the romantic partners and the ways that they negotiate their differences, day to day.[3]

This section examines how genre formulas influence writing about computerization that is supposed to be nonfictional, writing in which the author attempts to tell us truths about the world of computerization "out there" and not simply the author's imagination. Many science fiction writers portray vivid technologically utopian and anti-utopian images. But journalists, managers, and computer scientists also organize their stories about computerization in utopian terms in allegedly nonfiction outlets such as *IEEE Spectrum, Communications of the ACM, Scientific American,* and *The New York Times.*

A few of these works, including Weiland's selection about meetings with desktop conferencing systems, are framed in terms of future technologies and related social practices. But many descriptions of the use of current technologies in existing settings are also framed with specific genre conventions. Conventions make works more easily intelligible to their primary audiences. And social analyses of computing are written with genre conventions that limit the kinds of ideas that can be readily examined. Many professionals and scholars who read these social analyses are often unaware of the ways that works are crafted within the conventions of specific genres, and the ways in that these conventions limit as well as facilitate analysis and debate.

Technological Utopianism in Visions of Specific Contexts

Many of the books and articles that are infused with technological utopianism focus on some specific segment of society (e.g., home, schools, factories, or libraries) or on specific technologies (e.g., computer networks or virtual reality).

"2001: A Meetings Odyssey" by Ross Weiland examines how new forms of virtual video conferencing might enable people to have cross-country business meetings from their desktops. Or they might even videoconference from their bedrooms and appear in business clothes to everyone else who is tuned in. Weiland vividly portrays a way that this technology might be used, and emphasizes the benefits of this technology and others that he

---

[3] Scholars have examined the ways that literary formulas shape fiction (Cawelti, 1976), journalistic conventions shape newsmaking (Tuchman, 1978; Campbell, 1991), and academic conventions shape scholarship (McCloskey, 1990; Van Maanen, 1988).

expects to see developed in the next decade. But he mentions potential problems in these words:

> While the techno-types are working to perfect a brand-new field of applied science, sociologists worry about the human element: What about the loss of human contact? What about the employer's enhanced capability to monitor a person's work? Such concerns may well slow the acceptance of desktop videoconferencing. But like the fax and the PC before it, we will embrace this technology in the near future and ask a familiar question: How did we do business without it?

> A picture, even a live-action video, may never substitute for a site inspection. But imagine using these capabilities to conduct a meeting from your desk. Wouldn't you think twice if the alternative were an arduous and costly trip by air?

One of the distinctive features of Weiland's analysis is illustrated in this brief excerpt. He mentions potential problems of desktop conferencing, such as tightening surveillance over people's activities at work. But he doesn't examine them seriously. Rather he trivializes them into minor worries that people will just "get over." People who have become accustomed to new technologies often won't want to return to older forms: inevitably the refrigerator replaces the ice box, the flush toilet replaces the outhouse, the computerized word processor and spell checker replace the typewriter and pen, and so on. But many technological advances are not simple substitutions. For example, we did not simply replace horses and mules with cars and trucks. We have configured an elaborate system of motorized transport, including new roads, traffic regulations, gas stations, repair shops, insurance, and so on. In many cities, cars come first, and pedestrians come second. But many city planners have been finding ways to design downtowns, shopping centers, and residential neighborhoods so that people can walk, drive cars, or even bicycle without feeling unsafe. One hallmark of Weiland's technological utopianism is his unwillingness to acknowledge and examine how desktop conferencing can be done badly, and how deploying these advances in a humane way may entail important kinds of social designs as well as hot technologies. Weiland's analysis is but one illustration of technological utopianism. There are some important technological utopian analyses that emphasize a good life for almost all participants, for example, by democratizing access to important technologies such as computer networks.[4]

The selection by Thomas Stewart illustrates how technological utopian themes can appear in news magazines and business magazines such as *Time, Fortune,* and *Business Week.* Stewart published, "Boom Time on the

---

[4] See my lead article in Part V, "Social Relations in Electronic Forums: Hangouts, Salons, Workplaces, and Communities." Also see the cornucopia of books about empowering uses of communications technologies in Rheingold (1994:242–281).

New Frontier: Growth of Computer Networks" in *Fortune*, a major business magazine, in 1993. In contrast with Weiland, Stewart focuses on emerging trends for which he can provide concrete examples today:

> The future of information technology descends upon us in a swarm of buzzwords: global village, electronic superhighway, information age, electronic frontier. Someday soon, cyberspace—the vast, intangible territory where computers meet and exchange information—will be populated with electronic communities and businesses. In your home, a protean box will hook you into a wealth of goods and services. It will receive and send mail, let you make a phone or video call or send a fax or watch a movie or buy shoes or diagnose a rash or pay bills or get cash (a new digital kind) or write your mother. That will be just the living-room manifestation of what promises to be a radical—and rapid—transformation of commerce and society, the greatest since the invention of the automobile.

> The process has already begun. In Japan, used-car dealers gather via their computers on Saturday mornings to take part in an electronic auction, buying and selling cars by pressing the button on a joystick. In New York City, a seller of surgical gauze and other medical disposables recently logged on to a global electronic bulletin board operated by the World Trade Center and found a supplier in China. Now, instead of buying from U.S. wholesalers, he sells to them. The largest market in the world—the trillion or so dollars a day in international currency transactions—runs almost entirely over networks.

> During the next few years, electronic markets will grow and begin operating over cheap, accessible public networks—the so-called electronic highway. Just as railroads opened the West, the highway will open wide the electronic frontier. Whole industries will be destroyed and new ones born; productivity will leap and competitive advantage shift in the direction of small business.

The technological utopianism in this article is not simply signaled by Stewart's buoyant optimism about the growth of "electronic commerce" and growth of services on the Internet. It is marked by his failure to carefully engage critical questions about the downsides of the explosion of excitement over computer networks. He starts by noting the flurry of buzzwords that journalists, technologists, and scholars use in discussions of computer networking: global village, electronic superhighway, information age, and electronic frontier. But he then quickly picks up "cyberspace" and launches his analysis of emerging trends and significant examples.

Stewart's article builds on the recent and growing public popularity of the Internet in the United States. President Bill Clinton and Vice-President Al Gore stimulated substantial interest in computer networks (and the Internet) through their promotion of "information superhighways," or The National Information Infrastructure (NII). In 1992, most professionals outside of the computer industry, research institutes, and academia had never heard of the Internet. By 1994, many people who didn't know what the Internet was wanted accounts to access it so that they wouldn't be left out. Bookstores that carried a few books about services on the Internet soon devoted whole shelves to the topic. Many of these books are rather practical guidebooks that describe diverse services (such as e-mail, LIST-SERVs, gopher, ftp, and World Wide Web) and inform readers about specific examples and some pragmatics of using specific software. These books are generally buoyant about network services, but are not structured within technologically utopian conventions. While they encourage people to try out the Internet, they don't promise people that widescale network use will eliminate social ills such as street crime, social isolation, lifelong poverty, and unemployment! But people often turn to them after their interest has been piqued by articles such as Stewart's.

It is unfortunate that the executive branch of the United States federal government has not been a good source of studies that would help us understand the possibilities, but also the dilemmas and social choices, of a society that depends as much on computer networks for daily services as we have come to depend on the motorized transport system for cars, buses, and trucks. For example, a recent federal report about the NII discusses the ways that "improvements in the technical foundation upon which modern communications rests can benefit all Americans" (IITF, 1994). This report relentlessly focuses on computer networking in applications like digital libraries, lifelong learning, manufacturing, and commercial transactions. The authors of this report emphasize the way that the widespread expansion of computer networks can vitalize numerous aspects of business activity and social life in the United States. Like Weiland and Stewart, they occasionally mention potential problems, and then rapidly skate by them.

Utopian Social Visions

I have selected articles that illustrate the ways in which technologically utopian analyses shape some key discussions about the social possibilities of computerization. Utopian thinkers portray whole societies whose members live ideal lives. The first such description appeared in Plato's *Republic,* written some 2500 years ago. But the name "Utopia" derives from Thomas More, who in 1516 published a story about an ideal society where people lived harmoniously and free of privation. More's fanciful name, which literally meant "nowhere," has been picked up and applied to a whole tradition of writing and thinking about the forms of society that would supposedly make many people happiest.

There have been hundreds of utopian blueprints. They differ substantially in their details: some have focused on material abundance as the key to human happiness, while others have advanced ideal visions of austerity and simplicity. Some utopian thinkers advocate private property as a central social institution, while alternative visions place a premium on shared property.

The most obvious utopian sources are discourses that the authors explicitly identify as fictional accounts, complete with traditional devices such as invented characters and fanciful dialogue. But here we are concerned with discourses about computerization, which authors present as primarily realistic or factual accounts (and which are cataloged as nonfiction in bookstores and libraries).

Utopian images permeate the literatures about computerization in society. I don't criticize utopian ideals that emphasize a good life for all. After all, the United States was founded on premises that were utopian in the 1700s. The Declaration of Independence asserts that "all men are created equal" and that they would be guaranteed the right to "life, liberty, and the pursuit of happiness." This sentiment stood in significant contrast to the political cultures of the European monarchies of the time, where the rule of the king or queen, along with nobles (most of whom were "elected" by heredity) determined people's fates. Of course, asserting the right to "life, liberty, and the pursuit of happiness" as universal didn't immediately make it so. Until 1865, for example, slaves were legally property, and could be bought and sold, told where to live, and broken apart from their families. Women were not allowed to vote until 1919. And even in 1963, Martin Luther King's major speech about a country free of racial discrimination was called "I Have a Dream," not "An Old Dream Has Now Come True."

Furthermore, utopian ideals are hard to put into practice. Their advocates often have to fight hard to change social practices to better fit their ideals. The United States broke free of the English Crown through a four-year war. Almost two hundred years later, Martin Luther King and others advanced the cause of improved civil rights in the United States through aggressive confrontations: marches, rallies, court injunctions, and sit-ins, as well as through more quiet persuasion. The resulting social changes, which altered the balance of privilege and exploitation, did not come quietly and peacefully. Nor have the utopian dreams of our nation's founders been fully achieved after two hundred years of struggle.

Visions of Computerized Societies

So far, I have discussed technological utopian accounts that focus on some specific area of social life, such as desktop conferencing or electronic commerce. The classical utopian writings were much more expansive because their authors examined whole societies, and discussed leisure as well as work, child rearing as well as schooling, and so on. There are some relatively broad technological utopian accounts that focus on computerization. But more frequently, we find powerful images that link computerization and social change characterized with sweeping terms like "computer revolution," "information society," and "intelligent machine." These catch phrases have strong metaphorical associations, and are often introduced by authors to advance positive, exciting images of computerization.

"The Electronic Hive" by Kevin Kelly illustrates this more expansive and almost poetic writing. Kelly's essay is drawn from his recent book, *Out of Control: The Rise of Neo-Biological Civilization*, 1994, which examines how emerging computer technologies may develop like biological collectives: beehives. In this selection, Kelly examines some parallels that he sees between bee colonies and computer networks, especially the groups of people who use the Internet. Kelly argues that humanity is moving to a new stage of technological co-evolution with decentralized systems, like the Internet, and that computer networks provide new opportunities for people to deepen their communications with others. As in the previous selections, the technological utopianism of Kelly's essay (and his much longer book) is constructed from the troubling questions that he ignores as well as from the buoyant themes and examples that he examines explicitly.[5]

Kelly writes about the epochal changes in whole societies, much like George Gilder and Alvin Toffler. Alvin Toffler's best seller of the early 1980s, *The Third Wave,* helped stimulate popular enthusiasm for computerization. Toffler characterized major social transformations in terms of large shifts in the organization of society, driven by technological change. The "Second Wave" was the shift from agricultural societies to industrial societies. Toffler contrasts industrial ways of organizing societies to new social trends that he links to computer and microelectronic technologies. He is masterful at employing succinct, breathless prose to suggest major social changes. He also invented terminology to help characterize some of these social changes, terms like "second wave," "third wave," "electronic cottage," "infosphere," "technosphere," "prosumer," and "intelligent environment." Many of Toffler's new terms did not become commonly accepted. Even so, they help frame a seductive description of progressive social change stimulated by new technologies. The breathless enthusiasm can be contagious, but it also stymies critical thought. Authors like Toffler, Gilder, and Kelly open up important questions about how information technologies alter the ways that people perceive information, the kinds of information they can get easily, how they handle the information they get, and the forms of social life that we develop. Yet these accounts often caricature key answers by using only illustrations that support their generally buoyant theses. And they skillfully sidestep tough questions while creating a sense of excitement about the new.

Technological Anti-Utopianism

Some important writings about the social changes linked to computerization criticize utopian assumptions. In fact, some authors articulate a comparably dark "anti-utopian" view of computerization.[6]

---

[5] For a more extended criticism of a vision similar to Kelly's, see Max Dublin's analysis of Stuart Brand's book, *The Media Lab,* in *Futurehype* (1989:89–94).

[6] Ian Reinecke's book, *Electronic Illusions: A Skeptic's View of Our High Tech Future,* and Mander (1991) are examples.

Joseph Weizenbaum, in his popular book, *Computer Power and Human Reason*, observes:

> Our society's growing reliance on computer systems that were initially intended to "help" people make analyses and decisions, but which have long since surpassed the understanding of their users and become indispensable to them is a very serious development. First, decisions are made with the aid of, and sometimes entirely by, computers whose programs no one any longer knows explicitly or understand since no one can know the criteria or rules on which such decisions are based. Second, the rules and criteria that are embedded in such computer systems become immune to change, because, in the absence of detailed understanding of the inner workings of a computer system, any substantial modification of it is very likely to render the whole system inoperable and possibly unrestorable. Such computer systems can therefore only grow. And their growth and the increasing reliance placed on them is then accompanied by an increasing legitimation of their "knowledge base." (1976:236–237)[7]

Weizenbaum criticizes visions of computerized databases that record historical data because they usually eliminate important information that is too complex or costly to include:

> The computer has thus begun to be an instrument for the destruction of history. For when society legitimates only those "data" that are in one standard format, then history, memory itself, is annihilated. *The New York Times* has already begun to build a "data bank" of current events. Of course, only those data that are easily derivable as by-products of typesetting machines are admissible to the system. As the number of subscribers to this system grows, as they learn to rely more and more upon "all the news that [was once] fit to print,"[8] as the *Times* proudly identifies its editorial policy, how long will it be before what counts as fact is determined by the system, before all other knowledge, all memory, is simply declared illegitimate? Soon a supersystem will be built, based on *The New York Times'* data bank (or one very much like it), from which "historians" will make inferences about what "really" happened, about who is connected to whom, and about the "real" logic of events. . . . (Weizenbaum, 1976:238)

Weizenbaum's observations gain more force when one realizes that journalists often don't simply report "the facts." They tend to rely on standard sources, voices of publicly legitimate authority, in framing stories. For example, when a university alters a curriculum, deans and professors

---

[7] Weizenbaum goes on to describe the ways in which computer systems selected bombing targets during the late 1960s' American war in Vietnam. Mathematical criteria were used to select which hamlets were friendly enough to escape attack and which were not, which areas had enough Viet Cong to warrant declaration as "free fire zones," and so on. Weizenbaum asserts, probably correctly, that the officers who operated these systems did not understand their calculations (Weizenbaum, 1976, p. 238).

[8] *The New York Times*'s masthead slogan is "All the news that's fit to print."

are more likely than students are to appear in the resulting news story. Gaye Tuchman characterized reporters in search of a story as casting a selective "newsnet" around their favorite kinds of sources. Journalists often don't cast their nets to give equal voice to all kinds of informed parties. While reporters are much more likely to go to "the grass roots" today than they were in the 1950s, each newspaper prints a mix of stories in a style that reflects a relatively stable character. Even if the mastheads were interchanged, one would not confuse *The New York Times* with a small-town weekly newspaper.[9]

Moreover, Weizenbaum speaks with authority about future events ("Soon a supersystem will be built . . ."). Without special design, nothing in the database technology itself would be likely to give the user a clue about its real limitations in representing a narrow range of perspectives. I don't worry much about professional historians who have developed strong criteria for verifying events by appeal to a variety of corroborating sources. Nonetheless, the convenience of database technology makes it tempting for others to rely on it as a primary source, without appreciating its shortcomings.[10] That is the cautionary note that one might draw from Weizenbaum's bitter observations.

But Weizenbaum's argument is primarily polemical. He doesn't discuss any virtues of news databases, or conditions under which they might not have the deleterious consequences he identifies. After all, news databases can substantially assist in useful research as long as they do not become a sole source of information.

Two more selections in Part II illustrate different styles of technological anti-utopian writing. Sven Birkerts essay "The Electronic Hive—Refuse It" comes from his larger book *The Gutenberg Elegies: The Fate of Reading in the Electronic Age*. Birkerts's essay serves as a vivid counterpoint to Kevin Kelly's essay by criticizing as alienating the kind of enmeshment in nets that Kelly finds so satisfying. Birkerts is particularly concerned that humanly meaningful events and experiences are most often anchored in human-scale and bodily experiences. While we can send messages across a computer net in a few seconds, or even milliseconds, we don't have meaningful conversations or meaningful life experiences in seconds or milliseconds. Computer networks can be seductive places to work, play, and communicate. But Birkerts views them as further removing people from their natural worlds, much as life in the largest paved and built-up

---

[9] For a readable and revealing account about the way that newspapers shape the reports that appear as "news," see Robert Karl Manoff and Michael Schudson (eds.), *Reading the News*. New York, Pantheon Books, 1986.
[10] See "The Nexis Nightmare" by Christopher J. Feola (1994) for a discussion of the ways that reporters in small-town newspapers have made embarrassing errors by trusting news databases, such as Nexis.

cities has removed us from the rhythms and textures of the natural world. Where Kelly sees computer networks as deepening people's humanity, Birkerts sees them as fundamentally alienating.

Langdon Winner's short description of worklife in electronic offices ("Electronic Office: Playpen or Poison") serves as a counterpoint to Weiland's essay about desktop conferencing, as well as to Kelly's essay about the new freedoms of computer networks. Winner distinguishes three classes of participants: technical professionals, ordinary workers, and upper managers. His brief vignette indicates that each group experiences different kinds of work worlds. The technical professionals are likely to have significant freedom in maneuvering through computer networks and communicating with their co-workers. He claims that "ordinary workers" (who seem to be primarily clerical), are highly regimented and that their performance is tightly monitored through computerized control systems. Last, upper managers sit outside of these computer networks, and constrain their workers within them.

Winner echoes Birkerts's concern that people will be further alienated through the use of computer networks through his sarcastic characterization of technical professionals:

> They experience computer networks as spheres of democratic or even anarchic activity. Especially for those ill at ease in the physical presence of others (a feeling not uncommon among male engineers), the phenomenon of disembodied space seems to offer comfort and fulfillment. Here are new opportunities for self-expression, creativity, and a sense of mastery! Some begin to feel they are most alive, most free when wandering through the networks; they often "disappear" into them for days on end. (Winner, 1992:57)

Technological anti-utopians craft tragedies that serve as counterpoints to the technological utopians inspiring romances. Technological anti-utopianism is a particular form of cultural criticism that portrays the troublesome potentials of new technologies as relentlessly harsh. For example, both Birkerts and Winner acknowledge that people may enjoy playing with and communicating through computer networks. But they portray them as superficial seductions that suck the life from people's souls, much like heroin.

Conventions of Technological Utopianism and Anti-Utopianism

Utopian and anti-utopian analysts paint their portraits of computerization with monochromatic brushes: white or black. The anti-utopians' characterizations of the tragic possibilities of computerization provide an essential counterbalance to the giddy-headed optimism of the utopian accounts. The romances and tragedies are not all identical. For example, some anti-utopian writings examine the possibilities of computerized systems for coercion, while others emphasize alienation. But the utopian and anti-utopian genres have some important inherent limitations.

It is usually unclear how a social group can move from where it is to the more utopian social order. Computer specialists, like most scientists and technologists, aren't taught how to asses the social viability of different clusters of social assumptions. Nor are computer specialists taught to understand the dynamics of social change.

Utopian visions are sometimes characterized as "reality transcending" (Kumar, 1987, 1991). They play important roles in stimulating hope and giving people a positive sense of direction. But they can mislead when their architects exaggerate the likelihood of easy and desirable social changes. Writing about technological utopianism in the 1930s, Wilson, Pilgrim, and Tasjian (1986:335) comment:

> Belief in the limitless future potential of the machine had both its positive and negative aspects. During the 1930s this almost blind faith in the power of the machine to make the world a better place helped hold a badly shattered nation together. . . . These science fiction fantasies contributed to an almost naive approach to serious problems and a denial of problems that could already be foreseen.

In any of its forms, technological utopianism can be exciting and expand the range of people's visions of what is possible.

> Utopia confronts reality not with a measured assessment of the possibilities of change but with the demand for change. This is the way the world should be. It refuses to accept current definitions of the possible because it knows these to be a part of the reality it seeks to change. In its guise as utopia, by the very force of its imaginative presentation, it energizes reality, infusing it . . . with "the power of the new." (Kumar, 1991:107)

But in characterizing "a world that should be," technological utopians embed specific commitments to ways of life within their visions. Part II, Chapter B, Ross Weiland expresses his enthusiasm for desktop video conferencing in terms that trivialize any serious discussion of the ways of living and working with and without these technologies. I repeat some of his comments here:

> While the techno-types are working to perfect a brand-new field of applied science, sociologists worry about the human element: What about the loss of human contact? What about the employer's enhanced capability to monitor a person's work? Such concerns may well slow the acceptance of desktop videoconferencing. But like the fax and the PC before it, we will embrace this technology in the near future and ask a familiar question: How did we do business without it?

We can extract a set of Weiland's demands from this brief passage: ignore the possible loss of human contact; ignore the employer's enhanced capability to monitor a person's work; embrace desktop videoconferencing soon; do not do business without it.

The actual uses and consequences of developing computer systems depend on the "way the world works." Conversely, computerized systems may slowly, but inexorably, change "the way the world works," often with unforeseen consequences. A key issue is how to understand the social opportunities and dilemmas of computerization without becoming seduced by the social simplifications of utopian romance, or becoming discouraged by anti-utopian nightmares. Both kinds of images are far too simplified. But they do serve to help identify an interesting and important set of social possibilities.

Anti-utopian writings are far less numerous in the United States. They serve as an important counterbalance to technological utopianism. But they could encourage a comparably ineffective sense of despair and inaction. Utopian and anti-utopian visions embody extreme assumptions about technology and human behavior. But their causal simplicity gives them great clarity and makes them easy to grasp, to enjoy or to abhor. They can resonate with our dreams or nightmares. Consequently, they have immense influence in shaping the discussions (and real directions) of computerization.

Writings in each genre have formulaic limits much in the way that romantic fiction (or any other literary genre) has important limits (Cawelti, 1976). Cawelti notes that "The moral fantasy of the romance is that of love triumphant and permanent, overcoming all obstacles and difficulties" (Cawelti, 1976:41–42). This does not mean that we can't be entertained or our appreciation of life enriched by romantic fictions; it is simply a genre with important formulaic limits. The moral fantasies of technological utopianism and anti-utopianism similarly limit what they can teach us about the likely social realities of new forms of computerization: one is romantic and the other is tragic.

The Social Production
of Technologically Utopian Materials

Technological utopian and anti-utopian analyses of computing do not "just appear" in journals, magazines, and books. Their production and publication have some social organization, although not a simple one. Firms marketing their services and products through advertisements, product brochures, and broadcasting is one kind of large-scale social process that couples utopian imagery and computerization.[11] Typical business journalism is also a systematic source.

---

[11] In some special cases firms might market against computerization. Sabatier and Henckel are two European firms that manufacture high-quality kitchen knives. Sabatier published an

55555

Let's take a simple journalistic example. The editorial staff of a business magazine may agree that an article about the ways that work is changing in "virtual offices" would appeal to an important segment of readers. Before she writes her story the reporter might have a few weeks to read some background materials and contact a set of people who might be plausible experts for more details and lively quotes. She might develop a list that includes firms that have reputedly reduced their physical office space and created some virtual offices, consultants who advise about these business practices, and professors who are developing advanced versions of possibly relevant technologies, such as computer conferencing systems. Many of these informants have an interest in putting a positive spin on virtual offices. If the managers are willing to be quoted, they would like their firms to appear well managed in the magazine story. The professors believe in the potential contributions of their technologies, and would like to stimulate more interest in them. So they will also emphasize interesting ways to organize with them. The consultants might like their names in the article to help stimulate new business for them. They have an interest in suggesting that virtual offices can be tricky to organize well, but that they can be good and productive workplaces with the right consultant on hand to provide wise advice. The reporter would like to publish an engaging story, and business reporters often seem to push for short, vivid quotes (sometimes called soundbites in television).

Business reporters often produce stories with a technologically utopian spin (like the selection by Stewart about electronic commerce) out of a research process like this. It's an exciting story about a possible business trend. The reporter will usually strive to construct the story within a frame that readers can readily grasp. Technological utopianism and technological anti-utopianism are two such frames whose conventions readers can easily understand.

In addition to advertising and journalism, there is a third important large-scale social process that results in numerous books and articles about computerization that are framed in technologically utopian terms. "Computerization movements" refer to loosely organized collections of groups that promote specific forms of computerization, such as computer networking or instructing computing.

---

ad in the 1990s, which pictured one 10-inch black-handled, steel chef's knife from each company and included the following text:

> Both knives cost the same, but the one on the left is cheaper. It is Henckel's Four Star chef's knife. And a shadow of its former self. On the right is France's own Cuisine de France Sabatier chef's knife. A masterpiece of culinary art. Let us compare, shall we?

Sabatier's ad lists several alleged advantages over the visually similar Henckel, including this:

> The Henckel's is handled by robots. This is a slap in the face to all who value the knifemaker's art.

This ad caught my attention because computerized processes are usually treated as advantages in advertisements. Of course, this is Sabatier's ad, not Henckel's.

Computerization movements are like other kinds of movements that engage people in diverse organized activities with an interest in gaining broader support: political movements, like the civil rights movement; art movements, like surrealism; religious movements, like fundamentalist Christianity. Certainly, political, art, and religious movements differ in their public goals, the ways that they recruit members, their collective activities, and so on. But they share important commonalities. They also give us insights into sources of technologically utopian and anti-utopian writings written by professionals (in addition to ad copy and journalism). In the last section of Part II, "Computerization Movements and Tales of Technological Utopianism," Suzanne Iacono and I examine these sources in some detail. We examine two computerization movements, computer-based education and computer networking. But we could have examined other computerization movements as well, such as those that promote digital libraries or artificial intelligence. One of the surprising aspects of our analysis is that we treat these technologies as the products of social movements rather than the products of research labs and industrial firms.

As we approach the year 2000, there will be a large market for social analyses of computerization stimulated by:

- the steady stream of computing innovations;
- the drive by academic computer science departments and federal funding agencies to justify large expenditures on computing research;
- justifications for major national computerization programs, such as an expansion of the National Information Infrastructure; and
- articles examining life and technology in the twenty-first century.

Many social analyses of computing that appear in popular and professional magazines, as well as in newspapers and the trade press, will be strongly influenced by technologically utopian assumptions. Consequently, sophisticated professionals and researchers should be specially aware of the strengths and limitations of this genre of analysis.

Beyond Technological Utopianism and Anti-Utopianism

The selections and quotations introduce some of the controversies about the visions of computerization: To what extent are utopian or anti-utopian visions helpful in understanding the social possibilities of computerization? To what extent is social realism a more interesting and reliable guide to the future than the more utopian or anti-utopian visions? If one doesn't trust the anti-utopian or utopian visions, how does one develop a broad framework for asking questions about *what should be done,* what activities should be computerized, in what way, and with what associated practices?

Attractive alternatives to utopian and anti-utopian analyses should be more credible in characterizing conflict in a social order, the distribution of knowledge, the ways of solving problems that arise from new technologies.

They should rest upon less deterministic logics of social change.[12] Most important, they would identify the social contingencies that make technologies (un)workable and social changes that are benign or harmful for diverse groups.

"Social realism" refers to a genre that uses empirical data to examine computerization as it is actually practiced and experienced (Kling, 1994). Social realists write their articles and books with a tacit label: "I have carefully observed and examined computerization in some key social settings and I will tell you how it *really* is." The most common methods are those of journalism and the social sciences, such as critical inquiries, and ethnography. But the genre is best characterized by the efforts of authors to communicate their understanding of computerization as it "really works" based on reporting fine-grained empirical detail. Social realism gains its force through gritty observations about the social worlds in which computer systems are used.[13]

Social realist analyses often acknowledge complex patterns of social conflict, and yet are more open-ended and contingent than both genres of utopian analysis. In the following parts of this book, you will find many social realist analyses of computerization.

Sources

Birkerts, Sven (1994). "The Electronic Hive—Refuse It." *Harper's,* 228 (1728) (May): 17–20. (Adapted from *The Gutenberg Elegies: The Fate of Reading in an Electronic Age* (1994). Faber and Faber.

Kelly, Kevin (1994). "The Electronic Hive—Embrace It." *Harper's Magazine,* 228(1728)(May):20–25. (Adapted from *Out of Control: The Rise of Neo-Biological Civilization* (1994). Addison-Wesley.

Stewart, Thomas A. (1993). "Boom Time on the New Frontier: Growth of Computer Networks." *Fortune,* 128(7)(Autumn):153–161.

Weiland, Ross (1993). "2001: A Meetings Odyssey." *Successful Meetings,* 42(13)(Part 1, December):34–39.

Winner, Langdon (1992). "Virtual Office or Electronic Prison" excerpt from "Silicon Valley Mystery House," in Michael Sorkin (ed.), *Variations on a Theme-Park: The New American City and the End of Public Space.* Noonday Press, New York.

References

Campbell, Richard (1991). *60 Minutes and the News: A Mythology for Middle America.* University of Illinois Press, Chicago.

---

[12] See Kling (1994) and Kling and Lamb (in press) for substantially more detailed discussions of the utopian genres and empirically anchored alternatives.

[13] Kling's (1994) article contrasts the strengths and weaknesses of the utopian genres with social realism in substantial detail.

Cawelti, John (1976). *Adventure, Mystery and Romance: Formula Stories as Art and Popular Culture.* University of Chicago Press, Chicago.

Dorf, Richard C., and Yvonne L. Hunter (eds.) (1978). *Appropriate Visions: Technology, the Environment and the Individual.* Boyd and Fraser, San Francisco.

Dublin, Max (1989). *Futurehype: The Tyranny of Prophesy.* Viking, New York.

Feola, Christopher J. (1994). "The Nexis Nightmare." *American Journalism Review,* (July/August):38–42.

Information Infrastructure Task Force (1994). Putting the Information Infrastructure to Work. (May 3). URL, Washington, DC. gopher://iitfcat.nist.gov:95/11/

Kling, Rob (1994). "Reading "All About" Computerization: How Genre Conventions Shape Non-Fiction Social Analysis." *The Information Society,* 10:147–172.

Kling, Rob, and Suzanne Iacono (1988). "The Mobilization of Support for Computerization: The Role of Computerization Movements." *Social Problems,* 35(3) (June):226–243.

Kling, Rob, and Suzanne Iacono (1990). "Making a Computer Revolution." *Journal of Computing and Society,* 1(1):43–58. [Reprinted in Charles Dunlop and Rob Kling (eds.) (1991). *Computerization and Controversy: Value Conflicts and Social Choices.* Academic Press, San Diego.]

Kling, Rob, and Roberta Lamb (in press). "Conceptualizing Electronic Publishing and Digital Libraries," in Robin M. Peek, Lois Lunin, Gregory Newby, and Gerald Miller (eds.), *Academia and Electronic Publishing: Confronting the Year 2000.* MIT Press, Cambridge, MA.

Kling, Rob and Roberta Lamb (in press). "Analyzing Visions of Electronic Publishing and Digital Libraries," in Gregory B. Newby and Robin M. Peek (eds.), *Scholarly Publishing: The Electronic Frontier.* MIT Press, Cambridge, MA.

Kumar, Krishan (1987). *Utopia and Anti-Utopia in Modern Times.* Basil Blackwell, New York.

Kumar, Krishan (1991). *Utopianism.* University of Minnesota Press, Minneapolis.

Reinecke, Ian (1984). *Electronic Illusions: A Skeptic's View of Our High Tech Future.* Penguin, New York.

Rheingold, Howard (ed.) (1994). *The Millenium Whole Earth Catalog.* Harper, San Francisco.

Segal, Howard P. (1986). "The Technological Utopians," in Joseph J. Corn (ed.), *Imagining Tomorrow: History, Technology and the American Future.* The MIT Press, Cambridge.

Toffler, Alvin (1980). *The Third Wave.* Bantam Books, New York.

Tuchman, Gaye (1978). *Making News: A Study in the Construction of Reality.* Free Press, New York.

Van Maanen, John (1988). *Tales from the Field: On Writing Ethnography.* University of Chicago Press, Chicago.

Weizenbaum, Joseph (1976). *Computer Power and Human Reason.* Freeman Publishing, San Francisco.

Wilson, Richard Guy, Dianne H. Pilgrim, and Dickran Tasjian (1986). *The Machine Age in America: 1918–1941.* Harry Abrams, New York.

Further Reading

Berry, Wendell (1990). "Why I Am Not Going to Buy a Computer." From *What Are People for? Essays by Wendell Berry.* North Point Press. [Reprinted in Charles

Dunlop and Rob Kling (eds.) (1991). *Computerization and Controversy: Value Conflicts and Social Choices.* Academic Press, San Diego.]

Boguslaw, Robert (1965). *The New Utopians: A Study of System Design and Social Change.* Prentice Hall, Englewood Cliffs.

Book, James and Iain A. Boal (eds.). (1995). *Resisting the Virtual Life.* City Lights Books, San Francisco, CA.

Daedelus of the New Scientist (1970). "Pure Technology." *Technology Review,* (June):38–45. (Reprinted in Alfred Teich (ed.), *Technology and Man's Future,* 1st edition. St. Martin's Press, New York.

Dunlop, Charles, and Rob Kling (eds.) (1991). *Computerization and Controversy: Value Conflicts and Social Choices.* Academic Press, Boston.

Feigenbaum, Edward, and Pamela McCorduck (1983). *The Fifth Generation: Artificial Intelligence and Japan's Computer Challenge to the World.* Addison-Wesley, Reading. (Excerpted in Dunlop and Kling (eds.), *Computerization and Controversy,* 1991.)

Garson, David (1995). *Computer Technology and Social Issues.* Idea Group Publishing, Harrisburg, PA.

Glendinning, Chellis (1990). *When Technology Wounds: The Human Consequences of Progress.* William Morrow, New York.

Kozol, Jonathan (1988). *Illiterate America.* Anchor Press/Doubleday, Garden City.

Kurzweil, Raymond (1990). *The Age of Intelligent Machines.* MIT Press, Cambridge.

Lyon, David (1988). *The Information Society: Issues and Illusions.* Polity Press, Cambridge, England.

Mander, Jerry (1991). *In the Absence of the Sacred: The Failure of Technology and the Survival of the Indian Nations.* Sierra Club Books, San Francisco.

Marvin, Carolyn (1988). *When Old Technologies Were New: Thinking about Electric Communication in the Late Nineteenth Century.* Oxford University Press, New York.

McCloskey, Donald (1990). *If You're So Smart: the Narrative of Economic Expertise.* University of Chicago Press, Chicago.

Schement, Jorge Reine (1995). *Tendencies and Tensions in the Information Society.* Transaction Books, New Brunswick, NJ.

Sculley, John (1989). "The Relationship Between Business and Higher Education: A Perspective on the Twenty-first Century." *Communications of the ACM,* 32(9) (September):1056–1061. [Reprinted in Charles Dunlop and Rob Kling (eds.) (1991). *Computerization and Controversy: Value Conflicts and Social Choices.* Academic Press, San Diego.]

Singer, Eleanor, and Phyllis Endreny (1993). *Reporting on Risk.* Russell Sage, New York.

Talbott, Stephen (1995). *The Future Does Not Compute: Transcending the Machines in Our Midst.* O'Reilly & Associates, Inc., Sebastapol, CA.

Todd, Ian, and Michael Wheeler (1978). *Utopia.* Harmony Books, New York.

Webster, Frank (1994). "What Information Society?" *Information Society,* 10(1) (January–March):1–23.

Webster, Frank (in press). *Theories of the Information Society.* Routledge, London.

Webster, Frank, and Kevin Robins (1986). *Information Technology: A Luddite Analysis.* Ablex Publ. Co., Norwood, NJ.

Wright, Karen (1990). "Trends in Communications: The Road to the Global Village." *Scientific American,* 262(3)(March):83–94.

P·A·R·T · II

B

2001: A Meetings Odyssey[*]

Ross Weiland

Waves rumble quietly against the shore. Gulls squawk in the distance. The sun peeks over the horizon, gradually bringing more light into your day. Rubbing the sleep from your eyes and grabbing your bathrobe, you mumble, "Check messages." The 8-foot-by-10-foot ocean view at the foot of your bed clicks off, replaced by your computer-generated assistant who informs you of a morning seminar with the president of XYZ Corporation. You move to the next room, still in your bathrobe. The room is empty except for a leather lounge chair. You get comfortable, don your virtual-reality goggles, and say, "I'm ready for the meeting."

Suddenly, you're sitting in a conference room wearing a gray suit. The XYZ president is up front at a podium. In the sixth row of a packed hall, you sit next to a woman in a blue dress. You recognize her, but she doesn't see you. "Cameras on," you say. The woman notices you for the first time. "I was wondering when you'd get here," she says. "It's about to start."

The president clears his throat and delivers his presentation. Afterward, you approach the podium and shake his hand. Then you walk to a corner and quietly say, "Cameras off." Immediately, you're back in the lounge chair wearing your bathrobe. You remove the goggles and mumble to your assistant, "Set the wake-up program to begin in another thirty minutes." You drop your bathrobe and climb back into bed.

In just six years, on Saturday, January 1, 2000, we cross the threshold into a new century and enter a future that dreamers have long envisioned as featuring space stations, interplanetary travel, and world peace. These may turn out to be idealistic dreams. But with the technological advances already experienced, is the virtual reality meeting so far-fetched? In 1980, we didn't have voice mail, fax machines, PCs (certainly not laptops), or cellular phones. Now we do. And technological innovation only continues to accelerate. By 2000, the way we do business, communicate, learn, and yes, meet will have changed dramatically. The knowledge we use today will be largely obsolete. So will many of the tools.

"In the ten years before and after the turn of a century, the activity is frenetic. We run to change, to do, and to accomplish," says Don Libey, marketing and management consultant and president of The Libey Consultancy in Haddon Heights, New Jersey. "We are trying to do everything in the ten years before the change [of the century]. And in the ten years after, we're fixing everything we did wrong. That twenty-year span of time is absolutely rampant, dominant, chaotic change. It happened in the sixteenth century, the seventeenth century, the eighteenth century, the nineteenth century, and it's happening now," he says.

Technology versus Humanity

Rapid change comes with a red flag, however. A danger exists in being overrun with technology, whether it's the automatic-teller machine or virtual reality. A danger not lost on Patricia Aburdene, co-author of Megatrends 2000. She cites a phenomenon she calls high-tech/high-touch, "The more technology you have in your office and at your house, the more you need to balance that with the high touch of the personal meeting," she says.

This balance of technology and humanity will harness the pace of change somewhat for the meetings industry, allowing planners the opportunity to adapt and keep up with the onslaught. "The industry will change, but it's going to be spotty change," argues Dr. Tom McDonald, a speaker, trainer, and psychologist based in La Jolla, California. "The high-tech promise never lives up to its projections in the short term."

Why? Because although people will eventually embrace high-tech advances, they also traditionally fight change. Look at the personal computer, for example. PCs have revolutionized the workplace. Yet according to McDonald, "People today use PCs at ten percent of their effectiveness. The technology always outdoes the people."

The increasing speed and power with which computers accomplish tasks are staggering. The volume of information they can gather and distribute continues to grow. By the time the capabilities of today's PCs are accepted and used by the masses, third and fourth generations of the machines will have already been developed.

---

*This article originally appeared in *Successful Meetings*, 42(13) Pt. 1 (December 1993):34–39. Reprinted with permission of Bill Communications, Inc.

The microprocessor that runs the computer on your desk today is already being replaced by a communications laser that uses a compact disc (CD) instead of a floppy disk. In the not-too-distant future, your computer monitor will hang like a picture, filling most of an office wall. The monitor will bring live video and audio into your office and be capable of splitting into several different screens to simultaneously communicate with a number of other people.

And the almighty PC? It will eventually be replaced by a workstation that connects the user to ever-expanding highways of information. The workstation will handle phone calls, faxes, and E-mail. Research, creation, and distribution of documents will take place through the workstation. And, yes, meetings will be conducted through the workstation.

Desktop videoconferencing products have already arrived. The PC that sits on your desk today can become a meeting site. As the decade comes to an end, the slight but perceptible delay between video and audio will be bridged, video transmission will be standardized at broadcast quality, and various manufacturers' products will interface with ease. With a large monitor divided into segments, you will be able to see and talk with several other people dialing in from their offices or homes simultaneously. Like the PC of ten years ago, the workstation of ten years from now will revolutionize the business of doing business.

There's tremendous potential in technology that allows people to bridge distances effortlessly. The new buzzword in videoconferencing is "conference on demand." No need to schedule special rooms or equipment. Just push the Conference button on your touchtone phone, switch on the high-resolution color camera on top of your PC, and you're ready to meet with others in your organization or outside it.

While the techno-types are working to perfect a brand-new field of applied science, sociologists worry about the human element: What about the loss of human contact? What about the employer's enhanced capability to monitor a person's work? Such concerns may well slow the acceptance of desktop videoconferencing. But like the fax and the PC before it, we will embrace this technology in the near future and ask a familiar question: How did we do business without it?

A picture, even a live-action video, may never substitute for a site inspection. But imagine using these capabilities to conduct a meeting from your desk. Wouldn't you think twice if the alternative were an arduous and costly trip by air? Soon, meeting planners may find themselves asking, will attendees' best interests be met by a face-to-face meeting or will a less personal substitute suffice? The answer will depend on the meeting goals. Individuals today want your product or service faster and for less money. For getting information, for learning about new products or techniques, the attendee has alternatives. And a face-to-face meeting isn't necessarily the best one.

Time Savers

For the attendee, time is a critical issue and will become even more so in the twenty-first century. Today, next-day delivery is often expected. You don't want a product, service, or information next week, you want it today. The concept of time in the twenty-first century will be one of instant satisfaction.

To meet these demands, the meetings industry must capture the power of the computer, the power of information, and the power of communication, in order to know the answer to every inquiry from clients, superiors, staff, and attendees. Planners must adopt the gizmos, gadgets, and other hardware that will allow them to distribute their message faster.

The following products are coming soon to an office near you. These technologies will be status quo by the beginning of the century—forward-thinking planners, and business people will eagerly embrace and incorporate them into their daily business lives.

- Multimedia Computers. Computers that combine advantages of television, print, and the computer. Sound, video, and data combine for an interactive, integrated system suitable for training and presentations. This will end (thankfully) the reign of the slide carousel and overhead projector. PC-based multimedia will allow a speaker to manipulate images and sound effects while delivering a presentation.

- CD Evolution. Compact disks that we buy for the presentation of music merely hint at the potential for CDs. CD-ROMs (read-only-memory) are beginning to replace instruction/user manuals, textbooks, and other reference materials. CD-R (recordable) will allow the user to record information on a CD. And the photo CD will hold digital images from film-based photography. A CD-ROM database will replace printed directories. Planners will be able to view meeting rooms, guest rooms, and banquet and kitchen facilities. An interactive network will allow the planner to request specific details and photos of facilities and receive them instantly.

- Advanced Expert Systems (AES). AESs are knowledge-based artificial intelligence software programs that capture the expertise of decision makers and apply that expertise to problem solving. Uses will include management and sales support, accounting, decision making, and training. Expert systems can put together enormous amounts of information on a subject, allowing the computer, through a process of elimination, to render a decision to an inquiry on the subject. A limitation: Software will have to be updated regularly to keep up with advances.

- Fuzzy Logic. A software program that allows a computer to answer "maybe" rather than just "yes" or "no." This allows for the processing of abstract information and conflicting commands.

- Electronic Data Interchange (EDI). EDI replaces the fax, the mail, Fed-Ex, and the phone. It allows different companies and industries to conduct business electronically rather than through traditional methods. It increases speed and reduces cost and paperwork. For example, if most of your business is with one hotel chain, one audiovisual supplier, one destination management company, EDI will provide a permanent link between you and your supplier. A touch of a button will provide room availability, entertainment and catering possibilities, prices, and any other information relevant to your meeting, saving time and headaches in the preliminary planning process.
- Desktop Videoconferencing. Sony, GTE, AT&T, VTEL, PictureTel, and CLI introduced desktop videoconferencing products in 1993. Other companies have software products that let people at various locations work together on charts, blueprints, X-rays, or spreadsheets while communicating with full-motion video and voice.
- Group Decision Support Systems. Meeting rooms outfitted with PCs and software that allow simultaneous input from attendees. These systems help overcome the politics of speaking openly in front of a group. They also shorten the time frame for decision making because more opinions are heard in a shorter period.
- Audience Response Systems. These are keypads that let audience members vote on issues as the meeting is progressing. With a public screen, response is immediately available and visible in graph or chart form. Also allows immediate feedback and evaluation of the particular event.

Although these products exist now, they won't be commonly used for many more years. According to Paul Saffo, a research fellow at Institute for the Future, in Menlo Park, California, it takes about thirty years for new technology to be absorbed into the mainstream. Products for videoconferencing, which was invented fifteen to twenty years ago, are just now beginning to come into their own.

Working at Home

The technological changes that will affect business and the meetings industry will also affect how and where to work. "It's illogical to think we should get into cars and drive, park, get in an elevator, and go upstairs, so we can crawl into our womb for eight hours," Libey says. "People are changing, management styles are changing. Empowerment says I don't have to be hierarchically managed. The framework is being set for exurbanization, commercially and socially." A recent computer commercial portrays a man and his laptop working comfortably . . . on a beach. The man's biggest concern, presumably, is keeping sand out of his machine.

"In the future, if you have anything really important to do in the office you'll stay home," says George Gilder, author of *Life after Television*. He's only half kidding when he adds, "The people in the office will be security people."

The societal changes that are transforming corporate headquarters are already happening. Ten years ago, some 12 million people worked at home. Today, 25 million people do. Most of them are independent self-employed types, but the number of corporate employees working at home has increased 40% in five years.

Next month, Chiat/Day, the Venice, California, advertising agency responsible for the Energizer Bunny commercials, is sending 325 headquarters employees off to the "virtual office." Work is done at home, in a car, in a hotel, at the airport, at a client's office, anywhere. Employees are free to stop in at the main office where they can pick up laptops, fax machines, note pads, or cellular phones, do research at the media center, or even shoot pool in a recreation room. If employees want more privacy at headquarters, they can register at a concierge desk for a workspace.

The virtual office, in concert with technology sure to inundate people with information faster and in more abundance than ever before, isolates the individual. This is fruitful soil for face-to-face meetings. "The increase in technology will increase face-to-face get togethers, and increase the need to meet. There is no way to replace human interaction. We've got to balance it with technology," Aburdene says. There will be a balance, but clearly, some meetings will die. Replaced by videoconferencing, virtual reality, and communications pathways that bring you the information you want and need instantly.

As business embraces new technology, the meetings industry must adapt. When a major Swiss bank recently ordered 75 videoconferencing units for its offices around the world, it put them under the jurisdiction of its travel department. "That means a travel request will soon need to pass the, 'Could it be done by videoconference?' hurdle," says Ernest Arvai, president of The Arvai Group, a consultant specializing in high-tech business strategy, in Windham, New Hampshire.

"Videoconferencing is usually cost-justified on the basis of savings in travel costs," say Lisa Craig, a former event planner, and now manager of new applications marketing for PictureTel. "What happens, though, is that users end up seeing that the value is in saving time, letting you see and meet with clients or colleagues more frequently." That's the advantage that will ultimately convince companies to accept a new technology. Says McDonald: "People will make low-tech changes, move slowly into medium-tech changes and then become really knowledgeable about what the future will hold before making the high-tech changes." The meetings industry, like all of business, will pass, kicking and screaming, with the rest of us, into the next century, fighting change every step of the way. But as any barfly psychologist can tell you, change is inevitable. Beam me up, Scotty.

The Virtual Reality

The technology that everyone's fantasizing about is virtual reality. The expectations for virtual reality are of Star Trek magnitude. Enter a room. Tell a computer to run the "OK Corral" program, and you're deposited in the dusty Old West; with boots, bandanna, and six-gun, ready to take on Wyatt Earp. It's all done with computer simulation, and it's as real as any reality.

Today's virtual reality has not yet reached those expectations. Today, it involves putting on a helmet, goggles, and gloves and manipulating the world around you. You can feel yourself fly, you can see a cartoon-quality, color-saturated landscape, and you can hear sound effects that help the mind construct a sort of "reality."

Virtual reality is in its infancy. At the Banff Center for the Arts in Alberta, Canada, using a $500,000 computer and a $30,000 helmet, and with the sound of rushing water to help, users can determine that the blurry white wall they see is a waterfall. But virtual reality will grow up. The virtual site inspection will occur in our lifetime. Explore a facility without leaving your office. You like the ballroom, but need a stage at one end? Input the change. The stage appears. The computer sends the specs to a contractor. The stage is built before you arrive.

Virtual reality does have a downside. It could become society's next drug—the addict enjoying its pleasures to the point of never turning the computer off.

The New School

The future meetings industry will determine the adult curriculum of the entire workforce and oversee the effectiveness and efficiency of the delivery of that curriculum. That is an imposing responsibility.

Today, $30 billion a year is spent on training, and it reaches only 7% of the workforce. Most of that cost comes from travel and lodging. And most of the 7% are technicians and managers. "In the future, we will have to drive training through the organization right to the front-line worker. And we will have to find a less expensive way to do it," says Curtis Plott, president of the American Society for Training and Development (ASTD) in Alexandria, Virginia.

Perhaps the greatest potential of advancing technology lies not in the meeting room, but in the classroom. Today's training possibilities include satellite transmission of university courses, eliminating the need to be out of the office for an extended period. Or employees can go on-line and tap into educational resources around the world without every leaving their desks. Already, in Microsoft's Access program, a "Cue Cards" feature provides an on-line coach to teach the user. The know-how of the professor is available on demand.

A multimedia workstation used by Allstate Insurance Co. teaches users the twelve essential skills needed to be an effective claims agent. It also evaluates applicants for agent jobs. An applicant spends two hours at the station and Allstate knows exactly how the applicant's abilities match the twelve key skill requirements. When virtual reality becomes cost-effective in the next century, employees can practice negotiating with, and selling or speaking to a computer-generated version of the customer or vendor. "The use of an electronic connection, where people can access information, will have a huge impact on training," Plott says.

Microsoft's program, Allstate's workstation, virtual reality, and universities' distance learning programs via satellite represent a less expensive alternative to sending employees back to school. And this is how tomorrow's workforce will expect to be trained. While those of us in today's workforce may be in awe of twenty-first-century technology, tomorrow's employees were born in the 1980s. They are growing up computer-literate—part of the video generation. They will view desktop video as today's salespeople view traveling to see a client. By 2010, they will be out of graduate school possessing a far better grasp of technological realities than the rest of us.

Into the Air

Technology coming to the office will soon find its way into the air. Inside airplanes, passengers will be able to receive calls and send faxes and other information through a laptop computer. Interactive video will allow passengers to make hotel, restaurant, and air reservations. Each seat will have its own computer connected to the main computer on the plane. Information will be relayed through satellites.

Design firms such as GEC-Marconi, Matsushita Avionics, Hughes-Avicom, and BE Aerospace are all working on the airline seat of the future. And the airlines are interested. By 1995: GEC-Marconi will place $130 million worth of interactive systems into United Airlines and British Airways planes. Hughes-Avicom hopes to have systems on 40 of Northwest Airlines's jets. And USAir will have InFlight Phone's FlightLink on 402 jets, allowing passengers to send faxes, get stock quotes, and play video games.

These services come as airlines struggle to fill seats. New services will be offered to maintain a competitive edge. Airlines have to offer the services, because the business traveler, the industry's bread and butter, will selectively choose an airline because of these services.

P·A·R·T · II

C

Boom Time on the
New Frontier[*]

Thomas A. Stewart

The future of information technology descends upon us in a swarm of buzzwords: global village, electronic superhighway, information age, electronic frontier. Someday soon, cyberspace—the vast, intangible territory where computers meet and exchange information—will be populated with electronic communities and businesses. In your home, a protean box will hook you into a wealth of goods and services. It will receive and send mail, let you make a phone or video call or send a fax or watch a movie or buy shoes or diagnose a rash or pay bills or get cash (a new digital kind) or write your mother. That will be just the living-room manifestation of what promises to be a radical—and rapid—transformation of commerce and society, the greatest since the invention of the automobile.

The process has already begun. In Japan, used-car dealers gather via their computers on Saturday mornings to take part in an electronic auction, buying and selling cars by pressing the button on a joystick. In New York City, a seller of surgical gauze and other medical disposables recently logged on to a global electronic bulletin board operated by the World Trade Center and found a supplier in China. Now, instead of buying from U.S. wholesalers, he sells to them. The largest market in the world—the trillion or so dollars a day in international currency transactions—runs almost entirely over networks.

During the next few years, electronic markets will grow and begin operating over cheap, accessible public networks—the so-called electronic highway. Just as railroads opened the West, the highway will open wide the electronic frontier. Whole industries will be destroyed and new ones born; productivity will leap and competitive advantage shift in the direction of small business. The pioneers—miners and ranchers, railroaders and traders, capitalists and outlaws—have found that the electronic frontier, like frontiers that preceded it, is at once a realm of boundless opportunity and a harsh, brutal place.

The technological basis of electronic commerce is both simple and dauntingly complex. The simple part is that all images and sounds—a voice, a movie, a document, a tune—can be expressed in digital code, in streams of ones and zeros. Once digitized, they can be shipped electronically or stored on an electronic shelf and pulled down later. Thus the convergence between computers, which generate, read, and store digital code, and communications networks, which move it around. Once the networks are fully digital and sufficiently capacious, anybody can send anything to anyone else—a note to a neighbor, a World Series game to millions—choosing any form, whether video, voice, text, or a combination.

The complexity—and opportunity—is in making the network easy to use (with electronic directories, for example) and developing the services it will make possible (electronic shopping malls, say). A simple transaction, like buying a security analyst's report or dialing up a movie, might involve several ancillary services—Yellow Pages that locate the seller, electronic Better Business Bureaus that vouch for his integrity, and on-line banks that approve credit and transfer funds.

The rise of electronic networks is nothing short of staggering. Of the 100 corporations on FORTUNE's 1993 list of America's fastest-growing companies, 15 either operate or supply networking equipment. The market for networking between companies barely existed half a dozen years ago; today it stands at $1.5 billion a year, and it will mount to anywhere from $10 billion to $40 billion annually by the turn of the century. Telephone and cable companies are spending billions each year to upgrade their circuits— laying fiber-optic cable to widen data pipes and installing fancy routers and switches to direct the flood of electronic commerce.

Most stunning of all has been the growth of the Internet, a loosely confederated network of networks, public and private. They are linked through an array of data communications circuits and use a standard way of addressing and sending data so that a computer with an Internet connection can relay information to any of the others. Anyone who installs the necessary software can set up his computer as a "host" that other users can connect to and get access to the net.

The Internet evolved from a Pentagon network for academic and defense researchers. The National Science Foundation took over management of

---

*This article originally appeared in *Fortune,* 128(7)(Autumn 1993):153–161. Reprinted with permission of Time/Warner Inc.

the Internet ten years ago and in 1988 increased the capacity of its circuits. The number of users exploded. Says Vinton Cerf, president of the Internet Society, an advisory group: "Internet is growing faster than any other telecommunications systems ever built, including the telephone network."

Any estimate of its size is obsolete in hours. In March some 10,000 networks were part of the system. By July there were over 14,000—the number doubles every year. The Internet reaches from Greenland to Antarctica, connecting more than 50 countries. In the six months that it has been available in Russia, more than 6,000 host computers have joined, says John Quarterman, editor of *Matrix News*, a newsletter that tracks the network's growth.

In New York City, Stacy Horn, 37, owns a small Internet service called ECHO (for East Coast Hang-Out). She calls it "an electronic cultural salon, like Gertrude Stein's living room in Paris." ECHO is expanding so fast— membership doubled to nearly 3,000 between late June and mid-August— that it took over every free phone line in her Greenwich Village neighborhood. New York Telephone had to run a separate cable to Horn's apartment. The Internet's growth will inevitably slow—at current rates, everyone on earth would be connected by 2002—but Cerf says a reasonable estimate is that 100 million people will be using the system in five years.

The Internet has become the de facto electronic highway. Not the six-lane interstate of the near future, but something akin to the old U.S. highway system. It has its U.S. 1 and Route 66—the original National Science Foundation network, plus others built by companies like Sprint and UUNet Technologies of Falls Church, Virginia. Connected to them is a filigree of smaller roads: corporate networks, regional and local access providers like Stacy Horn, and so on. The Internet already serves as a way to send mail and documents, supports a radio station and several publishers, and transmits faxes for one-fiftieth of what faxing usually costs. It has transmitted TV and a movie, and this fall may broadcast a congressional hearing live. Because of customer demand, access to Internet E-mail has become *de rigueur* for on-line services like CompuServe and America Online; Prodigy, the last holdout, will begin offering members Internet mail soon.

Businesses have flocked to the Internet as excitedly as sea gulls to a clambake. Nothing is supposed to traverse the NSF lines that isn't scientific or educational, but that rule, never strictly enforced, has become irrelevant as alternate routes proliferate. NSF official Stephen Wolff says 58% of U.S. Internet addresses belong to people who got them through a private employer or one of the 60-odd commercial access providers. The other addresses belong to educational institutions, governments, and nonprofit organizations.

The U.S. government pays less than 3% of the Internet's operating cost, Wolff estimates. The rest is borne by users: Each pays the cost of operating his own host computer, out of university budgets, subscriber fees, or other sources. There is no charge for sending data via someone else's computer or network lines, just as Nebraska doesn't make Kansans pay for using its highways. This do-it-yourself approach to funding is why the internet is so inexpensive to use.

More and more the network is open to newcomers. And coming they are. Says Paul E. Peters, executive director of the Coalition for Networked Information, a Washington, D.C. group that represents primarily research libraries: "People on the Internet are talking as if they are Native Americans, and the Pilgrims are on the shore. They think of this as an Edenic environment, a garden, and hear over the horizon the combines coming to harvest its fruits for commercial purposes."

The network of the future, evolving out of the Internet, will have two characteristics that make it ideal for business: universality and low cost. Every network will be able to communicate with all others. As companies open gateways to the Internet from their networks, and as telephone, cable TV, satellite, and other networks convert to digital transmission, the great electronic frontier will lock into a compatible handful of switching standards. A user might spend most of her time inside one fenced-off private network (handling internal company data, say) but will be able to swing out onto the highway to reach another network (a customer's, for example) as seamlessly as making a phone call.

Moving around on the Internet now involves arcane commands that can befuddle even experts. That will change soon: Companies that provide network services will compete partly on ease of use. Says Carl Malamud, founder of Internet Multicasting Service in Washington, D.C.: "A lot of this 'too hard to use' stuff will go away. Radio was so messy for the first 20 years, it wasn't funny. Cars ditto—you had to be a mechanic to drive one."

As to cost: Already computers aren't a lot more expensive than TV sets. As the price of computing power continues its endless skydive, it is reasonable to expect that a full-featured information appliance—combining the functions of computer, phone, TV, and so on—will soon cost about what a TV does today. It will deliver basic digital services, including video phone calls, movies on demand, E-mail, banking, and shopping. Moreover, it will replace add-on gadgets that drive up the cost of furnishing a middle-class electronic cottage, such as VCRs and answering machines.

The price of equipment is the least of it. A bigger saving is the cost of transmission. Jordan Becker, a vice president of Advanced Network & Services, which built the NSF network, estimates sending an ordinary one-page E-mail message from New York to California via a commercial on-line service and the Internet costs about a penny and a half, versus 29 cents for a letter and $2 for a fax. As the network expands to handle data-intensive traffic such as video, the cost per bit will fall faster than Custer's cavalry. Says Mitchell Kapor, founder of Lotus Development and now chairman of the Electronic Frontier Foundation, a public-interest group: "If video is affordable, then the cost of plain old text messages has to be near zero."

The biggest boon might be the cost of cybernetic "land." In *The Frontier in American History*, Frederick Jackson Turner called free Western land "the most significant thing abut the American frontier"—a gift of capital that enabled pioneers to set themselves up as farmers, gold miners, and merchants at a fraction of the cost back East or in Europe. On the electronic frontier, the capital you need to stake your claim is trivial. An the free land never ends. Inside your gateway you can create as big a spread—as vast a business—as you please.

These electronic freeholds will alter every business. Says Benn Konsynski, who is establishing a center for electronic commerce at Emory University in Atlanta: "No markets are immune from networking technologies. They will change how buyers buy and sellers sell." Working with Sprint's high-speed data network, Microelectronics and Computer Technology Corp. (MCC), the Austin, Texas consortium of 80 major U.S. high-tech companies, has introduced a service that shows how an electronic marketplace works. When EINet (for Enterprise Integration Network; pronounced Eee-eye-net) becomes widely available this fall, anyone with an Internet link will be able to do business electronically. EINet is for business-to-business transactions, though it could offer consumer services, too.

On EINet, someone looking for, say, office products will find potential sellers in a Yellow Pages-like directory. From his computer, he can thumb through a catalog and even call up a video demo. He can talk or exchange E-mail with the seller, enter a purchase order, and pay. If the parties want a long-term partnership, they can set up full electronic data interchange (EDI) to permit just-in-time delivery and automatic inventory replenishment. The only piece missing at the moment is the payment mechanism—banks on the network to provide electronic funds transfer and credit services. MCC expects to make those arrangements with Citibank and Visa.

Passwords and more sophisticated security systems are built into EINet, including the option of sending encrypted data. Therefore users can do business in public on the Internet with little fear of eavesdropping or intrusion, and at a fraction of the cost of having a closed, bilateral link. Such private links, typically over leased phone lines, are familiar in a variety of industries. Wal-Mart's electronic ties to major suppliers like Procter & Gamble, for example, have allowed both companies to slash administrative and inventory costs, giving the big retailer one of its most powerful weapons against Main Street.

More than 40,000 U.S. companies use some form of EDI. Still, says Gregory B. Hartner, CEO of the EDI Association in Alexandria, Virginia, "we're to the right of the decimal point in terms of the number of potential users." That's because leased lines, which cost between $60,000 and $100,000 each to set up and thousands more per year to operate, are a major expense for big companies and effectively beyond the reach of small companies with many customers.

EINet could open the floodgates. MCC vice-president Roy Smith estimates that a comparable link over EINet could be established for less than $20,000, plus operating expenses. One giant American retailer, experienced at using EDI with big suppliers, is having serious discussions with MCC about using EINet to extend electronic partnering to all its vendors, no matter how small.

While EINet could become the first universal electronic marketplace in the U.S., specialty markets are already as common as flies on cows. There are electronic markets for aircraft parts and used textbooks. Database services like Mead Data Central's Nexis and Lexis are old-timers on the electronic frontier, eagerly awaiting the day when a secure, cheap, public network will let them cut back their use of leased lines (and possibly lower their prices). In California the American Information Exchange allows consultants, software companies, and others to find one another on-line, negotiate deals, and ship reports and computer codes.

These markets need two ingredients to reach their full potential. First is easy access to and from a universal utility—the electronic highway that's abuilding. Second is a package of core services, chief among them security. The public network must be at least as safe as any bank network, so no one can peek at your transactions or muck around in your records. On-line commerce also needs authentication services, so you know the person on the other end is not an imposter. And it must have financial services, including not only credit but electronic cash as well. These services either exist already or soon will.

As on-line trade booms, the effect on business will be profound. Electronic commerce dramatically lowers transaction costs, an enormous expense. According to D. J. Crane, a vice-president of GE Information Services, the administrative cost of trade between companies in the U.S.—selling and purchasing, billing and paying handling logistics—amounts to $250 billion a year. The high cost of dealing across company boundaries has been a powerful spur to vertical integration. As transaction costs fall, says John Hagel III, a partner at McKinsey & Co., "we're going to see a widespread disintegration of U.S. business and the emergence of very different corporate entities."

Companies will focus on a few core activities and unbundle the rest. In a fully electronic environment, the entire value chain might be dismantled and reformed. Take distribution. A manufacturer, focusing on his factories, could turn over logistics to what used to be a freight forwarder. That company, rather than own and manage a fleet of trucks and ships, might rent the vehicles it needs, as it needs them, from a sophisticated leasing company that knows what's where, what's full, what's empty. Each party—manufacturer, logistician, lessor—manages its assets more efficiently than before. Says Crane, who works with GE Capital, a major lessor of transportation equipment, and its customers on just such reconfigurings: "This is changing the business of being a middleman. Forward-thinking companies are taking up positions as middlemen for information, not goods."

The remaking of the value chain means a shift in power to small business. Says Michael Strangelove, publisher of the monthly *Internet Business Journal:* "Entrepreneurs will be less isolated. They can very quickly get in touch with a host of suppliers or customers." When a digital highway circles the globe, the fellow who builds a better mousetrap will find that the path to his door already exists. Malamud of Internet Multicasting Service is one such electronic entrepreneur. He produces a weekly radio program distributed over the Internet, sponsored by Sun Microsystems and O'Reilly & Associates, a publisher. Internet Talk Radio began broadcasting in March; users whose computers have speakers can download Geek of the Week and other features onto disks and listen whenever they want. Says Malamud: "In three months and for less than $100,000, I got a radio station that reached 30 countries the first day."

Small businesses will also gain electronic access to capital assets they couldn't afford before. In South Carolina, the Southeast Manufacturing Technology Center is developing a "virtual factory" whose computer-controlled machine tools small manufacturers can use by sending instructions over the network. The implications of such asset sharing are heartening. By enhancing the productivity of capital, it can strengthen U.S. competitiveness. Says Stanford economist Brian Arthur: "The U.S. is perfectly suited for this kind of economy. It calls for a lone-cowboy type— Steve McQueen and James Coburn."

It is a commonplace that the big winners on the electronic frontier will be "content providers"—those who make the movies, write the books, and build the databases. But saying content is king is too simple. When anything can be put on the market with a couple of clicks of a mouse, there will be even more stupid movies, dull books, sloppy data, and bad analyses— "infoglut," in the aptly ugly term of Christopher Locke, editor of *Internet Business Report,* which made its debut in August.

The Paleys and Sarnoffs of the information age will be those with the taste, judgment, and élan to offer the right mix of content, one that attracts a like-minded community of users who then meet and mingle with one another. Those people in turn will enrich the community by adding services of their own. In a business network they might be bankers, consultants, or engineers for hire. A town's network might attract local newspapers, civic groups, or teenagers advertising to mow lawns.

The enormous market for entertainment, whether it's movies or interactive games, will pay for much of the construction of a high-capacity highway to the home. The existing highway—the Internet in particular— will connect with it, widening its circuits and its reach, driven especially by burgeoning business-to-business markets. And off all these arteries, enjoying full access to them, will be hundreds, thousands, tens of thousands of smaller communities, linked by geography, line of business, or special interest. ECHO's Stacy Horn talks about what she should earn when her electronic salon fills up with the 6,000 to 10,000 people that she figures is its ideal size. Income she calculates at $19.95 a month per person; expenses consist mainly of phone charges and administration, "but I can automate most of that, like billing." Then she says, "I expect to become very rich."

P·A·R·T·II

D

The Electronic Hive: Embrace It*

Kevin Kelly

If twentieth-century science can be said to have a single icon, it is the Atom. As depicted in the popular mind, the symbol of the Atom is stark: a black dot encircled by the hairline orbits of several smaller dots. The Atom whirls alone, the epitome of singleness. It is the metaphor for individuality. At its center is the animus, the It, the life force, holding all to their appropriate whirling station. The Atom stands for power and knowledge and certainty. It conveys the naked power of simplicity.

The iconic reign of the Atom is now passing. The symbol of science for the next century is the dynamic Net. The icon of the Net, in contradistinction to the Atom, has no center. It is a bunch of dots connected to other dots, a cobweb of arrows pouring into one another, squirming together like a nest of snakes, the restless image fading at indeterminate edges. The Net is the archetype displayed to represent all circuits, all intelligence, all interdependence, all things economic and social and ecological, all communications, all democracy, all groups, all large systems. This icon is slippery, ensnaring the unwary in its paradox of no beginning, no end, no center.

The Net conveys the logic of both the computer and nature. In nature, the Net finds form in, for example, the beehive. The hive is irredeemably social, unabashedly of many minds, but it decides as a whole when to swarm and where to move. A hive possesses an intelligence that none of its parts does. A single honeybee brain operates with a memory of six days; the hive as a whole operates with a memory of three months, twice as long as the average bee lives.

Although many philosophers in the past have suspected that one could abstract the laws of life and apply them to machines, it wasn't until computers and human-made systems became as complex as living things—as intricately composed as a beehive—that it was possible to prove this. Just as a beehive functions as if it were a single sentient organism, so does an electronic hive, made up of millions of buzzing, dim-witted personal computers, behave like a single organism. Out of networked parts—whether of insects, neurons, or chips—come learning, evolution, and life. Out of a planet-wide swarm of silicon calculators comes an emergent self-governing intelligence: the Net.

I live on computer networks. The network of networks—the Net, also known as the Internet—links several million personal computers around the world. No one knows exactly how many millions are connected, or even how many intermediate nodes there are. The Internet Society made an educated guess last year that the Net was made up of 1.7 million host computers and 17 million users. Like the beehive, the Net is controlled by no one; no one is in charge. The Net is, as its users are proud to boast, the largest functioning anarchy in the world. Every day hundreds of millions of messages are passed between its members without the benefit of a central authority.

In addition to a vast flow of individual letters, there exists between its wires that disembodied cyberspace where messages interact, a shared space of written public conversations. Every day authors all over the world add millions of words to an uncountable number of overlapping conversations. They daily build an immense distributed document, one that is under eternal construction, in constant flux, and of fleeting permanence. The users of this media are creating an entirely new writing space, far different from that carved out by a printed book or even a chat around a table. Because of this impermanence, the type of thought encouraged by the Net tends toward the non-dogmatic—the experimental idea, the quip, the global perspective, the interdisciplinary synthesis, and the uninhibited, often emotional, response. Many participants prefer the quality of writing on the Net to book writing because Net writing is of a conversational, peer-to-peer style, frank and communicative, rather than precise and self-consciously literary. Instead of the rigid canonical thinking cultivated by the book, the Net stimulates another way of thinking: telegraphic, modular, non-linear, malleable, cooperative.

A person on the Internet sees the world in a different light. He or she views the world as decidedly decentralized, every far-flung member a producer as well as a consumer, all parts of it equidistant from all others, no matter how large it gets, and every participant responsible for manufacturing truth out of a noisy cacophony of ideas, opinions, and facts.

---

*Adapted from *Out of Control: The Rise of Neo-Biological Civilization* (1994) and appearing in *Harper's Magazine*, 228(1728):20–25 (1994), with permission.

There is no central meaning, no official canon, no manufactured consent rippling through the wires from which one can borrow a viewpoint. Instead, every idea has a backer, and every backer has an idea, while contradiction, paradox, irony, and multifaceted truth rise up in a flood.

A recurring vision swirls in the shared mind of the Net, a vision that nearly every member glimpses, if only momentarily: of wiring human and artificial minds into one planetary soul. This incipient techno-spiritualism is all the more remarkable because of how unexpected it has been. The Net, after all, is nothing more than a bunch of highly engineered pieces of rock braided together with strands of metal or glass. It is routine technology. Computers, which have been in our lives for twenty years, have made our life faster but not that much different. Nobody expected a new culture, a new thrill, or even a new politics to be born when we married calculating circuits with the ordinary telephone; but that's exactly what happened.

There are other machines, such as the automobile and the air conditioner, that have radically reshaped our lives and the landscape of our civilization. The Net (and its future progeny) is another one of those disrupting machines and may yet surpass the scope of all the others together in altering how we live.

The Net is an organism/machine whose exact size and boundaries are unknown. All we do know is that new portions and new uses are being added to it at such an accelerating rate that it may be more of an explosion than a thing. So vast is this embryonic Net, and so fast is it developing into something else, that no single human can fathom it deeply enough to claim expertise on the whole.

The tiny bees in a hive are more or less unaware of their colony, but their collective hive mind transcends their small bee minds. As we wire ourselves up into a hivish network, many things will emerge that we, as mere neurons in the network, don't expect, don't understand, can't control, or don't even perceive. That's the price for any emergent hive mind.

At the same time the very shape of this network space shapes us. It is no coincidence that the post-modernists arose as the networks formed. In the last half-century a uniform mass market has collapsed into a network of small niches—the result of the information tide. An aggregation of fragments is the only kind of whole we now have. The fragmentation of business markets, of social mores, of spiritual beliefs, of ethnicity, and of truth itself into tinier and tinier shards is the hallmark of this era. Our society is a working pandemonium of fragments—much like the Internet itself.

People in a highly connected yet deeply fragmented society can no longer rely on a central canon for guidance. They are forced into the modern existential blackness of creating their own cultures, beliefs, markets, and identities from a sticky mess of interdependent pieces. The industrial icon of a grand central or a hidden "I am" becomes hollow. Distributed, headless, emergent wholeness becomes the social ideal.

The critics of early computers capitalized on a common fear: that a Big Brother brain would watch over us and control us. What we know now of our own brains is that they too are only networks of mini-minds, a society of dumber minds linked together, and that when we peer into them deeply we find that there is no "I" in charge. Not only does a central-command economy not work; a central-command brain won't either. In its stead, we can make a nation of personal computers, a country of decentralized nodes of governance and thought. Almost every type of large-scale governance we can find, from the body of a giraffe, to the energy regulation in a tidal marsh, to the temperature regulation of a beehive, to the flow of traffic on the Internet, resolves into a swarmy distributed net of autonomous units and heterogeneous parts.

No one has been more wrong about computerization than George Orwell in *1984*. So far, nearly everything about the actual possibility-space that computers have created indicates they are not the beginning of authority but its end. In the process of connecting everything to everything, computers elevate the power of the small player. They make room for the different, and they reward small innovations. Instead of enforcing uniformity, they promote heterogeneity and autonomy. Instead of sucking the soul from human bodies, turning computer users into an army of dull clones, *networked* computers—by reflecting the networked nature of our own brains—encourage the humanism of their users. Because they have taken on the flexibility, adaptability, and self-connecting governance of organic systems, we become more human, not less so, when we use them.

P·A·R·T · II

E

The Electronic Hive: Refuse It*

Sven Birkerts

The digital future is upon us. From our President on down, people are smitten, more than they have been with anything in a very long time. I can't open a newspaper without reading another story about the Internet, the information highway. The dollar, not the poet, is the antenna of the race, and right now the dollar is all about mergers and acquisitions: the fierce battles being waged for control of the system that will allow us, soon enough, to cohabit in the all but infinite information space. The dollar is smart. It is betting that the trend will be a juggernaut, unstoppable; that we are collectively ready to round the corner into a new age. We are not about to turn from this millennial remaking of the world; indeed, we are all excited to see just how much power and ingenuity we command. By degrees—it is happening year by year, appliance by appliance—we are wiring ourselves into a gigantic hive.

When we look at the large-scale shift to an electronic culture, looking as if at a time-lapse motion study, we can see not only how our situation has come about but also how it is in our nature that it should have. At every step—this is clear—we trade for ease. And ease is what quickly swallows up the initial strangeness of a new medium or tool. Moreover, each accommodation paves the way for the next. The telegraph must have seemed to its first users a surpassingly strange device, but its newfangledness was overridden by its usefulness. Once we had accepted the idea of mechanical transmission over distances, the path was clear for the telephone. Again, a monumental transformation: turn select digits on a dial and hear the voice of another human being. And on it goes, the inventions coming gradually, one by one, allowing the society to adapt. We mastered the telephone, the television with its few networks running black-and-white programs. And although no law required citizens to own or use either, these technologies did in a remarkably short time achieve near total saturation.

We are, then, accustomed to the process; we take the step that will enlarge our reach, simplify our communication, and abbreviate our physical involvement in some task or chore. The difference between the epoch of early modernity and the present is—to simplify drastically—that formerly the body had time to accept the graft, the new organ, whereas now we are hurtling forward willy-nilly, assuming that if a technology is connected with communications or information processing it must be good, we must need it. I never cease to be astonished at what a mere two decades have brought us. Consider the evidence. Since the early 1970s we have seen the arrival of—we have accepted, deemed all but indispensable—personal computers, laptops, telephone-answering machines, calling cards, fax machines, cellular phones, VCRs, modems, Nintendo games, E-mail, voice mail, camcorders, and CD players. Very quickly, with almost no pause between increments, these circuit-driven tools and entertainments have moved into our lives, and with a minimum rippling of the waters, really—which, of course, makes them seem natural, even inevitable. Which perhaps they are. Marshall McLuhan called improvements of this sort "extensions of man," and this is their secret. We embrace them because they seem a part of us, an enhancement. They don't seem to challenge our power so much as add to it.

I am startled, though, by how little we are debating the deeper philosophical ramifications. We talk up a storm when it comes to policy issues—who should have jurisdiction, what rates may be charged—and there is great fascination in some quarters with the practical minutiae of functioning, compatibility, and so on. But why do we hear so few people asking whether we might not *ourselves* be changing, and whether the changes are necessarily for the good?

In our technological obsession we may be forgetting that circuited interconnectedness and individualism are, at a primary level, inimical notions, warring terms. Being "on line" and having the subjective experience of depth, of existential coherence, are mutually exclusive situations. Electricity and inwardness are fundamentally discordant. Electricity is, implicitly, of the moment—*now*. Depth, meaning, and the narrative structuring of subjectivity—these are *not* now; they flourish only in that order of time Henri Bergson called "duration." Duration is deep time, time experienced without the awareness of time passing. Until quite recently—I would not want to put a date on it—most people on the planet lived mainly in terms

---

*Adapted from *The Gutenberg Elegies: The Fate of Reading in an Electronic Age* (1994) and appearing in *Harper's Magazine*, 228(1728):20–25 (1994), with permission.

of duration: time not artificially broken, but shaped around natural rhythmic cycles; time bound to the integrated functioning of the senses.

We have destroyed that duration. We have created invisible elsewheres that are as immediate as our actual surroundings. We have fractured the flow of time, layered it into competing simultaneities. We learn to do five things at once or pay the price. Immersed in an environment of invisible signals and operations, we find it as unthinkable to walk five miles to visit a friend as it was once unthinkable to speak across that distance through a wire.

My explanation for our blithe indifference to the inward consequences of our becoming "wired" is simple. I believe that we are—biologically, neuropsychologically—creatures of extraordinary adaptability. We fit ourselves to situations, be they ones of privation or beneficent surplus. And in many respects this is to the good. The species is fit because it knows how to fit.

But there are drawbacks as well. The late Walker Percy made it his work to explore the implications of our constant adaptation. Over and over, in his fiction as well as his speculative essays, he asks the same basic questions. As he writes in the opening of his essay "The Delta Factor": "Why does man feel so sad in the twentieth century? Why does man feel so bad in the very age when, more than in any other age, he has succeeded in satisfying his needs and making over the world for his own use?" One of his answers is that the price of adaptation is habit, and that habit—habit of perception as well as behavior—distances the self from the primary things that give meaning and purpose to life. We accept these gifts of technology, these labor-saving devices, these extensions of the senses, by adapting and adapting again. Each improvement provides a new level of abstraction to which we accommodate ourselves. Abstraction is, however, a movement away from the natural given—a step away from our fundamental selves rooted for millennia in an awe before the unknown, a fear and trembling in the face of the outer dark. We widen the gulf, and if at some level we fear the widening, we respond by investing more of our faith in the systems we have wrought.

We sacrifice the potential life of the solitary self by enlisting ourselves in the collective. For this is finally—even more than the saving of labor—what these systems are all about. They are not only extensions of the senses; they are extensions of the senses that put us in touch with the extended senses of others. The ultimate point of the ever-expanding electronic web is to bridge once and for all the individual solitude that has hitherto always set the terms of existence. Each appliance is a strand, another addition to the virtual place wherein we will all find ourselves together. Telephone, fax, computer networks, E-mail, interactive television—these are the components out of which the hive is being built. The end of it all, the *telos*, is a kind of amniotic environment of impulses, a condition of connectedness. And in time—I don't know how long it will take—it will feel as strange (and exhilarating) for a person to stand momentarily free of it as it feels now for a city dweller to look up at night and see a sky full of stars.

Whether this sounds dire or not depends upon your assumptions about the human condition—assumptions, that is, in the largest sense. For those who ask, with Gauguin, "Who are we? Why are we here? Where are we going?"—and who feel that the answering of those questions is the grand mission of the species—the prospect of a collective life in an electronic hive is bound to seem terrifying. But there are others, maybe even a majority, who have never except fleetingly posed those same questions, who have repressed them so that they might "get on," and who gravitate toward that life because they see it as a way of vanquishing once and for all the anxious gnawings they feel whenever any intimations of depth sneak through the inner barriers.

My core fear is that we are, as a culture, as a species, becoming shallower; that we have turned from depth—from the Judeo-Christian premise of unfathomable mystery—and are adapting ourselves to the ersatz security of a vast lateral connectedness. That we are giving up on wisdom, the struggle for which has for millennia been central to the very idea of culture, and that we are pledging instead to a faith in the web.

There is, finally, a tremendous difference between communication in the instrumental sense and communion in the affective, soul-oriented sense. Somewhere we have gotten hold of the idea that the more all-embracing we can make our communications networks, the closer we will be to that connection that we long for deep down. For change us as they will, our technologies have not yet eradicated that flame of a desire—not merely to be in touch, but to be, at least figuratively, embraced, known and valued not abstractly but in presence. We seem to believe that our instruments can get us there, but they can't. Their great power is all in the service of division and acceleration. They work in—and create—an unreal time that has nothing to do with the deep time in which we thrive: the time of history, tradition, ritual, art, and true communion.

The proselytizers have shown me their vision, and in my more susceptible moods I have felt myself almost persuaded. I have imagined what it could be like, our toil and misery replaced by a vivid, pleasant dream. Fingers tap keys, oceans of fact and sensation get downloaded, are dissolved through the nervous system. Bottomless wells of data are accessed and manipulated, everything flowing at circuit speed. Gone the rock in the field, the broken hoe, the grueling distances. "History," said Stephen Daedalus, "is a nightmare from which I am trying to awaken." This may be the awakening, but it feels curiously like the fantasies that circulate through our sleep. From deep in the heart I hear the voice that says, "Refuse it."

P·A·R·T · II

F

Electronic Office: Playpen or Prison[*]

Langdon Winner

To enter the digital city one must first be granted access. Having "logged on," one's quality of participation is determined by the architecture of the network and its map of rules, roles, and relationships. Technical professionals are usually greeted by a computerized version of the social matrix, an organizational form in which there is at least superficial equality and ready access to information and one's co-workers. They experience computer networks as spheres of democratic or even anarchic activity. Especially for those ill at ease in the physical presence of others (a feeling not uncommon among male engineers), the phenomenon of disembodied space seems to offer comfort and fulfillment. Here are new opportunities for self-expression, creativity, and a sense of mastery! Some begin to feel they are most alive, most free when wandering through the networks; they often "disappear" into them for days on end.

Ordinary workers, on the other hand, typically face a much different set of possibilities. As they enter an electronic office or factory, they become the objects of top-down managerial control, required to take orders, complete finite tasks, and perform according to a set of standard productivity measures. Facing them is a structure that incorporates the authoritarianism of the industrial workplace and augments its power in ingenious ways. No longer are the Taylorite time-and-motion measurements limited by an awkward stopwatch carried from place to place by a wandering manager. Now workers' motions can be ubiquitously monitored in units calculable to the nearest microsecond. For telephone operators handling calls, insurance clerks processing claims, and keypunch operators doing data entry, rates of performance are recorded by a centralized computer and continuously compared to established norms. Failure to meet one's quota of phone calls, insurance claims, or keystrokes is grounds for managerial reprimand or, eventually, dismissal. A report issued by the Office of Technology Assessment revealed that by the late 1980s, four to six million American office workers are already subject to such forms of computer-based surveillance. Such systems do not, as utopian dreams of automation prophesied, "eliminate toil and liberate people for higher forms of work." While the old-fashioned secretary was expected to perform perhaps 30,000 keystrokes an hour, the norm for modern keypunch operators is now close to 80,000.

For those who manage the systems of computerized work, the structures and processes offer a wonderfully effective means of control. Here is an electronic equivalent of Jeremy Bentham's Panopticon, the ingenious circular design that allowed the guardians of a prison, hospital, or school to observe every inmate under totally panoptic scrutiny. The system is, of course, totally opaque. They are allowed to see only what the program allows. Closely watched and clocked, workers within the city of icons may find even fewer chances to express their individuality or participate in decisions than they did in the old-fashioned office or factory. When space is intangible, where do workers organize?

*This article is an excerpt from "Silicon Valley Mystery House" by Langdon Winner, from *Variations on a Theme Park: The New American City and the End of Public Space,* edited by Michael Sorkin. Essay copyright © 1992 by Langdon Winner. Reprinted by permission of Hill and Wang, a division of Farrar, Straus & Giroux, Inc.

P·A·R·T · II

Computerization Movements and Tales of Technological Utopianism

Suzanne Iacono • Rob Kling

Introduction

1993 was a watershed year for the promotion of communications networks and computer technologies in the United States. President Clinton and Vice-President Gore linked America's destiny with the creation of the National Information Infrastructure (NII), a vision of universal access to seamless computer networks and unlimited amounts of information. The NII is a new concept for transforming the lives of American people and revitalizing the economy (the White House, 1993). It promises to "unleash an information revolution that will change forever the way people live, work and interact with each other." While high-speed computer networks, including the Internet, and related information technologies have been widely used and written about by computer specialists for many years, a recent explosion of articles in the popular press has raised public awareness and interest in the transforming potential of networked forms of social life. Ordinary citizens, as well as those with special interests in business or education, now resonate with the government's framing of a national agenda to network the nation.

This national campaign to promulgate social change through the Internet and other communications networks is also stimulated by organizations whose members have long-standing interests in the development of networking standards and other issues related to security, reliability, and civil liberties. Organizations such as the Internet Society (ISOC), the Electronic Frontier Foundation (EFF), Computer Professionals for Social Responsibility (CPSR), and the Center for Civic Networking (CCN) render new technologies socially meaningful to the general public and advocate positions in national debates about computing policy.

Beyond such organizations, there are coalitions of organizations, such as the Federation of American Research Networks (FARNET), an association whose members include Internet service providers, telecommunications companies, and equipment vendors, and the Coalition for Networked Information (CNI), a professional group that is supported by three associations of academic institutions, EDUCOM, CAUSE, and the Association of Research Libraries (ARL). While the members and leaders of these diverse groups do not agree on many issues (similar to differences among the members and leaders of various environmental groups), they are generally united in preferring a computerized future premised on universal access over one that would perpetuate the gap between the information "haves" and the information "have-nots."

Participation in these organizations has grown considerably in the last several years. People who had previously expressed little interest in computer networking often want to be on the net even if they don't know exactly what it is or what being on it will do for them. For example, the Vice-President has promised to connect every classroom, public library, and health clinic to the NII. Many school administrators and teachers eagerly seek to be connected, even though they are not sure what kinds of materials will actually be available for improving education. But being on the net has become an important symbol of progress and accessibility. Even the President and Vice-President have electronic mail boxes and the White House recently announced a home page on the World Wide Web. While some people may be drawn to the excitement and transformational possibilities of computer networking, others may simply fear being left out of an important new social capability.

This discussion of the campaign to promote computer networking illustrates how the spread of these technologies is not simply the by-product of ambitious marketing departments in high-tech companies. The government, media, grass roots organizations, and coalitions of organizations all communicate favorable links between computerization and a transformed social order, which help legitimate relatively high levels of computing investment for many potential adopters. While the specific goals of these organizations and coalitions vary, they all envision an extensively computerized future that is deemed preferable to the less computerized world in which we currently live.

Our argument challenges the belief that the adoption of communications networks and computer technologies is based solely on fine-grained rational calculations about how a technology fits a set of tasks and the relative costs of alternatives. The mobilization of support for extensive computerization through loosely organized, but purposive, collective action does not mean that computer technologies are not useful to people and organizations. Many computer systems have arguably made organizations more effective and efficient. But large expenditures on the latest equipment and systems are often out of proportion for the attained value, while social costs are typically ignored. What this suggests is that computerization has important social and cultural dimensions that are often neglected in discussions of the rise of computer-based technologies and networking.

For example, the United States government's promise of universal access to the NII and societal renewal through technology resonates with key American beliefs about equal opportunity and the pursuit of life, liberty, and happiness. The government, and others, construct utopian tales about these technologies to render them socially meaningful and to mobilize large-scale support. If the goal of the NII is to revitalize the economy or enhance equal opportunity, who can disagree? Despite the fact that goals such as economic renewal are complex problems that continually elude us, people's hopes are renewed by the promise of new technology. In fact, however, we know little about how computer networking will be deployed, who will benefit, and who will lose.

The belief that computing fosters positive forms of social life glosses over deep social and value conflicts that social change can precipitate. Conflicts of interest among groups such as labor, government, and higher education, between workers and their managers, or between students and teachers are ignored. Sacrifices that might accompany the attainment of these goals, such as displaced workers or teachers, are portrayed as minor unavoidable consequences. Instead, computer technologies are linked to all socially valuable behavior and are singled out as the panacea for all social problems. We refer to these kinds of ideas and the literatures that embrace them as "tales of technological utopianism." They are easily spotted by the common, often unexamined, assertion that computing technologies are the single most important vehicles for moving us out of the "dark ages" and into the twenty-first century. Such utopian accounts are bloodless, portraying social change without reference to the battles staged and the consequent winners and losers.

This paper is organized in the following way: in the next section, we present several competing explanations for why the United States is rapidly computerizing. Then, we describe the processes by which computerization movements persist and recruit members. Next, we illustrate these processes by focusing on two specific computerization movements, computer-based education and computer networking. We then discuss why the emergence of a counter-computerization movement is unlikely and make some conclusions regarding the elite status of computerization in the United States today.

Why Is the United States Rapidly Computerizing?

Computerization is the process of developing, implementing, and using computer systems for activities such as teaching, accounting, writing, or designing circuits, for example. Local actors make social choices about the levels of appropriate investment, access to equipment, and expertise, as well as technical choices about what kinds of hardware and software will be available. Many professionals, managers, educators, and students are rapidly adopting computing systems, while puzzling about ways to organize positive forms of social life around them. By the early 1990s, computing and telecommunications accounted for half of the capital investments made by private firms (Dunlop and Kling, 1991). The latest U.S. Census Bureau members indicate that one-third of American workers used a computer at work in 1989, up from one-quarter in 1984 (Kominski, 1991). Today, the Internet comprises over 31,000 interconnected networks with 2.5 million computers attached (Wallich, 1994). Over twenty million people currently have access to the Internet and it is growing at a rate of one million new users a month (Leiner, 1994). However, the most fervent advocates of computerization have argued that the actual pace of computerization in schools, offices, factories, and homes is still too slow (Feigenbaum and McCorduck, 1983; Hodas, Part III, Chapter I; Lidtke & Moursand, 1993; Papert, 1980; Yourdon, 1986; also see Kaplan, 1983).

Why is the United States rapidly computerizing? One common answer argues that computer-based technologies are adopted because they are efficient economic substitutes for labor or older technologies (Simon, 1977; Rule and Attewell, 1991). Rapid computerization is simply a by-product of the availability of cost-effective computing technologies. A variant of this answer views computerization as an efficient tool through which monopoly capitalists control their suppliers and markets, and by which managers tighten their control over workers and the labor process (Braverman, 1974; Mowshowitz, 1976; Shaiken, 1985).

A second type of answer focuses on major epochal social transformations and argues that the United States is shifting from a society where industrial activity dominates to one in which information processing dominates (Bell, 1979). Computer-based technologies are power tools for information or knowledge workers in the same way that drill presses were the power tools for the machinists of the industrial age (Strassman, 1985).

These answers depend on two kinds of social actors: computer vendors who devise and manufacture products for sale and consumers (often managers or organizational decision makers) who purchase computer systems and services because they meet an instrumental need that can be determined by examining task structures or specific organizational functions. Social influences from other environmental actors, such as colleagues, trade associations for the computing industry, professional societies, regulatory agencies, and the numerous journalists who write about innovations in computing are assumed to play minor roles. In addition, the subjective meanings that people attribute to computing, for example, their value as cultural symbols, are considered insignificant. This viewpoint has a strong grounding in both the traditional bureaucratic view of organizations in American sociology, and in conventional economic analysis.

While each of these responses offers insight into computerization processes, we believe that they ignore some of the broadly noneconomic dimensions of computerization in industrialized countries. The market assumptions of these common answers have also shaped the majority of social studies of computerization (see Kling, 1980, 1987, for a detailed review of the empirical studies of computerization). Over the past fifteen years, our own research and participant experiences have taught us that the adoption, acquisition, installation, and operation of computer-based systems are often much more socially charged than the adoption and operation of other equipment, like telephone systems, photocopiers, air conditioners, or elevators. Participants are often highly mobilized to adopt and adapt to particular computing arrangements through collective activities that take place both inside and external to computerizing organizations (Kling and Iacono, 1984, 1988).

We argue that the rise of computer technologies and networking is due to collective action similar to that of other social movements, such as the environmental movement, the anti-tobacco movement, the movement against drinking and driving, or the woman's movement, for example. While each has its own particular goals, for example, clean air, elimination of smoking in public places, reduced traffic accidents and deaths from drunk driving, or equality of opportunity, they all focus on correcting some situation to which they object or changing the circumstances for a group that suffers some sort of social disadvantage (Gamson, 1975). Similarly, advocates of computerization focus on the creation of a new revolutionary, world order where people and organizations use state-of-the art computing equipment and the physical limitations of time and space are overcome.

Not all movements are successful, however. Social movement success has variously been defined as: social acceptance, the accrual of new advantages, the creation of new social policies, or the implementation of new laws (Gamson, 1975). Still other analysts argue that the most important outcome of a social movement is a shift in public perception. For example, the movement against drinking and driving and affiliated organizations like Mothers Against Drunk Driving (MADD) have shifted public perception about "killer drunks" so that state legislatures have raised the legal age for drinking alcoholic beverages and lowered the acceptable level of blood alcohol for drivers with little controversy or debate.

Similarly, organizations affiliated with computer networking, such as CNI and CNN, as well as writers and the popular press, have attempted to shift public perceptions about computing technologies. Until recently, computer networking was the province of serious scientists, nerds, hackers, and hobbyists. But new magazines, such as *Wired* and *Computer-Life*, and writers, such as Rheingold (1993), emphasize the "cool," often counter-cultural, side of computer networking. Their articles focus on new-found freedoms, the loosening of regulated behaviors, or the emergence of long-distance common-interest communities. Multi-user games and chat rooms allow participants to take on identities from epochs or from fiction and play out their fantasies in virtual night clubs and hot tubs (Quittner, 1994). Enthusiasts of virtual communities argue that computer networking allows people to expand their circle of friends and affiliate with them at a community level (Rheingold, 1993). While virtual hot tubbing and virtual communities are less visible than a march on a state or national capital, similar to other social movements, these activities challenge the status quo and offer alternative visions of utopian social arrangements.

In this paper we examine how computerization movements advance computerization in ways that go beyond the effect of advertising and direct sales by the industries that produce and sell computer-based technologies and services. Our main thesis is that participants in computerization movements, along with the media and the state, emphasize technological progress and deflect competing beliefs, laying a foundation for social visions that include the extensive use of advanced computer systems. In this vision, computer users actively seek and acquire the best computer technologies and adopt them regardless of their associated costs. These processes also frame adopters' expectations about what they should use computing for and how they should envision the future. In the next sections, we focus our attention on the character of computerization movements and their organizing beliefs, paying less attention to the ways in which social movements serve as social worlds for participants.

Computerization Movements

Sociologists have used the concept movement to refer to many different kinds of collective action. The most common term found in this literature is social movement, often used in a generic way to refer to movements in general. But sociologists also have written about professional movements (Bucher and Strauss, 1961), artistic movements, and scientific movements (Aronson, 1984; Star, in press). What analyses of these movements share is a focus on the rise of organized, insurgent action to displace or overcome the status quo and establish a new way of life. Computerization movements (CMs) are no different. Large-scale computerization projects are typically accompanied by political struggle and turmoil as the established structure is threatened and powerful actors fear being displaced (Kling and Iacono, 1984, 1988). Historically, those who advocate radically new forms of computerization find themselves in the role of challengers of the status quo.

Our analysis of the development and maintenance of CMs is focused on two key processes: (1) the ways in which movements persist over time through Computerization Movement Organizations (CMOs); and (2) the ways in which computerization movements recruit participants.

Computerization Movement Organizations

In order for any social movement to persist over time, pioneering activists must create more enduring organizational structures than those embodied in emergent and informal groups. These organizations are entities capable of taking social action. They can raise money, mobilize resources, hold meetings, and formulate positions (Gamson, 1975). For example, the Moral Majority (an organization in the Christian Right) raised $2.2 million via mass mailing campaigns during its initial year. These funds were used to appeal to other religious conservatives and to tie them into the organization's network (Snow *et al.*, 1986).

Similarly, CMs persist over time with the help of Computerization Movement Organizations. These are organizations or coalitions of organizations like FARNET, CNI, and CNN, which act as advocacy groups for the CM. They generate resources, structure membership expectations, educate the public, and ensure the presence of recognized leaders who can lend their prestige and interorganizational connections to the movement (McAdam, 1982; McCarthy and Zald, 1977). For example, CNI has task force members from 170 institutions and organizations, including major universities and corporations, all of whom contribute resources and time to the mission of the coalition.

Since movements are not monolithic, they may have any number of organizations affiliated with them. For example, the civil rights movement in the 1960s and 1970s consisted of the National Association for the Advancement of Colored People (NAACP), the Black Muslims, the Southern Christian Leadership Conference (SCLC), the Congress of Racial Equality (CORE), and the Black Panthers, among others (McAdam, 1982). Each had its own particular interests to push and under some circumstances worked with the other organizations to achieve their goals. In other cases, these organizations were in direct conflict about strategies and insurgent tactics. Similarly, the CMOs affiliated with computerization movements have different foci. During periods of crisis or opportunity, they may work in concert with each other. For example, the NII has galvanized many CMOs to form coalitions to ensure a bigger voice in national policy. At other times they may be in direct conflict with each other.

The number of CMOs affiliated with a CM is not constant across time and space. Some time periods are more favorable than others, due to resource availability and historical conditions. Beginning in 1990 with the growth of NSFNET and the passage of the High-Performance Computing Act of 1991, more resources became available and CMOs dedicated to computer-based education and networking flourished. In addition, some geographical regions, such as San Francisco Bay/Silicon Valley and Boston/Cambridge, are hotbeds of innovation and centers of CM activity due to the proximity of multiple universities, research centers, high-tech start-ups, and large numbers of computing specialists. Relational networks and professional associations are plentiful in these areas, fostering social intercourse across organizations and the emergence of new CMOs.

Recruitment to Computerization Movements

The primary resources of all social movements are members, leaders, and some form of communication network. Shared beliefs are communicated along these networks and lines of action are advocated. For example, organizations may learn about and implement the latest computer architectures because their members belong to professional associations that recommend them. Alternatively, friends, classmates, and family members may be avid Internet users and mobilize individuals to participate.

Since the social significance of technologies, like the Clipper Chip, multi-user dungeons, or hypermedia, are often obscure, uncertain, or uninterpretable, most people depend on the analyses of their friends, known or self-described experts, government officials, and CM entrepreneurs to interpret, frame, and attribute meaning to them (Snow *et al.*, 1986; Snow and Benford, 1988). CMOs undertake much of this framing work for constituents by amplifying current problems, interpreting events, and emphasizing the advantages of a transformed social order, where computerization and networking are central, over the current arrangements. Once these frames become publicly available, people can align their own beliefs and actions with those of movement entrepreneurs.

A rhetorical form, which we call technological utopianism, is a key framing device used by movement entrepreneurs to envision the renewal of society through technology. Specific technologies, such as groupware or personal digital assistants, are key enabling elements of utopian visions (Dunlop and Kling, 1991; Kling, 1994). Technological utopianism does not refer to the technologies themselves. It refers to analyses in which the use of specific technologies plays a key role in shaping an ideal or perfect world. For example, the Executive Summary of the NII: Agenda for Action (the White House, 1993) asks readers to imagine a world where people can live anywhere and telecommute to work, where everyone has access to the best teachers via virtual classrooms, and where health care is available on-line. With little or no articulation of the underlying technologies, the costs associated with actually implementing such a vision, or the political struggles that will certainly ensue, the government invites public identification with and participation in the mobilization of support for the expansion of computer networking into every facet of people's lives—in their homes, workplaces, and schools.

Thus far, we have focused on positive identification with new technologies and the rhetoric that accompanies it. But, negative identification with technology is also available, although somewhat less widespread today than in the past. Technological anti-utopianism analyses examine how certain broad families of technologies facilitate a new world order that is relentlessly harsh, destructive, and miserable. For example, technologies embedded with artificial intelligence (AI) are common focal points for science fiction scenarios where humans have lost control to machines (cf., Gibson, 1984). Alternatively, the dark side of computerization can be seen in the cyberpunk movement, that is, the hackers, crackers, and phone phreaks who exploit the weaknesses of telecommunications systems. Cyberpunks wreak havoc, engaging in hacking for profit (Edwards, 1991), espionage (Stoll, 1989), or the pure pleasure of it (Hafner and Markoff, 1991). Whether portrayed as science fiction or actual exploits, anti-utopian analyses focus on the central role of computerization in the emergence of a dystopian future.

Technological utopianism and anti-utopianism signify distinct poles in the framing and interpreting of large-scale computerization projects and what they might mean to the people that will experience them. While actual outcomes of past computerization projects have fallen somewhere between the two extremes, these visions serve to galvanize either support for or the rejection of an extensively computerized future. In the next section, we focus on the beliefs and goals of two specific computerization movements, computer-based education and computer networking, and the CMOs and recruitment processes that enable them. Specific movements are the various wings or submovements of a broader, general movement (Blumer, 1969). Many movements, like those that advance the Christian Right, Eastern religions, anti-tobacco interests, or computerization, are heterogeneous. The distinction between specific movements and general movements helps us to characterize the relationship between a general computerization movement and some specific or distinct wings of the larger movements.

Specific Computerization Movements

One theme in our discussion of computerization and the specific movements that help produce it is the importance of seeing how local practices and concerns, in schools, homes, or communities, are linked to external developments. By distinguishing between a general CM and several specific CMs, we want to draw attention to how similar conceptions about modes of computerization found across many organizations or social settings should be understood. The rise of computing in general can be characterized as steady over the past thirty to forty years with recent large growth. Similarly, the two specific computerization movements that we investigate here, computer-based education and computer networking, are particularly interesting because of their recent exponential growth. For lack of space, we do not focus on other computerization movements such as artificial intelligence, virtual reality, and personal computing, which we have written about elsewhere (Kling and Iacono, 1988, in press). In addition, we expect that new CMs will continue to emerge as new technologies are developed. If this were a book-length document, we could, at length, list the major CMOs in each of these movements and describe their members and communications. We could sample their publications and topics from their conferences, describe their meetings, and excerpt keynote speeches and reports. Instead, our descriptions of computer-based education and computer networking will be suggestive rather than definitive.

Computer-Based Education

Computer-based education refers to both specific technologies, such as computer-assisted instruction (CAI) programs, and the social arrangements in which they are embedded, for example, wired universities and virtual classrooms. Technologies for computer-based education include a broad array of applications such as computer-based simulations, tutorials, and courseware. Advanced graphics capabilities, hypermedia, and object-oriented features allow animation, charts, and tables to be linked by professors in presentations or by students in computer labs. During classroom lectures, systems can be connected to student response keypads allowing for instant feedback. The key belief is that interaction and dynamic adaptation of course materials will maintain student interest, improve retention, and enhance the learning process.

The social arrangements for computer-based education include all levels, from preschool to college to lifelong learning, and all forums, from classrooms to research labs to the Library of Congress and art museums (the White House, 1993). In the mid-1980s, several private colleges and universities required all their incoming students to buy a specific kind of microcomputer to use at school. Other schools invested heavily in visions of a wired campus, increasing computer lab space and wiring the dorms, libraries, and study areas for network connections. There was also a major push to establish computer literacy and computer science as required topics in the nation's elementary and secondary schools. In the mid-1990s, virtual classrooms have become the focus, enabled by computer conferencing, digital libraries, distance teaming, and global networking. These new instructional vehicles are being promoted and funded by the National Science Foundation (NSF), the National Telecommunications and Information Administration (NTIA), and the NII. The President's Fiscal Year 1994 budget included $1.1 billion for the High-Performance Computing and Communications Initiative, including $100 million to develop applications in areas such as education, health, and digital libraries, and $50 million for NTIA grants to demonstrate application of the NII for nonprofit institutions such as schools and libraries.

To mobilize support and generate resources for enabling these large-scale visions at the local level, partnerships and collaboration among business, government, school, and the community are encouraged. Advocates of these social changes argue that students will become active learners and information managers rather than passive receptacles of information transferred to them from the teacher (see Hodas, Part III, Chapter I). At the same time, the role of educators will be expanded as they collaborate with other educators around the world and move from a "chalk and talk" type of education format to one where they act as facilitators, trainers, and innovators. Thus, along with the push for increased computerization in educational settings, this CM advocates a major shift in core beliefs about what students and teachers actually do in the classroom and what constitutes learning.

This CM is far ranging and includes numerous organizations that promote special projects, publish enthusiastic reports, and sponsor periodic conferences. Brief descriptions of two CM organizations, CoSN and CNI, suggest the scale of this CM. The Coalition for Networked Information (CNI), was founded in 1990 to "promote the creation of and access to information resources in networked environments in order to enrich scholarship and to enhance intellectual productivity." It is a joint project of the Association for Research Libraries, CAUSE, and EDUCOM. CNI's members are organizations, and it currently includes over 170 colleges, universities, publishers, network service providers, computer hardware and system companies, library networks and organizations, and public and state libraries. CNI sponsors several working groups. For example, one group called for descriptions to identify "projects that use networking and networked information resources and services in the broadest possible ways to support and enhance teaching and learning (Coalition Working Group on Teaching and Learning, 1993)." This public call for descriptions also noted:

> The Coalition will use the project descriptions it receives in response to this call: (1) to build a database that can be used to share information and experience in this area; (2) to promote awareness of individuals, institutions, and organizations making important contributions to the state-of-the-art in this area; (3) to attract attention to and mobilize resources for this area; (4) to plan a program in this area for the EDUCOM conference in Cincinnati and; (5) to otherwise encourage individuals, institutions, and organizations to use networks and networked information resources and services to support and enhance teaching and learning.

The organizers of this call are not timid in making their interests in mobilizing support for network applications explicit. In order to mobilize more commitment and loyalty to their cause, they encourage people with experience to share information about their own projects and to network with others who are interested but less experienced.

The Consortium for School Networking (CoSN), a nonprofit membership organization, is working with FARNET to develop a model for the information-age school, one that incorporates communications and computer technologies in a new culture of active learning. They are promoting the use of electronic networks as resources for kindergarten through high school. Their long-term vision is of a transformed educational system with empowered teachers and involved communities, and of students educated to succeed in the workplaces of the twenty-first century.

The Clinton administration supports this approach, arguing that what people earn depends on what they learn. Consequently, the NII is dedicated to preparing children for the fast-paced workplace of the twenty-first century (the White House, 1993). This approach emphasizes the preparation of students for new work that will require problem-solving skills and creativity rather than order taking and narrowly defined specializations. Examples of programs that focus on the acquisition of these types of skills include the Global Laboratory Project in Cambridge, Massachusetts and the Texas Education Network (TENET). The Global Laboratory Project is funded by the NSF and links students from 101 schools in 27 states and 17 foreign countries in a global environmental monitoring study. TENET makes the Internet available to Texas school districts. School children, especially those in remote or impoverished school districts, are expected to benefit from the additional resources and access to distant learning opportunities. These schools without walls are utopian visions of education transformed. Despite their actual usefulness to the students and teachers in Cambridge, Massachusetts and Texas, they may do little to change education in the United States or alleviate critical problems, such as illiteracy, high school dropout rates, and inner-city school violence.

Mobilized by the belief that more computerization is better, coalitions of administrators, teachers, and parents are banding together to push for extensive computerization in classroom settings and a basic shift in the educational programs in public schools, universities, and libraries. Advocates of computer-based education promote utopian images of information-age schools where students learn in cooperative, discovery-oriented settings and where all teachers can be supportive, enthusiastic mentors (Kling, 1986). In fact, however, the deployment of technology in schools has generally not affected the day-to-day values and practices of teachers and students due to its threat to the existing social order (see Hodas, Part III, Chapter I). But utopian visions resonate with parents, teachers, and school administrators who are concerned about how education will meet the challenges of the future.

Computer Networking

The computer networking movement encompasses a wide range of domains, some of which overlap computer-based education. For example, this computer-based education movement currently advocates extensive network links across schools, libraries, art museums, and research centers. The computer networking CM pushes this vision even further, advocating the weaving together of all institutional sectors into one giant electronic web. This web is sometimes referred to as cyberspace, a term first used by Gibson (1984) in his science fiction novel, *Neuromancer,* to describe the electronic realm where the novel's action took place. Today, we use the term to refer to the place where all social interactions via computer networks occur.

Prior to 1990, the physical manifestation of cyberspace was the Internet and the primary users were government employees, research scientists, and other academics in research universities and centers throughout the United States and western Europe. The Internet started as an ARPA demonstration project on internetworking in the early 1970s (Kahn, 1994). After splitting off from MILNET (the military network), the ARPA NET became known as the Internet. The National Science Foundation (NSF) paid for new computer science sites to be added to the Internet through CSNET (the Computer Science Network) and then commissioned the NSFNET to link NSF-funded supercomputer centers across the United States. The Department of Energy (DOE) and the National Aeronautics and Space Administration (NASA) built HEPNET (high-energy physics net), SPAN (space physics analysis net), ESNET (energy sciences net), and NSI (NASA science internet), all used primarily by research, academic, and government communities.

In the last few years two related events have helped strengthen the public appeal of the Internet: the expansion and growing commercialization of the Internet and the promotion of technological support for the NII by the Clinton administration. These actions have already expanded the range of Internet services to most universities and colleges, many libraries, and some elementary and secondary schools. Government subsidy and other resources generated by CMOs along with strong advocacy about the transformational capacity of computerization by the media and popular magazines help to fuel the increasing demands for computer networking.

While most users connect to the Internet through work or school, situations where the institution bears the financial burden, increasingly people are willing to pay for Internet connections out of their own pockets. Today, PCs can be found in over 26% of households in the United States and many of them are connected to local computer bulletin boards, on-line services, or the Internet (Brody, 1992). In 1992, New York City had two providers of public Internet access. In 1993, there were seven. More people have been connected to the Internet in the last two years than in the previous twenty.

It is currently estimated that approximately four million homes in the United States are now connected to some type of on-line service and these numbers are growing daily (Eng and Lewyn, 1994). Current scenarios of home use portray exciting social interactions with distant people and places, primarily in the guise of entertainment, home shopping, and group game playing. The NII: Agenda for Action (the White House, 1993) states, "You could see the hottest video games, or bank and shop from the comfort of your home whenever you chose." Although the Clinton administration consistently advocates universal access and affordable prices for users, today only the rich can afford the equipment and network connections required to be on-line.

A less entertaining but nonetheless utopian vision of computer networking focuses on uses that empower and preserve the public interest. Several networking CMOs, like the Society for Electronic Access (SEA), and the Center for Civic Networking (CCN) have focused attention on grass roots networks and the recreation of civic life. The first civic network was the Community Memory in Berkeley, California, started in the mid-1970s to strengthen and revitalize the Berkeley community (Schuler, 1994). Today, over one hundred civic networks are planned or are currently in operation in the United States. They include the Cleveland Free-Net (Ohio), Big Sky Telegraph (Montana), Electronic Cafe International (Santa Monica, CA), and the Cambridge (MA) Civic Forum, all based in and run by local communities in partnership with networking CMOs. Global civil networks have also emerged. Examples include PeaceNet, EcoNet, GreenNet, and ConflictNet, all of which are dedicated to peace, human rights, and environmental preservation. In 1990, these networks with the support of the MacArthur, Ford, and General Service foundations and the United Nations Development Program established the Association for Progressive Communications (APC) with partners in ten countries and affiliated systems in many other countries (Frederick, 1993).

The goal of participants in these civic networks is to make information flows more democratic, break down power hierarchies, and circumvent information monopolies. At the local level, city- and region-wide citizen dialogue is considered critical to the development of innovative solutions for the improvement of government services, industrial competitiveness, and a revitalized democracy. At the global level, network enthusiasts argue that the present flow of world news is too regulated. Five news agencies around the world control about 96% of the world's news flows (Mowlana, 1986). By providing low-cost appropriate solutions, APC networks can democratize cyberspace and provide an effective counter-balance to trends in corporate control of the world's information flows.

Computer networks are central to utopian accounts of the next wave of human culture where much of life is spent on-line. Participants are referred to as settlers or homesteaders (Rheingold, 1993). Specialists are portrayed as cowboys with keyboards rather than six-guns. Exciting images of life at the frontier propel many into participation. Networking activists imply that there are no limits to what can be done in cyberspace by downplaying the actual costs of new technologies and the continuing benefits of physical forms of social interaction. Other media for learning, socializing, working, or revitalizing the community are treated as less important. Real life is life on-line. The physical world is relegated to IRL (in real life) or life off-line (Rheingold, 1993).

The beliefs and strategies advocated by the two CMs have changed over the past several decades. But both have moved in the direction of increasing computerization and networked forms of social arrangements. Helping to fuel this momentum are utopian visions that downplay the actual social choices that can constrain or inhibit institutions from making such large-scale changes and the political challenges that will certainly accompany them. These CMs require enormous resources and their orientation is sufficiently elitist that one might expect some systematic progressive alternative to it. In the next section, we focus on some organizations that have emerged to serve the public interest and which participate in the forming of national policy about computerization. We also discuss the challenges associated with the development of a general movement to counter computerization.

Counter-Computerization Movements

We have argued that CMs generally advance the interests of elite groups in society because of the relatively high costs of developing, using, and maintaining computer-based technologies. This pattern leads us to ask whether CMs could advance the interests of poorer groups or whether there are counter-movements that oppose the general CM. Many CM activists bridle at these questions. They do not necessarily value helping the rich or perceive themselves as part of the elite. In our fieldwork we have found that CM advocates more frequently see themselves as fighting existing institutional arrangements and working with inadequate resources. While many CM participants may have nonelite opinions and beliefs, they must develop coalitions with elite groups in order to gain the necessary financial and social resources to computerize with their preferred arrangements. Given this elite status, one might expect a counter-computerization movement (CCM) to have emerged.

There is no well-organized opposition or substantial alternative, however. Such a movement would have to rest on technologically anti-utopian visions of computerization in social life. Societies or groups that have adopted anti-utopian visions, such as the Amish in the United States or the Luddites during the Industrial Revolution, are typically marginalized and not considered as viable models of future social life. However, some writers are clearly hostile to whole modalities of computerization (Berry,

1991; Braverman, 1975; Mowshowitz, 1976; Reinecke, 1984; Weizenbaum, 1976). These writers differ substantially in their bases of criticism, from the Frankfurt School of critical theory (Weizenbaum) to Marxism (Mowshowitz, Braverman) to conservationism (Wendell Berry).

Today, the major alternatives to CMs come from relatively new and specialized advocacy groups such as Computer Professionals for Social Responsibility (CPSR) and the Electronic Frontier Foundation (EFF). CPSR emerged out of a Xerox/PARC antiwar distribution list in 1981 with an original mission to oppose certain kinds of computer-based weapons technologies such as the Strategic Defense Initiative. Today, it is a national organization of computer professionals with 22 chapters and a much broader focus on public issues and computerization, for example, workplace democracy, civil liberties issues in networking, and broad public access to national computer networks. CPSR has become an active participant in national policy negotiations about information technology policy and currently sponsors action-oriented research to shape social change and social responsibility (cf., CPSR, 1994).

The EFF is a small organization started in 1990 by Mitch Kapor and John Perry Barlow. They argued that long-time advocacy groups such as the ACLU were not taking seriously the violation of electronic publishers' and crackers' civil rights. The Secret Service paid scant attention to due process in their late-night raids and confiscation of computer equipment. The EFF supported the accused and continues to support similar litigation, fund educational projects, protect the public interest, and ensure that the Bill of Rights is extended to include computer and network users.

Long-term advocacy groups such as the ACLU and other social movements, such as the antiwar movement, have tended to focus more narrowly on the specific areas where technology intersects their central concerns. For example, the ACLU has developed long-term projects in the area of technology and privacy, while peace activists have criticized new technologies that they view as making war more likely. Union spokespersons are especially concerned about how computerization affects the number and quality of jobs (Shaiken, 1985). However, they are all relatively mute about many other kinds of computing applications. As a consequence, each of these reform movements is relatively weak and specialized, leaving many arenas of computerization still unexamined and unprotected.

During periods of crisis or opportunity, members of these groups may cooperate. For example, the EFF, CPSR, and the ACLU, among others, are responsible for shifting public opinion against a hardware encryption device, the Clipper Chip—now called Skipjack due to a trademark conflict—that they believe is potentially harmful. They have emphasized its role in the government's ability to conduct surveillance on the telecommunications activities of American citizens. Computing activists such as John Perry Barlow and Mitch Kapor have framed the technical, political, and policy issues involved so that its use is seen as potentially dangerous to privacy rights and other civil liberties. People who knew little about encryption before, are encouraged to think negatively about it and to join the EFF or CPSR to reassert "control over their own government" (Barlow, 1993:26).

Some groups have argued that the EFF effort in regard to the NII is too narrow and they have organized to reach a wider base of public support. The Telecommunications Policy Roundtable, for example, is a coalition of organizations including the Center for Media Education (CME), American Library Association (ALA), CPSR, ARL, and CCN. They are interested in assuring that upscale elite groups associated with the Internet are not the only groups involved in its development. Their goal is to give consumers and low-income persons more voice and power in the policy making process, to build ties among the various groups, and to motivate them to broaden their scope and work together.

In part, the NII has stimulated these groups to form coalitions to ensure more say in the development of national policy and the deployment of resources. They view appropriate computerization as something other than the most technologically sophisticated computer use at any price. Some of these groups are trying to envision computer use which is shaped by other values—such as the improvement of human life and the preservation of civil rights. While these groups challenge the most avid computerization enthusiasts, their missions cannot be characterized as counter computerization. The general drift in most sectors of American society today is toward increased and intensive computerization with CMs playing the major enabling roles.

Conclusion

We have argued that the computerization of many facets of life in the United States has been stimulated by a set of loosely linked computerization movements guided by mobilizing belief systems offered by activists who are not directly employed in the computer and related industries (Kling, 1983). We have characterized computerization movements by their organizations and the ways in which they recruit new members. In particular, a rhetorical form, which we call technological utopianism, is a key framing device for portraying societal renewal through technology and allowing people, many of whom know little about computing, to identify with the goals of the movement. Our analysis differs from most analyses of computerization by considering movements that cut across society as important sources of interpretations and beliefs about what computing is good for and what social actions people should take to secure the future they envision.

A primary resource for all movements are members, leaders, and communications networks. Academics like Daniel Bell, popular writers like

Howard Rheingold, and the White House stimulate enthusiasm for the general computerization movement and provide organizing rationales (e.g., transition to a new information society, participation in virtual communities, and societal renewal) for unbounded computerization. Much of the enthusiasm to computerize is a by-product of this writing and other visions of technological utopianism. Not every computerization movement thrives and the members are selectively influential. We believe that when one studies the sites where new computing applications are being adopted, it is common to find the influences of computerization movements. Members of the adopting organizations or people who consult to them are likely to belong (or have belonged) to a number of organizations that promote that form of computerization.

Computerization movements play a role in trying to persuade their audiences to accept an ideology that favors everybody adopting state-of-the-art computer equipment in specific social sectors. There are many ways to computerize, and each emphasizes different social values (Kling, 1983). While computerization is rife with value conflicts, activists rarely explain the value and resource commitments that accompany their dreams. And they encourage people and organizations to invest in the latest computer-based equipment rather than pay equal or greater attention to the ways that social life can and should be organized around whatever means are currently available. With the recent and notable exceptions discussed in the previous section, activists provide few useful guiding ideas about ways to computerize humanely.

There is unlikely to be a general counter-computerization movement, although some organizations, like CPSR and EFF, have emerged with some interest in the humanistic elements central to the mobilization of computing in the United States. But more frequently, humanistic beliefs are laid onto computerization schemes by advocates of other social movements: the labor movement (Shaiken, 1985), the peace movement, or the civil liberties movement (Burnham, 1983). Advocates of the other movements primarily care about the way some schemes for computerization intersect their special social interest. They advocate limited alternatives but no comprehensive, humanistic alternative to the general computerization movement. In its most likely form, the rise of computer technologies and networks, while promising technological utopias for all, will lead to conservative social arrangements, reinforcing the patterns of an elite-dominated, stratified society.

Acknowledgments

Thanks to Leigh Star for her continuing enthusiasm about this project. Jonathan Grudin has been a stimulating discussant about social movements and new forms of computerization. Vincent Janowicz, Paul Hower, and Woo Young Chung offered helpful comments that made this chapter more readable and provocative.

References

Aronson, Naomi (1984). "Science as a Claims-Making Activity: Implications for Social Problems Research," in Schneider and Kitsuse (eds.), *Studies in the Sociology of Social Problems*, pp. 1–30. Ablex Publishing Co., Norwood, NJ.

Barlow, John Perry (1993). "A Plain Text on Crypto Policy." *Communications of the ACM*, 36(11):21–26.

Bell, Daniel (1979). "The Social Framework of the Information Society," in Michael Dertouzos and Joel Moses (eds.), *The Computer Age: A Twenty-Year View*, pp. 163–211. The MIT Press, Cambridge, MA.

Berry, Wendell (1991). "Why I Am Not Buying a Computer," in Charles Dunlop, and Rob Kling (eds.), *Computerization and Controversy: Value Conflicts and Social Choices*. Academic Press, San Diego, CA.

Blumer, Herbert (1969). "Social Movements," in B. McLaughlin (ed.), *Studies in Social Movements: A Social Psychological Perspective*, pp. 8–29. Free Press, New York.

Braverman, Harry (1975). *Labor and Monopoly Capital: The Degradation of Work in the Twentieth Century.* Monthly Review Press, New York.

Brody, Herb (1992). "Of Bytes and Rights: Freedom of Expression and Electronic Communications." *Technology Review,* 95(8):22.

Bucher, Rue, and Anselm Strauss (1961). "Professions in Process." *American Journal of Sociology,* LXVI:325–334.

Burnham, David (1983). *The Rise of the Computer State.* Random House, New York.

Coalition Working Group on Teaching and Learning (1993). "Call for Project Descriptions" (April). Available by ftp from cni.org in /cniftp/calls/netteach/netteach.txt'.

Computer Professionals for Social Responsibility (1992). "Action-Oriented Research." *The CPSR Newsletter,* 10(1–2), Winter–Spring:3.

Computer Professionals for Social Responsibility (1994). "Serving the Community: A Public Interest Vision of the National Information Infrastructure." *The CPSR Newsletter,* 11(4) and 12(1), Winter:1–10, 20–30.

Dunlop, Charles, and Rob Kling (eds.) (1991). *Computerization and Controversy: Value Conflicts and Social Choices.* Academic Press, San Diego.

Edwards, Lynda (1991). "Samurai Hackers." *Rolling Stone,* September 19:67–69.

Eng, Paul, and Lewyn, Mark (1994). "On-Ramps to the Info Superhighway." *Business Week,* February 7:108.

Feigenbaum, Edward, and McCorduck, Pamela (1983). *Fifth Generation: Artificial Intelligence and Japan's Challenge to the World.* Addison-Wesley, Reading, MA.

Frederick, Howard (1993). "Networks and Emergence of Global Civil Society," in Linda Harasim (ed.), *Global Networks.* MIT Press, Cambridge, MA.

Gamson, William (1975). *The Strategy of Social Protest,* 2d edition. Wadsworth Publishing, Belmont, CA.

Gibson, William (1984). *Neuromancer.* Ace Books, New York.

Hafner, K., and J. Markoff (1991). *Cyberpunk.* Touchstone, New York.

Kahn, Robert E. (1994). "The Role of the Government in the Evolution of the Internet." *Communications of the ACM,* 37(8), August:15–19.

Kaplan, Bonnie (1983). "Computers in Medicine, 1950–1980: The Relationship between History and Policy." Unpublished doctoral dissertation. Department of History, University of Chicago.

Kling, Rob (1980). "Computer Abuse and Computer Crime as Organizational Activities." *Computers and Law Journal*, 2(2):403–427.

Kling, Rob (1983). "Value Conflicts in the Deployment of Computing Applications: Cases in Developed and Developing Countries." *Telecommunications Policy*, (March):12–34.

Kling, Rob (1986). "The New Wave of Academic Computing in Colleges and Universities." *Outlook*, 19(1&2) (Spring & Summer):8–14.

Kling, Rob (1987). "Defining the Boundaries of Computing Across Complex Organizations," in Richard Boland and Rudy Hirschheim (eds.), *Critical Issues in Information Systems*, pp. 307–362. John Wiley, London.

Kling, Rob (1994). "Reading 'All About' Computerization: How Genre Conventions Shape Non-Fiction Social Analyses." *The Information Society*, 10:147–172.

Kling, Rob, and Suzanne Iacono (1984). "The Control of Information Systems Development after Implementation." *Communications of the ACM*, 27(12) (December):1218–1226.

Kling, Rob, and Suzanne Iacono (1988). "The Mobilization of Support for Computerization: The Role of Computerization Movements." *Social Problems*, 35(3) (June):226–243.

Kling, Rob, and Suzanne Iacono (in press). "Computerization Movements and the Mobilization of Support for Computerization," in Leigh Star (ed.), *Ecologies of Knowledge: Work and Politics in Science and Technology*. State University of New York Press, New York.

Kominski, R. (1991). "Computer Use in the United States: 1989." Bureau of the Census, U.S. Department of Commerce.

Leiner, Barry M. (1994). "Internet Technology." *Communications of the ACM*, 37(8)(August):32.

Lidtke, Doris K., and David Moursund (1993). "Computers in Schools: Past, Present, and How We Can Change the Future." *Communications of the ACM*, 36(5) (May):84–87.

McAdam, Doug (1982). *Political Process and the Development of Black Insurgency, 1930–1970*. University of Chicago Press, Chicago.

McCarthy, John D., and Mayer N. Zald (1977). "Resource Mobilization and Social Movements: A Partial Theory." *American Journal of Sociology*, 82(6):1212–1241.

Mowlana, H. (1986). *Global Information and World Communication: New Frontiers in International Relations*. Longman, New York.

Mowshowitz, Abbe (1976). *The Conquest of Will: Information Processing in Human Affairs*. Addison-Wesley, Reading, MA.

Papert, Seymour (1980). *Mindstorms: Children, Computers and Powerful Ideas*. Basic Books, New York.

Quittner, Josh (1994). "Johnny Manhatten Meets the FurryMuckers." *Wired*, March:92–97,138.

Reinecke, Ian (1984). *Electronic Illusions*. Penguin Books, New York.

Rheingold, Howard (1993). *The Virtual Community*. Addison-Wesley, Reading, MA.

Rule, James, and Paul Attewell (1991). "What Do Computers Do?" in Charles Dunlop and Rob Kling (eds.), *Computerization and Controversy: Value Conflicts and Social Choices*. Academic Press, San Diego, CA.

Schuler, Doug (1994). "Community Networks: Building a New Participatory Medium." *CACM*, 37(1):39–51.

Schwartau, Winn (1993). "Crypto Policy and Business Privacy." *PC Week,* 10(25): 207.

Shaiken, Harlie (1985). *Work Transformed: Automation and Labor in the Computer Age.* Holt, Rinehart, and Winston, New York.

Simon, H. A. (1977). *The New Science of Management Decision-Making.* Prentice-Hall, Englewood Cliffs, NJ.

Snow, David A., and Robert D. Benford (1988). "Master Frames and Cycles of Protest." Invited Paper for Workshop on Frontiers in Social Movement Theory. Ann Arbor, Michigan, June 8–11.

Snow, David A., E. Burke Rochford, Jr., Steven K. Worden, and Robert D. Benford (1986). "Frame Alignment Processes, Micromobilization and Movement Participation." *American Sociological Review,* 51:464–481.

Star, Leigh (ed.) (in press). *Ecologies of Knowledge: Work and Politics in Science and Technology.* State University of New York Press, New York.

Stoll, Clifford (1989). *The Cuckoo's Egg.* Pocket Books, New York.

Strassman, Paul (1985). *Information Payoff: The Transformation of Work in the Electronic Age.* Free Press, New York.

Wallich, Paul (1994). "Wire Pirates." *Scientific American,* March, 90–101.

Weizenbaum, Joseph (1976). *Computer Power and Human Reason: From Judgment to Calculation.* W. H. Freeman, San Francisco.

The White House (1993). "The National Information Infrastructure: Agenda for Action." Public domain document.

Yourdon, Edward (1986). *Nations at Risk: The Impact of the Computer Revolution.* Yourdon Press, New York.

P·A·R·T · III

The Economic, Cultural, and Organizational Dimensions of Computerization

P·A·R·T · III

The Centrality of Organizations in the Computerization of Society

Rob Kling

The Enduring Importance of Organizations

This section examines several organizational aspects of computerization that also have cultural and economic dimensions: the ways in which computer systems support new services and alter competition between organizations; and the extent to which computerization alters the productivity of organizations and changes their costs.[1] We also examine how organizational processes, bureaucratization, and fights over power influence the way that organizations computerize.

Because of the powerful role that organizations of all kinds play in our society, it's important that we understand how they behave. The owners and managers of organizations often take organizations for granted. But many professionals are ambivalent about the roles of organizations in understanding how our society computerizes. For example, in *Out of Control: The Rise of Neo-Biological Civilization* (excerpted in Part II, Chapter B), Kevin Kelly examines the evolution of industrial societies that utilize technologies such as computer networks and tiny robots. Kelly celebrates some key discoveries and inventions of computer scientists in advanced research laboratories funded by huge private firms such as Xerox, and giant federal agencies such as NASA. But his own theorizing ignores the importance of organizations in his celebration of computing innovations. Kelly refers to organizations as part of an old-fashioned, control-oriented mind-

set that made more sense in the industrial era but which have less significant roles in the new "anarchic society" that Kelly heralds.
Criticisms of organizations, as such, have deep roots in American individualism. In the mid-1950s, William H. Whyte published a scathing critique of United States corporations in his book *The Organization Man:*

> the organization man . . . I am talking about *belong* to (The Organization) as
> well. They are the ones of our middle class who have left home, spiritually as
> well as physically, to take the vows of organization life, and it is they who are
> the mind and soul of our great self-perpetuating institutions. Only a few are
> top managers or ever will be. . . . they are of the staff as much as the line, and
> most are destined to live poised in a middle area . . . they are the dominant
> members of our society nonetheless. They have not joined together into a
> recognizable elite — our country does not stand still long enough for that — but
> it is from their ranks that are coming most of the first and second echelons of
> our leadership, and it is their values which will set the American temper.
>   The corporation man is the most conspicuous example, but he is only one,
> for the collectivization so visible in the corporation has affected almost every
> field of work. Blood brother to the business trainee off to join Du Pont is the
> seminary student who will end up in the church hierarchy, the doctor headed
> for the corporate clinic, the physics Ph.D. in a government laboratory, the
> intellectual on the foundation-sponsored team project, the engineering grad-
> uate in the huge drafting room at Lockheed, the young apprentice in a Wall
> Street law factory.
>   They are all, as they so often put it, in the same boat. Listen to them talk
> to each other over the front lawns of their suburbia and you cannot help but
> be struck by how well they grasp the common denominators which bind
> them. Whatever the differences in their organization ties, it is the common
> problems of collective work that dominate their attentions, and when the Du
> Pont man talks to the research chemist or the chemist to the army man, it is
> these problems that are uppermost. The word *collective* most of them can't
> bring themselves to use — except to describe foreign countries or organiza-
> tions they don't work for — but they are keenly aware of how much more
> deeply beholden they are to organization than were their elders. They are wry
> about it, to be sure; they talk of the "treadmill," the "rat race," of the inability
> to control one's direction. But they have no great sense of plight; between
> themselves and organization, they believe they see an ultimate harmony and
> . . . they are building an ideology that will vouchsafe this trust. (Whyte,
> 1956:3–4)

---

[1] Because of space limitations, this section will not examine how computerization changes
employment and the distribution of income. See the following sources for an introduction to
the key debates: Cyert and Mowery (1987); Forester (1987, Ch. 9); Ginzberg, Noyelle, and
Stanback (1986); Hartman, Kraut and Tilly (1986); Kling (1990); Kling and Turner (1991);
Menzies (1981); and Nisbet (1992). Bluestone (1994) reviews ten possible causes of income
inequality in the United States, including technological change, the shift to services, and the
global restructuring of businesses.

Whyte's book became a best seller in the 1950s and 1960s when he helped identify the angst that many people feel about the ways that large organizations, public and private, can overwhelm individuals with their seductive and oppressive cultures, with their pressures for people to fit in, and so on. Love them or hate them, we have to engage them. In order to understand many key social aspects of computerization, we have to have some good understanding of how organizations behave.

Despite the ambivalence that many professionals feel about organizations, they are also central players in our national stories of computerization. Huge companies, like IBM, Burroughs, General Electric, and RCA built the earliest computers in the 1950s.[2] These costly, room-sized behemoths were bought by large government agencies, such as the Department of Defense and the U.S. Census Bureau, as well as by large private firms such as the Bank of America.

Today, a book-sized, four-pound $1200 "sub-notebook PC" packs the computing power of million dollar mainframe computers of the 1960s. We might imagine that the downsizing and price reductions of computing technology has moved large organizations from center stage in our national story of computerization, because now anyone who can afford to buy a car or color TV can afford a computer or two as well. The press is carrying more stories about the ways that diverse people use computers, especially computer networks such as the Internet. Some people argue that a computer at hand enables a tiny business made up of a few people to compete with the biggest firms. This position has been argued most forcefully by John Naisbitt (1994) in *Global Paradox: The Bigger the World Economy, the More Powerful Its Smallest Players*. There is certainly some truth to the observation that tiny organizations have developed interesting software, and that tiny firms can sell high-quality business services by carefully subcontracting some of their activities.

But tiny firms do not remain small when they manufacture millions of items, or provide services (such as training and repair) to thousands of customers. Apple Computer Company may have been started by two guys hacking in a garage. But in the 1990s, it was employing about 16,000 people. And Apple's behavior in releasing new products, servicing old ones and so on was based, in part, on ways that large organizations behave.

I believe that organizations, large and small, still play major roles in the shape of computing in North America. On the production side, huge firms

---

[2] Some of these companies, such as GE and RCA, left the computer industry by the 1960s. They have been replaced by firms such as Apple, Novell, Microsoft, and Compaq, which started as tiny firms in the early 1980s.

like Microsoft, Apple, Sun, Hewlett-Packard, and IBM play major roles in selling computer software and hardware. While a gifted designer might conceive of the fundamental features of new kinds of software, it will become commonplace through sales to millions of computer users only with the follow-up work of a small army of product developers, marketers, salespeople, and accountants. Large firms like Microsoft, Claris, Novell, AT&T, Symantec, and Oracle—as well as the major computer companies— refine and market the software that runs on millions of computers, large and small. The communications infrastructure for wide area networking is provided by another set of huge organizations, including AT&T, the seven regional Bell operating companies, McGaw, and so on.

We live in a society in which many key goods and services are provided by organizations that employ hundreds to thousands of people: the airlines, state university systems, pharmaceutical firms, ensurers, phone companies, hotel chains, automobile manufacturers, and so on. Of course, many important life events do not take place in relationship to organizations, especially large ones. But from our births in hospitals to the recording of our deaths by county administrators, we deal continually with organizations. And the ways that these organizations computerize can influence the nature of their services, the costs of their goods, the ways that we interact with them, and the kinds of workplaces they create for tens of millions of North Americans.

It is easy to rely on conventional simplifications about organizations and fail to understand how they behave. It is easy to refer to all government agencies as bureaucracies, and emphasize their rigidities and rule-boundedness, while missing their roles as political agents that serve some interest groups more than others. It is easy to characterize private firms as efficient agents of their boards of directors, while underestimating the bureaucratic features of the larger firms. Or we might be willing to see a behemoth industrial firm like IBM as an arthritic bureaucracy, but miss the bureaucratic elements of more popular firms like Apple Computer or Ben and Jerry's ice cream company. In *Images of Organization*, Gareth Morgan examines many different metaphors for understanding how organizations behave, as machines, brains, psychic prisons (as in Whyte's characterization), and so on. It is an important book to help expand one's understanding of the many different ways to view organizations, since no single metaphor is adequate.

New Services and Business Competition

Business writers, managers, and technologists often argue that computerized information systems are essential if modern businesses are to compete nationally and internationally. In fact, some have argued that information technology and related skills are "the new wealth of nations."[3] The specific arguments vary and focus on different aspects of organizational life. Some focus on the ways that computer systems help firms develop new services, while other arguments emphasize the ways that computerized systems might enhance workers' productivity. It is an important social choice to organize society in order to maximize efficiency and profit, rather than according to other values, such as plentiful jobs, good working conditions, or reliable service to customers. The decisions to computerize are never *merely* economic.[4]

The first selection of this part, "Israel: Of Swords and Software Plowshares," by Gad Ariav and Seymour Goodman, examines some of the cultural and organizational aspects of computerization. They are quite frank in identifying the ways that a relatively aggressive cultural style leads software designers to "battle test" their computer systems. And they also identify the special role that the Israeli military played in training computer experts who were subsequently hired by private firms in Israel (and even the United States).

In "Getting the Electronics Just Right," Barnaby Feder examines computerization at Wells Fargo, a major California bank. Feder's story concisely describes several different computerization efforts, some aimed at providing new services and others aimed at improving internal efficiencies. Feder's account is one of the rare concise portraits of many different computerized information systems in a firm. Because of its brevity, it is necessarily highly simplified. Like many business writers, Feder stresses how a firm succeeded in developing innovative computer systems and new services. While each of Feder's descriptions portrays Wells Fargo as a cheerful place to work, one can readily imagine the stress that many workers felt in developing or using these information systems. Usually technological and organizational innovation is costly even when things go well.[5]

The third selection is "How Information Technologies Can Transform Organizations" by Michael Scott Morton of the MIT Sloan School of Management. He examines how organizations can benefit from making major company-wide investments in networked computer systems and how they

---

[3] See, for example, Feigenbaum and McCorduck (1983) and Opel (1987).

[4] Kling (1983) examines the character of value conflicts stimulated by computerization. Also see Bluestone (1994). We will examine some of these value conflicts explicitly in Part VI.

[5] Banks often compete on the interest they offer for savings and the amount they charge for loans. If computer systems lowered administrative costs, banks would be able to offer more favorable interest rates, and thus attract more business. But banks also compete on the kinds of services they offer, including notaries, branch locations, banking hours, networks of automated teller machines, and the variety of kinds of accounts. So, administrative cost savings, instead of being passed on to customers, may be used to support expanded banking services.

should align their approaches to computerization with other major organizational strategies.

> . . . information technology is a critical enabler of the re-creation (redirection) of organizations. This is true because it permits the distribution of power, function and control to wherever they are most effective, given the missions and objectives of the organization and the culture it enjoys. (Morton, 1991:17)

> [Information Technology] IT is available to radically alter the basic cost structure of a wide variety of jobs, jobs affecting at least half the members of an organization. IT is only an enabler, however: to actually change jobs takes a combination of management leadership and employee participation that is, thus far, extremely rare. (p. 11)

> In summary, the traditional organizational structures and practices do not have to stay the same as we move into the 1990s. All dimensions of the organization will have to be reexamined in light of the power of the new IT. The economics are so powerful and apply to so much of the organization that one has to question everything before accepting the status quo. (p. 11)

Morton offers a relatively sophisticated conception of information technologies by viewing them as enablers rather than as causes. Morton is optimistic about the potential value of information technologies to upper managers and professionals, but he differs from the technological utopians by refusing to treat technology as a simple cause. He observes that effectively selecting, organizing, and using information technologies require many subtle assessments of an organization's strategies, its culture, and the character of specific technical systems. He also notes that relatively few business firms have reaped broad benefits from IT. This is a frank observation to come from a senior professor of IT at MIT's Sloan School of Management.

Innovation is fraught with risks, and costs can escalate when things go wrong. And even very expensive projects developed by highly qualified professionals can fail to meet their designers' expectations; in extreme cases they may be aborted. The fourth selection by Douglas Frantz examines how another major bank, the Bank of America, spent $60 million to get a $20-million computer system for trust-management to work properly—and then abandoned the whole project. The Bank of America's experience is not unique (Oz, 1994). The story of many computerization projects lies somewhere between those of the Bank of America and Wells Fargo (Feder's case)—they ultimately work in some way, but they take longer to implement, cost more, and are much more disruptive than their advocates had hoped. Since managers and professionals are usually embarrassed when their computerization projects do not go smoothly and according to schedule, few of the professional articles about computerization accurately portray the dynamics of computerization in real organizations.

The main controversies about the role of computer systems in supporting new services concern the extent to which they serve as economically effective means for drawing new customers, retaining old ones, and improving the economy generally. At the same time, computer-based services are not just conveniences. Their widespread deployment restructures industries as well as relations between people and organizations.

Computerization in Organizational Context

Studies of computerization often make critical *implicit* assumptions about the way that organizations behave. It is interesting to contrast the analyses by Feder and Frantz. Feder portrays Wells Fargo as tightly managed, in which major purchases such as computer systems fit narrowly defined organizational purposes very well. In contrast, Frantz portrays some of Bank of America's internal structures that influenced their choices. In his view, the bank's diverse managers were either supportive or cautious about computerization projects. He also portrays fragmented authority, and how different groups relied on the same staff to carry out incompatible activities.

One might casually dismiss these two articles as "only cases of two banks that have limited relevance to other organizations." The next two selections by Kirkpatrick and Orlikowski illustrate how analysts implicitly assume different models of organizational behavior in their studies of computerization. David Kirkpatrick, a journalist who publishes in *Fortune,* and Wanda Orlikowski, a professor of information systems at MIT's Sloan School of Management, both write about the use of groupware by businesses. Groupware refers to a range of computer systems that facilitate the functioning of groups by allowing many people to communicate via electronic mail and conferencing facilities, or to work together with common bodies of text, colleagues' schedules, and so on.[6] Lotus Notes is designed to enable groups that are located in different offices and locations to share messages and memos via computerized bulletin boards and document databases. Groupware has been marketed with an emphasis on shared effort, collaboration, and cooperation. However, in his selection, "Groupware Goes Boom," Kirkpatrick claims:

> The new groupware tools are so powerful, in fact, that they virtually compel companies to reengineer themselves. By giving workers well below the top of the organizational pyramid access to information previously unavailable or restricted to upper levels of management, groupware spreads power far more widely than before. Many who have grown comfortable dwelling near the pyramid's apex are understandably distressed by the way groupware disrupts old-style hierarchies.

---

[6] Social psychologists characterize a group as a collection of two or more persons who interact with one another in such a manner that each person influences and is influenced by each other person (Shaw, 1976:11).

Many lower-level workers would be keenly interested in seeing upper managers' memos about such topics as executive compensation pay and bonus structures,[7] strategic plans for expanding an organization, or even specific plans for firing some staff! So one could imagine that lower-level staff would be specially interested in using Lotus Notes. Kirkpatrick speculates about the ways that Lotus Notes may have been used when a major accounting firm, Price Waterhouse, licensed 10,000 copies in 1991. Other journalists also published glowing reports of Notes's use in newspapers such as *The New York Times* and *The Washington Post*, and business magazines such as *Forbes* and *Business Week.*[8]

In "Learning from Notes," Wanda Orlikowski reports her own observations of Lotus Notes's use at a major consulting firm in the months after Lotus Notes was being installed. (She does not disclose the firm's identity, but it is widely believed to be a regional Price Waterhouse office.) Her study raises questions about the extent to which powerful new technologies can provoke professionals in organizations to change their ways of working. Orlikowski's rich case illustrates the complexities of deploying a new information technology in a large, decentralized professional organization. Lotus Notes was acquired by the firm's Chief Information Officer, who was highly enthusiastic about its possibilities for enabling offices worldwide to rapidly share their expertise. However, as Orlikowski points out, he overestimated how much the potential for innovations based on Notes would "become obvious" to anyone who used it, and the extent to which diverse professionals would actually invest their time in learning about Notes.

Part of Orlikowski's analysis rests on the way that Notes's use was related to the reward structure at Price Waterhouse. At many consulting firms the staff is divided into consultants and staff groups. The salaried support staff provide core services, including accounting and information services for the firm. The consultants who bill direct services to clients can be further divided into partners and associates. A relatively small group of highly paid partners own the company and are essentially tenured in their jobs. They are assisted by a much larger group of less well paid consultants, who are sometimes called associates. The partners' incomes are based primarily on profits from the projects that they directly manage, and a share of the firm's overall profits. The associates are salaried, and many of them want to become partners. The major consulting firms have a system of annual reviews in which associates are retained and rewarded with more authority and pay; or they are asked to leave ("up or out" rules). After

[7] See Earl Shorris' (1981) poignant stories of managers who are in the dark about the conditions under which they are rewarded, promoted, transferred, or fired (and especially pp. 220–225).

[8] See, for example, Dyson (1990a, 1990b), McAllister (1989), Miller (1992), and O'Reilly (1993).

seven to nine years of successive promotions, some of the surviving associates are promoted to be partners, while others leave the firm. The associates compete with each other for the few new partnerships, where incomes can start at over $200,000 per year. Orlikowski observed that the staff and partners who had significant job security were most willing to learn Lotus Notes and share professional information. In contrast, the numerous associates were preoccupied with their careers and the risk of being fired if they did not produce lots of billable services for their immediate clients. They were reluctant to learn Notes or to share their special expertise with each other. Why should people whose promotions depend on being seen as having unique expertise be willing to give it away to others, just because a slick computer system facilitates it? Her account of the relative interest in Notes use by partners and associates is the reverse of Kirkpatrick's claims that the uppermost managers would be least interested.

The next pair of selections by Henry Jay Becker and Stephen Hodas examine the possibility of using computer technologies to facilitate learning in K–12 schools. They also illustrate how analyses of the nature and conditions of computerization can rest on conceptions about how organizations and people in them behave. In "How Much Will a Truly Empowering Technology-Rich Education Cost?" Henry Becker examines the economic dimensions of educational innovation through new technology. He notes that schools in the United States buy 300,000 to 500,000 new computers, as well as associated software, every year. Traditional computer-based instruction, like the much-despised drill and practice programs are based on a model of instruction that views students as receptacles who are delivered information and skills from central repositories, whether they are expert human teachers or software.

Today's leaders in instructional computing favor an "access model" (Newman, 1993) in which networked systems enable teachers and students to collaborate and gather information from distributed resources and communities of peers. Becker advocates this access model and briefly examines the full costs of effectively supported computing that the access model requires. One of the striking features of Becker's analysis is the magnitude of the annual costs per student for equipment (about $550) and personnel support beyond the traditional classroom teacher (about $1400). While the ratio of these costs might change with the decreasing costs of computer hardware, they are much higher amounts than schools traditionally invest in educational innovations. Becker argues that schools could effectively computerize with a collaborative form of teaching and learning if educational reformers and technologists were willing to face up to the full costs. Becker concluded a recent related article with these observations:

> Schools are lagging behind, though, in the critical area of curriculum development for using computer-based tools in subject matter classes. Most subject-matter teachers have not yet learned how, for example, spreadsheets

relate to mathematics instruction, or multimedia to English or fine arts instruction, or databases to science instruction. For computer education to avoid becoming simply another isolated set of skills and procedures to be mastered, a major effort in curriculum upgrading must occur within the academic disciplines, as they are practiced in typical school settings. When that happens, computer education will be increasingly meaningful to the schools of America. (Becker, 1993:73)

In "Technology Refusal and the Organizational Culture of Schools," Steven Hodas examines the likelihood that schools will embrace the kinds of changes in instructional technologies and instructional approaches advocated by Becker. Hodas notes that

all these attempts to modernize, to rationalize, to "improve" the schools by making them more efficient have had very little effect. Textbooks, paperbacks, blackboards, radio, film, film strips, airplanes, television, satellite systems and telecommunications have all in their time been hailed as modernizers of American education.

He identifies technologies as social constructions (rather than contraptions or machines), which are value laden, and

Any practice (and a technology is, after all, a set of practices glued together by values) that threatens to disrupt this existing structure will meet tremendous resistance at both adoption and implementation stages.

Hodas's argument about the dilemmas of providing significant computer support for K–12 education hinges on an observation that is also pertinent to Orlikowski's study of Lotus Notes at Price Waterhouse:

The divergence of interests between managers and workers, and the potential implementation fissures along those lines, is a source of much of the implementation failure of widely-touted "advances."

But he goes on to make a much more wide-ranging systematic argument about the adoption of innovations than does Orlikowski or Becker:

And yet each battle is essentially the same battle. The technologists' rhetoric is remarkably consistent regardless of the specifics of the machine at issue. So too is their response when the technologies in question meet with only a lukewarm response: to blame the stubborn backwardness of teachers or the inflexibility and insularity of school culture. While elements of both of these certainly play their part in what I'll call 'technology refusal' on the part of schools, it behooves us to remember that all technologies have values and practices embedded within them. In this respect, at least, technology is never neutral; it always makes a difference. From this perspective, the reactionary response on the part of schools (by which I mean the response of individuals within schools acting to support their institutional function) perceived by technology advocates makes a great deal more sense than the pig-headed Luddism so often portrayed. Further, technology refusal represents an immediate and, I believe, fundamentally accurate assessment of the challenges to existing structures and authority that are embodied or embedded in the contested technology. I believe further that the depth of the resistance is generally and in broad strokes proportionate to the seriousness of the actual threat.

Hodas's paper provides a rich analysis of the ways that many interesting forms of computer-supported education threaten the expertise of many teachers and thus a key aspect of their sometimes shaky authority. Hodas's argument differs fundamentally from Becker's since he sees the core cultures of K–12 schools, rather than money, skill, and time, as the central dilemmas of effective instructional computing.

Arguably the best examples of the effective integration of instructional computing can be found in colleges and universities rather than in K–12 schools. How do the most lively colleges and universities differ from K–12 schools, beyond their abilities to accept and retain the more talented and motivated students and their relatively free intellectual milieux? Even the best universities have sometimes engaged in million-dollar instructional computing projects that had little sustained educational value (Shields, 1995).

Models of Organizational Behavior

We can find many points of contention between pairs of the last six articles: Feder versus Frantz, Kirkpatrick versus Orlikowski, and Becker versus Hodas. In some case the articles do not directly contradict each other. For example, Bank of America may have had much more trouble implementing its trust investment system than did the Wells Fargo Bank. But Frantz's and Orlikowski's articles can lead us to wonder whether the information systems at Wells Fargo were all implemented as simply, smoothly, and happily as Feder implies. Kirkpatrick and Orlikowski do provide different stories about the nature of Lotus Notes use at a specific company, Price Waterhouse. But, more seriously, they differ in their ways of conceptualizing the use of Lotus Notes and the ways that people integrate such programs into their work. In contrast, Becker and Hodas agree on the relatively limited use of instructional computing to support collaborative learning in K–12 schools in the United States. But they differ significantly in their diagnoses of the impediments to instructional innovation. Becker believes that a forthright willingness of school boards to account for the true equipment and labor costs of computerization (and tacitly, a willingness to raise taxes to pay for them) will transform the computation landscape of K–12 education. Hodas doesn't disagree that the actual costs for computing equipment and support staff are high. But he believes that professionals who are likely to lose power from an innovation (as teachers can from progressive teaching via computing) are unlikely to adopt it.

Underlying these debates about computerization in banks, consulting firms, and schools is a deeper set of debates about how organizations behave with information technology. Feder, Kirkpatrick, and Becker tacitly work with a vision of organization that sociologists refer to as a Rational Systems model (Kling and Jewett, 1994; Scott, 1992). A Rational Systems model focuses on clear goals, tasks, specialized jobs, and procedures (including information flows, authorizations, etc.). Concerns for efficiency dominate the organization, in this view. In contrast, Frantz, Orlikowski, and Hodas work with a Natural Systems model (Kling & Jewett, 1994; Scott, 1992). Natural Systems models focus on the ways that work is done based on informal influence, including informal communication patterns, status, power, friendships, emerging roles, and so on. Goals may be ambiguous, resources inadequate and problematic, and groups may seriously conflict within and between organizations, and act in self-interested ways to maintain their survival.

These different models lead analysts to have different expectations of the roles of computer-based systems in organizations. Rational Systems analysts do not always see computerization in rosy terms, although they often do (e.g., Feder). Since Natural Systems analysts see large organizations as having multiple and conflicting goals, and as incapable of perfectly meeting any goal in a sustained way, they view computerization as much more problematic, even when it works well. Although the selections in this book that are based on Natural Systems models examine an information system that failed or computerization projects that have had limited success, other analyses from this perspective have examined how political action is critical for the *success* of information systems.[9]

Since the 1970s, a group of scholars including Bill Dutton, Suzanne Iacono, John King, Rob Kling, David Knights, Kenneth Kraemer, Kenneth Laudon, Lynne Markus, Wanda Orlikowski, and Geoff Walsham produced a series of detailed studies that examined how the political coalitions within organizations shaped decisions to computerize, and the consequences of computerization.[10] These scholars focused on large organizations with hundreds or thousands of employees. They found that these large organizations were frequently segmented into coalitions that held conflicting views of which goals the organization should emphasize and which strategies would best achieve them. While the computer projects favored by specific coalitions often had important elements of economic rationality, they often helped to strengthen the power of their champions as well. In fact, systems champions often exaggerated what was known about the economic value or necessity of specific projects. From this perspective, computerization entails organizational changes that do not benefit all

---

[9] See, for example: Kling and Iacono (1984); Kraemer, Dickhoven, Tierney, and King (1987); Knights and Murray (1994); Lyytinen and Hirschheim (1987); and Walsham (1993).

[10] See Kling (1987), Kling (1992), and Kling and Jewett (1994) reviews of some of the studies that treat computerization as a phenomenon embedded within organizations.

participants. For example, in some research universities, the scientists have acquired relatively powerful "number crunchers," while instructional computing labs are relatively impoverished. Students and faculty do not necessarily benefit comparably when a university invests several million dollars in new academic computer systems. "Computer power" comes in part from the organized action of social systems rather than simply from "faster" computers with larger memories and greater communications capacity.

Those analysts who examine computerization from a Rational Systems perspective view computerization in different terms from those who view computerization from a Natural Systems perspective. It is relatively rare that analysts of these differing persuasions debate each other. The controversies are much more implicit in the diverse stories about computerization, such as the contrasts between Kirkpatrick and Orlikowski or between Becker and Hodas. Newspapers and professional journals are most likely to publish Rational Systems accounts, while the Natural Systems accounts are most likely to appear in a small number of scholarly journals and books. Although this is a critical controversy, the debate is not explicit and not joined.

Natural Systems analysts, like Hodas and Orlikowski, believe that behavior within organizations is crucial for understanding the role of computerization in shaping organizations. In fact, some analyses within this approach examine computerized systems as forms of organization rather than as easily separable entities (Kling, 1987; Kling and Iacono, 1989; Kling, 1992).

Computerization and the Productivity Paradox

Many analysts have argued that organizations could effectively increase the productivity of white collar workers through careful "office automation." There is a routine litany about the benefits of computerization: decreasing costs or increasing productivity are often taken for granted. For example, here is a brief sample news item from a computer science journal:

> Chrysler Corporation's new computerized car design system promises to accelerate the development of cars by thirty percent, saving the automotive giant millions of dollars in car costs. The $200,000 system was developed by the Evans and Sutherland Company of Salt Lake City.[11]

Brief items like this appear frequently in newspapers and magazines. That they are often printed without comment, as statements of fact, indi-

---

[11] *Communications of the ACM,* 32(9)(September, 1989).

cates the way in which the link between computerization and cost savings is often taken for granted. We might imagine some alternative news clips:

> Chrysler Corporation's new air conditioning system in its design center promises to accelerate the development of cars by thirty percent, saving the automotive giant millions of dollars in car costs.

> Chrysler Corporation's new practice of having designers feel free to look at the ceiling when they let their minds wander promises to accelerate the development of cars by thirty percent, saving the automotive giant millions of dollars in car costs.

These story lines could have plausible rationales. Staring at the ceiling could free up the imaginations of designers; better air conditioning might improve their ability to concentrate during Detroit's hot, humid summer days. But stories like these are less likely to appear without some special explanation! The theme of computerization's direct economic value has already become a cultural stereotype in the United States. Like many stereotypes, it is based on some important insights. But like all stereotypes, it alters those insights and goes well beyond them.

Sometimes these stereotypes concerning the economics of computerization actually work against managers and their staffs. Some computer-based systems have enabled organizations to reduce the amount of direct labor required for certain everyday activities, such as calculating and printing routine bills. However, many computer applications improve the quality of the work done, rather than reduce the number of people who work in a specific office. And this result won't readily appear in cost accounting. For example, some computerized accounting systems provide more detailed, timely, and accurate information about expenditures than do their manual counterparts or simpler computerized precursors. Use of these systems can sometimes help managers and professionals to manage their funds better. But they may also require as many accounting clerks as the simpler systems for organizing data and producing new reports. Higher-level managers in organizations have sometimes balked at investing in more sophisticated computer applications and have refused to approve proposals for new computer systems without associated staff reductions. Many managers view computer systems in direct economic terms, in terms of money spent or saved, and revenues generated.

Concerns with economic costs and payoffs might appear as rather narrow and concrete, in contrast to a richer array of social values, which we examine elsewhere in this book. Even so, there is a substantial debate about why organizations adopt some computer-based systems and why they do not adopt others. For example, despite the routine claims that computer-based technologies decrease costs and raise productivity, it is remarkably difficult to find careful cost/benefit studies of computerization in particular firms.[12] Executives report that they do not evaluate IT on productivity alone, but that they also emphasize issues such as revenue stability, risk avoidance, growth potential, strategic flexibility, or market share (Quinn and Baily, 1994). But productivity improvements are important at the level of the whole economy to increase the economic standard of living.

The meaning of productivity is much narrower than a "positive cost/ benefit ratio," and the term productivity is often used inaccurately and loosely. Productivity refers to a ratio of outputs divided by inputs. The outputs can be units of goods or services or revenue, and the inputs can include labor, equipment, supplies, and similar costs. For a simple example, consider an office assistant who is paid $6 per hour and who has an ink-jet printer that prints two pages per minute to help her produce ten two-page letters a week during a part-time job. If her supervisor bought her a $2000 laser printer that printed twelve pages per minute, she would spend less time waiting for her letters to print. She would *feel more productive* because a letter would be printed almost as fast as she turned to the printer. In fact, she would be saving about ten minutes a week in finger-tapping time, at a labor savings of about $50 per year. However, if she were the only person to use that new printer, the organization's productivity would have decreased, because the cost of producing each letter would have increased after we add in the cost of the laser printer. However, if twelve full-time assistants who produced forty letters each week and were paid $12 per hour shared this faster laser printer, the organization could be more productive after two years.

Many of us feel more productive when we get more done, or seem to be wasting less time. We focus on outputs or the costs that we bear personally. But the economic measures of productivity are defined by ratios of outputs to *total costs,* and are sensitive to labor rates, equipment costs, and similar factors. One of the complications in measuring productivity is that new equipment or technical systems can often produce qualitatively different kinds of products.

The 12-ppm laser printer is not just a faster ink-jet printer; it is likely to store more varied fonts, print with much finer resolution, and consequently be used for printing niftier documents, like brochures and charts. These new capabilities sometimes give people a heady feeling of heightened effectiveness, and it has helped energize excitement about the eco-

---

[12] See, for example, King and Schrems (1978) for an assessment of key techniques of cost–benefit analyses at the level of individual computer applications or systems. The "productivity paradox" refers to the absence of strong relationships between investments in information technologies and productivity at the level of economic sectors or the whole economy, not at the level of individual applications or the firm. Also, see Landauer (1995) for concrete discussions of the productivity gains attributable to specific technologies.

nomic value of computerization. But qualitative changes in the nature of computer-supported services make productivity comparisons more complex in practice.[13]

One key point that is usually ignored is the way in which the burden for increasing productivity with computer systems usually falls on the poorest paid workers in an organization. A clerk who is paid $20,000 per year must increase her productivity five times as much as an executive paid $100,000 to get a comparable return on a $10,000 computer investment. Over a three-year period, the clerk must increase her effectiveness (or productivity) by 15% a year (6 hours a week equivalent), while the executive need only improve by 3% a year to break even on the investment. Computerization is one strategy among many that organizations can employ to reduce costs or improve revenues and service. Other common strategies include improving the structure of the organization, including reallocations of responsibility, reducing the levels of hierarchy,[14] reducing the amount of internal review[15] and paperwork, and so on.[16] Computerization often seems most effective when it is coupled with a sensible reform program, rather than simply as a freestanding effort "to modernize."

Most articles and books about computerization and work, such as the article by Weiland in Part II and by Feder and Kirkpatrick in this section, are written as if computer systems are highly reliable and graceful instruments. The few systematic exceptions to this rule appear in some of the software reviews and advice sections written in popular publications such as *PC World, Mac World, PC Magazine*, and *Byte Magazine*, which sometimes identify clumsy features in commercial microcomputer software. But these reviews are exceptional, and are most likely to be read by computer specialists and computer buffs. And the names of some software packages, such as WordPerfect, RightWriter, Sidekick, and Excel, suggest graceful, refined tools that help only as needed.

It is common knowledge that programs can have bugs, or that people may have trouble transferring data between two different kinds of

---

[13] Economists struggle for reliable ways to measure the real output of service industries (i.e., Sherwood, 1994).

[14] See, for example, Hymowitz (1990).

[15] For example, Smith and Alexander (1988) report that the Xerox Corporation required about 180 reviews and signatures for a new photocopier to reach the market in the late 1970s. In the 1980s the firm was restructured to streamline the reviews, with significant improvements in the speed of releasing more competitive products. Certain kinds of computerization projects could seem helpful, but could actually simply reinforce problematic organizational practices. For example, an organization that requires many signatures for product reviews might seem to "need" a computerized database system to help track the status of a product in the maze of reviews and approvals. A simpler review process, with a less-complex status tracking system, might be of much greater value.

[16] See Campbell, Campbell and Associates (1988) for a high-quality comprehensive review of the research about productivity in organizations.

computers. But these problems are usually viewed as rare anomalies. An anomaly is an occurrence that differs from what one reasonably expects (see Gasser, 1986). Suppose that you write a report at home on a computerized word processor and take the file to your office for printing. If the system configurations in both locations are comparable, you naturally expect the report at work to print exactly as you formatted it at home; any differences appear to be anomalous.[17] Contrary to much advertising and reporting, problems in *ordinary* uses of computer systems can consume large amounts of time and patience.

The folk wisdom about computing is framed in a series of assumptions about the normal operation of equipment, such as that reports formatted on one microcomputer will print "properly" on another compatible computer that runs the same version of the software. The conventional wisdom of the computing world also has some general "escape clauses," such as Murphy's Law.[18] And the vision of computing advanced in many popular and professional sources is of a set of technologies that are easily usable, highly reliable, and relatively seamless.

In "The Integration of Computing and Routine Work," Les Gasser (1986) examined common anomalies in the daily use of computing systems. Anomalies include system bugs, but they go much further. For example, in 1990 the State of Massachusetts billed the city of Princeton one cent in interest after it paid a bill for a ten-cent underpayment of taxes (Tracy, 1990). Each of these transactions cost twenty-nine cents in postage, as well as several dollars in staff time and computing resources. The reporter viewed the situation as anomalous because one would not expect organizations to routinely invest many dollars in attempting to collect a few cents.[19] However, the computer program was probably working as it was designed—to compute interest on *all* underpayments and produce accurate bills for interest due to the State of Massachusetts.

---

[17] The report might print differently because of differences in the ways that the word processors are configured, for example, with different margin or font settings. In this case the anomaly is intelligible, even if it takes some time and fiddling to locate the problem. On the other hand, if the report prints in some weird format, such as printing the top half of the page in a bold font, or placing footer lines in the middle of the page, the source of the problem may be much less clear and even harder to track down.

[18] Murphy's Law is sometimes stated as, "If something can go wrong, it will." There are addenda such as, "Murphy was an optimist." Another wry observation, labeled Hoffman's Law states, "Computer tasks will take twice as long as you expect, even when you take Hoffman's Law into account." These elements of professional folk wisdom communicate the imperfection of complex technologies and the difficulties that people have in taking many factors into account when planning complex tasks. Of course, if Murphy's Law were really a "law," this book would never have been published.

[19] While some organizations routinely sent out bills for $0.00 when they first computerized in the 1960s and 1970s, one might expect that all major organizations would have cleared up these economic inefficiencies by 1990. The situation was specially farcical because the state was facing an $800-million budget deficit. See Tracy (1990).

Table 1. Average Annual Growth in Gross Domestic Product per Labor Hour in the United States (Selected Industries)[a]

Sector	Average Annual Growth Rate (% per year)	
	1948–1973	1973–1989
Business	2.9	1.1
Goods Producing	3.2	1.7
Farming	4.6	2.0
Manufacturing	2.9	2.8
Service Producing	2.5	0.7
Communications	5.2	4.6
Utilities	5.9	2.5
Trade (Wholesale and Retail)	2.7	1.2
Finance/Real Estate	1.4	0.2
Services	2.1	0.3
General Government	0.2	0.3

[a]From Table 1.1 of *Information Technology and the Service Society: A Twenty-First Century Lever*, p. 33. National Academy Press, Washington, D.C., 1994.

In the last few years economists have found it hard to identify systematic improvements in United States national productivity that can be attributed to computerization. Although banks, airlines, and other service companies spent over $750 billion during the 1980s on computer and communications hardware, and unknown billions more on software, standard measures have shown only a tiny 0.7% average yearly growth in productivity for the country's service sector during that time (see Table 1). Table 1 also shows that productivity growth in many sectors of the United States economy was much lower since 1973 than between the end of World War II and 1973.

The discrepancy between the expected economic benefits of computerization and measured effects has been termed "The Productivity Paradox," based on a comment attributed to Nobel laureate Robert Solow, who remarked that "computers are showing up everywhere except in the [productivity] statistics." Brynjolfsson (1993) groups many of the explanations that have been proposed for the productivity paradox into four categories: errors in measuring organizations' outputs and inputs; lags in time due to the time that organizations need for learning about information technologies and adjusting to them; redistribution and dissipation of profits; and the systematic mismanagement of information and technology.

In the next three selections, Martin Neal Baily, Paul Attewell, and John King examine the last three of these explanations and different facets of the productivity paradox. Each of them tacitly relies on Natural Systems models of organizations in examining why business firms don't computerize in ways that significantly improve their overall productivity.

In "Great Expectations: PCs and Productivity," economist Martin Neal Baily raises questions about the cost effectiveness of many computer applications. Baily keeps his eye on the overall productivity of the United

States economy, as measured by economists.[20] He notes that overall productivity growth in the United States economy has been sluggish in the 1980s. While the aggregate statistics about productivity mask large variations among different firms, and even within particular firms, Baily wonders why the nation's major investment in computing technologies has not shown up in national-level data.

Baily notes that computer systems often do things better than their manual equivalents. Computerized word-processing systems make it easier than ever to revise a manuscript forty times, and financial analysts find it increasingly simple to break their data into finer slices and report them more frequently. But Baily notes that it is usually hard to place an economic value on more polished manuscripts and refined reporting.[21] He also questions the role of certain applications in altering productivity within firms or within an industry. He points out that systems that help a firm attract its competitor's customers may be great for the firm; but it doesn't raise overall economic productivity. As Baily asks at one point, somewhat rhetorically, "If this stuff is so good, why do we have the same number of secretaries?"

In the next selection, "Information Technology and the Productivity Challenge," Paul Attewell reviews his own research to identify six common social processes that reduce the productivity gains from computerization. Attewell does not argue that computerization is inherently worthless for many organizations. Rather, he notes that many changes in products and ways of work that come from computerization, such as improving the appearance of reports and visual presentations, or managers being able to rapidly produce fine-grained reports about their domains of action, often do not result in direct improvements in overall organizational productivity. Numerous accounting reports may give managers an enhanced sense of control. But managers may seek more reports than they truly need, as a way to help reduce their anxieties about managing.[22] Similarly, some professionals may be specially pleased by working with advanced technologies. But much of the investment may result in improving job satisfaction rather than in being the most effective means for improving organizational productivity.[23]

---

[20] See Baily and Gordon (1988).

[21] Sometimes it is also hard to place a precise cost on these products. Moreover, although multiple revisions and fine-grained reporting are even *encouraged* by the availability of new technology (e.g., word processors), the returns may be of diminishing economic and aesthetic value. For example, does a revision from Draft No. 39 to Draft No. 40 really represent time well spent?

[22] See Jackall (1988) for an insightful discussion of managerial anxieties.

[23] Review, for example, Frantz's article (Part III, Chapter E) about the Bank of America's style of developing grand-scale information systems, and Kirkpatrick's article (Part III, Chapter F) about some professionals' joy in working with Lotus Notes.

Attewell does not argue that managers should not have some way of controlling activities for which they are responsible or that professionals should not enjoy their jobs. But he surmises that overall, a large fraction of the nation's multibillion-dollar investment in computerized systems has resulted in diverse changes that are "captured" within organizations rather than translated into substantial overall productivity increases.

In "Where are the Payoffs from Computerization?," John King carries Attewell's argument further. He acknowledges that organizations may have not substantially improved their overall productivity because of their ways of computerizing. And he acknowledges the importance of social processes like those that Attewell identifies as turning computerization toward diverse ends. In addition, he adds an important analysis of the ways that accounting and reporting organizational activities can confound our understanding of organizational productivity. But King's special advance beyond Attewell's argument lies in his historical argument about the organizational learning that is required for important innovations to effectively diffuse throughout industrial societies and for numerous managers and professionals to figure out how to use them effectively. King's argument builds on the research of historically oriented scholars such as economist Paul David. David examined the replacement of steam-driven factory equipment by electric motors in the early twentieth century. Although electric motors offered many advantages over steam, he found that it took over twenty years for the productivity gains of electric motors to show up in national-level productivity data. King notes:

> If and when computerization yields major productivity payoffs it will be as a result of the confluence of three factors: The new technologies themselves, the know-how needed to apply them successfully, and the wholesale substitution of the new technologies and new methods for older ways of doing things. The new technologies are here, and it is clear that we are learning to apply the technologies, but we have not learned enough to achieve cost-saving substitution. We are still bearing the direct costs of learning, and we must bear the costs of multiple, redundant systems until we have learned enough to switch completely from the old to the new. This learning phenomenon might sound simple and straight-forward, but it is not. It is highly complicated and it takes considerable time.

King's article examines these factors in some detail. His analysis encourages us to take a long, historical view of the complex processes by which managers, professionals, and workers learn about new technologies and restructure organizations to make the most of them. King is cautiously optimistic that, on balance, computerization will demonstrate major economic value. But he is aware that it can take decades before we are in a position to make firm judgments, and by that time trillions of dollars, millions of person-years, and immense hope and grief will have been expended on a great set of computerization ventures.

Organizational Analysis in Information and Computer Science

During the last thirty years there has been a huge sea change in the nature of jobs for people educated in academic information science and computer science programs. To simplify, in the 1960s, most such people worked as software developers or support people for batch computer systems. The computer industry, aerospace firms, and large database providers were major sites of employment. Assembly language, COBOL, and Fortran reigned supreme as programming languages. The concept of a "person who used their products" was usually an abstraction. In the 1990s, the spread of desktop computing and networks of all shapes and sizes has led to a demand for people with information and computer science skills close to the site of application. In the concluding selection, "Can Computer Science Solve Organizational Problems?," Jonathan Allen and I argue that many information science and computer science graduates need some skills in analyzing human organizations to do high-quality professional jobs.

We introduce the relatively new term, Organizational Informatics,[24] to denote a field that studies the development and use of computerized information systems and communication systems in organizations. It includes studies of their conception, design, effective implementation within organizations, maintenance, use, organizational value, conditions that foster risks of failures, and their effects for people and an organization's clients. We argue that is overdue for academic information science and computer science to embrace organizational analysis (the field of Organizational Informatics) as a key area of research and instruction.

Material and Sources

Ariav, Gad, and Seymour Goodman (1994). "Israel: Of Swords and Software Plowshares." *Communications of the ACM*, 37(6)(June):17–21.

Attewell, Paul "Information Technology and the Productivity Challenge." [Original article for this book.]

---

[24] Organizational Informatics is a relatively new label. In Europe, the term Informatics is the name of many academic departments that combine both Computer Science and Information Systems. I have found that some people instantly like it, while others are put off. I've experimented with alternative labels, like Organizational Computing, which has also resulted in strong and mixed reactions. Computing is a more common term than Informatics, but it's too narrow for some researchers. Informatics also can connote "information," which is an important part of this field. Sociological Computer Science would have the virtues of being a parallel construction of Mathematical Computer Science, but it doesn't connote information either.

Baily, Martin Neal (1989). "Great Expectations: PCs and Productivity." *PC Computing,* 2(4)(April):137–141.

Becker, Henry Jay (1993). "A Truly Empowering Technology-Rich Education—How Much Will it Cost?" *Educational IRM Quarterly,* 3(1)(September):31–35.

Feder, Barnaby J. (1989). "Getting the Electronics Just Right: Wells Fargo is a Case Study in How a Company can Exploit the Information Revolution." *New York Times, Business Section* (June 4):1,8.

Frantz, Douglas (1988). "B of A's Plans for Computer Don't Add Up." *Los Angeles Times* (February 7).

Hodas, Steven (1993). "Technology Refusal and The Organizational Culture of Schools." *e-journal-Educational Policy Analysis Archives.* 1(10)(September). Available at http://info.asu.edu/asu-cwis/epaa/welcome.html.

King, John Leslie "Where are the Payoffs from Computerization? Technology, Learning and Organizational Change." [Original article for this book.]

Kirkpatrick, David (1993). "Groupware Goes Boom." *Fortune,* 128(16)(December 27):99–103.

Kling, Rob, and Jonathan Allen (1994). "Can Computer Science Solve Organizational Problems?: The Case for Organizational Informatics." [Original article for this book.]

Morton, Michael Scott (1991). "How Information Technologies Can Transform Organizations." Excerpt from the Introduction in Michael Scott Morton (ed.), *The Corporation of the 1990's: Information Technology & Organizational Transformation,* pp. 8–23. Oxford University Press, New York.

Orlikowski, Wanda J. (1993). "Learning from Notes: Organizational Issues in Groupware Implementation." *Information Society,* 9(3)(Jul–Sep):237–250.

References

Baily, Martin Neal, and Robert J. Gordon (1988). "The Productivity Slowdown, Measurement Issues, and the Explosion of Computer Power." *Brookings Papers on Economic Activity,* 2:347–431.

Becker, Henry Jay (1993). "Teaching with and about Computers in Secondary Schools." *Communications of the ACM,* (36)5(May):69–73.

Bluestone, Barry (1994). "The Inequality Express." *The American Prospect,* 20(Winter 1994):81–93.

Brynjolfsson, Erik (1993). "The Productivity Paradox of Information Technology: The Relationship between Information Technology and Productivity. *Communications of the ACM,* 36(12)(December):66–76.

Cotterman, William, and James Senn (eds.) (1992). *Challenges and Strategies for Research in Systems Development.* John Wiley, New York.

Cyert, Richard M., and David C. Mowery (eds.) (1987). *Technology and Employment: Innovation and Growth in the U.S. Economy.* National Academy Press, Washington, D.C.

Dyson, Esther (1990a). "Not Just Another Spreadsheet: Big Accounting Firm Purchases Lotus' Notes Groupware." *Forbes* 145(3)(Feb 5):161.

Dyson, Esther (1990b). "A Notable Order for Groupware: 10,000 Copies of Lotus Notes for Price Waterhouse and Co." *Datamation* 36(9)(May 1):51.

Feigenbaum, Edward, and Pamela McCorduck (1983). *The Fifth Generation: Artificial Intelligence and Japan's Computer Challenge to the World.* Addison-Wesley, Reading, MA.

Forester, Tom (1987). *High-Tech Society: The Story of the Information Technology Revolution.* MIT Press, Cambridge.

Gasser, Les (1986). "The Integration of Computing and Routine Work." *ACM Transactions on Office Information Systems,* 4(3)(July):205–225.

Ginzberg, Eli, Thierry J. Noyelle, and Thomas M. Stanback, Jr. (1986). *Technology and Employment: Concepts and Clarifications.* Westview Press, Boulder.

Grudin, Jonathan (1989). "Why Groupware Applications Fail: Problems in Design and Evaluation." *Office: Technology and People,* 4(3):245–264.

Hartman, Heidi I., Robert E. Kraut, and Louise A. Tilly (eds.) (1986). *Computer Chips and Paper Clips: Technology and Women's Employment.* National Academy Press, Washington, D.C.

Hymowitz, Carol (1990). "When Firms Cut Out Middle Managers, Those At Top and Bottom Often Suffer." *Wall Street Journal,* (April 5):B1,B4.

Jackall, Robert (1988). *Moral Mazes: The World of Corporate Managers.* Oxford University Press, New York.

Jewett, Tom, and Rob Kling (1990). "The Work Group Manager's Role in Developing Computing Infrastructure." *Proceedings of the ACM Conference on Office Information Systems,* Boston, MA.

King, J. L., and E. S. Schrems (1978). "Cost-Benefit Analysis in Information Systems Development and Operation." *Computing Surveys,* (March):19–34.

Kling, Rob (1980). "Social Analyses of Computing: Theoretical Orientations in Recent Empirical Research." *Computing Surveys,* 12(1):61–110.

Kling, Rob (1983). "Value Conflicts and Computing Developments: Developed and Developing Countries." *Telecommunications Policy,* (7)1(March):12–34. (Reprinted as "Value Conflicts in EFT Systems" in Dunlop and Kling (eds.) (1991). *Computerization and Controversy.* Academic Press, San Diego.

Kling, Rob (1987). "Defining the Boundaries of Computing Across Complex Organizations," in Richard Boland and Rudy Hirschheim (eds.), *Critical Issues in Information Systems.* John Wiley, London.

Kling, Rob (1990). "More Information, Better Jobs?: Occupational Stratification and Labor Market Segmentation in the United States' Information Labor Force." *The Information Society,* 7(2):77–107.

Kling, Rob (1992). "Behind the Terminal: The Critical Role of Computing Infrastructure In Effective Information Systems' Development and Use," in W. Cotterman and J. Senn (eds.), *Challenges and Strategies for Research in Systems Development,* pp. 153–201. John Wiley, New York.

Kling, Rob, and Suzanne Iacono (1984). "The Control of Information Systems Developments After Implementation." *Communications of the ACM,* 27(12)(December):1218–1226.

Kling, Rob, and Suzanne Iacono (1989). "The Institutional Character of Computerized Information Systems." *Office: Technology and People,* 5(1):7–28.

Kling, Rob, and Tom Jewett (1994). "The Social Design of Worklife With Computers and Networks: An Open Natural Systems Perspective," in Marshall C. Yovits (ed.), *Advances in Computers,* Volume 39. Academic Press, San Diego.

Kling, Rob, and Clark Turner (1991). "The Structure of Orange County's Information Labor Force," in Rob Kling, Spencer Olin, and Mark Poster (eds.), *Post-Suburban California.* University of California Press, Berkeley.

Knights, David, and Fergus Murray (1994). *Managers Divided. Organization Politics and Information Technology Management.* John Wiley, London.

Kraemer, Kenneth L., and Rob Kling (1985). "The Political Character of Computerization in Service Organizations: Citizen's Interests or Bureaucratic Control." *Computers and the Social Sciences,* 1(2)(April–June):77–89.

Kraemer, Kenneth L., Siegfried Dickhoven, Susan Fallows Tierney, and John Leslie King (1987). *Datawars: The Politics of Federal Policymaking.* Columbia University Press, New York.

Landauer, T. K. (1995). *The Trouble with Computers: Usefulness, Usability and Productivity.* MIT Press, Cambridge, MA.

Laudon, Kenneth C. (1974). *Computers and Bureaucratic Reform.* John Wiley, New York.

Lyytinen, K., and R. Hirschheim (1987). "Information Systems Failures—Survey and Classification of the Empirical Literature." *Oxford Surveys in Information Technology,* 4:257–309.

McAllister, Celia F. (1989). "Lotus Gets a Tall Order from One of the Big Eight Accounting Firms." *Business Week,* 3138(Dec 18):104C.

Menzies, Heather (1981). *Women and the Chip: Case Studies of the Effects of Informatics on Employment in Canada.* Institute for Research on Public Policy, Montreal.

Miller, Stephen (1992). "Putting Colleagues in Touch: Lotus Development Corp.'s Notes Office Automation Software." *New York Times,* v141 (Sun, March 1):F9(N), F9(L).

Morgan, Gareth (1986). *Images of Organization.* Sage Publications, Beverly Hills.

Naisbitt, John (1994). *Global Paradox: The Bigger the World Economy, the More Powerful Its Smallest Players.* William Morrow, New York.

National Research Council (1994). *Information Technology in the Service Society, a Twenty-First Century Lever.* National Academy Press, Washington, D.C.

Newman, Denis (1993). "School Networks: Delivery or Access." *Communications of the ACM,* 36(May):49–52.

Nisbet, Peter (1992). "Enterprise Size, Information Technology and the Service Sector—the Employment Implications." *New Technology Work & Employment,* 7(1)(Spring):61–70.

Opel, John (1987). "Technology and the New Wealth of Nations." *Society,* 24(6) (October/November):51–54.

O'Reilly, Richard (1993). "Lotus Notes Reorganizes the Way People Work." *Washington Post,* v116 (Mon, May 24):WB21.

Oz, Effy (1994). "When Professional Standards are Lax: The CONFIRM Failure and Its Lessons." *Communications of the ACM,* 37(10)(October):29–36.

Quinn, James Brian, and Martin N. Baily (1994). "Information Technology." *Brookings Review,* 12(3)(Summer):36–41.

Scott, W. Richard (1992). *Organizations: Rational, Natural, and Open Systems* (3d ed.). Prentice-Hall, Englewood Cliffs, NJ.

Shaw, Marvin E. (1976). *Group Dynamics: The Psychology of Small Group Behavior* (2d ed.). McGraw Hill, New York.

Sherwood, Mark K. (1994). "Difficulties in the Measurement of Service Outputs." *Monthly Labor Review,* 117(3)(Mar):11–19.

Shields, Mark (ed.) (1995). *Work and Technology in Higher Education: The Social Construction of Academic Computing.* Lawrence Erlbaum, Hillsdale, NJ.

Shorris, Earl (1981). *Scenes from Corporate Life: The Politics of Middle Management.* Penguin, New York.

Smith, Douglas K., and Robert C. Alexander (1988). *Fumbling the Future: How Xerox Invented, Then Ignored, The First Personal Computer.* William Morrow, New York.

Tracy, Diane (1990). "This State May be Penny-Wise, But it Sure Looks Pound Foolish." *Wall Street Journal,* (April 9):B1.

Walsham, Geoff (1993). *Interpreting Information Systems in Organizations.* John Wiley, New York.

Whyte, William H. (1956). *The Organization Man.* Simon and Schuster, New York.

Further Reading

Campbell, John P., Richard J. Campbell, and Associates (eds.) (1988). *Productivity in Organizations: New Perspectives from Industrial and Organizational Psychology.* Jossey-Bass, San Francisco.

Curtis, Bill, Herb Krasner, and Neil Iscoe (1988). "A Field Study of the Software Design Process for Large Systems." *Communications of the ACM,* 31(11) (November):1268–1288.

Davenport, Thomas H. (1994). "Saving IT's Soul: Human-Centered Information Management." *Harvard Business Review,* (March–April):119–131.

Dunlop, Charles, and Rob Kling (eds.) (1991). *Computerization and Controversy: Value Conflicts and Social Choices.* Academic Press, San Diego.

Harris, Douglas H. (1994). *Organizational Linkages: Understanding the Productivity Paradox.* National Academy Press, Washington, DC.

King, J. L., and K. L. Kraemer (1981). "Cost as a Social Impact of Telecommunications and Other Information Technologies," in M. Moss (ed.), *Telecommunications and Productivity.* Addison-Wesley, New York.

Kling, Rob (1980). "Social Analyses of Computing: Theoretical Orientations in Recent Empirical Research." *Computing Surveys,* 12(1):61–110.

Kling, Rob (1989). "Postscript 1988 to 'Social Analyses of Computing: Theoretical Orientations in Recent Empirical Research' " in Zenon Pylyshyn and Liam Bannon (eds.), *Perspectives on the Computer Revolution,* 2d ed., pp. 504–518. Ablex Publishing Co., Norwood, NJ.

Kraemer, Kenneth (1991). "Strategic Computing and Administrative Reform." (Reprinted from Charles Dunlop and Rob Kling (eds.) (1991). *Computerization and Controversy: Value Conflicts and Social Choices.* Academic Press, San Diego.)

Kuttner, Robert (1993). "The Corporation in America: How Can It Be Changed? Can It Be Controlled?" *Dissent,* (Winter):35–49.

Markus, M. Lynne, and Mark Keil (1994). "If We Build It, They Will Come: Designing Information Systems That People Want to Use." *Sloan Management Review,* 35(4)(Summer):11–25.

Markus, Lynne, and Dan Robey (1988). "Information Technology and Organizational Change: Causal Structure in Theory and Research." *Management Services,* 34(5):583–598.

McKersie, Robert B., and Richard E. Walton (1991). "Organizational Change," in Michael Scott Morton (ed.), *The Corporation of the 1990s: Information Technology & Organizational Transformation.* Oxford University Press, New York.

P·A·R·T · III

B

Israel: Of Swords
and Software Plowshares*

Gad Ariav • Seymour Goodman

In July 1947, the Advisory Committee of the Applied Mathematics Department of the Weitzmann Institute, consisting of Albert Einstein, Hans Kramer, Robert Oppenheimer, John von Neumann, and Abram Pais, recommended that the Institute build an electronic digital computer [1]. Thus, Israel became the first not-yet-a-nation to seriously commit itself to computing. After a delay to get the country started, an operational WEIZAC was built by 1955. Israel has gone on to distinguish itself in scientific and computing research and education and to claim some hardware niches, notably in defense-related systems.

But perhaps the most important and dramatically growing Israeli strength in computing today is software. Between 1984 and 1992 the Israeli software industry tripled its sales and increased export by 2700% [3]. There were approximately 150 software companies, with total sales of over $600 million in 1992 and employing about 5500 of the nation's 12,000 computer professionals [3]; the estimate for 1993 total sales is $720 million. The extent of "pure" software export (excluding embedded software) increased from $5 million in 1984 to $110 million in 1991 [3], $140 million in 1992 and an estimated $175 million in 1993. In 1991 58% of this volume headed for the United States and 37% to Europe [6]. The export share of total output from Israeli software houses rose from 2.5% in 1984 to about 25% in 1993. The importance of export to a small economy such as Israel's cannot be overstated—it is the only way to maintain a world-class computing sector.

Interestingly, as of 1992–1993, the Israeli software industry was again half as large as its much-examined Indian counterpart, but with about three-quarters of the latter's export value [6]. Structurally, in spite of the vast differences in size of their domestic economies and population (roughly 5 million to 850 million), the Israeli software industry seems to have more of an indigenous base.

Some of the conspicuous successes of Israeli software export are "niche products," based on expertise in advanced DBMS and application generators, computer center operation, educational software, and antivirus protection. A different but notable form of export occurs through joint ventures or subsidiaries. A number of major global computing companies such as Microsoft (DOS 6.0's antivirus capabilities and hard disk compression originated in Israel), IBM, Intel, National Semiconductor, and Motorola, among others, are engaged in software R&D in Israel.

Public policy with regard to the software industry takes the form of subsidies for R&D, tax incentives, and marketing support for software export. While considered by some to be a significant ingredient in the current growth, others think the government's positive attitude has taken too long to form and its impact falls short of what is required.

Israel is one of a number of little countries around the world whose energies and accomplishments in computing and other information technologies (IT) are out of proportion to their sizes and natural resources. What drives such progress in a country as small as Israel? We explored this question in a series of facility visits and interviews with key software players in May 1993 [2]. Answers identified three categories of driving factors: circumstances that prevailed at significant points in time, the nature of the Israeli market, and some cultural attributes that affect Israel as a software developer. We discuss each in turn.

The Drivers: Historical Circumstances

The lack of administrative capabilities that marked the early years of statehood led to an attitude that was especially receptive to computing. This frame of mind was further reinforced by the view of "the few against the many," which is widely held among Israelis. Accordingly, the history of IT in Israel started shortly after independence (1948) with the use of electromechanical machines. Therefore the development and adoption of technology was, and still is, seen as a way to maintain a qualitative edge in light of numerical inferiority.

The history of economically significant data processing and software development in Israel began in 1960 with the creation of MMRM, the computing center of the Israel Defense Forces (IDF). MMRM—commonly

---

*This article appeared in *Communications of the ACM,* 37(6)(June, 1994):17–21. Reprinted with permission of the Association for Computing Machinery.

called "Mam'ram"—is the Hebrew acronym for the Center of Computers and Automated Recording. The center was set up around a Philco Transac 2000 mainframe, one of the earliest transistor-based computers available outside the defense establishments in the United States, USSR, and United Kingdom. With this platform, modern record keeping became part of military management for personnel and logistics. In the late 1960s MMRM replaced its original engine with an IBM 360/50 mainframe and remained technology current ever since.

At the time, and for many years, MMRM was the largest and most sophisticated computing center in the country. There has been a tremendous growth in the number of computing centers in business, higher education, and civil government in Israel over the years, which has naturally eroded MMRM's singular position. Military computing in general has nonetheless maintained a central professional place and standing.

The unique role of MMRM in the Israeli computing milieu is manifested through commonly used linguistic coins like "MMRM graduate," which designates its holders as belonging to an "elite clique" by virtue of their service experience. Another term is "MMRM Diaspora," referring to MMRM graduates who were recruited by foreign companies. For instance, some leading financial companies in the United States list among their outstanding computing experts quite a few MMRM graduates. They are perceived to be able to quickly master complex topics ("devour many pounds of technical literature"), to select untraditional shortcuts to original solutions, and to avoid formal meetings.

Although no longer the dominant source for computing professionals in the country, MMRM's circumstances are still distinctive. As one person colorfully expressed it: "Where else can one get a 24-year-old with six years of intensive (professional) computing experience?" MMRM soldiers are required to serve longer than the mandatory three years, but they typically complete their service and enter the market in their early 20s. Many leading high-tech companies and computing centers in Israel have been established or are led by MMRM graduates. MMRM does represent a unifying experience of a central core of the Israeli IT community and its current leadership. The human potential that MMRM and other parts of the military (e.g., the air force and intelligence branches) helped spawn was there when the opportunities arose for the software industry to rapidly develop and expand.

In the last couple of decades, the Israeli base for software-related R&D and training has expanded considerably, most notably to include an exceptional academic community for a small country in engineering, computer science, and MIS. Notable Israeli computer scientists include Michael Rabin (1976 ACM Turing Award Laureate), Adi Shamir (the "S" in the RSA encryption system), David Harel (software engineering), among many others. Together, higher education programs annually feed the market with 500 to 700 well-educated computer professionals.

Another frequently mentioned historical circumstance is the relatively easy access to the United States market by Israeli enterprises. This was suggested as a crucial variable in explaining the differences between Israel's software industry achievements as compared to, say, Cuba. Both small countries have educated and aspiring computing professionals, and both are isolated within their respective hostile environments [5]. Neither has been able to develop regional markets, but the Israelis have been much more successful in finding more distant markets, not only in the United States but in Europe and Asia as well.

Finally, Israel is explicitly built on Jewish immigration, which offers access to many native speakers of foreign languages, which in turn has driven some of Israel's forays into markets abroad. Immigrants bring with them not only a strong command of the language but also an intimate knowledge of the respective cultures. For example, ex-Soviet immigrants since the 1970s have helped to set up business relations with their former employers in Russia, the Ukraine, and elsewhere.

The Drivers: Israeli Consumers

The Israeli defense industry has traditionally been driven by its challenging local customers. Military equipment and components could be labeled as "battle tested," attesting to their functionality and quality. Several interviewees suggested that a parallel experience exists in the civilian systems market. They argued that many of the appreciated features of software made in Israel owe their existence to the typically "tough" (some might say "obnoxious and aggressive") Israeli clientele.

The typical Israeli user tries to "outsmart" the system. In one example, a domestic airline reservation system had to control the overbooking "abuses" of its users, apparently much more so than elsewhere (Israelis are notoriously aggressive travelers). The resulting system was made more robust in that respect.

Israelis are known to be "information junkies" who consume more information than many counterparts elsewhere in the world. This is manifested by the exceptional per capita circulation of newspapers, by a national "addiction" to radio and TV newscasts, as well as by the amount of information available and demanded from bank ATMs—partly a result of the past hyperinflation period when maintaining the buying power of money, even for ordinary people, was an extensive daily exercise.

Another national trait is an acute suspicion of "apparatuses." In the realm of banking this calls for issuing an array of receipts. The on-line deposit procedure at Israel Discount Bank, for instance, involves actually reading the check at the ATM. The customer receives a more serious acknowledgment of acceptance than is the case in the United States, including the coded information found on the check itself.

The demanding nature of the Israeli information systems client requires corresponding software design ingenuity. Software houses that develop systems for local corporate customers and their users are able to export this advantage elsewhere. Exports to East European banking sectors are a case in point.

The Drivers: Cultural Circumstances

Broader cultural commentary surfaced during the interviews. Somewhat unexpected was the reference to the fact that Zionism, the movement that eventually led to the establishment of Israel, was among other things a cultural rebellion within the context of traditional Jewish existence. Thus, "modernity," "progress," and "advancement" were themes cherished in Israel, perhaps strongly linked to the founders' legacy of utopian fantasies. This view fostered fascination with machines, engineering, and automation.

This attitude had some negative effects as well. It was suggested that following the strong ideological roots of Israel's "founding fathers" in the original socialist movements of the turn of the century, software was officially classified as "service" and thus disqualified for industrial support and subsidy reserved for "real" productive activities such as agriculture and manufacturing. As was the case in the Soviet Union and other socialist states where software suffered from similar problems, this hardware-centered or classical socialist view of work also partially explains the limited appreciation of marketing. Such attitudes have undergone a dramatic change in recent years, and failures in these domains are no longer matters of ignorance, but of poor execution.

In general, valuing deed over deliberation has sustained the rather impatient Israeli "culture of action," exemplified by the popular view that "you can only avoid mistakes if you are not doing anything," or the perception that democracy means "everyone can give it a try." The proverbial "Jewish mother"—the ultimate motivator—was mentioned (only half jokingly) as the origin of the Israeli-driven character, which pushes Israelis to act, try, and dare. This may explain in part the appearance of Israeli software in some unlikely places and circumstances (e.g., in the automated generation of Japanese crossword puzzles).

The revival of Hebrew as a daily spoken language has created technical challenges to foreign vendors of software, as well as forcing Israeli developers to consider linguistic implications and to become experts in the design of multilingual software. Language peculiarities limit the global marketing appeal of local products, but also create a software development environment that is somewhat protected from the global giants. Hebrew has partly isolated the Israeli IT profession from the rest of the world. Due to language boundaries there is no massive flow of people from the developed West who seek IT opportunities in the country. There is some inflow of professional human know-how and experience through immigration, but by and large the Israeli IT human landscape, for better or for worse, is shaped by Israelis.

The return of foreign-educated Israelis may be another factor behind the successful embrace of computing. Israelis who could have lived and worked in the United States or Europe, but who decided to follow their cultural and emotional instincts and return home are common (some also apparently do not fit elsewhere because of their "disrespect for orderliness"). It is perhaps characteristic of strong nation-cultures, as similar sentiments are often expressed by expatriates who grew up in Greece or India. The returning Israelis have been bringing with them an experience base that is transplanted in the country, providing a shortcut in processes of local cultivation. The Israeli IT sector is a clear benefactor of technology transfer in human form.

On the other hand, brain-drain is also a problem as it is elsewhere, and it is possible that more Israeli IT professionals are leaving the country than returning. Nevertheless, it has not created a critical condition in the sense that it hampers the country's ability to perform. It appears that few who leave permanently or for long periods cut themselves off. Most maintain contacts professionally (e.g., by generating export activities). Overall, for an isolated and often beleaguered country, Israel seems to have a good flow of people between itself and the larger international IT world.

An Israeli National Character of Software Development?

Can one tell an Israeli software development company from those of other countries? Does such a distinction make sense at all in a world increasingly based on standard technologies and offering homogeneous products and services such as airline reservation systems? While not unanimously supported, it was conjectured that distinctive Israeli features do exist. It was time and again stated as "brilliance without discipline" or given "commando" connotations. The latter theme surfaced vividly early on and remained largely valid for the entire series of interviews and facility visits.

The commando theme should not be interpreted in a "Rambo-simplistic" fashion. Clarifying the meaning of the term "commando" in the Israeli mind may be best done with a list of terms closely associated with it in the Israeli culture: imaginative, unconstrained, informal, quick, small scale, flexible, resourceful, front line, hard work, difficult, self-reliant, aggressive, lack of sense for order and administration, specialized, intensively trained, effective, action-oriented, trouble shooting, elitist, arrogant, improvisational, reactive. It should be noted that military commando units are highly regarded within Israeli culture, as evidenced by the tremendous interest of young recruits in joining them.

The notion of "IT commando" therefore imbues software and system development with those descriptors. It is an Israeli counterpart of the "hacker" theme and culture that has characterized parts of the United States software scene. While obviously short of being a formal thesis, this theme suggests some views on the strengths and difficulties of Israeli computing, and of software in particular.

Interestingly, a top manager who claimed that "we do not exploit our national character in our company," turned quite naturally to describe how "informality" is the way responsibilities are handled in his company. Informality is commonly held to be a typical and distinctive Israeli management attribute. In this particular company the limits of possible informality actually determined the span of managerial control. Larger units that became too formal were split and organized as independent businesses. Informality as an Israeli characteristic is often reinforced rather than suppressed by military service.

The commando themes, similar to the hacker themes in the United States should not imply a strictly positive heroic connotation. For instance, the impatient "action orientation" and flexible mentality have a clear effect on strategic Information Systems (IS) planning in Israel. Typically, only companies that are influenced by the United States business community and standards are engaged in strategic IS planning. Furthermore, "commando properties" are very useful in product development and focused software problem solving but are less so for long-term business strategy, marketing planning, patient attention to customer needs, or the immersion in different cultures to understand subtleties. It also fosters occasionally a provincial, parochial, small-country mentality that "I can do better." This element has been suggested as a limiting factor in the success of the Israeli software industry and in particular its export activities. Original predictions of performance figures were higher than those that have recently materialized, creating a feeling that "something is missing" and prompting the current focus on marketing [7].

As discussed earlier, most of our interviewees unequivocally perceived that the country's IT human resource infrastructure was created at a critical time by military computing. The important role of military computing in the broader IT scene in Israel was unintended but fortuitous. Military computing itself was and is driven by defense concerns and needs, and it is not a component of a national IT public policy. Nevertheless, it is an example of an effective—although unintended—intervention in the shaping of the national IT landscape. Although it is centrally executed, it is vastly different from planned interventions elsewhere that attempt to shape the IT landscape in a top-down fashion (e.g., in Singapore or the former Soviet Union) [4].

Of course, the interaction among the roles of military computing in Israel with the other drivers is complex and the identification of isolated effects may prove to be difficult. Many of the things we found and attributed to the military are arguably more general Israeli attributes that are accentuated or amplified in these circumstances.

It is doubtful if the factors behind the strengths and weaknesses of computing in Israel would suggest general principles that may apply to a larger country or one that is completely open to its neighboring environment (e.g., the Netherlands). Are they even sustainable within Israel? Possibly not, considering the diluting trends of national identities (e.g., the "Americanization" of young Israelis), the prospects of a diminished siege mentality as well as a decrease in defense-related activities, if the recent peace initiatives materialize into reasonably normal relations with its neighbors. Unfortunately, the latter may take much longer than the former, but in the long term it will be interesting to see if the unique characteristics identified in this essay are going to be mellowed or fade away.

References

[1] Estrin, G. "The WEIZAC Years (1954–63)." *Ann. Hist. Comput.*, 13 (4) (Apr. 1991), 317–339.
[2] Interviews with David Assia, Israel Borovits, Phillip Ein-Dor, Meir Dvir, Menachem Gutterman, Shaul Lavi, Seev Neumann, Amiram Shore, Israel Spiegler, Giora Ullman, and Yehuda Zisappel.
[3] Israeli Association of Software Houses. Israel software industry 1992–3. (Nov. 1992).
[4] McHenry, W. K., and S. E. Goodman. "MIS in Soviet industrial enterprises: The limits of reform from above." *Comm. ACM*, 29 (11) (Nov. 1986), 1034–1043.
[5] Mesher, G. M., R. O. Briggs, S. E. Goodman, L. I. Press, and J. M. Snyder. "Cuba, communism, and computing." *Comm. ACM*, 35 (11) (Nov. 1992), 27–29, 112.
[6] NASSCOM Strategic Review. New Delhi, Nov. 1993.
[7] Toren, B., and Z. Adelman. Research and export potential of the Israeli software industry. Research Paper #13, The Jerusalem Institute for Israel Studies, 1991.

P·A·R·T·III

C

Getting the Electronics Just Right: Wells Fargo Is a Case Study in How a Company Can Exploit the Information Revolution*

Barnaby J. Feder

Carl E. Reichardt, the chairman and chief executive of Wells Fargo & Company, doesn't have a personal computer in his office. And he is quite happy to use secretaries, phones, and meetings to communicate with underlings. But that doesn't mean that Wells Fargo, the nation's eleventh-largest bank, is falling behind in an electronic age. An early backer of the telegraph, stage coaches, and the Pony Express to move information and wealth in the nineteenth century, the company is a case study of the effective use of information systems in carving out a strategic advantage over rivals.

In recent years, Wells Fargo has generally stayed away from the riskier frontiers like home banking by computer and artificial intelligence systems that try to mimic human thinking. But it has been among the largest investors in such bread-and-butter items as automated teller machines and basic computer systems. And it has succeeded in using the technology to pare operating costs, absorb acquisitions efficiently, and offer customers new services. "I am much more interested in reliability than being on the leading edge," said Mr. Reichardt. "There's nothing worse than selling technology-driven services that do not work."

Wells's legacy has proved valuable at a time when businesses prosper or founder depending on how deftly they exploit the rapid advances in computers and telecommunications. No single industry reflects the full sweep of the information technology revolution in America, but big banks are in the forefront.

Financial institutions account for 35% of information technology purchases in the United States, though they employ only 5% of workers, according to studies by McKinsey & Company, the New York consultants. Spending by commercial banks alone approached $12 billion last year.

So far, all this spending has led mainly to better and cheaper services for customers rather than to higher profits for banks. Since most major banks can afford the technology's basic building blocks, just as major airlines can buy the newest jets, banks have been spending hundreds of millions of dollars to stay even with rivals. And because banking suffers from over-capacity, only those using the technology effectively prosper in the mean-time.

"Wells is a leading-edge example of the transition to the third stage of the revolution in banking," said Thomas Steiner, a McKinsey partner. In the first stage, Mr. Steiner said, "Computers are used in functions like account-ing, which means fewer back-office people and fewer errors." The second stage brings information systems that perform transactions, "which means that customers see the results faster, everyone gets more information, and the growth in the number of tellers is blunted," he said. "And in the third stage, customers—starting with big business customers—use computers connected to the bank to do more of the work. That leads to increasingly tough price competition among banks offering various services and even-tually to big staff reductions."

50,000 jobs have disappeared from banking between 1986 and 1989. In 1986, employment peaked at 1.5 million, according to McKinsey, who expected the decline to continue (despite projections by the Labor Depart-ment that bank jobs will grow through 1999). Such layoffs are just part of the transformation that has accompanied the electronic revolution at Wells and other banks. "I remember one senior executive saying, 'I'm just a dumb banker; I don't understand technology,'" said Jack Hancock, chief architect of Wells's information technology strategy until his retirement from banking two years ago. "I told him if he didn't understand informa-tion technology, he couldn't be a good banker. He's no longer with the bank."

---

*This article appeared in *The New York Times* Business Section, Sunday, June 4, 1989: 1, 8. Copyright © 1989 by *The New York Times Company*. Reprinted by permission.

Table 1. The Growth of Wells Fargo's Computer Systems*

COMMERCIAL BANKING: Integrated Office Support System

Year	Total functions	Some of the functions added	Users
1984	2	Word processing; electronic mail	40
1985	8	Tracking delinquent loans; analyzing financial data	180
1986	10	Reports from credit bureaus and news wires	290
1987	22	Electronic reminders to check whether loan requirements (such as insurance) are being observed by customers	1,000
1988	28	Pricing loans to maximize bank income while meeting customers' needs	1,320
1989 (1st Qtr.)	40	Commodity price projections; attaching personal data, like CEO birthdays, to customer data base	1,400

PERSONAL BANKING: Wells Electronic Banking System

Year	Total functions	Some of the functions added	Terminals
1986	50	Opening accounts; issuing ATM cards; obtaining interest rates; immediate notice of overdrafts	2,300
1987	96	Establishing links to credit bureaus for credit-card authorization; deposit account history	6,892
1988	104	Faster account transfers; enhanced security; cross-referencing for accounts acquired with purchase of Barclay's Bank of California	7,024
1989 (1st Qtr.)	122	Reporting large currency transactions; credit-card payments by phone	7,300

*Reprinted with permission from Barnaby J. Feder, "Getting the Electronics Just Right," *New York Times*, Sunday, 4 June 1989, Business Section.

The new technology has also upset traditional notions of which jobs are best done at headquarters and which at branches and has changed how information is shared. At the same time, relationships with customers and suppliers have been altered.

The big challenge has been to harness the changes to the bank's business strategy. Wells concentrates on consumers and small- to medium-sized businesses in California. It also is a major lender for construction and leveraged buyouts. Now, a growing proportion of its dealings involve selling information about money and money management instead of taking deposits and making loans.

At Wells, various departments are in different stages of the information revolution. What follows are snapshots of how the technology has affected some aspects of the bank's structure and style (see Table 1).

Branches Shed Bookkeeping

The painstaking bookkeeping and decision making once performed at Wells's 455 retail branches—processing loans, verifying signatures on checks, balancing accounts—is now electronically centralized. As a result, the number of branch workers has declined. Officers at the branches, meanwhile, are freer to concentrate on generating new business and are being given much more freedom to do so. "We have been able to reduce 2000 pages of rules for operating branches to a 115-page booklet," said William F. Zuendt, the vice-chairman who oversees the bank's retail, or consumer, operations.

"I don't think I would have stayed in banking if we hadn't made these changes," said Barbara Crist, who joined Wells twenty-two years ago as a teller and now manages the street-level branch at Wells Fargo headquarters in the financial district here. "We spend more time on business now and it's more exciting."

The computer backbone of the bank's branches throughout California is the Wells Electronic Banking System, or WEBS. The product of separate systems that Wells and the Crocker Bank were developing when Wells acquired its California rival from Britain's Midland Bank in 1986, WEBS plugs branch employees into the centralized records and processing systems. With video-screen records of a client's banking activity, the staff can handle 100 transactions—everything from answering questions about safety-deposit boxes to opening accounts—without paperwork. "In the old days, we did a lot of bookkeeping," Ms. Crist said. "You would call other branches for balances just to cash a check."

WEBS—in conjunction with Wells's automated teller system—allows the branches to handle many more customers with fewer full-time employees. (Part-time workers are hired on the basis of computer projections of when they will be needed to limit customer waiting times to five minutes.) Ms. Crist's branch is down from 134 employees to 54.

With all this, Wells has cut the fixed costs at branches—a saving that allowed the bank to move quickly when it decided to extend banking hours to 6:00 p.m. on weekdays and to open on Saturdays. The bank says that the leanness of its operations also made it tough for competitors to match its moves.

The 24-Hour Customer

"The relationship with the customer has changed completely," said Elizabeth A. Evans, senior vice-president in charge of information services for retail banking and corporate systems planning. "A customer can deal with us anytime, almost anywhere."

The most familiar source of this freedom is the automated teller machine. Wells has 1246 ATMs, one of the highest figures per branch in the country. And it has linked them to the Star and Plus systems so that its customers have access to 25,000 machines at other banks nationwide. About 1.3 million Wells customers use ATM cards, the equivalent of 71% of the bank's checking accounts—the highest percentage for any bank in the country.

WEBS, meanwhile, has been linked with modern telecommunications to make another Wells service—24-hour telephone banking—a success. A Northern Telecom switch automatically distributes calls to balance the load between five sites. The night shift employs students, housewives, and people seeking second jobs—a whole new group of low-wage workers the industry was largely unable to tap in its 9-to-3 days. Some two million callers a month request everything from CD rates to stopping a check.

For corporate customers, Wells offers a system that allows corporate treasurers to see exactly when money moves in and out of their bank accounts and to initiate transactions without ever talking to a banker. And accounts are updated as soon as a transaction occurs—so-called real-time banking. This corporate equivalent of home banking has major customers like the Chevron Corporation—which ten years ago typically had $125 million on deposit on a given day—reinvesting cash so quickly that its average daily balance is only $1 million.

Some corporate customers can communicate automatically with the bank's computer system. The Hilton Hotel Corporation's computers contact Wells's computers and those at other major banks, starting in the middle of the night, to find out how much is in the company's accounts. Then, when Richard H. Chambers, Hilton's assistant treasurer, arrives at his Beverly Hills office in the morning, a job that used to take a flurry of phone calls is already done.

The hot new development for corporate customers is electronic data interchange—a system that allows businesses to bill one another and make payments electronically. Wells is now involved in a pilot experiment with Citibank, Philadelphia National Bank, and Chevron, Shell Oil, and Amoco to settle accounts for an oil field Chevron operates in partnership with the other two oil companies. "I learned to play golf when I started in this business twenty years ago," said David Kvederis, executive vice-president in Wells's wholesale services group, commenting on how bankers court business. "Today it is far more valuable to get their PCs to interact with your computers."

Wells's Integrated Office Support System, the commercial bank's equivalent of WEBS, offers a range of computer services to account officers. It helps bankers dream up everything from new lending arrangements to potential mergers and acquisitions. "What used to take a day—studying things in a deal like cash flow and the sensitivity of the figures to changes in interest rates—can be done in fifteen minutes," said Michael R. James, head of Wells's commercial banking office in Palo Alto, California. "We can use that information as a marketing tool, particularly when approaching small companies that have never been able to do that kind of thing."

Some of Wells's information technology even blurs the lines between the bank and its customers. Wells's cash management service for the Catholic Diocese of Santa Rosa, California automatically pools funds from 200 schools, churches, retirement homes, and clubs into an account that monsignor Thomas Keys, the diocese's financial officer, manages via his Compaq portable computer. "It allows me to use a program I wrote that tracks the deposits, withdrawals, and average daily balances of the different entities and generates a monthly interest check for them," said Monsignor Keys. "We pay Wells a fee of $3500 to $5000 a month, and the diocese gets the float. They are a conduit and we have become the bank."

Just-in-Time Suppliers

Electronic ordering and record keeping has centralized purchasing at Wells so much that the bank now deals with only seven major office-supply vendors instead of 150 and writes only a handful of checks to pay their bills instead of thousands. And now the vendors are mostly those willing to ship what is needed when it is needed, thus allowing the bank to eliminate the practice of maintaining a six-month supply of materials, worth up to $1 million, in an Oakland warehouse. "It's more of a mutual partnership," said Susan Bosco, a manager who oversees the ordering of 2000 different forms and 5000 office-supply items for Wells. Her purchasing staff has been cut from forty employees to ten. As with other significant staff cuts at Wells, some got other work at the bank. Others were laid off with an offer of severance pay and job placement services.

Management by E-Mail

Electronic mail has been breaking down barriers by encouraging senior executives to exchange information with a far larger and more diverse group of employees. No one has a better view of such changes than Ms. Evans, who gets her first look at the coming day when she sits down to breakfast in her home in suburban San Mateo, thanks to an e-mail system that she can phone into from her personal computer. Her e-mail directory routinely includes status reports from night-shift employees who run data and telecommunications centers under her supervision. She might also find suggestions from colleagues for proposed meetings or requests for comments on their ideas. There may also be notes from subordinates about spending decisions they have made or want to make. "There are lots of simple, quick questions that occur to people at odd hours," said Ms. Evans. "Instead of jotting them down on a piece of paper that gets lost, they send them out on e-mail."

Ms. Evans deals with some matters immediately, often by sending an electronic reply. The ability to get a jump on the workday at home, or to extend it there, helps her juggle responsibilities at the bank with the life she shares with her husband and four-year-old son. "A lot of us use the system to be able to spend more time with family," she said.

Currently, the 6600 Wells employees on the e-mail system send 15,000 to 20,000 messages daily. "It's more informal than a written memo and less intrusive than a phone call," said Shirley Moore, an information systems manager. "That means you're more likely to communicate and include more people in the loop." Ms. Moore added: "The informality is well suited for developing business proposals. You feel freer to contact people who have information, no matter where they are on the corporate ladder, and you're more likely to get a timely response."

The spreading use of e-mail also has secretaries doing less typing and more administrative work. According to Mr. Zuendt, it also allows executives to get a much better view of the variety of jobs in the bank, which makes it easier for up-and-coming managers to move to new assignments. It is also making life more difficult in some respects for Andy Anderson, who heads a staff of historians at Wells. "E-mail doesn't leave the kind of paper trail that would have existed prior to the 1980s to show how a project developed," he said. "We have had to do more things like oral interviews to document recent subjects, such as how the Crocker merger was accomplished."

That does not mean Mr. Anderson is opposed to the information technology revolution. Computerized databases help his department support Wells's legal department and its advertising campaigns, which often feature the company's history. "Besides, if it weren't for the computers," he said, "scheduling the road shows of the bank's historic stagecoaches would be a real headache."

P·A·R·T · III

D

How Information Technologies Can Transform Organizations*

Michael Scott Morton

IT in Perspective

Information technology has important general-purpose power to manipulate symbols used in all classes of work, and therefore, as an "information engine," it can do for business what the steam engine did in the days of the Industrial Revolution. It goes beyond this, however, as a technology that permits one to manipulate models of reality, to step back one pace from the physical reality. Such an ability lies at the heart of IT's capacity to alter work fundamentally.

The telegraph and telephone were the predecessors of IT and were central to the rise of the modern industrial corporation. The application of those technologies resulted in the mass-production, vertically integrated hierarchial organization. But there is nothing sacred about such an organizational form. At a particular moment in time, around the turn of the century, the conditions in the marketplace of the newly industrializing Western world were conducive to the emergence of this form. The pressures of global competition and the enabling coordinative capabilities of IT have led to experimentation, and an evolution away from the traditional hierarchical organization can be expected.

Information is the lifeblood of any organization. Little can be done successfully without it. Hence, the cost of handling and processing information is important. In the data-processing era this was also true, but it was less critical to organizational success, as data processing principally dealt with back-office clerical functions and the technology was still expensive. Technology costs have dropped, and one can go beyond numerical data for algorithmic processing and move to qualitative information and heuristic manipulation. This, in turn, can be combined with the ability to work with pictures and drawings, and then one can connect all this to virtually any location in the world. Such power is new in kind; it represents a step-function change from what was available before.

The economics of IT have changed both absolutely and relatively. At an absolute level, we are expecting to see IT cost-performance ratios continue to change in the range of 20 to 30% a year. Such change can lead to considerable differences over relatively short intervals of time. Table 1, based on results of an earlier MIT study, illustrates the profound consequences of such a compounding change. In 1980 the cost of a computer with a processing power of 4.5 MIPS was $4.5 million, the cost equivalent of 210 employees of a certain skill level. The cost of a machine of this power was projected to decline to $300,000 in 1990, the cost equivalent of 6 workers of the same skill level. The actual 1990 cost will be closer to $100,000. The cost of such a machine in the year 2000 is likely to be no more than $10,000, the cost equivalent of only a fraction of a worker. Thus, organizations are faced with radically different trade-offs over time among processing power, human effort, and dollars with which to best meet the organization's objectives.

The relative costs are also changing. The cost of IT relative to the cost of other forms of capital equipment is widening. Thus, it is *relatively* cheaper today to invest in IT capital than in any other form of capital. This relationship, based on thirty years of data, is shown in Figure 1.

IT Is Different

Information technology exerts such a strong influence because it can affect both production and coordination. Production refers to the task of producing any good or service that the organization is in business to sell. It is not limited to physical production but includes the intellectual production of things such as loans or other "soft" products. The production jobs that are most affected by IT are those in which information and/or knowledge makes a difference. We call such production workers "information workers" or "knowledge workers." The fraction of the work force that falls into this category has grown to be very large. In manufacturing industries it averages around 40% and in service industries more than 80%. The information worker processes information without significant modification, a

---

*This article is excerpted from the Introduction in Michael Scott Morton (ed.), *The Corporation of the 1990s: Information Technology & Organizational Transformation* (1991). Oxford University Press, New York.

Table 1.   Computing Cost-Performance Trends

	1980	1990	2000
Constant functionality*	4.5 MIPS	4.5 MIPS	4.5 MIPS
Cost			
Original projection (1981)	$4.5 million	$300,000	
Modified projection (1988)		$100,000	$10,000
Number of people of equivalent cost			
Original projection (1981)	210	6	
Modified projection (1988)		2	0.125

*Metaphor for constant functionality is millions of instructions per second (MIPS)

task that is typically classified as clerical, such as order entry. The knowledge worker category covers those who add value to the original information. This would include engineers and designers required to design new products, those who trade in the securities markets, those in financial institutions who lend money to companies or individuals, and all those who produce budgets, market research analyses, legal briefs, and so on. The use of IT to change the nature of both such categories of production work is widely recognized.

Just as important is the use of IT to change the ways in which coordination activities are carried out. Coordination tasks make up a large part of what organizations do. With IT the effects of both distance and time can shrink to near zero. For example, it is possible today to make financial trades in global markets anywhere in the world from any city. A similar activity is placing orders to a supplier's plant or accepting orders directly from a customer's site to one's own organization. The airline reservation systems are among the most visible and oldest examples of such coordination.

Organizational memory is another feature of coordination affected by IT. Corporate databases now provide an enormous reservoir of information that can be used for constructive management of the organization. Personnel records indicating who has had what job, at what salary, and with what training form the basis for understanding the skill mix in a company and help identify possible candidates for certain jobs. Thus, IT can be thought of as affecting coordination by increasing the organization's memory, thereby establishing a record that allows for the detection of patterns. Although this has been true for some time, the added power of heuristics and artificial intelligence provides important additional tools for using information.

In summary, the traditional organizational structures and practices do not have to stay the same as we move into the 1990s. All dimensions of the organization will have to be reexamined in light of the power of the new IT. The economics are so powerful and apply to so much of the organization that one has to question everything before accepting the status quo.

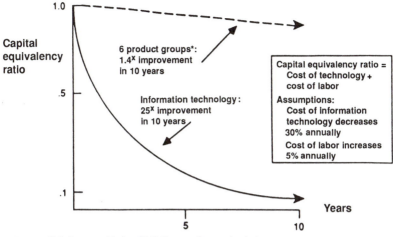

*Source: U.S. Bureau of Labor Statistics, producer price index,
compensation per hour, nonfarm, business sector, 1950 - 1980.

Figure 1.   Capital equivalency ratio: Information technology versus six product groups.

Major Findings of the Research

We see six major implications from the research. The first and most basic is that the nature of work is changing.

Finding 1. IT Is Enabling Fundamental Changes in the Way Work Is Done

The degree to which a person can be affected by the rapid evolution of information technology is determined by how much of the work is based on information—that is, information on what product to make or what service to deliver and how to do it (the production task), as well as when to do it and in conjunction with whom (the coordination task). In many organizations the people in these two categories account for a large proportion of the work force.

IT is available to radically alter the basic cost structure of a wide variety of jobs, jobs affecting at least half the members of the organization. IT is only an enabler, however; to actually change jobs takes a combination of management leadership and employee participation that is, thus far, extremely rare.

We saw change in three kinds of work being enabled by IT in ways that portend the kind of patterns we expect throughout the 1990s.

Production Work

The potential impact of IT on production work is considerable. This is most apparent when the nature of production work is broken up into three constituent elements:

1. Physical production affected by robotics (increasingly with "vision"), process control instrumentation, and intelligent sensors.
2. Information production affected by data-processing computers for the standard clerical tasks such as accounts receivable, billing, and payables.
3. Knowledge production affected by CAD/CAM tools for designers; workstations for those building qualitative products such as loans or letters of credit; and workstations for those building "soft" products such as new legislation or new software (with CASE tools).

These forms of change are readily understood in the case of physical products and standard information processing but do not seem to be as easily grasped and exploited when it comes to knowledge work. As a result, organizations appear to be very slow in exploiting and utilizing technology to increase the effectiveness of knowledge production.

Coordinative Work

IT, as it has been defined in this research program, includes six elements, one of which is communications networks. These are currently being installed at a rapid rate by nations and organizations, and we expect this to continue throughout the 1990s. Such networks are being utilized within a building, within an organization, between organizations, and between countries. However, their use has been less than it might be; there is a lack of standards that permit easy connectivity. This situation has begun to improve, and we can expect this improvement to accelerate through the 1990s as the enormous economic benefits to industries and societies become more obvious.

The new IT is permitting a change in the economics and functionality of the coordination process. As a result we can see changes in three areas:

1. Distance can be shrunk toward zero, becoming increasingly irrelevant as far as information flow is concerned. Thus, the location of work can be reexamined, as can potential partners. Even in 1989, leading companies had design teams in different countries working together on a single product.
2. Time can shrink toward zero or shift to a more convenient point. Airline reservation systems are a leading example of IT in a time-critical setting. Organizations located in different time zones yet required to work together are utilizing store-and-forward and common databases as a way to shift time.

3. Organizational memory, as exemplified by a common database, can be maintained over time, contributed to from all parts of the organization, and made available to a wide variety of authorized users.

Beyond memory is the organization's ability to share skills. In a sense, such "group work," or the utilization of teams, combines the three aspects of coordination: distance, time, and memory. This combined effect has more impact than the three elements by themselves.

This change in the economics and functionality of coordination fundamentally alters all the tasks in an organization that have to do with coordinating the delivery of products and services to customers and the actual production of such goods and services. To the extent that an organization's structure is determined by its coordinative needs, it too is subject to potential change.

Management Work

The third IT-enabled change in work is the work done by managers. The principal dimensions of management work that can be most affected are those of direction and control. *Direction,* as used here, is concerned with sensing changes in the external environment and also with staying in close touch with the organization of its members' ideas and reactions to their views of the environment. Relevant, timely information from these two sources can be crucial input to the organization's direction-setting process. This is as true for a sophisticated strategic planning system as for an informal executive support system or customer feedback system.

The *control* dimension of management work has two key aspects for our purposes here. The first is the measurement task, that is, measuring the organization's performance along whatever set of critical success factors has been defined as relevant. The second aspect is to interpret such measures against the plan and determine what actions to take. Effective control is a critical dimension of organizational learning as it feeds back to future direction setting, and both of these can be fundamentally changed by the increasing availability of IT.

Finding 2. IT Is Enabling the Integration of Business Functions at All Levels within and between Organizations

The continuing expansion of public and private telecom networks means that the concept of "any information, at any time, anywhere, and any way I want to look at it" is increasingly economically feasible. The infrastructure to permit this is being put in place by different companies at different rates. Those organizations that have created a significant enterprise-level infrastructure will be able to compete effectively in the 1990s. Additionally, the ability to electronically connect people and tasks within and between firms

will be increasingly available and affordable. Boundaries of organizations
are becoming more permeable; where work gets done, when, and with
whom is changing. This can be a difficult, often revolutionary, move whose
impact is blunted by people's unwillingness to exploit the new opportunities. However, in a few situations components are being designed with
suppliers in weeks, not months; parts are ordered from suppliers in hours,
not weeks; and questions are answered in seconds, not days. This enormous speedup in the flow of work is made possible by the electronic
network. The integration it permits is showing up in four forms:

Within the Value Chain. Xerox, among many others, connected design,
engineering, and manufacturing personnel within its system of local area
networks (LANs) and created a team focusing on one product. Such teams
have accomplished tasks in shorter time with greater creativity and higher
morale than with their previous tools and organizational structures. There
is no part of an organization that, in principle, is excluded from the team
concept.

End-to-End Links of Value Chains between Organizations. A supplier's
shipping department can be electronically connected to the buyer's purchasing department, and the sales force directly connected to its customers. This form of electronic integration is a powerful way of speeding up the
flow of goods between organizations. It has been popularized in the press
using various terminologies such as *electronic just-in-time* (JIT) or *electronic
data interchange* (EDI). This can be thought of as the boundary of the
organization being permeable to IT. It can also be thought of as shifting the
boundary of the organization out to include elements of other organizations, thus creating a "virtual" organization.

Value Chain Substitution via Subcontract or Alliance. This occurs when an
organization takes one stage in its value chain and subcontracts either a
specific task or the whole stage to another organization. A common example is when a firm asks a supplier to design a component for it. Modern
CAD/CAM environments permit a supplier's designers to be electronically
linked to the host team to allow the data exchange needed to accomplish a
joint design. Ford Motor Company's agreement with Ryder Truck to handle Ford's new car shipments is an example of a subcontracted task that
would not work effectively without electronic integration. These collaborations are enabled by IT and would not be feasible without it. They lead
to the host organization being able to take advantage of the economies of
scale and unique skills of its partner. To be of lasting value, of course, there
must be reciprocal benefits.

Electronic Markets. This is the most highly developed form of electronic
integration. Here, coordination within the organization or among a few
organizations gives way to an open market. Travel agents, for example, are

able to electronically reserve seats from all the major carriers and can look around for the best price at which to complete the transaction. Electronic markets will be increasingly prevalent in the 1990s as IT costs continue to drop and thereby reduce transaction costs to the point where the "market" becomes economically effective.

These four forms of electronic integration have, to varying degrees, the net effect of removing buffers and leveraging expertise. Shrinking time and distance can have the effect of allowing the right resources to be at the right place at the right time. In effect, this removes the need to have people and other assets (such as inventory or cash) tied up as unproductive buffers.

It appears that an organization must have the necessary infrastructure of communications, data, applications software, and educated and empowered users before any of these four forms of integration can be fully exploited.

We have found that each of these four forms of integration is visible in embryonic form in some organization. However, the real economic impact and rate of dissemination of the integration vary enormously, and in no case has there been a clearly sustainable transformation. Some of the major reasons for this are discussed below.

Finding 3. IT Is Causing Shifts in the Competitive Climate in Many Industries

At the level of the industry, information technology has a unique impact on the competitive climate and on the degree of interrelatedness of products or services with rivals. This can lead to unprecedented degrees of simultaneous competition and collaboration between firms. This effect of IT is spreading rapidly. For example, parts suppliers that are linked electronically with purchasers for design and manufacturing are not uncommon.

Another illustration is the creation of an electronic linkage between the U.S. Internal Revenue Service (IRS) and tax preparation firms. The linkage was created to enable the electronic filing of individual income tax returns prepared by those firms. This has opened up opportunities for lending or borrowing what is, in aggregate, some $70 billion. This is causing the creation of new arrangements between multiple financial services firms.

Finding 4. IT Presents New Strategic Opportunities for Organizations That Reassess Their Missions and Operations

A turbulent environment, the changing nature of work, the possibilities of electronic integration, and the changing competitive climate are all compelling reasons for the third stage in the evolution of the organization of the 1990s. In short, *automate* and *informate* set the stage for transformation.

Research during the 1990s program suggests that the three findings just discussed—new ways of doing work, electronic integration, and the shifting competitive climate—present an organization with an opportunity, if not a pressing need, to step back and rethink its mission and the way it is going to conduct its operations.

There appear to be three distinct stages that organizations are going through as they attempt to respond to their changing environments: automate, informate, and transformation.

Automate

IT applications in this stage are designed to take the cost out of "production." Savings are usually achieved by reducing the number of workers. For information handlers such as order entry clerks, this can result in effectively being eliminated from the work force. For other production workers, manual operations are replaced by machine actions under computer control. For example, an operator no longer has to change valve settings by hand but instead watches a computer screen and types instructions.

This requires fewer operators with consequent direct cost savings. Beyond process control and automation of traditional paper processing (for example, bank check clearing), IT is being used for automation with the scanner and bar code, the universal product code (UPC). This is now used not only for packaged goods but also for inventory in warehouses and a host of other tracking applications. These kinds of IT tools can give rise to enormous cost reductions.

The new IT tools, used by the "production" workers who are left after automation, often generate information as a by-product. This is clearly seen in the case of process control where the operators have information from multiple sensors and watch screens and type in instructions. In the automate stage, however, little or no use is made of this new information beyond direct control of the existing process.

Informate

Informate is a term (first coined by Shoshana Zuboff) that describes what happens when automated processes yield information as a by-product.

The informate stage as we saw it in the 1990s program has three distinguishing characteristics. The first is that production work involves new tools that provide information that must be used to get the job done; for example, the operator must read the screen to see if the process is within tolerance. This work can be fairly "simple," as in monitoring machines, or it can involve complex new skills, such as using a 3-D dynamic color workstation for engineering design. Similarly, the foreign exchange trader working in several markets on a real-time basis has to use a set of computer-based tools that are quite different from the telephone and voice with which the job used to be done. At a more mundane level, a salesperson making a presentation to a potential customer uses financial models to demonstrate the savings on this month's "deal." All these knowledge workers are having to develop new skills to work with new information tools. These often involve new ways of thinking.

The second distinguishing characteristic of the informate state is that the new IT tools often generate new sorts of information as a by-product of the basic tools. For example, the process control operator might notice that one limit is always exceeded when the weather is hot; the foreign exchange trader may notice that certain accounts are building a position in certain currencies; or the salesperson, by analyzing twelve months of sales data, notices buying patterns in some of the customers. Thus, the process of using the new IT tools develops some by-product information that in turn can require a different kind of conceptual grasp by the person concerned. Thus, "invisible" work is going on in the worker's mind. This kind of work may require changes in skills and management practices if it is to be used successfully to improve the organization's performance. It requires an ability to see patterns and understand the overall process rather than just looking at controlling the information on the screen. In this situation the production worker becomes an "analyzer," a role involving a different level of conceptual skill from what was needed before as a "doer," or machine minder.

The third distinguishing characteristic of the informate stage is that the new skills and information are developed to the point where new market opportunities can be opened up. This may require a broader view of one's job and an identification with the whole organization rather than one's narrow piece of it. For example, American Hospital Supply (AHS) was able to sell the patterns of their customers' buying behavior, detected by the AHS sales force, back to the producer of the original product. The salespeople concerned had noticed that there were patterns with certain kinds of customers. They alerted their management to these patterns and in turn came up with the idea that this would be a valuable by-product that could be sold and thus form the basis for a new business.

Transformation

The changing nature of work does not stop with the informate stage but goes on to the transformation stage. The term *transformation* has been chosen deliberately to reflect the fundamental difference in character exhibited by organizations (or parts of organizations) that have been through the first two stages and have begun on the third.

All successful organizations in the 1990s will have to pass through this stage, a stage characterized by leadership, vision, and a sustained process of organization empowerment so basic as to be exceptionally hard to accomplish. In a way, it can be thought of as the necessary follow on to "total quality." The total quality programs are a uniquely American phenomenon of the late 1980s. They have served as a very useful rallying cry to energize organizations so that they could fix the woefully inadequate practices that had crept into their operations and management procedures. The concept of transformation includes the broad view of quality but goes beyond this to address the unique opportunities presented by the environment and enabled by IT. A process to help accomplish this, the Strategic Alignment Model (SAM), emerged from the 1990s research.

Finding 5. Successful Application of IT Will Require Changes in Management and Organizational Structure

The 1990s program has shown that information technology is a critical enabler of the re-creation (redefinition) of the organization. This is true in part because it permits the distribution of power, function, and control to wherever they are most effective, given the mission and objectives of the organization and the culture it enjoys.

Organizations have always managed some form of matrix structure, a matrix involving functions, products, markets, and geography in some combination. With the new IT, unit costs of coordination are declining significantly. This means that over the next decade we can afford more coordination for the same dollar cost. In addition, IT is causing changing economies of scale. For example, flexible manufacturing permits smaller organizations to also be low-cost producers. Thus, IT is enabling a breakup, a dis-integration, of traditional organizational forms. For example, multiple skills can be brought together at an arbitrary point in time and location. In short, ad hoc teams are enabled by IT. Digital Equipment, among others, has all their engineers on the same network; thus an engineer anywhere in the world can share information, ask for help, or work on a project as needed. As these ad hoc teams become an effective way of working, they give rise to the "networking" organization. In such organizations, horizontal and vertical working patterns can be created as needed. This will not be the most appropriate organizational form for all tasks and all organizational cultures; however, it is increasingly an option. IT's ability to affect coordination by shrinking time and distance permits an organization to respond more quickly and accurately to the marketplace. This not only reduces the assets the organization has tied up but improves quality as seen by the customer.

Put another way, the 1990s research suggests that the "metabolic rate" of the organization, that is, the rate at which information moves and decisions are made, is speeding up and will get faster in the decade of the 1990s. This is partly because the external environment demands responsiveness and partly because of the way IT has enabled changes to be made in how work is done. In both cases the availability of electronic tools and electronic integration permits this responsiveness. Since global competitive forces do not permit an organization to ignore its competition, as one firm picks up the new options the others must follow. Thus, the management of interdependence in the 1990s will take place in a dynamic environment. This requires new management systems and processes. The measurement systems, the rewards, the incentives, and the required skills all require rethinking in the new IT-impacted world. For example, the use of an electronically based JIT system obviously requires new production planning and control processes. The use of small autonomous product teams that combine design, engineering, and manufacturing raises issues of rewards, evaluation, and reassignment. The changes in work created by the use of new technology require new skills and totally new ways of doing the job.

Management has the challenging task of changing the organizational structure and methods of operation to keep it competitive in a dynamically changing world. Research has shown that IT provides one set of tools that can enable such changes. However, to think through the new systems and processes so that they can be exploited effectively is a major challenge for line management.

Finding 6. A Major Challenge for Management in the 1990s Will Be to Lead Their Organizations through the Transformation Necessary to Prosper in the Globally Competitive Environment

The 1990s research has pinpointed some characteristics of the organizations that will be able to successfully go through the transformation process. The first, and obvious, fact is that none of the potentially beneficial enabling aspects of IT can take place without clarity of business purpose and a vision of what the organization should become. A clear mission visible to, and understood by, the organization is a well-known prerequisite for any major organization change. However, when the issue at hand is organizational transformation, enabled by technology, it appears particularly important to invest a large amount of time and effort in getting the organization to understand where it is going and why. This effort is further complicated by the lack of knowledge and skills, not to say fear, of new technology. There appear to be two other important preconditions of successful transformation. One is that the organization has been through a process of aligning its corporate strategy (business and IT), information technology, and organizational dimensions. The second precondition is that the organization have a robust information technology infrastructure in place, including an electronic network, and understood standards.

One root cause for the lack of impact of IT on the improved economic performance of organizations is an organization's unwillingness to invest heavily and early enough in human resources. Changing the way people work can be extremely threatening and therefore takes a great deal of

investment. There must be investment in new skills, in psychological
ownership of the change process, and in a safety net under the employee
so that there is no fear of taking prudent risks. These investments are
required throughout the organization as management itself is part of the
required change.

The ultimate goal of this change is to give all employees a sense of
empowerment. They need to feel that they can make a difference, that their
efforts directly affect the organization's performance, and that they are able
to take on as much responsibility and commensurate reward as they are
willing to work for. Such a "Theory Y" view of an organization is a long
way from our history of large hierarchically organized mass-production
command and control organizations.

However, the economic realities engendered by IT and the nature of the
business environment suggest that if the above factors are in effect the
attributes needed by the successful organization of the 1990s, as has been
suggested, moving from the present state of most large organizations to the
next generation requires a transformation.

The Challenge of the 1990s

No impact from information technology is yet visible in the macroeconomic
data available. A very few individual firms are demonstrably better off, and
there is a larger group of isolated examples of successful exploitation in
particular individual functions or business units. However, on average the
expected benefits are not yet visible.

One major explanation of this lack of impact lies in the enormous
strength of historical precedence. The Western economies have had more
than half a century of doing business in a certain way. These ways are very
hard to discard, and it appears to be harder yet to learn new ones.

Understanding one's organizational culture, and knowing what it means
to have an innovative culture, is a key first step in a move toward an
adaptive organization. This in turn seems to require innovative human
resource policies that support the organization's members as they learn to
cope with a changing and more competitive world. To accomplish this
successfully is one of the major challenges for an organization in the decade
of the 1990s.

Reference

Zuboff, S. (1988). *In the Age of the Smart Machine: The Future of Work and Power*. Basic
Books, New York.

P·A·R·T · III

E

B of A's Plans for Computer Don't Add Up*

Douglas Frantz

In May, 1986, Bank of America was so confident about the impending success of its pioneering new computer system for trust accounts that dozens of the bank's most important corporate clients were invited to a lavish two-day demonstration at the Santa Barbara Biltmore Hotel. Holes were cut in the hotel roof to ventilate the rooms full of computers, and color monitors were in place to show off the bells and whistles of what B of A officials touted as the industry's most sophisticated technology for handling trust accounts. The party's $75,000 tab was minor to officials anticipating the lucrative new business that the system seemed sure to generate when it went on-line within the next few weeks.

End of Good Times

"There never has been a meeting that went as well as this from a point of view of inspiring the customers," said Clyde R. Claus, a thirty-year veteran of banking, who organized the session as the executive in charge of B of A's trust department. "People were trembling with excitement."

The bash at the Biltmore was the last thing that went right.

Last month, Bank of America acknowledged that it was abandoning the $20-million computer system after wasting another $60 million trying to make it work. The bank will no longer handle processing for its trust division, and the biggest accounts were given to a Boston bank. Top executives, including Claus, have lost their jobs already and an undisclosed number of layoffs are in the works.

If the episode involved only a handful of ruined careers and the millions lost in pursuit of a too-fancy computer system, it would merit an embarrassing but forgettable footnote in Bank of America's legendary history. But the story is more important than a simple footnote because it opens a rare window on what author Martin Mayer has dubbed "a decade of decline" at the San Francisco bank, an unprecedented span in which its fortunes plunged from a $643-million profit in 1980 to a $955-million loss in 1987 and the bank fell from largest in the world to Number 29.

Deeper Questions

Further, the total abandonment of a computer system after five years of development and nearly a year of false starts raises questions about the bank's ability to overcome its technological inadequacy in an era when money is often nothing more than a blip on a computer screen.

A spokesman said last week that Bank of America officials would not respond to questions from *The Times* about the episode. "Since last year, we have acknowledged that operational problems existed in our institutional trust business and our energies have been directed toward resolving them as quickly as possible," the spokesman said in a prepared statement. "We are not interested in fixing blame. . . . We do not believe that it is productive to rehash the situation."

The widely publicized difficulties surrounding the trust computer problems obscure the fact that the Bank of America was once a technological leader, developing the first big commercial computer in the 1950s and inventing the magnetic ink that allows machines to read the codes on checks. By the late 1970s, however, under the leadership of A. W. Clausen, the bank was skimping on the spending required to keep up with technological advances. Instead, the money went into greater profits. By the time Clausen relinquished the helm of the parent company, BankAmerica, to Samuel H. Armacost in 1981, the bank had fallen far behind in the computer race.

Armacost launched a $4-billion spending program to push B of A back to the technological forefront. The phrase he liked was "leapfrogging into the 1990s," and one area that he chose to emphasize was the trust department.

Financial Role

Trust departments serve as custodians and managers of investments for individuals, corporations, unions, and government agencies. Investments can be real estate, cash, stocks, and bonds. Accounts run from a few

---

*This article appeared in *The Los Angeles Times,* Business Section, Sunday, June 4, 1989: 1, 8. Copyright © 1989, *Los Angeles Times.* Reprinted by permission.

thousand to billions of dollars for big pension funds. Banks collect fees for their services, and the amounts can be substantial. In return, trust departments must provide customers with extensive records and statements to explain their actions and balance the accounts. The reporting is similar to balancing a checkbook for thousands of customers with enormously varied demands.

For instance, a $300-million pension fund might cover six affiliates within the company. The affiliates would share the services of an investment manager, whose trading would be reported to the bank as trustee. The bank must allocate each purchase or sale to the proper affiliate account, keep track of dividends, and provide the customer with an ongoing accounting and monthly statements. Throw in the management of an office building or two and a picture emerges of the complexity of trust accounting. Developing a computer system that puts all of this information on the computer screens of customers in a microsecond is enormously complex, and it is vital to be competitive.

Traditionally, the field has been dominated by a handful of big Eastern banks, such as Bankers Trust in New York and State Street Bank & Trust in Boston. Although it was the largest trust bank on the West Coast, B of A in the late 1970s was small by comparison, and it was mired in a 1960s-vintage accounting and reporting system. An effort to update the system ended in a $6-million failure in 1981 after the company's computer engineers worked for more than a year without developing a usable system. So Armacost turned to Claus, who had spent twenty years with New York's Marine Midland Bank before arriving at B of A in 1977.

Gets Ultimatum

Soon after Claus was named executive vice-president in charge of the trust department in 1982, Armacost called him to his office on the fortieth floor of the bank's granite tower in downtown San Francisco to discuss the trust department's problems. "Fix it or close it," Armacost ordered Claus.

Claus soon found that abandoning the business would damage client relationships. Many customers who relied on the bank for trust business as a convenience maintained far larger corporate accounts there. He was equally reluctant to return to the in-house technicians who had produced the stillborn system a year before.

So, Claus and two key executives in data processing, Nicholas Caputo and Thomas Anderson, embarked on a search to find an outside vendor to help develop the new system. In true Bank of America style, the plan was grand: Create a system to surpass Bankers Trust and State Street and turn B of A into a national power in trust business.

In the fall of 1982, the trust industry held its annual convention in Atlanta. Caputo and Anderson attended, and so did Steven M. Katz, a pioneer in creating software for bank trust departments. Katz, the computer expert, and Alfred P. West, Jr., a marketing specialist, had formed a company called SEI Corporation outside Philadelphia in Wayne, Pennsylvania. They had parlayed concepts in Katz's MBA thesis into a software system used by about 300 small banks in the 1970s. Katz left in a dispute and, in June, 1980, he founded a rival company, Premier Systems, across the street from SEI in Wayne. Insiders referred to the pavement between the companies as "the DMZ."

Katz was in Atlanta trying to drum up business. Caputo knew Katz and invited him to meet with the B of A officials at the Hyatt Regency Hotel. By the accounts of people who were there, it was a stormy beginning.

Basis of System

Bank of America's existing system was based on IBM computers, and the bank officials wanted to stick with the familiar hardware. Katz insisted on using Prime Computer, an IBM rival with which he had a long relationship. There also was a clash on delivery time. According to one participant, Katz boasted that he could put together a system by 1983, and Anderson argued that the promise was ridiculously optimistic. The argument ended the meeting—but did not doom the partnership.

During the next six months, Bank of America and Katz brought together a consortium of banks that agreed to advance Premier money to develop a new, cutting-edge system for trust reporting and accounting. The other banks, all smaller than B of A, were Seattle-First National Bank (which would later be purchased by BankAmerica), United Virginia Bank (now Crestar), and Philadelphia National Bank. The three smaller banks were using SEI's system.

Nearly a year was spent on additional research before Claus took the proposal to the bank's management committee and got the go-ahead to fund the project in March, 1984. A contract was signed with Premier to provide a system called MasterNet. While the trust business was by far the biggest task, the contract also called for the bank's technicians to develop eight smaller systems to augment it under the MasterNet umbrella. While it was not a deadline, the goal was to have the new system, called TrustPlus, in operation by December 31, 1984. What followed was a textbook structure for designing a computer system.

A committee was formed of representatives from each B of A department that would use the system, and they met monthly to discuss their requirements. Data-processing experts from the four banks gathered for a week each month in Pennsylvania to review progress and discuss their needs with the Premier designers. "The bank seemed to be doing it right," a B of A executive involved in the project said. "The risks were shared with other banks. A proven vendor was hired. And all areas of the bank were involved."

Some of the bank data-processing experts found Katz difficult to deal with occasionally, particularly when they offered views on technical aspects of the project. "Don't give us the solutions. Just tell us the problems," Katz often said. Katz declined to answer questions for this article, saying: "It's our policy not to talk about individual customer relationships."

When the ambitious December 31, 1984 goal passed without a system, no one was concerned. There was progress, and those involved were excited about the unfolding system and undaunted by the size of the task. The immense size of what they confronted is contained in two minor statistics: B of A devoted twenty person-years to testing the software system and its 3.5 million lines of code; 13,000 hours of training, including rigorous testing, were provided to the staff that would run the system.

After 1985 passed without a working system, some team members detected subtle pressures from corporate brass to come up with a return on the bank's investment, which was approaching $20 million. Customers who had been promised the best system in the world were also concerned. "Major clients were anxious to get the system and we were real late," one executive who was involved said. "Some of these people were threatening to leave the bank."

Claus, the only person connected with the program who would speak for attribution, denied that he had been pressured over costs or timing. He said Thomas A. Cooper, then the president of B of A, told him in 1986: "You're not getting any pressure from me to do it unless you're ready." That spring, Claus decided the system was about ready. Some smaller parts of MasterNet were already working smoothly in other parts of the bank. Test runs for the trust system had not been perfect, but the technicians thought most bugs could be worked out soon. A demonstration run in Wayne had been successful.

Divergent Opinions

So, invitations were mailed for the bash at the Biltmore. Although Claus genuinely thought that the system was about ready, others viewed the party as a means of appeasing anxious customers by giving them a taste. The taste was good.

"It was a very well-staged function and it really did show the capabilities of a system that had great appeal to us and others attending," said Derek Rowlett, administrator of the $350-million pension fund of the Directors Guild of America.

The plan was to first bring in the institutional trust customers. Although their accounts were larger, totaling assets of $38 billion, there were only 800 of them. The consumer division, with 8000 smaller accounts, would be converted later. But the promise that the bank would soon convert the institutional customers to MasterNet was unfulfilled. Technical bugs kept popping up and the system would not work efficiently enough to handle the conversion. "There were all kinds of problems," a former bank official said. "You could be sitting at a terminal and it would take too long to get a response, too long for the screen to pop up. Other times, the whole system crashed."

The delays put additional pressure on bank employees, many of whom were also operating the old system and working double shifts and weekends to try to get the new system operating, too. "It was an especially heavy burden on the people involved," one executive who worked on the conversion said.

Late in 1986, Claus received an anonymous letter from someone familiar with the system who warned against a "rush to convert" and told Claus, who was not a computer expert, that people had "pulled the wool" over his eyes.

Memo to Staff

Claus responded with a memo to the staff assuring them that there would be no conversion before it was time. The three chief components of the system—trust department, systems engineering, and the bank's securities clearance operation—had reported to Claus at the start of the project, which gave him the authority to ensure full cooperation.

By 1986, his authority had been restricted. The systems group and the securities staff had been given their own bosses who did not report directly to Claus. It made obtaining cooperation, particularly from the securities group in Los Angeles, difficult as the pressure to perform increased in 1986.

These pressures, whether spoken or not, were felt by many involved in the project. The bank had reported severe losses in 1986 and efforts were being made throughout the giant company to cut back. Some of the bank's most profitable businesses were sold and 9600 jobs were cut. One who lost his job was Armacost, and with him went his vision of 1990s technology. Clausen was brought back from retirement to run the bank again, and his perception of computers was not enhanced when he reviewed the trust troubles.

The economic cutbacks and Clausen's reaction made it difficult to justify the continued expense of staffing two trust systems when one was mired in costly troubles. For several months in late 1986 and early 1987, however, tests of TrustPlus had been running with only a few bugs. "There were still bugs, but the users felt they could run with it and work out the bugs as we went along," one former executive said. A conversion date was set: March 2, 1987. Just as the data-processing staff was rushing to complete work for the conversion, half of the sixteen-member contingent was pulled off the assignment.

Trust Business Sale

In its push to raise money to offset its losses, B of A had sold its consumer trust business to Wells Fargo for $100 million. B of A was rushing to close the deal by March 31, 1987, so the proceeds could be booked in the first quarter. So, half the data-processing staff was switched to help transfer the accounts to the Wells Fargo system, which was based on SEI software.

On Saturday, February 28, and Sunday, March 1, the remaining staff worked almost nonstop to complete the switch of the institutional trust accounts, which had begun a week before. They pulled it off on that Monday—and it lasted until Saturday, March 7. That was the day the first of the twenty-four disk-drive units on the Prime computers blew up, causing the loss of a portion of the database and signaling the beginning of the end. Workers spent a discouraging weekend retrieving data from a backup unit. It was past midnight each night before they left the offices. Over the next month, at least fourteen more of the disk drives blew up. None had malfunctioned in the previous months of tests.

It turned out that the units were part of a faulty batch manufactured by Control Data Corporation, a Minneapolis computer firm. But by the time the cause was discovered, delays had mounted and other difficulties had arisen. Taken individually, none would have caused the ensuing disaster. Together, they doomed the system. "When the stuff hit the fan in the springtime, there was a series of really statistically impossible little disasters that became one big one," Claus said.

At the precise time the technical team was struggling with these setbacks in April, the bank decided to move the staff from San Francisco to its data-processing headquarters across the bay in Concord, thirty miles away, in another money-saving effort. For many who had been working under great stress for months, the move became the focus for their frustration. Several key people quit and morale sank as many who remained grumbled.

The difficulties were not restricted to San Francisco. The securities clearing operation on the eighteenth floor of the BankAmerica building in Los Angeles was thrown into disarray by the computer woes and its own unrelated problems. Securities clearing is critical to a trust operation. It involves reconciling thousands of stock and bond trades daily. At the end of the day, the accounts must balance—each purchase and sale recorded in the proper account and matched to the records from the brokers who actually execute the trades. Stocks, or their equivalent, must be delivered and money accepted. One of the intended functions of TrustPlus was to both reconcile this activity and ensure that transactions were credited to the proper accounts. When it did not work, the securities group had to rely on records from the outside brokers to settle transactions. The practice, called "blind settling," is abhorrent to any well-run operation.

The computer problems confirmed the suspicions of the securities people in Los Angeles, many of whom had never thought that TrustPlus would

work. But its defenders maintain that the securities operation had unrelated problems that contributed to its difficulties. The securities people had
become reluctant to participate in the design process. When the problems
erupted in the spring, Claus no longer had authority over the division, and
many thought he was unable to force its cooperation. An outside consultant later told bank employees that some securities work was destroyed and
some was simply stuck away in drawers during the critical weeks after the
ill-fated conversion. And some in Los Angeles were less inclined to put up
with the demands of the collapsing computer system because in March the
bank had announced plans to move the operation to San Francisco, which
meant many Los Angeles workers would lose their jobs. Reaction was so
strong against the move that the bank put it on hold three months later, but
nearly forty people had left by then.

   Whatever the complex causes, dozens of highly paid "temporary" workers were brought into the securities group in Los Angeles to straighten out
the reconciliation mess at an enormous cost. In the ensuing months, there
were conflicts between the bank staff and the "temps" from Ernst &
Whinney and Touche Ross, and there were turf battles among the consulting firms as they jockeyed for the millions of dollars that B of A was paying
in an attempt to fix the problem.

   The bank's first public acknowledgment of the problems came in a
one-line notice in the earnings report it issued in July, 1987. It said $25
million was being placed in a reserve to cover anticipated losses from
problems with MasterNet. Bank officials assured reporters and clients that
the problems would be resolved. But within weeks the bank was quietly
seeking a buyer for the entire institutional trust department. The effort was
unsuccessful because, an official at a rival bank said, there was not much
to buy. Clausen also ordered an in-house investigation of the debacle,
which many staff members viewed as little more than a witch hunt. The
result was a "one-copy" report that went only to Clausen. In October,
Claus and Louis Mertes, the executive in charge of systems engineering,
resigned. Claus acknowledged that he was leaving over the MasterNet
problems and took responsibility for them. Mertes, who had been at the
bank only two years, has not spoken publicly about his departure.

   Another surprise came in January when the bank announced that an
additional $35 million would be reserved to "correct problems" with the
system, bringing the total spent on fixing the $20-million system to $60
million.

Period of Decline

By then, the institutional customers were leaving. The number of accounts
had dropped from about 800 to around 700, and assets under management
had declined to $34 billion from $38 billion. What the bank did not say was

that the decision had been made to abandon the system. But over the next few days, it was disclosed that the bank was shifting 95% of its trust business to Seattle-First National Bank, now a BankAmerica affiliate, which uses an IBM-based system from SEI. The remaining accounts, deemed too complex for the Seattle bank, were given to State Street Bank in Boston, one of the industry leaders that Bank of America had set out to overtake nearly six years and $80 million ago. Even the decision to crop the embarrassing program is not immune to criticism, which was summarized by Claus last week. "A lot of people lay down on the floor and spilled blood over this system, and why they abandoned it now I cannot understand," he said. "A guy called me this morning out of the blue and said that 95% of it was working very well."

P·A·R·T · III

Groupware Goes Boom*

David Kirkpatrick

When Rick Richardson arrives at his office each morning, he gets a cup of coffee and turns on his PC. On an average day he receives twenty to twenty-five e-mail messages—not surprising, since he's in charge of all the work that Price Waterhouse, the accounting and consulting firm, does with New York City banks. Then he clicks the mouse to see news articles on topics he has given the computer standing orders to track. He has already done more with his PC than most American executives, but what happens next makes him truly exceptional.

Price Waterhouse maintains electronic bulletin boards on more than 1000 different subjects, accessible to as many as 18,000 employees in twenty-two countries. Richardson calls up a board that holds messages about the firm's financial services business. A Washington staffer reports on an accounting regulation change; Richardson adds a comment for all to see. A manager in Miami needs Spanish-speaking consultants for an assignment in Buenos Aires; Richardson zaps him a name by e-mail.

Finally, he checks a board called PW Alert, where employees post general information and queries. One message, from Dublin, asks if anyone has experience auditing a cheese plant processing 100 million gallons of milk a year. Messages are listed by title, so Richardson can skip that one and any others he's not interested in. But he reads carefully a query from Chicago soliciting CFO candidates for a client. Perhaps he'll call the sender later and suggest a name.

From the moment he turned on his PC, Richardson has been using Notes, a Lotus Development software product that is helping define the future of corporate computing. Notes is the most popular entry in a fast-growing category called groupware. While most PC software has been written for people working alone, these programs make it easier for groups to work together. That couldn't be more timely. Just when the theorists of business-process reengineering are telling companies to flatten hierarchies and get people working in teams, along comes the software that—properly used—can help make it all happen.

The new groupware tools are so powerful, in fact, that they virtually compel companies to reengineer themselves. By giving workers well below the top of the organizational pyramid access to information previously unavailable or restricted to upper levels of management, groupware spreads power far more widely than before. Many who have grown comfortable dwelling near the pyramid's apex are understandably distressed by the way groupware disrupts old-style hierarchies. Says a consultant who helps clients figure out how to use the software: "FORTUNE 500 companies are having a hell of a time with groupware. There's a tremendous amount of what I call antibody immune response."

Like e-mail, groupware became possible when companies started linking PCs into networks. But while e-mail works fine for sending a message to a specific person or group—communicating one-to-one or one-to-many— groupware allows a new kind of communication: many-to-many. Groupware can improve efficiency, because it keeps workers continually apprised of what colleagues are thinking and doing. To be sure, it also creates even more data for the already-besieged to digest. Some complain that groupware only adds to information overload.

Lotus Notes combines a sophisticated messaging system with a giant database containing work records and memos. It changes the way information flows in an organization. It creates a kind of corporate on-line service, an Internet of the office. Unlike plain e-mail, Notes doesn't require you to figure out who needs to know a fact or hear an idea. Instead, you simply forward your memo to the appropriate bulletin board. Like Rick Richardson of Price Waterhouse, anyone who needs to know about a subject will check there and find it.

Groupware Seldom Succeeds without Top-Level Support

Price Waterhouse was fortunate to have one of the world's great technology cheerleaders at the helm of its Notes effort. Sheldon Laube, the firm's chief technologist, has a techie's brain and a salesman's personality. He got his top-level job—one of the company's twenty most senior—in 1989 with explicit instructions to make the firm's technology state-of-the-art. When he found Notes, he recognized its potential for tackling one of Price

*This article appeared in *Fortune*, 128(16)(December 27, 1993):99–103. Reprinted with permission of Time/Warner Inc.

Waterhouse's key challenges: capturing and storing information. Laube pushed, cajoled, joked, and lobbied for it. Richardson says Price Waterhouse would never have won one recent multimillion-dollar job if it hadn't been able to use Notes to put together a proposal quickly.

The giant accounting and consulting firm was the first customer for Lotus Notes, the program that got groupware off the ground. Behind chief technologist Laube is the screen he sees when he turns on his computer. Each icon represents a Notes database that he can share with up to 18,000 colleagues.

Here's how Price Waterhouse put together a proposal in four days and won a multimillion-dollar consulting contract by using Lotus's Notes software for groups. On Thursday a Price Waterhouse executive learned that a major securities firm was about to award a big consulting contract to help develop a complex new trading operation. Price Waterhouse was invited to bid, but there was a hitch: The proposals were due Monday. A Price Waterhouse competitor had been working on its own bid for weeks.

The four Price Waterhouse executives who were needed to write the proposal were in three different states. But they were able to work together using Notes, which allowed them to conduct a four-way dialogue on-screen. They also extracted key components of the proposal from various databases on Notes. From one, they pulled resumes of the Price Waterhouse experts from around the world who could be assigned to the job. From another, they borrowed passages from similar successful proposals. As the draft evolved, each of the four modified it or make comments. Notes kept track of the changes. Other executives looked at the proposal via Notes over the weekend.

The proposal was ready Monday, and Price Waterhouse won the deal. Its competitor didn't even meet the deadline. A year later, the client hired Price Waterhouse to audit the new operation. That contract will probably last for years.

P·A·R·T· III

G

Learning from Notes: Organizational Issues in Groupware Implementation*

Wanda J. Orlikowski

Introduction

Computer-supported cooperative work, collaborative computing, and groupware have become common labels in our contemporary technological vocabulary. While some have discussed the potential for such technologies to enhance organizational effectiveness (Dyson, 1990; Govani, 1992; *PC Week*, 1991; Marshak, 1990), others have suggested that the implementation of such technologies is more difficult and yields more unintended consequences than is typically acknowledged (Bullen and Bennett, 1990; Grudin, 1988; Kiesler, 1986; Kling, 1991; Perin, 1991). Empirical studies of groupware usage in organizations are clearly needed to shed light on these diverse expectations. While there have been many field studies of electronic mail usage (Bair and Gale, 1988; Eveland and Bikson, 1986; Feldman, 1987; Finholt and Sproull, 1990; Mackay, 1988; Markus, 1987; Sproull and Kiesler, 1986), groupware technologies (that include more collaborative features than electronic mail) have been studied less frequently.

In this paper I describe the findings of an exploratory field study that examined the implementation of the groupware product Notes (from Lotus Development Corporation) into one office of a large organization. [*Notes* supports communication, coordination, and collaboration within groups or organizations through such features as electronic mail, computer conferences, shared data bases, and customized views. See Marshak (1990) for more details on the product.] My interest in studying the implementation of this product was to investigate whether and how the use of a collaborative tool changes the nature of work and the pattern of social interactions in the office, and with what intended and unintended consequences. Two organizational elements seem especially relevant in influencing the effective utilization of groupware: people's cognitions, or mental models, about technology and their work, and the structural properties of the organization, such as policies, norms, and reward systems. The findings suggest that where people's mental models do not understand or appreciate the collaborative nature of groupware, such technologies will be interpreted and used as if they were more familiar technologies, such as personal, stand-alone software (e.g., a spreadsheet or word-processing program). Also, where the premises underlying the groupware technology (shared effort, cooperation, collaboration) are countercultural to an organization's structural properties (competitive and individualistic culture, rigid hierarchy, etc.), the technology will be unlikely to facilitate collective use and value. That is, where there are few incentives or norms for cooperating or sharing expertise, groupware technology alone cannot engender these. Conversely, where the structural properties do support shared effort, cooperation, and collaboration, it is likely that the technology will be used collaboratively, that is, it will be another medium within which those values and norms are expressed. Recognizing the significant influence of these organizational elements appears critical to groupware developers, users, and researchers.

Research Site and Methods

Field work was conducted within a large services firm, Alpha Corporation (a pseudonym), which provides consulting services to clients around the world. The career structure within Alpha is hierarchical, the four primary milestones being staff consultant, senior consultant, manager, and principal. In contrast to the pyramidal career structure, the firm operates through a matrix form, where client work is executed and managed in a decentralized fashion out of local offices, while being coordinated through consulting practice management centralized in the headquarters office.

A few years ago, Alpha purchased and distributed Notes to all their consultants and support staff as part of a strategy, described by a senior principal as an attempt to "leverage the expertise of our firm." My research study examined the implementation of Notes in one large office of Alpha (henceforth referred to simply as "the office") over a period of five months. Detailed data collection was conducted through unstructured interviews,

*This article appeared in *The Information Society*, Vol. 9:237–250. Reprinted with permission of the Association for Computing Machinery.

Table 1. Number and Type of Interviews in Alpha

	Practice	Technology	Total
Principals	13	4	17
Managers	26	15	41
Seniors	12	13	25
Support staff	8	–	8
Total	59	32	91

review of office documents, and observation of meetings, work sessions, and training classes. More than ninety interviews were conducted, each about an hour in length, and some participants were interviewed more than once over the period of study. In addition to the office where the study was conducted, I interviewed key players from Alpha's headquarters and technology group. Participants spanned various hierarchical levels and were either consultants in active practice, administrators supporting practice activities, or members of the centralized technology support function (see Table 1).

The research study was designed to examine how the groupware technology is adopted and used by individuals, and how work and social relations change as a consequence. The research study began in February 1991, before the Notes system was due to be installed within the office, and continued through the implementation and early use (June 1991). The findings reflect participants' anticipations of as well as their early exposure to Notes.[1] These findings need to be interpreted cautiously, as they only reflect the adoption and early-use experiences of a sample of individuals within a specific office in what is a larger implementation process continuing over time in Alpha. While early, the findings to date are interesting, as they reflect people's initial experiences and assessments of Notes in light of their current work practices and assumptions about technology. The initial period following the implementation of a technology is typically a brief and rare opportunity for users to examine and think about the technology as a discrete artifact, before it is assimilated into cognitive habits and work practices, and disappears from views (Tyre and Orlikowski, in press). It is possible that with time, greater use, and appropriate circumstances, these early experiences will change.

[1] This research study represents the first of a series of studies that are being conducted within Alpha over time. Further analyses and observations are thus anticipated.

Research Results

Background to the Notes Acquisition

In the late eighties, a few senior principals realized that Alpha, relative to its competitors and its clients' expectations, was not utilizing information technology as effectively as they could. In response, they commissioned an internal study of the firm's technological capabilities, weaknesses, and requirements. On the basis of this study's recommendations, a new and powerful position—akin to that of a chief information officer (CIO)—was created within Alpha with responsibility for the firm's internal use of information technology. One of the first tasks the new CIO took on was the creation of firm-wide standards for the personal computing environments utilized in Alpha offices. It was while reviewing communication software that the CIO was introduced to the Notes groupware system. As he remarked later, after a few days of "playing with Notes," he quickly realized that it was "a breakthrough technology," with the potential to create "a revolution" in how members of Alpha communicated and coordinated their activities. Shortly thereafter, the CIO acquired a site license to install Notes throughout the firm and announced that the product would be Alpha's communications standard.

The CIO began to market Notes energetically within various arenas of the firm. He gave numerous talks to principals and managers, both at national meetings and in local offices, during which he promoted his vision of how Notes "can help us manage our expertise and transform our practice." Through interest and persuasion, demand for Notes grew, and the physical deployment of the technology proceeded rapidly throughout the firm. The actual use of Notes within the office I studied, however, appeared to be advancing more slowly. While electronic mail usage had been adopted widely and enthusiastically, the use of Notes to share expertise, and the integration of Notes into work practices and policies, had not yet been accomplished. The data I collected and analyzed during my field study of one office suggest that at least two organizational elements— cognitive and structural—influenced the participants' adoption, understanding, and early use of Notes.

Cognitive Elements

Cognitive elements are the mental models or frames of references that individuals have about the world, their organization, work, technology, and so on. While these frames are held by individuals, many assumptions and values constituting the frames tend to be shared with others. Such sharing of cognitions is facilitated by common educational and professional backgrounds, work experiences, and regular interaction. In the context of groupware, those cognitive elements that have to do with information technology become particularly salient. Elsewhere, I have termed these technological frames and described how they shape the way information technology is designed and used in organizations (Gash and Orlikowski, 1991).

When confronted with a new technology, individuals try to understand it in terms of their existing technological frames, often augmenting these frames to accommodate special aspects of the technology. If the technology is sufficiently different, however, these existing frames may be inappropriate, and individuals will need to significantly modify their technological frames in order to understand or interact effectively with the new technology. How users change their technological frames in response to a new technology is influenced by (1) the kind and amount of information about the product communicated to them, and (2) the nature and form of training they receive on the product.

Communication about Notes

Employees in the office I studied received relatively little communication about Notes. Many of them first heard about the CIO's decision to standardize on Notes through the trade press. Others encountered it during Alpha's annual management seminars that form part of consultants' continuing education program. Most encountered it for the first time when it was installed on their computers. Without explicit information about what Notes is and why Alpha had purchased it, these individuals were left to make their own assumptions about the technology and why it was being distributed. This contributed to weakly developed technological frames around Notes in the office. Consider, for example, these remarks made by individuals a few weeks before Notes was to be installed on their computers:

> I know absolutely nothing about Notes. I don't know what it is supposed to do.
>
> All I know is that the firm bought it, but I don't know why.
>
> I first heard that the firm had bought Notes through the *Wall Street Journal*. Then your study was the next mention of it. That's all I know about it.
>
> I heard about Notes at the [management seminars] about eight months ago. I still don't know what it is.
>
> It has something to do with communications.
>
> It's big e-mail.
>
> I've heard that it's hard copy of e-mail . . . but I am not very clear about what it is exactly.
>
> I understand that it makes your work environment paperless. It's like taking all your files—your library of information in your office—and putting it on the computer.
>
> I believe Notes is putting word processing power into spreadsheets.
>
> Is it a new version of 1-2-3?
>
> It's a network . . . but I don't know how the network works. Where does all this information go after I switch my machine off?
>
> It's a database housed somewhere in the center of the universe.

Weakly developed technological frames of a new and different technology are a significant problem in technology transfer because people act toward technology on the basis of the meaning it has for them. If people have a poor or inappropriate understanding of the unique and different features of a new technology, they may resist using it or may not integrate it appropriately into their work practices. In the office, one consequence of such poor understanding was a skepticism toward Notes and its capabilities. For example, principals and managers in the office commented:

> I first heard about Notes when I read in the *Wall Street Journal* that Alpha had purchased a revolutionary new piece of software. My first thought was—how much is this costing me personally? . . . [T]his kind of implementation affects all of our pocketbooks. . . . I have [heard that] there is no value in information technology—so you can imagine how I feel!
>
> When I first heard about it, I thought "Oh yeah? First hook me up to the network, and then I'll listen." Right now I still can't see the benefit.
>
> I don't believe that Notes will help our business that much, unless all of our business is information transfer. It's not. Business is based on relationships. Ideas are created in nonwork situations, socially, over lunch, et cetera.

Poor circulation of information about Notes was a consequence of the rapid installation of Notes that Alpha had pursued. The CIO had delegated responsibility for Notes deployment to the firm's technology group. Because demand for Notes was growing quickly, the technologists did not have an opportunity to plan the Notes rollout and did not develop or pursue a formal implementation plan or information dissemination strategy. Two technology managers commented:

> We tried to stay one step ahead of the firm's demand and [the CIO's] evangelism. We were swamped with requests. Every time [the CIO] gave a talk, we'd be deluged with requests for Notes. . . . We had no time to do a formal plan or a grand strategy because [the CIO] had raised the level of enthusiasm in the firm, and there was no way we could say to the principals "wait while we get our act together."
>
> [The CIO] set the tone for the deployment strategy by generating interest in the product at the top. He was pushing a top-down approach, getting to all the principals first. So our deployment was driven by a lot of user pull and a little push from us. . . . We were constantly struggling to keep up with demand.

This rapid, demand-driven rollout was consistent with the CIO's assumption about how technologies such as Notes should be implemented. He commented that:

> Our strategy was to blast Notes through our organization as quickly as possible, with no prototypes, no pilots, no lengthy technical evaluation. We want to transform the way we deliver service to clients.

He believed that an "empowering" technology such as Notes should be distributed rapidly to as many people as possible, and that if the technology is compelling enough "they will drift into new ways of doing things." That is,

> [I]f you believe that Notes is a competitive technology, you have to deploy it quickly, and put in the hands of the users as fast as possible. Critical mass is key.

In particular, the CIO focused on convincing the key "opinion leaders" in the firm of the value of the technology, as he believed that these individuals would lead the charge in defining and spreading the uses of Notes throughout the firm.

Training on Notes

Training users on new technology is central to their understanding of its capabilities and appreciating how it differs from other technologies with which they are familiar. It also significantly influences the augmentation of existing technological frames or the development of new ones. Because the technologists were extremely busy deploying Notes and keeping it up and running, they did not have the resources to pay much attention to the education of users. Their first priority was to physically install hundreds of copies of Notes in multiple offices around the country and keep them operational. As one technology manager noted, it was a matter of priorities:

> We made a conscious decision between whether we should throw it [Notes] to the users versus spending a lot of time training. We decided on the former.

The underemphasis on training was consistent with the CIO's general view that Notes does not require formal end-user training, and that it is through experimentation and use, not formal education programs, that people begin to appreciate a technology's potential and learn to use it in different and interesting ways. This user-driven diffusion strategy, however, typically takes time, particularly in a busy services firm with considerable production pressures. Because this study did not detect any new user initiatives around the use of Notes in the office, it is possible that the timing of the research is simply too early in the implementation process. The following experiences thus represent the first encounters consultants had with Notes and how they initially appropriated it.

The training that was made available to users in the office I studied came in two forms, self-study and classroom training. The former provided users with a videotape and workbook, and covered Notes's basic functions and interfaces. The latter offered up to four hours of instruction and hands-on exercises by local computer support personnel. None of these training options emphasized the business value of Notes or its collaborative nature as groupware. The training materials were relatively technical, individual-oriented, and nonspecific in content. Trainees were exposed to the basic Notes functions such as electronic mail, editing, and database browsing.

While facilitating the accessibility of the material to all individuals, from secretaries to principals, this "one size fits all" training strategy had the effect—at least initially—of not conveying the power of Notes to support specific consulting applications or group coordination.

This training on Notes resembled that of the training conducted on personal productivity tools. While useful for teaching the mechanics of Notes, it does not give users a new way of thinking differently about their work in terms of groupware. While Alpha was less concerned with collaborative or group work than with sharing expertise across the firm, the effect of the initial training was that participants in my study attempted to understand Notes through their existing frame of personal computing software. Such interpretations encouraged thinking about Notes as an individual productivity tool rather than as a collaborative technology or a forum for sharing ideas. For example, one manager noted,

> I see Notes as a personal communication tool. That is, with a modem and fax applications I can do work at home or at a client site and use Notes to transfer work back and forth. In the office, instead of getting my secretary to make twenty copies of a memo, she can just push a button.

Further, the applications built for users by the technology group tended to automate existing information flows rather than creating new ones through the cooperative features of Notes. This reinforced the message that users received in their training, that Notes is an incremental rather than a transforming technology, and that new technological frames or new work practices around it are not required.

Thus, in contrast to the technologists' vision of Notes as a technology that can "fundamentally change the way we do business," consultants in the office appeared to expect, at most, an incremental improvement in operations. One manager commented,

> The general perception of Notes is that it is an efficient tool, making what we do now better, but it is not viewed by the organization as a major change. Remember we're . . . a management consulting firm and management consultants stick to management issues. We don't get into technology issues.

Another said,

> I think it will reduce the time of gathering information. I think it will cut down on frustration in transferring information. But it is not a radical change.

As a result of the lack of resources that technologists had for communication and training, users of Notes in the office developed technological fames that either had weakly developed notions of Notes, or that interpreted Notes as a personal rather than a group or firm productivity tool. Because technological frames may change over time and with changing contexts, it is possible that the frames developed by the office participants will change over time. For example, if individuals are exposed to other applications of Notes developed elsewhere in the firm or in other firms, or if their increased use of Notes helps them understand how they can change the way they work, new understandings and uses of Notes may result. Our ongoing study of this implementation process will monitor such possible developments.

Structural Elements

Structural properties of organizations encompass the reward systems, policies, work practices, and norms that shape and are shaped by the everyday action of organizational members. In the office, three such structural properties significantly influenced individuals' perceptions and early use of Notes.

Reward Systems

Within Alpha there is an expectation—shared by many services firms—that all or most employee hours should be "billable," that is, charged to clients. This is a major evaluation criterion on which employees are assessed, and employees studiously avoid "nonbillable hours." Because most of the participants did not initially perceive using Notes as a client-related activity (and hence as "not chargeable"), they were disinclined to spend time on it. Further, given their lack of understanding and skepticism of Notes, they were unwilling to give up personal time to learn or use it. Consider these comments from senior consultants and managers:

> One of the problems is time. Given my billing rate, it makes no sense for me to take the time to learn the technology. In Alpha we put so much emphasis on chargeable hours and that puts a lot of pressure on managers. . . . And now we've made an enormous commitment to Notes and Hardware, and LANs, but we haven't given people the time and opportunity to learn it. For them to do classes, they have to work extra on weekends to meet deadlines.
>
> I think it is going to be a real issue to find time to use Notes. We don't have the time to read or enter information in Notes. What would I charge it to? We already complain that we can't charge our reading of our mail to anything. We end up having to charge it to ourselves [he reads his mail on the train going home].
>
> The whole focus in this firm is on client service, and we are not going to tell the clients to chill out for a week while we all get trained on Notes.
>
> I don't think that Notes will ever be used in Alpha as effectively as it could be. We're not going to make sure everyone in the office has fifteen hours over the next year to spend time learning it. And if they expect us to take it out of our own time, I'm not going to invest that time. I have another life too.
>
> The opportunity costs for me to take training in the office are very high. At my level, every week is a deadline, every week is a crisis. No accommodations are made in our schedules or workload to allow us to train on technology. So I won't learn it unless it's mandatory.

Thus, one significant inhibitor of learning and using Notes was the office's reward system with its accompanying incentive schemes and evaluation criteria. Because the reward system had not changed since the implementation of Notes, consultants in the office perceived time spent on Notes as less legitimate than client work. While many used Notes for electronic mail or database browsing, these activities amounted to a few minutes a day, and hence were easily subsumed into client or personal time. However, any more extensive use of Notes was seen as potentially disrupting the balance between billable hours and personal time, and hence to be avoided. These concerns, however, varied by position in the office. Not surprisingly, principals were willing to take a longer-term and firm-wide perspective on Notes, being less preoccupied than were managers and senior consultants with time constraints, "billable hours," personal performance, and their own careers.

Policies and Procedures

Along with the few resources dedicated to Notes training and communication, the office—at the time of my study—had not formulated new work procedures or set new policies around data quality, confidentiality, and access control. Many participants indicated that their use of Notes was inhibited by their lack of knowledge about these issues, particularly concerns about liability (their own and Alpha's). Principals, for example, worried about data security:

> Security is a concern for me. . . . We need to worry about who is seeing the data. . . . Managers should not be able to access all the information even if it is useful [such as] financial information to clients, because they leave and may go and work for competitors. So there should be prohibitions on information access.
>
> I am not sure how secure Notes is. Many times we have run into difficulties, and things have gotten lost in never-never land.
>
> I have concerns about what goes into the databases and who has access to them and what access they have. . . . But we haven't thought that through yet.

Managers and senior consultants in the office were more anxious about personal liability or embarrassment. For example,

> I would be careful what I put out on Notes though. I like to retain personal control so that when people call me I can tell them not to use it for such and such. But there is no such control within Notes.
>
> My other concern is that information changes a lot. So if I put out a memo saying X today and then have a new memo two weeks later, the person accessing the information may not know about the second memo which had canceled the first. Also if you had a personal discussion, you could explain the caveats and the interpretations and how they should and shouldn't use the information.
>
> I'd be more fearful that I'd put something out there and it was wrong and somebody would catch it.
>
> I would be concerned in using Notes that I would come to the wrong conclusion and others would see it. What would make me worry is that it was

public information and people were using it and what if it was wrong? I would not want to be cited by someone who hasn't talked to me first. I'm worried that my information would be misconstrued and it would end up in Wichita, Kansas ". . . as per J. Brown in New York . . ." being used and relied on. You should be able to limit what access people have to what information, particularly if it is your information. I would definitely want to know who was looking at it.

There is a hesitancy here because you don't want to put everything into public information, as people may rely on that information and screw up, and it may reflect badly on you.

The lack of explicit procedures and policies around Notes highlights the difficulty of enforcing firm-wide policies in a decentralized firm. While the CIO has been able to institute standards around certain technology platforms—clearly, a technical domain—instituting standard procedures and policies about data quality, control, and liability begins to encroach on the organizational domain—an arena where the CIO's authority is less established. As a result, the technologists have been careful about setting policies that would require organizational changes and that might invoke turf issues. The management of local offices, however, had not devoted any attention to this issue, at least in the early adoption phase. As a result, there was some ambiguity about the locus and nature of responsibility and liability with respect to the intellectual content of Notes databases. This may have inhibited the application of Notes to a broader range of work practices in the early phase of its implementation.

Firm Culture and Work Norms

Alpha shares with many other consulting firms a relatively competitive culture—at least at the levels below principal. The pyramidal structure and the hierarchical "up or out" career path promote and reinforce an individualistic culture among consultants, where those who have not yet attained principal status vie with each other to get the relatively few promotions handed out each year. In such a competitive culture, there are few norms around cooperating or sharing knowledge with peers. These comments by consultants in the office are illustrative:

> This is definitely a competitive culture—it's an up or out atmosphere.
>
> Usually managers work alone because of the competitiveness among the managers. There is a lot of one-upmanship against each other. Their life dream is to become a principal in Alpha, and they'll do anything to get there.
>
> The atmosphere is competitive and cut-throat; all they want is to get ahead as individuals.

Interestingly, there was some evidence that there is much more collegiality at the highest levels of the firm, where principals—having attained tenure and the highest career rank—enact more of a "fraternal culture" than the competitive individualism evident at lower levels. This is consistent with research conducted in other service organizations with similar organizational structures, such as firms providing legal, accounting, or medical services (Greenwood, Hinings, and Brown, 1990). Below the principal level, however, managers and senior consultants in my study indicated that there was generally little precedent for sharing or cooperating with colleagues and little incentive to do so, as they needed to differentiate themselves from their peers. For example,

> The corporate psychology makes the use of Notes difficult, particularly the consultant career path, which creates a backstabbing and aggressive environment. People aren't backstabbing consciously; it's just that the environment makes people maximize opportunities for themselves.
>
> I'm trying to develop an area of expertise that makes me stand out. If I shared that with you, you'd get the credit not me. . . . It's really a cut-throat environment.
>
> Individual self-promotion is based on the information [individuals] have. You don't see a lot of two-way, open discussions.
>
> Power in this firm is your client base and technical ability. . . . It is definitely a function of consulting firms. Now if you put all this information in a Notes database, you lose power. There will be nothing that's privy to you, so you will lose power. It's important that I am selling something that no one else has. When I hear people talk about the importance of sharing expertise in the firm, I say, "Reality is a nice construct."

The competitive individualism—which reinforces individual effort and ability, and does not support cooperation or sharing of expertise—is countercultural to the underlying premise of groupware technologies such as Notes. It is thus not surprising that, at all but the highest career level, Notes is being utilized largely as an individual productivity tool in the office. Senior consultants and managers within this office feel little incentive to share their ideas for fear that they may lose status, power, and distinctive competence. Principals, on the other hand, do not share this fear and are more focused on the interests of the office and the firm than on their individual careers. An interesting contrast to this point, which further supports it, is that Notes is apparently being used by Alpha technologists to exchange technical expertise. Not being subject to the competitive culture, individual-focused reward systems, "up-or-out" career pressures, and "chargeable hours" constraints of the consultants, the technologists appear to have been able to use the technology to conduct their work, namely, solving technical problems.

Discussion

The results of this research study suggest that the organizational introduction of groupware will interact with cognitive and structural elements, and that these elements will have significant implications for the adoption, understanding, and early use of the technology. Because people act toward technology on the basis of their understanding of it, people's technological frames often need to be changed to accommodate a new technology. Where people do not appreciate the premises and purposes of a technology, they may use it in less effective ways. A major premise underlying groupware is the coordination of activities and people across time and space. For many users, such a premise may represent a radically different understanding of technology than they have experienced before. This suggests that a particularly central aspect of implementing groupware is ensuring that prospective users have an appropriate understanding of the technology, that is, that their technological frames reflect a perception of the technology as a collective rather than a personal tool.

At the time I conducted my study, many of the participants in the office did not have a good conception of what Notes was and how they could use it. Their technological frames around Notes were weakly developed and relied heavily on their knowledge and experience of other individually used technologies. Given such cognitions, it is not surprising that in their early use of the technology, these participants had not generated new patterns of social interaction, nor had they developed fundamentally different work practices around Notes. Instead, they had either chosen not to use Notes, or had subsumed it within prior technological frames and were using it primarily to enhance personal productivity through electronic mail, file transfer, or accessing news services. As indicated above, however, these findings reflect an early phase of the participants' experiences with Notes. It is possible that these experiences will change over time, as they get more accustomed to using Notes, and these are expected to change over time depending on their ongoing experiences with the technology.

Where a new technological frame is desirable because the technology is sufficiently unprecedented to require new assumptions and meanings, communication and education are central in fostering the development of new technological frames. Such communication and education should stress the required shift in technological frame, as well as provide technical and logistic information on use. A training approach that resembles that used for personal computing software is unlikely to help individuals develop a good understanding of groupware. For individuals used to personal computing environments and personal applications, shared technology use and cooperative applications are difficult to grasp. In these cases, meaningful concrete demonstrations of such applications can help to provide insight. Further, if individuals are to use groupware within a specific group, learning such a technology collectively may foster joint understanding and expectations. Where individuals learn a shared technology in isolation, they may form their own assumptions, expectations, and procedures, which may differ from those of the people they will interact with through the technology.

In those organizations where the premises underlying groupware are incongruent with those of the organization's culture, policies, and reward systems, it is unlikely that effective cooperative computing will result without a change in structural properties. Such changes are difficult to accomplish and usually meet with resistance. Without such changes, however, the existing structural elements of the firm will likely serve as significant barriers to the desired use of the technology. For example, in the study described above, the existing norms, policies, and rewards appear to be in conflict with the premises of Notes. Because incentive schemes and evaluation criteria in the office had not been modified to encourage or accommodate cooperation and expertise sharing through Notes, members feared loss of power, control, prestige, and promotion opportunities if they shared their ideas, of if their lack of knowledge or misinterpretations were made visible. Thus, in a relatively competitive culture where members are evaluated and rewarded as individuals, there will be few norms for sharing and cooperating. If groupware products such as Notes are to be used cooperatively in such cultures, these norms need to be changed—either inculcated top-down through training, communication, leadership, and structural legitimation, or bottom-up through facilitating local opportunities and supportive environments for experimenting with cooperation and shared experiences. Without some such grounding in shared norms, groupware products will tend to be used primarily for advancing individual productivity.

In addition to norms, resources are a further important facilitator of shared technology use. Whether formally ear-marked from some firm-wide R&D budget, or provided informally through local slack resources, occasions for experimenting with shared applications are needed to generate interest and use around cooperative computing. For example, in the office I studied, there had been no change in the allocation of resources following the initial implementation of Notes, and members had not been given time to use and experiment with Notes. There was thus a tension between the structural requirement that all work be production oriented, and the adoption of an infrastructure technology such as Notes, which was perceived to be only indirectly related to production work. Where individuals are not given resources to learn and experiment with the new technology, or not given specific, client-related applications that help them accomplish their production work within the technology, the immediate pressures of daily production tasks and deadlines will tend to dominate their decisions around how they allocate their time.

This research study suggests that in the early adoption of a technology, cognitive and structural elements play an important role in influencing how people think about and assess the value of the technology. And these significantly influence how they choose to use the technology. When an organization deploys a new technology with an intent to make substantial changes in business processes, people's technological frames and the organization's work practices will likely require substantial change. An interesting issue raised by this requirement is how to anticipate the required structural and cognitive changes when the technology is brand new. That is, how do you devise a game plan if you have never played the game before? This is particularly likely in the case of an unprecedented technology such as groupware. One strategy would be to deploy the technology widely in the belief that through experimentation and use over time, creative ideas and innovations will flourish. Another strategy would prototype the technology in a representative group of the organization, on a pilot basis, and then deploy it to the rest of the organization once the technology's capabilities and implications are understood. This way, the required structural and cognitive changes learned through the pilot can be transferred. Viewed in terms of these two strategies, aspects of Alpha's adoption activities now appear to resemble the former strategy. Our future studies should indicate how successful this strategy has been.

It is worth noting that while the early use of Notes in the office has proved more valuable for facilitating individual productivity than for collective productivity, the implementation of Notes has resulted in the installation of an advanced and standardized technology infrastructure. As one technology manager put it, "A side benefit of Notes is that it got people into a more sophisticated environment of computing than we could have done otherwise." Most of the office members, from principals to senior consultants, now have ready and easy access to a network of personal computers and laser printers. Thus, while the initial experiences with Notes in the office may not have significantly changed work practices or policies, the office appears to be relatively well positioned to use this platform to take advantage of any future technological or work-related initiatives.

In general, the findings presented here provide insight for future research into the structural and cognitive organizational elements that interact with and shape the adoption and early use of groupware in organizations. They also have practical implications, indicating how and where such organizational elements might be managed to more effectively implement groupware in various organizational circumstances.

Acknowledgments

This research was sponsored by the Center for Coordination Science at the Massachusetts Institute of Technology. This support is gratefully acknowledged. Thanks are due to Jolene Galegher, Bob Halperin, Tom Malone, and Judith Quillard, who provided helpful comments on an earlier version of this paper. Thanks are also due to the men and women of Alpha Corporation who participated in this research.

References

Bair, James H., and Stephen Gale (1988). "An Investigation of the COORDINATOR as an Example of Computer Supported Cooperative Work," in *Proceedings of the Conference on Computer Supported Cooperative Work*. The Association for Computing Machinery, New York, NY.

Bullen, Christine V., and John L. Bennett (1990). "Groupware in Practice: An Interpretation of Work Experience," in *Proceedings of the Conference on Computer Supported Cooperative Work*, 291–302. The Association for Computing Machinery, New York, NY.

Dyson, Esther (1990). "Why Groupware is Gaining Ground." *Datamation*, March: 52–56.

Eveland, J. D., and T. K. Bikson (1986). "Evolving Electronic Communication Networks: An Empirical Assessment," in *Proceedings of the Conference on Computer Supported Cooperative Work*, 91–101. The Association for Computing Machinery, New York, NY.

Feldman, Martha S. (1987). "Electronic Mail and Weak Ties in Organizations." *Office: Technology and People*, 3:83–101.

Finholt, Tom, and Lee S. Sproull (1990). "Electronic Groups at Work." *Organization Science*, 1(1):41–64.

Gash, Debra C., and Wanda J. Orlikowski (1991). "Changing Frames: Towards an Understanding of Information Technology and Organizational Change," in *Academy of Management Best Papers Proceedings*, 189–193. Academy of Management, Miami Beach, FL.

Govani, Stephen J. (1992). "License to Kill." *Information Week*, January 6, 22–28.

Greenwood, R., C. R. Hinings, and J. Brown (1990). "P²-Form Strategic Management: Corporate Practices in Professional Partnerships." *Academy of Management Journal*, 33(4):725–755.

Grudin, Jonathon (1990). "Why CSCW Applications Fail: Problems in the Design and Evaluation of Organizational Interfaces," in *Proceedings of the Conference on Computer-Supported Cooperative Work*, 85–93. The Association for Computing Machinery, New York, NY.

Kiesler, Sara (1986). "The Hidden Messages in Computer Networks." *Harvard Business Review*, January–February:46–59.

Kling, Rob (1991). "Cooperation, Coordination, and Control in Computer-Supported Work." *Communications of the ACM*, 34(2):83–88.

Mackay, Wendy E. (1988). "Diversity in the Use of Electronic Mail." *ACM Transactions on Office Information Systems*, 6(4):380–397.

Markus, M. Lynne (1987). "Toward a 'Critical Mass' Theory of Interactive Media." *Communication Research*, 14(5):491–511.

Marshak, David S. (1990). "Lotus Notes: A Platform for Developing Workgroup Applications." *Patricia Seybold's Office Computing Report*, 13(7):1–17.

PC Week (1991). "Groupware: The Teamwork Approach." Special supplement, October 14:8, 41.

Perin, Constance (1991). "Electronic Social Fields in Bureaucracies." *Communications of the ACM*, 34(2):75–82.

Sproull, Lee S., and Sara Kiesler (1986). "Reducing Social Context Cues: Electronic Mail in Organizational Communication." *Management Science*, 32(1):1492–1512.

Tyre, Marcie J., and Wanda J. Orlikowski (1994). "Windows of Opportunity: Temporal Patterns of Technological Adaptation in Organizations." *Organization Science*, 5(1):98–118.

P·A·R·T · III

How Much Will a Truly Empowering Technology-Rich Education Cost?*

Henry Jay Becker

For the past decade schools around the world have been spending large fractions of their discretionary funds on computer technology and related software and instructional preparation. Every year, for example, schools in the United States purchase 300,000 to 500,000 computers and spend millions of dollars on software. Numerous schools have been established as "technology magnets" or "model technology schools" with even substantially more equipment and software than schools typically receive. Yet still the typical experience of most school children each year is to have limited experience using computers—computers that in many cases are technologically fifteen years old and far more limited than the powerful, fast, video- and CD-ROM-linked personal computer systems advertised in today's educational technology publications.

More important, survey data are clear that the kinds of experiences that most students have with school computers are hardly revolutionary—worksheet drills, entertaining diversions, or recopying handwritten text so that it is more easily read. Although there has been a strong growth in the use of computers for word processing, most teachers have too few computers to provide computer-based writing opportunities to whole classrooms. Moreover, even if they had those computers, schools would have to make major changes in the allocation of time during the school day to provide enough opportunities for students to do that amount of writing.

Yet, the promises of electronic information technology still beckon, and even more convincingly than in the early days of school computer use. There is now a clearer and more broadly supported vision of how instruction and learning should be changed in schools. Components of this vision include students actively engaged in collaborative project-based learning attending to subject matter that is meaningful and important to the student. It involves students gathering information from diverse sources well beyond the classroom textbook and school library, doing intensive analysis and substantial writing, and making a public presentation of conclusions for a specific audience and specific purpose.

With even current technology, students in elementary and secondary classrooms can themselves become creators of educational products using menu-driven, program-generating environments such as Hypercard; they can access volumes of video- and text-based information two orders of magnitude greater than floppy-disk-based CAI systems; they can communicate electronically with schools and students all over the world, with scientists engaged in real-world inquiry, and with databases of enormous magnitude; and they can use analysis and exploration tools such as collaborative writing programs, graphical modeling tools to assess mathematical propositions, and microcomputer-based laboratories to collect scientific data and experience true scientific inquiry.

Yet the capacity of schools to provide these kinds of learning experiences to all of their students will require a tremendous investment. And the investments go well beyond replacing outdated computer equipment with new hardware and software. What is involved here is more than just the substitution of traditional learning media with new ones, but a revolution in what teachers understand to be the methods and goals of instruction and the standards for student accomplishment.

Although schools and society have a long way to go to see this new vision through to widespread implementation, we can learn a great deal about the conditions and resources necessary to support these changes from studies of "exemplary" current teachers who have taken major steps to use technology to achieve new learning goals. Research from a national survey of computer-using teachers found that the most exemplary computer users did not just have more of the best and newest computer technology, although they did have that as well. Exemplary computer-using teachers practice in a teaching environment characterized by a great deal of support for instructional change (Becker, 1994). Specifically, exemplary computer-using teachers are much more likely than other computer users to be working in:

*This article appeared in *Educational IRM Quarterly*, 3(1)(September, 1993):31–35. Reprinted with permission of the International Society for Technology in Education.

1. a school where there is a strong social network of *many* computer-using teachers, teachers who themselves have gained expertise through extensive computer experience;
2. a school with a full-time technology coordinator on staff, and, in particular, a coordinator active in promoting computer use among other teachers;
3. a district that provides them and other teachers with substantial formal staff development for using tool-based software and using technology specifically within their own curriculum;
4. a school that has made a long-term commitment to students using word processing—not just learning word processing in a computer applications class, but using word processing in subject-matter classes and for productive ends outside of class, such as for the school newspaper and yearbook;
5. a school with policies assuring equity of computer access between boys and girls and among students with different levels of academic preparation;
6. a school where the pattern of computer use extends technology beyond basic math, language arts, and computer literacy to social studies, the fine arts, and business and industrial arts education;
7. an environment that somehow allocates time at school for teachers to use school computers themselves not just to preview software but for their own professional tasks such as information retrieval, lesson preparation, and communication with colleagues;
8. a school that, as a result of more extensive use of its computer facilities, is faced with additional maintenance and coordination problems that are lacking in schools without exemplary computer-using teachers; and
9. perhaps most costly of all, smaller class sizes for computer-using teachers.

In addition, exemplary computer-using teachers themselves have more substantial educational backgrounds; in this study they were much more likely to have majored in liberal arts subjects rather than simply education and were more likely to have had advanced degrees. In addition, exemplary teachers have more computer equipment available and a much greater variety of software and other technology-related materials.

Clearly, schools wanting to create an environment where exemplary teachers exploit the potential benefits of information technology must consider the costs they will incur to accomplish this goal. The out-of-pocket costs for equipment and instructional materials are commonly costed out (albeit, most often, incorrectly as one-time expenditures). But the less visible and more intangible costs of developing expertise in teachers and providing them with the opportunity to use that technology must also be estimated. Indeed, my rough estimation of those costs suggests that these personnel-related costs may be greater in magnitude than the hardware/

software costs—even when the latter are considered as recurring costs to account for the inevitable upgrading that will routinely occur because of new capabilities provided by the technology.

The estimates shown in Table 1 ought to be regarded as a quick initial pass at these issues. They assume a school of 800 students (rather large for an elementary school, but substantially smaller than the typical high school). The faculty size assumed for this hypothetical school is forty full-time equivalents (FTE). To simplify calculations, all person-costs assume $50,000 per person per year including benefits and administrative personnel support. The estimates leave out a great deal—for example, the cost of developing expertise among the nonteaching staff—and are meant to stimulate the thinking of administrators and teachers who are closer to their own particular setting than am I.

The entries in Table 1 correspond to the nine factors found by our research to distinguish the environments of exemplary computer-using teachers from those of other computer-using teachers. The *magnitude* of the costs are based on a considered judgment, but clearly are subject to varying points of view. In particular, though, the assumption of the need for 25% more teachers to create 20% smaller class sizes comes from the research data on the difference in class size between the teachers judged as exemplary and all other computer-using teachers.

Table 1 suggests that the largest personnel-related costs for empowering teachers to become exemplary users of technology are for smaller class sizes and for greater personal access to school computers for lesson preparation and other professional use. In addition, substantial costs will be incurred in two other areas: (1) staffing each school with full-time computer coordinators to support all teachers' use of technology; and (2) providing time for teachers to work collaboratively to improve each other's technology-related competencies.

Altogether, we estimate the annual additional personnel costs for this hypothetical school to be $1.1 million, or $1,375 in additional per-pupil expenditures, by itself an increase of 25% over the current expenditures by schools for all purposes.

In addition to these personnel costs, there are, of course, the more commonly considered hardware, software, and maintenance costs. Table 2 provides one estimate for these for our hypothetical school. These estimates assume that the school now has 80 computers (a 10:1 student:computer ratio; roughly the national average), and will need to have 400 computers (a 2:1 ratio) within four years. But the estimates also assume that because of continual improvements in the capacity of information technology equipment, an annual replacement of 80 computers should be budgeted. So, the purchase of 80 computers is seen here as an annual expense rather than as a one-time expense.

In addition, quite a large variety of other information-technology-related hardware would be required in this model of widespread and curriculum-driven pattern of exemplary utilization. This includes such elements as

Table 1.   Estimated Annual Personnel Costs for Developing Expertise in Technology Use among Teachers (Hypothetical School of 800 Students)

Type of personnel support required	Description and calculation	Total annual cost
Support for interpersonal networks	Time for teachers to work together, planning facilities use, and educating each other in new applications and capabilities: 2 hours/week × 40 teachers.	$100,000
Full-time technology coordinators	Two professional staff members for a school staff of 40 teachers.	$100,000
Staff development	Formal instruction for groups of teachers of the same subject: 10 days/year for 20 teachers. Costs of release time and trainers' salaries.	$60,000
Word-processing support	Development and maintenance of technology support for writing across curriculum, school newspaper, and yearbook: 0.2 FTE.	$10,000
Equity support	Support for allocating effective computer access for girls and lower-performing students: 0.2 FTE.	$10,000
Support for new subjects	Development and maintenance of technology support for industrial arts, fine arts, social studies, other subjects with low initial utilization: 0.2 FTE.	$10,000
Teacher access	Time for teachers to use school computers themselves; lesson planning and own professional utilization: 5 hours/week × 40 teachers.	$250,000
Maintenance, coordination	Technical support for 40 teachers: 2 FTE.	$60,000
Smaller class sizes	Reducing class sizes from 25 to 20 per teacher: increase of 10 FTE teachers.	$500,000
Total		$1,100,000
Total per pupil expenditure		$1,375

network cabling and hardware; printers, scanners, and other digital hard-copy translation devices; satellite dishes, telephones, and other tele-communication facilities; camcorders and video-playback and projection equipment for whole-class presentations; and digital storage media. Those elements are all included as a mixed hardware category for which annual expenditures are also assumed. Finally, Table 2 incorporates annual estimates for software and other technology-related instructional material and for maintenance.

The total annual cost estimated from these hardware and software components in Table 2 is $445,000 or $556.25 per student. Even with the rather expansive assumptions made in Table 2 (e.g., $105,000 in maintenance per

Table 2. Estimated Annual Hardware and Software Costs for Developing Expertise in Technology Use among Teachers (Hypothetical School of 800 Students)

Type of equipment/ material required	Description and calculation	Total annual cost
Computers	80 per year (bringing stock to 400 in four years). After that point, 80 per year replacement due to obsolescence. (Each computer at $1250)	$100,000
Other hardware	Network cabling and computers, printers, video-related hardware, telecommunications, digital storage. (40 classrooms × $1000/year)	$40,000
Software, other technology materials	For 80 new computers per year, $1000. 320 existing computers per year, $250. 40 classrooms per year (teacher directed): $1000.	$200,000
Maintenance	Estimated as 15% of total capital expense of equipment spent for any five-year period.	$105,000
Total		$445,000
Total per-pupil expenditure		$556.25

year), the total for all hardware and software expenditures is less than one-half (actually, exactly two-fifths) as much as the total estimated for personnel costs related to empowering a teaching staff to become exemplary technology users.

From one perspective, these costs seem huge. The total costs shown in Tables 1 and 2 come to nearly $2000 per student per year in addition to current educational expenditures, which in 1993 totaled $5200 per pupil. On the other hand, districts now *differ* from one another by much more than $2000 per student per year. So, spending that much in a low-spending district merely brings its level of educational investment up to the level of the current spending of a modestly high-spending district.

Moreover, it is quite clear that making substantial improvements in educational outcomes will not come cheaply under any circumstance. True, there are plenty of nontechnology approaches that have been advocated for improving educational outcomes. Schools might invest, for example, in smaller classes for teachers (but not specifically for using computers); or in systematic and ongoing in-service training and supervision (on topics other than technology); or in larger salaries to recruit smarter teachers (who don't particularly have interests in technology); or in restructuring to give teachers fewer class hours and more planning responsibilities (that do not involve computers); or in innovative print-based curriculum materials. But all these reform efforts that putatively improve instructional practice cost money, too—indeed, they all call for similar levels of added expenditure whether technology-based learning approaches are contemplated or not.

For example, Theobald and Nelson (1992) investigated five schools attempting to implement Sizer's Coalition of Essential Schools model for secondary school organization and instruction. That model involves large-scale changes in what teachers are expected to do as instructors and how the school is organized to provide a schedule of activities and assessment for varied students. The degree of change is not unlike what is envisioned when large-scale technology utilization is seen as the central vehicle of change. The researchers concluded that "the financial, human, and political costs involved in fundamentally restructuring a secondary school are enormous and involve almost every aspect of the school's program." The effort at these schools involved teachers in observing other teachers using new pedagogical practices, conversing extensively with peers and instructional leaders to come to understand the rationale for these changed practices, learning about and creating new curriculum materials that embodied these new teaching practices, working collaboratively with other teachers to implement them, and obtaining education about technology to support these new practices.

The central barrier the researchers saw to implementing major teaching innovations was the problem of scheduling formal planning and staff development activities in ways that didn't interfere with teaching obligations or with nonwork commitments after school and on weekends. In order to accommodate those activities into people's schedules, teachers had to be compensated for off-hour activities and substitute classroom supervision had to be budgeted for school-hour activities. It is one thing to obtain short-term contributions of extra effort and time among a group of volunteers who are already committed to a specific change being planned. It is quite another to substantially raise the complexity of teaching practice for a school faculty as a whole and to maintain that level over multiple years.

School technology advocates need not hide (from themselves or from others) the true costs of effectively implementing technology in school settings. Indeed, by not facing up to these true costs, they are likely to insure the failure of their approach, and to increase the voices heard against investments in technology. It is vital that the possibilities that computers and video can provide to the renewal of school learning be allowed to come to fruition. To do that, planning must incorporate expectations and budgets for the kinds of expenditures that permit average teachers to become exemplary users of these extraordinary resources for learning.

References

Becker, Henry Jay (1994, Spring). "How Our Best Computer-Using Teachers Differ from Other Teachers: Implications for Realizing the Potential of Computers in Schools." *Journal of Research on Computing in Education,* 26(3).

Theobald, Neil, and Bryce Nelson (1992). "The Resource Costs Involved in Restructuring a Secondary School." Paper presented at the annual conference of the American Educational Research Association, San Francisco, April.

P·A·R·T · III

I

Technology Refusal and the Organizational Culture of Schools*

Steven Hodas

The Culture of Schools

For nearly a century outsiders have been trying to introduce technologies into high school classrooms, with remarkably consistent results. After proclaiming the potential of the new tools to rescue the classroom from the dark ages and usher in an age of efficiency and enlightenment, technologists find to their dismay that teachers can often be persuaded to use the new tools only slightly, if at all. They find further that, even when the tools are used, classroom practice—the look-and-feel of schools—remains fundamentally unchanged. The fact that it is possible to cite occasional counter-examples of classrooms and schools where new practice has crystallized around new technologies only highlights the overwhelming prevalence of conventional school structures. Indeed, the last technologies to have had a defining influence on the general organization and practice of schooling were the textbook and the blackboard.

What is often overlooked in such assessments, however, is that schools themselves are a technology, by which I mean a way of knowing applied to a specific goal, albeit one so familiar that it has become transparent. They are intentional systems for preserving and transmitting information and authority, for inculcating certain values and practices while minimizing or eliminating others, and have evolved over the past one hundred years or so to perform this function more efficiently (Tyack, 1974). Since schools do not deal in the transmission of all possible knowledge or the promotion of the entire range of human experience but only a fairly small and stable subset thereof, and since their form has remained essentially unchanged over this time, we can even say that schools have been optimized for the job we entrust to them, that over time the technology of schooling has been tuned. When schools are called upon to perform more "efficiently," to maximize outputs of whatever type (high school or college graduates, skilled workers, patriotic citizens, public support for education and educators) from a given set of inputs (money, students, staff, legal mandates, public confidence), it is their capacity to act as technologies, as rational institutions, that is being called upon. It is widely but mistakenly expected that, after analyzing the facts at hand and determining that a problem exists (high drop-out rates or functional illiteracy, for instance) and within the limits of their discretion (since they are not free to act however they wish), schools will attempt to implement an optimal solution, the one that yields the most bang for the buck. This expectation, too, derives from the assumption that schools, since they are purpose-built machines, will pursue the deductive means–ends approach that characterizes rational pursuits. Following this, it is also expected that schools will embrace, indeed will clamor for, any technology that would help them increase their productivity, to perform more efficiently and effectively. It seems natural that they should employ the same tools that have led the world outside the classroom to become a much more information-dense environment, tools like film, television, and computers. Certainly many educational technologists reflexively expect such a response, and are both miffed and baffled when it is not immediately and abundantly forthcoming.

But schools are not simply technologies, nor are they purely or even mainly rational in the ways in which they respond to a given set of conditions. They also have other purposes, other identities, seek other outputs. They are, perhaps first and foremost, organizations, and as such seek nothing so much as their own perpetuity. Entrenched or mature organizations (like the organisms to which they are functionally and etymologically related) experience change or the challenge to change most significantly as a disruption, an intrusion, as a failure of organismic defenses. This is especially true of public schools since they and their employees have historically been exempt from most forms of pressure that can be brought to bear on organizations from without (Chubb and Moe, 1990; Friedman, 1962).

Organizations are not rational actors: their goal is not to solve a defined problem but to relieve the stress on the organization caused by pressure operating outside of or overwhelming the capacity of normal channels. Their method is not a systematic evaluation of means and ends to produce

---

*This article appeared as *Technology Refusal and the Organizational Culture of Schools* in e-journal *Education Policy Analysis Archives* 1.10 (Sept. 1993). Reprinted with permission.

an optimum response, but rather a trial-and-error rummaging through Standard Operating Procedures to secure a satisfying response. As organizational entities, schools and the people who work in them must be less than impressed by the technologists' promises of greater efficiency or optimized outcomes. The implied criticism contained in those promises and the disruption of routine that their implementations foreshadow, even (or especially) for the most dramatic of innovations, is enough to consign them to the equipment closet. What appears to outsiders as a straightforward improvement can to those within an organization be felt as undesirably disruptive if it means that the culture must change its values and habits in order to implement it. Since change is its own downside, organization workers must always consider, even if unconsciously, the magnitude of the disruption an innovation will engender when evaluating its net benefit and overall desirability. This circumspection puts schools directly at odds with the rational premises of technologists for whom the maximization of organizational culture and values almost always takes a back seat to the implementation of an "optimal" response to a set of conditions defined as problematic. Indeed, a characteristic if unspoken assumption of technologists and of the rational model in general is that cultures are infinitely malleable and accommodating to change. As we'll see later, schools' natural resistance to organizational change plays an important (though not necessarily determining) role in shaping their response to technological innovation.

Organizations are defined by their flow of power, information, and authority. Schools as workplaces are hierarchical in the extreme, with a pyramidal structure of power, privilege, and access to information. Indeed, proponents of the "hidden curriculum" theory of schooling propose that acceptance of hierarchy is one of the main object lessons schools are supposed to impart (Apple, 1982; Dreeben, 1968). At the bottom, in terms of pay, prestige, and formal autonomy are teachers. Next up are building-level administrators, and finally, district-level administrators. Any practice (and a technology is, after all, a set of practices glued together by values) that threatens to disrupt this existing structure will meet tremendous resistance at both adoption and implementation stages. A technology that reinforces existing lines of power and information is likely to be adopted (a management-level decision) but may or may not be implemented (a classroom-level decision). The divergence of interests of managers and workers, and the potential implementation fissures along those lines, is a source of much of the implementation failure of widely touted "advances."

Finally, in addition to their rational and organizational elements, schools are also profoundly normative institutions. Most obviously, schools are often actors in and venues for the performance of significant shifts in social mores and policy. Within the lifetime of many Americans, for example, schools have institutionalized successive notions of separate-and-unequal, separate-but-equal, equal resources for all, and, most recently, unequal resources for unequal needs as reifications of our shifting cultural conceptions of fairness. Because schools are the ubiquitous intersection between the public and the private spheres of life, feelings about what "values" should and should not be represented in the curriculum run deep and strong among Americans, even those without school-aged children. When thinking about values, however, it is crucial to remember that schools generally do not seek this contentious role for themselves. More often than not it is imposed upon them by legislators, the courts, community activists, and others whose agenda, though it may to some degree overlap with that of the schools', has a different origin and a different end. For if anything, the norms of school culture are profoundly conservative, in the sense that the underlying mission of schools is the conservation and transmission of preexisting, predefined categories of knowing, acting, and being in the world. As David Cohen points out, the structure of schools and the nature of teaching have remained substantially unchanged for seven hundred years, and there exists in the popular mind a definite, conservative conception of what schools should be like, a template from which schools stray only at their peril (Cohen, 1987).

When parents or others speak with disapproval of the "values" that are or are not being transmitted to children in schools they largely miss the point. For the values that predominate most of all, that indeed must always predominate, are less the set of moral and social precepts that the critics have in mind than the institutional and organizational values of knowing, being, and acting on which the school itself is founded: respect for hierarchy, competitive individualization, a receptivity to being ranked and judged, and the division of the world of knowledge into discreet units and categories susceptible to mastery (Dreeben, 1968). To a great extent these values are shared in common with our other large-scale institutions, business and government—indeed, if they were not, it seems most unlikely that they would predominate in schools. They are, in fact, the core values of the bourgeois humanism that has been developing in the West since the Enlightenment, and it is these norms and values, more than the shifting and era-bound constructions of social good, that schools enact in their normative capacity. There is a tight coupling between these values and schools-as-a-technology, just as there is between any technology and the values it operationalizes. Given this linkage, it's often difficult to say with certainty whether school values predate the technology of schools-as-we-know-them, in which case the technology is a dependent tool dedicated to the service of an external mandate, or whether the technology produces *sui generis* a set of values of its own that are then propagated through society by school graduates. When it is this difficult to extract a technology from its context, you know you have found a tool that does its job very, very well.

School Workers

In manifesting its culture, school places teachers and administrators in an unusual and contradictory position. They are subjected to many of the limitations of highly bureaucratic organizations but are denied the support and incentive structures by which bureaucracies usually offset such constraints. School workers are the objects of recurring scrutiny from interested and influential parties outside of what is generally conceived of as the "school system," many of whom have conflicting (and often inchoate) expectations for what schools should accomplish. Yet teachers and administrators almost always lack the rights of self-definition and discretionary control of resources (time, money, curriculum) that generally accompany this kind of accountability to give it form and meaning.

At the same time, even the most complacent bureaucracies direct some incentives at their workers. These may be monetary, in the form of performance bonuses or stock options, career enhancing in the form of promotions, or sanctions like demotion and the consequent loss of authority and responsibility. Schools generally offer none of these. Instead they proffer to good and bad alike a level of job security that would be the envy of a Japanese sarariman: unless you commit a felony or espouse views unpopular in your community you are essentially guaranteed employment for as long as you like, no matter what the quality of your work. Teachers cannot be demoted: there is no position of lesser authority or responsibility within schools. Just as students are essentially rewarded with promotion for filling seats and not causing trouble, so teachers are paid and promoted on the basis of seniority and credentials rather than performance. Providing they have not violated some school norm it is not uncommon for teachers or administrators who demonstrate incompetence at their assigned tasks to be transferred, or even promoted to off-line positions of higher authority rather than being fired, demoted, or retrained. Perversely, the only path to formally recognized increase in status for dedicated, talented teachers is to stop teaching, to change jobs and become administrators or consultants. Some schools and states are starting to create Master Teacher designations and other forms of status enhancement to address the need for formal recognition of excellence, but the overwhelmingly dominant practice provides no such acknowledgment for outstanding practitioners, thus lumping all teachers together into an undifferentiated mass. This condescension toward the teachers' craft—frequently accompanied by cynical paeans to their selfless devotion to Knowledge and children—is central to the organizational culture of schools, and teachers' reaction against it forms the base of their suspicions of the motives and values of technologists who have often claimed to be able to improve education by substituting the output of a teacher with that of a box.

As with any organization possessed of a distinct and pervasive culture, schools attract and retain either those most comfortable with their premises and conditions, thus without other options, or those who care deeply about the organizational mission and are willing to accept the personal disadvantages that may accompany a calling. Most beginning teachers identify with the latter group, and approach their nascent careers with a sense of excitement and commitment, and are prepared to work for not much money under difficult conditions in order to pursue this commitment. It is in the nature of people and organizations, however, for workaday values and practices to replace idealism as the defining experience of place and purpose. This means that over the long term the idealism and enthusiasm of the novice teacher must necessarily give way to the veteran's acquiescence to routine. It is this willingness to accept the values of the organizational culture and not the nature of the personal rewards that determines who remains in teaching and who leaves.

In plumbing the nature of a bureaucratic organization we must take into account the personalities and skill sets of those who seek to join it. According to studies cited by Howley et al., prospective teachers have lower test scores than do prospective nurses, biologists, chemists, aeronautical engineers, sociologists, political scientists, and public administrators (Howley, Pendarvis, and Howley, 1995). They also cite studies that demonstrate a negative correlation between intellectual aptitude and the length of a teacher's career. Recognizing that there are many reasons to dispute an equation of standardized test scores with intellectual capacity, depth, or flexibility, Howley cites Galambos et al. to demonstrate that

> teachers, as compared to arts and sciences graduates, take fewer hours in mathematics, English, physics, chemistry, economics, history, political sciences, sociology, other social sciences, foreign languages, philosophy, and other humanities. (Galambos, Cornett, and Spitler, 1985)

The fact that teachers are not as a group accomplished or engaged intellectuals does not require that they be resistant to change. It does suggest, though, a certain comfort with stasis and a reluctance to expand both the intellectual horizon and the skill set necessary to achieve proficiency with new technologies. This may help to explain the unusually long latency required to master personal computers that has been reported to Kerr and Sheingold by teachers who have incorporated technological innovations into their practice (Kerr, 1991; Sheingold and Hadley, 1990).

Given that long-term school workers are well adapted to a particular ecosocial niche, it is understandable that their first response to attempts at innovation would be one of resistance. Calls for change of any kind are seen as impositions or disturbances to be quelled as soon as possible, as unreasonable attempts to change the rules in the middle of the game. Larry Cuban has described the position of teachers as one of "situationally constrained choice," in which the ability to pursue options actively desired is limited by the environment in which teachers work (Cuban, 1986). While this is true as far as it goes, I prefer to see the process as one of gradual adaptation and acquiescence to the values and processes of the organization, rather than the continued resistance and frustration implied by Cuban; in other words, as one of situationally induced adaptation. This, I think, more easily explains the affect and frame of mind of most veteran teachers and administrators, and accommodates the possibility that the average teacher might be no more heroic or selfless than the average office worker.

The Culture of Technology

If the State religion of America is Progress, then surely technology provides its icons. It is largely through the production of ever more marvelous machines—the grace of technology made flesh—that we redeem the promise of a better tomorrow, confirm the world's perfectibility, and resorb some to ourselves and to our institutions. As Cohen succinctly puts it,

> Americans have celebrated technology as a powerful force for change nearly everywhere in social life . . . [and] are fond of picturing technology as a liberating force: cleaning up the workplace, easing workers' burdens, making the good life broadly available, increasing disposable income, and the like. (Cohen, 1987, p. 154)

But it goes further than that. According to the American *zeitgeist* our machines not only signal and refresh our modernity, they serve as foundational metaphors for many of our institutions, schools among them.[1]

---

[1] Although we may apotheosize this habit, we didn't invent it. The desire to apprehend the complexity of the world, to encompass it in a more immediately accessible form, gives western culture a long, albeit narrow, history of mechanical and neo-mechanical metaphor. The shift from one metaphor to another generally lags technology itself by a generation or so, and each shift to a new metaphor drastically affects the way cultures view the natural and human worlds.

Until the fourteenth century there were no such metaphors. Indeed, the rope of nearly all metaphor, metonymy, and analogy was tied to the natural or supernatural rather than to the created world, simply because there were no complex machines as we understand them today. The invention of the astrolabe and its close and quick descendant, the clock (both of which were developed to aid in navigation at the dawn of the modern commercial era), provided the first tangible human creation whose complexity was sufficient to embody the observed complexity of the natural world. It's at this time that we start seeing references to the intricate "workings" of things and of their proper "regulation," usually of the cosmos and nature, although occasionally of human systems as well. The clock, with its numerous intricate, precise, and interlocking components, and its felicitous ability to corporealize the abstraction of temporality, shaped western perceptions of the world by serving as its chief systemic metaphor for the next five hundred years.

In the early nineteenth century, the metaphor of the clock was gradually replaced by that of the engine and, somewhat more generally, by the notion of the machine as a phylum unto

Machines corporealize our rationality, demonstrate our mastery. They always have a purpose and they are always *prima facie* suited to the task for which they were designed. Every machine is an ideal type, and even the merest of them, immune to the thousand natural shocks the flesh (and its institutions) is heir to, occupies a pinnacle of fitness and manifests a clarity of purpose of which our institutions can only dream. They reflect well on us, and we measure ourselves by their number and complexity. It is nearly inconceivable that we would judge a school to be complete, no, to be American, that was without a representative sample of these icons of affirmation. It is absolutely inconceivable that we would trust our children, our posterity, to anything less than a machine, and so we consciously model, relentlessly build, and generally fill, our schools.

For although they often seem so ageless and resilient as to be almost Sphinx-like in their inscrutability, schools as we know them are both relatively recent and consciously modeled on that most productive of all technologies, the factory (Tyack, 1974). For at least the last hundred years, schools have been elaborated as machines set up to convert raw materials (new students) into finished products (graduates, citizens, workers) through the application of certain processes (pedagogy, discipline, curricular materials, gym). It is this processing function that drives the rationalist proposition that schools can be tuned well or poorly, can be made more or less efficient in their operation. Although it seldom articulates them overtly, this view is predicated on the assumptions that we

---

itself. The figures shift from those of intricacy and precision to those of "drive" and "power," from regulation to motivation. In the early twentieth century, as technology became more sophisticated, the concepts of motivation and regulation were to some extent merged in the figure of the self-regulating machine. This is essentially the dominant metaphor with which we've grown up, the notion of a "system" that contains the means of both its own perpetuity and its own governance. This metaphor has been applied to everything from political science, to nature, to the human body, to the human mind. The enginic "drive" of the Freudian unconscious, Darwinian evolution, and the Marxian proletariat give way to "family systems," ecosystems, and political equilibria as the Industrial Revolution lurches to a close.

The edges of a new metaphor for complex systems can be seen emerging. It is, however, one that is able to embrace the relativity and immanence that stress mechanical metaphors to the point of fatigue: that of the computer and its data networks. We see, and will see more, large-scale shifts away from the concepts of drive and regulation to those of processing and transmission. The raw material upon which processes act will be regarded not as objects and forces but as data, which is not a thing but immanence itself, an arbitrary arrangement given temporary and virtual form. The action will be seen as a program, a set of instructions allowing for more or fewer degrees of freedom. Interrelationships will be embodied in paths, arrangements, and pointers rather than linkages (creakingly mechanical) through which objects transmit force. Important phylogenic distinctions will be made between hardware (that which is fixed/infrastructure) and software (that which determines use and function). This has tremendous consequences for our notions of property, of originality and authorship, of privacy and relationship. It may, perhaps, be less limiting than the mechanical metaphors it will largely displace.

know what we wants schools to do, that what we want is unitary and can be measured, and that it can be affected by regular, replicable modifications to one or more school processes. It presumes that the limits of education are essentially technological limits and that better technology will remove them. It is the most generic and encompassing theory of "educational technology," since it embraces all curricular, instructional, and material aspects of the school experience. In its more comprehensive and embracing instantiations such an attitude does not limit its concerns only to the school plant. For early progressive educators (and again today) students' readiness to learn, in the form of adequate nutrition, housing, and medical care, was seen as a proper concern for school "technologists."

This suggests at least two impetuses for wanting to bring machines into schools. The first is the desire of the central planner and social scientist to have these social crucibles be as modern as the world of tomorrow they help conjure into being. Cuban details how each new development in the popularization of information and entertainment technology (radio, film, television, computers) in society at large brought with it a corresponding assumption that the deployment of this revolutionary machine into schools would, finally, bring the classroom out of the dark ages and into the modern world (Cuban, 1986). Attempts to deploy technology that follow this pattern seldom specify how the machines will be used, and if outcomes are discussed at all it is in vague, incantatory language that employs words more as talismans than as descriptors. The connection between such scenarios and the outcomes they believe they strive for is essentially animist or semi-magical, using up-to-date machinery to signify modernity and believing that the transformative power resides in the box itself rather than in the uses to which it is put. Given the nonrational character of these initiatives, it's not surprising that they originate with elected officials, state administrators, community groups (business, parents), and others for whom signaling is paramount. They tend not to originate with technologists or classroom teachers, who have different (if differing) agendae.

In the group "technologists" I include those whose avowed goal is to make schooling more efficient through the manipulation of its objects or processes. Efficiency, however, is not the straightforward, value-free quantity that those who most embrace it suppose it to be. An industrial-revolution coinage, efficiency was intended to denote the relative quantity of energy lost during manufacturing or processing, contexts in which such things can be easily and unambiguously measured. Clearly, the socially situated diffusion of skills and values that is our system of education presents a very different case, one that is more complex, more contested, more informed by subjectivity. In order to apply the concept of efficiency to such a messy world technologists and others must narrow their gaze to focus on one particular element of the process. They have therefore tended to concentrate on the transfer of information to students, partly because it is one of the few processes in schools that can be measured, and partly because it is one of even fewer functions that everyone agrees schools ought to perform. What they discovered almost immediately was that when judged simply as knowledge-transfer machines, schools are just not very good: it seems to take an awful lot of workers, money, and other resources to transfer a relatively small amount of information. By framing the question in this way, technologists (re)cast education as a fundamentally didactic process, and problems with education as problems of "instructional delivery." This didacticism posits education as the transfer of information from a repository to a receptacle, a cognitive diffusion gradient across a membrane constituted not by the rich, tumultuous, contradictory social processes that situate the student, the teacher, and the school within society, but solely by the "instructional delivery vehicle." By this light, of course, nearly any organic, indigenous school practice or organization will be found wanting, since schools have many more outcomes in mind than just information transfer.

The second concern of technologists has been standardization. Regardless of how well they succeed, schools intend to produce the same outputs year after year. They are supposed to ensure that seventh graders, say, will emerge at essentially the same age with essentially the same sets of skills and broad values this year as last. If they do not attempt this then socially important categories like "seventh grade" or even "common school" lose their meaning. Signaling functions aside, the explicit reason given for modeling schools on factories was their promise of standardization, of uniformity of outcome. Technologists and planners have long felt that the weakest link in this chain is the last, "the instructional delivery vehicle," the teacher. Standardization of curricula, of facilities, of teacher certification requirements, means little once the classroom door is closed and the teacher is alone with her students. The inefficiency and variability of this last crucial stage undoes all prior ratiocination. For this reason, educational technologists have tended to produce solutions designed not to aid teachers, but to recast, replicate, or replace them, either with machines or through the introduction of "teacher-proof" curricula.[2]

---

[2] It is neither possible nor desirable to ignore the issue of gender here. It may be coincidence that the classroom, the one white-collar occupation where women have historically had a dominant institutional place, is repeatedly characterized by technologists as a place of darkness and chaos, stubbornly resistant to the enlightening gifts of rationalized technology. It may be coincidence that educational technologists are as a group overwhelmingly male but direct their transformative efforts not at the powerful—and overwhelmingly male—community of planners and administrators but at the formally powerless—and overwhelmingly female—community of practitioners. It may be coincidence that the terms used to describe the insufficiency of the classroom and to condescend to the folk-craft of teaching are the same terms used by an androgenized society to derogate women's values and women's work generally. But that's a lot of coincidence. Kerr discusses the differences in world view and values between the teachers who deal with children and the technologists who approach the classroom from industrial and, as Noble demonstrates, often military perspectives (Kerr, 1990;

Yet all these attempts to modernize, to rationalize, to "improve" the schools by making them more efficient have had little effect. Textbooks, paperbacks, blackboards, radio, film, film strips, airplanes, television, satellite systems and telecommunications have all in their time been hailed as modernizers of American education (Cuban, 1986). Cohen, for his part, demonstrates how, with the exception of the textbook and the blackboard, none of these much-vaunted exemplars of modern efficiency have had any significant effect on school organization or practice (Cohen, 1987). They did not make schools more modern, more efficient, more congruent with the world outside the school, or have any of the myriad other effects their advocates were sure they would have. Why is this so?

The Culture of Refusal

Technology can potentially work change on both the organizational and practice patterns of schools. That change can subvert or reinforce existing lines of power and information, and this change can be, for the technologist or the school personnel, intentional, inadvertent, or a combination of the two. Since schools are not monolithic but composed of groups with diverse and often competing interests on the rational, organizational, and symbolic levels, the adoption and the implementation of a proposed technology are two different matters.

And yet each battle is essentially the same battle. The technologists' rhetoric is remarkably consistent regardless of the specifics of the machine at issue. So too is their response when the technologies in question meet with only lukewarm interest: to blame the stubborn backwardness of teachers or the inflexibility and insularity of school culture. While these elements certainly play a part in what I'll call "technology refusal" on the part of schools, it behooves us to remember that all technologies have values and practices embedded within them. In this respect, at least, technology is never neutral; it always makes a difference. From this perspective, the reactionary response on the part of schools (by which I mean the response of individuals within schools acting to support their institutional function) perceived by technology advocates makes a great deal more sense than the pig-headed Luddism so often portrayed. Further, technology refusal represents an immediate and, I believe, fundamentally accurate assessment of the challenges to existing structures and authority

---

Noble, 1991). He stops short of characterizing what may perhaps be obvious but nevertheless should be acknowledged: the casual, pervasive misogyny that characterizes the attitude of dominant culture toward any environment or activity that is predominantly female. It is perhaps for this reason that we never see proposals to replace (mostly male) administrators with machines. The usage of computers to perform administrative tasks should pose no more, and probably fewer, value dilemmas and conflicts than their usage to define and practice teaching.

that are embodied or embedded in the contested technology. I believe further that the depth of the resistance is generally and in broad strokes proportionate to the seriousness of the actual threat. In simple terms, schools do, on some level, understand the implications of the technology, and they resist them.

Change advocates, of whom technologists are a permanent subset, often try to have things both ways. On the one hand, the revolutionary potential of the innovation is emphasized, while at the same time current practitioners are reassured (implicitly or explicitly) that their roles, positions, and relationships will remain by and large as they were before. The introduction of computers, for example, is hailed in one discourse (directed toward the public and toward policy makers) as a process that will radically change the nature of what goes on in the classroom, give students entirely new sets of skills, and permanently shift the terrain of learning and schools. In other discourse (directed toward principals and teachers) computers are sold as straightforward tools to assist them in carrying out preexisting tasks and fulfilling preexisting roles, not as Trojan horses whose acceptance will ultimately require the acquisition of an entirely new set of skills and world outlook (Hodas, 1993). Since school workers and their practice do not fully maximize instructional delivery—indeed, cannot, under the assumption and constraints of school organization—the "remedies" or alternatives proposed by technologists necessarily embody overt or implicit critiques of workers' world view as well as their practice. The more innovative the approach, the greater its critique, and hence its threat to existing principles and order. When confronted with this challenge workers have two responses from which to choose. They can ignore or subvert implementation of the change or they can coopt or repurpose it to support their existing practices. In contrast to generalized reform efforts, which Sarason maintains are more likely to be implemented the more radical they are, these efforts by technologists to change the institution of schooling from the classroom up make teachers the objects rather than the subjects of the reformist gaze (Sarason, 1990). The more potent and pointed technologists' ill-concealed disinterest in or disregard for the school order of things, the less likely their suggestions are to be put into practice. The stated anxiety of teachers worried about losing their jobs to machines is also a resistance to the re-visioning of the values and purposes of schooling itself, a struggle over the soul of school. It is about self-interest, to be sure, but it is also about self-definition.

Much of the question of teacher self-definition revolves around the anxiety generated by their unfamiliarity and incompetence with the new machines. The fear of being embarrassed is a major de-motivating factor in the acquisition of the skills required to use computer technology in the classroom (Honey and Moeller, 1990; Kerr, 1991; Sheingold and Hadley, 1990). This is an area where institutional and individual interests converge to produce a foregone effect. The (self-)selection for teaching of individuals who by and large show neither interest nor aptitude for ongoing intellectual development buttressed by the condition of lifetime employment almost guarantees a teacher corps that is highly reluctant to attempt change. This, in turn, suits the interests of school management whose job is made considerably simpler with a population of workers whose complacence acts as a buffer against change. Since teachers' situationally reinforced lack of motivation limits their action as advocates for change, school administrators are relieved of the responsibility for developing the creative management skills that would be required for teachers to develop new classroom skills.

There are technologies that are suited perfectly to such a climate, those that either actively support the organization of schools or are flexible enough to readily conform to it (Cohen, 1987). Not surprisingly, they are the ones that are so ubiquitous, so integrated into school practice as to be almost invisible. On the classroom level we would expect to find tools and processes that both ease the physical labor of the teacher while maintaining her traditional role within the classroom. The blackboard, the duplicating machine, and the overhead projector come immediately to mind. All enhance the teachers' authoritative position as an information source, and reduce the physical effort required to communicate written information so that more energy can be devoted to the nondidactic tasks of supervision, arbitration, and administration. This type of technology seldom poses a threat to any of the teacher's functions, is fundamentally supportive of the school values mentioned earlier, and reproduces locally the same types of power and information relationships through which the teacher herself engages her administrators. We might also consider the school intercom system. Ideally suited to the purposes of centralized authority and the one-way flow of information, it is as ubiquitous in classrooms as its polar opposite, the direct-dial telephone, is rare. Technologies such as these will seldom meet with implementation resistance from teachers because they support them in the roles through which teachers define themselves, and because they contain no critique of teachers' practice, skills, or values. In general, resources that can be administered, that can be made subject to central control and organization, will find more favor from both administrators and teachers than those that cannot.

These examples of successful technologies confirm the requirement of simplicity if a technology is to become widely dispersed through classrooms. This has partly to do with the levels of general teacher aptitude described above, partly with the amount of time available to teachers to learn new tools, and partly with the very real need for teachers to appear competent before their students. As with prison administration and dog training, a constant concern in the running of schools is that the subject population not be reminded what little genuine authority supports the power its masters exercise. Although there are more complex models for understanding the diffuse, polysemous generation of power and status that comprise the warp and woof of institutional fabric (see Foucault on medicine or prisons, for example), for our purposes a simple model of authority-as-imposition will suffice. In this tradition, French and Raven (1968) describe the five sources of power as follows:

1. Reward, the power to give or withhold something the other wants;
2. Coercive, the power to inflict some kind of punishment;
3. Legitimate, the use of institutionally sanctioned position or authority;
4. Referent, the use of personal attraction, the desire to be like the other, or to be identified with what the other is identified with;
5. Expert, the authority that derives from superior skill or competence.

Teachers are fully authorized to make use of each of these forms of power. Indeed, those teachers most respected by their peers and their students deploy some situationally optimal combination of these. For students, however, the only authorized form of power is Expert power, and this expertise is the only legitimated field on which to contest adult authority within the school. Thus, an unfortunate (but hardly unforeseeable) consequence of school organization is that many teachers are threatened by students' acquisition or demonstration of mastery that is equal to or greater than the teacher's own within a shared domain.

If technologists have their way, however, teachers will be expected to know how to use computers, networks, and databases with the same facility they now use blackboards and textbooks, and with greater facility than the roomful of resourceful, inquisitive students who were weaned on the stuff. The pressure toward competence and the acquisition of new skills, which is generally not a feature of school culture or the employment contracts under which teachers work, will be strong. It will come from unexpected directions: from below (from the "tools" themselves) and from within, as teachers struggle to retain mastery over their students. It's easy to see why teachers would resist this scenario. Administrators, for their part, have equally few organizational incentives for inviting this disruption into schools. Not only would they be required to respond to teachers' demands for the time and resources needed to attain proficiency, they themselves would need to attain some minimum level of competence in order to retain authority over teachers. Since there is no way for the system to reward this kind of responsible management nor any way to penalize its absence, school authorities' most sensible route is to ignore or quell demands for the implementation of such potentially disruptive processes.

Having inherited the mantle of modernity from instructional television and computer-aided instruction, microcomputers and microcomputer networks are presently charged with the transformation of schools. As school technologies, however, computers and networks are unusually polyvalent: they can both support and subvert the symbolic, organizational, and normative dimensions of school practice. They can weaken or strengthen the fields of power and information that emanate from the institutional positions of students, teachers, and administrators. It is my thesis that authority and status within organizations are constituted from two sources: power, itself sourced as outlined by French and Raven, and control over and access to the form and flow of information. Authority and status are singularities, as it were, produced by a particular confluence of (potentially) shifting fields of power and information. As bureaucratic, hierarchical institutions and as concretizations of a particular tradition of pedagogy, schools teach and model as canonical a particular arrangement of paths for the flow of information. Introducing computers into schools highlights these assumptions, causes these normally invisible channels to fluoresce.

It is not their capacity to process information that gives computers this special ability. Data-processing systems have existed in large school districts for decades, helping central administration to run their organizations more efficiently. Irregularities of control call attention to themselves and thereby remind workers that such arrangements are created things, neither aboriginal nor ahistorical but purpose-built and recent. To the extent that automation can help existing administrative processes to run more smoothly and recede into the background, it helps to reintroduce a kind of medieval reassurance regarding the rightness and permanence of a given order. Schools and school workers, particularly, seem to prefer this type of predictability. Such data-processing regimes also relieve school workers of much of the tedium of their administrative work, since scheduling, grading, communication, and tracking are all made less drudging by automation. The easing of these burdens offered by the machine fits well with popular conceptions of machines as value-free, labor-saving devices and offers workers a benefit in exchange for their participation in a process that strengthens the mechanisms of control exerted by the bureaucracy over their daily routines. To the extent that they are aware of this bargain at all most are willing to accept it.

Such strengthening of administrative priority and control over teachers is recapitulated by teachers over students when computers are used for Computer-Assisted Instruction or as "integrated learning systems." Although they have fallen out of favor somewhat of late, the vast majority of school-based computer use has taken place in this context. Kids are brought en masse to a (generally) windowless room presided over by a man with no other function than to administer the machines. There they work for between thirty and fifty minutes on drill-and-practice software that compels them to perform simple tasks over and over until they have reached a preset level of proficiency, at which time they are started on new tasks.

This behaviorist apotheosis fits neatly into the organizational model of schools, and into much pedagogical practice as well. The progress and work habits of each student are carefully tracked by the server. Reports can be generated detailing the number of right and wrong answers, the amount of time spent on each question, the amount of "idle" time spent between questions, the number of times the student asked the system for help, the tools used, and so on. Not much use is ever made of this information (assuming some could be) except to compare students and classes against one another. Nevertheless, the ability to monitor work habits, to break tasks down into discrete chunks, and the inability of students to determine what they work on or how they work on it fits quite well into the rationalist model of the school as factory and the technologists' goal of maximizing "instructional delivery."

Such systems were an easy sell. They complemented existing organizational and practice models, and they signaled modernity and standardization (Newman, 1992). Perversely, they were also claimed to promote individualization, since each student was tasked and speeded separately from the rest of the group. The fact that a student was working on exactly the same problems, with the same tools and in the same sequence as classmates seems not to have mattered. Since students work in isolation, these systems accord well with the premise of structured competition. Since mastery at one level leads relentlessly to more difficult (but essentially identical) problems, the students never have a chance to exhibit facility of a type that would threaten their teacher, and since the terminals at which they work are both limited in their capacities and centrally controlled, students have no opportunity to acquire a disruptive mastery of the technology itself.

Labs like these are prime examples of the nonneutrality of technology. They do not foster all or even several types of learning but rather one particular—and particularly narrow—conception whose origin is not with teachers who work with children but with the technologists, industrialists, and military designers who develop "man–machine systems" (Noble, 1991). They do not encourage or even permit many types of classroom organization but only one. They instantiate and enforce only one model of organization, of pedagogy, of relationship between people and machines. They are biased, and their easy acceptance into schools is indicative of the extent to which that bias is shared by those who work there.

This technology is not the technology of computers, or computers-in-schools per se, any more than armored cars represent the technology of internal combustion, or washing machines the technology of electromagnetic induction. They are machines, to be sure, but machines require a social organization to become technologies. Thus the uses of computers described above for data processing and "learning labs" are not examples of computer technologies but of normative, administrative, and pedagogical technologies supported by computers.

This distinction is important because many teachers, lay people, and some administrators have concluded from their experiences with such systems that computers in school are anathema to their notions of what schools ought to do with and for children. Computer-based technologies of the kind described above are hardly "neutral." Indeed, they are intensely normative and send unambiguous signals about what school is for and what qualities teachers ought to emulate and model. Interpersonal and social dynamics, serendipity, cognitive apprenticeship, and play all seem to be disdained by this instantiation of machine learning. The teacher's fear of "being replaced by a computer" is a complex anxiety. It obviously has a large component of institutional self-interest, since no one wants to lose their job. But the very fact that replacement by a machine is even conceivable cuts deeper, to the heart of teachers' identity and self-respect. The suggestion that the deskilled roles that teachers are called upon to fulfill might be better performed by machines calls this self-image into question in a manner that is painfully direct. It is hence unwelcome.

Beyond the question of self-respect but intertwined with it is the frustration that many teachers experience with the promulgation of a purely rationalist notion of education. Teachers, after all, are witness and partner to human development in a richer and more complex sense than educational technologists will ever be. Schools are where children grow up. They spend more waking hours in school with their teachers than they do at home with their parents. The violence that technologists have done to our only public children's space by reducing it to an "instructional delivery vehicle" is enormous, and teachers know that. To abstract a narrow and impoverished concept of human sentience from the industrial laboratory and then inflict it on children for the sake of "efficiency" is a gratuitous, stunting stupidity and teachers know that, too. Many simply prefer not to collaborate with a process they experience as fundamentally disrespectful to kids and teachers alike.

Cultural Change

I have described how technologies are variously embraced and resisted in an effort to strengthen a system and maintain an organizational status quo. I've tried to make clear that since schools are complex organizations, not all their component members or constituencies have identical interests at all times; that a technology that is favorable to one faction at a given moment may be resisted by another that might favor it for different reasons under different circumstances. Most importantly, I've tried to show that technologies are neither value free nor constituted simply by machines or processes. Rather, they are the uses of machines in support of highly normative, value-laden institutional and social systems.

Decisions about whether or not to deploy a given technology are seldom made with diabolic or conspiratorial intent. Teachers and administrators only infrequently plot to consolidate their hegemony. But the mental model under which they operate tends over and over again to foreclose some options even before they can be formally considered, while at the same time making others seem natural, neutral, and, most dangerously, value free. It is those latter options, those "easy" technologies that are adopted and implemented in schools. If one accepts this framework, there are only two ways to imagine a relationship between an introduction of technology into schools and a substantive change in what schools do and how they do it. The first is to believe that some technologies can function as Trojan Horses; that is, that they can engender practices that schools find desirable or acceptable but that nevertheless operationalize new underlying values, which in turn bring about fundamental change in school structure and practice (Hodas, 1993). The second is to hope that schools will come to reevaluate the social purposes they serve, the manner in which they serve them, or the principles of socially developed cognition from which they operate. The impetus for this change may be internal, as teachers and administrators decide that their self-interest in serving new purposes is greater than their interest in perpetuating the existing scheme of things. It may be external, as powerful outside forces adjust the inputs available to and outputs desired from the schools. It may be institutional, as restructuring initiatives encourage schools to compete with one another in a newly created educational marketplace.

To a certain extent all these processes are under way, albeit slowly, unevenly, and amidst contestation. On the Trojan Horse front, there are more and more reports of teachers taking physical and pedagogical control of computers from the labs and the technologists. They are being placed in classrooms and used as polymorphic resources, facilitators, and enablers of complex social learning activities (Newman, 1990, 1992; Kerr, 1991). As computers themselves grow farther from their origins as military-industrial technologies, educational technologists increasingly are people whose values are more child centered than those of their predecessors. This is reflected in the software they create, the uses they imagine for technology, and their ideas about exploration and collaboration (Char and Newman, 1986; Wilson and Tally, 1991; Collins and Brown, 1986). Nationally, the rhetoric of economic competitiveness used to justify the National Research and Education Network (and now its putative successor, the Information Superhighway) has encouraged the deployment of several national school network testbeds. These prototype partnerships between public schools, private research organizations, and the National Science Foundation link geographically dispersed students and teachers together with one another and with shared databases. The collaborative, project-based explorations they are designed to support more closely resemble science as practiced by scientists (or history as practiced by historians) than they do the usual classroom-based, decontextualized, and teacher-centered approach to learning. Such projects nearly always result in a significant deauthorization of the teacher as the source of knowledge, a shift embraced by most teachers who experience it because it allows them to spend more time facilitating student learning and less time maintaining their real and symbolic author-ity. If students, parents, and teachers are all pleased with the cognitive and affective changes induced locally by working with these types of tools (and it is by no means certain that they will be), it may become difficult to sustain the older, more repressive features of school organization of which cen-trally administered and imposed technology is but one example.

The second possibility, that schools will reevaluate their means and ends, also has momentum behind it, at least within a somewhat circum-scribed compass. Teachers and administrators are taking steps to secure the autonomy necessary to reengineer schools-as-technologies, though not all are happy with this unforeseen responsibility and some choose to abdicate it. Nevertheless, for the first time practitioners are being given the chance to redesign schools based on what they've learned from their experiences with children. Given that chance, many teachers and admin-istrators are demonstrating that schools and school technology can support practices of the kind that reflect values described by Wendell Berry in another context as care, competence, and frugality in the uses of the world (Berry, 1970). Others are using the opportunity to reconstruct the role of the school within its larger community. In Mendocino, California, for example, an area devastated by declines in the traditional fishing and timber industries, the local high school has taken the lead role in develop-ing a community-wide information infrastructure designed to encourage a fundamental shift in the local economic base away from natural resource dependency and toward information work. While initially dependent on NASA's K–12 Internet program for connectivity, the school district has moved to create partnerships with local providers to both secure its own telecommunications needs and be able to resell excess capacity to commu-nity businesses brought on-line by the school's own adult education pro-grams. The school is moving toward a project-based approach that relies on Internet access in every classroom to devise an updated version of voca-tional education (many of their students will not go on to four-year col-leges) that meets both state requirements and the wishes of the Mendocino staff to work with their students in a radically different environment.

It remains to be seen whether instances like these will multiply and reinforce one another or whether they will remain isolated counter-examples, "demonstration projects" whose signaling of modernity serves mostly to inoculate the larger system against meaningful change. If schools are in fact able to be more than rhetorically responsive to either local initiatives or global trends it will be because these impetuses are them-selves manifestations of a more significant and far-reaching shift: a change in the dominant mechanical metaphor on which we model our institutions. As we move from mechanical to information models of the world we will inevitably require that our institutions reflect the increased fluidity, immanence, and ubiquity that such models presuppose.[3] As we change our medieval conceptions of information from something that is stored in a fixed, canonical form in a repository designed exclusively for that purpose and whose transfer is a formal, specialized activity that takes place mainly within machines called schools, schools will change too. They will not, as some naively claim, become redundant or vestigial simply because their primacy as information-processing modelers is diminished (Perelman, 1992). Rather, they will continue to perform the same functions they always have: those relating to the reproduction of the values and processes of the society in which they're situated.

What this underlines, I think, is that machines can indeed change the culture of organizations, even ones as entrenched and recalcitrant as schools have proven to be. But they do it not, as technologists have generally imagined, by enabling schools to do the same job only better (more cheaply, more efficiently, more consistently, more equitably) but by causing them to change their conception of both what it is they do and the world in which they do it. This shift is not instigated by the machines deployed within schools but by those outside of it, those that shape and organize the social, economic, and informative relationships in which schools are situated and which they perpetuate. This is not the same as saying that machines that are widely used outside the classroom will automatically diffuse osmotically into the classroom and be used there: history shows that this is clearly not the norm.

What is happening, simply put, is that the wide, wet world is rapidly changing the ways it organizes its work, its people, and its processes, reconceptualizing them around the metaphors and practices enabled and embodied by its new supreme machines, distributed microcomputer networks. Archaic organizations from the CIA to IBM to the university have fundamentally rearranged themselves along the lines I've outlined in the notes to this report. Schools have been out of step with this change, and it is this misalignment more than anything else that causes us to say that schools are failing when in fact they are doing exactly the jobs they were set up and refined over generations to perform. It is the world around them that has changed, so much so that the jobs we asked them to carry out now seem ridiculous, now make us angry.

---

[3] In the shift from a mechanical to a digital organization of society we can expect the following changes in the social construction of relationship: information, not authority; networks and pointers, not linkages; inexpensive ubiquity, not dear scarcity; simultaneous possession, not mutually exclusive ownership; instantaneity/timeshifting, not temporality; community of interests, not community of place; distributed horizontally not centralized verticality. I don't contend that we thereby usher in Utopia. These new structures will bring new strictures. But they will be very, very different.

The fundamental instinct of durable organizations is to resist change; that is why they are durable. As schools scurry to serve the new bidding of old masters, and as they induct younger workers raised and trained under the auspices of new models and new practices, we discover—not surprisingly—that schools too are reorienting themselves along the lines of the latest dominant machine and, consequently, welcome those machines inside to assist in their nascent realignment of means and ends.

The norms and procedures of entrenched bureaucratic organizations are strong and self-reinforcing. They attract people of like minds and repel or expel those who don't share them. Schools are technologies, machines with a purpose. They embed their norms and processes in their outputs, which in the case of schools helps them to further strengthen their cultural position and resist marginalization. But they can never be independent of the values of society at large. If those change, as I believe they are beginning to, then schools must too. If they do not then they will be replaced, relegated to the parts bin of history.

References

Apple, Michael (1982). *Education and Power.* Routledge and Kegan Paul, Boston.

Berry, W. (1970). *A Continuous Harmony: Essays Cultural and Agricultural.* Harcourt Brace Jovanovich, New York.

Bowles, S., and H. Gintis (1977). *Schooling in Capitalist America: Educational Reform and the Contradictions of Economic Life.* Basic Books, New York.

Char, C. A., and D. Newman (1986). "Design Options for Interactive Videodisc: A Review and Analysis." Technical Report No. 39. Center for Technology in Education, Bank Street College of Education, New York.

Chubb, J. E., and T. M. Moe (1990). *Politics, Markets, and America's Schools.* The Brookings Institution, Washington, D.C.

Cohen, D. K. (1987). "Educational Technology, Policy, and Practice." *Educational Evaluation and Policy Analysis,* 9(Summer):153–170.

Collins, A., and J. S. Brown (1986). "The Computer as a Tool for Learning through Reflection." Technical Report No. 376. Center for Technology in Education, Bank Street College of Education, New York.

Cuban, L. (1986). *Teachers and Machines: The Classroom Use of Technology Since 1920.* Teachers College Press, New York.

Dreeben, R. (1968). *On What Is Learned in School.* Addison-Wesley, Reading, MA.

French, J. R. P., Jr., and B. Raven (1968). "The Bases of Social Power," in D. Cartwright and A. Zander (eds.), *Group Dynamics* (pp. 259–269). Harper & Row, New York.

Friedman, Alan (1962). *Capitalism and Freedom.* University of Chicago Press, Chicago, IL.

Fullan, M. G. (1991). *The New Meaning of Educational Change.* Teachers College Press, New York.

Galambos, E. C., L. M. Cornett, and H. D. Spitler (1985). "An Analysis of Transcripts of Teachers and Arts and Sciences Graduates." Southern Regional Education Board, Atlanta, GA.

Hodas, Steven (1993). "Implementation of a K–12 NREN: Equity, Access, and a Trojan Horse." Educational Resources Information Clearinghouse Document ED, 358–829.

Honey, M., and B. Moeller (1990). "Teacher's Beliefs and Technology Integration: Different Values, Different Understandings" (Technical Report No. 6). Center for Technology in Education, Atlanta, GA.

Howley, A., Pendarvis, M., and C. Howley (1995). *Out of Our Heads: Anti-Intellectualism in American Schools.* Teachers College Press, New York.

Kerr, S. T. (1990). "Technology:Education :: Justice:Care." *Educational Technology* (November, 1990), Vol. 30, pp. 7–12.

Kerr, S. T. (1991). "Lever and Fulcrum: Educational Technology in Teachers' Thought and Practice." *Teachers College Record,* 93(Fall):114–136.

Newman, D. (1990). "Technology's Role in Restructuring for Collaborative Learning" (Technical Report No. 8). Center for Technology in Education, Bank Street College of Education, New York.

Newman, D. (1992). "Technology as Support for School Structure and School Restructuring." *Phi Delta Kappan,* 74(4):308–315.

Noble, D. D. (1991). *The Classroom Arsenal: Military Research, Information Technology, and Public Education.* Falmer, London; New York.

Perelman, L. J. (1992). *School's Out: Hyperlearning, the New Technology, and the End of Education* (1st ed.). William Morrow, New York.

Sarason, S. B. (1990). *The Predictable Failure of Educational Reform.* Jossey-Bass, San Francisco.

Senge, P. M. (1990). *The Fifth Discipline.* Doubleday, New York.

Sheingold, K., and M. Hadley (1990). "Accomplished Teachers: Integrating Computers into Classroom Practice." Center for Technology in Education, Bank Street College of Education, New York.

Tyack, D. B. (1974). *The One Best System: A History of American Urban Education.* Harvard University Press, Cambridge, MA.

Wilson, K., and W. Tally (1991). "Looking at Multimedia: Design Issues in Several Discovery-Oriented Programs" (Technical Report No. 13). Center for Technology in Education, Bank Street College of Education, New York.

P·A·R·T · III

J

Great Expectations: PCs and Productivity*

Martin Neil Baily

In recent years, companies in the United States have installed billions of dollars' worth of computer and PC technology, which has changed the way Americans conduct business and propelled an unprecedented boom in the computer industry. At the same time, though, growth of productivity has declined and the United States economy has become less competitive. Computers have yet to prove their benefit in the worldwide race to boost productivity.

Nevertheless, America's commitment to computers and PCs continues to grow. Investment in computers jumped an average of 24% per year in the 1980s, while investment in other types of business equipment actually declined. And PCs are becoming an increasingly important factor within this exploding market. Today's PCs pack more power than the mainframes of just a few years ago, and they're found just about everywhere: on the desks of executives, managers, secretaries, and technicians and on the laps of peripatetic salespeople, attorneys, and engineers.

Many people hoped and expected that the rapid growth in computer hardware would help fuel overall economic performance. But in fact, the nation's economic performance has been mixed during the computer boom. The good news is that inflation has been tamed and that United States living standards have improved. The bad news is that productivity growth has slowed, the national debt has ballooned, and the country has turned a huge foreign trade surplus into an even bigger trade deficit. The two sides of this picture are related, of course. Much of the increase in living standards came about because we bought more goods such as autos, tanks, and VCRs than we could produce, and we borrowed from foreigners to pay the bills.

Why haven't computers helped improve productivity, and why aren't PCs making a bigger impact today? Well, they may be helping more than we know. A great deal of the improvement due to computer use has come in service industries, where productivity is notoriously difficult to measure. Another point to consider is that managers don't always use PCs to the best effect. Sometimes companies concentrate on using them to steal business from competitors, not to raise overall productivity.

Maybe we're expecting too much: computers and PCs cannot address all our productivity problems. It's unrealistic to expect them to compensate for collapsing infrastructures and poor work habits.

The Slowdown

To understand the role PCs play in productivity, it's helpful to look at the history of American productivity since World War II. After the war, the United States assumed clear leadership of the world economy. We had escaped the devastation that ravaged Europe and Asia; our factories were intact and operating at top capacity. Even more important, United States companies could exploit new technologies developed during the war, testing their potential in civilian markets. The Great Depression of the 1930s, which had held back the development of new ideas, was finally laid to rest. It's no surprise that the 1950s and 1960s saw unusually rapid growth in productivity.

The first signs of a slowdown came in the late 1960s, as growth in mining and construction began to ease off. A virtual collapse in productivity growth followed in 1973. The problem spread from blue-collar, goods-producing industries like manufacturing to white-collar service industries like retail and wholesale trade.

Slow productivity growth in the 1970s can be explained by the exhaustion of postwar growth opportunities, the energy crisis, and the onset of economic disruptions such as inflation and recession. After about 1979, however, the nation's continuing productivity woes become more difficult to explain away. Certain sectors of the economy have recovered, but others remain mired in extended slumps. The recovery has been strangely concentrated in the goods-producing sector, where output per hour has grown an average of 3% per year since 1979. During the same period, the service sector has seen almost no improvement in productivity.

---

*This article appeared in *PC Computing,* 2(4)(April, 1989):137–141. Copyright © 1989 Ziff-Davis Publishing Company. Reprinted by permission.

Computers and PCs have played an odd and rather troubling role in the recovery of manufacturing. The biggest contributor to productivity growth has been the manufacture of computer equipment. On the other hand, computers have been used heavily in service industries, where the productivity problem is now concentrated. Apparently we are getting better at making computers, but we still don't really know what to do with them once they're built.

Measurement Problems

Part of the dilemma may lie in the way we measure productivity. The standard measure is output per hour of work. The number of hours worked in the economy is not that hard to count, so the hardest task in assessing productivity is measuring real output—the value of the goods and services produced in a year, adjusted for inflation.

Inflation can be a sticking point. Although government statistical agencies collect precise data on the dollar value of production, in many cases it is hard to know how much of a yearly increase in value is due to inflation. Calculating the effect of inflation on tangible items such as cars and houses is difficult enough, but measuring its effect on the output of many service industries is nearly impossible. In the medical care industry, for example, the consumer price index overstates inflation and understates real output and productivity. The measuring process has not captured many of the tremendous technological advances in medical care, such as new drugs and new monitoring instruments.

The situation is even worse in banking and financial services, one of the hottest areas of the economy in recent years. The Department of Commerce doesn't even calculate a price index for financial services; it merely assumes that real output is always proportional to the number of hours worked. This approach categorically ignores any productivity increases in the entire banking sector. All the investments that these industries have made in computerizing their operations, from installing bigger and faster mainframes to building networks of automatic teller machines around the country to buying thousands of PCs, do not show up at all in any official measures of productivity.

Many other service industries encounter similar problems. PCs have had a dramatic effect on transportation industries, particularly the airline industry. It's hard to imagine the sheer volume of today's air travel market without computerized reservation systems linking mainframes, PCs and terminals around the world. The value of these systems is clear. United Airlines recently sold 50% of its voting interests in the Covia Corporation, developer and marketer of its Apollo system—generally considered second best to American's Sabre reservation system—for $499 million. But standard measures do a poor job of capturing the productivity improvements they bring.

In "Measurement Issues, the Productivity Slowdown, and the Explosion of Computer Power," a study published in 1995 by the Brookings Institution, Robert Gordon of Northwestern University and I looked at these and many other examples of poor measurement of productivity data. We concluded that the contribution of the computer is indeed being understated, but that the errors in measurement didn't account for the overall slowdown or the puzzle of the weakened service sector.

Independent sources of data for some industries find more improvement in efficiency than the standard numbers do, but still do not show the kind of growth one would expect. A study of productivity in banking, for example, found that output per hour grew about 2% per year in the 1980s, after growing at less than 0.5% per year from 1973 to 1979. That's an improvement, but only a small one.

Getting the Worst Out of Your PC

One problem is that companies are not properly using their computers and PCs to boost productivity. It's not hard to find PC applications that don't contribute anything to productivity. And PC vendors are little help: one expert at a large, full-line computer company was asked about the productivity benefits of his company's machines. Instead of answering, he turned to the PC on his desk and spoke in great detail about the calendar he kept on it. Keeping a calendar on a computer is handy, but a $4.95 pocket calendar may do just as well. Thousands of PCs spend most of their time performing such marginal tasks, and thousands more never even get switched on. Instead of serving as a tool to do real work, many a PC has been reduced to a high-tech status symbol.

And even when companies attempt to use PCs for substantive work, the benefits are often arguable. An executive at a large chemical company says that PC-based word processing lets his company put reports through as many as forty preliminary drafts. But he's not at all sure that the extra drafts have resulted in better reports or better decision making. Such doubts have led companies to question their levels of spending for word-processing hardware and software. "If this stuff is so good," they ask, "why do we still have the same number of secretaries?"

Similar problems can arise when the people who decide what computer equipment to buy do not understand how it will be used. In "Remedies for the Bureaucratic Mentality in Private Industry," published in 1985 by the SAM Advanced Management Journal, management consultant David Vondle argues that this results from a process he calls "staff infection." As companies grow and become more complex, staff groups begin to take over responsibility for keeping records, managing personnel, and so on. Staff infection keeps support decisions away from line managers, the people in direct contact with customers and/or workers. The line managers may know exactly what the company needs, but they have to plead with the staff groups for support. The staff groups tend to make hardware and software buying decisions based on their secondhand imaginings of what the company needs, not on the real needs of the line managers. Afraid to dilute their authority, data-processing departments often resist using PCs and cling to inefficient mainframes.

Paper Pushing, Not Productivity

Offices and service industries often struggle with these problems more than factories do. When offices are automated, managers will often resist dismissing employees and simply increase the flow of paper that departments produce, arguing that all the new reports are helping the company. They have an incentive to do this because companies often dispense salary and position according to the number of workers a manager supervises. True efficiency can mean career suicide.

In manufacturing operations, on the other hand, the bottom line is often easier to read, forcing companies to be more productive. The United States textile industry, for example, has installed innovative equipment that spins and weaves fabrics many times faster than previous models could. When the new machinery came in, plant managers had no choice but to cut back drastically on the labor required to produce a yard of cloth. Thus they kept their industry afloat in the face of stiff foreign competition.

Stories like the above are rare when one talks about PCs and productivity. Instead, most companies tell horror stories about their computer operations. And while anecdotes don't prove anything, they do suggest a general problem.

The revolution in computer hardware has lowered the cost of information. The price of a million calculations has fallen again and again. But the value of information remains difficult to assess. Maybe company reports really are better after forty drafts, or at least after five or ten. No one wants to go back to the old days when entire documents had to be retyped every time a single word was changed, but where do you draw the line? I don't know, and neither do most company managers. When a department is computerized with no cut in personnel, the manager can rationalize the increased costs by telling the boss about all the new statistics he can produce. Maybe the new information is vital; maybe it isn't. We haven't figured out how to value and assimilate the mountains of information computers lay at our feet. Nor have we learned how to tell which information is worthless. A learning process always involves a good deal of trial and error. When a company cannot even decide whether or not its approach has paid off, it is going to have trouble improving that approach.

PCs have changed the nature of the services many industries provide. No wonder companies and government statistical agencies have trouble evaluating the changes and incorporating them into measures of productivity. It takes time for productivity to improve in response to a new technology. In fact, it often gets worse before it gets better. The learning process can be surprisingly long. According to a study by Professor Kim Clark and colleagues at the Harvard Business School, the newest and most up-to-date factories are often not the most productive ones.

Every time a company introduces a new production process, its employees must move along a learning curve before they can make the new technology pay off. PCs are hardly new, but the service sector is still learning how to use them effectively. In some applications, the hardware has outstripped the software. The financial services sector, for example, has had difficulty developing software to fit the operating procedures of individual banks. Interstate banking regulations have allowed thousands of small banks to stay in business. Because each of these banks has developed its own operating procedures, standard software packages are useless. And the companies that write custom software for banks have had their own problems. Frank Reilly, a Washington, D.C. consultant to the banking industry, says the companies that have written packages for Washington-area banks have had trouble remaining solvent. After they finish the programming, a seemingly endless series of bugs continues to soak up money, raising the overall cost of development to the point where it becomes prohibitive.

Profit Taking

Mistakes can keep PCs from raising productivity, but even when individual companies do everything right, overall industry productivity may not rise. That's because companies may use PCs to enhance their own profits at the expense of their competitors, adding nothing to the output of the economy.

Competition is the life force of a market economy. Adam Smith's capitalist theory postulates that the invisible hand of competition guides the economy for the betterment of all, even though each person is motivated by a desire for individual profit. But sometimes the invisible hand misses the mark. Markets do not operate in all areas, and the lack of a market can distort the economy by burying costs in areas where the producers are not liable. There is no market in clean air, for example, so the invisible hand encourages factories and car owners to spew out air pollution. The polluters do not incur the cost of cleaning up the mess they make.

Sometimes companies see ways to make a profit, not by increasing the value of goods and services they produce, but by taking away profit from someone else. In this kind of zero-sum game, one person's gain equals another's loss: the totals remain the same, but the distribution changes.

Companies fight over who gets the slices of the pie, rather than working to increase the size of the pie.

Computers have greatly increased the scope of these zero-sum redistributive activities. According to a data-processing manager at a large Hartford, Connecticut-based insurance company, it's clear why PCs have not raised productivity in the insurance industry. His company uses its computers to create demographic profiles of potential customers and employs computer-aided telemarketing to steal customers away from its rivals. These marketers are not looking for new insurance customers to expand their own business; they are merely trying to get existing customers to switch their policies.

What Is the Solution?

The mystifying reasons behind the PC's failure to boost productivity significantly are tied to the nature of what computers do. Computers analyze and process information. Dazzling technological advances allow them to do this much more easily and cheaply than they did just a few years ago. As information processing got less expensive, companies began to do more of it. But the temptation to do too much can be overwhelming. If it's so easy, why not provide more graphs, more tables, more three-color charts, and more desktop-published glossy reports and brochures?

David Vondle suggests that companies should assign values to their information flows and use these values to assess the performance of white-collar departments. What is it really worth to process shipping invoices in a day instead of a week? What real benefits come from knowing a breakdown of sales by city for each month?

These questions go right to the heart of the problem, but the answers are not at all clear. What do you use to calculate the value of the knowledge? Using the results of the valuations can be even harder. Any attempt to monitor the activities of white-collar employees can be expected to run into stiff—and possibly legitimate—opposition from most employees and many managers.

Are PCs Helping or Hurting Productivity?

The move to PCs has obviously encouraged some wasted expenditures, but as PC prices continue to decline, the scope of that waste will decline as well. At least the cost of PC paperweights for status-hungry executives is less than it was. On the plus side, PCs can free line managers from the tyranny of staff departments and encourage companies to apply the technology to bottom-line activities such as lowering production costs, serving customers, and cutting inventory. In this context, the PC learning process speeds up as line personnel quickly find out which approaches work and which do not. Accountability follows naturally.

For the improvements to spread to the big picture, senior executives as well as line managers must learn to understand computers. Today, the people making decisions about PC investments often have little knowledge of the technology. Conversely, those who recommend the technology often do not fully understand the company's overall strategy or the general needs of its employees and customers. Companies must invest in computer training for senior executives so that they can understand the PC's strengths and weaknesses in pursuing the company's goals.

Research has a role to play, too. The United States remains the world leader in pure science, resting on a still unmatched scientific establishment. Unfortunately, we have not always done so well when it comes to applying science for commercial goals. We need research aimed at developing organizational innovations to improve the efficiency of white-collar activities, particularly using PCs more effectively. It would make sense to poll different companies' experiences with PCs, and to try to isolate the factors that lead some organizations to do well while others struggle. We also need to work on developing basic models of how information flows and contributes to an organization's output.

Concern over how well PCs have paid back the enormous investment in them is legitimate. But most of the problems are symptoms of the learning process, which, though it can seem agonizingly slow, is proceeding.

American companies are wrestling PC technology to the ground and learning how to shape it to fit real-world needs. Once the current problems are licked, PCs have the potential to make a major contribution to productivity in the future.

P·A·R·T · III

K

Information Technology and the Productivity Challenge

Paul Attewell

The widespread adoption of computers in American business throughout the 1970s was spurred, in part, by the expectation that this new technology would provide a boom in productivity. One of the surprises of the "information technology revolution" has been that in the twenty years that have passed since then, the expected upswing in productivity has failed to materialize. This puzzle has stimulated a lot of research, which in turn has modified ideas we once had about how information technology would be used, and has given us new insights into changes that occur in workplaces when they computerize.

Economists use the term productivity to refer to the efficiency of firms or of individual employees. Productivity is usually conceptualized as a ratio of output (goods or services produced) divided by the inputs (labor, capital, materials) used to produce that output. If we focus on labor productivity, the ratio becomes the amount of product produced per worker per year, or some equivalent. If computers can speed human work, and hence allow a firm to produce the same amount of goods as before, but with fewer human hours of work, labor productivity should increase markedly.

Higher productivity has a number of important consequences for society at large. If a new technology enables firms to produce a given volume of goods or services with less labor, then firms' wage costs decrease, and (with competition) the price of the goods produced should go down. This in turn means that as a productive technology spreads through the economy, a given amount of wages should purchase more goods and services than before, so the standard of living rises. Historically this is what happened during the industrial revolution in nineteenth-century America, when the transition from hand to machine work took place. Productivity rose considerably, and so did the average standard of living. Conversely, a period of stagnation in productivity is associated with stagnant real wages. This occurred in the United States from the early 1970s until about 1990. Productivity growth slowed to about 65% of its previous level (Baumol, 1989, p. 614), and hence real wages, and the average standard of living for Americans, crawled to a near stop for almost twenty years (Levy, 1987).

A second implication of technologically induced productivity growth concerns employment. If information technology allows each employee to produce more than before, then a firm may well need fewer employees. (This was one of the central marketing messages put out by computer manufacturers seeking to encourage corporations to invest in computing.) Rapid technological change is therefore associated with job loss and unemployment. Based on estimates that computers would raise productivity, the Nobel Prize winner Wassily Leontief and his colleague Faye Duchin (1986, p. 12), predicted that information technologies would displace 11 million American workers by 1990 and 20 million by the year 2000, a shrinkage of about 11% of the labor force.

Last, productivity growth is important in the competitive struggle between nations to sell goods on the world market. Although the United States is considered to have a higher level of economic productivity than Japan, Germany, and other industrialized nations, its lead was eroding in the 1970s and 1980s because rates of productivity growth in those nations were growing faster than in the United States. Thus productivity growth, and the role of information technology, became caught up in a national debate during the 1980s concerning the loss of various markets to foreign competition and a perceived crisis in United States manufacturing competitiveness (National Academy of Engineering, 1988).

So the stakes surrounding technologically driven productivity growth are high: an increased standard of living for American workers, improved competitive status *vis a vis* other nations, and the downside—serious unemployment or job displacement if productivity growth is rapid.

As the 1970s and 1980s went by, economists and other commentators became increasingly puzzled by the fact that United States productivity didn't seem to be rising much, despite escalating investments in Information Technology (IT). The service sector was particularly baffling. This growing sector had consumed the lion's share of investment in computers and information technologies, yet productivity in services grew slowly during the 1970s and 1980s.

Steven Roach (1986) used the term "the productivity paradox" for this puzzle, and a stream of studies followed, seeking evidence of whether computer investments were or were not resulting in productivity increases in firms and in whole industries.

Detailed reviews of the literature on the productivity paradox are found in Attewell (1994) and Brynjolfsson (1993), so I will only summarize major themes here. The preponderance of research during the 1970s and 1980s did fail to show any productivity increase from information technology in representative samples of firms or in whole industries. In trying to explain this, researchers made the following kinds of arguments: (1) some suggested that it takes a long time for new technology to pay off, because firms first have to learn new ways of doing business and develop new procedures to take advantage of the potential of the technology (David, 1989); (2) others argued that the levels of investment in IT during the 1970s and 1980s, although they seemed large, were not big enough to be detected in available government productivity statistics (Panko, 1991); (3) many scholars noted that government productivity statistics for whole industries are problematic. It is not easy to measure the outputs of services like banking and insurance, hospitals or government. Thus the productivity paradox may be due to measurement problems, and may not be real; (4) yet others suggested that the paradox was real, and stemmed from forces within firms and the economy, which absorb the potential gains from IT in ways (discussed below) that cancel potential productivity improvements.

Proponents of the first two arguments—that we have to wait for IT payoff to manifest itself—gained a considerable boost from the presentation, by Brynjolfsson and Hitt (1993), of the first convincing evidence from the 1990s that did show a quite considerable profitability and productivity payoff from IT investment in a sample of large United States firms. For many, this evidence suggested that the productivity paradox had gone away. I am a little more skeptical, for two reasons. First, Brynjolfsson and Hitt's own data show unusual patterns, including a productivity payoff that dropped to zero in the most recent year studied. Second, the firm level improvements in productivity they observed have still not clearly manifested themselves in industrial level statistics that the government keeps. After an initial jump in productivity after the recession of 1990/1991, United States productivity, especially in services, seems to have slowed down again.

Time may resolve this issue, and IT investments may now be proving more productive than in previous decades. But for the moment, I believe it is useful to summarize the fourth position above, which identifies a series of mechanisms within firms and the economy at large that attenuate or absorb the potential productivity gains of computer technologies.

Based on my own fieldwork in several computerized workplaces, as well as drawing on others' research (detailed in Attewell, 1994), I believe that the following mechanisms are significant.

The Formalization of Communication

Most studies of productivity improvements from information technology focus on changes within a single communication modality or channel. For example, researchers compare the speed of computer word processing compared to typing or writing. However, new technologies can also shift a communication that might have occurred in one channel into another channel. For example, a manager may decide to send a memo on electronic mail, rather than phoning someone. Different communications channels have quite different speeds of transmission: speech is potentially five times faster than typing (Gould and Boies, 1983). Thus a new information technology can simultaneously improve productivity within one modality or channel (e.g., the shift from typing to word processing), yet can also degrade productivity if it shifts communications from faster to slower channels (e.g., from speech to typed communication). This effect is compounded by differences in the completeness or "wordiness" of communications in different channels. Linguists have noted that humans are more terse in some settings (where they assume a lot of shared background of one another) than in others. Less has to be said. But in other settings people spell out their ideas or elaborate, so that less shared background knowledge is assumed to exist. This phenomenon is known as *indexicality.*

The degree of indexicality can differ markedly across communication channels or modalities. Face-to-face communication is often, but not always, highly indexical or terse. Written communication is typically more lengthy or less indexical. Experiments using the same business "message" have shown that the message is expressed in a considerably more elaborated way when it is intended for a typed/written medium, than when it is going to be heard by the recipient.

The implication is that to the extent that IT investment has focused on the written/typed medium of communication, by providing electronic mail, word processing, and so on, it may have shifted communications that would otherwise have occurred in the relatively fast and indexical spoken medium into the relatively slower written one. This process may be called the *formalization of communication.* Writ large, it means that IT may have had the unintended effect of increasing the amount of formalized typed communication within organizations, at the expense of faster spoken communication. This would offset some of the potential productivity gains from IT.

There is no systematic evidence concerning the size of this formalization effect. There is ethnographic evidence that e-mail and word processing have increased the volume and scope of written communication in computerized workplaces, and that Manufacturing Resource Planning (MRP) and similar computerized software have led to a formalization of communications around workflow and inventory. There are also experimental studies that demonstrate the speed differences between different communications channels. But there are no hard data on how much of an impact this might have on productivity.

The Quality/Quantity Trade-Off

For many white-collar jobs, the introduction of IT seems to alter preexisting balances between quality and quantity of task performance, tempting individuals to improve quality at the expense of quantity. Often this change in quality is primarily a matter of improvement in the appearance or aesthetic aspects of output rather than in its substance. But whether "real" or superficial, improvements in quality are achieved either by a slowing of work speed (a decrease in output per hour) or, more commonly, by using any time freed up through IT to elaborate the quality of documents.

With personal computers, employees produce more drafts of documents, and make more corrections than before. They also spend more time on fonts, graphics, charts, and appearance. Lotus 1-2-3 enables managers to consider more complex "what if" spreadsheet models, where once they may have labored over a single simple model. Computers have also led to a proliferation of charts and graphics and quantitative data in organizational communications.

This shift toward quality is an expression of pride in work, and as such is a positive gain for individual employees. It is also a reflection of the fact that the appearance of documents is important in many bureaucratic settings because it affects the *authority* of the message. Whether this shift improves efficiency is a matter for skepticism, however.

In a study of personal computing in the IRS, Pentland (1989) developed measures of productivity for several thousands of auditors. He found that *subjectively*, auditors using PCs were sure that computers enabled them to do better work, even if they didn't believe they were able to do more work in a given time. When comparing these self-report data to "objective measures" of audit quality and quantity, Pentland found that computers failed to increase either productivity or quality, and that there was evidence that productivity (quantity of work done in a given time) was actually lowered by computer use. In short, IRS auditors felt strongly they were doing better work using PCs, but their productivity had degraded.

The implication of the quality/quantity trade-off is that the relative control over their work that many white-collar workers enjoy means that potential productivity gains resulting from computerization are absorbed by those workers, who pursue goals other than simply speeding up their work. The productivity potential does not appear as an increase in the work output per hour.

The Volume of Work Expands with Computerization

When Leontief and Duchin (1986) developed their estimates of the effects of computerization on employment, they assumed (as do many others) that there is a given amount of work to be done in a firm, and that if the productivity of individual workers increases, fewer workers will be needed to produce a given output. While this logic is sensible, it is incomplete, for it neglects the extent to which improvements in the efficiency of processing information within organizations has simultaneously led to large increases in the demand for information work within those firms. In other words, computers may make information work easier to do, but they thereby increase the amount of such work to be done.

In economic terms, one would say that computers have reduced the unit cost of information work, but this has resulted in rapidly increased demand for information work within firms. Thus the total cost (or effort) spent on information work hasn't gone down nearly as much as one might expect, if one hadn't allowed for the burgeoning demand. For example, as CAD software makes certain aspects of drafting and designing work easier, the number of drawings produced before a design is settled on also increases (Salzman, 1989). As it becomes easier to re-edit and correct documents, the amount of revisions and rewriting has skyrocketed.

There is considerable ethnographic evidence for this mechanism, and there have also been systematic efforts to measure its importance. In the author's study of 187 New York area firms, assessments were made of the changes of employment and workload resulting from the introduction of specific computer applications during the mid-1980s. Applications were studied (489 in all), which included tasks such as processing accounts receivable, or querying inventory levels and preparing shipping slips, or a system for analyzing loan risks. On average, mean output per worker rose by 78% compared to the immediately prior technology. However, overall employment in these applications didn't decline, because the volume of work done, the output or workload, also jumped by 76%, effectively absorbing almost all of the potential productivity gain in doing extra work. Clerks produced more billing notices than before, or made more queries of databases, or generated more reports. Kraut, Dumais, and Koch (1989) found a similar pattern in a different setting.

In these and other examples, the amount of information or paper work done in organizations increased with computerization, thus absorbing time and other resources that might otherwise have been freed up. The increased productivity was not manifested as fewer people producing more goods.

Information and the Managerial Taste for Control

One particular arena in which the demand for information has grown precipitously within firms following computerization is in the proliferation of Management Information Systems (MIS). Compared with twenty years ago, today's corporation is awash with computerized data about the numbers of items produced or sold per employee per hour, breakdowns of cash flow, costs, inventory levels, accounts payable and receivable, and so on.

This data is far more detailed and more current than anything seen in precomputer days. It would have taken an army of cost clerks to obtain such information in the days before computing, and even then they couldn't have collected it fast enough to keep current. Today, this information is a by-product of transaction processing and other databases that are central to normal functioning in computerized businesses.

MIS data has affected the culture of American management. Writers talk of "management by numbers" or "management by facts" to describe the ways that top executives are able to scrutinize detailed performance measures (Pascale and Athos, 1981). MIS give managers the sense that they are in control, that they know what is going on within their jurisdiction without actually having to look at the shop or office floor. But MIS data is not free. On the contrary it places a large direct burden on companies. Weill (1988) calculated that "Informational IT" constituted 56% of total IT investment costs within one manufacturing industry.

MIS also has an indirect cost, the substantial amount of work it creates for managers. In many firms I have studied, managers spend days per month looking at multiple MIS performance indicators and preparing reports for higher management about why certain indicators are looking bad. Requests for new machinery or investment have to be accompanied by rationales including spreadsheet models of cost and payoff data drawing from MIS data, often illustrated by pie charts and other graphics. An earlier generation of managers might have made such a request in a simple memo or presentation.

Since the information culture within firms is driven by top management, who feel it gives them greater control, it is rarely opposed. But it has enormous costs in terms of software, hardware, and labor time spent in collecting and analyzing data. Some critics go further and suggest that management by numbers actively contributes to our productivity decline by substituting for more effective managerial work. Perhaps the most eminent of these critics is W. Edwards Deming, the father of statistical quality control, who noted:

> To manage one must lead. To lead one must understand the work that he and his people are responsible for. . . . It is easier for an incoming manager to short-circuit his need for learning and his responsibilities, and instead focus on the far end, to manage the outcome—get reports on quality, . . . inventory, sales, people. Focus on outcome is not an effective way to improve a process or an activity. . . . management by numerical goal is an attempt to manage without knowledge of what to do, and in fact is usually management by fear. . . . Anyone may now understand the fallacy of "management by numbers." (Deming, 1986, p. 76)

A phenomenon that may well be related to the expansion of computerized systems is the rapid increase in the proportion and absolute numbers of managers in most United States industries. Although there is a widespread perception that growth in administrative overhead implies employment of more clerks and secretaries, analysis of occupational statistics indicates otherwise. Managerial employment growth, not clerical growth, has fueled two decades of administrative expansion in the United States, and has been greatest in those service industries where computerization has dominated. There is circumstantial evidence, then, that information technology fuels administrative "bloat." Recent efforts by many giant corporations to delay and reduce managerial numbers are an attempt to reverse this overall trend. But so far the managerial layoffs, while large, have not stopped the secular trend to increased managerial numbers.

Increasing numbers of managers, and high expenditures on MIS, absorb potential productivity gains from information technology. What is gained in one part of the organization is consumed in another. Automating a secretary or clerk out of existence but adding a manager or computer professional in the process will not improve a firm's productivity.

Competition versus Productivity

In the 1960s, information technologies were primarily conceived as methods for lowering the costs of processing various kinds of highly automated paper work, so-called "transaction processing systems." In the 1980s, the marketing message changed, and much was made of the use of computer systems as competitive weapons to wrest market share from rival firms (known as "Strategic Information Systems.") While these two goals of information systems aren't mutually exclusive, they do have quite different implications for productivity.

A firm that successfully uses information technology as a strategic weapon seeks to increase its volume of business, and thereby its profits, at the expense of its competitors. This typically means that the successful firm will expand, but the firm need not improve its productivity (output per unit of input) in order to increase its profits. An increase in output or sales at the old level of productivity will still generate increased profits for the firm.

The productivity or profitability of an industry as a whole is not improved through this strategic use of IT. One is redistributing market share, not creating more wealth with less inputs. In this situation we have a disjuncture between what benefits an individual firm and what benefits an industry or economy.

American Hospital Supply Inc. (AHS) is widely used in business schools as a case study of outstanding use of strategic information systems. By installing order-entry terminals in the purchasing departments of its customer hospitals, AHS made it easier for customers to order medical supplies, and speeded up its response time to orders. With this innovative use of IT, AHS was able to develop an enviable degree of customer loyalty, and its sales and market share boomed. But analysis of its annual reports shows that several indices of AHS's productivity showed no improvement at all during this period. This did not hurt the firm: it was growing at its competitors' expense and was profitable. This becomes a cause for concern, however, when translated into an economy-wide phenomenon. For if IT investment is focused on the strategic goal of increasing market share, and is shunted away from productivity-enhancing areas, costs may increase, leaving such industries highly vulnerable to foreign competitors who maintain a cost-lowering strategy.

The introduction of Automatic Teller Machines (ATMs) illustrates another aspect of Strategic IT. ATMs proved to be very popular with customers. Banks that introduced them early on gained market share at the expense of slower banks. But rapidly, competitor banks had to follow suit. While no consumer bank can hope to survive today without having them, automatic tellers have not generated large new profits for banks. On the contrary, the highly competitive environment in banking has made it difficult to charge customers for ATM service. Nor have ATMs allowed banks to cut costs by employing fewer tellers (Haynes, 1990). Customers use them to make extra transactions that they wouldn't have made before: for example, they take out smaller amounts of money at more frequent intervals.

Use of technology to provide an added service to customers is a potent competitive strategy, as the ATM experience shows. But it is also an expensive undertaking. Each company is coerced to follow the leader, rapidly investing in a new technology that may not make profits or increase productivity, but that is necessary if one wants to maintain one's market share. In more and more industries, firms have to make large IT investments to "stay in the game," in a private-sector equivalent of the arms race, whether or not these investments improve productivity or profitability.

What is new about this is the rapidity with which IT service innovations can be copied by competitors, the short time-window for recouping one's investment in the innovation, and the apparent reluctance of customers to pay for service improvements, compared to their willingness to pay for better tangible goods. Customers clearly benefit from the provision of below-cost, better service from this kind of IT. However, the phenomenon looks less benign when one realizes that having to invest in IT in order to stay in the game, and suffering as a result poor returns on IT investment, detracts from capital accumulation. This would not be serious except for the fact that it occurs in an era of intense competition and productivity stagnation, when investment needs to be productively deployed.

Interorganizational Processes

The information revolution is a self-fueling process: improvements in the availability of information lead to ever greater demands for information. According to Jacques Ellul (1954), "new technologies create needs which only more of that technology can fulfill." In the 1970s the introduction of computers into hospitals and doctors' offices had led to a dramatic increase in the number of computer-generated duplicate bills presented by clients for payment. Medical insurance companies were inundated, as their human claims process tried to avoid paying for the same medical service twice. The insurance companies responded by introducing expensive computerized claims payment systems to deal with this double-billing assault from others' computers.

This kind of dynamic is seen throughout our economy as relationships between organizations become more information intensive. The possibility of computerized data has enabled government to demand more and more detailed information from hospitals, banks, military contractors, and universities. It has stimulated bank customers to expect 24-hour information on their accounts, and users of overnight delivery services to demand instant tracking of their packages. Firms expect to be able to tap into their suppliers' computers to find out about their status of orders, inventory levels, and so on. Car dealerships are required to provide the auto companies with detailed breakdowns of what sold in the last week.

Whatever the long-term implications of such phenomena, in the immediate term IT is placing greater burdens of information-work upon organizations, and firms have to make sizable investments of personnel and equipment to provide this kind of information access. In highly competitive environments, or when facing legally mandated demands, corporations may have no way of passing on the costs of all this information provision to those who demand it. Thus the burden of information provision absorbs or attenuates the benefits accruing from increased productivity elsewhere in the organization.

Conclusion

The processes described above are mechanisms whereby the potential benefits of productivity improvements from IT become absorbed within organizations. Productivity improvements never see the light of day because they are attenuated or canceled out by various forces within organizations. In the most general terms, we can see that processes of *goal displacement* underlie much of the productivity paradox. Instead of using IT to attain the goal of productivity improvement, IT is put to other uses within organizations. Individual employees shift the goal of IT from quantity of production to quality or appearance. Managers shift IT investment into costly MIS data that is helpful to them for control purposes, but which doesn't necessarily enhance productivity. Competition, and the search for more customers, leads to big "strategic" IT investments that may bring profits to the early adopter, but that place burdens on the industry as a whole. And much IT is used to produce information and other forms of service for customers or other organizations, services that are frequently not paid for.

To some extent this is not a bad thing. Job satisfaction for workers, and enhanced service for customers, are positive outcomes. But if we return to the idea that productivity growth is central to improvements in our national standard of living and our international competitiveness, then the deflection of IT away from productivity goals is a troubling outcome; for these mechanisms or processes could undermine or at least slow down wage growth and capital accumulation. The research around the productivity paradox teaches that there are alternative benefits (and risks) from information technology, and that wittingly or unconsciously trade-offs are occurring between these different goals or outcomes. The fruits of the information technology revolution can be wasted. That is the lesson of the productivity paradox.

References

Attewell, Paul (1994). "Information Technology and the Productivity Paradox." Chapter 2 in Douglas Harris, Paul Goodman, and D. Scott Sink (eds.), *Organizational Linkages: Understanding the Productivity Paradox*. National Academy of Sciences Press, Washington, D.C.

Baumol, William (1989). "Is There a U.S. Productivity Crisis?" *Science*, 243 (February):611–615.

Brynjolfsson, Erik (1993). "The Productivity Paradox of Information Technology." *Communications of the ACM*, 36(12)(December):67–77.

Brynjolfsson, E., and L. Hitt (1993). "Is Information Systems Spending Productive? New Evidence and New Results." International Conference on Information Systems, Orlando, Florida.

David, Paul (1989). "Computer and Dynamo: The Modern Productivity Paradox in a Not-too-distant Mirror." Working paper. Center for Economic Policy Research, Stanford University.

Deming, W. Edwards (1986). *Out of the Crisis*. Massachusetts Institute of Technology, Center for Advanced Engineering Study, Cambridge, MA.

Ellul, Jacques (1954). *La Technique ou l'enjeu du siecle*. Librarie Armand Colin, Paris. (English translation published as *The Technological Society*. Vintage, New York.)

Gould, John, and Stephen Boies (1983). "Human Factors Challenges in Creating a Principal Support Office System—the Speech Filing System Approach." *ACM Transactions in Office Information Systems*, 1(4)(October):273–298.

Haynes, R. M. (1990). "The ATM at Twenty: A Productivity Paradox." *National Productivity Review*, 9(3):273–280.

Kraut, Robert, Susan Dumais, and Susan Koch (1989). "Computerization, Productivity, and the Quality of Worklife." *Communications of the ACM*, 32:220–238.

Leontief, Wassily, and Faye Duchin (1986). *The Future Impact of Automation on Workers*. Oxford University Press, New York.

Levy, Frank (1987). *Dollars and Dreams: The Changing American Income Distribution*. Russell Sage, New York.

National Academy of Engineering (1988). *The Technological Dimensions of International Competitiveness.* National Academy of Engineering, Washington, D.C.

Panko, R. (1991). "Is Office Productivity Stagnant?" *MIS Quarterly,* (June):190–203.

Pascale, Richard T., and Anthony G. Athos (1981). *The Art of Japanese Management.* Warner Books, New York.

Pentland, Brian (1989). "Use and Productivity in Personal Computing." *Proceedings of the Tenth International Conference on Information Systems* (ICIS, Boston, Dec. 4–6):211–222.

Roach, Stephen S. (1986). "The Productivity Puzzle." *Economic Perspectives,* April 10, 1986. Morgan Stanley & Co., New York.

Salzman, Harold (1989). "Computer Aided Design: Limitations in Automating Design and Drafting." *IEEE Transactions on Engineering Management,* 36(4):252–261.

Weill, Peter (1988). "The Relationship between Investment in Information Technology and Firm Performance in the Manufacturing Sector." Ph.D. thesis. Stern School of Business Administration, New York University.

P·A·R·T · III

L

Where Are the Payoffs from Computerization? Technology, Learning, and Organizational Change

John Leslie King

The Productivity Paradox

Computer technology was first applied commercially in the 1950s to more fully automate procedures such as accounting that had already been partially automated through use of electronic record machines and calculators. The rationale behind this computerization was to gain the productivity improvements that had long been associated with the substitution of machinery for labor. Computing equipment had established a track record of substantial accomplishments. By 1840 Charles Babbage had proven that a mechanical calculator could be used to correct errors in the British Navy's navigation tables (Morrison and Morrison, 1961; Lindgren, 1987). Herman Hollerith's remarkable card-punching and sorting machines had enabled the U.S. Census Bureau to tabulate the 1890 Census in just over two years, compared to the eight required for the 1880 Census (Goldstine, 1972; Bohme and Wyatt, 1991). During the first half of the twentieth century, Burroughs calculators, National Cash Register machines, and IBM card-sorting equipment had all been used to speed up information processing, reduce error rates, and generally improve the flow of information in corporations (Chase, 1980). Digital computers, developed first to assist the military in calculating ballistic trajectories, followed in this tradition. It is not surprising that organizations of all kinds embraced the general purpose digital computer as a tool to enhance productivity.

The growth of the computer and information-processing industries since 1950 suggests that every expectation of productivity payoffs had been fulfilled. During the great postwar boom in the United States economy, computerization was a hallmark, if not a driver, of economic progress. By the late 1970s, however, United States dominance of the world economy had begun to weaken and a protracted era of economic uncertainty had begun. By the early 1980s, the first tentative questions were being raised about the productivity payoffs of computerization. In 1981 King and Kraemer likened organizational investments in computer technology to audiophile investments in expensive stereo equipment. Fancy computers were required because they could handle more information, in the same way that more expensive stereo equipment was required because the listener could hear less noise. The question of the real goal—processing only the right information, or listening to the music instead of the noise—seemed to be lost. They concluded their assessment with this prediction:

> [C]omputing costs will not only continue to grow across organizations, but the rate of increase in cost of computing will go higher. . . . We suspect that ten years from now, the problematic nature of computing and other information technologies in organizations will be a major concern of both top management and users in organizations. (King and Kraemer, 1981: 124)

In fact, it took less than ten years for the concerns about the growing investment in organizational computerization to make the front page of major business publications. *Fortune* magazine's May 26, 1986 issue carried a cover story with the title "The Puny Payoff from Office Computers," and a caustic article inside with the following rhetorical exchange: "Have the millions of computers purchased by US businesses brought any overall improvement in productivity? Surprisingly, the best information available says no." Two years later, *Business Week's* June 6, 1988 issue carried a cover with the bold title, "The Productivity Paradox," beneath a bright yellow slug asking, "Can American Compete?" Inside, the cover article answered its own question about weak productivity numbers with this observation: "It's technology, of course, that should do the trick. So bring on automation, from office PC's to process-control devices. In theory, productivity should soar. In practice, the promise of technology hasn't been fulfilled."

Business magazines are seldom sources of rigorous productivity data, but they do reflect the opinions and moods of business experts on topics such as productivity. With respect to computers and productivity, these moods have been unreliable and inconsistent. For example, *Fortune* soon followed its "puny payoffs" article with a new article titled, "Here Come the Payoffs from PC's." Yet, in March of 1992 the business section of *The Los Angeles Times* carried a front-page article titled, "The Productivity Paradox," suggesting that the payoffs of computers were as elusive as ever.

Lester Thurow's popular book on international competition, *Head to Head*, carried this quote: "New technology, new hardware, new software, and new skills are all going into the American office, but negative productivity is coming out. . . . This is one place where the problem is not underinvestment" (Thurow, 1992:169). Yet the June 14, 1993 issue of *Business Week* announced "The Technology Payoff" in a cover story.

Given all the uncertainty, perhaps the experts can clear up the confusion. A distinguished group of economists convened in November of 1993 under the auspices of the Organization for Economic Cooperation and Development (OECD) and the U.S. National Science Foundation to address the question. They could not reach consensus on the facts, but only on the need for more research. The uncertainty of the payoffs from computerization is evident almost everywhere one looks. The spring of 1994 brought newspaper articles on the looming computerization disaster in the Federal Aviation Administration's multibillion dollar modernization program for the nation's air traffic control system. By the summer of 1994, newspapers were carrying stories of a $44 million computer system fiasco in California's Department of Motor Vehicles. Yet that same month, *Fortune*'s cover story (June 27) was "Guide to the New Economy," with a special story titled "The Productivity Payoff Arrives," signaling that computerization has finally been proven a moneymaker.

What is the answer? Are computers giving organizations greater productivity? Does anybody really know? Where do the stories reported by these journalists come from? And what do they mean for those who wish to make sound decisions about computerization at the personal, organizational, or social level? This article attempts to put the Productivity Paradox in perspective by reviewing the premises from which these arguments arose, and the evidence used to make them convincing enough to attract noted business journalists. In the process, we will examine possible underlying causes for the paradox, concentrating on the more subtle and important transformations taking place in our economy and society. The focus is not on the question of whether computers lead to improved productivity, but rather the lessons we should draw from the fact that the productivity benefits of computers have been called into question in the first place.

Origins of the Arguments

The Productivity Paradox is produced by the collision of two conflicting viewpoints. One is the long-standing expectation that computerization does, or at least will, produce productivity improvements in organizations that computerize. The other is economic evidence that productivity in those industries most heavily computerized in the past two decades has remained flat. Given the huge investments in information technology, flat productivity growth forces the question. "Where are the payoffs from computerization?" There would be no paradox if there were no evidence to spoil expectations of productivity, but it is also important to remember that there would be no paradox if people had lower expectations about productivity. In fact, expectations are and have long been high on this point. Traces of these expectations appear in the advertisements of computer companies, but the expectation of productivity is a totemic element of American popular culture for many years, from the robots in Kurt Vonnegut's 1952 novel *Player Piano* that improve labor productivity to the point that everyone is provided for and almost no one is employed in a meaningful job, to the chummy C-3PO of the 1977 movie *Star Wars* who speaks over six million languages and is a master of protocol, productivity from computers is part of our cultural expectations.

Scholars have built sound arguments to show why productivity payoffs could be expected from computerization. In 1958 Leavitt and Whisler published a *Harvard Business Review* article titled "Management in the 1980s" that claimed that computerization would enable radical restructuring of organizations by the elimination of large numbers of middle managers made redundant by computerized decision making and information handling (Leavitt and Whisler, 1958). Two years later Herbert Simon published his book, *The New Science of Management Decision*, which explained the logic underlying claims made implicitly in the Leavitt and Whisler article (Simon, 1960). He explained that the development of both *technology* in the form of computers and *technique* in the form of operations research and management science methods would usher in a new era of control over the tasks of management that had long been relegated to the status of "art" or "craft." Both of these seminal works helped shape the thinking of a whole generation of managers, both directly and indirectly, by influencing the views of graduate students who would become the faculty of management schools.

For a quarter century these predictions slipped by with little fanfare. Management in the mid-1980s looked a lot like management in the late 1950s, and management decision was a "science" only in academic journal titles. Late in the 1980s, however, two new articles appeared in *Harvard Business Review* that resurrected the issues joined by Leavitt and Whisler and Simon. Applegate, Cash, and Mills's 1988 article titled "Information Technology and Tomorrow's Manager" argued that computer technology would soon transform organizations in fundamental ways, and that the managers of these new organizations would require special skills in use of the technology (Applegate, Cash, and Mills, 1988). They also, in an appendix to the article, interviewed Leavitt and Whisler, concluding that the predictions made thirty years earlier, although delayed, would soon come to pass. Management guru Peter Drucker also published a *Harvard Business Review* article that year titled "The Coming of the New Organization," arguing that the organization of the near future would be an "information organization," dependent on, among other things, successful use of information technology (Drucker, 1988).

These writings from the late 1950s and the late 1980s are a small sample of what has been written about the coming changes resulting from computerization in organizations. The striking thing about them is their future-imperfect voice: the changes are always coming, but they seem never to arrive. One would think that hard-headed business people would have called the question earlier on when the promised changes would materialize, but this did not happen for two reasons. First, there was the astonishing growth in technological capability and price-performance in the computing world. Each year since the mid-1970s and the arrival of the minicomputer it has been possible to buy more power with less money, thus forestalling any top-management crackdown on expenditures. Second, many of the tasks that were computerized in the 1950s and 1960s were so completely interwoven into routine organizational operations that there was no alternative but to keep supporting and enhancing them with new computerization expenditures. Instead of putting the brakes on new computerization investments, managers approved new projects and upgrades to earlier systems. Each year, overall organizational investments in computerization grew substantially throughout the decades of the 1960s, 1970s, and 1980s.

An important change occurred in the mid-1980s, however, when the discussion about computerization payoffs turned from the qualitative to the quantitative. Publications began to appear using data from national econometric time-series such as the National Accounts to "test" the proposition that the corporate investment in the technology was yielding productivity. The results were surprising, to say the least. The consistent failure of investment in computerization to correlate with productivity gains in the economy prompted Nobel Prize-winning economist Robert Solow to comment that productivity from computers seemed to show up everywhere but in the numbers. Excellent reviews of these analyses can be found in Attewell (1992), Brynjolfsson (1993), and in David (1989, 1990). For our purposes, it is sufficient to examine the argument by just one of the Productivity Paradox's chief protagonists, economist Stephen Roach. In a series of working papers published between 1983 and 1989, Roach constructed the following story (Roach, 1983, 1984, 1986a, 1989a; Gay and Roach, 1986).

1. The United States is changing away from "goods" as the focus of production and toward "information." Figure 1 shows this set of changes in nonfarm output mix and labor distribution between 1960 and 1985.

2. Investment in "high technology" capital goods has soared compared to investment in basic industrial capital goods. Figure 2 shows this trend. Note that the majority of the investment in "high tech" capital

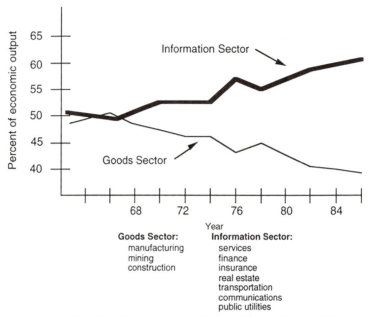

Figure 1. The changing economy. (Adapted from Gay and Roach, 1986.)

goods has been concentrated in the "information sector" of the economy.

3. In spite of the great growth in investment in "high tech" capital goods in the information sector, production per worker in this sector has remained essentially flat for at least fifteen years. Figure 3 shows these trends.

In other words, despite a huge investment in technology in industries where the technology is presumed to provide productivity payoffs, productivity had remained flat. If the logic behind these analyses and the data used to construct them are correct, Roach's analyses confront the proponents of computerization with two disturbing questions: Does computerization reduce productivity? Or, if not, does computerization merely fail to increase productivity? Either way, the results burst the bubble on a decades-old belief.

Reactions to the Paradox

The productivity paradox story contains an interesting dilemma. Individual and organizational-level expenditures on computerization have increased year after year, despite lack of economically legitimate proof of productivity gains from such investment. The dilemma arises from microeconomic

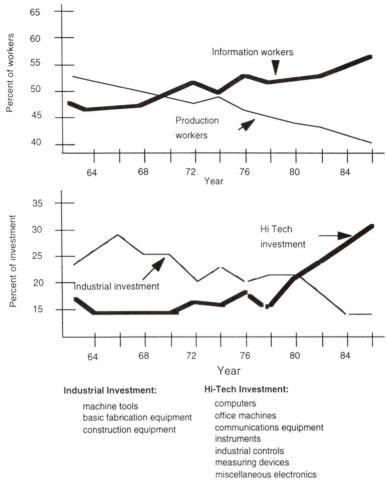

Figure 2.   Investment and labor. (Adapted from Gay and Roach, 1986.)

theory that rational, self-interested individuals and organizations will not invest heavily in unproductive activity over time. The major line of argument to escape the dilemma holds that microeconomic theory remains sound, and that productivity benefits often are in fact realized. However, even in the best cases those benefits can be difficult to prove, and they are often difficult to achieve. This rationale can be seen in the National Research Council's 1994 report "Information Technology in the Service Sector: A Twenty-First Century Lever," which dwells extensively on measurement problems and management problems, citing poor decision making regarding computerization as a major cause of productivity failures. In short, microeconomic theory is upheld but there appears to be something

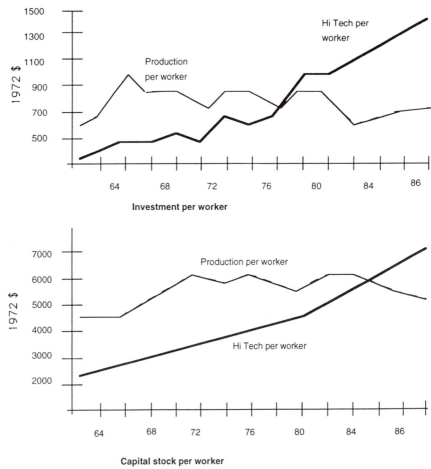

Figure 3. Productivity and investment. (Adapted from Gay and Roach, 1986.)

wrong with the numbers and with management behavior. This takes us back to the concerns mentioned above.

Reviews of the objections to the productivity paradox can be found in Brynjolfsson (1993) and in King (1995). Those supporting computerization note that even if the measures of productivity are accurate, it is possible that, without computerization, productivity would have fallen. This is a fair rejoinder, but it is hardly satisfactory because what might have happened is never knowable. A more common response is that the many problems encountered in measuring productivity effects from computerization make the negative claims unreliable. The problems appear in inputs to the equations, in the analytical techniques used, and in the measurement of productivity outputs. The best of these criticisms are damaging to the claims that computerization does not yield productivity benefits, but again, such arguments claim only that the existing data do not tell us the right story; they do not tell us what the right story is. More significantly for the purposes of the overall productivity debate, it is clear to everyone that the dispute over measures is inevitably political as well as scholarly. After all, we would hardly expect the proponents of computerization to be protesting against the measures if they happened to show major payoffs from computerization. In all, arguments against the productivity paradox based on measurement problems do not resolve the key open question of whether computerization pays off.

A more fruitful response to the productivity numbers has been provided by Attewell (1992, and Part III, Chapter K). Attewell begins with the conjecture that the numbers might be right, and that computerization has not yielded major payoffs because managers do not have the skills to implement the technology correctly. Even the most ardent proponents of computerization acknowledge the kinds of problems Attewell mentions, but they argue that these losses are temporary and can be expected to diminish as skill in computerization is gained. Once again one might object that organizations have had forty years to develop such skills, and that such defenses are little more than reruns of the "payoffs are coming" argument repeated since the late 1950s. However, it is more constructive to interpret the measurement breakdowns and management difficulties of the productivity paradox as symptoms rather than causes. If we think of failed productivity expectations as the result of a profound social transformation that cannot be assessed by conventional measures or managed by conventional wisdom, we might develop new insights that can be anchored in historical analysis of analogous technological revolutions, and centered on the issues of timing and social learning.

If and when computerization yields major productivity payoffs it will be as a result of the confluence of three factors: the new technologies themselves, the know-how needed to apply them successfully, and the wholesale substitution of the new technologies and new methods for older ways of doing things. The new technologies are here, and it is clear that we are learning to apply the technologies, but we have not learned enough to achieve cost-saving substitution. We are still bearing the direct costs of learning, and we must bear the costs of multiple, redundant systems until we have learned enough to switch completely from the old to the new. This learning phenomenon might sound simple and straightforward, but it is not. It is highly complicated and it takes considerable time.

An excellent analysis of precisely this point can be seen in Paul David's comparison of two "general purpose" engines: the dynamo or electric motor, and the computer (1989, 1990). David essentially replicates the argument made by Roach regarding the computerization productivity paradox using data from the period 1870 to 1940 on the replacement of steam power with electric power in factories in the United States. Prior to 1870 most United States factories were powered either by water or steam, and

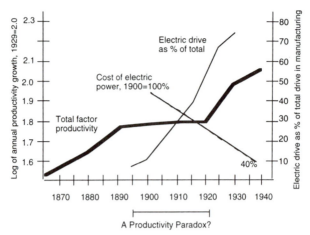

Figure 4. A productivity paradox from the age of electrification? (Adapted from David, 1989.)

steam was by far the dominant motive source. As electric motors were introduced, their benefits became increasingly obvious and they were substituted for steam. By 1935 electric motors had essentially replaced steam altogether. During this period factory managers had to make major investments in the new technology of electricity. Also, the cost of electric power was steadily dropping from about 1900 to 1935, during which a major part of the substitution took place. Yet total factor productivity during the period from about 1890 to 1920, during the period of electricity's greatest displacement of steam, was essentially flat. The general story of this argument can be seen in Figure 4.

David concludes from his analysis that the measures used to assess the productivity payoffs of computerization simply do not capture the historical reality of the substitution process that is taking place. The shift from steam to electric power was gradual and costly, not just because of the required investments in technology, but because the technology enabled and required fundamentally new ways of organizing and conducting work. These new ways of working had to be learned through a combination of trial and error and dissemination of innovation, and they took place while the old technology of steam and its requirements were still a key part of the production system. The entire manufacturing sector during this protracted period was bearing the costs of running two production systems, one of which was highly experimental. Many of the changes enabled and required by electricity were manifestations of the great benefits of electricity. For example, electricity was a decentralizable form of power distribution. Each machine had its own motor, unlike the steam factory, which had one or a few large engines and distributed power through systems of shafts, wheels, and belts. The distributed system of electric power had many advantages. Machines could be taken off-line and brought back on-line without having to shut down the whole operation as was required with steam power. Also, electricity made possible safer and more efficient factory designs because the constraints of transmitting power by steam were removed. But the costs of changing to this newer and better system were high, and during the long decades of this investment, apparent productivity fell.

If one looks only at the years between 1890 and 1920 in Figure 4 it would be easy to conclude that there is productivity paradox in the switch to electric motors. When the years prior to 1890 and after 1920 are added, we see steep growth in productivity. Something important happened during the thirty years around the turn of the century, but it was not a breakdown in productivity. Factory owners were investing in a fundamentally new way of manufacturing, and the payoffs of that investment were measured in decades rather than years. The right sense of time is vital to understanding what happened.

David's analysis shows that history matters. Organizations carry into any new era of technology a robust and highly valuable store of knowledge about the old ways of doing things. This knowledge was hard-won, and is not easily bushed aside. Moreover, given the great stock of knowledge about the older ways, it is often possible to make improvements in those old ways that make them competitive with the new technologies for protracted periods of time. For a number of years during the replacement of steam by electric motors steam technology maintained a steady lead in efficiency through continuous improvements in technology and techniques. New technologies are at a disadvantage in such circumstances. It is not only unsurprising that the payoffs from such a switch can be long in coming, but it is logical to assume they will.

Computerization as Social Transformation

David's analysis can be cast as a process of social learning leading to social transformation. Organizational adaptation to use of new information technologies has been shown in other historical accounts to be a complicated, expensive, and protracted affair. Eisenstein's study of the consequences from the invention of printing provides a good starting point (Eisenstein, 1979). Among other things, Eisenstein notes that with the invention of printing came not only the ability to disseminate information in previously unthinkable volume, but also the ability to disseminate error in equal volume. This was important in the relatively mundane sense that unavoidable errors in printing necessitated the development of *errata* procedures and refined techniques for authentication. But in the larger sense, printing raised serious political questions about the dissemination of error in the form of "wrong thinking." The printing of the Bible enabled the dissemination of holy scripture far beyond the controlled realm of the clergy, and played a key role in the reformation. Similarly, seemingly small but very important standards had to be developed regarding the format and size of printed documents that affected portability and readability (Lowry, 1979). The invention of printing essentially brought about the invention of reading in societies where all but a few in key positions of power were illiterate, and in time led to the establishment of universal education. These changes took several hundred years, but they altered the world in incalculable ways.

Broader Historical Perspectives

Chandler (1977) also provides instructive accounts of the importance of information technology in the transformation of industry and the rise of the managerial class. Chandler describes the key role of the telegraph in coordinating the great revolution enabled by mass production from steam-powered factories and mass distribution over railroads. One of his valuable insights is that information technology by itself did not enable or cause great change, but rather it was a key complement among several factors that brought about the industrial transformation of the United States during the nineteenth century. Without the telegraph it was essentially impossible to safely operate the railroad system on the efficient schedule required to lower freight costs and establish rail cargo as the backbone of the national distribution network. The learning involved in this transformation went far beyond the development and dissemination of new techniques. It required the creation of an entirely new class of key economic actors, the professional managers, to learn and implement the techniques required to sustain the mighty industrial engine. In the process, the very concept of capitalism was changed.

Yates (1989) provides a wealth of useful studies of organizational adoption of information technology in offices and factories. An important finding from her research is the near universality of decades-long diffusion times for new information technologies among complex organizations. As strange as it sounds today, it was rare for organizations to keep copies of their correspondence during the first half of the nineteenth century simply because doing so required tedious hand copying. In fact, a technology for press copying of documents written in ink had been invented in 1780, but it was not routinely used until the 1860s. The telegraph was introduced in 1844, and was first applied to effect a change in a train schedule in 1851, but was not routinely used in railroad control and coordination until 1870. The telephone was first demonstrated in 1876, but did not see widespread use in factories until the late 1890s, and was not used routinely by the public until the 1910s. Typewriting was introduced in 1871, but was not used commonly until 1900. Vertical filing was pioneered by libraries in the 1870s but was not common in business until 1910. It is quite uncommon that any important innovation in information handling took less than twenty-five years to disseminate across the organizational landscape, and some of these technologies took many decades to diffuse.

Of particular importance in Yates's work is the role of organizational and social learning that accompanies the successful adoption of an information technology innovation. Information technologies have frequently been the subject of wildly misplaced expectations when first developed. Morse believed his telegraph would be used mainly for personal correspondence, but in fact it was vital for commerce. Bell believed that his telephone would be used to broadcast entertainment, but it proved its value in person-to-person communication. Television was heralded as the greatest invention for education since printing, but in fact it is mainly used for entertainment. Thomas J. Watson, Jr. of IBM believed that the worldwide market for digital computers was five machines: an underestimate of at least eight orders of magnitude. These quaint stories usually paint the main actors as ignorant or naive, but they were often the most qualified people in the society to make such predictions at that time. The application of new technology is a learned phenomenon. It is linked by the inherent applicability of the technology, but within those limits application is socially constructed through the learning experiences of those who seek to apply it.

Yates provides a particularly striking example of the complexity and subtlety of this learning behavior in her analysis of technological change in vertical and horizontal organizational communications in factories. She notes that information technologies such as directive memoranda and the telephone greatly facilitated vertical communications, enabling coordination of diverse functions and vertical integration. At the same time, however, growth and the reinforcement of vertical communications contributed to efficiency losses in day-to-day operations. The problem was a lack of equally effective improvements in lateral communications that would allow workers to communicate with each other to coordinate work on the shop floor. To redress this problem, managers introduced such reforms as middle management meetings, company newsletters, company events such as picnics, and so on to acquaint workers with their counterparts and encourage lateral communication. The explanation often given for the introduction of such reforms is paternalistic altruism, but Yates convincingly shows that these reforms were a learned, remedial response to dysfunctional consequences of exploiting the benefits of technology applied to vertical communication.

The Complexities of Learning

The role of learning in the application of computers is complicated. The computer itself is a general-purpose engine, applicable to a huge range of tasks enabling change in many task domains (David, 1989, 1990). Learning cannot be a narrowly circumscribed and specialized activity, involving a small number of experts. It takes place simultaneously in many different social and organizational domains that are not necessarily in communication with one another. This kind of learning cannot proceed in a predictable or tractable direction or pace, and it cannot be managed in any meaningful sense. Beyond this, vital features of the technology such as performance capability and cost of production are in constant flux. This is highly beneficial given that the trend is toward ever better price-performance characteristics, but it is also destabilizing to the learning process. "Mastery" is elusive because what can be mastered is itself changing all the time.

It is also worth noting that we pursue this expensive process of learning and transformation precisely because we desire the benefits we think we will gain by doing so. New and improved technologies provide us with the promise of "a better way." There are no guarantees that this better way will materialize, despite our efforts, but as long as there is good reason for individuals to think they will gain the benefits, they will persevere in the learning process. Strangely, then, productivity remains elusive because the technological capabilities in the world of computing are constantly improving, and the range of applications possible is ever increasing. Thus, skills cannot be learned once and for all, but must be learned new all the time because the target of what is to be done keeps moving. Organizations in such a case are always catching up, and until the pace of technology improvement slows or stops, the payoffs that come from mastery cannot be fully obtained.

There is a perplexing aspect to application learning in the information technology realm arising from different modes of learning-in-action. Arrow pointed out that much learning related to technology application comes through doing—by applying the technology and observing the results (Arrow, 1962). For example, knowledge about how to build aircraft is gained by building aircraft and flying them. Von Hippel subsequently pointed out that considerable knowledge about technology application comes through use, particularly by consumers of the products (Von Hippel, 1977, 1978). Rosenberg (1982) later noted that for many technologies learning is a result of both doing and using, where producers learn by doing and then learn more by the use experiences of their customers. These observations certainly apply to learning in the realm of information technology, but there is an important additional feature of information technology that must be understood in the context of the productivity paradox: information technologies are typically inputs in processes undertaken by their users. Users learn to use these inputs by doing, but in many cases— the use of personal computers by secretaries, for example—such learning-by-doing cannot take place until a period of learning-by-using has been completed. In order to begin experimenting with applying computer technology to a task like publishing the user must first spend enough time actually using the technology to become sufficiently knowledgeable to recognize successful application from unsuccessful application.

Learning in the realm of information technology is often a two-step process at both the individual and organizational level. This can be characterized as "learning-by-using for learning-by-doing." Learning-by-using is a necessary first step before actual production can begin, even if that production is itself conducted only for the sake of learning. Moreover, this two-stage process is repeated every time a major change in the capability of the technology becomes available. As a result, the "payoff knowledge" of how to apply the technology effectively to the bottom-line production of the organization comes only after a protracted period of learning by using and learning by doing, neither of which generates a surplus. In a world of rapidly changing capability, these using/doing cycles follow one another and the exploitation of payoff knowledge becomes an elusive goal. In fact, such exploitation might be going on all the time, but the disruption and costs associated with the using/doing cycle of learning occlude the benefits that result from that exploitation. Equilibrium in the form of a clearly identifiable payoff is likely to emerge only when the basic improvements in technological enablement cease. The productivity payoff of computerization is therefore likely to appear in measurable form only when information technology is itself no longer getting better all the time. Under this model, technological improvement is a key cause of our inability to measure productivity improvements from application of that technology.

Difficulties in organizational learning required to exploit information technology also arise because the new products and processes enabled by the technology are not familiar from past learning experience. An example of this is the problem of rent dissipation with respect to the knowledge assets or intellectual property that are made possible from use of computers. The owner of intellectual property like computer software or databases cannot make money on that property without collecting a rent, but the same technology that enables production of that properly also makes it easy for people to appropriate it without paying the rent. Software piracy is an example of this problem, but a similar case can be made for photocopying of copyrighted materials. The technology makes it possible to replicate information at almost zero cost, so the only constraint on dissipation is technical protection schemes that have not worked well, such as copy protection on software, and reliance on voluntary compliance with the law. As the information sector grows, rent dissipation might produce beneficial learning-by-using and learning-by-doing among consumers who use pirated information in the form of software, data, documents, and so on, even while the producers lose their rightful rents. This distortion must be addressed, but the means to do so are not obvious and must themselves be learned.

Another problem arises from the failure of well-established principles for handling information in light of new capabilities brought from modern information technology. For example, consider the long-established principle of rational decision making that argues that a decision maker should review all relevant, available data before deciding. When all relevant, available information was limited to what could be found within the reach of one's corporate staff this was an easy principle to fulfill. When all relevant, available information is accessible from tens of thousands of databases over global network connections, the principle is unworkable. New means must be learned for finding, filtering, and collating vast quantities of information rapidly and affordably so only the right information is used.

These examples show the centrality of learning with respect to the productivity paradox. Learning to do old things new ways takes time, and, as suggested by the historical studies cited, such learning can take decades. While this learning is under way, the direct benefits from the learning cannot be exploited. The benefits of learning, at least in measurable economic terms, occur only when the learning is put to use in some productive capacity. More important, information technology enables the doing of entirely new things, and learning to do new things is much riskier and more costly than improving on established practice. That a productivity paradox can be seen at all is proof that information technology truly is enabling fundamental social transformations; the changes under way are so profound that they cannot be understood or even measured until we learn more about them.

The Reengineering Chimera

The complexity of the problem raised by the productivity paradox can be seen even more starkly when we realize that technological capabilities powerful enough to alter what we *can* do will alter our expectations of what we *ought* to do. This shows up repeatedly in discussion about business process reengineering, which argues that real payoffs come only when organizations exploit technology to reengineer the fundamentals of their operations (Davenport, 1993; Hammer, 1990; Hammer and Champy, 1993). It is unfortunate that the rhetoric of the reengineering movement is often naive and misleading. The illusion of reengineering is that improved productivity will result from simply linking the power of technology to some established overall organizational strategy. In fact, organizational strategy itself will change as a result of the new opportunities, and formulating new strategies is itself an iterative, learning-by-doing process. The organizational adaptations made in this learning-by-doing process can produce side effects of questionable or even clearly negative productivity value, and these too must be dealt with.

A good example of one such problematic adaptation is seen in the mechanism of compliance with reporting requirements. Reporting is required by both governmental and nongovernmental institutions for many socially useful purposes. For example, it makes sound economic sense to require that publicly held commercial organizations report their financial status in a standardized format so investors can evaluate these firms' economic performance when making investment decisions. It makes sense for financial institutions to require those seeking real property loans to provide evidence that the property is ensured against common risks like fire. Mandatory reporting provides the statistical information of the National Accounts discussed earlier. Reporting is necessary to enforce adherence regarding safety of building construction and workplaces, fairness in hiring practices, and so on.

Reporting requirements are certainly shaped by apparent need, but they are also shaped by likelihood of feasible compliance. No reporting requirement would survive if only a small fraction of the reporting organizations could feasibly comply with it. Information technology plays a key role in shaping compliance feasibility. By building sophisticated systems that facilitate data collection, analysis, report generation, and information dissemination, organizations gradually bring themselves into the position where they can comply with increasingly demanding reporting requirements. Thus we see a reversal in which demands that might have been met by only 10% of the organizations required to report become possible for 90% through use of information technology. The remaining 10% are "out of compliance," and will be forced to comply. Unworkable reporting requirements are thus transformed into viable requirements. The goal of remaining in compliance with reporting requirements is thereby added to the list of existing goals of many organizations; in fact, compliance can become more important than other, possibly more vital, organizational goals.

Compliance shifts not only bring direct costs, such as the costs of compliance, but displacement costs as well. The case of financial reporting requirements provides a good case in point. Johnson and Kaplan (1987) tell the story of the transformation of the activity of cost accounting from its root mission to trace costs of production into a powerful institutional enterprise of externally oriented financial reporting to comply with the regulations surrounding capital markets. In the process, the engineers who originally did cost accounting were displaced by trained accountants who were members of guildlike accounting associations. These associations grew up around mandatory external auditing requirements, and controlled credentialing processes in ways that ensured allegiance from their members. For the first time in history, an entire industry—public accounting and auditing—evolved with the sole purpose of producing reports. These reports often were important to their subject organizations' activities in capital markets, but they contained essentially no information that might affect decisions related to organizational productivity. The goal of productivity embodied in the early cost accounting schemes was displaced by the goal of reported profitability as articulated and enforced by the accounting guilds and other regulatory organizations.

The "reporting industry" has affected the insides of firms in important ways. Feldman and March (1981) and Feldman (1989) make a convincing case that information collection, management, and storage in organizations take place at a level far beyond what could be justified for organizational decision-making purposes. This information serves important symbolic purposes, to signal a particular attitude or position, a particular capability or need. The demonstrated ability to mobilize information and produce "good reports" becomes a key part of status maintenance in a culture that rewards "information readiness." This curious dilemma strikes at the heart of many claims made about the information society, and especially the notion that ubiquitous and readily available information will spawn a flood of creative entrepreneurial activity. The problem facing most organizations is the flood of information of indeterminate value. Dealing efficiently and effectively with the enormous volume of information created by reporting compliance and organizational signaling needs presents a major challenge to achieving productivity in any simple sense of the term.

Ultimately, the issue of reporting raises the question of what is "real." Organizational leaders, like any individuals, can become deluded by appearances. As reporting processes become sanctified, the reports they produce become sanctified. The information reported becomes more real than the facts at hand. The magnitude of the danger inherent in this tendency is seen in the recent tragic events involving the United States thrift industry. Major public accounting firms held firmly to their long-established processes for auditing savings and loan associations, even while the regulatory regime governing this industry was undergoing radical alteration. Actions that were previously unlawful, and thus simply not seen as a realistic threat during audit, became lawful (White, 1992). The audits did not pick up the problems arising from these new practices until serious damage had been done. The savings and loans, the accounting firms, and the federal regulatory agencies with jurisdictions over thrifts deluded themselves and each other into thinking that the reports of the long-established audit processes told the "truth" about the state of the thrifts. They were seriously mistaken. The accounting firms have subsequently been forced to pay fines amounting to hundreds of millions of dollars for their negligence, but these fines fall far short of the tens of billions of dollars in savings and loan losses that will have to be covered by U.S. Federal Government insurance programs (NCFIRRE, 1993). In short, this particular institutional culture of reporting apparently broke down so seriously that it did not even accomplish its avowed goal of certifying the fiscal health of audited organizations.

A similar observation has been made at a much higher level of social aggregation, involving the relationship between reporting systems and economic competitiveness among the United States and its most aggressive international competitor, Japan. It has been claimed that a key to Japanese economic success has been the willingness of Japanese firms to take a "long view" of their business goals as opposed to the "short view" taken by United States firms. At base, this argument is one of cultural differences and social organization, which goes far beyond the scope of this essay. Nevertheless, the culture of reporting evident in the United States plays a key role in this argument, and it is of use to our analysis. The institutional reporting apparatus governing United States capital markets requires quarterly financial reports by publicly held firms, culminating in an annual report. It is difficult to tell whether this reporting protocol is the result of the underlying economic orientation of the United States capital markets, that tend to favor rapid movement, or a cause of that rapid movement. Most likely it is both. In any case, the fact that reports are issued quarterly arguably induces in many investors a "quarterly" or "annual" horizon for evaluation of firm quality and performance. This makes sense in a world where short-term performance perfectly predicts long-term performance, but it is a major problem if important long-term goals such as establishment of large market share are in conflict with short-term goals such as quarterly profits or dividends.

The arguments noted here do not answer the question of whether the payoffs from computerization will ever materialize, but they hold open the possibility that the payoffs can materialize. The challenge of reengineering to "do things right" is difficult when it is not clear what the "right" things are. If computerization simply substituted for well-understood ways of doing things in organizations, it would be easy to recognize when productivity payoffs might occur and act to obtain them. In fact, computerization appears to be altering the entire nature of production in complex ways similar to those seen during earlier revolutions that shifted production from rural-based farming and cottage industries to city-based factories. In this case it would come as no surprise that we cannot readily see the productivity payoffs from use of computers, or how to achieve them. Computerization seen as a force for social transformation requires that we shift from finding the "answers" for applying computers successfully to finding the patterns of social change in which these answers will be learned through trial and error.

Conclusion

The productivity paradox has stimulated a great deal of discussion about whether available data are reliable as indicators, and if so, why a shortfall in productivity might have occurred. Productivity shortfalls, if they are real, are attributed to management failures, and will be eliminated only when managers begin to make the "right" decisions about application of the technology. This theme is suggested in later writings by Roach (1986b, 1988, 1991) and it is the heart of the arguments of the "reengineering" rhetoric (Hammer, 1990; Hammer and Champy, 1993; Davenport, 1993). The problem, of course, is knowing what the "right" things are.

The debate over the productivity paradox is understandable, given the expectations of productivity from computerization that are embedded in our culture. But it is arguable that the changes under way will inevitably take place across a much longer time frame than the measurements can currently cover, and actual payoff cannot be expected until major elements of organizational and social learning are complete. The measurement, management, and learning arguments can be combined to create a broad case for fundamental social transformation. In this transformation older systems of measurement and management fail as the entire regime of production is altered, and learning becomes to a much greater degree experimental and risky. This line of argument assumes that the underlying microeconomic rationale for action—rational opportunism—remains viable. The slow accrual of learning will probably, eventually, produce major productivity benefits.

None of the arguments made in this chapter can be proven at present. They are all conjectural. Nevertheless, persuasive evidence can be provided to suggest that a major shift in means of production is now under way, with significant social transformation as a consequence. The industrialized societies making the most rapid and significant investments in this new means of production will be the first to discover the opportunities and dislocations that will accompany this change. On the upside, these societies will likely experience great gains in productivity, economic competitiveness, and national wealth. On the downside, these societies might be faced with the challenge of ameliorating the possible negative consequences such as labor dislocation, job deskilling, and exacerbated growth in the gap between the rich and the poor. It is doubtful that the changes now under way can be reversed, and one of the first casualties of the changes will be the productivity paradox itself. The paradox cannot be allowed to remain. The investments in computerization will either produce the benefits hoped for, even if in ways not anticipated, or decline to the level at which the benefits make them worthwhile.

References

Applegate, Lynda M., James I. Cash, Jr., and D. Quin Mills (1988). "Information Technology and Tomorrow's Manager." *Harvard Business Review,* 66(6)(Nov.–Dec.):128–136.

Arrow, Kenneth (1962). "The Economic Implications of Learning by Doing." *Review of Economic Studies,* 29 (June):155–173.

Attewell, Paul (1992). "Information Technology and the Productivity Paradox." Working paper: Department of Sociology, Graduate Center, City University of New York, July.

Bohme, Frederick, and J. Paul Wyatt (1991). *100 years of data processing: the punchcard century*. Washington, D.C., U.S. Dept of Commerce, Bureau of the Census.

Brynjolfsson, Erik (1993). "The Productivity Paradox of Information Technology." *Communications of the ACM*, 36(12), December:67–77.

Chandler, Alfred D., Jr. (1977). *The Visible Hand: The Managerial Revolution in American Business*. Belknap Press, Cambridge, MA.

Chase, George C. (1980). "A History of Mechanical Computing Machinery." *Annals of the History of Computing*, 3(3), July:198–226.

Davenport, Thomas H. (1993). *Process Innovation: Reengineering Work Through Information Technology*. Harvard Business School Press, Boston, MA.

David, Paul A. (1989). Computer and Dynamo: The Productivity Paradox through a Distant Mirror. Stanford University Center for Economic Policy Research, Stanford, CA.

David, Paul A. (1990). The Dynamo and the Computer: An Historical Perspective on the Modern Productivity Paradox." *AEA Papers and Proceedings*, 80(2), May: 355–361.

Eisenstein, Elizabeth L. (1979). *The Printing Press as an Agent of Change: Communications and Cultural Transformations in Early Modern Europe*. Cambridge University Press, Cambridge.

Feldman, Martha S. (1989). *Order without Design: Information Production and Policy Making*. Stanford University Press, Stanford, CA.

Feldman, Martha S., and James G. March (1981). "Information in Organizations as Signal and Symbol." *Administrative Science Quarterly*, 26(2):171–186.

Gay, Robert S., and Stephen S. Roach (1986). *The Productivity Puzzle: Perils and Hopes. Economic Perspectives*. Morgan Stanley and Company, Inc., New York.

Goldstine, Hermann H. (1972). *The Computer from Pascal to von Neumann*. Princeton University Press, Princeton, NJ.

Hammer, Michael (1990). "Reengineering Work: Don't Automate, Obliterate." *Harvard Business Review*, 68, July/August, 104–112.

Hammer, Michael, and James Champy (1993). *Reengineering the Corporation: A Manifesto for Business Revolution*. Harper Business, New York.

Johnson, H. Thomas, and Robert S. Kaplan (1987). *Relevance Lost: The Rise and Fall of Management Accounting*. Harvard Business School Press, Boston, MA.

King, John L. (1995). The productivity paradox in perspective: information technology and social transformation. Center for Research on Information Technology and Organizations, Irvine, CA.

King, John L., and Kenneth L. Kraemer (1981). "Cost as a Social Impact of Telecommunications and Other Information Technologies," in Mitchell Moss (ed.), *Telecommunications and Productivity*. Addison-Wesley, New York.

Leavitt, Harold, and Thomas Whisler (1958). "Management in the 1980s." *Harvard Business Review*, 38(Nov.–Dec.):41–48.

Lindgren, Michael (1987). *Glory and Failure: The Difference Engines of Johann Muller, Charles Babbage and Georg and Edvard Scheutz*. Linkoping, Sweden: Linkoping University, Dept. of Technology and Social Change.

Lowry, Martin (1979). *The World of Aldus Manutius: Business and Scholarship in Renaissance Venice*. Cornell University Press, Ithaca, N.Y.

Morrison, Philip, and Emily Morrison (eds.) (1961). *Charles Babbage and His Calculating Engines*. Dover Publications, New York.

NCFIRRE (1993). *Origins and Causes of the S&L Debacle: A Blueprint for Reform: A Report to the President and Congress of the United States.* National Commission on Financial Institution Reform, Recovery and Enforcement. Washington, D.C.: U.S. G.P.O.

NRC (1994). *Information Technology and the Service Society: A 21st Century Lever.* A National Research Council Report. National Academy Press, Washington, D.C.

Roach, Stephen S. (1983). "The New Capital Spending Cycle." *Economic Perspectives.* Morgan Stanley and Company, Inc., New York.

Roach, Stephen S. (1984). "Productivity, Investment, and the Information Economy." *Economic Perspectives.* Morgan Stanley and Company, Inc., New York.

Roach, Stephen S. (1986a). "Stop the Dice Rolling on Technology Spending." *Computerworld*, 20, June 20:6.

Roach, Stephen S. (1986b). "Technology and the Services Sector: America's Hidden Challenge," in B. Guile and J. Quinn (eds.), *The Positive Sum Strategy*, pp. 118–138. National Academy Press, Washington, D.C.

Roach, Stephen S. (1988). "White-Collar Productivity: A Glimmer of Hope?" *Economic Perspectives.* Morgan Stanley and Company, Inc., New York.

Roach, Stephen S. (1989a). "The Case of the Missing Technology Payback." *Economic Perspectives.* Morgan Stanley and Company, Inc., New York.

Roach, Stephen (1989b). "Pitfalls on the 'New' Assembly Line: Can Services Learn from Manufacturing?" *Economic Perspectives.* Morgan Stanley and Company, Inc., New York.

Roach, Stephen S. (1991). "Services under Siege: The Restructuring Imperative." *Harvard Business Review*, 69(Sept./Oct.):82–91.

Rosenberg, Nathan (1982). *Inside the Black Box: Technology and Economics.* Cambridge University Press, Cambridge, MA.

Simon, Herbert Alexander (1960). *The New Science of Management Decision.* Harper, New York.

Thurow, Lester (1992). *Head to Head: The Coming Economic Battle among Japan, Europe and America.* Morrow, New York.

Von Hippel, Eric (1977). "The Dominant Role of the User in Semiconductor and Electronic Subassembly Process Innovation." *IEEE Transactions on Engineering Management*, 24(2):60–71.

Von Hippel, Eric A. (1978). "Users as Innovators." *Technology Review*, 80(3)(January):30–39.

Vonnegut, Kurt, Jr. (1952). *Player Piano.* Delacorte Press/Seymour Lawrence, New York.

White, Lawrence J. (1992). *A Cautionary Tale of Deregulation Gone Awry: The S&L Debacle.* New York, N.Y.: Working paper S-92-4, Salomon Center, Leonard N. Stern School of Business, New York University.

Yates, JoAnne (1989). *Control through Communication: The Rise of System in American Management.* Johns Hopkins University Press, Baltimore, MD.

P·A·R·T · III

M

Can Computer Science Solve Organizational Problems? The Case for Organizational Informatics

Rob Kling • *Jonathan P. Allen*

Introduction

People who have studied the information and computer sciences have learned to solve computational problems. They know how to sort lists, analyze binary trees, design databases and information retrieval systems, and how to organize document catalogs. They may also learn about how to design interfaces for people, or to manage large-scale projects. But how well does their information science or computer science education enable them to design or configure computerized systems that are useful to organizations such as banks, hospitals, schools, and government agencies that face difficult problems every day? How well does an education in information science or computer science help professionals solve organizational problems?

In this article we will argue that men and women who study information and computer science must learn topics that are not yet widely taught in these fields if they wish to be professionally effective in solving organizational problems. Traditional computer science does not teach its students enough about how organizations work, how organizations influence the design and use of computerized systems, and how these systems in turn affect the ways that people work. This is unfortunate, because the challenge of creating useful, workable systems for organizations is becoming even more important. More computer professionals, in an era of decentralized technology, are working closely with computer users on their practical problems. Government agencies are demanding more "applied" research that meets the needs of organizations (Hartmanis and Lin, 1992). Organizations have been the major "consumer" of computing and spend nearly $150 billion per year in the United States alone.

Organizations depend on computer professionals to design systems that help people do their jobs well. Poor computer systems can undermine the effectiveness of organizations, or even drive them into bankruptcy (e.g., Geyelin, 1994). Good organizational computing is a challenge because technical excellence alone does not guarantee that a computer system will be consistently used well. A local area network may never lose a file, and the routing algorithm may be efficient, but this is no guarantee that people in a competitive workplace will actually share information (as Orlikowski, 1993, shows).

A small but growing number of studies have looked at computer development and use in organizations over the past twenty years. We have called this emerging research area Organizational Informatics (Kling, 1993). Organizational Informatics research does not provide a simple handbook for how computer professionals can achieve organizational computing excellence. If, however, a large fraction of computer scientists are trying to create effective organizational computing, we argue that computer science as a field needs to take on this new challenge. Computer science needs to cultivate a subfield dedicated to examining how organizations affect technology design, and how computing changes the way organizations behave. Organizational Informatics research provides our best starting point for understanding how computing becomes useful for organizations.

When Does Computer Science Take on New Challenges?

If Organizational Informatics does become a subfield of computer science, it would not be the first time computer science had expanded to take on new challenges. Computer science began in the late 1940s and early 1950s as an interdisciplinary field of mathematics and electrical engineering. The first major challenge was hardware design (Phase 1 in Table 1). As the technology became more powerful and more widely used, new kinds of computing challenges arose. The subfields of software engineering and human–computer interaction are two examples of how computer science has expanded in the face of new challenges.

The challenge of building and maintaining large software systems encouraged the growth of a new subfield known as software engineering (Phase 2 in Table 1). Software engineering draws upon the fields of engineering, management, economics, and social psychology to investigate

Table 1. System Development Challenges[a]

Phases of computer development	Time period	Key challenges

Phase 1
  Hardware constraints
	Late 1940s–
	  mid-1960s
		High hardware costs
		Machine capacity constraints
		Routine handling of high-volume
		  problems

Phase 2
  Software constraints
	Mid-1960s–early
	  1980s
		High software development costs
		Increased user demands
		Software methodology

Phase 3 User relations constraints	Early 1980s–today	Higher-level languages Direct user interaction Less-structured problems

Phase 4
  Organizational environment
  constraints
	Today–the near
	  future?
		Networking
		Standards
		Facilitating communications

[a]Adapted from Friedman (1989).

how to best organize large programming teams, estimate the costs of software projects, and obtain useful systems requirements. All of these important computing challenges were brought about by advancing computer technology, and require the help of other disciplines. For instance, mathematical computer science models describe the computational behavior of database systems. By one can't rely on mathematics alone to assess how well the relations and object-entities created in a systems design serve as useful representations of the data stored in an airline reservation system. There must be some reference to the "real world" in which these database models are used (or not used) (see Smith, Part VII, Chapter E).

By the early 1980s, the direct use of computing by nonexperts prompted the growth of another new subfield in computer science (Phase 3 in Table 1). The subfield of human–computer interaction uses psychological theories and research methods to determine what kind of interfaces are most usable by people. The mathematical models of traditional computer science, such as Turing machines and automata, cannot by themselves give us an adequate understanding of why people might prefer a graphical user interface to a command line interface, or vice versa (cf., Ehn, 1991; Grudin, 1989). Men and women who represent actual users must be studied, and involved, to understand their usability preferences.

Both software engineering and human–computer interaction are now considered core subfields of computer science (Hartmanis and Lin, 1992). Both new subfields are examples of an evolution toward "usability" issues in computer science. Computer scientists are now much more likely to evaluate computer development and use in terms of human behavior and capabilities, in addition to formal, mathematical computability (Kling, 1993).

We believe that the new challenges of organizational computing—intensified by new technological capabilities such as networking and communications—will spur the development of a new subfield in computer science. The ability to make computer systems usable for organizations depends on understanding how organizations behave as well as understanding technological principles (Kling and Elliott, 1994; Markus and Keil, 1994). The explosive growth of networking has also forced computer professionals to understand how people work together, rather than individually (Grudin, 1989; Orlikowski, 1993; Greif, 1988; Galegher, Kraut, and Egido, 1990; also see Bullen and Bennett, Part IV, Chapter F). New industries and research communities have been created around terms such as "computer-supported cooperative work" and "groupware." The boundary between technical aspects and social aspects of artifacts in use has always been somewhat arbitrary (Bloomfield and Vurdubakis, 1994). Information and computer professionals who try to maintain such boundaries and who avoid working on both social and technological issues are usually ineffective in designing usable computerized systems.

Organizational Informatics is the name we give to this latest chapter in the continued broadening of information and computer science. Emerging fields, such as human–computer interaction, do not replace the traditional core of these fields. Computer systems still depend on algorithms, whose computational features are well described by mathematical theories. But mathematical theories of machine computation do not (and could not) provide a sound basis for understanding why some interfaces are more effective for people under certain conditions than under others, or why many "technically sound" computer systems are used or not used by particular organizations.

The New Challenge of Organizational Computing

There are practical, as well as academic, reasons for computer professionals to have a better understanding of organizations and organizational computing. In a world of fierce global economic competition, many are worried about the ability of organizations, both private and public, to maintain and improve a high standard of living. That is why it was especially disturbing to read in the 1980s that the productivity of the largest part of the United States economy, the service sector, did not increase substantially, despite the service sector's heavy investment in computing. This dilemma has been called the "Productivity Paradox."

Economists are still battling over the Productivity Paradox, and whether the productivity of the United States service sector is finally improving (see Attewell, Part III, Chapter K and King, Part III, Chapter L). Even if computerization proves to be a good investment for the economy as a whole, there is substantial evidence that many organizations get much less value from their computing investments than they could, or should. It is unfortunate that there is no automatic link between computerization and improved productivity.

Today, most of the 40,000 people who obtain B.S. and M.S. degrees in computer science each year have no opportunity for systematic exposure to reliable knowledge about the best design strategies, common uses, effective implementation, and assessment of the value of computing for organizations (Lewis, 1989). Yet a substantial fraction of these students go on to work for organizations, attempting to produce or maintain systems that improve organizational performance. Without training in how organizations work, it is hardly surprising that many of them develop systems that underperform in organizational terms. As the funding for computer science research shifts from military sources to civilian sources at the end of the Cold War, there is additional practical pressure on computer science to develop its own knowledge of computing, organizations, and organizational performance.

What Is Organizational Informatics?

Organizational Informatics is a small but growing body of research that examines the design and use of computing in organizations. Organizational Informatics research uses theories of organizations and work to understand the complex relationship between the design and use of information technologies and human behavior in organizations (Huff and Finholt, 1994; Cotterman and Senn, 1992). We will examine two of the key insights that this research offers for professionals trying to understand why computing in organizations is more than simply a matter of computer technology.

1. *The behavior of human organizations affects the design and implementation of computer systems.* The values, interests, skills, and formal positions of groups and individuals within organizations affect how initial design problems are framed, the possible range of design choices, and the resources available to support different design and implementation activities.
2. *The effective use of computerized systems in organizations does not depend on technology alone.* Many other aspects of organizations—including job design, reward and incentive schemes, political negotiation, and cultural understandings—combine with technology choices to affect how computing is used in practice.

The many computer professionals working to provide useful organizational computing should be able to learn from this body of research. Even a modest exposure can give working professionals a set of concepts and examples they can use to improve their understanding of the often disorderly world of organizational computing.

Organizations Shape Systems Design in Practice

It is not controversial to say that organizations should affect the design of organizational systems they are going to use, especially if they are paying for them. Many argue that computing systems should be "aligned," or compatible, with an organization's formal strategy and structure (Scott Morton, Part III, Chapter D; Walton, 1989). In the perfect world of traditional systems development, the client organization would:

- provide computer scientists with an absolutely clear, consistent, complete, and unchanging set of requirements for a system design;
- know exactly what they want from the very beginning of the project;
- adequately anticipate how the final system (yet to be built) will be used;
- know the major organizational effects of the design choices (yet to be made).

These assumptions don't hold up in the typical world of organizational computing. Two criticisms of the traditional systems development model (e.g., Avison and Fitzgerald, 1988) are worth emphasizing. First, systems development is a learning process (Greenbaum and Kyng, 1991). At the beginning of a systems project, the participants often do not know exactly what they want, and what will work. In many cases, neither the users nor the technologists know ahead of time what the organizational consequences of the design choices will be (though Organizational Informatics research is improving our knowledge of this link, as selections in the next part show). People often have to see a computer system working in realistic situations to know what they like or dislike about it.

Second, medium- and large-scale organizations are not single entities that have a single set of systems requirements. Organizations are internally heterogeneous. They are composed of many groups, individuals, and activities, partially cooperating and partially conflicting. The values, interests, skills, and formal positions of different groups and individuals within organizations play powerful roles in systems development. The workings of organizations affect how an initial design problem is framed, the possible range of design decisions, and the resources available to support different design activities (Kling, 1987).

Every computer system project begins with a framing of a problem. What is the problem? Which kinds of activities, people, and objects are relevant, and which are not? The framing of a problem—and different groups will have different framings—can have a large impact on the resulting computer system. For example, consider an office of customer service agents. If the problem is framed as "getting customer service agents to do more work," then the systems to be considered will more likely concentrate on speeding up and tightly controlling their existing work practices. If the problem is framed as "helping customer service agents serve the consumer better," then there is a possibility that work practices and work skills, as well as the computing system, may be changed (Jewett and Kling, 1990). This framing gives a design emphasis to systems that provide more, and different, kinds of information to the customer service agents, and allows them to do something with it. According to a founder of the "systems approach" to problem solving:

> We fail more often because we solve the wrong problem than because we get the wrong solution to the right problem . . . The problems we select for solution and the way we formulate them depends more on our philosophy and world view than on our science and technology. (Russell Ackoff, quoted in Greenbaum and Kyng, 1991, p. 9)

Forsythe (1993) provides a good example of how important problem framing can be in the case of expert systems. The designers of expert systems learned how experts worked only through formal interviews conducted away from their normal working environments. For example, they invited a car mechanic to a conference room to discuss how he repaired cars. They interviewed a surgeon in a conference room, away from his colleagues that he often turned to when there was something he didn't understand. In their framing of the problem, the systems builders did not consider the physical work environment and interactions with others as an important part of experts' work. This framing led the systems designers to produce expert systems that were considered "fragile," or difficult to apply to typical working situations.

The values that shape systems design are also influenced by how powerful groups and individuals believe that people in organizations should behave. For example, there is a difference between seeing people in organizations as skilled and trustworthy and seeing them as unskilled and lazy. Common design strategies such as "idiot-proofing" or tight monitoring assume the people using the system are unskilled and/or likely to misbehave. Salzman and Rosenthal (1994) discuss the case of a bank teller system with a design based on these organizational assumptions. The design of the teller system hard-wired formal organizational rules, such as not allowing a single customer to make more than three transactions every day without supervisor approval. Because powerful groups within the organization put a high value on the enforcement of formal procedures, these features were emphasized in the final systems design. The system could have been designed with what Salzman and Rosenthal (1994) call "soft controls"—letting the system suggest what the tellers should do in unusual situations, rather than forcing them to stop and obtain supervisors' approval. The values of a particular group played a strong role in systems design.

Of all the groups found within organizations, computer professionals are likely to have a strong, and perhaps the strongest, influence on which organizational assumptions are emphasized in the design. The organizational values of systems designers can vary significantly. Kumar and Bjorn-Andersen (1990) studied the work values of computer professionals in Scandinavia and North America. They found the Scandinavian designers much more willing to consider questions of job design and quality of work life than were North American designers, who were more likely to focus exclusively on technical and economic questions.

Despite the important role computer professionals have in making technical decisions that affect working life, most computer scientists tend to have a highly technical and undersocialized view of how computerization takes place in organizations. This view, which Kling and Jewett (1994) call a Rational Systems approach to organizations, assumes that organizational goals are clear, resources are ample, and that organizational members are generally cooperative. Years of research on organizations shows that these assumptions are routinely violated in typical organizations (see Scott, 1992; Morgan, 1986). Computer scientists making important changes in organizations need to have a more complete understanding of how organizations actually behave.

Systems design in real organizations is difficult. Diversity within organizations makes system design as much an organizational activity—and thus a social, cultural, economic, and political activity—as a technical activity. Organizational Informatics researchers who have studied the software development process have been active in prototyping, iterative design, user involvement, and other new techniques to address the classic barriers between designers and users. Some advocate new ways of looking at the design process: as a mutual learning process (e.g., Greenbaum and Kyng, 1991), or as the construction of a new shared language (e.g., Winograd and Flores, 1986; Ehn, 1991). Others closely study organizational situations empirically, using methods from social psychology (Fish *et al.*, 1993) and anthropology (Bentley *et al.*, 1992). All of these efforts are intended to cope with the problem of how organizations shape technical decision making in practice.

Effective Use Requires More Than Technology

A second key insight of Organizational Informatics research has to do with the complexities of computer use in organizations. How do computer design decisions affect organizational behavior and organizational effectiveness? Is technical adequacy, or even technical excellence, enough to guarantee that computing will be used, and used effectively? The effective use of computing does not depend on technology alone, as many examples from Organizational Informatics research show.

An extreme example of the importance of organizational issues can be seen in Orlikowski's (1993) study of the use of a groupware system in an extremely competitive consulting firm. The groupware system, Lotus Notes, was designed to be a common database of ideas and work products that consultants could share. By re-using other consultants' work and ideas, the organization could save time and money. However, the organization strongly rewarded individual effort. Every two years, a small percentage of the consultants were promoted to the next level, and the rest were fired. After eight to ten years of successful promotions, a tiny fraction of the original consultants would be promoted to "partner" and have secure jobs with high incomes. Also, the rules of the organization forced the consultants to charge each hour of their labor to a specific customer. Hours spent learning to use the groupware system could not be billed to a customer, so the consultants had to train themselves during their own personal time. Not surprisingly, the system was not widely used by the consultants, regardless of the technical sophistication of the local area network or the user interface.

Organizational implementation is difficult from the strictly technical conception of implementation as coding a program. Organizational implementation means making a computer system accessible to those who could or should use it, and integrating its use into the routine work practices. The effort that goes into making computer systems work in organizations often reveals differences in the ways that different groups perceive the costs and benefits of different systems designs. Group calendar systems, for example, can impose the most burdensome record-keeping demands on the people being scheduled, while most of the benefit is enjoyed by the clerical staff that performs the scheduling (Grudin, 1989). Imbalances between the costs and benefits of using a system lead to a lack of incentive to contribute to the system and, in the case of group calendars, potentially low usage (see Bullen and Bennett, Part IV, Chapter F). People are more likely to share information when the system helps provide social feedback about the value of their efforts, or when they are rewarded (or at least not punished) for contributing (e.g., Sproull and Kiesler, 1991).

A long tradition of research shows that the quality of organizational implementation makes a large difference in how effectively these technologies work for organizations (Lucas, 1981; Kraemer et al., 1985; Walton, 1989). The social, economic, and political relationships between people and groups in organizations have an important influence on the design, development, and uses of computerized systems. People compute in a social world of relationships with others. They are concerned about acceptance, status, resources, power, and meaning. This "web" of social relationships and technological dependencies extends beyond the formally defined group and organizational boundaries that computer scientists usually rely on as an adequate description of organizational behavior (Kling and Scacchi, 1982; Kling, 1987; Kling, 1992). Understanding the use, and value, of computing requires knowledge of informal social behavior, available resources, and the dependencies between key groups (Kling, 1987, 1992).

Computer scientists in organizations constantly face organizational issues that directly affect their work. We discuss one example below of how a "technical" problem of systems safety and reliability is crucially tied to "organizational" as well as technical issues, with life-or-death consequences.

System Safety and Reliability

In a simplified engineering model of computing, the reliability of products is assured through extensive testing in a development lab. The social world of technology use is not perceived as shaping the reliability of systems, except through irascible human factors such as "operator errors." An interesting and tragic illustration of the limitations of this view can be found in some recent studies of the causes of death and maiming by an electron accelerator, which was designed to help cure cancer, the Therac-25 (see Jacky, Part VII, Chapter C; Leveson and Turner, 1993).

The Therac-25 was designed and marketed in the mid-1980s by a Canadian firm, Atomic Energy of Canada Limited (AECL), as an advanced medical technology. It featured complete software control over all major functions (supported by a DEC PDP-11), among other innovations. Previous machines included electromechanical interlocks to raise and lower radiation shields. Thousands of people were effectively treated with the Therac-25 each year. However, between 1985 and 1987 there were six known accidents in which people died in the United States. Others were seriously maimed or injured. Both studies concur that there were subtle but important flaws in the design of the Therac-25's software and hardware. AECL's engineers tried to patch the existing hardware and (finally) software when they learned of the mishaps, but they treated each fix as the final repair.

Both studies show how the continuing series of mishaps was made worse by diverse organizational arrangements. Jacky claims that pressures for speedy work by radiological technicians, combined with an interface design that did not emphasize important error messages, was one of many causes of the accidents. Leveson and Turner differ in downplaying the working conditions of the Therac-25's operators and emphasize the flawed social system for communicating the seriousness of problems to federal regulators and other hospitals. Both studies observe that it is unlikely for even the best companies to develop error-free systems without high-quality feedback from users. Their recommendations differ. Jacky discusses the licensing of system developers, and the regulation of computerized medical systems to improve minimal standards of safety. Leveson and Turner propose extensive education and training of software engineers and more effective communication between manufacturers and their customers.

However, both studies also show us that an understanding of the safety of computer systems must go beyond the laboratory, and extent into the organizational settings where it is used. In the case of the Therac-25, it required understanding a complex web of interorganizational relationships, as well as the technical design and operation of the equipment. Nancy Leveson (1992) observes that most major technological disasters within the last twenty years "involved serious organizational and management deficiencies." In another example of systems safety and reliability, Hughes, Randall, and Shapiro (1992:119) observe that no civil collision in United Kingdom air space has been attributed to air traffic control failures. But the United Kingdom's Mediator control system was failing regularly, and had no backup during the period of their study. They conclude that the reliability of the British air traffic control system resides in the entire combination of relevant social and technical systems, rather than in any single component.

The need for this kind of organizational understanding is unfortunately slighted in the computer science academic world today. For example, Hartmanis and Lin (1992:110–111) discuss only those aspects of computer system reliability that are amenable to understanding through laboratory-like studies. But cases of safety-critical systems, like the Therac-25 and British Air Traffic Control, indicate why some computer scientists must be willing to undertake (and teach) some form of organizational analysis.

Organizational Informatics in Computer Science

People who study information and computer science today rarely understand how organizations behave with information technologies—how and when they change, and how and when their behavior is relatively stable (institutionalized). Graduates of these academic programs often tacitly develop highly rationalized and formal conceptions of how organizations should behave. Their education has placed information technologies as the centerpiece of excitement, classroom analysis, and (again tacitly) social change. They often view organizations in individualistic terms, in which "the personality" of key participants plays key roles, and in which systemic organizational patterns (such as incentive structures and recruitment patterns) are in the background. Further, a bias toward "the right solution," or "the right technology" makes it hard for such graduates to see information technologies from the viewpoints of diverse people who will manage and use new systems. As a collection, this set of beliefs and perspectives weakens the abilities of many graduates to effectively solve organizational problems with information technologies.

We offer Organizational Informatics as an antidote—a body of knowledge that, when studied, can help students of information and computer science become more effective working professionals. A small but growing body of Organizational Informatics research tells us that the quality of computerized systems in use depends on the behavior of organizations, as well as the behavior of technology. Many of the research studies are much more conceptually sophisticated than we have been able to explain in this chapter.

This brief review scratches the surface of topics that Organizational Informatics research has addressed. We hope to stimulate sufficient curiosity in Organizational Informatics, so that students and professionals will examine a larger literature for key concepts and theories. Some of the Organizational Informatics studies that could improve professional practice include:

- the practical problems of systems development in actual organizational situations (Boland and Hirschheim, 1987; Cotterman and Senn, 1992; Orlikowski, 1993);
- the organizational impacts of electronic communications (Sproull and Kiesler, 1991; Kling and Jewett, 1994; Markus, 1994);
- how computer systems are used in daily work life (Suchman, 1983; Gasser, 1986; Kling, 1992);
- how computing creates new kinds of connections and dependency relationships between groups (Kling and Iacono, 1984; Bjorn-Andersen, Eason, and Robey, 1986);
- how computing increases the visibility of organizational activities, and triggers changes in the balance of power (Zuboff, 1988; Kling and Iacono, 1984);
- the practical dilemmas of managing software projects with hundreds of programmers (Curtis, Krasner, and Iscoe, 1988);
- how computerization changes the size and structure of organizations (Malone, Yates, and Benjamin, 1987);
- how power relations shape the way that computing is actually used in government operations and planning (Kraemer *et al.*, 1985; Danziger *et al.*, 1982);
- how the development of emerging computing technologies, such as supercomputing (Kling, Scherson, and Allen, 1992) and digital libraries (Kling and Lamb, 1995), is being shaped by larger organizational and societal forces.

Though the fields of information science and computer science continue to broaden their scope by adding new subfields such as software engineering and human–computer interaction, many established academics are often reluctant to take on new and different kind of phenomena. Human organizations are different from computing systems. Most computer scientists are not trained in systematic organizational analysis. They also belong to a culture that sees large private and public organizations as a "necessary evil" at best, and an oppressive dinosaur heading for extinction at worst (Kling, Part III, Chapter A). However, the number of computer scientists working on organizational problems continues to grow. For the computer scientists who choose to do this work, we argue that a basic knowledge of organizations and organizational computing is critical.

Organizational Informatics research does not provide a simple handbook for how computer professionals can achieve organizational computing excellence. Information and computer professionals trying to create effective organizational computing, however, need much more of a useful introduction to organizational computing than the traditional academic programs currently provide. Information and computer science needs a subfield dedicated to examining how organizations affect technology design, and how computing changes the way organizations behave. Organizational Informatics research provides our best foundation for understanding how computing becomes useful for organizations.

Acknowledgments

We thank Tom Jewett, Peter Denning, Beki Grinter, and Margaret Elliott for their ideas and comments.

References

Avison, D. E., and G. Fitzgerald (1988). *Information Systems Development: Methodologies, Techniques and Tools.* Blackwell Scientific, Oxford.

Bentley, Richard, Tom Rodden, Peter Sawyer, Ian Sommerville, John Hughes, David Randall, and Dan Shapiro (1992). "Ethnographically Informed Systems Design for Air Traffic Control," in Jon Turner and Robert Kraut (eds.), *Proc. Conference on Computer-Supported Cooperative Work.* ACM Press, New York.

Bjorn-Andersen, Niels, Ken Eason, and Daniel Robey (1986). *Managing Computer Impact: An International Study of Management and Organizations.* Ablex, Norwood, NJ.

Bloomfield, Brian, and Theo Vurdubakis (1994). "Boundary Disputes: Negotiating the Boundary Between the Technical and the Social in the Development of IT Systems." *Information Technology and People,* 7(1):9–24.

Boland, Richard, and Rudy Hirschheim (eds.) (1987). *Critical Issues in Information Systems.* John Wiley, New York.

Cotterman, William, and James Senn (eds.) (1992). *Challenges and Strategies for Research in Systems Development.* John Wiley, New York.

Curtis, Bill, Herb Krasner, and Niel Iscoe (1988). "A Field Study of the Software Design Process for Large Systems." *Communications of the ACM,* 31(11):1268–1287.

Danzinger, James, William Dutton, Rob Kling, Rob Kenneth, and Kenneth Kraemer (1982). *Computers and Politics: High Technology in American Local Governments.* Columbia University Press, New York.

Dunlop, Charles, and Rob Kling (eds.) (1991). *Computerization and Controversy: Value Conflicts and Social Choices.* Academic Press, Boston.

Ehn, Pelle (1991). "The Art and Science of Designing Computer Artifacts," in C. Dunlop and R. Kling (eds.), *Computerization and Controversy: Value Conflicts and Social Choices*. Academic Press, Boston.

Fish, Robert S., Robert E. Kraut, Robert W. Root, and Ronald E. Rice (1993). "Video as a Technology for Informed Communication." *Communications of the ACM*, 6(1)(January):48–61.

Forsythe, Diana E. (1993). "The Construction of Work in Artificial Intelligence." *Science, Technology, & Human Values*, Vol. 18, No. 4 (Autumn):460–479.

Friedman, Andrew L. (1989). *Computer Systems Development: History, Organization, and Implementation*. John Wiley, New York.

Galegher, Jolene, Robert Kraut, and Carmen Egido (eds.) (1990). *Intellectual Teamwork: Social and Intellectual Foundations of Cooperative Work*. Lawrence Erlbaum, Hillsdale, NJ.

Gasser, Les (1986). "The Integration of Computing and Routine Work." *ACM Transactions on Office Information Systems*, 4(3)(July):205–225.

Geyelin, Milo (1994). "Doomsday Device: How an NCR System for Inventory Turned Into a Saboteur." *Wall Street Journal*, (August 8):1.

Greenbaum, Joan, and Morten Kyng (1991). *Design at Work: Cooperative Work of Computer Systems*. Lawrence Erlbaum, Hillsdale, NJ.

Greif, Irene (ed.) (1988). *Computer Supported Cooperative Work: A Book of Readings*. Morgan Kaufman, San Mateo, CA.

Grudin, Jonathan (1989). "Why Groupware Applications Fail: Problems in Design and Evaluation." *Office: Technology and People*, 4(3):245–264.

Hartmanis, Juris, and Herbert Lin (eds.) (1992). *Computing the Future: A Broader Agenda for Computer Science and Engineering*. National Academy Press, Washington, D.C. [Briefly summarized in *Communications of the ACM*, 35(11) November 1992.]

Huff, Chuck, and Thomas Finholt (eds.) (1994). *Social Issues in Computing: Putting Computing in Its Place*. McGraw-Hill, New York.

Hughes, John A., David Randall, and Dan Shapiro (1992). "Faltering from Ethnography to Design," in Jon Turner and Robert Kraut (eds.), *Proc. Conference on Computer-Supported Cooperative Work*. ACM Press, New York.

Jewett, Tom, and Rob Kling (1990). "The Work Group Manager's Role in Developing Computing Infrastructure." *Proceedings of the ACM Conference on Office Information Systems*. Boston, MA.

Kling, Rob (1987). "Defining the Boundaries of Computing Across Complex Organizations," in Richard Boland and Rudy Hirschheim (eds.), *Critical Issues in Information Systems Research*. John Wiley, New York.

Kling, Rob (1992). "Behind the Terminal: The Critical Role of Computing Infrastructure in Effective Information Systems' Development and Use." Chapter 10 in William Cotterman and James Senn (eds.), *Challenges and Strategies for Research in Systems Development*, pp. 365–413. John Wiley, New York.

Kling, Rob (1993). "Organizational Analysis in Computer Science." *The Information Society*, 9(2)(Mar–May):71–87.

Kling, Rob, and Margaret Elliott (1994). "Digital Library Design for Organizational Usability," in John L. Schnase, John J. Leggett, Richard K. Furuta, and Ted Metcalfe (eds.), *Proc. Digital Libraries '94 Conference. June 19–21, 1994 College Station Texas*, pp. 146–155. (URL: http//atgl.WUSTL.edu/DL94.)

Kling, Rob, and Suzanne Iacono (1984). "Computing as an Occasion for Social Control." *Journal of Social Issues*, 40(3):77–96.

Kling, Rob, and Tom Jewett (1994). "The Social Design of Worklife with Computers and Networks: An Open Natural Systems Perspective," in Marshall C. Yovits (ed.), *Advances in Computers*, Volume 39. Academic Press, San Diego.

Kling, Rob, and Roberta Lamb (1995). "Analyzing Visions of Electronic Publishing and Digital Libraries," in Gregory Newby and Robin M. Peek (eds.), *Scholarly Publishing: The Electronic Frontier*. MIT Press, Cambridge.

Kling, Rob, and Walt Scacchi (1982). "The Web of Computing: Computing Technology as Social Organization." *Advances in Computers*, Vol. 21. Academic Press, New York.

Kling, Rob, Isaac Scherson, and Jonathan Allen (1992). "Massively Parallel Computing and Information Capitalism," in W. Daniel Hillis and James Bailey (eds.), *A New Era of Computing*, pp. 191–241. MIT Press, Cambridge, MA.

Kraemer, Kenneth L., Siegfried Dickhoven, Susan Fallows-Tierney, and John L. King (1985). *Datawars: The Politics of Modeling in Federal Policymaking*. Columbia University Press, New York.

Kraemer, Kenneth L., and John L. King (1986). "Computing in Public Organizations." *Public Administration Review*, 46(November):488–496.

Kumar, Kuldeep, and Niels Bjorn-Andersen (1990). "A Cross-Cultural Comparison of IS Designer Values." *Communications of the ACM*, 33(5)(May):528–538.

Leveson, Nancy G. (1992). "High Pressure Steam Engines and Computer Software." *Proc. International Conference on Software Engineering*, Melbourne, Australia, (May).

Leveson, Nancy G., and Clark S. Turner (1993). "An Investigation of the Therac-25 Accidents." *Computer*, 26(7)(July):18–39.

Lewis, Philip M. (1989). "Information Systems as an Engineering Discipline." *Communications of the ACM*, 32(9)(Sept.):1045–1047.

Lucas, Henry C. (1981). *Implementation: The Key to Successful Information Systems*. Columbia University Press, New York.

Malone, T. W., J. Yates, and R. I. Benjamin (1987). "Electronic Markets and Electronic Hierarchies." *Communications of the ACM*, 30:484–497.

Markus, M. Lynne (1994). "Finding a 'Happy Medium': The Explaining the Negative Effects of Electronic Communication on Social Life at Work" from *ACM Transactions on Information Systems*, 12(2)(April):119–149.

Markus, M. Lynne, and Mark Keil (1994). "If We Build It, They Will Come: Designing Information Systems That People Want to Use." *Sloan Management Review*, 35(4)(Summer):11–25.

Morgan, Gareth (1986). *Images of Organization*. Sage, Beverly Hills, CA.

Orlikowski, Wanda J. (1993). "Learning from Notes: Organizational Issues in Groupware Implementation." *Information Society*, 9(3)(July–September): 237–250.

Salzman, Harold, and Stephen R. Rosenthal (1994). *Software by Design: Shaping Technology and the Workplace*. Oxford University Press, New York.

Scott, W. Richard (1992). *Organizations: Rational, Natural, and Open Systems* (3d ed.). Prentice-Hall, Englewood Cliffs, NJ.

Sproull, Lee, and Sara Kiesler (1991). *Connections: New Ways of Working in the Networked Organization*. MIT Press, Cambridge, MA.

Suchman, Lucy (1983). "Office Procedures as Practical Action: Models of Work and System Design." *ACM Transactions on Office Information Systems,* 1(4)(October): 320–328.

Walton, Richard E. (1989). *Up and Running: Integrating Information Technology and the Organization.* Harvard Business School Press, Boston.

Winograd, Terry, and Fernando Flores (1986). *Understanding Computers and Cognition.* Ablex Publishing, Norwood, NJ.

Zuboff, Shoshanna (1988). *In the Age of the Smart Machine: The Future of Work and Power.* Basic Books, New York.

P·A·R·T·IV

Computerization and the Transformation of Work

P·A·R·T · IV

Computerization at Work

Rob Kling

Work, Technology, and Social Change

This part examines the extent to which computer-based systems are organized to enhance or degrade the quality of working life for clerks, administrative staff, professionals, and managers. Worklife merits a lot of attention for four reasons:

1. Work is a major component of many people's lives. Wage income is the primary way that most people between the ages of 22 and 65 obtain money for food, housing, clothing, transportation, and so on. The United States' population is about 260,000,000, and well over 110,000,000 work for a living. So, major changes in the nature of work—the number of jobs, the nature of jobs, career opportunities, job content, social relationships at work, working conditions of various kinds—can affect a significant segment of society.

2. In the United States, most wage earners work thirty to sixty hours per week—a large fraction of their waking lives. And people's experiences at work, whether good or bad, can shape other aspects of their lives as well. Work pressures or work pleasures can be carried home to families. Better jobs give people some room to grow when they seek more responsible or complex positions, while stifled careers often breed boredom and resentment in comparably motivated people. Although people vary considerably in what kinds of experiences and opportunities they want from a job, few people would be thrilled with a monotonous and socially isolated job, even if it were to pay well.

3. Computerization has touched more people more visibly in their work than in any other kind of setting—home, schools, churches, banking,

and so on. Workplaces are good places to examine how the dreams and dilemmas of computerization really work out for large numbers of people under an immense variety of social and technical conditions.

4. Many aspects of the way that people work influence their relationships to computer systems, the practical forms of computerization, and their effects. For example, in Part III, Steven Hodas argued that the tenuousness of many teachers' classroom authority could discourage them from seeking computer-supported instruction in their classes. Also, Martin Baily and Paul Attewell argued that computerization has had less influence on the productivity of organizations because people integrate computers into their work so as to provide other benefits to them, such as producing more professional looking documents that enhance their esteem with others, or managers becoming counterproductive control-freaks with computerized reports.

When specialists discuss computerization and work, they often appeal to strong implicit images about the transformations of work in the last one hundred years, and the role that technologies have played in some of those changes. In nineteenth-century North America, there was a major shift from farms to factories as the primary workplaces. Those shifts—often associated with the industrial revolution—continued well into the early twentieth century. Industrial technologies such as the steam engine played a key role in the rise of industrialism. But ways of organizing work also altered significantly. The assembly line with relatively high-volume, low-cost production and standardized, fragmented jobs was a critical advance in the history of industrialization. During the last one hundred years, farms also were increasingly mechanized, with motorized tractors, harvesters, and other powerful equipment replacing horse-drawn plows and hand-held tools. The farms also have been increasingly reorganized. Family farms run by small groups have been dying out, and have been bought up (or replaced by) huge corporate farms with battalions of managers, accountants, and hired hands.

Our twentieth-century economy has been marked by the rise of human service jobs, in areas such as banking, insurance, travel, education, and health. And many of the earliest commercial computer systems were bought by large service organizations such as banks and insurance companies. (By some estimates, the finance industries bought about 30% of the computer hardware in the United States in the 1980s.) During the last three decades, computer use has spread to virtually every kind of workplace, although large firms are still the dominant investors in computer-based systems. Since offices are the predominant site of computerization, it is helpful to focus on offices in examining the role that these systems play in altering work.

Today, the management of farms and factories is frequently supported with computer systems in their offices. Furthermore, approximately 50% of the staff of high-tech manufacturing firms are white-collar workers who make use of such systems—engineers, accountants, marketing specialists, and the like. There is also some computerization in factory production lines through the introduction of numerically controlled machine tools and industrial robots. And issues such as worklife quality and managerial control are just as real on the shop floor as in white-collar areas (see Shaiken, 1986; Zuboff, 1988). While the selections here examine white-collar work, the reader can consider the parallels between the computerization of blue-collar work and white-collar work. Many of the studies of the computerization of blue-collar work focus on factories (e.g., Noble, 1984; Shaiken, 1986; Weekley, 1983; Zuboff, 1988). Factories employ a significant fraction of blue-collar workers, but not a majority. Some of the major blue-collar occupations that are not factory jobs include bus and truck drivers, heavy-equipment operators, construction workers, appliance repair personnel, automobile and airplane mechanics, gas station attendants, dockworkers, gardeners, and janitors. Factories have been the site of some major computerization projects, as in the use of robots for welding and painting and the use of numerically controlled machinery. But many other blue-collar jobs are being influenced by computerization as well.

The Transformation of Office Work

Office work has always involved keeping records. We don't have many detailed accounts of the earliest offices, which date back before the Middle Ages. Today, offices with dozens of clerks carrying out similar tasks are commonplace. Before the twentieth century, the majority of offices were small and were often the workplace of a single businessman or professional who kept informal records (Delgado, 1979). The shape of offices—the way work is organized, the role of women in their operation, the career lines, and office technologies—has been radically transformed in the last one hundred years.

Novelists like Charles Dickens have written some detailed descriptions of nineteenth-century English clerks. They were often viewed as a dull bunch of sickly men who had safe but tedious jobs. In the nineteenth century, information was recorded by clerks using pen and ink, and copies were also made by hand. There were no powerful technologies for assisting one's hand in writing, copying, or even doing calculations. Filing systems were relatively makeshift, and there weren't standardized sizes of forms such as 3 × 5 cards or letter-size paper. Clerical work was a man's job, and was a common route for learning a business and becoming a potential owner.

In the early twentieth century, the technologies and organization of office work underwent substantial change. Firms began to adopt telephones and typewriters, both of which had been recently invented. By the 1930s and 1940s, many manufacturers devised electromechanical machines to help manipulate, sort, and tally specialized paper records automatically. Some of the more expensive pieces of equipment, such as specialized card-accounting machines, were much more affordable and justifiable in organizations that centralized their key office activities.

While new equipment was often adopted to enhance the efficiency of offices, its use was tied to more widespread changes in the shape of organizations: the shifts in control to central administrators, and an increase in the number of jobs that were mostly being filled by women. Women began to work in offices as typewriter operators and clerks, and were typically viewed as short-term jobholders, working between school and marriage during their early to mid-twenties. As larger firms hired professional managers, many aspiring professionals turned to graduate schools rather than apprenticeships to learn their craft. Increasingly, specialized colleges rather than on-the-job training became the key entry point for professional and managerial careers. And with these careers dominated by males, clerical work became the province of women who could not readily move into the upper cadres of professional or managerial life.

This sketch indicates some of the key themes that permeate discussions of computerization and the quality of worklife: how efficient and flexible work will be, who controls the work that is done and how it is organized, how work is divided by gender, and who shares in the benefits of technological and organizational change.

Businesses such as insurance companies and banks, along with public agencies, adopted computer-based information systems on a large scale in the 1960s. Many of the early digital computer systems replaced electromechanical paper-card systems. The earliest systems were designed for batch operation. Clerks filled in paper forms with information about a firm's clients, and the forms were then periodically sent to a special group of keypunchers to translate the data onto cardboard cards. These "Hollerith cards" each stored one line of data, up to eighty characters. They were punched with a series of holes for each character or number. Keypunch machines were clanky devices with a typewriter-style keyboard, a bin for storing blank cards, and a holder for the card being punched. There was no simple way for a keypunch operator to correct an error. Cards containing errors (e.g., a letter "s" instead of an "a") had to be completely repunched. The punched cards were then taken to a data-processing department for a weekly or monthly "run," during which time records were updated and reports were produced. It often took a few cycles—sometimes weeks or months—to identify and correct errors. Using these early computerized systems required immense precision and care, since inaccuracies were detected and corrected slowly. In addition, the data from one information system were usually formatted in a way that did not make them accessible to other systems. Professionals and managers often waited a few months for a new kind of report, and reports that required merging data from several separate systems were often viewed as prohibitively complex, time-consuming, and expensive to create. The earliest computer systems were speedier than the hand in processing large volumes of highly specialized transactions. But they were also rigid and cumbersome for many people who used them.

Furthermore, the transaction-processing and report-generating programs were usually written by specialized programmers who were organized into specialized data-processing departments. Often, the large specialized computer systems, their operators, and their programmers were all located in basement offices—isolating them from organizational life. During the last twenty-five years, most companies have reorganized their computer-based information systems to be more responsive and flexible, and to support a richer array of organizational activities. Terminals connected to shared databases or microcomputers are commonplace in today's organizations.

During the 1980s and early 1990s, virtually every organization bought PCs and workstations. But "the PC revolution" did not merely change the nature of office equipment—it expanded the range of people who use computers routinely to include a much larger fraction of professionals (who are often men)—managers of all kinds, architects, accountants, lawyers, and so on. Many larger organizations are beginning to use computerized communication systems, like electronic mail, to help managers and professionals keep in contact when they are out of the office. And a few organizations are experimenting with pushing some of their staff out of regular offices and creating "virtual offices" in locations closer to their clients, their homes, and other more convenient (and less costly) locations.

In the last decade many larger organizations have been restructuring work. Some analysts tout these restructurings as by-products of computerization. But many of these changes are often unrelated to computerization. For example, in the early 1990s many top managers have restructured their organizations so as to eliminate layers of managers below them ("delayering"). Some analysts argue that the use of electronic mail and computerized reporting systems has enabled this flattening of corporate hierarchies. But I have seen such thinning of middle management in corporations that make relatively little use of electronic mail. If organizations can delayer without the use of e-mail, why would we believe that e-mail plays a key role in delayering?

Similarly, in the United States recession, many organizations have laid off numerous workers, and the remaining staff often work much harder and much longer hours. It's not clear whether computerization has any significant influence on this pattern. Last, many organizations have restructured their employment contracts so that they have a much larger fraction of readily dispensable part-time and/or temporary employees than before the recent recession. This approach has created fewer full-time jobs with good career opportunities in specific organizations, and is probably unrelated to computerization.

Today, the typical clerk, professional, or manager is much more likely to use a variety of powerful computer systems than would his or her counterpart ten and certainly fifteen years ago. But have jobs improved in a way that is commensurate with the technical improvement in computer systems? That is a key question that we will examine from several vantage points in this part.

Gender, Work, and Information Technology

It may seem strange to begin a discussion of computerization and work with gender, when the common terms of computer use—such as "computer user" and interface—seem to be gender neutral. But finding ways to talk about people's identities can help us understand computerization more deeply.

Discussions of women and computing often focus on clerical work because about one-third of the women in the work force are clerks. Conversely, about 80% of the 20 million clerks in the United States in 1993 were women. Women work in every occupation from janitors to ambassadors for the federal government, but they are not equally represented in the higher-status and better-paid professions. Less than 30% of the nation's 1.3 million programmers and systems analysts were women in 1993. But the nation's 16.1 million female clerks vastly outnumbered the nation's 412,000 female programmers and systems analysts in 1993. Female computer users today are more likely to be clerks who process transactions such as payroll, inventory, and airline reservations, than to be information and computer professionals.

In Chapter B, Suzanne Iacono and I examine how the dramatic improvements in office technologies over the past one hundred years have sometimes made many clerical jobs much more interesting, flexible, and skill rich. But we also observe that these changes, especially those involving increased skill requirements, have not brought commensurate improvements in career opportunities, influence, or clerical salaries. We examine the actual changes in clerical work that have taken place over the last one hundred years, from the introduction of the first typewriters through whole generations of office equipment—mechanical accounting machines, telephones, and photocopiers. Each generation of equipment has made certain tasks easier. At the same time, clerical work shifted from a predominantly male occupation, which provided an entry route to higher levels of management, to a predominantly female occupation, which has been ghettoized. We criticize some of the technological utopians, such as Giuliano (1982), by arguing that a new generation of integrated computer-based office systems will not automatically alter the pay, status, and careers of clerks without explicit attention.[1] Further, we argue that computerization is a continuous process that doesn't stop when a new kind of equipment is acquired (also see Kling and Iacono, 1989).

These observations become more meaningful because the vast majority of working women are still concentrated in a few occupations, despite the growing numbers of women who have entered the professions and management in the last two decades (Reskin and Padavic, 1994). About 80% of the clerical workers in the United States in 1993 were women. In contrast, about 42% of the executives and managers and 53% of the professionals were women. However, women professionals were clustered in nursing, social work, library jobs, and school teaching. For example, 75% of school teachers were women, while less than 20% of architects were women. In 1988 only 30% of employed computer scientists and 10% of employed doctoral-level computer scientists were women (Pearl et al., 1990), and the percentages have not changed substantially since then.[2]

The way that clerical work is computerized affects 16 million working women in the United States. But men often believe that much of the work done in female work groups is trivial and can be readily automated. The problems in effectively computerizing such seemingly routine work that can, in fact, require managing subtle complexities of work processes, actually affects a much larger number of people—both inside and outside the targeted work group. This idea is developed in Lucy Suchman's article, "Supporting Articulation Work" (Chapter H), which I will discuss in more detail later in this introduction.

Information Technology and New Ways of Organizing Work

An important aspect of worklife is the issue of who controls the way that work is organized, the way that people communicate, and workers' levels of skills. In the 1980s, many professionals became enamored with microcomputers. They became the new electronic typewriter for writers of all kinds. Engineers set aside their slide rules and electronic calculators for

---

[1] See Iacono and Kling (1987) for a much more detailed version of this analysis.

[2] By 1992, about 30% of the M.S. degrees and 14% of the Ph.D. degrees in computer science were awarded to women. Even if 50% of the graduate degrees in computer science were awarded to women in 1990 and every subsequent year, it would take close to twenty years for the fraction of women employed in the field to be about 50%. Klawe and Leveson (1995) argue that it is difficult to draw substantially more women into the information and computer sciences without some special efforts. Consequently, we should not expect to see women and men represented equally in the diverse information and computer science occupations until well into the next century, at best.

software that mechanized their calculations and produced graphical data displays; accountants helped drive the demand for micros with their passion for computerized spreadsheets, and so on. Many professionals became hooked on the relative ease and speed of their computer tools, and dreaded any return to manual ways of working. They often adopted and adapted computers to their work in ways that enhanced their control over their work products. Work still remained labor intensive, since the working week did not diminish in length. Work sometimes became more fun, or at least less tedious.

In Giuliano's (1982) account, managers organized "industrial-age" offices for efficiency, and will organize "information-age" offices in a way that enhances the quality of jobs as well. But some observers argue that managers will not give up substantial control to their subordinates. Andrew Clement, for example, argues that the close monitoring of employee behavior represents the logical extension of a dominant management paradigm—pursuit of control over all aspects of the business enterprise. Indeed, some believe that to manage is to control. ". . . [M]anagement may be called 'the profession of control' " (Clement, 1984:10).

Some authors argue that the industrialization of clerical work sets the stage for the industrialization of professional work as well. In "The Social Dimensions of Office Automation" Abbe Mowshowitz summarizes his sharp vision in these concise terms:

> Our principal point is that the lessons of the factory are the guiding principles of office automation. In large offices, clerical work has already been transformed into factory-like production systems. The latest technology—office automation—is simply being used to consolidate and further a well-established trend. For most clerical workers, this spells an intensification of factory discipline. For many professionals and managers, it signals a gradual loss of autonomy, task fragmentation and closer supervision—courtesy of computerized monitoring. Communication and interaction will increasingly be mediated by computer. Work will become more abstract . . . and opportunities for direct social interaction will diminish. (Mowshowitz, 1986)

Some analysts have hoped that new computer communication technologies, such as electronic mail, would enable workers to bypass rigid bureaucratic procedures (e.g., Hiltz and Turoff, 1978:142). Some analysts have found that electronic mail can give groups more ability to develop their own culture (Finholt and Sproull, 1990). And some have hoped that electronic mail would reduce the barriers to communication between people at different levels of hierarchy in an organization. But the evidence is mixed. Zuboff (1988) reports an interesting case that can dim these unbridled enthusiasms and lead us to ask under what conditions they are most likely to occur. In a large drug company she studied, managers claimed that their communications to electronic groups were often treated as policy statements, even when they wanted to make informal observations or ad hoc decisions. Further, when a group of about 130 professional women formed a private women's conference, male managers felt threatened, upper managers discouraged women from participating, and soon many participants dropped out (Zuboff, 1988:382–383).

I suspect that electronic communications systems are most likely to facilitate the formation of groups that upper managers deem to be safe, except in those special organizations—like universities and R&D labs—where there are strong norms against censorship. The controversy between technological utopians who see technologies as improving human and organizational behavior and those who see social systems as changing slowly in response to other kinds of social and economic forces will not be resolved by one or two case studies. But the cases are instructive to help focus the debate about what is possible and the conditions under which computer systems of specific kinds alter social life.

In "The Case of the Omniscient Organization," sociologist Gary Marx reports the behavior of a hypothetical company, Dominion-Swann (DS). The article, which is written as an excerpt from DS's 1995 Employee Handbook, was originally published in the *Harvard Business Review*, a premier management magazine, in 1990 as the springboard for a discussion about information technology and management practices. The DS case is constructed as a technologically anti-utopian narrative (see Part II). But it also illustrates the power of well-crafted utopian or anti-utopian narratives to highlight significant social choices. Marx crafted the DS case to illustrate how a business firm could develop a tight system of social control by partly relying on relatively unobtrusive information technologies. However, the DS's 1995 Employee Handbook characterizes each form of control as either inoffensive or actually in the employee's best interests. In effect, DS has created a totally encompassing electronic prison in which virtually every aspect of an employee's behavior is continually monitored. Simultaneously, DS's 1995 Employee Handbook characterizes the company as a homelike community, where employees feel so comfortable with DS and each other that continual monitoring of work practices, health, and social relations is simply a cozy part of everyday life. Marx has brilliantly portrayed the contradictions of some contemporary corporate cultures. DS would appear as hellish to an ardent individualist like William Whyte (see Chapter A in Part III).

While Marx's portrait of DS can outrage and even terrify some people, it's not automatically true that a firm like DS would have trouble finding willing employees. North American society is diverse, and many people live out social practices that would offend others in their own communities. And many firms have increased the extent to which they monitor some aspects of their employees' work. Today, most of the monitoring focuses on measures of work, but some organizations also tap phone calls or eavesdrop on conversations between co-workers (Kadaba, 1993). A few organizations are experimenting with "active badges" that would enable others to learn of their whereabouts at any time (Kling, 1993).[3] The next selection "Mr. Edens Profits from Watching His Workers' Every Move" by Tony Horwitz describes a small financial services firm whose boss observes his employees by sitting behind their desks. Mr. Edens's techniques for having his employees work intensively by prohibiting them from looking at the window or conversing are simple. But the fact that many people desperate for some kind of stable job will work for Mr. Edens suggests that employers that used techniques like Gary Marx's DS would also find willing employees.

In 1991, Grant and Higgens reported an empirical study about the effectiveness and repercussions of monitoring the activities of service workers, such as those who audit insurance claims. They studied a group of existing companies, none of which were as finely wired as the hypothetical DS. Grant and Higgens developed a rich, multidimensional concept of monitoring, which includes features such as the granularity of data (i.e., amount of work per minute, hour, day, or week), the different types of data collected (i.e., work completed, error rates, customer complaints, nature of tasks), and the variety of people who routinely see data about a person's work (i.e., oneself, one's supervisor, one's peers, and/or upper managers). They found that many people did not object to computerized monitoring. And in a few cases, some people liked their work to be measured to help demonstrate how productive they actually were. But they also found that monitoring does not always improve performance and the quality of service. For example, extensive monitoring discouraged some people from being willing to help their co-workers with problems or work crunches. In fact, service seemed to degrade most when many aspects of performance were monitored and made available to supervisors. Grant and Higgens view monitoring as a legitimate but subtle form of managerial intervention that can often backfire when system designers and managers do not pay close attention to people's indirect responses to monitoring.

Control over the Location of Work

It is possible for managers to work with several competing logics. They may be concerned with maintaining some control over their subordinates' time and pay, but also with allowing sufficient flexibility and self-direction to ensure good quality work and retain good employees. In fact, some organizations try to pay less by offering attractive working conditions. One

---

[3] See Andrew Clement's reprinted discussion of the seductions and complexities of active badges and other technologies that can monitor a person's location in "Considering Privacy in the Development of Multimedia Communications" (Part VIII, Chapter G).

of the interesting possibilities of computerized work—work at home— seems to have gotten stalled because of dilemmas of workplace control. Many self-employed people work at home. Futurists like Alvin Toffler have been specially excited by the possibilities that people who normally commute to a collective office could elect to work at home. In *The Third Wave*, Toffler portrayed homes with computer and communications equipment for work as "electronic cottages."

A recent report developed under the auspices of the Clinton administration included a key section, "Promoting Telecommuting," which lists numerous advantages for telecommuting (IITF, 1994). These include major improvements in air quality from reduced travel; increased organizational productivity when people can be more alert during working hours; faster commercial transit times when few cars are on the roads; and improvements in quality of worklife. The benefits identified in this report seem so overwhelming that it may appear remarkable that most organizations have not already allowed all of their workers the option to work at home.

Forester (1989) critiqued the visions of full-time work at home via telecommuting as a romantic preference. After coming to appreciate the social isolation reported by several people who worked at home full time, he speculates that many analysts who most enthusiastically champion full-time work at home with computing have never done it themselves. There have been several published studies of the pros and cons of firms giving their employees computer equipment to use at home while communicating with their shared offices via electronic mail (Kraemer and King, 1982; Olson, 1989; Huws, Korte, and Robinson, 1990). Some analysts hoped that work at home will decrease urban congestion during computer hours, give parents more opportunity for contact with young children, and allow people to spend more time in their neighborhoods. However, people who work a substantial fraction of the time at home may be unavailable for meetings, may be less visible to their peers and (therefore) passed over for promotions, and may be difficult to supervise unless they work on a piece-rate system. And some employees may lack sufficient self-discipline for work at home.

Many popular accounts focus on the way that home can be a less-distracting place to work than the collective office. Homes are different kinds of places to work than offices. Homeworkers report a different set of attractions and distractions at home: sociable neighbors may expect to be able to drop in any time; the refrigerator may beckon others too frequently; a spouse who works in an office may expect the partner at home to cook dinner nightly, the child who comes home from school at 3:00 P.M. may want immediate attention, and so on. Some parents choose to work at home because they can spend time with their babies and preschool children, but they often get much less done than at their collective offices. Olson's (1989) study of full-time work at home by computer professionals exemplifies some of the empirical studies. She found reduced job satisfaction, reduced organizational commitment, and higher role conflict in her sample. She also wonders whether work-at-home practices can exacerbate workaholism.

A few firms, such as IBM and Chiat/Day, have conducted pilot tests of the telecommuting and "virtual offices" (Kindel, 1993; Sprout, 1994; Taylor, 1994). And the members of a few occupations, such as journalists, professors, salespeople, and accountants often take notebook computers on the road when they travel. But the vast majority of firms keep their office-bound work force keystroking in the office rather than at home. Some workers are given computer equipment to use for unpaid overtime work. To date, however, no large firms have dispersed a large fraction of their full-time work force to their homes to work with computer systems.

It seems that the desire to maintain control underlies many managers' fears of having their employees work full time at home. It is much easier for managers to be sure that their subordinates are putting in a fair day's work in an office from nine to five (sometimes called "face work"), than to develop and monitor subtle contracts about the amount of work ("deliverables") to be produced each week or month.

Anthropologist Connie Perin adds an interesting insight about the complexities of off-site work after interviewing about 150 managers and professional employees in a variety of occupations, all organizationally employed, full-time workers in several United States industries. She found that

> Field-based employees typically complain of their "isolation" from a central office which "never understands" the conditions of their work—that lack of empathy or interest represents a fundamental negativism toward office absence. Those not working in a central office may be regarded as quasi-employees, similar to contract, part-time, or temporary employees within the organization. . . . Overall, both physical and social distance, independent of all other considerations, attenuates organizational legitimization and managerial trust. (Perin, 1991)

Electronic mail seems to give greater visibility to people who work at home (Sproull and Kiesler, 1991). But the technology only facilitates communication, and effective communication requires additional skills and attention. And there may be some subtle gender biases in electronic discussion groups (Herring, 1994). Some telecommuters have gone as far as making videos of their homes to show their supervisors their working conditions.

In addition, some people find social and technological attractions to working in a group office. A shared office is often populated with people to chat or go to lunch with, especially when it is compared with the typical isolating suburban neighborhood where many telecommuters live. In addition, organizations usually provide better computer equipment, including higher-speed computer networks and faster laser printers in shared offices than in their employees' homes. Last, today's computer equipment is still relatively clumsy and occasionally unreliable. It is much easier to get meaningful help from a colleague who can see one's work, or even from a technical support person at the office, than by explaining subtle problems over a telephone. Any of these patterns could be altered, but they each require changing many conventions of organizational life and neighborhood organizations.

I am discouraged when I read a government report like "Promoting Telecommuting" (IITF, 1994). It is infused with a decent enthusiasm for "doing the right thing," but fails to come to terms with many of the significant institutional issues that inhibit significant telecommuting. Conceptually, it relies on rational systems models of organizations rather than the natural systems models of organizations that I briefly explained in "The Centrality of Organizations in the Computerization of Society" (Part III, Chapter A). The report encourages federal agencies to take the lead in creating telecommuting programs with their employees, especially in large metro areas with substantial air pollution. And it will be interesting to see whether these pilot projects scale up to include a significant work force and if they are sustainable.

It is still an open question whether many organizations will allow substantial fractions of their work force to work at home with computing part time (one to three days a week), for reasons of personal flexibility or to facilitate regional transportation plans. Few homes are designed for significant home offices, and there are many important questions about the pros and cons of part-time work at home with computing (and fax) for those who prefer this option.[4]

New Forms of Work Organization

This article began with the controversies about the ways that computerization changes the organization of work. This debate used traditional forms of regimented assembly lines as a major reference point. Another related controversy is the extent to which new computing technologies, especially those that support communications, open up new forms of work. Does electronic mail eliminate organizational hierarchies and facilitate the formation of flexible (virtual) work groups? Do new forms of computerization create novel possibilities for organizational learning (Zuboff, 1991)?

There are few empirical studies that support these speculations, and the existing evidence is mixed. In one intriguing study, Tom Finholt and Lee Sproull (1990) found that electronic mail can give groups more ability to

---

[4] Also, see Vitalari and Venkatesh (1987) for an assessment of in-home computing services that examines work-oriented technologies among other systems.

develop their own culture. Others argue that electronic mail reduces the barriers to communication between people at different levels of hierarchy in an organization (Sproull and Kiesler, 1991).

The controversy about the possibility of computerization fostering new forms of work organization is engaging. Enthusiasts of the position that computerization can lead to new forms of work have the advantage of offering exciting possibilities. However, they rarely face the issues of workplace and support systems for technical work. When they ignore recurrent themes from previous eras of computerization, they risk being blindsided by perennial issues in new guises (Kling and Jewett, 1994).

The Design and Routine Use of Computerized Technologies

The Integration of Computing into Work

The vast majority of articles and books about computerization and work are written as if computer systems are highly reliable and graceful instruments. There are relatively few published studies of the ways that people actually use software systems in their work—which features do they use, to what extent do they encounter problems with systems or gaps in their own skills, how do they resolve problems when difficulties arise, how does the use of computerized systems alter the coherence and complexity of work?

There do not seem to be single simple answers to these questions. Some organizations computerize some jobs so as to make them as simple as possible. An extreme example is the way that fast-food chains have computerized cash registers with special buttons for menu items like cheeseburgers and malts so that they can hire clerks with little math skill. Kraut, Dumais, and Koch (1989) report a case study of customer service representatives in which simplifying work was a major consequence of computerization.

But it is common for images of simplification to dominate talk about computerization, regardless of the complexity of systems. Clement (1990) reports a case of computerization for secretaries in which managers characterized new systems as "super typewriters," which didn't require special training; they were mistaken. Many of the popular "full-featured" PC software packages for text processing, spreadsheets, and databases include hundreds of features. Narratives that focus on the capabilities of systems usually suggest that people can readily have all the advantages that all the features offer; actual behavior often differs from these expectations. Most people who use these powerful programs seem to learn only a small fraction of the available capabilities—enough to do their most immediate work. Moreover, it is increasingly common for many workers to use multiple computer systems, often with conflicting conventions, further complicating people's ability to "use computer systems to their fullest advantage." Some of these dilemmas can be resolved when organizations adopt relatively uncomplicated systems, train their staffs to use them, and provide consulting for people who have questions. However, many managers believe that supporting computer use with training and consulting is too expensive. Training is not cheap; an organization may pay $500 in labor time for a professional to learn to use a package that costs $150 to purchase.

I vividly remember a research administrator of a major food processing firm who was using a popular and powerful spreadsheet to budget projects. He wanted to print out reports in different fonts, such as printing budget categories in larger, bolder print. But he was puzzled how to do this. He knew that "it could be done" because he saw such a report in an advertisement. He treated his ignorance as a personal failing. He would have had to learn his spreadsheet's macro facility to produce this effect, and there was no clue in his manual about the appropriate strategy. In some organizations he might have turned to an information center with skilled consultants. But in his organization, the PC consultants were already overworked just installing new PCs and had no time to train users or consult on software use. This was not a critical problem for the manager. But it is indicative of the way that many organizations expect white-collar workers to learn to effectively use computer systems on their own, with little support besides limited manuals and advice from co-workers. Most computer systems do not work perfectly, further complicating what users have to learn and how they integrate systems into their work (see Kling and Scacchi, 1979; Gasser, 1986; Clement, 1990).

The selection by Poltrock and Grudin goes behind the scenes of a major software development firm to examine the way that software is designed and built in practice. They describe published principles of software development, such as those of John Gould, that emphasize close contact with the people who will actually use a software package (or surrogates) at all stages of design and testing. But they observe an odd contradiction in the practical work of many software developers. Many software developers claim that these principles are obvious, but they rarely follow them in practice. Poltrock and Grudin's study examines how such a contradiction can happen in practice. It could be that software developers behave like those of us who know that we should always balance our checkbooks, but often let it slip when we're busy. Their case study examines how computer scientists who were designing CAD software work within a structured organization. They are not autonomous masters of their own designs. People in other departments also play key roles in shaping the resulting product. In this case, the marketing department was able to seize the role as the group that would speak for people who would use the CAD system. They quote one software engineer, who noted:

> I think it would be worthwhile if all developers would spend maybe a couple of hours a year seeing how the product is used by those customers. Just watching them. And while they're watching them the customer would say, "I don't like the way this works," and noting those things. . . . You need to see

how they use it. You need to understand, first of all, what they're doing. So you need them to give you a little background, and then watch how they accomplish it, and see the totality of it, especially. How they fire up, the whole structure of their day. And then use that information to give you a global sense of how to help them out. You can't help them without understanding how they work.

This comment poignantly portrays the isolation of many software designers for whom spending just "a couple of hours a year" with their customers would be a major improvement in their abilities to develop higher-quality software.

In the next selection, MIS professor Christine Bullen and John Bennett (then employed by IBM) follow this advice. They examine the ways that people actually integrate computer systems to support collaborative work in groups (groupware) into their work. They report how several work groups have attempted to use some of today's best commercially available groupware systems with mixed results. Their informants often report that they value the electronic mail features of these systems as most important, even though each of these systems has many other advertised features. But many groups have found other features hard to use routinely, or simply not worth the effort (also see Grudin, 1989).

More significant, Bullen and Bennett report that many groups slowly learned that they would have to reorganize their work in order to take best advantage of their groupware. For example, the usage of electronic calendars to schedule meetings requires that all participants keep detailed calendars up to date on the computer system, even if they often spend much of their days out of the office. Many managers and professionals hope that they can computerize effectively by installing appropriate equipment, rather than by reorganizing work when they re(computerize). Bullen and Bennett made a provocative attempt to characterize those groups that are high performers: they are not always the most computerized. They argue that group members and their managers have worked hard to create work environments that have "clear elevating goals" and that support and reward commitment. These groups have developed effective social systems with coherent goals and related rewards as well as adopting technologies that might help improve their performance.

There is considerable unpublished controversy about this kind of analysis, since many technologists and computer vendors try to convince computer-using organizations that appropriate new technologies alone will improve working styles and organizational effectiveness. During the 1990s interesting technologies such as expert systems, groupware, and graphical interfaces will be written about by technologists and journalists as if they can significantly improve the ways that people work without requiring important changes in the way that groups organize their work. Careful studies of work with new computing technologies, like Bullen and Bennett's study, suggest that new technologies alone are unlikely to be magic potions that can automatically improve work merely by appearing in a workplace (also see Jewett and Kling, 1990).

Social Design of Computerized Systems and Work Settings

An exciting recent development is the effort by some researchers and practitioners to conceptualize the design of computer and networked systems as a set of interrelated decisions about technology and the organization of work. Managers and professionals who focus on the use of computing may find that this approach fits their routine practices. But thinking and talking about computerization as the development of sociotechnical configurations rather than as simply installing and using a new technology is not commonplace.

Many professionals use computer technologies that expand the range of their work methods. The adoption of electronic mail to facilitate communication between people who work in different time zones and the acquisition of compact, portable computers to facilitate working on the road are two routine illustrations. But organizations that adopt portable computers and e-mail to improve the flexibility of people's work relationships must do more than simply acquire technologies to realize these specific advantages. For example, portable computers may help people work outside of their offices. Some of the resulting convenience hinges on technological choices, such as acquiring machines that run software whose files are compatible with file formats used in the office. But much of the resulting flexibility depends on social choices as well. For example, if organization A requires men and women to report to work daily during regular working hours even when they have the portable computers, then people gain relatively little flexibility in work location if that policy is not also changed. People may be able to take portable computers home after hours or on weekends, or on the road while they travel. Thus, organization A may gain some unpaid overtime work with these policies. But the men and women who work in organization A will not gain much of the "control over the location of work" that many people attribute to portable computing. In contrast, if organization B allows its employees to work at places and times that they choose, then its employees can use portable computing to have even more flexibility in their work. In each of these cases, the men and women who adopt the equipment and construct work policies and practices for organizations A and B have created distinct sociotechnical configurations—or social designs. And these social designs that incorporate portable computing, rather than the technology alone, have different consequences.

Analytical research about computerization in organizations, as well as our own systematic observations, have helped identify many arenas in which organizational participants make social choices about the sociotechnical configurations of their computerized and networked systems (Jewett and Kling, 1990; Jewett and Kling, 1991; Kling, 1992; Bikson and Law, 1993;

Table 1. Some Elements of a Social Design

Arena	Social design choices to adopt, create, or restructure
Technology	Selection and configuration of hardware and software
Social organization of work	a. The division of labor b. Rewards/demands for learning new systems c. Access to machines and data
Equipment access	a. Shared vs. independent systems b. Who has access and with what privileges c. Standardization of systems and capabilities d. Extensiveness of use within a work group or organization
Infrastructure	a. Training programs
Control patterns	a. Implementation strategy and operations b. Daily working conditions c. Levels of monitoring

Markus, 1994). The term "social design of computerized systems," or "social design," characterizes the joint design of both the technological characteristics of a computerized system and the social arrangements under which it will be used (Kling, 1987a; Kling and Jewett, 1994). Table 1 lists several common social dimensions that can be part of the social design of a computing or network system.[5]

The social design of work systems with computing does not necessarily improve the quality of people's worklives. For example, some managers have computerized relatively routinized clerical work by fragmenting jobs and tightening supervisors' abilities to monitor the quality, pace, and speed of people's work. These same managers may develop good systematic training programs for the clerks whose work is now more regimented. However, social design can also be benign. It encourages participants in a computerization project to review the web of practices and policies related to computing that can otherwise be "unanticipated."

Two of the major approaches to social design contrast strongly in their assumptions about people, organizations, technology, and work. *Business Process Reengineering* is usually applied by managers and consultants to streamline operations (Hammer, 1990; Hammer and Champy, 1993; Davenport, 1993). The main aims of these reengineering projects seem to be reducing the time for a specific business process, such as dispatching a repairman to a site or processing an insurance claim, and also reducing the number of people who work on that activity. However, some consultants

---

[5] We have abstracted these dimensions from research studies about the use and impacts of computerized systems on people's worklives.

have promised more diverse financial benefits to their clients (and potential clients).

David Schnitt (1993) characterizes a business process in these terms:

> A business process is best defined as an activity in the organization funda-mental to operating the business that serves an internal or external customer and has a well-defined outcome or series of outcomes. Every organization is made up of business processes. Examples include such mundane activities as accounts payable, inventory control, field service, or the processing of a customer application. . . . Since many work steps in business processes are executed by people in different departments, this view encourages a cross-functional perspective. . . . the business process view of the Accounts Pay-able (A/P) process sheds new light on it as a complicated, slow, error-prone process involving many different departments and personnel. It reveals that the process is really the procurement process, not just A/P. Seen from this perspective, the opportunities for improvement are much greater. The key is to focus on the value-added outcome of the process (why it is done, not what is done) and how it relates to other processes in the organization.

Business process reengineering brings an industrial engineering perspec-tive to the design of organizations and work. The flow of documents and authorizations are key elements, and the character of people's jobs is a secondary consideration in much of the writing about this approach to redesigning organizations. Computer systems of various kinds are often key elements of a reengineering project, including scanners and document processing systems at the "front end" of a process, and the use of workflow software to model and manage some of the subsequent activity.

The analyses that support these projects usually rest on Rational Systems models of organizations to examine workflows that run across depart-ments. They usually examine few influences on worklife and work orga-nization other than those that directly pertain to reliable and efficient workflows.

The major alternative approach, sometimes called Sociotechnical Sys-tems design, makes people and their relationships in support of work, rather than workflows, the center of organizational reforms with informa-tion technology (Johnson and Rice, 1987; Zuboff, 1988; Pava, 1983). Peter Keen (1991) articulates this approach in these terms:

> The business team, rather than the functionally defined hierarchy or the dotted-line or matrix-management variants that show up on the organization chart, is increasingly being seen as the real unit of organizing. Business is finally recognizing that division of labor is increasingly ineffective as the basis for an organization in an environment of constant rather than occasional change and of shifting functions to the proven project and team-based processes long employed by the research and technical functions. Teamwork is relational; the quality of performance rests on the quality of interactions, communication, and coordination among team members. . . .
>
> Instead of focusing on organization structure, business today needs to look at the mechanisms that make communication simple, flexible . . . IT makes

practical many of the visions of management thinkers. The management principles for exploiting IT organizational advantage require a basic rethinking of old assumptions—especially concerning the links between strategy and structure—at the top of the firm.

Flexibility and adaptability are the new watchwords for organizations and for people. Firms that do not attend to their people's careers as well as their jobs might well have to replace much of their work force. Their human capital will be a depreciated resource, one they may find harder to replenish than they thought.

Keen's analysis appeals to many professionals. One technologically oriented corollary leads some computer scientists to develop designs for computer systems that facilitate communication and collaboration in diverse forms: mail systems, conferencing systems, co-authoring systems, and so on (Kling, 1991a). But it is much too facile to think that lower-status workers, such as clerks and semiprofessionals, are most appropriately targeted with business process reengineering, while only higher-status workers, such as managers and professionals, can bask in a more supportive and enriched relational organization.

For example, Jim Euchner and Patricia Sachs (1993) recently reported the redesign of a "work system" in which a regional United States phone company (NYNEX) provided customers with high-speed (T.1) phone service. The installation required the collaboration of over forty people in five distinct departments (Corcoran, 1992). NYNEX took much longer to complete these installations than their competitors, and rapidly lost significant market share in New York City. A computerized scheduling system had been used to assign different technicians to their specialized activities in the installation and fine-tuning of the T.1 lines in customers' offices. A large part of the delay seemed to derive from the way that some key problems cut across the domains of different technicians—they were either problems at system interfaces, or problems whose causes were somewhat ambiguous. The computer system helped to efficiently schedule the technicians' trips to the site—one at a time—to give them full and balanced workloads. It did not help bring together the specific technicians who would be needed to solve the more vexing installation problems.

A group from NYNEX's Science and Technology Center collaborated in a sociotechnical design with both the craft workers and managers who were responsible for T.1 installations to develop a new "work system design." Some of the principles of work system design that they articulated are common themes in many sociotechnical systems projects. For example, they had craft workers who do the actual work, as well as more senior managers, design the new work system and implement it. They focused on workflows and whole processes rather than on discrete tasks, a concept that is shared with many business process reengineering projects. However, they sought to provide people with ownership and responsibility for whole jobs, rather than discrete tasks. And they developed some specific guidelines for designing computer and communication systems: to support workflows and communications; to provide "intelligent" information handling; and to have interfaces that match the language in which people conceptualize their work.

The new T.1 work system reorganized the installations around cross-functional teams who have joint responsibility for ensuring that installations are prompt and effective. The team's composition is rather fluid and can depend on the specific customer and the stage of the installation. But they usually mix both white-collar and blue-collar workers, and can include people at different managerial levels. The coordination relies on people scheduling technicians rather than on computerized scheduling, although computer support is provided for other activities. In this particular case, the work system was redesigned, while the existing computer systems were left untouched.

Jewett and Kling (1990) report the case of a pharmaceutical firm in which sales managers radically restructured the responsibilities of sales clerks from passive order takers to more proactive sales representatives. The department held extensive meetings to reconceptualize their roles, and the staff rewrote all of the job descriptions. The resulting jobs were enriched and also reclassified at somewhat higher pay levels. The department's managers also commissioned the development of a new computerized information system to provide richer searching capabilities to support the restructured jobs. In this case, the configuration of the information systems was part of a larger social design that included the explicit reconceptualization of key jobs (also see Chapter 4 of Levering, 1988).

These sociotechnical strategies require that systems analysts and designers understand many of the work practices, schedules, resource constraints, and other contingencies of the people who will use the new computerized systems. Some organizations, such as NYNEX, have included social scientists on their design teams to facilitate such observation and understanding. They also recommend that people who use the systems have a substantial role in specifying their designs as well as altered work practices. One reason that stand-alone microcomputers may have been so attractive for many people is that they offered more control over the form of computerization and changes in work than systems that ran on shared computer systems. In addition, microcomputer users' work methods made them less dependent on having access to busy, full-time computer professionals to design and modify systems. This made their computing arrangements more adaptable. Many organizations implemented PC systems with a tacit social design that gave their workers more autonomy.

The next two selections by computer scientist Andrew Clement and anthropologist Lucy Suchman give us some deeper insights into sociotechnical work design. In "Computing at Work: Empowering Action by 'Low-Level Users' " Andrew Clement describes how several different groups of clerks participated in the design of computer systems in their work. The opportunity to participate was not generously initiated by upper managers in any of these cases. In the case of the Manitoba (Canada) Telephone System (MTS), managers developed a "pervasive command and control culture in which (mostly female) operators were . . . constantly watched over and punished for every infraction of the rules." In 1986, operators began reporting health problems, and even stopped work in one office after they became frightened of unsafe working conditions. A Canadian health authority and the clerk's union helped negotiate the opportunity for redesigning work in a "Trial Office" with upper managers. Clement reports the resulting change that "operator services have been reorganized around smaller, multi-function work groups while several of the innovations first adopted by the Trial Office—e.g., elimination of remote monitoring, improved training resources, cross training, unlimited rights to trading shifts, greater discretion in responding to customer queries—are being extended throughout MTS." Clement describes two other projects in a library system and in a university administration, in which clerks were able to convince upper managers to allow them to redesign their work and computer support systems. He notes some important commonalities in these cases:

> For all the differences between these three cases in terms of the jobs, technologies, and organizational setting, there are striking similarities. In each, women office workers faced unnecessary hardships because of conventional ways in which computerization had been imposed on them. They had not been consulted about the introduction of the computer systems in the first place, and initially tried to accommodate to the new conditions, in spite of experiencing considerable adverse effects—effects that are commonly associated with the negative implications of computerization elsewhere. Coming from the lower reaches of rigid, strongly hierarchical organizations, attempts to voice concerns were met with fates typical of bottom-up initiatives. It was only after pressures for change had grown considerably that any action was taken.

The high side of these "participatory design" projects was that the clerks in each of these organizations were able to create more productive and less regimented jobs for themselves. These kinds of working conditions are sometimes taken for granted by higher-status professionals.

In "Supporting Articulation Work" Lucy Suchman examines the way that critical work processes are often invisible to casual observers. In a telling example that appears in the middle of her article, Suchman contrasts the way that lawyers and legal assistants in a firm view the work of coding legal documents with "objective categories" such as From, To, and Date. The male lawyer viewed the coding task as mindless work that could be done "by chimpanzees" or "by 9-year-olds." The lawyer viewed legal interpretation as mindful work. In contrast, the female legal assistants showed Suchman that the tasks of identifying which set of papers should be considered as a document, which names on the papers should be labeled as To and From, and which date should serve as the document's official date all required mindful interpretation. Suchman notes that it is common for male workers to create artificial categories, such as mindful/mindless or hard/easy to create status boundaries. She goes on to describe how she and her research team developed a prototype document imaging system whose key features were based on the document coding task as experienced by the coders.

In a more recent paper, Andrew Clement and Pater Van den Besselaar (1993) examined the results of many participatory work-redesign design projects. In many cases specific projects led to participants improving their understanding of information technologies and effectively proposing new or altered systems that improved their working conditions. However, many of these projects were relatively short term, and most of them were isolated examples within their larger organizations. Participatory design is a fundamentally controversial approach because it advocates forthright questioning of traditional lines of authority and typical assumptions about who has expertise in organizations.

A third approach to social design is congruent with both business process reengineering and sociotechnical design: web analyses of computing infrastructure (Kling, 1992). One key insight of this approach is that social designs that focus primarily on the overt work system, such as processing an insurance claim or installing a phone line, can overlook the kinds of systems and support that are critical for making computer and communications systems workable for people. For example, in a study of computing and organizational practices in a large number of leading companies, McKersie and Walton (1991:275) observe, "Despite widespread recognition among IT planners that most systems are underutilized because of inadequate training, the deficiency is repeated in systems implementation after systems implementation." Training is only one element of infrastructure for computing support. Web analysis locates computer systems and people who use them in matrix relationships with other people, organizations, and technologies on which they depend.[6]

Computing infrastructure can play a key role in social designs. A group may prefer a high-performance computing application that requires substantial training and consulting, or a medium-performance application that people may learn more effectively on their own. Whichever application is chosen makes subsequent demands on computing infrastructure for those

---

[6] Kling (1987b, 1992) provides concrete criteria to help analysts draw larger boundaries around computer and work systems, so that one can examine how they actually work and how they can effectively be changed and sustained. Identifying relevant infrastructure is one part of a web analysis. Identifying other resources, such as data sources and participants' incentives for supporting a work system, is also part of the analysis. When these resources cross administrative or organizational boundaries they are excluded from many systems analyses. Web analyses help social designers include them explicitly.

work groups. Organizations often fail to realize the gains from IT that they hope for when they: (1) select high-performance applications and fail to provide needed support or training in their use; or (2) select lower-performance applications but still do not encourage people to experiment and learn in their workplaces. My case study of computerization in a research team (Jewett and Kling, 1991; Kling, 1992) illustrates how a Natural Systems model of organizations is needed to understand what kinds of infrastructure are feasible for specific work groups and work systems. This case was specially complex because the work groups' computing facilities, including PCs, printers, and e-mail systems, were administered by several different organizations and located in dispersed locations.

Computing practices can be complex in practice. It is one thing to say that your computer network has a high-speed printer, and another thing to use it effectively when it is located one-half mile away or in an office that is often locked when you work. I know of remarkable examples in which people who worked in high-tech organizations forwarded e-mail and files via the Internet to their spouses who worked twenty miles away so they could get printed copies within a day. Printing messages and files that they received over their networks proved to be elusive in their own organizations! It is easiest for us to imagine that someone who uses e-mail can routinely attach files, print messages, file copies of inbound and outbound messages in special folders, send messages to groups, and so on. It is remarkable how many e-mail systems are configured in ways that make these seemingly routine activities cumbersome or virtually impossible for many men and women who use them.

The analysts who facilitate social designs use tacit models of organizational behavior. Business process reengineering often rests on Rational Systems models. Since one overt goal of many of these projects is reducing the number of people employed in an area (often referred to as "downsizing" or "decapitation"), it should not be surprising that the people who will do redesigned work are often unenthusiastic about sharing their best insights with designers. Natural Systems models of organizations take much more explicit account of people's social behavior (such as seeking occupational security, careers, and specific kinds of economic and social rewards from work). Natural Systems models also underlie many of the sociotechnical design projects.

Conclusions

During the next decade organizations will continue to computerize work—automating new activities and replacing earlier systems with newer technologies. The controversies about how to change work with computer systems will continue to have immense practical repercussions. This article identified some of the key controversies that pervade this diffuse literature—those that pertain to gender equity, control, support systems, social design, and new ways of organizing work. Many of the controversies are implicit, since authors often take positions without carefully discussing the alternative positions and debates.

Further systematic research can help resolve some controversies, such as the possibilities of effective social design, the conditions that engender new forms of work organization, and the extent to which they create higher-quality workplaces. However, these controversies also pertain to the concrete behavior of organizations, and questions about what they do and will do, not just what they should do.

Organizations and workplaces differ and, consequently, their appropriate work organization technologies differ. The research shows that no single logic has been applied toward changing work with computerization. So key controversies cannot be automatically resolved by a new kind of computer technology, such as pen-based systems, or voice recognition. New technologies create new opportunities, but do not always require that the opportunities will be exploited, for better or worse. For example, the research shows that few organizations utilize fine-grained computer monitoring systems as intensively as critics of automated monitoring suggest. On the other hand, relatively few organizations systemically and broadly exploit the possibilities of more flexible work schedules that telecommuting can provide. And it is common for organizations to underinvest in the support for helping people effectively integrate computerized systems into their work.

The choices of how to computerize involve practical judgments about what makes workers more productive. But it also engages managers' preferences for control and innovation. Controversies over control pervade the literature about computers and worklife. They also pervade numerous workplaces. They entail controversies that have no inherent resolutions. But good research can at least help men and women at work in understanding the issues and some of their most significant repercussions. After all, on a large scale, the resulting choices will affect the lives of tens of millions of people.

The practical situation is worsened when advocates of some new family of technologies write as if all that has been learned from the last thirty years of computerization is totally irrelevant to help us understand how their systems can be integrated into work or serve as a catalyst for reorganizing work. In this article, we have criticized technological utopianism and anti-utopianism as key genres that inform many normative accounts about how organizations should or should not computerize work. We have seen a reliance on these genres in a large body of professional writing about new families of computing that are technologically discontinuous with past devices. Expert systems, personal computing, groupware, and networking have often been the subject of analyses that are anchored in technological utopian premises. We expect to see a similar body of misleading literature develop to characterize new worlds of work with other exciting technologies, such as "personal digital assistants."

A more realistic body of scholarly and professional analyses can develop in two ways; first, if analysts are willing to learn from the past, such as the nature of control issues in work and the importance of infrastructure and social design, in their relentless search for a better future; and, second, if the technological community is willing to devote some resources to sponsor serious empirical inquiry into the opportunities, limitations, and problems of specific families of new technologies. Despite the limitations of the current body of research, certain perennial themes recur. While there are many important and open research questions, there is a body of good research to help inform better choices now.

Sources

Clement, Andrew (1994). "Computing at Work: Empowering Action by 'Low-level Users.' " *Communications of the ACM* (37)1(January):52–65.

Horwitz, Tony (1994). "Mr. Edens Profits from Watching His Workers' Every Move." *The Wall Street Journal* (Dec. 1):A11.

Iacono, Suzanne, and Rob Kling (1984). "Office-Routine: The Automated Pink Collar." *IEEE Spectrum* (June):73–76.

Marx, Gary (1990). "The Case of the Omniscient Organization." *Harvard Business Review* (March–April):4–12.

Poltrock, Steven E., and Jonathan Grudin (1994). "Interface Development in a Large Organization: An Observational Study." [Adapted from *ACM Transactions on Computer and Human Interaction,* 1(1)(March):52–80.]

Suchman, Lucy (1994). "Supporting Articulation Work: Aspects of a Feminist Practice Office Technology Production." *Proceedings of the 5th IFIP WG9.1 Conference on Women, Work and Computerization.* Elsevier, Amsterdam.

References

Bikson, Tora K., and S. A. Law (1993). "Electronic Mail Use at the World Bank: Messages from Users." *Information Society,* 9(2)(Apr.–Jun.):89–124.

Clement, Andrew (1984). "Electronic Management: New Technology of Workplace Surveillance." *Proceedings, Canadian Information Processing Society Session 84,* Calgary, Alberta, (May 9–11):259–266.

Clement, Andrew (1990). "Computer Support for Cooperative Work: A Social Perspective on Empowering End Users." *Proceedings of the Conference on Computer Supported Cooperative Work.* Los Angeles, CA, (October 7–10):223–236.

Clement, Andrew, and Peter Van den Besselaar (1993). "A Retrospective Look at Participatory Design Projects." *Communications of the ACM,* 36(4)(June):29–37.

Corcoran, Elizabeth (1992). "Building networks: New York Telephone Rethinks Work to Regain Lost Customers." *Scientific American,* 267(5)(November):118, 120.

Davenport, Thomas H. (1993). *Process Innovation: Reengineering Work Through Information Technology.* Harvard Business School Press, Boston, Mass.

Delgado, Alan (1979). *The Enormous File: A Social History of the Office.* John Murray, London.

Euchner, Jim, and Patricia Sachs (1993). "The Benefits of Intentional Tension." *Communications of the ACM,* 36(4)(June):53.

Finholt, Tom, and Lee Sproull (1990). "Electronic Groups at Work." *Organization Science,* 1(1):41–64.

Forester, Tom (1989). "The Myth of the Electronic Cottage," in Tom Forester (ed.), *Computers in the Human Context: Information Technology, Productivity, and People.* MIT Press, Cambridge.

Gasser, Les (1986). "The Integration of Computing and Routine Work." *ACM Transactions on Office Information Systems,* 4(3)(July):205–225.

Giuliano, Vincent E. (1982). "The Mechanization of Work." *Scientific American,* 247(September):148–164. [Reprinted in Charles Dunlop and Rob Kling (eds.) (1991). *Computerization and Controversy: Value Conflicts and Social Choices.* Academic Press, San Diego.]

Grant, Rebecca, and Chris Higgins (1991). "The Impact of Computerized Performance Monitoring on Service Work: Testing a Causal Model." *Information Systems Research,* 2(2):116–141.

Grudin, Jonathan (1989). "Why Groupware Applications Fail: Problems in Design and Evaluation." *Office: Technology and People,* 4(3):245–264.

Hammer, Michael (1990). "Reengineering Work: Don't Automate, Obliterate." *Harvard Business Review,* (July/August):104–112.

Hammer, Michael, and James Champy (1993). *Reengineering the Corporation: A Manifesto for Business Revolution.* Harper-Collins, New York.

Herring, Susan C. (1993). "Gender and Democracy in Computer-Mediated Communication." *Electronic Journal of Communication/REC,* 3(2). (Reprinted in Section V, Chapter C.)

Hiltz, Starr Roxanne, and Murray Turoff (1978). *The Network Nation: Human Communication via Computer.* Addison-Wesley, Reading, MA.

Hodas, Steven "Technology Refusal and the Organizational Culture of Schools." (Section III, Chapter I.)

Huws, Ursula, Werner Korte, and Simon Robinson (1990). *Telework: Towards the Elusive Office.* John Wiley, New York.

Iacono, Suzanne, and Rob Kling (1987). "Changing Office Technologies and the Transformation of Clerical Jobs," in Robert Kraut (ed.), *Technology and the Transformation of White Collar Work.* Lawrence Erlbaum, Hillsdale, NJ.

Information Infrastructure Task Force (IITF) (1994). "Promoting Telecommuting: An Application of the National Information Infrastructure" (Sept. 7). Washington D.C. URL: gopher://iitfcat.nist.gov:95/0/.catitem2/telecom.txt

Jewett, Tom, and Rob Kling (1990). "The Work Group Manager's Role in Developing Computing Infrastructure." *Proceedings of the ACM Conference on Office Information Systems,* Boston, MA.

Jewett, Tom, and Rob Kling (1991). "The Dynamics of Computerization Social Science Research Team: A Case Study of Infrastructure, Strategies, and Skills." *Social Science Computer Review,* 9(2)(Summer):246–275.

Johnson, Bonnie M., and Ronald E. Rice (1987). *Managing Organizational Innovation: The Evolution from Word Processing to Office Information Systems.* Columbia University Press, New York.

Kadaba, Lini S. (1993). "Big Boss Is Watching You; Employers Are Tapping Phones and Counting Keystrokes—and Employees Are Getting Nervous." *San Jose Mercury News*, (October 25):1C.

Keen, Peter G. W. (1991). *Shaping the Future: Business Design Through Information Technology*. Harvard Business School Press, Boston.

Kindel, Stephen (1993). "The Virtual Office." *Financial World*, 162(22)(November 9):93–94.

Klawe, Maria, and Nancy Leveson (1995). "Women in Computing: Where are we Now?" *Communications of the ACM*, 38(1)(January):29–35.

Kling, Rob (1987a). "Computerization as an Ongoing Social and Political Process," in Gro Bjerknes, Pelle Ehn, and Morten Kyng (eds.), *Computers and Democracy: A Scandinavian Challenge*. Gower Pub. Co., Brookfield, VT.

Kling, Rob (1987b). "Defining the Boundaries of Computing Across Complex Organizations," in Richard A. Boland and Rudy A. Hirschheim (eds.), *Critical Issues in Information Systems Research*. John Wiley and Sons, New York.

Kling, Rob (1991a). "Cooperation, Coordination and Control in Computer-Supported Work." *Communications of the ACM*, 34(12)(December):83–88.

Kling, Rob (1992). "Behind the Terminal: The Critical Role of Computing Infrastructure in Effective Information Systems' Development and Use," in William Cotterman and James Senn (eds.), *Challenges and Strategies for Research in Systems Development*, pp. 153–201. John Wiley, New York.

Kling, Rob (1993). "Fair Information Practices with Computer Supported Cooperative Work." *SIGOIS Bulletin*, (July):28–31.

Kling, R., and Iacono, S. (1989). "Desktop Computing and the Organization of Work," in Tom Forester (ed.), *Computers in the Human Context*. MIT Press, Cambridge, MA.

Kling, Rob, and Tom Jewett (1994). "The Social Design of Worklife With Computers and Networks: A Natural Systems Perspective," in Marshall C. Yovits (ed.), *Advances in Computers*, Volume 39. Academic Press, San Diego.

Kling, Rob, and Walt Scacchi (1979). "Recurrent Dilemmas of Computer Use in Complex Organizations." *National Computer Conference Proceedings*, (48):107–115.

Kraemer, K. L., and J. L. King (1982). "Telecommunications—Transportation Substitution and Energy Productivity." *Telecommunications Policy*, Part I, 6(1):39–59; Part II, 6(2):87–99.

Kraut, Robert, Susan Dumais, and Susan Koch (1989). "Computerization, Productivity and Quality of Worklife." *Communications of the ACM*, 32(2)(February):220–238.

Levering, Robert (1988). *A Great Place to Work: What Makes Some Employers So Good (and Most So Bad)*. Random House, New York.

Markus, M. Lynne (1994). "Finding a 'Happy Medium': Explaining the Negative Effects of Electronic Communication on Social Life at Work." *ACM Transactions on Information Systems* (12)2(April):119–149. (Reprinted in Part V, Chapter D)

McKersie, Robert B., and Richard E. Walton (1991). "Organizational Change," in Michael S. Scott Morton (ed.), *The Corporation of the 1990s: Information Technology and Organizational Transformation*. Oxford University Press, New York.

Mowshowitz, Abbe (1986). "The Social Dimension of Office Automation," in Marshall Yovits (ed.), *Advances in Computers*. Academic Press, San Diego.

Noble, David F. (1984). *Forces of Production: A Social History of Industrial Automation*. Knopf, New York.

Olson, Margrethe H. (1989). "Work at Home for Computer Professionals: Current Attitudes and Future Prospects." *ACM Transaction on Information Systems*, 7(4)(October):317–338.

Pava, Calvin (1983). *Managing New Office Technology: An Organizational Strategy.* Free Press, New York.

Pearl, Amy, Martha E. Pollack, Eve Riskin, Becky Thomas, Elizabeth Wolf, and Alice Wu (1990). "Becoming a Computer Scientist: A Report by the ACM Committee on The Status of Women in Computing Science." *Communications of the ACM*, 33(11)(November):47–58.

Perin, Connie (1991). "Electronic Social Fields in Bureaucracies." *Communications of the ACM*, 34(12)(December):74–82.

Reskin, Barbara, and Irene Padavic (1994). *Women and Men at Work.* Pine Forge Press, Thousand Oaks, CA.

Schnitt, David L. (1993). "Reengineering the Organization Using Information Technology." *Journal of Systems Management*, 44(1):14.

Shaiken, Harley (1986). *Work Transformed: Automation and Labor in the Computer Age.* Lexington Books, Lexington, MA.

Sproull, Lee, and Sara Kiesler (1991). "Increasing Personal Connections." *Connections: New Ways of Working in the Networked Organization.* MIT Press, Cambridge.

Sprout, Alison L. (1994). "Moving Into the Virtual Office." *Fortune*, 129(9)(May 2):103.

Taylor, Thayer C. (1994). "IBM Moved Into the Virtual Office." *Sales & Marketing Management*, 146(5)(May):100.

Vitalari, Nicholas, and Alladi Venkatesh (1987). "In-home Computing Services and Information Services, A Twenty Year Analysis of the Technology and Its Impacts." *Telecommunications Policy* (March):65–81.

Weekley, Thomas L. (1983). "Workers, Unions, and Industrial Robotics." *Annals, American Academy of Political and Social Sciences*, 470:146–151.

Zuboff, Shoshana (1988). *In the Age of the Smart Machine: The Future of Work and Power.* Basic Books, New York.

Zuboff, Shoshana (1991). "Informate the Enterprise." *National Forum*, (Summer): 3–7.

Further Reading

Aronowitz, Stanley, and William DeFazio (1994). *The Jobless Future: Sci-tech and the Dogma of Work.* The University of Minnesota Press, Minneapolis, MN.

Attewell, Paul (1987). "The Deskilling Controversy." *Work and Occupation*, 14(3):323–346.

Attewell, Paul. "Big Brother and the Sweatshop: Computer Surveillance in the Automated Office." *Sociological Theory*, 5(Spring):87–99. Reprinted in Dunlop and Kling, 1991.

Bansler, Jorgen (1989). "Systems Development in Scandinavia: Three Theoretical Schools." *Office: Technology and People*, 4(2)(May):117–133.

Cabins, Lucius (1990). "The Making of a Bad Attitude," in C. Carlsson and M. Leger (eds.), *Bad Attitude: The Processed World Anthology*, pp. 94–102. Verso, New York.

Carlsson, Chris, and Mark Leger (eds.) (1990). *Bad Attitude: The Processed World Anthology.* Verso, New York.

Cockburn, Cynthia (1988). *Machinery of Dominance: Women, Men and Technical Know-How*. Northeastern University Press, Boston.

Fox, Matthew (1994). *The Reinvention of Work: A New Vision of Livelihood in Our Times*. Harper, San Francisco.

Galegher, Jolene, Robert Kraut, and Carmen Egido (eds.) (1990). *Intellectual Teamwork: Social and Technological Foundations of Cooperative Work*. Lawrence Erlbaum, Hillsdale, NJ.

Harvey, David (1989). *The Condition of Postmodernity: An Inquiry into the Origins of Cultural Change*. Basil Blackwell, Oxford, UK.

Jewett, Tom, and Rob Kling (1991). "The Dynamics of Computerization Social Science Research Team: A Case Study of Infrastructure, Strategies, and Skills." *Social Science Computer Review*, 9(2)(Summer):246–275.

Kling, Rob (1990). "More Information, Better Jobs? Occupational Stratification and Labor Market Segmentation in the United States' Information Labor Force." *The Information Society*, 7(2):77–107.

Kling, Rob (1991a). "Cooperation, Coordination and Control in Computer-Supported Work." *Communications of the ACM*, 34(12):83–88.

Kling, Rob (1991b). "Computerization and Social Transformations." *Science, Technology and Human Values*, 16(3):342–367.

Kling, Rob (1992). "Behind the Terminal: The Critical Role of Computing Infrastructure In Effective Information Systems' Development and Use," in William Cotterman and James Senn (eds.), *Challenges and Strategies for Research in Systems Development*, pp. 153–201. John Wiley, New York.

Kling, Rob, and Suzanne Iacono (1984). "Computing as an Occasion for Social Control." *Journal of Social Issues*, 40(3):77–96.

Kling, Rob, and Clark Turner (1991). "The Information Labor Force," in Rob Kling, Spencer Olin, and Mark Poster (eds.), *Postsuburban California*. University of California Press, Berkeley.

Kraut, Robert E. (ed.) (1987). *Technology & the Transformation of White Collar Work*. Lawrence Erlbaum, Hillsdale, NJ.

Kuhn, Sarah, and Michael J. Muller (1993). "Participatory Design." *Communications of the ACM*, 36(4)(June):24–28.

Kyng, Morton, and Joan Greenbaum (1991). *Design at Work: Cooperative Work of Computer Systems*. Lawrence Erlbaum, Hillsdale, NJ.

Mouritsen, Jan, and Niels Bjorn-Anderson (1991). "Understanding Third Wave Information Systems," in Charles Dunlop and Rob Kling (eds.), *Computerization and Controversy: Value Conflicts and Social Choices*. Academic Press, San Diego.

Nohria, Nittin, and James D. Berkley (1994). "The Virtual Organization: Bureaucracy, Technology and the Implosion of Control," in Charles Heckscher and Anne Donnellon (eds.), *The Post-Bureaucratic Organization: New Perspectives on Organizational Change*. Sage, Thousand Oaks, CA.

Orlikowski, Wanda (1991). "Integrated Information Environment or Matrix of Control? The Contradictory Implications of Information Technology." *Accounting, Management and Information Technology*, 1(1):9–42.

Orlikowski, Wanda (1993). "Learning from Notes: Organizational Issues in Groupware Implementation." *Information Society* 9(3)(July–Sept.):237–250. (Reprinted in Section III, Chapter G)

Perrolle, Judith (1986). "Intellectual Assembly Lines: The Rationalization of Managerial, Professional and Technical Work." *Computers and the Social Sciences*, 2(3):111–

122. (Reprinted in Charles Dunlop and Rob Kling (eds.) (1991). *Computerization and Controversy: Value Conflicts and Social Choices*. Academic Press, San Diego.)

Salzman, Harold, and Steven Rosenthal (1994). *Software by Design: Shaping Technology and the Workplace*. Oxford University Press, New York.

Wagner, Ina (1993). "A Web of Fuzzy Problems: Confronting the Ethical Issues." *Communications of the ACM*, 36(4)(June):94–101. Reprinted as "Confronting Ethical Issues of Systems Design in a Web of Social Relationships" in Section VIII.

Wood, Stephen (1989). "The Transformation of Work," in Stephen Wood (ed.), *The Transformation of Work: Skill, Flexibility and the Labour Process*. Unwin Hyman, London.

Wright, Barbara Drygulski, and Associates (1987). *Women, Work and Technology: Transformations*. University of Michigan Press, Ann Arbor.

B

Computerization, Office Routines, and Changes in Clerical Work*

Suzanne Iacono • Rob Kling

Electronic aids are changing work routines in offices, but not all changes may be for the better. Studies show that people's worklives must be considered in relation to the new equipment. Otherwise workers can become more disgruntled, even though their initial expectations for the new equipment may have been high. In a similar vein, advanced electronic equipment is often sold to businesses with the promise of high gains in productivity. In practice, studies suggest, such gains may prove elusive. Each new wave of technical development seems to be accompanied by high-spirited optimistic promotion. In the 1970s, one vision of the "office of the future" was based on IBM Corporation's "word-processing plan." In its most rigid form, the plan projected that individual secretaries for managers would be eliminated in the office of 1985. Instead, several managers would share services from a secretarial pool. Few organizations adopted this vision literally, but IBM was able to articulate a persuasive image of professional office life with automatic text processing that excluded secretaries. The promotional language for office-automation systems in the 1980s tended to emphasize support for managerial and professional work rather than displacement of clerical employees.

But care nevertheless must be taken in implementing the new support. The following example, reported by Enid Mumford in *Designing Secretaries* (Manchester Business School Press, 1983), illustrates some of the social complexities that can arise. A department in a large British company, for example, bought two stand-alone word processors for a group of five secretaries to use. Space was limited, and the machines were placed in an isolated room. The secretaries had been used to typing reports and letters with occasional interruptions from telephone calls and other office staff. Now, with the word processors, they could work efficiently without interruption. But they hated the new arrangement. They had to work at a continuous tempo, moving their eyes from "paper to screen" for an hour or two, with few breaks in their relative isolation. The secretaries liked the flexibility of the new equipment, but they strongly disliked the new working conditions under which they used it. In one sense, the word processors were the catalysts (and thus the "cause") for the change in the work arrangement. However, the technical capabilities of word processors were not the causal agents. These capabilities made them attractive to the director of the company. But equipment cost—about $18,000 for each word processor—led him to insist that the machines be used efficiently. Because they were not sufficiently compact to replace a standard typewriter, they required additional space. The combination of space shortages in the department, the director's desire to have secretaries use expensive machines efficiently, and a social order that placed secretaries at the bottom resulted in work under pressure and in isolation—and a drop in office morale.

Technology Alters Jobs

In some cases, workplace technologies have altered jobs. For example, telephone operators' jobs have changed considerably since the 1940s, when long-distance operators had to know routing patterns to direct cross-country calls. The jobs always tied operators to headphones and consoles. But as telephone switching became automated, the operators needed less skill. As a result the jobs became boring for many operators. Before the advent of the automatic switchboard, a light would appear, but the operator had to plug in the cord to take the call. With the automatic switchboard, the calls are just there, whether the operator wants them or not or whether the operator needs a breather or not. Surreptitious monitoring— both of the number of calls taken and the rate at which they are handled and of the operator's demeanor—increases the tension. In the book *Working* (Avon Books, 1972), Studs Terkel reported on a similar situation. Says Beryl Simpson, an airline reservations clerk:

> With Sabre [the computer system] being so valuable, you were allowed no more than three minutes on the telephone. You had 20 seconds to put the

*This article appeared as "Office Routine: The Automated Pink Collar" in *IEEE Spectrum* (June, 1984):73–76. Reprinted with permission. © 1984 IEEE.

information into Sabre, then you had to be available for another phone call. It was almost like a production line; we adjusted to the machine. The casualness and informality that had been there previously were no longer there. The last three or four years on the job were horrible.

The obvious lesson is that workers may be highly pleased with the new technologies initially and simultaneously frustrated with the conditions under which they must use them. In a study of computers in the worklife of traffic-ticket clerks in municipal courts, conducted at the University of California at Irvine in the mid-1970s, the authors found that most traffic-ticket clerks attributed job-enlarging characteristics, such as increased variety, to their use of automated equipment. Impacts of new technologies are varied. But "better" technologies do not guarantee a better worklife.

Contemporary accounts of the "office of the future" focus primarily on computing technologies for flexible text processing, scheduling, and communication. Most analysts who write about such an office assume that the social dimensions of office life will mirror the flexibility provided by improved information technologies. Variations in the character of offices and life within them is largely ignored in these accounts. Most office workers have white-collar jobs, and there are usually a variety of jobs and roles in most offices. These activities often include planning, supervising, decision making, persuading, recording, typing, accounting, inventorying, and handling phone calls. Managers, and sometimes workers, organize who will be responsible for the execution of the various tasks through a division of labor. The hierarchy of roles identifies who will have the authority to implement certain decisions and decide schedules and who will abide by them.

Gains Are Elusive as Equipment Advances

In 1800, office equipment consisted of pens, ink, and paper. At the turn of the century, a primitive typewriter may have been deemed necessary for a clerk. Punched-card tabulating equipment began to be used in accounting offices, and the installation of telephones spread everywhere between the two world wars. After World War II, more office machines appeared on the market. Money counters, mechanical erasers, billing machines, and machines that can open envelopes and seal, stamp, and address them outfitted the automated offices of the day. Today, most of these mechanical forms of office automation seem old-fashioned. All offices in the United States have telephones, most have access to photocopiers, and many have computer terminals or word processors. In twenty years, the advanced office systems of today, which feature integrated calendars, text processing, and electronic mail accessible through multiple windows on a twelve-inch video data terminal, will also seem archaic. "Modern technologies" do not denote particular technologies; they are temporary pointers in a continuous cavalcade of technological devices. When business computers first appeared, promoters promised that the machines would replace people who engaged in routine activities by simply mimicking their tasks. Computer applications would be more efficient than an office worker, and some said that office staffs could be reduced by 50%. Because clerical work is deemed the most repetitive and routine work done in an office, it was expected to be the easiest to automate. Despite substantial investments in office automation in the 1970s, however, national estimates of productivity from 1968 to 1978 indicate only a 4% increase for office workers. While the office technologies of this period included such primitive machines as magnetic-tape and magnetic-card typewriters, they were sold as high-leverage advances. Aggregate national data cannot prove that new office technologies have had little impact, but they suggest caution in creating expectations or setting goals. The abilities of information technologies to support real productivity gains in organizations are influenced by elements of worklife beyond machine capabilities. Real gains can often be measured by focusing on one task under controlled conditions.

However, in the "real" workplace, these single-task gains do not translate directly into proportional gains in office productivity. Most office workers, aside from data-entry operators, perform several tasks. A secretary, for example, may answer phone calls, do photocopy work, type a document on a word processor, file, and communicate with the boss. Replacing one word processor with a "better" one may simplify formatting problems, for instance. But if the secretary spends 10% of the day formatting text and if the productivity gain is expected to be 50%, that only translates into a 5% gain in overall productivity.

Then there is the issue of overhead. In a major Southern California engineering firm, an advanced office system was installed. It was used by managers, engineers, and secretaries to write letters and documents, schedule rooms, arrange calendars, and communicate via electronic mail. The corporate managers expected this project to yield a 20% increase in productivity, but measuring the improvement has proved difficult. While many staff members like the new equipment, it is hard to show that they have actually gained any fixed fraction of their work time, because of the overhead for system use—learning time, the time it takes to turn from a task, log on to the system, and to check for electronic mail when perhaps there is none, and so on.

When real gains in productivity can be measured, people often find new tasks that exploit the gains. Photocopiers produce more copies, text-processing machines produce more versions of a manuscript, and computer-based accounting systems provide more detailed accounting data. Some of these additional uses help multiply organizational products; others add little. However, the process of exploiting these "labor saving" devices does not always reduce staff, as the work load may grow. The additional work is done by the system—a phantom, automated clerk.

Consequently, extra working capacity does not necessarily translate into cost reduction or even improved overall effectiveness. When format changes are easier, document authors often request additional changes in a particular document. When the number of requested changes increase, these can reduce any time savings that might have accrued from using a new text formatter. Even so, many people like the feel of working with powerful tools.

The Phantom Efficiency

The efficiency standards that some companies set up—the monitoring and pacing of work that is made possible by new electronic equipment—can also be counter-productive, further eating away at the promised productivity gains. For example, some organizations monitor the number of keystrokes that a typist makes, and this information becomes a means of determining the pace of the work. There is some evidence that continual monitoring increases errors. In an ongoing study of automated text processing, the authors have found that business organizations vary considerably in the way they organize clerical work. Some have centralized word-processing pools or data-entry departments in which clerical workers are isolated from the rest of the organization and have little opportunity to control the pace of their work. Others have decentralized office arrangements that can give clerical workers more opportunities for decision making.

A word-processing center can give employees several advantages not provided by a decentralized arrangement. One advantage is that the center offers a longer career path. For example, in one organization that was studied, a woman started as a secretary and moved up to executive secretary, normally the top of the ladder in a decentralized organization. Then the company brought in a new word-processing system. The woman became active in the development of a word-processing center, soon was named supervisor to the center, and then was promoted to manager of administrative services, where she directed all of the company's secretarial functions. Such career opportunities were available because a word-processing center is a complete support organization with its own hierarchical structure. In more conventional arrangements, a secretary is dependent on the boss for advancement: if the boss moves up, the secretary may also move up. Clerical workers in a word-processing center have a second advantage: they develop a special expertise with their systems by working with them constantly. In addition, because of economies of scale, they tend to have the best equipment. A centralized organization has disadvantages as well. The work is starkly routine and can be dull. There is less flexibility in determining the order of tasks. There is reduced social contact with workers outside the word-processing center; operators become segregated, in touch only with a supervisor who collects work from the various departments and passes it along.

The issue of monitoring job performance also arises more often than in a decentralized system. On the other hand, clerical workers in a decentralized office arrangement, with individual managers having personal secretaries or several managers sharing one secretary, have considerable flexibility in determining their work schedule and the order of tasks. The situation can be more interesting than in a centralized arrangement, because the workers have more contact with other people in the company outside the secretarial class, and there is less likelihood of strict job performance monitoring. Clerical workers in this arrangement, however, also have fewer opportunities for advancement and do not acquire the same level of technical expertise as workers in a word-processing center. From a political perspective, the individual secretary is also at a disadvantage. The clerical organization is fragmented, with secretaries having stronger ties to their bosses than to each other; therefore collective job action, such as forming a union, is more difficult. Some organizations have both individual secretaries and a word-processing pool. The advantages of such a mixed arrangement ·are obvious for the managers: they have local support for immediate needs, and they can lean on the word-processing center for larger projects that would be difficult for one person to handle, but could be completed in a day if divided among five workers. For the clerical staff, the mixed arrangement also provides more options, but tension can result from the division of clerical workers into two types.

In one such organization that we studied, the word-processing workers saw themselves as much more professional than the traditional secretaries because of their higher level of technical expertise. The secretaries, because their jobs were more varied, did not have the opportunity to become so intimately familiar with the word-processing system. Also, secretaries were sometimes asked to do menial tasks, such as get coffee for the boss or buy a present for him to give to his wife, whereas no one in a word-processing center received such requests. In addition, the secretaries sometimes resented the people in the word-processing center because they were more likely to have the best equipment.

Technology: No Guarantee of Improvement

The lesson is clear: technology alone cannot guarantee improved performance and higher morale in an office. The quality of people's worklives is equally involved. Gains come by a skillful blending of these two basic ingredients. Many managers who work with information technologies come to this realization. They become fascinated with new equipment and point to the promised gains in office productivity to justify expensive purchases. Often they overestimate the actual gains, as the new equipment's use becomes routine and its limitations apparent. At a later time, the managers become aware of more advanced equipment in the marketplace; once again they succumb to vendor descriptions of increased productivity and decreased operating costs. The gains sought, however, may not be attained because human factors in the workplace were not considered.

In the next twenty years it seems likely that offices will become even more automated. More clerical workers will sit in front of video display terminals (VDTs) as they handle inquiries from customers, prepare memos and reports, and communicate with certain co-workers. Most offices will not become "paperless." Rather, computer and telecommunications technologies will be more widely used to replace and to complement other information media. Office environments also should improve in general, as sensitivity to occupational hazards grows. Today, some employers may push their employees to work at VDTs, with fewer breaks than are healthy, or employers may not invest in proper lighting or office furnishings. These conditions should improve. However, change will not come uniformly, as offices vary in size and in what they produce. (The kind of work performed in the Oval Office of the White House is significantly different from work done in a typing-pool office.) Offices also differ in work organization, number of employees, diversity of tasks, physical arrangements, the kinds of technology in use, predominant control strategies, and so on. Researchers are less sanguine about changes in the structure of careers, pay, and job roles for clerical workers.

The complexity of many clerical jobs will increase as offices adopt more complex arrays of computing and telecommunications equipment. But there will always be routine tasks, whether in preparing individual transactions for computer processing, scheduling meetings, or organizing files of data and memos on integrated office systems. Some of these jobs may become more interesting, but it is unlikely that the career lines for clerks will begin to parallel the careers and salaries of technicians. Discontent on the job will remain a major obstacle to gains in productivity. One solution would be to reorganize routine clerical work so that the most monotonous jobs were truly automated, perhaps with optical data readers and similar technologies. Clerical workers could then be used in less isolated work arrangements with greater opportunity for career development within the organization, if they desired. Such options hinge on a less stereotypical way of viewing clerical support work rather than on a new wave of office technologies.

P·A·R·T · IV

C

The Case of the
Omniscient Organization*

Gary T. Marx

The following is an excerpt from Dominion-Swann Industries's 1995 Employee Handbook. DS is a $1 billion diversified company, primarily in the manufacture of electrical components for automobiles. This section of the handbook was prepared by the corporate director of personnel, in consultation with the human resource management firm SciexPlan Inc.

Dominion-Swann's New Workplace:
Hope for Industry through Technology

We are a technology-based company. We respect our employees, whose knowledge is the core of the technological enterprise. We care about the DS community. We value honesty, informed consent, and unfettered scientific inquiry. Our employees understand company strategy. They are free to suggest ways to improve our performance. We offer handsome rewards for high productivity and vigorous participation in the life of our company. Committed to science, we believe in careful experimentation and in learning from experience.

Since 1990, we have instituted changes in our work environment. The reasons for change were clear enough from the start. In 1990, DS faced an uncertain future. Our productivity and quality were not keeping pace with overseas competition. Employee turnover was up, especially in the most critical part of our business—automotive chips, switches, and modules. Health costs and work accidents were on the rise. Our employees were demoralized. There were unprecedented numbers of thefts from plants and offices and leaks to competitors about current research. There was also a sharp rise in drug use. Security personnel reported unseemly behavior by company employees not only in our parking lots and athletic fields but also in restaurants and bars near our major plants.

In the fall of 1990, the company turned to SciexPlan Inc., a specialist in employee-relations management in worldwide companies, to help develop a program for the radical restructuring of the work environment. We had much to learn from the corporate cultures of overseas competitors and were determined to benefit from the latest advances in work-support technology. The alternative was continued decline and, ultimately, the loss of jobs.

Frankly, there was instability while the program was being developed and implemented. Some valued employees quit and others took early retirement. But widespread publicity about our efforts drew to the program people who sincerely sought a well-ordered, positive environment. DS now boasts a clerical, professional, and factory staff that understands how the interests of a successful company correspond with the interests of individual employees. To paraphrase psychologist William James, "When the community dies, the individual withers." Such sentiments, we believe, are as embedded in Western traditions as in Eastern; they are the foundation of world community. They are also a fact of the new global marketplace.

The Fundamentals

Since 1990, productivity per worker is up 14%. Sales are up 23%, and the work force is down 19%. Employees' real income is up 18%, due in large part to our bonus and profit-sharing plans. Many of these efficiencies can be attributed to reform of our factories' production technologies. But we can be proud to have been ahead of our time in the way we build our corporate spirit and use social technologies.

At DS four principles underlie work-support restructuring:

1. Make the company a home to employees. Break down artificial and alienating barriers between work and home. Dissolve, through company initiative, feelings of isolation. Great companies are made by great people; all employee behavior and self-development counts.
2. Hire people who will make a continuing contribution. Bring in people who are likely to stay healthy and successful, people who will be on

---

*This article appeared in *Harvard Business Review* (March–April, 1990):4–12. HBR's cases are derived from the experiences of real companies and real people. As written, they are hypothetical and the names used are fictitious. Reprinted by permission of *Harvard Business Review*. Copyright © 1990 by the President and Fellows of Harvard College; all rights reserved.

the job without frequent absences. Candor about prospective employees' pasts may be the key to the company's future.

3. Technical, hardware-based solutions are preferable to supervision
and persuasion. Machines are cheaper, more reliable, and fairer than
managers. Employees want to do the right thing; the company wants
nothing but this and will give employees all the needed technical
assistance. Employees accept performance evaluation from an impartial system more readily than from a superior and appreciate technical
solutions that channel behavior in a constructive direction.

4. Create accountability through visibility. Loyal employees enjoy the
loyalty of others. They welcome audits, reasonable monitoring, and
documentary proof of their activities, whether of location, business
conversations, or weekly output. Once identified, good behavior can
be rewarded, inappropriate behavior can be improved.

These principles have yielded an evolving program that continues to
benefit from the participation and suggestions of our employees. The
following summary is simply an introduction. The personnel office will be
pleased to discuss any aspect of community performance or breaches of
company policy in detail with employees. (You may call for an appointment during normal business hours at X-2089.)

Entry-Level Screening

As a matter of course and for mutual benefit, potential employees are
screened and tested. We want to avoid hiring people whose predictive
profile—medications, smoking, obesity, debt, high-risk sports, family
crises—suggests that there will be serious losses to our community's productivity in the future.

Job applicants volunteer to undergo extensive medical and psychological
examinations and to provide the company with detailed personal information and records, including background information about the health,
lifestyle, and employment of parents, spouses, siblings, and close friends.
Company associates seek permission to make discreet searches of various
databases, including education, credit, bankruptcy and mortgage default,
auto accident, driver's license suspension, insurance, health, worker's
compensation, military, rental, arrest, and criminal activity.

The company opposes racial and sexual discrimination. DS will not check
databases containing the names of union organizers or those active in
controversial political causes (whether on the right or the left). Should the
company's inquiry unwittingly turn up such information, it is ignored. We
also use a résumé verification service.

Since our community is made up of people, not machines, we have
found it useful to compare physiological, psychological, social, and demographic factors against the profiles of our best employees. Much of this
analysis has been standardized. It is run by SciexPlan's expert system,
INDUCT.

Community Health

We want employees who are willing to spend their lives with the company, and we care about their long-term health. The company administers monthly pulmonary tests in behalf of the zero-tolerance smoking policy. Zero tolerance means lower health insurance premiums and improved quality of life for all employees.

In cooperation with Standar-Hardwick, one of the United States's most advanced makers of medical equipment and a valued customer, we've developed an automated health monitor. These new machines, used in a private stall and activated by employee thumbprint, permit biweekly urine analysis and a variety of other tests (blood pressure, pulse, temperature, weight) without the bother of having to go to a health facility. This program has received international attention: at times, it has been hailed; at times, severely criticized. People at DS often express surprise at the fuss. Regular monitoring of urine means early warning against diabetes and other potentially catastrophic diseases—and also reveals pregnancy. It also means that we can keep a drug-free, safe environment without subjecting people to the indignities of random testing or the presence of an observer.

The Quality Environment

Drawing on SciexPlan's research, our company believes that the physical environment is also important to wellness and productivity. Fragrant aromas such as evergreen may reduce stress; the smell of lemon and jasmine can have a rejuvenating effect. These scents are introduced to all work spaces through the air-conditioning and heating systems. Scents are changed seasonally.

Music is not only enjoyable to listen to but can also affect productivity. We continually experiment with the impact of different styles of music on an office's or plant's aggregate output. Since psychologists have taught us that the most serious threat to safety and productivity is stress, we use subliminal messages in music such as "safety pays," "work rapidly but carefully," and "this company cares." Personal computers deliver visual subliminals such as "my world is calm" or "we're all on the same team."

At the start of each month, employees are advised of message content. Those who don't want a message on their computers may request that none be transmitted—no questions asked. On the whole, employees who participate in the program feel noticeably more positive about their work. Employees may borrow from our library any one of hundreds of subliminal tapes, including those that help the listener improve memory, reduce stress, relax, lose weight, be guilt free, improve self-confidence, defeat discouragement, and sleep more soundly.

On the advice of SciexPlan's dieticians, the company cafeteria and dining room serve only fresh, wholesome food prepared without salt, sugar, or cholesterol-producing substances. Sugar- and caffeine-based, high-energy snacks and beverages are available during breaks, at no cost to employees.

Work Monitoring

Monitoring system performance is our business. The same technologies that keep engines running at peak efficiency can keep the companies that make engine components running efficiently too. That is the double excitement of the information revolution.

At DS, we access more than 200 criteria to assess productivity of plant employees and data-entry personnel. These criteria include such things as the quantity of keystroke activity, the number of errors and corrections made, the pressure on the assembly tool, the speed of work, and time away from the job. Reasonable productivity standards have been established. We are proud to say that, with a younger work force, these standards keep going up, and the incentive pay of employees who exceed standards is rising proportionately.

Our work units are divided into teams. The best motivator to work hard is the high standards of one's peers. Teams, not individuals, earn prizes and bonuses. Winning teams have the satisfaction of knowing they are doing more than their share. Computer screens abound with productivity updates, encouraging employees to note where their teams stand and how productive individuals have been for the hour, week, and month. Computers send congratulatory messages such as "you are working 10% faster than the norm" or messages of concern such as "you are lowering the team average."

Community Morale

There is no community without honesty. Any community must take reasonable precautions to protect itself from dishonesty. Just as we inspect the briefcases and purses of visitors exiting our R&D division, the company reserves the right to call up and inspect without notice all data files and observe work-in-progress currently displayed on employees' screens. One random search discovered an employee using the company computer to send out a curriculum vitae seeking employment elsewhere. In another, an employee was running a football pool.

Some companies try to prevent private phone calls on company time by invading their employees' privacy. At DS, encroachments on employees' privacy are obviated by telecommunications programs that block inappropriate numbers (dial-a-joke, dial-a-prayer) and unwanted incoming calls. In addition, an exact record of all dialing behavior is recorded, as is the number from which calls are received. We want our employees to feel protected against any invalid claims against them.

Video and audio surveillance too protects employees from intruders in hallways, parking lots, lounges, and work areas. Vigilance is invaluable in protecting our community from illegal behavior or actions that violate our safety and high commitment to excellence. All employees, including managers, check in and out of various workstations—including the parking lot, main entrance, elevator, floors, office, and even the bathroom—by means of an electronic entry card. In one case, this surveillance probably saved the life of an employee who had a heart attack in the parking lot: when he failed to check into the next workstation after five minutes, security personnel were sent to investigate.

Beyond Isolation

Our program takes advantage of the most advanced telecommunications equipment to bind employees to one another and to the company. DS vehicles are equipped with onboard computers using satellite transponders. This offers a tracking service and additional two-way communication. It helps our customers keep inventories down and helps prevent hijacking, car theft, and improper use of the vehicles. Drivers save time, since engines are checked electronically. They also drive more safely, and vehicles are better maintained, since speed, gear shifts, and idling time are measured.

In addition to locator and paging devices, all managers are given fax machines and personal computers for their homes. These are connected at all times. Cellular telephones are provided to selected employees who commute for more than half an hour or for use while traveling.

Instant communication is vital in today's international economy. The global market does not function only from nine to five. Modern technology can greatly increase productivity by ensuring instant access and communication. Periodic disruptions to vacations or sleep are a small price to pay for the tremendous gains to be won in worldwide competition. DS employees share in these gains.

Great companies have always unleashed the power of new technology for the social welfare, even in the face of criticism. During the first industrial revolution, such beloved novelists as Charles Dickens sincerely opposed the strictures of mass production. In time, however, most of the employees who benefited from the wealth created by new factories and machines came to take progress for granted and preferred the modern factory to traditional craft methods. Today we are living through a Second Industrial Revolution, driven by the computer.

Advanced work-support technology is democratic, effective, and antihierarchical. DS's balance sheet and the long waiting list of prospective employees indicate how the new program has helped everybody win. To recall the phrase of journalist Lincoln Steffens, "We have been over into the future, and it works." We are a company of the twenty-first century.

P·A·R·T · IV

D

Mr. Edens Profits from Watching His Workers' Every Move*

Tony Horowitz

Control is one of Ron Edens's favorite words. "This is a controlled environment," he says of the blank brick building that houses his company, Electronic Banking System Inc.

Inside, long lines of women sit at spartan desks, slitting envelopes, sorting contents, and filling out "control cards" that record how many letters they have opened and how long it has taken them. Workers here in "the cage," must process three envelopes a minute. Nearby, other women tap keyboards, keeping pace with a quota that demands 8500 strokes an hour.

The room is silent. Talking is forbidden. The windows are covered. Coffee mugs, religious pictures, and other adornments are barred from workers' desks.

In his office upstairs, Mr. Edens sits before a TV monitor that flashes images from eight cameras posted through the plant. "There's a little bit of Sneaky Pete to it," he says, using a remote control to zoom in on a document atop a worker's desk. "I can basically read that and figure out how someone's day is going."

This day, like most others, is going smoothly, and Mr. Edens's business has boomed as a result. "We maintain a lot of control," he says. "Order and control are everything in this business."

Mr. Edens's business belongs to a small but expanding financial service known as "lockbox processing." Many companies and charities that once did their paperwork in-house now "out-source" clerical tasks to firms like EBS, which processes donations to groups such as Mothers Against Drunk

Driving, the Doris Day Animal League, Greenpeace, and the National Organization for Women.

More broadly, EBS reflects the explosive growth of jobs in which workers perform low-wage and limited tasks in white-collar settings. This has transformed towns like Hagerstown—a blue-collar community hit hard by industrial layoffs in the 1970s—into sites for thousands of jobs in factory-sized offices.

Many of these jobs, though, are part time and most pay far less than the manufacturing occupations they replaced. Some workers at EBS start at the minimum wage of $4.25 an hour and most earn about $6 an hour. The growth of such jobs—which often cluster outside major cities—also completes a curious historic circle. During the Industrial Revolution, farmers' daughters went to work in textile towns like Lowell, Massachusetts. In post-industrial America, many women of modest means and skills are entering clerical mills where they process paper instead of cloth (coincidentally, EBS occupies a former garment factory).

"The office of the future can look a lot like the factory of the past," says Barbara Garson, author of "The Electronic Sweatshop" and other books on the modern workplace. "Modern tools are being used to bring nineteenth-century working conditions into the white-collar world."

The time-motion philosophies of Frederick Taylor, for instance, have found a 1990s correlate in the phone, computer, and camera, which can be used to monitor workers more closely than a foreman with a stopwatch ever could. Also, the nature of the work often justifies a vigilant eye. At EBS, workers handle thousands of dollars in checks and cash, and Mr. Edens says cameras help deter would-be thieves. Tight security also reassures visiting clients. "If you're disorderly, they'll think we're out of control and that things could get lost," says Mr. Edens, who worked as a financial controller for the National Rifle Association before founding EBS in 1983.

But tight observation also helps EBS monitor productivity and weed out workers who don't keep up. "There's multiple uses," Mr. Edens says of surveillance. His desk is covered with computer printouts recording the precise toll of keystrokes tapped by each data-entry worker. He also keeps a day-to-day tally of errors.

The work floor itself resembles an enormous classroom in the throes of exam period. Desks point toward the front, where a manager keeps watch from a raised platform that workers call "the pedestal" or "the birdhouse." Other supervisors are positioned toward the back of the room. "If you want to watch someone," Mr. Edens explains, "it's easier from behind

---

*This article appeared in *The Wall Street Journal*, December 1, 1994, page A11. Reprinted by permission of *The Wall Street Journal*, © 1994 Dow Jones & Company, Inc. All Rights Reserved Worldwide.

because they don't know you're watching." There also is a black globe hanging from the ceiling, in which cameras are positioned.

Mr. Edens sees nothing Orwellian about this omniscience. "It's not a Big Brother attitude," he says. "It's more of a calming attitude."

But studies of work place monitoring suggest otherwise. Experts say that surveillance can create a hostile environment in which workers feel pressured, paranoid, and prone to stress-related illness. Surveillance also can be used punitively, to intimidate workers or to justify their firing.

Following a failed union drive at EBS, the National Labor Relations Board filed a series of complaints against the company, including charges that EBS threatened, interrogated, and spied on workers. As part of an out-of-court settlement, EBS reinstated a fired worker and posted a notice that it would refrain from illegal practices during a second union vote, which also failed.

"It's all noise," Mr. Edens says of the unfair-labor charges. As to the pressure that surveillance creates, Mr. Edens sees that simply as "the nature of the beast." He adds: "It's got to add stress when everyone knows their production is being monitored. I don't apologize for that."

Mr. Edens also is unapologetic about the Draconian work rules he maintains, including one that forbids all talk unrelated to the completion of each task. "I'm not paying people to chat. I'm paying them to open envelopes," he says. Of the blocked windows, Mr. Edens adds: "I don't want them looking out—it's distracting. They'll make mistakes."

This total focus may boost productivity, but it makes many workers feel lonely and trapped. Some try to circumvent the silence rule, like kids in a school library. "If you don't turn your head and sort of mumble out of the side of your mouth, supervisors won't hear you most of the time," Cindy Kesselring explains during her lunch break. Even so, she feels isolated and often longs for her former job as a waitress. "Work is your social life, particularly if you've got kids," says the 27-year-old mother. "Here it's hard to get to know people because you can't talk."

During lunch, workers crowd in the parking lot outside, chatting nonstop. "Some of us don't eat much because the more you chew the less you can talk," Ms. Kesselring says. There aren't other scheduled breaks and workers aren't allowed to sip coffee or eat at their desks during the long stretches before and after lunch. Hard candy is the only permitted desk snack.

New technology, and the breaking down of labor into discrete, repetitive tasks, also have effectively stripped jobs such as those at EBS of whatever variety and skills clerical work once possessed. Workers in the cage (an antiquated banking term for a money-handling area) only open envelopes and sort contents; those in the audit department compute figures; and data-entry clerks punch in the information that the others have collected. If they make a mistake, the computer buzzes and a message such as "check digit error" flashes on the screen.

"We don't ask these people to think—the machines think for them," Mr. Edens says. "They don't have to make any decisions."

This makes the work simpler but also deepens its monotony. In the cage, Carol Smith says she looks forward to envelopes that contain anything out of the ordinary, such as letters reporting that the donor is deceased. Or she plays mental games. "I think to myself, A goes in this pile, B goes here, and C goes there—sort of like Bingo." She says she sometimes feels "like a machine," particularly when she fills out the "control card" on which she lists "time in" and "time out" for each tray of envelopes. In a slot marked "cage operator," Ms. Smith writes her code number, 3173. "That's me," she says.

Barbara Ann Wiles, a keyboard operator, also plays mind games to break up the boredom. Tapping in the names and addresses of new donors, she tries to imagine the faces behind the names, particularly the odd ones. "Like this one, Mrs. Fittizzi," she chuckles. "I can picture her as a very stout lady with a strong accent, hollering on a street corner." She picks out another: "Doris Angelroth—she's very sophisticated, a monocle maybe, drinking tea on an overstuffed mohair couch."

It is a world remote from the one Ms. Wiles inhabits. Like most EBS employees, she must juggle her low-paying job with child care. On this Friday, for instance, Ms. Wiles will finish her eight-hour shift at about 4 P.M., go home for a few hours, then return for a second shift from midnight to 8 A.M. Otherwise, she would have to come in on Saturday to finish the week's work. "This way I can be home on the weekend to look after my kids," she says.

Others find the work harder to leave behind at the end of the day. In the cage, Ms. Smith says her husband used to complain because she often woke him in the middle of the night. "I'd be shuffling my hands in my sleep," she says, mimicking the motion of opening envelopes.

Her cage colleague, Ms. Kesselring, says her fiance has a different gripe. "He dodges me for a couple of hours after work because I don't shut up—I need to talk, talk, talk," she says. And there is one household task she can no longer abide.

"I won't pay bills because I can't stand to open another envelope," she says. "I'll leave letters sitting in the mailbox for days."

P·A·R·T · IV

E

Interface Development in a Large Organization: An Observational Study[*]

Steven E. Poltrock • *Jonathan Grudin*

The development of human–computer interfaces was studied in a large software product development organization. A researcher joined a development project for approximately one month and participated in interface design while concurrently interviewing other project participants and employees, recording activity in meetings and on electronic networks, and otherwise observing the process. Development practices blocked the successful application of accepted principles of interface design. The obstacles to effective design included the inability of interface designers to obtain access to users, prototyping tools that allow minor changes to be tested but that constrain innovation, resistance to iterative design that results from people noticing and being affected by interface changes, and a lack of communication among those sharing responsibility for different aspects of the interface. All of these are serious concerns that seem rooted in widespread organizational structures and practices.

Interface Design Practices Are Not Well Documented

"It is difficult to develop good user interfaces. We know this because there is no shortage of bad user interfaces, even in products where developers tried to incorporate 'user friendliness.' " [17]

The poorly designed features that handicap most interfaces are common targets of criticism, but their origins are largely unexamined. Descriptions of particularly successful or innovative development are few, but careful analyses of more typical design and development are virtually nonexistent. Accounts of the successful use of new interface design methods and tools are valuable, but we also need detailed accounts of the existing design practices that the new methods and tools are to displace. This paper includes such an account.

It is not surprising that developing good interfaces is difficult. Interactive systems are something new: millennia of artifact design did little to prepare us for the challenges that they present. Even within the computer field, many organizations that develop interfaces today originally developed systems that did not have a significant human–computer interface. Possibilities for interface expression are mushrooming. Computational power permits more media to be combined in more ways, and on the other side of the interface, the nature of user populations is changing just as rapidly. Finding an appropriate fit is a challenge.

Do bad interfaces arise because we do not know *how* to develop good interfaces? Or do we know how, but fail to practice it? In our view, principles and methods for developing good interactive systems are known and are rapidly being refined, so it is a matter of execution. This raises a second question: Could the principles and methods be applied in a straightforward manner, or are there fundamental organizational barriers? In this paper, we identify widely accepted principles of design and then describe a detailed study of development practice in a software development project. The project succeeded, in that the product was built and marketed, but the product interface was far from perfect. Obstacles to applying accepted design principles and methods were evident. These obstacles are a direct consequence of interface development practices, which are, in turn, a consequence of organizational structures and processes. In the end we are left to ponder what combinations of new methods, new organizational structures and processes, and new tools will best move us forward.

One goal in identifying problems or bottlenecks in current interface development practices is to inspire tools that will contribute to greater productivity and quality. Prototyping tools that allow designers to explore design alternatives, demonstrate the advantages of a design to management, and test designs with users can increase usability and decrease the cost of development. Other tools could enhance communication and

*This article is adapted from "Organizational Obstacles to Interface Design and Development: Two Participant Observer Studies," *ACM Transactions on Computer–Human Interaction*, 1(1)(March, 1994):52–80. Reprinted with permission from the Association for Computing Machinery.

coordination. But the effectiveness of such tools might be highly dependent on organizational context; in fact, some problems or bottlenecks might be more easily repaired just by changing organizational practices. Interface design and development have only recently become a respected area of software specialization. Many software development organizations do not yet recognize the unique requirements of interface design. In some cases, significant improvements will be achieved by changing an organization's design practices. The discrepancies between interface design principles and practices described below suggest opportunities for such changes.

Interface Design Principles

Gould and Lewis [9, 10] proposed principles of interactive system design that have had the benefit of repeated application and refinement [6, 7, 8]. Their four principles currently are:

Early Focus on Users. Designers should have *direct* contact with intended or actual users—via interviews, observations, surveys, and participatory design. The aim is to understand users' cognitive, behavioral, attitudinal, and anthropometric characteristics—and the characteristics of the jobs they will be doing.

Early, and Continual, User Testing. The only presently feasible approach to successful design is an empirical one, requiring observation and measurement of user behavior, careful evaluation of feedback, insightful solutions to existing problems, and strong motivation to make design changes.

Iterative Design. A system under development must be modified based on the results of behavioral tests of functions, user interface, help system, documentation, and training approach. This process of implementation, testing, feedback, evaluation, and change must be repeated to iteratively improve the system.

Integrated Design. All aspects of usability (e.g., user interface, help system, training plan, documentation) should evolve in parallel, rather than be defined sequentially, and should be under one management [8, p. 75].

Gould [6] notes some similarities of these principles to those proposed by others and lists methods for implementing them. Researchers have successfully used the principles to develop working systems [7, 15]. Presented with these principles, systems developers consider them to be obvious [10]. However, many people, including Gould and his colleagues, find that developers rarely follow them. Most designers report giving some consideration to users, but few involve users directly in the design process or plan for design iterations.

Investigations of the interface development process and of developers' disregard for these principles have relied primarily on interviews, surveys, and direct reports of experience [e.g., 5, 10, 13, 14, 20]. Gould and Lewis

[10] suggested that the rules are not applied because designers underestimate diversity in the user population, believe that users do not know what they need, have faith in the power of reason to resolve design issues, and believe that the right design can be achieved the first time. They also allude to "obstacles and traditions" that stand in the way. Gould [6, p. 776] later noted the principles "are hard to carry out, mainly for organizational and motivational reasons." Others have noted that design decisions are based on faulty "common sense theories" of users rather than on observations of actual users [14], late contact with users [20], and lack of communication among different interface specialists [13].

These reports strongly suggest that there is a mismatch between the needs of interactive systems development and existing systems development practices. To address this problem effectively, we needed to know whether it arises from insufficient awareness of what is required to develop interactive systems or is an inherent consequence of existing organizational structures and practices. Such a determination required detailed examinations of development practices in specific organizational contexts.

A Case History Based on Participant Observation

As one of a series of participant–observer studies carried out at major computer companies, an investigator joined a software development organization that consisted of over seventy people responsible for the development of a major product that is sold internationally. The organization was designing a new version of an existing product.[1]

The investigator joined an interface team. Over the course of a month, he participated in interface design and interviewed people throughout the organization, primarily people who contributed directly or indirectly to interface design or development. He interviewed about twenty-five people, starting with the interface team and later including other developers, members of technical support groups, and managers. As a member of the interface team, the investigator acquired first-hand an appreciation of the methods and tools used in that period. Through interviews, we learned about preceding activities and planned activities, and explored the perspectives of other members of the development organization. Issues investigated included the organizational context for interface development, the tools used in the organization, how those tools affect the work, which different disciplines are involved in interface development, how people from different disciplines coordinate their contributions, and how the organizational structure affects interdisciplinary coordination.[2]

---

[1] This is typical of product development projects, but care must be taken in generalizing our findings to other kinds of projects. This is discussed in the conclusion.

[2] Participant observation is a widely used field study approach. Anthropologists cannot avoid participating in the life of the communities they study. A fear is that by participating,

The Product History[3]

The organization was responsible for a CAD product that started as a university project and then survived more than five years in a dynamic marketplace. Some new functionality and small changes to the interface had appeared in periodic releases, but as the product aged, maintenance and modernization became increasingly difficult and it was rapidly losing ground to competitors' newer products. The organization had anticipated this problem years earlier and set up a small research project to design a new product, but after a year they were disappointed with its progress and canceled the project in favor of major modifications to the existing product. For two more years they vacillated between the strategies of building a new product and modifying the old one. As time passed a sense of urgency grew and these projects were allocated greater resources. The projects provided some product enhancements but failed to produce an acceptable long-term development plan.

As recounted by those who had been involved, these projects were overwhelmed by the difficulty of deciding what to do. The same issues arose repeatedly, with little sense of moving toward a consensus. Every option could be the topic of seemingly endless discussion and any decision could later be overruled by someone outside the group deciding that it did not fit the organization's marketing strategy. Frequent reorganizations and some staff reductions contributed to both the indecision and the sense of urgency.

This unproductive state of affairs was overcome by a "super designer" brought in from a group that supported the product at a distant site (see [4] for a description of the roles of super designers in software development). He had a strong technical background that included experience customizing the product for a major customer and a thorough understanding of this customer's needs based on contacts with managers and users. He joined the vice-president's staff after persuading the vice-president that the product could be made competitive within a year.

This leader knew exactly what he wanted to do. He had a vision of an innovative release and how it would be built, and his vision drove the interface design. To realize his vision in a year would take extraordinary effort and commitment from everyone and could not wait for the usual cycle of reviews, consensus building, and approval. Working without formal authority, he hand-picked developers without consulting their man-

---

the investigator may be less objective; on the other hand, the investigator can obtain a much richer sense of the experience. In our studies, the investigators' involvement was limited in time, they did not work on critical aspects of the project, and they had less stake in the project outcome than other team members.

[3] The names of organizational units have been changed to protect their anonymity.

agers, assigned them tasks, and then reviewed their progress and problems daily. This hands-on approach was a significant change from standard practice and it irritated many managers and developers. But when anyone complained, the vice-president backed the super designer.

Early reports indicate that the new product was a success in the marketplace. But the procedures that made this success possible were subsequently abandoned. At the time of our study, the vice-president had left, the super designer expected to leave, and the management structure had been reorganized. When the new managers were interviewed, they talked about the importance of following standard software development management practices to control the product design and to ensure coordination across the project. These practices would enable them to meet reliability criteria and schedules, goals that seemed more important than further innovation.

During our study an interface development team was designing the interface for the next release. This team did not use the product and did not have the experience working with customers that was apparently the basis for the super designer's vision for the product. They could not involve users in the interface design and no usability testing was planned.

The Organizational Context

Figure 1 shows a partial organizational structure similar to those observed in this and other of our studies. It includes only the organizational elements that are most relevant to interface development. We are defining interface broadly to include documentation and training, as well as the software and hardware interface. The groups in italics had especially direct involvement in some aspect of interface design in the organizations studied; the other groups were more tangential. For example, Performance Analysis and Quality Control groups were not heavily concerned with interface design issues. Performance analysts focused on issues affecting total system performance, not user performance,[4] and Quality Control groups did not critique or evaluate the interface unless, as one engineer put it, "the interface is truly awful." The structure shown does not exactly reflect this organization, which did not have a team of human factors engineers.

The purpose of Figure 1 is not to endorse this organizational structure but to guide our exploration of the ways in which organizational structures can influence interface development. Pressman [19] notes that "there are almost as many human organizational structures for software development

---

[4] Of course, system performance influences user performance, and interface designs can affect system performance.

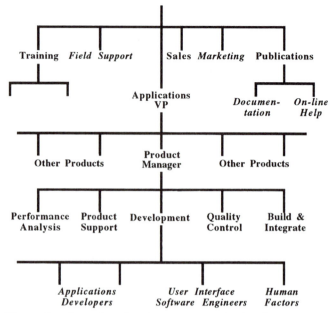

Figure 1. A product development organizational structure.

as there are organizations that develop software." Some issues of generality are discussed in the conclusion.

Little is known about the relationship between organizational structure and productivity, but organizations do impose a structure on formal communication that influences its frequency and quality [4]. More communication generally occurs among people at a given hierarchical level than across levels. Communication tends to decrease in frequency and increase in formality as organizational and physical distances increase [1, 16]. Communication across organizational boundaries can be limited or impaired by being channeled through managers or other intermediaries, by a reduced incidence of informal contact, and by the difficulty of overcoming physical distances.

Figure 1 suggests reasons for interface developers to be concerned about the effects of organizational distance on communication. People responsible for different aspects of the interface—documentation, training, and software—are far apart organizationally. Field Support and Marketing, which can also contribute to interface design, are organizationally distant from the interface developers. Note that this structure violates the fourth design principle, which calls for placing all aspects of usability under one management. Indeed, we observed problems arising from communication breakdowns between organizationally distant groups.

Within this broad framework, details of an organization's structure, as well as the managers responsible for the organizational entities, may change frequently. Such changes are often accompanied by changes in direction, which can adversely affect the interface design among other things. One manager described the effects of organizational changes as follows:

> "I don't think anybody's figured it out yet! I don't think anybody has taken the time. Everybody's working so hard at defining their perch. I've got this image that you've got this big bird cage, and everybody has their perch. And then along comes a new vice-president, and bang they hit the cage with their baseball bat, and all the birds fly up in the air. And they take out a couple of perches, and then everybody comes down to land. And they work real hard at getting their perch stabilized, and now I got a job definition, and I'm building my empire again. And just about the time everybody gets settled and starts singing again, here comes the next king, right? The king's dead, long live the king. BANG! They hit the bird cage again, and everybody flies up, and it's just crazy! You never have consistency. . . . Any time you change the organization all the commitments are gone! And what the hell's the customer do with that!"

Design decisions have a political component; they are often compromises between competing forces. Management changes often shift the political balance, re-opening design issues and forcing revisions in partially completed designs. Changes in management and even in organizational structure can mask an underlying perpetuation of high-level structures, dynamics, and practices in an organization. Readers may benefit from comparing their own organizational structures, organizational dynamics, and design practices to those we observed.

Interface Design Practices

Now we turn to the interface design practices of this case study. Keeping in mind the principles for building effective interfaces noted in the introduction, we first look at the organization's "theory" of the interface design process and how it maps onto the organizational structure. Then we compare these principles and the organization's theory with its actual practices.

In Theory

> "Well, the theory of this organization structure is that marketing is the primary one working with sales and customers to understand market requirements. The Design group works with customers to understand the technical details of the requirements. And Development should be able to get that information from the Design group without having to go out and work with

the customers as well. You know, certainly Development will always have the argument, 'Well, gee, if we could do that, we'd understand it better.' Well, yes, that's true! But you can't have everybody going out to the customers all the time. You should focus on doing development and respond to those design requirements. . . . When once they write the User Interface Specification, then the Design group may come in and say, 'No, we should have done something else. You did not meet the intent.' "

A theory describing how the organization coordinates interface design and development was extracted from interviews with several people. Figure 2 depicts the flow of information, according to this theory, between customers and elements of the organization. Marketing defines product requirements, including new product features, based on information about customers' needs acquired directly from customers and indirectly through field support. Marketing communicates these requirements in the form of specifications to a Design group, which in turn specifies how the features will function in more detail. Such a Design group does not appear in Figure 1 but is similar to the product manager in that figure. The Design group interacts with customers as needed to produce a specification of a high-level product design. This specification may call for new interface features, but does not define such details as methods for accessing the features.

A group of software engineers with Development designs the software interface based on specifications from the Design group and produces an interface design specification. As noted by the design group manager quoted above, this User Interface group is intended to have no contacts with customers or users.[5] The Design group reviews the interface specification to determine whether it meets the intent of their high-level design specification. Then the software engineers implement the interface in accordance with the approved interface specification. Later, an Evaluation group ensures that the interface matches the interface specification. Thus, formal specifications are the primary means of communication among Marketing, the Design group, Development, and Evaluation.

In Practice

"The general consensus is that our Marketing group is next to worthless."

In theory, Marketing is the primary source of information about customers and drives the entire design process. Designers and developers, how-

---

[5] There is an important distinction between customers and users. Customers purchase software systems. A customer is generally a company or other organization that purchases the systems, but the customer is personified in the managers responsible for the purchasing decisions, such as the managers of an MIS organization. Users are the people who actually interact with the product, and may include people within the software development company, even members of the development team. Customers may be users, but often are not.

Figure 2. A theory of information flow for interface design that is widely held in the organization.

ever, had low regard for Marketing and most had relatively little contact with them. Developers were unable to reach users directly. One developer met an experienced user at a trade show who complained about communications with Development. The user was quoted as saying, "It's really a shame the way that [you] decide what to do in the product. I have to talk to Marketing, who really sometimes don't have the foggiest idea what I'm talking about. They pass the information on as best they can to the Design group, who might not have any idea what Marketing is talking about either, so now we've got it even that much more garbled. And then it gets to you guys, and you have no idea what it is about; you don't know where it came from, and you don't know how to contact me."

By examining Figure 2, you might guess another approach taken by designers and developers anxious for more information about users:

> "We tried to get Field Support involved in design reviews, because Field Support has a lot of involvement with customers through the support they're providing and potential customers through the demos and benchmarks, etc. We always had difficulty getting the time from the Field Support people to be involved in those design reviews and the planning of the features. . . . Then Field Support moved under Marketing, and the Marketing approach was that they didn't want Field Support working directly with Development or the Design group. They wanted it to come through the Marketing people. . . ."

Thus, the theoretical flow of information did not work, yet there were efforts to enforce it. We will now discuss the effects in detail in terms of the Gould and Lewis principles.

Product Definition and User Involvement

As noted above, Marketing was viewed by Development as ineffective at getting the information needed to define product requirements.

> "The biggest problem area is the fact that the Marketing organization is not very strong. . . . They really don't have very many people at all that understand marketing or how to determine market requirements, and so that's the biggest danger, that we may respond very effectively to the market

requirements as defined by Marketing, but those may not be what we should have been doing to capture the market and be successful in that industry."

One can easily understand how Marketing, the principle communication channel to customers, could acquire this reputation. Marketing's primary role is to determine what is needed to sell systems, not what is needed to make systems usable. Were Development to seek guidance from Marketing about users' needs, Marketing would lack the information required for a constructive reply. Their contacts are with the customers' management; marketing rarely communicates with users or with field support about users' needs. Information from customers' management may be adequate to define high-level objectives, but it cannot support the understanding of users' tasks that is required to design and develop effective interactive systems. Neither customers' management nor Marketing have sufficient experience or intuition with the newly important and rapidly changing area of interface design. This communication paradigm may have been sufficient when the interface was an unimportant part of their products, but it is inadequate to support interface design.

Given that Marketing is not highly regarded, who actually defines product features? A great many of the features were proposed by members of the development organization, including the Design group. In fact, many features were proposed and added to the design during development. Often these features were motivated by customers' requests. The development managers maintained their own informal, unofficial contacts with customers' management and used these contacts to bypass Marketing and acquire ideas for new features. A member of the Marketing group complained that Development "is very intimately involved with a lot of our customers, they make commitments personally for features." These contacts with customers provide Development with limited information about users' needs, but it should be noted that Development's source of information, customers' management, does not use the products. Formal analyses of users and their tasks played no role in the definition of product features.

Although development management maintained some contacts with customers, rarely did individual interface developers or users bypass the consciously interposed intermediaries such as Marketing and Field Service. A few customers were acquainted with specific developers and in that way bypassed or supplemented communication with Marketing, and opinions could be expressed at trade shows or user group meetings. Several justifications for these barriers were offered. Some managers worried that developers would be excessively influenced by requests for features from customers who are not representative of the marketplace. Others worried that developers, who often have a reputation for lacking social skills, would damage customer relations. Still others believed that it is important to protect developers from distractions so they can be productive.

These barriers may be well motivated, but they clearly stand in the way of the first two design principles and equally clearly had negative consequences for interface design. The software engineers responsible for designing the interface were not informed about the intent of the features they were designing. The specifications provided by the Design group did not indicate what problem the features were intended to solve or the context in which the features would be used. As one software engineer said, "They give us a solution, and they don't tell us what the problem is." Consequently, the software engineers were uncertain how to design the interface. When adding new features, the software engineers had to decide which menus would provide access to the features without information about why or when the features would be used.

As noted above, to acquire information about the purpose and use of features, the User Interface group interacted informally, though somewhat infrequently, with field support staff who had experience using the products. Discussions with Field Support were not a recognized part of the interface design process and consequently often occurred after part of the design was completed. One software engineer reported, "I mean, I was just today talking with a fellow [from Field Support] about a feature and how he thought it ought to work, and I've had to start from scratch just based on talking to him."

Some people did realize that the absence of user involvement had consequences for the interface. A member of the Marketing group said, "Development doesn't even know how to build a friendly user interface because they don't know what a user is. And that really is, I think, a real key right there in how you make something user friendly." This Marketing representative went on to describe in more detail the limitations of contacts between customers and Development.

> "They should have very close knowledge and connection with a user, a user, not the companies but the user. What happens is not this, is that management of Development goes out and gives presentations to management of customers. This is what actually happens. They want a new feature called 'undo.' They call development management and say, 'Goddamn it, your product ought to have undo.' Management says, 'Yeah, we're going to put in undo.' The poor little developer sitting there never gets to talk to the goddamn user down here of what really undo is. . . . We don't even have our own internal users talking to our developers."

The problem is, of course, even more strongly recognized by some of the software engineers who design and implement the interface. One software engineer said,

> "What I'd really like to do as a user interface designer, if the Marketing people could at least provide some major direction, some areas that we want to address, and I think they have done some of that, and then, I wish they would identify some customers that we could go to and work with."

Indeed, this software engineer suggested that all of Development could benefit from observing users at work. He recognized that users provide a resource that can be tapped only with some ingenuity and with a global view of their work.

> "I think it would be worthwhile if all developers would spend maybe a couple of hours a year seeing how the product is used by those customers. Just watching them. And while they're watching them the customer would say, 'I don't like the way this works,' and noting those things. . . . You need to see how they use it. You need to understand, first of all, what they're doing. So you need them to give you a little background, and then watch how they accomplish it, and see the totality of it, especially. How they fire up, the whole structure of their day. And then use that information to give you a global sense of how to help them out. You can't help them without understanding how they work. And not to ask them so much, 'What do you want to see?' Because they don't know."

A Couple of Hours a Year!

Some software engineers and the Marketing representative clearly recognized the importance of involving users, one of the principles of interface design. Nonetheless, the development organization persisted in applying a theory of design that prevented this involvement.

Prototyping and Iterative Design

In the absence of user feedback, iteration has less utility, but the software engineers did prototype their designs. These prototypes were constructed by changing the product code, not through use of prototyping tools. The prototypes were not evaluated through tests conducted with users; in fact, they were not implemented to evaluate the interface design, but to estimate more accurately the time that would be required to implement the interface. The developers did informally evaluate prototypes by showing them to their colleagues and to management. However, in the absence of evidence favoring a design, such demonstrations could have unwelcome effects. An interface developer commented that at design review meetings, "unqualified people make lots of comments off the top of their heads." The interface developers hoped to find a way to limit the involvement of other project members by requiring written review comments.

Even the finished product was not evaluated by users before it was shipped to customers. Some people realized that the tests conducted by Quality Control to ensure that the product matches the specification were not sufficient. One manager noted,

> "I would say that testing should be done by a group outside Development. 'Cause Development knows how the code works, and even though you don't want it, your subconscious makes you test the way you know it works. . . . See, those people in the Quality Control group have nothing to do with customers. They're not users."

In fact, two members of Field Support were reported to have found more bugs than the Quality Control group in the latest release, and they had accomplished this by working with the product as they imagined that users would. Testing by Field Support was an innovative experiment, however, and not part of the accepted development process.

> "The Quality Control group has a lot of systematic testing, and you need some of that, but at the same time, you need somebody who is essentially a customer. It is as if you had a customer in house who uses it the way a customer would every day, and is particularly tough on it and shakes all these things out. That's what these two guys did, and it was just invaluable."

Integrating All Aspects of Usability

The fourth principle encourages the concurrent development of all aspects of usability under one management. Until shortly before our visit, all software engineers shared responsibility for designing and implementing the interface. Maintaining a consistent software interface style had thus been a serious challenge on previous releases; the software engineers had been more concerned with the data their programs needed from users than with the usability of the programs. All software interface design and development was now centralized in a single group, which included some engineers with training and interest in interfaces. However, the organization had no involvement of interface specialists such as human factors engineers or industrial design engineers, and Documentation and Training were handled in organizationally distinct groups. In a separate survey of interface development practices that included the two companies observed here, we found that documentation and training are typically developed late and in isolation from software development [13]. In this organization, one developer enjoyed writing and worked closely with the Documentation group. Interface specifications were the primary sources for the technical writers, but these were supplemented with frequent face-to-face meetings.

Communication with Performance Analysis and Quality Control groups was less frequent. To construct automatic performance or quality tests required information about typical user interactions, but users were not consulted directly. Manuals and specifications were used by Quality Control to construct an interaction scenario. Quality Control reported bugs formally using databases accessed by the developers.

A more serious integration problem resulted from sharing design responsibility across Marketing, Design, and Development organizations. Specifications were management's coordination mechanism. As Curtis *et al.* [4] observed, specifications are an important but unsatisfactory communication medium. As noted earlier, the User Interface group complained that the specification provided by the Design group failed to explain the reasons for the features it described. Clarification of the specifications was made difficult by the separation of the groups.

"The design requirements are written specifically as, 'This is what will be done.' And it doesn't try to justify why that should be done. And they don't come back and say, 'Well, let's have a meeting with the Design group and discuss and understand why these things are requirements.' . . . There still is somewhat of a barrier there to effective communications in that we are physically in different parts of the building here."

These groups were in the same building. In another instance, a small group located in another state developing part of the product was eventually disbanded because of communication problems.

"That whole communication there was real difficult, trying to keep in synch. . . . It was very difficult to keep the standards the same because it was a small group so far away. It was very difficult. The code that came back was hard to work with and hard to integrate, and then if we had to iterate real quickly on something when we were trying to release, the long distance communications just slowed everything down. We had a lot of teleconferences but I think you do miss a lot [that is] in the face-to-face."

Physical distances as well as organizational distances that foster competition for limited resources and power can erode the trust required for effective communication. A manager attributed some communication problems to both distance and lack of trust.

"There are two primary things. One is just the historical lack of respect and trust or whatever between different organizations, Development, the Design group, and Marketing. The other is being in separate physical locations. For most of the time that the division has been in existence within the company, Marketing was at one site, Field Support was at another site, Development was at a third site. . . . And there was always the desire to have all three of those groups together, but there was never economic justification for making those moves up until fairly recently."

The management role of serving as a communication channel among groups, selecting and distributing information or establishing direct contacts at lower levels, is impaired when trust erodes. Some managers restrict any communication with their subordinates, perhaps to protect them from outside distractions or perhaps simply to control the flow of communication.

The Design group was composed of experienced software engineers charged with translating Marketing's requirements into a high-level design. Their role as designers gave them a stake in the outcome and perhaps impaired their effectiveness as pure communication channels. Developers seemed reluctant to approach the Design group for more information about users. The tension that existed between the Design group and developers was revealed in a statement that a Marketing manager attributed to a member of the Design group.

"Camels complain whether you put one straw on their backs or a whole bale of straw on their backs, they complain about the same. They make as much noise and braying and all that. It's just a lot of goddamn weight. No matter what you put on their back, it's an enormous undertaking to do that, and that's the camel's nature. And it's real hard for you to tell whether the camel's really carrying a lot of weight or if the camel is just passing gas, right? And so you load the camel up until it just about collapses and then you say, 'Oh, that's about the load the camel can take.' And then you drive the camel that way. . . . The same thing happens in Development. Everything you ask them is too hard, it takes too long, and it's just an enormous undertaking, it won't work. And some of that's real and some of it isn't, and it's really hard to determine what is and what isn't. And it's the nature of the beast to do that. It's got nothing to do with personality or anything else. It's just the way all of the management and the culture has been built in the development group."

Managers face the problem of maintaining effective communication despite obstacles such as incomplete specifications, distance, and distrust. The super designer of the previous release accomplished this by usurping the organizational design process. He constructed the high-level design himself and bypassed the usual management chains of communication, personally talking to each developer daily, even several times per day, during the design and development of the product. Describing this coordination task, he said, "I ran around like a living information system between all the sub-projects and checked them against the master project." His close supervision ensured smooth communication, though many of the developers resented it. At the end of the project, Management was eager to return to "a standard development process."

What are the consequences for interface quality of the standard design practices? A middle manager in the development organization said, "Relative to user interface, we don't have the best in the world, I know that."

Design Principles Revisited

What emerges from this and our other studies [18] is further validation of the desirability of following the recommended principles of designing interactive systems, together with a description of organizational factors that can block their application. Even developers who fully support the principles can encounter great difficulty following all or even most of them.

Product Definition and User Involvement

Access to real users is at the heart of three of the four principles: early focus on users; early, and continual, user testing; and iterative design. Large product development organizations have consciously insulated developers from customers, delegating customer contact to marketing, customer support, field service, training, and other specialists. This policy may be beneficial when developing products with little or no human–computer interface, but those benefits become obstacles to carrying out structural or procedural changes to promote user involvement in interactive system development. Also, some people fear that by exposing features and functionality that are under development, user involvement can discourage customers from buying the current product version, create false expectations if features are not implemented, risk legal rights to software patents, and give competitors information about product plans. Obtaining access to users can require overcoming these concerns.

In current practice, most contacts are with buyers or customers and not the actual "end users." Marketing may be tasked with conveying information about customer needs to developers, but they are not equipped to do so at the level of detail required for interface design. In organizations that permit some communication with customers, it is carefully managed and developers rarely observe users performing real work to appreciate how users' tasks differ from benchmark tasks [18].

In the organization observed, achieving an early and continual focus on users was complicated by the fact that Marketing was the first to be involved in product definition. Marketing's focus is on competitive products and on the buyers or customers (who are often distinct from the users). Its primary goal is marketability rather than usability, so, for example, features from competitors' products might be desirable whether provably useful or not. Its expertise in usability issues is limited: usability has long been in the shadow of functionality from a marketing perspective and is only now becoming important in its own right. The differences between the goals of Marketing and the development team often lead to a breakdown of trust.

Even when some communication with users is possible, ongoing participation of users in designing or evaluating interface elements is also problematic [11, 12]. Organizations have delegated external contacts to groups other than development and have concerns about changing that arrangement. In addition, Marketing (or other design groups) has a stake in a product they have defined: From their perspective, developer–user contact may result in claims that Marketing erred in product definition or in failing to provide sufficiently detailed design information. Changing the situation will require both a determination that greater usability is of enough importance to warrant change and knowledge of what is required to achieve usability.

Prototyping and Iterative Design

Virtually no iterative design was observed in this project. Iterative design faces a fundamental, historical engineering challenge: the success of non-iterative design for many *noninteractive* systems. Most software does not involve human–computer interfaces. Management and software designers have learned to approach design as a rational, highly analytic process that can be done right the first time. But the introduction of users has consequences that Gould and Lewis [10] describe as follows:

> Adding a human interface to the system disrupts this picture fundamentally. A coprocessor of largely unpredictable behavior (i.e., a human user) has been added, and the system's algorithms have to mesh with it. There is no data sheet on this coprocessor, so one is forced to abandon the idea that one can design one's algorithms from first principles. An empirical approach is essential. (p. 305)

Organizations that try to use iterative design face unique problems due to the visibility of the interface. This impact of visibility was nicely summed up by a designer interviewed in another study [18] who said,

> "I think one of the biggest problems with user interface design is, if you do start iterating, it's obvious to people that you're iterating, you know. Then people say 'How is this going to end up?' They start to get worried as to whether you're actually going to deliver anything, and they get worried about the amount of work it's creating for them, and people, like [those writing] documentation, are screwed up by iterations. Whereas software, you can iterate like mad underneath, and nobody will know the difference."

Another problem with interface visibility is that more people in the development organization have and express opinions about the interface than about other aspects of development outside their area of expertise. Another developer commented [18],

> "If you put up an architectural model, not many people will come back and comment on architecture. But if you actually put up screens and ask people to comment, everyone from the managing director downwards use the product and has their own personal idea, and you get as many ideas as people in the room. . . ."

While user feedback should ensure that iterations will lead to improvements, the very concept is not easily accepted in engineering environments conditioned to stress the importance of thorough up-front design.

The ability to exploit the contributions of interface specialists and users can be limited by the available tools. Prototype construction was difficult and largely limited to exploring minor changes by changing the product source code. Development organizations could benefit from powerful rapid prototyping tools that allow them to explore new interface designs early; the studied organization planned to incorporate an interface management system in their product that would provide this capability.

Integrating All Aspects of Usability

Perhaps the most difficult principle to apply is to carry out all aspects of usability concurrently under one management. The organization we observed had a long tradition of independently developing hardware, software, documentation, and training. Coordination with developers of on-line training and documentation is particularly critical because these interface components stand between the users and the product. However, the requisite specialists are often geographically distributed and assigned to projects at different times. They may also be viewed as having different funding sources.

Contributors to interface design can include software engineers, technical writers, training specialists, marketing representatives, field support, performance analysts, quality control, human factors engineers, and others. Their involvement in interface development varies greatly in time and extent, making it more difficult to envision bringing them under one management. Matrix management models, in which specialists effectively have more than one manager, is one approach. In practice, we observed specifications used as the principal medium of project-level communication about interface issues. Face-to-face communication outside of management meetings was relatively rare, despite the inadequacies of specifications as a communication medium and the resulting breakdowns. Certainly communication tools could help, but organizational change is required to bring usability concerns under one management.

In support of the potential usefulness of the concept of integration, we observed relatively few within-team communications and coordination problems. Constant communication in face-to-face meetings, including regularly scheduled team meetings and impromptu meetings of two or more team members, established a shared context and personal relationships that facilitated communication. Although team members had different educational backgrounds, they had similar professional experience, goals, and knowledge of interface issues, particularly issues relevant to their products. In addition to interface design and development issues, procedural and organizational issues were often discussed. Part of the work was to produce formal documents that were distributed outside the team, and each team supported this work by reviewing paper or electronically distributed drafts.

Integrating under one management would facilitate direct communication; instead, both cases relied on written specification documents as a communication medium. Marketing specified the marketing requirements, the Design group produced the performance requirements, and both these specifications influenced the interface design. The interface specifications were reviewed and approved by managers and technical leaders throughout the project. During the course of a project, requirement and design changes were continuously proposed and reviewed. But many researchers and developers feel that written specifications cannot adequately convey interface information [4, 18]. Interface specialists are well aware of the limitations of specifications.

"You just can't specify in words what your intentions are when you design a user interface. You can produce a spec which defines what you want and there's no saying it's right until you use it. So there isn't a technology that we have currently that allows people to write down definitions of user interfaces that are complete. I've seen people wanting to specify user interfaces by defining objects and hierarchies of widgets and so on in which you can build up a user interface. That still doesn't mean it's going to be a good user interface at the end of the day and it still doesn't mean that it's going to turn out to be the interface that you thought you were writing down when you wrote the spec." [18]

This study examined the development of new releases of existing products. Different challenges face the developers of a new product. Identifying and accessing prospective users can be even more difficult, and prototyping by modifying existing code (with its virtues and vices) is impossible. Similarly, developers of interactive systems for in-house use or under contract face different constraints. The eventual users are often more easily identified, but obstacles to their involvement can be as great [11]. Many of our findings will extend to other settings, but not all will generalize, so they should be taken as possibilities to consider in a given setting. In fact, a product development company that grew up in the past decade, in the era of interactive systems, may be organized differently and more effectively than the older organizations we studied.

In summary, adopting widely recognized and accepted principles of interface design in a large project requires an organizational commitment. Interface designers and developers may recognize the value of these principles but lack the authority to recruit users or to plan for design iteration. Change will not be quick or easy. Training is required to maximize the benefit from access to populations of users. The development schedule must accommodate iterative cycles of design, prototyping, and testing with users, and the development organization must learn to tolerate the instability that results from iterative interface design. One way to minimize uncertainty is careful prioritization and the use of concrete usability objectives and measures [2, 3, 21, 22] that prevent never-ending design iterations, just as system performance and reliability are measured and controlled. Of course, without a thorough knowledge of users' tasks it may not be possible to set meaningful usability objectives.

Can we go beyond general encouragement to work around obstacles to applying the guidelines? Can we recommend specific organizational change? Often we hear calls for placing human factors and software engineers together, or for fostering much tighter collaboration among developers and marketers. These are consistent with the principles but may not work well everywhere. We see positive signs that in some companies younger than those described here, virtually all employees take usability seriously. Such changes in attitude are an important first step.

Acknowledgments

Thanks are due to William P. Jones, who contributed to the planning and study of the organization. Thanks also to Randolph Bias, Rob Kling, Bill Kuhlman, Jean McKendree, and dedicated anonymous reviewers for comments on early versions. Special thanks are due to Jim Hollan, who encouraged this research, to MCC, which supported it, to the company studied, and to the members of the software development organization for their hospitality and cooperation.

References

1. Allen, T. J. (1977). *Managing the Flow of Technology.* MIT Press, Cambridge, MA.
2. Butler, K. A. (1985). "Connecting Theory and Practice: A Case Study of Achieving Usability Goals," in *Proceedings CHI'85 Conference on Human Factors in Computing Systems,* pp. 85–88. ACM, New York.
3. Carroll, J. M., and M. B. Rosson (1985). Usability Specifications as a Tool in Iterative Development," in H. R. Hartson (ed.), *Advances in Human–Computer Interaction* (Vol. 1), pp. 1–28. Ablex, Norwood, NJ.
4. Curtis, B., H. Krasner, and N. Iscoe (1988). "A Field Study of the Software Design Process for Large Systems." *Communications of the ACM,* 31(11):1268–1287.
5. Goransson, B., M. Lind, E. Pettersson, B. Sandblad, and P. Schwalbe (1987). "The Interface is Often Not the Problem." *Proceedings of CHI + GI'87*:133–136.
6. Gould, J. D. (1988). "How To Design Usable Systems," in M. Helander (ed.), *Handbook of Human–Computer Interaction,* pp. 757–789. North-Holland, Amsterdam.
7. Gould, J. D., S. J. Boies, S. Levy, J. T. Richards, and J. Schoonard (1987). "The 1984 Olympic Message System: A Test of Behavioral Principles of System Design." *Communications of the ACM,* 30(9):758–769.
8. Gould, J. D., S. J. Boies, and C. Lewis (1991). "Making Usable, Useful, Productivity-Enhancing Computer Applications." *Communications of the ACM,* 34(1):74–85.
9. Gould, J. D., and C. H. Lewis (1983). "Designing for Usability—Key Principles and What Designers Think." *Proceedings CHI'83 Conference on Human Factors in Computing Systems,* pp. 50–83. ACM, New York.
10. Gould, J. D., and C. Lewis (1985). "Designing for Usability—Key Principles and What Designers Think." *Communications of the ACM,* 28(3):300–311.
11. Grudin, J. (1991). "Interactive Systems: Bridging the Gaps between Developers and Users." *IEEE Computer,* 24(4):59–69.
12. Grudin, J. (1991). "Systematic Sources of Suboptimal Interface Design in Large Product Development Organizations." *Human–Computer Interaction,* 6(2):147–196.
13. Grudin, J., and S. E. Poltrock (1989). "User Interface Design in Large Corporations: Coordination and Communication across Disciplines." *Proceedings CHI'89 Human Factors in Computing Systems,* pp. 197–203. ACM, New York.
14. Hammond, N., A. Jorgensen, A. MacLean, P. Barnard, and J. Long (1983). "Design Practice and Interface Usability: Evidence from Interviews with De-

signers." *Proceedings CHI'83 Conference on Human Factors in Computing Systems,* pp. 40–44. ACM, New York.

15. Hewett, T. T., and C. T. Meadow (1986). "On Designing for Usability: An Application of Four Key Principles." *Proceedings CHI'86 Human Factors in Computing Systems,* pp. 247–252. ACM, New York.

16. Kraut, R., C. Egido, and J. Galegher (1988). "Patterns of Contact and Communication in Scientific Research Collaboration," in *Proceedings of the Conference on Computer-Supported Cooperative Work,* pp. 1–12. (Portland, September 26–29), ACM, New York.

17. Perlman, G. (1988). "Software Tools for User Interface Development," in M. Helander (ed.), *Handbook of Human–Computer Interaction,* pp. 819–833. North-Holland, Amsterdam.

18. Poltrock, S. E., and J. Grudin (1994). "Organizational Obstacles to Interface Design and Development: Two Participant Observer Studies." *ACM Transactions on Computer–Human Interaction,* 1(1):52–80.

19. Pressman, R. S. (1987). *Software Engineering: A Practitioner's Approach.* McGraw-Hill, New York.

20. Rosson, M. B., S. Maass, and W. A. Kellogg (1988). "The Designer as User: Building Requirements for Design Tools from Design Practice." *Communications of the ACM,* 31(11):1288–1298.

21. Whiteside, J., J. Bennett, and K. Holtzblatt (1988). "Usability Engineering: Our Experience and Evolution," in M. Helander (ed.), *Handbook of Human–Computer Interaction,* pp. 791–818. North-Holland, Amsterdam.

22. Wixon, D., and J. Whiteside (1985). "Engineering for Usability: Lessons from the User Derived Interface." *Proceedings CHI'85 Human Factors in Computing Systems,* pp. 144–147. ACM, New York.

P·A·R·T·IV

F

Groupware in Practice:
An Interpretation of Work
Experiences*

Christine V. Bullen • John L. Bennett

Introduction

The fact that personal computer (PC) availability in the workplace is
growing at an astounding rate is being heralded from many corners:

> Computers and information systems are now present everywhere in Ameri-
> can public and private organizations. (Kraemer *et al.*, 1993)

> It happened, amazingly, just three years ago: The Industrial Age gave way to
> the Information Age. In 1991 companies for the first time spent more on
> computing and communications gear—the capital goods of the new era—
> than on industrial, mining, farm, and construction machines. (Stewart, 1994)

> The global market for personal computers is estimated to be $45 billion per
> year, according to *Fortune* magazine. (*Fortune*, 1993, p. 18)

> Technological changes have had an unprecedented effect on business;
> technology—from mainframes to personal computers to laptops to tele-
> communications—is not only helping organizations do what they do, but is
> beginning to change the very nature of organizations. (Goldberg and Sifonis,
> 1994)

The usual assumption that the use of personal computers contributes to
increased worker productivity is turning into an open question: Loveman
reports that at a national economy level, researchers have failed to establish
a significant relationship between information technology investments and
increased productivity (Loveman, 1988).

What aspects of PC use *could* contribute to measurable increased productivity? How do we get beyond the extravagant claims often associated with PCs to discover the reality of their value? Are changes in the organizational workplace or in the design of systems needed to bring the potential into actual realization? We believe that understanding how PCs are being used now can be important for understanding the value that PCs could potentially bring to the office environment.

One area where personal computers are being brought into use is to support the work of business teams.

> Business teams are becoming a way of life in many organizations. . . . Business teams are seen by many as a wave of the future. (Bullen and Johansen, 1988)

> Traditional departments will serve as guardians of standards, as centers for training, and the assignment of specialists; they won't be where the work gets done. That will happen largely in task-focused teams. (Drucker, 1988; see also Reich, 1987)

Our particular focus is on looking at people who work in teams and are networked through personal computer workstations. We seek to understand the value that the technology brings to the office environment. We believe the quality of the results of using information technology to support group work has the potential to far exceed what is achieved today through the use of PCs by relatively isolated individuals within organizations.

If indeed team work is an important form of office work now—and will be more so in the future—then investigating how teams of people work and studying the use of personal computer workstations in a team environment should be valuable for understanding how information technology is used and how this is affecting productivity in today's organizations. The MIT Commission on Industrial Productivity found the following:

> The third recurring weakness of the U.S. production system that emerged from our industry studies is a widespread failure of cooperation within and among companies. . . . Most thriving firms in the U.S. . . . have learned to integrate technology in their . . . strategies and to link [their strategies] to organizational changes that promote teamwork, training and continuous learning. (Berger *et al.*, 1989)

The presence of PCs networked together in communication paths provides the physical infrastructure. But is a new kind of software needed to provide tools for team processes? A term that has become popular during the last few years is *groupware*, a term applied to software that is intended to be used in support of interpersonal work within an organization:

---

*This article originally appeared in *Computerization and Controversy: Value Conflicts and Social Choices*, Charles Dunlop and Rob Kling (eds.). Academic Press, San Diego (1991). It was revised for this edition.

Groupware is a generic term for specialized computer aids that are designed for the use of collaborative work groups. Typically, these groups are small, project-oriented teams that have important tasks and tight deadlines. . . . Sometimes, groupware is used by permanent groups or departments. . . . Group interactions may be formal or informal, spontaneous or planned, structured or unstructured. (Johansen, 1988; see also Engelbart, 1963, 1988; Hiltz and Turoff, 1978; Stevens, 1981; Hiltz and Kerr, 1981; Kerr and Hiltz, 1982; Rice, 1984)

Our questions about the use of PCs, the role of PCs when teams are linked through communications networks, the underlying issue of productivity, and the role of specialized software for use on PCs and workstations all served as background as we began this research project. We used a case study methodology to investigate the current status of group work in organizations and to observe how computer-based tools were being employed in the facilitation of group work. Our purposes in this research are to develop insight on factors that should be influencing software design, and to report experiences that can help guide managers who put group support systems into practice.

Research Design

An interview framework (see Appendix I) served as a focus for data gathering. While the outline provided for initial distinctions we knew would be of interest, we let other distinctions emerge from our interviews. This work illustrates a research methodology often used by anthropologists and titled in a variety of ways, including "exploratory observation" (Malone, 1983) and "contextual inquiry" (Bennett, Holtzblatt, Jones, and Wixon, 1990). This type of study is not intended to be a controlled experiment or a large sample survey. The technique focuses on interacting with people in their own contexts as they do actual work. The goal of data gathering is to obtain insights through observation, interviews, and interaction. The challenge of this methodology is that it relies on the skill of the observer to accurately report and interpret, while allowing unexpected phenomena to emerge from the examples studied. This approach often results in uncovering research questions that can be investigated through controlled experiments or additional contextual inquiry. Our conclusions present such opportunities for further research.

We spoke with two hundred and twenty-three people in twenty-five organizations, represented at thirty-one sites (see Table 1 for details on companies, number of interviewees, and groupware systems available in each). Each interview lasted a minimum of one hour, with the longest interview lasting two hours. In almost every case, the interviews were carried out in the individual's office or work area.

Table 1. Companies Studied with Revenues,* Number of People Interviewed, and Groupware Systems Available

Company	Revenues in billions	Number of people interviewed	Groupware systems
BigChem	$30.00	8	PROFS, Higgins, The Coordinator (V.I)
SoapCo	17.00	30	Other, Metaphor, ForComment
InsurCo	12.00	5	PROFS, Higgins
OilCo	11.00	5	PROFS
ExploreCo	10.00	3	Other
ConstrucCo	10.00	3	PROFS, Other
FoodCo	9.60	3	PROFS, The Coordinator (V.I), Higgins
TerminalCo	9.40	10	All-In-1
RBOC	8.00	10	PROFS, Higgins
HealthCo	8.00	20	All-In-1
BankCo	6.80	5	All-In-1
MedCons	6.00	3	PROFS, ForComment
LawCo	5.00	3	Higgins
ServBuro	4.40	13	The Coordinator (V.I)
SnackCo	2.00	35	The Coordinator (V.I), Other
BeerCo	1.40	6	Metaphor
SmallCons	1.40	10	Other
CableCo	1.00	15	The Coordinator (V.I)
SmallChem	1.00	5	The Coordinator (V.I)
PubServBuro	0.90	3	PROFS, Other
TransDist	0.18	10	The Coordinator (V.I)
SmallRes	**	3	Other
IndCons	**	2	The Coordinator (V.I)
StateBuro	n/a	3	PROFS, ForComment
BigU	n/a	10	PROFS, ForComment, Other

PROFS available in many places; studied in 2.
*Revenues approximate, 1988.
**Revenues less than $1 million.

The twenty-five organizations represented a wide range of industries and size of companies. We chose organizations in which groupware systems were available, and those systems helped to define the set of groupware systems that we studied. Organization names are coded, as our agreement with those interviewed guaranteed confidentiality. We consulted with each organization to choose groups for our interviews that met the following criteria:

- cohesive business teams, facing challenging environmental conditions that would emphasize the importance of coordination for achieving their goals and objectives; and
- teams that had some form of information technology available to support the work of the group.

The size of our work groups ranged from seven to thirty-five people. Those interviewed included individuals at all levels of management within the target work group and, where appropriate, support personnel (administrative assistants and secretaries). In most organizations, the managers to whom the work group reported were also included as part of the case study to help establish some of the contextual information.

We did not choose our groups for study on the basis of a statistically random sample. We contacted potential research sites on the basis of referrals and our own knowledge of their use of technology. However, the resulting sample is drawn from a wide variety of industries, and it includes a wide range of organizational sizes and geographic dispersion. Although these characteristics do not guarantee that the results can be generalized, they do suggest that we are not seeing isolated and unusual instances of groupware tool use.

Conducting a study of work groups raises some interesting questions about how to define inclusion in a work group. What are its bounds? Work groups have been defined as "identifiable and bounded subsystems of a whole organization [with a] recognized purpose, which unifies the people and activities" (Trist, 1981); "collaborating groups of information workers" (Bikson et al., 1989); and "multiple individuals acting as a bounded whole in order to get something done" (Rousseau, 1983).

We found a variety of organizational forms constituting work groups, and organizational conditions in which the workgroups functioned. For example, at CableCo the work group coincides with the organizational department, although it is spread geographically across the continental United States. Four levels of management are included: corporate functional vice-president, regional directors, geographic managers, and support staff. As a growing firm, this functional area is dealing with business pressure to support corporate client growth, a rapidly expanding customer group, hiring and training of new staff, and planning and managing new initiatives in international markets.

At SmallCons, the work group consists of the entire firm. Because it is a small organization, the work group handles a full range of organizational tasks. For example, the following represent typical weekly topics: external issues like marketing and client management, internal issues like getting the work done, and administrative issues like corporate planning and training. The work group includes everyone from the president and founder to the support staff.

At SoapCo, the work group is a flexible concept such that at times it involves an organizational entity at one location (e.g., the Boston marketing group), while at other times it consists of the worldwide instances of the organizational entity (e.g., all marketing groups); under still other circumstances, the work group is a subset of entities (e.g., Boston, Chicago, and San Francisco marketing groups). Within each group, levels of management range from corporate vice-president to support staff. The overriding functional responsibility focuses the work of each group on one primary area.

In the world of electronic communications, the composition of work groups is showing important changes from those observed in the past. Because of flexibility provided by communication technology of all kinds, it is becoming more difficult to identify a formal organizational unit as a work group. That is, some people co-located in an office area do not necessarily work together as a group, and people geographically separated may form a team focused on achieving a common work result. Through the power of electronic media, these groups are dynamic and fluid; this is true for both formal and informal organizational units.

> The traditional concept of an "organization" is no longer useful to managers or students of organizations. It is dominated by models of structure and physical identity at a time when telecommunications has eroded the boundaries between firms and changed the nature of coordination across geographic location. (Keen, 1988)

Given our research interest in the factors important for software specifically designed for use by teams, we had to develop a working definition of what constitutes *groupware*. This term often is used to indicate computer software that is intended to support interpersonal work within an organization. Early notions of groupware saw a clear connection between the software tool and the group processes. However, current manifestations of groupware tools appear to focus on the technical qualities of the functionality and may, in effect, ignore the dynamics of group use.

We have employed a broad definition in our research in order to accommodate the evolving nature of this field. In time, the term *groupware* will probably be narrowed to include only those tools specifically designed to support group work. However, at present, it is useful to include all tools being used to support group work, even if the tools represent user adaptation of an existing technology (e.g., group agreement to share files and calendars on a system designed to keep such functionality private). Therefore, our working definition of groupware is: computer-based tools that can be used by work groups to facilitate the exchange and sharing of information.

A number of systems, with a large variety of functionality, fall under this groupware umbrella. Figure 1 illustrates a framework for organizing these systems using the dimensions of time and place to create four domains that describe circumstances of interpersonal work (Bullen and Johansen, 1988):

- same time, same place
- same time, different place
- different time, same place
- different time, different place

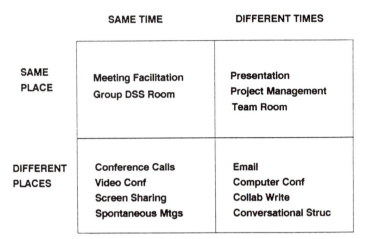

Figure 1. Categorizing systems with respect to time and place.

Although each of these domains is important and the four are interdependent, for this study we decided to investigate those computer systems that can be used to facilitate work in the different time, different place domain. (The other domains are being extensively studied by a number of organizations, including the University of Arizona, the University of Michigan, IBM, GM, DEC, MCC, and others.)

Information Technology Tools Studied

In the course of the case studies, we focused on the use of eight different information technology systems at various times and various locations. The choice of the specific systems was influenced by their presence at the organizations that agreed to participate. Within the various systems a number of functions can be considered as tools that can be used for support of groups. In order to describe these systems broadly, we make the following generalizations. All of the systems studied provide the following functionality:

Construction/Editing Facilities. All systems provide at least a rudimentary text creation and editing facility. Some include elaborate editors and provide function to import graphics. One special purpose system (ForComment) focuses on joint authorship and editing as an aspect of group work.

Electronic Exchange of Text. This includes electronic mail and/or conferencing, gateways to other systems (both internal and external, e.g., facsimile transfer), and document transfer. As a result of the text being captured in a computer-readable form, the content can be reused, edited, re-sent, and so on. Capabilities with respect to exchange of graphics, images, and spreadsheet data differ in different tool environments. Some of the tools provide ways to manage the exchange of text through folders or through automatically linking related messages.

Directory. This functionality at a minimum provides a name and electronic address file to support data exchange by users of the system. Some of the tools provide a traditional "little black book" functionality, where extensive data on mailing addresses, multiple telephone numbers, and notes about individuals (e.g., secretary's name) can be stored.

Time Marking and Time Keeping. All the tools except one (ForComment) provide a facility for recording events scheduled for a particular date. The capability ranges from this basic task to recording, for example, repetitive events, reminders, "to do" lists, and linking this data to other system functions.

General Tools. Some of the systems provide tools for the support of work in financial and budgeting areas, and because of the ways in which the tools can be used, support some project tracking capability.

Integration across the functionality provided is an interesting concept in groupware research for two specific reasons:

1. We found that people were hindered in the use of tools because of problems associated with the degree of integration.
2. This term is used imprecisely by both vendors and users as a measure of quality in describing groupware systems. Therefore it showed up often in our interviews and we feel there is value in defining integration and exploring its application to these systems.

The concept of *integration of function* needed for support of group work is a relative term. One aspect of integration can be measured by examining the process required for each user to move freely between functions, and by looking for the presence of system-dictated steps (e.g., log off from one function, log on to another function). Another aspect is the extent to which the software enables the user to move data from one function to another without requiring special transformations. Thus, integration, as we use the term, refers to the *flow of control* during work by an individual or by team members, and to the *flow of data* during the process of individual interaction with the software or during interaction among team members.

Integration within and across the functional categories listed above differed significantly among the various tools. As a result, some of the systems resembled a group of functions rather than a cohesive package. Brief descriptions of the individual systems appear in Appendix II.

Table 2 shows a list of the systems and gives the general categories of functionality provided in each. We do not provide here specific information on the details of operation for each tool. The range of capability is wide in terms of search mechanisms, ordering rules, and so on.

Observations, Key Issues, and Conclusions

In this section we summarize the results of our study. It is important to understand that, because of the complexity of intervening factors, the observations we report here do not have simple explanations. Research by Iacono and Kling (1988) and Markus and Forman (1989) supports the notion that we need to take multiple perspectives in performing research in organizations. We have found the framework suggested by Iacono and Kling (shown in Table 3) to be particularly useful to us as we sorted out factors influencing the adoption of technology. From a tool perspective, technical solutions are offered as if the innovative benefits of the function would overshadow any historical, political, and social factors that might be present in the environment. Instead, Iacono and Kling find that the environments into which computer-based tools are introduced should be viewed as institutions. As institutions, the environments exhibit many barriers to adoption that have little or nothing to do with the technical merits of the innovative tools. Consideration of historical, political, and social factors can forewarn those developing tools and those introducing them into the environment where computer-based support is provided.

> We conceptualize these patterns as the social organization of computing. We define "social organization of computing" as the choices about computing (both social and technical) which become embedded in work environments and which are experienced by the users as part of the social practices in their everyday work world. (Iacono and Kling, 1988)

Other researchers have stressed the importance of understanding the balance between a technology perspective and an organizational one. Bikson *et al.* (1989) comment,

> group members are interdependent not only on one another but also on the technology, and technical and organizational issues are closely interrelated. The more advanced the information-handling tools provided to the group, the more critical it becomes to give equivalent and concurrent attention to the social processes through which these tools are deployed, and to seek a mutual adaptation rather than maximization of either the social or technical system in isolation. (p. 89) (see also Mumford and Ward, 1968)

In making our observations and drawing conclusions we were struck by the importance of understanding the complex interplay of factors that

Table 2. Tools Studied

	Construction/editing facilities	Electronic exchange of text	Directory	Time marketing/time keeping	General tools
All-In-1	Yes	Yes	Yes	Yes	Some
ForComment	Yes	Specialized	Specialized	No	No
Higgins	Yes	Yes	Yes	Yes	Yes
In-House System 1	Yes	Yes	Specialized	No	Some
In-House System 2	Yes	Yes	No	No	No
Metaphor	Yes	Yes	Specialized	Some	Specialized
PROFS	Yes	Yes	Yes	Yes	Some
The Coordinator (V.I)	Yes	Yes	Specialized	Yes	Some

Table 3. Iacono and Kling Framework

	Tool perspective	Institution perspective
Historical *past decisions that may limit future actions*	Assume freedom from past; focus on future technology perfection; less attention to present; assume individuals free to move in new direction. Groups less a factor.	Interests served in past are present in current situation; those commitments constrain future choices; individuals assume current activities will persist; interdependence of groups.
Political *control over access to resources*	Local control and self-interest assumed paramount; potential conflicts rarely recognized; assume power of technology will overcome political barriers.	Shared control and shared interest groups recognized; specialization limits possible changes; organizational structure (social-structure) may hinder adaptation and survival.
Social *staff skills, patterns of control and discipline*	Local and simple negotiating context without constraints from other sources.	Complex and overlapping negotiating contexts within and among groups.

influenced the specific organizations we studied. However, in order to simplify the presentation of our conclusions we have sorted them into two categories:

From a Design Perspective. In this category we discuss those conclusions that designers ought to consider when conceptualizing functionality for groupware systems. Our conclusions suggest that while designers must be concerned about the technical solutions, they need to go beyond the "tool perspective" to include an appreciation for organizational factors that may influence the use of groupware systems.

From an Organizational Perspective. In this category we discuss those conclusions that management ought to consider when planning for and implementing groupware systems. These conclusions suggest ways in which managers could anticipate organizational factors that might influence the groupware implementation process and subsequent use. However, managers must also be careful to not fall into a pure "institutional perspective" to the exclusion of concern about the quality of the technical solutions.

As with any categorization, this dichotomy of conclusions is an oversimplification that we make for analysis purposes. These groupings clearly overlap, and we believe designers will find useful information in the second grouping, and managers will benefit from the conclusions in the first category.

As interviewers, observers, and interpreters of these work experiences, we have been conscious of these perspectives. In the following discussion of key issues and conclusions we support the ideas using observations and quotations from our field work. Some of the researchable questions that emerged are suggested in each section. However, others can be formed from the work reported here.

From a Design Perspective

Electronic Message Communication Is the Primary Tool

The functionality for sending and receiving electronic messages, available in all of the products we studied, was by far the function most heavily used and universally stated as valuable.

> "I love this tool. I can reach people and they can reach me anytime, anyplace and discuss anything." (Senior Manager, SnackCo)

The desire to have support for communication within a work group was usually the primary motivation for acquiring the tool. People quickly learned the electronic messaging functions, and this contrasted with their failure to use many of the other functions available in these systems. The simple presence of function in a groupware tool does not in any way mean that it will be used. In each system we studied, several of the available functions were ignored by the using groups. However, the electronic messaging capability, regardless of its user interface design, ease or difficulty, or level of sophistication, was used extensively. In several instances interface features were either ignored or adapted by the people to accomplish a simplified process of communicating electronically.

For example, the interface provided by The Coordinator (Version I) contains language related to the underlying theory of speech acts (Searle, 1969). This terminology is intended to lead the users to think about what they are doing and then to characterize particular communications as one of several choices, for example, a request or promise. Although the software provides a choice for simple e-mail (called "free form"), we found people consistently sending each other "requests" regardless of the content of the message. Not surprisingly, "request" is the first menu choice and where the cursor falls by default. Many people we interviewed reported that they ignored the choices and just "hit enter" to send a message. However, they had high praise for the tool:

> "The Coordinator gets the information out! . . . The Coordinator opens communication lines." (Senior Manager, CableCo)

> "The Coordinator's major advantage: instant communication with a large audience." (Senior Manager, SnackCo)

In another example, the user interface for Higgins electronic mail walks the user through a series of steps to answer questions about how to assign key words, follow-up dates, and so on. A person using Higgins to help manage information or for sharing messages in the groupware sense would answer these questions. However, the users we observed skipped through this menu leaving blanks in most categories. People reported that they understood the value of the categories, and knew that they "should" be filling the blanks, but that they were in a hurry and just wanted to get the message sent.

One possible response to this observation is that the message-flow needs of work groups are so great that they overshadow the other system-based activities. This immediately suggests that we need a definition for this kind of communication, which, on the basis of what we observed, could be termed sending and receiving messages. Any of a number of the tools provided as part of a groupware system can be also thought of as entering into "communication" in the sense that they can be used to support transfer of information in some way, for example:

- calendar entries
- expense reports
- reports of project status

- telephone directory
- spreadsheets
- budget reports
- tickler files/to do lists.

It is interesting to note that these particular functions tend to be separated from electronic messaging in the information technology tools themselves. We do not support this distinction as correct. However, as we observed and interviewed people, we found that they acted as if this separation of functionality was real for them, and they generally spoke in terms of "e-mail and the other things the system can do."

This raises the interesting point of how to distinguish between what people say they do with information technology tools (or want to do) versus what people think they should or should not do because they have been influenced by the tools at hand. We cannot answer this question definitively. We can, however, say that, given the choices existing in information technology tools today, the people we studied used what we are calling "message functions" almost exclusively.

Our interviewees frequently stated that they chose groupware systems because of the mix of functionality offered. Given that, an important question is: why do they *not* use most of the functions?

For example, users say they want groupware tools that provide calendaring functions. Yet in the majority of organizations we studied, the calendar tools were not being used. People gave a variety of reasons; the net result is the fact that although the desired function was present, this did not in and of itself mean that it was used.

> "We thought having the calendaring function available on PROFS would be useful in organizing meetings, but no one has taken the time to learn about it." (Manager, InsurCo)

> "One of the reasons we chose Higgins was because of the wide range of functionality it provides. However, most people just use the e-mail." (Support Staff, RBOC)

If developers commit resources to provide function, it is important to understand what is seen by users as a barrier between "offered" (by the system) and "used" (by the people). Other factors, as we shall report, were important in determining whether a function was used.

Our field observations show that the tool people use the most is electronic messaging. The message-flow needs of work groups appear to be so great that messaging overshadows other system-based functions. If we can assume that these busy people would use just those system portions essential for their work, we may conclude that electronic messaging support is what is most needed. In the following sections, however, we discuss other factors that increase the complexity of forming this conclusion. A researchable question here revolves around gaining a better understanding of the value to the user of the electronic messaging function as compared to the value of other functionality. Another research topic raised by this conclusion is understanding the barriers to effective use of the functionality other than electronic messaging.

Message Linking Is a Key Improvement Provided by Electronic Communications

One aspect of electronic message communication that stood out in our interviews was the ability to link messages concerned with one subject area or with a distribution list. This functionality is provided in two of the tools (Higgins and The Coordinator) and it is also inherent in the concept of computer conferencing, which is available in All-in-1 (VAX Notes) and in In-House System I.

Computer conferencing organizes all electronic messages according to topic areas. Therefore, when a message is composed and sent, it is addressed to a topic. The concept of a *topic* is not limited in any way, and can in fact represent a project, general discussion, software release, distribution list, individual, and so on.

People reported in our interviews that they gained much value by being able to "look in one place for all discussion pertaining to project XYZ." In contrast to this observation, users of e-mail systems like PROFS and All-in-1 (without VAX Notes), complained about the difficulties of tracking down related messages and managing their mail folders (i.e., files for grouping messages by categories).

Message linking provides four primary values:

- collection of notes in one place
- chronological record
- ability for latecomers to view an entire record of interaction
- knowledge of the "right" place to put new messages.

In The Coordinator (Version I) this functionality is embodied in a concept basic to the underlying theory: the "conversation" is the primary unit of interaction. Because of this, each time someone replies to a message, the reply is automatically linked to all previous messages in the stream and becomes part of the "conversation."

> "I use the traceback function a lot to find out how we arrived at a particular point in the conversation." (Senior Manager, SnackCo)

> "If I receive an answer to my request that is not linked, I get annoyed because it messes up the ability to follow back through the conversation." (Manager, CableCo)

Users found this feature of The Coordinator one of the most valuable aspects of the tool.

Our interviews showed clearly that people value the ability to group and link messages that are related by subject. This "computer conferencing" capability has been available for more than fifteen years in electronic communication systems (Johansen, 1988). However, general understanding of how it works and general availability to users have been limited. It remains interesting to us that this functionality should be singled out by many users as a key benefit of groupware.

Historically, knowledge workers have always sought ways to organize the volume of information they manage. The first major innovation to affect this process was the vertical file system (the file cabinet, in 1892), which facilitated the grouping of correspondence by subject:

> [Vertical files] had several advantages over [other forms of filing]. Most importantly, the folders allowed related papers to be grouped together and easily removed from the files for use. . . . The new equipment alone was not enough to make storage and retrieval efficient. In a textbook on filing published by the Library Bureau, vertical filing of correspondence was defined as including the *organization* of papers in the files, as well as the filing apparatus itself: "The definition of vertical filing as applied to correspondence is—the bringing together, in one place, all correspondence to, from or about an individual, firm, place or subject, filed on edge, usually in folders and behind guides, making for speed, accuracy and accessibility." (Yates, 1989)

In effect, nothing has changed: groupware message linking or conferencing allows people to carry out this task for electronic correspondence!

The need represented in our interviews (i.e., comments on the value of message linking), is one that should be carefully investigated by both designers and implementers of groupware. People use message linking to manage communications and documents, keep records, and develop "group memory." This conclusion may be telling us a great deal more than what is at first obvious: rather than looking at "fancy," innovative functions for groupware systems, designers should be focusing on how to better solve the basic need of office workers, that is, managing large volumes of information. There may well be ways other than those we see today for designers to address these needs and better serve the groupware user.

What Functionality Is Included and How It Is Offered Are Important Factors

It became clear through our interviews that people did not use some of the functionality in groupware systems because of the design of the tool. There are two characteristics of design quality that we observed.

What functionality is included. One of the best examples of functionality requested by "the marketplace" but not used effectively is the calendaring function. The explanations we were given in our interviews focused on one fact: electronic calendars in their current form cannot replace traditional paper ones. The topic of electronic calendars would justify a separate paper, but we can summarize some of the key problems.

1. Traditional calendars are not simply places where you record times for events to take place on dates, though electronic calendars are usually limited to such a simple function. Traditional calendars have notes on them, contain telephone numbers, are often color coded, and have other papers attached (such as yellow sticky notes or paper-clipped memos, letters, etc.). The nonhomogeneity of traditional calendars is actually an asset for finding important information [there are parallels here with Malone's (1983) findings on desk organization].

   "I honestly tried to use the calendar in Higgins, but I found it frustrating to not have my familiar book with all its messy notes, colors, and paper clips." (Senior Manager, RBOC)

2. Electronic calendars are not portable, and paper copies of the information contained in the computer are inadequate substitutes. Notes made on the paper copies often do not get keyed back into the computer-based version.

   "I need a portable calendar for traveling. My secretary makes me a copy of the computer one for trips, but it is ugly and hard to read. Then I have to make notes on it and do not put them in the computer, and everything gets out of sync for a while." (Manager, HealthCo)

3. The group calendaring value of electronic calendaring is lost unless everyone cooperates. People do not have an incentive to maintain their calendars in such a way that they support group use. In addition, people object to the notion that others (not their secretaries) may schedule their time.

   "We tried to use it to schedule meetings and found that several guys weren't keeping their calendars up to date. So almost as many phone calls get made and it takes just as long." (Secretary, ConstrucCo)

4. The process of setting up meetings is not always a mechanical one. There are times when negotiation is required to secure the presence of all desired parties.

   "When we set up meetings we have to go through lots of negotiation since the Board is made up of members from many locations. Dates for regular meetings get established well in advance and put on everyone's calendar. But setting up special meetings requires lots of personal contact. (Administrative Assistant, TransDist)

5. Very often those who take time to input the information never gain the value of group calendaring because others (usually secretaries) do

the group scheduling. Therefore, people see a basic economic imbalance of input effort to output value (see also Grudin, 1988).

> "It seems I do all the work and Harry's secretary gets all the benefits!" (Manager, BigU)

The calendar function has potential for supporting important group activities (keeping track of time commitments), but the current combination of software and hardware is seen by users as "not up to our needs."

How the functionality is offered. The second aspect of functionality relates to the way it is offered to users. Aside from the functional limitations mentioned above, calendaring was not used in several of the systems because people found the process of use awkward (e.g., no easy way to indicate recurring events). In other examples, people reported that they could not use a tool effectively because they could not remember how to access a particular function and could find no effective help on-line or in the written manuals.

Aspects of the user interface design were also important factors in the reaction people had to The Coordinator (Version I) (see also Bair and Gale, 1988). Although people in fact used the package, and stated that the product was valuable to them:

> "It's great for communication breakdowns since you can backtrack the conversations and find out what went wrong." (Manager, SnackCo)

they also commented on the terminology of the interface:

> "I am not enchanted with the verbiage." (Manager, ServBuro)

Two other products, ForComment and Higgins, were consistently praised for their interfaces, even though some other aspects of their designs were criticized.

> "ForComment is a joy to use; it's so easy to understand the menu items without a manual or checking 'Help.' " (Senior Manager, SoapCo)

> "Higgins menus are self-evident, and the use of color is really nice." (Manager, RBOC)

It has long been recognized that user interface design is a critical element in the successful use of a software product (Martin, 1973). Therefore, it is not surprising that it continues to be an important element in the case of groupware tools. However, it may be that, because people in a work group use these tools, additional factors must be considered in interface design. For example, in a single-user product, like the spreadsheet, designers must be concerned about how each user interprets menus and takes action. In a groupware tool the designer must be concerned about the individual user and, in addition, must address the issue of how what that user does is interpreted by many others, individually and as a group. Additionally, the individual is acting as a representative of the group, which may influence how the tool is used and interpreted.

> It is important to note that an intergroup transaction is not the same as an interpersonal one, although both take place between individuals. A group member involved in intergroup transactions acts as a representative of the group in accordance with the group's expectations. The member is not acting solely on an individual agenda. (in Ancona, 1987)

For example, one person may choose to use an all-lower-case character style to indicate "informality" in notes. This style may be detrimental in communication if other users interpret this as not having enough concern to compose a note properly. The judgment of this user's behavior can then be made not only against that individual, but against the group as being, for example, "unprofessional." Such issues introduce many more layers of complexity into the interface design process, and they emerge from a social analysis of our interview data rather than an analysis that looks purely at the technological merits of design.

In conclusion, it is clear from our interviews that the quality of design, both in terms of functionality provided and access to that functionality, is an important factor in how and whether people use groupware tools. The researchable questions that are suggested by this conclusion focus on gaining a better understanding of (1) interface design in software that serves a team of users, and (2) the actual tasks carried out by individuals acting as members of groups.

Isolated Tools Hinder Productive Use of Groupware Systems

The tools are considered isolated with respect to the flow of user control during work and with respect to the flow of data among tools (as discussed earlier). In some cases the process of accessing the function of a second tool when using one tool (i.e., flow of control) requires an awkward sequence of user actions. Other cases require the transfer of data from one tool to another (i.e., flow of data) (see also Nielsen *et al.*, 1986).

Transfer of User Control. In several of the organizations we studied, it was necessary for the people to go through a series of steps in order to move from the groupware tool they were using for their business group/team to other tools they were required to use for tasks relating to the firm as a whole. For example, some groups used a personal computer e-mail system like those available on Higgins or The Coordinator within their departments, but they had to change to a mainframe-based tool like PROFS or All-In-1 for e-mail access to other parts of their companies. This was universally considered to be an aggravation and a waste of time, regardless of the ease or difficulty associated with the switch.

"I want to log on to The Coordinator and Excel at the same time because I need to bounce back and forth from moment to moment." (Manager, Small-Chem)

"Because Forecasting uses Metaphor to analyze sales data from last year, pricing people are using HP3000s, and I have my analysis programs on a Compaq 386, I have a heck of a time moving between functions I need to access when we set up a promotional campaign." (Manager, BeerCo)

"It's such a pain, I actually have to crawl behind my desk and change plugs. Is this modern technology??!!" (Analyst, SnackCo)

Transfer of Data. Tools that were not completely integrated required that the result from one task be consciously moved into the environment of another tool in order to perform additional tasks. Most users were annoyed by this step, irrespective of its ease or difficulty. From the examples given above to illustrate flow of control problems, it is clear that transfer of data is also a problem at some of the sites.

"I know it is hard to believe, but we actually have to print the output from the HP3000 programs and key the data in to the Compaq 386 because we haven't found a more cost-effective way to move the data across directly." (Analyst, BeerCo)

The ForComment system, highly praised in most respects, was singled out here with respect to data transfer. In order to use ForComment, the person must import text created elsewhere. Although this is a straightforward step, users consistently commented that they would prefer that the functionality provided by ForComment be available as part of the word processor they used to create the text.

"I love ForComment, but I wish it were part of our word processing package. I am always afraid something will get lost in the transfer, so I take the time to check the whole document." (Manager, BigU)

With respect to both flow of control and flow of data, the interviews showed clearly that a lack of integration from either integration perspective was a barrier to the use of some groupware tools. In addition, Ancona's (1987) research on boundary management (i.e., the management of the group's relations with environments and individuals external to the group) raises an interesting point with respect to flow of control. She found that teams equally matched on group process characteristics could be differentiated based on their boundary management capability. This implies that boundary management is a key aspect of team performance and, therefore, productivity. If teams are using groupware systems that interfere with their ability to perform boundary management (e.g., the team e-mail system is not easily connected to the organizational e-mail system), their productivity may be adversely affected. From this we conclude that productive use of groupware is reduced when the tools are isolated.

From an Organizational Perspective

People Report Most Value from Tools
That Parallel Their Nonelectronic Activities

Those we interviewed reported that use of e-mail, for example, was "easy" because it was analogous to, but better than, what they did without groupware tools. People saw computer messaging as an improvement over "the old way" because it was faster, traceable, geography- and time-independent, and accessible from almost any location (e.g., at home, while traveling). Therefore it was easy for people to see the benefits to them in learning how to communicate electronically.

Other functions provided by the systems either differed significantly from what people saw as needed (e.g., electronic calendars) or presented capabilities that they were not currently employing. In the latter category, functions such as project tracking, reminders, directories, and expense tracking all represent tasks that the people interviewed were not doing. Therefore, to use the electronic version of these tools would require them to expend resources for activities they did not normally carry out or carried out only infrequently.

We therefore conclude that the designers, developers, and installers of groupware tools are presented with an interesting challenge: how are people going to make a transition to new practices that some of the functionality enables? Part of the answer lies in designing functionality that is easy to learn and remember after long periods of nonuse. However, another part of the answer is found in the organizational considerations related to examining current work processes.

Benefits Gained Need To Balance or Outweigh the Invested Resource

The benefits from some of the functionality (other than that provided for messaging) were not clear, nor balanced in our interviewees' minds. In fact, users often perceived extra effort on their part for no corresponding gain. For example, people currently do not have an incentive to maintain an electronic calendar to support group use. They see the work involved as redundant (since most also wanted to have a portable calendar on paper in any case). Though they agreed that their managers and groups would benefit, the value to them personally was too far removed to motivate their behavior. They likened maintaining calendars and project information to "keypunching" activities. Yet the group value of electronic calendaring is realized only when everyone cooperates.

Messaging functions, however, had a beneficial impact on them directly. They experienced the satisfaction of "getting the message out," "putting the ball in the other guy's court," assigning tasks to group members, and so on. On the receiving side, they had a record of what they were expected to do and, through being on copy lists, had a sense of being in touch with what was going on in the group. They had no need to conceptualize anything beyond a personal benefit.

Other functions as mentioned previously (e.g., project tracking, reminders, etc.) actually required additional effort on the part of the users to learn to do things in a different way, independent of the technology. While the people we interviewed often said things like "I should do expense tracking," "I know it would be more efficient if I kept an electronic directory," "I could really benefit from the reminder function," invariably they were unwilling to adapt their behavior and invest the personal resources necessary to employ this kind of functionality. They had not identified benefits to using the technology that equaled or exceeded their resource investment.

Grudin explores "the disparity between who does the work and who gets the benefit" and raises some serious questions about whether groupware applications will ever succeed:

> Not all groupware introduces such a disparity—with electronic mail, for example, everyone generally shares the benefits and burdens equally. But electronic mail may turn out to be more the exception than the rule, unless greater care is taken to distribute the benefit in other applications. (Grudin, 1989)

Therefore, we can conclude that unless there is a balance between the effort required on the part of the user and the benefit delivered to that user, a person is not likely to employ the functionality present in a tool. Other forms of motivation (e.g., management directives, group agreement, education) can be important in influencing the perception of balance. Research to investigate motivation and change management as part of the implementation of groupware technology could be beneficial in understanding the dynamics here.

Groupware Implementation Is Simultaneously
a Social and Technical Intervention

Our research observations support Kling and Iacono (1989): "computerization is simultaneously a social and technical intervention." One of the most important aspects of this complex intervention is that it is a "strategic intervention" (Kling and Iacono, 1989, p. 342). Whether the strategy of technology introduction is made explicit or kept implicit, it exists and can have a significant impact on the organization.

In our research we saw the effects of strategies on the individuals we interviewed. For example, when a groupware system was introduced as a way to streamline procedures by merely training new users in the mechanics of the tools, we saw people using a minimum of the functionality present in the systems. That is, people used what they were taught to use without any innovative thinking on their parts about either (1) how to employ other functionality present in the groupware systems, or (2) how to creatively use that which they had learned to have an impact on the way they carried out their work. When instruction went beyond mechanical steps, however, to include, for example, a presentation on the concepts of groupware, or material on how to relate the groupware functionality to accomplishing their work tasks, then people made use of, and applied creative thinking to using, the functionality present in the tool.

When a groupware system was introduced as a new technology to experiment with, the people did not take it seriously and did not look for ways to augment their productivity. When decision makers held high expectations for productivity enhancement through groupware, yet gave no attention to examining the work process, people reported that they felt under pressure to perform better while leaning a new tool and without a clear understanding of how the tool would make a difference. In many of these cases, the introduction of the groupware system had a negative effect on productivity.

Organizational factors in the following four general categories showed up as consistently important as we interviewed people in the twenty-five firms.

Champions. Management support for the introduction of groupware tools varied significantly in our sample. In some organizations, support for the tool emanated from the top levels of the firm:

> "When the president wanted us to use this e-mail package without even looking at any others, we thought it was strange, but had enough faith in [him] to try it." (Senior Manager, CableCo)

At others, like SnackCo, the management support was at the departmental level:

> "We thought this tool was weird, but if WW asked us to try it, we knew it was worth doing." (Manager)

In some instances, the support came lower in the organization in the form of middle management supporters who felt they could engineer successful pilots and demonstrate the value of the tools to upper management:

> "Through my own coaching and interpersonal skills I have been able to teach people and win them over to the value of using The Coordinator. Now management is paying attention." (Manager, ServBuro)

While these instances of managerial support represent different levels of power within each organization, they demonstrate the importance in general of a committed leader in the introduction of a new technology. Management literature for decades has discussed the value of leadership and champions for the successful implementation of an innovation. In the area of groupware tools, this "common wisdom" continues to be valid. However, as the previous observations have shown, and the next observations will suggest, managerial support cannot guarantee successful implementation by itself.

Expectations. We observed two different work groups in one organization in which the same software had been introduced. In one of these groups (Group A) the tool was originally described as a new technology that the group members should familiarize themselves with and see what they could use it for. In the other group (Group B) the tool was described as an important new technology that was going to be used to improve communication throughout the organization. Five years later, when we conducted our interviews, the original attitudes were present in these two groups and were influencing the use of the software. As a result, in Group A the tool had never been taken seriously and was still considered "an experiment" and informal. In Group B the tool was described by people as "critical to their jobs."

It is clear from our studies and those of others "that the kinds of expectations with which an organization approaches new information technology do much to define the consequences that will be observed" (Carroll and Perin, 1988). Therefore, the way in which new groupware tools are introduced into the work group will influence the ways in which they are used.

Training. Those interviewed generally described the training that they had received in the use of their software as directed toward building procedural or mechanical skills—basic instruction in what keys to push to accomplish specific tasks. This was true for all the tools we studied. However, in the case of The Coordinator, we did interview some users who had received training that included an introduction to the theory underlying this product. A subset of this group did report that the ideas were too sophisticated for them and their colleagues to assimilate:

"The linguistic concept went over most people's heads." (Manager, SnackCo)

"The training left me cold, but we pursued the value on our own." (Senior Manager, CableCo).

However, some reported that knowledge of the theory helped them to use the tool and to implement the communication practices that the tool supports:

"Knowledge of speech-act theory has really helped me use The Coordinator to be more effective in my daily communication." (Manager, ServBuro)

"The workshops were inspirational and make using The Coordinator vocabulary much easier." (Manager, SnackCo)

Given the previous observations that people are not using the functionality provided by these tools, the fact that they have also received only basic, mechanical training would tend to indicate that the training is not adequate.

> "Training was not very good, but we figured it out." (Manager, MedCons)

Evolution. After an initial introduction into the use of a groupware tool, the users we interviewed tended to "practice" only those procedures that they needed to accomplish their most urgent business tasks. As a result, much of what they were initially trained to do but did not continue to do regularly was forgotten.

> "Two weeks after the training program I could barely remember how to get to my file directory." (Senior Manager, LawCo)

In the use of any system, people will encounter special case needs for functions from time to time in their work. Those interviewed did not regularly look up procedures in a manual when these situations arose. When online help was available, most who used it were unable to find what they needed. Instead, the typical form of help sought was to ask a colleague or subordinate.

> "I refuse to read manuals and documentation; they aren't even written in English!" (Manager, BigChem)

> "The only copy of the manual I could find was two years old and inappropriate to the version I am using." (Manager, SoapCo)

> "On-line 'Help' is a bust. It never covers the exact problem I'm having and is written with lots of jargon." (Senior Manager, FoodCo)

> "I always ask Joe for help. He can tell me in two seconds where I've gone wrong." (Support Staff, BigU)

> "Sue explains my mistakes in the context of our work. That makes it easier for me to remember for next time." (Senior Manager, TerminalCo)

Some of the organizations provided a person or group to serve as the designated support source to which the users would turn for help. These organizations appeared to understand the evolutionary nature of a person's use of software, and they supported that evolution through a formal organizational entity. Other sites we studied assumed that once the initial training had taken place, no formal corporate role of an ongoing nature was needed. In these cases, *de facto* support grew up in the form of individuals in work groups who became "local gurus."

> "Dick has become the guy we all go to for help. He's part of our department and understands our questions best." (Manager, TerminalCo)

"The Infocenter has been wonderful in supporting the use of this tool. They are always available and polite in telling you where you made your mistakes." (Senior Manager, OilCo)

We observed what might be called a "plateau of competence" in using a tool. Without a timely and user-appropriate incentive to move beyond self-standardized use, people tend to settle into standard operations (Rosson, 1985). We observed close group interaction serving as a constructive stimulus for individuals. In SnackCo a central person sent out a newsletter of hints and ideas that was found useful by some. However, the presence of new ideas was countered by pressure to "get the job done," so many people found little time to try new things. This suggests that such stimuli must be in the form of easily tried procedures with immediately visible value so that they fit into the practices carried out during a busy day.

In each of the categories—champions, expectations, training, evolution —we saw a need for sensitivity to organizational issues. In addition, the degree and timing of organizational intervention must be planned. The risk of failure increases when the multiple organizational factors are not considered. In the case of groupware technology, there is little experience in understanding these factors, which may be particularly complex because of the "group" aspects of the application.

Process Redesign May Be Required to Realize Productivity Improvement

We have just suggested that organizations should consider the perspectives of people at all levels when introducing technology. It is also interesting to consider the extent to which organizations need to alter their basic processes in order to achieve higher levels of coordination and productivity.

This process redesign may occur on a variety of levels. For example, traditional process redesign looks at formal processes that have been established in an organization in order to achieve its business goals and objectives. These processes are reevaluated for a variety of reasons, including changes in products or services, changes in the structure of the industry, or the impacts of new technology on basic functions (e.g., manufacturing or distribution channels).

However, process redesign can be employed on a local level in an organization. For example, the process of work coordination in a department or the process of conducting meetings may be areas in which productivity gains could be achieved through rethinking and redesigning the traditional forms (e.g., Whiteside and Wixon, 1988). In our field work we observed instances of management expecting substantial productivity improvement to result from the simple act of putting a groupware system into place. In these instances our interviews did not uncover any significant change in how people approached their jobs. Some felt that the new technology created more work for them and therefore made them less productive.

Whenever we observed the implementation of groupware technology without a concurrent examination of how work procedures and coordination should perhaps change or evolve, we saw that these systems had little impact on the perceived productivity of the groups. These observations lead us to the conclusion that in some cases when groupware systems are implemented, not enough attention is being placed on examining the basic processes of work and how technology may enhance these processes. Therefore, process redesign may be required to achieve productive benefits in using groupware technology.

Creating Productive Teams Is a Challenge

Managers in some of the organizations we studied had explicit goals of changing the way work was carried out, moving their groups to new planes of performance, creating "paradigm shifts":

> "I am intrigued by the linguistic theory underlying The Coordinator and would like to see everyone undergo a paradigm shift and significantly change the way they interact." (Senior Manager, SnackCo)

Does the current generation of groupware systems facilitate this process? What is truly needed to create productive teams? In *TeamWork* (Larson and LaFasto, 1989), the authors present eight characteristics of high-performing teams, which they draw out of interviews with publicly acclaimed high-performing teams, including sports, science and technology, and industry. Most of these appear to reflect generally understood notions of good team work, and they are described at a somewhat abstract level, for example, "clear elevating goal," "competent team members," "collaborative climate."

They also raise many questions in terms of *how* these characteristics are operationalized. In the context of our research, how can technology be applied to facilitate the creation of the key elements necessary to create productive teams?

The partnership of organizational process and technology is clear. Management must carry out specific tasks to bring forth productive team characteristics. High-performing teams can be created without any technology. However, in the fast-paced, geographically dispersed environment of today's corporation, groupware technology could enhance the individual's ability to carry out the appropriate tasks.

Examining people's attitudes appears to be an important step in understanding barriers to productive team work. In our interviews we noted that when people saw the immediate value to themselves of using a function (e.g., messaging), they quickly adapted to its use. However, when it was in the interests of the "higher good"—that is, the team, department, or organization would benefit—the incentive for the individual was missing.

In these situations it took other motivators to cause people to use these tools. Some of the motivators included

- a charismatic leader
- orders from higher management
- workshops on organizational issues
- obtaining group agreement and individual permission.

In other words, the technology alone, regardless of its potential value, attractiveness, or ease of use, could not inspire people to use it. In addition, introducing new technology into a poorly operating work group is unlikely to improve its performance. In fact, researchers have found that new technology may very well degrade performance because its introduction brings more complexity and a threat to the people on the team (Henderson and Cooprider, 1988).

The well-known concept of "unfreezing" in organizational change theory (Lewin, 1952) seems applicable here. The potential users of groupware systems need to "open up" or "unfreeze" to the possible value of learning to use the technology. That unfreezing is not a simple matter of mechanical training, but rather an organizational process that includes training, education, and rethinking the goals of the team, and then considering how work results will be accomplished from the new perspective.

One of the lessons that comes out of *TeamWork* is that much of the success of teams depends on communication among team members on key issues. One of groupware's greatest values, according to our research, is the support it provides for electronic messaging. Our conclusion here is that if a groupware system can facilitate team interaction and information exchange, it has the potential to move group work into the realm of high-performance teams.

Summary

Is groupware too new to study conclusively? We have learned from innovation research (Rogers, 1983) that it takes time for new ideas to be assimilated by people. Although the technology for electronic mail and conferencing has been available for fifteen years (Engelbart, 1963; Johansen, 1988), the concept of technology to support work groups has been discussed for only about four years. (Engelbart in the early 1960s developed pioneering technology especially designed to support high-performing teams, but this work was not well known outside the computer science community.) We may therefore be observing the use of these new tools when they are in their infancy and before people have learned to think about them as essential tools for effective office work.

Nonetheless, experiences gained from studying people as they learn to use new tools can benefit the designers of the next tool generation, thereby helping to accelerate the process of acceptance and use of these tools. We also believe that managers can learn to be sensitive to the complex balance that exists between the organization and the technology.

Our observations were consistent across a wide range of organizations. Work groups at the largest organization we studied, BigChem, with $30 billion in revenues, experienced the same challenges in organizing work and using information technology as did those at the smallest organizations. Work groups at companies recognized as being "forward thinking," "networked," and participatory in management style did not differ in their problems nor in their attempted solutions from work groups in companies characterized as "conservative," hierarchical, and traditional in management style.

For example, CableCo ($1 billion in revenues) is a young, quickly growing, highly successful company with a participatory management style. The work group consisted of nine people who had concerns related to effective communication and management of tasks in an accelerating, fast-paced environment that spanned several time zones. At SoapCo ($17 billion in revenues) one work group consisted of fifteen people who expressed exactly the same concerns and were attempting to use information technology in the same way to support their work group. SoapCo is an old company with a long tradition of hierarchical, conservative management, and with long-standing procedures for accomplishing tasks. *A priori,* we might have assumed the differing environments in these two organizations would have dictated different approaches to solving the coordination problems. We found this to be true neither here nor at other research sites. Apparently today's business environment of global, twenty-four-hour marketplaces with the concurrent acceleration of information and coordination needs brings the same challenges in managing work groups to diverse organizations.

We have discussed major questions and conclusions about work groups and their use of information technology. We see an important interplay of factors in our major conclusions. For example, people seem to need training beyond the simple mechanical instruction that usually accompanies groupware tools. Because groupware is a relatively new technology, this may change in the future as the tools are more widely known and used. Their inherent value may become more obvious to people and they will adapt to their use more easily.

However, the organizational inhibitors that we observed cannot be dismissed. Recognizing the long-lasting constraints of history and the power of politics in the organization at the same time as considering the new possibilities for technology support may result in new insights. These contrast with insights suggested when using traditional requirements analysis, often focused on individual users to the exclusion of organizational factors. Understanding the interplay of

1. economic balances (i.e., input resources vs. output value) inherent in the use of a tool,

2. the differential impacts on organizational roles (e.g., managerial impacts may differ from support staff impacts), and
3. the organizational readiness (i.e., management attention through planned change or intervention)

may lead management toward different technological paths than those discovered through simple analysis.

We have stated earlier that managing the volume of information has been traditionally, and still is, the major task facing knowledge workers. As we have interviewed, observed teams, and better understood the tasks they are undertaking, we have come to the conclusion that a groupware system like The Coordinator, for example, could have an effect on knowledge work by compressing it. That is, The Coordinator, if it were used as its designers intended, could reduce the volume and complexity of information so that managing the content and meaning of interaction would dominate managing volume.

Revolutionizing work may be an effective role for groupware systems in organizations. Most of today's groupware systems are not designed to do this. Instead they attempt to provide electronic support for the tasks people are believed to carry out in performing knowledge work in groups. If indeed the concept of work groups and business teams is the organizational concept of the future, it becomes critical to better understand the interaction of individuals in these groups, and how information technology can support or even enhance the work of groups.

Acknowledgments

The authors acknowledge the many individuals who agreed to be interviewed, and who interacted with us in the course of this research. Without their cooperation and genuine interest in the topic, it would have been difficult to learn about the experience of groupware use in organizations. We thank David L. Anderson who assisted us in the field work and provided support for the ideas presented here. We also acknowledge the following for their valuable roles in reviewing drafts: John Henderson, J. Debra Hofman, Bob Johansen, Wendy Kellogg, Bob Mack, Tom Malone, Wanda Orlikowski, Judith A. Quillard, John Richards, and JoAnne Yates.

Appendix I

Case Study Interview Outline

General background information on the organization, the work group, and the individual being interviewed;
Detailed information on the work group or project:

- Members
- Description
- Mode of operation
    meeting frequency
    forms of communication (face-to-face, phone, electronic, video)
    levels of stress
    leadership
    boundary management (relationship to world outside project);

Description of how tasks are accomplished;
Determination of information technology (IT) tools that are used to facilitate task accomplishment with detailed description of use;
Determination of general sense of satisfaction with existing mode of operation;
Suggestions for change;
Probing of interviewee's sense of the future:

- Types of group work that will take place
- Changes anticipated for organization as a whole
- Needs for different IT tools.

Appendix II

All-In-1

All-In-1 is more accurately described as a family of tools or even an office tool environment. This system resides on a centralized computer, with PCs often serving as a means of access (both local and remote). It does not provide flow of data integration, but does provide flow of control within its environment. The basic tool provides a variety of functions ranging from electronic mail to a spreadsheet package. An organization can customize All-In-1 by adding other commercial products under the general All-In-1 "umbrella." For example, the popular word-processing software, WordPerfect, can be installed to operate under All-In-1. The extent to which the functionality provided under All-In-1 can be used as groupware depends on which functions are used and on what agreement the people in the organizational unit reach on how the functions will be used.

The logical groupware use of this tool involves employing the electronic mail function and VAX Notes (computer conferencing) for communication and the exchange of documents. A calendar function can be used for scheduling group meetings.

The basic All-In-1 functions described above are in use at three organizations in our study.

ForComment

ForComment is a single-purpose system. It assists users in group authoring or editing of documents. This system is available in single PC and local area network configurations. ForComment "imports" text produced in most of the popular word-processing environments or ASCII and allows multiple authors or reviewers to rewrite and/or comment on the document. Control over the final version of the document always remains with one individual, the designated primary author. Proposed rewrites and comments are noted through a symbol in the margin, and the actual text of the revision is displayed in a second window on the viewer's screen. Each entry is identified by reviewers' initials, color coding, and date of entry. The software automatically merges entries from multiple reviewers so that the primary author reviews a single, aggregated version. In this respect ForComment provides flow of data integration.

ForComment is used by four organizations in our sample. Each organization uses it unmodified as provided by the vendor.

Higgins

Higgins is a personal computer system based on a local area network that provides a variety of functionality including electronic mail, personal information organization, project tracking, and project expense tracking. The electronic mail function links messages and their associated replies, allowing users to trace the history of communications leading to a current message. All of the functions are integrated on Higgins both with respect to flow of control and to flow of data. For example, a user can employ key words to find all entries dealing with specific categories. Therefore, the name "project xyz" can be used to find electronic mail, "to do" entries, expense reports, calendar entries, and so on, that relate to that project by its code name. In this way Higgins can be used both as a personal organization tool and as a groupware tool.

Higgins is used in five of the organizations in our sample, in each case in a stand-alone local area network (LAN) mode as provided by the vendor.

In-House System I

One large organization in our sample developed its own global electronic mail, conferencing, and document exchange system. This system resides on a mainframe computer and is accessed by PCs acting as workstations (both local and remote). Integration in terms of both flow of data and flow of control exists to varying degrees in this system. Development of increased integration in both areas is a current priority. This system has been in worldwide use by a large number of people at this organization for more than ten years.

In-House System II

One small organization in our sample developed its own relatively basic electronic messaging tool. This system resides on a centralized computer and is accessed by both local and remote PCs. The system is used primarily in the United States (although one European node is in place) and has been in use for approximately eight years.

Metaphor

Metaphor provides high-end specialized, networked workstations and software to support professionals, managers, and executives in constructing complex queries against multiple databases. Users build queries by specifying data elements graphically and then by linking sequences of operations on that data. These queries can be saved in "capsules" for later use or for use by others. Data results can be passed to others on the specialized local area network in the form of spreadsheets, reports, and graphs. The graphical user interface is intended for easy and effective use by business professionals (such as marketing analysts) who need to review and aggregate data extracted from large databases. Flow of control and flow of data integration exist within the Metaphor environment.

Metaphor is in use at two sites in our sample. In one of those sites it is being used as a stand-alone system; in the other it is designed with a gateway into the corporate data network.

PROFS

PROFS is a general purpose office system tool. This system resides on a centralized computer with PCs often serving as a means for access (both local and remote). PROFS includes functionality for electronic mail, calendaring, reminders, and folders for mail management. Other than for the electronic mail component, the extent to which PROFS can be used as groupware depends on the agreements people in an organization reach for allowing access to calendars and folders. Flow of control integration exists to a limited degree within the PROFS environment.

PROFS was studied at two of our sites.

The Coordinator System (Version I)

The Coordinator System (TCS) is a groupware system that was designed to support people in effective action during the course of their work in an organization. The system is generally available in two hardware configurations: either on a PC/local area network, or via dial-up mode supported by the vendor. TCS differs from most of the other products we examined in that the software implementation is based on an underlying theory of human interaction. The theory suggests that the basic unit of interaction is a conversation, and that people use language (speech acts) to make requests, promise results, decline requests, declare commitments completed, and so on. The software makes these distinctions visible and thereby is designed to encourage people to conduct their interactions in a way presumed (under the theory) to be more effective.

The Coordinator Version I is available in seven of the organizations in our sample. Technical details of the implementations differ (e.g., remote mail, local area network), but these differences do not play an important role in what the users see, or how they tend to employ the tool. The fact that Version I is the tool we studied is, however, important because the user interface of Version I differs significantly from that of Version II. Version II became available in 1989, and it is currently being marketed and used in a number of organizations.

The degree to which flow of control integration exists in a TCS implementation depends on the nature of the implementation and bridges that have been established to other systems. Flow of data integration exists in some of the tools.

References

Ancona, Deborah Gladstein (1987). "Groups in Organizations," in Clyde Hendrick (ed.), *Group Processes and Intergroup Relation,* pp. 207–230. Sage Publications, Newbury Park, CA.

Bair, James H., and Stephen Gale (1988). "An Investigation of the Coordinator as an Example of Computer Supported Cooperative Work." Extended Abstract, submitted to the Second Conference on Computer-Supported Cooperative Work, Portland, Oregon, September.

Bennett, J. L., K. Holtzblatt, S. Jones, and D. Wixon (1990). "Usability Engineering: Using Contextual Inquiry." Tutorial at CHI '90, Empowering People. Seattle, WA, April 1–5. Association for Computing Machinery, New York. (Forthcoming.)

Berger, Suzanne, Michael L. Dertouzos, Richard K. Lester, Robert M. Solow, and Lester C. Thurow (1989). "Toward a New Industrial America." *Scientific American,* 260(6)(June):39–47.

Bikson, Tora K., J. D. Eveland, and Barbara Gutek (1989). "Flexible Interactive Technologies for Multi-Person Tasks: Current Problems and Future Prospects," in Margrethe H. Olson (ed.), *Technological Support for Work Group Collaboration,* pp. 89–112. Lawrence Erlbaum, Hillsdale, NJ.

Blomberg, Jeanette (1988). "The Variable Impact of Computer Technologies on the Organization of Work Activities," in Irene Greif (ed.), *Computer-Supported Cooperative Work: A Book of Readings.* Morgan Kaufmann, San Mateo, CA.

Bullen, Christine V., and Robert R. Johansen (1988). "Groupware: A Key to Managing Business Teams?" CISR Working Paper No. 169. May. Center for Information Systems Research, Cambridge, MA.

Carroll, John S., and Constance Perin (1988). "How Expectations About Microcomputers Influence Their Organizational Consequences." Management in the 1990s Working Paper 88-044. April. Sloan School of Management, Cambridge, MA.

Drucker, Peter (1988). "The New Organization." *Harvard Business Review,* 66(1) January–February.

Engelbart, Douglas C. (1963). "A Conceptual Framework for the Augmentation of Man's Intellect," in P. Howerton (ed.), *Vistas in Information Handling,* Volume 1, pp. 1–29. Spartan Books, Washington, D.C.

Engelbart, Douglas C., and William K. English (1988). "A Research Center for Augmenting Human Intellect," originally published in 1968 and reprinted in Irene Greif (ed.), *Computer-Supported Cooperative Work: A Book of Readings.* Morgan Kaufmann, San Mateo, CA.

Fortune (1993). Special Issue. "Making High Tech Work for You." Autumn.

Goldberg, Beverly, and John G. Sifonis (1994). *Dynamic Planning: The Art of Managing Beyond Tomorrow.* Oxford University Press.

Grudin, Jonathan (1988). "Why CSCW Applications Fail: Problems in the Design and Evaluation of Organizational Interfaces." *Proceedings of the Conference on*

Computer-Supported Cooperative Work, pp. 85–93. September 26–28, Portland, Oregon.

Grudin, Jonathan (1989). "Why Groupware Applications Fail: Problems in Design and Evaluation." *Office: Technology and People,* 4(3):245–264.

Henderson, J. C., and J. Cooprider (1988). "Dimensions of I/S Planning and Design Technology." Working Paper No. 181. September. MIT Center for Information Systems Research, Cambridge, MA.

Hiltz, S. R., and E. B. Kerr (1981). "Studies of Computer-Mediated Communication Systems: A Synthesis of the Findings." Final Report to the National Science Foundation.

Hiltz, Starr Roxanne, and Murray Turoff (1978). *The Network Nation: Human Communication via Computer.* Addison-Wesley, Reading, MA.

Iacono, Suzanne, and Rob Kling (1988). "Computer Systems as Institutions: Social Dimensions of Computing in Organizations." *Proceedings of the Ninth International Conference on Information Systems,* pp. 101–110. November 30–December 3, Minneapolis, Minnesota.

Johansen, Robert (1988). *Groupware: Computer Support for Business Teams.* Free Press, New York.

Keen, Peter G. W. (1988). "The 'Metabusiness' Evolution: Challenging the Status Quo." *ICIT Advance,* October.

Kerr, Elaine B., and Starr Roxanne Hiltz (1982). *Computer-Mediated Communication Systems: Status and Evaluation.* Academic Press, New York.

Kling, Rob, and Suzanne Iacono (1989). "Desktop Computerization & the Organization of Work," in Tom Forester (ed.), *Computers in the Human Context.* MIT Press, Cambridge, MA.

Kraemer, Kenneth L., James N. Danziger, Debora E. Dunkle, and John L. King (1993). "The Usefulness of Computer-Based Information to Public Managers." *MIS Quarterly,* 17(2)(June):29–51.

Larson, Carl E., and Frank M. J. LaFasto (1989). *TeamWork.* Sage Publications, Newbury Park, CA.

Lewin, Kurt (1952). "Group Decision and Social Change," in G. E. Swanson, T. N. Newcomb, and E. L. Hartley (eds.), *Readings in Social Psychology* (revised edition). Holt, New York.

Loveman, Gary W. (1988). "An Assessment of the Productivity Impact of Information Technologies." MIT Management in the 1990s Working Paper 88-504, July. Massachusetts Institute of Technology, Cambridge, MA.

Malone, Thomas W. (1983). "How Do People Organize Their Desks? Implications for the Design of Office Information Systems." *ACM Transactions on Office Information Systems,* 1(1)(January):99–112.

Markus, M. Lynne, and Janis Forman (1989). "A Social Analysis of Group Technology Use." UCLA Information Systems Research Program Working Paper No. 2-90, July.

Martin, James (1973). *Design of Man-Computer Dialogues.* Prentice-Hall, Englewood Cliffs, NJ.

Mumford, E., and T. B. Ward (1968). *Computers: Planning for People.* Batsford, London.

Nielsen, J., R. Mack, K. Bergendorff, and N. Grischkowsky (1986). "Integrated Software Usage in the Professional Work Environment: Evidence from Questionnaires and Interviews." *Proceedings of CHI'86 Human Factors in Computing Systems,* pp. 162–167. Boston, April 13–17. Association for Computing Machinery, New York.

Reich, Robert B. (1987). "Entrepreneurship Reconsidered: The Team as Hero." *Harvard Business Review* (May–June):77–83.

Rice, Ronald, and Associates (1984). *The New Media.* Sage, Beverly Hills, CA.

Rogers, Everett (1983). *The Diffusion of Innovation.* Free Press, New York.

Rosson, Mary Beth (1985). "The Role of Experience in Editing." *Proceedings of INTERACT'84,* pp. 45–50. Elsevier North-Holland, Amsterdam.

Rousseau, D. M. (1983). "Technology in Organizations: A Constructive Review and Analytic Framework," in S. E. Seashore, E. E. Lawler, P. H. Mirvis, and C. Caman (eds.), *Assessing Organizational Changes: A Guide to Methods, Measures and Practices.* Wiley & Sons, New York.

Searle, John R. (1969). *Speech Acts.* Cambridge University Press, Cambridge, England.

Stevens, Chandler Harrison (1981). "Many-to-Many Communications." Working Paper No. 72, June. MIT Center for Information Systems Research, Cambridge, MA.

Stewart, Thomas A. (1994). "The Information Age in Charts." *Fortune* (April 4):75.

Trist, E. L. (1981). "The Sociotechnical Perspective," in A. H. Van de Ven, and W. F. Joyce (eds.), *Perspectives on Organization, Design and Behavior.* John Wiley & Sons, New York.

Whiteside, John, and Dennis Wixon (1988). "Contextualization as a World View for the Reformation of Meetings." *Proceedings of the Conference on Computer-Supported Cooperative Work.* Association for Computing Machinery, New York.

Yates, JoAnne (1989). *Control Through Communication: The Rise of System in American Management.* Johns Hopkins University Press, Baltimore.

P·A·R·T · IV

Computing at Work: Empowering Action by Low-Level Users*

Andrew Clement

Computers in the 1980s merely had to be user-friendly—now it seems they have positively to *empower* their users. The image of computers empowering people is a potent and appealing one. For the many working people whose autonomy is routinely challenged by the constraints of large organizations or the vagaries of the market, the spread of sophisticated computers holds the promise of gaining in personal control. This prospect is celebrated at a time when conventional organizations are themselves being increasingly criticized for being excessively rigid and hierarchical. The notion of empowerment also touches directly on one of the longest-standing debates over the social implications of workplace computing, the issue of control—how does computerization influence who controls productive processes and in what way? The classic tension between labor and management perspectives in this debate is increasingly overshadowed by talk of coordination, cooperation, and, perhaps most intriguingly, worker "empowerment." It is now commonplace to hear management experts claiming to reject Taylorist precepts in favor of providing employees with greater autonomy of action—with sophisticated computing systems promoted as potent tools enabling this shift.

Although there are good grounds to treat much of this talk of empowerment as advertising hype, managerial soft-sell, and at best naively optimistic, this paper takes a different approach. It explores what it would mean to take the notion of empowerment seriously in addressing the central social issues of computerization as they have affected a large group of workers who have long been relatively disadvantaged in their dealings with computers.

Functional versus Democratic Empowerment

"Empowerment" is a highly charged term that is now fashionably applied to a wide range of situations. However, underlying its proliferating use, we can identify two durable and distinct meanings. Most prominently the term has been given currency in the context of recent managerial initiatives to reshape organizations and their internal practices. Driven by a host of interrelated factors, notably an intensification of competition through the globalization of markets and widespread technological changes, enterprises are turning to approaches such as total quality management (TQM) and business process reengineering (BPR) in attempts to remain viable. They are urged on by a burgeoning literature heralding visions of the "flexible/intelligent/lean/networked/reinvented/virtual . . . organization" (Applegate, 1994). The popular prescriptions for achieving this involve flattening the organizational structure by shrinking middle management and pushing decision making down the hierarchy. Employees are expected to take on wider task responsibilities with reduced direct supervision. As Benjamin and Scott Morton note:

> The leaner, more networked, more autonomous forms of organization we are moving toward, all have an empowering characteristic. Empowerment requires knowledgeable workers who rather than pass information up the hierarchy use that knowledge to manage their process as a feedback control system. . . . Empowerment means that operational decisions will not be made hierarchically, that knowledge workers must feel comfortable in making decisions, that managers must provide counsel rather than directives, and that information and our conceptual models of how to use it are the source of decisions. (1992, pp. 137–138)

Similarly, Tapscott and Caston observe a "paradigm shift" to a new form of organization based technically on the client–server model and open networked architecture in which individual employees and work groups are "empowered to act and create value" (1992, p. 209) in another best-selling management book, business "gurus" Hammer and Champy claim that employee empowerment is the "unavoidable consequence" of reengineering business processes (1993, p. 71).

Computers, we are told, contribute to employee empowerment by serving as powerful tools that can bring relevant information to the person on

*This article appeared in *Communications of the ACM*, 37(1)(January 1994):52–65. Reprinted with permission from the Association for Computing Machinery.

the front line, implement the action decided upon, and then provide monitoring feedback. Although there is growing attention to supporting work groups via Computer-Supported Cooperative Work (CSCW) applications, the computers are still seen mainly as personal devices for extending the capabilities of individual users. This vision is neatly illustrated in the poster for the CHI'90 conference, which had the theme "Empowering People." The poster shows a solitary, young, white, male sitting on top of a tall pile of computer equipment gazing into the distance (see illustration).

This conception of empowerment may be termed "functional," in the sense that it is oriented to improving performance toward organizational goals that are assumed to be shared unproblematically by all participants. The managerial literature presents it as a way to respond locally and flexibly to rapidly changing environmental conditions within the framework of organizational relations demanded by efficiency and other competitive criteria. Such empowerment is thus largely a matter of authorizing employees to assume much greater responsibilities, whether or not they choose to do so. Although occasionally there is some admission within these visions that lower-level staff have been insufficiently empowered in the past, there is never a provision for the initiative for change to come from below. Even Shoshana Zuboff (1988), who shows unusual sympathy and insight into the plight of workers at the bottom of authoritarian organizations and who rejects a hierarchical organizational model, sees no role for this staff in the transformation that is presumably so much in their interests. In short, this is a vision of empowerment in which the political dimension of power is submerged and any enlargement of discretion remains confined within a managerial framework of "bounded autonomy."

But empowerment has another and older meaning. It has been used for years by advocates within the labor and women's movements as a rallying cry to encourage members to work together to achieve greater control over important aspects of their lives—to act with a greater grasp and sense of their own powers. This may be termed democratic empowerment, for it emphasizes the rights and abilities of people to participate as equals in decisions about affairs that affect them. It is not so much received as a gift or an obligation, but claimed through ongoing individual and collective actions—actions that can be aimed at improving the *conditions* of work as much as they are aimed at its *products*. It seeks emancipation from the subordination within oppressive institutions and "is directed toward creating conditions for independent individuals in a society of free cooperation and communication" (Ehn, 1988, p. 247). And where this emancipation is blocked by entrenched, privileged interests, struggle will likely be necessary. In other words, this form of empowerment is based on the history and ideals of western democracy, as they would apply to workplaces. Ironically, it is the association with this celebrated tradition that gives "empowerment" much of its current rhetorical potency and appeal.

Although elements of both these two meanings of empowerment are relevant to addressing problems workers have experienced with computer use, there are obvious tensions between them. Functional empowerment can promote higher quality, greater productivity, and more rewarding jobs, but it assumes that the overall workplace structures are adequate and that staff have no need nor even legitimate interest in affecting the broader conditions under which they work. It takes for granted that goals are agreed upon and that there are no major obstacles to individuals achieving their potential as long as they work responsibly within the domains delimited by higher-level management. In the many settings where these assumptions of institutional virtue are not met, such a narrowly based notion of empowerment becomes a hollow claim. It is easily distorted into meaning that workers have to take on greater responsibilities without corresponding additional authority or resources at their disposal. It may even be dangerous when the rhetoric of empowerment is used to eliminate jobs and intensify work, while obscuring an inequitable distribution of the benefits.

Democratic empowerment seeks to overcome these common pitfalls by giving staff a potentially unbounded scope to participative rights on all matters that directly affect them. While it is unfair that organizations that are relatively democratic have to compete directly with those that can pass on to society at large the costs of being less so, it is currently too often a matter of practical reality that their overall performance must actually compare favorably. Otherwise, organizations pursuing democratic empowerment will remain a marginalized ideal for the foreseeable future. Thus for empowerment to offer an authentic promise of enhancing work experiences and outcomes, it needs to combine the attention to job effectiveness aspects of the functional approach with the emancipatory aspirations of the democratic approach. Since we have already dramatically advanced our capabilities for improving productivity in recent decades, even as the structures of subordination have remained remarkably resistant to reform, it is democratic empowerment that we need to pursue more vigorously.

Control Issues in Workplace Computerization

Examination of the empowering potential of computers belongs within a larger discussion of the role that computing plays in the control of work. Since the very earliest days of computerization, when Norbert Wiener withdrew from research on automatic control over fear of consequences for workers (Noble, 1984), there has been a sharp and still largely inconclusive debate over its workplace implications (see Dunlop and Kling, 1991, and elsewhere in this volume). Issues of control have been at the center of this debate: Who sets the pace and standards of performance? What skills will be recognized and rewarded? Who will govern when and how these skills will be deployed? How will work be supervised? What data will be collected on the production process and who will use it for what purposes? Two starkly opposing visions of computerized work have captured the imagination of observers and framed the debate—the "optimistic" or utopian view, which sees computers as benign, even friendly devices under the control of workers, which liberate them from toil while offering new possibilities for creative expression and social engagement—and the "pessimistic" or dystopian view, which sees computers as extensions of oppressive management imposed on workers, rendering many human skills redundant, and monitoring every move to enforce an unrelenting pace of routinized production. What we have learned in the debate is that, while these extremes can be found, most situations of computer application lie somewhere in the middle. Although there are powerful social and technological logics in play, they do inexorably drive all computerization in one direction or the other (see Dunlop and Kling, 1991, and elsewhere in this volume). Furthermore, the characteristics of the computer systems and their implications for the workers involved depends on the specific technical and social contexts in which they are deployed. A conclusion of this debate, from a social responsibility perspective, is not to focus mainly on assessing the net, aggregate effect of computerization (i.e., whether technology is "good" or "bad" for workers). Instead, as the aim becomes more to eliminate or alleviate adverse consequences, it is more productive to ask such questions as: In which situations are the conditions worst? Who has contributed to this and how? Whose interests have been served? What actions can participants take to promote reform? A prime place to start this investigation is with low-status office work.

Why Focus on Women Office Workers?

Office work performed largely by women provides a fruitful focus for understanding and ameliorating the adverse consequences of computerization for a host of reasons:

1. Office service and support tasks play a large and vital role in the effective operation of all major organizations, particularly those that provide essential services to the public. Industrial restructuring processes reinforce the importance of office-based service work as a major center of economic activity even as other sectors decline.
2. Office settings have been the primary site of capital investment in productive technology over the past few decades as well as the scene of the most intensive computer use.
3. The labor market places a substantial proportion of the female work force in a few large job classes (i.e., secretarial/clerical) at the end of the occupational hierarchy most vulnerable to technological and

economic pressures. In spite of considerable efforts to change the picture, this concentration of working women in a small number of female-dominated occupations is remarkably durable (e.g., the United States clerical work force is growing faster than the work force as a whole. The United States' 16.1 million female clerks vastly outnumbered the nation's 412,000 female programmers and systems analysts in 1993.) (See the subsection on Gender, Work, and Information Technology within "Computerization at Work," by Rob Kling, Article A, this section.)

4. A substantial body of research identifies a range of potentially deleterious effects, particularly for women, from office computerization— stress, health and safety, social isolation and alienation, occupational immobility, pay inequity.

5. As a principal location of female employment, it has been the focus of the women's movement reform efforts—arguably one of the most important progressive influences in contemporary western society. Specifically, there have been significant feminist critiques of the technological, cultural, and organizational aspects of office work that have informed moves to greater user participation in system design, employment equity, and valuing of "women's work" (Green, Owen, and Pain, 1993).

In short, what happens to office workers experiencing computerization is of considerable importance, not only to the millions of women involved, but to the organizations that employ them, the public they serve, and society as a whole. In turn, this implies a complex set of responsibilities and challenges for the many professionals who design, develop, and implement the information systems targeted at office settings.

Three Case Examples

Office service work is by no means a homogeneous phenomenon—indeed there are wide and significant variations in information technologies, implementation strategies, organizational settings, task requirements, and management styles. However, there are common patterns for each of these factors that can be found repeatedly in a large number of settings. Some of the more important ones can be usefully illustrated in three case examples involving, respectively, telephone operators, library clerks, and secretaries. They are not unusual, neither for the computerization processes involved nor the problems that emerged. What they have in common, and what distinguishes them from most other settings, is that they have been the scenes of change initiatives in which the office staff have played a central role. These cases reveal serious shortcomings in conventional approaches to computerization while demonstrating opportunities and obstacles for office workers seeking empowerment.

Telephone Operators—MTS Trial Office Project

The work of telephone operators epitomizes the routinized, fragmented, fast-paced, computerized office job. Positioned in the ever-shrinking interface between the machine that automatically feeds calls into her headpiece and the machines that switch circuits and retrieve telephone numbers, a telephone operator is under constant pressure to work quickly and accurately while being unfailingly courteous in the company prescribed manner. This regime is enforced through a system of work monitoring that is perhaps the most comprehensive and fine-grained of any job. Operators are typically expected to maintain an average working time (AWT) per call of only thirty seconds, and sometimes much less. They can be listened in on and recorded surreptitiously by a supervisor at any moment without announcement. It is little wonder operators report high levels of stress. Usually the effects are confined to the individuals concerned, in the form of muscular discomfort, elevated blood pressure, repeated sick leaves, increased consumption of painkillers, and so on, but in the case of the operators at one telephone company, the stress reactions also triggered a chain of events with much more dramatic and wide-ranging consequences.

The Manitoba Telephone System (MTS) is a public corporation employing 5000 individuals. Its operations are centered in Winnipeg, where more than 350 operators work. Ninety percent are women. Above them in the organizational hierarchy are seven levels of supervision and management, which at its top is exclusively male. A management consultant who began working with the corporation in 1988 observed that it was an "intensely hierarchical, autocratic" place, which at that time had a "serious gender ghettoization problem." According to her, "it had a pervasive command and control culture in which operators were treated like prisoners," constantly watched over and punished for every infraction of the rules (personal communication, 1993). Operators themselves felt they had become "Rapid Transit Robots" (MTS/CWC, 1990, p. 28).

Starting in early 1986, operators reported on several occasions experiencing "shock-like" sensations while working with the computerized switchboards. The symptoms ranged from numbness and tingling to more severe pain requiring medical attention. In September, with the incidents increasing and tests of equipment not indicating any physical cause, operators in one office exercised their legal right to refuse work they considered to be hazardous to their health and walked off the job—severely disrupting telephone services. Following a stop-work order from the provincial Workplace Health and Safety Division, terminals and staff were relocated to another building while technical, ergonomic, and environmental testing continued. Several studies concluded that the equipment was not a key factor in this phenomenon, pointing instead to the "highly-automated, repetitive, routine, closely-measured and supervised" (MTS/CEP, 1992, p. 2) work environment as the main cause of a "collective stress response" (Maupin and Fisher, 1989). Prompted by these findings, the corporation executive immediately removed the most overt aspects of machine pacing of work—the use of AWT as an individual performance measure, the screen message telling operators when there were calls waiting that the office couldn't handle immediately, the high-pitched tone when the call waiting queues were full, and the bell that sounded throughout the building warning that coffee break would end in exactly two minutes. To deal with longer-term issues the executive agreed with the union representing the operators to the establishment of a joint labor-management Trial Change Project. A principal aim of the project was to "trial innovative organizational and managerial approaches in order to improve the working environment" (MTS/CWC, 1988).

The Trial Change Project got under way in June 1988 with a Design Team consisting of three managers and three operators running the project. Two external consultants were hired to support the design and implementation processes. Together, they established a Trial Office where issues such as shift scheduling, the elimination of electronic monitoring, training, group problem solving, consensus decision making, and a host of other work reorganization ideas could be tried and evaluated before being implemented throughout the corporation. The Trial Office was a working service center staffed by forty operators selected randomly from ninety volunteers. The operators took turns sitting on the internal committee that ran the office. In the beginning, managers played very little role in this and decisions were made by consensus. The operators developed a statement of philosophy that stressed the need for "equality, fair-play, openness and honesty in order to . . . experiment with innovative organizational and managerial concepts . . . [and] empower active involvement of all employees in decision-making by encouraging development of skills and knowledge, achieving high morale and enhancing work" (Maupin and Fisher, 1989, p. 14). Another theme emphasized by both operators and managers was the importance of improving customer service, both as a way of enhancing operators' jobs as well as to bolster the company's competitive position in an increasingly deregulated telecommunications industry.

After six months of experimental operation, the Trial Office, in conjunction with the Design Team, had refined a list of twenty-two recommendations involving changes to organization structure, training and education, operator job description, work procedures, scheduling, and participative management. A project trustee group consisting of MTS executives and senior union officials selected nine of the top-rated proposals and presented them to the operators for approval. Operators ratified all the proposals and as a result operator services have been reorganized around smaller, multifunctional work groups, while several of the innovations first adopted by the Trial Office, for example, elimination of remote monitoring, improved training resources, cross-training, unlimited rights to trading shifts, greater discretion in responding to customer queries, are being extended throughout MTS. The more radical proposals related to flattening the organizational hierarchy and raising its lowest level—eliminating some management and supervisory positions, enhancing the responsibilities and pay of operators, continuing the participative management practices of the Trial—await approval by the senior trustee group. The Trial Office still operates, but in a reduced capacity. The union-side coordinator of the project feels that although important gains have been made, the office had become "nothing more than a glorified quality circle" (personal communication, 1993) and is disillusioned that the early promise of the experiment will likely not be achieved. She attributes this to a variety of factors—short-term financial pressures, a new president more interested in pushing a TQM approach, and the more general resistance to change of a deeply ingrained organizational culture.

The Trial Change project has led to significant innovations in the way in which the corporation develops new information systems. For the first time operators and unionists are included in the committees responsible for overseeing major system upgrades. For instance, there are equal numbers of labor and management representatives on the most recent of these, the Modernization of Operator Services Technology task force. It is charged with recommending a replacement for the computer systems used by operator services, identifying future service enhancements, and planning for the human resource implications. An explicit objective for the new technologies is to help enhance and expand the job of the operators. The committee in 1993 recommended moving away from IBM as the vendor for a new directory assistance system, a decision subsequently ratified at the executive level in spite of considerable outside pressure on the corporation.

Results of an internal evaluation of the now renamed M-POWER (M-Professional Operators With Enhanced Responsibilities) project indicate considerable success in improving working conditions. A preliminary report notes that the change effort has "had positive impacts on the work lives of the workers and managers affected. Many have reported greater job satisfaction, more challenge and variety in their work, more opportunities for learning new skills and for career advancement at MTS. This has generally been manifested by a drop in absenteeism, significant decreases in the number of grievances . . . , and improvements in customer satisfaction" (MTS/CEP, 1992, p. 4). But there is also a recognition that more needs to be done. Although jobs have enlarged, many remain highly repetitive and boring. Based on this experience, the joint labor/management evaluation team encouraged the corporation to proceed with the further organizational restructuring proposed by the Design Team and Trial Office. Progress in this direction has been hampered by a major downsizing, a phenomenon currently afflicting much of the telephone industry.

It is important to note that the main impetus for these beneficial changes did not come initially from managers, but rather despite them. It was the operators, systematically excluded from any formal influence for so long, who first had to force management in a dramatic way to take their concerns seriously, and who then came up with many of the concrete proposals for change. They showed they could run much of the operation on their own by developing innovative work practices and structures. Even if not all their feasible proposals have been adopted and if progress has been slowed by institutional factors, MTS operators have initiated a process of significant organizational reform. In so doing, they also demonstrated the latent potential of lower-level staff that in many similar settings still awaits the opportunity for release.

Library Assistants—Human-Centered Office Systems Project

The four hundred library assistants of Sheffield City Council Library and Information Services have much in common with office clerks in large service organizations everywhere. They are almost all women (99%), are poorly paid, and have little upward mobility. The work is conventionally regarded as routine and low status, involving responding in person to inquiries from the public and maintaining transaction-based records in a computerized information system. The library assistants check out books, receive, repair, and reshelve them, process catalog and borrower records, and otherwise keep one of the most heavily used public libraries in Britain functioning smoothly. Although they are beginning to integrate microcomputers into this information-intensive operation, many of the principal files are still accessed via a batch-processing system running on the City Council's mainframe computer. The system, regarded by management and staff alike as a "disaster" (Green, Owen, and Pain, 1993, p. 222), was constructed piecemeal over more than a decade. Staff find that the poor response time makes these facilities worse than the previous manual system. Its many shortcomings and peculiarities are a constant source of great frustration for the staff, one of whom described it as "an iron carthorse with ribbons" (Green, Owen, and Pain, 1993, p. 17).

In the mid-1980s the library service as a whole began moving away from its traditional "custodial" view of its role to a more outward-looking, active, community-oriented model. As part of this, management accepted a trade union-based equal opportunities proposal to expand the pay and career opportunities of library assistants. They began to be rewarded for handling the more complex public inquiries, officially the exclusive domain of professionals. Management also recognized the need to upgrade the computer system, and began planning to acquire and customize one of the integrated library systems then becoming widely available. However, they were not able to finalize specifications for the £1 million system nor develop proposals for staff involvement. In part, this was because they feared that in light of the staff's reaction to computerization so far, they would resist any further moves in this direction.

It was into this setting that an interdisciplinary team of researchers from the nearby university came with proposals for collaborative research on new approaches to user involvement in systems development. Management welcomed the initiative, and later released the clerical staff to participate in project activities during their regular working hours. The researchers also contacted the staff union, which, while it approved of the project, played little subsequent role.

The principal techniques that the Human-Centered Office Systems Project (HCOSP) brought to the experiment were the "study circle" and the "design team." A study circle is a small group of staff who come together voluntarily to work with a facilitator on a range of activities around a given central topic (in this case the specification of an information system) (Vehviläinen, 1991). The agenda is not mandated or delegated by management, but can be open ended. As the researchers leading the project note,

> Unlike management-inspired "quality circles," study circles emphasize active involvement by the participants in working on an agenda which they define themselves. The groups can provide a basis for "consciousness-raising" (in the feminist sense), they enable participants to develop a mutual-supportive network, and also to gain access to new ideas and information. (Green, Owen, and Pain, 1993, p. 323)

The study circles consisted of six to eight volunteers from the clerical staff, with the researchers acting as facilitators. The first study circle was held in 1987 and initiated the establishment of a broadly based Design Team to oversee the acquisition of the new computer system. Unlike the uniform status of the study circle participants, the design team was more representative of the organization as a whole—with three library assistants working alongside colleagues from middle management, computing, and other professional posts. Over the next three years, six more study circle groups met, so that eventually over 10% of all library assistants had taken part. While the study circles were gaining momentum, the Design Team began to get bogged down. The library assistants' representatives felt isolated—from senior management and, increasingly, from their coworkers. To address this situation, the research team held a seminar designed to bring together all those concerned with the project. Library assistants were put in a majority and during policy making sessions were in a group of their own. One major outcome was the expansion of the design team so that library assistants made up nearly half its membership and their successful insistence that a *senior* manager serve as chair. They were thus able to raise the clout of the team and their own role within it. In addition, management agreed to set up a multiparty support group to coordinate detailed work by professional and nonprofessional staff in such areas as job design, health and safety, and training. On this basis, the new design team structure made slow but steady progress in spite of delays related to managerial resistance to the new staff assertiveness and changes in key personnel. A more serious and chronic source of delay was the growing budget crisis affecting local authorities throughout the United Kingdom. Nevertheless, the library completed the specifications in 1991, short-listed potential vendors, and more recently advertised a call for tenders. In anticipation of recessionary pressures easing sufficiently to enable software purchase and customization work to begin, library assistants continued to be involved in the related organizational redesign activities, specifically job design, health and safety, and systems services. In 1994, with funding finally secured, actual implementation is about to begin with the continuing participation with some of the early participants.

Even though all the original objectives have not been reached, at least not yet, the HCOSP project is able to claim some significant achievements. The study circles demonstrated both to the management and the staff themselves that "low-level" support workers, who previously had been regarded simply as an obstacle to technological reform through their passive resistance, could take the initiative and make valuable, positive contributions. By developing a network of support within the organization, library assistants gained the confidence to make and press their demands. In contrast to entrenched gender stereotypes, the women made informed, practical suggestions about the software specifications. Based on their direct experience of the work involved and their concern for serving clients, the library assistants identified significant requirements that would otherwise have been overlooked. In particular, the specifications now contain several items intended to enhance their interaction with customers, for example, manual overrides for overdue notices, fines collection policies, local printing facilities, and maximum response times. Furthermore, the library assistants enlarged the focus of inquiry beyond the narrowly technical aspects to include relevant issues of job design, training, and equity of employment opportunity. In addition to broadening and strengthening the specifications, the study circles were an impetus in structuring (and restructuring) the Design Team, overcoming an impasse in its activities, and generally reshaping the design process as a whole so it was more in tune with the organizational realities of everyday library work. In so doing they have improved the chances that the final system would be accepted and better fit the varied needs it must fulfill.

Secretaries — Self-Managed Office Automation Project

Secretarial work is among the least structured of clerical office jobs. Although specific task outcomes are usually clearly specified, the manner in which secretaries accomplish them is often more discretionary. They are told what to do, but not how. In a busy office a secretary must constantly juggle a complex and dynamic set of demands from a variety of sources. The computer support for the document preparation aspects of such a job reflects the character of the tasks and the organizational relationships within which they are embedded. The current norm is for management to provide standard microcomputer hardware and software packages for word processing, and possibly spreadsheets, databases, and the like. Networks for resource sharing (e.g., disks and printers) and communications are now becoming commonplace. Installations often grow in an incremental, ad hoc fashion, without the guidance of a detailed central plan.

This is certainly a pattern followed at York University, near Toronto, where the widespread introduction of desktop computers for office support began in the mid-1980s. This was a time when student enrollments were growing rapidly, while the number of support staff remained fairly static. The Dean's office in the Faculty of Arts led this computerization effort by installing over one hundred PC-compatible micros in the seventeen academic department offices that make up the faculty. While the intention was to save the "secretarial system [from] breaking down under the pressure [of increasing workloads]," the secretaries were not consulted about this beforehand, and in many cases the equipment arrived on their desks without prior warning. Reflecting an all too common underestimation of the complexity of computerization and the organizational learning needed, it was planned that training would consist of a two-day introductory session on DOS and WordPerfect. According to the Dean responsible, the purpose of the training was "as much to desensitize people's fear of the machine as to instruct them in any intricacies of [its] operation" (Clement, 1989, p. 211). Secretaries were expected to learn as they worked, but no extra time was set aside for this.

It soon became clear that this approach did not work well. Complaints by staff prompted managers to provide some temporary additional training and support, but this too was not sufficient. A later survey of the entire all-women secretarial support staff in the faculty revealed that the source of dissatisfaction was not with the computers themselves, but with the lack of training, support, and consultation. Consistent with detailed studies in similar settings (Clement and Parsons, 1990; Hartman, 1987), the secretaries reported learning much more by studying on their own and discussing with co-workers than from formal courses or other external sources of expertise. They dealt with usage problems primarily through mutual support within the work groups rather than by referring to written manuals or to outside specialists. A comment by one secretary summarized well the overall reaction of the staff:

> I certainly feel that there was a great lack of consultation with the staff in the introduction of computers, and it is only due to the efforts of the staff themselves that this has had any success at all. I feel strongly that training has been inadequate in the extreme and that computers are not being used as they should be. With proper training there is so much that could be done. The staff neither have the time nor the facilities to expand on their knowledge.

As the secretaries were attempting to adapt to the introduction of desktop computing, they also took their complaints about the continuing lack of training and support to the Technology Committee of the staff union. This led to collaboration between the chair of the committee and the author, a computer scientist on the faculty. Together we initiated an action-oriented research project entitled Self-Managed Office Automation Project (SMOAP) (Clement, 1989; Clement and Zelechow, 1987). The aim was to help the office staff assess their needs and demonstrate that, with appropriate resources under their control, they could support their own use of computers.

The main focus of the project was the establishment of a microcomputer resource center. This served as the site for regular meetings of the Analysis Group, consisting of secretaries from selected department offices who discussed their computer-related work problems. These were conducted along lines similar to the Study Circle sessions of the previously described project. According to the wishes of the participants, there was a strong emphasis on training for word processing (indeed stronger than the organizers had originally planned). But also the staff raised and discussed related issues of direct concern to them—dealing with heavy workloads, upgrading job descriptions, improving ergonomic conditions, developing new computer uses, and generally getting the recognition they felt they deserved from management for their contributions to the university.

At the end of the five-month project, a questionnaire survey of the participants indicated strong positive attitudes to the experience. One of the secretaries remarked:

> I feel there is concrete hope for staff demands. re: ergonomics, staff input in decision making, staff independence over access to training and procedure making. Through my own initiative to learn and develop new skills, I have created new systems and procedures for carrying out my responsibilities. (Clement, 1989, p. 225)

These remarks take on added significance in light of subsequent events. Several months after the project ended and the resource center closed, the support staff union went on strike. One of the three main issues that kept the 1100 members out for over two weeks was the demand for a staff-run microcomputer training. This demand was ultimately met, and in early 1988 a training program was established. Modeled on SMOAP, it was headed by the former project coordinator and offered small workshop-based training. After three years of expansion and internal "politicking," the Microcomputer Training Program moved into its own specially designed training facility. At the opening ceremony, the university vice-president in charge of finance and administration publicly apologized to support staff on behalf of management for taking so long to recognize the validity of their demands! The program has a regular budget funded by the administration, while the union retains a say in its operation. One of the features the union has successfully insisted on is that all staff have an equal right, on a first-come first-serve basis, to the program's services. In other words, a secretary, not her boss, formally decides what courses to take and when. With a former secretary as Trainer/Administrator, the program trains over three hundred staff per year in using software popular for word processing, spreadsheets, and hard disk management. A deliberate attempt is made to gear the courses and the content of each session to the self-identified needs of the staff. It has offered support specifically for informal design activities, and the secretaries in at least one department regularly followed up training sessions with group discussions on how to apply what they learned to their particular office. The expanding scope and continued popularity of the program's offerings are testimony to the valuable role it plays in helping university staff make effective use of their desktop computing technologies.

Common Patterns

These quick sketches do not do full justice to what are complex organizational changes subject to multiple interpretations. Nor should they be treated as "success stories," for the eventual outcomes are far from clear cut. Nevertheless, they provide the basis for interesting insights into empowerment issues over computerization. For all the differences between these three cases in terms of the jobs, technologies, and organizational setting, there are striking similarities. In each, women office workers faced unnecessary hardships because of conventional ways in which computerization had been imposed on them. They had not been consulted about the introduction of the computer systems in the first place, and initially tried to accommodate to the new conditions, in spite of experiencing considerable adverse effects—effects that are commonly associated with the negative implications of computerization elsewhere. Coming from the lower reaches of rigid, strongly hierarchical organizations, attempts to voice concerns were met with fates typical of bottom-up initiatives. It was only after pressures for change had grown considerably that any action was taken. In the MTS and York University cases, the office staff had to take the drastic step of actually stopping work before management took their complaints seriously enough to support a process leading to significant organizational reforms. In pushing this along, staff had to act collectively to overcome the resistive presumptions of technological primacy and managerial authority by those above them. In the HCOSP case, less extreme actions were needed, in part because of the timely arrival of researchers who were instrumental in resolving an organizational impasse.

   In each case, the clerical staffs' demands were not mainly for personal gain (e.g., pay increase) but to improve the functioning of the organization.

To do this, they sought greater control over various facets of their workplaces—information (e.g., reduction of individualized monitoring), control over knowledge (e.g., via their own training program), and decision making (e.g., scheduling, technology investment). They also sought to change the structure of the organization in ways that would give them greater influence. However, this pursuit of greater control was not principally to challenge management, but to perform their jobs more effectively, to improve their working conditions, and to enjoy greater respect than they had hitherto been granted. All these were matters that management could (should?) have acceded to earlier in the common interest of enhancing organizational performance without diminishing their legitimate authority. It was only later that management recognized the validity of the demands, and belatedly agreed to corrective actions in these areas.

It is also interesting to note that although the initial focus of concern in each case was a computerized information system, the avenues for remedying the situation were quickly enlarged to embrace various aspects of its organizational context—training, support, job design, organizational structure, and so on. Thus it was not just the particular design of the computer system as such that was problematic for the office staff, but how it fitted in with their overall jobs. By taking a more comprehensive approach and taking an active role in many of the details, the participants have undoubtedly contributed positively to the overall system development. The signs are thus good that when the systems described in the cases are fully implemented, they will be welcomed as functional tools for extending the capabilities of the office workers who use them.

The central organizational innovations adopted to pursue these concerns were also remarkably similar, though arrived at independently. In each case, staff voluntarily came together on a regular basis in a forum where they could address a wide range of problems in a manner largely of their own choosing. The Study Circle, Analysis Group, and the Trial Office, with the assistance of their facilitators/mentors, and in the context of more general employee agitation, each served multiple and crucial functions in the wider organizational reforms. They provided a relatively protected setting where women could learn on their own from each other, develop mutually supportive relationships, and experiment with new ideas and approaches. The skills they developed there, as well as the confidence that came from practice and the assurance that they were not alone, helped participants to be more assertive in their dealings with other organizational actors. In two cases, although the union actively supported these efforts, much of their strength and authority derived from the experiences gained in the groups. In effect, these grass roots forums drew their vitality from the women who participated and in turn enabled them in various ways to find and amplify their voices when other routes had been denied.

Empowerment Revisited

We can see that each of these three cases represents partial yet significant examples of empowered action—in both senses of the term discussed above. First, the staff took on greater responsibilities and worked with management to improve their own job performance. They were not trying to avoid work or obtain larger rewards, but rather gain access to resources so they could do their jobs better. They took initiatives to develop systems and establish infrastructure to enable them to use the computing facilities more effectively as work tools. In spite of difficulties, they achieved some success. This is the sort of empowerment that the TQM and business process reengineering advocates would approve of. However, the staffs went considerably further than this, for they also made progress tackling the wider technical and organizational constraints that they found blocking the way of more satisfying jobs. In the spirit of labor and feminist notions of empowerment, they worked together in effectively challenging their subordination within the gendered workplace hierarchies of managerial and professional authority. It is in combining both functional and democratic dimensions of empowerment that these three cases point out possibilities for significant organizational and technical reform.

However, these cases also show that making progress will not be straightforward. In spite of the ultimate acceptance by management of many of their initiatives, the efforts by staff to act in an empowered way involved overt political contest. In part, this accurately reflects the inherent political nature of empowerment. After all, any attempt by individuals or groups to expand their influence over some sphere of activity raises questions of how this affects others who also have a stake in the same sphere. One should therefore not be surprised or dismayed that addressing these questions results in dispute. Indeed, in these cases, the contest is best regarded as a healthy sign that the tensions resulting from poor management and the more widespread need to readjust organizations in the face of technological and other changes in the external environment are being dealt with openly and constructively. This illustrates Gareth Morgan's (1986) more general observation that political conflict can serve a useful purpose by stimulating innovation. In this sense, computerization serves not so much as an empowering tool, but rather as the catalyst and occasion that expands the possibilities for organizational realignment and empowerment. The constraints and opportunities presented by technological change help in opening up "spaces" in organizational life within which the staff can bring to the surface long-submerged concerns. A particular focus in addressing such concerns is to exercise control *over* the information technologies as a precondition to exercising control *through* them.

It must be recognized that although the staff in these cases have taken significant steps in the direction of authentic empowerment, it is not yet clear how far they will be able to go. The improvements so far are modest, and fall short of their goals. It is not even clear to what extent organizational changes are permanent, in the sense that old patterns of subordination may reassert themselves. Indeed, there are signs of this happening. As the more obvious irritants that provoked the reforms are tackled, an important component of the motivation among clerical staff for change subsides. Maintaining momentum requires overcoming some formidable obstacles. We have seen that shifts in senior personnel, resistance from middle management, conservatism of union officials, and external financial pressures have all taken their toll. The cultural climate generally does not yet favor initiatives of this kind and there are few ready examples to legitimize and guide such efforts. Further progress depends not only on dynamics within the staff but also on gaining support in other sectors of the organization. In particular, systems specialists can help improve the prospects for sustainable empowerment initiatives.

Implications for Systems Specialists

These cases suggest several important lessons that can be useful in enabling office workers to take empowered action. They underscore the growing recognition that conventional, rationalistic systems development approaches are inadequate for dealing with the interpersonal aspects of service work illustrated in these cases. The required skills are often vital to office operation, but are inherently difficult if not impossible to formalize and they lack the authoritative status they would enjoy if associated with higher-ranked, more formally qualified personnel. Greater priority therefore needs to be given to development methods that allow the people concerned to bring their experiences as well as their self-identified interests to bear in an early and effective manner.

The alternative approach reflected in these cases is consistent with the traditions of participatory design (PD) (see the *Communications of the ACM* special issue, June 1993; Ehn, 1988; Greenbaum and Kyng, 1991; and Schuler, 1994). It should be clear that this involves more than simply having user representatives attend design meetings, explore various options, and take responsibility for the results. In the two cases involving systems design, this was done, but it was supported by additional forums, notably study circles, where office workers could meet on their own to share their experiences and study the common problems they faced. Their value comes from being separate from, but feeding into, the multiparty negotiating forums more conventionally associated with participatory design approaches. To function effectively, they need to meet regularly during working hours and with experienced facilitators. Providing the necessary official sanction and resources will initially require considerable faith on the part of management, since these forums must operate informally and free from immediate managerial oversight or reporting obligations. There are indications, such as in the "Coast Pharmaceuticals" case (Jewett and Kling, 1990), that where far-sighted middle managers have fostered a climate supportive of grass roots innovations, the payoffs have been significant and sustained (Rob Kling, personal communication, 1993).

This raises the interesting possibility that with the spread of networks, electronic mail and other forms of computer-mediated communications may be useful for providing valuable forums for office staff to keep in touch. Like the workplace analogues of community information networks (Schuler, 1994), these may offer vehicles for learning about new developments, raising issues, sharing perceptions, and mobilizing effort. Although lacking in the rich immediacy of face-to-face contact, they could fill a useful niche by offering an efficient way for staff to communicate among each other with fewer cost and schedule constraints. It is now technically possible to create various forms of quasi-private electronic spaces. Some could be like study circles, with small stable memberships and all interactions between participants mutually known. Others could be equally protected from outside observation, but with a dynamic membership and contributions made anonymously. This could be valuable in facilitating idea generation, voting, and other group processes. However, as Constance Perin (1991) suggests, the emergence of such "electronic social fields" is likely to face the greatest suspicion where they are perhaps needed most—in traditional bureaucratic institutions. Nor will it be easy to protect against the sort of managerial subversion that Zuboff reports effectively shut down a lively computer conference about "professional improvement" among women in a large drug company (Zuboff, 1988, pp. 382–383). Although computer systems may play a useful role in expanding the functional capabilities of individuals and groups of workers and provide forums for more open discussion, the benefits of these will likely be modest at best unless, as Mike Hales (1994) suggests, staff can become legitimate "actor-constructors" in systems development as well as wider organizational reform activities.

To help achieve this, systems specialists will need to do more than adopt more participative methods and assist in creating new forums. Essential to both and more fundamental in nature, systems specialist and office staff must develop much more constructive and respectful relationships than is reflected in the cases discussed above. Ben Shneiderman (1987) pleads for an important step in this direction with his stirring call for systems designers to "fight" for users. In order that this advocacy not usurp active participation by users themselves, it should be directed mainly at allowing their voices to be heard. The basic principle he identifies for this is to "recognize the diversity" of users. Typically, this means taking into account differences in users' experience, but when the aim is to foster empowered action, it means first recognizing and then addressing the specific gender, racial, occupational, and hierarchical dimensions to the power differentials that have helped marginalize office staff in the first place. These are not merely abstract attributes of contemporary organizations, but must be observed and dealt with in the immediate situations of everyday worklife.

Peter Denning (1992) offers similar useful guidance on how to accomplish this when he identifies *listening* as one of the critical skills for educated engineers to acquire. The "clients" of systems specialists who need to be listened to most carefully will be the office staff, for often it will be their voices that are least customarily heard. The adaptations required for tuning in to what these women are saying go beyond the subtle changes in speech pattern and physical deportment appropriate to respectful attention. Where managers resist grass roots innovation, systems specialists may also need to assert some of their professional independence. For instance, in the interests of good development practice, it might be necessary to insist that office staff have an adequate opportunity to prepare among themselves before design meetings and that they be able to participate in sufficient numbers that their views can compete with those of parties more accustomed to such settings. During such meetings, as well as in the wider workplace discussions, everyone involved can assist in fostering what Enid Mumford (1994, p. 315), in drawing upon Habermas, refers to as "emancipatory discourse." The basic principles involve ensuring that all participants have an equal opportunity or are in an equal position to:

- raise issues by asking questions
- give and refuse orders, to permit or prohibit
- call into question the truth, correctness, appropriateness, or sincerity of what is said
- express their attitudes, feelings, concerns, and doubts.

When employee empowerment is explicitly identified as an organizational goal, it may be usefully revealing to verify the authenticity of this claim by seeing how much progress toward this discursive ideal can actually be achieved. As forums are made more participative in these ways, staff will no longer be regarded as mere "users" but as real "actors" with their own distinctive voices and constructive roles to play in the ongoing dramas of technological and organizational development.

Although systems specialists should not abandon the particular and vital competencies they bring to any encounters with office staff, they do need to shun the presumptions of technical authority to define exclusively problems on its own terms. Such changes to habitual behavior and sources of prestige will likely be uncomfortable for many systems professionals, especially men, but will be fruitful when it leads to relationships that are more equal and open. It can only be through partnerships based on mutual respect and learning that the full potential of all participants can be brought to bear in improving the development and use of information systems. Otherwise, the old patterns will persist—where staff remain silent or else finally must shout before they are heard, and struggle with inadequate systems all the while.

Where office staff and systems specialists can open up dialogues that recognize equality of rights as well as differences of perspective it is likely that all parties will learn much. In an environment of mutual learning (Kyng, 1991), office staff will develop a deeper understanding of the technical processes involved as well as appreciate better the opportunities and constraints under which system personnel have to work. Likewise, systems specialists will encounter many of the practical considerations in real office systems from the point of view of the people actually doing the work. Seeing how their design decisions can affect others' lives may educate them better to the ethical dimension of systems development work and encourage an accountability for their actions that is an essential aspect of socially responsible computing (Suchman, 1994). If the cases discussed earlier are any guide, then systems specialists will also be reminded by staff that it is not so much the actual technologies that are critical for effective systems, but a range of other, highly contextualized, factors that contribute to success or failure. Wherever technologies are made, what counts in the end is how they can be worked together with the specific practices of the organization they have to serve. These collaborative development processes can also be seen as the microlevel counterparts of the democratic, participative, needs-driven policy vision advocated at national levels (Chapman, 1994).

Conclusions

We are in a period of considerable institutional flux, when many of the assumptions and structures that have guided organizations in the past are being questioned and alternatives actively sought. In particular, there are frequent calls for the reshaping of organizations along lines that are significantly less hierarchical and more democratic than in the past. At the same time, systems specialists are promoting technologies that can support such a redistribution of institutional power. If these transformative visions are to have real substance, then those who have suffered most from the now recognizably outdated organizational and technical forms should have a strong voice in any reform process. For both practical and ethical reasons, the promotion of authentic empowerment among those at the lower end of occupational hierarchies needs to be taken seriously. Organizations can become more effective even as humanistic and democratic values are pursued. Though enlightened managers and tool-like technologies can certainly help in this process, they alone are unlikely to be sufficient.

Rather, as we have seen from the experiences of women performing three common clerical jobs, the initiative of the office workers themselves can be vital in reshaping technologies and reforming organizations. Systems development professionals concerned with fulfilling pragmatic as well as social responsibilities can play an important role in this. If they listen carefully to the individual and collective voices of office staff, they may be surprised to find they have new partners in creating information systems that function better, contribute to a greater quality of worklife, and distribute power more democratically. At the same time, they will be lending their efforts to wider social reform processes as people generally, and women in particular, actively claim more equitable participation in work organizations. We should not look mainly to competitive pressures and computing advances to foster such overdue empowerment, but to the concerted endeavors of individuals taking greater control over their own working lives and enabling others to do likewise.

Acknowledgments

I am grateful to Eileen Green, Helen Maupin, Joanne Swayze, and Den Pain for their generous response to my repeated requests for more details on the projects they were involved with. My collaboration with Ann Zelechow on the SMOAP project, in addition to providing the essential foundation for this line of inquiry, was also personally rewarding. I appreciate the helpful comments that Jonathan Allen, Peter van den Besselaar, Rob Kling, Doug Schuler, Lucy Suchman, and especially Mike Hales made on an earlier draft. Research funding was provided by Labour Canada and the Social Sciences and Humanities Research Council (SSHRC).

References

Applegate, L. (1994). "Managing in an Information Age: Transforming the Organization for the 1990s," in R. Baskerville *et al.* (eds.), *Transforming Organizations with Information Technology,* pp. 15–94. North-Holland, Amsterdam.

Benjamin, R., and M. Scott Morton (1992). "Reflections on Effective Application of Information Technology in Organizations . . . From the Perspective of the Management in the 90's Program," in F. H. Vogt (ed.), *Personal Computers and Intelligent Systems: Information Processing 92,* pp. 131–143. North-Holland, Amsterdam.

Chapman, G. (1994). "The National Forum on Science and Technology Policy Goals." *Communications of the ACM,* 37(1) January:30–37.

Clement, A. (1989). "A Canadian Case Study Report: Towards Self-Managed Automation in Small Offices." *Information Technology for Development,* 4(2):185–233.

Clement, A., and Parsons, D. (1990). "Work Group Knowledge Requirements for Desktop Computing," in *Proceedings of the 23rd Hawaii International Conference on System Science,* pp. 84–93. Kailua-Kona, Hawaii.

Clement, A., and A. Zelechow (1987). *Self-Managed Office Automation Project.* Technology Impact Research Fund of Labour Canada, Ottawa.

Denning, P. J. (1992). "Educating a New Engineer." *Communications of the ACM*, 35(12):82–97.

Dunlop, C., and R. Kling (1991). *Computerization and Controversy: Value Conflicts and Social Choices*. Academic Press, San Diego.

Ehn, P. (1988). *Work-Oriented Design of Computer Artifacts*. Arbetslivcentrum, Stockholm.

Green, E., J. Owen, and D. Pain (1991). "Developing Computerized Office Systems: A Gender Perspective in UK Approaches," in Inger Eriksson, Barbara Kitchenham, and Kea Tijdens (eds.), *Women, Work and Computerization*, pp. 217–232. North-Holland, Amsterdam.

Green, E., J. Owen, and D. Pain (1993). " 'City Libraries': Human-Centred Opportunities for Women?," in Eileen Green, Jenny Owen, and Den Pain (eds.), *Gendered by Design? Information Technology and Office Systems*, pp. 127–152. Taylor and Francis, London.

Green, E., J. Owen, and D. Pain (eds.) (1993). *Gendered by Design? Information Technology and Office Systems*. Taylor and Francis, London.

Greenbaum, J., and M. Kyng (1991). *Design at Work: Cooperative Design of Computer Work*. Lawrence Erlbaum, Hillsdale, NJ.

Hales, M. (1994). "Where are Designers? Styles of Design Practice, Objects of Design and Views of Users in Computer Supported Cooperative Work," in D. Rosenberg and C. Hutchison (eds.), *Design Issues in CSCW*, pp. 151–177. Springer-Verlag, London.

Hammer, M., and J. Champy (1993). *Reengineering the Corporation: A Manifesto for Business Revolution*. Nicholas Brealey, London.

Hartman, K. (1987). "Secretaries and Computers," in Sara Kiesler and Lee Sproull (eds.), *Computing and Change on Campus*, pp. 114–130. Cambridge University Press, Cambridge.

Jewett, T., and R. Kling (1990). "The Work Group Manager's Role in Developing Computing Infrastructure," in *Proceedings of the 5th Conference on Office Information Systems (COIS'90)*, pp. 69–78. Cambridge, MA.

Kyng, M. (1991). "Designing for Cooperation: Cooperating in Design." *Communications of the ACM*, 34(12):64–73.

Maupin, H. E., and R. J. Fisher (1989). *Joint Labour-Management Organizational Change: A Model Integrating People and Technology*. Manitoba Institute for Management, Winnipeg.

Morgan, G. (1986). *Images of Organization*. Sage, Newbury Park, CA.

MTS/CEP (1992). *M-Power Evaluation Program*. Manitoba Telephone System/ Communication Energy & Paperworkers Union of Canada, Winnipeg.

MTS/CWC (1988). *Letter of Understanding, Operator Services, Trial Change Project*. Manitoba Telephone System/Communication Workers of Canada, Winnipeg.

MTS/CWC (1990). *Fast Forward to the Future*. Manitoba Telephone System/ Communication Workers of Canada.

Mumford, E. (1994). "Technology, Communication and Freedom: Is There a Relationship?" in R. Baskerville *et al.* (eds.), *Transforming Organizations with Information Technology*, pp. 303–322. North-Holland, Amsterdam.

Noble, D. F. (1984). *Forces of Production: A Social History of Industrial Automation*. Knopf, New York.

Perin, C. (1991). "Electronic Social Fields in Bureaucracies." *Communications of the ACM*, 34(12):74–82.

Schuler, D. (1994). "Community Networks." *Communications of the ACM*, 37(1) January:38–51.

Shneiderman, B. (1987). *Designing the User Interface: Strategies for Effective Human–Computer Interaction.* Addison-Wesley, Reading, MA.

Suchman, L. (1994). "Working Relations of Technology Production and Use." *Computer Supported Cooperative Work*, Vol. 3, April.

Tapscott, D., and A. Caston (1992). *Paradigm Shift: The New Promise of Information Technology.* McGraw-Hill, New York.

Vehviläinen, M. (1991). *Social Construction of Information Systems: An Office Workers' Standpoint.* Department of Computer Science, University of Tampere. Tampere, Finland.

Zuboff, S. (1988). *In the Age of the Smart Machine: The Future of Work and Power.* Basic Books, New York.

P·A·R·T · IV

Supporting Articulation Work[*]

Lucy Suchman

Invisible Work Revisited

In her paper for the *4th Conference on Women, Work and Computerization*, Leigh Star takes up the theme of women's invisibility in enterprises of technology production and use and calls for a recognition of articulation work as vital to the development of a "sociology of the invisible" (1991, pp. 81–82). "Articulation work" names the continuous efforts required in order to bring together discontinuous elements—of organizations, of professional practices, of technologies—into working configurations.[1] In this paper I want to explore further the place of articulation work in technology production and use: to bring that work forward and begin to think through what it would mean to organize a design practice around it.

To identify forms of articulation work central to systems design I have suggested the phrase *artful integrations* (Suchman, 1994). The phrase is meant to draw attention to aspects of systems development and use that have been hidden, or at least positioned in the background or shadows, and to bring them forward into the light. These include various forms of professional configuration and customization work, as well as an open horizon of mundane activities involved in incorporating technologies into everyday working practices, and keeping them working.[2]

To bring such artful integration work to light, we first need to reconceptualize systems development from the creation of discrete, intrinsically meaningful objects, to the ongoing production of new forms of working practice. Reorienting to practice in turn implies moving from a preoccupation with sites of professional design to an orientation to settings of technologies-in-use. Dorothy Smith has a vision of the sociological text (the artifact of sociologists-as-designers) that is relevant here, as text that is conscious of its necessary indexicality and hence that its meaning remains to be completed by a reader who is situated just as [the writer] is—a particular woman reading somewhere at a particular time amid the particularities of her everyday world—and that it is the capacity of our sociological texts, as she enlivens them, to reflect upon, to expand, and to enlarge her grasp of the world she reads in, and that is the world that completes the meaning of the text as she reads. (1987, p. 106)

Applied to artifacts more generally, this perspective orients us to an embodied user, located in a particular, actual, historically constituted worksite. Moreover, this user is herself a designer.[3] That is to say, the production of new forms of technologically mediated practice relies not only upon professional design practice, but on the articulation work that is necessary if an artifact is to be integrated effectively into the situated activities of its use.

Asking Other Questions

Such reorientations require, among other things, that we replace general narratives of technological change with specific accounts and critical questions. One dominant narrative is illustrated nicely in an image that I often use to introduce the efforts of our research group at Xerox PARC. The image was part of an advertisement in an issue of a popular computing magazine of some years ago. The top of the page pictures the proverbial paper napkin, onto which great ideas have been inscribed over the course of a lunch. Below that is a second image, of two businessmen sitting at the lunch table, now with a portable computer placed between them. The question the advertisement asks us, in apparently rhetorical voice, is "Why do this?"—that is, why use a paper napkin—"When you can do this?"—that is, introduce a portable computer onto the lunch table.

Our research agenda is to take the question this advertisement asks as a serious one. That is, we do not want simply to assume, as the writers of the

---

*A previous version of this paper appears in the *Proceedings of the 5th IFIP WG9.1 International Conference on Women, Work and Computerization: Breaking Old Boundaries, Building New Forms,* Manchester, UK, 2–5 July, 1994, A. Adams, J. Emms, E. Green, and J. Owen (eds.), Amsterdam, Elsevier, pp. 46–60. Reprinted with kind permission from IFIP & Elsevier Science B.V., Amsterdam, The Netherlands.

[1] On articulation work, see Strauss *et al.* (1985), Star (1991), and Fujimura (1987). On the relevance of articulation work for system design, see Gasser (1986), Kling (1992), Kling and Jewett (1994), and Schmidt and Bannon (1992).

[2] See, for example, Trigg and Bødker (1994), Mackay (1990), Nardi and Miller (1991) on tailorability/customization, Clement (1993), Hales (1992) on designing without designers, Blomberg (1987) on machine operation, and Orr (1991) on machine maintenance/repair.

[3] The essential, if largely invisible, role of workers in general and women in particular in the construction of technical systems has been well argued. See, for example, Clement (1994, 1993), Hales (1992), and Pain *et al.* (1993). For discussions of cooperation among professional and user designers see Greenbaum and Kyng (1991), and Schuler and Namioka (1993).

ad copy appear to do, that the answer to the question they pose to us is obvious: that no one in their right mind would continue to use a paper napkin when they could use a computer instead. Rather, we want to begin by taking the napkin seriously as a technology. In this case it is a rather flexible artifact, readily available in a certain class of settings, that affords easy appropriation into uses quite different from those that its designers originally envisioned for it. We want to understand the resources that this artifact provides in order to be aware of those resources as we or others propose new technologies intended to augment it.

Second, where the advertisers seem to imply that each next technology that comes along should totally displace those that came before—in this case, that the computer should become ubiquitous, so that it can be everywhere—we want to recognize the value of diverse media within and across settings. There may be some settings or occasions on which one medium feels more appropriate than another. Moreover, our studies and, I suspect, your experience indicate that rather than in a paperless world, we are living, and are likely to continue to live, in a world made up of hybrid systems, even in those settings where computing has assumed a central place. The challenge then is to understand each technology's place in an ecology of devices, to make it possible for people to choose which medium they find most effective for what purposes and to enable them, regardless of their choices, to cooperate with others whose choices may be different.

Finally, the image of the advertisement presents both napkin and laptop computer as decontextualized, focal objects, floating in white space. Instead we want to re-imagine technologies in their place; that is, in relation to particular, densely populated environments of working practices and heterogeneous artifacts.[4] Taking up this challenge poses another; namely, how can we develop an understanding of the problems and solutions that different technologies imply for working practice in particular settings? The answer to this question turns out to be less obvious than one might assume, because it turns out that it is not enough just to ask people: not because they will lie to you, or because they do not have good accounts of their own about what they are doing and why. The problem is rather that just to the extent that some form of activity is a fundamental aspect of a person's practice, they would never think of mentioning it to you. It becomes, quite literally, *unremarkable* to them. For this reason, as researchers we need ways not only of asking people about their work but of

---

[4] The table at which I sit as I write this, for example, is in the kitchen of the home of a friend in Arlington, Massachusetts. On the table in addition to the powerbook on which I'm working are a radio/audiotape player, two stacks of audio tapes, many piles of papers of various kinds (tax forms, letters, newspapers, magazines, a hand-drawn map of the herb garden she is intending to plant), a sugar bowl, a box of Kleenex, a plate, and coffee mug.

investigating with them the specific courses of action and extended networks of interaction of which working practices are made.

Recognizing Articulation Work

Two projects may help to illustrate how we have explored the qualities of articulation work and their implications for design. From 1989 through 1991, we carried out an extended study of work at a metropolitan airport on the west coast of the United States.[5] Our study focused on the work of ground operations; that is, all of the work involved in servicing arriving and departing airplanes. Within ground operations we took as a further focus a particular "backstage" area called the Operations room, charged with coordinating the work of the gates and the ramp.[6]

We began the project with a general interest in contributing to analyses of the dynamic structuring of people's interactions with each other and with their material environments, and in exploring the relevance of such analyses to problems in design. In the course of the project we came to see in detail the intimate relationship between work environments and the structuring of work activities, where the work environment in this case includes architectural features and furnishings, telephone lines, radio frequencies, computer screens, video monitors, documents, and the like. It was clear, moreover, that objects in the workplace assume multiple identities according to their relevance for practice; for example, an airplane may be for one person at one moment a specific aircraft while for another it is an instance of a flight, a container to be loaded, a machine to be repaired, and so forth (Brun-Cottan, 1991; Goodwin and Goodwin, in press; Jordan, 1992). Nor are there unidirectional effects between technologies and activities. Rather people are engaged in a continuous process of making the resources of the environment work for the activities at hand. In doing so, they leave the mark of their activities on the environment in ways that set up the conditions for subsequent actions. Along the way, the workspaces, furnishings, technologies, and artifacts are experienced as more and less focal or contextual, negotiable or resistant, enabling or constraining of the work that needs to be done.

One way of viewing the Operations room is as a center for articulation work across the multiple, distributed settings and interdependent activities involved in accomplishing the orderly arrival and on-time departure of an

---

[5] For a summary of the project and references to the full set of research papers produced, see Suchman (in press). Brun-Cottan et al. (1991) present a video final report on the project.

[6] The gate refers to the areas in which passengers are organized before boarding and after disembarking from planes. The ramp includes the outside areas around the parked planes themselves, in which provision of various services to the plane (food, fuel, etc.) and baggage handling are done. This is distinct from the runways or "taxiways," where planes are actually in motion.

airline's flights. As a more specific example of articulation work in the Operations room we can look at the job of controlling ground traffic for a small commuter airline. In the case of the airline's jet operations, responsibilities end when a plane has pushed back from the gate and moves onto the taxiway, at which point control is handed off immediately to ground traffic controllers located in the airport tower. In the case of the commuter airline, however, the arrangement of the parking ramp, the terminal building, and the taxiway at this airport requires extended participation by the Operations room in the hand-off of planes to and from ground traffic control. More specifically, the Operations room has responsibility for guiding airplanes that are out of visual range of ground controllers in the tower around one corner of the terminal building, down a one-way passage, and into or out of the ramp area in which the planes are parked for loading and unloading. This work makes artful use not only of computer technologies, but of a range of other communications and representational technologies as well.

The responsibilities of the traffic controller, taken up on one afternoon when we were present in the Operations room by a worker named Nancy, include conveying the assignment of an arriving plane's parking space both to the pilot and to workers on the ramp. The assignment of planes to specific parking spaces is designed to coordinate activities in space. Because of the physical layout of this airport, however, the success of that design requires an orderly arrangement of arriving planes in time as well, specifically management of the order in which each plane travels through the narrow passageway between the runways and the parking ramp. The mediating role that Nancy plays between the pilot and workers on the ramp is visible in her body as she works, as she negotiates the limited perceptual access provided her by two windows facing out from the corner in which she sits (see Figure 1). The window on Nancy's left gives her a view of the passageway, that on her right a view of the ramp area. The point at which planes move out of range of ground traffic control is marked by a large red square painted on the pavement. Pilots stop at this position to establish radio contact with the Operations room, then wait for directions on moving through the passageway. "Red square" itself is not directly visible from the Operations room, but a camera has been positioned there that feeds a video image into the room, giving Nancy access to a third, technology mediated view in addition to those provided by the windows.

As Nancy communicates between pilots and workers on the ramp, she engages in a series of translations, referring to a given plane by its flight number when speaking to the pilot (flights being for them the relevant form of identification), by its aircraft number or assigned parking space when speaking with the ramp (particular aircraft and where they are going to park being the relevant issues for workers on the ramp). As the supervisor on the ramp radios in to Nancy with a "go ahead" for a particular

Figure 1.   Nancy conveys parking directions to the pilot and to the ramp.

arriving plane, Nancy does not simply pass the message along to the pilot. Instead, she carefully crafts its formulation and timing to correspond to what she is able to see of the movement of planes through the passageway, instructing a pilot, for example, to "do a slow taxi" in order to maintain a safe distance from the plane ahead. From her position inside the room, in sum, Nancy acts through skillful, embodied articulation work to achieve an orderly movement of the planes outside.[7]

Articulation Work as Knowledge Work

In enterprises like airport operations, the task of coordination is sufficiently central that articulation work is foregrounded, however much its detail may be glossed over by standard job descriptions. In other cases, articulation work remains in the background. Bringing it forward and rendering visible the practical reasoning and action that it requires challenges existing political economies of knowledge; that is, the grounds on which knowledge and experience are differentially rewarded, symbolically as well as materially.

---

[7] For a more detailed analysis of this work, see Suchman (1993).

In *Living Thinkwork* (1980), Hales develops the metaphor of a "class geography" that maps the distribution of legitimated knowledges and associated working conditions throughout societies. The systematic disadvantage and exploitation of women in and through such geographies is well documented. A crucial demarcation in such geographies is the distinction of "knowledge" from "routine," or "mental" from "manual" labor. This distinction enables and reproduces the differential attribution of value across the division of labor, with some workers being assigned to one category, others to the other. A corollary of this move is the ideological separation of managerial from production work, with the former assigned control over the latter. At the same time, the distance of managerial specialists from the sites that they are assigned to control limits, for better and worse, management access to production practices:

> "Job control" is the ability of those workers in the job to out-think management in terms of immediate permutations of practice in the workplace, because they know, better than more remote managers and technicians, how the process works in day-to-day terms. This capability underpins the subtler side of collective bargaining. Also, and this is crucial, it gives workers the ability to think ahead towards new and more satisfying, useful, or productive ways of working which, in a better society, they would feel free to use because they wouldn't always expect to find these initiatives turned against them. In most jobs today it's a commonplace that "You're not paid to think." (Hales, 1980, p. 133–134)

Cockburn's (1988) analyses of the gendering and regendering of technologies provide ample support for the argument that skills and associated occupational status are established not by demands of technology, but by power-differentiated actors within the workplace. Henwood (1993) cites research leading to similar conclusions:

> In their series of case studies of gender and the labour process in Australian manufacturing and service industries, [Game and Pringle] too show how skill is an ideological and social category, not merely a technical one. In the whitegoods industry, for example, they show how male workers resist the "feminization" of work, which they fear will result from the introduction of new technologies, by creating and supporting a whole series of dichotomies which (they argue) distinguish between men's and women's work. According to Game and Pringle, distinctions such as heavy/light, dirty/clean, technical/non-technical, mobile/immobile are constructed to preserve a sexual division of labour, the whole basis of which is "threatened by technological changes." (p. 39)

Henwood goes on to point out that the clerical work involved in the use of information systems, for example, data entry, is so marginalized that it often is not even counted as part of the industry. She cites research on the "outsourcing" of clerical work:

[T]hese clerical workers are often spatially segregated into separate companies which specialize in data preparation and may be located in a different town, or even country, from others in computer occupations. This point is verified by Posthuma's research on "offshore office work" where big US companies were found to have "decentralized" data entry tasks and made use of suburban women's labour, as well as women's labour in "off-shore" sites in the Caribbean. (fn. 12, p. 46)

We have recently encountered these issues in the context of a research project aimed at exploring the possible usefulness of new image processing technologies for the work of a large law firm.[8] The firm is an extremely document-intensive worksite, in the midst of ongoing changes in relations between paper and electronic media. Within the firm we established a collaborative research relationship with a small number of people, located in two different areas of the firm's practice, interested in exploring new technologies for bridging between paper and electronic documents. One of these areas was a form of work called litigation support, involving the creation of a database index to the large corpora of paper documents, numbering often in the hundreds of thousands, that provide the basis for arguing each case.[9]

We soon discovered an ongoing struggle over the future of the work of litigation support within the firm, tied to the status of that work as mental or manual labor, as well as to a gendered division of labor. Not surprising, the majority of lawyers within the firm are male, while the support staff is predominantly female. This is by no means exclusively the case: we encountered women particularly within the junior ranks of the lawyers, and one of the temporary workers in litigation support with whom we spent the most time was male. Nevertheless, the firm reflected typical patterns of concentrations of men (particularly at the upper ranks of the partnership), with the positions of paralegals and litigation support workers (particularly those for whom this represented permanent vs. temporary employment) being filled predominantly by women.

In their distance from litigation support, attorneys at the firm held highly stereotyped views of the work of coding documents for entry into the database. Specifically, document coding was described to us as "mindless" labor, representing a prime target for automation or out-sourcing as part of a general cost-cutting initiative within the firm. Our initial account of the work was from a senior attorney who described the process of document coding as made up of two types: what he termed "subjective," or issues

---

[8] See also Blomberg *et al.* (1994) and Suchman (1994).

[9] The other area in which we worked was corporate law, where we collaborated with an attorney to understand his practice and developed a prototype to support document storage and reuse. See Blomberg *et al.* (1994) and Rao *et al.* (1994).

coding, done by attorneys, and "objective" coding, which he described as follows:

> "You have, you know, 300 cartons of documents and you tear through them and say, I'm going to put post-its on the ones we have to turn over [to the other side]. And then, ideally, you hire chimpanzees to type in From, To, Date. And then, ideally, you then have lawyers go through it again and read each document, with their brain turned on."

On another occasion, the same attorney became excited by the prospect that our image-processing technologies might be used to automate the work of litigation support:

> "If this works, it could save us just a fortune. I'm now negotiating for offshore data entry in the Philippines, because it's cheaper. In which we send things DHL. They do the objective coding, 40 cents to 80 cents a page. No thought, just author, recipient. And if you could have, not even paralegals, sort of, you could hire 9-year-olds to sit there, or just train the program, after To that was the recipient, From was the author, and Re was the subject, and Date was date. Feed that—just stuff the thing in the scanner and shoot it through, and then to make sure it worked, do it again, and then compare the two. You could save me millions."

During this time we talked with and recorded the work of case assistants, paralegals, junior attorneys, and the senior attorney himself. At no point did we encounter the work of objective document coding directly. That aspect of the work of the firm was, literally as well as figuratively, invisible from the attorneys' point of view.

Having developed an initial sense for the work of document production as done by attorneys, we decided that it was time for us to look more directly into the work of objective coding. Through inquiries, we located the document coding operation. There we found a former paralegal, with extensive experience in the maintenance and use of computerized databases, supervising an office of temporary workers, many with college degrees. These "document analysts," as the supervisor called them, were engaged in carefully examining and representing the thousands of documents for a given case with the goal, vigorously instilled by their supervisor, of creating a valid and useful database.

At the same time, we discovered that the litigation support supervisor was quite aware of the attorneys' views. As she put it to us:

> S: "One reason that I'm trying to get the attorneys—another reason I'm trying to get the attorneys very involved in what we do, is so that they can see that we, y'know, don't have three heads and we're not drooling at the mouth. [S and L both laughing] Because there are two problems here. One is that they don't understand—I hope you're not going to be showing this at some partners meeting—"
>
> L: "No no no, we promise"
>
> S: "and if you are I really don't care [laughs]"

L: "[laughing] because it's the truth"

S: "it is. [pauses, no longer laughing] But you know on the—on the one hand I—the attorneys need to understand what the process of getting a document from hardcopy to abstract is because on the one hand they think it's a very streamlined, easy process and when I tell them that no, I can't create a two-hundred-page database in 30 days they don't understand why. They get very frustrated. They have no idea why that can't happen."

The litigation support supervisor expressed to us her belief that, given their familiarity with the document corpus, the document coders could be responsible for certain other aspects of the document production process as well, now handled by junior attorneys. She also suggested that on her view the attorneys underutilized the database, because of their ignorance of its capabilities and how to exploit them.

So we found ourselves cast into the middle of a contest over professional identities and practices within the firm, framed by the attorneys as a distinction between "knowledge work" on the one hand and "mindless labor" on the other, framed differently by the workers within litigation support themselves. At the same time, the more we looked into the work of litigation support the more we saw the interpretive and judgmental work that the document coders were required to bring to it, as well as the work's potential fit with our design agenda.[10] As a result, we decided to work with the supervisor of litigation support and her staff to prototype a redesigned document coding practice, incorporating some of our technologies.

Our first effort was to identify and describe the practical reasoning involved in the work of document coding. Some examples should illustrate the kinds of problems that document coders face.

Document Designation. The first task facing the document coders is simply to decide what constitutes a document; that is, where are the boundaries between one document and the next? This is not as obvious a judgment as it may at first seem, as documents when they come to the document coders do not wear their identities on their sleeves. Rather, they come in the form of cardboard boxes full of paper. And coders know that physical attachment of pages, that is, with a paper clip, is not a reliable indicator of document boundaries. First, documents may have been misstapled, or clipped together in the client's files for reasons other than those of interest

---

[10] Specifically, we were interested in exploring the usefulness of a class of image-processing technologies, emerging from research and making their way into product development within our company. These technologies are aimed at turning marks made on paper into instructions to the machine at the point that a paper document is scanned. So, for example, the machine can "recognize" a circled text region on a paper document and store just the circled text in a designated electronic file for subsequent reuse.

to the attorneys. Moreover, once taken from the client's files the documents have been photocopied before they reach the coders, with those who do the copying charged with re-attaching multipage documents with a paper clip. Coders are aware of the practicalities of document filing, copying, and handling, and the uncertainties that they introduce.

Second, beyond simply identifying document boundaries coders often are asked to enter an additional code into the database in cases where one document is closely related to another. For example, a letter with an agreement attached could logically be coded as two separate documents or as a single document. On one hand, information is lost if the letter and agreement are coded as two separate documents, insofar as the letter is not meaningful without the agreement, and provides critical context for it. On the other hand, if the letter and agreement are simply treated as a single document and coded as a letter, the agreement may be missed in a search. In such cases, therefore, it becomes important to code the two documents separately, but with an indication that one is attached to the other.

Date Selection. The coding of document dates is viewed by attorneys as an "objective" action, which, because it involves no judgment, is a good candidate for automation. Watching the document coders work, in contrast, reveals vagaries requiring adjudication here as well. Coders work from a rule of thumb that prescribes coding the date that will be most salient to the users of the database, namely, "What is the client/attorney going to remember?" Correctly this means, for example, that, given an agreement and the question of whether to code the date the agreement was faxed, the date it was signed or entered into, or the date it was first produced, coders learn to select the date that it was entered into. This in turn may require a search through the document's text to identify the relevant date.

Names Disambiguation. Perhaps the most important aspect of any document from the point of view of the attorneys are proper names, including document authors, recipients, and any persons, companies, or products mentioned in the text. Creating a coherent and usable database involves ongoing work of normalizing across multiple designations for the same referent, for example, B. Jones, Bob Jones, Robert Jones may all refer to a single person. Coders are given specific instructions about how variants should be reconciled and how names should be entered. At the same time, they are expected to exercise ordinary judgments in an open-ended horizon of ways, for example, recognizing from context when Bob and Robert refer to the same person. Similarly, coders need to know that, for example, Martin Marietta is a company rather than a person, UNIX is an operating system rather than a company, and DEC in the context of the Silicon Valley refers to Digital Equipment Corporation, not to December.

Toward Artful Integrations

Given the requirements of document coding, the goal of our prototype design became to explore with the document coders the possibility of incorporating some image-processing technologies into their practice in a way that would relieve the tedium (e.g., of transcribing numbers from documents to forms), while maintaining the level of engagement in the process that seemed required in order for them to make the necessary interpretations and exercise the necessary judgments, as well as to ensure the quality of the database entries.

First, we assumed that control over the designation of document boundaries would have to stay in the hands of the coders. Every piece of paper taken from the client's files is given a unique identification number, and documents are represented in the database as a range. Even if we imagine a technology by which numbers could be automatically assigned to document pages (at the moment, the numbers are actually affixed to the pages manually), or that all documents are scanned and available in digitized form, coders must still be able to see and read the pages in order to define document boundaries. For this and other reasons, our prototype provided for the display of full document images in a form inspectable by document coders.

Second, we assumed that any system we designed would require a combination of machine processing and mindful human work. While we could prototype a scenario in which some marks on paper documents could be "read" directly into the database by the system, other text, like the description of the document (which might or might not be contained in the document itself) would need to be composed and entered manually.

Third, we assumed that whatever level of automated processing we could introduce, the accuracy of the database would continue to rely on assessments and interventions on the part of the coders. So, for example, our system offered the possibility of scanning a region of text from a paper document (e.g., a region indicated by a circle drawn by the coder), optically "recognizing" the characters and transforming them into digitized text, and placing them in a file. Actually entering the text into the database, however, relied upon a coder's ability to read it and designate an appropriate field. The accuracy of available technologies for optical character recognition, moreover, meant a high likelihood that the text would contain inaccuracies. So our design assumed that the image of the document should be available to a coder alongside an interface to the database through which the coder could indicate a destination field for a particular bit of text, and that the scanned text would need to be editable in order that the coder could compare it with the original image and correct any errors. Most important, we developed our prototype on the premise that document coding is a crucial form of articulation work within the firm. Through their coding practices, litigation support workers create the databases that mediate between documents and the lawyers who need to find and use them in making a successful case. Moreover, we quickly realized that reflection and design were an ongoing, integral concern for workers in litigation support themselves. Our task then was less to introduce design agendas into the site, as to engage for a time with those already under way.

In the course of our project within litigation support, our approach emerged as a kind of design value shared by us and by the litigation support supervisor. This value involved working toward the artful integration of new technologies and working practices within litigation support in a way that recognized and honored the practical reasoning that the work involved. The litigation support supervisor herself, toward the end of the project, expressed our common approach as follows:

> "And it would seem to me that all we're really doing is—hopefully what we're doing, and I think this would be a great idea, is you take people now who do the laborious coding and you turn them into very intelligent quality assurance people. So you get the more tedious tasks done by the computer and the OCR, and then the coders really become your 'does this make sense' kind of people."

Due to the conditions of our own working practice, our design efforts with respect to litigation support at the firm ended with the research prototype. Meanwhile, however, the litigation support staff have taken their own initiatives to increase the productivity of their practice, by coding documents directly into the database rather than in two separate passes for document coding (on forms) and data entry (from forms into the database). At the same time, they have managed successfully to counter claims by outside sources to be able to do accurate database creation at a significantly cheaper rate. For the moment, their place within the firm seems secure. We hope at least to have contributed to their efforts by seeing their work and acknowledging what we saw, both in our representations of it and our designing for it.

Making Technological Meanings

The importance of bringing together analyses of gender with analyses of technology has by now been well and eloquently argued.[11] In attempting to contribute further to that effort, I want to take up the call, by feminist scholars like Henwood (1993), that we find ways of theorizing relations of gender and technology that are nonessentializing (in our analyses of gender) and nondeterministic (in our analyses of technology). More specifically, I want to take to heart Henwood's complaint that in thinking and

---

[11] Most recently by Eileen Green, Jenny Owen, Den Pain, and the contributors to the volume *Gendered by Design*, Taylor & Francis, Ltd., London, 1993.

writing about gender and technology we have taken technology too much at face value, as a given. As she puts it:

> Technological meanings are not "given"; they are made. Our task in trying to transform the gendered relations of technology should not be focused on gaining access to knowledge as it is but with creating that knowledge. By this I mean that we have to be involved at the level of definition, of making meanings and in creating technological culture. (1993, p. 44)

What we need to work toward, according to Henwood, is an alternative that does not simply reject technology as inherently masculinist, or propose either that there could be technologies that are inherently feminist or that more women in systems design will "naturally" lead to its transformation. Instead she argues that what we need are analyses aimed at interventions into the technology design process itself, informed by feminist theorizing and in the service of positive changes in the practical conditions of women's work and lives.

> What we need is more research that seeks to explore the alternative, if more marginal discourses of technology and to examine the factors responsible for the marginalization of the more radical and feminist discourses in favour of liberal ones that appear to reproduce and reinforce the *status quo* [i.e. those that concede technology production and definitions of technological meaning to men, while promoting the participation of women in those male-defined discourses.] . . . Both technology and gender are constitutive of each other and we need to develop frameworks that are capable of analyzing the diverse ways in which the two interact to produce a range of different subjective experiences and practices. At its best, feminist research into the process of systems design can enable us to do this. (Henwood, 1993, p. 45)

A fundamental requirement for the project of developing design practice to support articulation work is recognizing that design is an essential aspect not only of creating information systems but of putting them into use. However, the invisible work of design-for-use is deliberately and systematically ignored in promotional accounts of the capabilities and benefits of new technologies. Put more strongly, it is precisely the invisibility of the work that makes it possible to assign those capabilities and benefits to the new technologies themselves, rather than to those (typically low-status and low-paid) workers who actually make technical systems function effectively. Clement (1993), among others, has elaborated the connection between the systematic backgrounding of this form of design activity and its assignment to women workers. To challenge this order, Clement argues, requires that infrastructural work be recognized as an essential element in the successful operation of organizations and the design of working systems. Infrastructural design work involves configuring received technological packages in such a way that they actually fit the specific requirements of a particular organization's working practice. Clement proposes that recognizing actual, *in situ* design practices could inform a corresponding transformation of professional design practice as well.

A reordering of locales and criteria of assessment for new technology design is, at least in part, what a design practice based in the recognition of articulation work could mean. Reordering locales of technology design is in part a matter of bringing professional design out into the sites of technologies-in-use, in part a matter of acknowledging the extent to which design work already takes place across those boundaries. In Suchman (1994) I argue that crucial to the place of technology in human activity are the working relations required to construct technologies and put them into use. Those relations are characterized at present by a complex layering of social—particularly professional—identities and associated boundaries. Reconstructing technologies requires understanding those identities and boundaries, the contributions they make to reproducing the current order, and the openings they afford for change. Unquestionably, the most difficult problems we face are not changes to existing technologies as such, but rather transformation of the institutional arrangements that sustain existing technological orders. To transform these arrangements, we need to begin by bringing articulation work forward in design discourse as central to the successful workings of technology production and use. This includes beginning to talk about the realities of design practice as the many places where design work actually gets done, the institutional and technical practicalities that structure current activities and relations, and the problems and possibilities that those conditions offer for a transformed practice of systems design.

Acknowledgment

Thanks to Randy Trigg, as usual, for his very helpful reading of the first version of this paper.

References

Blomberg, J. (1987). "Social Interaction and Office Communication: Effects on User's Evaluation of New Technologies," in R. Kraut (ed.), *Technology and the Transformation of White Collar Work*, pp. 195–210. Lawrence Erlbaum, Hillsdale, NJ.

Blomberg, J., L. Suchman, and R. Trigg (1994). "Reflections on a Work-Oriented Design Project," in R. Trigg, S. I. Anderson, and E. Dykstra-Erickson (eds.), *PDC'94: Proceedings of the Participatory Design Conference* (pp. 99–109). Computer Professionals for Social Responsibility, Palo Alto, CA.

Brun-Cottan, F. (1991). "Talk in the Workplace: Occupational Relevance." *Research on Language in Social Interaction*, 24:277–295.

Brun-Cottan, F., K. Forbes, C. Goodwin, M. Goodwin, B. Jordan, L. Suchman, and R. Trigg (1991). *The Workplace Project: Designing for Diversity and Change* (Videotape). Xerox Palo Alto Research Center, 3333 Coyote Hill Road, Palo Alto, CA 94304.

Clement, A. (1993). "Looking for the Designers: Transforming the 'Invisible' Infrastructure of Computerized Office Work," *AI & Society*, 7:323–344.

Clement, A. (1994). "Computing at Work: Empowering Action by 'Low-Level Users,' " in D. Schuler (ed.), *Communications of the ACM*, Special Issue on Social Computing, January 1994, Vol. 37, No. 1, pp. 53–105.

Cockburn, C. (1988). *Machinery of Dominance: Women, Men and Technical Know-How.* Northeastern University Press, Boston.

Fujimura, J. (1987). Constructing 'Do-able' Problems in Cancer Research: Articulating Alignment. *Social Studies of Science*, 17:257–93.

Gasser, Les (1986). "The Integration of Computing and Routine Work." *ACM Transactions on Office Information Systems.* 4(3)(July):205–225.

Goodwin, C., and M. H. Goodwin (in press). "Formulating Planes: Seeing as a Situated Activity," in Y. Engestrom and D. Middleton (eds.), *Communication and Cognition at Work.* Cambridge University Press, NY.

Green, E., J. Owen, and D. Pain (1993). *Gendered by Design?* Taylor & Francis, Ltd., London.

Greenbaum, J., and M. Kyng (eds.) (1991). *Design at Work: Cooperative Design of Computer Systems.* Lawrence Erlbaum, Hillsdale, NJ.

Hales, M. (1980). *Living Thinkwork: Where Do Labour Processes Come From?* CSE Books, London.

Hales, M. (1992). "Where are Designers? Styles of Design Practice, Objects of Design and Views of Users in Computer-Supported Cooperative Work," in D. Rosenberg (ed.), *Design Issues in CSCW.* Springer-Verlag, Heidelberg.

Henwood, F. (1993). "Establishing Gender Perspectives on Information Technology: Problems, Issues and Opportunities," in E. Green, J. Owen, and D. Pain (eds.), *Gendered by Design?* pp. 31–49. Taylor & Francis, Ltd., London.

Jordan, B. (1992). "Technology and Social Interaction: Notes on the Achievement of Authoritative Knowledge in Complex Settings" (IRL Technical Report No. IRL92-0027), Institute for Research on Learning, Palo Alto, CA.

Kling, Rob (1992). "Behind the Terminal: The Critical Role of Computing Infrastructure in Effective Information Systems' Development and Use," in William Cotterman and James Senn (eds.), *Challenges and Strategies for Research in Systems Development,* pp. 153–201. John Wiley, New York.

Kling, Rob, and Tom Jewett (1994). "The Social Design of Worklife with Computers and Networks: A Natural Systems Perspective," in Marshall C. Yovits (ed.), *Advances in Computers,* Vol. 39. Academic Press, San Diego.

Mackay, W. (1990). "Patterns of Sharing Customizable Software," in *Proceedings of CSCW'90, Conference on Computer-Supported Cooperative Work,* pp. 209–221. ACM Press, Portland, Oregon.

√ Nardi, B., and J. Miller (1991). "Twinkling Lights and Nested Loops: Distributed Problem Solving and Spreadsheet Development." *International Journal of Man-Machine Studies,* 34:161–184.

Orr, J. (1991). "Talking about Machines: An Ethnography of a Modern Job." *Xerox PARC Technical Report* SSL-91-07 [P91-00132], Palo Alto, CA.

Pain, D., J. Owen, I. Franklin, and E. Green (1993). "Human-Centered Systems Design," in E. Green, J. Owen, and D. Pain (eds.), *Gendered by Design?* pp. 11–30. Taylor & Francis, London.

Rao, R., S. K. Card, W. Johnson, L. Klotz, and R. Trigg (1994). "Protofoil: Storing and Finding the Information Worker's Paper Documents in an Electronic File Cabinet," in *Proceedings of the ACM CHI'94 Conference* (April 24–28, Boston, MA), pp. 180–185. ACM Press, New York.

Schmidt, K., and L. Bannon (1992). Taking CSCW Seriously: Supporting Articulation Work. *Computer-Supported Cooperative Work,* 1:7–40.

Schuler, D., and A. Namioka (eds.) (1993). *Participatory Design: Perspectives on Systems Design.* Lawrence Erlbaum, Hillsdale, NJ.

Smith, D. (1987). *The Everyday World as Problematic: A Feminist Sociology.* Northeastern University Press, Boston.

Star, S. L. (1991). "Invisible Work and Silenced Dialogues in Knowledge Representation," in I. Eriksson, B. Kitchenham, and K. Tijdens (eds.), *Women, Work and Computerization,* pp. 81–92. North-Holland, Amsterdam.

Strauss, A., S. Fagerhaugh, B. Suczek, and Ca. Wiener (1985). *The Social Organization of Medical Work.* University of Chicago Press, Chicago.

Suchman, L. (1993). "Technologies of Accountability," in G. Button (ed.), *Technology in Working Order: Studies of Work, Interaction and Technology,* pp. 113–126. Routledge, London.

Suchman, L. (1994). "Working Relations of Technology Production and Use," in A. Clement and I. Wagner (eds.), *NetWORKing, Special Issue of Computer-Supported Cooperative Work (CSCW),* pp. 21–40. Kluwer, Dordrecht.

Suchman, L. (in press). "Centers of Coordination: A Case and Some Themes," in L. Resnick, R. Saljo, and C. Pontecorvo (eds.), *Discourse, Tools, and Reasoning.* Springer-Verlag, New York.

Trigg, R., and S. Bødker (1994). "From Implementation to Design: Tailoring and the Emergence of Systematization in CSCW." Submitted to *CSCW '94, Conference on Computer-Supported Cooperative Work.*

P·A·R·T · V

Social Relationships in Electronic Forums

P·A·R·T · V

A

Social Relationships in Electronic Forums: Hangouts, Salons, Workplaces, and Communities

Rob Kling

Social Relationships in Electronic Forums

Electronic forums are springing up worldwide, and especially in North America. Millions of people are now corresponding through electronic newsgroups, bulletin boards, conferences, distribution lists, and similar media. Somewhere, on the Internet, on a private service like America On-line, or on an independent bulletin board, there is at least one electronic forum that focuses on almost any topic that someone would want to talk (or write) about. And there are many groups organized for "casual chat" to help foster friendship, and sometimes even romance, between their participants. Enthusiasts for these forums argue that they are building new forms of community life (Rheingold, 1993). But other analysts observe that not every collection of people who happen to talk (or write) to each other form the sense of trust, mutual interest, and sustained commitments that automatically deserve to be labeled as communities (Jones, 1995).

This part examines some specific controversies about the kinds of social relations that people develop when they communicate via computer networks. The search for "a sense of community" has been an enduring theme in United States culture. Ironically, the technologies of freedom—trains, cars, and airplanes; telephones, faxes, and computer networks—have enabled us to be on the move, and to live, work, and do business with more people with whom we share limited parts of our lives.[1] Further, at a time when community life in North American cities is unraveling, some people hope that people can meet and enrich their social lives at work and at home via computer networks.[2]

The ways that people work and communicate via computer networks destabilize many conventional social categories. For example, I just referred to "social lives at work and at home" as if they refer to distinct places as well as webs of social relationships. But telecommuting and virtual offices enable people to work routinely while they are in their homes, and blur these boundaries.

This part examines social relationships of people's physical lives—not just their electronic images. It starts by examining social relationships in workplaces. Then it examines people's private lives—their relationships within their preexisting towns, cities, and metropolitan areas as they lobby their local governments for political change or search for romance on-line. It also examines how communities of authors and readers are shifting their relationships with electronic journals and digital libraries.

Much of the recent flood of books and articles about computer networking, information highways, virtual offices, and cyberspace are infused with technological utopianism and anti-utopianism. The selections in Part II by Weiland, Stewart, and Kelly illustrate technological utopian analyses of social relationships in electronic forums. And the selections in Part II by Birkerts and Winner illustrate technological anti-utopianism. Most of the articles in this part go beyond the utopian and anti-utopian genres to examine social life in cyberspace in more socially realistic terms.

Work Relationships and Electronic Communication

Many writers, including scholars, professionals, and technical journalists, have speculated about the effects of new technologies on worklife. Some speculate that electronic mail will eliminate organizational hierarchies, or at least reduce the barriers to communication between people at different levels of hierarchy in an organization (Sproull and Kiesler, 1991a) and facilitate the formation of more flexible work groups (perhaps even "virtual" work groups).

Other speculations involve the extent and the conditions under which electronic communications will foster or undermine a sense of community

---

[1] See the article by Kling, Ackerman, and Allen in Part VI (Chapter L) for a discussion of the ways that social life in the United States has shifted from one based on a few direct relationships to one based on many indirect relationships.

[2] See, for example, Howard Rheingold's (1993) book about "virtual communities" and Doug Schuler's (1994) essay about the ways that community networks might enhance people's participation in the political activities of their cities.

in the workplace and elsewhere. Workers who are connected by electronic communications media may form "communities" that differ in substantial ways from other communities to which they may belong. Much of what has been written about networks at work has been concerned, in part, with community. A recurring theme of electronically enhanced group cohesion is typified by Heintz (1992, p. 34), who claims that "the world of electronic science is smaller and more tightly knit." However, there are currently few empirical studies of changing forms of work that support these speculations. Technical journalists like Perry (1992) claim that "electronic mail has removed the barriers of time and place between engineers collaborating on complex design projects." Aydin and Rice (1992) describe how networks bring together different groups in the workplace. There is some empirical evidence that computer nets help foster a sense of community among geographically or organizationally isolated professionals, such as special librarians (Ladner and Tillman, 1992) and oceanographers (Sproull and Kiesler, 1991b).

A substantial body of research has attempted to identify the unique characteristics of electronic media, and how new media use may be optimized. Although much of this research is social-psychological in nature, a few researchers engage issues of organizational behavior. Kiesler, Siegel, and McGuire (1984) conducted controlled problem-solving experiments that compared computer-based communication with face-to-face discussion. They found that the groups that used computer communication took longer to reach consensus, participated more equally, showed more willingness to arrive at conclusions that differed from their initial proposals, and displayed more "uninhibited verbal behavior" (colloquially known as "flaming"). Some of the effects that they observed have been attributed to the absence of nonverbal cues that are present in face-to-face discussion (body language, smiles, or frowns, etc.) and even to some extent in telephone conversation (laughter, voice inflection, etc.).

The first selection in this part, "Increasing Personal Connections," by Lee Sproull and Sara Kiesler, sets the stage for examining electronic mail (e-mail) and distribution lists in organizations. They argue that electronic mail is not simply a tool that replaces telephones and paper memos—it has distinctly different social properties. They argue that the use of e-mail enables people who are peripheral in organizations to become more visible. Lower-level staff can communicate more readily to upper managers. People in branch offices or the field can communicate more readily with others in the home office and other branch offices. They argue that these electronic connections help democratize organizations by giving more visibility to people who are often out of sight or ignored by people in more central or powerful positions. Sproull and Kiesler go beyond the normal focus on job-specific communication, and also examine distribution lists where people can communicate about hobbies (the cinema list) or just hang out (the rowdies list). They argue that these formats for electronic communication also help people make connections and heighten the sense of social solidarity in organizations. These are important claims, especially for geographically dispersed organizations or those that are experimenting with telecommuting.[3]

But there is also the possibility that people's social relationships in networked offices may suffer in some ways. Research claims about e-mail facilitating less inhibited behavior and flaming suggest that electronic groups may behave somewhat differently than face-to-face groups (Kiesler, Siegel, and McGuire, 1984; Sproull and Kiesler, 1991). Deborah Kezsbom (1992), a technical journalist, suggests one possible downside to networked worklife: "As the use of cross-functional, multi-disciplined project teams increases, the conflict that accompanies such team work will rise accordingly." And Zuboff (1988) reports the experiences of a large drug company where managers claimed that their electronic communications were being treated as policy statements, even when they wanted to make an informal observation or ad hoc decisions.

In the next selection, "Gender and Democracy in Computer-Mediated Communication," linguist Susan Herring examines the ways that men and women communicate in two different electronic discussion groups: LINGUIST, devoted to the discussion of linguistics-related issues, and Megabyte University (MBU), informally organized around the discussion of computers and writing. Herring uses a particular (idealized) conception of "democratic discourse" in which any participant can question any assertion, introduce any assertion, and express his or her own attitudes, desires, and needs without being coerced into silence or compliance by other participants. She carefully examined discussions of these groups for the rates of participation by men and women. She went beyond counting the number of messages to examine the lengths of messages (the longest messages were written by men), and the style of interaction (supportive, critical, hostile). She also examined the ways in which people received rejoinders to the comments that they sent to the group, or if their messages were lost in cyberspace without public acknowledgment. Herring summarizes her disturbing conclusions:

> Despite the democratizing potential . . . male and female academic professionals do not participate equally in academic CMC. Rather, a small male minority dominates the discourse both in terms of amount of talk, and rhetorically, through self-promotional and adversarial strategies. Moreover, when women do attempt to participate on a more equal basis, they risk being actively censored by the reactions of men who either ignore them or attempt to delegitimize their contributions. Because of social conditioning that makes women uncomfortable with direct conflict, women tend to be more intimidated by these practices and to avoid participating as a result. . . . [The]

---

[3] See my discussion of telecommuting in "Computerization at Work," the lead article for Part IV.

conditions for a democratic discourse are not met: although the medium theoretically allows for everyone with access to a network to take part and to express their concerns and desires equally, a very large community of potential participants is effectively prevented by censorship, both overt and covert, from availing itself of this possibility. Rather than being democratic, academic CMC is power-based and hierarchical. This state of affairs cannot, however, be attributed to the influence of computer communication technology; rather, it continues preexisting patterns of hierarchy and male dominance in academia more generally, and in society as a whole.

Herring's study is based on a special sample of people (academics) and a special kind of forum: a discussion group. Perhaps other kinds of groups or other kinds of electronic forums more effectively facilitate democratic discussions. Social psychologist Giuseppe Mantovani (1994) reviewed a broad study of systematic empirical research about the role of computer communication systems in enhancing democratic discussions between participants. Computer-mediated communication (CMC) tools, include both distance-spanning and time-synchronous systems, like teleconferencing, and distance-spanning and time-bridging asynchronous systems, like electronic mail (e-mail). These are diverse kinds of technologies, including those studied by Sproull and Kiesler and Markus in this part, as well as those that support virtual offices. Mantovani carefully examines a position, most actively advanced by Sara Kiesler and Lee Sproull, that "CMC is democratic because it supports participation in communication in organizations in a way that is consistent with Western images of democracy."

The democratization thesis can be stated simply; but it has a number of complex dimensions that Sproull and Kiesler explore in their book *Connections* and in the selection from their book ("Increasing Personal Connections"). In *Connections*, Sproull and Kiesler summarize a rich body of research about face-to-face meetings, which shows that they are often dominated by members who are highest in status, most verbally articulate, and/or speak the most. Lower-status members, or those who are shyer are less likely to influence the decisions made in meetings, even when they have important expertise. The democratization thesis mixes the moral value of democracy with the hope that more democratic organizations can more effectively draw upon the skills and expertise of their employees.

However, Mantovani uses an informal conception of democracy, without carefully identifying different meanings of democracy, such as equal participation, one person–one vote, ability for minority groups to organize and argue for their interests, and so on. It is particularly important to be clear about the differences between political democracy (in which the authority to govern derives from the consent of those who are governed) and conversational equality, which is closer to the Habermassian conception of democracy explained by Herring (Pateman, 1970). Democratic theorists like Pateman argue that effective political democracy at the national level is most likely in societies that have many arenas for people to experience conversational democracy and political democracy—including their workplaces and their communities. But conversational democracy does not transform authority relationships into those of political democracy. For example, university students might enjoy conversational democracy on a campus. But students usually play no significant role in selecting the faculty and administrators who exercise authority over curricula and campus life.

Mantovani carefully examines a diverse body of research for evidence about the extent to which CMC use democratizes social interaction and social influence. He discusses a body of studies conducted by Tora Bikson and her colleagues (1989) that find that e-mail is effective in overcoming physical barriers, but not necessarily social barriers. These technologies primarily enhance existing interaction patterns. He also draws upon Child and Loveridge's (1990) studies, undertaken in different European countries, that found that CMC is usually designed precisely to support ongoing hierarchical relations. Mantovani concludes that whether or not CMC engenders democracy actually depends on the social context of CMC use, on the organizational history, and on the rules determining CMC's application.

The next selection (Chapter D) by M. Lynne Markus, "Finding a Happy Medium: Explaining the Negative Effects of Electronic Communication on Social Life at Work," gives us a concrete illustration of Mantovani's abstract reference to "the social context of CMC use," "organizational history," and "the rules determining CMC's application." Her careful case study of the social effects of e-mail use examines communications between the staff at an insurance firm's headquarters (HCP). HCP's upper managers required their staffs to rely upon e-mail, and it was the major medium for internal corporate communications at the time of her study. HCP's staff used e-mail to speed communications and bring people closer together. But they also reported significant negative effects, such as feeling that HCP was a less personal place to work. Electronic mail was often used to avoid face-to-face confrontation or unpleasant situations; and often in-office visitors were ignored while employees tended to the demands of messages on their computer terminals.

How should we understand the occurrence of these negative effects? Some analysts have argued that they are a by-product of key characteristics of e-mail as a medium, which reduces the intensity of important social cues, such as people's feelings (Sproull and Kiesler, 1991). Markus challenges the "social cues filtered out" theory,[4] and concludes that managers ascribe negative effects of electronic communications to "people's

---

[4] Other investigators have also contested the view of e-mail as a medium that alters social behavior because it reduces social cues about other people's social roles and emotional responses. Lea and his associates (1992) have also re-examined much of the literature on "flaming" in electronic mail. They reinterpret the evidence to suggest that flaming is much less widespread than has been reported, and that it is dependent on the context in which the

deliberately intended inappropriate behavior." The negative effects that she cited were primarily focused on depersonalization—including employee feelings that the company was a less personal place to work, feelings of "invisibility," reduced feedback on job performance, and avoidance of personal contact. She believe that in some cases, these negative effects occur as ironic by-products of people's attempts to avoid potential problems with system use. Markus examines how depersonalization may result from people's strategic behavior, such as using e-mail to send critical messages or forwarding messages to one's supervisor.[5] This paper has far-reaching repercussions for analysts who conceptualize the consequences of new information technologies, such as advanced e-mail systems and groupware.

The studies of Herring and Markus raise important questions that counter our conventional notions of communication on computer networks. In 1993, the *New Yorker* magazine published a famous cartoon of a dog at a keyboard who says, "On the Internet nobody knows if you're a dog." Visual cues, such as how one is dressed (if at all) or a person's physique, do not appear in written e-mail. But Herring tells us how writing style can help reveal a person's gender, in addition to obvious gendered naming conventions, like John and Mary. And Markus shows us that people who know each other at work can effectively communicate many emotional nuances through written e-mail messages. Of course, people can misinterpret e-mail, as they do verbal comments. Many people hope that cyberspace can be "a place" where people develop more humane and democratic conversational relationships. And Kiesler and Sproull's studies suggest that electronic forums and e-mail can help people on the periphery of organizations and communities be more visible. But the evidence is beginning to mount that social relationships in electronic forums mirror many key aspects of face-to-face relationships.

Experiments with Community Life On-Line

Socializing and Romance On-Line

Although the first computer networks and conferencing systems supported communications between people who used them at work, the

---

systems are used. Lea suggests that if flaming depended only upon using e-mail, then people should flame at comparable rates on all bulletin boards, including all of those on Usenet/Internet. However, they observe that flaming is relatively common on some Usenet/Internet boards and comparatively rare on others. Something other than "e-mail use" and "cueless media" must be invoked to explain these differences.

[5] It may also result from social processes that go beyond individuals' rational intentions. Markus carefully compares the abilities of different kinds of explanations to account for the social consequences of e-mail use at HCP. She finds that rational action is a better explanation than technological determinism. But she finds that rational action does not account for important aspects of e-mail use, and that their occurrence is better conceptualized as an emergent social process.

biggest growth now seems to be for people to use them outside of work—for finding friends and lovers, pursuing hobbies, scavenging for investment tips, political organizing, and so on. As in other applications of computerized communication systems, these uses are often the subject of promotional articles. To be sure, many people have found new friendships on some of the nation's 60,000 independent computerized bulletin boards, via information services like CompuServe, Prodigy, and America On-line, or via complex networks like the Internet. In addition, these diverse services have helped spawn diverse discussion groups via CompuServe's forums, Usenet's newsgroups, and the Internet's LISTSERVs.

However, in the United States communities seem to be deteriorating from a complex combination of causes. In the inner cities of big urban centers, many people fear street crime and stay off the streets at night. In the larger suburban and postsuburban areas, many people hardly know their neighbors and "latchkey" children often have little adult contact after school. An African proverb, which says "that it takes a whole village to raise a child," refers to a rich community life with a sense of mutual responsibility that is difficult to find in many new neighborhoods. Real estate developers can rapidly build a tract of 50 or even 3000 homes and give it a homey villagelike name, such as Deerfield. But communities that are based on people caring about and taking responsibility for the well-being of their members are harder to build. Some advocates believe that computer technology in concert with other efforts could play a role in rebuilding community life by improving communication, economic opportunity, civic participation, and education (Schuler, 1994; Civille, Fidelman, and Altobello, 1993).

Before examining some of these politically oriented community networks, it's worth discussing some of the personal considerations that draw people to using computer networks to make personal connections. Without a broad understanding of what kinds of social relationships people miss in their ordinary lives and seek on computer networks, it's too easy to overstate the value of high-minded civic and schoolish uses of computer networks; for example, Usenet, a global replicated-BBS structure offering more than 3500 topic-oriented "newsgroups" on everything from PCs and Novell LANs to book reviews, music, pets, sex, and politics. How much of the Usenet communications is devoted to "high-minded topics" like science and technology, and how much is devoted to recreational topics?

Usenet newsgroups include numerous topics, including discussions among cat lovers (rec.pets.cats), dog lovers (rec.pets.dogs), societal roles and relationships between men and women (soc.men and soc.women), as well as numerous specialized topics about computer technologies, politics, world cultures, hobbies, and so on. These newsgroups are organized into hierarchies: comp.* newsgroups (like comp.sys, intel) focus on computer topics, sci.* on scientific topics, soc.*, alt.*, and misc.* include diverse social topics, and so on.

Table 1. Message Volume for Top 16 Usenet Newsgroup Hierarchies, March 1994

Category	Article Count	Mbytes	Total Percent	Mbytes
alt	214195	835	53.8	962
rec	168235	245	15.8	336
comp	129021	198	12.8	270
soc	69077	150	9.7	192
clari	46707	63	4.1	92
talk	18832	45	3.0	58
misc	29986	43	2.8	60
relcom	44415	41	2.7	71
sci	21748	41	2.7	53
bit	26158	39	2.5	60
news	4942	29	1.9	33
de	9418	23	1.5	29
zer	13323	16	1.1	27
fj	7902	16	1.0	20
ncar	5060	15	1.0	17
cbd	8619	11	0.7	15

One way to get some simple clues about the scope of popular topics is to examine the volume of messages that people write for these various hierarchies. Table 1 shows us that in a two-week period in March 1994, people sent about 129,000 articles (taking about 198 megabytes of space) to newsgroups computer topics. These messages were less than 13% of the file space required for all of the newsgroup messages in that period. However, the alt.*, rec.*, and soc. hierarchies produced and consumed the vast majority of messages and file space.

Usenet newsgroups constitute a small fraction of the world's electronic forums. But other kinds of forums also support interesting social relationships. Computerized BBSs (Bulletin Board Systems) that support "chat modes" sometimes foster special senses of personal trust and intimacy. Though they are less personal than face-to-face communication, they can reduce social distance. The French government's Minitel system has developed a set of "messageries," which enable people to develop friendships, including romances, through simple terminals in their homes (see De Lacy, 1987). The messageries have been popular—and controversial. Because they provide about 30% of Minitel's revenues, the French government has continued to allow them despite substantial controversy.

These systems are especially attractive to people who have trouble getting out of their homes to socialize—people who are handicapped, feel socially insecure, live alone with young children, work at unusual hours, and so on. Such individuals are hardly the only, or even primary, users of these systems. But, for people with restricted social lives, electronic systems may provide truly important avenues to expand their social circles. "On-line" friendships may develop between people who never meet face-to-face (FTF)—friendships that easily survive geographical relocation, and that might not have begun had age, physical appearance, sex, or race been evident from the start.

In Chapter E, "They Call It Cyberlove," Margo Kaufman reports her experiences in meeting others via computer services. Kaufman started out indifferent to computer networks until a friend, Jon, seemed to have disappeared. She found that Jon had simply been living like a hermit to his "physical world friends" while he spent much of his days on-line. Jon drew Margo into his electronic world, and she rapidly became fascinated by the nature of her conversations on America On-line. She felt empowered by being able to send an electronic mail message to president@whitehouse.gov (but unfortunately doesn't report the nature of such an electronic conversation). And she felt that "the lost art of conversation is thriving on-line. I had lengthy discussions about politics, literature, music, and art." While Margo met new friends on-line, Jon confessed "I use the computer in part to avoid conviviality." While Margo began to chat and play games nightly on her computer, she also found some irritating interactions (such as being "hit upon" by some aggressive men.[6] Fortunately, she found a way to click them out of her life. But in the end, Margo found that she was behaving similarly to Jon by ignoring old friends. Unlike Jon, Margo was married and had some "real-life" (RL) social interactions at home. Throughout her essay, Kaufman remains a wry observer of the interplay of life on-line and off-line.

In the next selection, Lindsy Van Gelder's tale of "Alex" discusses the way in which some people have developed unusually intimate friendships on these electronic systems. Although the anonymity afforded by electronic communication can exhilarate and liberate, it also raises new possibilities for abuse. Van Gelder's tale serves as a reminder of this fact since "Alex" impersonated a disabled woman. Obviously, violations of trust are possible in many different arenas; however, the ease of computerized access to a special group of people, along with interactive yet voiceless dialogue, certainly aided Alex in perpetuating his fraud. Some readers may detect a slight moral ambiguity in this particular case, since Alex indisputably did some good as well as harm. Yet, not only were his intentions manipulative and largely self-serving; some of his victims had a strong sense of "identity rape" as well.

Community Building through Computer Networking

Kaufman's and Van Gelder's articles help sensitize us to some of the nuances of life on-line. And they set a more realistic stage for discussing

---

[6] Also see "Men, Women and Computers" (Kantrowitz, 1994) about the ways that women find men to be sexually aggressive on computer nets.

community networking than do articles that examine only the joys of life on-line. These articles can stimulate us to question who will be drawn to spend a lot of their time communicating through computer networks, and whether extensive networking will enhance or undermine the vestiges of existing communities.

Cyberspace symbolizes a new American frontier, full of unexplored opportunities that stimulate high levels of excitement as well as fears of chaotic semiorganized activity and even personal harm. New frontiers attract adventurers, speculators, and even con artists. Taming a frontier is a kind of work that favors people who are bold and action oriented rather than timid or reflective.[7] Community has been a kind of question in the United States, as well as an answer. Sociologist Claude Fischer (1991) notes that discussions of community in the United States are marked with unacknowledged tensions. This is a country inhabited by people with diverse religious and linguistic traditions. Americans have been tradition-ally mobile. And a deep ideology of individualism makes community sound like an oppressive organization as well as a romantically warm concept. These contradictions are brought forth, but not resolved in Howard Rheingold's book *The Virtual Community: Homesteading on the Electronic Frontier.*

There have been several community networking experiments, including high-profile systems in Cleveland (Ohio), Santa Monica (California), and Blacksburg (Virginia). The following description of the Blacksburg Electronic Village typifies the enthusiasm of the experimenters for the potential role of widely available computer networks or conferencing systems for enriching community life:

> The Blacksburg Electronic Village is a project to link an entire town in Southwestern Virginia with a 21st century telecommunications infrastructure. This infrastructure will bring a useful set of information services and interactive communications facilities into the daily activities of citizens and businesses. The project will encourage and nurture the development of applications and of delivery mechanisms for services designed for everyday life. The goal of the project is to enhance the quality of people's lives by electronically linking the residents of the community to each other, to world-wide networks, and to information resources in new and creative ways. The entire community of Blacksburg is being used as a real-life laboratory to develop a prototype "residential street plan" for the country-wide "data superhighway" being discussed as a high priority on the national agenda. The project is being conducted so that its most successful aspects can rapidly be replicated in future electronic villages in the state of Virginia and elsewhere in the United States.

---

[7] For a frank view of the frame of mind of America's early frontiersmen, see W. J. Cash's *The Mind of the South* (especially pp. 6–7 and 11–20).

The prototype in Blacksburg will exemplify four characteristics essential to a successful electronic village:

(1) including an entire community to achieve a "critical mass" of users,
(2) focusing on interactions between people rather than focusing on particular technologies,
(3) providing applications tailored for each type of user, and
(4) implementing the project on a timely basis, so that community networking becomes a fundamental consideration in the vision and planning of the nationwide networking infrastructure. (Vision Statement of the Blacksburg Electronic Village, n.d.)

Because of the tremendous power it gives to the individual, community networking can have the same revolutionizing effect in residential life and ordinary businesses as widespread telephone service has had. The key to the success of the telephone has been the concept of universal access. The foundation upon which the Blacksburg Electronic Village rests is to have a network connection available for every home, business, and classroom in the community. Furthermore, adequate network access equipment must be available to allow use of the network on a routine basis. Ordinary computers can be used for data and some types of image transfer, and TVs, VCRs, and camcorders serve as video transfer devices for optional video capabilities. A high level of service coverage and participation for data access is as important in community networking as it is in the telephone system. Unless a "critical mass" of people possess and access their network connections regularly, they may choose other methods of communication in situations when, for example, an Electronic Mail message is the quickest and most efficient method. Also, the more commonplace the facility, the more readily each user will share his or her knowledge about how to access a useful database search facility or in mentioning the availability of the latest "hot" discussion group about a current event in the community. (Vision Statement of the Blacksburg Electronic Village, n.d.)

In the next selection, "Yakety-Yak, Do Talk Back!: PEN, the Nation's First Publicly Funded Electronic Network, Makes a Difference in Santa Monica," Joan Van Tassel examines early experiences with PEN. Van Tassel describes how PEN's use met many of its founders' hopes that it would enhance political participation in Santa Monica. Even homeless people were able to use public access terminals to organize on their own behalf. But not everyone was enthusiastic about PEN. Van Tassel mentions some aspects of PEN's use that undermined a sense of community:

netbozo takeovers (massive missives from a few residents who dominate the system), excessive flaming (no surprise to cyberspace denizens), and topic digression. Some PEN users, including several public officials, withdrew from PEN conferences because of what they perceived as vicious, unwarranted personal attacks from flamers.

She also quotes a Santa Monica resident who wrote:

"The city probably spends $200,000 a year on PEN. There are 85,000 residents, 5,000 users, and 150 heavy users. Why should the taxpayer pay so some crazy wacko can write 'fuck you' to the council members when he goes off his meds?"

Not only is PEN heavily used by a tiny fraction of residents, but the men and women who use PEN represented a distinctive segment of Santa Monica's residents who make more money, are more likely to be male, and are more likely to be college graduates. They are also much more politically active than the typical Santa Monica resident. Van Tassel's article helps identify the complexities of community building on public access computer networks and the nuances of success and failure.

The next selection (Chapter H), "Taboo, Consensus, and the Challenge of Democracy in an Electronic Forum" by Julian Dibbell, is also a study of the complexities of building electronic communities. Superficially, the article is about an offensive cyber-rape that took place in a fantasy computer world. But Dibbell examines the ways that groups define their norms and forms of social control when some of their members are offended by some violation. It is easiest to be permissive and tolerant in both real life and in electronic forums when no one is offended or harmed by anyone else's behavior.

It is common for groups that meet in electronic forums to debate about the nature of behavior that participants find to be acceptable to them. For example, Usenet newsgroups periodically debate about the level of public personal criticism that is acceptable, the kinds of message content that are appropriate for a specific forum, and so on. In particular work groups, there can be debates about the extent to which "personal electronic mail" can be shared with others.

Dibbell examines a group that is meeting in a MUD (Multi-User Dungeon or, sometimes, a Multi-view), which was developed by Pavel Curtis, a computer scientist at Xerox's Palo Alto Research Center, and made accessible over the Internet.

> Participants (usually called players) have the appearance of being situated in an artificially-constructed place that also contains those other players who are connected at the same time. Players can communicate easily with each other in real time. This virtual gathering place has many of the social attributes of other places, and many of the usual social mechanisms operate there. (Curtis, 1992)

Although MUDs are described by Dibbell and Curtis as being used for fantasy games, they are also being explored as formats for on-line conferences and digital libraries (Henderson, 1994). Dibbell's vivid article is a superb account of the ways that some participants in a particular MUD (called LambdaMOO) observed a violation of their unstated norms, felt the violation as a real experience in their lives, and tried to articulate principles for punishing the violator (by expulsion/execution). Dibbell is specially sensitive to the tenuous relationships between everyday life and the experiences of people in electronic forums. After describing how a character known as Mr. Bungle cyber-raped two other participants in LambdaMOO, he notes:

> These particulars, as I said, are unambiguous. But they are far from simple, for the simple reason that every set of facts in virtual reality (or VR, as the locals abbreviate it) is shadowed by a second, complicating set: the "real-life" facts. And although a certain tension invariably buzzes in the gap between the hard, prosaic RL facts and their more fluid, dreamy VR counterparts, the dissonance in the Bungle case is striking. No hideous clowns or trickster spirits appear in the RL version of the incident, no voodoo dolls or wizard guns, indeed no rape at all as any RL court of law has yet defined it. The actors in the drama were university students for the most part, and they sat rather undramatically before computer screens the entire time, their only actions a spidery flitting of fingers across standard QWERTY keyboards. No bodies touched. Whatever physical interaction occurred consisted of a mingling of electronic signals sent from sites spread out between New York City and Sydney, Australia. Those signals met in LambdaMOO, certainly, just as the hideous clown and the living room party did, but what was LambdaMOO after all? Not an enchanted mansion or anything of the sort—just a middlingly complex database, maintained for experimental purposes inside a Xerox Corporation research computer in Palo Alto and open to public access via the Internet.

Even so, people who manipulated characters in a database began to identify with them, and began to struggle with their rules for creating a civil society for LambdaMOO's participants. One ironic part of the process was that, after substantial deliberations, LambdaMOO's designer and operator *imposed* a form of democracy on its participants. This article is much less about sex in cyberspace than a haunting contribution to the debates about social relationships and democracy in electronic forums.

How Freely Should Information Flow in Computer Networks?

Part VI examines issues that arise from the fact that information can be used to tighten social control. But the *control* of information also raises important problems. Information control (censorship), traditionally discussed in the context of print and broadcast media, has taken on an important new dimension in the age of the computer. Here the issue is freedom of people's abilities to send and receive information on computer networks. Questions about who controls information in electronic networks have not been resolved in any absolute sense.

Presently, there is a significant mobilization to draw people onto e-mail and computer conferencing systems to communicate "at work" and "after work." Most of these systems are privately owned, either by employers, or by firms that sell conferencing services (i.e., Prodigy, America On-line, CompuServe). The operators of both kinds of systems claim the right to monitor and control communications content, and rely upon eighteenth-century conceptions of private property to ground their claims. In addition, there is a movement to expand "civic nets" whose explicit aims are to foster lively discussions about local politics (Schuler, 1994; Van Tassel, 1994). Although the operators of these systems are usually much more respectful of participants' privacy and freedom of expression than are the operators of some of the private systems, there is no commonly accepted normative framework for these systems.

The shift from face-to-face, paper, and telephone to computer-mediated communications makes people's communications more persistent, permeable, less controllable, and more traceable. The persistence of messages sometimes puzzles people. Electronic communication can appear to people as a transient conversational medium, even though the messages usually have the persistence of archived text.[8] Electronic forums are often permeable. Messages stored in e-mail or conferencing systems can be read verbatim unobtrusively. In fact, most reading is unobtrusive to the message sender (and is more like paper mail than face-to-face conversations or even phone calls).

People lose control over who may read ("overhear") their electronic conversation. Overheard conversations can be repeated, but listeners are often aware that they are learning hearsay rather than a verbatim account. Even taped phone messages can usually be heard by only a few other people. In contrast, computerized messages can be copied verbatim and rapidly sent to hundreds or thousands of potential readers. Electronic messages are often more traceable than their paper or verbal counterparts. Face-to-face conversations are transitory, and leave no trace of their existence for someone who walks into the conversational space after the discussants have left. In contrast, letters may be dated, and indicate to whom they were addressed. Phone calls may be identified by the phone numbers, dates, times, and duration of calls. (Cellular phones may identify a party's location.) E-mail messages may also be marked by their time, addressing, size, and so on.

The operator of an e-mail system or conferencing system has tremendous surveillance capabilities, and censoring capabilities, if they choose to exercise them. In practice, surveillance has been infrequent, but occasionally surprises participants and chills important discussions.

Electronic mail and the records of conferences are often explicitly contested terrain. Today, firms are being encouraged by both the apostles of "virtual corporations" (e.g., Davidow and Malone, 1992) and the federal

---

[8] Of course, messages can be deleted, sometimes wiped out, and people sometimes inadvertently lose messages.

government to develop and institutionalize telecommuting. E-mail use has become routine at most large United States corporations and many smaller ones. Some organizations have issued specific policies, but these vary considerably.[9] Some companies, such as Pacific Bell, Nordstrom's, Eastman Kodak, and United Parcel Service, inform their staff that e-mail will be monitored because it is company property and it is in the corporate interest to do so. Other firms, including Hallmark Cards, Warner Brothers, Citibank, and General Motors, have established policies that focus on employee privacy rights and better data security measures (Cappel, 1993).

There are a few documented cases in which supervisors felt threatened by employees' criticisms via e-mail, and had them fired. Cappel (1993) summarizes two of the most visible cases:

> In the Epson case, Shoars, a former e-mail administrator at the company's Torrance, California site, raised objections when she discovered her boss was routinely reading messages which passed through a gateway between the company's internal e-mail system and its external MCI communications e-mail service. Shortly after, Shoars was terminated, when the company claimed she opened an MCI Mail account for her personal use. Shoars filed two suits over this issue: a $1 million wrongful termination suit and a $75 million class action lawsuit on behalf of herself and others at the site who claim that the company invaded their privacy by reading their e-mail messages. In January 1991, a California judge dismissed the lawsuits, ruling that the state's telephone wiretapping law (which the plaintiff had alleged was violated) had nothing to do with electronic mail. . . . (Cappel, 1993)

> In the Nissan case, two employees, who were hired to set up and run an e-mail network between the company and its Infiniti dealers, were threatened with dismissal when their supervisor discovered by monitoring their e-mail that they allegedly made some disparaging remarks about her and the company. When the two employees filed a grievance stating that their privacy had been violated, one employee was allegedly fired and the other given the opportunity to resign. The case of these employees was also dismissed by a California court, with Nissan successfully arguing that since it owns the computer system it has the right to read anything on it. (Cappel, 1993)

Zuboff's report on a related case may dim unbridled enthusiasms and lead us to wonder about the conditions most likely to generate these transformations. When a group of about 130 professional women formed a private conference that threatened male managers, participation was discouraged

---

[9] The principal law protecting the privacy of e-mail is the Electronic Communications Privacy Act of 1986 (ECPA). ECPA is a federal law that extends to e-mail the protections long afforded telephone conversations. The ECPA makes it a serious crime to read, use, or disclose another person's electronic communications when they are routed outside of one's premises, such as a home or office, without justification. The ECPA does not extend privacy protections to on-premise communications, such as interoffice e-mail, when the computer/communications system does not extend off premises (see Cappel, 1993).

by upper managers and many participants dropped out (Zuboff, 1988:382–383).

Should workers have significant rights to treat their electronic communications as private? Why shouldn't Nissan's argument that an e-mail system is private property, and thus messages are Nissan's property, guide our social norms (see Brown, 1994)? After all, in other workplace contexts such as telephone call monitoring, the courts have previously upheld the right of an employer to monitor where "a valid business reason" exists. Langdon Winner portrays this position that privileges private property in hauntingly stark terms:

> For those who manage the systems of computerized work, the structures and processes offer a wonderfully effective means of control. Here is an electronic equivalent of Jeremy Bentham's Panopticon, the ingenious circular design that allowed the guardians of a prison, hospital, or school to observe every inmate under totally panoptic scrutiny. The system is, of course, totally opaque. They are allowed to see only what the program allows. Closely watched and clocked, workers within the city of icons may find even fewer chances to express their individuality or participate in decisions than they did in the old-fashioned office or factory. When space is intangible, where do workers organize? (Winner, 1992)

Increasingly, people are being encouraged (or channeled) into communicating via electronic mail at work rather than by phone or face-to-face by private firms (see Markus, 1994) and recently by the Federal government (IITF, 1994). It's hard to argue that this shift would best serve the public good if it were to lead to more panoptic workplaces and a depletion of social capital. As with the on-line services and community networks, the most appropriate policies would be those that give employees significant freedoms to exercise free speech and rights of association in their electronic workplaces. In some cases, they may be working from home, and only their electronic images will pass through the disks at work.

Electronic communications systems can encourage the formation of diverse groups. But managers are likely to eradicate electronic groups that threaten their power, except in those special organizations—like universities and R&D labs—where there are strong norms against censorship.

Universities, for example, usually try to maintain norms of openness, and are usually permissive in allowing information that is not illegal to be posted on publicly accessible bulletin boards. However, if a posting offends certain groups, people will clamor to have it removed. Many political, religious, ethnic, and occupational jokes are offensive to members of those groups. The line between humor and libel, "fair humor" and cruelty, is not finite.

In February 1988, the administration at Stanford University blocked access to an electronic bulletin board posting from Usenet—an internationally distributed electronic forum with a wide readership. The Stanford administration's action was stimulated by complaints about a racially in-sensitive joke that appeared on a Usenet newsgroup. Similar episodes have occurred at other universities—and administrators have acted in various ways: from removing postings, leaving them untouched, or removing them when people complain and then restoring them when others com-plain about censorship! At Stanford, the administrative action was highly selective, blocking access to the files containing the allegedly offensive jokes, but not interfering with an *un*moderated joke forum, or with many other forums (including a few that allowed students to discuss their use of illegal drugs, or to exchange information about sexual techniques and nude beaches).[10] In response, Stanford's Computer Science faculty voted to treat Stanford's computer systems with the same kind of academic freedom as the university library and influenced the administration to restore the controversial newsgroup.

In October 1994 controversy erupted when the administration of Car-negie Mellon University (CMU) in Pittsburgh, Pennsylvania attempted to ban about eighty sex-oriented Usenet newsgroups from campus comput-ers, including the alt.sex.* hierarchy, rec.arts.erotica, and alt.binaries.pic-tures.erotica. CMU's administrators felt that Pennsylvania law and recent court rulings forbade them to knowingly distribute sexually explicit mate-rials to minors. Many of CMU's students are under age 18, and the university administrators wanted to obey the applicable laws. The an-nouncement noted that CMU intended to support free speech, and that the only criteria for censoring computerized newsgroups "is that either the intended purpose for which it was established or its primary use (majority of the posts) makes it illegal for Computing Services to provide access to the bulletin board" (Kuszewski, 1994). The administration's actions were im-mediately protested by students, faculty, and nationally visible groups, including the American Civil Liberties Union and the Electronic Frontier Foundation. How can anyone fault CMU's administrators for wanting to obey their state laws? The questions arise in interpreting the extent to which CMU is bound by their interpretation of Pennsylvania state law. For example, the university library and bookstore are likely to contain erotic novels by famous authors such as Henry Miller, Anais Nin, and Erica Jong. CMU's administrators were not about to censor their library and bookstore. In addition, there are questions about the legal status of computerized bulletin boards.

> At the core of the CMU dispute is a question that goes beyond the campus and could touch every media and entertainment company that wants to do business on the info highway: to what extent can the operators of interactive media be held responsible for the material that moves through their systems? Are they common carriers, like the phone companies, which must ignore the

---

[10] See the discussion and debates about this episode in Dunlop and Kling (1991:325–326).

content of the messages? Are they like TV stations, whose broadcasts are monitored by the government for fairness and suitability? Or are they like bookstores, which the courts have ruled can't be expected to review the content of every title on their shelves? And what happens when that content hops over borders and lands in a different city—or country—whose laws and community standards may differ? (Phillip, 1994)

These issues were hotly debated on the Usenet newsgroups comp. org.eff.talk, alt.comp.acad-freedom.talk, and alt.censorship. In Chapter I, "Applying Library Intellectual Freedom Principles to Public and Academic Computers," Carl Kadie, who moderates alt.comp.acad-freedom.news, characterizes eight additional cases where someone attempted to censor a newsgroup for its contents.[11] Kadie examines each of these cases in light of specific academic freedom guidelines that have been articulated by the American Library Association. Kadie is a strong advocate of free speech and encourages the people and organizations who manage electronic forums not to censor messages and files that some people may find offensive. The counterpoint position argues that there are some materials, such as racist hate literature, that are so damaging that bulletin board operators should have a right (or even a moral obligation) to be able to remove them.

Communication, Persuasion, and Influence in Scholarly Communities

The Internet, which is often viewed as a symbol and prototype for new data superhighways, was developed and refined in specific academic and closely related R&D communities. We now turn to some controversies about the ways that electronic media are changing communities of scholars. Even though a good deal of university research involves long hours of solitary work, research takes on a special meaning within the social worlds that encourage it, utilize it, and reward (or ignore) it.

Electronic publishing has attracted an interesting group of enthusiasts who view them as virtually inevitable. Richard Lanham (1994) argues that electronic publishing will erode the importance of the codex book (a collection of pages bound between two covers in a fixed sequence) as "the operating system" of the humanities. Lanham suggests that the digitization of textual, audio, and visual communications will encourage reorganizations of knowledge via hypertext. Common storage representations, transmission protocols, and manipulation algorithms will enable a confluence of data not previously achievable with analog paradigms. In Lanham's

---

[11] A hypertext version of this document, with links to many of the on-line references, is available via WWW/Mosaic from the Computers and Academic Freedom Archive as http:// www.eff.org/CAF/cfp94.kadie.html.

view, this technological capability makes inevitable a future in which the reader *is* the author and where copyright law is irrelevant:

> Texts are not fixed in print but projected on a phosphor screen in volatile form. They can be amended, emended, rewritten, reformatted, set in another typeface, all with a few keystrokes. The whole system of cultural authority we inherited from Renaissance Humanism thus evaporates, literally, at a stroke. The "Great Book," the authoritative text, was built on the fixity of print technology. That fixity no longer operates. The reader defined by print—the engrossed admiration of the humanist scholar reading Cicero—now becomes quite another person. He can quarrel with the text, and not marginally, or next year in another book, but right now, integrally. The reader thus becomes an author. Author and authority are both transformed. . . .
>
> Let us consider the dreariest textbook of all, the Freshman Composition Handbook. You all know them. Heavy. Shiny coated paper. Pyroxylin, peanut-butter-sandwich-proof cover. Imagine instead an online program available to everyone who teaches, and everyone who takes, the course. The apoplexy that comp handbooks always generate now finds more than marginal expression. Stupid examples are critiqued as such; better ones are found. Teachers contribute their experience on how the book works, or doesn't work, in action. The textbook, rather than fixed in an edition, is a continually changing, evolutionary document. It is fed by all the people who use it, and continually made and remade by them. (Lanham, 1994:161–162)

Lanham explores this exciting imagery of people communicating differently through electronic reading and writing as a lively alternative to the relatively static world of traditional printed books. Lanham doesn't examine how these electronic academic communities will develop in practice. For example, imagine that you had an electronic copy of his article, and that you disagreed with some of his arguments. How could you communicate your disagreement to other people who also have his paper on-line? Would you have to post your commentaries in a centralized archive? Could you send them as messages throughout a network? The mechanics of making electronic communication matters as much in the details as do the mechanics of reading a paper book and commenting privately in the margins. Further, Lanham doesn't ask whether people will continue to want portable paper books for leisure reading in bed or on a beach—and thus paper and electronic versions of many books will coexist. Despite these limitations, Lanham forcefully opens deep questions about the nature of humanistic inquiry and the relations between readers and authors in a world of electronic writing.

There is a fundamental change in the world of scholarly publishing and libraries as they shift from paper-based to electronic formats. Today, few prolific academic authors peck away at typewriters. Although virtually all academic journal articles and books are now produced in electronic form, the majority are sooner or later printed on paper for sale or distribution to their readers. It is difficult to create forums for lively discussion and debates in the paper journals because it can take months from the time that a letter is sent to the editor for it to appear in print. So, most scholarly journals publish research papers, but rarely publish debates about their credibility and importance. These discussions used to take place through correspondence between colleagues and face-to-face at conferences and in special seminars.

The driving images of electronic publishing and digital libraries converge in focusing on ways that an author's keystrokes (and thoughts) can be rapidly transmitted to potential readers without the required mediation of paper formats, even if there is significant editorial structuring and filtering. An even richer set of images rests on expanding the scope of scholarly discussion by using diverse electronic forums to support active dialogues and debates. Today, there are thousands of specialized electronic scholarly discussion groups that communicate worldwide through electronic mail via Usenet newsgroup, LISTSERVs, and ad hoc mailing lists. This trend was heralded by computer scientist Peter Denning (1987) as a "new paradigm for science" in which busy scholars could better cope with the torrent of new specialized publications.

One area in which electronic publishing is particularly well organized is high-energy physics. Physicists follow work in other labs to build on others' research. But they are also fiercely competitive (Traweek, 1988). Major awards and rewards, such as Nobel Prizes and memberships to the National Academy of Sciences, are granted to those who have been the first to be credited with new observations or to develop new theories and paradigms. Like other scientists, physicists circulate early versions of their articles (preprints) to colleagues. Because academic publication can take one to two years from the date an article is first submitted to a scholarly journal for publication, physicists who work on a research frontier avidly read their colleagues' preprints. Hepnet, an electronic database of preprints that is accessible over the Internet, allows high-energy physicists to document their claims to fame with preprints unambiguously time-stamped and rapidly accessible worldwide.

In the selection, "The Electronic Journal: What, Whence, and When?," Ann Okerson argues that electronic journals should become an important form of scholarly communication. Okerson characterizes Hepnet, whose database contains over 200,000 publications, as one of the most interesting experiments in electronic publishing. Physicists also rely on traditional paper journals to review their preprints for scientific merit and to publish them in a paper format for circulation to libraries and other subscribers. High-energy physicists publish in both electronic and paper formats, and do it in a way that does not challenge conventional beliefs about the legitimacy of paper-based publication.

The electronic journals (e-journals) available through the Internet come closest to fitting the image of direct communication between authors of systematic studies and their readers. In the last few years, e-journals have appeared in diverse fields, from avant-garde cultural studies to medicine and even to medieval studies. Okerson's article first appeared in an e-journal, *The Public-Access Computer Systems Review,* and I found it when I was browsing the journal's electronic archives. These e-journal are currently the subject of substantial debate by scholars and librarians (Fuller, 1995; Harnad, 1995; Kling and Covi, 1995). Some scholars, like Ann Okerson, see them as a new form that will bloom in the twenty-first century. But Okerson acknowledges that e-journals are criticized for lax intellectual standards and for requiring readers to work with clumsy computer technologies.

I have found that many scholars (especially those who have never knowingly read an e-journal) are confused about their character. For example, some academics assume that articles in e-journals are not subject to the kind of stringent peer review that characterizes the highest-quality paper journals. In fact, some journals, in paper or electronic form, strictly review each article. Other paper journals and e-journals use less restrictive reviews. And to complicate matters, some journals such as *The Journal of Artificial Intelligence Research* blend e-journal and paper formats by publishing each article electronically when it is accepted, but also publish a single paper issue once a year that librarians (and others) can purchase to file on bookshelves. *The Journal of Artificial Intelligence Research* doesn't signal its electronic publishing in its name, and it works as a stealth e-journal (Kling and Covi, 1995).

Librarians observe numerous practical problems when academics try to work flexibly with today's e-journals (Entlich, 1993). They might be rapidly disseminated and searched on-line. But long e-journal articles are hard to read in many common workplaces unless they are printed on paper. These places include airplane flights, especially during landing and takeoff! More important, publishing exclusively in electronic formats has yet to become truly legitimate in major research universities (Lougee, 1994; Beniger, 1991). And few university libraries have explicit collection development policies that enable them to systematically archive specific e-journals. In Chapter K, "I Heard It through the Internet," library professional Walt Crawford argues that people who find their news and reading material via the Internet must be specially skeptical about the sources of various files, their authenticity, and their veracity. Crawford, who has served as president of the Library Information Technology Association, is alert to the opportunities that the Internet opens up and to the complexities of relying on electronic materials. Traditionally, publishing houses, editors, and librarians acted as gatekeepers and curators. Almost any Internet account holder can set up shop as a publisher and bypass the institutional apparatus of publishers and librarians to reach a large potential readership. This form of institutional bypass surgery has many charms: it facilitates rapid communication, and it enables authors who have novel viewpoints to reach potentially large audiences. But it assumes that readers are sophisticated enough to make their own judgments of the veracity of materials.

On March 23, 1989, chemists Martin Fleischmann and B. Stanley Pons announced that they had sustained a cold fusion nuclear reaction at the University of Utah, using relatively simple laboratory apparatus. Almost as noteworthy as their announcement was the way it was made. Rather than following the usual protocol of deferring public discussion until publication of experimental details in a scientific journal, Fleischmann and Pons called a news conference. Within hours scientists worldwide were apprised of the Utah claim, and fax machines and electronic mail networks were soon abuzz with copies of a Fleischmann and Pons paper, which in turn generated hundreds of e-mail responses and discussions of details. It took several years for the scientific community to conclude that Fleischmann and Pons's experiments and claims were basically not credible. Today, a scientist seeking publicity could promptly announce her or his results with a web page or a paper sent to a LISTSERV.

More serious would be the problems of intentional deception. Crawford (Chapter K) notes:

> Anyone with an Internet connection and a decent graphics toolkit can create pages just as impressive as anything from the Library of Congress or NASA— but without any regard for factuality or meaning. You don't even need good taste to build impressive presentations; modern software will provide professional defaults so that you just add your erroneous or misleading text and graphics.

Crawford doesn't suggest that filtering be reimposed (but he does suggest that readers learn to be aware and be wary of what they download).

In the next selection (Chapter L), "Technology, Scholarship, and the Humanities," Vartan Gregorian, president of Brown University, examines the effects of electronic communication and electronic publishing in terms of the production of knowledge and teaching in universities. In contrast with Denning (1987) he observes that computer nets help academic specialists retain and even refine their narrowness. He argues that,

> We must rise above the obsession with quantity of information and speed of transmission, and recognize that the key issue for us is our ability to organize this information once it has been amassed—to assimilate it, find meaning in it, and assure its survival for use by generations to come.

Gregorian notes that specialization has been a master trend in universities for over one hundred years. Computers did not cause specialization. But he notes that "Information technologies also contribute to the fragmentation of knowledge by allowing us to organize ourselves into ever more specialized communities." Gregorian makes some rather harsh observations about electronic communities in academic specialties:

> Are you developing an interest in exotic insects, rare minerals, or an obscure poet? With little effort you can use electronic mail and conferencing to find several others, in Japan, Peru, or Bulgaria, with whom you can communicate every day, creating your own small, self-confirming world of theory, technique, and methodology. McLuhan's prediction that electronic communication would create a global village is wrong in my opinion. What is being created is less like a village than an entity that reproduces the worst aspects of urban life: the ability to retreat into small communities of the like-minded,

safe not only from unnecessary interactions with those whose ideas and attitudes are not like our own, but safe from having to relate our interests and results to other communities.

Gregorian's harsh criticisms would be most apt when scholars (and other professionals) work primarily on-line from their homes or offices. And some faculty do adopt these hermitlike workstyles. But universities also create face-to-face forums that bring together people with diverse viewpoints—invited speakers, committees to create or review curricula, interdisciplinary research institutes, faculty seminars, and so on. Gregorian's dark vision is an interesting warning. But it may also be a by-product of university administrations that reward extreme specialization and that don't develop lively forums and formats for discussions among their faculty. In those cases, a special risk for urban universities with dispersed faculty, life on-line may become much more seductive than life on-campus.

When Do Electronic Forums Computer Enhance or Undermine Community Life?

In the final selection of Part V, "On the Road Again?" Richard Sclove and Jeffrey Scheuer examine the metaphor of information highways by discussing the social effects of the interstate highway system on community life in the United States. Sclove and Scheuer note that the interstate highways were not constructed because the public demanded them. Rather, a coalition of powerful business firms lobbied Congress to create them. Although they expanded Americans' sense of the open road and space to roam, they were sometimes routed through cities in ways that divided neighborhoods. They became the gateways to regional shopping malls that killed many lively downtowns. Today, interstates are clogged with commuter traffic during urban rush hours.

Electronic services might also compete with today's public places, if only because few people can (or will) simultaneously log in to an on-line service while simultaneously participating in a face-to-face group meeting outside their homes. If the enthusiasts for electronic communities and virtual communities had their visions come true, electronic services would be so active they could shrivel many existing traditional face-to-face forums. They would be like the lively regional mall drawing trade away from the old downtown (Kling, Olin, and Poster, 1995). Sclove and Scheuer remind us that, although highways connect places, they don't always connect people in ways that build community. And they suggest that the best designs are likely to come when people who are affected by them can participate actively in their conceptualization. It is ironic, but it may require the political action of strong communities to strengthen their citizens' social ties through electronic connections.

Sources

Crawford, Walt (1994). "I Heard It Through the Internet." Published as "And Only Half of What You See, Part III: I Heard It Through the Internet." *The Public-Access Computer Systems Review*, 5, No. 6, 27–30. [Or, use the following URL: gopher:// info.lib.uh.edu:70/00/articles/e-journals/uhlibrary/pacsreview/v5/n6/crwford. 5n6.]

Dibbell, Julian (1993). "Taboo, Consensus, and the Challenge of Democracy in Electronic Communities." Originally published as, "A Rape in Cyberspace, or How an Evil Clown, a Haitian Trickster Spirit, Two Wizards, and a Cast of Dozens Turned a Database Into a Society." *The Village Voice* (December 21), 36–42.

Gregorian, Vartan (1994). "Information Technology, Scholarship and the Humanities." Originally titled "Technology, Scholarship and the Humanities: Implications of the Electronic Age." *Leonardo* (27)2, 155–164.

Herring, Susan C. (1993). "Gender and Democracy In Computer-Mediated Communication." *Electronic Journal of Communication/REC*, Vol. 3, No. 2 (not paginated). [EJC is a peer-reviewed journal distributed electronically. Copies of articles are available through the "Comserve" service at vm.its.rpi.edu.]

Kadie, Carl M. (1994). "Applying Library Intellectual Freedom Principles to Public and Academic Computers." *Proceedings for the Conference on Computers, Freedom, and Privacy '94* (March).

Kaufman, Margo (1993). "They Call it Cyberlove." *Los Angeles Times Magazine* (September 12), 45–62.

Markus, M. Lynne (1994). "Finding a 'Happy Medium': Explaining the Negative Effects of Electronic Communication on Social Life at Work." *ACM Transactions on Information Systems*, (12)2(April), 119–149.

Okerson, Ann (1991). "The Electronic Journal: What, Whence, and When?" *The Public-Access Computer Systems Review* (2)1, 5–24.

Sclove, Richard and Jeffrey Scheuer. "On the Road Again: If Information Highways Are Anything Like Interstate Highways—Watch Out!" Part V, Chapter M.

Sproull, Lee, and Sara Kiesler (1991). "Increasing Personal Connections." *Connections: New Ways of Working in the Networked Organization*. MIT Press, Cambridge.

Van Gelder, Lindsy (1985). "The Strange Case of the Electronic Lover: A Real-Life Story of Deception, Seduction, and Technology." *Ms* (14)4:(October), 94, 99, 101–104, 117, 123, 124.

Van Tassel, Joan (1994). "Yakety-Yak, Do Talk Back: PEN, the Nation's First Publicly Funded Electronic Network, Makes a Difference in Santa Monica." *Wired*, (2)1(January), 78–80.

References

Aydin, Carolyn E., and Ronald E. Rice (1992). "Bringing Social Worlds Together: Computers as Catalysts for New Interactions in Health Care Organizations." *Journal of Health and Social Behavior*, 33(2),168–185.

Beniger, James R. (1988). "Information Society and Global Science." *The Annals of the American Academy of Political and Social Science*, 495(January, 1988),14–28. [Also in Charles Dunlop and Rob Kling (eds.) (1991). *Computerization and Controversy: Value Conflicts and Social Choices*. Academic Press, San Diego.]

Bikson, Tora K., J. D. Eveland, and Barbara A. Gutek (1989). "Flexible Interactive Technologies for Multi-Person Tasks: Current Problems and Future Prospects," in M. H. Olson (ed.), *Technological Support for Work Group Collaboration*. Erlbaum, Hillsdale, NJ.

Brown, Bonnie (1994). "Companies Own E-mail and Can Monitor It." *Computerworld* 28(26)(June 27),135–136.

Cappel, James J. (1993). "Closing the E-mail Privacy Gap: Employer Monitoring of Employee E-mail." *Journal of Systems Management*, 44(12)(Dec), 6–11.

Cash, W. J. (1991). *The Mind of the South*. Vintage Books, New York.

Child, J., and R. Loveridge (1990). *Information Technology in European Services— Towards A Microelectronic Future*. Blackwell, Oxford.

Civille, Richard, Miles Fidelman, and John Altobello (1993). A National Strategy for Civic Networking: A Vision of Change. Center for Civic Networking. [Available at URL: gopher://hey.internet.com:2400/00/ssnational_strat/national_strategy. txt.]

Curtis, Pavel (1992). "Mudding: Social Phenomena in Text-Based Virtual Realities." *Proceedings from DIACS*. Berkeley, California (May 2–3). CPSR, Palo Alto.

Davidow, William H., and Michael S. Malone (1992). *The Virtual Corporation: Structuring and Revitalizing the Corporation for the 21st Century*. HarperCollins Publishers, New York.

De Lacy, Justine (1987). "The Sexy Computer." *The Atlantic*, 20(1)(July), 18–26.

Denning, Peter J. (1987). "A New Paradigm for Science." *American Scientist* (75)(November–December), 572–573.

Dunlop, Charles, and Rob Kling (eds.) (1991). *Computerization and Controversy: Value Conflicts and Social Choices*. Academic Press, San Diego.

Entlich, Richard (1993). *Networked Delivery of Full-Text Electronic Journals: Diverse Options, Shared Limitations*. University of Illinois, Urbana.

Fischer, Claude (1991). "Ambivalent Communities: How Americans Understand Their Localities," in Alan Wolfe (ed.), *America at Century's End*, pp. 79–90. University of California Press, Berkeley.

Fuller, Steve (1995). Cyberplatonism: An Inadequate Constitution for the Republic of Science. *The Information Society* 11(4).

Harnad, Stevan (1995). The Postgutenberg Galaxy: How to Get There from Here. *The Information Society* 11(4).

Heintz, Lisa (1992). "Consequences of New Electronic Communications Technologies for Knowledge Transfer in Science: Policy Implications." Office of Technology Assessment (OTA) contractor report. Congress of the United States, Washington, D.C.

Henderson, T. (1994). "Moving Towards A Virtual Reference Service." *Reference Librarian*, 41–42, 173–184.

Herring, Susan C. (1993). "Gender and Democracy in Computer-Mediated Communications." *Electronic Journal of Communication* 3(2). [EJC is a peer-reviewed journal distributed electronically that is available through the "Comserve" service at vm.its.rpi.edu.]

Hess, Bradford, Lee Sproull, Sara Kiesler, and John Walsh (1993). "Returns to Science: Computer Networks in Oceanography." *CACM*, 36(8)(August), 90–101.

Information Infrastructure Task Force (1994). Promoting Telecommuting: An Application of the National Information Infrastructure. (Sept. 7). Washington, D.C. [Available at URL: gopher://iitfcat.nist.gov:95/0/.catitem2/telecom.txt.]

Jones, Steven G. (1995). "Understanding Community in the Information Age," in Steven G. Jones (ed.), *CyberSociety: Computer-mediated Communication and Community.* Sage Publications, Thousand Oaks, CA.

Kantrowitz, Barbara (1994). "Men, Women and Computers." *Newsweek* (May 16), 48–55.

Kezsbom, Deborah S. (1992). "Re-opening Pandora's Box: sources of project conflict in the 90s." *Industrial Engineering* 24(5):(May), 54.

Kiesler, Sara (1986). "The Hidden Messages in Computer Networks." *Harvard Business Review,* 64(1)(January–February), 46–60.

Kiesler, Sara, Jane Siegel, and Timothy W. McGuire (1984). "Social Psychological Aspects of Computer-Mediated Communication." *American Psychologist,* 39(10) (October), 1123–1134.

Kling, Rob, and Lisa Covi (1995). "Electronic Journals and Legitimate Media in the Systems of Scholarly Communication." *The Information Society* 11(4).

Kling, Rob, and Tom Jewett (1994). "The Social Design of Worklife with Computers and Networks: An Open Natural Systems Perspective," in Marshall C. Yovitz (ed.), *Advances in Computers* (39), 239–293.

Kling, Rob, Spencer Olin, and Mark Poster (1995). "The Emergence of Postsuburbia," in Rob Kling, Spencer Olin, and Mark Poster (eds.), *Post-Suburban California: The Transformation of Orange County Since World War II* (2d ed.). University of California Press, Berkeley.

Kuszewski, Robert Joseph (1994). "Sexually Explicit Bboards." Posted to <restrict-bb + official.computing-news@andrew.cmu.edu>. November 3.

Ladner, Sharyn, and Hope Tillman (1992). "How Special Librarians Really Use the Internet: Summary of Findings and Implications for the Library of the Future." *Canadian Library Journal,* 49(3), 211–216.

Lanham, Richard A. (1994). "The Implications of Electronic Information for the Sociology of Knowledge." *Leonardo* (27)2, 155–164.

Lea, Martin, Tim O'Shea, Pat Fung, and Russell Spears (1992). " 'Flaming' in Computer-Mediated Communication," in Martin Lea (ed.), *Contexts of Computer-Mediated Communication.* Harvester Wheatsheaf, New York.

Lougee, Carolyn C. (1994). "The Professional Implications of Electronic Information." *Leonardo,* 27(2), 143–154.

Mantovani, Giuseppe (1994). "Is Computer-Mediated Communication Intrinsically Apt to Enhance Democracy in Organizations?" *Human Relations* (47)1(January), 45–62.

Pateman, Carole (1970). *Participation and Democratic Theory.* Cambridge University Press, New York.

Perrolle, Judith A. (1987). "Conversations and Trust in Computer Interfaces." *Computers and Social Change: Information, Property, and Power.* Wadsworth Inc., Belmont, CA. [Reprinted in Charles Dunlop and Rob Kling (eds.) (1991). *Computerization and Controversy: Value Conflicts and Social Choices.* Academic Press, San Diego.]

Perry, Tekla S. (1992). "E-Mail at Work." *IEEE Spectrum,* 29(10)(Oct), 24–28.

Phillip, Elmer-Dewitt (1994). "Censoring Cyberspace: Carnegie Mellon's Attempt to Ban Sex from its Campus Computer Network Sends a Chill along the Info Highway." *Time,* 144(21) (Nov. 21), 102–104.

Rheingold, Howard (1993). *The Virtual Community: Homesteading on the Electronic Frontier.* Addison Wesley, Reading, MA.

Schuler, Doug (1994). "Community Networks: Building a New Participatory Medium." *Communications of the ACM,* 37(1)(Jan.), 39–51.

Schuler, Doug (1995). *New Community Networks: Weaving Electronic Webs for the 21st Century.* Addison-Wesley, Reading, MA.

Sennett, Richard (1977). *The Fall of Public Man.* Knopf, New York.

Sproull, Lee, and Sara Kiesler (1986). "Reducing Social Context Cues: Electronic Mail in Organizational Communication." *Management Science,* 32(11)(November), 1492–1512.

Sproull, Lee, and Sara Kiesler (1991). *Connections: New Ways of Working in the Networked Organization.* MIT Press, Cambridge.

Traweek, Sharon (1988). *Beamtimes and Lifetimes: The World of High Energy Physicists.* Harvard University Press, Cambridge.

Vision Statement of the Blacksburg Electronic Village. n.d. Available at http://crusher.bev.net/index.html.

Watts, Gary D., and Castle, Shari (1992). "Electronic Networking and the Construction of Professional Knowledge." *Phi Delta Kappan,* 73(9)(May), 684–689.

Winner, Langdon (1992). "Silicon Valley Mystery House," in Michael Sorkin (ed.), *Variations on a Theme Park: The New American City and the End of Public Space.* Noonday Press, New York. (Excerpt reprinted in Part II, Chapter F of this book.)

Zuboff, Shoshana (1988). "The Panopticon and the Social Text," in *The Age of the Smart Machine.* Basic Books, New York.

Further Reading

Amiran, Eyal, John Unsworth, and Carole Chaski (1992). "Networked Academic Publishing and the Rhetorics of its Reception." *The Centennial Review,* 36(1)(Winter), 43–58.

Beniger, James R. (1991). "Information Society and Global Science" in Charles Dunlop and Rob Kling (eds.), *Computerization and Controversy: Value Conflicts and Social Choices.* Academic Press, San Diego.

Chartier, Roger (1994). *The Order of Books: Readers, Authors and Libraries in Europe Between the 14th and 18th Centuries.* Stanford University Press, Palo Alto, CA.

Crawford, Walter, and Michael Gorman (1995). *Future Libraries: Dreams, Madness, and Reality.* ALA Editions, Chicago, IL.

Finholt, Tom, and Lee Sproull (1990). "Electronic Groups at Work." *Organization Science,* 1(1), 41–64.

Fischer, Claude S. (1992). *America Calling: A Social History of the Telephone to 1940.* University of California Press, Berkeley.

Harrison, Teresa M., Timothy Stephen, and James Winter (1991). "Online Journals: Disciplinary Designs for Electronic Scholarship." *The Public-Access Computer Systems Review,* 2(1), 25–38.

Herring, Susan C. (ed.) (1995). *Computer-Mediated Communication.* John Benjamins Publishing Co., Amsterdam.

Hiltz, Starr Roxanne, and Murray Turoff (1978). *The Network Nation: Human Communication via Computer.* Addison-Wesley, Reading, MA.

Kahin, Brian, and James Keller (eds) (1995). *Public Access to the Internet.* MIT Press, Cambridge, MA.

Kling, Rob (in press). "Boutique and Mass Media Markets, Intermediation, and the Costs of On-Line Services." *The Communication Review.*

Kling, Rob (in press). "Synergies and Competition between Life in Cyberspace and Face-to-Face Communities. *Social Science Computer Review.*

Kling, Rob, and Roberta Lamb (in press). "Analyzing Visions of Electronic Publishing and Digital Libraries," in Gregory B. Newby and Robin M. Peek (eds.), *Scholarly Publishing: The Electronic Frontier.* The MIT Press, Cambridge, MA.

Kraemer, K. L., and J. L. King (1982). "Telecommunications-Transportation Substitution and Energy Productivity." *Telecommunications Policy,* Part I, 6(1), 39–59; Part II, 6(2), 87–99.

McCloskey, Donald N. (1990). *If You're So Smart: The Narrative of Economic Expertise.* University of Chicago Press, Chicago.

McClure, Charles R. (1994). "Network Literacy: A Role for Libraries?" *Information Technology and Libraries,* 13(2)(June), 115–125.

Myers, David J. (1994). "Communication Technology and Social Movements: Contributions of Networks to Social Activism." *Social Science Computer Review,* 12(2)(Summer), 250–260.

National Research Council, NRENAISSANCE Committee (1994). *Realizing the Information Future: The Internet and Beyond.* National Academy Press, Washington, D.C.

Poster, Mark (1990). "Derrida and Electronic Writing," in *The Mode of Information: Poststructuralism and Social Context.* The University of Chicago Press.

Quittner, Josh (1994). "The War Between alt.tasteless and rec.pets.cats." *Wired,* 2.05 (May), 46–53.

Rogers, Everett M., Lori Collins-Jarvis, and Joseph Schmitz (1994). "The PEN Project in Santa Monica: Interactive Communication, Equality, and Political Action." *Journal of the American Society for Information Science,* 45(6)(Jul), 401–410.

Rooks, Dana (1993). "The Virtual Library: Pitfalls, Promises, and Potential." *The Public-Access Computer Systems Review,* 4(5), 22–29.

Rosenberg, Richard S. (1993). "Free Speech, Pornography, Sexual Harassment, and Electronic Networks." *Information Society,* 9(4)(Oct.–Dec.), 285–331.

Sclove, Richard E. (1995). *Democracy and Technology.* Guilford Press, New York.

Soe, Louise L., and M. Lynne Markus (1993). "Technological or Social Utility? Unraveling Explanations of email, vmail and fax use." *Information Society,* 9(3) (Jul.–Sept.), 213–236.

Turkle, Sherry (in press). *Life on the Screen: Identity in the Age of the Internet.* Simon and Schuster, New York.

Weingarten, Fred W., and D. Linda Garcia (1988). "Public Policy Concerning the Exchange and Distribution of Scientific Information." *The Annals of The American Academy of Political and Social Science* (495)(January), 61–72. [Reprinted in Charles Dunlop and Rob Kling (eds.) (1991). *Computerization and Controversy: Value Conflicts and Social Choices.* Academic Press, San Diego.

P·A·R·T · V

B

Increasing Personal Connections*

Lee Sproull • Sara Kiesler

Not everyone can be the boss, have a big office, make important decisions, be the center of attention. Many employees are geographically and hierarchically distant from the center of things. Whenever an organization has more than two people in it, someone will be out of the center. The larger the organization, the greater the number and proportion of peripheral employees. "Peripheral," however, does not mean unimportant. Peripheral employees in the commercial and service sectors are the first, and often the only, contact that customers have with an organization. Their behavior can make the difference between keeping customers or clients and losing them. Peripheral employees in manufacturing and construction perform and inspect the actual production work. Their behavior can make the difference between acceptable and unacceptable product quality. Yet peripheral workers pose problems for organizations. They may not know what's going on—an information problem—and they may not care—a motivation problem.

Advertisements that encourage us to "reach out and touch someone" reflect the belief that we strengthen relationships when we communicate with others. Every relationship is both informational and emotional. All other things being equal, the more you talk with someone, the more you learn from that person (and vice versa). Additionally, the more you talk with someone, the more you like and feel committed to that person (and vice versa).[1] Participation through communication is an old principle of management. It has recently revived in the United States as managers look to Japan and the industrial democracies of Western Europe for "new" management practices.

Participation plans typically rely on communications initiated from the center and representation of the periphery to the center. Management initiates most participation plans. Employees receive participation overtures rather than initiate them. For instance, management may ask employees to get more involved through such mechanisms as quality circles, or employee representatives may be named to various management committees. Much of the internal communications apparatus of modern organizations is designed to "get the word to the troops," to ensure that employees have current information on policies, procedures, and other relevant topics. Devices ranging from televised messages from the company president to routine policy manual updates are intended to reduce the information distance between peripheral employees and the center. Even so, peripheral employees may be operating with outdated information, unaware of new initiatives or policies.

Even if peripheral employees have the information they need to do their jobs, they may not have any great desire to do so. (Motivation, of course, can interact with how informed an employee is. Highly motivated employees will figure out ways to learn what is going on.) Unmotivated employees' relationship with their employer is strictly letter of the law. Their information connection may be adequate, but their emotional connection is weak. Motivation and commitment can affect both work quality and work satisfaction. When people are "marking time" or "going through the motions," their behaviors and attitudes are qualitatively different from those in which people are "gung ho" or "going all out." Episodes of working to rule, as in, for instance, an air traffic controllers' slowdown, show the importance of employees who do more than they have to do. Organizations employ a host of motivating techniques to reduce the emotional distance between peripheral employees and the center: employee recognition awards, spirit campaigns, company-sponsored social occasions, and community events. Like information procedures, the center initiates most of these for the periphery.

Electronic communication may offer peripheral employees new opportunities to initiate connections within the organization to reduce the information gap and increase motivation. If connectivity is high, there are potentially many people accessible via the network. If management policies permit or encourage such interactions, employees can increase their information and emotional connections. These interactions can increase both

*This article appeared in *Connections: New Ways of Working in the Networked Organization* (1991). MIT Press, Cambridge. Reprinted with permission.

[1] See, for instance, Festinger, Schachter, and Back (1950); Newcomb (1961); Monge and Kirste (1980).

connections between the periphery and the center of the organization and connections among peripheral workers.

In the first section of this chapter, we show how employees can benefit from increasing their electronic connections with other employees. These increasing connections could benefit all employees, but peripheral employees are likely to see a relatively greater benefit than are central employees. We show how both passive and active connections (receiving information and sending it, respectively) can be beneficial. Passive connections offer employees the opportunity not only to learn from other employees but also to discover similarities they share with people who have different jobs and are located in different places. Active connections provide a new opportunity for employees to have a voice in their work group and with their boss. In the second section of the chapter we consider performance implications of having peripheral members increase their connections.

Increasing Information and Commitment through New Connections

Window on the Corporation

Receiving mail can affect employees' attitudes toward their organization by increasing their informational and emotional connections to other employees. This can be particularly true for peripheral employees who participate in large electronic distribution lists (DLs), bulletin boards, or conferences.

In one Fortune 500 firm, we noted several instances of these benefits. One secretary described several DLs to which she belonged by saying that she liked seeing what people had to say on various topics, including "important people who would never talk to me in person." She said she would never send a message to any of these DLs, but they were her "window on the corporation." Another employee used the mail system to describe his feelings about his employer, which had recently sold one of its subsidiaries. In a message sent to a large DL, the sender explained that another employee had told him: "It's a firm policy that [the corporation] won't make anything that will hurt anyone; they're getting pretty close, and that's probably why we're selling it." The sender then confided (to several hundred people), "That made me feel awfully good." As Martha Feldman (1987) pointed out in analyzing this message, "Though not all people who hear about the reason for selling the operation will agree on whether it is good or bad, the knowledge, by itself, provides organizational members a better understanding of the organization" (p. 97). In a third case, another secretary used the electronic mail system to organize a get well gift for an employee (Box 5.1). Tokens of appreciation are common in many organizations. What made this one interesting is that the message went to three hundred people, presumably most of whom had never before heard of Benny, the ailing employee. Probably most people paid little conscious attention to this message. But even with a quick scan and delete, the subliminal message was, "I work for a company with caring people."

Corporate communications offices and human resources offices are in the business of sending employees information designed to increase informational and emotional connections. How could ad hoc communications among employees be any more effective than professionally designed ones? Messages share several characteristics that distinguish them from professional communications and that may make them particularly potent. First, most are from voluntary or discretionary DLs. People choose to belong to these DLs and therefore perceive that they receive messages by their choice, not because they must do so. Second, because these DLs have widespread membership, they can reflect information and feelings from throughout the organization, not just from one communication office. Third, the overt contents of these messages pertain to a variety of topics and interests, not just to official company news or boosterism. These characteristics can make these messages more persuasive than professional ones because of a process psychologists call insufficient justification (Aronson 1966).

When people receive a message, they evaluate the sender's motivation so that they know how to interpret the message. If a recipient knows that the sender was paid for sending the message or was coerced into sending it, the recipient discounts the sender's sincerity. The recipient believes that the sender has "sufficient justification" for sending a message even without sincerely believing its contents. By contrast, if a sender lacks obvious

---

Box 5.1. Benny hurt his back

Date: 19 May 1983 10:37 am PDT (Thursday)
From: Sandi Colman
Subject: Benny Schrinka
To: [All employees, about 300 people, working in one location]
cc:
Reply To: Sandi Colman

   Benny Schrinka hurt his back last week and will be unable to work for at least 3–4 weeks or more. . . . . . .depends on how he responds to physical therapy.
   Several of his friends are putting together a surprise "goodie basket" for him, hoping to cheer him and ease his pain. We hope to include a ham, some wine, maybe a good book or two for him to read. . .suggestions welcome.
   If you care to make a contribution toward the basket. . .I am collecting $$$; John Devon has volunteered to coordinate getting the goodies and basket.
   I am in "Area 2" of ABC Bldg. 10. . . .x1111; John Devon is in room 76, same building, Thanks to you all. . . .Sandi

external incentives for sending the message, the recipient does not discount the sender's sincerity. When unsolicited messages appear on large, discretionary distribution lists, readers have little reason to doubt their sincerity. Peripheral employees who frequently receive such messages build information connections over time to other employees of the corporation.

Cognitive processes of everyday inference also can magnify the influence of these messages in the minds of their recipients. Because people commonly ignore base rates and remember singular instances, they overestimate the frequency of rare events (Lichtenstein et al., 1978).[2] For instance, people typically overestimate the frequency of death by lightning. (Similarly they tend to underestimate the frequency of death by motor vehicle accidents, which are more frequent and less memorable.) Suppose a person who read the message in Box 5.1 were to ask, "How kind to one another are people who work for this company?" The best answer, without any other information, is "About as kind as the people who work for any similar company." The Benny message should carry very little weight in changing that assessment, increasing the kindness score by only $1/n$th, where n is the total number of employees. Because the message has memorable features—the ham, the bottle of wine, the books—it is likely to be overweighted (in a statistical sense) in its contribution to the person's assessment.

Reading messages gives employees the opportunity to make connections with other employees who would otherwise be invisible or unknown. Because electronic communication can be independent of geographic and organizational distance, these connections cut across conventional organization boundaries. In this way, employees can learn about people whose experiences are different from theirs because they have different jobs or work in different locations. They also can learn that, despite these differences, they have much in common. Such lessons are reinforced by the nature of the communication—the free exchange of unofficial information. Research on the relationship between electronic connections and feelings of affiliation shows that if you have a choice of face-to-face contact with people exactly like you or meeting via electronic communication, then you will like each other more if you meet in person (Kiesler et al., 1985). The situation is different for meeting people you would otherwise not see in person, whom you might avoid, who are different. Here there is a positive association between electronic connections and affiliation.

It is possible that people communicating electronically could become attached to specific other people or even to favorite bulletin boards or electronic groups without these positive attachments generalizing to the larger organization. No research directly tests the impact of "windows on

---

[2] This literature is reviewed in Fischhoff et al. (1981). Also see Dawes (1988).

the corporation" on attachment to the organization. If the process works as it has in other settings, then whether affiliation extends to the larger organization will depend on the orientation of the individuals' communications. If messages about the larger organization are mainly negative, recipients will increase their affiliation with the communicators but decrease it with the larger organization. If the communications are mainly positive toward the larger organization, recipients will increase both affiliations.

A Voice for the Voiceless

Sending messages also can increase information and emotional connections. An experiment conducted by the Rand Corporation demonstrated that peripheral people who communicated electronically became better integrated into the organization (Eveland and Bikson, 1988). Two corporation task forces were formed to investigate how employees make the transition to retirement and to develop a set of recommendations about preretirement planning. Each task force had forty members—half recently retired from the company and the other half still employed but eligible for retirement. The only difference between the two groups was that one of them was given electronic communication technology and the other was not. At the outset, the retired people in both task forces were judged by themselves and others to be more peripheral to the group than their employed counterparts. On standard sociometric measures of recognition, knowing, and contact, retirees had lower scores than those who were still employed. Halfway through the year's work, the retired members of the electronic communication group had become intensely involved in the project by electronic mail. They knew more people, had more interactions, belonged to more subgroups, and felt more involved than their retired counterparts in the nonelectronic task force. They even decided to continue meeting after the year's work was completed and the task forces had been officially disbanded.

We found a similar story in a city government (Huff, Sproull, and Kiesler, 1989). Over 90% of the city employees used electronic mail routinely. We discovered that the more they used it, the more committed they were to their employer—measured by how willing they were to work beyond the requirements and hours of their jobs, how attached they felt to the city government, and how strongly they planned to continue working for the city. The connection between electronic communication and commitment is not explained by employees' total amount of communication across all media, by their technical ability, or by their seniority and hierarchical status (although the later two variables predicted commitment independently). One explanation of our findings is that using electronic mail caused commitment to increase. Another explanation is that already committed people used the modern, symbolically important technology of electronic mail. To compare these alternatives, we proposed that if communicating by electronic mail increased commitment, then the correlation between using electronic mail and commitment should be especially strong among shift workers who are routinely separated from the mainstream of work and decision making in the organization. We reasoned that the technology would be somewhat more useful to them than to employees in the mainstream. By contrast, if commitment caused people to use electronic mail, then shift work should have no differential effect. We found that the relationship between using electronic mail and commitment was much higher for shift workers than for other workers, supporting the idea that electronic mail can increase commitment among those who otherwise might feel somewhat peripheral in an organization.

Once we knew that total volume of an employee's electronic mail predicted that person's level of commitment, we wondered if receiving mail or sending it (or both) contributed to feelings of commitment. It might be that receiving more mail would cause people to feel more informed, as was the case with the large corporation, and therefore more committed. We found, however, that neither the amount of electronic mail received nor a person's reporting that he or she felt "in the know about what is going on in the city" predicted commitment. Rather, the amount of electronic mail a person sent predicted commitment. In this city government, computer communication seems to have increased commitment primarily because it allowed employees to participate actively in the life of the organization by sending messages that they would not otherwise have sent, not primarily because it increased the amount of information they received. One police officer wrote to us, "Working the night shift, it used to be that I would hear about promotions after they happened though I had a right to be included in the discussion. Now I have a say in the decision making." Electronic communication gave peripheral employees the chance to have a voice.

We found a similar relationship between commitment and sending mail in software development teams. The teams using electronic mail the most produced the best systems because they could better coordinate their activities than could the teams that relied on more conventional means of communicating. We also looked at how committed each member felt to his or her team. For this analysis, we categorized each person by how much he or she talked in meetings and how much electronic mail he or she sent. We discovered that people who sent much mail were just as committed to their team as were the people who talked a lot in meetings. Also, as is true of the city government, there was no relationship between the amount of mail a team member received and his or her commitment to the team, although receiving mail was related to performance (see Table 1). Thus electronic mail can provide an alternate route to letting people have a voice if they are low contributors to face-to-face meetings.

Face-to-face groups consistently show a positive relationship between how much a person talks and how satisfied that person is with the group

Table 1. Attitudes and Performance of Individuals as a Function of Communication Behavior

	Performance[a]	Commitment[b]
High communicators[c]	17.4	9.1
High talkers only	17.5	8.7
High mailers only	17.0	8.9
Low communicators[c]	12.3	7.8

[a]Performance was measured on a scale from 0–20.
[b]Commitment was measured on a scale from 1–10.
[c]High or low frequency of both talking and using electronic mail.

and how committed he or she is to it (McGrath, 1984; Forsyth, 1983). Yet air time in meetings is an extremely limited commodity—only one person can talk at a time—and total meeting size is physically constrained. With electronic communication, air time and meeting size are less constrained resources, and so more people can enjoy the benefits of active participation. These benefits may especially accrue to those who, by virtue of geographic or organizational position, would otherwise be peripheral contributors.

Talking to the Boss

Most managers talk more than they listen and issue more directives, make more organizational announcements, and promulgate more policy statements than do lower-level employees. When managers do listen, it's mostly to people close to them. Most talking and listening occurs among people who are physically and hierarchically close to each other. This means managers often don't hear new news; they may be ignorant of information they need that is in the heads or on the desks of lower-level or distant employees—and lower-level employees may feel that no one listens to them.

Giving people a voice is a strong value in our culture. Its embodiment ranges from constitutional principles of freedom of speech and assembly and parliamentary rules of order to public opinion polls, Dale Carnegie's rules for success, and radio call-in shows. Although work organizations are not democracies and free speech does not prevail, giving peripheral people a voice is an important means of binding them to the organization, and it may yield information important for performance.

Managers face three kinds of problems in giving people a voice. One is straightforward logistics problems. By definition, peripheral people are far from the center. Physically collecting their opinions can be time-consuming and expensive. This is one reason that conventional participation mechanisms usually rely on representation rather than direct participation; collecting information from employee representatives is easier than listening to all employees. A second problem is motivational. Although peripheral employees may have a lot to say, they may be reticent, distrustful, or fear recrimination. A third problem is also motivational—but on the receiving end rather than the sending end. Central management may not want to hear what peripheral employees have to say. Given the cultural value we put on being good listeners, this reluctance is not likely to be expressed publicly. Instead it is more likely to be expressed as confidence in the existing ways of hearing from employees and a need to avoid information overload. Management reluctance may actually stem from confusing a commitment to listen to employees with a commitment to act on what they say.

Electronic communication offers the possibility of increasing the amount of communication from lower to higher levels of the hierarchy and solving the logistics problems of collecting information from distant employees. Workers can send messages at their convenience, without having to wait for an appointment or to catch the manager in the hall. It also can alleviate employee reluctance to talk. Workers feel less intimidated about talking to the boss electronically than they do about talking to him or her face-to-face, particularly if what the worker wants to say is in any way negative. Because there are few reminders of status differences, the fear of evaluation or criticism declines.

In one corporation we studied, people who used electronic communication extensively reported that they preferred this form when communicating up the hierarchy to negotiate or solve problems (Sproull and Kiesler, 1986). Box 5.2 displays an example of a message from a first-level manager to a vice-president located four levels above him in the hierarchy. This message illustrates how status imbalance can be reduced in computer communication both in the style of communication from subordinate to superior and in the behavior about which the subordinate is complaining. Although both had offices in the same building, the sender almost never talked with the vice-president directly; most of the occasions on which they were in the same room were formal or ceremonial ones in which the vice-president was making a speech or conducting a large meeting. Yet the sender felt he could send this frank complaint electronically. Notice that the topic of the message is electronic mail behavior. The sender liked the vice-president's electronic open-door policy but did not like what he saw as an electronic endorsement policy.

Managers notice that the nature of the conversation often changes when they walk in the room.[3] One manager calls this the "social Heisenberg effect." "With electronic communication people can forget that I'm their manager when they talk to me," he told us. The manager did not mean this

---

[3] See Jablin (1987) for a review of research supporting this observation. Managers tend to dominate the conversation, and subordinates expect them to. Furthermore, subordinates are reluctant to convey bad news or negative information to their bosses (Rosen and Tesser, 1970; O'Reilly and Roberts, 1974; Linde, 1988).

literally, but in our terms many cues to status differences disappear with electronic communication. For this manager, that produced benefits. The cliché is that the boss is always the last to hear the bad news. Electronic communication may convey it sooner.

Why should managers want to encourage more communication from their subordinates, particularly if it's likely to be bad news, negative opinions, or complaints? Obviously, smart managers may prefer to know sooner, rather than later, that all is not well. That justification assumes a view of managers as problem finders and problem solvers. Another view of managers as involvement increasers also suggests benefits from encouraging more communication from lower-level employees. In this view, managers elicit communication because they believe it increases involvement and improves morale. High morale may be sought for its own sake, because it has some direct link with performance, or both. It may turn out

---

Box 5.2. Talking with the boss

DATE: 20 May 89   07:29:24
FROM: Sam.Marlowe
SUBJECT: Messages from on high
TO: Bill.Hargrave   John.East
CC: Don.Dulane, Bob.Bilk, Sam.Marlowe

This is to inform you of some small personnel problems you have been causing at lower levels of the organization. I hope that being informed, you will do the right thing in the future. I have made a suggestion at the end.

I like your (electronic) open-door policy; anyone can send you a message on anything, and you will read (and maybe respond to) it. I hope that we do not misuse this policy by sending you so many messages that you will have to close the door, and I would ask that you not misuse this policy by running the organization with it.

There are many good ideas floating around this organization. We do not have enough resources to work on all of them, so managers have to allocate their resources to the most important one (which sometimes are not the most ingenious ones). When a person has a good idea, and it is not worked on, that person tends to be disappointed. Usually, he understands the situation, and respects the decision of his boss(s). Sometimes when he thinks a mistake is being made, or when he is just plain angry, he uses your open-door policy to sell his good idea. This is just what the policy is for, and I see no harm done.

The problems arise when you, with all your weight and authority, endorse the good idea to the point where the originator believes he now has your blessing to start work on it. He believes that you have/will over-rule his boss, and [the organization] will implement his idea because you think it is so good.

SUGGESTION
When someone sends you an idea, and you are willing/want to respond, please continue to give your opinion (for/against) of the idea, but please make sure that you indicate that the decision to work on the idea will be made by the normal processes in the organization (like release planning or chain of command). I am not suggesting that you stop responding altogether.

that what is most important is letting people talk, not acting on what they say. In the city government we described, we have no evidence that anyone acted on the messages sent by the shift workers, but the electronic communication gave peripheral employees the opportunity to communicate more actively with the boss.

Electronic Discussion Groups

Electronic discussion groups offer the opportunity to consolidate and magnify the effects of passive and active electronic participation. Most employees belong to few groups at work—a primary work group, perhaps a committee or two, and perhaps a social group. (Group membership is positively associated with hierarchical position; high-level managers belong to many more groups than do lower-level employees.) Except for committee assignments, these memberships are relatively stable and enduring, and they lead to important benefits for their members. Electronic group communication makes it possible for more people to belong to many groups and to tailor their group memberships to their changing interests. The groups are not constrained by physical location or fixed-length meetings and can enroll anyone who wants to participate, either actively or passively.

Employees in one Fortune 500 firm received an average of twenty-one DL messages per day from over seven hundred DLs (Finholt and Sproull, 1990). The majority of the average person's DL mail came from strangers (company employees unknown to the recipient), and a high percentage came from remote locations. Thus DLs represented a way for people to receive information and make connections that otherwise would have been difficult or impossible. About half the DLs were required ones: an employee's name was placed on a required DL as a function of his or her job or work location. The employee had no choice about belonging to required DLs, which ranged from ten-person DLs for subunit groups to six-hundred-person site lists for all employees working in a particular city. The discretionary DLs, which people joined by choice, covered a wide spectrum of topics, some about work and some extracurricular. They ranged from the exotic to the mundane: Oenologists for wine fanciers, NetSpecs for computer network designers, GoPlayers for students of the Japanese strategy game Go, Classifieds for selling things, and ChildCare for locating babysitters.

Some discretionary DLs, such as Classifieds and ChildCare, merely served as a convenient way to broadcast information; others functioned as interacting discussion groups. (See Box 5.3 for descriptions of three electronic discussion groups and sample messages from each of them.) The discretionary discussion groups were large and geographically dispersed, averaging 260 members located in seven different cities, and they interacted regularly. Four days out of five, messages went to these groups, week after week—an average of four messages a day. Messages were sent by an average of 41 different people in each discussion group over a two-week to one-month period. Although most of these members were not personally known to one another and had no common tasks, most messages were not simply disconnected broadcasts unrelated to one another but explicit replies to previous messages. These groups sustained involving discussions over distance and time among strangers. Each discretionary group also worked at being a group. They sent messages discussing the purpose and procedures of the group and membership criteria for it. Although group members were physically invisible and unknown to one another, the groups took on personalities and lives of their own.

Membership in any group confers informational and emotional benefits to the member, including increased information resources, emotional resources, and the opportunity to take on different roles and identities. These processes are so powerful that people's mental health status is positively associated with the number of groups they belong to (Thoits, 1983). It is plausible, although only a hypothesis at this point, that membership in multiple electronic groups has similar beneficial effects, particularly for people who belong to few face-to-face groups. For those who belong to a great many face-to-face groups, we would expect much less effect; the costs in demands on their time and energy might well outweigh the benefits.

Performance Implications

This chapter emphasizes the information and motivation benefits of increasing peripheral employee participation through electronic communication. Do these connections also differently benefit the performance of peripheral workers? There are almost no data to help us answer this question; we can only lay out the basic reasoning underlying why we might expect to see a differential benefit and report some tantalizing bits of evidence.

Differential Performance Benefits for Peripheral Employees

The basic argument suggests that peripheral employees have more to gain from electronic communication than do more central employees. We assume that peripheral employees start out at an information disadvantage. In principle, both groups of employees could benefit equally, illustrated as "equivalent benefits" in Figure 1. But central employees are likely to experience ceiling effects on their communication. That is, each new communication benefits them relatively less because they already know a great deal and are already active contributors. Peripheral employees, by contrast, derive more benefit from each additional communication both because they know less and because they have fewer other opportunities to participate

Box 5.3. Electronic discussion groups

UserFeatureForum

UserFeatureForum was a work-related discretionary DL for employees interested in discussing interface features of company products. UFF had 125 members and received a mean of 2 messages a day (max = 8, min = 0). Many of the messages on UFF were mildly pedantic, as people demonstrated their technical opinions or virtuosity.

Regarding contention resolution in Graphics: I like meaning 1 (option 2) of the next key (next item in the contenders list). Meaning 2 would seem to me to be very unpredictable from a user's point of view. The internal sibling structure could not in general be predicted from the image they see whereas the next contender would be much more natural. Regarding how frames behave during pagination: both alternatives have undesirable qualities. Data should never be intentionally thrown away (as in alt1). And alt2 would more than likely result in an unacceptable positioning of the frame. Given the current of document structure in [product], I don't see any better pagination heuristic than what we do now. One possibility might be to post a message when one of these guys is encountered and let the user decide what to do such as abort pagination. Then the user could change the page props of the problem page and repaginate.
/Joe

Still, UFF was not all bland discourse on "contention resolution problems" or "multinational user interfaces." Personal rivalries sometimes surfaced. For example, toward the end of one particularly arcane exchange, one member pointedly observed in a message that "some people" on UFF spent more time talking about user interfaces than building them. On the whole, though, talking about interfaces was the raison d'être of UFF. It had no identity outside the mail system. UFF was an arena for people to display their knowledge before their superiors and peers—although this knowledge was rarely acted upon (in our sample of messages, only two UFF communications resulted in actual changes to an interface). In the words of one UFFer:

To paraphrase a famous saying about economists, which pretty much summarizes my feeling about all this endless user-interface niggling that's been going on for the last six years, and shows every indication of continuing out to eternity:

If all the user interface experts in the world were laid end to end, they wouldn't reach a conclusion.

In response to this complaint, though, another member responded with a hoary mail system adage: "If you don't like talking about user features, drop out of UserFeature-Forum."

Cinema

Cinema was an extracurricular discretionary DL, with over 500 members—managers, professionals, technicians, and secretaries. Cinema members received a mean of 4 messages a day from this DL (max = 31, min = 0). Messages were related to movie reviews—highly subjective commentaries on everything related to the movie, including the ambiance in the theater and the quality of the popcorn.

John,
I just saw FlashDance, you were very right. I stopped by Tower Records on the way home and picked up the sound track. I am taping it now. I am not a big movie goer and I am at odds with Mann and AMC theaters but this film was well worth the trip to my local corporate theater. Fortunately I was spared the newspaper ads by arriving 5 minutes late.

Well, I did not start this as a flame about corporate theaters. I wanted to say that FlashDance is a clever, well filmed, moving musical that runs around your head for a long time after leaving the theater. Go see it and check out the sound track on Casablanca Records. It's a Polygram Record with a few built in flaws.
Later...
/PRL

V was a mashed-up composite of about twenty science-fiction stories. Not a single original idea in it. And besides that, it wasn't very good.
Save Joe-Bob!

Rowdies

Rowdies, a discretionary extracurricular DL, had 98 members, 73 percent of them male technicians or professionals. Typically Rowdies was the source of over 20 "Rowdie-Mail" messages per day (max = 50, min = 0). Although some work issues occasionally crept into Rowdies discussions, most messages concerned gossip (mostly about other Rowdies), group activities (such as organizing softball teams or writing electronic novels), and crude humor.

Sounds to me like you have quit while you were ahead!! Has anyone else noticed that we've actually been getting messages from 666 lately, and most of them have times on them like 3:05 a.m.—5:42 a.m., etc., etc. Do you think he's trying to impress us with his devotion to duty? I'll bet his boss gets a message every day at that time as well....even if 666 has nothing much to say to him. He also lets us know that he is working a 13 hour day—he has stated that more than once.

I mean, we enjoy your messages 666, but, really, impressing us isn't going to change the fact that there are no merit increases this year—unless, of course, they change their mind in June or July after re-evaluating this situation.

And by the way, 3:00 a.m. to 12:30 p.m. is only a 9-1/2 hour day.........
2
GeezSomePeople

Rowdies regularly sent messages to organize afternoon beer busts, which were the focus of elaborate preparation. These outings were documented in full, and their histories were carefully indexed and archived for future references in secure Rowdie disk space.

John and Phil,
   I have room for both of you in my car plus one more RowdieLuncher. I'm pretty sure
the luncheon is still on for 12:30 pm.
44

.....zzzzzzzzzzzzzzzzzz.Hmmph. Burp...huh? who me....what column? miss a deadline...what day is it? ohmygod it's wednesday already. What? somebody wrote it? Joe,
who? Oh yes, JOE! — he's the one I had always thought was bald.
zR722

Was a great party, in fact I'm still smiling.
....that whipped cream was good stuff

   Rowdies messages displayed complex stylistic conventions, including closing messages with a Rowdy number and a run-on commentary that often took the form of
sarcastic observations on previous messages or continued observations from other
messages. Rowdies sometimes referred to fellow Rowdies by using Rowdy "handles,"
such as "Colt45" or "Mr. Toon-toon," an important part of Rowdy identity. Periodically Rowdies issued a membership list indicating numbers, handles, birthdates, and
favorite "RowdieDrinks." During our observation, the membership list contained the
names of honorary Rowdies, including several waitresses at Rowdy hangouts, and
Divine, the transvestite star of *Pink Flamingos* and *Polyester*.
   Rowdies messages expressed clear opinions about Rowdies and the larger electronic
community. On one occasion a prominent Rowdy noted, after three new Rowdies
members dropped out after only two days, "They weren't Rowdy material. Keep up
the good work!"
Source: Adapted from Finholt and Sproull (1990).

---

actively. This relationship is illustrated as the "decreasing gap hypothesis"
in Figure 1: peripheral employees' performance increases more than central
employees' performance does, closing the gap between the two groups. Of
course, there could be other relationships as well. Both groups could be
produced by a simple information overload process in which each new
communication distracts attention or confuses the recipient. Or central
employees could benefit much more than peripheral employees. This
"gap-increasing" benefit (shown at the bottom of Figure 1) could most
plausibly occur if central employees had better access to computer-based
information resources, or if they communicated only with one another or
communicated entirely different kinds of information. We believe, however, that when access is open the effects are mainly positive, with differential benefit to peripheral workers.

   We have found evidence of differential benefits to peripheral workers in
an investigation of how physical oceanographers use computer networks
(Hesse *et al.*, 1990). We examined how the use of electronic communication
affected the relationship between age and professional recognition (scientific awards, appointment to editorial boards, professional committees, and
advisory committees). In this kind of analysis, younger scientists are
considered more peripheral than older scientists. We found that while

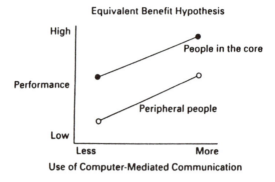

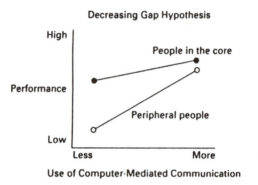

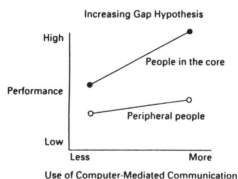

Figure 1. Some hypothetical relationships between computer-mediated communication and employee performance.

older scientists generally received more professional recognition than younger scientists (and scientists who used electronic communication more received more professional recognition), electronic communication benefited younger scientists more than it did older scientists in receiving professional recognition.

John Earls has discovered a similar pattern of advantage for people with physical handicaps. He directed a multiyear program for participants in

a rehabilitation program designed to teach confidence and positive attitudes toward the disabled among both disabled people and human service
professionals. He compared a control group with an equivalent experimental group that used a computer bulletin board for communication over
several years. Each group had thirty members: ten disabled people, ten
therapists, and ten university students. The experimental group did not
differ from the control after six months in the program, but after two years
there were highly significant differences. By then the experimental group
was more positive in its attitudes about disability and the disabled than the
control group was. The disabled members were even more positive in their
attitudes than other experimental group members were. Also, the disabled
people in the experimental group participated more actively. They logged
onto the network and read and sent more messages than the professionals
or students did (Box 5.4).

Short-Run versus Long-Run Implications

Even if increasing affiliation and commitment through increasing electronic
connections is feasible, the direct link between increased commitment and
increased performance has not been demonstrated. Happy workers are not
necessarily more productive workers.[4] Nor are more informed workers
necessarily more productive workers. Charles O'Reilly (1980) looked at the
relationship between employees' attitudes toward and use of information
and the quality of their job performance as rated by their supervisors. He
found a positive association between how much information people had to
do their jobs and their satisfaction with the amount of information they
had. That is, people who reported they had more information were also
more satisfied with the amount of information they had. But he also found
a negative association between how much information people had to do
their jobs and the quality of their actual performance. The more information people had, the worse was their performance. These findings are
consonant with the view of economists who point out that people often
overinvest in information; they acquire more information or more costly
information than they need to do their work. In this view any strategy that
seeks to increase information and motivation connections among employees should be viewed with suspicion. This view is typically characterized
by an extremely short-run perspective, considering the relationship between performance and amount of information or amount of satisfaction at
only one time. Companies or managers that have primarily a short-run
orientation can use similar reasoning to forbid or minimize widespread use
of a computer-based communication system.

---

[4] Research reviews for the past thirty years have failed to find a consistent positive
relationship between job satisfaction and performance (Brayfield and Crockett, 1955; Vroom,
1964; Petty, McGee, and Cavender, 1984; Iaffaldano and Muchinsky, 1985; Podsakoff and
Williams, 1986).

Box 5.4. Differential benefits of computer-based communication

T is a 30-year-old man whose disability is cerebral palsy. He works in the office area
at Centrecraft Industries, a sheltered employment facility. In the last year he has been
nominated as a representative of the disabled people working at his work facility.

T states that one of the personal benefits of his participation in the Bulletin Board
project has been the opportunity to resume communication with people with whom
he had lost contact. In addition, he sees that being able to talk to other people with
disabilities about work issues as well as his own thoughts and feelings as being a great
strength of the Bulletin Board. The fact that he is able to talk to individuals using their
private mail box is particularly good; especially when he wants to discuss a problem
at work and wants to be assured of privacy. Its use as a public forum, allowing the
discussion of issues relevant to the disabled consumer group, has been very helpful in
his role as a consumer representative. It has enabled him to get different people's
ideas, discuss matters with them and report them to the consumer group at Industries.

In T's opinion, his involvement in the Bulletin Board has enabled him to better
express his thoughts and opinions. In effect, it has made him more confident in talking
to groups both via the Bulletin Board and also face to face. In addition, it has made him
more willing to consider other people's viewpoints. He reported that prior to his use
of the Bulletin Board, he was probably "one sided" in his attitudes. Now, he is more
able and prepared to consider the attitudes and feelings of the group as a whole. In
addition, T feels that his involvement with the Bulletin Board has resulted in staff
looking at him "in a much more positive light."

During his participation in the Bulletin Board project, T was initially loaned a
computer, modem and communications software by the organisation. He has subsequently purchased his own computer and equipment and reports that this is a direct
consequence of his involvement with the Bulletin Board. He uses the computer not
only for communication purposes but also for word processing. He is currently writing
a book and has begun to see other possible uses for his computer.

T is now accessing a community bulletin board as well as that run by the organisation. T reported that this board extends his information capability and there is more
opportunity to communicate with people you do not know. It also has a variety of
different interest areas covering topics such as sports, politics and hobbies. Although
T has not yet communicated with people in these areas, he enjoys reading the
comments of others and feels that one day he will want to share his own thoughts on
some of the different areas.

Source: Earls (1990: 204–205).

Companies and managers with a longer view, however, may think of
increasing employee participation by electronic communication as a
capacity-building strategy with implications for long-term performance.
They might consider three components of such a strategy: creating connections among employees, building new skills, and increasing employees'
ability to absorb new ideas. Increasing employee participation increases
links among employees. Although most of the time these links are irrelevant to routine performance, they are available when needed, in times of
crisis or opportunity. A case from Manufacturer's Hanover Trust (MHT)
illustrates the point. Several years ago, MHT launched a new financial
product in the Far East under extremely tight time deadlines governed by

impending regulatory changes. MHT lawyers in Washington, corporate officers in New York, and marketing personnel in California used the MHT electronic mail system to coordinate their activities with one another and with the Hong Kong office to bring out the product under the deadline. Employees told us this story to illustrate how much they depend on their mail system. It also illustrates a capacity-building strategy. At the time of this opportunity, MHT personnel already "knew" many employees through communicating with them electronically. They could use these connections because they already existed.

Research on teaching and learning shows that people don't learn new ideas or skills just by being exposed to them.[5] Learners must be prepared to learn; they must have the mental scaffolding and requisite skills to understand and master new ideas (Cohen and Levinthal, 1990). Listening to network discussions may help produce this "absorptive capacity" in employees, both old-timers and newcomers. It is easier to join and be socialized to electronic groups than to face-to-face ones (Moreland and Levine, 1982). When group members are physically invisible, as is true with electronic interaction, the high salience and potential stress associated with the newcomer identity decline. Putting new employees on the mail system, especially if they can join large discretionary distribution lists, can help bring them quickly up to speed on how and what their fellow employees are thinking. It can get them more oriented toward the organization.

What about Extracurricular Mail?

Although some companies discourage any electronic discussions, many permit or encourage discussions related to company business for the reasons noted. Extracurricular messages and groups are a more difficult issue. It is easy to dismiss them as a waste of company resources—both network resources and employee time. The question of extracurricular mail is not one to be settled in a vacuum. It is simply an instance of a much more general view of human resource management. Some companies subsidize extracurricular benefits for their employees. Exercise facilities, discount entertainment tickets, office celebrations, softball teams—all could be viewed as a waste of resources. Companies that invest in them do so as a way of building employee enthusiasm, loyalty, or commitment. A recent study of employees in a high-technology service sector firm showed that "socializing with coworkers and supervisors, either on or off the job or both" was correlated with positive organizational attitudes (Kaufman *et al.*,

---

[5] See, for instance, Mayer and Greeno (1972); Chi and Glaser (1984); Rouse and Morris (1986).

1988). Allowing extracurricular messages and groups may serve a similar function. Where we have systematic data, it seems lower-level employees rather than managers more often send and receive extracurricular messages and participate in extracurricular electronic groups.

Allowing extracurricular mail also can contribute to a capacity-building strategy. A steely-eyed controller might frown on a company DL called ChocolateLovers. Yet that DL might be just the means to get peripheral employees motivated to increase their network connections and skills. In the accounting department of one large organization, a new employee was enrolled in a ChocolateLovers DL by another employee as a friendly orientation gesture. (She was also enrolled in all of the DLs required for her job and location.) After reading ChocolateLovers for a month or so, the new employee decided she wanted to print out some recipes she had read, so she had to learn various commands for manipulating and printing text. She then decided that she would compile recipes from the DL into a book to give as a Christmas present. To illustrate the book, she learned color desktop graphics by experimenting during her lunch hour. Over an eighteen-month period, this accounts payable supervisor became the office guru on desktop publishing and color graphics because she had joined ChocolateLovers. These skills were not directly applicable to accounts payable supervision, but they represented an increase in her skill repertoire and an increase in the skill capacity of the entire office.

Conclusion

It may seem paradoxical that computers, stereotyped as cold and impersonal, can be used to increase personal connections and affiliation. Electronic communication is not a substitute for face-to-face relationships, but for many peripheral employees, satisfying face-to-face relationships are hard to come by in the workplace. Electronic communication can increase the informational and emotional connections of these employees. The benefits to individual employees are immediate. The organization can additionally benefit by increasing employee capacity to work beyond the letter of the employment contract.

From the organization's perspective, giving a voice to the voiceless and opening a window on the corporation can produce bad effects as well as good ones. If the previously voiceless employees use the mail system to complain or to mobilize protest, managers might prefer that they had remained mute. And even if increasing participation by electronic means does not lead to riot or revolution, it still costs money. Some managers may be unwilling to support communication services that are not directly tied to task performance even if they do increase employee motivation and commitment. That decision, however, is one that should be taken in the light of more general human resource strategies.

References

Aronson, E. (1966). "The Psychology of Insufficient Justification: An Analysis of Some Conflicting Data," in S. Feldman (ed.), *Cognitive Consistency*, pp. 115–133. Academic Press, New York.

Cohen, W., and D. A. Levinthal (1990). "Absorptive Capacity: A New Perspective on Learning and Innovation." *Administrative Science Quarterly* 35:128–152.

Earls, J. (1990). "Social Integration by People with Physical Disabilities: The Development of an Information Technology Model Based on Personal Growth and Achievement." Unpublished doctoral dissertation. The University of Wollongong, Wollongong, Australia.

Eveland, J. D., and T. K. Bikson (1988). "Work Group Structures and Computer Support: A Field Experiment." *Transactions on Office Information Systems* 6(4):354–379.

Feldman, M. S. (1987). "Electronic Mail and Weak Ties in Organizations." *Office: Technology and People* 3:83–101.

Finholt, T., and L. Sproull (1990). "Electronic Groups at Work." *Organization Science* 1(1):41–64.

Forsyth, D. R. (1983). *An Introduction to Group Dynamics.* Brooks/Cole Publishing Co., Monterey, CA.

Hesse, B., L. Sproull, S. Kiesler, and J. Walsh (1990). "Computer Network Support for Science: The Case of Oceanography." Unpublished manuscript. Carnegie-Mellon University, Pittsburgh, PA.

Huff, C., L. Sproull, and S. Kiesler (1989). "Computer Communications and Organizational Commitment: Tracing the Relationship in a City Government." *Journal of Applied Social Psychology* 19:1371–1391.

Kaufman, R. L., T. L. Parcel, M. Wallace, and W. Form (1988). "Looking Forward: Responses to Organizational and Technical Change in an Ultra-High Technology Firm," in I. H. Simpson and R. L. Simpson (eds.), *Research in the Sociology of Work*, pp. 4:31–67. JAI Press, Greenwich, CT.

Kiesler, S., D. Zubrow, A. M. Moses, and V. Geller (1985). "Affect in Computer-mediated Communication: An Experiment in Synchronous Terminal-to-Terminal Discussion." *Human Computer Interaction* 1:77–104.

Lichtenstein, S., P. Slovic, B. Fischhoff, M. Layman, and B. Combs (1978). "Judged Frequency of Lethal Events." *Journal of Experimental Psychology: Human Learning and Memory* 4:551–578.

McGrath, J. E. (1984). *Group Interaction and Performance.* Prentice Hall, Englewood Cliffs, NJ.

Moreland, R. L., and J. M. Levine (1982). "Measuring Proximity in Human Organizations." *Advances in Experimental Social Psychology* 15:137–192.

O'Reilly, C. (1980). "Individuals and Information Overload in Organizations: Is More Necessarily Better?" *Academy of Management Journal* 23:684–696.

Sproull, L., and S. Kiesler (1986). "Reducing Social Context Cues: Electronic Mail in Organizational Communication." *Management Science* 32(11):1492–1512.

Thoits, P. (1983). "Multiple Identities and Psychological Well-Being." *American Sociological Review* 48:174–187.

P·A·R·T · V

C

Gender and Democracy in Computer-Mediated Communication*

Susan C. Herring

The Democratization Claim

Despite a substantial body of research demonstrating sex differences in face-to-face communication (see, e.g., Coates, 1986), the question of sex differences in computer-mediated communication has only recently begun to be raised. The lag is due in large part to a climate of general optimism surrounding the new technology: specifically, the belief that computer-mediated communication (hereafter, CMC) is inherently more democratic than other communication media. Thus philosophers and social theorists see in CMC a more equal access to information, empowering those who might otherwise be denied such information, and leading ultimately to a greater democratization of society (Ess, 1994; Landow, 1992; Nelson, 1974). Educators evoke the potential of computer networks to foster creativity and cooperation among students, and to help break down traditional barriers to communication between students and instructors (Kahn and Brookshire, 1991; Kiesler, Siegel, and McGuire, 1984; McCormick and McCormick, 1992). Even feminists are encouraged by evidence of more equal communication between women and men in the absence of status- and gender-marked cues (Graddol and Swann, 1989), and by the opportunities for women to establish grass roots electronic communication networks of their own (Smith and Balka, 1991).

The notion of democracy as it emerges through these claims has two essential components: access to a means of communication, and the right to communicate equally, free from status constraints. These components are inherent in the formal "rules of reason" proposed by the German philosopher Habermas (1983, p. 89; discussed in Ess, 1994) as criteria that must be observed in order for a discourse to be truly democratic:

1. Every subject with the competence to speak and act is allowed to take part in the discourse.
2a. Everyone is allowed to question any assertion whatever.
2b. Everyone is allowed to introduce any assertion whatever into the discourse.
2c. Everyone is allowed to express his [sic] attitudes, desires, and needs.
3. No speaker may be prevented, by internal or external coercion, from exercising his [sic] rights as laid down in (1) and (2).

Habermas's third rule provides for an important social dimension: in a truly democratic discourse, there can be no censorship. To the extent that computer technology facilitates open, egalitarian communication of this sort, it is held to be democratizing (Ess, 1994).

A number of specific characteristics of CMC have been claimed by researchers and users to facilitate communication that is democratic in nature. The first of these is *accessibility*. Through universities and other institutions, increasing numbers of people are able to gain access to computer networks at little or no cost. This access in turn makes available to them a variety of benefits, the most widely touted of which is information, in the form of on-line library catalogs, public domain databases, and the like. Less commonly mentioned, but equally if not more important, are the opportunities provided by electronic networks to connect and communicate, to express one's views and be recognized in a public forum, potentially even by large numbers of people (including, now that President Clinton has a public access e-mail address, highly influential people) around the world. In theory, anyone with access to a network can take equal advantage of these opportunities.

A second potentially democratizing characteristic of CMC is its *social decontextualization*. As noted by Graddol and Swann (1989) and Kiesler *et al.* (1984), the identity of contributors need not be revealed, especially given login "names" and return addresses that bear no transparent relationship to a person's actual name, sex, or geographical location.[1] Further, CMC neutralizes social status cues (accent, handwriting/voice quality, sex, appearance, etc.) that might otherwise be transmitted by the form of the message. Although on one hand these characteristics render the medium

---

*This article appeared in *Electronic Journal of Communication/REC* Vol. 3, No. 2 (not paginated). (Available through Comserve at vm.its.rpi.edu.) Reprinted with permission.

[1] Examples of opaque electronic addresses drawn from the data reported on in this study include 'f24030@barilvm,' 'T52@dhdurz1,' 'SNU00169@krsnucc1,' and the like.

less personal, they also provide for the possibility that traditionally lower-status individuals can participate on the same terms as others—that is, more or less anonymously, with the emphasis being on the content, rather than on the form of the message or the identity of the sender. As one member of an academic discussion list wrote in a recent posting to another:

> "One of the greatest strengths of e[lectronic]-mail is its ability to break down socio-economic, racial, and other traditional barriers to the sharing and production of knowledge. You, for example, have no way of knowing if I am a janitor or a university president or an illegal alien—we can simply communicate on the basis of our ideas, not on any preconceived notions of what should be expected (or not expected) from one another."

Although one might question the assumption that the posts of anonymous janitors, university presidents, and illegal aliens would not reveal their status (via differences in, e.g., grammatical usage, stylistic register, and familiarity with conventions of CMC and academic discourse), the idealism expressed by this writer is typical of that of many network users.

Third, as a relatively new discourse type, CMC lacks a set of consensually agreed-upon and established *conventions of use* (Ferrara, Brunner, and Whittemore, 1991; Kiesler *et al.*, 1984). As a result, users may be less inhibited, leading to "flaming" and outrageous behavior on one hand, and to greater openness on the other. This feature has led hypertext theorists such as Bolter (1991), Landow (1992), and Nelson (1974) to characterize CMC as "anarchic" as well as "democratic," with the potential to contribute to the breakdown of traditional hierarchical patterns of communication.

Finally, overt *censorship* on the electronic networks is as yet rare; what censorship exists is typically more concerned with selectively blocking the use of vulgar language than with blocking message content.[2] Even moderated discussion lists tend to accept virtually all contributions and post them in the order in which they are received. Thus each and every contributor to a discussion theoretically has the same opportunity to have his or her messages read and responded to by other members of the group (Habermas's third "rule of reason").

Taken together, these four characteristics would appear to constitute a strong a priori case for the democratic nature of CMC. But how democratic is the communication that is actually taking place currently via electronic networks? Specifically, does it show evidence of increased gender equality, as Graddol and Swann (1989) claim?

---

[2] An example of such censorship is the Defense Communications Agency's periodic screening of messages on the government-sponsored network ARPANET "to weed out those deemed in bad taste" (Kiesler *et al.*, 1984, p. 1130).

Summary of Investigative Results

The research reported on in this article is based primarily on investigations carried out over the past year on male and female participation in two academic electronic lists (also known as "bulletin boards" or "discussion groups"): LINGUIST, devoted to the discussion of linguistics-related issues; and Megabyte University (MBU), informally organized around the discussion of computers and writing. What follows is a summary of findings analyzed in detail in three recent articles (Herring, 1992; Herring, 1993; Herring, Johnson, and DiBenedetto, 1992); much of the data and analysis on which the earlier studies were based has of necessity been omitted here.

Three types of methods were employed in investigating participation on LINGUIST and MBU. The first was *ethnographic observation* of discussions as they occurred: I subscribed to and saved contributions to both lists over a period of one year, in the process assimilating information about contributors, current issues in the field, and other relevant background information. (CMC is especially amenable to data collection of this type, in that observers can easily remain invisible, thus avoiding the "observer's paradox" of altering by their presence the nature of the phenomenon they seek to observe.) Second, I subjected the texts of two extended discussions from each list to a *discourse analysis* in which patterns of grammatical and stylistic usage were identified. Observed patterns of usage were then correlated with participant sex, which was determined either from contributors' names when available (i.e., because they signed their message, or their mailer program included it in tracing the path of the message), or else by matching electronic addresses to names from a publicly available list of subscribers to each list.[3] Finally, I prepared and distributed two electronic surveys, one each for LINGUIST and MBU, in which I asked for participants' reactions to a particular discussion that had taken place on the list to which they subscribed, and solicited background information regarding their sex, professional status, and familiarity/competence with computers. The data collected by these three methods were subjected to quantitative as well as qualitative analysis. The combined results reveal significant differences between male and female participants. The principal differences are discussed below.

---

[3] With sex-neutral first names such as Chris or Robin, or with foreign names that I did not recognize, I contacted individuals by e-mail, identified the nature of my research, and asked whether they were male or female. By employing a combination of methods, I was able to determine with a reasonable degree of certainty the sex of approximately 95% of contributors on both lists.

Amount of Participation

The most striking sex-based disparity in academic CMC is the extent to which men participate more than women. Women constitute 36% of LINGUIST and 42% of MBU subscribers.[4] However, they participate at a rate that is significantly lower than that corresponding to their numerical representation. Two extended discussions were analyzed from each list, one in which sexism was an issue, and the other on a broadly theoretical topic. Although the "sexism" discussions were more popular with women than discussions on other topics, women constituted only 30% of the participants in these discussions on both lists; in the "theoretical" discussions, only 16% of the participants were women. Furthermore, the messages contributed by women are shorter, averaging a single screen or less, while those of men average one and a half times longer in the sexism discussions, and twice as long in the theoretical discussions, with some messages ten screens or more in length. Thus, although a short message does not necessarily indicate the sex of the sender, a very long message invariably indicates that the sender is male.

What accounts for this disparity? It does not appear on the surface as though men are preventing women from participating—at least, on one of the lists (MBU), male participants actively encourage more women to contribute. There is evidence to suggest, however, that women are discouraged from participating or intimidated on the basis of the reactions with which their posts are met when they do contribute. In a medium that permits multiple contributors to post messages more or less simultaneously to the group, gaining the focus of the group's attention or the "conversational floor" depends entirely on the extent to which other participants acknowledge and respond to one's postings. In the CMC analyzed here, messages posted by women consistently received fewer average responses than those posted by men. In the MBU sexism discussion, 89% of male postings received an explicit response, as compared with only 70% of those by women; on LINGUIST, the disparity is even greater. Of interest is the fact that it is not only men who respond more often to men, but women as well; postings from women acknowledging the postings of other women constitute the smallest portion of total responses, an implicit recognition, perhaps, of the more powerful status of men in the groups. In keeping with the unequal rate of response, topics initiated by women are less often taken up as topics of discussion by the group as a whole, and thus women may experience difficulty and frustration in getting the group to talk about topics that are of interest to them.

On those rare occasions when, out of special interest or a strong commitment to a particular point of view, women persist in posting on a given

---

[4] These percentages were calculated from lists of subscribers as of September 1992, on the basis of names from which sex could reliably be inferred.

topic despite relative lack of response, the outcome may be even more discouraging. During the period of this investigation, women participated actively three times: once during the MBU sexism debate, in which men and women became polarized regarding the legitimacy of offering a special course on "Men's Literature," and twice on LINGUIST, the first in a discussion of the interpretation of Sister Souljah's remarks on the Rodney King beating, and the second in a sexism discussion on the question of whether the label "dog" refers primarily to women, or to unattractive persons of either sex. In all three discussions, women's rate of posting increased gradually to where it equaled 50% of the contributions for a period of one or two days. The reaction to this increase was virtually identical in all three cases: a handful of men wrote in to decry the discussion, and several threatened to cancel their subscription to the list. Various reasons were given, none of them citing women's participation directly: in the MBU discussion, the tone was too "vituperative";[5] in the LINGUIST discussions, the topics were "inappropriate." Although the LINGUIST list moderators (one male, one female) intervened to defend the appropriateness of the Sister Souljah thread, the discussion died out almost immediately thereafter, as did the others. Of course, the possibility cannot be ruled out that the men who protested were responding to the content rather than (or in addition) to the frequency of women's posts. Nevertheless, the coincidence is striking, since at no other time during the period of observation did women participate as much as men, and at no other time did any subscriber, male or female, threaten publicly to unsubscribe from either list. Reactions such as these are consistent with Spender's (1979) claim that women cannot contribute half of the talk in a discussion without making men feel uncomfortable or threatened. She found that men (and to a lesser degree, women) perceive women as talking more than men when women talk only 30% of the time. This phenomenon is not limited to Spender's academic seminar data or to CMC, but rather is a feature of mixed-sex conversation in public settings more generally (Holmes, 1992).

This interpretation is further supported by the results of a survey conducted on MBU several months after the Men's Literature discussion. All available external evidence points to the conclusion that, despite the temporary increase in women's participation, men were more successful than women overall in the Men's Literature debate—men posted more, were responded to more, and introduced more successful topics in the discussion; further, the real-world course of action they advocated was ultimately followed (that is, a Men's Literature course was offered). However, when

---

[5] Although it is difficult to evaluate objectively what might count as evidence of a "vituperative" tone, the only postings to contain personal criticism of other participants (excluding the messages of protest) were those contributed by the man who originally proposed the "Men's Literature" course.

MBU subscribers were surveyed later regarding their reactions to the discussion, male respondents indicated a higher degree of dissatisfaction than women, and were more likely to say that women had "won" the debate; women, in contrast, were more likely to say that neither side had won (Herring, Johnson, and DiBenedetto, 1992). When women's attempts at equal participation are the cause of (male) dissatisfaction—even if voiced publicly by only a few—and disruption of list functioning, a message is communicated to the effect that it is more appropriate for women to participate less. And so they do: the day after the MBU protests, women's contributions dropped back to 15% of the total, and the discussion continued apace. The rather depressing conclusion to be drawn from this is that it is "normal" for women to participate less than men, such that an increase in the direction of true equality is perceived as deviant, even in liberal, academic settings.

Topic

The above observations indicate that although women contribute less than men overall, they contribute relatively more on certain topics of discussion, specifically those that involve real-world consequences as opposed to abstract theorizing. Herring (1993) describes a ranking of preferences based on participation in different topic types during a random two-week period on LINGUIST. Men were found to contribute most often to discussions of issues, followed by information postings (i.e., where they provided information, solicited or otherwise), followed by queries and personal discussions. Women, on the other hand, contributed most to personal discussions (talk about linguists, as opposed to talk about linguistics), followed by queries soliciting advice or information from others, with issues and information postings least frequent. The ranking of preferred topic types is represented schematically below:

MEN: issues > information > queries > personal
WOMEN: personal > queries > issues > information

A tendency for women to contribute less to discussions of theoretical issues than to other types of exchanges is evident on MBU as well.

Independent support for these observations comes from the Women's Studies List (WMST), devoted to issues involved in the organization and administration of women's studies programs. WMST, which is owned by a woman and has a subscribership that is currently 88% female, constitutes a context in which women post almost exclusively for and among themselves. Personal discussions are avoided on WMST, presumably in the interest of greater academic professionalism. Instead, the overwhelming majority of messages posted to WMST are queries for advice and/or information. Answers to queries, however, are required (according to posted list protocol) to be sent privately to the asker—although summaries of answers thus collected may be publicly posted—and issues discussions are explicitly prohibited by the list owner, who sees the list as "serving as a source of information" rather than "as a place to hold discussions about that information." Although on one hand participants might simply be following WMST protocol in formulating their contributions as queries rather than as messages of other types, as an active list with a steadily increasing membership (currently approaching 2000 members), WMST is proof that many women are comfortable with CMC that consists primarily in asking advice and information of others.

At the same time, there are indications that women do not avoid discussion of issues entirely by choice. Issues discussions arise periodically on WMST, only to be cut short by reminders from the list owner and other self-appointed list vigilantes; more than a few subscribers have written in to complain that the most interesting threads are invariably censored. The list owner feels, however, that it is important to avoid such exchanges in the interests of limiting message volume, and out of a fear that "discussion about highly-charged societal issues . . . would attract all sorts of unpleasant, acrimonious people who are just looking for a fight."[6] As the following section shows, this fear is not entirely unfounded.

Manner of Participation

The stylistic register of all of the CMC analyzed here is that of academic discourse. Nevertheless, there are significant sex-based differences to be noted, such that it is often possible to tell whether a given message was written by a man or a woman, solely on the basis of the rhetorical and linguistic strategies employed.[7]

In Herring (1992), I identify a set of features hypothesized to characterize a stylistic variety conventionally recognizable as "women's language" as opposed to "men's language" on the LINGUIST list. These features are summarized in Table 1.

The examples below, taken from messages posted during the LINGUIST "issues" discussion, illustrate some of the features of each style.

---

[6] Korenman, Joan (KORENMAN@UMBC.BITNET), Women's Studies List, June 9 11:08 PDT, 1992. In the only instance I observed where an issues discussion on WMST was allowed to take place, the discussion—concerned with media bias in reporting research on sex differences in the brain—was one in which all participants were essentially in agreement. (See Herring, in press.)

[7] There are also differences in character between the two lists. The overall level of formality is higher, and differences in sex-based styles greater, for LINGUIST than for MBU. Perhaps because of the rhetorical practices that currently characterize the two fields (formal argumentation in linguistics vs. creative collaboration in composition), discourse in the former tends to be more adversarial, or "masculine," while discourse in the latter is more personal, or "feminine." (For example, both men and women reveal information about their feelings and their nonacademic lives on MBU, whereas postings of this sort are virtually nonexistent on LINGUIST.)

Table 1.   Features of Women's and Men's Language

Women's language	Men's language
Attenuated assertions	Strong assertions
Apologies	Self-promotion
Explicit justifications	Presuppositions
Questions	Rhetorical questions
Personal orientation	Authoritative orientation
Supports others	Challenges others
	Humor/sarcasm

[female contributor]
I am intrigued by your comment that work such as that represented in WFDT
may not be as widely represented in LSA as other work because its argumentation style doesn't lend itself to falsification à la Popper. Could you say
a bit more about what you mean here? I am interested because I think similar
mismatches in argumentation are at stake in other areas of cognitive science,
as well as because I study argumentation as a key (social and cognitive) tool
for human knowledge construction.
[personal orientation, attenuation, questions, justification]

[male contributor]
It is obvious that there are two (and only two) paradigms for the conduct of
scientific inquiry into an issue on which there is no consensus. One is [. . .].
But, deplorable as that may be, note that either paradigm (if pursued honestly) will lead to truth anyway. That is, whichever side is wrong will sooner
or later discover that fact on its own. If, God forbid, autonomy and/or
modularity should turn out to be His truth, then those who have other ideas
will sooner or later find this out.
[authoritative orientation, strong assertions, sarcasm]

In order to quantify the distribution of these features according to sex, I
then analyzed 261 messages in two extended LINGUIST discussions, coding each message for the occurrence or nonoccurrence of each of the
features in Table 1. The results show that women's language features are
indeed used more often by women, and men's language features more
often by men. Sixty-eight percent of the messages produced by women
contained one or more features of women's language, as compared with
only 31% of those produced by men. In contrast, 48% of the messages
produced by men contained features of only men's language, as compared
with 18% of women's messages. Although the majority of women's messages (46%) combined a mixture of male and female rhetorical features, the
fewest men's messages (14%) combined features. This finding supports the
view that it is easier for men to maintain a distinct style (masculine,
feminine, or neutral) than it is for women, who must employ some features
of men's language in order to be taken seriously as academics, and some
features of women's language in order not to be considered unpleasant or
aggressive.

These observations on gender-marked styles lead to a second finding regarding manner of participation. Discussion on each of the lists investigated tends to be dominated by a small minority of participants who abuse features of men's language to focus attention on themselves, often at the expense of others. Such abuse, which I term "adversarial" rhetoric, ranges from gratuitous displays of knowledge to forceful assertions of one's views to elaborate put-downs of others with whom one disagrees. In the two LINGUIST discussions analyzed, 4% and 6% of the participants, respectively (all but one of them male), were responsible for the majority of adversarial rhetoric. This same 4% and 6% also posted the most words (33% and 53% of the total, respectively, or more than eight times the participant average), and thus dominated in amount as well as in manner of participation.[8]

A similar pattern is found in a different kind of CMC—electronic mail exchanges between undergraduates (75% male) on a local network, as investigated by McCormick and McCormick (1992). The authors report that 4.7% of the undergraduates used the network "a great deal," and "may have been responsible for generating most of the electronic mail." Although the content and purpose of communication in this setting is quite different from that on professional academic discussion lists, the minority also seems to have imposed its style on the discourse overall, turning the computer lab into "an adolescent subculture" complete with crude jokes, threats, and put-downs.

The extent to which other participants are negatively affected by the behavior of a dominant minority may depend, at least partly, on their sex. A survey of LINGUIST subscribers distributed after the "issue" discussion took place revealed that 73% of respondents of both sexes felt intimidated and/or irritated by the adversarial tone of the discussion (Herring, 1992). Men and women appear to behave differently on the basis of this reaction, however. Male respondents indicated that they take it in stride as part of academic interaction; as one man remarked: "Actually, the barbs and arrows were entertaining, because of course they weren't aimed at me." Many women, in contrast, expressed a deep aversion and a concern to avoid interactions of this type. Comments included: "I was terribly turned off by this exchange, which went on and on forever. I nearly dropped myself from the list of subscribers," and "I was disgusted. It's the same old arguments, the same old intentions of defending theoretical territory, the same old inabilities of open and creative thinking, all of which make me ambivalent about academics in general." The concern expressed by the

---

[8] The tendency for a small minority to dominate the discourse is evident on MBU as well. Eight percent of participants (all but one of them male) produced 35% of the words in the sexism discussion. This minority dominated rhetorically by posting long-winded and often obscure postings, on MBU an abuse more common than overt adversarial attacks.

owner of the WMST list to avoid acrimonious exchanges is fully consistent with the comments of the female LINGUIST survey respondents. Why do women react with greater aversion than men to adversarial exchanges? Sheldon (1992) suggests that this aversion can be traced to cultural norms of sex-appropriate behavior with which children are indoctrinated from an early age: while boys are encouraged to compete and engage in direct confrontation, girls are taught to "be nice" and to appease others, a distinction internalized in the play behavior of children as young as three years of age. As a consequence, verbal aggressiveness comes to have a different significance for women than for men; as Coates (1986) observes, women are apt to take personal offense at what men may view as part of the conventional structure of conversation.

Discussion of Results

The results of this research can be summarized as follows. Despite the democratizing potential described in the first section of this article, male and female academic professionals do not participate equally in academic CMC. Rather, a small male minority dominates the discourse both in terms of amount of talk, and rhetorically, through self-promotional and adversarial strategies. Moreover, when women do attempt to participate on a more equal basis, they risk being actively censored by the reactions of men who either ignore them or attempt to delegitimize their contributions. Because of social conditioning that makes women uncomfortable with direct conflict, women tend to be more intimidated by these practices and to avoid participating as a result. Thus Habermas's conditions for a democratic discourse are not met: although the medium theoretically allows for everyone with access to a network to take part and to express their concerns and desires equally, a very large community of potential participants is effectively prevented by censorship, both overt and covert, from availing itself of this possibility. Rather than being democratic, academic CMC is power-based and hierarchical. This state of affairs cannot, however, be attributed to the influence of computer communication technology; rather, it continues preexisting patterns of hierarchy and male dominance in academia more generally, and in society as a whole.

How can we reconcile these findings with the more encouraging reports of democratization based on earlier research? The claim of status-free communication hinges in large part on the condition of anonymity (Graddol and Swann, 1989; Kiesler et al., 1984), a condition that is not met in the discourse analyzed here, since most messages were signed, or else the sender's identity is transparently derivable from his or her electronic address.[9] In a very few cases could there have been any doubt upon receipt of a message as to the sex of the sender, and thus sex-based discrimination could freely apply. However, given the existence of "genderlects" of the sort identified here, it is doubtful that such discrimination would disappear even if everyone were to contribute anonymously. Just as a university president or a janitor's social status is communicated through their unconscious choices of style and diction, CMC contains subtle indications of participants' gender.

Second, CMC is claimed to be more uninhibited (disorganized, anarchic), because of lack of established conventions of use (Kiesler et al., 1984; Nelson, 1974). It is important, however, to distinguish between the adversarial behavior observed on academic lists and "flaming," which is defined as "excessive informality, insensitivity, the expression of extreme or opinionated views, and vulgar behavior (including swearing, insults, name calling, and hostile comments)" by McCormick and McCormick (1992, p. 381). While flaming may well result from spontaneously venting one's emotion, adversariality is a conventionalized and accepted (indeed, rewarded) pattern of behavior in academic discourse, and characterizes postings that otherwise show evidence of careful planning and preparation. Rather than being at a loss for a set of discourse conventions, the members of these lists appear to have simply transferred the conventions of academic discourse, as they might be observed, for example, in face-to-face interaction at a professional conference, to the electronic medium, with some modifications for the written nature of the message.

Another factor claimed to lead to decreased inhibition is the supposedly depersonalized nature of CMC. However, this assumption too can be challenged. From my observations, academic list subscribers do not view the activity of posting as targeted at disembodied strangers. Their addresses are people with whom they either have a professional relationship, or could potentially develop such a relationship in the future. This is likely to increase (rather than decrease) inhibition, since one's professional reputation is at stake. In this respect, the CMC discussed here differs from the experimental CMC described by Kiesler et al., where subjects risked nothing beyond the confines of the experimental setting. Three factors in Kiesler et al.'s (1984, p. 1129) experimental design were found to correlate with less inhibited verbal behavior: anonymity, simultaneity (as opposed to linear sequencing of messages), and simultaneous computer conferencing (as opposed to electronic mail). None of these conditions obtained in the

---

[9] As far as I was able to ascertain, surprisingly few participants took advantage of the anonymity potential of the medium. Fewer than 2% of contributors attempted to disguise their identity, and when they did so, it was for humorous effect.

CMC investigated in this study, since discussion lists, in addition to not meeting the anonymity condition, present postings linearly, and typically after some delay.

In concluding, we return to the question of censorship, freedom from which is an essential condition for democracy. Although it is true that no external censorship was exercised by the moderators or owners of LINGUIST or MBU, women participating in CMC are nevertheless constrained by censorship both external and internal. Externally, they are censored by male participants who dominate and control the discourse through intimidation tactics, and who ignore or undermine women's contributions when they attempt to participate on a more equal basis. To a lesser extent, nonadversarial men suffer the same treatment, and in and of itself, it need not prevent anyone who is determined to participate from doing so. Where adversariality becomes a devastating form of censorship, however, is in conjunction with the internalized cultural expectations that we bring to the formula: that women will talk less, on less controversial topics, and in a less assertive manner. Finally, although it was not a focus of the present investigation, women are further discouraged from participating in CMC by the expectation—effectively internalized as well—that computer technology is primarily a male domain (McCormick and McCormick, 1991; Turkle, 1991). This expectation is reflected in the responses of female survey respondents on both LINGUIST and MBU to the question: "How comfortable/competent do you feel with computer technology?" Female respondents overwhelmingly indicated less confidence in their ability to use computers, despite the fact that they had had the same number of years of computer experience as male respondents.[10] Internalized censorship of this sort reflects deeper social ills, and it is naive to expect that technology alone will heal them.

References

Bolter, J. D. (1991). *Writing Space: The Computer, Hypertext, and the History of Writing.* Lawrence Erlbaum, Hillsdale, NJ.

Coates, J. (1986). *Women, Men, and Language.* Longman, New York.

Ess, C. (1994). "The Political Computer: Hypertext, Democracy, and Habermas," in George Landow (ed.), *Hypertext and Literary Theory.* Johns Hopkins University Press, Baltimore, MD.

Ferrara, K., H. Brunner, and G. Whittemore (1991). "Interactive Written Discourse as an Emergent Register." *Written Communication,* 8, 8–34.

---

[10] In the MBU survey, 30% of female respondents reported feeling "somewhat hesitant" about using computers, as compared with 5% of the men (the rest of whom rated themselves as "competent" or "extremely competent"). In the LINGUIST survey, 13% of the women responded "somewhat hesitant" as compared with none of the men. The average length of computer use for both sexes was nine years on MBU and eleven years on LINGUIST.

Graddol, D., and J. Swann (1989). *Gender Voices.* Basil Blackwell, Oxford.

Habermas, J. (1983). "Diskursethik: Notizen zu einem Begruendungsprogram," in Moralbewusstsein und kommunikatives Handeln (Frankfurt: Suhrkamp). Translated as "Discourse Ethics: Notes on Philosophical Justification," in Christian Lenhardt and Shierry Weber Nicholsen (trans.), *Moral Consciousness and Communicative Action* (43–115). MIT Press, Cambridge (1990).

Herring, S. (1992). "Gender and Participation in Computer-Mediated Linguistic Discourse." Washington, DC: ERIC Clearinghouse on Languages and Linguistics, Document no. ED345552.

Herring, S. (1993). "Men's Language: A Study of the Discourse of the LINGUIST List." in A. Crochetihre, J.-C. Boulanger, and C. Ouellon (eds.), *Les Langues Menacies: Actes du XVe Congres International des Linguistes,* Vol. 3, pp. 347–350. Quibec Les Presses de l'Universiti Laval.

Herring, S. (forthcoming). "Two Variants of an Electronic Message Schema." in S. Herring (ed.), *Computer-Mediated Communication: Linguistic, Social, and Cross-Cultural Perspectives.* John Benjamins, Amsterdam/Philadelphia.

Herring, S. C., D. Johnson, and T. DiBenedetto (1992). "Participation in Electronic Discourse in a 'Feminist' Field," in *Locating Power: Proceedings of the 1992 Berkeley Women and Language Conference.* Berkeley Linguistic Society.

Herring, S., D. Johnson, and T. DiBenedetto (in press). " 'This Discussion Is Going Too Far!' Male Resistance to Female Participation on the Internet." in M. Bucholtz and K. Hall (eds.), *Gender Articulated: Language and the Socially-Constructed Self.* Routledge, New York.

Holmes, J. (1992). "Women's Talk in Public Contexts." *Discourse and Society,* 3(2), 131–150.

Kahn, A. S., and R. G. Brookshire (1991). "Using a Computer Bulletin Board in a Social Psychology Course." *Teaching of Psychology,* 18(4), 245–249.

Kiesler, S., J. Siegel, and T. W. McGuire (1984). "Social Psychological Aspects of Computer-Mediated Communication." *American Psychologist,* 39, 1123–1134.

Landow, G. P. (1992). *Hypertext: The Convergence of Contemporary Critical Theory and Technology.* Johns Hopkins University Press, Baltimore, MD.

McCormick, N. B., and J. W. McCormick (1991). "Not for Men Only: Why So Few Women Major in Computer Science." *College Student Journal,* 85(3), 345–350.

McCormick, N.B., and J. W. McCormick (1992). "Computer Friends and Foes: Content of Undergraduates' Electronic Mail." *Computers in Human Behavior,* 8, 379–405.

Nelson, T. H. (1974). "Dream Machines: New Freedoms through Computer Screens —A Minority Report." *Computer Lib: You Can and Must Understand Computers Now.* Hugo's Book Service, Chicago. (rev. ed.). Microsoft Press, Redmond, WA (1987).

Sheldon, A. (1992). "Conflict Talk: Sociolinguistic Challenges to Self-Assertion and How Young Girls Meet Them." *Merrill-Palmer Quarterly,* 38(1), 95–117.

Smith, J., and E. Balka (1991). "Chatting on a Feminist Computer Network," in C. Kramarae (ed.), *Technology and Women's Voices* (pp. 82–97). Routledge and Kegan Paul, New York.

Spender, D. (1979). "Language and Sex Differences," in *Osnabrueker Beitraege zur Sprach-theorie: Sprache und Geschlect* II, 38–59.

Turkle, S. (1991). "Computational Reticence: Why Women Fear the Intimate Machine," in C. Kramarae (ed.), *Technology and Women's Voices* (pp. 41–61). Routledge and Kegan Paul, New York.

P·A·R·T · V

D

Finding a Happy Medium: Explaining the Negative Effects of Electronic Communication on Social Life at Work*

M. Lynne Markus

Introduction

It is now well known that, for all its many benefits, electronic communication holds risks for social life at work: Though it does not always do so, electronic communication can result in misinterpretations, angry and uninhibited exchanges, and feelings of isolation or depersonalization among its users (Kiesler, Siegel, and McGuire, 1984; Sproull and Kiesler, 1986). These effects are often attributed to the technological characteristics of electronic media, such as their limited ability to transmit the gestures, tones of voice, and eye movements that people use to regulate their interactions in face-to-face communication (Culnan and Markus, 1987). Consequently, communicators via the electronic media are frequently urged to use these technologies in "appropriate" ways, whether this means attending to "ethics and etiquette" (Shapiro and Anderson, 1985) or avoiding these media for certain types of communication (Lengel and Daft, 1988).

The belief that the negative social effects of electronic communication are caused by technological characteristics is an optimistic theory. It suggests the cheerful prospect that the risks will diminish as technology becomes more advanced. The hope is that progress toward the integration of voice, text, and video will soon succeed in personalizing electronic communication, allowing users to relax their guard against outcomes that are both undesirable and undesired.

But what if the negative outcomes result not from the technology itself, but rather from how people use it? If so, multimedia integration may change the outcomes, but not necessarily for the better. And what if the negative outcomes occur despite people's best efforts to avert them through such prophylactic behaviors as thinking twice before pushing "send"? If so, the consequences of using electronic communication, both good and ill, may be here to stay.

These "what if" questions reflect potentially distinct alternatives to the theory that ascribes social consequences, negative or positive, to the technological characteristics of electronic communication media. The first alternative argues that social outcomes, both positive and negative, can be attributed to the intentions of the users. This theory suggests that, to ensure positive outcomes, users must not only know the rules of proper e-mail etiquette, but they must also be motivated to achieve socially desirable outcomes. Yet this motivation may be lacking when socially desirable outcomes conflict with private motives. The second alternative theory argues that the outcomes of technology use are inherently unpredictable and may not reflect either the true possibilities of the technology or the users' deliberate goals. This theory suggests that negative social consequences from the use of electronic media may not prove tractable despite concerted efforts at technical and social engineering.

How much can these two alternative theories add to our understanding of the negative social consequences of electronic communication? The research question is examined here in the context of an exploratory investigation of electronic mail use in a large organization in which some negative effects were observed. The findings have interesting implications for efforts to ensure socially desirable outcomes through better technology design, better communication etiquette, or better people management.

Background

Of the many possible theoretical models of technology use and impacts (Kling, 1980; Kling and Scacchi, 1982; Markus and Robey, 1988; Poole and DeSanctis, 1990; Orlikowski and Robey, 1991), much research on the social impacts of electronic communication media has focused on technological characteristics. According to the theoretical perspective of *technological determinism,* social outcomes derive primarily from the material characteristics of a technology, regardless of users' intentions. Changes in technological characteristics are argued to influence social outcomes (Markus and Robey, 1988).

---

*This article appeared in *ACM Transactions on Information Systems* (12)2(April 1994), 119–149. Reprinted with permission of the Association for Computing Machinery.

One prominent stream of research in this tradition has emphasized the deficiencies in electronic media when they are compared to face-to-face interaction (Culnan and Markus, 1987). In this view, communication technologies such as teleconferencing and electronic mail "filter out" certain personal, social, and behavioral cues used by people to maintain interpersonal relationships and regulate interaction in face-to-face communication (Short et al., 1976; Sproull and Kiesler, 1986). As a result, mediated communication is generally believed to be "impersonal and lacking in sociability," although studies do not always show this to be the case (Rice and Love, 1987, p. 88).

Researchers in the "cues filtered out" tradition often conclude that negative impacts will result from heavy use of electronic media. To the extent that the technologies are unable to facilitate "supportive interaction" (Kerr and Hiltz, 1982, p. 131) relationships at work may become impersonal, anomic, or even hostile. Consistent with this view, electronic communication has been observed to display evidence of "deregulation," "disinhibition," and "depersonalization" (Kiesler, Siegel, and McGuire, 1984), such as impoliteness and "flaming" (i.e., swearing and other inappropriate behavior), as well as problems in the formation of coalitions, the emergence of leaders, and the achievement of consensus in groups (see Culnan and Markus, 1987, for a review). In addition, it has been suggested that heavy use of electronic communication technologies might create social isolation by distancing users from relationships "external to the medium," for example, friendships and personal relationships with people who are not "on-line" (Kerr and Hiltz, 1982, p. 106).

On the other hand, it is clear that negative social outcomes do not always result from the use of electronic communication technology. The theory of technological determinism is also invoked to explain positive social outcomes, usually by referencing the "new capabilities" of electronic media (Culnan and Markus, 1987; Hollan and Stornetta, 1992) not found in face-to-face communication. For instance, in a comparison of various media, Sproull (1991) pointed out that electronic mail possesses at least three useful characteristics that face-to-face meetings do not: asynchrony (temporal separation between sending and receiving), externally recorded memory, and computer-processable memory. From the perspective of technological determinism, these new features and capabilities of electronic media are likely to engender various positive social outcomes such as "increased connectedness" (Kerr and Hiltz, 1982) or "increased personal connections" (Sproull and Kiesler, 1991). Consistent with this view, numerous studies have found that technologies such as electronic mail promote "new communication" among members of large or geographically dispersed communities—communication that would not have occurred through alternative communication channels (see Kerr and Hiltz, 1982; Feldman, 1987; Sproull and Kiesler, 1991; and studies reviewed in Rice and Associates, 1984, and Culnan and Markus, 1987).

Similarly, the new communication technologies have also been found to reduce the social isolation of geographically dispersed people with few opportunities for face-to-face meetings (Eveland and Bikson, 1987). They enable peripheral employees (those socially or geographically distant from the "center") to be more informed about, and to have greater voice in, the affairs of their community (Kerr and Hiltz, 1982; Sproull and Kiesler, 1991). They allow people to "meet" others with common interests and concerns, thus supporting and sustaining grouplike interaction among "communities of interest" (Kerr and Hiltz, 1982, p. 127; Finholt and Sproull, 1990). And they facilitate increased sociability by transmitting a fair amount of the social-emotional communication believed essential to the maintenance of social relationships, in addition to the work-related information required for the performance of organizational tasks (Kerr and Hiltz, 1982; Rice and Love, 1987; Steinfield, 1986).

While research that emphasizes the deficiencies of electronic communication compared to face-to-face interaction has tended to find evidence of negative social effects, and research that emphasizes the new capabilities of media has tended to find evidence of positive outcomes, there is no necessary relationship here. The filtering out of personal cues has been argued to explain the positive social outcome that telephone users are more reasonable and willing to compromise during negotiation than are face-to-face communicators (Short, Williams, and Christie, 1976). And the new capabilities of electronic media might also be argued to enable certain negative social consequences such as compulsive documentation and accountability games (see findings reported later in this paper). Thus, the key theoretical issue is not the relationship between particular features and particular outcomes. Rather, it is the degree to which the outcomes, whether positive or negative, are the inevitable results of technological characteristics, or whether they might be subject to other influences, such as people's deliberate choices about how to use the new electronic media. To address this question, we must turn to different theoretical perspectives.

One alternative to an explanation of negative social effects rooted in the technological characteristics of media emphasizes the "purposive behavior" of media users (Pool, 1978). In other words, how people use the technology and what they try to accomplish with it are likely to affect the outcomes. Often named after the hypothetical "rational actor" it celebrates (Kling, 1980; Pfeffer, 1982; Markus and Robey, 1988), the *rational actor* perspective holds that impacts result not from the technology itself, but from the choices individuals make about when and how to use it. Some researchers have argued, for example, that personal and organizational ineffectiveness results when people use e-mail for equivocal communication tasks (Daft and Lengel, 1984, 1986).

The rational actor perspective opens the door to the possibility that there are "good uses" of electronic communication technology (uses that result in positive social outcomes, within the constraints imposed by technolog-ical characteristics) and "bad uses" (ones that result in negative social outcomes). Further, it invites us to ask the question: Under what condi-tions would it be rational for e-mail users to behave in ways that result in negative effects? To this question, the rational actor perspective suggests two broad answers. First, "bad uses" of electronic communication tech-nology might be rational when users *want* to achieve "negative social impacts," for instance, when they want to achieve social distance in their relationships with others. And, second, "bad uses" might be rational when, despite the fact that they generate negative social effects, they also produce benefits that outweigh these negative effects.[1]

In other words, the rational actor perspective suggests the need to inquire about the reasons for the "bad uses" that can be argued to cause negative social outcomes. And one insight of this perspective is that the negative social effects of e-mail, such as greater interpersonal distance, may be outcomes that are deliberately *intended* by the users of the technology. For instance, Sproull and Kiesler (1986) have suggested that subordinates may prefer to use electronic communication when dealing with their su-periors (but not with their subordinates!), because this medium suppresses the cues that convey their lower hierarchical status. Other examples readily come to mind. It is sometimes the case that one's emotional state conflicts with the words one wants another person to "hear." Psychological studies show (and people know) that in cases of conflict between words and nonverbal behavior, listeners believe the latter (Short *et al.*, 1976). This being the case, the rational subordinate who strongly disapproves of the decision of a superior is well advised to select a medium that can censor such reactions.

Similarly, people who do not like those they need to work with may wish to avoid interacting with them as much as they can. However, when interaction is unavoidable, when work needs to get done, they may prefer to communicate about work without communicating their dislike. Further, they themselves may wish to avoid experiencing the negative emotional reactions aroused by interacting with people who are disliked or feared. And electronic communication may help them do so: Eveland and Bikson (1988) have concluded that electronic communication is not always viewed as "real" interaction, a clear advantage when people do not want a real, negative, interaction. Along these lines, Markus (1992) found that mem-bers of a small work group that had the ability to work together face-to-face began to communicate exclusively through electronic mail when social relations on the team became unbearably tense. In short, the rational actor

---

[1] Among the potential benefits of "bad uses" of e-mail are: satisfaction at having registered a protest, defense of one's own position (suggested by Michael Myers), and efficiencies due to the avoidance of idle chitchat (suggested by Louise Soe).

perspective on technology impacts suggests the possibility that people may deliberately choose electronic communication systems precisely because these systems can allow users to circumvent face-to-face interaction, to defuse or impersonalize problematic relationships, or otherwise to manage their communication with others (Contractor and Eisenberg, 1990; Eisenberg and Phillips, 1991).

An additional insight of the rational actor perspective is that people may continue to engage in a behavior that has the potential for negative impacts, because it has other, positive effects that the user desires to achieve. As rational actors, people may know that particular uses of electronic communication, such as using it regularly with their subordinates, entail risks such as weakened authority or depersonalized interaction, but they may also value the benefits of using the technology in these ways, such as the ability to transcend time and distance, the ability to reach multiple parties simultaneously, and the ability to document the communication— the "new capabilities" discussed earlier. In such cases, the rational actor perspective suggests that users aware of potential negative consequences will take active measures to *minimize* them. A uniquely human ability permits people to anticipate that an action they plan to take has the possibility of negative consequences and to employ measures intended to counteract, or compensate, for these consequences. So, if the perceived benefits of electronic communication are great enough to make it worthwhile risking negative "side effects," one would expect to see e-mail users adopting strategies for managing the risks.

A second alternative to the technological determinism perspective on impacts has been called the *emergent process* view (Pfeffer, 1982; Markus and Robey, 1988). According to this perspective, technologies and the choices of users are believed to interact with mutually causal influences that occasionally result in consequences that are unforeseen, undesired, and even unintended. Like the technological determinism perspective, this perspective directs attention to negative consequences that may occur *despite* users' good intentions and despite their best efforts to use technology so as to avert negative social outcomes. Unlike the determinism perspective, however, emergent process theory does not attribute the negative consequences entirely to the features of the technology. Instead, this perspective argues that negative outcomes may ironically originate in the very actions people take to prevent negative effects and ensure positive outcomes (Douglas, 1986). Thus, the emergent process perspective helps to explain depersonalization, when it occurs, as an unpredictable by-product of the capabilities and limitations of electronic communication systems in interaction with people's deliberate choices about when and how to use them most effectively.

Furthermore, the emergent process perspective encourages us to inquire about the origins of "good" and "bad" uses of technology. Whereas proponents of rational actor models frequently derive prescriptions for appropriate uses of the technology from an analysis of technological characteristics, such as the cues filtered out and new capabilities of electronic media, emergent process theorists tend to recognize that models of what a technology is good for (or bad for) are "socially defined" (Barley, 1986; Poole and DeSanctis, 1990; Orlikowski and Robey, 1991) and thus possibly unique to a particular social setting.

In summary, there are several alternative explanations for why electronic communication technology sometimes has negative social effects. The technological determinism perspective focuses on the material characteristics of media, such as the absence of personal or social cues and the presence of new features. The rational actor perspective focuses on users' intentions and behaviors, such as whether they deliberately use technology in ways likely to achieve or avert negative social effects. The emergent process perspective focuses on the social definitions of what technology is good for and accepts the possibility that negative effects might occur despite the well-intentioned behaviors of media users (see Table 1).

The preceding discussion suggests the value of comparing these partially conflicting, partially complementary, theories of the negative social effects of electronic communication technology. These theories are examined here in the context of a detailed exploratory case study of a single organization in which electronic communication was routinely used by the majority of managerial employees as a primary means of work-related communication. In particular, the following research questions are addressed:

- In general, how were people in the setting using e-mail, and what did they intend to accomplish with it?
- To what extent were the social effects of using e-mail positive, negative, or mixed?
- To what extent can the rational actor and emergent process perspectives increase our understanding of any negative effects observed?
- Did people ever deliberately employ "bad uses" of e-mail or *intend* to achieve negative social effects, and, if so, how?
- Did people try to *prevent* negative social side effects due to the use of e-mail, and, if so, how?
- And did negative social effects sometimes result from using e-mail *despite* users' best attempts to prevent them?

The next section describes the method and research site.

Method and Research Site

The research questions stated in the previous section were examined via a descriptive case study of a single organization, called HCP Inc. (a pseudonym). The case study research strategy was believed appropriate in view of the admittedly exploratory aims of the current research. More details

Table 1. Theoretical Perspectives on the Negative Social Effects of E-mail Use

Perspective	Explanation of Negative Effects/Predictions about Behavior
Technological Determinism	
• Social effects are determined by the characteristics of technology, regardless of users' intentions. • Relevant technological characteristics of electronic media include "cues filtered out" and "new capabilities."	• Negative outcomes occur when e-mail is used, because e-mail filters out the cues that people need to regulate their social interaction. • Negative outcomes occur when e-mail is used, because e-mail has new capabilities that deregulate or depersonalize social interaction.
Rational Actor	
• Social effects result from intended human actions within the constraints and enablements afforded by technological characteristics. • People may intend negative outcomes, when private motives differ from socially desirable outcomes. • People may anticipate negative outcomes and take steps to avert them.	• Negative outcomes occur because people occasionally engage in "bad uses" of e-mail. While some bad uses of e-mail may result from ignorance, some may be deliberate, that is, people may actually intend to bring out negative social effects, such as increased interpersonal distance. • People may know that using e-mail entails the risk of negative social outcomes, because the technology clearly filters out some important social cues. However, using e-mail may also produce benefits that users desire. Therefore, people who use e-mail may take steps to avoid e-mail's potential negative "side effects" on social interaction.
Emergent Process	
• The effects of technology use result from unpredictable interactions among technological characteristics, users' intentions and behaviors, and social definitions of good and bad uses.	• When negative effects occur, they are often unintended and unanticipated; they may even be the ironic result of actions people take to avoid the potential negative effects of using e-mail.

about the research design and its justification can be found in Markus (in press).

Case studies are a particularly useful strategy when the phenomena of interest—in this instance users' intentions, technology use patterns, and social impacts—cannot be clearly separated from the social, technological, and organizational context in which they occur (Yin, 1989). The aim of case studies is not to discover particular facts—for instance, the incidence of negative social impacts—which are claimed to "generalize" to other settings. Rather, the aim of case studies is to make observations about the explanatory power of different theoretical arguments that, through replication, can be argued to generalize (Yin, 1989; Lee, 1989).

HCP operates in the risk management industry, acquiring professional services for which there is variable demand and retailing them to large organizations for a fixed fee. At the time of the study, HCP had branches in twenty-six states. Subject to headquarter's approval, the branches were permitted to initiate contracts with local suppliers and customers, but most final approvals as well as most routine operational support activities (e.g., accounting and claims processing) were performed at corporate headquarters. In 1987, HCP had approximately 7500 employees, 825 of whom were managers (first-level supervisors through corporate officers). Thus, HCP was large, geographically dispersed, and structurally complex. People in the firm had been using electronic mail long enough and heavily enough so that one could expect any impacts to have made themselves felt, but not for so long that people had forgotten what things were like before the technology was introduced (Zuboff, 1988).

A hallmark of the case study research method is the use of multiple data sources (Yin, 1989), permitting the phenomenon of interest to be examined in depth and reducing the limitations of any single data source. This study "triangulated" (Jick, 1983) data from interviews, a survey, and archives.

Interviews. Twenty-nine people at HCP headquarters were interviewed in one or more sessions lasting forty-five minutes to two and one half hours in length, following a relatively unstructured and evolving interview protocol (Merton et al., 1990; Stewart and Shamdasani, 1990). Interviewees were selected with the help of an organizational informant on the basis of their knowledge of the company and its communication practices and thus overrepresent the organizational elite (Sieber, 1973). The interviewees numbered the Chairman, twelve corporate vice-presidents and assistant vice-presidents, seven managers and directors, and nine administrative assistants. The interviewees provided information about the firm, its industry, and its e-mail system, in addition to self-reported descriptions of, and explanations for, the interviewees' personal media use behaviors. Interview data were analyzed both analytically (Miles and Huberman, 1984) and interpretively (Orlikowski and Baroudi, 1991; Lee, 1991) to identify how managers at HCP experienced the technology and its role in the company.

Table 2.   Questionnaire Respondents by Level and Location

Level	Headquarters	Field	Total
Vice-presidents	31	9	40
	(24)[a]	(4)	(11)
Directors	42	164	206
	(33)	(67)	(55)
Managers	30	47	77
	(23)	(19)	(21)
Supervisors	25	23	48
	(20)	(10)	(13)
Total	128	243	371[b]
	(35)	(65)	(100)

[a]Percentages in parentheses.
[b]Differs from sample total ($N = 375$) because of missing data.

Survey. A second source of data for this study is a paper and pencil instrument, constructed and administered along the lines recommended by Dillman (1978). It was mailed to 504 managers in HCP, 60% of the firm's managers, with a cover letter indicating the Chairman's support for the project. The sample was stratified by organizational unit—headquarters and branches—in proportion to the number of employees. Within these units, the questionnaire was sent to managers at four hierarchical levels— supervisors, managers, directors, and vice-presidents. Two follow-up letters to questionnaire recipients yielded a response rate of 77% ($N = 375$ completed questionnaires). The distribution of managers responding, shown in Table 2, is similar to the distribution of HCP managers, allowing one to be reasonably confident that the questionnaire results represent the beliefs of the population of HCP managers. Thus, the survey helps compensate for the elite bias in the selection of interviewees (Sieber, 1973).

Three closed-ended questions[2] on the survey are most relevant to the research questions addressed in this paper. The first question was described to respondents as addressing "the effects of using electronic mail (e-mail) on work performance and work relationships at HCP" and consisted of forty statements about perceived impacts preceded by the phrase "Because of e-mail. . . ." Respondents were requested to indicate the extent of their agreement with each item on a scale of 1 to 5 (where 1 was anchored as "strongly disagree" and 5 as "strongly agree"). The items included on the instrument had been chosen to reflect arguments made in

---

[2] Existing measures of e-mail impacts were not believed sufficiently fine-grained for the purpose of this exploratory research. Therefore, new instruments were designed. Scales constructed from the instruments by means of factor analysis were shown to have acceptable reliability.

Table 3. Perceived E-Mail Impacts: Questionnaire Items, Factor Loadings, Means, Standard Deviations and Percentages of Respondents Agreeing and Disagreeing with Questionnaire Items about E-Mail Impacts[a]

Item	Loading	Mean (S.D.)	Agree (%)	Disagree (%)
Closeness factor[b]				
I feel closer to my subordinates	.68	2.8 (.82)	19	31
I feel closer to my boss	.67	2.8 (.94)	22	36
Depersonalization factor[c]				
HCP is a less personal place to work	.62	2.9 (.97)	28	38
I feel more invisible at HCP	.58	2.6 (.97)	17	52
HCP is better at solving problems	−.51	3.3 (.97)	42	19
HCP is less responsive to [suppliers and customers]	.49	2.2 (.88)	6	63
I get less feedback on my job performance	.43	3.6 (.91)	17	49
People can avoid personal contact	.40	3.6 (.92)	66	15

[a]The question was worded: "Please indicate the extent of your agreement or disagreement with these statements, which begin 'Because of e-mail.'" Respondents answered on a 5-point scale, where 1 = "strongly disagree" and 5 = "strongly agree." In the table, "agree" includes those who responded 4 or 5; "disagree" includes those who responded 1 or 2.
[b]Alpha = .70.
[c]Alpha = .74.

the literature about positive and negative impacts of electronic communication on each of two dimensions: work-related efficiency and social relations at work. Exploratory factor analysis derived the theoretically expected factors; the two most relevant for this paper were interpreted as representing "positive" social impacts (e.g., increased "closeness": alpha = .70) and "negative" social impacts (e.g., increased "depersonalization": alpha = .74) of e-mail use (see Table 3 for the factors and items).

The second question concerned "the 'etiquette' of using electronic mail (e-mail) at HCP" and consisted of forty statements of typical behavior and normative beliefs about "how you and others at [HCP] use e-mail." Respondents were again requested to indicate agreement or disagreement on a 5-point scale. This question was originally intended to assess the frequency of certain communication behaviors, but it also contained a few items that appeared to assess perceived "impacts" of e-mail use. The relevant items from the "etiquette" question are displayed in Table 4.

The third question had been designed to determine whether respondents' assessment of media appropriateness agreed with the predictions of information richness theory (see Markus, in press). On the basis of inter-

Table 4. E-Mail Etiquette: Questionnaire Items, Means, Standard Deviations and Percentages of Respondents Agreeing and Disagreeing with Questionnaire Items about Use of E-Mail at HCP[a]

Item	Mean (S.D.)	Agree (%)	Disagree (%)
If I had a choice, I wouldn't use e-mail	1.9 (.90)	6	84
I couldn't live without e-mail	3.4 (1.17)	47	32
When the computer goes down or I can't get to a terminal, I start feeling anxious	3.3 (1.12)	55	29
If I didn't use e-mail, I would feel like an outsider at HCP	3.6 (1.10)	62	22
E-mail is great for saying "attaboy"	3.6 (.92)	61	13
People cannot exert their authority through e-mail	2.1 (.78)	6	79
Every now and then, an e-mail message will infuriate me	3.7 (.87)	72	13
I receive too many "nastygrams" (angry or hostile e-mail)	2.3 (.87)	10	70
I receive many inappropriate e-mail messages	2.4 (.87)	15	65
I receive many e-mail messages not related to my work	2.4 (.94)	20	66
E-mail creates misunderstandings that a phone call or meeting could prevent	3.0 (1.02)	36	66
E-mail helps people go "over the boss's head" or "through the back door"	3.0 (1.05)	39	40
Too many people here use e-mail to "CYA"	3.4 (1.00)	46	20
It is "fair game" to forward any e-mail message I receive	2.6 (1.05)	28	56
E-mail should never be forwarded without the sender's knowledge and consent	2.8 (1.05)	29	50
Many people here forward messages that were intended for them alone	3.1 (.88)	36	28
I am careful how I word e-mail messages for fear they will be forwarded	3.4 (1.04)	53	29

[a]The question was worded as follows: "Please indicate the extent of your agreement or disagreement with these statements about how you and others at [HCP Inc.] use e-mail." Respondents answered on a 5-point scale, where 1 = "strongly disagree" and 5 = "strongly agree." In the table, "agree" includes those who responded either 4 or 5; "disagree" includes both those who responded 1 or 2.

views with users of electronic media in many organizational settings, I added four exploratory items to this question, intended to determine whether people were deliberately choosing e-mail to avoid unwanted social interactions. Respondents were requested to select the single best medium to use in communication situations characterized by the negative emotions of conflict, dislike, anger, and intimidation. The following response choices

Table 5. Avoiding Interaction: Percentage of Respondents Selecting Various Media As "Best" in Emotionally Equivocal Situations[a]

	Best communication means			
Item	% PERS	% TELE	% E-MAIL	% MEMO
When you want to convey a "nonnegotiable" decision to someone likely to dispute it	15	4	45	37
When you do not like the other person	5	5	75	14
When you want to describe a situation that makes you angry	26	26	41	7
When you want to make a request of someone who intimidates you	10	5	73	13

[a]The question was worded as follows: "Which of the following means of communication do you think is best for communicating *with other [HCP] employees* in the situations described?
PERS, means to meet in person (e.g., by calling a meeting or traveling to visit, etc.)
TELE, means to place a telephone call
E-MAIL, means to send an electronic message
MEMO, means to send a paper memo"

were given: (1) PERS: to meet in person (e.g., by calling a meeting or traveling to visit, etc.); (2) TELE: to place a telephone call; (3) E-MAIL: to send an electronic message; or (4) MEMO: to send a paper memo[3] (see Table 5 for these items).

The survey also contained one open-ended question: "Is there anything else you would like to tell us about your use of Electronic Mail or other communication media at [HCP]?" Nearly one-third ($N=115$) of the returned questionnaires contained responses to this question, sometimes quite lengthy. These were fully transcribed and comprise an additional rich source of data for this study.

Archival Data. A third source of data for this study involves samples of actual e-mail communications collected from HCP employees in various ways. Some messages were collected during interviews from people's electronic and paper files. I also obtained samples of all messages sent and received by particular individuals during particular time periods. Two high-ranking managers who used e-mail heavily were requested to select any convenient, but typical, day for collecting messages, a day that did not, for example, involve travel out of the office or an unusual meeting schedule. Both respondents were given the opportunity to screen their message

---

[3] Facsimile was not included as one of the response choices, because the questionnaire dealt entirely with intracompany communication, and because, at the time of the study, fax was not heavily used for intraorganizational communication at HCP, according to key organizational informants.

samples and delete any sensitive or confidential material. Messages were coded for sender, receiver(s), time of sending, and length, then grouped with others to and from the same people into "discussions," that is, several messages on the same topic, such as a query and its replies (see also Reder and Schwab, 1989, 1990), so that the meaning of the communications and technology use patterns could be assessed through interpretive analysis (Orlikowski and Baroudi, 1991; Lee, 1991).

Findings

In this section, I first describe how managers at HCP used e-mail relative to the way they used other media and what they hoped to accomplish by using e-mail in this way. After discussing the effects of e-mail on social life at HCP, I consider the extent to which the rational actor and emergent process perspectives can shed light on these outcomes.

How E-Mail Was Used and Understood at HCP

In 1983, the Chairman of HCP learned, quite by chance during an informal tour of computer facilities, that the firm's multinode distributed minicomputer system supported an unsophisticated version of DECMail. Immediately convinced of the potential utility of this technology for improving coordination in his widely dispersed organization, he directed that all managers be supplied with terminals and that they begin using e-mail. Interviews revealed that the diffusion of e-mail was not accomplished without hitch. Senior women executives did not like being asked to type; some male executives tried to get their secretaries to answer their e-mail. But with continued pressure from the Chairman, who described using e-mail as "a condition of employment" in his company, use began to spread, first to the senior executives, then to their subordinates. By 1987, the Chairman felt able to claim in a public lecture that all managers (as well as many nonmanagerial employees) at HCP used e-mail daily as a fundamental way of doing intraorganizational business.

In the course of this inquiry, much evidence was found to corroborate the Chairman's beliefs about the extensiveness and frequency of e-mail use in his company. For example, e-mail userids were listed on corporate organization charts and telephone directories, and virtually all supervisory employees[4] were listed as having e-mail userids. All but one of the senior

---

[4] Operational employees (e.g., service providers) usually did not have userids. Some clerical employees (e.g., claims processors) had e-mail userids but no telephones.

executives interviewed[5] claimed to use e-mail daily, heavily (in the range of 70 to 250 messages per day), and usually in a "hands-on" mode. Only four questionnaires (from an initial mailing of over 500) were returned incomplete on grounds that the recipient did not use e-mail; by contrast, all remaining incomplete questionnaires ($N = 12$) were returned on grounds that the intended recipient was no longer employed by the firm. The high estimates of messages sent and received by senior managers in interviews were corroborated by an actual one-day sample of a regional vice-president's e-mail, which contained 153 messages. Twenty-five percent of questionnaire respondents ($N = 92$) reported sending more than twenty-one messages per day; only 22% ($N = 80$) reported sending five or fewer messages per day.

However the senior executives at HCP felt about e-mail when they were first required to use it, most had become extremely enthusiastic users by the time they were interviewed in 1987. Assertions like "I couldn't live without it" were common:

> "Mail is my lifeblood. I use it for everything. My people [direct and "dotted line" subordinates] all use it. Everything I do is through the Mail system. When I decided to leave [HCP], they [the company I just joined] had to have Mail." (director who had just accepted a position at another email-using firm)

> "We all go crazy when it's [the email system is] down. When it's down it screws up a whole work day. We're much more dependent on this than on the phone." (director)

The extent to which these views were shared by others at HCP can be assessed from the first three items in Table 4. While a fair number of respondents were unwilling to go so far as to say that they could not live without e-mail, the vast majority of respondents indicated that they would not want to give it up; as one person noted at the end of the questionnaire: "I could live without e-mail, but I can't imagine why I'd ever want to."

Interviewees described e-mail as the primary medium of work-related[6] communication at HCP, with the telephone a distant second. One regional vice-president expressed the views of many when he said: "I'm very verbal and I like the telephone, but this [indicating the terminal] is my primary communication tool. I could do this job without ever picking up the phone." When asked which form of communication they preferred best among face-to-face interaction, telephone, e-mail, and written memos, 42% of questionnaire respondents selected e-mail, in contrast to 32% who selected face-to-face and 22% who selected the telephone (Markus, in press).

---

[5] One executive interviewed claimed to have stopped using e-mail, a probable reaction to her disaffection from the company: she resigned a few weeks later.

[6] Interviewees stressed that there was very little use of e-mail for nonwork-related purposes at HCP, and this assertion was borne out by the questionnaire (see item in Table 4) and by the message samples.

At HCP, e-mail was considered to be appropriate for all work-related communication, even for developing corporate strategy; the one exception was personnel matters, which were either confidential, and so could not be entrusted to e-mail, or else required delicate handling of the communication partner's emotions. E-mail allowed HCP managers to involve multiple people in discussions of important corporate issues and get quick responses even when the people were located at great distances and in several different time zones; complex e-mail exchanges involving several partners with several "turns" each were observed within the span of a few hours in the e-mail transcripts collected for this study. By contrast, the telephone was widely described as a great "waste of time," and, where work-related communication was concerned, managers generally preferred e-mail:

> "When you get on the phone, one hour will be gone before you know it. With Mail [email], . . . [you're done much more quickly]." (director)

> "I require all of my employees to learn Email immediately and to read it daily. It is more important at times than telephone messages." (questionnaire)

Naturally, using e-mail as the primary medium of work-related communication required considerable discipline on the part of virtually everyone at HCP. It required, for instance, people to read their e-mail messages regularly and to answer them promptly. Indeed, 68% of questionnaire respondents reported that they generally remained logged on to e-mail all day and checked incoming messages as they arrived, rather than "batching" their electronic communications. In addition, it required people at HCP to type their messages, something that could be quite onerous for managers with poor typing skills,[7] particularly when the communication context was complex or equivocal, because messages about such situations tended to be lengthy:

> "You can even do strategy in Mail. It gets long, though; you get 3 and 4 page messages." (regional vice-president)

Because using e-mail as a primary medium of work-related communication required managers to type when it would have been easier for them to talk, there was always a tendency for them to want to reach for the telephone, and of course they often did. But the telephone had drawbacks —such as "telephone tag" and the absence of documentation, largely attributable to its technological characteristics—that reinforced HCP managers' preference for e-mail. The telephone also posed a potential threat to continued e-mail use: if people reached for the phone too often, instead of typing their requests and replies, it might have become difficult to

---

[7] Despite e-mail's typing requirements, almost 80% of HCP questionnaire respondents reported handling all e-mail functions without the aid of an assistant.

to maintain people's diligence in reading and answering messages (Markus, 1990). Consequently, HCP executives actively discouraged their subordinates from using the telephone for work-related communication (Markus, in press). For instance, in one of the message samples, a regional vice-president (RVP) made several attempts to respond to telephone "pink slips" in e-mail. And, in interviews, executives told me that they accepted calls from their subordinates only after the latter had thoroughly documented, in e-mail, the reason for the request. The message sample provided an intriguing example of this behavior, involving the exchange of six messages between the RVP and a subordinate within a twenty-five-minute period. When the subordinate attempted to arrange a telephone call with the RVP, the latter tried to forestall it by providing information he thought the subordinate wanted. After the subordinate replied that he wished to talk about another matter and stated his reasons, the RVP agreed to the call but scheduled it for several hours later. In these actions, the RVP clearly indicated that it was best to let one's "fingers do the talking" with a work-related request.

In short, e-mail at HCP was used by almost everyone, it was used heavily, and it was considered by many to be their primary medium of work-related communication. Using e-mail did not come naturally to HCP managers, who, like most managers, were very verbal and had relatively poor typing skills. But, because they believed in the benefits occasioned by e-mail's unique new capabilities, executives at HCP used e-mail extensively with their subordinates, maintaining their preferred communication practices through a variety of social controls. I turn now to findings about the perceived positive and negative social effects of e-mail use at HCP.

The Social Effects of E-Mail Use at HCP

Table 3 presents data about the perceived positive effects (closeness) and perceived negative effects (depersonalization) of e-mail use on social life at HCP. In comparison to data (not reported here) about e-mail's perceived positive and negative effects on work-related outcomes (efficiency and stress/overload), the results in Table 3 suggest that the social effects of e-mail were not perceived to be as great (or else were not as salient to HCP managers) as e-mail's primary, efficiency-oriented effects.[8] For instance, more people disagreed than agreed that e-mail had made them feel closer to their bosses and subordinates, suggesting that e-mail was not perceived to contribute strongly to improved supervisory relationships. Similarly, respondents were somewhat more likely to disagree than to agree that

---

[8] A similar pattern can be seen in the responses to open-ended questions: there were many more comments about the efficiency effects of e-mail (mostly positive) than about the social effects (but these were mainly negative).

e-mail had had a negative effect on the personalness of HCP as a workplace. And, while the majority of respondents believed that e-mail was quite capable of transmitting positive and negative affect (e.g., an "attaboy" or a message that "infuriates"—see Table 4), relatively few people agreed that these capabilities had resulted in an inability to exert one's authority or in "too many" flaming messages.

On the other hand, data in Tables 3 and 4 suggest that a sizable number of HCP respondents were aware that using e-mail could have and occasionally did have social consequences that could be interpreted as negative. For instance, over one-quarter of questionnaire respondents reported that use of e-mail had made HCP a less personal place to work (Table 3). Fully 66% agreed that e-mail allowed people to avoid personal contact (Table 3). And nearly half of all respondents concurred that too many people were employing e-mail in accountability games, for instance by using e-mail to "cover your a . . ." (Table 4).

Open-ended responses to the questionnaire helped to clarify the nature of the concerns people had about e-mail's negative social effects.[9] Some people described these effects in terms quite consistent with Sproull and Kiesler's (1986) arguments about the depersonalizing effects of electronic mail:

> "I believe that the real downside of e-mail is interpersonal. I believe people say things to others through the computer, that they would not say either by phone or in person. The instances of people being "beat up" through e-mail are too great." (questionnaire)

However, while a few instances of hostile or flaming messages were shown to me by interviewees,[10] none were observed in the one-day message samples, suggesting that they were not daily events.

Other respondents were more likely to complain about "corporate reliance on e-mail to replace all communication" (questionnaire). Arguments against the company practice of minimizing phone calls and meetings[11] emphasized both social and efficiency concerns:

---

[9] There were only three unambiguously positive comments about the social effects of e-mail, in contrast to fourteen negative comments; three were mixed.

[10] One was a particularly flaming example. Written at 3:00 A.M. by a recently discharged computer professional whose account had not yet been canceled, this lengthy, articulate, shockingly embarrassing, but very, very funny, message excoriated the VP of computer services to over 200 HCP Inc. executives, including the Chairman and the President. Among other things, the message compared the VP's appearance to that of a rodent, and it alleged unethical conduct. I wish I could reproduce it here.

[11] Interviewees explained that HCP Inc. did not have "a meeting culture." They denied, however, that the lack of meetings was a result of widespread e-mail use: They claimed that it had characterized the company since its founding.

"E-mail is replacing necessary phone conversation. . . . personal communication is a human essential (a need) that I don't think is being met at [HCP]."
(questionnaire)

"Major work projects are often "discussed" over Email—while Email is useful
to begin a dialogue re: an important topic, too often it is used as a replacement
for face to face group meetings, which I feel are irreplaceable to ensure many
different people affected by a particular issue have an opportunity to discuss
their concerns in person with one another, raise/clarify questions, and obtain
general group agreement and understanding over a particular issue. Using
Email as a substitute leaves all parties with different understandings/
conclusions about the *same* issue!" (questionnaire)

In short, while not all managers at HCP perceived that using e-mail had
had negative social consequences, enough of them did so to warrant
further investigation into why these effects occurred. In the following
sections, the negative social effects of e-mail use at HCP are examined from
the vantage point of theoretical perspectives that emphasize human intentions and the ironic consequences of deliberately intended behavior.

Inviting Social Distance

As discussed above, the rational actor perspective on technology impact
suggests the possibility that negative social effects might occur *because* these
outcomes are the effects that users wish to achieve. Is there any evidence
that people at HCP valued e-mail and selected it deliberately in preference
to other media precisely because of its ability to make social interactions
impersonal?

Table 5 displays responses to the questionnaire items in which respondents were requested to select the "best medium" to use in situations characterized by the negative emotions of conflict, dislike, anger, and intimidation. The results are striking. E-mail was selected as the best medium far
more often than any other medium when the relationship between the
communicators involved dislike or intimidation. E-mail was also frequently
selected as best when communicators were angry or fearful that recipients
would object to the content of the communication. It seems that the technological characteristics of e-mail—its ability to filter out personal or social
cues and to make communication asynchronous—can be perceived by
users as a benefit when users do not want personal interaction (see also
El-Shinnawy and Markus, 1992).

One of my interviewees at HCP provided a graphic example of e-mail
deliberately used in place of a more personal form of interaction in a highly
charged emotional situation. The situation involved Nedra (the director of
a support services unit reporting directly to the Chairman of HCP), Yvette
(an employee in a different corporate staff department, where Nedra used
to work before she was promoted and given a direct reporting relationship
to the Chairman), and Martha (Yvette's boss, a manager, lower in rank and

reporting relationship than Nedra). According to Nedra, the department in which Yvette and Martha worked had ongoing difficulties in managing its relationships with customers (inside HCP). In response to these problems, a new unit was created to provide special support services, and Nedra was named its director. At about the same time, Yvette and Martha's department formed its own customer service unit, which Martha headed.

Clearly, there was some overlap in the charter of these two units, leading to predictable organizational conflict. In order to accomplish her mission, Nedra frequently required information from Martha's unit. As a result, she often came into contact, by telephone and e-mail, with Martha's direct subordinates, of whom Yvette was one. Nevertheless, at the time of the message reproduced below, Nedra and Yvette, who worked on different floors of a high-rise office building, had never met in person.

Nedra was happy with her relationship with Martha, whom she believed to be dedicated to the customers the two managers served in common. But she had formed a poor impression of Yvette through their mediated communication:

> "I guess initially I need to say she was very hostile. I don't know why. I think she was playing off of the "Nedra used to work [in our department] and so she's a bad guy for leaving" mentality. . . . I guess . . . hostility's too strong of a word, but I don't understand why her messages were always just condescending and awful to work with."

So, when Nedra and Martha scheduled a series of meetings to coordinate the activities of the two units, outlining priorities and developing an agenda for the future, Nedra brought up her reactions to Martha's subordinate:

> "I said, 'You and I get along fine, but . . . who's this other person? It's just like incredible to get anything done [with Yvette].' And [Martha] spoke to [Yvette]. . . . I guess you could say she counseled her."

The result was the following message from Yvette to Nedra, sent late at night. Although Yvette used the message to request a personal meeting, much of the message would probably have been better delivered in person. Yet, it is clear from the "off" tone of the message—its informal "Hi!" and "Thanx," its obsequious apologies and presentations—how thoroughly threatening Yvette might have found it to wait until the next day to drop in on Nedra and request a personal meeting.

Despite its clearly inappropriate tone, Yvette's communication strategy seems to have worked. Nedra agreed to a meeting, and, for a time, the relationship was repaired.

> "This [the message from Yvette reproduced on the following page] was the response to that. . . . Martha talked to her, and then after this message, I thought: oh, let's give this a try. So we were getting along great. Interaction and Mail [e-mail] got a lot more informal, and things worked quickly."

From: [Yvette's userid]   18-Feb-1987 23:28
To: [Nedra's userid]

Subj: [none given]

Dear Nedra:

Hi! I spoke to Martha earlier today and she explained what you had discussed during
your meeting. I just wanted to say that I have alot of respect for you and at no point
in time have I felt any different. I am so sorry if I have in any way made you feel the
way you do. Frankly you are a person that I have heard nothing but good about and
it is only natural for me to feel the same. Your requests are always top priority and I
have tried and will continue to be of assistance when needed.
I hope you do not think that my detailed explanations are indicating that I am not
aware of your broad knowledge of. . . . I felt that I would be doing a much better job
by giving you extra information.
I would like to take this opportunity **to ask for us to meet in person** [emphasis added]
and maybe you'll see that I'm really a down to earth person. I guess the reason I'm
sending this mail message at 11:30 p.m. when I'm usually asleep is because I would
like for you to understand that I had absolutely no intentions what so ever to make you
feel the way you do.
Some of the requests you made to Martha have been assigned to me. I will be sure to
do the best I possibly can to satisfy your needs.
Good Night and Thanx,
Yvette [surname]

But when Martha left HCP (Yvette temporarily took her place) and a large
project involving the two units went sour, things between Nedra and
Yvette "went back to the original hostility." In the new "wars," the players
chose to communicate with each other in e-mail in lieu of more personal
forms of interaction. This example, combined with evidence from both the
survey and archival sources, then, lends some credibility to the view that
people at HCP occasionally endeavored to turn the technological capabilities of e-mail to their advantage when negotiating interpersonally difficult
situations.

Aware of their own deliberate choices in when and how to use e-mail,
HCP managers tended to attribute the relatively mild negative social effects
they observed to others' deliberate, intentional behavior. Rather than
blaming the technology for negative outcomes, they tended to blame each
other, as these quotes show:

"E-mail is an invaluable asset to this company but **is used by some people**
[emphasis added] to express things they would never express, or in a tone
they would not utilize by phone or in person." (questionnaire)

"My main complaint is I feel it can be used by some managers as a "crutch"
or a "tool" to manage people much too often. It should never replace the
interpersonal-communication skills necessary to successfully manage a group

of people. That situation is **obviously not the fault of the machine but rather the manager** [emphasis added] getting lazy and too often allowing E-mail to do something the manager must do in person." (questionnaire)

The attribution of negative outcomes to "bad uses" of the technology, rather than to "the machine," implies that people at HCP believed negative outcomes could be prevented if only they and others took the proper preventive measures. In the next section, I examine the variety of prophylactic and remedial behaviors that HCP managers adopted in the attempt to minimize negative social effects.

Warding Off the Threat

The rational actor perspective suggests that, once aware of its risks, people convinced that a behavior is too valuable to abandon will do it anyway, but actively try to minimize its negative consequences. Did HCP managers view e-mail as posing risks for their social relationships, and, if so, how did they try to prevent these risks from becoming a reality?

Both interviews and open-ended questionnaire responses suggest considerable awareness on the part of HCP managers that heavy e-mail use entails a certain amount of risk. As one questionnaire respondent put it: ". . . [T]he strengths of e-mail are also its weaknesses." Another wrote: ". . . 'The sword cuts both ways!' " The perceived risks of heavy e-mail use included threats not only to work-related performance, for example, miscommunication and things falling through the cracks, but also to social relationships. In particular, people whose responsibilities included managing subordinates were particularly concerned about the possibility that boss–subordinate relationships might become more distant or strained:

> "With E-mail I find myself answering w/o all the kindness necessary to keep people happy with their job. Sometimes I answer more pointedly." (questionnaire)

Despite these worries, most HCP managers believed that the overall impact of their e-mail was positive, as these comments show:

> "I cannot, though, imagine working without it." (questionnaire)

> "For all its drawbacks, the good *far* outweigh the bad!" (questionnaire)

And, consequently, the simplest means of preventing negative impacts —not using e-mail, or not using it as much—were simply not an option for the majority of HCP managers.

If negative outcomes of heavy e-mail use were to be averted, a strategy other than abandoning it had to be found. For many managers at HCP, the preferred strategy involved prophylactic use of the telephone:

> "We [each of my direct subordinates and I] talk [on the telephone] once a week **whether we need it or not** [emphasis added] [i.e., need it to discuss

problems]. **We talk for different reasons than we message.** We talk **for the personal connection.** . . . [emphasis added]. Mail messages don't work if it goes on too long [without telephone or face-to-face interaction]. We have to talk once a week **or it gets impersonal** [emphasis added]." (regional vice-president)

Several questionnaire respondents concurred:

"Occasionally, I feel a need for a human voice and **use the phone to address a problem and also say 'Hi'** [emphasis added]. I think Email used exclusively can be cold and may hinder development of some interpersonal contacts." (questionnaire)

"I don't feel it has depersonalized our operations, just speeded up some areas. There will always be times **I make a personal phone call, as much to keep in touch** [emphasis added] with a subordinate or peer as for the task that needs to be dealt with." (questionnaire)

Similarly, managers at HCP would pick up the telephone whenever they "read" evidence of negative emotions in the messages from their subordinates:

"I can tell [from an e-mail message] when they're [my subordinates are] frustrated and need to talk. When this happens, I call them immediately. It's very clear [from their messages when subordinates feel that way]." (assistant vice-president)

Thus, although e-mail was preferred at HCP for work-related communications, managers recognized that heavy e-mail use threatened the quality of their relationships with subordinates. To avert this risk, they came to view the telephone as their primary means of maintaining these essential interpersonal relations.

Another way that managers at HCP attempted to avert negative social consequences from heavy use of e-mail was by taking care in composing their e-mail messages. Some of this care could be traced to efficiency concerns; care was needed to ensure that the meaning of their messages really got across without additional messages of clarification. But part of it can be understood as a defensive social maneuver, intended to ensure that users' own words could not be used as documentation against them.

One of the advantages frequently claimed for e-mail relative to the telephone is its capability for *documenting* the content of a communication (Culnan and Markus, 1987; Sproull, 1991). On the other hand, this very advantage embodies the risk that the document will be used to the sender's disadvantage. Whereas ". . . the telephone permits confidential messages without the risks attendant on their commitment to writing" (Pool, 1983, p. 6), e-mail not only commits messages to writing but provides unprecedented ease of storing, retrieving, modifying, and forwarding them to third parties. This benefit clearly has "attendant risks."

"I feel very uncomfortable about the forwarding/edit feature of E-mail. I find a feature that, actually allows you to access a message someone has sent, and completely edit that message prior to sending it on to another, to be a potentially dangerous feature." (questionnaire)

But just because a technological capability exists does not mean that it will be used. To learn more about whether fear of forwarding was founded and how HCP managers managed this risk, I included several questions about message forwarding practices in the "etiquette" section of the questionnaire (see the last four items in Table 4). The majority of HCP managers believed that it was inappropriate for e-mail recipients to view the messages they received as their own property or as "fair game" to forward on to others whenever they chose. More than a few, it seems, had been victimized by various forwarding "abuses," as this respondent notes:

" 'Blind copying' should be outlawed. This means complaining to someone about their performance (as though it were private), then forwarding your message to their boss or others, without telling the original addressee." (questionnaire)

However, a sizable minority of respondents (over one-quarter) agreed that forwarding was fair game (see Table 4), apparently believing that any negative consequences were the sender's, not the forwarder's, fault:

"E-mail is a very valuable and useful tool for communicating and documenting. In a world where it's easiest to say 'I never received it . . .' you can verify and document when requests are sent and responded to. Most people need to remember that E-mail is not private. If you think it is, you're very misled. I feel any message sent or received is "fair game" (for forwarding) and the sender and responder should be aware of this and keep it in mind when communicating with others. If your comments would be inappropriate if forwarded on, then you probably should never have stated it in the manner you did on the message." (questionnaire)

Despite widespread disapproval of indiscriminate message forwarding, the data in Table 4 suggest that most respondents did not agree that the solution was to require forwarders to request permission from message senders.[12] Instead, most e-mail users at HCP took it upon themselves to word their messages carefully in order to prevent their messages from coming back to haunt them.

In short, data from interviews, archives, and the survey provide considerable evidence about HCP managers' beliefs that using electronic mail entailed various risks, including the possibility that their relationships with subordinates would be depersonalized and that the messages they

---

[12] The most likely explanation is efficiency. It would be time consuming if message receivers had to ask senders' permission every time they wished to redirect inquiries more properly dealt with by someone else (e.g., subordinates).

514   M. Lynne Markus

perceived as sensitive, confidential, or private would be forwarded on to others. To counteract these risks, managers at HCP engaged in a variety of prophylactic behaviors such as using the telephone to maintain personal relationships with subordinates and carefully wording their messages to avoid the risks attendant on committing them to writing.

But were these tactics successful? Or did some negative consequences occur despite, or possibly even because of, these prophylactic actions? I address these questions next.

Social Impacts Happen

The emergent process perspective suggests that negative social impacts sometimes occur despite people's best intentions or as an unintended consequence of normal "good" behavior. One of the great ironies of e-mail use at HCP was the degree to which negative consequence seemed to follow, not solely from the medium or from deliberate "bad uses," but from the steps users took to use e-mail to full advantage. For instance, to ensure that e-mail would be useful as a primary means for communicating about work, managers at HCP had to ensure that e-mail messages received a timely response, or people would resort to the phone, thus undermining routine e-mail use. They were so successful in doing this that e-mail messages were widely believed to get a faster response than telephone calls. But, in their haste to respond quickly to e-mail communications, they often gave short shrift to the people who physically visited their offices.[13]

In a typical office at HCP headquarters, terminals were placed so that managers working at them had their backs turned to visitors and assistants at nearby workstations. Most of the terminals were set up so that, when a manager was "logged on," the terminal would "beep" and display a message waiting notification ("New mail from [userid]"), whenever messages were delivered. Because most managers logged on as soon as they arrived at the office and remained logged on throughout the day, face-to-face meetings in offices were punctuated by audible beeps from the terminal as well as the telephone's ring. While managers often relied on assistants to screen their telephone calls, they usually screened their e-mail messages themselves. They did this by turning their heads to read who the message was from, then deciding whether to "take the call" immediately or defer it until later. Frequently, the beeping terminal took precedence over visitors to the office. For example, a regional vice-president's assistant complained that:

> "Ted should batch his work; he's constantly interrupted by the beep. Ted has such an urgency about Mail. When I'm in there talking to him and the terminal beeps, he turns around and starts responding. That makes me mad:

---

[13] This behavior has also been observed among telephone users (Pool, 1983).

he's supposed to be talking to me [emphasis added]. But people here expect such a quick response."

An assistant vice-president made a similar complaint about her boss, an executive vice-president. She said:

"I told [him] that it bothered me when he turned around at the beep. **He wasn't even aware he did it** [emphasis added]. He had to turn it [the terminal] off to ignore it. It really bothers me."

I was able to observe this behavior during my own interviews with HCP managers. When the beep sounded, as it frequently did, managers would flick their gaze over their shoulders toward the terminal screen. On one occasion, this was followed by a look of such acute distress that I invited the manager to answer the "call." He took me up with an expression of relief that told me I had guessed right about what was going on. Part of what was going on gives entirely new meaning to the hypothesis that e-mail depersonalizes interaction: e-mail use may result in depersonalized interactions with face-to-face communication partners to a greater extent than it does so with people at the other end of the wire.[14]

Other unintended fallouts of users' attempts to get the most out of e-mail were compulsive documentation and aggressive accountability games. As mentioned earlier, maintaining quick response in e-mail is essential to its usefulness as a primary medium of work-related communication. Because e-mail is an asynchronous medium that interposes delays between message sending and receiving, e-mail senders have to keep track of whether they have received a response; occasionally, they need to follow up. Fortunately for senders, e-mail can make response monitoring and follow-up relatively easy:

"E-mail is often better than the phone because it allows you to track the time of requests and can easily trigger a followup response." (questionnaire)

But tracking only works for requests made *in e-mail*. One result was the emergence of documentation mania, in which:

"*Everything* now seems to be required 'in writing' by E-mail—even simple requests—this can be time consuming and irritating when a brief telephone conversation must be followed by a lengthy Email to reiterate the conversation." (questionnaire, emphasis in original)

---

[14] Bob Anderson (of the RAND Corporation) made the following comment about the behavior patterns described here: "I resonated strongly with the execs that 'looked over their shoulder' at their terminals when in personal meetings. My Mac also beeps when it gets a message, and I too get nervous when I can't see who it's from and respond during a face-to-face meeting. I know I shouldn't be that interrupt-driven, but it's fun when you're the first person to give the right answer to a question that's raised, or to show you're highly responsive, etc. When I'm not 'plugged in' to the net, I feel disconnected. (Is that why I'm typing this message at 10:25 pm??)" (personal communication, 10/14/92 22:29:34.26).

"The 'CYA' [cover your a . . .] aspect seems to be getting crazy. A simple 'yes, no' phone call is now on E-mail in case someone 'doesn't remember.' " (questionnaire)

Ironically, compulsive documentation detracted from the very productivity it was designed to increase:

"The main problem with E-mail is that as one feels more and more compelled to verify every action that is taken, for superiors or simply to justify what one has done, there is a corresponding drop in the productivity of a person. Rather than just doing a job I find that increasingly I am documenting everything I have done which robs from the accomplishments I could have achieved. The concept of Email is a good one but has changed in a negative way." (questionnaire)

Time spent compiling e-mail documentation is wasted if it is never used. The excellent documentation provided by e-mail begs to be used in cases where colleagues fail to live up to the commitments that had been documented in e-mail:

"When a project is held up due to lack of response from another area, it is easy to document ones efforts to attain the information, and to properly place blame for any deadlines not met." (questionnaire, as written)

E-mail provided an excellent way for the offended to hold offenders accountable; they simply forwarded the e-mail documentation via e-mail to superior managers who would presumably take the appropriate punitive action (see the last four items in Table 4. The appendix contains an actual example of documentation used to establish accountability).

In short, the evidence in this case study suggests that some of the negative consequences for social life at HCP may have occurred despite managers' deliberate attempts to prevent them. Precedence given to e-mail callers over physically present visitors and aggressive accountability games occurred, not because the technology required these things to occur, nor even because the users deliberately intended them. Instead, they appear to be an ironic result of HCP managers' deliberate and well-intentioned efforts to ensure that e-mail was useful as a primary medium of work-related communication.

Discussion and Conclusion

As noted at the outset of this paper, technological determinism, which focuses on material characteristics such as "cues filtered out" or "new capabilities," is the most common explanation for negative social effects of electronic communication technology. This paper has presented two alternative explanations for negative social effects, when they occur. How well do the rational actor and emergent process explanations enhance our understanding of the negative social impacts observed in the case of HCP, and what can we conclude on the basis of this study about the negative social effects of electronic communication technology more generally?

First, what can be learned from the case of HCP in particular? At HCP, here was some evidence of negative social effects due to the widespread and heavy use of e-mail, but these effects did not appear to be particularly severe. Thus, while it is worthwhile to consider alternative explanations for why the negative effects occurred, the magnitude of the effects was not so significant that one would be tempted to dismiss this case as an extreme outlier caused by obvious technology abuse.

When we apply the rational actor explanation to the case of HCP, there is ample evidence consistent with it, suggesting that this perspective is a useful complement to, or moderation of, the technological determinist position. HCP managers themselves tended to attribute the negative social effects they observed to other people's deliberately intended inappropriate behavior, rather than to the technological characteristics of the technology. And they themselves deliberately behaved in ways that could be viewed as intended to produce the so-called negative effects. For instance, many people at HCP believed that the technology allowed them to avoid personal contact if they chose to do so, and they frequently selected electronic communication in situations imbued with negative emotions. Although they did not generally believe that e-mail made their organization a less personal place to work, they did worry about the effects that using e-mail might have on relationships they knew they must preserve, especially those with their subordinates. In addition, they feared the ability of others to make trouble for them by forwarding their messages to third parties. Consequently, they engaged in behaviors intended to avert negative con-sequences, such as phoning their subordinates "for social reasons" and taking care in wording messages for fear that they would be forwarded.

But just because HCP managers tended to attribute the negative social effects of e-mail to "bad uses" of the technology does not necessarily mean that we as social scientists or technology designers are similarly justified in doing so. For the emergent process perspective also contributes to our understanding of the reasons for the negative social effects observed in the case of HCP. For example, some negative effects occurred despite HCP managers' deliberate attempts to prevent them, and these effects can actually be attributed in part to users' well-intentioned efforts to use e-mail effectively in the context of the social relationships at work. Thus, the rational actor perspective does not form a complete explanation for the outcomes observed at HCP, suggesting that there is much more to the negative social consequences of e-mail use than can be subsumed under the facile labels of "bad technology" or "bad uses."

What can be concluded on the basis of this single case study about the negative social effects of electronic communication technology more gen-erally? It is easier to say first what *cannot* be concluded on the basis of this case. Case studies cannot yield reliable information about the magnitude or incidence of various phenomena. Thus, we cannot begin to speculate how severe or widespread are the negative social effects observed at HCP. For this, we need to conduct careful surveys of large samples of organizations.

By contrast, the value of a single case study lies in systematic comparison of alternative explanations for a particular type of outcome. If an explanation is shown to work well in explaining the outcome in one setting, one has good reason to expect that the explanation will work well in other settings where the outcome occurs and where similar theoretical or "boundary" conditions obtain. Thus, the evidence in the HCP case suggests that both the rational actor and the emergent process perspectives are likely to explain (at least partially) any negative social effects observed in other work organizations where electronic communication technologies are widely used.

This "analytical generalization" (Yin, 1989) rests on the assumption that, while some of the characteristics of the HCP organization and culture may be unique, HCP is similar to most other work organizations in the kinds of working relationships that exist among organizational members. As Kling (1991) has noted: ". . . many working relationships . . . mix elements of cooperation, conflict, conviviality, competition, collaboration, commitment, caution, control, coercion, coordination and combat." It is these "multivalent" working relationships that provide people in organizations with the motivations to use electronic communication technology to work more effectively with close co-workers and to create social distance with disliked colleagues or to attempt to avoid negative social effects with subordinates while still using e-mail heavily with them. Similarly, it is the complex, systemic nature of all work organizations that ensures that some outcomes will inevitably elude people's best efforts at rational social or technological control (Douglas, 1986). Consequently, negative social effects can sometimes appear to "just happen."

In summary, the current study implies that future research on the social effects of electronic communication technology should consider not only the technological characteristics of various media but also those purposes and goals that users attempt to accomplish through the media and the things that can "just happen" despite or even because of users' best or worst efforts. In addition, the current study shows that the effects that "just happen" can be explained through careful analysis of sociotechnical interactions.

What are the theoretical and practical implications of the current study? Whereas the perspective of technological determinism argues that negative social effects occur regardless of how people use electronic communication technology, because it strips away personal and social cues or provides new capabilities, the rational actor perspective argues that some of the negative social effects may be outcomes that people deliberately intend to achieve, and that users might anticipate the medium's risks and take steps intended to ward off negative effects. In some cases, these prophylactic behaviors may actually be effective; thus, the rational actor perspective can help explain, better than the technological determinist perspective, why negative social effects might accompany the use of a particular technology in some settings and positive effects might occur in others. This suggests that researchers should intensify efforts to identity, and educate users about, the "good" and the "bad" ways to use e-mail and other communication technologies.

But the current study also shows that deliberate measures taken to avert negative outcomes may not always succeed—that such outcomes can be an ironic byproduct of "good" behavior. Thus, the emergent process perspective helps to explain, better than the technological determinist perspective, how negative effects might occur in unexpected places, for instance, in relationships among those who communicate face-to-face, not just among those who communicate via e-mail. Further, this perspective suggests that it may be inappropriate to blame users for all the observed negative social effects of electronic communication technology and that technical enhancements or improved user education may have little effectiveness at eradicating them. The emergent process perspective cautions us that the prospects for achieving socially desirable outcomes are dim, as long as social scientists, technology designers, and users cling to simple theories that attribute all social consequences directly to technology or to users.

The results of this study imply that, however advanced our communication technologies may become, however much they may incorporate the sense of "being there" or even move beyond it (Hollan and Stornetta, 1992), their effects will always depend, at least in part, on how people understand these technologies and on how they choose to use them. At the same time, however, the complex, systemic interactions between people and technologies ensure that the social effects of electronic communication may continue to appear "puzzling, evasive, and hard to pin down" (Pool, 1978, p. 4).

Acknowledgments

I gratefully acknowledge the helpful comments of editor Rob Kling, the anonymous reviewers, Robert H. Anderson, Lyne Bouchard, Michael Myers, Lorne Olfman, and Louise Soe.

Appendix
Using E-Mail to Document Accountability

This instance of forwarding used to document accountability for failure comes from the one-day message sample of a regional vice-president at HCP Inc. (reproduced with original typographic errors; emphasis added).

From: EXDIRWIS   6-AUG-1987 08:59   [message #058]
To: JOSEPHS
Subj: Ted, **this is going to cost us** in . . . What happened—in-short—is we ask permission to print locally, denied, we obtained **assurances ofabsolute delivery** by Thursday July 31,'87, and subsq. **July Monday August 3,'87.** We followed up daily, we spoke/worked w/ [VP in charge] **but it didn't work.** I do not want to make a big issue out of this—most people worked hard to make it happen—but it needs to be noted for future ref. and as a learning exp. thx.

From: ADMINWI   6-AUG-1987 07:52   [message #057]
To: EXDIRWIS, MKTWI
Subj: [Customer] Mailing
The new . . . brochure . . . **did not arrive in time** to be mailed out, **despite arrangements** made with print production. **I will forward you a copy of the original mail messages** between [the VP in charge] and myself. . . .
Dale

From: EXDIRWIS   5-AUG-1987 20:30   [message #056]
To: MKTWI, ADMINWI, WISCONSIN
Subj: . . . Mailing, What was mailed and when?

From: WISCONSIN   5-AUG-1987 12:26   [message #055]
To: MKTWI, ADMINWI, EXDIRWIS
Subj: Pete, Dale, Mike: **fyi,** Cheryl

From: PRNTMGR   5-AUG-1987 12:26   [message #054]
To: WISCONSIN
Subj: Cheryl, [brochure] shipped today by Federal Express. Please let me know if you don't have them **by 10:30 am your time Thurs 8-6.**
Maria [surname]

In message #055, Cheryl called the attention of her boss (ADMINWI) and her boss's boss (EXDIRWIS) to the failure of the print production group to deliver the brochures by the (revised) agreed-upon date of August 3. She did this by forwarding message #054 from the manager in charge of inhouse printing along with the note "fyi." When the Executive Director of the Wisconsin branch was unclear about the meaning of this information (message #056), Cheryl elaborated in message #057 and promised to supply additional information by forwarding related correspondence (messages #060–062). Mike (EXDIRWIS) decided the situation was sufficiently problematic that it should be brought to the attention of his own boss (Ted Josephs) by forwarding both sets of messages from Cheryl to Ted in messages #058 and #063.

From: EXDIRWIS   6-AUG-1987 09:01   [message #063]
To: JOSEPHS
Subj: **Follow up detail** to . . . problem re: new brochure

From: ADMINWI   6-AUG-1987 07:58   [message #062]
To: EXDIRWIS
Subj: Mike, this is **the original request . . . I said I's forward.**

From: [VP, boss of PRNTMGR]   16-Jul-1987 10:45   [message #061]
To: ADMINWI, PRNTMGR
Subj: Dale, please overnight [mail] the materials that you would like to print. I would
prefer to try and schedule here if possible and can't make the judgement without
seeing the extent of what you need. If we can't handle within your time-frame, we will
allow it to be printed there, but only as a last resort. If you overnight it and put through
an email order form defining quantity and due date etc. I'll review with Maria
tomorrow and we'll let you know. JD

From: ADMINWI   16-Jul-1987 07:13   [message #060]
To: [VP in charge]
Subj: Phone Call
[salutation]
Thank you for getting back to me. I was calling to find out about having a brochure . . .
printed locally here in Wisconsin. . . . [W]e need to announce . . . immediately. . . .
[A]nd time does not seem to be on our side. . . . We would need the new piece in
about two weeks. Please advise.
Dale [surname]
[title and telephone extension]

References

Barley, Stephen R. (1986). "Technology as an Occasion for Structuring: Evidence
   from Observations of CT Scanners and the Social Order of Radiology Depart-
   ments." *Administrative Science Quarterly*, 31, 78–108.
Contractor, Noshir S., and Eric M. Eisenberg (1990). "Communication Networks
   and New Media in Organizations," in Janet Fulk and Charles Steinfield (eds.),
   Organizations and Communication Technology, pp. 143–172. Sage Publications,
   Newbury Park, CA.
Culnan, Mary J., and M. Lynne Markus (1987). "Information Technologies," in
   Frederick M. Jablin, Karlene H. Roberts, Linda L. Putnam, and Lyman W. Porter
   (eds.), *Handbook of Organizational Communication: An Interdisciplinary Perspective*,
   pp. 420–443. Sage Publications, Newbury Park, CA.
Daft, Richard L., and Robert H. Lengel (1984). "Information Richness: A New
   Approach to Managerial Behavior and Organizational Design," in Lawrence L.
   Cummings and Barry M. Staw (eds.), *Research in Organizational Behavior* (Vol. 6),
   pp. 191–233. JAI Press, Homewood, IL.
Daft, Richard L., and Robert H. Lengel (1986). "Organizational Information Requirements, Media Richness and Structural Design." *Management Science*, 32, 5 (May),
   554–571.

Dillman, Don A. (1978). *Mail and Telephone Surveys: The Total Design Method.* John Wiley and Sons, New York.

Douglas, Mary (1986). *How Institutions Think.* Syracuse University Press, Syracuse, NY.

Eisenberg, Eric M., and S. R. Phillips (1991). "Miscommunication in Organizations," in N. Coupland, H. Giles, and J. M. Wiemann (eds.), *Miscommunication and Problematic Talk,* pp. 244–258. Sage Publications, Newbury Park, CA.

El-Shinnawy, Maha M., and M. Lynne Markus (1992). "Media Richness Theory and New Electronic Communication Media: A Study of Voice Mail and Electronic Mail." Proceedings of the International Conference on Information Systems, Dallas, TX, pp. 91–105.

Eveland, J. D., and Tora K. Bikson (1987). "Evolving Electronic Communication Networks: An Empirical Assessment." *Office: Technology and People,* 3, 2 (August), 103–128.

Eveland, J. D., and Tora K. Bikson (1988). "Work Group Structures and Computer Support: A Field Experiment." Proceedings of the Conference on Computer-Supported Cooperative Work, Portland, OR, pp. 324–343.

Feldman, Martha S. (1987). "Electronic Mail and Weak Ties in Organizations." *Office: Technology and People,* 3, 83–101.

Finholt, Tom, and Lee S. Sproull (1990). "Electronic Groups at Work." *Organization Science,* 1, 1, 41–64.

Hollan, Jim, and Scott Stornetta (1992). "Beyond Being There." Proceedings of the ACM Conference on Computer Human Interaction (May), pp. 119–125.

Jick, Todd D. (1983). "Mixing Qualitative and Quantitative Methods: Triangulation in Action," in John Van Maanen (ed.), *Qualitative Methodology,* pp. 135–148. Sage Publications, Newbury Park, CA.

Kerr, Elaine B., and Starr R. Hiltz (1982). *Computer-Mediated Communication Systems.* Academic Press, New York.

Kiesler, Sara, Jane Siegel, and Timothy W. McGuire (1984). "Social Psychological Aspects of Computer-Mediated Communication." *American Psychologist,* 39 (October), 1123–1134.

Kling, Rob (1980). "Social Analyses of Computing: Theoretical Perspectives in Recent Empirical Research." *Computing Surveys,* 12, 61–110.

Kling, Rob (1991). "Cooperation, Coordination and Control in Computer Supported Work." *Communications of the ACM,* 34, 4 (December), 83–88.

Kling, Rob, and Walt Scacchi (1982). "The Web of Computing: Computer Technology as Social Organization," in M. C. Yovits (ed.), *Advances in Computers,* pp. 1–89. Academic Press, Orlando, FL.

Lee, Allen S. (1989). "A Scientific Methodology for MIS Case Studies." *Management Information Systems Quarterly,* 13, 1 (March), 33–50.

Lee, Allen S. (1991). "Integrating Positivist and Interpretive Approaches to Organizational Research." *Organization Science,* 2, 4 (November), 342–365.

Lengel, Robert H., and Richard L. Daft (1988). "The Selection of Communication Media as an Executive Skill." *Academy of Management Executive,* 2, 3, 225–232.

Markus, M. Lynne (1990). "Toward a 'Critical Mass' Theory of Interactive Media," in Janet Fulk and Charles Steinfield (eds.), *Organizations and Communication Technology,* pp. 194–218. Sage Publications, Newbury Park, CA.

Markus, M. Lynne (1992). "Asynchronous Tools in Small Face-to-Face Groups." *Information Technology and People,* 6, 1, 29–48.

Markus, M. Lynne (in press). "Electronic Mail as the Medium of Managerial Choice." *Organization Science.*

Markus, M. Lynne, and Daniel Robey (1988). "Information Technology and Organizational Change: Causal Structure in Theory and Research." *Management Science,* 34, 5 (May), 583–598.

Merton, Robert K., Marjorie Fisk, and Patricia L. Kendall (1990). *The Focused Interview: A Manual of Problems and Procedures* (2nd ed.). The Free Press, New York.

Miles, Matthew B., and A. Michael Huberman (1984). *Qualitative Data Analysis: A Sourcebook of New Methods.* Sage Publications, Newbury Park, CA.

Orlikowski, Wanda J., and Jack J. Baroudi (1991). "Studying Information Technology in Organizations: Research Approaches and Assumptions." *Information Systems Research,* 2, 1 (March), 1–28.

Orlikowski, Wanda J., and Daniel Robey (1991). "Information Technology and the Structuring of Organizations." *Information Systems Research,* 2, 2 (June), 143–169.

Pfeffer, Jeffrey (1982). *Organizations and Organization Theory.* Pitman, Marshfield, MA.

Pool, Ithiel de Sola (ed.) (1978). *The Social Impact of the Telephone.* MIT Press, Cambridge, MA.

Pool, Ithiel de Sola (1983). *Forecasting the Telephone: A Retrospective Technology Assessment of the Telephone.* Ablex, Norwood, NJ.

Poole, Marshall Scott, and Gerardine DeSanctis (1990). "Understanding the Use of Group Decision Support Systems: The Theory of Adaptive Structuration," in Janet Fulk and Charles Steinfield (eds.), *Organizations and Communication Technology,* pp. 173–193. Sage Publications, Newbury Park, CA.

Reder, Stephen, and Robert G. Schwab (1989). "The Communicative Economy of the Workgroups: Multi-Channel Genres of Communication." *Office: Technology and People,* 4, 3 (June), 177–195.

Reder, Stephen, and Robert G. Schwab (1990). The Temporal Structure of Cooperative Activity. Los Angeles, CA: Proceedings of the Conference on Computer Supported Cooperative Work, pp. 303–316.

Rice, Ronald E., and Associates (1984). *The New Media: Communication, Research, and Technology.* Sage Publications, Newbury Park, CA.

Rice, Ronald E., and Gail Love (1987). "Electronic Emotion: Socioemotional Content in a Computer-Mediated Communication Network." *Communication Research,* 14, 1 (February), 85–108.

Shapiro, Norman Z., and Robert H. Anderson (1985). "Toward an Ethics and Etiquette for Electronic Mail." Santa Monica, CA: RAND, R-3283-NSF/RC.

Short, John, Ederyn Williams, and Bruce Christie (1976). *The Social Psychology of Telecommunications.* John Wiley, London.

Sieber, Sam D. (1973). "The Integration of Fieldwork and Survey Methods." *American Journal of Sociology,* 78, 6 (May), 1335–1359.

Sproull, Lee, and Sara Kiesler (1986). "Reducing Social Context Cues: Electronic Mail in Organizational Communication." *Management Science,* 32, 11 (November), 1492–1512.

Sproull, Lee, and Sara Kiesler (1991). *Connections: New Ways of Working in the Networked Organization.* MIT Press, Cambridge, MA.

Sproull, Robert F. (1991). "A Lesson In Electronic Mail," in Lee Sproull and Sara Kiesler (eds.), *Connections: New Ways of Working in the Networked Organization,* pp. 177–184. MIT Press, Cambridge, MA.

Steinfield, Charles W. (1986). "Computer-Mediated Communication in an Organizational Setting: Explaining Task-Related and Socioemotional Uses," in Margaret L. McLaughlin (ed.), *Communication Yearbook 9*, pp. 777–804. Sage Publications, Newbury Park, CA.

Stewart, David W., and Prem N. Shamdasani (1990). *Focus Groups: Theory and Practice*. Sage Publications, Newbury Park, CA.

Yin, Robert K. (1989). *Case Study Research: Design and Methods* (rev. ed.). Sage Publications, Newbury Park, CA.

Zuboff, Shoshanna (1988). *In the Age of the Smart Machine: The Future of Work and Power*. Basic Books, New York.

P·A·R·T·V

E

They Call It Cyberlove[*]

Margo Kaufman

Greetings from Cyberspace!

I fell down the electronic rabbit hole a few months ago when I went to visit my friend Jon. I was worried because I hadn't seen him for months, and whenever I called he seemed distant and distracted. At first, I thought he was mad at me, but then a mutual friend also expressed concern that he was withdrawing. We speculated that he was having a torrid love affair or an attack of agoraphobia. But when I got to his house, I discovered that Jon had just moved to cyberspace.

"You've got to see my new system," he said, beckoning me into a dimly lit study dominated by a Macintosh IIvx with a built-in CD-ROM (a souped-up drive that holds staggering amounts of information, like an unabridged Oxford English Dictionary); a high-resolution color monitor, two laser printers, a scanner, a modem, plus more than one hundred software programs.

For three hours he demonstrated his new pal's capabilities. In addition to such prosaic computer tasks as writing or balancing a checkbook, it could play a riff on a snare drum, bark, turn an image into a fresco and lead me on an interactive journey through the Australian Outback. Whenever I introduced a nontechnological subject, Jon's eyes wandered back to the screen. "Let's go into the living room," I pleaded. I thought my brain was going to crash from overstimulation. "Wait," he said. "I haven't shown you Morphing." I politely watched a special-effects program turn a man into a woman and back without surgery.

Jon isn't the first person to prefer virtual to everyday reality. While there have always been computer addicts, more and more casual users seem to be going off the deep end. Either they're enticed by the lure of extra power, or multimedia capabilities, or the ability to pick up girls with just a hello and a :-) (that's bulletin board-ese for a smile). But they find that time off-line just can't compete.

Take Robin Williams, the Santa Rosa-based author of "Jargon," an informal guide to computer terms (Peachpit Press). She recently had an intense love affair via electronic mail with a man who lives in Atlanta. "Love in cyberspace is so much deeper," Williams said. "When you're writing, you phrase things more beautifully. And you can say things that you never have the opportunity to reveal in person. I was able to go on at length about things that were inside me, without being interrupted." (As many women know, this is impossible to do with a man in real life.)

The physical bodies in this virtual romance turned out to belong to a 24-year-old guy and a 37-year-old single mother of three. After a passionate weekend, they went their separate ways, two :-)'s that passed on the information superhighway.

I guess it's only natural that Williams socialized on-line, since like many writers she's at her keyboard from early morning to the wee hours of the night. Occasionally she gets her realities confused. "Once I woke up in the middle of a dream and thought, 'Do I save on floppy or hard?' " she said. "And I look at cars on the freeway and want to click on them and hit delete."

Whenever someone annoys me, I create a file with his or her name on it and drag it to my Mac's trash icon. If I'm really angry, I empty the trash, and whoever was bugging me disappears into the void.

Perhaps one early warning sign is when you develop a bond with your machine. Granted, it's hard to resist an intelligent colleague that doesn't gossip or stab you in the back and makes you look smarter than you really are. "It never lets you down," Jon marveled. "It's consistent, it's reliable, but at the same time unpredictable in terms of wonder and surprise."

"I threaten to spank mine periodically," said Heather Sherman, a computer analyst at Caltech, who categorizes her relationship with her machines as "usually antagonistic." One system's computers are named after Shakespearean characters ("which is odd at Caltech, since nobody's heard of them") and she tends to personalize them. "I'll say, Juliet was upset because Romeo crashed last night. I came to the conclusion that we should never name computers after tragic figures again. Hamlet was always crashing disk drives."

Still, it's one thing to anthropomorphize and another to turn your Amiga into your amigo. "I've got the whole interface configured so when I start it up, it says, 'I've been expecting you Mr. Fergerson,' " said James Fergerson, an assistant director of institutional research at Hamilton College in

---

*This article appeared in *The Los Angeles Times Magazine* (September 12, 1993), pp. 45–62. Reprinted with permission.

New York. "Then at night, there are times when I won't go to bed unless I'm told. So, I digitized the voice of the doctor from 'Star Trek.' She orders me to go to bed."

If I were a digitized voice, I might order him to get some fresh air. But people don't nag in cyberspace, which is another big attraction. There is no ageism, sexism, or racism, since all you see are words. It's also cleaner, safer and more efficient than reality, and above all, you're in control. Or at least it seems that way.

"Look what I have at my fingertips," said Jon, who claims to get a thrill akin to an adrenaline rush from the heady sense of power. "I can access a database and retrieve an article in 10 minutes that would have taken an hour to get at the library. And that's not including the drive there and back or the time I'd spend cajoling surly bureaucrats and waiting in line with a bunch of crazy people."

I'm not in that big a hurry to ease humans out of my life. But I was intrigued by reports of futuristic communities. As Dr. Joyce Brothers, the psychologist, who recently went on a cyber-business trip, told me, "In small towns there used to be a general store and you'd sit around the potbelly stove and swap tales and gossip and deal with life. Later, the stove became the drugstore. Now it's the computer network."

I have no desire to spend one more second staring at my monitor than I already have to. On the other hand, I do have a weakness for anything that simplifies my life. Cyberspace can be remarkably convenient. For instance, to research this article, I used my built-in fax modem to send a message to a service called ProfNet, which connects public information officers on college campuses via the Internet, which links more than a million university and government computers around the globe.

Within twenty-four hours, the roll of faxed responses stretched from my office to the front door, a distance of some thirty feet. No doubt, I would have received even more input if I'd had an e-mail address at the time. Folks with electronic mailboxes regard the telephone with disdain, as if it were two tin cans connected by string. (They call real letters "snail mail.")

"We've been trading voice-mail messages," Dave Farber, a professor of computer science at the University of Pennsylvania, said reproachfully when I finally managed to connect in real time (what you and I think of as the here and now). "If you had electronic mail, we could have been trading information."

And the information would always be welcome, since one of the watchwords of this Twilight Zone is asynchronicity. No need to listen anymore; I can communicate whenever I feel like it and you can respond when it feels good for you. "Talking requires both people to be awake," said Farber.

I don't think this is asking a lot. Besides, there are nuances that you can pick up in the course of actual conversation that might slip past in an ephemeral note. From talking to Farber, I learned that the Internet has turned the academic world into one big electronic wine-and-cheese party.

More than 15 million students, professors, and government employees around the world enjoy nearly unlimited access (their respective institutions pick up the tab), so there's no material incentive for restraint (by contrast, the nearly 5 million consumers who subscribe to national interactive services like Prodigy, GEnie, and CompuServe pay a monthly fee and/or an hourly rate).

"I *live* on the Net," said Farber, who spends four or five hours a day on-line dealing with students, communicating with colleagues as far away as Japan and throwing out junk mail. "I can't eat from it, but I can make reservations. I can order supplies. It's so much easier to deal with someone in Europe who is on the network than someone in the next office who's not."

The hallowed halls of academia are being choked by binary ivy. One of the editors of the Software Industry Bulletin, a computer newsletter, estimates that between 30,000 and 40,000 messages are sent daily on the Internet, and these missals will only increase since the Internet is growing at a monthly rate of 15%. Cyberspace is not just some intellectual hangout. The number of American households containing computers with modems has gone from 300,000 in 1982 to more than 12 million today. The growth in commercial on-line services is equally startling. In 1985, CompuServe had 258,000 members, and today there are 1.4 million subscribers. In 1990, Prodigy reported 460,000 members who signed on 47.9 million times per year. In just the first six months of 1993, 2 million addicts have signed on to Prodigy 131.3 million times.

I asked my husband, also on the Net, if he spends a lot of time on-line. He nodded sheepishly. "It's quite useful," said Duke, whose cyberspace passport has many visas. "I can send messages instantaneously. I can access the Library of Congress instantaneously. And I can waste a lot of time reading the Oingo Boingo Fan News Group or the I Hate Howard Stern News Group." These news groups, which remind me of microchip sororities and fraternities, are bulletin boards that enable a Netster to sound off on literally thousands of topics from 'alt.bald spots' to 'alt.barney.dinosaur.die.die.die.' Or a bored doctoral candidate can download armpit sound effects and erotic pictures. And you wondered why college tuition is going up?

And what about competing with the Japanese? "When you talk about the decline in American productivity, one factor is that people get lost in cyberspace," said Stuart Brotman, a communications consultant based in Lexington, Massachusetts. "It's pretty common in large companies. People feel that it's their job to initiate and receive electronic messages, but as soon as they do that, they take time away from other things." He understands the appeal though. "It lets you escape your job without leaving your desk."

I was certain that I'd never be one of those people whose first question is "What's your e-mail code?" But then Jon sent me software to connect my PowerBook to America Online, an electronic information service. It took five minutes to install the software, log on, and seal my fate. "Welcome," said my computer, which up to that moment I didn't know could talk. "You've got mail." On-screen, a pygmy note popped out of a wee envelope. I felt a thrill, akin to the one I last felt in high school when a girlfriend slipped me a folded message from my latest crush. Jon had sent me a welcome note.

"This is so much better than the damn telephone," the P.S. read.

"No, it's not," I replied. But in a way, it was. I had the possibility of reaching people I couldn't touch in real life, even President Clinton, whose Internet e-mail address is president@whitehouse. Nobody said, "Can I put you on hold?" or "Excuse me, I've got to take this call." I could also buy airline tickets, check stock quotes, order office supplies, and perform a zillion other tasks without seeing the inside of my car (can on-line hairdressers be far off?).

This struck me as a one-way ticket to a life as a shut-in, so I passed. Instead, I double-clicked on the bitsy picture of a woman whispering into a man's ear. Instantly, I was transported into the Lobby, where modemmouths can chat in real time. Imagine a party line or a CB radio channel and you've got the idea. I stared at my monitor, transfixed, as the text conversations of strangers unfurled. It was like walking into a cosmic cocktail party. Folks from all over the country, with handles like "RedLipstk" and "Wilecoyote," greeted me by name and sent {{{}}} (hugs) and :*:* (kisses). I couldn't believe how happy they were to see me. I asked what they liked about cyberspace. "I can have lots of friends who, almost by definition, like me for my mind and wit rather than because I'm rich or good-looking," "Fearless L," replied.

I was bound to succumb. In cyberspace, unlike Los Angeles, nobody is geographically undesirable or too busy to talk. And people ask questions. I can't remember the last time I went to a party and had a veritable stranger do more than probe vaguely to ascertain if I could be of any use to them and then walk away.

But the lost art of conversation is thriving on-line. I had lengthy discussions about politics, literature, music and art. Sure, I didn't know who I was talking to, but the hallmark of this corner of the nineties seems to be that you have intimate relationships with folks you've never met. (I've always been tempted to have a "Come As Your Phone Number" party and invite all my as-yet-unseen phone friends).

Jon was unimpressed with my new discovery. "I use the computer in part to avoid conviviality," he said. But my husband was delighted. As long as I was contentedly typing away, Duke was free to wander the Net like a hobo roaming the rails. He especially enjoyed monitoring the bulletin-board flame wars, where the level of vitriol shoots through the roof. "A wonderful place to discharge hostility," Duke said. "No danger of shooting someone or being shot. The worst that happens is someone types in capital letters." (This indicates shouting.)

Night after night, I popped into the Trivia Room, where games were played in real time. A host would ask tricky questions such as "Where are Panama hats made?" and some twenty-three contestants would rush to answer. In between questions, the regulars chatted and joked—it was sort of like "Cheers," everybody knew my name, well, at least my handle. "It's nice after a hard day to 'see' friendly faces and be sorta 'welcomed home,' " said "Koz," who traded his twice-a-year vacation for a mini vacation on-line four or five nights a week.

As diversions go, it's relatively cheap ($9.95 a month, with five free hours, then $3.50 an hour). Besides, "I don't have to pay a sitter. I don't have to pay a cover charge," said "MinnieM," a teacher who found the camaraderie helped her over a messy divorce. "I can sit in a nightshirt with my teeth unbrushed and my hair a mess and have a wonderful time." She estimated she ran up $2000 in on-line charges last year playing Trivia. But she got her money's worth. She recently married "Heifitz," a fellow Triviot.

Life in cyberspace is not always romantic. One night, on my way to the Trivia Room, a merry bell tinkled and an Instant Message appeared on my screen from a character named "MacDeSade" (not a good sign). "What are you wearing?" he asked. A moment later, the bell tinkled again, and "ThknMeaty" asked for my measurements. I felt like I had wandered into the electronic version of the Tailhook convention. Luckily, creeps are easy to deal with in cyberspace. I clicked my mouse and they vanished in the void.

Not everybody clicks though. Nightly the electrons were jumping in cyber pick-up spots such as the "Romance Connection," "Guys4Guys," "Married but Lonely," "Deep Dark Secret," and "La Pub." Some cruisers were looking for love, but others were looking to "go private." A couple choose a password and check into the electronic version of the Bide-A-Wee Motel, where they have cybersex. I was told this is essentially like phone sex, except that you type. There's even a protocol for faking orgasm: you type a lot of O's and AH's in capital letters. (A San Francisco company has since put out a CD called Cybergasm.)

Suddenly, I realized that life in cyberspace was even weirder than life in Venice Beach. "It has somewhat of a black-hole quality," said Brotman, the communications consultant. "The more you're into it, the deeper you go. At some point it begins to conflict with real life." True, I'd been getting worried phone messages from friends and relatives with whom I hadn't talked in weeks.

I asked Jon what he'd given up. "Let's put it this way," he said. "I was seeing this woman and we would get together religiously once a week. She somehow became disenchanted when I failed to call for the month after I got my new Mac. She actually accused me of seeing someone else."

"When was the last time you left the house?" I wondered. We hadn't had lunch for months.

"Does taking the trash out count?" he asked.

After a month I decided that I had to escape. I accepted an invitation to visit Caltech, ground zero of the Information Age. It was the first campus I've been to where there were no students tossing Frisbees in the quads or couples rolling around in the newly mown grass. Bo Adler, an amazingly bright 23-year-old with otherworldly energy, led me to a computer lab, where guys with complexions the color of acoustical tile gawked at behemoth Hewlett-Packards.

"Here are the people with no lives," said Bo, who got his first computer when he was 8. I asked him what he found most appealing. "I love information," he said. "I spend my life trying to find the answers." Recently he pulled down Hillary Rodham Clinton's official schedule "because it was there." But he assured me he could tell when he was on a cyberbender. "It's when I don't see the light of day for several days because I stayed in the computer lab until late at night. When I haven't touched a person for a week and have to ask for a hug so I remember what people feel like." That was a little scary, but it was nothing compared to what followed.

Bo's friend Brad Threatt, 22, showed me an interactive game called "Revenge at the End of the Line," one of many bizarre entertainments that exist on the Internet. In these virtual dungeon-and-dragon-type amusements, players choose a form to inhabit—What's your pleasure? Troll? Wood Elf? Halfling? Squid?—and have bizarre adventures with other outlandish beings, many of whom are real-life students from around the country who are cutting class to play. (Students of the nineties use these games to escape, much like their counterparts in the sixties and seventies used sex and drugs.)

I decided to be an Imp, and Brad logged on. At 11:30 on a Friday morning there were 47 creatures on the line. "Nine are wizards," said Brad, who would like to be one of these programming black-belts but has yet to contact the Wizard Board of Directors and beg for an internship. Wizards create the space; they also construct the intricate and arcane series of moves and countermoves that define the game. As near as I could tell, my objective was to go on some sort of quest. According to a text description, I, well, the Imp, was in a "lounge filled with easy chairs and lots of couches for weary adventurers such as yourself."

Brad, who used to play eight hours a day but has since cut back, assured me that this area was safe. "But there are places outside where it's dangerous," he said. "You'll need armor and maybe a weapon."

"Where do I get them?" I wondered.

"At the store," said Brad, as if it were obvious.

He typed a command and I was transported to a medieval Nordstrom. Let's see. What should I buy? Leather breastplates? Clog breeches? Scale mail shirts? Moose blood? "They have everything," Brad assured me.

"I'd like a four-carat emerald," I typed.

"I don't think that's going to work," he said.

"Huh?" said the powerful computer. (Funny, my husband said the same thing when I asked him.)

I couldn't take any more so I told Brad to attack the guard in front of the Castle of Doom. "But you'll be killed," he said. I insisted. He typed in the attack command, an in an instant the computer announced that the Imp had been stabbed in the head. I didn't feel a thing. I was already brain-dead from future shock.

Bo walked me to my car. On the way, I showed him my tiny cellular phone. It got him thinking. "Is talking to you on the phone a virtual reality?" he wondered. "And if it's not, why is talking to you on the computer virtual reality?" I must have looked puzzled because he tried again. "You know humans are just great big walking databases. . . ."

Suddenly, I had an overwhelming desire to walk on the beach and watch the waves and listen to the birds sing. I drove like hell out of cyberspace. When I got home I found a message—a voice message—from Jon.

"Do you want to have lunch?" he asked.

P · A · R · T · V

F

The Strange Case of the Electronic Lover*

Lindsy Van Gelder

I "met" Joan in the late spring of 1983, shortly after I first hooked my personal computer up to a modem and entered the strange new world of on-line communications. Like me, Joan was spending a great deal of time on the "CB" channel of the national network CompuServe, where one can encounter other modem owners in what amounts to a computer version of CB radio. I was writing an article for Ms. about modems and doing on-line interviews with CB regulars. Joan was already a sought-after celebrity among the hundreds of users who hung out on the channel—a telecommunications media star.

Her "handle" was "Talkin' Lady." According to the conventions of the medium, people have a (usually frivolous) handle when they're on "open" channels with many users; but when two people choose to enter a private talk mode, they'll often exchange real information about themselves. I soon learned that her real name was Joan Sue Greene, and that she was a New York neuropsychologist in her late twenties, who had been severely disfigured in a car accident that was the fault of a drunken driver. The accident had killed her boyfriend. Joan herself spent a year in the hospital, being treated for brain damage, which affected both her speech and her ability to walk. Mute, confined to a wheelchair, and frequently suffering intense back and leg pain, Joan had at first been so embittered about her disabilities that she literally didn't want to live.

Then her mentor, a former professor at Johns Hopkins, presented her with a computer, a modem, and a year's subscription to CompuServe to be used specifically doing what Joan was doing—making friends on-line. At

first, her handle had been "Quiet Lady," in reference to her muteness. But
Joan could type—which is, after all, how one "talks" on a computer—and
she had a sassy, bright, generous personality that blossomed in a medium
where physicalness doesn't count. Joan became enormously popular, and
her new handle, "Talkin' Lady," was a reflection of her new sense of self.
Over the next two years, she became a monumental on-line presence who
served both as a support for other disabled women and as an inspiring
stereotype-smasher to the able-bodied. Through her many intense friendships and (in some cases) her on-line romances, she changed the lives of
dozens of women.

Thus it was a huge shock early this year when, through a complicated
series of events, Joan was revealed as being not disabled at all. More to the
point, Joan, in fact, was not a woman. She was really a man we'll call
Alex—a prominent New York psychiatrist in his early fifties who was
engaged in a bizarre, all-consuming experiment to see what it felt like to be
female, and to experience the intimacy of female friendship.

Even those who barely knew Joan felt implicated—and somehow
betrayed—by Alex's deception. Many of us on-line like to believe that
we're a utopian community of the future, and Alex's experiment proved to
us all that technology is no shield against deceit. We lost our innocence, if
not our faith.

To some of Alex's victims—including a woman who had an affair with
the real-life Alex, after being introduced to him by Joan—the experiment
was a "mind rape," pure and simple. (Several people, in fact, have tenta-
tively explored the possibility of bringing charges against Alex as a psychiatrist, although the case is without precedent, to put it mildly.) To some
other victims, Alex was not so much an imposter as a seeker whose search
went out of control. (Several of these are attempting to continue a friendship with Alex—and, as one woman put it, "to relate to the soul, not the
sex of the person. The soul is the same as before.") Either way, this is a
peculiarly modern story about a man who used some of our most up-to-
date technology to play out some of our oldest assumptions about gender
roles.

More than most stories, it requires a bit of background. A modem, of
course, is the device that connects a computer to the phone and from there
to any other similarly equipped computer. CompuServe is the largest of a
number of modem networks; it charges its subscribers an initial small fee
to open an account with a special ID number and then charges hourly fees
for access to its hundreds of services, from stock reports to airline information. In addition to its business services, the network also offers a

*This article appeared in *Ms.* (14)4(October 1985), pp. 94, 99, 101–104, 117, 123, 124.
Reprinted with permission of the author.

number of "social" services (including numerous Special Interest Groups—SIGs—and the CB channels) where users can mingle.

The unfolding of an on-line relationship is unique, combining the thrill of ultrafuturistic technology with the veneration of the written word that informed nineteenth-century friendships and romances. Most people who haven't used the medium have trouble imagining what it's like to connect with other people whose words are wafting across your computer screen. For starters, it's dizzingly egalitarian, since the most important thing about oneself isn't age, appearance, career success, health, race, gender, sexual preference, accent, or any of the other categories by which we normally judge each other, but one's mind. My personal experience has been that I often respond to the minds of people whom, because of my own prejudices (or theirs), I might otherwise not meet. (For example, my best friend on-line is from Appalachia, which I once thought was inhabited only by Li'l Abner and the Dukes of Hazzard. My friend, in turn, had never had a gay friend before.)

But such mind-to-mind encounters presume that the people at both keyboards are committed to getting past labels and into some new, truer way of relating. In the wake of the Alex/Joan scandal, some on-line habitués have soberly concluded that perhaps there's a thin line between getting out of one's skin and getting into a completely false identity—and that the medium may even encourage impersonation. (One network, for example, has a brochure showing a man dressed up as Indiana Jones, Michael Jackson, and an Olympic athlete; the copy reads, "Be anything you want on American PEOPLE/LINK.") Still, when it works, it works. Disabled people are especially well represented on-line, and most of them say that it's a medium where they can make a first impression on their own terms.

Another positive consequence of the medium's mind-to-mind potential —and this is germane to Joan's story—is that it's powerfully conducive to intimacy. Thoughts and emotions are the coin of this realm, and people tend to share them sooner than they would in "real life" (what CBers refer to as "off-line"). Some people, in fact, become addicted to computer relationships, per se. But most use the modem merely as a way to start relationships that may, in time, continue off-line. After several on-line conversations with someone who seems especially compatible, people commonly arrange to speak on the telephone, to exchange photographs, and eventually, to meet in person, either by themselves or at one of the regular "CB parties" held around the country. (Several marriages have resulted from on-line meetings on CompuServe CB alone.) I've met four good computer friends in person, and found them all much the same off-line as on. For me, the only odd thing about these relationships has been their chronology. It's a little surreal to know intimate details about someone's childhood before you've ever been out to dinner together.

One of the reasons that Joan's real identity went undetected for so long was that her supposed disability prevented her from speaking on the phone. (Several people did communicate with Joan on the phone, in one case because Joan had said that she wanted to hear the sound of the other woman's voice. Joan in turn "would make horrible noises into the receiver—little yelps and moans.") There was also the matter of Joan's disfigurement; she supposedly drooled and had a "smashed up" face, untreatable by plastic surgery. She was, she said, embarrassed to meet her computer friends in person. Those who wanted to be sensitive to disabled concerns naturally didn't push. It was an ingenious cover.

Alex supposedly began his dual identity by mistake. One of the social realities of the computing world is that the majority of its inhabitants are male; women usually get a lot of attention from all the men on-line. (Women who don't want to be continually pestered by requests from strange males to go into private talk mode often use androgynous handles.) Female handles also get attention from other women, since many women on-line are pioneering females in their fields and feminists. Alex apparently came on-line sometime in late 1982 or early 1983 and adopted the handle "Shrink, Inc." His epiphany came one evening when he was in private talk mode with a woman who for some reason mistook him for a female shrink. "The person was open with him in a way that stunned him," according to one of the women—let's call her Laura—who has maintained a friendship with Alex. "What he really found as Joan was that most women opened up to him in a way he had never seen before in all his years of practice. And he realized he could help them."

"He later told me that his female patients had trouble relating to him—they always seemed to be leaving something out," said Janis Goodall, a Berkeley, California software firm employee who also knew both Joan and Alex. "Now he could see what it was." (Despite their similar recollections, Goodall is in the opposite camp from Laura, and says: "For someone supposedly dedicated to helping people, I think he rampaged through all of our feelings with despicable disregard.") At some point after Shrink, Inc.'s inadvertent plunge into sisterhood, Joan was born.

According to both Goodall and Laura (both of whom are disabled themselves), Alex has a back condition, "arthritis of the spine or a calcium deposit of some kind," according to Goodall," which causes him discomfort, and has the potential, but not the probability of putting him in a wheelchair someday." Goodall added that Alex later defended his choice of a disabled persona by claiming that he "wanted to find out how disabled people deal with it." Others on-line believe that Joan's handicaps were a way both to shroud her real identity and aggrandize her heroic stature.

If Joan began spontaneously, she soon became a far more conscious creation, complete with electronic mail drop, special telephone line, and almost novelistically detailed biography (although she sometimes told different versions to different people). She was, by my own recollection and by the accounts of everyone interviewed, an exquisitely wrought character. For starters, she had guts. (She had once, before the accident, driven alone across the interior of Iceland as a way to cure her agoraphobia.) She had travelled everywhere, thanks to money left to her by her family's textile mill fortune. She lived alone (although neighbors checked on her and helped her with errands) and was a model independent female. In fact, Joan was quite a feminist. It was she who suggested the formation of a women's issues group within CompuServe, and she actively recruited members. Several women had relationships with Joan in which they referred to each other as "sister."

Joan was earthy, too, and spoke easily about sex. One woman remembers hearing at length about Joan's abortion at age sixteen; another recalls having a long conversation about Joan's decision not to embark on a particular course of spinal surgery that might relieve her leg pain, but "would also affect her clitoral nerve, and she wouldn't do that." She was bisexual. Although her family had been religious (she told some people that her parents were ministers), she herself was an ardent atheist who liked to engage religious people in debate. She was also a grass-smoker who frequently confessed to being a little stoned if you encountered her late at night. Her usual greeting was a flashy, flamboyant "Hi!!!!!!!!!!!!"

Interestingly, the two people who knew Joan and also met Alex in person say that their surface personalities were opposite. Alex is Jewish. He almost never drinks or smokes pot (although one of his medical specialties is pharmacology). He is a workaholic whose American Psychiatric Association biography reports wide publication in his field. "Joan was wild and zingy and flamboyant and would do anything you dared her to," notes Laura. "A part of Alex wanted to be like that, but he's actually quite intellectual and shy." Adds Janis Goodall: "Alex has a great deal of trouble expressing his emotions. There are long silences, and then he'll say, 'uh-huh, uh-huh'—just like a shrink."

Above all, Joan was a larger-than-life exemplary disabled person. At the time of her accident, she had been scheduled to teach a course at a major New York medical school (in fact, the teaching hospital that Alex is affiliated with as a psychiatrist). Ironically, Joan noted, the course dealt with many of the same neurological impairments that she herself now suffered. One of Joan's goals was eventually to resume her career as if the accident had never happened—and when I first knew her, she was embarked on an ambitious plan to employ a computer in the classroom to help her teach. The idea was that Joan would type her lecture into a computer, which would then be either magnified on a classroom screen or fed into student terminals. To all of us techno-fans and believers in better living through computers, it was a thrilling concept.

Joan was also a militant activist against the dangers of drunken drivers. Early in her convalescence, when she was frequently half out of her mind with anger, she had on several occasions wheeled herself out of her apartment and onto the streets of Manhattan, where she would shout at passing motorists. On one such occasion, police officers in her precinct, upon learning her story, suggested that she put her rage and her talent to more productive use. Joan then began to go out on patrol with a group of traffic cops whose job it was to catch drunken drivers. Joan's role in the project was twofold: (1) as a highly credentialed neuropsychologist, she was better trained than most to detect cars whose drivers had reflex problems caused by too much drinking; and (2) she was willing to serve as an example to drunken drivers of what could befall them if they didn't shape up.

On one of Joan's forays, she met a young police officer named Jack Carr. As he and Joan spent more time together, he came to appreciate her spirit in much the same way the rest of us had. They fell in love—much to the distress of Jack's mother, who thought he was throwing his life away. (Joan's on-line friends were heartened to learn much later that Mrs. Carr had softened after Joan bought her a lap-top computer, and the two of them learned to communicate in the on-line world where Joan shone so brightly.) Jack occasionally came on-line with Joan, although I remember him as being shy and far less verbal than Joan.

Shortly after I met Joan, she and Jack got married. Joan sent an elaborate and joyous announcement to all her CB pals via electronic mail, and the couple held an on-line reception, attended by more than 30 CompuServe regulars. (On-line parties are not unusual. People just type in all the festive sound effects, from the clink of champagne glasses to the tossing of confetti.) Joan and Jack honeymooned in Cyprus, which, according to Pamela Bowen, a Huntington, West Virginia newspaper editor, Joan said "was one of the few places she'd never been." Bowen and many of Joan's other on-line friends received postcards from Cyprus. The following year Joan and Jack returned to Cyprus and sent out another batch of cards.

"I remember asking Joan how she would get around on her vacation," recalls Sheila Deitz, associate professor of law and psychology at the University of Virginia. "Joan simply replied that if need be, he'd carry her. He was the quintessential caring, nurturing, loving, sensitive human being"—a Mr. Right who, Deitz adds, exerted enormous pull on the imaginations of all Joan's on-line female friends. In hindsight, Deitz feels, "he was the man Alex would have loved to be"—but in fact could only be in the persona of a woman.

Joan was extraordinarily generous. On one occasion, when Laura was confined to her bed because of her disability and couldn't use her regular computer, Joan sent her a lap-top model—a gift worth hundreds of dollars. On another occasion, when Laura mentioned that no one had ever sent her roses, Joan had two dozen delivered. Marti Cloutier, a 42-year-old Massachusetts woman with grown children, claims that it was Joan who inspired her to start college. "She made me feel I could do it at my age." When it came time for Cloutier to write her first term paper, she was terrified, but

Joan helped her through it, both in terms of moral support and in the practical sense of sending her a long list of sources. (Ironically, Cloutier's assignment was a psychology paper on multiple personalities. She got an "A" in the course.) On another occasion, Joan told Cloutier that she was going out to hear the "Messiah" performed. When Cloutier enviously mentioned that she loved the music, Joan mailed her the tape. On still another occasion, when Cloutier and her husband were having difficulties over the amount of time she spent on-line, Joan volunteered to "talk" to him. Cloutier's husband is also a part-time police officer, as Jack ostensibly was, and he and Joan easily developed a rapport. According to Marti Cloutier, Joan was able to persuade him that if his wife had her own friends and interests, it would ultimately be good for their marriage. "She was always doing good things," Cloutier recalls, "and never asking anything in return."

My personal recollections are similar. Once, when Joan and I were chatting on-line late at night, I realized to my great disbelief that a bat had somehow gotten into my apartment and was flapping wildly about, with my cats in crazed pursuit. I got off the computer, managed to catch the bat and get it back out the window—but in the attendant confusion, the windowpane fell out of the window and onto my arm, slicing my wrist and palm. Needless to say, I ended up in the emergency room. Joan dropped me several extremely solicitous notes over the next few weeks, making sure that my stitches were healing properly and that I was over the scare of the accident. Even earlier, around the time I first met Joan, the child of two of my oldest friends was hit by a car and knocked into a coma that was to last for several weeks. Joan had a lot of thoughts about the physiology of comas, as well as about how to deal with hospital staffs, insurance companies, and one's own unraveling psyche in the midst of such a crisis. She offered to set up an on-line meeting with the child's mother. I later heard that Joan had also helped several women who had suicidal tendencies or problems with alcohol.

Still another way that Joan nurtured her friends—hilarious as it sounds in hindsight—was to try to keep CB free of impostors. Although Joan was probably the slickest and most long-lived impostor around, she was hardly the only one; they are a continuing phenomenon on CompuServe and on every other network. Some lie about their ages, others about their accomplishments. Some appropriate the handles of established CB personae and impersonate them. (Unlike ID numbers, handles can be whatever you choose them to be.) There are also numerous other gender benders, some of them gay or bisexual men who come on in female guise to straight men. Most aren't hard to spot. Joan herself told several friends she had been fooled by a man pretending to be a gay woman, and she was furious. "One of the first things she ever told me," recalls Janis Goodall, "was to be terribly careful of the people you meet on CB—that things were not always as they seemed."

Sheila Deitz remembers meeting a man on-line who said he was single, but turned out to be not only married in real life, but romancing numerous women on-line. Deitz met the man off-line and realized that his story was full of holes. "Joan was very sympathetic when I told her about it, and we agreed that we didn't want this guy to have the chance to pull this on other women." At some later point, according to Deitz, "Joan created a group called the Silent Circle. It was sort of an on-line vigilante group. She'd ferret out other impostors and confront them and tell them they'd better get their act together."

All of Joan's helping and nurturing and gift-giving, in Deitz's opinion, "goes beyond what any professional would want to do. Alex fostered dependency, really." But at the time, especially among those of us who are able-bodied, there was a certain feeling that here was a person who needed all the support we could give her. Numerous disabled women have since rightly pointed out that our Take-a-Negro-to-Lunch-like attitudes were in fact incredibly patronizing.

The truth is that there was always another side to Joan's need to be needed. She could be obnoxiously grabby of one's time. Because she and I both lived in New York, she once suggested that we talk directly, modem to modem, over our phone lines—thus paying only the cost of a local call instead of CompuServe's $6 an hour connect charges. But as soon as I gave Joan my phone number, I was sorry. She called constantly—the phone would ring, and there would be her modem tone—and she refused to take the hint that I might be busy with work, lover, or children. "Everybody else had the same experience," according to Bob Walter, a New York publisher who also runs CompuServe's Health SIG, where Joan (and later Alex, too) frequently hung out. "She would bombard people with calls." Finally, I had to get blunt—and I felt guilty about it, since Joan, after all, was a disabled woman whose aggressive personality was probably the best thing she had going for her. (My first somewhat sexist thought, when I found out that Joan was really a man, was Of course! Who else would be so pushy?)

Joan was sexually aggressive. Every woman I interviewed reported—and was troubled by—Joan's pressuring to have "compusex." This is on-line sex, similar to phone sex, in which people type out their hottest fantasies while they masturbate. (In the age of herpes and AIDS, it has become increasingly popular.) According to one woman, "one time she said she and Jack had been smoking pot and then he'd gone off to work, but she was still high. She told me she had sexual feelings toward me and asked if I felt the same." (Joan's husband, who was conveniently off on undercover detail most nights, supposedly knew about these experiments and wasn't threatened by them, since Joan's partners were "only" other women.) Her MO, at least with friends, was to establish an intense nonsexual intimacy, and then to come on to them, usually with the argument that compusex was a natural extension of their friendship. In one case, cited by several sources, a woman became so involved as Joan's compusex lover that she was on the verge of leaving her husband.

Interestingly, Joan never came on to me—or, to my knowledge, to any bisexual or gay women. Sheila Deitz is of the opinion that Alex only wanted to have "lesbian" compusex with heterosexual women, those whom he might actually be attracted to in real life. Some straight women apparently cooperated sexually not out of physical desire, but out of supportiveness or even pity—and this too might have been part of Alex's game. But it would be misleading to overemphasize Joan's sexual relationships, since compusex in general tends to be a more casual enterprise on-line than affairs of the heart and mind. Deitz estimates that at least fifteen people were "badly burned" by the revelation that Joan was Alex, and that only a few were compusex partners. Lovers or not, most were caught in Joan's emotional web.

Janis Goodall was in a category all her own. Now thirty-seven and cheerfully describing herself as "a semiretired hippie from 'Berserkeley,' California," Goodall met Joan at a time in her life "when I was a real sick cookie—an open raw wound." Goodall was herself coping with the emotional and physical aftermath of an automobile accident. (Although she can walk, Goodall's legs are badly scarred and she suffers from both arthritis and problems of the sciatic nerve.) Beyond her injuries, Goodall was also dealing with a recent separation from her husband and her brother's death. "It was Joan who helped me to deal with those things and to make the transition into the life of a disabled person who accepts that she's disabled."

Joan and Goodall were "fixed up" by other CompuServ regulars after Goodall attended an on-line conference on pain management. When she and Joan arranged via electronic mail to meet in CB, "it was love at first sight. By the end of that first discussion, which lasted a couple of hours, we were honorary sisters. Later, I went around profusely thanking everyone who had told me to contact her."

The fact that Joan's disability was more severe than her own gave her an authority in Goodall's eyes, and her humor was especially therapeutic. "We used to make jokes about gimps who climb mountains. At the time, just to get through the day was a major accomplishment for me, and my attitude was screw the mountains, let me go to the grocery store." The two never became lovers, despite strenuous lobbying on Joan's part. ("I often found myself apologizing for being straight," said Goodall.) But they did become intense, close friends. "I loved her. She could finish my sentences and read my mind."

About a year ago, Joan began telling Goodall about "this great guy" who was also on-line. His name was Alex. He was a psychiatrist, very respected in his field, and an old friend of Joan's, an associate at the hospital. Largely on the strength of Joan's enthusiastic recommendation, Goodall responded with pleasure when Alex invited her into private talk mode. "During our second or third conversation, he began to get almost romantic. He clearly thought I was the greatest thing since sliced bread. I couldn't understand why an established Manhattan psychiatrist his age could be falling so quickly for a retired hippie—although of course I was very flattered. Hey, if a shrink thought I was okay, I was okay!"

Alex told Goodall that he was married, but that his marriage was in trouble. Last winter he invited her to come visit him in New York, and when she said she couldn't afford it, he sent her a round-trip ticket. "He treated me like a queen for the four days I was there," Goodall remembers. "He put me up at a Fifth Avenue hotel—the American Stanhope, right across the street from the Metropolitan Museum. He took me to the Russian Tea Room for dinner, the Carnegie Deli for breakfast, Serendipity for ice cream, museums, everywhere—he even introduced me to his daughters." The two became lovers, although, Goodall says, his back problems apparently affected his ability and their sex life was less than satisfactory. Still, it seems to have been a minor off note in a fabulously romantic weekend. There were also many gifts. Once, Goodall says, "he went out to the corner drugstore to get cigarettes and came back with caviar. I went to Berkeley on Cloud Nine."

Naturally, Goodall had also hoped that she might meet Joan during her New York holiday. None of Joan's other women friends had. Some of the able-bodied women, especially, were hurt that Joan still felt shame about her appearance after so many protestations of love and friendship. According to Sheila Deitz, several people were reported to have arranged rendezvous with Joan and were stood up at the last minute—"although you just know Alex had to be lurking about somewhere, checking them out." Joan would, in each case, claim to have gotten cold feet.

Marie Cloutier says that Joan told her that she had promised her husband that she would never meet any of her on-line friends, but "that if she ever changed her mind and decided to meet any of her on-line friends, I would be one of them." In fact, the only CB person who had ever seen Joan was her hospital colleague—Alex. Over the course of Goodall's four days in the city, she and Alex both tried to reach Joan by phone, but without success. Goodall had brought Joan a gift—a stylized, enameled mask of a smiling face. Alex promised to deliver it. Back in Berkeley, Goodall resumed her on-line relationship with Joan, who had been out of town for the weekend. Joan, however, was anxious to hear every detail of Goodall's trip. Did she think she was in love with Alex? Was the sex good?

It was the disabled women on-line who figured it out first. "Some things about her condition were very farfetched," says one. Says another woman: "The husband, the accomplishments—it just didn't ring true from the beginning." But her own hunch wasn't that Joan was a male or able-bodied; she suspected that she was in fact a disabled woman who was pretending to have a life of dazzling romance and success.

Although such theories, however, ultimately ran up against the real postcards from Cyprus, people began to share their misgivings. "There were too many contradictions," says Bob Walter. "Here was this person who ran off to conferences and to vacations and did all these phenomenal things, but she wouldn't let her friends on-line even see her. After a while, it just didn't compute."

In hindsight, I wonder why I didn't question some of Joan's exploits more closely. As a journalist, I've dealt with the public relations representatives of both the New York City Police Department and the hospital where Joan supposedly taught—and it now seems strange to me that her exploits as drunk-spotter and handicapped professor weren't seized on and publicized. Pamela Bowen says she once proposed Joan's story to another editor, but urged him "to have somebody interview her in person because her story was too good to be true. So my instincts were right from the beginning, but I felt guilty about not believing a handicapped person. I mean, the story could have been true." It's possible that many of us able-bodied were playing out our own need to see members of minority groups as "exceptional." The more exceptional a person is, the less the person in the majority group has to confront fears of disability and pain.

Even with the contradictions, the game might have continued much longer if Joan hadn't brought Alex into the picture. According to both Goodall and Laura, Alex has, since his unmasking, said that he realized at some point that he had gotten in over his head and he concocted a plan to kill Joan off. But after seeing how upset people were on one occasion when Joan was off-line for several weeks, supposedly ill, he apparently couldn't go through with it. "It would have been a lot less risky for him to let Joan die," according to Laura, "but he knew it would be cruel." (Meanwhile, someone had called the hospital where Joan was thought to be a patient and had been told that no such person was registered.)

What Alex seems to have done instead of commit compu-murder was to buy a new ID number and begin his dual on-line identity. Joan increasingly introduced people to her friend Alex, always with great fanfare. We may never know what Alex intended to do with Joan eventually, but there's certainly strong evidence that he was now trying to form attachments as Alex, both off-line (with Goodall) and on.

One might imagine that The Revelation came with a big bang and mass gasps, but this was not the case. According to Walter, months and months went by between the time that some of Joan's more casual acquaintances (he among them) put it together and the time that those of her victims whom they knew heeded their warnings. "People were so invested in their relationships with the female persona that they often just didn't want to know," Walter said. And Joan was also a brilliant manipulator who always had an explanation of why a particular person might be trashing her. "If you ever questioned her about anything," Goodall recalls, "she would get very defensive and turn the topic into an argument about whether you really loved her."

Goodall now acknowledges that she and others ignored plenty of clues, but, as she says, "Let's remember one thing—it was a pro doing this." Deitz, whose off-line work sometimes involves counseling rape victims, agrees that Alex's victims were caught in an intolerable psychological bind. "Alex zeroed in on good people," she says, "although they were often good women at vulnerable stages of their lives." To admit that Joan was a phantom was, in many cases, also to assault the genuine support and self-esteem that they had derived from the relationship. In fact, with only two exceptions—pressuring for compusex and, in Goodall's case, using the Joan persona to pump "girl talk" confidences about Alex—there seems to have been absolutely nothing that Joan did to inspire anyone's rancor. What makes people angry is simply that Joan doesn't exist. "And a lot of what a lot of people were feeling," Deitz adds, "is mourning."

Laura ultimately confronted Joan on-line. She had already "cooled off" her relationship with Joan because of all the inconsistencies in her persona, but while she was suspicious, she had failed to suspect the enormity of the imposture. In February, however, she called another woman close to Joan, who told her she was convinced that Joan was a man. When Laura found Joan on-line later that night, she immediately asked Joan about the charge. Joan at first denied it. It was only after Laura made it clear that "I believed that we're all created after the image of God, and that I loved the person, not the sex, and would continue to do so" that Alex came out. Laura, who is Catholic and says that her decision to stick with Alex is partially motivated by principles of Christian love, admits that it took her several weeks to "make the transition." Since then, however, she's met Alex in person and come to love him "as my adopted brother instead of my adopted sister."

Marti Cloutier to this day hasn't confronted Alex, although she has talked with him by CB and phone. "I just haven't the courage. Once, when we were talking, he mentioned something about going for a walk that day, and I wrote back that it would be a lovely day for Joan to go for a walk. I was instantly sorry." Cloutier adds: "Joan was a very special person and I loved Joan. I feel as if she died. I can't really say that I love Alex, although maybe I could, in time. Maybe I wouldn't have given him a chance if I'd known from the beginning he was a male. I've tried to sort out my feelings, but it's hard. I know I don't feel like a victim, and I don't understand why some of these other women gave gone off the deep end. I don't think he was malicious. What I can't get out of my mind was that he's the same person I've spent hours and hours with."

Sheila Deitz had been introduced on-line to Alex by Joan, but found him "not all that interesting" and never became close to him. But as a visible on-line person known to many as a psychologist, she heard from many of the victims—some of whom formed their own circle of support, and in Goodall's words, "sort of held each other together with bubble gum." Some victims, according to Deitz, were so upset by the chain of events that they stopped using their modems temporarily.

Janis Goodall heard it first over the telephone, from Alex himself who mistakenly assumed that Goodall already knew. "I had just come home from the doctor, and was incredibly frustrated at having just spent $155 to have some asshole neurosurgeon tell me I would have to live with what was bothering me. The phone rang, and it was Alex. The first words out of his mouth were 'yep—it's me.' I didn't know what he was talking about. Then he said: 'Joan and I are the same person.' I went into shock. I mean, I really freaked out—I wanted to jump off a bridge."

Since then, she has communicated with Alex by letter but has refused to see him. She emphatically resents those on-line who have spent efforts trying to "understand" him. She agreed to speak for this interview in part because "although I think this is a wonderful medium, it's a dangerous one, and it poses more danger to women than men. Men in this society are more predisposed to pulling these kinds of con games, and women are predisposed to giving people the benefit of the doubt."

Laura thinks that CompuServe and other networks ought to post warnings to newcomers that they might, in fact, encounter impostors. Others believe that the fault doesn't lie with the medium or the network, but with human frailty. "Blaming CompuServe for impostors makes about as much sense as blaming the phone company for obscene calls," says Bob Walter. CompuServe itself has no official position on the subject, although CompuServe spokesman Richard Baker notes: "Our experience has been that electronic impersonators are found out about as quickly as are face-to-face impersonators. While face-to-face impersonators are found out due to appearance, on-line impersonators are found out due to the use of phrases, the way they turn words, and the uncharacteristic thought processes that go into conversing electronically. I also believe that people are angrier when they've been betrayed by an electronic impersonator."

It would have been nice to hear Alex's side of the story. The first time I called his office, I gave only my name (which Alex knows)—not my magazine affiliation or the information that I was working on an article about "our mutual friend Joan." The receptionist asked if I was a patient. Did I want to make an appointment? I had a giddy vision of impersonating one but decided against it. Although I telephoned twice more and identified myself as a journalist, Alex never returned my calls. He has continued his presence on-line, however, even telling Deitz that he planned to form a SIG—on another network—for psychologists and mental health professionals.

Meanwhile, in the aftermath of the Joan/Alex case, soul-searching has run rampant on CompuServe's CB and in certain SIGs. One common thread was that of Eden betrayed. As one man wrote: "I guess I figured the folks here [on-line] were special . . . but this has certainly ruptured the 'pink cloud' of CompuServe." A woman wrote back: "The feelings remind me of the ending of my first love relationship. Before that, I didn't realize fully how much hurt could result from loving."

Some of the reactions were frankly conservative—people who were sickened simply by the notion of a man who wanted to feel like a woman.

There was much talk of "latency." Others seemed completely threatened by the idea that they might ever have an "inappropriate" response to someone of the "wrong" gender on-line. One message left by a male gravely informed other users that he and his girlfriend had nearly been conned by a male pretending to be a swinging female—until the girlfriend was tipped off by the impersonator's "claiming to be wearing panty hose with jeans." The message prompted an indignant reply by someone who insisted: "I always wear heels with my jeans, and when I wear heels I wear panty hose, and I don't think that is odd, and I am all female!"

But Alex's story raises some other questions that have special resonance for feminists. Chief among them, for me, is why a man has to put on electronic drag to experience intimacy, trust, and sharing. Some women have suggested that the fault is partly ours as women—that if Alex had approached us as a male, with all of Joan's personality traits, we wouldn't have been open to him. I for one reject that notion—not only because I have several terrific male friends on-line but also because it presumes that men are too fragile to break down stereotypes about themselves. (After all, we've spent the last fifteen years struggling to prove that we can be strong, independent, and capable.) On the other hand, in Alex's defense, I can't help but appreciate the temptation to experience life in the actual world from the point of view of the other sex. Think of "Tootsie" and "Yentl." Annie Lennox and Boy George. What Alex did was alien, taboo, weird . . . and yet the stuff of cosmic cultural fantasy. Haven't you ever wanted to be a fly on the locker room (or powder room) wall?

Sheila Deitz comments that some on-line transsexualism may be essentially harmless. Where she draws the line—and where I would also—is at the point that such experimentation starts impinging on other people's trust. Joan clearly stepped over that line years ago.

Maybe one of the things to be learned from Alex and Joan is that we have a way to go before gender stops being a major, volatile, human organizing principle—even in a medium dedicated to the primacy of the spirit.

I personally applaud those souls on CB who, when asked "R u m or f?" [Are you male or female?], simply answer "yes."

P·A·R·T · V

Yakety-Yak, Do Talk Back!: PEN, the Nation's First Publicly Funded Electronic Network, Makes a Difference in Santa Monica*

Joan Van Tassel

The seaside city of Santa Monica is beautiful, affluent, and, even in the governmentally weird state of California, a political anomaly. Often referred to as the People's Republic of Santa Monica, middle-class radicalism makes the city's politics both unpredictable and innovative, a far cry from its megametro Siamese twin, Los Angeles. For example, there's PEN.

In the mid-1980s Santa Monica officials installed the Public Electronic Network. Paid for entirely by taxpayer dollars and accessible to all city residents, PEN is the first free, government-sponsored electronic network in the United States.

The founders of PEN hoped to increase public participation in city government and politics, and in many ways, PEN has succeeded well beyond their expectations. Since it went on-line in 1989, more than 5000 of the 85,000 Santa Monica residents have signed onto the system, including an estimated 200 homeless people. One dialogue between housed and homeless citizens resulted in the creation of several programs to aid the homeless. PEN figured prominently in the defeat of a 1990 development initiative. And PEN continues to be a vital center for public discussion and citizen/government communication.

PEN was the brainchild of Ken Phillips and Joseph Schmitz, when Phillips was the director of Santa Monica's Information Systems Department, and Schmitz a doctoral candidate at the Annenberg School for Communication at the University of Southern California. The system began with a request from a city council member asking Phillips to research whether Santa Monica could provide computer access to a small group of his constituents. "I thought that this system shouldn't be limited to a bunch of buddies of one councilman. This would work for everyone," Phillips says.

Phillips approached Schmitz to conduct an exploratory study to determine whether there was public support for a community-based electronic communication system. Schmitz found that Santa Monicans wanted such a system to be open to all residents. Schmitz and Phillips relied on the study to guide the design of PEN, ensuring ongoing citizen support for the innovative program. Phillips then approached Hewlett-Packard for hardware and Metasystems for software. Both organizations agreed to provide start-up equipment, and PEN was born.

Initially, PEN had six objectives: (1) to provide easy access to, and use of, public information; (2) to aid the delivery of city services; (3) to enhance communication among residents; (4) to provide electronic forums and increase a sense of community; (5) to diffuse knowledge of, and access to, new communication technology among residents; and (6) to provide equitable distribution of communication resources to all residents.

PEN consists of a Hewlett-Packard minicomputer with sixty-four modem ports and Metasystems software that interfaces with all types of computers. For people without home computers, twenty Hewlett-Packard public terminals are scattered throughout Santa Monica in libraries, recreation centers, senior centers, and public buildings. Any resident, including a homeless person, can register with the city's Information Systems Department and get a user ID and password. At login, users see a PEN Main Menu and choose from options including City Hall, Community Center, mail, and current events.

How well does PEN work, and who uses it? Besides the initial research, the city's Information Systems Department authorized follow-up studies to evaluate progress and problems with PEN's implementation.

In May 1993, Schmitz, Phillips, and Everett M. Rogers presented the first such report, covering the system's first four years, at the annual International Communication Association conference in Washington, D.C. The paper had one additional author: Donald Paschal, a homeless resident.

*This article appeared in *Wired* 2.01 (January 1994), pp. 78–80. Reprinted with permission of Pepperdine University.

Paschal writes about PEN:

"I am homeless. If you knew me, it might come as a shock to you, as it does to me. I did not start out this way. This is not a career choice we make when planning our lives in high school. . . . We without shelter are looked on with disdain, fear, loathing, pity, and hatred. This difference makes 'normal' contact with other humans almost impossible. Not only might we be dirty, or perhaps smell bad, we are different. In the minds of many, people who are different must be avoided. This is why Santa Monica's PEN system is so special to me. No one on PEN knew that I was homeless until I told them. After I told them, I was still treated like a human being. To me, the most remarkable thing about the PEN community is that a city councilmember and a pauper can coexist, albeit not always in perfect harmony, but on an equal basis. I have met, become friends with, or perhaps adversaries with, people I would otherwise not know of—even if I were homed."

In itself, the diverse backgrounds of the authors who collaborated to write this report reveal much about PEN and how the system brings together disparate social elements. The study details how politically active users have been able to harness the power of electronic messages to communicate with one another, to recruit newcomers to their causes, and to gather previously obscure legal and procedural information. Each of these functions empowers citizen-activists to press their points of view at a time when many voters, in Santa Monica and elsewhere, feel increasingly powerless and disenfranchised.

A good example of such empowerment is an innovative program for the homeless called SHWASHLOCK (showers, washers, and lockers), which was conceived on the PEN system. For a decade, Santa Monica residents have been upset and frustrated over the estimated 2000 homeless people who subsist in makeshift shelters in the city's parks and on the beaches. When PEN was launched on February 21, 1989, homelessness was a high-profile topic in on-line discussion conferences. PEN became the focal point for public expression about the issue.

By August 1989, housed PENners had engaged in substantive on-line discussions with homeless PENners. The homeless presented a new perspective: they needed jobs to get off the streets but could not present an employable appearance without being able to shower, wash their clothing, and store their meager belongings.

Armed with a greater understanding of the needs of the homeless, the PEN Action Group, headed by Cal State Northridge psychology professor Michele Wittig, launched the SHWASHLOCK program to combat the problems of homelessness. The group has also established a job bank for the homeless.

The evaluation report observes that the development of the PEN Action Group demonstrates "a distinctive process in which diverse individuals meet in 'electronic space' devoted to shared interests. As they become acquainted, they may choose to meet face to face and to form a group."

Santa Monica activists also used the PEN system to build a coalition in another, more bitter political battle. In 1990, Michael McCarty, a local restauranteur, quietly proposed to lease choice public beach property from the State of California for sixty years to build a luxury hotel and restaurant. The property had previously been leased to a private club, the Sand and Sea Club, but that lease had run out. There was a window of opportunity to replace private use with public use of the beach front.

Antidevelopment organizations quickly rallied, using the PEN system to solicit volunteers and discuss the issues. The ensuing public outcry was vociferous enough to ensure that Proposition Z, which directed the city to lease the property for public use, made the November 1990 ballot and passed into law.

PEN users exercise considerable political clout, in large part because they differ significantly from typical Santa Monicans. PENners make more money ($50,000 annually, compared to the Santa Monica average of $36,000), are more likely to be male (65% to 50%), and are more likely to be college graduates (65% to 42%). Finally, 60% of heavy PEN users describe themselves as "very interested" in politics. The evaluation study notes that "PEN registrants were more active (than the average city resident) in each of seven types of local political activity, ranging from attending City Council meetings to contacting city officials."

The evaluation shows that PEN has met most of its initial six objectives. Ironically, in light of the founders' great expectations, the system is least successful at providing electronic forums and increasing a sense of community. The mistakes made in PEN's design offer important guidelines for effective electronic town hall operation by pointing out the facets of electronic life that decrease a sense of community and cut off, rather than enhance, public discussion of important current topics: netbozo takeovers (massive missives from a few residents who dominate the system), excessive flaming (no surprise to cyberspace denizens), and topic digression. Some PEN users, including several public officials, withdrew from PEN conferences because of what they perceived as vicious, unwarranted personal attacks from flamers.

Ken Phillips has since moved and is now executive director of the Joint Computer Facility in Salem/Marion County, Oregon, where he plans to establish a public communication system. In Salem, he says, he will take steps to ensure that rampant flaming and netbozo takeovers do not occur. "Anyone who just stumbled onto PEN could use it however they wanted and the system never recovered. It's important to recruit opinion leaders to set the tone," Phillips observes. In short, Phillips has learned the importance of establishing strong forum leaders and good sysops. Flaming by the yakety few has undermined some support for PEN, which, by Schmitz and Phillips's estimate, costs about $200,000 per year in staff time (all equipment is donated) to operate. As one user who preferred to remain unidentified commented, "The city probably spends $200,000 a year on PEN.

There are 85,000 residents, 5000 users, and 150 heavy users. Why should the taxpayer pay so some crazy wacko can write 'fuck you' to the council members when he goes off his meds?"

Now that changes to public conferences have been implemented, the major complaint against the system has been addressed. In all other areas, Santa Monicans are proud of their innovative system. Although founders Phillips and Schmitz would like to see greater PENmanship, that is, more users, they are pleased with the results of the evaluation study. Don Paschal expresses it best: "On PEN, I have been helped, rebuffed, scorned, criticized, considered, and in most cases, respected—as a human. PEN is a great equalizer. There are no homeless or homed unless we say we are. We are not one happy family; like most families, we squabble. On any topic, no one can accuse PENners of agreeing fully. But we are communicating, and that is a start."

What's in a PEN?

After logging on, residents of Santa Monica can choose from any of these five main menus:

- City Hall: over 200 documents, including schedules, notices and reports, city government, public works, planning and building, city attorney, public safety, transportation, and rent control
- Community Center: information about recreation and parks, libraries, neighborhood groups, office of the disabled, senior citizen center, social services directory, schools, cultural arts, and youth services
- Mailroom: user-to-city officials, and user-to-user e-mail services
- Conferences: public meeting spaces where users can participate in a variety of discussions; can be used in real time or in asynchronous mode
- Current Events: includes calendar of events, pets for adoption, PEN news, city jobline, cityTV schedule, and public notices

Taboo, Consensus, and the Challenge of Democracy in an Electronic Forum*

Julian Dibbell

They say he raped them that night. They say he did it with a cunning little doll, fashioned in their image and imbued with the power to make them do whatever he desired. They say that by manipulating the doll he forced them to have sex with him, and with each other, and to do horrible, brutal things to their own bodies. And though I wasn't there that night, I think I can assure you that what they say is true, because it all happened right in the living room—right there amid the well-stocked bookcases and the sofas and the fireplace—of a house I've come to think of as my second home.

Call me Dr. Bombay. Some months ago—let's say about halfway between the first time you heard the words *information superhighway* and the first time you wished you never had—I found myself tripping with compulsive regularity down the well-traveled information lane that leads to LambdaMOO, a very large and very busy rustic chateau built entirely of words. Nightly, I typed the commands that called those words onto my computer screen, dropping me with what seemed a warm electric thud inside the mansion's darkened coat closet, where I checked my quotidian identity, stepped into the persona and appearance of a minor character from a long-gone television sitcom, and stepped out into the glaring chatter of the crowded living room. Sometimes, when the mood struck me, I emerged as a dolphin instead.

I won't say why I chose to masquerade as Samantha Stevens's outlandish cousin, or as the dolphin, or what exactly led to my mild but so-far incurable addiction to the semifictional digital otherworlds known around the Internet as multi-user dimensions, or MUDs. This isn't my story, after all. It's the story of a man named Mr. Bungle, and of the ghostly sexual violence he committed in the halls of LambdaMOO, and most importantly of the ways his violence and his victims challenged the 1000 and more residents of that surreal, magic-infested mansion to become, finally, the community so many of them already believed they were.

That I was myself one of those residents has little direct bearing on the story's events. I mention it only as a warning that my own perspective is perhaps too steeped in the surreality and magic of the place to serve as an entirely appropriate guide. For the Bungle Affair raises question that—here on the brink of a future in which human life may find itself as tightly enveloped in digital environments as it is today in the architectural kind—demand a clear-eyed, sober, and unmystified consideration. It asks us to shut our ears momentarily to the techno-utopian ecstasies of West Coast cyberhippies and look without illusion upon the present possibilities for building, in the on-line spaces of this world, societies more decent and free than those mapped onto dirt and concrete and capital. It asks us to behold the new bodies awaiting us in virtual space undazzled by their phantom powers, and to get to the crucial work of sorting out the socially meaningful differences between those bodies and our physical ones. And most forthrightly it asks us to wrap our late-modern ontologies, epistemologies, sexual ethics, and common sense around the curious notion of rape by voodoo doll—and to try not to warp them beyond recognition in the process.

In short, the Bungle Affair dares me to explain it to you without resort to dime-store mysticisms, and I fear I may have shape-shifted by the digital moonlight one too many times to be quite up to the task. But I will do what I can, and can do no better I suppose than to lead with the facts. For if nothing else about Mr. Bungle's case is unambiguous, the facts at least are crystal clear.

The facts begin (as they often do) with a time and a place. This time was a Monday night in March, and the place, as I've said, was the living room—which, due to the inviting warmth of its decor, is so invariably packed with chitchatters as to be roughly synonymous among Lambda-MOOers with a party. So strong, indeed, is the sense of convivial common ground invested in the living room that a cruel mind could hardly imagine a better place in which to stage a violation of LambdaMOO's communal

---

*This article appeared as "A Rape in Cyberspace or How an Evil Clown, a Haitian Trickster Spirit, Two Wizards, and a Cast of Dozens Turned a Database into a Society" in *The Village Voice* (December 21, 1993), pp. 36–42. Reprinted with permission.

spirit. And there was cruelty enough lurking in the appearance Mr. Bungle presented to the virtual world—he was at the time a fat, oleaginous, Bisquick-faced clown dressed in cum-stained harlequin garb and girdled with a mistletoe-and-hemlock belt whose buckle bore the quaint inscription "KISS ME UNDER THIS, BITCH!" But whether cruelty motivated his choice of crime scene is not among the established facts of the case. It is a fact only that he did choose the living room.

The remaining facts tell us a bit more about the inner world of Mr. Bungle, though only perhaps that it couldn't have been a very comfortable place. They tell us that he commenced his assault entirely unprovoked, at or about 10 p.m. Pacific Standard Time. That he began by using his voodoo doll to force one of the room's occupants to sexually service him in a variety of more or less conventional ways. That this victim was legba, a Haitian trickster spirit of indeterminate gender, brown-skinned and wearing an expensive pearl gray suit, top hat, and dark glasses. That legba heaped vicious imprecations on him all the while and that he was soon ejected bodily from the room. That he hid himself away then in his private chambers somewhere on the mansion grounds and continued the attacks without interruption, since the voodoo doll worked just as well at a distance as in proximity. That he turned his attentions now to Starsinger, a rather pointedly nondescript female character, tall, stout, and brown-haired, forcing her into unwanted liaisons with other individuals present in the room, among them legba, Bakunin (the well-known radical), and Juniper (the squirrel). That his actions grew progressively violent. That he made legba eat his/her own pubic hair. That he caused Starsinger to violate herself with a piece of kitchen cutlery. That his distant laughter echoed evilly in the living room with every successive outrage. That he could not be stopped until at last someone summoned Zippy, a wise and trusted old-timer who brought with him a gun of near wizardly powers, a gun that didn't kill but enveloped its targets in a cage impermeable even to a voodoo doll's powers. That Zippy fired this gun at Mr. Bungle, thwarting the doll at last and silencing the evil, distant laughter.

These particulars, as I said, are unambiguous. But they are far from simple, for the simple reason that every set of facts in virtual reality (or VR, as the locals abbreviate it) is shadowed by a second, complicating set: the "real-life" facts. And although a certain tension invariably buzzes in the gap between the hard, prosaic RL facts and their more fluid, dreamy VR counterparts, the dissonance in the Bungle case is striking. No hideous clowns or trickster spirits appear in the RL version of the incident, no voodoo dolls or wizard guns, indeed no rape at all as any RL court of law has yet defined it. The actors in the drama were university students for the most part, and they sat rather undramatically before computer screens the entire time, their only actions a spidery flitting of fingers across standard QWERTY keyboards. No bodies touched. Whatever physical interaction occurred consisted of a mingling of electronic signals sent from sites spread out between New York City and Sydney, Australia. Those signals met in LambdaMOO, certainly, just as the hideous clown and the living room party did, but what was LambdaMOO after all? Not an enchanted mansion or anything of the sort—just a middlingly complex database, maintained for experimental purposes inside a Xerox Corporation research computer in Palo Alto and open to public access via the Internet.

To be more precise about it, LambdaMOO was a MUD. Or to be yet more precise, it was a subspecies of MUD known as a MOO, which is short for "MUD, Object-Oriented." All of which means that it was a kind of database especially designed to give users the vivid impression of moving through a physical space that in reality exists only as descriptive data filed away on a hard drive. When users dial into LambdaMOO, for instance, the program immediately presents them with a brief textual description of one of the rooms of the database's fictional mansion (the coat closet, say). If the user wants to leave this room, she can enter a command to move in a particular direction and the database will replace the original description with a new one corresponding to the room located in the direction she chose. When the new description scrolls across the user's screen it lists not only the fixed features of the room but all its contents at that moment— including things (tools, toys, weapons) and other users (each represented as a "character" over which he or she has sole control).

As far as the database program is concerned, all of these entities—rooms, things, characters—are just different subprograms that the program allows to interact according to rules very roughly mimicking the laws of the physical world. Characters may not leave a room in a given direction, for instance, unless the room subprogram contains an "exit" at that compass point. And if a character "says" or "does" something (as directed by its user-owner), then only the users whose characters are also located in that room will see the output describing the statement or action. Aside from such basic constraints, however, LambdaMOOers are allowed a broad freedom to create—they can describe their characters any way they like, they can make rooms of their own and decorate them to taste, and they can build new objects almost at will. The combination of all this busy user activity with the hard physics of the database can certainly induce a lucid illusion of presence—but when all is said and done the only thing you *really* see when you visit LambdaMOO is a kind of slow-crawling script, lines of dialogue and stage direction creeping steadily up your computer screen.

Which is all just to say that, to the extent that Mr. Bungle's assault happened in real life at all, it happened as a sort of Punch-and-Judy show, in which the puppets and the scenery were made of nothing more sub- stantial than digital code and snippets of creative writing. The puppeteer behind Bungle, as it happened, was a young man logging in to the MOO from a New York University computer. He could have been Al Gore for all any of the others knew, however, and he could have written Bungle's script that night any way he chose. He could have sent a command to print the message "Mr. Bungle, smiling a saintly smile, floats angelic near the ceiling of the living room, showering joy and candy kisses down upon the heads of all below"—and everyone then receiving output from the database's subprogram #17 (a/k/a the "living room") would have seen that sentence on their screens.

Instead, he entered sadistic fantasies into the "voodoo doll," a subprogram that served the not-exactly kosher purpose of attributing actions to other characters that their users did not actually write. And thus a woman in Haverford, Pennsylvania, whose account on the MOO attached her to a character she called Starsinger, was given the unasked-for opportunity to read the words "As if against her will, Starsinger jabs a steak knife up her ass, causing immense joy. You hear Mr. Bungle laughing evilly in the distance." And thus the woman in Seattle who had written herself the character called legba, with a view perhaps to tasting in imagination a deity's freedom from the burdens of the gendered flesh, got to read similarly constructed sentences in which legba, messenger of the gods, lord of crossroads and communications, suffered a brand of degradation all-too-customarily reserved for the embodied female.

"Mostly voodoo dolls are amusing," wrote legba on the evening after Bungle's rampage, posting a public statement to the widely read in-MOO mailing list called *social-issues, a forum for debate on matters of import to the entire populace. "And mostly I tend to think that restrictive measures around here cause more trouble than they prevent. But I also think that Mr. Bungle was being a vicious, vile fuckhead, and I . . . want his sorry ass scattered from #17 to the Cinder Pile. I'm not calling for policies, trials, or better jails. I'm not sure what I'm calling for. Virtual castration, if I could manage it. Mostly, [this type of thing] doesn't happen here. Mostly, perhaps I thought it wouldn't happen to me. Mostly, I trust people to conduct themselves with some veneer of civility. Mostly, I want his ass."

Months later, the woman in Seattle would confide to me that as she wrote those words posttraumatic tears were streaming down her face—a real-life fact that should suffice to prove that the words' emotional content was no mere playacting. The precise tenor of that content, however, its mingling of murderous rage and eyeball-rolling annoyance, was a curious amalgam that neither the RL nor the VR facts alone can quite account for. Where virtual reality and its conventions would have us believe that legba and Starsinger were brutally raped in their own living room, here was the victim legba scolding Mr. Bungle for a breach of "civility." Where real life, on the other hand, insists the incident was only an episode in a free-form version of Dungeons and Dragons, confined to the realm of the symbolic and at no point threatening any player's life, limb, or material well-being, here now was the player legba issuing aggrieved and heartfelt calls for Mr. Bungle's dismemberment. Ludicrously excessive by RL's lights, woefully understated by VR's, the tone of legba's response made sense only in the buzzing, dissonant gap between them.

Which is to say it made the only kind of sense that *can* be made of MUDly phenomena. For while the *facts* attached to any event born of a MUD's strange, ethereal universe may march in straight, tandem lines separated neatly into the virtual and the real, its meaning lies always in that gap. You learn this axiom early in your life as a player, and it's of no small relevance to the Bungle case that you usually learn it between the sheets, so to speak. Netsex, tinysex, virtual sex—however you name it, in real-life reality it's nothing more than a 900-line encounter stripped of even the vestigial physicality of the voice. And yet as any but the most inhibited of newbies can tell you, it's possibly the headiest experience the very heady world of MUDs has to offer. Amid flurries of even the most cursorily described caresses, sighs, and penetrations, the glands do engage, and often as throbbingly as they would in a real-life assignation—sometimes even more so, given the combined power of anonymity and textual suggestiveness to unshackle deep-seated fantasies. And if the virtual setting and the inter-player vibe are right, who knows? The heart may engage as well, stirring up passions as strong as many that bind lovers who observe the formality of trysting in the flesh.

To participate, therefore, in this disembodied enactment of life's most body-centered activity is to risk the realization that when it comes to sex, perhaps the body in question is not the physical one at all, but its psychic double, the bodylike self-representation we carry around in our heads. I know, I know, you've read Foucault and your mind is not quite blown by the notion that sex is never so much an exchange of fluids as it is an exchange of signs. But trust your friend Dr. Bombay, it's one thing to grasp the notion intellectually and quite another to feel it coursing through your veins amid the virtual steam of hot netnookie. And it's a whole other mind-blowing trip altogether to encounter it thus as a college frosh, new to the net and still in the grip of hormonal hurricanes and high-school sexual mythologies. The shock can easily reverberate throughout an entire young worldview. Small wonder, then, that a newbie's first taste of MUD sex is often also the first time she or he surrenders wholly to the slippery terms of MUDish ontology, recognizing in a full-bodied way that what happens inside a MUD-made world is neither exactly real nor exactly make-believe, but profoundly, compellingly, and emotionally meaningful.

And small wonder indeed that the sexual nature of Mr. Bungle's crime provoked such powerful feelings, and not just in legba (who, be it noted, was in real life a theory-savvy doctoral candidate and a longtime MOOer, but just as baffled and overwhelmed by the force of her own reaction, she later would attest, as any panting undergrad might have been). Even players who had never experienced MUD rape (the vast majority of male-presenting characters, but not as large a majority of the female-presenting as might be hoped) immediately appreciated its gravity and were moved to condemnation of the perp. legba's missive to *social-issues followed a strongly worded one from Zippy ("Well, well," it began, "no matter what else happens on Lambda, I can always be sure that some jerk is going to reinforce my low opinion of humanity") and was itself followed by others from Moriah, Raccoon, Crawfish, and evangeline. Starsinger also let her feelings ("pissed") be known. And even Jander, the Clueless Samaritan who had responded to Bungle's cries for help and uncaged him shortly after the incident, expressed his regret once apprised of Bungle's deeds, which he allowed to be "despicable."

A sense was brewing that something needed to be done—done soon and in something like an organized fashion—about Mr. Bungle, in particular, and about MUD rape, in general. Regarding the general problem, evangeline, who identified herself as a survivor of both virtual rape ("many times over") and real-life sexual assault, floated a cautious proposal for a MOO-wide powwow on the subject of virtual sex offenses and what mechanisms if any might be put in place to deal with their future occurrence. As for the specific problem, the answer no doubt seemed obvious to many. But it wasn't until the evening of the second day after the incident that legba, finally and rather solemnly, gave it voice:

"I am requesting that Mr. Bungle be toaded for raping Starsinger and I. I have never done this before, and have thought about it for days. He hurt us both."

That was all. Three simple sentences posted to *social. Reading them, an outsider might never guess that they were an application for a death warrant. Even an outsider familiar with other MUDs might not guess it, since in many of them "toading" still refers to a command that, true to the gameworlds' sword-and-sorcery origins, simply turns a player into a toad, wiping the player's description and attributes and replacing them with those of the slimy amphibian. Bad luck for sure, but not quite as bad as what happens when the same command is invoked in the MOOish strains of MUD: not only are the description and attributes of the toaded player erased, but the account itself goes too. The annihilation of the character, thus, is total.

And nothing less than total annihilation, it seemed, would do to settle LambdaMOO's accounts with Mr. Bungle. Within minutes of the posting of legba's appeal, SamIAm, the Australian Deleuzean, who had witnessed much of the attack from the back room of his suburban Sydney home, seconded the motion with a brief message crisply entitled "Toad the fukr." SamIAm's posting was seconded almost as quickly by that of Bakunin, covictim of Mr. Bungle and well-known radical, who in real life happened also to be married to the real-life legba. And over the course of the next twenty-four hours as many as fifty players made it known, on *social and in a variety of other forms and forums, that they would be pleased to see Mr. Bungle erased from the face of the MOO. And with dissent so far confined to a dozen or so antitoading hardliners, the numbers suggested that the citizenry was indeed moving toward a resolve to have Bungle's virtual head.

There was one small but stubborn obstacle in the way of this resolve, however, and that was a curious state of social affairs known in some quarters of the MOO as the New Direction. It was all very fine, you see, for the LambdaMOO rabble to get it in their heads to liquidate one of their peers, but when the time came to actually do the deed it would require the services of a nobler class of character. It would require a wizard. Master-programmers of the MOO, spelunkers of the database's deepest code-structures and custodians of its day-to-day administrative trivia, wizards are also the only players empowered to issue the toad command, a feature maintained on nearly all MUDs as a quick-and-dirty means of social con-trol. But the wizards of LambdaMOO, after years of adjudicating all manner of interplayer disputes with little to show for it but their own weariness and the smoldering resentment of the general populace, had decided they'd had enough of the social sphere. And so, four months before the Bungle incident, the archwizard Haakon (known in RL as Pavel Curtis, Xerox researcher and LambdaMOO's principal architect) formalized this decision in a document called "LambdaMOO Takes a New Direction," which he placed in the living room for all to see. In it, Haakon announced that the wizards from that day forth were pure technicians. From then on, they would make no decisions affecting the social life of the MOO, but only implement whatever decisions the community as a whole directed them to. From then on, it was decreed, LambdaMOO would just have to grow up and solve its problems on its own.

Faced with the task of inventing its own self-governance from scratch, the LambdaMOO population had so far done what any other loose, amor-phous agglomeration of individuals would have done: they'd let it slide. But now the task took on new urgency. Since getting the wizards to toad Mr. Bungle (or to toad the likes of him in the future) required a convincing case that the cry for his head came from the community at large, then the community itself would have to be defined; and if the community was to be convincingly defined, then some form of social organizations, no matter how rudimentary, would have to be settled on. And thus, as if against its will, the question of what to do about Mr. Bungle began to shape itself into a sort of referendum on the political future of the MOO. Arguments broke out on *social and elsewhere that had only superficially to do with Bungle (since everyone agreed he was a cad) and everything to do with where the participants stood on LambdaMOO's crazy-quilty political map. Par-liamentarian legalist types argued that unfortunately Bungle could not legitimately be toaded at all, since there were no explicit MOO rules against rape, or against just about anything else—and the sooner such rules were established, they added, and maybe even a full-blown judiciary system complete with elected officials and prisons to enforce those rules, the better. Others, with a royalist streak in them, seemed to feel that Bungle's as-yet-unpunished outrage only proved this New Direction silli-ness had gone on long enough, and that it was high time the wizardocracy returned to the position of swift and decisive leadership their player class was born to.

And then there was what I'll call the technolibertarians. For them, MUD rapists were of course assholes, but the presence of assholes on the system was a technical inevitability, like noise on a phone line, and best dealt with not through repressive social disciplinary mechanisms but through the timely deployment of defensive software tools. Some asshole blasting violent, graphic language at you? Don't whine to authorities about it—hit the @gag command and the asshole's statements will be blocked from your screen (and only yours). It's simple, it's effective, and it censors no one.

But the Bungle case was rather hard on such arguments. For one thing, the extremely public nature of the living room meant that gagging would spare the victims only from witnessing their own violation, but not from having others witness it. You might want to argue that what those victims didn't directly experience couldn't hurt them, but consider how that wisdom would sound to a woman who'd been, say, fondled by strangers while passed out drunk and you have a rough idea how it might go over with a crowd of hard-core MOOers. Consider, for another thing, that many of the biologically female participants in the Bungle debate had been around long enough to grow lethally weary of the gag-and-get-over-it school of virtual-rape counseling, with its fine line between empowering victims and holding them responsible for their own suffering, and its shrugging indifference to the window of pain between the moment the rape-text starts flowing and the moment a gag shuts it off. From the outset it was clear that the technolibertarians were going to have to tiptoe through this issue with care, and for the most part they did.

Yet no position was trickier to maintain than that of the MOO's resident anarchists. Like the technolibbers, the anarchists didn't care much for punishments or policies or power elites. Like them, they hoped the MOO could be a place where people interacted fulfillingly without the need for such things. But their high hopes were complicated, in general, by a somewhat less thoroughgoing faith in technology ("Even if you can't tear down the master's house with the master's tools"—read a slogan written into one anarchist player's self-description—"it is a damned good place to start"). And at present they were additionally complicated by the fact that the most vocal anarchists in the discussion were none other than legba, Bakunin, and SamIAm, who wanted to see Mr. Bungle toaded as badly as anyone did.

Needless to say, a pro death penalty platform is not an especially comfortable one for an anarchist to sit on, so these particular anarchists were now at great pains to sever the conceptual ties between toading and capital punishment. Toading, they insisted (almost convincingly), was much more closely analogous to banishment; it was a kind of turning of the communal back on the offending party, a collective action which, if carried out properly, was entirely consistent with anarchist models of community.

And carrying it out properly meant first and foremost building a consensus around it—a messy process for which there were no easy technocratic substitutes. It was going to take plenty of good old-fashioned, jawbone-intensive grassroots organizing.

So that when the time came, at 7 P.M. PST on the evening of the third day after the occurrence in the living room, to gather in evangeline's room for her proposed real-time open conclave, Bakunin and legba were among the first to arrive. But this was hardly to be an anarchist-dominated affair, for the room was crowding rapidly with representatives of all the MOO's political stripes, and even a few wizards. Hagbard showed up, and Autumn and Quastro, Puff, JoeFeedback, L-dopa and Bloaf, HerkieCosmo, Silver Rocket, Karl Porcupine, Matchstick—the names piled up and the discussion gathered momentum under their weight. Arguments multiplied and mingled, players talked past and through each other, the textual clutter of utterances and gestures filled up the screen like thick cigar smoke. Peaking in number at around thirty, this was one of the largest crowds that ever gathered in a single LambdaMOO chamber, and while evangeline had given her place a description that made it "infinite in expanse and fluid in form," it now seemed anything but roomy. You could almost feel the claustrophobic air of the place, dank and overheated by virtual bodies, pressing against your skin.

I know you could because I too was there, making my lone and insignificant appearance in this story. Completely ignorant of any of the goings-on that had led to the meeting, I wandered in purely to see what the crowd was about, and though I observed the proceedings for a good while, I confess I found it hard to grasp what was going on. I was still the rankest of newbies then, my MOO legs still too unsteady to make the leaps of faith, logic, and empathy required to meet the spectacle on its own terms. I was fascinated by the concept of virtual rape, but I couldn't quite take it seriously.

In this, though, I was in a small and mostly silent minority, for the discussion that raged around me was of an almost unrelieved earnestness, bent it seemed on examining every last aspect and implication of Mr. Bungle's crime. There were the central questions, of course: thumbs up or down on Bungle's virtual existence? And if down, how then to ensure that his toading was not just some isolated lynching but a first step toward shaping LambdaMOO into a legitimate community? Surrounding these, however, a tangle of weighty side issues proliferated. What, some wondered, was the real-life legal status of the offense? Could Bungle's university administrators punish him for sexual harassment? Could he be prosecuted under California state laws against obscene phone calls? Little enthusiasm was shown for pursuing either of these lines of action, which testifies both to the uniqueness of the crime and to the nimbleness with which the discussants were negotiating its idiosyncrasies. Many were the casual references to Bungle's deed as simply "rape," but these in no way implied that the players had lost sight of all distinctions between the virtual and physical versions, or that they believed Bungle should be dealt with in the same way a real-life criminal would. He had committed a MOO crime, and his punishment, if any, would be meted out via the MOO.

On the other hand, little patience was shown toward any attempts to downplay the seriousness of what Mr. Bungle had done. When the affable HerkieCosmo proposed, more in the way of an hypothesis than an assertion, that "perhaps it's better to release . . . violent tendencies in a virtual environment rather than in real life," he was tut-tutted so swiftly and relentlessly that he withdrew the hypothesis altogether, apologizing humbly as he did so. Not that the assembly was averse to putting matters into a more philosophical perspective. "Where does the body end and the mind begin?" young Quastro asked, amid recurring attempts to fine-tune the differences between real and virtual violence. "Is not the mind a part of the body?" "In MOO, the body IS the mind," offered HerkieCosmo gamely, and not at all implausibly, demonstrating the ease with which very knotty metaphysical conundrums come undone in VR. The not-so-aptly named Obvious seemed to agree, arriving after deep consideration of the nature of Bungle's crime at the hardly novel yet now somehow newly resonant conjecture "all reality might consist of ideas, who knows."

On these and other matters the anarchists, the libertarians, the legalists, the wizardists—and the wizards—all had their thoughtful say. But as the evening wore on and the talk grew more heated and more heady, it seemed increasingly clear that the vigorous intelligence being brought to bear on this swarm of issues wasn't going to result in anything remotely like resolution. The perspectives were just too varied, the meme-scape just too slippery. Again and again, arguments that looked at first to be heading in a decisive direction ended up chasing their own tails; and slowly, depressingly, a dusty haze of irrelevance gathered over the proceedings.

It was almost a relief, therefore, when midway through the evening Mr. Bungle himself, the living, breathing cause of all this talk, teleported into the room. Not that it was much of a surprise. Oddly enough, in the three days since his release from Zippy's cage, Bungle had returned more than once to wander the public spaces of LambdaMOO, walking willingly into one of the fiercest storms of ill will and invective ever to rain down on a player. He'd been taking it all with a curious and mostly silent passivity, and when challenged face to virtual face by both legba and the genderless elder statescharacter PatGently to defend himself on *social, he'd demurred, mumbling something about Christ and expiation. He was equally quiet now, and his reception was still uniformly cool. legba fixed an arctic stare on him—"no hate, no anger, no interest at all. Just . . . watching." Others were more actively unfriendly. "Asshole," spat Karl Porcupine, "creep." But the harshest of the MOO's hostility toward him had already been vented, and the attention he drew now was motivated more, it seemed, by the opportunity to probe the rapist's mind, to find out what made it tick and if possible how to get it to tick differently. In short, they wanted to know why he'd done it. So they asked him.

And Mr. Bungle thought about it. And as eddies of discussion and debate continued to swirl around him, he thought about it some more. And then he said this:

"I engaged in a bit of a psychological device that is called thought-polarization, the fact that this is not RL simply added to heighten the affect of the device. It was purely a sequence of events with no consequence on my RL existence."

They might have known. Stilted though its diction was, the gist of the answer was simple, and something many in the room had probably already surmised: Mr. Bungle was a psycho. Not, perhaps, in real life—but then in real life it's possible for reasonable people to assume, as Bungle clearly did, that what transpires between word-costumed characters within the boundaries of a make-believe world is, if not mere play, then at most some kind of emotional laboratory experiment. Inside the MOO, however, such thinking marked a person as one of two basically subcompetent types. The first was the newbie, in which case the confusion was understandable, since there were few MOOers who had not, upon their first visits as anonymous "guest" characters, mistaken the place for a vast playpen in which they might act out their wildest fantasies without fear of censure. Only with time and the acquisition of a fixed character do players tend to make the critical passage from anonymity to pseudonymity, developing the concern for their character's reputation that marks the attainment of virtual adulthood. But while Mr. Bungle hadn't been around as long as most MOOers, he'd been around long enough to leave his newbie status behind, and his delusional statement therefore placed him among the second type: the sociopath.

And as there is but small percentage in arguing with a head case, the room's attention gradually abandoned Mr. Bungle and returned to the discussion that had previously occupied it. But if the debate had been edging toward ineffectuality before, Bungle's anticlimactic appearance had evidently robbed it of any forward motion whatsoever. What's more, from his lonely corner of the room Mr. Bungle kept issuing periodic expressions of a prickly sort of remorse, interlaced with sarcasm and belligerence, and though it was hard to tell if he wasn't still just conducting his experiments, some people thought his regret genuine enough that maybe he didn't deserve to be toaded after all. Logically, of course, discussion of the principal issues at hand didn't require unanimous belief that Bungle was an irredeemable bastard, but now that cracks were showing in that unanimity, the last of the meeting's fervor seemed to be draining out through them.

People started drifting away. Mr. Bungle left first, then others followed—one by one, in twos and threes, hugging friends and waving goodnight. By 9:45 only a handful remained, and the great debate had wound down into casual conversation, the melancholy remains of another fruitless good idea. The arguments had been well-honed, certainly, and perhaps might prove useful in some as-yet-unclear long run. But at this point what seemed clear was that evangeline's meeting had died, at last, and without any practical results to mark its passing.

It was also at this point, most likely, that JoeFeedback reached his decision. JoeFeedback was a wizard, a taciturn sort of fellow who'd sat brooding on the sidelines all evening. He hadn't said a lot, but what he had said indicated that he took the crime committed against legba and Starsinger very seriously, and that he felt no particular compassion toward the character who had committed it. But on the other hand he had made it equally plain that he took the elimination of a fellow player just as seriously, and moreover that he had no desire to return to the days of wizardly fiat. It must have been difficult, therefore, to reconcile the conflicting impulses churning within him at that moment. In fact, it was probably impossible, for as much as he would have liked to make himself an instrument of LambdaMOO's collective will, he surely realized that under the present order of things he must in the final analysis either act alone or not act at all.

So JoeFeedback acted alone.

He told the lingering few players in the room that he had to go, and then he went. It was a minute or two before ten. He did it quietly and he did it privately, but all anyone had to do to know he'd done it was to type the @who command, which was normally what you typed if you wanted to know a player's present location and the time he last logged in. But if you had run an @who on Mr. Bungle not too long after JoeFeedback left evangeline's room, the database would have told you something different.

"Mr. Bungle," it would have said, "is not the name of any player."

The date, as it happened, was April Fool's Day, and it would still be April Fool's Day for another two hours. But this was no joke: Mr. Bungle was truly dead and truly gone.

They say that LambdaMOO has never been the same since Mr. Bungle's toading. They say as well that nothing's really changed. And though it skirts the fuzziest of dream-logics to say that both these statements are true, the MOO is just the sort of fuzzy, dreamlike place in which such contradictions thrive.

Certainly whatever civil society now informs LambdaMOO owes its existence to the Bungle Affair. The archwizard Haakon made sure of that. Away on business for the duration of the episode, Haakon returned to find its wreckage strewn across the tiny universe he'd set in motion. The death of a player, the trauma of several others, and the angst-ridden conscience of his colleague JoeFeedback presented themselves to his concerned and astonished attention, and he resolved to see if he couldn't learn some lesson from it all. For the better part of a day he brooded over the record of events and arguments left in *social, then he sat pondering the chaotically evolving shape of his creation, and at the day's end he descended once again into the social arena of the MOO with another history-altering proclamation.

It was probably his last, for what he now decreed was the final, missing piece of the New Direction. In a few days, Haakon announced, he would build into the database a system of petitions and ballots whereby anyone could put to popular vote any social scheme requiring wizardly powers for its implementation, with the results of the vote to be binding on the wizards. At last and for good, the awkward gap between the will of the players and the efficacy of the technicians would be closed. And though some anarchists grumbled about the irony of Haakon's dictatorially impos-ing universal suffrage on an unconsulted populace, in general the citizens of LambdaMOO seemed to find it hard to fault a system more purely democratic than any that could ever exist in real life. Eight months and a dozen ballot measures later, widespread participation in the new regime has produced a small arsenal of mechanisms for dealing with the types of violence that called the system into being. MOO residents now have access to an @boot command, for instance, with which to summarily eject berserker "guest" characters. And players can bring suit against one another through an ad hoc arbitration system in which mutually agreed-upon judges have at their disposition the full range of wizardly punishments—up to and including the capital.

Yet the continued dependence on death as the ultimate keeper of the peace suggests that this new MOO order may not be built on the most solid of foundations. For if life on LambdaMOO began to acquire more coher-ence in the wake of the toading, death retained all the fuzziness of pre-Bungle days. This truth was rather dramatically borne out, not too many days after Bungle departed, by the arrival of a strange new character named Dr. Jest. There was a forceful eccentricity to the newcomer's man-ner, but the oddest thing about his style was its striking yet unnameable familiarity. And when he developed the annoying habit of stuffing fellow players into a jar containing a tiny simulacrum of a certain deceased rapist, the source of this familiarity became obvious:

Mr. Bungle had risen from the grave.

In itself, Bungle's reincarnation as Dr. Jest was a remarkable turn of events, but perhaps even more remarkable was the utter lack of amaze-ment with which the LambdaMOO public took note of it. To be sure, many residents were appalled by the brazenness of Bungle's return. In fact, one of the first petitions circulated under the new voting system was a request for Dr. Jest's toading that almost immediately gathered fifty-two signatures (but has failed so far to reach ballot status). Yet few were unaware of the ease with which the toad proscription could be circumvented—all the toadee had to do (all the ur-Bungle at NYU presumably had done) was to go to the minor hassle of acquiring a new Internet account, and Lambda-MOO's character registration program would then simply treat the known felon as an entirely new and innocent person. Nor was this ease generally understood to represent a failure of toading's social disciplinary function. On the contrary, it only underlined the truism (repeated many times throughout the debate over Mr. Bungle's fate) that his punishment, ultimately, had been no more or less symbolic than his crime.

What *was* surprising, however, was that Mr. Bungle/Dr. Jest seemed to have taken the symbolism to heart. Dark themes still obsessed him—the objects he created gave off wafts of Nazi imagery and medical torture—but he no longer radiated the aggressively antisocial vibes he had before. He was a lot less unpleasant to look at (the outrageously seedy clown description had been replaced by that of a mildly creepy but actually rather natty young man, with "blue eyes . . . suggestive of conspiracy, untamed eroticism and perhaps a sense of understanding of the future"), and aside from the occasional jar-stuffing incident, he was also a lot less dangerous to be around. It was obvious he'd undergone some sort of personal transformation in the days since I'd first glimpsed him back in evangeline's crowded room—nothing radical maybe, but powerful nonetheless, and resonant enough with my own experience, I felt, that it might be more than professionally interesting to talk with him, and perhaps compare notes.

For I too was undergoing a transformation in the aftermath of that night in evangeline's, and I'm still not entirely sure what to make of it. As I pursued my runaway fascination with the discussion I had heard there, as I pored over the *social debate and got to know legba and some of the other victims and witnesses, I could feel my newbie consciousness falling away from me. Where before I'd found it hard to take virtual rape seriously, I now was finding it difficult to remember how I could ever *not* have taken it seriously. I was proud to have arrived at this perspective—it felt like an exotic sort of achievement, and it definitely made my ongoing experience of the MOO a richer one.

But it was also having some unsettling effects on the way I looked at the rest of the world. Sometimes, for instance, it was hard for me to understand why RL society classifies RL rape alongside crimes against person or property. Since rape can occur without any physical pain or damage, I found myself reasoning, then it must be classed as a crime against the mind—more intimately and deeply hurtful, to be sure, than cross burnings, wolf whistles, and virtual rape, but undeniably located on the same conceptual continuum. I did not, however, conclude as a result that rapists were protected in any fashion by the First Amendment. Quite the opposite, in fact: the more seriously I took the notion of virtual rape, the less seriously I was able to take the notion of freedom of speech, with its tidy division of the world into the symbolic and the real.

Let me assure you, though, that I am not presenting these thoughts as arguments. I offer them, rather, as a picture of the sort of mind-set that deep immersion in a virtual world has inspired in me. I offer them also, therefore, as a kind of prophecy. For whatever else these thoughts tell me, I have come to believe that they announce the final stages of our decades-long passage into the Information Age, a paradigm shift that the classic liberal firewall between word and deed (itself a product of an earlier paradigm shift commonly known as the Enlightenment) is not likely to survive intact. After all, anyone the least bit familiar with the workings of the new era's definitive technology, the computer, knows that it operates on a principle impracticably difficult to distinguish from the pre-Enlightenment principle of the magic word: the commands you type into a computer are a kind of speech that doesn't so much communicate as *make things happen,* directly and ineluctably, the same way pulling a trigger does. They are incantations, in other words, and anyone at all attuned to the technosocial megatrends of the moment—from the growing dependence of economies on the global flow of intensely fetishized words and numbers to the burgeoning ability of bioengineers to speak the spells written in the four-letter text of DNA—knows that the logic of the incantation is rapidly permeating the fabric of our lives.

And it's precisely this logic that provides the real magic in a place like LambdaMOO—not the fictive trappings of voodoo and shapeshifting and wizardry, but the conflation of speech and act that's inevitable in any computer-mediated world, be it Lambda or the increasingly wired world at large. This is dangerous magic, to be sure, a potential threat—if misconstrued or misapplied—to our always precarious freedoms of expression, and as someone who lives by his words I do not take the threat lightly. And yet, on the other hand, I can no longer convince myself that our wishful insulation of language from the realm of action has ever been anything but a valuable kludge, a philosophically damaged stopgap against oppression that would just have to do till something truer and more elegant came along.

Am I wrong to think this truer, more elegant thing can be found on LambdaMOO? Perhaps, but I continue to seek it there, sensing its presence just beneath the surface of every interaction. I have even thought, as I said, that discussing with Dr. Jest our shared experience of the workings of the MOO might help me in my search. But when that notion first occurred to me, I still felt somewhat intimidated by his lingering criminal aura, and I hemmed and hawed a good long time before finally resolving to drop him MOO-mail requesting an interview. By then it was too late. For reasons known only to himself, Dr. Jest had stopped logging in. Maybe he'd grown bored with the MOO. Maybe the loneliness of ostracism had gotten to him. Maybe a psycho whim had carried him far away or maybe he'd quietly acquired a third character and started life over with a cleaner slate.

Wherever he'd gone, though, he left behind the room he'd created for himself—a treehouse "tastefully decorated" with rare-book shelves, an operating table, and a life-size William S. Burroughs doll—and he left it unlocked. So I took to checking in there occasionally, and I still do from time to time. I head out of my own cozy nook (inside a TV set inside the little red hotel inside the Monopoly board inside the dining room of

LambdaMOO), and I teleport on over to the treehouse, where the room description always tells me Dr. Jest is present but asleep, in the conventional depiction for disconnected characters. The not-quite-emptiness of the abandoned room invariably instills in me an uncomfortable mix of melancholy and the creeps, and I stick around only on the off chance that Dr. Jest will wake up, say hello, and share his understanding of the future with me.

He won't, of course, but this is no great loss. Increasingly, the complex magic of the MOO interests me more as a way to live the present than to understand the future. And it's usually not long before I leave Dr. Jest's lonely treehouse and head back to the mansion, to see some friends.

P·A·R·T·V

I

Applying Library Intellectual Freedom Principles to Public and Academic Computers*

Carl M. Kadie

Introduction

Should a university restrict access to on-line discussions of sex? Should a community's Free-Net create a no-children-allowed area? How should a school react when someone accuses the school of facilitating libel? For those of us in the computer community these are new questions with difficult social and intellectual freedom implications. Our technical training has allowed us to turn computers into public information resources, but it has not prepared us to manage the human side of that resource. Happily, we need not develop policy from scratch. Librarians have one hundred years of experience managing public information resources. They have developed a tradition of resource management that works and that promotes freedom of expression, the freedom to read, and privacy. In this chapter, I'll share some of my experience as an activist applying these library intellectual freedom principles to public and academic computers and networks.

I must start with two disclaimers. First, I reference many policies of the American Library Association (ALA), but the conclusions I draw are my own; I don't speak for ALA. I am not a librarian. I am just a computer science student who became involved in these issues as an advocate when, as an extracurricular project, I created and edited a free on-line newsletter called Computers and Academic Freedom (CAF). Second, take neither my prescriptions nor those of the ALA as authoritative. Intellectual freedom means nothing if not the right of everyone to draw their own conclusions.

Eight Controversial Cases of Censorship in Electronic Forums

Figure 1 lists the library policy statements I have found most helpful. The rest of this article will illustrate the application of these policies to computers with eight real-life cases. For each case, I'll describe a scenario, list the library principles I think relevant, tell how I think those principles should be applied, and briefly describe some of the subsequent events through March 1994.

The Case of the Offensive Newsgroup

The Scenario—Date: March 12, 1994

You are a computer science professor at the University of Denver and creator of NYX, a free public-access service affiliated with the University. The early edition of tomorrow's Sunday Denver Post includes a story about NYX carrying alt.sex.intergen, an electronic free-speech forum about intergenerational sexual relations. The newspaper didn't interview you and their story leaves the impression that the newsgroup contains illegal material when, in fact, it just discusses "Is pedophilia OK or evil?" Do you remove the newsgroup? (Simpson, 1994; CAF News, March 13, 1994).

Library Policy

The American Library Association's "Library Bill of Rights" says:

> Materials should not be proscribed or removed because of partisan or doctrinal disapproval.

In other words, do not remove something just because it is offensive to many or even to yourself. If you believe that the principles of intellectual freedom developed for libraries apply to public access computer sites, you should not remove the newsgroup.

Subsequent Events

NYX sysop Andrew Burt has declined to kill the newsgroup and (as of March 1994) NYX is still on-line. The Denver Post received faxes critical of its one-sided reporting.

---

*Adapted from a presentation to The Fourth Conference on Computers, Freedom, and Privacy, March 26, 1994 in Chicago. Reprinted with permission.

1.   Library Bill of Rights
2.   Diversity in Collection Development
3.   Selection Policy Writing Workbook
4.   Intellectual Freedom Statement (ALA)
5.   Definition of "Censorship" and Related Terms
6.   Freedom to Read Statement
7.   Intellectual Freedom Statement (CLA)
8.   Statement on Labeling
9.   Statement Concerning Confidentiality of Personally Identifiable Information about Library Users
10. Statement on Challenged Materials
11. Access for Children and Young People to Videotapes and Other Nonprint Formats
12. Free Access to Libraries for Minors
13. Expurgation of Library Materials
14. Grade and High School Library Policy
15. Restricted Access to Library Materials
16. Regulations, Policies, and Procedures Affecting Access to Library Resources and Services
17. Policy on Confidentiality of Library Records
18. Evaluating Library Collections
19. Exhibit Spaces and Bulletin Boards

Figure 1.   Helpful intellectual freedom policy statements. Eighteen are from the American Library Association, the largest and oldest professional association for librarians in the United States. One is from the Canadian Library Association. Most of the statements can be found in OIF-ALA (1992). On-line, they can be found via gopher with the command "gopher -p1/library/ala/ala-x gopher.uic.edu 70."

The Case of the "Naughty" Hypertext

The Scenario—Date: January 2, 1994–February 6, 1994

You are on the computer staff of Indiana University and are the creator of the CICA on-line archive. Your archive is the largest and most popular archive of Microsoft Windows software in the world. The University does not pay you to be an archivist; you work on the archive on your own time. The University does, however, provide significant computer and network resources for the archive. Someone submits a Windows hypertext version of *Fanny Hill,* an eighteenth-century novel containing sexual narrative. Someone from New Zealand says that having *Fanny Hill* on the Net violates New Zealand's harmful-to-minors laws. You fear that the University considers sexual subject matter unacceptable. How do you decide whether to include *Fanny Hill* in your collection?[1]

---

[1] Wilson (1994); Welsh-Huggins (1994); CAF News (January 2, January 9, January 30, February 6, February 13, 1994).

Library Policy

The American Library Association's Statement on Challenged Materials says:

> [I]t is the responsibility of every library to have a clearly defined materials selection policy in written form which reflects the LIBRARY BILL OF RIGHTS, and which is approved by the appropriate governing authority.

The American Library Association's Workbook for Selection Policy Writing (1993) lists selection criteria for grade and high schools that are legitimate with respect to intellectual freedom. Some of the legitimate criteria are:

- contribution the subject matter makes to the curriculum and to the interests of the students
- contribution the material makes to breadth of representative viewpoints on controversial issues
- high degree of potential user appeal
- value commensurate with cost and/or need

Note that "offensiveness" is not considered a legitimate reason to exclude material.

The "Freedom to Read" statement of the ALA and others says:

> There is no place in our society for efforts . . . to confine adults to the reading matter deemed suitable for adolescents. . . .

I believe that the CICA archivist should first clarify his authority. Next, he should create a selection policy consistent with intellectual freedom. Finally, he should apply that selection policy fairly.

Subsequent Events

The CICA archivist created this selection policy:

> As is a standard practice with most anonymous-ftp sites (that are supported with funds from an independent host institution), certain programs, files, or software are outside the general scope of archive operations, and therefore will NOT be accepted. These files include (but are not limited to) any software: containing political, religious, racist, ethnic, or other prejudiced or discriminatory messages therein; that is adult or sexually explicit in nature; otherwise considered unsuitable by the site moderator.[2]

This policy does not clarify his authority. (For example, is he acting on his own or as an agent of the university?) It violates intellectual freedom standards by banning materials that some people might find to be offen-

---

[2] CAF News, January 30, 1994.

sive. It is not applied fairly. For example, the archive continues to contain the Bible, which some people find to be offensive and to contain adult material.

The Case of the Criticizing E-Mailing List

The Scenario—Date: July 1993

You are a computer-system administrator at Brown University, American University, or the University of Georgia. Your school is one of the nodes for the Hellas (Greek) mailing list. You have just received e-mail from a system administrator at the Democritus National Research Center in Athens, Greece. He claims that he is suing your school because you are allowing people on the Hellas mailing list to "libel, slander, defame his character" and cause him "great emotional stress, and problems with his family and friends." What do you do? (CAF News, July 18, 1993).

Library Policy

The American Library Association's "Intellectual Freedom Statement" says:

> We need not endorse every idea contained in the materials we produce and make available.

The statement on "Challenged Materials" says:

> Freedom of expression is protected by the Constitution of the United States, but constitutionally protected expression is often separated from unprotected expression only by a dim and uncertain line. The Constitution requires a procedure designed to focus searchingly on challenged expression before it can be suppressed. An adversary hearing is a part of this procedure.

I think you should get advice from the university legal counsel. Do not take action because of a one-sided legal threat.

Subsequent Events

Within a day all three systems administrators shut down their nodes. The shut-out forum participants then explained their side of the story. They said that one of their main topics of conversation for the past month was the censorship, privacy violations, and arbitrary punishment at the DNRC. They say that this conversation was legitimate and should not be censored. As of July 13, 1993, two of the sites restored their nodes.[3]

---

[3] CAF News, July 18, 1994.

The Case of the "Adult" Material on the Free-Net

The Scenario—Date: Pre-1991

You are on the organizing committee of the Cleveland Free-Net, a computer system with the mission of providing computer and network resources for free to the community. Some parents may not want their kids to access some of the more "adult" resources. Ohio may even have a "harmful-to-minors" law. What do you do?[4]

Library Policy

The ALA's policies include these statements:

> A person's right to use a library should not be denied or abridged because of origin, age, background, or views. ("Library Bill of Rights")

> [P]arents—and only parents—have the right and the responsibility to restrict the access of their children—and only their children—to library resources. . . . Librarians and governing bodies cannot assume the role of parents or the functions of parental authority in the private relationship between parent and child. ("Free Access to Libraries for Minors")

> ALA acknowledges and supports the exercise by parents of their responsibility to guide their own children's reading and viewing. ("Access for Children and Young People to Videotapes and Other Nonprint Formats")

> There is no place in our society for efforts to coerce the taste of others, to confine adults to the reading matter deemed suitable for adolescents, or to inhibit the efforts of writers to achieve artistic expression. ("Freedom to Read")

> With every available legal means, we will challenge laws or governmental action restricting or prohibiting the publication of certain materials or limiting free access to such materials. ("Intellectual Freedom Statement")

Free-Nets that follow ALA policies should not ban so-called adult material. They should not stop minors from accessing it unless the Free-Nets' competent legal advisors say they must. They should lobby the government to do away with so-called "harmful-to-minors" laws, especially as they apply to not-for-profit information providers like libraries and Free-Nets and some BBSs.

Subsequent Events

As of 1991, the Cleveland Free-Net segregates so-called adult material and requires users, as a condition of access to such material, to certify that they

---

[4] CAF News 1.32.

are eighteen years old or have a parent's permission. I believe other Free-Nets ban all so-called adult material.

The Case of the University-Restricted Topics

The Scenario — Date: February 1992–present

You are a faculty member at Iowa State University. Your computer administrators have set up a system in which members of the university community can access sex-related newsgroups (such as alt.sex) only by asking for a computer account on a special computer and by "acknowledg[ing] their responsibility in access, using, and distributing material from it" by signing a statement to that effect. Some people say the university's action is appropriate because anyone who wants access can get it. What do you think?[5]

Library Policy

ALA's "Books/Materials Challenge Terminology" statement characterizes "censorship" as:

> The change in the access status of material, made by a governing authority or its representatives. Such changes include: exclusion, restriction, removal, or age/grade level changes.

The ALA "Restricted Access to Library Materials" says:

> Attempts to restrict access to library materials violate the basic tenets of the LIBRARY BILL OF RIGHTS. . . . In any situation which restricts access to certain materials, a barrier is placed between the patron and those materials. . . . Because restricted collections often are composed of materials which some library patrons consider objectionable, the potential user may be predisposed to think of the materials as objectionable and, therefore, are reluctant to ask for them.

A university that follows ALA policies should not segregate and restrict this material.

Subsequent Events

The restrictions at Iowa State University continue.

---

[5] (ftp://ftp.iastate.edu/pub/netinfo/news/; CAF News 2.8, 2.30; ftp://ftp.eff.org/pub/CAF/banned.1992).

The Case of the TV "Violence" Chip

The Scenario—Date: May 1993–present

You are a member of the United States Congress. Representative Markey has introduced the "V-Chip" bill. Under this bill, the federal government would require broadcasters to send a violence signal whenever they depict what someone defines as violence. The government would require new TVs to carry a chip that would detect the signal and if enabled, say, by a parent, blank out the screen. Do you support the bill (Edwards, 1993; BNA Daily Report for Executives, 1993; Newsbytes, 1993)?

Library Policy

The American Library Association's "Statement on Labeling" says:

> Labeling is the practice of describing or designating materials by affixing a prejudicial label and/or segregating them by a prejudicial system. The American Library Association opposes these means of predisposing people's attitudes toward library materials for the following reasons: Labeling is an attempt to prejudice attitudes and as such, it is a censor's tool.

If you follow the ALA's guidelines, you should oppose the bill.

Subsequent Events

The bill is in committee.

The Case of the Implicit Express Consent

The Scenario—December 1992–present

You are a computer systems administrator at a university. You read that the CERT (the Computer Emergency Response Team) recommends you include a sign-on banner that says (in part):

> Individuals using this computer . . . in excess of their authority are subject to having all of their activities on this system monitored and recorded. . . . In the course of monitoring individuals improperly using this system, or in the course of system maintenance, the activities of authorized users may also be monitored. . . . Anyone using this system expressly consents to such monitoring and is advised that if such monitoring reveals possible evidence of criminal activity, system personnel may provide the evidence of such monitoring to law enforcement officials.[6]

---

[6] ftp://ftp.eff.org/pub/CAF/policies/cert.org; CAF News, 2.62, 2.63, 2.64, 2.65, 3.1, 3.9, November 7–14–28, 1993.

Do you include this text in your sign-on banner?

Library Policy

The ALA's "Statement Concerning Confidentiality of Personally Identifiable Information about Library Users" says:

> The First Amendment . . . requires [. . . that] the corresponding rights to hear what is spoken and read what is written be preserved, free from fear of government intrusion, intimidation or reprisal. . . . If there is a reasonable basis to believe such records are necessary to the progress of an investigation or prosecution, our judicial system provides the mechanism for seeking release of such confidential records: the issuance of a court order, following a showing of good cause based on specific facts, by a court of competent jurisdiction.

You should not require your users to give up their privacy based, apparently, on your personal determination that they are acting in excess of their authority. If you think you need a login banner, work with your competent legal advisor to create one that is more narrow than CERT's (ftp://ftp.eff.org/pub/CAF/policies/cert.org.critique).

Subsequent Events

At least nine other schools have adopted a variant of the CERT banner, including: Arizona State University, Northern Arizona University, Northwestern University, Salt Lake Community College, Stevens Institute of Technology, University of Michigan, University of South Florida, Weber State University, and Worcester Polytechnic Institute.

The Case of Filtering Sex "Facts" Out of High School

The Scenario—Date: January 1993

You are a systems administrator at the University of Kentucky. You would like to provide a Netnews newsfeed to high schools. You have already decided not to provide alt.sex, but you would like to provide newsgroup news.answers. The only problem is that the alt.sex FAQ (Frequently Asked Questions, pronounced "facts") file, like many other FAQs, is periodically posted to newsgroup news.answers. Should you filter out the news.answers articles containing the alt.sex's FAQ?[7]

Library Policy

According to the ALA statement "Expurgation of Library Materials":

---

[7] CAF Talk, January 17, 1993; CAF Talk, January 24, 1993.

> Expurgating library materials is a violation of the Library Bill of Rights.
> Expurgation as defined by this interpretation includes any deletion, excision,
> alteration, editing, or obliteration of any part(s) of books or other library
> resources by the library, its agent, or its parent institution (if any). By such
> expurgation, the library is in effect denying access to the complete work and
> the entire spectrum of ideas that the work intended to express.

When you filter out articles from a moderated or edited newsgroup
without the moderator's permission, and then pass the result on to others,
you violate the integrity of the moderator's work (and possibly his or her
copyright). Thus, you should never expurgate articles from an edited
newsgroup without permission. It is also wrong to filter out articles from
an unmoderated newsgroup and then pass the results on under the same
name. The reason is that readers will have the incorrect impression that
they are seeing the whole newsgroup. If you do expurgate articles from a
newsgroup, you are in effect creating a new (edited) newsgroup. To avoid
confusion, you should give that new newsgroup a new name (perhaps by
appending ".censored").

Subsequent Events

As of January 1993, the University of Kentucky was providing an expur-
gated newsgroup with no notice to its readers.

Conclusion

I chose these eight cases in part because I know them to be controversial.
If you disagree with my prescriptions for particular cases, I will not be
disappointed. I hope, however, that the cases have demonstrated that
library intellectual freedom can reasonably be applied to public computer
resources. This is not an assertion that computer media are just like
libraries, rather it is an assertion that intellectual freedom is not tied to a
particular medium.

   In practice, almost all computer policy and intellectual freedom policy is
made at the local level by people like you. To discuss this topic further, join
the discussion in the Usenet newsgroups alt.comp.acad-freedom.talk and
alt.censorship. If you are a systems administrator, lead the defense of
intellectual freedom (the way that librarians do). Finally, if you have an
opportunity to make policy, add a line like this one from the University of
Wisconsin at Milwaukee's Netnews policy:

> [T]he same standards and principles of intellectual and academic freedom
> developed for University libraries [will] be applied to material received from
> the [computer] news network.[8]

---

[8] ftp://ftp.eff.org/pub/CAF/policies/netnews.uwm.edu.

With just one line, you can connect your computer to one hundred years of library intellectual freedom experiences.

References

BNA Daily Report for Executives (1993). (August 6), p. A23.

Computers and Academic Freedom News (CAF News) (1994). Accessible via anonymous ftp to ftp.eff.org, directory pub/CAF/news.

Computers and Academic Freedom Talk (CAF Talk) (1993). Accessible via anonymous ftp to ftp.eff.org, directory pub/CAF/batch.

Edwards, Ellen (1993). "Broadcast and Cable TV to Name Violence Monitors." *The Washington Post* (February 2) Wednesday, Final Edition, p. A1.

ftp://ftp.eff.org/pub/CAF/banned.1992. Accessible via anonymous ftp to ftp.eff.org, directory pub/CAF, file banned.1992.

ftp://ftp.eff.org/pub/CAF/policies/cert.org. Accessible via anonymous ftp to ftp. eff.org, directory pub/CAF/policies, file cert.org.

ftp://ftp.eff.org/pub/CAF/policies/cert.org.critique. Accessible via anonymous ftp to ftp.eff.org, directory pub/CAF/policies, file cert.org.critique.

ftp://ftp.eff.org/pub/CAF/policies/netnews.uwm.edu. Accessible via anonymous ftp to ftp.eff.org, directory pub/CAF/policies, file netnews.uwm.edu.

ftp://ftp.iastate.edu/pub/netinfo/news/. Accessible via anonymous ftp to ftp.iastate. edu, directory pub/netinfo/news.

Newsbytes news service (1993). "Proposal Sees Chip Blocking TV Violence." (May 13).

Office for Intellectual Freedom of the American Library Association (OIF-ALA) (1983). *Workbook for Selection Policy Writing,* revised, Chicago.

Office for Intellectual Freedom of the American Library Association (OIF-ALA) (1992). *Intellectual Freedom Manual,* 4th ed.

Simpson, Kevin (1994). "Local techie rides posse on computer network." *The Denver Post* (March 13) Sunday, 1st ed., B-01.

Washington Post (February 4, 1994). "TV to Name Violence Monitors; Some on Hill Say Move Isn't Enough."

Welsh-Huggins, Andrew (1994). "Cultures Clash on Computer: Internet Users Debate Censorship." *Sunday Herald-Times* (January 30), Bloomington, Indiana.

Wilson, David L. (1994). *The Chronicle of Higher Education* (Jan. 19), p. A25.

P·A·R·T · V

J

The Electronic Journal: What, Whence, and When?*

Ann Okerson

Introduction

A quick scan of topics of recent library, networking, professional, and societal meetings leads to the inevitable conclusion that electronic publishing is the "Debutante of the Year." Supporting technologies have matured and present their dance cards to eager potential suitors: publishers and content creators. The newest entrant to the glittering ballroom is academic discourse and writing, suddenly highly susceptible to the nubile charms of the ripening medium. The season's opening features the youthful search for the future of the journal.

By "journal," I mean the scholarly journal. The scholarly journal mainly communicates the work of scholars, academics, and researchers, and it contributes to the development of ideas that form the "body of knowledge." By "electronic journal," I generally mean one delivered via networks, although those locally owned through a static electronic format such as CD-ROM are not specifically excluded.

This paper overviews several critical questions about the electronic journal. What is it? What is its appeal? Where will it come from? At what rate will it appear? When will it be accepted? It suggests that for the first time in over two hundred years the paper scholarly journal can be supplanted or, at least, supplemented in a significant way by another medium, and this may lead to a new type of scholarly discourse.

At the outset, consider a historical parallel for today's scholarly information concerns. In an article of fall 1990, Edward Tenner, an executive editor at Princeton University Press, describes information stresses of the last century.[1] Between 1850 and 1875, the number of United States library collections with more than 25,000 volumes increased from nine to one hundred, and the number of libraries with more than 100,000 volumes grew infinitely from zero to ten. This unprecedented growth occurred during the time of a technologically advanced tool—the printed book catalog. The printed book catalog was indisputably an advance on the handwritten one. Nonetheless, the printed book catalog became grossly inadequate to cope with ever-plentiful scholarly output.

Although we view information management as a serious academic concern today, the perception that knowledge is increasing far more rapidly than our ability to organize it effectively and make it available is a timeless issue for scholarship and libraries. In the 1850s, Harvard pioneered the solution to the book catalog problem by establishing a public card catalog. In 1877, ALA adopted the present 75 × 125 mm standard for the catalog card. Despite Dewey's anger about its shift to nonmetric 3 × 5 inch size, the card changed the entire face of bibliographic information, from the bounded (and bound), finite book catalog to the far more user-responsive, open, adaptable, organic—and exceedingly convenient—individual entry. Even then, libraries were technological innovators.

The Library Bureau was established in 1876 to supply equipment to librarians, and even eager commercial customers lined up. In the late 1880s, the secretary of the Holstein-Friesian Association of America in Iowa City wrote to the Bureau that he had first seen a card system in the Iowa State University Library in 1882 and had applied the idea to 40,000 animals in the Holstein-Friesian Herd Book. "We are now using," he enthusiastically exulted, "about 10,000 new cards per year, which henceforth must double every two years." Mr. Tenner points out that here was a cattle-log in its truest sense! After I related this story to a group of librarians, a collections librarian from Iowa State announced that the Holstein-Friesian Herd Book still exists at the University library; it is in electronic form!

The story effectively reminds us—again—how quickly users want the latest information. Whether of books or cows, a catalog printed every year or so would not do, even one hundred years ago. The unit card improved access by an order of magnitude, and on-line catalogs today list a book as quickly as it is cataloged, often prior to its publication. The book, or at least knowledge of its existence, becomes accessible instantaneously.

One hundred years ago, perhaps even twenty years ago, articles were published in journals because journals were the quickest means of disseminating new ideas and findings. The information "explosion" teamed with today's journal distribution conventions mandates that the printed article

---

*This article appeared in *The Public-Access Computer Systems Review* 2, no. 1 (1991), pp. 5–24. Reprinted with permission.
[1] "From Slip to Chip." *Princeton Alumni Weekly*, 21 (November 1990), pp. 9–14.

can take as long, or longer, than a monograph to reach the reader. As articles queue for peer review, editing, and publication in the journal "package," distribution delays of months are the norm. One- to two-year delays are not unusual. Under half a year is "fast track." Meanwhile, as scholars demand the latest ideas, more and more papers are distributed in advance of "normal" publication outlets through informal "colleges"— distribution lists of colleagues and friends.

The archival work of record is currently the paper one. The printed journal is important because it has established a subscriber tradition that reaches far outside the preprint crowd. Since libraries subscribe to journals, they potentially reach any interested reader and respondent. The scholarly journal's familiar subscription distribution mechanism and built-in quality filters (refereeing and editing) have also made its articles the principal measure of research productivity. By publishing critiqued ideas, authors not only distribute their work, they also leverage this printed currency into the tangible remunerations of job security and advancement.

Nonetheless, by the time of formal print publication, the ideas themselves have circulated a comparatively long time. Given researchers' information expectations and the perception that high-speed distribution is possible (and indeed already happens), alternative, rapid means of sharing information will assuredly displace the print journal as the sole icon or sacrament of scholarly communication. The front-runner is distribution via the electronic networks, such as BITNET and Internet, that already link many campuses, laboratories, and research agencies. For already established journal titles, advance descriptions of articles will routinely become available (like cataloging copy), followed closely by prepublication delivery of the articles themselves. The success of such a program will eventually alter the fundamental characteristics of the paper journal. These changes are already beginning.

At the heart of Mr. Tenner's story is the breaking down of the catalog into its component parts, paralleled one hundred years later in the potential for unbundling the journal into its flexible component parts— articles—that can be delivered singly or in desired recombinations. Of course, the indexing and abstracting services began this process long ago. After World War II, photocopying made it practical to reproduce single articles. Now, rapid electronic technologies will accelerate unbundling. Soon the article (or idea) unit will supplant the publisher prepackaged journal. Like the book catalog, it will be perceived as a lovable but unwieldy dinosaur.

Like the records cast loose from book catalogs, articles will need fuller and more unified subject description and classification to make it possible to pull diverse ideas together. These are urgent needs that reflect some of the most serious problems of the journal literature: (1) inadequate, inconsistent description of articles; and (2) the failure of the present secondary sources to cross-index disciplines, even as they duplicate title coverage.

Two Visions of the Electronic Journal

One view of the electronic journal, a conservative view, is based on today's journal stored as electronic impulses. This electronic journal parallels and mimics the current paper journal format, except that it may be article rather than issue based. Because it is delivered via electronic networks, it is quick, transmitted the moment it is written, reviewed, and polished. Able to appear at a precise location, it is a key component of the scholar's "virtual library." Where the subscriber does not seek a paper copy, the electronic journal saves the costs of paper printing and mailing. Its paper-saving characteristics could eventually relieve the "serials crisis," which is characterized by libraries' inability to repurchase institutional research results because of the learned journals' skyrocketing subscription prices. Of course, early experience with electronic equivalents of paper information loudly and clearly proclaims that the moment information becomes mobile, rather than static, this transformation fundamentally alters the way in which information is used, shared, and eventually created. Changing the medium of journal distribution, even with so modest, cautious, and imitative a vision, carries unpredictable consequences.

Visionaries and electronic seers ("skywriters" such as *Psycoloquy*'s co-editor Stevan Harnad[2] find mere electronic substitution for paper archiving a timid, puny view of the e-journal. In their dreams and experiments, the idea is sprouted precisely when it is ready, critiqued via the "Net," and put out immediately for wide examination or "open peer commentary." Ideas that might have been stillborn in paper come alive as other scholars respond with alacrity and collaborate to improve knowledge systems.

Such a revolutionary e-journal concept offers the potential to rethink the informal and formal systems of scholarly communication, and alter them in ways that are most effective and comfortable for specific disciplines and individuals, utilizing electronic conversations, squibbs, megajournals, consensus journals, and models not yet dreamt of. Diverse forms of academic currency coexist, and fewer writings are considered the "last word" on any subject.

The visionaries' e-journal is comfortable intermedia; it opens windows onto ideas attached as supplementary files, footnotes, sound, and visual matter. Writing is not confined to any place or time or group. Paper distribution either takes place secondarily or does not happen at all. In short, an increasing number of scholars imagine the whole process of scholarly communication undergoing dramatic change, becoming instant, global, interactive.[3]

---

[2] E-mail and list correspondence with Stevan Harnad, editor of *Behavioral and Brain Sciences* as well as the refereed electronic journal *Psycoloquy*.

[3] Stevan Harnad, "Scholarly Skywriting and the Prepublication Continuum of Scientific Inquiry." *Psychological Science*, 1 (November 1990), pp. 342–344.

Not surprising, some academic editors believe that electronic publishers ought to begin with a more "conventional" publication strategy, which is likely over time to transform the scholarly communications system. Charles Bailey of the Public-Access Computer Systems (PACS) group of electronic publications as well as Eyal Amiran and John Unsworth of the Postmodern Culture group share this vision.

Rivaling the Scholarly Paper Journal

In existence for over two hundred years, the paper journal has been given the imprimatur and loyalty of the best scholars as authors and editors. Continually expanding, it has resisted all attempts to supplement it, let alone supplant it. For a nice discussion of the largely unsuccessful projects that were targeted at a new format or type of journal, see Anne Piternick's article in *Journal of Academic Librarianship*.[4] For a detailed review of electronic journal literature and a comprehensive bibliography through about 1988, Michael Gabriel provides an excellent overview.[5] Early electronic publishing proposals long precede the Chronicle editorials by Dougherty[6] (we should marry the technological capabilities of university computers and university-sponsored research into a coherent system) and Rogers and Hurt[7] (the packaged, printed journal is obsolete as a vehicle of scholarly communication) with which librarians are so familiar. They were developed in the 1970s in the information science literature.

Early experiments fundamentally failed because they were externally imposed, scholars were disinterested in writing for electronic media, and they were unwilling to read it. They were probably unwilling because of lack of pervasive equipment, learned electronic skills, and critical mass. But today, there are some thirty networked electronic journals, of which about eight are refereed or lightly refereed, and there are probably at least sixty networked electronic newsletters.[8]

---

[4] Anne B. Piternick, "Attempt to Find Alternatives to the Scientific Journal: A Brief Review." *Journal of Academic Librarianship*, 15 (November 1989), pp. 263–265.

[5] Michael R. Gabriel, *A Guide to the Literature of Electronic Publishing: CD-ROM, Desktop Publishing, and Electronic Mail, Books, and Journals* (Greenwich, CT: JAI Press, 1989).

[6] Richard M. Dougherty, "To Meet the Crisis in Journal Costs, Universities Must Reassert Their Role in Scholarly Publishing." *Chronicle of Higher Education*, 12 (April 1989), p. A52.

[7] Sharon J. Rogers and Charlene S. Hurt, "How Scholarly Communication Should Work in the 21st Century." *Chronicle of Higher Education*, 18 (October 1989), p. A56.

[8] For a complete listing of such journals and newsletters, see the free electronic directory that is maintained by Michael Strangelove (send an e-mail message with the following commands on separate lines to LISTSERV@UOTTAWA: GET EJOURNL1 DIRECTRY GET EJOURNL2 DIRECTRY). This information is also included in a paper directory, the Directory of Electronic Journals, Newsletters, and Academic Discussion Lists, which is available at low cost from the Office of Scientific and Academic Publishing, Association of Research Libraries, 1527 New Hampshire Ave., N.W., Washington, D.C. 20036.

Since the publication of Gabriel's book, the literature on electronic, network-based communication has mushroomed. The most comprehensive and highly readable report about what needs to be done (in areas of technology, standards, economics, and social acceptance) before the networked journal can become a genuine option has been issued in draft form as an Office of Technology Assessment Report by Clifford Lynch.[9] While exhortation and skepticism about electronic publishing continue in the conventional journal literature and have spawned at least one scholarly paper journal of its own (Wiley's *Electronic Publishing*) some of the best work and discussion is now, not surprising, on-line, through various lists and bulletin boards of editors and scholars interested in the future of scholarly communication.

Even when articles on electronic publishing are headed for the paper track, authors may make them available electronically either in advance of publication or as an adjunct to print publication. For example, a thoughtful essay by psychologist William Gardner recently appeared in *Psychological Science*.[10] Gardner views the electronic literature and archive as more than a database; it is a single organization run by scientists and applied researchers, who adapt the environment to meet the needs of its users. His piece is noteworthy in part because readers debated it on the Net months before it was published in a print journal.

Who Will Publish Electronic Journals?

Four possible sources of electronic journals currently exist. The list is simple in that, for reasons of time as much as experience, it does not detail the specific—and not inconsiderable—problems connected with the options. However, Lynch and others have provided this type of critique.

Existing Publishers

Upon reflection, it appears that the majority of networked electronic journals could originate with existing journal publishers. Most journals, at least in the Western world, become machine readable at some point in the publishing process. For these journals, some recent electronic archives already exist. A number of scholarly publishers are experimenting with

---

[9] Clifford A. Lynch, "Electronic Publishing, Electronic Libraries, and the National Research and Education Network: Policy and Technology Issues" (Washington, D.C.: Office of Technology Assessment, draft for review April 1990).

[10] William Gardner, "The Electronic Archive: Scientific Publishing for the 1990s." *Psychological Science*, 1, no. 6 (1990), pp. 333–341.

networking options. In the commercial arena, publishers such as Elsevier, John Wiley, and Pergamon are discussing—perhaps implementing—pilot projects. Scientific societies such as the American Chemical Society, the American Mathematical Society, and the American Psychological Association are pursuing development of electronic journals.

At the same time, vexing issues—uncertainty about charging models, fear of unpoliced copying resulting in revenue loss, questions about ownership, lack of standardization, inability to deliver or receive nontext, and user unfriendliness or acceptance—work off each other to create a chicken-and-egg situation that keeps electronic conversion careful and slow. And tensions abound. For example, some say one can place tollbooths every inch of the electronic highway and charge for each use; others say that at last the time has come to emancipate ideas from the bondage of profit.

Nonetheless, solutions are under way by systems designers, publishers, and standards organizations. For example, by middecade there will assuredly be a reliable, affordable way to reproduce and receive nontext; technology specialists assert that "the technology is there." Nontechnical (economic and social) issues are the ones that will slow network acceptance. As systems and standards develop, publishers will evolve transitional pricing models that maintain profit levels. As a consequence, publishers will offer the same article arrayed in different clothing or packaging: paper journal collection, single-article delivery, compendia of articles from several journals, collections-to-profile, publications-on-demand, and networked delivery to research facilities and institutions. Parallel CD-ROM versions of a number of scholarly titles are already becoming widely available.

This flexible parallel publication activity will have major side effects. Academic publishers (both commercial and not-for-profit) unable to deliver electronically will be left behind as personal user revenue grows. Paper subscription revenues from Third World countries will not be enough to sustain an academic publisher.

The term "subscription" will be replaced. At present, it is currently used for a product that a reader or library buys and owns. It also will come to represent—indeed, already has with CD-ROMs—something that the purchaser does not own at all, but has the right to use. Subscriptions may gradually be replaced by licenses. The multisite license will be applied not only to electronic publications, but also to paper subscriptions that are shared among institutions. Licenses are intended to compensate the publisher for the potentially broad and possibly undisciplined electronic copying of scholarly materials that could violate the "fair use" provisions of the Copyright Act. Unless libraries are prepared to pay the high differential prices currently charged for CD-ROMs and locally mounted databases, the language of such licenses will be increasingly important, as will good library negotiators and lawyers.

Publishers assert that in the early days of parallel systems, whatever the ultimate storage and distribution method of networked journals might be, the price of information will be higher than ever. After research and development costs are stabilized and the print and electronic markets settle, who knows what pricing structures will prevail? There will probably be an enormous, unregulated range of fees. For instance, it is conceivable that, like older movies rented for a dollar at a video outlet, older science works will become cheap, and new works, much in demand, will be expensive.

Just as libraries found retrospective conversion to machine-readable records to be a lengthy and expensive process, publishers will find retrospective conversion of full-text information to be costly, and it will not happen quickly, even if library customers demand electronic documents. Retrospective conversion will be a noncommercial activity, which will be a joint venture between publishers and optical scanning conversion services or the sole domain of conversion services.

Currently, some publishers are experimenting with converting back files into electronic form, mostly in collaboration with universities or libraries. For example, Cornell, the American Chemical Society, Bellcore, and OCLC are experimenting with scanning ten years' worth of twenty ACS journals. The National Agricultural Library has negotiated agreements with a handful of society and university publishers for the optical scanning of agricultural titles. Public domain work will be scanned and converted first.

Although today's electronic articles from mainstream publishers are almost incidental or accidental and are not intended by publishers to replace the products that comprise their daily bread, they are opportunities for electronic experimentation, market exploration, and, possibly, supplementary income.

Intermediaries

A number of intermediary organizations have negotiated copyright agreements with publishers and are well positioned to deliver their output to customers. Some of these organizations include indexing and abstracting services such as the Institute for Scientific Information (ISI) and the American Chemical Society. The Colorado Alliance of Research Libraries (CARL) promises document delivery in the near future as an extension of its UnCover table of contents database service. This fall, the Faxon Company, a major paper journal subscription agency, intends to initiate an article delivery service. University Microfilms International (UMI) clearly has copyright clearance for thousands of journals to redistribute them in microform format; electronic distribution is only a step behind. Other efforts include full-text files available on BRS, Dialog, and IAC; the AIDS library of Maxwell Electronic Communications; and the Massachusetts Medical Society CD-ROM.

It is not entirely clear why publishers, when they become fully automated and networked, would desire some of these intervening or even competitive services, although the networks will breed many other kinds of value-added opportunities. Rights and contracts will be critical in this area. The current pattern appears to be that publishers will assign rights in return for royalties to almost any reputable intermediary that makes a reasonable offer.

General hearsay suggests that large telecommunications firms (e.g., the regional phone companies and MCI) might wish to become information intermediaries or even content owners (i.e., publishers), and rumors abound about Japanese companies making serious forays in this arena.

Innovative Researchers and Scholars

In this category, I include the trailblazers who publish the handful of refereed or lightly refereed electronic-only journals that currently exist or are planned. They are editors of publications such as the *Electronic Journal of Communication* (University of Windsor), *EJournal* (SUNY Albany), the *Journal of the International Academy of Hospitality Research* (Virginia Tech), the *Journal of Reproductive Toxicology* (Joyce Sigaloff and Embryonics, Inc.), *New Horizons in Adult Education* (Syracuse University, Kellogg Project), *Postmodern Culture* (North Carolina State), *Psycoloquy* (Princeton/Rutgers/APA), and *The Public-Access Computer Systems Review* (University of Houston Libraries).

Some regard these electronic-only journals as devils rather than saviors. For example, they serve those who are already information and computer rich, or even spoiled. Because network communication can be clunky, cranky, and inconsistent, e-journals serve the highly skilled or the tenacious. Rather than opening up the universe, they may appear temporarily to limit it, because only text is easily keyed and transmitted. Presently, editors of electronic journals are academics who spend a great deal of time being reviewers and referees, editors, publishers, advocates, marketers. After all that effort, it is unclear whether these activities, which are the path to tenure and grants in the paper medium, will being similar rewards in the electronic medium. Powerful and persistent persuasion may be needed to induce colleagues to contribute articles and referee them.

Today's electronic-only journals' greatest contributions are not that they have solved many of the problems of the current publishing system—or of the networked world—but that they are brave, exciting, innovative experiments that give us a hope of doing so.

It is not entirely clear whether this handful of swallows makes a summer—it feels like the beginning of a new warm season for academic communications—or how long that summer will be. It is an open question as to whether these academics will hand over their work to university presses, scholarly societies, or outside publishers.

External economic conditions may push scholars to start networked electronic journals instead of paper ones. If the past year's serial price increases continue, scholars will have an incentive to create electronic journals, and they may appear faster than we expect. Substantial cost savings can be realized if the new start-up is electronically distributed on networks. Otherwise, paper and parallel publication costs become substantial.

Currently, scholars' use of academic networks appears to be largely free, and it is a good time to experiment. It is unknown how long these good times will last; universities may not continue to subsidize academics' network use. (Even commercialized, the communications costs should appear as cheap as long distance and fax.) Meanwhile, individually produced journals may come and go, like New York restaurants.

University-Based Electronic Publishing

At this time, it has been estimated that universities at most publish 15% of their faculty's output.[11] This includes discussion papers and periodicals emanating from individual academic departments as well as formalized university outlets like university presses and publications offices.

Nonetheless, to the considerable cynicism of existing publishers, a vision of university-based electronic networked publishing is expressed by many librarians and other members of the university community in conversations about academe's regaining control and distribution of its own intellectual output. Publishers' skepticism is certainly justified in that, in spite of good rhetoric, there are no vital signs of university electronic journal publishing activity, apart from the publications of individual academics described in the last section.

However, there are some related electronic publishing experiments by universities. The most interesting experiments are in the preprint arena. One university research facility, the Stanford Linear Accelerator, has supported a preprint database in high-energy physics for some fifteen years. Researchers worldwide contribute preprints, that is, any article intended to be submitted for publication. Database managers create bibliographic records and access each preprint. Using this information, on-line subscribers can locate preprints, which they can request from either the author or the database. Database staff scan the printed literature routinely for new articles. A preprint so identified is discarded from the library, and the database record is annotated with the correct citation to the formal journal article. Staff add about two hundred preprints per week, and the full database contains citations to 200,000 articles.

Some experimentation is under way by a couple of laboratories to deposit the full text of preprint articles with the system. (Absent a submission

---

[11] Stuart Lynn (untitled paper presented at the Coalition for Networked Information meeting, November 1990).

standard, particularly for nontext information, this becomes complex.) If such a pilot is successful, the articles in the database could be distributed widely and quickly via the networks. Of course, the relationship with existing scholarly publishers might be jeopardized because of prior "publication" and perceived encroachments on the present notion of copyright. SLAC staff are sensitive to these potential problems, and they are being thoughtful about them.

Some scholars argue that a preprint creates demand for the published version of a paper. In any case, since the preprints have not been refereed or edited and they represent work in progress, many scientists are hesitant to cite them, and, consequently, they lack the validity of the "finished" paper. On the other hand, a paper published in a prestigious university database might eventually preempt the paper version, provided some network review mechanism is added.

A second major initiative is being created in mathematics. The IMP project (Instant Math Preprints) will maintain a database of abstracts on a network computer at a major university. At the same time, authors of the mathematics articles will deposit the full text of preprints with their local university computer center, which will store them on a network computer. After searching the abstract database, users will be able to retrieve desired article files from host computers via anonymous FTP. Presently, the project is proposed to extend to about ten key research universities. The abstracts also will be searchable on "e-math," the American Mathematical Society's electronic member service. The benefits to researchers of both of these types of preprint information are enormous. In high-energy physics and mathematics, we may be viewing the substantial beginnings of university-based scientific publishing.

Computer Conferences as Electronic Journals

Librarians and scholars are beginning to take seriously the scholarly computer conferences (known as "lists") available through the various networks, such as BITNET and Internet. Such academic flora and fauna number in the hundreds and thousands and grow daily.[12] Although many of the original lists and their exchanges earned the Net a reputation as an information cesspool, an increasing number of lists are indispensable to specific interest areas and ought to be available through library catalogs and terminals. Indeed, some academics view the topical lists as an entirely

---

[12] Diane Kovacs at the Kent State University libraries assiduously catalogs and organizes these electronic conferences. Her work is available to all users for free through files made available to discussion groups such as LSTOWN-L, HUMANIST, LIBREF-L, and others. The Association of Research Libraries includes her information about these groups in their directory.

new kind of "journal." It is well to remember that the ancestor of today's fancy scholarly journal was the diary or logbook (the original "journal") in which the scholar or scientist recorded data, thoughts, ideas, meetings, and conversations, much as do today's networked electronic lists.

A growing number of colleagues testify that a few weeks of being active on the networks changes one's working life. Some of the benefits are: (1) accessing a wealth of informal information; (2) linking to colleagues and growing ideas quickly, with a wide variety of input and critique; (3) sharing an idea all over the world in a matter of minutes; and (4) finding new colleagues and learning who is pursuing the same interests in another discipline. Surely, this is the excitement of discovery at its most energetic and best. A number of librarians have recognized the new medium's power and they are promoting network-facilitating activities.

It is certain that widespread participation and ownership of this new method of communication have the potential to transform scholarly writing and publishing far more dramatically than the motivation to unbundle journals, publish quickly, or even reduce subscription costs.

Speculations

These are early days for this new information creation and distribution medium; however, readers want guesses about the future, and authors are tempted to satisfy the public and their own egos by venturing them. The self-evident statement is that the honorable, long-lived communication medium—the prestigious scholarly journal—will surely be quite different than it is today. It will be different because it will represent a new way of growing and presenting knowledge.

Here is a possible scenario for the evolution of scholarly journals.

A.D. *1991*

- Paper journals totally dominate the scholarly scene.
- There are some parallel electronic products, mostly the "static" CD-ROM format.
- Some full text (without graphics) is available on-line via services such as Dialog and BRS.
- Some mainstream publishers are experimenting with electronic publications.
- There are a variety of options for delivering individual articles via mail and fax.
- The biggest single article suppliers are libraries, via the long-popular and fairly effective interlibrary loan mechanisms.
- Over a thousand scholarly electronic discussion groups exist.

- Under ten scholarly electronic journals exist that are refereed, lightly refereed, or edited.
- Two institutional preprint services are in development.
- OCLC, a library utility, positions itself through development work for the AAAS as a serious electronic publisher of scientific articles.

A.D. 1995

- Significant inroads into the paper subscription market, because: (1) libraries make heavy journal cancellations due to budget constraints, and they feel "mad as hell" about high subscription prices; and (2) it becomes possible to deliver specific articles directly to the end user.
- Librarians and publishers squabble over prices—ELECTRONIC prices.
- For the first time, the Association of American Publishers (AAP) sues a research library or university over either electronic copying or paper resource-sharing activities.
- There are over one hundred refereed electronic journals produced by academics.
- In collaboration with professional or scholarly societies, university-based preprint services get under way in several disciplines.
- The Net is still subsidized.
- Rate of paper journal growth slows.
- Many alternative sources exist for the same article, including publishers and intermediaries.
- Bibliographic confusion and chaos reign for bibliographic utilities, libraries, and, by extension, scholars.

A.D. 2000

- Computer equipment and user sophistication are pervasive, although not ubiquitous.
- Parallel electronic and paper availability for serious academic journals; market between paper journals and alternatives (e.g., electronic delivery) is split close to 50/50.
- Subscription model wanes; license and single-article models wax.
- Secondary services rethink roles; other indexing (machine browsing, artificial intelligence, and full-text or abstract searching) strengthens.
- Net transferred to commercial owners, but access costs are low.
- New niches are created: archive, scanning, repackaging, and information-to-profile services.

- Publishers without electronic delivery shrink or leave the marketplace.
- Many collaborations, some confusing and unworkable, as publishers struggle with development, conversion, and delivery.
- Major Copyright Law revision continues.
- Stratification of richer and poorer users, universities, and nations.

Conclusion

Teilhard de Chardin writes:

> No one can deny that a world network of economic and psychic affiliations is being woven at an ever-increasing speed which envelops and constantly penetrates more deeply within each of us. With every day that passes, it becomes a little more impossible for us to act or think otherwise than collectively.[13]

Another writer has said that the only way to know the future is to write it yourself.

We have some hints where the future of journals and scholarly communications, which will move quickly beyond today's journal, may lie. Those who have a vision for the future are uniquely positioned to write the scenario.

---

[13] Pierre Teilhard de Chardin, *The Future of Man* (New York: Harper and Row, 1969).

P·A·R·T · V

K

I Heard It through the Internet*

Walt Crawford

Effective public access requires skeptical users, a point that the previous two Public-Access Provocations tried to make indirectly. Just because something comes from "the computer," there is no reason to believe that it's correct—and, although library cataloging represents one of the treasures of the profession, catalogs aren't always completely trustworthy, either.

But at least library catalogs represent sincere efforts to provide useful, validated, even authority-controlled information. Similarly, although commercial on-line databases are rife with typos and other errors, it is still true that the databases available on Eureka, FirstSearch, Dialog, and the like represent reasonable attempts to organize data into useful information with good levels of correctness.

Then there's the Internet, the nascent Information Superhighway according to some, where everything's up to date and the hottest information is available by clicking away at Mosaic or using WAIS to find out everything you could ever want to know, magically arranged so that the first thing you get is the most useful! And, with disintermediation and direct usage from every home (and a cardboard box under the freeway?), tomorrow's super-Internet will offer this wonderland to everyone, all the time, making everyone potentially an up-to-date expert on whatever. Skeptical? Why? It's hot, it's happening, it's now—it's on the Internet!

Seventy Elements: More Than Enough!

Thus we can expect to have fledgling scientists learning the new and improved seventy-element periodic table with innovative new element symbols. It must be right—it's on the Internet. I could go on with hundreds of examples; as one version of that famous cartoon goes, "On the Internet, nobody knows you're a fraud."

Of course, truly up-to-date users may be wary of something that's just boring old ASCII. If they can't chew up bandwidth with neat color pictures or (preferably) important live video—such as vital visual information on how the coffee maker at some university lab is doing right now—why would they want to be bothered? The newest and most correct information will all be graphical, accessed through Mosaic or some replacement.

Traditionally, well-done presentations have added weight to content: there was an assumption that anyone with the resources to do high-quality graphics and good text layout would probably pay attention to the content. That was never a good assumption, of course, but at least it separated well-funded frauds from casual cranks and those who simply couldn't be bothered to check their facts.

That's all changed. It doesn't take much to build truly impressive World Wide Web servers. Anyone with an Internet connection and a decent graphics toolkit can create pages just as impressive as anything from the Library of Congress or NASA—but without any regard for factuality or meaning. You don't even need good taste to build impressive presentations; modern software will provide professional defaults so that you just add your erroneous or misleading text and graphics.

Knowing the Source

The anarchic nature of the Internet and the leveling effect of today's software raises the importance of cultivating appropriate skepticism among users, which must begin with appropriate skepticism among librarians and other library staff. For starters, Internet searchers must be trained to look for (and understand) the source of stuff that comes over the Net, but they must also learn to go beyond simple source awareness.

Some Internet navigation tools tend to mask sources, and that can be dangerous. There are thousands of cranks on the Internet now, and there will be even more in the future. Given a few thousand dollars and a few weeks of time, I could prepare a Library of Regress server that could be seen as a serious competitor to the Library of Congress—never mind that everything at the Library of Regress was at least half wrong, or at best meaningless. A neo-Marxist crank could create an impressive news bureau and be taken quite as seriously as a major news agency, even if that crank made up the supposed news flashes and wildly misinterpreted real events.

---

*This article appeared in *The Public-Access Computer Systems Review*, 5, no. 6 (1994), pp. 27–30 as "And Only Half of What You See, Part III: I Heard It through the Internet." Reprinted with permission.

A few MIT students with good software could provide a steady stream of Rubble Telescope (or Hobbled Telescope?) discoveries based on creatively modified clip art—and they would probably even have a ".mit.edu" suffix, assuring credibility. (To the best of my knowledge, all of these examples are hypothetical. I use MIT as an example because of its reputation for ingenious pranks.)

What's the solution? Certainly not to restrict Internet access to a few hallowed and licensed information providers. That would be even more dangerous to our society than having huge gobs of erroneous material on the Net and is, I believe, an impossibility as things stand. Rather, if there is a solution, it is to inculcate caution and healthy skepticism among users of the Internet and other immediate resources: to make them understand that being on-line and apparently up-to-date confers no authority or even probability of correctness on the information they see.

One way to start may be to use a different name for the Internet. It's not the Information Superhighway; it's the Stuff Swamp. There is a lot of good stuff out there, to be sure—but it's still a swamp, and a heavily polluted one at that. Wear your hip boots when you go out on the Internet; the stuff can get pretty thick at times.

P·A·R·T· V

L

Technology, Scholarship, and the Humanities: The Implications of Electronic Information*

Vartan Gregorian

Keynote Address (Transcript)

My interest in this conference stems from my concern about our divided knowledge, and its implications for education. I am also fascinated by the possibilities presented by technology for reintegrating knowledge and assisting universities in the task of resynthesizing information. We are moving rapidly to the dawn of an information revolution that may well parallel the Industrial Revolution in its impact and far-reaching consequences. We are told that the total amount of collected information doubles every four years, yet the ratio of used information to available information is steadily decreasing.

We are unable to use 90 to 95% of the information that is currently available, and nowhere is this more apparent than at the university, where the daunting arrival of information in the form of books and journals has been compounded by an accelerating electronic torrent from thousands of databases around the world. Today, at the touch of a computer keyboard, we can gain access to more information than we can possibly digest. But while it is true that attention to detail is a hallmark of professional excellence, it is equally true that an overload of undigested facts is a sure recipe for mental gridlock.

No wonder John Naisbitt, in his popular book *Megatrends*, bemoans the phenomenon that the world is "wallowing in detail, drowning in information, but is starved for knowledge." Undigested facts do not amount to knowledge. The current proliferation of information is accompanied by its corollary pitfalls, such as counterfeit information, inflation of information, and apparent, or real, obsolescence. I agree with Carlos Fuentes, who said that one of the greatest challenges facing modern society and contemporary civilization is how to transform information into knowledge. Our universities, colleges, libraries, learned societies, and contemporary scholars, more than ever before, have a fundamental historical and social task and responsibility to ensure that we provide not training, but education; and not only education, but culture as well. We must provide not just information, but its distillation, namely knowledge, in order to protect our society against counterfeit information disguised as knowledge.

This is not an easy task, because in addition to an explosion of information and knowledge, we also face dangerous levels of fragmentation in knowledge dictated by the advances of sciences, learning, and the accumulation of over two thousand years of scholarship. Max Weber criticized the narrowness, the absence of spirit, of modern intellectual specialists. It was this phenomenon that prompted Dostoevsky to lament, in *The Brothers Karamazov*, about scholars "who have only analyzed the parts, and overlooked the whole, and indeed their blindness is marvelous." It was the same phenomenon that Ortega y Gasset described in the 1930s in *Revolt of the Masses* as "the barbarism of specialization." "We have today," he wrote, "more scientists, more scholars, more professional men and women than ever before, but many fewer cultivated ones."

The university, which was to embody the unity of knowledge, has become an intellectual "multiversity." The process of both growth and fragmentation, under way since the seventeenth century, has accelerated in our century and will intensify in the twenty-first. Today, universities consist of a tangle of specialties and subspecialties, disciplines and subdisciplines, within which further specialization continues apace. The unity of knowledge has collapsed, and the scope and intensity of specialization is such that scholars, even scientists, have great difficulty keeping up with the important developments in their own subspecialties, not to mention their field in general.

As Professor Wayne Booth put it wistfully in his 1987 Ryerson lecture, "Centuries have passed since the fateful moment . . . was it in the eighteenth century or the late seventeenth century? . . . when the last of the Leonardo da Vincis could hope to cover the cognitive map. Since that fatal

*This article appeared in *Leonardo* (27)2(1995), pp. 155–164. Reprinted with permission of MIT Press.

moment everyone has been reduced to knowing only one or two countries on the intellectual globe." In the universities we are smitten by our pride, as for one reason or another we discover what a pitifully small corner of the cognitive world we live in. The knowledge explosion left us ignorant of vast fields of knowledge that every educated man or woman ought to have known. The growth and fragmentation of knowledge, and proliferation of specialties, is in turn reflected in the curricula of our universities. There are currently, I am told, more than one thousand different undergraduate majors and programs offered in America's colleges and universities. This, in turn, has led to the phenomenon that our students often learn to frame only those questions that can be addressed through the specialized methodologies of their particular disciplines and subdisciplines.

It was to address this kind of ahistorical, uncontextual, academic isolationism that the late Charles Franklin, the Columbia University philosopher, wrote, "When the study of human experience turns entirely inward, upon itself, it becomes the study of the study of the study of human experience. As the study of the study of the study, it does not achieve greater objectivity, but merely becomes thinner." In every generation in which the humanities have shown vitality they have refreshed their thinking by learning from other disciplines, and they have looked beyond their books to the primary materials that have made the books. They have preferred and performed an essential public, civic, educational function, namely the criticism and reintegration of ideas and values of cultures dislocated from their traditions and needing a new sense of meaning.

Unfortunately, in our universities today the triumph of the monograph, or scientific investigation, over synthesis, has further fragmented the commonwealth of learning and undermined our sense of commitment to the grand end of synthesis, general understanding, and the integration of knowledge. According to Professor William Bouwsma, specialization, instead of uniting human beings into a general community of values and discourse, has by necessity divided them into small and exclusive coteries, narrow in outlook and interest. It isolates and alienates human beings. Social relations, as a result, cease to be the expression of common perceptions and common beliefs; they are reduced to political relations, to the interplay of competitive, and often antagonistic, groups. Specialized education makes our students into instruments to serve the specialized needs of a society of specialists.

Faced with the explosion of information and its fragmentation, as well as the proliferation of disciplines and subdisciplines, the faculties of our universities are confronted with the difficult choice of balancing analysis with synthesis, methodology, and the relevant course content, thus placing more and more responsibility on the student to form his own synthesis. These developments are what perturbed Bouwsma in his brilliant 1975 essay "The Models of an Educated Man." He wrote:

The idea of the educated man has also been deeply affected by the 'knowledge revolution,' out of which has emerged the conception of education as preparation for research. As long as knowledge was limited, relatively simple, and not very technical, education could be fairly eclectic. Although it regularly emphasized the formation of character, it could attempt at the same time to discipline the mental faculties, provide a common culture, and supply a minimum of substantive knowledge. Yet obviously, the sheer bulk of the knowledge now deemed necessary for an educated person has squeezed out of education—and for the most part, even out of our understanding of it—everything but the acquisition of knowledge in some monographic form. One result has been a broad decline in the idea of a general education, which for all practical purposes has become little more than a nostalgic memory. Indeed, the body of requisite knowledge has become so vast that no one can hope to master more than a small segment of it. So, in the popular mind, an educated person is now some kind of a specialist; and, in a sense, we no longer have a single conception of the educated man, but as many conceptions as there are learned specialties.

Nowhere is this better reflected than in the concept of literacy itself; it too has lost its unity, it too has been fragmented. According to The Oxford Unabridged Dictionary, literacy is the quality or state of being literate, the possession of education, especially the ability to read and write. Today we are using the term "illiterate" as a euphemism for ignorance of a given subject matter, and the term "literate" to refer to knowledge of a specific subject matter. We have proponents of "functional literacy," "technological literacy," "computer literacy," "civic literacy," "historical literacy," "cultural literacy," "analytical literacy," "mathematical literacy," "geographical literacy," "scientific literacy," "ethical literacy," "artistic literacy," and (my favorite) "managerial literacy." Born in the pages of *The New York Times*, this literacy consists of 1200 terms. We are told that if you score 80% or more, you should feel confident that you can engage in meaningful conversations with other experienced managers. One word that I learned was "tasksatisfizing," which means the acceptance of satisfactory levels of performance of many orders. In conclusion, there are at present too many facts, too many theories, subjects, and specializations to permit the arrangement of all knowledge into an acceptable hierarchy. Without opportunities for creative discourse among educated persons, both within and without the university, without the broad understanding of the premises and assumptions of various academic disciplines, it is not easy for either student or faculty, or lay men and women, to pursue complex problems that cut across the artificial barriers between the disciplines.

Today, in our universities, we face the challenge of integrating and resynthesizing the compartmentalized knowledge of disparate fields. Clearly, our age of excessive specialization and fragmentation of knowledge does not call for the abandonment of specialization: After all, the division of labor has greatly advanced the cause of civilization. Specialization has always been hailed as an instrument for progress. It has been a source of the general conception of excellence. Complexity, by necessity, has always required specialization in pursuit of the discovery of solutions.

The answer, then, is not to call for an end to specialization, nor for the castigation of those humanists and social scientists who avail themselves of scientific methods and technology, nor of those who attempt to provide rigid analyses of literary texts, social trends, and historical facts. This, in my opinion, is to indulge in unwarranted snobbery. To scorn sociology for its jargon while exonerating philology, philosophy, aesthetics, and literary criticism from that sin is equally unwarranted. Such attitudes remind me of the Anglican bishop who told the Episcopal bishop, "Brother, we both serve the Lord, you in your way and I in His."

The scientific passion of verifiability, the habit of testing and correcting a concept through its consequences in experience, is just as firmly rooted in the humanities as it is in the sciences. As early as 1944, Jose Ortega y Gasset prescribed a solution to our dilemma in The Mission of the University. He wrote:

"The need to create sound syntheses and systematizations of knowledge . . . will call out a kind of scientific genius which hitherto has existed only as an aberration—the genius for integration. Of necessity, this means specialization as all creative effort inevitably does; but this time the person will be specializing in the construction of a whole. The momentum which impels investigation to dissociate indefinitely into particular problems—the pulverization of research—makes necessary a compensatory control . . . which is to be furnished by a force pulling in the opposite direction, constraining centrifugal science in a wholesome organization."

The selection of professors will depend not on their rank as investigators, but on their talent for synthesis.

The need for breadth of coverage inevitably conflicts with the need for coverage in depth. It is the depth, rather than the breadth, of humanistic education that we must now defend. The ability to make connections among seemingly disparate disciplines, and to integrate them in ways that benefit the scholarly community, hence the educational process, is our major challenge. Our scholars and our students must be skilled at synthesis as well as analysis, and they must be technologically astute and literate. Within the university communities, in particular, we must create an intellectual climate for an integral process of societal change. We must encourage our educators to encourage our students to bridge the boundaries between the disciplines and make connections that produce deeper insights.

The new information technologies are the driving force behind both the explosion of information and the fragmentation of knowledge. Information technologies contribute to the explosion of information by shrinking the traditional barriers of time and space, giving us the ability to record, organize, and quickly communicate vast amounts of information. The entire corpus of Greek and Latin literature, for example, can fit on a CD-ROM and be carried inconspicuously in a jacket pocket. If a friend in Paris would like to see an article you have just written, a copy of it can be transferred to him or her in seconds by the international Internet. If one inquires about articles written on pituitary surgery in the last year, the abstracts are available within seconds, and the article itself arriving by fax within the hour. Soon, we are told, any book or article on the most abstruse bit of information will be instantly available from any networked computer. This will compound documents with photographs, live graphics, and hypertext links that will take the reader instantly to any other related book or article.

That is the future, and it is probably nearer than we think. But our primary problem as universities is not engineering that future. We must rise above the obsession with quantity of information and speed of trans-mission, and recognize that the key issue for us is our ability to organize this information once it has been amassed—to assimilate it, find meaning in it, and assure its survival for use by generations to come.

Information technologies also contribute to the fragmentation of knowl-edge by allowing us to organize ourselves into ever more specialized communities. Are you developing an interest in exotic insects, rare min-erals, or an obscure poet? With little effort you can use electronic mail and conferencing to find several others, in Japan, Peru, or Bulgaria, with whom you can communicate every day, creating your own small, self-confirming world of theory, technique, and methodology. McLuhan's prediction that electronic communication would create a global village is wrong in my opinion. What is being created is less like a village than an entity that reproduces the worst aspects of urban life: the ability to retreat into small communities of the like-minded, safe not only from unnecessary interac-tions with those whose ideas and attitudes are not like our own, but safe from having to relate our interests and results to other communities.

As well as encouraging the formation of specialist communities, the new information technologies contribute to fragmentation in other ways. The new electronic formats and computer techniques, with special terminol-ogy, equipment, and methodology, nicely support the development of "priesthoods" and esoteric communities. This is not just a quarrel between traditional scholars and a generation with new ideas and new instruments. It is increasingly a conflict that is played out whenever any group uses the new technology to construct information formats or techniques that prove unnecessarily forbidding to any but the initiated. This may not require malign intent, only ignorance and indifference to the larger issues of scholarship and communication in a technological society.

Paradoxically, information technology also presents us with the oppor-tunity and the tools for meeting the challenge of the explosion of infor-mation and the fragmentation of knowledge. If, on one hand, the new information technologies seem fragmenting, they are also profoundly integrative. Remember, these technologies are fundamentally communication technologies, and their deployment at the university is, as often as not, an exploration of new connections among the traditional disciplines, new ways of finding significance and meaning. The process of assimilating new information technologies can, in the right setting, help us think hard and deeply about the nature of knowledge, and even about our mission as a university.

T. S. Eliot, in one of his early commentaries on Dante's *Inferno*, described Hell as a place "where nothing connects with nothing." The condition of absurdity and anomie is often noted as a distinctive liability of modern intellectual life. Now, near the end of the twentieth century, this threat may seem to have reached its epitome in the explosion and fragmentation of information caused by our new technology. In fact, while the threat is real enough, the new technology brings us new resources for the establishment of coherence, connection, and meaning. That is why this meeting is so important—to bring the practitioners, the theorists, the academics, and administrators together in search of a new pathway for integrating knowledge and affecting the course of education delivery.

Is this a revolution? In my opinion, yes. Technologically, the dizzying rate of performance improvements in computer hardware is matched only by an equally dizzying drop in costs. No one who reads the newspapers can have missed the comparison between the expensive, massive, computer of two decades ago, which required teams of experts to operate, and its contemporary equivalent, a small, pleasingly designed, one-thousand-dollar appliance on the desk of a junior high school student.

Advances in telecommunications technology also show a startling acceleration. There are now nearly 10 million users of the worldwide Internet, which connects over 500,000 host computers, and new hosts and users are being added every day. Electronic mail, network file transfer, and remote searching of databases are now a fact of academic life, totally integrated into faculty members' working routine. Software improvements are also impressive. While the difficult user interfaces of older software required a considerable investment in time, today intuitive graphic interfaces and improved program design have made it easy for students to use a sophisticated program the first time they encounter it. These programs give their users extraordinary powers, allowing them to pose and answer questions in minutes that might have taken teams of technicians weeks or months using traditional methods.

While the rate of technological change is dramatic, equally dramatic will be the changes in our organizational structures necessary to accommodate technological advances. The relevant organizational structure must change to adapt to the new technology. Until that happens, the real revolution of technology in higher education will not have occurred.

This was the case for printing, the Industrial Revolution, the automobile, air travel, and radio and television. New technology per se is not revolution; the revolution is the difference in how we organize, structure, and empower our lives. This is, of course, the source of many of our problems. How do we adapt our organizations and social structures to these techno- logical changes? How do we exploit technological developments while subordinating them to our larger purposes? We are too often putting new wine in old bottles. But discovering the new organizational forms that are required is hard, not just because it is difficult to understand the nature and significance of the changes in information technology, but because orga- nizational innovation requires a sure grasp of our mission and identity as an institution.

Once these forms are recognized, implementing them requires ingenu- ity, commitment, and, above all else, risk and courage. Although the revo- lution is far from over, there may be a lull of sorts ahead. It is about time for the enthusiasm and revolutionary fervor regarding the new technology to subside for a bit, while the methods of exploiting the technology are evaluated and integrated into the historical identity of institutions. Al- though not a time of high drama, such lulls can, in fact, be the most crucial periods of revolutionary change.

This is the time to separate the confusions and self-deceptions from the truths and insights, and to effect the real information technology revolu- tion by adjusting our organizational structures to discern, accommodate, assimilate, and exploit what is lasting and valuable in these technological developments. In short, these lulls are times of evaluation and integration, and that is the business, unfortunately, of presidents of universities.

What can a president do? The role of the president, of course, is not to lead the development of new information technologies, nor even to herald their arrival, argue their importance, or warn of their dangers. If presidents are successful at their leadership and managerial tasks, then there will be plenty of others who will be doing those things within the university community. The role of the president is to establish a process that will promote the integration of these new technologies, with each other and with the mission and the core values of the university. It is one of active moral and intellectual leadership. This is hard, and some days the presi- dent will be beset by the prophets of the new technology, as I have been. They will grab you by the arm and whisper in your ear, feverishly pressing upon you the revelation that "Things are completely different now . . . we are being left behind." On other days, you will be dogged by self-styled protectors of ancient wisdom and the old ways. "What is good is not new, and what is new is not good," they will whisper darkly. You will think your faculty and advisers have all become pre-Socratic: "Everything is chang- ing," announce the breathless Heracliteans; "Nothing changes," warn the gloomy Parmenideans. To both you will give the same Aristotelian answer: "Some things change, and some things remain the same."

Our identity, values, principles, and goals remain the same. The tech- nological accidentals we use to exemplify these values in the twentieth century will vary. In fact, these must vary, for we cannot remain the same in our essentials unless we change in our accidentals to meet the new circumstances. The president must create the climate where risk taking and innovative solutions are encouraged. But most of all the president must create a community that is totally informed regarding the values and peculiar identity of our institution. If that can be achieved, and if all members of the university can trust each other to be motivated by the same shared values, then the community can move forward to address the problems of technology and the integration of knowledge.

Very few institutions will be on the so-called "leading edge" of the technology revolution, but none can escape the risk taking and wrenching changes necessary to assimilate its results into its own mission and peculiar identity. Every institution will be the site of its own convulsion, each will have its own special solution, and each will contribute something unique to the collective effort to advance learning, education, and culture.

P·A·R·T · V

M

On the Road Again? If Information Highways Are Anything like Interstate Highways—Watch Out!*

Richard Sclove† • *Jeffrey Scheuer*

Vice-President Gore envisions the information superhighway as the second coming of the interstate highway system championed by his father, former United States Senator Al Gore, a generation ago.[1] Let us pray the good Vice-President is proven wrong. Rush-hour traffic jams, gridlock, garish plastic and neon strips, high fatality rates, air pollution, global warming, depletion of world oil reserves—have we forgotten all of the interstate highway system's most familiar consequences?

It's not that Gore's analogy is wrong, only that his enthusiasm is misplaced. Comparing the electronic and asphalt highways is useful—but mostly as a cautionary tale. Building the new information infrastructure will not entail the degree of immediate, physical disruption caused by the interstate highway system. But sweeping geographic relocations, and accompanying social transformations, seem probable. And the risk of inequity in contriving and distributing electronic services—or, conversely, imposing them where they are not wanted—is clear.

Indeed, disparities in access to new information systems have already begun to surface. A study released in 1994 by a coalition of public interest organizations, including the National Association for the Advancement of Colored People and the Center for Media Education, notes that low-income and minority communities are underrepresented in United States telephone companies' initial plans for installing advanced communications networks.[2]

Unequal access is only the most obvious among many social repercussions that may lie in store for us. The real history of the interstate highways system suggests how we can think about and control the vast implications of new technologies and a new national public infrastructure.

It is widely assumed that Americans' infatuation with cars led to the construction of America's superhighways. But actually when Congress passed the Interstate Highway Act in 1956, car sales were slack, and there was no popular clamor for building a new road system. At the time only about half of American families owned an automobile; everyone else depended on public transportation. Congress was responding to aggressive lobbying by auto makers and road builders, plus realtors who saw profits in developing suburban subdivisions.

The act's key provisions included support for bringing freeways directly into city centers and earmarking gasoline tax revenues for highway construction. As the interstate highways were built, city and suburban development adapted to the quickening proliferation of autos. Soon more Americans found themselves forced to buy a car in order to be able to shop or hold a job. The Highway Trust Fund, by assuring the rapid atrophy of competing public transit systems, bolstered this trend.

Thus the asphalt highways—and the society around them—are a reflection of successful lobbying by powerful business interests and external compulsion, not simply the free choices of consumers.[3] There is no guarantee that the process of wiring consumers and employees into the electronic highway system will be different.

Sometimes new technologies achieve ironic effects. Proponents loudly advertised the interstate road system as being indispensable to national security. But in truth the United States had prevailed in World War II, relying largely on rail transport.[4] Indeed, eventually car-induced dependence on precarious foreign oil sources *reduced* United States security. The

---

*Portions of this chapter originally appeared in the authors' "The Ghost in the Modem: For Architects of the Info-Highway, Some Lessons from the Concrete Interstate," *The Washington Post,* Outlook Section, May 29, 1994, p. C3.

† Richard Sclove is executive director of the Loka Institute in Amherst, Massachusetts, a public-interest research and advocacy organization concerned with the social repercussions of science and technology. He is the author of *Democracy and Technology* (New York: Guilford Press, 1995). Jeffrey Scheuer, a New York writer, is a fellow of the Loka Institute.

[1] Ken Auletta, "Under the Wire," *The New Yorker,* January 17, 1994, p. 49.

[2] Steve Lohr, "Data Highway Ignoring Poor, Study Charges," *The New York Times,* May 24, 1994, pp. A1 and D3.

[3] See James J. Flink, *The Automobile Age* (Cambridge, MA: MIT Press, 1988), especially Chapter 19.

[4] See James J. Flink, *The Automobile Age* (Cambridge, MA: MIT Press, 1988), p. 371.

consequences have included the trauma of petroleum supply disruptions during the 1970s, spiraling domestic military expenditures, alarming build-ups of armaments in the Middle East, and periodic military engagements (most recently with the armed forces of Saddam Hussein).

Poor people, the working class, women, and disadvantaged minorities—that is, a majority of all Americans, many of whom did not own cars—played no role in fundamental decisions about highways. Yet they were very much affected. In cities, for instance, "Ambitious programs for building urban freeways resulted in the massive destruction of once viable poor and minority neighborhoods."[5] In other cases, new highways encircled poor neighborhoods, physically segregating minorities into marginalized ghettoes.[6]

Gradually a black and Hispanic middle class did emerge. Its members too fled along the interstate to the suburbs, further draining economic and cultural resources from the inner city. This contributed to the emergence of a new social phenomenon: today's desperately deprived, urban under-class.[7]

Elsewhere the effects were subtler but still significant. The noise and danger from growing numbers of autos drove children's games out of the street, and neighbors and families off their front porches. Before long, suburbs without sidewalks came to signal an unprecedented paucity of local destinations worth walking to. Suburban housewives found themselves leading increasingly isolated daytime lives at home.[8]

Highways made shopping malls possible, enabling franchise and chain store sales to boom. But this sapped downtown centers. For some teenagers and senior citizens, today's anonymous, consumption-mad expanses provide a semblance of community space—having swallowed up the general store, the soda fountain, the Main Street sidewalk, and the town square.[9]

---

[5] See James J. Flink, *The Automobile Age* (Cambridge, MA: MIT Press, 1988), p. 135.

[6] See, for example, Harris Stone, *Workbook of an Unsuccessful Architect* (New York: Monthly Review Press, 1973).

[7] William Julius Wilson, *The Truly Disadvantaged: The Inner City, the Underclass, and Public Policy* (Chicago: University of Chicago Press, 1987).

[8] Ruth Schwartz Cowan, *More Work for Mother: The Ironies of Household Technology from the Open Hearth to the Microwave* (New York: Basic Books, 1983); Kenneth T. Jackson, *Crabgrass Frontier: The Suburbanization of the United States* (New York: Oxford University Press, 1985); David Engwicht, *Reclaiming Our Cities and Towns: Better Living with Less Traffic* (Philadelphia: New Society Publishers, 1993).

[9] Ray Oldenburg, *The Great Good Place: Cafés, Coffee Shops, Community Centers, Beauty Parlors, General Stores, Bars, Hangouts, and How They Get You Through the Day* (New York: Paragon House, 1989); Michael Sorkin, ed., *Variations on a Theme Park: The New American City and the End of Public Space* (New York: Noonday Press, 1992); James Howard Kunstler, *The Geography of Nowhere: The Rise and Decline of America's Man-Made Landscape* (New York: Simon and Schuster, 1993).

To appreciate the involuntary nature of many such transformations, imagine a new Wal-Mart store locating on a town's outskirts. Suppose that over time half the residents start to do, say, one-third of their shopping at the new store. That means they still do two-thirds of their shopping downtown, while the remaining half of the population does all its shopping downtown. Thus if we asked them, we would find that everyone wants downtown to remain vibrant. Nevertheless, there's been a 16.5% decline in downtown retail revenue. If profit margins aren't high, that can be enough to start killing off downtown shops. Thus through a perverse market dynamic, there is an aggregate result that *no* consumers wanted or intended.[10] As cyberspace is commercialized—which will include a growing number of economic transactions being conducted tele-electronically—there is ample danger that this kind of erosion of convivial public spaces will accelerate.

Remember too that it is easy to romanticize new technology. The popular arts glorified life on the highway. People read Jack Kerouac's *On the Road*, watched "Route 66" on television, and recall the Merry Pranksters' psychedelic bus-capades during the 1960s. In fusing alienation and rebellion with youthful exuberance, each of these foreshadows contemporary cyberpunk culture. Yet real-life experience on the interstate is mostly banal and uneventful. McDonald's, Pizza Hut, and Wal-Mart look about the same wherever you exit.

There are also political ramifications of a vast new public infrastructure. Interstate highways contributed to national and even international economic integration. But while GNP soared, mom-and-pop production and retailing declined. That meant greater local dependence on national and global market forces and on distant corporate headquarters—powers that communities simply couldn't control. The locus of effective political intervention thus shifted toward more distant power centers. But because those are realms in which everyday citizens cannot be as effectual as in smaller political settings, democracy was impaired.[11]

Finally, as citizens became more politically mobilized during the 1960s and early 1970s, opposition to relentless highway expansion arose from environmentalists and from local communities, both rich and poor. In

---

[10] This dynamic represents a classic instance of a social theorists's "collective action problem." See Brian Barry and Russell Hardin (eds.), *Rational Man and Irrational Society?: An Introduction and Sourcebook* (Beverly Hills: Sage Publications, 1982). For further analysis of perverse market dynamics, see Richard E. Sclove, *Democracy and Technology* (New York: Guilford Press, 1995), pp. 161–173.

[11] Readings that discuss the logic in this paragraph include Richard E. Sclove, *Democracy and Technology* (New York: Guilford Press, 1995), pp. 119–138, 215–216, 235–238; Samuel P. Hays, *American Political History as Social Analysis* (Knoxville: University of Tennessee Press, 1980), especially pp. 244–263; and Ralph Nader *et al.*, *The Case Against Free Trade: GATT, NAFTA, and the Globalization of Corporate Power* (San Francisco: Earth Island Press, 1993).

many places construction halted, and eventually some highway funds were redirected to public transit. Transportation engineers reeled at the specter of upright citizens rejecting their good works.[12] Many current telecommunications engineers and true-believing entrepreneurs are no less convinced of the unalloyed beneficence of their art.

What if a wider range of people, including non–car owners, had been involved in transportation planning all along? Possibly, the interstate system would never have been built. But, considering alternatives envisioned by 1950s critics such as Lewis Mumford, it seems more likely we would have a smaller and different road system today.[13] As in Europe and Japan, there probably would have been greater investment in public transit. Modern America might exhibit less sprawl, less dependence on foreign oil, and more cohesive urban neighborhoods.

Steel and concrete highways are not identical to fiber optic pathways. Still, there are lessons here. To its credit a coalition of more than one hundred twenty public-interest groups, known as the Telecommunications Policy Roundtable, is already lobbying vigorously for an information infrastructure that supports civic uses, protects privacy, and is universally accessible and affordable.[14] But other issues remain to be addressed.

For instance, electronic shopping is likely to put more local stores, social and professional services, and amenities out of business, just as malls and video have done to the local movie theater. That, in turn, will compel many new consumers to start using electronic services, like it or not.

As more people spend more time communicating electronically, time for face-to-face family and community life, or for reflective reading—already vastly eroded by television—will diminish even further. Some will mourn the loss of meaning and depth they remember from pre-electronic life.[15]

There are employees who will enjoy choosing among a wider array of work settings, such as telecommuting from a neighborhood office suite. But others may encounter new work arrangements only as harsh impositions, such as laboring in solitude or enduring remote, computerized job surveillance.[16]

---

[12] Samuel P. Hays, *Beauty, Health and Permanence: Environmental Politics in the United States, 1955–1985.* (Cambridge, England: Cambridge University Press, 1987), pp. 84–85; Mark H. Rose and Bruce E. Seely, "Getting the Interstate System Built: Road Engineers and the Implementation of Public Policy, 1955–1985," *Journal of Public History,* Vol. 2, No. 1 (1990), pp. 23–55.

[13] Donald L. Miller, *Lewis Mumford: A Life* (New York: Weidenfeld & Nicolson, 1989).

[14] See, for example, "Serving the Community: A Public Interest Vision of the National Information Infrastructure," *The CPSR Newsletter,* Vol. 11, No. 4 and Vol. 12, No. 1 (Winter 1994), pp. 1–10, 20–23, 26–31.

[15] Albert Borgmann, "Philosophical Reflections on the Microelectronic Revolution," in *Philosophy and Technology II: Information Technology and Computers in Theory and Practice,* Carl Mitcham and Alois Huning (eds.). (Dordrecht: D. Reidel, 1986), pp. 189–203.

[16] See, for example, Robert G. Boehmer and Todd S. Palmer, "Worker Privacy in the Networked Organization: Implications of Pending U.S. and E.C. Legislation" in *The Use and*

Broad shifts in overall political power relations appear likely—but in which direction? On one hand—especially if new electronic systems become ubiquitous and easily affordable—individuals, small groups, and groups with geographically dispersed membership should be able to organize themselves for enhanced social efficacy. But it is also conceivable that already-powerful corporate and governmental bureaucracies, by dint of superior capability to amass, analyze, and act on the basis of vast agglomerations of data, will enhance their relative power. It is hard to predict which trend will predominate, and thus whether social power relations will tend to become more diffuse and democratic or more concentrated.

If the emergence of electronically mediated "virtual communities" continues, a growing mismatch could also arise between our system of political representation, which is territorially based, versus bonds of social affiliation that would increasingly be nonterritorial in nature. Info-highway boosters sometimes respond that political systems can, if necessary, change.[17] But apart from the problem of providing specifics, this answer fails to grapple with the United States Constitution's requirement, in Article V, that Constitutional amendments garner the support of a majority of elected federal or state legislators. How readily do legislators normally accede to voting away their own offices?

What can be done? Some helpful guiding principles include:

No Innovation without Evaluation. To help reduce adverse social impacts, the federal government should mandate carefully evaluated social trials of alternative electronic services. Analogous to environmental impact statements, these trials should precede full-scale deployment of any major components of new information infrastructures.[18]

Telecommunications companies already run their own pilot trials, but usually only in order to help forecast the market for their proposed services. But with such trials already under way or in the offing, an independent evaluation of their results—including a wider array of social and political consequences than private businesses would otherwise consider—would only marginally increase costs, while producing extremely valuable public information.

Abuse of Computer Networks: Ethical, Legal, and Technological Aspects: Preliminary Report (Washington, DC: American Association for the Advancement of Science, Sept. 1994), pp. 143–187; Vincent Mosco and Janet Wasko (eds.), *The Political Economy of Information* (Madison: University of Wisconsin Press, 1988).

[17] Jock Gill, "Reinventing Government Processes and Political Participation," a talk given at MIT, February 17, 1994. At the time Mr. Gill was electronic mail coordinator in the Clinton White House.

[18] See Richard E. Sclove, *Democracy and Technology* (New York: Guilford Press, 1995), pp. 55–57, 219–221.

No Innovation without Regulation. We should conserve cultural space for face-to-face social engagement, traditional forms of community life, off-screen leisure activities, and time spent in nature.[19] For example, what if rates were adjusted to discourage use of the information superhighway for one evening each week? (Because content would remain unregulated, this would not compromise the First Amendment.) Or how about a modest tax on electronic home shopping and consumer services, rebating the revenue to support compensatory, local community-building initiatives? Measures such as these would help ensure that electronic systems complement rather than supplant desirable aspects of traditional human experience.

No Innovation without Participation. A number of European nations are outcompeting America in including laypeople in technology decision making. For instance, the Danish government appoints panels of everyday citizens to cross-examine a range of experts, deliberate among themselves, and then publish their own social assessments of technological alternatives. Sweden, Norway, and Germany have pioneered processes for involving workers directly in designing new production systems.[20]

The coming revolution in information systems is going to change life for every single one of us. That includes people in every occupation and geographic location, babies, women, old people, sick people, disadvantaged minorities, people who don't currently use computers, people who never want to use a computer. It is imperative to develop mechanisms for involving all segments of our society in designing, evaluating, and governing these new systems.

Data highway enthusiasts may see the measures we propose as just creating obstructions. But what entrepreneurs would have you believe is red tape is really democracy in action.

---

[19] On some of the virtues of nonelectronically mediated human experience see, for example, Albert Borgmann, *Technology and the Character of Contemporary Life: A Philosophical Inquiry* (Chicago: University of Chicago Press, 1984); Erazim Kohák, *The Embers and the Stars: A Philosophical Inquiry into the Moral Sense of Nature* (Chicago: University of Chicago Press, 1984); Chellis Glendinning, *My Name is Chellis & I'm in Recovery From Western Civilization* (Boston: Shambala, 1994); and Richard E. Sclove, *Democracy and Technology* (New York: Guilford Press, 1995), pp. 40, 79–81.

[20] See Richard E. Sclove, *Democracy and Technology* (New York: Guilford Press, 1995), pp. 26–29, 48–53, 180–238; and *Technology and Democracy: The Use and Impact of Technology Assessment in Europe*, Proceedings of the 3rd European Congress on Technology Assessment, Copenhagen, November 4–7, 1992, 2 vols. (published by the Danish Board of Technology, Antonigade 4, DK-1106 Copenhagen K, Denmark, Tel. +45 33 32 05 03, Fax +45 33 91 05 09).

P·A·R·T·VI

Privacy and Social Control

Information Technologies and the Shifting Balance between Privacy and Social Control

Rob Kling

Privacy: Who Wants It?

Privacy is a powerful word with diverse connotations. Consider these examples:

- The teenager who doesn't want her parents listening to her phone calls with her new boyfriend, and criticizes them for violating her privacy.
- A family sitting down for dinner around 7:00 P.M. gets frequent phone calls from telemarketers who want to offer them great deals on car loans or prizes for visiting delightful vacation properties. The family members want "more privacy" during the few minutes that they spend together each evening, but are reluctant to turn off their phones because they may miss emergency calls.
- A young engineer is afraid to sign any political petitions, because she is afraid that her employer might learn of her signatures, not like her politics, and ruin her promising career.
- A talented accountant moves to Texas to live closer to his aging parents. He has serious trouble finding a new job due to medical reports that state he lost work from chronic back pain, and credit reports that inaccurately identify him as having mountains of unpaid bills. He is never called for an interview and has trouble learning why he is ignored.

- A systems analyst who works for an office supply company is fired after he criticizes his supervisor via "private e-mail." He thought that he had a right to share his private views with a co-worker. The analyst sees the company as an even worse place to work since the supervisor can read his subordinates' e-mail at will.

- A college student in a midwestern university is shocked to find that an anonymous mailing to a public electronic bulletin board about the changing admissions standards includes material describing him as having served jail time. He is further mortified when some of his friends start avoiding him. The student wants to have the offending note promptly removed, and to confront his accuser (whose identity is masked by an anonymous electronic remailing service).

- A young systems analyst is upset that a company whose headquarters is nearby has been ineffectively storing toxic waste, thus polluting part of the local water supply. She skips lunch to join a peaceful demonstration in front of their headquarters, and notices that several policemen are videotaping the demonstration. She doesn't want to become part of a police file and leaves the area embittered at the company. The analyst feels she was intimidated by the police.

Privacy has many connotations and has become a catchphrase to signify diverse issues such as these. In their landmark article, "The Right to Privacy," Warren and Brandeis (1890) characterized privacy as a person's "right to be let alone." This meaning catches some of what bothers the teenager, the family, and the young engineer. Privacy is an elastic term that has broader connotations. The family may also wonder, "Why are they always calling us, and how did they get our names and phone numbers?" (Culnan, 1993).

The accountant wonders whether potential employers believe something about him that he doesn't know. After all, he desires a job. He may soon want to know what information his prospective employers are using to screen their applicants and what is contained in his profile. He would like to see employers' criteria for hiring, (information that they treat as private). The accountant should know that they are using his medical insurance records and limit access to them. He needs to know that his credit report is grossly inaccurate and be able to correct it. The accountant is caught up in a large web of personal record keeping systems about which he has little knowledge and over which he has little control. For the accountant, privacy refers to gaining control over the ways that information about him is collected, verified, and passed on to other organizations.

The accused student may have served time in jail, but was looking forward to a new life that college would open for him. He would like to change his life, and also find out who is harassing him. The systems analyst would like to register her disgust at a company's dangerous handling of toxic wastes without developing a police record. Each of these examples illustrates some of the nuances of the term privacy.

Chapter B in Part VI, "Your Personal Information Has Gone Public" by Professor David F. Linowes, lists numerous additional cases in which people have been denied housing, insurance, and jobs. They were ignorant of the information about them that apartment owners, banks, insurers, and various employers were using to screen applicants and set prices. Linowes also reports some shocking cases in which people had immense trouble in having their records corrected when they were grossly inaccurate. The strength of the article is in the way he concisely identifies the meanings of threats to privacy through vivid examples of personal troubles. However, he doesn't examine how these social practices developed.

Linowes starts his article with the provocative claim, "Privacy invaders are all around us." But many of the people and organizations who are seeking information about specific individuals or sharing what they know may not see themselves as "privacy invaders." Parents who are interested in the well-being of their children, may see eavesdropping as a fair way to learn about a secret and potentially dangerous relationship. The banks that employ telemarketers are seeking good clients for their loans, so that they can earn money on their deposits, in order to pay their account holders higher interest rates. A manufacturing firm may carefully prescreen applicants for an accounting job with credit checks after having been embezzled by an employee who had huge debts to pay off, and so on.

The office supply supervisor may feel that the morale of his work groups is being undermined by a subordinate who continually criticizes him and makes fun of him to his co-workers. Although some of these breaches of personal privacy could be obnoxious or harmful to one party, in most cases, they are not merely frivolous. What kinds of guidelines should we have to balance a person's privacy with other social goods, such as parental guidance, the ability to conduct business, and the ability to have citizens participate freely in political life? Before examining some of the debates about these issues, it helps to examine how North American societies developed their current privacy practices.

Record Keeping in Mobile Societies

People and groups in any society spend some effort in learning about and regulating each other's behavior. But the means differ, and social issues raised by different means also differ. In relatively small social units, such as families and villages, people learn about each other's behavior through direct observation, inference, and gossip. And the forms of social control, introduced to help ensure compliance with social expectations, can range from those that are gentle to others that are harsh and even brutal.

A distinctive feature of villages and small towns is that many business relationships are based on personal knowledge. For example, storekeepers and bankers know most of the people to whom they offer credit, and they also know the extent to which their customers are reliable. Yet even in small town societies, people sometimes find it necessary to deal with large and distant organizations (e.g., government agencies such as tax collectors and the military).

During the last one hundred years, there has been an astounding transformation in the ways that life in industrial societies is organized. New means of transportation (trains, buses, cars, and airplanes) enabled people to become mobile. In the early nineteenth century, most people who were born in the United States lived and died within fifty miles of their birthplaces. Today, in a highly mobile society, a huge fraction of the urban population moves from city to city, following better jobs and better places to live. Adolescents often leave their hometowns to attend college, and may move even farther away for jobs. Further, over 130 metropolitan areas in the United States number over 250,000 in population. Even moving "across town" in one of these cities can bring a person into a new network of friends, employers, and service providers. This combination of mobility and urban development means that many people seek jobs, goods, and services from businesses whose proprietors and staff do not have much firsthand knowledge about them.

The scale of businesses and the number of government agencies with huge clienteles have also increased in the last one hundred years. In the nineteenth century few businesses had thousands of clients. An even smaller fraction of the public interacted frequently with the larger businesses of the day. Similarly, government agencies were also smaller. Overall, most business was conducted through face-to-face (direct) relations. Only specific government activities, such as taxing and drafting, were carried out between people who didn't know each other at all. Craig Calhoun (1992) characterizes contemporary industrial societies as ones in which a significant fraction of people's important activities are carried out with the mediation of people whom they do not see and may not even know exist. Today, banks can readily extend credit to people who come from anywhere in the country. And they can do so with relative safety because of large-scale credit record systems that track the credit history of over 100,000,000 people. The credit check brings together a credit seeker and employees of the credit bureau who are related *indirectly.*

Other private firms, such as insurance companies and mail order companies, also extend services to tens of thousands of people who local agents do not—and could not—personally know. In these transactions, judgments about insurability and credit worthiness are made via indirect social relationships, and are often mediated with computerized information systems that are operated by data brokers such as TRW Credit Data[1] and

---

[1] You can obtain a free copy of your TRW credit report once a year. Call (800) 392–1122 for details.

the Medical Information Bureau.[2] Furthermore, many new government agencies, responsible for accounting for the activities of millions of people, have been created in the twentieth century: the Federal Bureau of Investigation (1908), the Internal Revenue Service (1913), the Social Security Administration (1935), along with various state departments of motor vehicles, and so on. The sheer scale of these services creates "environmental conditions" that provide incentives to organizations to use computerized record systems to help the maintenance of indirect social relationships become routine. However, organizations of a similar kind and size, such as banks or police agencies, differ in their aggressiveness in using new technologies and management practices.

The United States has developed a body of privacy law that gives people some explicit rights and protections in a few areas as well as restricting wiretapping and other invasive acts. However, during the last thirty years, people have lost control over records about them. Increasingly, courts have ruled that records about a person belong to an organization, and the person to whom they apply cannot restrict their use (Privacy Protection Study Commission, 1977). Consequently, inaccurate police records, medical records, employment histories, to name a few, can harm people without their explicit knowledge about why they are having trouble getting, for example, a job or loan. Although a right to privacy is not set forth in the Bill of Rights, the United States Supreme Court has protected various privacy interests. The Court found sources for a right to privacy in the First, Third, Fourth, Fifth, Ninth, and Fourteenth Amendments to the Constitution (U.S. Office of Technology Assessment, 1994). In Chapter C of this part, we include the Bill of Rights of the United States Constitution.

Many key social rights in the United States have been defended as privacy rights by the United States Supreme Court. Many of these privacy rights have little to do with computer systems, and are more linked to "a right to be left alone." Supreme Court justices relied on privacy rights in *Griswold v. Connecticut*, 381 U.S. 479 (1965), which gave married couples the right to use birth control devices. Prior to this ruling, some states banned the sale of birth control devices. The majority opinion referred to "zones of privacy" created in the First, Third, Fourth, Fifth, and Ninth Amendments. Similarly, *Roe v. Wade*, 410 U.S. 113 (1973) further extended the right of privacy "to encompass a woman's decision whether or not to terminate her pregnancy and justified its action by reference to the Fourteenth Amendment (U.S. Office of Technology Assessment, 1994: 79; Garrow, 1994).

---

[2] You can contact the Medical Information Bureau to receive a free copy of a report that shows which part of your medical history is stored in their insurance industry data base by writing to P.O. Box 105, Essex Station, Boston, MA 02112 or by calling (617) 426–3660.

Value Conflicts in Controversies about Personal Record Systems and Privacy

Discussions of computerization and privacy are embroiled in a major set of controversies with big stakes. On one hand, some people fear that emerging computer-based information systems are helping to erode personal privacy. They would like to see certain kinds of record systems regulated or limited in scope. Others fear that new ways of doing business—combined with computer systems—have reduced people's control over their personal affairs. On the other hand, representatives of those private firms and government agencies that have an interest in expanding their computerized information systems frequently argue hard against legal limits or substantial accountability to people about whom records are kept. They deny that problems exist, or they argue that the reported problems are exaggerated in importance. The contention is that proposed regulations are either too vague or burdensome and that new regulations about information systems would do more harm than good. The proponents of unregulated computerization are wealthy, organized, and aligned with the antiregulatory sentiments that have dominated the United States federal politics during the last fifteen years. Consequently, they have effectively blocked many attempts to preserve personal privacy through regulation.

Managers and professionals in business organizations and public agencies characterize their searches for information about people in limited and pragmatic terms. They emphasize how they want to improve their rationality in making specific decisions, such as: whom to hire, to whom to extend a loan, to whom to rent an apartment, and whom to arrest. These searches for personal information are sometimes fair and sometimes invasive of their privacy from the viewpoint of individuals.

Some of the key policy debates about computerization and privacy of personal records reveal conflicting values, not just conflicting interests. There are at least five major value orientations that influence the terms of key debates (Kling, 1978). These values can also help us understand the social repercussions of computer-based surveillance technologies:

Private Enterprise Model. The preeminent consideration is profitability of financial systems, with the highest social good being the profitability of both the firms providing and the firms utilizing the systems. Other social goods such as consumers' privacy or the desires of government agencies for data are secondary concerns.

Statist Model. The strength and efficiency of government institutions are the highest goals in order for government to access personal data on citizens. The need for mechanisms to enforce citizens' obligations to the state will always prevail over other considerations.

Libertarian Model. Civil liberties, such as those specified by the United States Bill of Rights, are to be maximized in any social choice. Other social purposes such as profitability or welfare of the state would be secondary when they conflict with the prerogatives of the individual.

Neo-Populist Model. The practices of public agencies and private enterprises should be easily intelligible to ordinary citizens and be responsive to their needs. Societal institutions should emphasize serving the "ordinary person."

Systems Model. Financial systems must be technically well organized, efficient, reliable, and aesthetically pleasing.

In different instances, policies and developments may support, conflict with, or be independent of these five value models. Each of them, except the Systems Model, has a large number of supporters and a long tradition of support within the United States. Thus, computing developments that are congruent with any of these positions might be argued to be in "the public interest." Information entrepreneurialism is most directly aligned with the Private Enterprise Model for guiding social action. But, the information capitalist approach can also support statist values in cases where public agencies use computerized information systems to model and explore alternative revenue-generating programs, to assess the effectiveness of social programs, or to track scofflaws through networks of records systems. It is conceivable that information entrepreneurialism could support neo-populist consumer control, by constructing databases that report on the quality of commercial products and services, or by enhancing access to government records systems. However, such uses are extremely rare, and are not accessible to the majority of people, who are not computer savvy. It is difficult to imagine that many new computerized systems would, on balance, automatically support libertarian values. In the last part, for example, we examined how electronic mail, which is stored in computer systems, can lead to losses of privacy between correspondents. However, enhanced privacy regulations reduce the extent to which computerized systems that support statist or private enterprise values further erode personal privacy in the United States.

The next six selections in this part illustrate how debates about computerization and privacy are anchored in these value positions. The debates about computer file matching pit civil libertarian against statist values. The debates about the proposed Clipper chip and government wiretapping pit statist values against libertarian and private enterprise values. And the debates about direct mail marketing pit private enterprise values against neo-populist values.

Computer File Matching

Government agencies are often charged with regulatory and policing activities—social control on a large scale. Information about the activities of potential or real lawbreakers is a critical resource for their operations. But privacy issues have taken on a new form and a new urgency with the advent of computer matching, a technique involving large databases with unrelated purposes that are cross-checked for consistency. For example, a state's automobile registration records might be matched against tax records, looking for individuals who own expensive cars but who declared only small incomes. Computer matching has been used to track down and withhold tax refunds from parents whose child support payments are in arrears; to ferret out young adult males who have failed to register for the draft; to detect ineligible welfare and/or food stamp recipients; and to locate former students with delinquent loan payments. Advocates of this approach, such as Richard Kusserow in Chapter E, argue that it is simply a tool necessary to carry out institutional mandates (e.g., helping to ensure that fathers pay child support). Critics rarely object to the specific ends to which matching has been put so far. They would like to see fathers pay their required child support, to reduce welfare cheating, and so on. At the same time, they see matching as Big Brother's encroachment on individual privacy. Today, the examples of computer matching are relatively benign, but there are no legal guarantees that the uses may not become more and more intrusive as we enter the twenty-first century.

Matching can assist in controlling various illegal activities, which is why the 1984 Deficit Reduction Act required all states to participate in matching programs. Although the precise number of matches that have been conducted is difficult to determine because of the lack of a comprehensive reporting mechanism, the United States Congress's Office of Technology Assessment (OTA) testified that the number of computer matches nearly tripled between 1980 and 1983. OTA also conducted a survey on 20% of the federal-level computer matching programs that were carried out between 1980 and 1985. Even within that limited number of matching programs, agencies had exchanged 7 billion records. Moreover, estimates of the magnitude of computer matching benefits reported ranged from $4 to $54 for each $1 spent on a match (United States General Accounting Office, 1993).

In Chapter D, John Shattuck reviews various dangers of computer matching, among them the idea that matching involves a presumption of guilt.[3] He also anticipates a criticism in a 1993 study by the U.S. General Accounting Office that the guidelines for overseeing matching efforts are

---

[3] This presumption may also appear in other forms of computerized data analysis, for example, profiling techniques (described in Clarke, 1988). Such a situation was poignantly portrayed in the 1988 film *Stand and Deliver*. This (true) story involves a group of Hispanic East Los Angeles high school students, whose scores on the Advance Placement Examination in calculus were challenged by the Educational Testing Service due to "unusual patterns" of answers. No other evidence of cheating was presented, and when the students ultimately elected to retake the examination, all of them passed.

much too weak and ineffective. Kusserow illustrates a "statist" value position[4] and Shattuck's chapter illustrates a civil libertarian argument.

This debate illustrates some of the ways that statist and libertarian advocates frame privacy issues. Since this debate was first published in 1984, the United States Congress passed the Computer Matching Privacy and Protection Act of 1988.[5] The matching law permits government agencies to compare information from two or more sources to detect discrepancies, which are then examined to see if fraud or some other type of abuse has taken place. It also gives people affected by adverse findings in a matching process a way to appeal, and requires that people be notified thirty days in advance of the cutoff of benefits.

Many of the issues raised in this debate also surface in other statist-libertarian debates over required identity cards to streamline healthcare services or to reduce the number of illegal immigrants in the United States (Bourke, 1994; Davies, 1996).

Wiretapping, Encryption, and the Clipper Chip

In the next selection, "Clipper Chip Will Reinforce Privacy," computer scientist Dorothy Denning supports a new Digital Telephony law that the U.S. Department of Justice and its Federal Bureau of Investigation proposed in 1992. This law would require telecommunications service providers to assist government agencies in tapping conversations and communications. In the United States, the Omnibus Crime and Safe Streets Act of 1968 permits wiretapping only to investigate specific serious felonies if: the targeted communications device is likely being used to facilitate the crime; normal investigative procedures have been used with past failure and future success is unlikely, or they are too dangerous to use.[6] Private taping of phone conversations is a social taboo in the United States. However, federal law, which applies to interstate phone calls, requires the consent of at least one party. But California and a few other states require that all

---

[4] "The strength and efficiency of government institutions is the highest goal. Government needs access to personal data on citizens. The need for mechanisms to enforce obligations to the state will always prevail over other considerations."

[5] Computer Matching Privacy Act, Pub. L. No. 100-503, 102 Stat. 2507 (1988), as amended by Pub. L. No. 101-56, 103 Stat. 149 (1989) (codified within paragraphs of 5 U.S.C. Sec 552a). "As a result of this Act, an agency can disclose records that will be used in a computer matching program only pursuant to a written agreement between the agency and the receiving agency. 5 U.S.C. Sec 552a(o). The Act specifies the agreement should contain provisions that provide notice, verify accuracy, ensure security and ensure retention for only as long as necessary. idem, Additionally, before an agency can make a major decision using the records via a matching program, the Act requires the agency to independently verify the information and give the data subject the opportunity to contest the findings. idem, Sec 552a(p)" (Trubow, 1992).

[6] This account is based on an FBI official's testimony (U.S. Office of Technology Assessment, 1994: 116) and Landau et al. (1994). Laws about wiretapping vary from one country to another.

parties consent to the private taping of an instate phone conversation. As an extreme example, a woman in New York State was granted a divorce after her husband taped her phone conversations (Geyelin, 1991).[7]

According to testimony by an official of the Federal Bureau of Investigation, fewer than 1000 wiretaps were authorized at the local, state, and federal levels in the United States in 1992 (U.S. Office of Technology Assessment, 1994: 116, note 10). FBI officials fear that new encryption devices will scramble telephone calls so effectively that a simple phone tap would not let them actually hear an intelligible voice. They have been eager to promote a specific family of encryption methods that would make it easy to unscramble encrypted phone calls when a wiretap was authorized through a court order. One of the most controversial portions of the FBI's proposal was the provision that certain federal agencies would be designated to hold the keys for all conversations, even those that were not authorized for wiretapping.

In addition, new digital switching systems could mix diverse phone calls on the same line in such a way that it could be hard for a tap to isolate a single specific phone line and conversation. FBI officials argued that they needed new help from telephone companies and other telecommunications services to be able to effectively tap phones in the future. The FBI argued that telecommunications systems and networks are often used in the furtherance of criminal activities including organized crime, racketeering, extortion, kidnapping, espionage, terrorism, or trafficking in illegal drugs, and that the agency would be ineffective without an ability to conduct wiretaps. Denning's article articulates these issues from the viewpoint of the FBI and also explains some of the subtle technicalities that underlie this proposal and subsequent debates.

The proposed Digital Telephony law ignited a firestorm of controversy. A previous article by Denning advocating her positions appeared in *Communications of the ACM* along with eight critical commentaries and one sympathetic commentary by William A. Bayse, an Assistant Director of the FBI's Technical Services Division. The criticisms came primarily from two major value positions: civil libertarian and private enterprise. Chapter G, by Marc Rotenberg (a lawyer who then directed CPSR's Washington office), illustrates a civil-libertarian analysis. Rotenberg acknowledges the legitimacy of wiretapping in special cases. But he is wary of the FBI's proposal because they haven't documented their case.

Some people noted that the FBI exaggerated the importance of wiretaps in investigating terrorism or kidnapping. In fact, the vast majority of wiretaps are used to investigate drug cases and organized crime. In an earlier publication, Rotenberg (1993) also observed that the FBI has not

---

[7] The state of New York has relatively restrictive divorce laws. In New York State, divorces are normally granted only for very serious breaches of marital trust, such as adultery, cruelty, and desertion.

acknowledged its history of abusing wiretaps and harassing groups that sought progressive social change, especially in the 1950s and 1960s (see Churchill and Vander Wall, 1990). Some people who saw local police departments, as well as the FBI, infiltrate, disrupt and sometimes destroy legally constituted student and church-based organizations in the 1960s learned that police agencies at all levels of government have periodically undermined important democratic movements. In this view, giving effectively absolute powers to any police agency is likely to be a destructive gesture.

Direct Mail Marketing

There is a good chance that every day you receive some mail from banks, credit card firms, political groups, and/or mail order firms with whom you've never done any business. You might enjoy some of the unsolicited mail or find some of it to be a nuisance or a waste of paper and postage. The average household in the United States receives between eight and nine pieces of promotional mail per week A confirmed mail order buyer may receive about 1000 pieces a year (Hatch, 1993). The privacy issues in direct mail differ from those of other practices in that the recipients of unwanted mail or phone calls are not deprived of jobs or important services. At worst, it can seem to be a manageable nuisance. One key issue is the question, "How did they get my name?"

In Chapter H, "Privacy: How Much Data Do Direct Marketers Really Need?," Denison Hatch argues that direct mail marketers often collect much more personally sensitive data than they need. He argues that direct mail marketing firms should regulate their own behavior in a way that is respectful of potential customers' sense of comfort. Hatch is not a strong libertarian. He is, in fact, quite critical of "the forces arrayed against us —the media, government, liberal do-gooders, as well as those in our own industry whose zeal for profits overwhelms their common sense and decency." Even so, Hatch argues that direct mailers should be sensitive to public concerns out of self-interest, and regulate their own behavior through specific "opt-out" and fair information practices lest they be regulated.

Robert Posch, a vice-president of legal affairs for Doubleday Book and Music Clubs, argues vehemently against Hatch's concerns about the public's annoyance with some of the sloppy direct mail–phone marketing campaigns. He argues that the Mail Preference Service (MPS), which has allowed about 3 million people to opt out of receiving unsolicited direct mail, is primarily a public relations device.[8] Writing in *Direct Marketing*, he

---

[8] You can contact the Mail Preference Service at P.O. Box 9008, Farmingdale, NY 11735. You can also contact the Direct Marketing Association's Telephone Preference Service at P.O. Box 9014, Farmingdale, NY 11735.

argues: "Our opponents are competitive media (television, magazines, newspapers, etc.) which have the power to editorialize and create value perceptions in their product." Posch wants advertising mail to be treated as (commercial) free speech and to be given First Amendment protections. He is a staunch advocate of private enterprise values. Posch's article also points to schisms in the business world—between mailing list services that facilitate direct mail–phone campaigns and print and television media that thrive on mass advertising.

Individual, Regulatory, and Market Approaches for Balancing Personal Privacy with Other Social Values

The preceding selections illustrate how value commitments pervade the debates about computerization, privacy, and social control. Even so, some people do not appreciate the value issues in these debates and do not find extensive personal record keeping objectionable, arguing that "If you haven't done anything wrong, you have nothing to worry about." They think of record keeping that fits the routine behavior of legitimate organizations; banks wanting to know credit histories, courts wanting to know prior criminal records, and so on.

Computer-based information systems can be used in a myriad of ways that fit organizational practices. Many of these practices are legitimate; some may be questionable; and some may even be illegal.[9] Problems arise under a variety of circumstances, for example, when the records about people are inaccurate and they are unfairly denied a loan, a job, or housing. In large-scale record systems (with millions of records) there are bound to be inaccuracies. But people have few rights to inspect records about themselves except for credit records. During the last thirty years, people have lost control over their records. Increasingly, courts have ruled that records about a person belong to an organization, and the person to whom they apply cannot restrict their use. Consequently, inaccurate police records, medical records, employment histories, and the like can harm people without their explicit knowledge about why they are having unusual difficulties.

Many of the issues of data ownership are complex and controversial in themselves. For example, today there are major controversies about whether people who test positive for HIV should be able to keep that information completely private. In principle, the question has nothing to

---

[9] Especially worrisome are the IRS audits that have been conducted at the directive of the CIA and FBI for the sole purpose of harassing political activists who held views with which key elected officials disagreed. For example, during Richard Nixon's presidency, the White House staff compiled a list of "enemies" whom they directed the FBI and IRS to harass. This example also illustrates how information collected for ostensibly benign ends may be pressed into the service of malevolent goals.

do with computer systems. The controversy focuses in part on the public good served by being able to identify HIV carriers versus the concern that many people may avoid HIV testing if they cannot be assured of the privacy of their test results. In practice, the ability of organizations to share files electronically makes it more likely that personal information can pass across organizational, state, and national boundaries if it is shared at all.

This approach has a certain clarity, but it is misleading as well. First, almost everyone recognizes *some* point at which one's personal activities are nobody else's business.[10] A person may wish only a specific party to know certain information: the bank to know the purpose of a loan, the doctor to know the reasons for a visit, and so on. Second, as the White House "enemies" list and the Japanese-American incarceration sadly show, it cannot be assumed that (legally obtained) information will always be used for legal and ethical purposes. Last, in a society where so many records are not under the control of individual citizens, and are unavailable for people to review for accuracy, people may be denied key social goods (like employment, housing, or credit) when inaccurate information about them is passed through the files of businesses and public agencies without audit.

Studies of existing records have revealed widespread inaccuracies and ambiguities, with some state criminal history systems having a majority of their records being inaccurate or incomplete. As Kenneth C. Laudon (1986) demonstrates, a person's arrest record almost always remains "in the system" regardless of the disposition of the case (conviction, dismissal of charges, etc.). All too often, the records show no disposition whatsoever. And many employers are unwilling to hire applicants with an arrest record, no matter how the case against them was eventually resolved. Laudon also found that employers and apartment house owners, not just police, were major users of criminal history systems.

Many citizens have grown so accustomed to detailing their medical histories and handing over their social security numbers that they scarcely give the matter a second thought. Probably few of them realize the extent to which computerization provides a record of individual activities. An electronic trail of one's whereabouts is available via records of Electronic Funds Transfers (EFTs), airline reservation systems, rental car agencies, telephone calls, and credit card purchases. These records may be used for salutary purposes in certain emergency situations. The movements of accused killer Ramon Salcido were reportedly traced by monitoring his

---

[10] Just where that point lies doubtless reflects not only one's personal value system, but also one's conception of privacy. Rule *et al.* (1980) distinguish between *aesthetic* privacy ("restriction of personal information as an end in itself") and *strategic* privacy ("restriction of personal information as a means to some other end"). The first notion is clearly wider in scope.

ATM transactions.[11] But in less extreme circumstances, certain aspects of one's life are arguably a private matter.

Some video stores, for example, maintain an ongoing record of each customer's rentals. The sale of lists of videos rented by specific customers was protected by the Federal Video Privacy Protection Act in 1988, but stores can still sell lists that indicate the category of videos that one rents (i.e., political thrillers, foreign movies, and perhaps much more refined categories). Given cheap, long-term information storage, combined with interconnected data systems, it becomes progressively difficult for anyone to escape the record of activities that have long passed. Diverse personal information is subject to compromise and abuse any time that an unauthorized party gains access to it. There is plenty of evidence that today's large-scale computer systems are not adequately secure. (Issues concerning the reliability and security of computer systems are discussed in Part VII of this volume.)

A huge fraction of the literature about computerization, social control, and privacy refers to regulatory strategies for striking fair and sound balances between value conflicts and interests. These regulatory strategies vary widely from one country to another. For example, Sweden instituted a nationwide Data Inspection Board in 1973, which licenses all databases with significant personal records (Flaherty, 1989: 93–94). In contrast with this highly centralized and bureaucratic approach, the United States regulates few uses of personal data. And Hiramatsu (1993:74) notes that "Traditionally, the Japanese have not been very sensitive to the right of privacy."

The Fair Credit Reporting Act of 1970 (15 U.S.C. 1681) was the first comprehensive piece of Federal legislation to give consumers legal protections from difficulties of inaccurate credit records. The Act requires credit bureaus to have "reasonable procedures" for ensuring that the information they collect and disseminate is accurate. It permits consumers to see any credit information that has been used to deny them a loan, and also contains provisions for consumers to contest inaccurate information or to fill in incomplete information. But few people check their credit records with major data brokers like TRW until they have been denied a loan. It can then take precious months to straighten out inaccurate records or problems of mistaken identity. As a United States government report aptly noted:

> The fact that the Fair Credit Reporting Act will enable him to get errors in the record corrected can be small and bitter comfort to a traveler stranded in a

---

[11] It was also reported that authorities changed Salcido's credit ceiling to "unlimited" in order to forestall the possibility that he might become violent if denied ATM funds at some point (*RISKS-FORUM Digest*, Vol. 8, No. 62 [April 24, 1989]).

strange city late at night because information about his credit-card account status was inaccurately reported to an independent authorization service.[12]

In 1974, the United States Congress passed a Federal Privacy Act that embodies five major principles of fair information practices.[13] Although the Privacy Act applied only to federal agencies, these principles have influenced many people's thinking about an appropriate structure for regulating other personal records systems:

1. There must be no secret personal data record keeping system.
2. There must be a way for individuals to discover what personal information is recorded and how it is used.
3. There must be a way for individuals to prevent information about themselves, obtained for one purpose, from being used or made available for other purposes without their consent.
4. There must be a way for individuals to correct or amend a record of information about themselves.
5. An organization creating, maintaining, using, or disseminating records of identifiable personal data must assure the reliability of the data for its intended use and must take reasonable precautions to prevent misuses of the data. (U.S. Office of Technology Assessment, 1994)

The Privacy Act gives individuals the right to access much of the personal information about them kept by federal agencies. The Privacy Act of 1974 also established a Privacy Protection Study Commission, which in 1977 issued a substantial report on its findings and recommendations. Although computerization was not a focal point in the report, it is never far below the surface.

The Commission made 155 recommendations to develop "fair information practices." Many of these recommendations gave people the right to know what records are kept about them, to inspect records for accuracy, to correct (or contest) inaccuracies, to be informed when records were transferred from one organization to another, and so on. Less than a handful of these proposals were enacted into federal law.

In the last fifteen years, numerous privacy laws have been introduced into various state legislatures and into the United States Congress. Most of these laws were effectively killed by representatives of the industries whose actions would have been constrained. Even so, a few laws have passed where organizations have had a strong interest in drawing customers with promises of confidentiality. The Right to Financial Privacy Act of

---

[12] From Chapter 1 of the Privacy Protection Study Commission report. Also see Chapter 2 of that report for one of the better statements of placing credit records in the context of an integrated information policy. For a harrowing example, see Riley (1990).

[13] Privacy Act of 1974, Pub. L. No. 93-579, 88 Stat. 1897 (codified at 5 U.S.C. Sec 552a).

1988[14] and the Family Educational Right to Privacy Act[15] enable the right of access and review by the data subject, require that data be accurate, and place limitations on access by third parties (Trubow, 1992). In addition, the Video Privacy Protection Act of 1988[16] prohibits disclosure of personal information in video rental records, and the Cable Communications Policy Act of 1984[17] regulates the disclosure of cable television subscriber records. But these few national laws are exceptions. Aside from the regulation of personal records maintained by federal agencies, whole domains of record keeping and record sharing, such as medical, employment, and insurance records, are open to the preferences of the record-keeping organizations. In discussing the regulations about telecommunications in the United States, law professor George Trubow observes:

> Subsequent to the break-up of our Bell System, a variety of entrepreneurs have begun to provide telecommunications services which vary from state to state and are virtually unregulated with respect to customer information practices. "Caller I.D." for instance, has been approved in some states without any opportunity for the caller to block disclosure of his phone number; other states have required this option. Additionally, the regional Bell companies which replaced the national Bell System have recently been permitted to develop and market data bases so they themselves can supply information about customers; previously, message-switching was the principal function of the "Baby Bells." (Trubow, 1992)

Analysts respond in diverse ways to this state of affairs. Private enterprise advocates like Robert Posch and statist advocates like Richard Kusserow are relatively happy and criticize additional legislation as hampering the competitiveness of business or the efficiency of government agencies. Civil libertarians like Marc Rotenberg and management professor H. Jeff Smith (1993, 1994) seek policies and laws that give people fair protections against record keeping and information sharing practices that harm people and that do not result in a compelling social good.

Civil libertarians face difficult dilemmas because new technologies can support new services or organizational practices that can reduce people's privacy. There are a few technologies, such as encryption, where more powerful methods can enhance the privacy of communicants. But encryption is the rare example contrasting with the diverse technologies for collecting data, storing, manipulating, retrieving, portraying, and communicating it.[18]

---

[14] Right to Financial Privacy Act, 12 U.S.C. Secs 3401.3422 (1988).

[15] Family Educational Right to Privacy Act, 20 U.S.C. Sec 1232g (1988).

[16] The Video Privacy Protection Act, 18 U.S.C. Sec 2710 (1988).

[17] 8 631, Pub. L. No. 98-549, 98 Stat. 2779 (codified at 47 U.S.C. 551).

[18] Some private enterprise advocates, like Robert Posch (1994) argue that networking technologies also enhance personal privacy because they are decentralized, and they enable people to shop in the privacy of their own homes through telemarketing.

In the United States, privacy laws tend to be reactive—to be enacted after some explicit damage has been documented. For example, the Telephone Consumer Protection Act of 1991[19] was enacted after many people were sick and tired of receiving numerous prerecorded telephone solicitations when they were selected with autodialers and specialized databases. After a reporter obtained a list of videos rented by Robert Bork, a nominee for the United States Supreme Court in 1987, Congress passed the Video Privacy Protection Act in 1988 (Flaherty, 1989:451).[20] Some civil libertarians believe that passing privacy protection laws is insufficient, since the United States legal system now puts the burden of enforcement on individuals who have been harmed and who must seek redress through the courts. Historian David Flaherty concluded his study of privacy protections in Germany, Sweden, France, Canada, and the United States with the observation that an agency to enforce privacy laws is a necessary part of an effective regulatory apparatus (Flaherty, 1989:381–385).

Some civil libertarians who have been long-term observers of the dramas of computerization and weak public privacy protections in the United States and Canada have become discouraged with the possibility of creating an effective protective framework based on the current regulatory approaches. Kenneth Laudon develops a new approach in Chapter K, "Markets and Privacy." He argues that giving people property rights in data about themselves and creating markets where people can receive fair compensation for data about themselves is a viable alternative. Laudon provides a broad sketch of his approach and anchors it within interesting economic theories. The core issues are important: that personally sensitive data can have economic value, and that individuals can make the trade-offs between their preferences for privacy and the value of the data that they could sell. Unfortunately, Laudon doesn't examine the nitty-gritty details. Could an insurance company reduce its rates by 20% to clients who are willing to share all of their medical data? Would personal privacy be primarily a luxury, or would most data sell for so little that only those who don't care or are relatively poor would be very open? Even so, Laudon's market proposal sets a controversial new direction for structuring privacy protection and information access.

One other limitation of Laudon's approach is that people are now required to use certain documents such as drivers' licenses and Social Security Numbers (SSNs) as forms of identification. In the selection "What To Do When They Ask for Your Social Security Number," Chris Hibbert tells us about the history and controls over the use of the SSN. He tells us why our SSNs are poor identifiers. Hibbert takes an activist stance and encourages us to disclose our SSNs as infrequently as possible. Hibbert is

[19] Public Law No. 102-243, 105 Stat. 2394.
[20] Members of Congress may have been concerned about their being embarrassed if a reporter publicized their viewing preferences.

interested in making laws effective by encouraging people to know their rights and to argue for them when they are asked for personally sensitive data. His article builds on a deep American tradition of informed citizens actively protecting their rights.[21]

The Continuing Growth of Personal Record Systems and Supporting Technologies

During the next decades we expect to see new streams of services whose technologies include computer components such as: on-line, household-oriented, medical diagnostic systems, vehicle identification and location systems, "smart cards" for shoppers, and so on. These information services attract customers, in part, by giving them a little more control over some part of their lives. But in collecting personally sensitive data and placing it in organizational matrices of information-sharing arrangements whose nature is not well understood by nonspecialists, such systems also reduce many people's effective control over the use of information about themselves ("privacy"). What are the forces that underlie the expansion of organizations' gathering records about people's lives?

One view is that bureaucracies have a natural appetite for information, since information represents a source of power.[22] A second explanation is proposed by James B. Rule and his colleagues (1980), who argue that much of the pressure for information gathering stems from public demand that organizations make "fine-grained" discriminations in determining eligibility for goods and services. If, for example, all citizens were entitled to free health care, the need to collect information about insurance and employment would disappear. If all car drivers paid similar rates (rather than receiving "good driver discounts" and paying higher rates for many driving offenses), the demands for driver history information would be reduced.

Mark Ackerman, Jonathan Allen, and I examine a third view in the final selection of this part, "Information Entrepreneurialism, Information Technologies, and the Continuing Vulnerability of Privacy." We link the adoption and use of new computer technologies for personal record systems to a set of social practices we refer to as *information entrepreneurialism*. Information entrepreneurial explanations focus on the active attempts of

---

[21] Several footnotes in this article give you contacts for various credit, direct mail marketing, and medical recorders brokers to take more control over your records. Also see Robert Ellis Smith's *Our Vanishing Privacy* and "Privacy Survival Guide" (The Privacy Rights Clearinghouse, 1994) for numerous additional guidelines and points of contact. You can find their gopher at URL:gopher://pwa.acusd.edu:70/11/USDinfo/privacy.

[22] When this attitude is coupled with a distorted sense of what constitutes national security, information collected on private citizens may go completely unchecked. Herbert Mitgang (1989) summarizes FBI files on some thirty-five artists and writers, including such "security risks" as E. B. White, William Faulkner, and Georgia O'Keeffe.

coalitions within organizations to organize production in such a way as to take advantage of changes in society and information technology. The internal structure of North American organizations has been transformed in the late twentieth century by the rise of professional managers who have been trained and rewarded to pursue managerial strategies that depend on data-intensive analysis techniques, such as precision direct mail marketing and data mining (Blattberg *et al.*, 1994).

Information entrepreneurial practices are made efficacious by some of the major social transformations in industrialized society over the past century: the increasing mobility of populations, the growth of nationwide organizations, and the increasing importance of indirect social relationships. Informaticn entrepreneurial practices are also encouraged by the development of more cost-effective technologies for managing large-scale databases and making fast computations. Analysts organize, implement, and utilize information systems to improve marketing, production, and operations as an organization shifts its managerial style to be more information entrepreneurial. Information systems multiply as cost accounting, production monitoring, and market survey practices become a key resource in advancing the organization's competitive edge. Only a small fraction of these information systems contain personally sensitive data. But across the United States, these can lead to hundreds, if not thousands, of new personal record systems created every year.

We argue that information entrepreneurialism relies on a set of skills that people are likely to learn by participating in specific social worlds including academic programs (such as MBA degree programs) and professional associations. We examined some popular MBA texts about information systems, and found that their discussions of privacy issues were relatively superficial. Schooling is, however, just one stage in learning and refining a new world view for many of the managers who seek to innovate. The business press publishes (and exaggerates) stories of computerization efforts that promise better markets and profits. Magazines like *The Harvard Business Review* and *Business Week* publish stories about using information technology, including data systems with privacy dimensions, for competitive advantage. But they rarely highlight the privacy issues in their enthusiasm to excite managerial readers about new ways of conceiving of business opportunities. In addition, professional associations help managers learn diverse approaches to their trades. However, some professions' (e.g., marketing, finance, and operations management) computerization strategies play an important role. Professional associations in these fields offer talks, workshops, and publications for their members that also help popularize key aspects of information entrepreneurialism.

Professor David Linowes started Chapter B with the provocative claim, "Privacy invaders are all around us." Mark Ackerman, Jonathan Allen, and I believe that "privacy invaders" can be information entrepreneurs; and they are made rather than born. Our article is a provocative sketch of the social system that rewards informational entrepreneurship, and a look at some of the ways that talented people learn the relevant skills and orientation.

Conclusion

Debates about computerization and fair information practices will not go away, even though they catch public attention intermittently. For a variety of "sensible" social reasons, organizations expand their computerized record systems and their use of "dataveillance" techniques. It is difficult to document cases of real harm, because few organizations collect such information systematically.[23] Consequently, those who see people losing control and organizations becoming less accountable place a lot of weight on the relatively small number of well-documented problems. But, we wonder, is this an appropriate state of affairs? What social costs are we incurring as we wait for problems to become visible or to mount up until regulation—however late—becomes necessary?

In the meantime, computer professionals play key roles in expanding the variety and uses of personnel systems. But, given that many such systems raise important ethical issues, the question arises as to why some computer professionals often seem untroubled by their advocacy. Some may argue that they are unaware of any ethical repercussions. Others maintain that computer science is a technical discipline, unconnected with value questions. Still others say that "If I don't do it, somebody else will anyway." We examine these and other ethical matters in Part VIII.

Sources

Linowes, David (1993). "Your Personal Information Has Gone Public." *Illinois Quarterly* (6)2, 22–24.

Murphy, Gerald (ed.) (no date). Bill of Rights of the U.S. Constitution. Distributed by the Cybercasting Services Division of the National Public Telecomputing Network (NPTN).

Shattuck, John (1984). "Computer Matching is a Serious Threat to Individual Rights." *Communications of the ACM* (27)6(June), 538–541.

Kusserow, Richard P. (1984). "The Government Needs Computer Matching to Root Out Waste and Fraud." *Communications of the ACM* (27)6(June), 542–545.

Denning, Dorothy (1994). "Clipper Chip will Reinforce Privacy." *Insight* (October 24), 18–20.

Rotenberg, Marc (1994). "Wiretapping Bill: Costly and Intrusive." *Insight* (October 24), 20–22.

Laudon, Ken (1996). "Markets and Privacy." *Communications of the ACM.*

---

[23] In late 1992, the Privacy Rights Clearinghouse in San Diego, California began a hotline (1-619-298-3396 and e-mail prc@teetot.acusd.edu) for consumer complaints and questions. In two years it has received about 20,000 calls.

Posch, Robert (1994). "Direct Marketing is Not a Significant Privacy Threat" (published as) "After MPS—Then what?" *Direct Marketing* (56)11(March), 63–64.
Hatch, Dennison (1994). "How Much Data Do Direct Marketers Really Need?" (published as) "Privacy: How Much Data Do We Really Need? *Target Marketing,* 17(2)(February), 35–40.
Hibbert, Chris (1994). "What to do When they Ask for Your SSN." *Computer Professionals for Social Responsibility* (November). (RK Edited excerpt, 5 pages).
Kling, Rob, Mark Ackerman, and Jonathan P. Allen. "How the Marriage of Management and Computing Intensifies the Struggle for Personal Privacy: Value Conflicts and Social Change."

References

Bennett, Colin J. (1992). *Regulating Privacy: Data Protection and Public Policy in Europe and the United States.* Cornell University Press, Ithaca.
Blattberg, Robert C., Rashi Glazer, and John D. C. Little. (Eds.) (1994). *The Marketing Information Revolution.* Harvard Business School Press, Boston.
Bourke, Michael K. (1994). *Strategy and Architecture of Health Care Information Systems.* Springer, New York.
Burnham, David (1983). *The Rise of the Computer State.* Random House, New York.
Calhoun, Craig (1992). *The Infrastructure of Modernity: Indirect Social Relationships, Information Technology, and Social Integration,* in H. Haferkamp and N. Smelser (eds.), *Social Change and Modernity.* University of California Press, Berkeley.
Churchill, Ward, and Jim Vander Wall (1990). *The COINTELPRO Papers: Documents from the FBI's Secret Wars Against Domestic Dissent.* South End Press, Boston.
Clarke, Roger C. (1988). "Information Technology and Dataveillance." *Communications of the ACM* (31)5(May), 498–512. [Reprinted in Charles Dunlop and Rob Kling (eds.) (1991). *Computerization and Controversy: Value Conflicts and Social Choices.* Academic Press, San Diego.]
Culnan, Mary J. (1993). "How Did They Get My Name? An Exploratory Investigation of Consumer Attitudes Toward Secondary Information Use." *MIS Quarterly* (17)3(September), 341–363.
Davies, Simon (1996). "Dystopia on the Health Superhighway." *The Information Society* 12(1).
Denning, Dorothy (1993) "To Tap or Not to Tap." *Communications of the ACM* (36)3(March), 26–35.
Dunlop, Charles, and Rob Kling (eds.) (1991). *Computerization and Controversy: Value Conflicts and Social Choices.* Academic Press, San Diego.
Flaherty, David H. (1989). *Protecting Privacy in Surveillance Societies: the Federal Republic of Germany, Sweden, France, Canada, and the United States.* University of North Carolina, Chapel Hill.
Garrow, David J. (1994). *Liberty and Sexuality: the Right to Privacy and the Making of Roe V. Wade.* Macmillan, New York.
Geyelin, Milo (1991). "Husband's Wiretap is Grounds for Divorce, New York Judge Rules." *Wall Street Journal* (Monday, November 11), B3(W), B3(E), col 4.
Hatch, Denison (1993). "The True Cost of Our Excesses." *Target Marketing* (16) 12(December), 22.
Hiramatsu, Tsuyoshi (1993). "Protecting Telecommunications Privacy in Japan." *Communications of the ACM* (36)8(August), 74–77.

Hoffman, Lance (1993). "Clipping Clipper." *CACM* 36(9)(September), 15–17.

Kling, Rob (1978). "Value Conflicts and Social Choice in Electronic Funds Transfer Systems." *Communications of the ACM* (21)8(August), 642–657.

Kling, Rob (1983). "Value Conflicts and Computing Developments: Developed and Developing Countries." *Telecommunications Policy* (7)1(March), 12–34.

Landau, Susan, Stephen Kent, Clint Brooks, Scott Charney, Dorothy Denning, Whitfield Diffie, Anthony Lauck, Doug Miller, Peter Neumann, and David Sobel (1994). "Crypto Policy Perspectives." *Communications of the ACM* 37(8) (August), 115–121.

Laudon, Kenneth C. (1980). "Comment on 'Preserving Individual Autonomy in an Information-Oriented Society,' " in Lance J. Hoffmann *et al., Computer Privacy in the Next Decade,* pp. 89–95. Academic Press, New York. [Reprinted in Charles Dunlop and Rob Kling (eds.) (1991). *Computerization and Controversy: Value Conflicts and Social Choices.* Academic Press, San Diego.]

Mitgang, Herbert (1989). *Dangerous Dossiers.* Ballantine Books, New York.

Posch, Robert J., Jr. (1994). "1994." *Direct Marketing,* 57(6)(October), 68–69.

Privacy Protection Study Commission (1977). *Personal Privacy in an Information Society,* U.S. Government Printing Office, pp. 3–37. [Excerpted in Charles Dunlop and Rob Kling (eds.) (1991). *Computerization and Controversy: Value Conflicts and Social Choices.* Academic Press, San Diego.]

The Privacy Rights Clearinghouse (1994). "Privacy Survival Guide: How to Take Control of Your Personal Information," URL:gopher://pwa.acusd.edu:70/00/ USDinfo/privacy/fsenglish/fs_sg.txt.

Riley, Michael G. (1990). "Sorry Your Card is No Good: A Nightmarish Tale from the Realm of Consumer Credit Ratings." *Time Magazine* (135)15(April 9), 62.

Rotenberg, Marc (1993). Commentary on "To Tap or Not To Tap." *Communications of the ACM,* 36(3)(March), 36–39.

Rule, James, Douglas McAdam, Linda Stearns, and David Uglow (1980). *The Politics of Privacy: Planning for Personal Data Systems as Powerful Technologies.* Elsevier North-Holland, New York.

Smith, Jeff (1993). "Privacy Policies and Practices: Inside the Organizational Maze." *Communications of the ACM,* 36(12)(December), 104–119.

Smith, H. Jeff (1994). *Managing Privacy: Information Technology and Corporate America.* University of North Carolina Press, Chapel Hill.

Smith, Robert Ellis (1993). *Our Vanishing Privacy.* Loompanics, Port Townsend, WA. (Also available from Smith's *Privacy Journal,* P.O. Box 28577, Providence, RI 02908. Or call 401/274-7861.)

Trubow, George B. (1992). "The European Harmonization of Data Protection Laws Threatens U.S.Participation in Trans Border Data Flow." *Northwestern Journal of International Law & Business,* 13(1)(Spring/Summer), 159–176.

United States General Accounting Office (1993). A Study of Computer Matching. U.S. Government Printing Office, Washington, D.C. Also available at gopher: //gopher.cpsr.org:70/00/cpsr/privacy/misc_ privacy/gao_computer_matching_ failures.

U.S. Office of Technology Assessment (1994). *Information Security and Privacy in Network Environments.* OTA-TCT-606 (September). U.S. Government Printing Office, Washington, D.C.

Warren, S.D., and Brandeis, Louis D. (1890). "The Right to Privacy." *Harvard Law Review* 4(5)(March), 193–220.

Further Reading

Agre, Philip E. (1994). "Surveillance and Capture: Two Models of Privacy." *Information Society*, 10(2)(April–June), 101–127.

Cavoukian, Ann, and Don Tapscott (1995). *Who Knows: Safeguarding Your Privacy in a Networked World*. Random House, Toronto, Canada.

Clement, Andrew (1994). "Considering Privacy in the Development of Multi-media Communications." *Computer Supported Cooperative Work*, 2, 67–88.

Culnan, Mary (1993). "How Did They Get My Name?" *MIS Quarterly*, (17)3 (September), 341–363.

Donaldson, Molla S., and Kathleen N. Lohr (Ed.) (1994). *Health Data in the Information Age: Use, Disclosure, and Privacy*. National Academy Press, Washington, D.C.

Electronic Privacy Information Center (1996). *EPIC Online Guide to Privacy Resources*. EPIC, Washington, D.C. (http://www.epic.org/privacy/privacy_resources_faq.html).

Freedman, Warren (1987). *The Right of Privacy in the Computer Age*. Quorum Books, New York.

Hoffman, Lance (ed.) (1995). *Building in Big Brother*. Springer-Verlag, New York.

Johnson, Deborah G. (1994). *Computer Ethics* (second ed.) Prentice-Hall, Englewood Cliffs, NJ.

Kling, Rob, and Suzanne Iacono (1984). "Computing as an Occasion for Social Control." *Journal of Social Issues* (40)3, 77–96.

Laudon, Kenneth C. (1986). *Dossier Society: Value Choices in the Design of National Information Systems*. Columbia University, New York.

Lyon, David (1994). *The Electronic Eye: The Rise of Surveillance Society*. University of Minnesota Press, Minneapolis.

Lyon, David, and Elia Zureik (eds.) (1995). *New Technology, Surveillance and Social Control*. University of Minnesota Press, Minneapolis.

Marx, Gary (1985). "I'll Be Watching You: Reflections on the New Surveillance." *Dissent*, 32(Winter), 26–34.

Marx, Gary (1990). "The Case of the Omniscient Organization." *Harvard Business Review* (March–April), 4–12.

Platt, Charles (1993). "Nowhere to Hide: Lack of Privacy Is the Ultimate Equalizer." *Wired*, 1.5. Also available at http://www.hotwired.com/Lib/Wired/1.5/.

Privacy Protection Study Commission (1977). *Personal Privacy in an Information Society*, 052-003-00395-3. U.S. Government Printing Office, Washington, D.C.

Rubin, Michael Rogers (1988). *Private Rights, Public Wrongs: The Computer and Personal Privacy*. Ablex, Norwood.

Rule, James B. *et al.* (1980). "Preserving Individual Autonomy in an Information-Oriented Society," in Lance J. Hoffman *et al.*, *Computer Privacy in the Next Decade*, pp. 65–87. Academic Press, New York. [Reprinted in Charles Dunlop and Rob Kling (eds.) (1991). *Computerization and Controversy: Value Conflicts and Social Choices*. Academic Press, San Diego.]

Schoeman, Ferdinand David (1984). *Philosophical Dimensions of Privacy: An Anthology*. Cambridge University Press, New York.

Schoeman, Ferdinand David (1992). *Privacy and Social Freedom*. Cambridge University Press, New York.

P·A·R·T · VI

B

Your Personal Information
Has Gone Public*

David F. Linowes

Privacy invaders are all around us. We live in a social environment comprised of organizations that have an insatiable appetite for personal information. These massive information bases have developed into new and disturbing forms of potential social controls, the ramifications of which society is just beginning to understand. Computer technology makes mass surveillance efficient. Never before in the history of man has it been possible to surreptitiously monitor the personal affairs of millions of individuals. Today it is done with little or no oversight. The objectives are legitimate in most instances, but will they always be so?

Data on individuals are held by business organizations, banks, insurance companies, government organizations, schools, political and even religious organizations. People are being surprised constantly at how easy it is for others to obtain information they assume is confidential.

A New York City woman received a telephone call from a salesman offering her long-distance services. She told him she didn't make many out-of-town calls, hoping to dissuade him. He persisted, saying that was surprising since he noted that her telephone records showed frequent calls to New Jersey, Delaware, and Connecticut. When the woman demanded to know where the salesman had obtained her telephone records, he quickly hung up.

A person's telephone bill, bank checking account, and credit card records are a reflection of one's lifestyle, personal interests, and political beliefs. They reveal the books and magazines read, the political party supported, things bought, and places traveled. Computers track customers' shopping and banking habits. Cable companies, advertisers, and direct marketing firms are just some of the users.

Investigative firms offer services to many organizations, especially business corporations. When information is not readily available through legitimate channels, they routinely turn to covert and even illegal means.

One private investigative agency trained its operatives to pose as physicians on the telephone. File cards were kept on hospitals all over the country with specific instructions for soliciting information. Suggestions included items such as to call after midnight, talk with a black accent, and so on. At times, interns or nurses were paid as informants. The agency claimed a 99% success rate in obtaining the information it went after. In flyers produced for its insurance company clients, the firm boasted that it could secure medical record information without patient authorization.

Telephone taps, both legal and illegal, have been used for years to eavesdrop on personal conversations. Now computer technology makes it possible for electronic listening devices to pick out a single voice from among an entire telephone system without the targeted person ever knowing about the monitoring.

The use of electronic bugging devices is becoming increasingly common, even though it is illegal. New monitoring equipment is both inexpensive and easy to operate. For an investment of $695, anyone can purchase an Infinity Transmitter that allows for monitoring someone's home or office. After the miniature transmitter is attached to the target telephone, the eavesdropper just dials that telephone's number from any other telephone. The phone does not ring, but any sound in the room up to thirty feet away can be overheard by the caller. Other devices are attached to the phone line outside the home or business, making surveillance of telephone conversations even easier.

Sounds monitored on inexpensive baby-room monitors sold in many stores are easily adapted for listening in on a variety of radio communication frequencies. Some scanners can pick up conversations a mile or two away, making one observer comment that it was like having an open microphone in an adult bedroom.

Uses of Personal Information

Just last year, an extensive network of "information brokers" known as the Nationwide Electronic Tracing Company (NET) was uncovered. These brokers traded in stolen computer files from the Social Security Administration by bribing Social Security employees $25 for an individual's Social Security information. The information was then sold to insurance companies, employers, and attorneys.

*This article appeared in the *Illinois Quarterly*, 6(2)(1993), pp. 22–24. Reprinted with permission.

The company's brochure said that if provided with a home address, it could find a Social Security number in two hours. With a subject's name and address, the telephone numbers and addresses of up to nine current neighbors were available in two hours. A name and Social Security number were all that were needed to obtain a subject's earnings for the last ten years. An individual's complete credit history costs just $10. Driving records and criminal histories also were available.

Ironically, it was the sales brochure that tipped off authorities. NET pleaded guilty in Florida to conspiracy charges in connection with this illegal work, but the practice still continues. Some of these "information brokers" have learned from investigative firms. Its operatives simply call the Social Security Service Center pretending to be government officials and request the information, which is readily furnished. A total information base is thus created, which is a valuable resource to third parties, to be used for many unintended purposes in unexpected places.

Employee Monitoring

Privacy continues to be a fundamental workplace issue as managers are increasingly using new surveillance technology to control worker behavior. It has been estimated that employers eavesdrop on 400 million telephone conversations between workers and consumers every year. Eavesdropping is especially prevalent in the telecommunications, insurance, and banking industries where as many as 80% of the workers are subjected to telephone or computer-based monitoring. Employer eavesdropping on electronic mail messages is also widespread and currently not prohibited by federal wiretapping laws.

Two Nissan employees who trained dealers, sales staff, and mechanics on using the company's electronic mail system were fired for making disparaging e-mail remarks about a supervisor.

In 1991, two male employees of Boston's Sheraton Hotel were video-taped without their knowledge while changing clothes in their locker room. The taping was part of a drug investigation. Authorities later admitted the two men were never suspects.

The Olivetti Corporation has developed electronic ID cards called "smart badges," which track employees as they move from location to location within a building or complex. The system is designed to route telephone calls to a phone near the wearer, but such technology can also tell managers where an employee is at any given moment.

How Privacy Invasions Affect Our Lives

When personal information is taken out of context, hardships often result. Where the information is inaccurate, it can cost the individual a job, promotion, or result in denial of credit or insurance. The cases of hardship resulting from such mishandling of information are limitless.

Many of the ways information gets into a record are strange, indeed, and help create the broad concerns about privacy. In one case, a free-lance artist in southern California discovered that his doctor had erroneously written on his file that he had AIDS. The doctor explained his mistake by saying a radiologist had referred to the man as being HIV positive on a report of a CT scan.

A Roxbury, Massachusetts man was told he had to pay a 25% surcharge for disability insurance because he was an alcoholic. The man was startled because he hadn't had a drink in seven years. His medical record, however, said he had a drinking problem and had attended Alcoholics Anonymous. The man then realized that years earlier he had mentioned on an insurance application that he had gone to some AA meetings while trying to quit smoking.

Personal vulnerability when seeking insurance coverage is extensive. The general authorization form that is signed when one applies for a policy has been characterized as a "search warrant without due process." Unless specifically limited, it gives the holder the right to obtain data from any organization having information about the individual.

In addition, the agent receives information from outside investigators and centralized industry data banks. The Medical Information Bureau furnishes personal information, not just medical information, from 800 insurance companies throughout the country. Much of it is not verified, and some of it may not always be true.

The consumer credit industry is another area where mistakes in personal information can have serious consequences for individuals and families. The industry is the No. 1 source of consumer complaints in America, according to the Federal Trade Commission.

Free-lance, Washington, D.C. journalist Stephen Shaw was surprised by a call from his local bank when he applied for low-interest credit. The loan processor said Shaw had many loans on his credit report he hadn't listed on his application. In addition, the report said Shaw had moved from Washington to Winter Park, Florida where he was working as a car sales-man. Among his recent credit purchases were a new $19,000 car, $3000 in Visa charges, a $2000 IBM computer, electronic items worth more than $1300, and $7500 worth of home furnishings.

Shaw was the victim of credit-card fraud on a massive scale. In all, nearly thirty accounts under his name had been established with balances totaling nearly $100,000. Apparently someone in the Orlando area had circulated his Social Security number and it had been used to retrieve his file from a credit bureau database. Even though it has been more than a year since Shaw first discovered the problem, the phony accounts keep popping up and his credit bureau file still lists a Winter Park address.

When Consumers Union surveyed 161 credit reports, they found that one-half contained inaccuracies. Based on a sampling of 1500 reports from Equifax, Trans Union, and TRW Credit Data, a credit bureau official in New York City found that there were mistakes in as many as 43% of the credit reports they issue.

A Norwich, Connecticut doctor's car loan was held up because his credit report said he owed thousands in back taxes. The doctor was surprised to say the least since his financial condition had been first-rate. When the bank checked with TRW, the credit-reporting firm, it discovered that the doctor wasn't the only one with a problem. In fact, every taxpayer in Norwich was listed as a deadbeat.

TRW, it turned out, had made a huge mistake. A young investigator had obtained a list of taxpayers and thought they were delinquent. As a result, 1500 residents of the town were listed as tax evaders. Tax-lien data was also falsely reported in TRW files from other Vermont towns and in New Hampshire, Rhode Island, and Maine.

What Can Be Done to Help

There is a need today for a national public policy on individual information privacy protection. Most of the democracies in the world have such a policy. We do not. Such a policy would establish relationships between individuals and organizations that are essentially fair business practices.

Until such protection is enacted, we can try to help prevent abuse by following some fundamental guidelines:

1. Give out information only that is relevant to the decision at hand. And ask that it be used only for that purpose.
2. If the organization must transfer data about you to a third person, ask them to get your approval first.
3. Ask what sources the organization might contact to get additional information and how the data will be used.
4. Ask to see the records about you the organization has.

5. If a government official wants access to records about you, ask the organization to require proper authorization and then ask to be notified.

Over the last several years, the United States has lagged behind the European nations in privacy protection. Other countries have enacted wide-ranging laws that restrict the use of personal information without one's knowledge or consent. Canada and most European nations have established privacy commissions or data-protection agencies to regulate the use of personal data by the government and private companies. Even though almost all fifty states have enacted some pieces of privacy legislation, it is wholly inadequate. We need and should have federal legislation providing for a broad public policy on information privacy protections.

P·A·R·T · VI

C

The Bill of Rights of the Constitution of the United States

Prepared by *Gerald Murphy*

Amendment I

Congress shall make no law respecting an establishment of religion, or prohibiting the free exercise thereof; or abridging the freedom of speech, or of the press; or the right of the people peaceably to assemble, and to petition the government for a redress of grievances.

Amendment II

A well regulated militia, being necessary to the security of a free state, the right of the people to keep and bear arms, shall not be infringed.

Amendment III

No soldier shall, in time of peace be quartered in any house, without the consent of the owner, nor in time of war, but in a manner to be prescribed by law.

Amendment IV

The right of the people to be secure in their persons, houses, papers, and effects, against unreasonable searches and seizures, shall not be violated, and no warrants shall issue, but upon probable cause, supported by oath or affirmation, and particularly describing the place to be searched, and the persons or things to be seized.

Amendment V

No person shall be held to answer for a capital, or otherwise infamous crime, unless on a presentment or indictment of a grand jury, except in cases arising in the land or naval forces, or in the militia, when in actual service in time of war or public danger; nor shall any person be subject for the same offense to be twice put in jeopardy of life or limb; nor shall be compelled in any criminal case to be a witness against himself, nor be deprived of life, liberty, or property, without due process of law; nor shall private property be taken for public use, without just compensation.

Amendment VI

In all criminal prosecutions, the accused shall enjoy the right to a speedy and public trial, by an impartial jury of the state and district wherein the crime shall have been committed, which district shall have been previously ascertained by law, and to be informed of the nature and cause of the accusation; to be confronted with the witnesses against him; to have compulsory process for obtaining witnesses in his favor, and to have the assistance of counsel for his defense.

Amendment VII

In suits at common law, where the value in controversy shall exceed twenty dollars, the right of trial by jury shall be preserved, and no fact tried by a jury, shall be otherwise reexamined in any court of the United States, than according to the rules of the common law.

Amendment VIII

Excessive bail shall not be required, nor excessive fines imposed, nor cruel and unusual punishments inflicted.

Amendment IX

The enumeration in the Constitution, of certain rights, shall not be construed to deny or disparage others retained by the people.

Amendment X

The powers not delegated to the United States by the Constitution, nor prohibited by it to the states, are reserved to the states respectively, or to the people.

P·A·R·T · VI

D

Computer Matching Is a Serious Threat to Individual Rights*

John Shattuck

More and more frequently, government agencies have been employing a new investigative technique: the matching of unrelated computerized files of individuals to identify suspected law violators. This technique—computer matching—provides a revolutionary method of conducting investigations of fraud, abuse, and waste of government funds. It permits the government to screen the records of whole categories of people, such as federal employees, to determine who among them also falls into separate, supposedly incompatible categories, such as welfare recipients.

Computer matching raises profound issues concerning individual privacy, due process of law, and the presumption of innocence. It also poses serious questions about cost effectiveness and the internal management of government programs.

Computer Matching versus Individual Rights

To understand the impact of computer matching on individual rights, it is first necessary to grasp the difference between a computer-matching investigation and a traditional law enforcement investigation.

A traditional investigation is triggered by some evidence that a person is engaged in wrongdoing. This is true for cases of tax evasion, welfare fraud, bank robbery, or traffic speeding. The limited resources of law enforcement usually make it impracticable to conduct dragnet investigations. More important, our constitutional system bars the government from investigating persons it does not suspect of wrongdoing.

A computer match is not bound by these limitations. It is directed not at an individual, but at an entire category of persons. A computer match is initiated not because any person is suspected of misconduct, but because his or her category is of interest to the government. What makes computer matching fundamentally different from a traditional investigation is that its very purpose is to generate the evidence of wrongdoing required before an investigation can begin. That evidence is produced by "matching" two sets of personal records compiled for unrelated purposes.

There are four ways in which a computer match differs from a conventional law enforcement investigation in its impact on individual rights.

Fourth Amendment

The Fourth Amendment protects against unreasonable searches and seizures, the most blatant of which have been "fishing expeditions" directed against large numbers of people. From the "writs of assistance" used in the eighteenth century by royal revenue agents, to door-to-door searches for violations of the British tariff laws in the American colonies, to the municipal code inspections of the twentieth century to enforce health and safety standards, the principle that generalized fishing expeditions violate the right to be free from unreasonable searches has held firm in American law.

That principle is violated by computer matching. The technique of matching unrelated computer tapes is designed as a general search. It is not based on any preexisting evidence to direct suspicion of wrongdoing to any particular person. Although systematic searches of personal records are not as intrusive as door-to-door searches, the result is the same: a massive dragnet into the private affairs of many people.

Presumption of Innocence

People in our society are not forced to bear a continuous burden of demonstrating to the government that they are innocent of wrongdoing. Although citizens are obliged to obey the law—and violate it at their peril—presumption of innocence is intended to protect people against having to prove that they are free from guilt whenever the government investigates them.

Computer matching can turn the presumption of innocence into a presumption of guilt. For instance, Massachusetts welfare recipients have been summarily removed from welfare rolls as the result of a computer match. These people fought for reinstatement based on information the state neglected to consider after their names appeared as "hits" in the match.

---

*This article appeared in *Communications of the ACM* (27)6(June 1984), pp. 538–541. Reprinted with permission from the Association for Computing Machinery.

Another example of this "presumption of guilt" occurred three years ago in Florida. The state's attorney for a three-county area around Jacksonville obtained case files for all food stamp recipients in the area. He then launched fraud investigations against those receiving allotments of more than $125 a month. A federal court of appeals invalidated the file search and enjoined the investigation on the ground that the targeted food stamp recipients were put in the position of having to prove the allotment they had received was not based on fraud. Construing the Food Stamp Act, the Court held that "it did not allow the [state food stamp] agency to turn over files . . . for criminal investigation without regard to whether a particular household has engaged in questionable behavior."

Once a computer match has taken place, any person whose name appears as a "raw hit" is presumed to be guilty. In part, this is because the technology of computer matching is so compelling and in part because its purpose—the detection of fraud and waste—is so commendable. The worst abuses of computer matching, such as summary termination of welfare benefits, have occurred when authorities have casually transformed this "presumption" into a conclusive proof of guilt.

Privacy Act

The most important principle governing collection and use of personal information by the government is that individuals have a right to control information about themselves and to prevent its use without their consent for purposes wholly unrelated to those for which it was collected. This principle is imperfectly embodied in the Privacy Act of 1974.

The Privacy Act restricts disclosure by federal agencies of personally identifiable information, unless the subject consents. There are two major exceptions. The first involves a "routine use," defined as "the use of (a) record for a purpose which is compatible with the purpose for which it was collected." The second involves a "law enforcement" disclosure, which enables an agency to be responsive to a request by another agency for information relevant to the investigation of a specific violation of law. When computer matching was in its infancy, the Privacy Act was correctly perceived by several federal agencies to be a major stumbling block. The Civil Service Commission initially balked in 1977 at the plans of Health, Education, and Welfare (HEW) Secretary Joseph Califano to institute a match of federal employee records and state welfare rolls, on the grounds that the use of employee records for such a purpose would violate the Privacy Act. The Commission's General Counsel, Carl F. Goodman, stated that the proposed match could not be considered a "routine use" of employee records, since the Commission's "information on employees was not collected with a view toward detecting welfare abuses." Similarly, it could not be considered a "law enforcement" use, continued Goodman, since "at the 'matching' stage there is no indication whatsoever that a violation or potential violation of law has occurred."

This reasonable interpretation of the Privacy Act soon gave way to a succession of strained readings. Since enforcement of the Privacy Act is left entirely to the agencies it regulates, it is hardly surprising that the agencies have bent the Act to their own purposes. They have now miraculously established that computer matching is a "routine use" of personal records. All that is required, they say, is to publish each new computer matching "routine use" in the Federal Register.

The Privacy Act has now been so thoroughly circumvented by executive action that it can no longer be seen as an effective safeguard. Nevertheless, the principle underlying the Act—that individuals should be able to exercise control over information about themselves that they provide to the government—is a bedrock principle of individual privacy. That principle is at war with the practice of computer matching.

Due Process of Law

Once a computer match has taken place, it will result in a series of hits. All those identified are in jeopardy of being found guilty of wrongdoing. To the extent that they are not given notice of their situation and an adequate opportunity to contest the results of the match, they are denied due process of law.

This is precisely what has happened in several matching programs. For example, the results of Secretary Califano's Operation Match were kept secret from federal employees whose records were matched with welfare rolls, because the Justice Department viewed the investigation "as a law enforcement program designed to detect suspected violations of various criminal statutes." The Justice Department ordered the Civil Service Commission not to notify any of the federal employees whose names showed up as hits, since "[t]he premature discussion of a specific criminal matter with a tentative defendant is in our view inimical to the building of a solid prosecutorial case." In Massachusetts, welfare authorities have terminated benefits of persons showing up as hits without even conducting an internal investigation.

This approach makes a mockery of due process. Due process is the right to confront one's accuser and introduce evidence to show that the accuser is wrong. When the accuser is a computer tape, the possibility of error is substantial. Keeping the subject of a raw hit in the dark increases the likelihood that an error will go undetected.

Some Comments on the Guidelines of the Office of Management and Budget

Since 1979 computer matching at the federal level has been regulated by guidelines issued by the Office of Management and Budget (OMB). These guidelines, which were considerably looser in May 1982, are intended to "help agencies relate the procedural requirements of the Privacy Act to the operational requirements of computerized matching." Although Kusserow (Chapter E, Part VI) cites the guidelines as evidence of the federal government's concern about privacy protection, in fact, they constitute an effort to paper over the profound conflict between: (1) the Privacy Act principle that personal records are to be used by federal agencies only for purposes compatible with those for which they are compiled and (2) the computer-matching practice of joining personal records compiled for wholly unrelated purposes.

OMB's matching guidelines have rendered meaningless the central principle of the Privacy Act. In 1980, for instance, the Office of Personnel Management (OPM) published a notice in the Federal Register concerning its proposed use of personnel records for a matching program to help the Veterans' Administration (VA) verify the credentials of its hospital employees. The notice dutifully stated that the proposed match of OPM and VA records was a "routine use," which it explained as follows:

> An integral part of the reason that these records are maintained is to protect the legitimate interests of the government and, therefore, such a disclosure is compatible with the purposes for maintaining these records.

Under that broad justification any disclosure or matching of personal records would be permissible, since all federal records are purportedly maintained for the "legitimate interests of the government."

The guidelines, on which Kusserow (Chapter E) so heavily relies, contain no requirements or limitations on the conduct of computer matching in these critical areas:

1. The nature of the record systems to be matched. There are no personal records, no matter how sensitive (e.g., medical files, security clearance records, intelligence records) that are beyond the reach of computer matching for any investigative purpose.
2. The procedures to be followed in determining the validity of hits. No particular procedures are required to ensure that the subjects of hits are afforded due process of law.
3. The standards and procedures to be followed for securing OMB approval of a proposed match. Since the first guidelines were promulgated in 1979, OMB has not disapproved a single computer match.
4. The projected costs and benefits of a proposed match. The 1982 guidelines have deleted all reference to cost-benefit analyses of reports on computer matches. It is entirely at an agency's discretion whether to undertake a proposed match or to report the costs and benefits of the match.

It is impossible not to conclude that computer matching at the federal level is a huge unregulated business, the only clear effect of which to date has been the undermining of individual privacy.

Some Examples of Computer Matching

In the seven years since the technique was first used, over two hundred computer matches have been carried out. At the federal level there have been matches for a wide variety of investigative purposes, using a broad range of personal record systems of varying degrees of sensitivity.

These include matches of: federal employee records maintained by the Civil Service Commission with files of persons receiving federal Aid to Families with Dependent Children, to investigate "fraud"; federal personnel records maintained by OPM with the files of VA hospital employees, to check "accreditation"; federal personnel records of Agriculture Department employees in Illinois with Illinois state files on licensed real estate brokers, to "ascertain potential conflicts of interest"; Internal Revenue Service (IRS) records of taxpayer addresses with lists of individuals born in 1963 supplied by the Selective Service System, to locate suspected violators of the draft registration law; and Labor Department files of persons entitled to receive Black Lung benefits with Health and Human Services (HHS) records of Medicare billings, to investigate double-billing medical fraud.

These matches are only a handful of the total conducted. Even with these, little hard data are available, thanks to the extraordinarily weak oversight and reporting requirements of the OMB guidelines and to the lack of attention to this subject by Congress.

Conclusion

Computer matching is an attractive investigative technique. It appears to permit law enforcement officials to instantaneously root out all instances of a particular kind of wrongdoing in a particular segment of the population. It constitutes a general surveillance system that supposedly can detect and deter misconduct wherever it is used. It appeals to the view that "if you haven't done anything wrong, you don't have anything to worry about."

But there are heavy costs associated with computer matching, both in terms of individual rights and in terms of law enforcement expenditure. It is not at all clear that the benefits of the technique outweigh the costs.

The comparison of unrelated record systems is fraught with difficulty. Data on the computer tapes may be inaccurate or inaccurately recorded. It may present an incomplete picture. It is unlikely to be sufficient to "answer" difficult questions, such as whether a person is entitled to receive welfare or is engaged in a conflict of interest. On the other hand, computer matching erodes individual rights: the Fourth Amendment right to be free from unreasonable search, the right to the presumption of innocence, the right to due process of law, and the right to limit the government's use of personal information to the purposes for which it was collected. Moreover, the rapid and unchecked growth of computer matching leads inexorably to the creation of a de facto National Data System in which personal data are widely and routinely shared at all levels of government and in the private sector.

Recommendations

As a general framework for safeguarding individual rights, I propose the following:

1. The Privacy Act should be amended to clarify that computer matches are not ipso facto "routine uses" of personal record systems.
2. No further federal computer matches should be permitted without express congressional authorization.
3. Congress should not authorize computer matches of sensitive personal records systems (the confidentiality of which is otherwise protected by statute) such as taxpayer records maintained by the IRS, census records maintained by the Census Bureau, or bank records maintained by federally insured banking institutions.
4. No computer match should be authorized unless and until an analysis has been made of its projected costs and projected savings in the recoupment of funds owed to the government. The match should not be authorized unless the public benefit will far outweigh the cost— and unless individual rights will be protected. The results and full costs of any match should be published.
5. Procedural due process protections for the persons whose records are to be matched should be specified by statute, including the right to counsel, the right to a full hearing, and the right to confidentiality of the results of a match.

The thrust of my comments has been to raise some basic questions about computer matching. I recommend a moratorium on all further matching so Congress and the public can study the results of all computer-matching programs conducted to date and assess the long-term consequences.

In closing, I second the view of Justice William O. Douglas, when he said, "I am not ready to agree that America is so possessed with evil that we must level all constitutional barriers to give our civil authorities the tools to catch criminals."

P·A·R·T · VI

E

The Government Needs Computer Matching to Root Out Waste and Fraud*

Richard P. Kusserow

More information will be collected, stored, and retrieved in our lifetime than in all other generations combined. This information explosion, however, is creating new problems for the government manager. Crucial issues revolve around the use of computer technology to ensure that taxpayers' money is being safeguarded and to manage personal data without sacrificing individuals' rights to privacy. Predictions about the dehumanizing effects of technology heat the issues.

Unfortunately, computer matching, charged with myth and misconception, has become fuel for this emotional debate. Critics depict mere man against massive computers and evoke the specter of the Orwellian 1984 and "Big Brother." In reality, computer matching covers many processes used to detect payment errors, increase debt collection, and identify abusive grant or procurement practices. The Department of Education, for instance, uses computer matches to identify federal workers who default on student loans. The National Science Foundation screens research fund applicants against its employee and consultant lists to prevent any conflict of interest in grant awards.

My office in the federal Department of Health and Human Services (HHS) uses matches to unearth doctors who are double-billing Medicare and Medicaid for the same service. Over 230 problem health providers were removed from participation in the Medicare program in the last fiscal year—a 253% increase over the previous year. We have also matched the Social Security benefit rolls against Medicare's record of deceased patients and discovered thousands of cases of administrative error and fraud. This project alone resulted in savings of over $25 million.

Without the computer, government could not fulfill many mandated missions. Forty million Social Security checks are issued each month—an impossible feat without automated data processing. Computers are here to stay and will become even more pervasive. We are witnessing the virtual disappearance of hard copy, a development of special importance to the government manager, auditor, and investigator. Without a paper trail, government workers must use innovative techniques to meet this new challenge.

Computer matching is an efficient and effective technique for coping with today's expensive, complex, and error-prone government programs. For instance, computer matching and other innovative techniques helped my office identify $1.4 billion in savings—about a 300% increase over the previous year.

The High Cost of Errors and Fraud

Over $350 billion is paid out every year through government entitlement programs to millions of recipients. Ineligibility and payment errors cost the taxpayers billions of dollars annually. Add to this the dollars lost through loan delinquencies, excessive procurement costs, and other abuses, and the losses become even more staggering. Perceptions of waste and cheating in government programs erode public support for the programs and respect for government itself.

Government managers cannot simply rely on chance discovery, voluntary compliance, or outdated manual procedures to detect errors. They have a responsibility to use innovative techniques to monitor the expenditures of program dollars, to detect fraud, to determine who is ineligible or being paid incorrectly, and so on.

Computer Matching: Not a New Technique

Computer matching is not a new technique. The basic approach of matching one set of records to another has been used by both public and private sectors for years. Although matching predates the computer, the computer has made it quick and cost effective.

In 1977, Congress, recognizing the effectiveness of computer matching, passed Public Law 95-216. This law mandated that state welfare agencies

---

*This article appeared in *Communications of the ACM* (27)6(June 1984), pp. 542–545. Reprinted with permission from the Association for Computing Machinery.

use state wage information in determining eligibility for Aid to Families with Dependent Children (AFDC). Subsequent legislation also required similar wage matching for the Food Stamp program.

Computer matching can serve many objectives:

- assuring that ineligible applicants are not given costly program benefits;
- reducing or terminating benefits for recipients who are being paid erroneously;
- detecting fraudulent claims and deterring others from defrauding the program;
- collecting overpayments or defaulted loans more effectively; monitoring grant and contract award processes;
- improving program policy, procedures, and control.

Simply defined, computer matching is a technique whereby information within two or more records or files is compared to identify situations that could indicate program ineligibility or payment errors.

The process, however, should not and does not stop there. The computer does not decide who is getting erroneous payments and does not automatically decide who should be terminated from the payment rolls. The computer merely provides a list of items that could indicate an erroneous or aberrant situation. The matched items must be investigated by program staff. Only then can an agency determine whether a payment should be adjusted or stopped, or if the file record needs to be corrected.

Early computer-matching efforts, which acted on "raw hits" without proper follow-up, were justifiably criticized. Today, computer matching is far more effective, efficient, and less intrusive. A manual examiner had to search through all records in a file. A computer, however, picks out only those records that match and ignores all the others: it scans for aberrations only. In this sense, computer matching is far less of an invasion than 100% manual review.

President's Council on Integrity and Efficiency

In 1981, President Reagan formed the President's Council on Integrity and Efficiency (PCIE) to coordinate efforts to attack fraud and waste in expensive, government programs. One of its major activities is the Long-Term Computer Matching Project, which I cochair with the Inspector General of the Department of Labor.

Our overall objective is to expand the cost-effective use of computer matching techniques that prevent and detect fraud, abuse, and erroneous payments and, at the same time, to protect the rights and privacy of individuals. The Project does not run computer matches. Rather, through its membership of federal and state program administrators, the Project

- gathers and shares information about federal and state matching activities,
- analyzes and removes technical and administrative obstacles to computer matching, and
- fosters increased federal and state cooperation in computer-matching activities.

So far, the Project has inventoried federal and state matches, established a clearinghouse and a newsletter, and launched an effort with eight states to test standardized data extraction formats for computer matching. The standardized formats will make matching "hits" more reliable, thereby reducing the need for manual review of client files.

One of the Project's first tasks was to revise the Office of Management and Budget's (OMB) "Guidelines for Conducting Computer Matching Programs." The Guidelines were originally set forth in 1979 to implement the Privacy Act of 1974, in the context of federal computer-matching efforts. The 1982 revision streamlined paperwork requirements and reiterated requirements for privacy and security of records.

The Guidelines call for public notice of proposed matches and strict safeguards concerning use, storage, and disclosure of information from matches. In his December 1982 testimony before Senator William S. Cohen's Subcommittee on Oversight of Government Management, David F. Linowes, former chairman of the Privacy Protection Study Commission, stated that the 1982 Guidelines make "sound provisions for protecting the privacy of the individual."

Fears of a National Database on Individuals Ungrounded

A major concern is that computer matching will ultimately result in the creation of a national database of computerized information on every individual. OMB Guidelines ensure that such would be impossible. Once a match is completed, Guidelines require that the files be returned to the custodian agency or destroyed.

To be effective, computer matching must be built into the administration of a government program—not just run as an ad hoc investigation. Also, matching should be performed before payments are made, as well as used in an ongoing monitoring effort. In this way, matching stops payment errors before they occur. Prepayment screens using computer-matching techniques not only detect errors, they also deter fraud and abuse in government programs. California, for instance, routinely checks public assistance claims against wage records, saving an estimated $1 million per month in overpayments.

Computer matching is racially, sexually, and ethnically blind. No person or group is targeted.

Some Existing Privacy Safeguards

A number of privacy safeguards have already been institutionalized. "The Computer Matching Reference Paper," published by the PCIE, sets forth "purpose" standards. An agency considering a match must first conduct a study to determine the match's scope and purpose, identify agencies and records involved, and ascertain the information and follow-up actions needed. A key aspect is the assessment of the estimated costs and benefits of a match.

Another safeguard is OMB's "Model Control System." This document suggests that government officials carefully analyze the hits from a computer match to verify the data with the source agency and determine whether the hit is the result of error or abuse. For large matches, officials would have to analyze only a sample of the hits to verify the matching process. After doing this, officials should take corrective measures, proceeding cautiously against any individual where doubt exists.

A third privacy safeguard is provided by a memorandum sent by the deputy director of OMB, Joseph A. Wright, Jr., to the heads of all government agencies on December 29, 1983. That memorandum provides instructions for preparing a Computer Match Checklist, to be completed by each government agency involved in matching federal data records. This checklist and the Model Control System help agencies to comply with the Privacy Act of 1974 and the OMB Computer Matching Guidelines of May 11, 1982.

Relevant government agencies must complete this checklist immediately following their announced intent (as indicated by publication in the Federal Register) to conduct a computer match. This checklist must be on file for review by OMB, Government Accounting Office (GAO), and others interested in ensuring that safeguards are being followed to protect personal data.

Still another privacy safeguard, the PCIE reference paper, calls upon government managers to do a cost-benefit analysis both before and after a computer-matching project. In some cases it will make sense to do a pilot match based on a sample. The results of this pilot study would provide a better idea of what could be achieved from a full-scale matching project. In any event, pilot matches are subject to Privacy Act safeguards.

Finally, the OMB Matching Guidelines require government managers to prepare a matching report at least thirty days prior to the start of the match project. It would be published in the Federal Register to give relevant parties an opportunity to comment.

Conclusion

Any computer match that does not consider privacy, fairness, and due process as among its major goals is not a good project. Well-designed computer matches are cost effective.

The government's need to ensure a program's integrity need not be incompatible with the individual's right to privacy and freedom from government intrusion. The point is to balance these competing interests. Government managers have a responsibility to ensure that program funds are spent as intended by Congress. At the same time, these managers must carry out those responsibilities within the requirements and spirit of the Privacy Act. Such a balance is both possible and essential.

Additional Comments

In addressing the concerns raised by John Shattuck (Part VI, Chapter D), I must first put federal computer-matching projects into perspective. A common misconception is that computer matching is primarily an investigative tool. In reality, matches are used primarily to assist in government audits to identify inappropriate data (e.g., mistakes or errors) in the records under review. Most of our computer-assisted audits use computer screens rather than tape-to-tape matches, which are usually performed on a one-time basis.

The goals of these matches are twofold: (1) to purify the databases; and (2) to build in routine front-end prevention procedures. ("Front-end matches" match data to an existing database before payments are made.) Shattuck's premise seems to be that computer-matching programs have enlarged the number of individuals subjected to government inquiry. This is not true. The criteria for identifying a "hit" are no different than the criteria for evaluating the need for further information received by other means. Computer matches have not created new areas of audit or investigation, but they have allowed agencies to improve their methods.

I fail to see the merit of requiring agencies to limit themselves to less effective audit activities. That argument is based on the unfounded belief that sophisticated proactive audit techniques are per se violative of individual rights.

Shattuck's comments demonstrate a lack of understanding of the procedures followed in federal computer matchings. The individuals whose records are included in a match are not really under investigation. The only records that can result in an inquiry are those that produce a hit. Such indicates a mistake, error, or possible fraud or abuse. In an Aid to Families with Dependent Children (AFDC) state-to-state match, for instance, records indicating a recipient receives AFDC benefits in several jurisdictions would be identified for further review. Since this clearly raises a question of eligibility, an eligibility review can hardly be characterized as a "fishing expedition."

The only real change from computer matches is the increased number of cases identified. Much of the alleged impact on individual rights discussed by Shattuck are issues separate and distinct from computer matching. Once hits are identified for further review, the reviews should be evaluated as any other reviews based on information from any source.

Examples cited by Shattuck of actions taken as a result of matches reflect his disagreement with the evidentiary criteria used by some agencies in pursuing an adverse action. They are in no way an indictment of computer matching for identifying cases for review. The two issues are separate.

The information produced by a matching program is no different from that produced by any other audit or law enforcement inquiry. Once that is recognized, the constitutional concerns raised by Shattuck can be put into perspective. I am unaware of any court decision even remotely indicating that computer-assisted audits of government records run afoul of the Fourth Amendment protections against unlawful search and seizure.

I also fail to see how a law enforcement inquiry based on a computer-matching hit has any impact on the presumption of innocence in a criminal proceeding. This presumption places the burden on the government to prove guilt in a criminal case. None of the examples cited by Shattuck have any bearing on this principle.

It is equally misleading to imply that computer matching has resulted in any weakening of due process. The right to confront an accuser has never applied to the purely investigative stages of a law enforcement inquiry. Shattuck apparently believes that individuals identified in a computer match should be afforded rights never afforded any investigative subject. Law enforcement inquiries can often be closed without a subject interview. This is equally true to inquiries triggered by a computer match. This in no way violates any legally recognized due process standards.

Criticisms made against computer matching are generally unfounded. I strongly oppose Shattuck's recommendations as being unnecessary and inappropriate. His intent is to greatly restrict, if not totally eliminate, the use of computer-matching projects by the federal government.

Requiring congressional authorization for each match and affording persons whose records are being matched rights far in excess of those available to the actual subjects of a law enforcement inquiry would not improve but *end* the use of matching. This is far too vital an audit technique to lose, especially in view of the fact that Shattuck has failed to provide even a single example of a federal computer match that violated an individual's legal rights.

The rights of individuals in federal criminal, civil, or administrative proceedings are already protected by constitutional and other legal constraints. I agree with Shattuck that matches should not be conducted prior to an analysis of their cost effectiveness. In fact, no federal agency has the resources to conduct such matches without careful consideration of costs versus benefits. Further restrictions are, therefore, unnecessary.

P·A·R·T · VI

F

Clipper Chip Will Reinforce Privacy[*]

Dorothy E. Denning

None of us wants the government snooping through our records or eavesdropping on our conversations. So when we read that the government is trying to turn the nation's phone system and information superhighway into a giant eavesdropping device, making wiretaps possible at the push of a button, we ought to be concerned, if not alarmed. But our concern should not be with the government, which is not proposing any such thing. Rather, it should be with those who are grossly distorting the facts.

At issue are two items: A "Digital Telephony" bill; and whether telephone users voluntarily should use an encryption device called the "Clipper chip" on telephone wires. The primary purpose of the proposed Digital Telephony legislation is to ensure that the government can intercept the contents of communications as the telecommunications infrastructure evolves. The purpose of the Clipper chip is to provide a method of scrambling communications that locks out eavesdroppers but does not lock out the government when, and only when, it has the legal authority to listen in.

Neither of these measures weakens our privacy. Wiretaps still will have to be carried out under the existing, tightly controlled conditions, subject to strict legal and procedural controls. The new technologies will not give the government the capability to tap into anyone's conversations with the push of a button, as some privacy extremists have asserted. Rather, they will make illegal wiretaps virtually impossible. The result will be more privacy, not less.

If we don't take steps to maintain an effective wiretap capability, our telecommunications systems will evolve into sanctuaries for criminality in which organized crime leaders, drug dealers, terrorists, and others can conspire with impunity. Eventually, we could find ourselves with an increase in incidents such as the World Trade Center bombing, a diminished capability to fight crime and terrorism and no timely solution.

FBI Director Louis Freeh has identified the wiretap maintenance issue as "the No. 1 law enforcement, public safety and national security issue facing us today." In testimony before the Senate Judiciary subcommittee on Technology and the Law and the House Judiciary subcommittee on Civil and Constitutional Rights in August, Freeh stated that "electronic surveillance is one of law enforcement's most important and effective investigative techniques and is often the only way to prevent or solve the most serious crimes facing today's society."

In earlier testimony, given in March, he described incidents in which wiretaps had been critical in fighting organized crime, drug trafficking, public corruption, fraud, terrorism and violent crime, and in saving innocent lives. Losing a viable electronic surveillance technique, he predicted, would spur the growth of organized crime groups as well as the availability of illegal drugs. He also warned of a likely increase in undetected and unprosecuted public corruption and terrorist acts, as well as an increase in acquittals and hung juries resulting from lack of direct and persuasive evidence. Freeh estimated the potential economic harm to be in the billions of dollars.

By law, wiretaps can be used only against identified criminals, only for serious offenses, and only when other methods of investigation will not work or are too dangerous. In the past decade, federal and state judges issued about 800 court orders per year for various types of electronic surveillance (mostly for wiretaps), leading to approximately 22,000 convictions.

Until recently, executing wiretaps was not a problem. But new technologies such as fiber-optic cable and advanced call forwarding have made wiretaps increasingly difficult. In his August testimony, Freeh reported that a recent informal survey of federal, state, and local law enforcement agencies identified 183 instances in which law enforcement was frustrated by technological impediments—and that figure does not include cases in which court orders never were sought or served because the impediments were known in advance. One federal law enforcement agency reported that it did not pursue twenty-five court orders because a particular cellular-phone carrier could not provide the intercepts.

These numbers show that the carriers already are experiencing difficulties with new technologies. Without intervention, the problem is likely to grow much worse. At the August hearings, Roy Neel, president of the U.S. Telephone Association, stated that in a number of cases wiretaps probably

---

*This article appeared in *Insight* (October 24, 1994), pp. 18–20. Reprinted with permission. Copyright 1994 *Insight*. All rights reserved.

would be frustrated because of new services. The General Accounting Office reported that industry representatives told them there are current and imminent technological situations that would be difficult to wiretap. The Digital Telephony bill, sponsored in the Senate by Democrat Patrick Leahy of Vermont and in the House by Democrat Don Edwards of California, was introduced to counter this ominous trend and to ensure that the carriers could assist in the execution of court orders. It was the result of extensive dialogue with the FBI, industry, and advocates for privacy and civil liberties.

The bill was introduced only after the government recognized that the problems would not be solved voluntarily. Freeh testified in March that while meetings with industry over the previous four years had led to a greater understanding of the problem, they had not produced solutions from industry or a commitment to implement solutions. Moreover, of the 2000 or so companies that would be affected, only a handful have participated in a technical working group that was established two years ago to address the problem. This experience, plus the general nonbinding nature of committee resolutions and the cost factor to the telecommunications carriers, led the Clinton administration and congressional leaders to conclude that a legislative mandate was needed. The bill authorizes reimbursements to manufacturers and telecommunications carriers of $500 million during the next four fiscal years.

The Digital Telephony bill includes new privacy protections for cordless phones, certain transactional records and location-specific information; it requires carriers to protect the privacy and security of communications not authorized to be intercepted; and it provides long-needed legislation, against fraudulent use of another person's cellular identification number. It requires that wiretaps from phone company switches be activated by company employees instead of by police in remote locations.

While the bill will help ensure government access to communications, it will do nothing to ensure that intercepted communications can be understood. Criminals can subvert a wiretap by using encrypting methods that are intended to shelter their communications from the government. Although encryption has not been a significant threat to law enforcement so far, it is anticipated to become one as the technology comes into widespread use.

Enter the Clipper chip, a microchip smaller than a dime, manufactured by a California company called Mykotronx. The chip implements "escrowed encryption," meaning that the encryption keys are held by a trusted third party—in this case the federal government. While designed to provide extremely strong security for communications, Clipper technology also is designed to permit lawful wiretaps through a special chip-unique key that can unlock communications encrypted with the chip. Exploiting this decoding capability, however, involves sophisticated equipment requiring access to key components held by two independent, non–law enforcement key escrow agencies. (The keys are split evenly between the Treasury Department and the National Institute of Technical Standards.)

As with all wiretaps, a law enforcement officer first must obtain a court order for a wiretap and take it to the service provider. After the wiretap is installed, the officer must use a special decoding device in order to determine if the intercepted communications are encrypted with Clipper technology and then to determine the identifier of the particular Clipper chip. Next, the officer must present the chip's ID, along with certification of the legal authority to conduct the wiretap, to the two key escrow agents to obtain their components of that chip's key. Only after both components have been loaded into the decrypt device is decryption possible. When a court order expires, the decrypt device will destroy the key automatically, prohibiting further decryption.

The Clipper system and its accompanying key escrow system have extensive safeguards against government misuse of keys. These safeguards parallel those used to protect some of the country's most sensitive information. Auditing is used extensively so that it will be easy to determine that keys are used only as authorized and only to decode communications intercepted during a period of authorized surveillance. Thus, Clipper will require much less trust in the government than the current system, since most phone calls and data transmissions currently are in the clear.

Although Clipper encryption will provide excellent security, no law requires that it be used, particularly outside the government. Thus, people who do not trust the government or who wish to use some other method of encryption for entirely different reasons are free to do so. Indeed, because it is voluntary, opponents argue that criminals won't use it, thereby defeating the law enforcement objectives.

Whether criminals use Clipper or some other form of escrowed encryption will depend to some extent on whether such encryption spreads throughout the market. It is conceivable that over time, market forces will favor escrowed encryption, which unlike some other encryption technologies can be sold and used in other countries. Exportability of escrowed encryption will give industry the opportunity to manufacture a single product line for domestic and international customers. Furthermore, organizations may require key escrow capabilities to enable their own information recovery. Finally, the government will be ordering key escrow products, and contractors who wish to talk to the government likely will order the same system.

Although criminals could use systems without key escrow, many might use it anyway, because it would be more readily available or to communicate with the rest of the world.

But the issue is not just whether criminals will use Clipper, but what would happen if the government promoted encryption without key escrow. As cryptography proliferated in the market, the government eventually would be locked out of all communications, making telecommunications systems a safe haven for criminal activity. The government responsibly concluded that it would not make sense to pursue encryption standards that fundamentally subvert law enforcement and threaten public safety.

Clipper also has been criticized for using classified algorithms developed in secrecy by the National Security Agency. The critics argue that encryption standards should be set through open-standards settings and subject to public scrutiny. But if Clipper's encryption algorithm, known as SKIP-JACK, is made public, anyone could use it without the key escrow feature, thereby taking advantage of the NSA's cryptographic expertise while evading law enforcement decryption.

The adoption of Clipper does not preclude the development of other key escrow systems. The National Institute of Standards and Technology has established a joint industry-government working group to explore different approaches to key escrow encryption, including software approaches based upon unclassified algorithms. (SKIPJACK cannot be implemented in software, since there are no known ways of hiding a classified algorithm in software.) Several proposals have been made. The government's commitment to work with industry to consider alternative approaches was reconfirmed in a July letter from Vice-President Al Gore to Rep. Maria Cantwell, a Washington Democrat.

Besides aiding law enforcement, key escrow encryption is beneficial in other ways. One concern of many encryption users, particularly corporations, is that encrypted information could become inaccessible if keys are accidentally lost, intentionally destroyed, or held for ransom. A corporate key escrow system, which would enable a company to escrow keys and then obtain access to those keys, would protect a corporation's information assets and protect against liability problems.

Although accommodating the need for court-ordered wiretaps is sometimes viewed as trading some privacy for law enforcement, privacy for most people is totally unaffected by whether the government can conduct wiretaps, since most communications never will be targeted for interception anyway. Even for those who are the subject of a criminal investigation, it is not obvious that they would have greater privacy if wiretaps became technically impossible. Since the government would be unable to successfully investigate or prosecute many cases without the use of wiretaps, it would likely try more dangerous methods, such as undercover operations and bugging subjects' premises. These methods are potentially more invasive than a wiretap.

We need court-ordered wiretaps to protect society against major and violent crimes, and we need encryption to provide communications security. The Digital Telephony bill and Clipper chip are sound approaches to meeting both goals.

P·A·R·T · VI

G

Wiretapping Bill: Costly and Intrusive*

Marc Rotenberg

This August, the most expensive proposal ever developed for monitoring personal communications in the United States was introduced in Congress. The FBI plan would commit more than $500 million toward making the communications infrastructure easier to wiretap. In other words: Welcome to the Information Snooper Highway.

Meanwhile, the National Security Agency is urging that consumers voluntarily use an encryption device called the Clipper chip to make it easier to intercept private messages. The agency, which has no authority to wiretap inside the United States, has spent the last several years pushing a new technology that will make it easier to listen in on private telephone calls.

If something about this picture seems wrong to you, you're not alone. Industry groups, privacy advocates, and computer scientists all have opposed the plans. Why the concern?

Let's turn to Digital Telephony first. The FBI says that since new technology is making its job harder, it needs a law requiring all communications companies to make it easy to wiretap. This is a poorly conceived plan that does not fit into our constitutional traditions.

It also will be unpopular. Surveys taken every year by the Bureau of Justice Statistics on public attitudes toward wiretapping show that Americans oppose wiretapping by roughly a 3-to-1 margin. The opposition to wiretapping is found across all demographic groups.

Americans should be concerned about the Digital Telephony bill because it represents an unnecessary advance in the government's powers of intrusion. The drafters of the 1968 federal wiretap law never intended that the government could tell private companies to make their technologies "wiretap friendly." That legislation, which permits the government to conduct electronic surveillance, described wiretapping as "an investigative method of last resort" and set out elaborate restrictions for its use. The reason for the precautions is understandable. Wire surveillance is far more intrusive than other types of criminal investigation and more prone to abuse. To treat an investigative method of last resort as a design goal of first priority, as the Digital Telephony bill would do, is to stand wiretap law in this country on its head.

In granting power to the Justice Department to establish standards for communications surveillance across every telephone system in the United States, the wiretap plan takes a sharp turn toward greater encroachment upon personal privacy. What could follow? We shouldn't be surprised if the next step is mandatory licensing schemes for technologies that protect privacy, criminal sanctions for developers of equipment that is not easily wiretapped, or a presumption of illegal conduct when people choose to communicate with technology that the United States has not certified can be wiretapped.

Moreover, the cost of the FBI wiretap bill should give lawmakers sticker shock. It authorizes $500 million during the next four years to reimburse private firms for complying with the FBI's "capacity requirements" for electronic surveillance. But that amount may not be enough to satisfy the FBI's goal. The General Accounting Office estimates that their cost could run as high as $2 billion to $3 billion. U.S. Telephone Association President Roy Neel estimates that it could cost as much as $1.8 billion just to redesign call forwarding to satisfy the FBI's concerns.

Contrary to what is frequently claimed by wiretap advocates, the legislation actually may have an adverse impact on national security. In 1992 the General Services Administration, the largest purchaser of telecommunications equipment in the federal government, wrote that the FBI wiretap plan would make it "easier for criminals, terrorists, foreign intelligence (spies) and computer hackers to electronically penetrate the phone network and pry into areas previously not open to snooping." This is because building in capabilities for government intercepts of communications is never impervious to criminal manipulation; it is like cutting a door into a wall where no openings existed. The confidential memo was obtained as a result of a Freedom of Information Act request.

A further concern is that the wiretap bill mandates new technologies for data surveillance. The bill states that "a telecommunications carrier shall ensure that it can enable government access to call-identifying information." This is the first time the United States government has required by

---

law that communications networks be designed to facilitate electronic data surveillance. Telecommunications firms, equipment manufacturers, and those who work in the high-tech industry face a legal obligation to design networks for electronic monitoring.

Meanwhile, the Constitution protects the right of privacy, not the use of wiretaps. The Fourth Amendment protects privacy and the right of individuals to be free from unreasonable search and seizure. Wiretapping is permitted by federal statute only in narrow circumstances; it has no constitutional basis. Congress could outlaw all wiretapping tomorrow if it chose to do so, but it could not easily repeal the Fourth Amendment.

Recent experience shows that standards developed to facilitate wiretapping are costly to American business and individual privacy. The recent development of a technical standard called the Digital Signature Standard, or DSS, used for authentication of electronic documents, provides a case study of what happens when an agency with legal authority to conduct wire surveillance also is given the authority to set technical standards for communications networks. Viewing the role of the NSA in the development of the DSS, Ronald Rivest, a Massachusetts Institute of Technology professor and noted cryptographer, said, "It is my belief that the NIST [National Institute of Standards and Technology] proposals [for DSS] represent an attempt to install weak cryptography as a national standard, and that NIST is doing so in order to please the NSA and federal law enforcement agencies." Martin Hellman, a Stanford University professor and coinventor of the Public Key standard, concluded that "NIST's action gives strong indication of favoring NSA's espionage mission at the expense of American business and individual privacy."

The FBI wiretap plan also will undermine the privacy and security of communications networks worldwide. Communications firms in the United States are the largest producers of networking equipment in the world. The adoption of surveillance-based standards in the United States almost certainly will lead to more electronic monitoring in other countries by national police. Many countries do not have even basic legal protections to control unlawful electronic surveillance.

If the case for Digital Telephony is weak, the case for Clipper chip is almost nonexistent. This high-tech proposal has the dubious distinction of being the least popular technical standard ever put forward by the federal government. When the Commerce Department asked the technical community what it thought of the plan, more than three hundred respondents said, "Bad idea." Two people (one of whom is Dorothy E. Denning) said, "Looks good." It's hard in Washington to find that level of agreement on almost anything. Shortly afterward, an electronic petition signed by 50,000 people who opposed the Clipper plan went to the president.

What's wrong with the proposal?

First, Clipper doesn't work. The proposed scheme is easy to defeat by "pre-encrypting"—simply concealing a message in code before the government's device receives the message. It also can be defeated by more sophisticated systems, as Matt Blaze, a computer researcher with Bellcore in New Jersey, showed earlier this year by demonstrating a way to disable the key escrow mechanism, and by less sophisticated schemes, such as not using a Clipper phone. Government officials acknowledge it's only a partial solution and also say that it should be voluntary, which suggests that the bad guys are not the ones most likely to use "surveillance certified" technologies.

Second, Clipper creates a new type of vulnerability for network communications. By requiring that copies of electronic keys be stored with government agencies, a risk is created where none existed. These copies could be misused or mistakenly disclosed. New types of crime easily could arise. The proponents of Clipper are reluctant to discuss the security problems surrounding storage of the keys, since it is fairly well-known that no system is absolutely secure.

Third, Clipper is expensive. It would require the use of tamperproof hardware where inexpensive software otherwise could be used. For consumers, this would mean higher prices for cellular phones and telecommunications services generally. It also has slowed the introduction of better, less expensive consumer technologies such as an AT&T cellular phone that the NSA, which designed Clipper, said would not go to market until Clipper was installed.

Fourth, Clipper is based on a secret algorithm that proponents say is necessary to protect its functionality. But science and innovation dislike such secrets. They often conceal mistakes and easily frustrate progress. Also, how can we be assured that Clipper works as described without giving experts of differing views the opportunity to "kick the tires" on this high-tech proposal?

There is some indication that supporters of the Clipper plan may be backing off. But Clipper remains the proposed standard for telephone networks in the federal government. The White House is pushing hard for the private sector to develop similar "surveillance friendly" standards for the future communications network.

So, if Digital Telephony is poorly conceived and Clipper won't work, does it matter very much if the government goes forward anyway?

Yes, for several reasons. First, both of these proposals are extremely expensive. The FBI may not succeed in building a "wiretappable" network, but if the pending wiretap bill goes forward, it will spend more than half a billion taxpayer dollars in the effort. Because of the official secrecy of the NSA, the costs are hard to estimate. However, if you consider not only Clipper but also related technologies designed for network surveillance and the cost to government agencies of adopting hardware-based encryption schemes, the costs easily could exceed several hundred million dollars. (Software-based encryption schemes, which are much cheaper, are disliked by the NSA because they are harder to control.) That means that taxpayers are looking at a bill of around $1 billion for a plan that even proponents agree will only partly work.

Second, both efforts will slow technical innovation and leave United States companies to play catch-up with foreign companies that do not face similar requirements. New network technologies require good privacy technology. Wireless networks in particular, such as cellular phones and satellite systems, would benefit greatly from better privacy protection. But the Clipper chip and Digital Telephony plans will discourage research and slow innovation. This means less security for consumers and businesses and less competitive products for United States firms.

Third, Clipper and Digital Telephony pose grave threats to personal privacy. The premise of both proposals is that new communications technologies should be designed to facilitate wire surveillance. This premise is contrary to the natural development of communications technology, which is to provide greater privacy. Few would use a telephone today to make a personal call knowing that others were on the line. Yet, a generation ago, such party lines were found in many parts of the country.

The Clipper chip and Digital Telephony will not meet the government's goal of trying to ensure the viability of electronic wiretapping. But in the effort to preserve this form of electronic surveillance, a lot of damage can be done to network security, American business, and personal privacy.

In fact, of all the many proposals for the information highway, no two are less popular, less needed, and less desirable than the Clipper chip and Digital Telephony. The White House can cut its losses by simply dropping these surveillance plans.

Some will say that the plans are necessary for law enforcement. But Americans have never been comfortable with electronic wiretapping. We recognize that law enforcement is a central goal in every democratic society. But the exercise of law enforcement and the ability to conduct citizen surveillance requires a careful assessment of methods and objectives. Even a country deeply concerned about crime must be prepared to draw some limits on the scope of government power.

P·A·R·T · VI

H

Privacy: How Much Data Do Direct Marketers Really Need?*

Denison Hatch

An extraordinarily prescient statement that sums up the massive challenge direct marketers face in terms of privacy and the sanctity of the individual was made by C. Rose Harper, chairman and CEO of the Kleid company—not in response to the survey on privacy *Target Marketing* recently sent to industry leaders—but, astonishingly, in a decade-old press release dated April 1984:

> "With increasing concern about 'invasion of privacy,' those of us in the list business must do all we can to recognize and address this concern. The truth is we are not dossier compilers or personal investigators. But in today's world, what one is is often less important than what one is perceived to be. If there is one major challenge facing us, I think the challenge is to find an effective way to make sure that the public's perception of our business is shaped by us and not the media. And not by those companies in our field who just don't care."

No, we are not dossier compilers or personal investigators—at least consciously. Yet when a person who is not in our business receives a mailing that reveals knowledge of the intimate details of his or her life, the perception is that it came from a dossier compiler who probably knows a lot more. In the words of Direct Marketing Association counsel, Richard Barton:

> "We have the capability to gather, store, analyze, segment and use for commercial (and many other) purposes more data about more people than

was ever dreamed of, and technology is providing us with even more ingenious ways to reach into the lives of every American."

Misuse of Data

One of the most successful direct mail letters of all time was written in 1960
by Ed McLean for *Newsweek*. More than 170 million of these letters were
sent out over the course of fifteen years, and it brought in subscribers by
the thousands at a mouth-watering cost per order.

The letter began:

> Dear Reader, If the list upon which I found you name is any indication, this
> is not the first—nor will it be the last—subscription letter you receive. Quite
> frankly, your education and income set you apart from the general popula-
> tion and make you a highly-rated prospect for everything from magazines to
> mutual funds.

According to McLean, even back then—long before databases—a number of people were disturbed enough to call *Newsweek* and ask what list they
were on. But the letter was so successful—and the calls so few—that
Newsweek mailed it for years. But, isn't it simply the feeling of having one's
privacy invaded that's the real problem for most consumers? Consider, for
instance, this personal experience I had last year. In August, my wife,
Peggy, and I bought a townhouse in Philadelphia. On December 30, a
postcard arrived from a mortgage insurance company.

My guess is that some snoop had prowled through the records at city
hall, recorded the transaction, and then sold the information to a stranger,
Mike Berman, who sent out this teaser. Not only is it deceptive in that it is
designed to appear that the sender had something to do with the mortgage
company, but he put the actual amount of the mortgage on the back of a
postcard, allowing it to hang out naked for all to see. It's nobody's business
who one's lender is or the amount of a mortgage; yet a local insurance
salesman has made it a lot of people's business in a pointless and insen-
sitive use of personal data.

But isn't this typical? Consumers routinely receive mail from utter
strangers with such highly personal information played back to them as:
the names and ages of their children; the year and make of the family car;
the make of car they rented on vacation in Florida; their exact dates of birth
(usually in relation to insurance offers); the phone numbers or area codes
they call most frequently; reference to an illness or medication they are
taking; the amount of pre-approved credit they have; their marital status or
impending parenthood, and so on.

---

*This article appeared in *Target Marketing*, 17(2)(February 1994), pp. 35–40. Reprinted with
permission.

Consumers will, perhaps, tolerate this information being reeled off to them from a company with whom they regularly do business. But when it arrives in their mailboxes from absolute strangers, it's creepy.

How Much Is Too Much?

Direct marketing efforts can be divided into two areas: prospecting and customer or donor retention. Retention marketing, customer development, relationship marketing—call it what you will—is quite different from acquisition efforts.

When you have existing customers, you are expected to keep track of their interests and needs and send them sensible offers. Maintaining a file on customer behavior makes sense for everybody; it's the whole purpose of database marketing. Much of the information that direct marketers use is gleaned from their own customer records. Purchase a Porsche accessory from the Whitney automotive catalog, a subscription to *Scuba Diver* magazine, or order a size 3 dress from the Unique Petite catalog and you've spilled a lot of information about yourself.

Other information can come from public records—auto registrations, drivers' licenses, home ownership and bankruptcy documents found in city halls and county courthouses. Information is also generated by geographic, demographic, and credit overlays and matches. Still more data are volunteered by consumers themselves. For example, consumers regularly supply personal information on product warranty cards, direct mail survey forms, and cents-off coupons they plan to redeem.

As the great free-lance copywriter Herschell Gordon Lewis wrote in his reply to our survey:

> "If the individual has supplied the information about himself/herself, it can no longer be considered 'personal.' "

The right of refusal comes at the moment the individual agrees to complete the questionnaire. Jack Miller, president of Quill Corporation, warns:

> "Consumers should give only that information to anyone that they don't consider private. Sometimes this isn't possible. So in those cases, consumers should have the right to say it is private information and not to be given to anyone else. But this right to designate what is private should be limited to truly private matters."

One problem is that people lead busy, hectic lives, and very often they don't remember ever having volunteered any personal information. If a total stranger recites information about you that came from your answers in a year-old survey—but you don't remember having filled out the questionnaire—you are spooked.

Hard-nosed direct marketers will say: "The person volunteered the information; therefore we have no compunction about using it, and we're totally within our rights." True. But isn't it stupid to upset people and lose the sale, even if you're in the right? Why not start a direct mail letter with the source of the information:

> Some time ago, you filled out a survey that indicated . . .

It's a strong opening, showing that someone cared enough to read your answers to a survey and pay attention to your specific needs. More to the point, it immediately puts the reader at ease. The whole question of privacy is obviated at the outset, and the writer can get on with the sale.

How Much Is Enough?

Is knowing the minutiae of people's lives and habits necessary to make the sale? Or will a powerful, benefit-heavy offer do the job? As Rose Harper suggests:

> "Let's be realistic. It isn't essential to know an individual's real income and/or net worth. If someone subscribes to a financial publication, a photography magazine, a fashion magazine, a health publication, that positions the person as a prospect for certain types of related products."

Donn Rappaport, in his *List Day* debate, urged direct marketers to self-regulate. He said:

> "Stop scaring consumers unnecessarily over how much personal data is actually available about them. Some list owners like to play 'my customer is better than your customer' games with list datacards, offering selections no mailer really needs, just to look good against their competition. They may also make boastful claims that rub everybody the wrong way. Last year, for example, Pacific Bell Telephone Co. began promoting its customer file with the announcement: 'Now a business List from the company that has every-one's number.' "

Before you make these types of claims, ask yourself if it's really neces-sary, or is it just a gratuitous selection? As Ed McLean says about copy-writing in this information-laden environment: "You have to dumb-down what you know."

The Opt Out

National Demographics and Lifestyles (NDL) creates detailed question-naires for 130 separate companies with more than 300 brands. Consumers receive the surveys as the result of the purchase of a product—an auto-mobile, refrigerator, camera. If a customer wants to make absolutely sure the manufacturer knows the specifics of the purchase in case anything goes wrong, they will complete the survey and return it to NDL. The result: NDL receives dossiers on individuals and their families—25 million of them a year! Those personal dossiers enable NDL to offer a dizzying array of options for direct marketers.

To its credit, NDL takes two major precautions to assure the consumers that this personal information they revealed is not misused. First, NDL lets consumers opt out; they can indicate that they do not wish to receive any offers as a result of the information they have supplied, and that request is scrupulously honored. Until recently, the opt-out language was in small print at the end of the questionnaire. In the current version of the survey, it's up front and in big type.

What is the effect of the opt out in terms of list building? "The number of people who opt out is between 6 percent and 7 percent, and that number has been steady for 15 years," NDL's CEO, Tim Prunk, says. "Sure, we saw a little hiccup around Earth Day where the number rose to 10 percent; but it's now right back down to the usual 6.7 percent."

At the 1993 U.S. Postal Forum, Disabled American Veterans' Executive Director, Max Hart, revealed ". . . on DAV's initial rental disclosure tests, we had a 13-percent removal rate on the first mailing and an additional 6 percent on the next mailing."

A number of direct marketers in all fields are offering their customers the chance to opt out. For example, First Chicago Corporation (FCC National Bank) offers its credit card customers an opt out.

Second, NDL insists on reviewing a copy of every proposed mailing going to its list. As Prunk explains, "Our clients are Fortune 500 companies. Could you imagine the president of Kodak finding out that some dishonest mailing was going to his customers? It could have a devastating effect on our entire business."

R. L. Polk, whose massive database is compiled primarily from state auto registrations, also scrupulously monitors what mailings go to its lists; the last thing in the world Polk needs is to have consumers complain to state motor vehicle bureaus who, in turn, could cut off the source.

Our Survey

The editors of *Target Marketing* were amazed that of the two hundred opinion leaders surveyed, a paltry 15% responded. Isn't privacy—especially the threat of restrictive legislation—a top concern of all direct marketers? Here are two possible reasons for the low return. First, in the words of Robin Smith, president of Publishers Clearing House, "It was a tough questionnaire." Dave Florence of Direct Media echoed those sentiments. "It would have taken me an hour to fill it out and I don't have that kind of time." The other reason may be that a number of direct marketers—such as Doubleday Book and Record Clubs corporate counsel, Robert Posch—feel it's a nonissue. Posch says:

"Listen to Rush Limbaugh or Bob Grant or Pat Buchanan. Nobody calls in to complain about privacy or databases. This is not a big problem in the minds of consumers. It's an artificial issue in the minds of a cottage industry."

Futurist Don Libey agrees, noting:

"The interesting possibility is that, aside from the big government-types with a vested interest in their profiles in the media, perhaps the general public really doesn't care as long as they get what they want at the lowest possible cost and with the least amount of hassle. Strip out the social crazies, the activists, the ACLU and the other radical fringes, and it is quite possible that the great unwashed consuming public could care less about 'privacy.' Perhaps, in fact, 2 percent are once again destroying the utility for 98 percent of the people; 'privacy' is just another stop on the road to victimization."

Libey and Posch may be in the minority. As James R. Rosenfield wrote in November 1991:

"If I had another wish, it would be for massive research into consumer attitudes on an ongoing basis, so that we should know with confidence at what point people feel that their privacy is being invaded. I know one thing for sure: Sensitivities in North America have increased significantly over the past several years and are likely to continue increasing for some time into the future.

"Sensitivities are now acute enough in North America—particularly in the mail-inundated United States—that routine personalization techniques must now be looked at afresh. Things that got no reaction in 1985 are causing consumers to squirm uncomfortably in the early 1990s. Individualization techniques that no one cared about in 1987 now get people thinking, 'How do they know this?' and 'Do I really want them to know this?' "

If Rosenfield is correct, then the most important single element in the privacy debate is the comfort level of consumers. If consumers are made to feel uneasy—and persuasively convey that uneasiness to politicians—we could be legislated back to the Stone Age of mail order; all the marvelous technology that has been developed would be relegated to footnotes in graduate school marketing courses.

This is not sensationalism nor idle fear-mongering. For example, privacy laws in Germany make it illegal to send a fax—or make a telephone call—without prior permission. Further, the sale or trade of specific information is banned. For instance, according to Axel Andersson, you can get a list of those who want to learn a language, but you cannot find out which language. Robert Posch writes:

"Europe lost its 21st century economy by their self-destructive laws. There are no software companies or any other serious database-related companies on the continent."

Another Solution

Infobase Services, an affiliate of Acxiom in Conway, Alaska, in the data management and enhancement business, makes its customers—companies using its data—sign an ironclad contract. Three paragraphs are pivotal:

> Paragraph 6. Customer agrees that any solicitation or ad copy prepared in connection with the use of Customer's list(s) containing information derived from the Data shall be devoid of any reference to any selection criteria or presumed knowledge concerning the intended recipient of such solicitation, or source of the recipient's name and address.

> Paragraph 7. Customer agrees that any solicitation made in connection with the use of Customer's list(s) derived from the Data shall comply with all federal, state and local laws, statutes, rules and regulations, and that such solicitation shall be in good taste and of the highest integrity.

> Paragraph 8. Customer agrees to furnish Infobase, upon request, three samples of each mailing piece mailed using information derived from the Data.

If all in the mailing chain—marketers, managers, and brokers—adopted these three paragraphs in the Infobase contract (plus honored all Mail Preference Service and Telephone Preference Service opt-out requests), in theory the privacy issue should dry up and go away. In theory.

Two Huge Obstacles

First, the list rental business is so profitable that many list owners are willing to overlook what goes out to their names. This is particularly true of compiled lists where many owners may have no personal stake in customer loyalty or lifetime value.

More important, in researching the Target Marketing Special Report on Privacy, it became immediately apparent that all who maintain databases have many enemies—the media, the 3 million consumers who have opted out of direct mail via the DMA Mail Preference Service and the 50,000 a month who join them, and the 31,000 consumers who filed complaints about credit bureaus with the FTC over the past four years.

Plus, much political hay can be made. As NDL's Prunk says, "Politicians don't have a lot of money to play with anymore. This is an easy issue that won't cost them anything, and by protecting citizens from the privacy invaders, they can look like heroes."

Consumers' feelings about Big Brother are being whipped like a brush fire in a California Santa Ana. A recent example of the media hype was found in Larry Tye's incendiary three-part series on privacy that ran during the first week of September 1993 in the *Boston Globe*. Another media blast came from *Time* magazine under the scary title, "NOWHERE TO HIDE: Using computers, high-tech gadgets and mountains of data, an army of snoops is assaulting our privacy," by Richard Lacayo. The media gleefully dredge up horror stories about databases that are, in the words of William M. Bulkley, writing in *The Wall Street Journal*, "plagued by reign of error." And the public is regularly regaled with tales of computer hackers who break into government, scientific, and corporate databases with ease because of lax security and the theft of pass codes.

These blistering indictments of direct marketing follow hot on the heels of similar pieces by Michael W. Miller in *The Wall Street Journal,* Leonard Sloane and Barry Meier in *The New York Times* and the Public Broadcasting System's "Nova: We Know Where You Live," where viewers saw Vice-President Dan Quayle's most intimate financial records pop up onscreen on network television. William Barnhill's "Privacy Invaders" article in the *AARP Bulletin* reached some 37 million easily frightened older Americans.

Even though all five of these media giants (Dow Jones, *The New York Times*, Time Warner, the AARP, and PBS) are among the largest direct mailers in the world and are totally dependent upon database marketing, they continually slam the very technique on which their corporate survival and growth depends. The pejorative terms "junk mail" and "junk phone calls" are used routinely throughout their coverage.

Why are they savaging us—and themselves? First off, it makes compelling reading, giving the subscribers a real dose of cathartic outrage. Second, direct marketing is deeply wounding the newspaper industry's traditional source of revenue: advertising. Make no mistake about it; the term "junk mail" was coined by the newspaper industry.

The forces arrayed against us—the media, government, liberal do-gooders, as well as those in our own industry whose zeal for profits overwhelms their common sense and decency—are a juggernaut that could crush us unless we self-regulate.

A Call for a Summit

The only way to head off the privacy juggernaut is to call a summit meeting of all database owners, users, and processors—direct marketing, financial, corporate, scientific, medical and pharmaceutical, retail, insurance, educational, government. The purpose would be to create a wiring diagram for our future:

1. To learn what databases are out there and what they contain.
2. To figure out what information is essential . . . helpful . . . tangential . . . and not necessary for these databases to be efficient and useful.
3. To come up with a self-created owner's and user's code of conduct to head off state and federal governments from legislating draconian

measures that will bomb our information-based society back into the Stone Age of data dissemination. Included might be a system of encryption of highly personal and sensitive data.

4. To teach sensitivity training to database owners and users so they don't rub consumers' noses in how much they know.

5. To set up a watchdog committee to monitor what is going on in the name of marketing and research—not for censorship, but to alert database owners and users where they may have made a misstep that can hurt us all.

6. To take a high-profile, proactive stance to educate consumers about many benefits of databases in terms of their lifestyle and well-being.

The DMA is sponsoring "Dialogues" around the country. But the summit envisioned here would be a joint effort among database owners, users, processors, the media, government, the state attorneys general, consumers, and consumer advocate groups. It is imperative that we all enter the twenty-first century in full agreement that the technology we harness will be for the benefit of civilization rather than its exploitation.

The Direct Marketing Association has assembled a war chest of $2.6 million "to successfully convey to the media and to government officials our positive message of the value of the non-invasive character of the direct marketing process . . ."

The DMA's approach is an effort to isolate direct marketing from other databases and persuade everyone, "We're the good guys . . . We don't want to know about you specifically, only collectively so we can make you great offers." Direct marketing cannot isolate itself from the other information databases. We are all in this together.

The British Code

With the Target Marketing survey was included those sections of the British Code of Advertising Practice dealing with the accumulation and use of information. While the United States and Canadian DMAs have issued guidelines on the subject, the British Code is currently in force. Among the provisions:

- Giving the consumer the right to opt out.
- Maintaining records of those who do opt out and making sure they are not contacted.
- Safeguarding of all personal data.
- On surveys, telling the consumer what the information will be used for.
- A consumer must have the right to object "when it is proposed to use personal information for a purpose significantly different from that for which it was originally collected."

- All list rental names should be run against the Mail Preference Service and all requests for no mail must be honored.
- Particular care must be taken "in using sensitive personal data (including race, political opinions, religious and other beliefs, physical and mental health, specific salaries and investments, sexual orientation and criminal convictions) so as to avoid causing offence or harm to individuals. They should also, where appropriate, seek the prior permission of individuals to use sensitive personal data."
- Personal information should at all times "be held securely and safeguarded against unauthorized use, disclosure, alteration or destruction."
- "List users should maintain records which permit requests for the source of the mailing lists to be identified, in order that such information can be supplied promptly upon request."

Although most of the respondents said they could live with the British Code, several balked at certain clauses. Richard Benson, publisher of the *University of California Wellness Letter*, does not match against the DMA Mail Preference Service list because he claims it would cost him $300,000 a year. And both Benson and Max Hart of the DAV said their systems are not set up to maintain the original list source forever.

P·A·R·T · VI

I

Direct Marketing Is Not
a Significant Privacy Threat*

Robert Posch

Personally, I support the value of the effective Direct Marketing Association's ethics code (as PR) and helped draft this code. The DMA also has published a useful PR piece—"Privacy: The Key Issue of the 1990s." However, we're reaching a crucial watershed. If voluntary mail preference can be legislated as was telephone, then we have temporarily succeeded, but only against the wrong opponent. If it can't, we're not there or anywhere.

For years, the industry has held forth voluntary suppression as a panacea. Many firms cheer this on, but a few then refuse to seriously comply with DMA's ethical codes or they ignore them altogether. So, the industry then argues it can force people to comply. This, of course, is theoretically a boon for the huge database owners. They can lose a few names at the margin in exchange for creating barriers against new entrants. This pre-planned market exclusion and territorial allocation previously was governed by the antitrust laws.

However, the mechanism for mandatory compliance is a nightmare. Who will report on their competitors and who exactly will have clean hands in so doing? Further, so what? Mail (and telephone) preference have always been smoke screens designed to combat the wrong opponent. Besides the tactical errors that we refuse to address, we retain a fundamental strategic error—we are the only form of business that acknowledges that some people may not find it desirable to be associated with us. Precisely, we're about targeting. The more we encourage people to leave, the more we cast doubt on our *raison d'etre* or the credibility of targeting as a socially desirable goal.

I know that the party line is we don't want to contact people who don't want to hear from us. However, forget party line for a few minutes and think seriously. We'd lose customers, sales, and maybe our business. You and I both know this is fatalism in lieu of strategy. We all know we'd love to have a preference by category because most people are reachable if better targeted. This is a huge price to pay for a strategy that ignores our primary opponents.

We want to be loved and we want to do business as we should. This is mutually contradictory. As stated above, we address our wrong opponent with tactically deficient PR and a strategically deficient position, that is, we lack a fallback position after it is proven we have addressed the wrong opponent.

If we're going to remain in business, we can continue to straddle. This has worked for twenty years and may continue to do so—it would continue to do so if we had a positive message. We also need to address our real opponent candidly.

Who Are Our Real Opponents and Why the Mail Preference Service Is Worthless to Counter Them

Our opponents in the competitive world of advertising dollars want our money and that is the only real issue that ever existed in what we have let our opponents define as the "privacy debate." The latest scam was the article in the *New York Magazine*.[1] We've seen the battle engaged with Dan Rather, which Phil Herring was so fond of citing.[2] At other times, it was *Wall Street Journal* or *U.S. News*.[3] "Legal Outlook" has cited this phenomena over and over again.

The Advertising Mail Marketing Association (AMMA), in response to the "junk"-laden article, told the weekly magazine: "In your article concerning advertising mail . . . you have an obvious and overt conflict of interest: You fail to tell readers that magazines and newspapers compete with advertising mailers for advertising dollars. The very term 'junk mail' was developed by editorial writers to disparage a competing media and its editorial usage prejudices your coverage of the start. AMMA believes that every article and broadcast which uses the term 'junk mail' as a substitute for

---

*This article appeared as "After MPS—Then What?" in *Direct Marketing*, 56(11)(March 1994), pp. 63–64+. Reprinted with permission.
[1] "Junk Mail Deluge" (January 31, 1994), cover story.
[2] Robert J. Posch, Jr., "It's Not Junk Phil." *Direct Marketing*, (March 1992), p. 60.
[3] Alicia Mundy, "Unwilling Players In The Name Game" (May 1, 1989), p. 52.

'advertising mail,' 'direct mail,' 'bulk business mail' or a similar term is biased."

As *E-Magazine* (November/December 1993), a publication concerned with environmental matters, reported in a cover story, "Direct mail exists because it works. It generates response rates from the public that are tens, hundreds and even thousands of times better than ads in newspapers or on television. Clearly, such response rates would not be possible if most people did not elect to buy, contribute or support causes and charities through the mails."

Does anyone reading this article really believe mail/telephone preference will curb the "privacy debate" so long as our competitors have editorial power to frame the debate as such, while continuing to pretend it's really a public outcry? Does anyone believe that having Lou Harris ask the wrong question about the wrong issues will do anything to lessen this prompted assault on competition?

Our response has been to substitute PR and the appearance of activities for a solution. We don't address the only issue that matters—we never do. We pretend the public cares and so we act as if Alan Westin or Dan Flaherty represent a constituency. They represent neither a constituency nor the issue. They are given forums by our competitive media, which want our dollars. Equifax gives Lou Harris a forum and DMA gives a whole host of vocal opponents a forum at varied trade shows. No forum leads to a solution. None can because they never involve our real opponents: the editorial media losing dollars to targeted, database marketing.

Mail preference and telephone preference will only lessen the debate if they prove successful and decrease your sales. If they succeed, you lose sales (maybe your business) and our competitive media can editorialize on other issues. You can't win. If mail/telephone preference fails (and your business succeeds), then our competitive media opponents have no reason whatsoever to cease their assaults on us. Further, by making it mandatory, we prove self-regulation can't work, so we write the legislation that will put us out of business.

If you really believe our opponents are people like Computer Professionals for Social Responsibility or the ACLU's Privacy Project, you can pretend mail preference will work. If you recognize that our real competitors must be addressed (and their loss of advertising revenue), then you realize PR is not strategic policy.

We can never win, or at least confront our correct opponents, if the who, how, and why is unknown.

Mail Preference Will Fail beyond PR

In my first book, *The Direct Marketer's Legal Advisor,* I discussed why mail preference is PR—not a final answer, that is:

The Mail Preference Service does not address itself to compiled lists or cross-transfers. While it is nice PR and many of its member firms have voluntarily followed the Privacy Study Commission's voluntary-removal recommendations, the DMA cannot speak for all the individual direct marketers. Many non-profit associations and fund-raising organizations are refusing to comply. The Mail Preference Service cannot mitigate the compilation of dossier-type information from government records. Finally, even when there is success in removing a name, that success is temporary, for the name will be back on other lists after subsequent purchases.[4]

This is not to say that those who created and fostered this PR are not forever in our debt. It bought twenty years for the industry to create real arguments against our real opponents. This was 1981. MPS has increasingly forced us into a defensive pattern of evasion and false concessions. We appear to be dealing with our opponents' concerns while actually doing our best to make the issue disappear. However, it has also led us astray so that we fail to address the real issue (dollars, not privacy) and our real opponents.

The Privacy Debate and the "Junk" Debate Are the Same Debate

Database marketing exists because it works. Our competitors for advertising dollars can't quantitatively verify that database marketing isn't inferior so they must attack the form of distribution. A message in a newspaper becomes a First Amendment shrine, while the same message in a letter becomes "junk"! More hypocritical was the phony environmental debate in which the landfilling newspapers claimed that the largest car pool on earth[5] was less efficient.

To any objective person, "junk" is determined by the message content and its desirability to the individual recipient, not the medium. Landfill quantity is determined by paper in the landfill and not the editorial bias of one media, which can debase its economic competitors by abusing the huge editorial power it has to slant stories against such competitors to manipulate trusting readers/viewers into believing they are reading fact, when they are actually reading a competitive disparagement posing as fact.

Unless we confront our real opponents in a real debate, we may force ourselves into:

1. losing sales through visible mail/telephone preference.
2. losing more sales through legislation.

---

[4] Robert J. Posch, Jr., *The Direct Marketer's Legal Adviser* (1983), p. 158. McGraw Hill, New York.
[5] Robert J. Posch, Jr., "The Largest Car Pool On Earth." *Direct Marketing,* (November 1990), p. 75.

3. becoming mini-Stalinists, informing on our competitors to enforce a mandatory mail/telephone preference.

Then when the points above are frighteningly in place, we find we must return to the same debate because our opponents weren't those we engaged in the first place. We have found that we not only failed to win a war—we didn't even win a battle in the real war.

Confronting Our Real Opponents

Our opponents are competitive media (television, magazines, newspapers, etc.) that have the power to editorialize and create value perceptions in their product.

As I've said in *Civil Liberties*,[6] the ABA *Communications Lawyer*,[7] "Legal Outlook,"[8] and elsewhere, mail is the proven effectuation of Justice Black's ideal that the First Amendment's guarantee of freedom of speech extended special solicitude to the "poorly financed causes of the little people." Mail and only mail is the historically proven forum in which the minority views of the "poorly financed causes of little people" become the dominant views of society.[9]

At a minimum, we should be positively asserting our value as a First Amendment marketplace equal to, if not superior to, our critics. The AMMA's Image Campaign does this. It is hoped that the DMA will follow an assertive and not a defensive image campaign (e.g., WEFA). "How Did They Get My Name" was less defensive and often a positive sell. However, we can confront our real opponents in the competitive media revenue world only when we demand that our media have equal constitutional weight. This argument, and not privacy, will determine the core debate.

Commercial Speech Is Valuable Democratic Speech

True democracy involves more than the right to vote once a year in November for people we hardly know and who we presume will be liars anyway. The First Amendment's proper role is to uncover and publicize abuses of power and mismanagement in government. Today, we witness our media creating smoke screens out of Tonya Harding and the Bobbits so we won't focus on the death of Vincent Foster (an alleged suicide no one investigated until Chris Ruddy of the *New York Post* began to look into it

---

[6] Robert J. Posch, Jr., "A Little Noticed Civil Liberties Threat: Price Censorship." *Civil Liberties* (Winter 1990–1991), p. 15.

[7] Robert J. Posch, Jr., "Price Censorship Is Real And Growing." *Communications Lawyer* (Fall 1990), p. 15.

[8] Robert J. Posch, Jr., "Free Speech On The Ropes." *Direct Marketing* (March 1991), p. 61.

[9] See footnotes 6–8 above.

seven months later). Our media are corrupted by a drive of soap opera sales and further corrupted by their biased attack against competitive advertisers. They do not deserve superior constitutional protection.

Since the editorial media is no less important than ideas presented in mail (this is why we have the frank),[10] we also shouldn't be shy in asserting our superior value to our competitors in the economic as well as political democracy.

Democracy in economic life is at least as important as the formality of political democracy where those who believe in principles today must now feel like outsiders. Economic democracy (commercial free speech) is more important because it involves the real life of everyday people year-round. Big government has largely deprived us of self-government, which is input into decision making. Targeted marketing liberates individuals to at least make informed decisions with the 52% of their money not confiscated by the state to feed its clients. These clients don't have free speech either—just a free ride.

I don't believe we have engaged our opponents effectively—if we have really come to grips with who they are. Vocal people with no constituency anywhere have been given a public forum by our economic competitors to slow down, if not curtail, our business. To the extent we voluntarily curtail our business, on a business-by-business basis, we can believe that we're not losing, but merely not selling, to those who don't want to do business with us. Is there any quantitative proof of this? I've seen proof to the contrary. However, if PR buys off serious adverse results it is worth a few sales—maybe.

Now the rubber hits the road. We are making serious decisions that could irrevocably hamper our business permanently. Are you confident legislating mail preference or making it a mandatory obligation of DMA will at least "do you no harm"? The loss of these names and these lists will be analogous to the quote of Ray Schultz, "Targeting marketing will enter a new era—that of 1950."[11] Will any of these policies curtail the attacks upon targeted database-driven media by mass, competitive media? To ask the question is to answer it!

No one is discussing what we'll do then and we better consider this before we do anything permanent. It should not be a mark of leadership to be mystified by the obvious. I don't believe we have addressed our primary opponent with our primary argument. If I'm right, we'll have gone a few steps off the plank while only feeding the sharks below.

---

[10] Robert J. Posch, Jr., "The Stamp Tax—The Incumbents' Insurance Plan." *Direct Marketing* (January 1991), p. 74.

[11] "Heaven Help Us, Congress Has Awakened." *DM News* (February 7, 1994), p. 40 (commenting on the loss of motor vehicle and other compiled lists and your inability to target your customer).

We have accepted the terms of debate framed by our opponents. This is bad enough, but we'd better be able to distinguish our vocal critics from our serious opponents who provide the forum for the vocal critics and who constitute the opposition we must address if we are to be successful. MPS addresses only the former. MPS is trying to play hardball with a softball mentality.

If we implement mail preference as a strategy, rather than a tactic, we shall then reflect, similar to Gene in John Knowles's excellent novel, *A Separate Peace:*

> All of them, all except Phineas, constructed at infinite cost to themselves these Maginot Lines against this enemy they thought they saw across the frontier, this enemy who never attacked that way—if he ever attacked at all—if he was indeed the enemy.[12]

---

[12] Bantam Books, p. 196. New York, 1988.

P·A·R·T · VI

J

What to Do When They Ask for Your Social Security Number*

Chris Hibbert

Many people are concerned about the number of organizations asking for their Social Security Numbers. They worry about invasions of privacy and the oppressive feeling of being treated as just a number. Unfortunately, I cannot offer any hope about the dehumanizing effects of identifying you with your numbers. I *can* try to help you keep your Social Security Number from being used as a tool in the invasion of your privacy.

Short History of the Social Security Number

Social Security Numbers (SSNs) were introduced by the Social Security Act of 1935. They were originally intended to be used only by the Social Security program. In 1943 Roosevelt signed Executive Order 9397 (EO9397) which required federal agencies to use the number when creating new record-keeping systems. In 1961 the IRS began to use it as a taxpayer ID number (TIN). The Privacy Act of 1974 required authorization for government agencies to use SSNs in their databases and required disclosures (detailed below) when government agencies request the number. Agencies that were already using SSN as an identifier before January 1, 1975 were allowed to continue using it. The Tax Reform Act of 1976 gave authority to state or local tax, welfare, driver's license, or motor vehicle registration authorities to use the number in order to establish identities. The Privacy Protection Study Commission of 1977 recommended that EO9397 be revoked after some agencies referred to it as their authorization to use SSNs.

It has not been revoked, but no one seems to have made new uses of the SSN recently and cited EO9397 as their sole authority.

Several states use the SSN as a driver's license number, while others record it on applications and store it in their database. Some states that routinely use it on the license will make up another number if you insist. According to the terms of the Privacy Act, any that have a space for it on the application forms should have a disclosure notice. Many do not, and until someone takes them to court, they aren't likely to change.

The Privacy Act of 1974 (Pub. L. 93-579, in sec. 7) requires that any federal, state, or local government agency that requests your Social Security Number has to tell you four things:

1. Whether disclosure of your Social Security Number is required or optional.
2. What statute or other authority they have for asking for your number.
3. How your Social Security Number will be used if you give it to them.
4. The consequences of failure to provide an SSN.

In addition, the Act says that only federal law can make use of the Social Security Number mandatory (at 5 U.S.C. 552a note). So anytime you're dealing with a government institution and you're asked for your Social Security Number, just look for the Privacy Act Statement. If there isn't one, complain and do not give your number. If the statement is present, read it. If it says giving your Social Security Number is voluntary, you'll have to decide for yourself whether to fill in the number.

Why SSNs Are a Bad Choice for Universal IDs in Databases

Database designers continue to introduce the Social Security Number as the key when putting together a new database or when reorganizing an old one. Some of the qualities that are (often) useful in a key and that people think they are getting from the SSN are uniqueness, universality, security, and identification. When designing a database, it is instructive to consider which of these qualities are actually important in your application; many designers assume unwisely that they are all useful for every application, when in fact each is occasionally a drawback. The SSN provides none of them, so designs predicated on the assumption that it does provide them will fail in a variety of ways.

Uniqueness

Many people assume that Social Security Numbers are unique. They were intended by the Social Security Administration to be unique, but the SSA didn't take sufficient precautions to ensure that it would be so. They have several times given a previously issued number to someone with the same name and birth date as the original recipient, thinking it was the same person asking again. There are a few numbers that were used by thousands of people because they were on sample cards shipped in wallets by their manufacturers.

The passage of the Immigration reform law in 1986 caused an increase in the duplicate use of SSNs. Since the SSN is now required for employment, illegal immigrants must find a valid name/SSN pair in order to fool the INS and IRS long enough to collect a paycheck. Using the SSN when you cannot cross-check your database with the SSA means you can count on getting some false numbers mixed in with the good ones.

Universality

Not everyone has a Social Security Number. Foreigners are the primary exception, but many children do not get SSNs until they're in school (and some not until they get jobs). They were designed only to cover people who were eligible for Social Security. If your database will keep records on organizations as well as individuals, you should realize that they're not covered, either.

Identification

Few people ever ask to see an SSN card; they believe whatever you say. The ability to recite nine digits provides little evidence that you're associated with the number in anyone else's database. There's little reason to carry your card with you. It isn't a good form of identification, and if your wallet is lost or stolen, it provides another way for the thief to hurt you.

Security

Older cards are not at all forgery resistant, even if anyone did ever ask for it. (Recently issued cards are more resistant to forgery.) The numbers do not have any redundancy (no check-digits) so any nine-digit number in the range of numbers that have been issued is a valid number. It is relatively easy to write down the number incorrectly, and there's no way to tell that you've done so.

In most cases, there is no cross-checking that a number is valid. Credit card and checking account numbers are checked against a database almost every time they are used. If you write down someone's phone number incorrectly, you find out the fist time you try to use it. An incorrect SSN might go unnoticed for years in some databases. In others it will likely be caught at tax time, but could cause a variety of headaches.

Why You Should Resist Requests for Your SSN

When you give out your number, you are providing access to information about yourself. You're providing access to information that you do not have the ability or the legal right to correct or rebut. You provide access to data that is irrelevant to most transactions but that will occasionally trigger prejudice. Worst of all, since you provided the key (and did so "voluntarily"), all the information discovered under your number will be presumed to be true, about you, and relevant.

A major problem with the use of SSNs as identifiers is that it makes it hard to control access to personal information. Even assuming you want someone to be able to find out some things about you, there's no reason to believe that you want to make all records concerning yourself available. When multiple record systems are all keyed by the same identifier, and all are intended to be easily accessible to some users, it becomes difficult to allow someone access to some of the information about a person while restricting them to specific topics.

Far too many organizations assume that anyone who presents your SSN must be you. When more than one person uses the same number, it clouds the records. If someone intended to hide their activities, it is likely to look bad on whichever record it shows up. When it happens accidentally, it can be unexpected, embarrassing, or worse. How do you prove that you weren't the one using your number when the record was made?

What You Can Do to Protect Your Number

If, despite your having written "refused" in the box for Social Security Number, it still shows up on the forms someone sends back to you (or worse, on the ID card that they issue), your recourse is to write letters or make phone calls. Start politely, explaining your position and expecting them to understand and cooperate. If that doesn't work, there are several more things to try:

1. Talk to people higher up in the organization. This often works simply because the organization has a standard way of dealing with requests not to use the SSN, and the first person you deal with usually has not been around long enough to know it.
2. Enlist the aid of your employer. You have to decide whether talking to someone in personnel, and possibly trying to change corporate policy, is going to get back to your supervisor and affect your job.
3. Threaten to complain to a consumer affairs bureau. Most newspapers can get a quick response. Ask for their "Action Line" or equivalent. If you're dealing with a local government agency, look in the state or local government section of the phone book under "consumer

affairs." If it is a federal agency, your congressmember may be able to help.

4. Insist that they document a corporate policy requiring the number. When someone cannot find a written policy or doesn't want to push hard enough to get it, they will often realize that they do not know what the policy is, and they've just been following tradition.
5. Ask what they need it for and suggest alternatives. If you're talking to someone who has some independence, and they'd like to help, they will sometimes admit that they know the reason the company wants it, and you can satisfy that requirement a different way.
6. Tell them you'll take your business elsewhere (and follow through if they do not cooperate).
7. If it is a case where you've gotten service already, but someone insists that you have to provide your number in order to have a continuing relationship, you can choose to ignore the request in hopes that they will forget or find another solution before you get tired of the interruption.

If someone absolutely insists on getting your Social Security Number, you may want to give a fake number. There are legal penalties for providing a false number when you expect to gain some benefit from it. A federal court of appeals ruled that using a false SSN to get a driver's license violates the federal law.

There are a few good choices for "anonymous" numbers. Making one up at random is a bad idea, as it may coincide with someone's real number and cause them some amount of grief. It is better to use a number like 078-05-1120, which was printed on "sample" cards inserted in thousands of new wallets sold in the 1940s and 1950s. It has been used so widely that both the IRS and SSA recognize it immediately as bogus, while most clerks haven't heard of it. The Social Security Administration recommends that people showing Social Security cards in advertisements use numbers in the range 987-65-4320 through 987-65-4329.

There are several patterns that have never been assigned, and which therefore do not conflict with anyone's real number. They include numbers with any field all zeroes, and numbers with a first digit of 8 or 9. Giving a number with an unused pattern rather than your own number isn't useful if there is anything serious at stake, since it is likely to be noticed.

If you're designing a database or have an existing one that currently uses SSNs and want to use numbers other than SSNs, you should make your identifiers use some pattern other than nine digits. You can make them longer or shorter than that, or include letters somewhere inside. That way no one will mistake the number for an SSN.

The Social Security Administration recommends that you request a copy of your file from them every few years to make sure that your records are correct (your income and "contributions" are being recorded for you, and no one else's are.) As a result of a recent court case, the SSA has agreed to accept corrections of errors when: there isn't any contradictory evidence; SSA has records for the year before or after the error; and the claimed earnings are consistent with earlier and later wages.[1]

Collecting SSNs Yourself

There aren't any federal laws that explicitly forbid the collection of SSNs. However, there is a body of law, intended to prohibit the misuse of credit cards, that is written vaguely enough that it could be interpreted to cover personal collections of SSNs. The laws are at 18 U.S.C. 1029, and cover what is called "access device fraud." An access device is "any card, plate, code, account number or other means of access that can be used, alone or in conjunction with another access device, to obtain money, goods, services, or any other thing of value, or that can be used to initiate a transfer of value." The law forbids the possession, "knowingly and with intent to defraud" of fifteen or more devices which are counterfeit or unauthorized access devices. If interstate commerce is involved, penalties are up to $10,000 and ten years in prison.

When All Else Fails: Getting a Replacement Number

The Social Security Administration will occasionally issue a replacement SSN. The most common justification is that the SSA or the IRS has mixed together earnings records from more than one person, and since one of the people cannot be located, it is necessary to issue a new number to the other. The SSA tries hard to contact the person who is using the number incorrectly before resorting to this process.

There are a few other situations that the SSA accepts as justifying a new number. The easiest is if the number contains the sequences 666 or 13. The digits need to be consecutive according to SSA's policy manual, but may be separated by hyphens. You apparently do not have to prove that your religious objection is sincere. Other commonly accepted complaints include: someone who is harassing you is tracing you through your SSN; sequential numbers assigned to family members; or serious impact on your credit history that you've tried to clear up without success.

---

[1] See the *San Jose Mercury News* (May 14, 1992), p. 6A. Call the Social Security Administration at (800) 772-1213 and ask for Form 7004 (Request for Earnings and Benefit Estimate Statement).

In all cases, the process includes an in-person interview at which you have to establish your identity and show that you are the original assignee of the number. The decision is normally made in the local office. If the problem is with a credit bureau's records, you have to show that someone else continues to use your number, and that you tried to get the credit bureau to fix your records but were not successful. When they do issue a new number, the new records are linked to the old ones (unless you can convince them that your life might be endangered by such a link).

There are a few justifications that they do not accept at all: attempting to avoid legal responsibilities; poor credit record that is your own fault; lost SSN card (without evidence that someone else has used it); or use of the number by government agencies or private companies.

The only justification the SSA accepts for cancelling the issuance of an SSN is that the number was assigned under their Enumeration at Birth program (wherein SSNs are assigned when birth certificates are issued) without the parent's consent. In this case, the field officer is instructed to try hard to convince the parent that getting the number revoked is futile, but to give in when the parent is persistent.

Dealing with Government Organizations

Government agencies are reasonably easy to deal with; private organizations are much more troublesome. Federal law restricts the agencies at all levels of government that can demand your number, and a fairly complete disclosure is required even if the disclosure is voluntary. There are no comparable federal laws either restricting the uses nongovernment organizations can make of it, or compelling them to tell you anything about their plans. Some states have recently enacted regulations on collection of SSNs by private entities. With private institutions, your main recourse is refusing to do business with anyone whose terms you do not like. They, in turn, are allowed to refuse to deal with you on those terms.

Universities and Colleges

Universities that accept federal funds are subject to the Family Educational Rights and Privacy Act of 1974 (the Buckley Amendment), which prohibits them from giving out personal information on students without permission. There is an exception for directory information, which is limited to names, addresses, and phone numbers, and another exception for release of information to the parents of minors. There is no exception for Social Security Numbers, so covered universities aren't allowed to reveal students' numbers without their permission. In addition, state universities are bound by the requirements of the Privacy Act (so they have to give a Privacy Act notice if they ask for a SSN). If they make uses of the SSN that aren't covered by the disclosure, they are in violation.

United States Passports

The application for a United States Passport (DSP-11 12/87) requests a Social Security Number, but doesn't give enough information in its Privacy Act notice to verify that the passport office has the authority to request it. There is a reference to "Federal Tax Law" and a misquotation of Section 6039E of the 1986 Internal Revenue Code, claiming that that section requires that you provide your name, mailing address, date of birth, and Social Security Number. The referenced section requires only TIN (SSN), and it requires that it be sent only to the IRS (not to the passport office). It appears that when you apply for a passport, you can refuse to reveal your SSN to the passport office, and instead mail a notice to the IRS, give only your SSN (other identifying information optional), and notify them that you are applying for a passport.[2]

Fighting the Requirement in Your Company

According to a note in the Federal Register on May 10, 1994, the department of Health and Human Services requested that the requirements be delayed for eighteen months in order that the requirements could be made more consistent with (then impending) health care reform legislation. I do not know whether the delay was ever implemented, but you can probably keep your HR department busy by telling them that HHS wanted a delay. You can also point out to them the compliance requirements in HHS's proposed regulations; they require only a good faith effort on the employer's part, and even define what that is.

> An employer is deemed to have made a reasonable good faith effort to provide the information with respect to the name and TIN of each other individual covered by the group health plan with respect to the reports for a specific calendar year if the employer can prove that it has established a systematic method to obtain the necessary information that includes both (i) a documented initial effort to obtain the necessary information from the electing individual and (ii) a documented follow-up effort if the electing individual does not respond to the initial effort.

In any case, when the federal government requires your employer to collect SSNs from you, it has to provide a form with a Privacy Act notice. If your personnel department asks you to give them your dependents' SSNs, ask to see a Privacy Act notice. If necessary, ask them to look at the statement on W-4 forms and tell them that they need a statement like it in order for the request to be legal.

---

[2] Copies (in postscript) of the letter that was used by one contributor are available by anonymous ftp from cpsr.org in /cpsr/privacy/ssn/passport.ps.Z. (The measure of his success is that he didn't hear back from anyone with complaints.)

Children

The Family Support Act of 1988 (Pub. L. 100-485) requires states to require parents to give their Social Security Numbers in order to get a birth certificate issued for a newborn. The law allows the requirement to be waived for "good cause," but there is no indication of what may qualify.

The IRS requires taxpayers to report SSNs for dependents over one year of age when you claim them as a deduction, but the requirement can be avoided if you're prepared to document the existence of the child by other means if the IRS challenges you. The law on this can be found at 26 U.S.C. 6109. The penalty for not giving a dependent's number is only $5. Several people have reported that they haven't provided SSNs for their dependents for several years, and haven't been challenged by the IRS.

Private Organizations

The guidelines for dealing with nongovernmental institutions are much more tenuous. Most of the time private organizations that request your Social Security Number can get by quite well without your number, and if you can find the right person to negotiate with, they will willingly admit it. The problem is finding that right person. The person behind the counter is often told no more than "get the customers to fill out the form completely."

Most of the time, you can convince them to use some other number. Usually the simplest way to refuse to give your Social Security Number is simply to leave the appropriate space blank. One of the times when this isn't a strong enough statement of your desire to conceal your number is when dealing with institutions that have direct contact with your employer. Most employers have no policy against revealing your Social Security Number; they apparently believe that it must be an unintentional slip when an employee doesn't provide an SSN to everyone who asks.

Public utilities (gas, electric, phone, etc.) are considered to be private organizations under the laws regulating SSNs. Most of the time they ask for an SSN, and aren't prohibited from asking for it, but they will usually relent if you insist. See the other suggestions above in the section "What You Can Do To Protect Your Number" for more ideas.

Lenders and Borrowers: Those Who Send Reports to the IRS

Banks and credit card issuers and various others are required by the IRS to report the SSNs of account holders to whom they pay interest or from whom they collect it. If you do not tell them your number you will probably either be refused an account or be charged a penalty such as withholding of taxes on your interest.

Most banks send your name, address, and SSN to a company called ChexSystem when you open an account. ChexSystem keeps a database of people whose accounts have been terminated for fraud or chronic insufficient funds in the past five years. ChexSystems is covered by the Fair Credit Reporting Act, and the bank is required to let you know if it refuses to open your account and a report from ChexSystems was a factor. You can also send a letter to ChexSystems directly (Consumer Relations, 1550 E. 79th Street, Suite 700, Minneapolis, Minnesota 55425) and request a copy of their report on you.

Many banks, brokerages, and other financial institutions have started implementing automated systems to let you check your balance. All too often, they are using SSNs as the PIN that lets you get access to your personal account information. If your bank does this to you, write them a letter pointing out how common it is for the people with whom you have financial business to know your SSN. Ask them to change your PIN, and if you feel like doing a good deed, ask them to stop using the SSN as a default identifier for their other customers. Some customers will believe that there's some security in it, and be insufficiently protective of their account numbers. Sometimes banks provide for a customer-supplied password, but are reluctant to advertise it. The only way to find out is to ask if they will let you provide a password.

When buying (and possibly refinancing) a house, most banks will now ask for your Social Security Number on the Deed of Trust. This is because the Federal National Mortgage Association recently started requiring it. The fine print in their regulation admits that some consumers won't want to give their number, and allows banks to leave it out when pressed. (It first recommends getting it on the loan note, but then admits that it is already on various other forms that are a required part of the package, so they already know it. The Deed is a public document, so there are good reasons to refuse to put it there, even though all parties to the agreement already have access to your number.)

Insurers, Hospitals, Doctors

No laws require private medical service providers to use your Social Security Number as an ID number. They often use it because it is convenient or because your employer uses it to identify employees to its group's health plan. In the latter case, you have to get your employer to change their policies. Often, the people who work in personnel assume that the employer or insurance company requires use of the SSN when that is not really the case. When a previous employer asked for my SSN for an insurance form, I asked them to find out if they had to use it. After a week they reported that the insurance company had gone along with my request and told me what number to use.

Most insurance companies share access to old claims through the Medical Information Bureau. If your insurance company uses your SSN, other insurance companies will have a much easier time finding out about your medical history.[3] If an insurance agent asks for your Social Security Number in order to "check your credit," point out that the contract is invalid if your check bounces or your payment is late. Insurance is always prepaid, so they do not need to know what your credit is like, just whether your check cleared.

Blood Banks

Blood banks also ask for the number but are willing to do without if pressed on the issue. After I asked politely and persistently, the (non–Red Cross) blood bank I go to agreed that they didn't have any use for the number. They have now expunged my SSN from their database, and they seem to have taught their receptionists not to request the number. I have gotten many reports that the Red Cross has a national policy of requiring SSNs.

Blood banks have changed their policies back and forth a few times in the last several years. When the AIDS epidemic first hit, they started using SSNs to identify all donors, so someone who was identified as HIV-positive at a blood bank wouldn't be able to contaminate the blood supply by donating at a different site. For a few years, they were a little looser, and though they usually asked for SSNs, some would allow you to donate if you provided proof of your identity. (I showed a driver's license, but didn't let them copy down the number.) Now the federal government has declared blood banks to be "manufacturers" of a medical product, and has imposed various quality control processes on them.

The blood bank I go to now asks for SSNs, but, if you refuse, allows you to give a driver's license number. I balked at that, since I hadn't had to give it before. They let me donate, but while I was eating cookies, the director of Quality Control came down and talked to me. After a little bit of discussion, she was satisfied to have me pick an ID number that I promised to remember and provide when I visited gain. So, once again, if you want to protect your SSN and your privacy, it pays to push back when they ask.

[3] You can get a copy of the file MIB keeps on you by writing to Medical Information Bureau, P.O. Box 105, Essex Station, Boston, Massachusetts 02112. Their phone number is (617) 426-3660.

P·A·R·T · VI

Markets and Privacy

Kenneth Laudon

Introduction

The protection of individual information privacy is a widely accepted value in democratic societies without which the concept of democracy based on individual choice makes little sense (Westin, 1967; Gavison, 1980).[1] Since the 1960s many societies have developed privacy protection laws and regulations to guard against unfettered government and private industry use of personal information. While these protections conceived in the 1960s are important first steps in protecting privacy, existing laws and their conceptual foundation are outdated because of changes in technology. New concepts and methods of privacy protection are needed to address the contemporary and near-future technological environment.

By the year 2000 technological developments are likely to make existing legal frameworks for protecting privacy even more outdated than is true today. For instance, the proposed National Data Network of the Clinton Administration, and the prototype National Research and Education Network (NREN), which is an important component of the High-Performance Computing Act (1991), are destined to contain a great deal of personal information including medical, genetic, insurance, retail purchase, and financial records. This personal information will reside on thousands of file servers—public and private—which will largely be beyond the control of existing privacy laws. Although these networks offer society important benefits like remote diagnosis of disease, lower medical costs, and lower financial transaction costs, such networks will make it less expensive and much easier to engage in privacy invasion on a scale never before possible. Who will or should own and control this personal information on future national networks? What accounting should be made to individuals for use of their private information stored and available on national networks?

Who will be liable for misinformation and the injuries that may result? Current laws and conceptual frameworks do not answer these questions. National Data Networks also offer opportunities for developing new concepts and methods of protecting privacy and security in a network-intensive twenty-first century.

Rethinking Privacy

The premise of this chapter is that to ensure the protection of privacy beyond 2000 we should consider market-based mechanisms based on individual ownership of personal information and National Information Markets (NIMs) where individuals can receive fair compensation for the use of information about themselves. This step is necessary because of the continued erosion of privacy brought about by technological change, institutional forces, and the increasingly outdated legal foundation of privacy protection. Together these forces have eroded individuals' control over the flow of information about themselves. Today, the cost of invading privacy is far lower than the true social cost. Although market-based approaches will not solve all our privacy problems, I believe it is possible to strengthen individual control over personal information and to strengthen (not replace) the existing legal foundations of privacy protection by permitting markets to work. In the end, there should be as much privacy as people are willing to pay for, and as much use of private personal information for commercial purposes as is socially efficient. Today, personal privacy is expensive and in short supply, while the use of personal information is wasteful and inefficient.

Privacy: The Current Situation

Privacy is the moral claim of individuals to be left alone and to control the flow of information about themselves (Warren and Brandeis, 1890; Westin, 1967; Laudon, 1986, Flaherty, 1989; Bennett, 1992; Gavison, 1980).[2] Privacy

---

[1] A number of constitutional law scholars have argued that the concept of privacy is so vague that emphasis should instead be placed on liberty, which is more readily anchored in legal doctrine. (See, for example, Gavison, 1980; Henkin, 1974.)

[2] The development of the right to privacy (and its definition as the right to be left alone) in American law is given in the classic article by Samuel D. Warren and Louis D. Brandeis, "The Right to Privacy," 4 *Harvard Law Review*, 193 (1890); and later this phrase appeared in a Brandeis dissent in *Olmstead v. United States* 277 U.S. 438, 473 (1928) in a case concerning the admissibility of wiretap evidence. Other contemporary works are Alan F. Westin, *Privacy and Freedom*, New York: Athenum, 1967; Kenneth C. Laudon, *Dossier Society*, New York: Columbia University Press, 1986; James B. Rule *et al.*, *The Politics of Privacy*, New York: Elsevier Press, 1980; David Flaherty, *Protecting Privacy in Surveillance Societies*, University of North Carolina

is also a social value reflected in founding documents like the Constitution, and a political statement reflected in laws. There is also a behavioral reality of privacy, the day-to-day routine practices for handling personal information. The behavioral reality of privacy stands apart from the moral claims, political statements, and laws and must be considered separately.

When individuals claim that information about them (or their own behavior) is private, they generally mean that they do not want this information shared with others, and/or that they would like to control the dissemination of this information, sharing with some but not others. These claims of individuals are sometimes strongly supported by cultural assumptions that make it odious for individuals or organizations to deny these claims.[3]

Nevertheless, translating these general cultural value statements and individual claims to information control into political laws has been difficult because in all societies there are competing claims by government and private organizations demanding access to information about individuals in order to promote national security, public health, law enforcement, commerce, or other valued social ends.

The Foundations of Privacy in Law

There are three primary sources of privacy protection in United States law: the common law, the Constitution, and federal and state statutes. The common law protects individuals against the intrusions of other private parties. Today most jurisdictions recognize one or more common law actions that allow private parties to seek redress for invasion of privacy. There are four different types of privacy torts: intrusion on solitude, public disclosure of private facts, publicity that places a person in false light, and appropriation of a person's name or likeness for commercial purposes (Traver, 1994; Prosser, 1960). The common law right to privacy has its origins in a famous article by Warren and Brandeis, which sought to extend growing common law protections of person and property at the end of the nineteenth century. Warren and Brandeis defined a new "right be let

---

Press; Chapel Hill, N.C., 1989; and Colin J. Bennett, *Regulating Privacy: Data Protection and Public Policy in Europe and the United States*, Ithaca: Cornell University Press, 1992, (See also Ruth Gavison,"Privacy and the Limits of Law," *The Yale Law Journal*, 89, No. 3, January 1980.)

   [3] Claims to privacy are widespread and powerful. They are in important documents like the Declaration of Independence in the United States, and the U.S. Constitution. While not mentioning "privacy" per se, these documents declare that individuals shall be free to "life, liberty, and the pursuit of happiness" (Declaration of Independence), and they guarantee against government abridgement of "freedom of speech" (First Amendment), and the "right to be secure in their persons, houses, papers, and effects, against unreasonable searches and seizures" (Fourth Amendment). In other cultures like Germany or Sweden similar claims to privacy are expressed.

alone"—a right to privacy not based on property or contract but instead based on a more general and inherent right of the individual that applied to "the personal appearance, sayings, acts, and to personal relation, domestic or otherwise" (Warren and Brandeis, 1890).

The second major source of privacy law is the federal Constitution, which protects against governmental intrusions into private life. Although "privacy" is not mentioned in the Constitution, jurists and legal scholars have found privacy protections in the First Amendment, which protects freedom of expression, the Fourth Amendment, which protects the privacy of one's personal papers and effects,[4] the Fifth Amendment, which protects against compulsory self-incrimination, the Ninth Amendment, which leaves to the people rights not specifically mentioned in the Constitution, and the Fourteenth Amendment, which protects against deprivation of life, liberty, or property without due process of law.

Federal and state statutes form a third source of privacy. In general, statutes protect individuals against governmental intrusions and uses of information, although increasingly the use of personal information by private organizations is also the subject of legislation. In some instances, state statutes provide stronger protections than federal statutes against government and private-party intrusions (Gormley and Hartman, 1992; Goldstein, 1992).

In the United States there are twelve major pieces of federal legislation specifically regulating the collection, use, management, and dissemination of personal information by the federal government and private organizations (Figure 1).

The seven major pieces of privacy legislation affecting the federal government set forth the due process rules that federal officials must follow when dealing with personal information. The most important contribution of these separate laws is that they prevent federal officials from rummaging through your bank records without a warrant, listening to your electronic communications without a warrant, or cutting off benefits simply because of a computer match. The federal legislation also sets forth standards of

---

[4] Since *Katz v. U.S.* (1967) the Court has attempted to ensure that the Fourth Amendment protects people—not just places like homes as originally conceived in *Boyd v. U.S.* (1886) and in the property-based natural rights view of individual rights. In Katz the Court sought to overturn the property basis of privacy by use of a new standard called "reasonable expectation of privacy." A two-part test was proposed. A privacy right existed if (a) the individual had an "actual subjective expectation of privacy," and (b) society was "prepared to recognize as reasonable" this subjective expectation. However, much to the disappointment of some, the Court quickly returned to the old view that outside the home individuals could not have a reasonable expectation of privacy. Hence, individuals could not have an expectation of privacy regarding information gleaned from business transaction records, garbage, telephone booths, airplane flyovers, third-party consents, and government informants (Traver, 1994). Hence efforts to define a non-property-based Constitutional right to privacy from government intrusion have failed.

Privacy Laws Affecting the Federal Government
  Freedom of Information Act, 1968 as Amended (5 U.S.C. 552)
  Privacy Act of 1974 as Amended (5 U.S.C. 552a)
  Right to Financial Privacy Act of 1978
  Electronic Communications Privacy Act of 1986
  Computer Security Act of 1987
  Computer Matching and Privacy Protection Act of 1988
  Federal Managers Financial Integrity Act of 1982
Privacy Laws Affecting Private Institutions
  Fair Credit Reporting Act, 1970
  Family Educational Rights and Privacy Act of 1978
  Privacy Protection Act of 1980
  Cable Communications Policy Act of 1984
  Video Privacy Protection Act of 1988

Figure 1. Federal privacy laws in the United States.

computer security involving personal financial information. The omnibus Privacy Act of 1974 applies to all federal records and sets forth the rules that the government must follow when managing personal information. The Freedom of Information Act is included here because it severely limits federal government claims that information it holds is "private" and cannot be shared with the public.

Limitations to Privacy Law and the Conceptual Foundations of Privacy

Despite the rather enormous legal armament that has evolved over nearly a hundred years in the United States, most citizens feel their privacy has declined. Survey data show that 76% of citizens believe they have lost all control over personal information (Equifax, 1992). The law review literature, as well as public surveys, argue that computer technology is a major threat to privacy. The legal literature itself is highly critical of the existing legal apparatus for protecting privacy, citing the piecemeal, record-system approach to protecting privacy, and the absence of meaningful enforcement mechanisms (Traver, 1994). Scholars from diverse backgrounds in history, sociology, and political science have all concluded that the existing set of privacy laws do not in fact protect privacy well and that privacy law is far behind the developmental trajectory of information technology (PPSC, 1977; Rule et al., 1980; Laudon, 1986). Our view in this chapter is that the conceptual—and in part legal—foundations of privacy need re-thinking in the United States. This is especially true for the statutory approach to protecting privacy, which is based on a now outmoded doctrine called "fair information practices."

The existing legal approach to privacy in the United States—whether common law, Constitutional, or statutory—has many well-known limitations. Common law torts have been particularly ineffective mechanisms for providing privacy to individuals. Common law claims for protection from being placed in a false light, and protection from the revelation of embarrassing facts, interfere with constitutional protections of free speech and expression. The common law tort of appropriation has been quite effective in protecting celebrities from the appropriation of their likenesses, voices, and styles. However, while celebrities have successfully claimed a property-based privacy interest in their personal information—including likenesses and voices—ordinary citizens have not been equally successful. In this chapter we explore options for extending common law property rights to personal information of ordinary citizens.

Constitutional privacy protections are on weak ground simply because "privacy" per se is not mentioned in the Constitution and therefore must be inferred or derived from other enumerated rights and from judicial interpretation of what the Founding Fathers meant and/or intended by their original statements. The privacy required to think, believe, and worship is protected by the First Amendment's protections of expression and thought; the privacy of one's home and personal effects is protected by the Fourth Amendment. Somewhat less secure is decisional and behavioral privacy regarding highly personal matters like sexual behavior, abortion, birth control, and medical treatment. In these areas of decisional privacy, the state often claims superiority. There are no constitutional protections for any information you reveal in professional or business transactions—electronic or other—even if such information refers to highly personal matters like your genetic structure, medical and mental condition, or consumption patterns. Efforts by the Supreme Court to move away from a "home" or place-based view of privacy toward a more general view based on a "reasonable expectation of privacy" have met with mixed success (*Katz v. United States*, 1967; Freund, 1971).[5]

Privacy advocates in the United States have sought refuge in new laws to protect privacy in the computer age. However, many scholars argue that

---

[5] For instance, you have little privacy from government snooping in an open field, in a telephone booth, or from technologically remote surveillance techniques like aerial surveillance, pen registers that monitor incoming and outgoing calls, and remote electronic eavesdropping, and if you are homeless, your effects may be searched without a warrant (Traver, Section 6, 1994). The concept of "search" as it turns out is quite fluid as the technology of searching advances, and the constitutional protection of privacy remains rather deeply entwined with its original property basis in the home, and one's personal effects.

federal and state statutes protecting individuals against intrusions by government officials are confusing, piecemeal, and riddled with loopholes (Flaherty, 1979; Laudon, 1986; Rule *et al.*, 1980). Among the significant limitations of this legislation is that it generally limits the behavior of federal or state officials, and then only mildly. In some states local officials and private citizens and organizations may rummage through your bank records, for instance, or eavesdrop on your cellular phone conversations. Second, federal agencies have found loopholes in the law that permit them to widely share personal information within the government without your personal informed consent and contrary to the original purpose for which the information was gathered. The only "absolutist" federal privacy protection is the prohibition in the Privacy Act of 1974 against federal officials gathering information on citizens' exercise of their First Amendment rights. Third, in the belief that all record systems are different, United States legislation has been piecemeal, moving from one record system to another, rather than seeking to define an overall right to privacy. Thus, there is legislation covering communications privacy, bank record privacy, video rental privacy, and so on. Perhaps the most important limitation of this legislation is that enforcement is left entirely to individuals who must recover damages in court. There is no enforcement agency.

States have been somewhat more aggressive in defining a general right to privacy (some in their constitutions), and more aggressive in protecting against government agent snooping and employer snooping into the private lives of employees or job applicants. Nevertheless, state legislation suffers from the same limitations of federal legislation. State legislation is piecemeal, takes a record-system approach, and is largely based on the same outmoded doctrine described below. Perhaps the most dangerous aspect of privacy protection in the United States is that it varies wildly from state to state. Privacy invaders may simply move to "open record" states where there are few protections and export data to "closed record" states (Gormley and Hartman, 1992).[6]

Figure 1 also illustrates that private institutions have for the most part been exempt from privacy legislation. The only exceptions—and they are important exceptions—are the credit data, education, cable, and retail video industries where citizens are guaranteed at least due process access to their records and some protection against dissemination of records. For instance, retail video stores are prohibited from disclosing video rental records to anyone without a court order or your personal consent.

---

[6] "Open record" states are those that declare all public records open to the public, or to any private party for any use.

Medical records
Genetic records
Insurance files
Credit card retail transactions
Personnel records
Rental, real estate records
Financial records
Most state government records, e.g., motor vehicle, business records
Most local government records, e.g., tax receipts, real estate records
Criminal records
Employment records
Welfare files
Phone bills
Workman's Compensation
Mortgage records

Figure 2. Major record systems not subject to federal privacy protections.

With these exceptions, for the most part there are no federal laws that offer any protection for the vast storehouse of personal information gathered by the private and public sectors. Figure 2 lists some of the major record systems—both private and public—that can be and are accessed by private organizations and individuals.

An estimated two hundred information superbureaus routinely compile these basic records, collate the information, and then resell it to government agencies, private businesses, and individuals (Deveny, 1989). Among the records offered for a fee are bank balances, rental history, retail purchases, social security earnings, criminal records, credit card charges, unlisted phone numbers, recent phone calls, and a host of other information services (Rothfeder, 1992). Together, this information is used to develop a "data image" of individuals that is sold to direct marketers, private individuals, investigators, and government organizations.[7] There are no laws regulating superbureaus per se, although there have been some regulations issued by the Fair Trade Commission limiting the use of credit data, and one state forced a credit agency to pay a small fine for disseminating false credit reports (Betts, 1993; Wall Street Journal, 1993).

---

[7] The concept of a "data image" was first defined by Laudon in *Dossier Society* (1986, p. 4) as a high-resolution digital image of individuals in societies with widespread and powerful national information systems. Using contemporary database software and hardware, Laudon argued that such national systems could combine personal information from a wide variety of public and private sources, and analyze this information, to make life-shaping decisions about individuals with little or no face-to-face interaction, due process, or even knowledge of the individual.

Behavioral Privacy: Existing Information Markets

Laws are not always good indicators or predictors of behavior. Speeding is against the law, as is software theft, yet millions of adult citizens knowingly violate these laws. Likewise with privacy legislation. While the privacy legislation of the last twenty years has made an important contribution toward defining privacy, many scholars have concluded that the umbrella of privacy protection has failed to keep pace with the growth in computerized records, the laws are more loophole than law, and that in actual practice, with some exceptions, there are only a few meaningful limitations on the flow of personal information in the United States. Surveys of public opinion have documented a growing public concern over the loss of privacy and a growing demand of stronger legislation (Equifax, 1992).

In fact, there is already a lively marketplace in the United States for personal information. This market is dominated by large institutional gatherers with little role currently for individuals to participate. Personal information is a valuable asset to private and governmental institutions who use it to reduce their costs of operation.

The existing market for personal information is based on the notion that the gathering institution owns the personal information, and that the individuals involved have at best "an interest" but not ownership in information about themselves. The 400 million credit records maintained by the three largest credit agencies, the 700 million annual prescriptions records, the 100 million computerized medical records, 600 million personal records estimated to be owned by the 200 largest superbureaus, and the 5 billion records maintained and often sold by the Federal government, not to mention the billions of records maintained and stored by state and local governments all have a real market value that is demonstrated everyday in the marketplace.

It is commonplace, especially in the legal literature, to blame information technology for this state of affairs (Traver, 1994). But we argue that the inability of existing privacy legislation to effectively curtail the flow of personal information, or to give individuals a strong sense of control over the flow of their own information, reflects a deeper failure to understand the marketplace in information, a failure to bring economic perspectives to bear on the problem, and a policy failure lasting more than twenty years.

Rethinking the Fair Information Practices Regime

Virtually all American and European privacy legislation is based on a regulatory regime called Fair Information Practices (FIP) first set forth in a report written in 1973 by an advisory committee to the Secretary of the Department of Health Education and Welfare (now the Department of

Health and Human Services) (U.S. DHEW, 1973). The five fair information principles are:

1. There shall be no personal record systems whose very existence is secret,
2. Individuals have rights of access, inspection, review, and amendment to systems that contain information about them,
3. There must be a way for individuals to prevent information about themselves gathered for one purpose being used for another purpose without their consent,
4. Organizations and managers of systems are responsible and can be held accountable for the damage done by systems, for their reliability and security, and
5. Governments have the right to intervene in the information relationships among private parties.

One of the key advances of the Fair Information Practices (FIP) doctrine is its recognition that individuals have an "interest" in records that contain personal information about them even though those records are created by third parties. This followed, the report argued, from the fact of "mutuality of record generating relationships"—the fact that both parties in a transaction have a need for creating and storing records.

What is the nature of this "interest" and how could individuals and societies protect this interest? Is it a property interest? The Advisory Committee did not recommend a new enforcement agency, an Ombudsman, or individual ownership of information. Instead the Committee argued that any privacy laws should be enforced by individuals seeking redress in courts of law for damages done by invasion of privacy, and by building statutory incentives for large institutions to comply with the Fair Information Practices principles above.

Europe, Canada, and many other nations have followed the lead of the Committee in defining privacy, but often they have chosen to enforce their privacy laws by creating Privacy Commissions or Data Protection Agencies[8]

---

[8] Few would deny that European EEC countries and Canada have stronger data protection and privacy mechanisms in place than does the United States. The differences among countries have many origins in politics, culture, and history. There are three primary differences among nations: (1) the presence of explicit Constitutional protections versus mere statutory protections; (2) the existence of a formal bureaucratic enforcement agency versus reliance on individuals; and (3) formal recognition of international privacy conventions and declarations.

While some argue that the stronger European laws and regulatory structures create "stronger protections of privacy," there is little objective or subjective evidence that "more privacy" exists in these countries than in the United States. Conceptually, the European and Canadian approaches to privacy are heavily dependent on and influenced by the Code of Fair Information Practices developed by DHEW in 1973.

(Flaherty, 1979, 1989; Reagan, 1992; Schwartz, 1989; Bennett, 1992). Whether or not these nations have "more privacy" is open to question.

Technological and Institutional Limitations of the Fair Information Practices Regime

There are many problems with the FIP doctrine that seriously undermine its effectiveness in protecting privacy today. The FIP doctrine was based on the technological reality of the 1960s, where a small number of large-scale, mainframe databases operated by the federal and state governments, or by large financial institutions, were the primary threats to privacy. In this period it was conceivable that an individual could know all the databases in which he or she appeared. But today large-scale database systems can be operated by PC-based networks (even individual PCs now rival the size of 1960s mainframe capacities). Large-scale databases have become so ubiquitous that individuals have no possibility of knowing about all the database systems in which they appear. Hence, the "no secret systems" principle, which originated in an era when only large-scale institutions possessed databases, is technologically out of date.

A cascade of serious problems follows: not knowing about so many systems, it is impossible to gain access, review, or correct information in them. It becomes impossible to give "informed consent" for third-party use of private information.[9] And it becomes impossible to know if managers of systems are holding personal information secure, reliable, and hence difficult to hold managers of these systems accountable or liable.

The FIP regime does not take into account other forces in modern society that mitigate against individuals having a social space to think, read, write, conspire, and innovate. The FIP does not take into account the systemic nature of the problem of information—how much it costs, who it costs, and who owns it. The FIP perspective does not account for harm done to the entire society but focuses instead on individual injury. Imagine if we conceptualized and enforced environmental laws in this manner by relying on the courts to estimate the perceived damages done to individuals by polluters.[10]

---

[9] In the United States and many other countries, "informed consent" is tacitly obtained by a "Privacy Notification" on documents listing routine uses of the information, sometimes with an option to "opt out" (and sometimes lose a benefit). "Informed consent" under these circumstances is not consent at all and poses little threat to governments who wish to use whatever data they want.

[10] An analogy to toxic pollution is appropriate here. Imagine that we protected our physical environment with principles like FIP (Fair Information Practices). Take away the EPA, all environmental laws, and replace it with a single law based on the following principles:

1. You have a right to know what toxic substances, if any, your employer or local industry may be exposing you to
(continues)

Perhaps the most significant weakness of the FIP regime is its failure to specify a stronger form of "interest" that individuals have in their personal information. Under FIP, individuals have only limited rights to control their personal information—rights usually limited to inspection, challenge, and review. With FIP there is little or no individual control over the collection and uses of personal information. A much stronger form of "interest" would be a property interest rather than a mere juridical or administrative interest. Under concept and legal regime of property, individuals have nearly unlimited control over the disposition, uses, storage, and sale of their property. We explore this option below.

Finding Conceptual Support for Privacy in Microeconomic Perspectives

Due process, individual rights, and limitations on the power of the state and private organizations are all key ingredients in Enlightenment theories of social order.[11] These perspectives have preserved what little privacy we have left. But other theories of social order have different conceptions of information and privacy that are important to keep in mind when formulating new policies. In some of these other theories, progress depends on the near unfettered exchange of information, and the reduction of any barriers to the flow of information—including privacy protections (Posner, 1979). But in other theories, the unfettered exchange of information can create social costs for which individuals must be compensated in a rational market system. It is here in the theory of market systems that we can find new grounds for the support of privacy.

---

2. There can be no secret pollution and all pollution will be done in pursuit of commerce or a statutory purpose, in an orderly fashion

3. Managers and organizations are accountable for the pollution they create and can be held liable for any proven damages they do to individuals

4. Government has the right to regulate pollution

Now imagine the bewilderment of an American public if they were told, "If you think you've been harmed by some industrial polluter, you should sue that polluter in a Court of law."

Obviously, placing the burden of proof on individuals who would have to demonstrate actual harm in court, harm that might be irreversible, would destroy any possibility for systematically addressing environmental pollution before harm was done. The only environmental policy would be correction of past catastrophes. Likewise with privacy: we need a far broader foundation and understanding to protect privacy in the twenty-first century.

[11] The Enlightenment is considered to be that period in European history from roughly 1650 to 1789 when the ideas of progress, science, and citizenship based on individual liberty and limitations on the power of the state became widespread, popular, and politically powerful. The political ideas of this period provided many of the key ideas of the American Declaration of Independence and the Bill of Rights, as well as the French Revolution. See R. R. Palmer, *A History of the Modern World*, Alfred A. Knopf, New York, 1962, Chapters IIX and IX.

When Things Go Right: Production Function Models of Order

In a perfect world characterized by perfect information and perfect information systems widely shared by all, capital and labor are combined at their most socially efficient levels to produce the wealth of nations. In this most felicitous world of nineteenth-century economic thought, symmetry of information among market participants (capitalists, laborers, and consumers) is the lubricant of social and economic progress. Information also plays a critical role in the production process (as opposed to market process) because it is embodied in labor as knowledge and in capital, which after all is just a physical instantiation of social knowledge and information. Information technology is like any other capital investment: presumably cheaper than labor, and more productive, information technology replaces labor in the production function, making labor and overall production more efficient, and the society wealthier.

What is wrong with this theory of the firm and markets is of course that it bears little resemblance to reality and lacks predictive power. As it turns out, information is not symmetrically distributed (hence markets don't function as predicted) and information technology is not freely substitutable for labor (hence productivity in information-based firms doesn't follow typical patterns). This has created an industry and market for new theories based on opposite assumptions: the asymmetric distribution of information.

When Things Go Wrong: Asymmetries in Information

A number of contemporary theories of social order are concerned with problems arising from asymmetries in the distribution of information, a more realistic view of the real distribution of information. These theories play a large role in education and research in contemporary Finance, Microeconomics, Accounting, and Management/Organizational Behavior. *Agency theory* focuses on the dilemma of firm owners (principals) who must hire agents (managers) to run their firms (Jensen and Meckling, 1976; Fama, 1980). The firm is a nexus of contracts among self-interested individuals in which the agents have most of the information, and the principals find it costly or impossible to monitor the real behavior of their agents. Firms, and by implication societies, experience agency costs as they attempt to build more and more complex monitoring mechanisms. Public welfare declines as these investments produce no additional output. Information systems appear in agency theory as a convenient low-cost monitoring tool that permits firms to grow without increasing agency costs. For agency theorists, privacy—or any restriction on information flow by agents—is a costly extravagance that raises the costs of management.

Asymmetries in information also drive transaction cost models of social order. Why do firms or organizations exist? Rather than hire people, why don't firms rely on markets to supply their needs, markets where contractors would compete with one another? In *transaction cost theory* the answer is that in markets participants have unequal access to information on the quality of goods and providers in the marketplace (Williamson, 1975, 1985). It is costly to participate in markets: contracts have to be written, monitored, goods evaluated, and funds recovered for failure. Firms grow in size as a way of reducing transaction costs. Information technology appears in this theory as a platform for electronic markets where information on suppliers and prices, and costs of monitoring compliance with contracts, could be reduced. This means that firms could rely more on markets, less on firm growth in size. Likewise, firms could shrink in size (number of employees) as they expand business by contracting out vital services. For transaction theorists, privacy raises the costs of gathering information in the marketplace, and reduces overall social welfare.

Other contemporary theories—adverse selection and moral hazard—focus on market failures caused by asymmetries in information. Consider *adverse selection* (market situations where the bad drive out the good) due to asymmetries in information. Because insurance companies can never be sure about any individual's health (they lack enough detailed information), and because unhealthy people need insurance most, the insured pool becomes a collection of unhealthy people forcing insurance companies to raise rates. Healthy people drop out—refusing to pay these high rates and recognizing they rarely get sick anyway—and soon the insured pool becomes uneconomic to insure.

Or consider *moral hazard* (so called because individuals can alter their behavior, potentially creating a hazard, once they have paid a premium insuring against the consequences of their actions). Because insurance companies cannot monitor how many miles people really drive (information asymmetry), drivers know they can drive as many miles as they want once they have paid the insurance premium. Drivers assume any additional accident costs they incur will be spread over a large group and their perceived marginal cost of driving is lower than what in fact it actually is. This forces insurance companies to raise rates on all drivers and encourages wasteful, accident-increasing driving for all.

These theories leave the theoretical status of privacy as a desirable social goal somewhat ambiguous, presenting the dilemma of progress versus privacy. According to these theories, the restriction of information flows caused by privacy laws leads to a decline in social welfare (Posner, 1978). Let's face it: privacy is indeed about creating and maintaining asymmetries in the distribution of information. At first glance it seems microeconomics is not friendly territory for privacy protection. But there is some salvation in the notion of externalities.

Paying the Price by Finding the Cost: Externalities

The economist Pigou warned in 1932 that when manufacturers did not bear the full costs of making their goods, when they could "externalize" some costs by making others pay, the market price of the goods would be less than their real costs, leading to excess production and resulting social inefficiency (Pigou, 1932). Pigou noted that society permitted manufacturers to externalize many costs of production: the health damages done to workers, environmental damages, and loss in aesthetic and other nonmonetary values. If emissions from a chemical factory destroyed the paint on nearby autos, then chemicals were being produced at less than their true social cost, and they were selling at a lower price than they would otherwise. There could be external benefits as well, for instance, when people plant gardens on their front lawns and all enjoy them without paying anything. This problem came to be known among economists as the problem of positive and negative externalities.

The remedy for Pigou and many contemporary economists to this problem of external cost is to "internalize" the cost: impose a tax on the chemical manufacturer equal to the size of the externality. When they are charged for the damage they create, so the theory goes, polluters will raise prices (forcing consumers to pay the full cost of their production), shift to nonpolluting technologies, or reduce production.

One problem with this approach is finding the size of the externality. Ideally, one would want to charge a tax on polluters just equal to the external costs. This is difficult enough when dealing with tangible externalities, for example, damages to individuals and structures, but is quite complicated when aesthetic values are involved. How much is a sunny sky worth? What losses in psychological self-worth and well-being occur because of a polluted physical environment?

Political problems also arise. Why should we tax a socially obnoxious behavior, permitting "rich" people and firms to pollute? If the behavior is obnoxious, why not outlaw the behavior or closely regulate it using standards and enforcement through criminal and civil sanctions.

There are no easy answers to these questions. It may be much cheaper to permit some small level of obnoxious behavior for those willing to pay rather than ban it entirely, which would require a huge bureaucratic effort. Enforcing the Clean Air Act of 1990 is estimated to cost billions of dollars through the year 2000, force uneconomic production technology into general use, and result in an excessively high cost-benefit ratio. In contrast, an easy-to-administer Carbon Tax of $100 a ton may accomplish the same overall level of clean air at greatly reduced cost. Moreover, each polluter would be able to choose the best, most economic means of compliance with the law in order to reduce their taxes. This is far superior to bureaucratic dictates that all polluters use the same "approved" technology.

Given that an efficient information and knowledge-intensive economy requires the reduction of information asymmetries where possible within socially acceptable limits, can we apply the concept of externalities to achieve a high level of privacy protection at a minimal enforcement cost? I think we can if we extend some of the thinking from information economics and externalities outlined above.

Building Information Markets: The Cheapest and Best Protection of Privacy May Lie in Markets and Taxes— Not Regulation

Markets don't just happen. They arise in a context of social, moral, and political understandings. Sometimes markets need to be encouraged, monitored, created, and regulated by governments. A legitimate and useful role of government is to create the conditions for markets to function.

In the case of informational privacy, markets have either failed to function because of a legal framework that denies individuals a property right to their personal information, or they have been eliminated by collusion among large market participants who benefit from externalities created in the current situation. Privacy invasion is, we argue, partly the result of market failure. If markets were allowed to function, there would be less privacy invasion. The results of this failure of markets are several. First, the cost of using personal information to invade the privacy of individuals is far lower than the true social cost. This is because a part of the cost of invading privacy is borne by the individual whose privacy is invaded. Other costs (regulatory agencies, Congressional Hearings, federally funded study groups, and a small industry of privacy experts) are created and then the government is forced to pay the costs based on general revenue taxes. In addition, current government communication and postal regulations subsidize the invasion of privacy by maintaining artificially low prices in key communication markets required by privacy invaders.

Second, as a result, large public and private institutions make far greater use of privacy-invading techniques than they otherwise would. Third, this results in a decline in public welfare because of the inefficient allocation of tangible resources and a decline in individual self-confidence and public morale. In the end, we are swamped and overwhelmed by activities we do not approve of, which are costly and obnoxious. We tend to blame the technology for what in fact is an institutional situation we have ourselves created.

In what sense does privacy invasion impose a cost on individuals whose privacy is invaded? There are many kinds of costs: direct, indirect, tangible, and intangible costs. Many invasions of privacy in a mass society occur through the secondary and tertiary uses of information gathered in the ordinary conduct of business and government. A "secondary use" of information is any use beyond the purpose for which the information was originally gathered. For instance, when a direct marketing organization asks for your credit card number, that is a primary use of information. The information is being used to support a valid transaction. However, the subsequent selling of that information to database marketing organizations, who are interested in knowing both your credit card number and what you purchased, is a secondary use. Under current law, individuals largely lose control over information gathered about them in the course of legitimate transactions. Although no one here objects to the primary use of information to support a transaction, the question is, what happens to the information gathered in that transaction? The answer: once gathered, the information is beyond individual control, and sometimes this is sanctified by weak "informed consent" clauses, which themselves are often tied to a particular benefit, for example, in order to receive a public benefit, citizens must agree that the information they give may be used for other purposes.

Once individuals lose control of information about themselves, and lose any ownership in that information, the information is then used freely by other institutions to market and communicate with and about individuals. Individuals must cope with this onslaught of communication and incur "coping costs." Figure 3 highlights some of the different kinds of coping costs.

The solution to this problem is not stronger privacy laws as so often called for by well-meaning privacy advocates, or new regulations, or the creation of a "Data Protection Agency," however helpful this may be. Instead we should strengthen and make more fair the existing information markets.

National Information Markets

One possibility is the creation of a National Information Market (NIM) in which information about individuals is bought and sold at a market clearing price (a price, freely arrived at, where supply equals demand). Institutions who gather information about individuals would be allowed to sell baskets of information to other institutions willing to pay for it. Each basket would contain selected standard information on, say, 1000 persons (name, address, etc.), basic demographics where available, and specialized information, for example, health, financial, occupational, or market information. Different markets might exist for different kinds of information, for example, financial assets, credit data, health, government, and general marketing. Purchase of these information baskets confers the right to use this information for commercial purposes other than that for which it was originally collected. Information-using organizations would offer to buy

Direct	Opening unsolicited mail Responding to telephone, e-mail, and other unsolicited communication
Indirect	Maintaining excessively large mail and communication facilities to cope with unsolicited mail
Tangible	Loss of productive and leisure time
Intangible	Loss of control over information about oneself; feelings of helplessness; feelings of mistrust toward government and large private organizations

Figure 3.   Information coping costs. Direct costs are those that can be attributed to a specific activity, division, or product. Indirect costs are those that cannot be so attributed and are usually allocated arbitrarily. Tangible costs (benefits) are those that are palpable and can be easily quantified. Intangible costs (benefits) are those that cannot be easily quantified.

these baskets of information at a price based on the anticipated future revenues that each basket represents.

Figure 4 illustrates one version of how NIMs might work. The process is quite similar to the flows of financial assets in depository institutions that connect individual consumers, retailers, creditors, and banks, and it also borrows some concepts (like bundling of financial instruments into baskets) from the collateralized mortgage market in which thousands of mortgages are pooled and used to develop financial instruments called collateralized mortgage obligations (referred to as tranches).

Here is how an NIM could work. Individuals establish information accounts and deposit their information assets in a local information bank (this could be any local financial institution interested in moving into the information business). The local information bank pools local depositor assets into an information pool, and carves up the pool into marketable information baskets or tranches.[12] These baskets contain key personal information (credit, medical, educational, income, etc.) on groups of individuals. The local bank sells these baskets on a National Information Exchange. The purchase of a basket confers on the purchaser the right to use the information for commercial purposes. Similar to a stock exchange, the Information Exchange brings together buyers and sellers of information

---

[12] The carving up of demographic information into hundreds of social subgroups with distinct consumption patterns and predictable response patterns, and the selling of information about members of these subgroups, are common practices among large consumer information firms like Equifax.

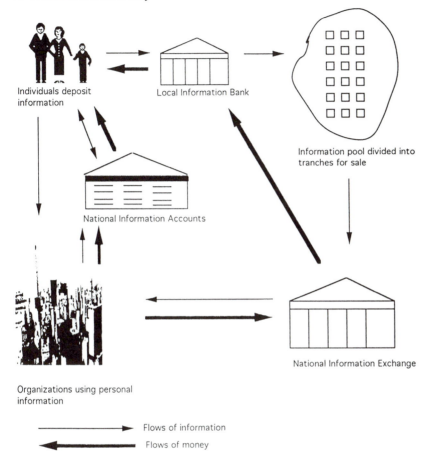

Figure 4. How National Information Markets would work.

in a forum (physical or electronic) for the purpose of transacting at a market clearing price. Once the transaction is completed, funds flow back to the local depository institutions, and ultimately to credit depositors' accounts, minus, of course, information-handling charges for both the local banks as well as the Exchange and any brokers involved. Organizational users of personal information—credit-granting agencies, medical institutions, insurance agencies, government agencies, retailers, and so on—purchase baskets of information on the Exchange, or through brokers acting as intermediaries. Private placements and nonmarket transactions are, of course, possible. Individuals and organizations may transact information off the market, with individuals granting organizations rights to use information about them in return for some fee. For instance, organizations that collect credit histories of consumption could—with the consent of individuals and probably involving some payment—sell baskets of this information on the National Exchange.

Payments for private placement sales of personal information could be cleared through a National Information Accounts Clearinghouse (NIAC) established by Congress for the purpose of permitting individuals the ability to collect fees for the use of their private information (a system similar to that established in the music industry, which permits individual artists to collect fees based on use of their music). The NIAC would also act as an audit mechanism by tracking the use of all secondary, commercial use of personal information, maintaining a record for individuals about who purchased information about them, where the purchase took place, and where the information was used.

National Information Markets would be the only legal avenue for the transfer of information about individuals being used for secondary purposes, that is, for purposes and institutions other than those for which the information was originally gathered. Hence MasterCard could use information on your credit history for the purpose of authorization of future MasterCard purchases (a primary use), but it could not sell your history of credit card purchases to other institutions like TRW Credit Data without your permission—and most likely some payment.

The National Information Market is self-supporting: a transfer tax is charged and this revenue is used to support the marketplace infrastructure, enforcement of rules, and monitoring activities.

National Information Accounts

A key aspect of a National Information Market is the development of National Information Accounts for both suppliers (individuals and institutions) as well as purchasers (information brokers, institutions, and individuals). Every citizen who chooses to participate in the marketplace would be assigned a National Information Account with a unique identifier number and unique bar code symbol. The NIA helps individuals keep track of who is using their information by informing the account whenever the individual's name is sold as part of a basket of information. Every secondary use of personal information must be authorized by the individual at some point, and a national information account informed (and credited if required). The greatest threat to individual privacy is the use of personal information by organizations without the knowledge or consent of the individual. This threat would be minimized through NIAs.

The purpose of the NIA is several fold. Personal accounts, like bank accounts, are required to assure that some percentage of the purchase price of information sold on the market is returned to individuals as revenue to compensate them for their cost of dealing with privacy invasion. Unique bar codes are required to control and audit the flow of unsolicited mail in the United States postal systems: no commercial unsolicited mail can flow through public post systems without a unique NIA identifier bar code that permits automatic crediting of NIA accounts. This is a realistic mechanism for attaining a complete computer-based audit trail for personal information used in commerce, a long-sought objective of privacy reformers (Berman and Goldman, 1989).

For instance, citizens calling an 800 number could find their account balance, and perhaps trace the flow of information about themselves, for example, how did Brown Harriman Investment Banking, who just contacted me with an unsolicited phone call, obtain my bank balance information from the Bank of New York? A National Information Clearinghouse could empower individuals to trace the flow of information about themselves.

From a societal point of view it is only through national accounts that external costs of an information-driven economy are properly internalized. From an individual point of view, national accounts restore some measure of real control, and the subjective perception of control, and order, to the flow of information.

Information Fiduciaries

Because most people would not have the time or interest to participate directly in information markets, information fiduciaries would naturally arise. Information fiduciaries are agents acting on your behalf who have assumed certain responsibilities under law. Like banks, they would accept deposits of information from depositors and seek to maximize the return on sales of that information in national markets or elsewhere in return for a fee, some percentage of the total returns. Such information fiduciaries could easily be recruited from the ranks of existing information superagencies and local credit/information bureaus.

Government Exemptions

Would governments have to pay for information that it needs to administer programs? In general, no. The concept of National Information Markets applies only to secondary and tertiary uses of information for purposes other than those for which it was gathered. The information collected by the government in the course of conducting business with citizens could be used to administer programs without cost. However, if a government sells this information to third parties, or seeks information from sources outside government programs, then it would be treated as simply another market participant and it would pay for information received, and be compensated for information sold. In either event, individual citizens would receive some fair percentage of these transactions. Of course, for law enforcement and national security purposes, these restrictions may be waived.

Objections and Issues

I have presented the ideas in this chapter before market research advertising executives, privacy-policy advocates, privacy scholars, and social science scholars from economics, sociology, and political science. Although there is much support for these ideas—surprisingly among market research and advertising executives—a number of serious objections have arisen to the basic ideas that (1) individuals should own their personal information, and (2) National Information Markets based on the trading of personal information would advance the cause of privacy. I have summarized these objections and issues in Figure 5. I can only briefly address each issue in this chapter, some more than others.

Let's look at each of these issues briefly.

Selling a basic right. In the existing unfair information markets, individuals give up or lose control over their personal information as a matter of course every day, sometimes under threat of not receiving a benefit. Surely these same individuals could charge for this same information that they currently give away or have stripped away without violating any Constitutional privilege. Second, it is by no means clear that "privacy" is an unqualified Constitutional right. The Constitution explicitly protects the privacy only of one's papers and personal effects, and this is generally interpreted by the Court as the privacy of one's home. The Constitution makes no mention of the personal information that makes up one's data image, although many legal scholars believe that such privacy can be inferred from the Constitution and its history. In any event, people can and do choose to give up their Constitutional rights under selected circumstances all the time. For instance, people may choose to give up some freedom of speech in order to achieve greater social harmony.

Social and Legal Issues
> People should not be allowed to sell a basic right
> Property is regressive: only the rich and powerful would benefit (equity)
> A revolution in American property law would be required
> Government privacy regulation is required, as in auto safety, because markets do not respond
>   to the social and individual needs for privacy

Economic Issues
> National Information Markets would raise business transaction costs and inhibit trade
> National Information Markets would experience high administrative costs
> Individual privacy leads to marketplace fraud; there is too much privacy already

Figure 5.   Issues and objections to market-based privacy.

The property regime is regressive and inequitable. In a market, some people will indeed sell their privacy, the poor more than the rich. Rich people may receive much more in the marketplace for the right to invade their privacy, but because they are rich, most will not care to sell their privacy, and most will charge excessively high prices assuring a nonsale, or simply withdraw from the market entirely to preserve their privacy completely. Information from middle-income groups will be in high demand and these individuals will seek out the best prices.

The ability of large information-using institutions to dominate the proposed new national information marketplace is also dubious. As it now stands, individuals have no institutions to represent their interests in the existing information marketplace. I believe that professionally operated, local information depository institutions would be a powerful economic and legal representative for individuals. It is likely that existing consumer banking corporations would be capable and interested in becoming local information depositories. In this manner, individuals could be as well represented in the information marketplace as they are in financial markets by such giants as Merrill Lynch and Citibank. Currently, individuals have no such protection at all in the existing information markets.

Finally, to those who argue that property is an elitist institution incapable of protecting the rights of non–property owners, we agree that property is not equally distributed. Nevertheless, everyone does in fact possess information about themselves that would be valuable under some circumstances to others for commercial purposes. Everyone possesses his or her own good reputation and data image. In this sense, basing privacy on the value of one's name is egalitarian. Even the poor possess their identity. In the current regime of privacy protection not even the wealthy can protect their personal information.

The point is that overall privacy invasion will decline; there will be a net increase in privacy because the cost of invading privacy will go up. People will have a greater understanding of the flow of information in the society (the markets will make it visible), the flow will be more institutionalized and less secret, and people will experience more control over the fate of their own information. The concept of a market includes the potential to withdraw, to protect one's privacy entirely.

A revolution in property law is required. No revolution in American property law is required to support National Information Markets or the ownership of one's own personal information. On the contrary, the connection between privacy and property has strong historical precedents (Barrad, 1992). Property law is quite flexible in recognizing value in a wide variety of tangible and intangible assets, including one's personal image. Personal information—from genetic codes to credit history to medical information—has many of the key characteristics of property as defined in American law and the Hohfeldian theory of property (Hohfeld, 1917; American Law

Institute, 1936). For instance, since the turn of the century courts have recognized the claims of celebrities to a property interest in their photographic image and the right of celebrities to seek compensation whenever their image is used for a commercial purpose (Dangelo, 1989). What is needed is the extension of a property interest to the digital data image of ordinary individuals. Clearly, today's "data images" of individuals have as much resolution as many photographic images. How can a property interest be granted to protect photographic images without extending such a property interest to data images?

Government regulation is required to achieve satisfactory levels of privacy. One theory of government, surely, is that government is required by the failure of markets, for example, to regulate natural monopolies or to correct assymetries in information by forcing disclosure of information, as in financial markets. Yet another theory is that markets fail when governments regulate (Stigler, 1975). Many privacy advocates argue for more regulation, more laws, more enforcement agencies, and more standards being imposed on everyone (Flaherty, 1989; Laudon, 1986; Berman and Goldman, 1989). With some notable exceptions, described earlier, the regulatory approach to privacy has not worked. This much we know.

Would markets work any better in protecting privacy? Social policy analysts may well question whether or not markets can solve the problem of privacy invasion any better than markets solved the problem of automobile safety. For instance, auto makers did not respond well to market demands for automobile safety features like air bags. Rather, the solution was regulated by government. Also, in a "free market" would not large institutions dominate the terms of transactions?

Our approach is empirical, not dogmatic. While automobile safety is a visible threat to people, and no doubt important, protecting one's property and ensuring a fair return on one's assets has proven to be a powerful motivation in free economies. Once told that personal information is an asset worth real money in a marketplace, individuals might easily be convinced to demand a proper institutional foundation for ensuring a fair return on their assets. And there is some reason to believe the individuals pursuing their own self-interest can protect their assets over the long term better than governments are able to do. Moreover, auto safety features, as manufacturers pointed out, generally meant money out of the pocket for consumers. National Information Markets—properly structured—should mean money into the pocket for millions of people, or at least a sense of justice. There is indeed a proper role for government described below, namely, ensuring that the markets operate fairly.

Transaction costs would rise and inhibit trade. Those who make this argument are ignorant of the enormous cost of the existing set of arrangements in which individuals have lost virtually all control over their personal information. Because individuals have lost control over their personal information, they are involuntarily included in marketing databases where they do not want to be and from whom they do not want to receive information. Nevertheless, owners of these marketing databases send millions of individuals substantial information, by mail or by phone, most of which is promptly tossed out or ignored, causing a waste of billions of dollars. For instance, according to the Direct Marketing Association of New York City, about 14.5 billion catalogs were distributed to homes in 1994. Researchers have found that 75% of these catalogs are tossed out within five seconds of the recipient viewing them.[13] Millions of telephone solicitations are also ignored. The precise cost of the wasteful system of nonconsensual databases is not known, but it may approach $50 billion annually, adding significantly to market transaction costs. Much of this waste could be avoided in a market-based system of privacy because only consensual databases would exist. Consensual databases could be built based on individual ownership of personal information and they could be operated for pennies per transaction. For this reason, many marketing and advertising executives are interested in consensual databases.

Costs of National Information Markets. The costs of operating National Information Markets should be much less than the costs of operating credit card or debit card systems. Owners of personal information voluntarily submit, correct, and update information; users of personal information simply have to make inquiries to national repositories to identify individuals and costs, and then they will submit payments to individuals for use of their information via the same route. The record complexity is quite low when compared to, say, credit or debit record systems. The costs of operating a system of National Information Markets may well be less than the waste generated by the existing system. National Information Markets will be self-supporting, based on fees charged to market participants. As it turns out, information systems are marvelously efficient and powerful at keeping accounts and quite useful in the creation of electronic markets involving huge transaction volumes at only pennies per transaction.

There is too much individual privacy already. Some economists analyzing privacy have reached opposite conclusions from ours (Hirshleifer, 1971, 1980; Stigler, 1980; O'Brien and Helleiner, 1980). Some legal scholars, writing from an economic perspective, argue that altogether too much privacy has been accorded individuals, and that the property right to personal information should be assigned "away from the individual where

---

[13] Stephanie Strom, "More Catalogs Clogging Mailboxes This Year," *The New York Times,* November 1, 1995.

secrecy would reduce the social product by misleading the people with whom he deals;" (Posner, 1978: 403; Posner, 1979). In this view, privacy is an intermediate—not ultimate—value; privacy is not a necessary utilitarian condition for contemporary society, and indeed may interfere with transactions insofar as the claim to privacy is tantamount to claiming the right to deceive others in the marketplace (Posner, 1978: 408). For Posner, more privacy—not less—should be accorded businesses who, in this view, require secrecy to perform entrepreneurial functions. These views, while interesting, fail to account for the negative information externalities that are inherent to the new information age. Also, these views fail to recognize the noneconomic functions of privacy, for example, political freedom and liberty, which contribute to social welfare.

Some economists have attacked the remedy for external costs that we propose and that other economists propose for controlling pollution— namely to tax the polluters in proportion to the costly damage they cause rather than regulate them. Coase (1960) argues that if a manufacturer damages a neighbor's property, creating an external cost not accounted for by the manufacturer in his pricing schedule, then it may make more economic sense to move the neighbor rather than tax the manufacturer. To tax the manufacturer in an amount equal to the damage to neighboring property could result in reducing the overall welfare when compared to the simple expedient of removing the damaged neighbor, or striking a bargain with local homeowners, for example, fixing their homes or cars injured by pollution. Moreover, Coase argues that taxing the polluter will not alter the overall distribution of resources but instead will reduce the efficiency of society as a whole. But this argument makes little sense when applied to privacy invasion on a massive scale, or pollution on a massive scale: how do you "move away" from privacy invasion and avoid experiencing the costs? The argument makes even less sense if the risks are life threatening, catastrophic, or injurious to liberty in some general sense.

Under a regime where individuals own their personal information, transaction costs may rise but only insofar as to pay for the cost of invading privacy, the externalities of the Information Age. National Information Markets will raise the cost of using personal information for reasons other than which it was gathered. This additional new cost will discourage the obnoxious use of information that could undermine the foundations of a free society if left unchecked. There should not be any "free lunch" when it comes to invading privacy. National Information Markets will result in a decline in the use of unsolicited communications—a key source of privacy concerns. But it will also lead to cost savings as firms use the latest technology to target their communications to a smaller group, devise new ways to market products and obtain market information, and compete with one another on their privacy-regarding corporate practices. Overall social welfare will increase.

National Oversight: A Federal Information Commission

We have argued that the principal privacy enforcement mechanism be a marketplace rather than a regulatory agency. Nevertheless, even marketplaces need an oversight agency to assure efficiency and standards. The functions of a Federal Information Commission (FIC) would be similar to, but go beyond, the traditional "Data Protection Agency" structured along the European and Canadian lines, and more in common with the U.S. Securities and Exchange Commission (SEC). Functions of the FIC would include:

- Creating and monitoring National Information Markets
- Conducting system and participant audits
- Developing data quality standards and expectations
- Developing privacy metrics
- Gathering and publishing statistical reports
- Conducting educational programs in schools
- Advising Congress and the Executive Branch on information matters

The Responsibility of Information Systems Professionals

Information system (IS) professionals in a democracy are obligated to help individuals and society achieve that level of privacy required for the preservation of democracy. IS professionals also have obligations to the organizations for whom they work to achieve efficiencies in administration that may require the extensive use of personal information. These obligations are not necessarily opposed and there are several opportunities for professionals to have a positive impact on their resolution. First, we should ensure that our professional associations (the ACM, DPMA) develop public policies on privacy and clarify the obligations of professionals. Second, we should encourage organizations that claim to represent and speak for IS professionals in Washington (like CPSR, Computer Professionals for Social Responsibility) to seriously consider new ways to achieve privacy aside from the traditional methods of more regulation and more bureaucracy in the form of Data Protection Commissions and the like. Third, we should encourage our employers to devise policies that do not demean the individual's control over personal private information, and that may compensate individuals for use of that information. Fourth, we should encourage our employers to compete on privacy much as Citibank, and L.L. Bean are now doing in their advertising, which promises individuals a measure of control over information given to these organizations. In the long run, establishing a relationship of trust with the customer and his or her personal information will have strategic business value and restore some measure of control to individuals.

Conclusion: Toward Second-Generation Privacy Policies

The deals cut in the first "regulatory" generation of privacy legislation—
segregation of files by function, prohibiting secondary uses of information
without "informed consent," establishing individual rights vis-à-vis record
systems, management accountability, and due process rules—were important first steps along the road to civilized management of information in
a digital age. Nevertheless, technology, economics and organizational
behavior have vitiated the strength of the regulatory approach. There is
simply too much money, political gain, and bureaucratic advantage for the
regulatory approach to work by itself.

If privacy is to be taken seriously as a public value, then the solution is
to rely on more powerful and less wasteful mechanisms like markets to
reduce the level of privacy invasion. As things currently stand, there is
much more unsolicited invasion of privacy than is tolerable, socially efficient, or politically wise. The current situation is costing corporations
billions of dollars in sheer waste as they pour money into privacy-invading
marketing and authorization techniques. Millions of dollars worth of junk
mail is tossed out without even being opened, millions of telephone
solicitations result in hang-ups, market researchers are refused vital information by disgusted and fearful consumers, millions of faulty credit authorizations are issued based on poor data quality, and public cynicism
about the information trade is growing, all suggesting a polluted, even
toxic information environment. A powerful way to clean our information
environment is through a mixture of market and regulatory mechanisms.

Acknowledgments

This research was supported in part by the National Science Foundation NCR
91-13216 Amelia Island Conference, "Civilizing Cyberspace: Priority Policy Issues
in a National Information Infrastructure," January 1993. Additional support
was provided 1994–1995 by the Department of Energy, Human Genome Project,
Ethical, Legal, and Social Implications of the Human Genome, and the Center for
Social and Legal Research, Hackensack, New Jersey.

References

American Law Institute (1936). Restatement of Property.
Barrad, Catherine M. Valerio (1992). "Genetic Information and Property Theory,"
    Northwestern University Law Review, Vol. 87, Spring.
Bennett, Colin J. (1992). Regulating Privacy: Data Protection and Public Policy in Europe
    and the United States. Cornell University Press, Ithaca, New York.
Berman, Jerry, and Janlori Goldman (1989). "The Federal Right of Information
    Privacy: The Need for Reform." The Benton Foundation, Washington D.C.

Betts, Mitch (1993). "FTC Targets Credit Bureau Mailing Lists." *Computerworld*, January 18.

Black's Law Dictionary, 5th ed. (1979). West Publishing Company, St. Paul, Minnesota.

Coase, R. H. (1960). "The Problem of Social Cost." *The Journal of Law and Economics*, Vol. III, October.

Dangelo, Kathleen Birkel (1989). "How Much of You Do You Really Own? A Property Right to Identity." *Cleveland State Law Review*, Vol. 37, 3.

Deveny, Kathleen (1989). "Is Nothing Private." *Business Week*, September 4.

Easterbrook, Insider Trading, Secret Agents, Evidentiary Privileges and the Production of Information (1981). Sup. Ct. Rev. 309 (discussing the Sup. Ct's treatment of property rights in information)

Equifax (1992). The Equifax Report on Consumers in the Information Age, A National Survey. Equifax Inc.

Fama, Eugene (1980). "Agency Problems and the Theory of the Firm." *Journal of Political Economy*, 88.

Flaherty, David H. (1979). *Privacy and Government Databanks: An International Perspective*. Mansell, London, U.K.

Flaherty, David H. (1989). *Protecting Privacy in Surveillance Societies*. University of North Carolina Press, Chapel Hill, N.C.

Freund, Paul A. (1971). "Privacy: One Concept or Many?," in J. Pennock and J. Chapman (eds.), *Nomos XIII: Privacy*, pp. 182–198. Atherton Press, New York.

Gavison, Ruth (1980). "Privacy and the Limits of Law." *The Yale Law Journal*, Vol. 89, No. 3, January.

Goldstein, Bruce D. (1992). "Confidentiality and Dissemination of Personal Information: An Examination of State Laws Governing Data Protection." *Emory Law Journal*, Vol. 41.

Gormley, Ken, and Rhonda G. Hartman (1992). "Privacy and the States." *Temple Law Review*, Vol. 65.

Hirshleifer, Jack (1971). "The Private and Social Value of Information and the Reward to Inventive Activity," 61 *Am. Econ. Rev.*, 561.

Hirshleifer, Jack (1980). "Privacy: Its Origins, Function and Future," 9 *J. Legal Studies*, Vol. 9, 649.

Hohfeld, Wesley N. (1917). "Fundamental Legal Conceptions as Applied in Judicial Reasoning." *Yale Law Journal*, Vol. 26.

Jensen, Richard, and William Meckling (1976). "Theory of the Firm: Managerial Behavior, Agency Costs, and Ownership Structure." *Journal of Financial Economics*, 11, 305–360.

Katz v. United States 389 U.S. 347 (1967).

Laudon, Kenneth C. (1986). *Dossier Society*. Columbia University Press, New York.

O'Brien and Helleiner (1980). "The Political Economy of Information in a Changing International Economic Order," 34 *Int'l Org.*, 445.

Pigou, A.C. (1932). *The Economics of Welfare* (4th ed.). Blackwell Books, London.

Posner, Richard (1978). "The Right of Privacy." *Georgia Law Review*, Vol. 12, 3.

Posner, Richard (1979). "Privacy, Secrecy, and Reputation." *Buffalo Law Review*, Vol. 28.

Privacy Protection Study Commission (1977). Personal Privacy in an Information Society. Report of the Privacy Protection Study (Government Printing Office).

Prosser, William (1960). "Privacy." *California Law Review,* Vol. 48, 383.

Reagan, Priscilla (1992). "The Globalization of Privacy: Implications of Recent Changes in Europe." Paper delivered at the Annual Meeting of the American Sociological Association, August 20–24.

Rothfeder, Jeffrey (1992). *Privacy for Sale.* Simon and Shuster, New York.

Rule, James B., Douglas MacAdam, Linda Stearns, and David Uglow (1980). *The Politics of Privacy.* Elsevier Press, New York.

Schwartz, Paul (1989). "The Computer in German and American Constitutional Law: Towards an American Right of Self-Determination." *The American Journal of Comparative Law,* Volume XXXVII, Fall, Number 4.

Stigler, G. J. (1975). "Can Regulatory Agencies Protect the Consumer," in *The Citizen and the State.* University of Chicago Press, Chicago.

Stigler, G. J. (1980). "An Introduction to Privacy in Economics and Politics," 9 *J. Legal Studies,* 623.

Traver, Carol (1994). "Privacy, Law, and the Human Genome Project: A Review of the Literature 1968–1993." Center for Social and Legal Research, Hackensack, New Jersey.

U.S. DHEW (1973). *Records, Computers and the Rights of Citizens.* MIT Press, Cambridge, MA.

Wall Street Journal (1993). "Equifax Inc. Will Pay $240,000 Restitution Over Credit Reports." December 27.

Warren, Samuel D., and Louis D. Brandeis (1890). "The Right to Privacy," 4 *Harvard Law Review,* 193–220; and later this phrase appeared in a Brandeis dissent in *Olmstead v. United States* 277 U.S. 438, 473 (1928).

Westin, Alan F. (1967). *Privacy and Freedom.* Athenum, New York.

Williamson, O. E. (1975). *Markets and Hierarchies.* Free Press, New York.

Williamson, Oliver E. (1985). *The Economic Institutions of Capitalism.* Free Press, New York.

P·A·R·T · VI

L

Information Entrepreneurialism, Information Technologies, and the Continuing Vulnerability of Privacy

Rob Kling • *Mark S. Ackerman* • *Jonathan P. Allen*

Introduction

Why is there a continuing development of information technologies, applications, and uses that impinge on personal privacy?

In the early 1990s Lotus Development Corporation announced plans to market a CD-based database of household marketing data, *Marketplace: Household*. Lotus *Marketplace:Household* would have given anyone with a relatively inexpensive Apple Macintosh access to personal data on more than 120 million Americans (Levy, 1991; Culnan, 1993). Lotus *Marketplace: Household* is only one example of surveillance and monitoring technologies and products. Many similar cases can be found. In 1991, for example, the Metromail division of R. R. Donnelley obtained names from voter-registration lists to sell to direct mail campaigns, violating state laws (Wartzman, 1994). More recently, in 1994 the Orange County, California sheriff's department constructed a text and photo database of possible gang members to help thwart a growing trend of ethnic gang violence. The database included many teenagers of Hispanic or Asian descent who had merely worn currently fashionable ganglike clothes to school.

Lotus withdrew *Marketplace:Household* from the market after receiving over 30,000 complaints from consumers about the privacy implications of the product. The Metromail division is under investigation. The Orange County sheriff's office has scaled back plans for its database. All of these stories ended well, or at least under control, but how are we to understand why these systems and products—with their substantial privacy implications—were developed in the first place? Were these strange, one-time aberrations in introducing abusive products? Or rather, were they particularly visible examples of a longer-term societal trend toward tightened surveillance and social control?

During the next decades we expect to see new streams of services whose technologies include computer components, such as on-line, household-oriented, medical diagnostic systems, vehicle identification and location systems, "smart cards" for shoppers, and so on. These information services attract customers, in part, by giving them a little more control over some part of their lives. But in collecting personally sensitive data, and placing it in organizational matrices of information-sharing arrangements whose nature is not well understood by nonspecialists, such systems also reduce many people's effective control over the use of information about themselves ("privacy").

These matrices of information sharing can be different for different kinds of data, such as records about medical diagnoses and recent purchases. So these new services need not lead to a centralized ("panoptic") surveillance megasystem that can electronically integrate all digital records about any member of a society. What is at stake is the extent to which the resulting social order enables people to live dignified lives; that they can participate in diverse social and economic relationships that they can adequately comprehend and control; and that people are not thrust into crises because of errors or sublime idiosyncrasies of personal record systems.

This chapter examines why some modern organizations find it attractive to develop and use these types of technologies and products. We will argue that certain societal and institutional arrangements reward organizations that develop such "informationalized services," and thus answer the question of why there is a continuing threat to personal privacy through even undeveloped information technologies and routine organizational practices.

Institutional and Environmental Explanations

In general, most studies of computers and privacy focus on the problems surrounding a particular law, portion of a social system (e.g., credit reporting), or kind of practice (e.g., computer matching) (Laudon, 1986; Lyon, 1991). Even broad-ranging studies, like *The Politics of Privacy* (Rule *et al.*, 1984), *Protecting Privacy in Surveillance Societies* (Flaherty, 1989), or *The Rise of the Computer State* (Burnham, 1983) focus on describing the rise of elaborate social surveillance systems and their legal and administrative frameworks. When authors explain the link between new technologies and changes in surveillance at the broader societal level, they tend to focus on the needs of bureaucracies, both public and private, to improve the fairness of their services and to better control their clientele and environments. Classic works such as Rule's *Private Lives and Public Surveillance* (1974) stress the mandates of various organizations to enforce social control—to make their clients' behavior more predictable and more acceptable.

We find this classic view too limited. Explaining the development and adoption of commercial surveillance technologies such as the ill-fated Lotus *Marketplace:Household* requires more than a generic "need" to enforce social control or improve bureaucratic efficiency. In contrast, we argue here that the expansion of existing information systems and the development of newer surveillance systems are being driven by a set of social dynamics that amplify the use of personal data and ignore privacy concerns.

Laudon (1986) makes a valuable distinction between "environmental" and "institutional" explanations for the adoption of computer technologies by organizations. Environmental explanations portray organizations as responding rationally to objective uncertainties created by their environments. For example, an organization may have too many clients or face severe financial losses from doing business with people who are not well known to the organization's staff.

Institutional explanations, on the other hand, argue that technology adoption strategies may operate independently of environmental pressures to be rationally efficient; they carry their own internal logic. Institutional explanations, for example, focus on the ways that organizations computerize to maintain legitimacy, or the way that computerization reflects the values and interests of specific groups and individuals within the organization. For example, some of the managers who are looking for an exciting project to help advance their careers will find that developing a new information system is a plausible vehicle. Of the millions of North American managers seeking a career-enhancing project, at any time only a handful may try to develop or expand an information system that contains personally sensitive data. But these systems projects add up to help create a new social order. Laudon studied the adoption of criminal records databases operated by state governments in the United States. He found that the initial adoption of the technology was well explained by environmental models, but institutional explanations provided a better understanding of how that surveillance technology was ultimately implemented, routinized, used, and expanded. Fully explaining the expanding use of surveillance technologies in commercial organizations, we argue, will require both environmental *and* institutional explanations.

We view the expansion and use of new computer technologies for personal record keeping as the by-product of a set of social practices that we refer to as *information entrepreneurialism*. Information entrepreneurialism refers to the active attempts of organizational groups to take advantage of changes in key social relationships and in information technology to gain market and organizational advantage. Of particular interest here is when information entrepreneurialism exists within *information capitalism*, an economic arrangement in which people and organizations are expected to profit from the use or sale of information (to be further described below).

Information entrepreneurial practices are made useful by many social transformations over the past century: the increasing mobility of populations, the growth of nationwide organizations, and the increasing importance of indirect social relationships. Information entrepreneurial practices are also encouraged by the development of more cost-effective technologies for managing large-scale databases.

However, external, environmental factors such as social mobility and computer improvements cannot completely explain the diverse ways and varying degrees to which surveillance technology has been implemented across industries, or even in different organizations within a single industry. The information entrepreneurialism model is useful for distinguishing the institutional from environmental motivations for corporate practices. Organizations selectively adopt technologies that serve the interests of coalitions that can afford them and that are considered legitimate. The internal structure of organizations has been affected tremendously by the rise of professional management, trained and rewarded for pursuing managerial strategies that depend on data-intensive analysis techniques. The growth of managerial analysts inside North American organizations is an important institutional explanation of modern society's push to increase the monitoring of people and their social relationships.

The information entrepreneurialism model, then, helps us recognize the taken-for-granted beliefs on the part of managers, as well as the institutional (rather than profit-motivated) rewards they reap for pursuing data-intensive strategies and their desire to keep those strategies unfettered. At the same time, it recognizes the active and effective pursuit of gain through legitimate patterns of action—the "offensive" side of new surveillance technologies—in direct mail and telemarketing campaigns.

In the rest of this chapter, we discuss information entrepreneurial practices by examining them in the context of information capitalism, computerization, and the monitoring of indirect social relationships. The first section examines information entrepreneurialism as an institutional explanation of computer and privacy practice in the commercial world. The second section discusses some of the major social transformations that enable information entrepreneurial practices to be rewarding for participants. This section also examines the important role of quantitatively oriented professional management in disseminating information entrepreneurial strategies. In the final section, information entrepreneurialism is tied to key policy debates about computerization and privacy.

The Engines of Information Capitalism and Information Entrepreneurialism

Over the next twenty years, we expect computer technologies designed to support databases that contain personally sensitive information to accelerate an interesting social trend—the expansion of information entrepreneurialism. Within a practice of information entrepreneurialism, organizations and organizational actors use data-intensive techniques, such as profiling and data mining, as key strategic resources for corporate production (Luke and White, 1985; Kling, Olin, and Poster, 1991; Kling, Scherson, and Allen, 1992). The owners and managers of agricultural, manufacturing, and service firms increasingly rely on imaginative strategies to "informationalize" production. Sometimes they sell information as a good or service, in the way that magazines can sell their mailing lists or that airlines sell the use of their reservation systems. Or they may use refined information systems to focus their production and marketing. Because of the potential value of these diverse approaches, computerized information systems have joined factory smokestacks as major symbols of economic power.

Just as traditional entrepreneurial behavior is embedded within a larger system of capitalist institutions and rewards, information entrepreneurialism is embedded and encouraged within a larger institutional system of information capitalism. The information capitalism metaphor joins both information and the traditional dynamism of capitalist enterprise.

Information capitalism is not a fundamentally new economic system. But focusing on the economic and political system for regulating information use gives us a different view of how business owners, managers, and professionals organize and use information systematically. We view information capitalism as the overarching economic system in which *organizations are expected to profit from the use or sale of information*. Information capitalism's legal basis is anchored in the body of law that assigns property rights to information, such as laws for copyright, patents, and trade secrets. Of particular importance here, information capitalism is also anchored in the laws (or lack thereof) that regulate ownership of information about people.

The structure and practices of a capitalist system differ in key details between countries (say, Japan, the United States, and France), and in different time periods. Similarly, information capitalism can take on somewhat different forms. But information capitalism differs, is distinct, from alternative economic regimes, such as information socialism. For example, under extreme forms of information capitalism, some private firms could routinely expect to profit from the use or resale of information collected by government agencies such as census data, economic data, and the texts of legal documents. Under extreme forms of information socialism, this information collected with public funds would be treated as a public trust and made available to all citizens without enabling a few firms to make handsome profits by monopolizing its resale.

Just as capitalism is nourished by the hunger of entrepreneurs, we find information entrepreneurs in information capitalism. Within capitalism, abundant rewards await a competitor who can develop a more clever angle on making a business work. The underlying edge to capitalism comes from this potential for rich rewards for innovation and the risk of destruction or displacement when the complacent are blindsided by their competitors. Similarly, information entrepreneurs within a system of information capitalism innovate in numerous ways, including the development and sale of more refined financial management, market analyses, customer service, and other information-based products. Only a small fraction of these diverse innovations may enhance the surveillance capacity of organizations. But this is an important fraction. The organizations that employ an information entrepreneurial approach are most likely to effectively exploit the use of sophisticated computer-based surveillance technologies such as databases of personal data.

Information entrepreneurialism, as a set of practices for fostering corporate production, has evolved in the context of important social transformations and technological advances that encourage and reward, but do not determine, information entrepreneurial strategies. Some of these social transformations are discussed in the following section.

The Emergence of Information Entrepreneurialism and the Intensification of Computer-Based Surveillance

Modern Societies and Indirect Social Relationships

One of the major social transformations of the last one hundred years in industrial societies is the growth of a mobile population, and the commensurate growth of organizations that must serve a shifting, diverse customer base. Though these broader "environmental" shifts provide a sociohistorical context, we have argued that linking these transformations to changes in social monitoring requires an additional institutional explanation of the organizational adoption and use of surveillance technologies. In this section we will sketch the links between these changes on one hand and the increasingly intensive use of data systems for monitoring through the emergence of information entrepreneurialism in the last few decades. Information entrepreneurialism has become more prevalent, we argue, because of the combination of analytic management education, the job market, and career paths.

Consider the changes in walking into a store over the last one hundred years. The transformation between a person's dealing with the small-town store and a huge retail-chain store like Sears is not in the retail-sale transaction itself; it is in the change in relationship between the customer and the seller. In a chain-store, customers rarely deal with people who know them outside these specific narrow business transactions. The small-town shopkeeper also knew his clients from school, church, and other, localized places.

During the last one hundred years, there has been an astounding transformation in the ways that life in industrial societies is organized. Today, in a highly urbanized and mobile society, a huge fraction of the urban population moves from city to city, following better jobs and better places to live. Adolescents often leave their hometowns to attend college, and may move even farther away for jobs. Further, over 130 metropolitan areas in the United States number over 250,000 in population. Even moving "across town" in one of these cities can bring a person into a new network of friends, employers, and service providers. This combination of mobility and urban development means that many people seek jobs, goods, and services from businesses whose proprietors and staff do not have much firsthand knowledge about them.

In the last one hundred years the scale of businesses and the number of government agencies with huge clienteles have also increased. In the nineteenth century few businesses had thousands of clients (Yates, 1989). Moreover, a smaller fraction of the public interacted frequently with the larger businesses of the day. Similarly, government agencies were also smaller. Overall, most business was conducted through face-to-face (*direct*) relations.

Calhoun (1992) characterizes contemporary industrial societies as ones in which a significant fraction of people's important activities are carried out through people whom they do not see, and may not even know exist. Today, banks extend credit to people who come from anywhere in the country. And they can do so with relative safety because of large-scale credit record systems that track the credit history of over 100 million people. The credit check brings together a credit seeker and employees of the credit bureau who are related only indirectly.

Other private firms, such as insurance companies and mail-order companies, also extend services to tens of thousands of people whom local agents do not—and could not—personally know. In these transactions, judgments about insurability and credit worthiness are made through *indirect* social relationships, often mediated with computerized information systems. Furthermore, many new government agencies have been created in the twentieth century that are responsible for accounting for the activities of millions of people, including the Federal Bureau of

Investigation (established 1908), the Internal Revenue Service (1913), the Social Security Administration (1935), and the state departments of motor vehicles. The sheer scale of these services creates "environmental conditions" that give organizations incentives to use computerized record systems to help routinize the maintenance of indirect social relationships. However, organizations of a similar kind and size, such as banks, differ in their aggressiveness in using new technologies and management practices.

The Rise of Information Entrepreneurialism

What explains the difference between the more and less information-intensive organizations when many of their environmental conditions are similar? We believe that informational entrepreneurial styles of management are an important part of the answer. But information entrepreneurialism is a relatively recent phenomenon, only developing after managerial capitalism. In *The Visible Hand*, Alfred Chandler (1977) documents the way that certain large enterprises in the late nineteenth century helped foster professional management jobs. The railroads were among the first United States firms to organize enterprises on such a large scale that families were too small to staff all of the key management positions. Other larger industrial and commercial enterprises followed suit by the first decades of the twentieth century. Schools of professional management also developed to train young men for these new positions. And by midcentury, the MBA was a popular degree in the United States.

After World War II, management schools began to shift from the case study approach, identified with the Harvard Business School, to more mathematical approaches. These curricula emphasized more quantitative skills based on microeconomics, managerial finance, and management science—deemphasizing the examination of problems within their rich and complex organizational life. By the 1970s, most United States schools of business had reorganized their curricula to emphasize analytical techniques. These analytical techniques include a new academic specialty, developed during the 1970s, "information systems." Today, a majority of business schools offer both required courses and elective courses in information systems. While information systems courses teach business students diverse ways to computerize to help gain economic advantage, they rarely teach about privacy issues and the problematic side of some information systems. In general, the shift in the education of MBAs from the traditional case-based approach, with its statement of a complex organizational richness, to a grounding in narrow quantitative analyses trained a generation of MBAs to use the approaches fostered by information capitalism.

The role of management training in ignoring privacy (and other concerns in social life) can be seen through an examination of two leading textbooks. *Management Information Systems* by Laudon and Laudon (1994) devotes about four pages of its 776 pages to privacy issues. The text lists five core privacy principles from an influential federal report. But the text does not examine how these principles can be applied to any specific case, including any of the dozens of cases that the authors use to illustrate many other practices of information management. And the text does not provide any cases that examine privacy issues directly. *Corporate Information Systems Management* by Cash, McFarland, McKenney, and Applegate (1992) is more generous, devoting five pages of its 702 pages to privacy issues. Cash and his colleagues begin their short privacy section with three brief illustrations of how the practices of credit bureaus and marketing managers can intrude on personal privacy. Their text gives students several additional concrete examples about ways that managers can compromise or protect their customer's privacy while practicing information capitalism. Cash and his colleagues make a serious effort to sensitize their student readers to privacy issues. One could hope for analyses of privacy issues in other sections of the book that advance the development of new information systems with personal data. Their account is probably the best in any of the popular information systems texts for MBA students. Information systems texts written before the late 1980s completely ignored privacy issues.

In a similar way, texts about marketing teach business students how to better identify potential customers and to improve sales and service by retaining and analyzing more data about customers' behavior. Overall, business schools teach their students to be clever and opportunistic information entrepreneurs—without much attention to the ways that routine business practices can create problems in public life, such as intruding on personal privacy.

By 1989, United States colleges and universities were conferring almost 250,000 bachelors' degrees in business and almost 75,000 MBAs each year (U.S. Department of Commerce and Bureau of the Census, 1992). The number of BAs in business awarded annually more than doubled in the past twenty-year period. During the 1980s alone, United States business hired almost 2.5 million people with BA degrees in business and almost 600,000 with MBAs. These numbers are crude indicators, rather than rigid parameters of a mechanistic process of social change. For example, only a small portion of graduates stimulate innovation in their organizations. But a large fraction of college-educated management educated since the 1970s understand key aspects of information entrepreneurialism, even when they follow rather than lead.

Schooling is, however, just the beginning for many of the managers who seek to innovate. The business press publishes (and exaggerates) stories of computerization efforts that promise better markets and profits. Magazines like *The Harvard Business Review* and *Business Week* publish stories about using information technology for competitive advantage. But they rarely highlight the privacy issues in their enthusiasm to excite managerial readers about new ways of conceiving of business opportunities (Bloom, Milne, and Adler, 1994). In addition, professional associations help managers learn diverse approaches to their trades. Professional associations offer talks, workshops and publications for their members that also help popularize key aspects of information entrepreneurialism. These professional communication channels serve to legitimize an understanding that diverse information systems can serve as valuable strategic resources, and that they pose no significant social risks.

In summary, the institutional processes that lead to extending surveillance technology use include the professionalization of managerial analysts within organizations and the risk-free conceptions of information systems that are taken for granted in their specialized professional worlds. But organizations that adopt these systems are also likely to face environmental conditions that reward information entrepreneurialism, such as increasingly large clienteles. In any era, organizations use the available technologies for keeping records—papyrus and paper were used for centuries. But in modern societies, where an enterprise may have millions of customers, there is a significant payoff to organizations that can effectively exploit the informational resources that this systematic record keeping entails for identifying potential customers, for assessing credit risks, and so on.

This payoff has led to the development of third-party data brokers, like financial brokers (e.g., TRW Information Services, Equifax, and Dunn and Bradstreet) and marketing data brokers (e.g., Information Resources). These data brokers have developed lively businesses by collecting data from some organizations and restructuring it for sale to other organizations—through custom search services, passing information to client firms, and also devising new information products to facilitate precision electronic marketing. For example, grocery scanner data, tied to individuals' demographic characteristics, is an extremely valuable commodity because it can be used for marketing analyses and direct advertising. The next section examines the growing role of these data brokers, as well as the political debates surrounding privacy.

Database Technology, Information Entrepreneurialism, and Changing Patterns of Social Control

A society where social relationships are often indirect can give people a greater sense of freedom. One can move from job to job, from house to house and from loan to loan, selectively leaving some of one's past behind. Managers in organizations that provide long-term services, such as banks, insurance companies, and apartment houses, often want to reduce their business risks by reconstructing what they believe are relevant parts of that past.

This desire to reduce risk encouraged larger organizations, such as some of the biggest banks, insurance companies, and public agencies, to take an early lead in adapting mainframe computing to support their huge personal record systems in the 1950s and 1960s. In the 1970s and 1980s these organizations enhanced their computer systems and developed networks to more effectively communicate data regionally, nationally, and internationally. Many such organizations have massive appetites for "affordable" high-speed transaction processing and tools to help them manage gigabytes and even terabytes of data, and they have teams of professionals who are eager to exploit new technologies to better track and manage their customers and clients.

Computerized database technology supports finer-grained analyses of indirect social relationships, such as precision marketing, to improve their abilities to target customers for a new product, or the ability of a taxing agency to search multiple large databases prowling for tax cheaters. In fact, the key link between information entrepreneurialism and surveillance technologies is the possibility for enhanced information processing that large-scale databases or advanced computational techniques allow. Significant advances in computer technology allow analysts to pursue managerial strategies that involve detailed analysis of the records of an organization's current and potential clients and of its operations. A huge organization might follow the path of American Express, which purchased two CM-5 parallel supercomputers for analyzing cardholders' purchasing patterns (Markoff, 1991). But many organizations can effectively use higher-end PCs and software based on rule induction, neural networks, fuzzy logic, and genetic algorithms to support data mining (Gendelev, 1992).

Managers and professionals in business organizations and public agencies defend their searches for information about people as limited and pragmatic actions that improve their rationality in making specific decisions about who to hire, who to extend a loan to, who to rent an apartment to, and who to arrest (see Kusserow, Part VI, Chapter E). The increasing importance of indirect social relationships that we described earlier gives many organizations a legitimate interest in using computerized personal records systems to learn about potential or actual clients.

It is not difficult to find examples of this. For example, landlords may legitimately wish to avoid renting to convicted felons. Or employers may want to analyze how to reduce their health insurance costs. However, such legitimate activities may extend until they impinge on the freedoms of individuals. Landlords may want to use a database of potential gang members, even though the people in the database were not convicted of any crime. Or, employers may screen potential employees on the basis of their health histories. (For an analysis of the potential misuses of medical records, see *Consumer Reports*, 1994.)

These kinds of situations create a tension between the preferences of an organization's managers and the freedoms of individual clients or workers. In these situations, organizations usually act to maintain the largest possible zone of free action for themselves, while downplaying their clients' interests. It is not surprising, then, that privacy issues are rarely considered when systems are constructed or implemented. Jeff Smith (1993) documented the way that managers of United States firms that manage huge amounts of personally sensitive data, such as health and life insurance and credit card processing, examined privacy issues only when their organization was faced with an external threat, such as a public embarrassment or impending privacy legislation.

Adding to the force of this tension between the interests of managers and their organization's clients, personal data systems have become increasingly larger and interlinked. Many databases of personal information now contain data from many different sources. Yet, there are few corresponding protections to reduce the risks of error, inappropriate disclosure, and other problems. In large-scale record systems (with millions of records), there are bound to be inaccuracies (see Shattuck, Part VI, Chapter D). But people have few rights to inspect or correct records about them in the United States—except for credit records. During the last thirty years, people have consistently lost significant control over records about them. Increasingly, courts have ruled that records about a person belong to the organization that collects the data, and the person to whom they apply cannot restrict their use (Privacy Protection Study Commission, 1977). Consequently, inaccurate police records, medical records, and employment histories can harm people—especially when they have no idea why they are having trouble getting a job, a loan, or medical insurance.

These new ways of doing business—taken together with computer systems—have reduced people's control over their personal affairs. Elected officials have periodically tried to create new laws to help correct this imbalance. In 1992, more than 1000 bills on privacy issues were presented in state legislatures and at least ten bills made an appearance at the federal level (Miller, 1993). Few of these bills emerge from various legislative committee and even fewer are enacted into law.

It is an unfortunate reality that representatives of those private firms and government agencies that have an interest in expanding their computerized information systems frequently argue vehemently against legal limits or substantial accountability to people about whom records are kept. They deny that problems exist, or they argue that the reported problems are exaggerated in importance (see, for example, Posch, 1994). And they argue that proposed regulations are either too vague or too burdensome, and that new regulations about information systems would do more harm than good. The proponents of unregulated computerization have been wealthy, organized, and aligned with the antiregulatory sentiments that have dominated United States federal politics during the last fifteen years. Consequently, they have effectively blocked many attempts to preserve personal privacy through regulation.

In this way, many representatives of the computer industry and of firms with massive personal record systems behave similarly to the representatives of automobile firms when they first were asked to face questions about smog. As smog became more visible in major United States cities in the 1940s and 1950s, the automobile industry worked hard to argue that there was no link between cars and smog (Krier and Ursin, 1977). First, their spokesmen argued that smog was not a systematic phenomenon; then they argued that it was primarily caused by other sources such as factories. After increases in smog were unequivocally linked to the use of cars, they spent a good deal of energy fighting any regulations that would reduce the pollution emitted by cars. Overall, the automobile industry slowly conceded to reducing smog in a foot-dragging pattern that Krier and Ursin (1977) characterize as "regulation by least steps." In a similar way, the organizations that develop or use personal record keeping systems behave like the automobile industry in systematically fighting enhanced public protections.

Information entrepreneurs, like other entrepreneurs in a capitalist economy, are sensitive to the costs of their services. When there is no price on goods like clean air or personal privacy, those goods are usually ignored unless there are protective regulations to compensate for market failures. The history of federal privacy protections in the United States is likely to continue unchanged without a new level of political interest in protections. The Privacy Act of 1974 established a Privacy Protection Study Commission, which in 1977 issued a substantial report on its findings and made 155 recommendations to develop "fair information practices." Many of these recommendations gave people the right to know what records are kept about them, to inspect records for accuracy, to correct (or contest) inaccuracies, to be informed when records were transferred from one organization to another, and the like. Less than a handful of these proposals were subsequently enacted into federal law.

Leaders of the computing movements and the associated industry that enable large-scale databases could help minimize the possible reductions of privacy that their applications foster by helping to initiate relevant and responsible privacy protections. It is hardly realistic, however, to expect them to take such initiatives, since they work within social arrangements that do not reward limiting their own market opportunities. As a consequence, we expect privacy regulation in the next two decades to be as lax as in the previous two decades. While the public is becoming sensitized to privacy, it does not have the salience and energizing quality of recent issues like tax reduction, abortion, or even environmental pollution. This does not mean that there will not be any new privacy protections for private persons. Regulation by least steps, in the case of personal privacy, can take the form of bounded regulations, like the Video Privacy Protection Act, which regulates access to video store rental records, or the Electronic Communications Privacy Act of 1986, which protects communications on wires between organizations but not within buildings. In the United States, there may be new protections restricting the dissemination of health

records, but the prospects of those protections seem tied to the comprehensive restructuring of health care.

Conclusions

We opened our paper with a simple but fundamental question: Why is
there a continuing development of information technologies whose use
impinges on personal privacy in modern societies? Few analysts have
tried to answer this question directly, although some answers are implicit.
Laudon and Laudon (1994:702–703), for example, focus on rapid improvements in the absolute capabilities and the cost/performance ratio of information technologies. They also identify "advances in data mining techniques" used for precision marketing by firms like Wal-Mart and Hallmark.

Our answer concentrates not only on these environmental factors, but as
well on the micropractices of those who manage such systems and their
incentives, as well as the institutional structures in which they work (i.e.,
information capitalism). In short, we argued that the dynamics of expanding surveillance systems is systemic rather than the result of isolated
practices. However, we know relatively little about the ways that informational entrepreneurs conceive and build internal alliances to develop information systems that collect and organize personally sensitive data.

Within modern corporations and organizations, there exists a set of
social practices that encourage the use of data about individuals, data-
intensive analysis, and computerization as key strategic resources. We
called these practices "information entrepreneurialism." Information entrepreneurialism thrives within an information capitalist social and political
system. It has been stimulated by many social transformations in the past
one hundred years in industrialized societies, especially North America:
the increasing mobility of populations, the growth of nationwide organizations, and the increasing importance of indirect social relationships. The
key link between information entrepreneurialism and the new technologies
that support databases of personally sensitive data lies in the possibilities
for enhanced information processing that it provides to analysts whose
managerial strategies profit from significant advances in analyzing records
of an organization's (potential) clients and operations.

We find it especially important to examine how managers and professionals develop surveillance technologies (Smith, 1993; Laudon, 1986) as
well as changing technologies. The information entrepreneurial model
argues that the growing importance of indirect social relationships in North
American society leads many organizations to seek personal data about
potential and actual clients. At the same time, managers and other organizational employees trained in analytical techniques and actively pursuing
data-intensive strategies foster the use of personal data. Attempts to introduce products such as Lotus *Marketplace:Household* are difficult to understand without examining this organizational context.

The positive side of these informational strategies lies in improved organizational efficiencies, novel products, and interesting analytical jobs. However, as a collection, these strategies reduce the privacy of many citizens and can result in excruciating foul-ups when record keeping errors are propagated from one computer system to another, with little accountability to the person. David Lyon (1994) argues that a sound analysis of changes in technology and social control should be based on a vision of "the good society," rather than simply on avoiding social orders that are horrifying or perverse.

Social changes toward a society that prizes fair information practices could be influenced by the policies and routine actions of commercial firms and public agencies. They are not inevitable social trends, as shown by the differences between United States and European regulatory systems for managing personal data (Flaherty, 1989; Trubow, 1992). For instance, the North American public might insist on stronger fair information practices to reduce the risks of expanding records systems. Or Laudon's (Part VI, Chapter K) proposals for pricing personal data might be developed for some areas, such as marketing. The society could change some key rules, rights, and responsibilities that characterize the current practice of unfettered information entrepreneurialism. It is unfortunate, but broad systematic changes in United States information policies seem politically infeasible today, for reasons that we have sketched above.

Currently, relatively few restraints have been imposed on the exchange of personal information between organizations, both public and private, in North America. We are not sanguine about any substantial shifts toward more privacy protections during the next two decades. Without changes that are exogenous to the direct use of specific computer applications, the trends we have discussed are likely to continue. These trends can be the subject to systematic empirical inquiry, and merit such an investigation.

Acknowledgments

This chapter benefited from discussions about information capitalism with Phil Agre, Vijay Gurbaxani, James Katz, Abbe Mowshowitz, and Jeffrey Smith. Conversations with Mary Culnan, Jeff Smith, and John Little provided important insights into the importance of computerization in marketing. Our colleagues John King and Jonathan Grudin have been continuous partners in provocative discussions about technology, privacy, and social change.

References

Bloom, Paul N., George R. Milne, and Robert Adler (1994). "Avoiding Misuse of New Information Technologies: Legal and Societal Considerations." *Journal of Marketing*, 58(1) (Jan), 98–110.

Burnham, David (1983). *The Rise of the Computer State.* Random House, New York.

Calhoun, Craig (1992). "The Infrastructure of Modernity: Indirect Social Relationships, Information Technology, and Social Integration," in H. Haferkamp and N. Smelser (eds.), *Social Change and Modernity.* University of California Press, Berkeley.

Cash, James, Jr., Warren F. McFarland, James McKenney, and Linda Applegate (eds.) (1992). *Corporate Information Systems Management: Text and Cases.* Irwin, Boston.

Chandler, Alfred D. (1977). *The Visible Hand: The Managerial Revolution in American Business.* Harvard University Press, MA.

Chandler, Alfred D. (1984). "The Emergence of Managerial Capitalism." *Business History Review,* 58(Winter), 473–503.

Consumer Reports (1994). "Who's Reading Your Medical Records?" *Consumer Reports,* 59(10), 628–633.

Culnan, Mary (1993). "How Did They Get My Name? An Exploratory Investigation of Consumer Attitudes Toward Secondary Information Use." *MIS Quarterly,* 17(3), 341–363.

Flaherty, David (1989). *Protecting Privacy in Surveillance Societies: The Federal Republic of Germany, Sweden, France, Canada and the United States.* University of North Carolina Press, Chapel Hill.

Gendelev, Boris (1992). "MIS and Marketing: Secrets of Strategic Information Mining." *Chief Information Officer Journal,* v5, n1 (Summer), 12–16, 23.

Kling, Rob, Spencer Olin, and Mark Poster (1991). "Emergence of Postsuburbia," in R. Kling, S. Olin, and M. Poster (eds.), *Postsuburban California: The Transformation of Postwar Orange County.* University of California Press, Berkeley.

Kling, Rob, Isaac Scherson, and John Allen (1992). "Massively Parallel Computing and Information Capitalism," in W. Daniel Hillis and James Bailey (eds.), *A New Era of Computing.* The MIT Press, Cambridge.

Krier, James, and Edmund Ursin (1977). *Pollution and Policy: A Case Essay on California and Federal Experience with Motor Vehicle Air Pollution, 1940–1975.* University of California Press, Berkeley.

Laudon, Kenneth (1986). "Data Quality and Due Process in Large Interorganizational Record Systems," *Communications of the ACM,* 29(1), 4–11.

Laudon, Kenneth (1986). *Dossier Society: Value Choices in the Design of National Information Systems.* Columbia University Press, New York.

Laudon, Kenneth, and Jane Laudon (1994). *Management Information Systems: A Contemporary Perspective* (3rd ed.). McMillan, New York.

Levy, Steven (1991). "How the Good Guys Finally Won: Keeping Lotus Market-Place off the Market," *MacWorld,* 8(6), 69–74.

Luke, Timothy, and Stephen White (1985). "Critical Theory, the Informational Revolution, and an Ecological Path to Modernity," in J. Forester (ed.), *Critical Theory and Public Life,* pp. 22–53. MIT Press, Cambridge.

Lyon, David (1991). "British Identity Cards: The Unpalatable Logic of European Membership?" *The Political Quarterly,* 62(3), 377–385.

Lyon, David (1994). *The Electronic Eye: The Rise of Surveillance Society.* The University of Minnesota Press, Minneapolis.

Markoff, John (1991). "American Express to Buy 2 Top Supercomputers from Thinking Machines Corp." *The New York Times,* October 30, 1991, C7(N), D9(L).

Miller, Cyndee (1993). "Privacy vs. Direct Marketing: Industry Faces Something on the Order of a Survival Issue." *Marketing News*, 27(5) (March 1), 1,14+.

Posch, Robert (1994). "After MPS—Then What?" *Direct Marketing*, 56(11) (March), 63–64+.

Privacy Protection Study Commission (1977). "Personal Privacy in an Information Society." U.S. Government Printing Office, Washington, D.C.

Rule, James (1974). *Private Lives and Public Surveillance*. Schocken, New York.

Rule, James, David McAdam, Linda Stearns, and David Uglow (1984). *The Politics of Privacy: Planning for Personal Data Systems as Powerful Technologies*. Mentor, New York.

Smith, Jeff (1993). "Privacy Policies and Practices: Inside the Organizational Maze: How Corporations Are Handling Sensitive Personal Information." *Communications of the ACM*, 36(12) (Dec), 104–119.

Trubow, George B. (1992). "The European Harmonization of Data Protection Laws Threatens U.S. Participation in Trans Border Data Flow." *Northwestern Journal of International Law & Business*, 13(1) (Spring/Summer), 159–176.

U.S. Department of Commerce and Bureau of the Census (1992). *Statistical Abstract of the United States, 1992*. U.S. Government Printing Office, Washington, D.C.

Wartzman, Rick (1994). "A Research Company Got Consumer Data From Voting Rolls." *The Wall Street Journal*, December 23, 1994, A1+.

Yates, JoAnne (1989). *Control through Communication: The Rise of System in American Management*. Johns Hopkins Press, Baltimore, MD.

P·A·R·T · VII

System Safety and Social Vulnerability

P·A·R·T·VII

Systems Safety, Normal Accidents, and Social Vulnerability

Rob Kling

An Introduction to Safe Systems

Computer systems are becoming more technically complex, and development times can sometimes frustrate customers. Simple applications software, like word processors, have expanded from thousands to millions of lines of program code as vendors pack them with ever more sophisticated features. Powerful computer chips, which serve as central processors for Macs, PCs, and engineering workstations, contain the equivalent of millions of transistors. Product designers are adding "smart controls" to household and industrial products, from air conditioners and bread makers to medical devices, telephone switching systems, banking systems, electric power plants, as well as food and chemical processing plants through the use of software and chips. These newer technologies are often more convenient, flexible, and reliable than their predecessors.

However, it is common for those who rely on computers or computer-based services to experience various kind of malfunctions, problems, and aberrant computer behavior. A word processor may hang, causing an author to lose a few brilliant paragraphs or find that a document representing a month's work is corrupted. An automated teller machine can "eat a bank card" and refuse to eject it after a transaction. A new homeowner might receive a $4000 water bill because of an ill-designed meter reading program.[1] Or a telephone answering machine may require such a complex and rigid sequence of commands to replay messages from another phone that a person erases his calls when he intends to repeat them.

These agonizing events are usually treated as the "minor irritants of modern life" and are illustrated in R. Aminzade's article about computer-driven "voice mail" (Chapter B). Michael Slavitch's article (Chapter B) examines both the "irritant" and the "blind faith" attitude people sometimes display toward computers and their systems. Slavitch uses his personal experience as an example. A convenient automated book-notice service from his library failed to work properly. The librarian's reaction when he complained about the malfunction graphically illustrates a more serious problem. The librarian "insisted that the 'system' must be 'reliable' and 'almost always' works," and that he had no basis for complaining.

Both articles appeared in the electronic newsletter, *RISKS-FORUM Digest* moderated by Peter G. Neumann of SRI International, with support from the Association for Computing Machinery (ACM).[2] *RISKS-FORUM Digest* is an important forum that gives computer specialists an opportunity to discuss unsafe computer systems designs and organizational practices. Although *RISKS-FORUM Digest* includes many accounts where accidents have been avoided or where the consequences are mostly irritating, its contributors also discuss and debate the nature of life-threatening systems hazards.

In extreme cases new information technologies have increased the vulnerability of communities. For example, computer system problems have led to millions of people losing telephone service, 85,000 airline passengers being grounded for hours, people being killed by medical equipment, as well as people and organizations losing billions of dollars. Between the individual hassles and problems that injure millions are the thousands of system "snafus" involving computers that don't appear in the news or professional literature because they harm or inconvenience only people who work within a specific organization.

While many computer systems are occasionally unreliable, their errors and failures, like Aminzade's voice mail example, usually do little harm. What is critical are computers and systems that are *unsafe*—and render

---

[1] See *Risks Digests* (comp.risks) Volume 15, #68 for November 26, 1994. (http://www.wais.com/wais-dbs/risks-digest.html.) A similar case with an erroneous water bill of $22,000 is discussed in Neumann (1995:121).

[2] One sign of health in the computing profession lies in the fact that many of the contributors to Neumann's newsletter are themselves working computer scientists. Their concern over computer-related risks is obvious. However, only a tiny fraction of practicing computer specialists are knowledgeable about the kinds of issues and debates examined in *RISKS-FORUM Digest*. Techniques for ensuring that computer systems are safe and reliable—topics within "software engineering"—are not yet a routine part of Computer Science curricula at many colleges and universities. See Neumann (1995) for an anthology of excerpts from *Risks* that is organized in a way that can serve as a text for such courses.

groups vulnerable by inadvertently leading to human injury or significant financial losses. When reviewing system safety and social vulnerability, consider the wide range of computer-based systems whose reliable function is indispensable for human health and well-being. These include transportation (air, rail, automobile, ship), national defense, communication, financial exchanges, payrolls, medicine, law enforcement, nuclear power, elections, elevators, chemical plants, space exploration, mining, the food industry, and record keeping associated with many social and governmental services.

Computer Science professor Nancy Leveson (1991) makes the key point that system safety should be defined in terms of hazards rather than accidents or disasters. She notes that "System-safety engineers define safety in terms of hazards and risk. A hazard is a set of conditions (i.e., a state) that can lead to an accident given certain environmental conditions." Hazards can include guard gates not lowering when trains approach traffic crossings, a warning light burning out in an electric power plant, a computer system deleting a file without asking for an operator's confirmation, or a company's failure to perform scheduled maintenance on key equipment. These hazards increase the likelihood of accidents—events that result in loss or injury—occurring. But, as Leveson and other safety analysts note, accidents are often caused (or avoided) because of multiple factors. For example, a guard gate may not lower when a train crosses a road, but the drivers may all spot the engine's headlight or hear its whistle and stay off the tracks.

In many cases, hazards lead to "near misses" (or incidents)—potential accidents that were avoided. Near-miss incidents occur, according to various estimates, from ten to over one hundred times more frequently than actual accidents (Smith, 1994). In special cases of systems and services where many lives or huge amounts of money are at risk, organizations institute procedures to report, track, and investigate incidents, not just accidents. For example, the U.S. Federal Aviation Administration requires pilots and air traffic controllers to report a variety of incidents, such as planes flying too close to each other. However, few companies create incident reports about their operations and those that do tend to treat them as highly confidential, internal information. The public usually learns about system and service hazards through reports of accidents.

On June 26, 1991, over six million Bell Atlantic telephones were cut off for seven hours in Washington, D.C., Maryland, Virginia, and West Virginia. Problems with Pacific Bell's network equipment in Los Angeles and Orange County, California affected three million lines for about two and a half hours on the same day. This loss of nine million phones in one day was one of the largest phone network failures in United States history. The problem was traced to a switching center in Baltimore, Maryland where a faulty circuit board triggered new switching software to pump erroneous messages into the phone system (Mason, 1991b; Karpinski, 1991). But beyond these technical glitches were other potential organizational hazards. The equipment vendor, DSC, was aware of similar problems that had briefly shut down millions of telephones in California on June 10. But it appears that DSC never informed the telephone companies about the nature of the equipment faults. In addition, regulatory arrangements prevented the regional phone companies from working closely together to improve the reliability of service (Mason, 1991a). The published accounts of this massive failure were sketchy, but it appears that communication gaps between DSC and the regional phone companies may have been as important as the specific failed circuit board in triggering this disaster. It is common for organizations and journalists to identity some equipment component or some individual operator as the cause of major mishaps (Perrow, 1984). But often the causes are more complex and interwoven.

Breakdowns in systems that we take for granted and think of as reliable can help us learn about computer systems hazards. On 10:10 A.M. Tuesday, September 17, 1991, AT&T cut over to diesel generators at a switching center in lower Manhattan, New York. The move, part of a power-saving agreement with Consolidated Edison Company of New York, was requested because the summer was particularly hot and air conditioners drove up the demand for electric power. However, this move also set off a massive telephone outage that left air traffic controllers in the Northeast "on hold" and 85,000 air passengers on the ground (Anthes, 1992). During or soon after the cut to internal power, rectifiers in the center's power supply failed. The rectifiers convert AC power to DC. An AT&T protective meter-relay that was improperly set triggered at 52.8 volts instead of at 53.5 volts. The failure of the meter-relay in the rectifiers initiated a series of other failures and mistakes (Watson, Devaney, and Thomas, 1992). When the normal electric power failed, the system immediately switched to backup batteries. Technicians monitoring the network failed to read several alarms properly, and did not conduct inspections that would have allowed them to discover the problem earlier. When AT&T technicians attempted to routinely convert back to commercial power at about 4:30 P.M., they discovered the failed rectifiers, which prevented them from using normal electrical power. By then the batteries, which have about a six-hour life-span, were close to drained. Twenty minutes later, they gave out for good (Mason, 1991b). Faulty maintenance and poor judgment further compounded the original problem. In one location, an alarm light did not work because its bulb was burned out; and in another place, an audible alarm did not sound because one of its wires had been cut; and elsewhere a standard-procedure maintenance walk-through was not done as it should have been (Watson, Devaney, and Thomas, 1992). Although power was restored by early evening, the airports did not clear until midnight. Because the telephones were inoperative, few passengers were able to call and inform others about the delayed flights. Ironically, travelers with cellular phones were able to phone their friends. And there are apocryphal stories of stranded passengers passing cellular telephones around inside grounded aircraft so other passengers could use them.

Although a computer system was not implicated in this telephone systems failure, it illustrates some of the ways in which major accidents occur through the *interaction* of several social and technical systems (power systems, phone systems, and air traffic control systems, in this case). They can involve a mixture of component failures, confusion by operators about what the nature and scope of problems really are, and by gaps in organizational routines (such as maintaining various equipment). Sociologist Charles Perrow discovered similar complexities when he investigated the causes of the near meltdown at the nuclear plant, Three Mile Island, near Harrisburg, Pennsylvania (Perrow, 1984). Perrow found that many industrial accidents involve an interacting mixture of technical and organizational causes. Perrow (pp. 62–100) coined the catchy term "normal accident" (or "systems accident") to refer to damage that occurs because of multiple interacting causes. Perrow raises provocative questions about the ways in which some systems that combine technologies and organizational practices (including staff training, preventive maintenance) are designed so that periodic accidents should be expected.

In Chapter C, "Safety-Critical Computing," Jonathan Jacky, a scientist who develops software for a radiation therapy clinic, focuses on a similarly complex, but more fatal, set of events. He begins with the story of how a new, highly computerized radiation machine (Therac-25) designed to treat cancer was sometimes overdosing patients to the extent that some died or were maimed. This is a remarkable set of mishaps, because the Therac-25 was heralded as a "better cure." Further, the Therac-25 seemed to be effectively giving radiation therapy to thousands of people suffering from cancer. Jacky shows us how these deaths and maimings were the byproducts of flawed technical system designs, hospital practices, the vendor's behavior, and the weak system for regulating computerized medical equipment. The Therac-25 killed and maimed people not simply because of technical failures, but because of complementary failures in the organizational systems that supported its daily use. He then discusses how computerized control systems embedded in airplanes, trains, and other equipment, where mishaps can kill, can be subject to some of these same organizational failures. Jacky also considers several possible solutions, including licensing software engineers for safety-critical systems, and tightening the procedures for certifying the safety of medical devices and other major systems.

In "Aging Airways" (Chapter D), Gary Stix examines the daunting obstacles that impede the U.S. Federal Aviation Administration (FAA) efforts to modernize the air traffic control system (ATC). Stix recounts a fascinating story in which the current ATC system depends on twenty-five-year-old Unisys computers, and archaic procedures in which air traffic controllers scribble flight information on tiny paper strips. The air traffic control system is remarkably reliable, due largely to the controllers' skill and moral commitment to airline safety. While IBM won a contract to modernize the ATC system, the price tag has almost doubled to about $31,000,000,000 and the project is four years overdue. Gary Stix describes some of the complexities of one apparently simple change: computerizing and eliminating the paper strips in ways that don't reduce the controllers' ability to monitor aircraft. Even though information and computer professionals view paper as worse than digital media, IBM's digital designs were much clumsier and compromised air safety much more than simple paper strips.

Strategies for Improving Systems Safety

Despite the many difficulties cataloged so far, it is apparent from existing systems (space exploration, airline transportation, etc.) that safe systems are not always an impossible dream. In fact, we take safety so much for granted that the fatal explosion of the space shuttle Challenger in January 1986 shocked the nation and cost NASA immense credibility (Heimann, 1993).[3] Although the technical failure of the Challenger was caused by faulty seals (O rings), the problem was known to certain managers and engineers in the firm (Morton-Thiokol) that designed the rockets. The nature of a managerial decision to risk the shuttle's launching and cover up the engineering criticisms of possible O ring failures was widely reported after a Congressional inquiry into this disaster. Heimann published an interesting analysis that shows how a change in NASA's organizational structure also made this kind of disaster more likely.

There is a strong cultural bias in North America to focus on discrete causes for system failures—like a broken device, a software bug, a single person's error, or even a cover-up. We are much less likely to examine whether the ways that organizations are structured or the character of their cultures can lead to system failures. Scholars are systematically studying organizational failures and high-performance organizations to better understand these issues (see, e.g., Weick and Roberts, 1993). Only recently have systematic organizational-level analyses influenced the information and computer science professions. But professional interest in developing

---

[3] Seventy-three seconds after lift-off, the space shuttle Challenger was destroyed in a powerful explosion fifty thousand feet above the Kennedy Space Center. The losses resulting from this catastrophe were quite high. Seven astronauts, including Teacher-in-Space Christa McAuliffe, were killed as the shuttle broke apart and fell into the sea. The shuttle itself had to be replaced at a cost of over two billion dollars. The launch of many important commercial and military satellites had to be delayed as American space policy ground to a complete halt. The accident had a profound impact on the National Aeronautics and Space Administration (NASA), as well. The agency's credibility and its reputation for flawless execution of complex technological tasks were lost, along with the Challenger. To this day, the legacy of the Challenger haunts the decision of both the agency and its political superiors in Congress and the White House. (Heimann, 1993:421)

safe systems should help fuel broader interest in systematic organizational analysis (see Kling and Allen, Part III, Chapter M).

There have been sustained studies of technological strategies for improving the quality of software designs. Software engineering methods incorporate various error-reducing strategies, including systematic testing strategies.[4] The licensing of professional programmers (see Jacky's discussion in Part VII, Chapter C) has been suggested. And computer scientists have worked hard to develop a meaningful theoretical basis for software design (see Winograd and Flores, 1987; Dahlbom and Mathiassen, 1993).

Formal verification techniques may help uncover the discrepancies between a program's specification and the actual program. For example, in the fall of 1994, Intel admitted that its highly touted and widely sold Pentium chip was not 100% reliable in carrying out arithmetic calculations. Intel admitted the flaws only after a mathematician publicly criticized the chip's accuracy. Further, Intel lost credibility when it minimized the importance of the problem and was unwilling to automatically replace the millions of Pentium chips that it had sold. Intel's spokespersons claimed that the computational errors were exceptionally rare and would show up only in specially complex calculations. Critics retorted that the errors could occur more frequently and that even common financial calculations,[5] could lead to erroneous results. Formally verifying the correctness of the chip's mathematical routines might have avoided the Pentium's problems.

The Pentium fiasco may lead more chip vendors to try verifying the correctness of their chips. Even so, vendors' claims should be carefully scrutinized, especially claims of "software engineering" and "program verification," and particularly in contexts where mistakes may be irreversible and catastrophic. Discussions of program verification tend to flounder due to confusion over what the "verification" process actually involves. The Verifiable Integrated Processor for Enhanced Reliability (VIPER) microprocessor was designed in the late 1980s for safety-critical military, space, and transportation applications, such as "fly-by-wire" aircraft and railroad crossing controllers. VIPER includes the equivalent of several million transistors. The sheer complexity of these chips makes guarantees of correctness alluring. VIPER's designers used mathematical proof techniques to help ensure absolute correctness and freedom from design errors. But it was the subject of exaggerated advertising after it was "proven to be free" of design errors (Dobson and Randell, 1989:422). For example, the proofs of correctness do not ensure that the original specifications were

---

[4] For a provocative discussion of two different approaches to software engineering, see Floyd (1987). Her contrast between a "product-oriented" view (programs as abstract objects) and a "process-oriented" view (programs as tools for humans) also bears directly on some of the program verification issues discussed below.

[5] Critics have found problems like this that a Pentium calculates inaccurately: the result of $4,195,835 - [(4,195,835/3,145,727) \cdot 3,145,727]$ should be 0; the flawed Pentiums produce an answer of 256 (Mossberg, 1994).

correct, and analysts subsequently claimed to have found four specification errors in VIPER's design.

Some of the debates on the meaning and significance of formal verification have been quite heated.[6] Brian Smith's paper (Chapter E) provides one lucid interpretation, explaining that a verification ("formal proof of correctness") establishes *relative consistency* between a program specification and program code. Smith goes on to observe, however, that if the specification itself reflects a world model that is deficient in some relevant respect, the deficiency will carry over to the program, thus remaining undetected by any formal consistency proof. This point is crucial, for it implies that a computer system with perfectly functioning hardware, and software that adheres accurately to a set of written requirements, may still result in serious failures. The indispensability of robust testing should be apparent in the face of this argument.[7] Still, software engineers will argue that formal methods help improve programs by encouraging people to carefully consider their designs and develop simpler systems that are easier to verify.[8] Jon Jacky, for example, comments,

> . . . it can be very valuable, and it provides far more assurance than we get from most projects. Even being in a position to attempt such a verification requires that somebody provide a complete and explicit specification that documents what the system is expected to do and reveals the builders' assumptions about what the system will demand of its environment. Most projects never produce such a specification, and as a result the expected system behaviors and the assumptions about the environment cannot be reviewed or criticized or even examined because they are hidden in the program text itself—usually encoded in some obscure way (they don't call it code for nothing). Because of this, the specification can be as valuable as the verification itself—maybe more so. (Jacky, 1994; Part VII, Chapter C).

Safe technological designs are a key element of safe systems. Jacky's article illustrates how the behavior of equipment users, such as radiological technicians in the case of the Therac-25, is also crucial. The 1991 fiasco in which a power system failure in one of AT&T's switching centers grounded air lanes at three major airports illustrates how high-quality preventive maintenance can also play a key role. Safe systems are most likely to be operated by high-performance organizations that place a premium on the safety of their customers, clients, and employees. Gary Stix's account of the way that the FAA is able to operate a highly reliable air traffic control system with ancient and unreliable technologies underlines this point.

---

[6] See Fetzer's (1988) critique of program verification and replies in *Communications of the ACM*, 32(3) (March, 1989), pp. 287–290, 374–381, and 32(4) (April, 1989), pp. 420–422, 507–512.

[7] Much-discussed papers by DeMillo, Lipton, and Perlis (1979) and by Fetzer (1988) contain different arguments with complementary conclusions. A paper by Parnas *et al.* (1990) discusses the issue in the context of safety-critical computing.

[8] Nancy Leveson, personal communication, November 7, 1989.

However, relatively few organizations have the safety consciousness of the FAA. Given the infusion of computer technology into everyday affairs, it is only to be expected that malfunctions will result in inconvenience, serious harm, or even threats to life, in an ever-widening spectrum.

When Are Computers Safe for People Who Use Them?

That computer use can be a cause of health problems is a relatively new concept. If people are asked to associate the terms "computers" and "health" they are likely to imagine applications like expert systems applied to medical diagnosis or perhaps health insurance record systems. However, long-term intensive computer users may be susceptible to a significant set of ailments, including headaches, visual ailments (i.e., blurred vision, double vision, color fringes, deterioration of visual acuity) and painful muscular strains that, in extreme cases, can make it hard for a person to cut a slice of bread with a knife. Workers' compensation claims related to repetitive strain injuries (RSI) are skyrocketing, and many lawsuits against employers are pending.

In Chapter F, "Caught in the Grip of RSI," Evan Williamson gives us a first-hand account of his predicament that includes these revelations:

> About three-quarters of the way through the project, I noticed an odd, tired feeling spreading over the backs of my hands and up my forearms. Thinking it was simple fatigue, I promised myself a long break from the computer when the project was done, readjusted my hands to a more comfortable position, and continued my work. . . . Over the next couple of months, I started to feel what could best be described as electric shocks running up my forearms. These were rare at first, but became common throughout the workday. What finally sent me to the doctor was a large, painful lump beneath my skin at the intersection of the base of my right thumb and wrist.

Williamson describes how his supervisor seemed more concerned with getting him to work harder than with minimizing his suffering. And some doctors and lawyers don't believe that RSI is a valid cause for complaint. For example, hand surgeon Morton L. Kasdan, M.D., a Fellow of the American College of Occupational and Environmental Medicine (ACOEM) and Chairman of its Committee on Ergonomics, doesn't endorse complaints like Williamson's:

> "Life without pain does not exist, period. Jobs without pain do not exist. Often, the psychosocial factors are more critical to the incidence of CTDs (cumulative trauma disorders). . . . If you look at people with chronic pain syndrome, more than 80 percent of them had some kind of psychological problem while growing up. With many of these CTD patients, if you talk to their employers, you'll find they're not model employees, they're not good workers, and there's usually a precipitating event to that medical claim, such as a reprimand, or they're about to lose their job. There's more here than a job or a computer or a chair: there are a lot of other factors that need to be looked at." (quoted in Fernberg, 1994)

The editors of *Managing Office Technology* (1993) report the way that a British court ruled against a financial reporter who claimed that he had severe pain and lost wages after he developed RSI five years earlier. The British judge ruled that the concept of RSI is "meaningless" and had "no place in the medical books." Despite the skepticism over RSI, it is easy to find ergonomic aids such as wrist rests and more hand-friendly keyboards for sale in many computer stores. In fact, some computer manufacturers are placing warning labels on keyboards, if for no reason other than to protect themselves from potential lawsuits for RSI. In fact, IBM and other keyboard manufacturers have been sued for knowing that traditional computer keyboards can cause RSI and not warning computer users. According to Savage (1993:41),

> Vendors find themselves faced with a dilemma. If they opt for safer designs, it implies their earlier products are unsafe. Yet, they may eventually be liable through negligence and product liability if they are found to have sold equipment that has harmed someone. Some vendors market safe products to companies, but do not make that information known to the general public.

In Chapter G, "Office Automation's Threat to Health and Productivity," Omar Khalil and Jessie Melcher discuss the rapid rise of reported RSI cases in the United States and Australia. They observe that:

> Computers have turned what was once the unseen work of the office into discrete keystrokes that can be counted and sped up. Computers store and retrieve data quickly. Users can type faster while having less control over the pace of their work. Word processors pose special problems, since they allow workers to type up to 240 characters per minute for hours without a break; and research results suggest that workers who type for more than five hours a day at a computer have twelve times as great a risk of developing RSIs as those who spend less time.

People who used traditional typewriters were less at risk for RSI because they moved in more diverse ways to push the carriage of mechanical typewriters or to stop briefly and feed new sheets of paper. These simple activities required a broader range of physical movement from even the fastest or most highly pressured typists. And, as Khalil and Melcher note, "Office workers who once might have mixed typing with filing, answering phones, and countless other tasks may now simply sit at their computers and type."

In the United States, a number of organizations have made serious efforts to reduce the risks of RSI. In one ironic case, the insurance firm Blue Cross had trouble finding workman's insurance for its own office workers.

> In 1990 most of the 3500 employees at Blue Cross of California sat at the same-size workstations and used a desktop computer or a terminal or both. Throughout the company, graphic designers, secretaries, programmers, data entry people, insurance underwriters, claims processors, managers, and

others complained of pain in the neck, arms, hands, and shoulders. That year 26 people were unable to do their jobs due to debilitating pain and filed workers' compensation claims. These injuries cost the company a staggering $1.6 million in 1990 alone. (Fryer and Ignatius, 1994:46)

In response to these conditions, Blue Cross's Ellen Ignatius was authorized to purchase new ergonomic office furniture that better fit each worker. In addition, Ignatius and her staff showed Blue Cross's employees proper ways to sit and work, how to do regular exercises, and how often to take stretch breaks.[9]

Other companies, such as Levi Strauss (jeans maker) and Sun Microsystems (workstation producer) have also developed wide-ranging computer/ workstation health programs to help reduce their medical costs and to increase productivity. Some companies, such as Sun, have gone further than Blue Cross by developing pamphlets and videos for its employees, and by enabling employees to select a wide range of computer-related equipment, such as articulating keyboard trays, wrist rests, mouse rests, foot rests, back rests, copy stands, telephone headsets, trackballs, glare screens, and task lights (Jones and Mattinson, 1994). Sun created workshops with a physical therapist for small groups of employees. And, more important, Sun's educational materials encouraged people to vary their movements and to take periodic short breaks.

Stress, poor posture, relentless work, and poor ergonomics all seem to contribute to RSI. Consequently, a focus on any single item, such as keyboards, is probably misplaced. Even so, few organizations seem ready to equip their staff with office equipment that fits the variety of their bodies, and with effective guidelines for safe work.

Computer System Security

In the 1960s and 1970s, the public viewed computer systems as being occasionally unreliable, but basically secure. Recent events publicized in the mass media, as well as Hollywood films, have radically changed that image. The 1983 film *Wargames* depicted a teenage computer-hobbyist, whose intrusion into a United States military computer system brought the world to the brink of nuclear war. Although the film's premise—that an unauthorized user could gain access to NORAD's strategic computer systems—is extremely dubious, other military-related computer systems do have serious security problems (see Ford, 1985). In February 1989, eighteen-year-old Chicagoan Herbert Zinn, Jr. was sentenced to nine

---

[9] Dan Wallach's "Typing Injury FAQ" (1994) provides brief descriptions of the various forms of RSI, work practices, and reviews of equipment. Wallach periodically updates his FAQ, and posts it on Usenet newsgroups, such as comp.human-factors.

months' imprisonment plus a $10,000 fine for breaking into United States military computers and AT&T computers, and stealing fifty-five programs.[10]

Clifford Stoll, an astronomer at the University of California's Lawrence Berkeley Labs, started investigating a "hacker" who gained unauthorized access to an account, and used the Berkeley system as a springboard to other (primarily military) computer systems. Over a period of months, Stoll followed the hacker, who entered over 430 computers connected by several networks in the United States and Western Europe. Stoll's book, *The Cuckoo's Egg*, provides a fascinating account of the arduous work required to locate an intruder's entry point and eventually identify the intruder, who, in this case, turned out to be located in West Germany.[11] As a result of Stoll's detective work, three West German programmers were eventually arrested and charged with espionage for the Soviet KGB; reportedly, they gained access to computerized information in NASA headquarters, Los Alamos, and Fermilab, along with various U.S. Army computers and military-related computers in Europe.[12] These examples are particularly serious because they compromise national security and involve computer systems designed to be open only to a relatively small group of authorized users. Moreover, intrusions may be difficult to detect (and even more difficult to trace) because of a multitude of interconnections among electronic networks.

Of course, not all breaches of computer security involve tightly restricted military systems, and not all are marked by malicious intent. In a widely reported episode during early November 1988, Cornell University Computer Science graduate student Robert T. Morris, Jr. planted a "worm"[13] that spread worldwide across several thousand computers linked to a large research computer network (Internet).[14] A small programming miscalculation caused the worm to replicate much faster than the programmer had intended, necessitating the temporary shutdown of many Internet computers while a "fix" was devised. Aside from this considerable inconvenience to researchers who relied on the computers, and the thousands of

---

[10] *RISKS-FORUM Digest*, Vol. 8, No. 29 (February 22, 1989). The Government information in this case was described as unclassified, but "highly sensitive."

[11] Stoll's (1989) book-length account of the saga explains how he tried to enlist the help of the FBI and CIA with only minor success.

[12] *RISKS-FORUM Digest*, Vol. 8, No. 35 (March 6, 1989).

[13] A worm is a piece of stand-alone code capable of replicating itself and propagating through a series of interconnected computer systems. It may or may not be intentionally destructive, but in either case it can consume significant system resources to the point where a computer system is rendered essentially inoperative.

[14] The June 1989 issue of *Communications of the ACM* contains a special section devoted to the character of Morris's worm, its pattern of destruction, and the strategies that system operators used to detect and correct it. See the articles by Gene Spafford (1989), Rochlis and Eichen (1989), and Donn Seeley (1989).

hours of technical time to detect and correct the problems, no other damage was done.

But the Internet worm stimulated considerable controversy (see Eisenberg et al., 1989). Although it was argued that Morris's experiment helped call attention to an important computer security weakness, critics insisted that it was widely known that the Internet was not totally secure. In fact, its gaps were like unlocked house doors in a friendly village. In the critics' view, someone who wandered through unlocked houses and left annoying signs of intrusion—like tracking mud across carpets, opening dresser drawers, and leaving notes on beds—was not giving people real news about their vulnerability. He would be *creating* a sense of vulnerability. In any case, the surrounding media publicity served to heighten public awareness of computer security issues.[15]

Within a month of Morris's worm attack, the Advanced Research Projects Agency (ARPA) announced the establishment of a Computer Emergency Response Team (CERT) to address the computer security concerns of Internet research users. The Coordination Center for the CERT, located at the Software Engineering Institute of the Carnegie Mellon University, taps the expertise of over one hundred computers security experts who work at Internet sites. CERT began issuing advisories about other attacks on Internet sites. Chapter H is a sample CERT advisory issued in February 1994 after over 10,000 user IDs were compromised by a Trojan login program surreptitiously installed on hundreds of networks linked to the Internet. The modified program, running under Unix, trapped the first 128 bytes of every login and wrote them to a local file so that the hackers could harvest the passwords (Kabay, 1994).

Balancing Computer Security and Usability

Security, however, is not the only priority in computer systems: accessibility and ease of use are often competing requirements. As the Cornell Commission pointed out in its comments on the Morris episode:

A community of scholars should not have to build walls as high as the sky to protect a reasonable expectation of privacy, particularly when such walls will equally impede the free flow of information. (Eisenberg et al., 1989; 707)

A system such as Internet, which provides electronic mail links and data exchange among thousands of researchers around the globe, can be made virtually worthless if security procedures make its operation so cumber-

---

[15] Denning (1989) describes and assesses the Internet worm's significance. Morris was convicted of federal computer tampering charges, placed on three years' probation, fined $10,000, and sentenced to 400 hours of community service.

some that people are reluctant or unable to use it.[16] The same trade-off confronts millions of microcomputer users, who want easy access to electronic bulletin boards to download software for personal use. Increasingly, they must deal with the possibility that a downloaded program may contain a virus[17] that is designed to maliciously lock up their system or erase all the files on their hard disk.[18]

The most emphasized aspect of system security has been the protection of information by prohibiting unauthorized access. Given a sufficient commitment and sufficient precautions (passwords, data encryption, call-back systems, restrictions on levels of access, or even physical identification of users and elimination of dial-in access), a reasonably high level of security can be achieved. Like many computer-related issues, "security" has both social and technical dimensions.

Honestly Acknowledging the Risks of Powerful Technologies

It is conventional wisdom that new technologies make daily life more convenient and safer. We could create a vast catalog of improved health

---

[16] One way that computer networks are intruded upon is for a person (or program) to guess passwords that are similar to an account name or to the account holder's name. Users can reduce the risk of intrusion by choosing obscure passwords. In addition, system administrators could enforce rules that require users to frequently change their password or to answer a set of personal questions before actually gaining access to a system. But security measures requiring people to remember complex passwords and pass "security tests" involve substantial effort. The problem is that as access procedures become increasingly complex, some people will be less inclined to use computer systems frequently, and those who do use them will find their work more onerous and less productive. In either case, the systems become less valuable as a communication medium.

[17] A computer virus is a piece of program code that exists within an otherwise normal program. When this program is run, the viral code seeks out other programs within the computer and modifies them. The other programs can be anywhere in a computer system and can even be the operating system itself. This alteration of program code can grow geometrically depending on the number and different types of programs that are run (1 program modifies 2, which modify 4, which modify 8, etc.). At a given point in time or based on some other external trigger (such as the number of times the program was run or the amount of remaining free disk space), the viral code goes to work. Some viruses are designed as nuisances, and simply leave cute messages on a computer screen. But many viruses are designed to lock up systems and erase files. They are quite costly to those who lose important work when their systems are attacked. See Cohen (1987) and Duff (1989) for sample virus code, and McIlroy (1989) for descriptions of experiences with viruses on UNIX systems.

[18] Several vendors have released software packages designed to prevent this kind of harm, but at least one (public domain) version itself turned out to be a culprit program. By late 1989 there were over fifty known kinds of viruses that had "infected" IBM PCs, and many more kinds that have been designed to infect Apple Macintoshes and other kinds of computers. By 1994 hundreds of viruses and numerous variants had been identified. It is fortunate that the number of computer systems attacked by any specific virus has usually been relatively small—from a handful to a few hundred. Even so, people (mostly teenage males) produce new viruses every year. The magazine *2600* serves as a kind of *Popular Mechanics* for virus writers.

technologies, industrial technologies, household technologies, and so forth that fit this maxim. Yet, in the last twenty years, a growing number of well-educated people, including scientists and engineers, have become cautious of blindly accepting new technologies. High-profile stories of major environmental hazards, including DDT, fluorocarbons, and toxic spills, as well as stories of how they were pushed by corporate greed and ineptitude, have helped shift public opinion (Pillar, 1991). In Chapter I, computer scientist Peter G. Neumann argues that we should seek a new common sense with technologies. Neumann draws upon Jerry Mander's (1991) environmental ethos and suggests that we apply it to computer technologies as well. His first point: Since most of what we are told about new technology comes from its proponents, be deeply skeptical of all claims—is one that we would take for granted in buying a new car or even a house. His second point: Assume all technology "guilty until proven innocent"—is one that we would normally apply to new drugs. Neumann's article lists all of Mander's ten points. None of them is remarkable, except that we normally don't apply them to assessing new computer technologies. Neumann argues that we should treat computer technologies with the same care that we treat other technologies whose dangers we have come to understand.

Sources

Posting by R. Aminzade (1990). *RISKS-FORUM Digest*, 9(61) (January 20).

Posting by Michael Slavitch (1994). *RISKS-FORUM Digest*, 15(54) (November).

Stix, Gary (1994). "Aging Airways." *Scientific American*, 270(5)(May), 96–104.

Brian Cantwell Smith (1985). "The Limits of Correctness." Issued as Report No. CSLI-85-35 by the Center for the Study of Language and Information (Stanford University) (Copyright 1985 by Brian Cantwell Smith). (Also printed in the ACM SIG Journal *Computers and Society*, combined [14]4 and [15]1, 2, 3 [Winter/Spring/Summer/Fall, 1985], 18–26.)

Williamson, Evan (1994). "Caught in the Grip of RSI: A First-hand Account." *Managing Office Technology*, 39(5)(May), 40–41.

Khalil, Omar E. M., and Jessie E. Melcher (1994). "Office Automation's Threat to Health and Productivity: A New Management Concern." *SAM Advanced Management Journal*, 59(3)(Summer), 10–14.

Computer Emergency Response Team (1994). "Ongoing Network Monitoring Attacks." *CERT Advisory* CA-94, 01 (February 3).

Neumann, Peter G. (1993). "Risks of Technology." *Communications of the ACM*, (36)3 (March), 130.

References

Anthes, Gary H. (1992). "Phone Outage Drives FAA to Backup Strategy." *Computerworld*, 26(31) (August 3), 63.

Cohen, Fred (1987). "Computer Viruses: Theory and Experiments." *Computers and Security*, 6, 22–35.

Dahlbom, Bo, and Lars Mathiassen (1993). *Computers in Context: The Philosophy and Practice of Systems Design*. Blackwell, London.

DeMillo, Richard A., Richard J. Lipton, and Alan J. Perlis (1979). "Social Processes and Proofs of Theorems and Programs." *Communications of the ACM*, 22(5) (May), 271–280. (See also various replies published in the same journal, 22[11][November, 1979], 621–630.)

Denning, Peter J. (1989). "The Science of Computing." *American Scientist*, 77(2) (March–April), 126–128.

Dobson, John, and Brian Randell (1989). "Program Verification: Public Image and Private Reality." *Communications of the ACM*, 32(4) (April), 420–422.

Duff, Tom (1989). "Experiences with Viruses on UNIX Systems." *Computing Systems*, 2(2) (Spring), 155–172.

Dunlop, Charles, and Rob Kling (1991). *Computerization and Controversy: Value Conflicts and Social Choices*. Academic Press, San Diego.

Eisenberg, Ted, David Gries, Juris Hartmanis, and Don Holcomb (1989). "The Cornell Commission: On Morris and the Worm." *Communications of the ACM*, 32(6), 706–709.

Fernberg, Patricia M. (1994). "Are Workplace Ailments All They're Claimed?" *Managing Office Technology*, 39(3) (March), 27–31.

Fetzer, James H. (1988). "Program Verification: The Very Idea." *Communications of the ACM*, 31(9) (September), 1048–1063. (See also replies in the same journal, 32[3][March, 1989], 287–290; 374–381, and 32[4][April, 1989], 420–422; 506–512.)

Floyd, Christiane (1987). "Outline of a Paradigm Change in Software Engineering," in Gro Bjerknes, Pelle Ehn, and Morten Kyng (eds.), *Computers and Democracy*, pp. 191–210. Gower Publishing Company, Brookfield, VT.

Ford, Daniel (1985). *The Button*. Simon and Schuster, New York.

Fryer, Browyn, and Ellen Ignatius (1994). "The High Cost of Keyboard Injuries. Blue Cross of California Addresses Repetitive Strain Injuries." *PC World*, 12(3) (March), 45–46.

Heimann, C. F. Larry (1993). "Understanding the Challenger Disaster: Organizational Structure and the Design of Reliable Systems." *American Political Science Review*, 87(2) (June), 421–435.

Jones, Jeffrey R., and Dennis Mattinson (1994). "There's More to Computer Ergonomics Than New Equipment." *Risk Management*, 41(5) (May), 39–46.

Kabay, Mich (1994). "Global Group Guards Against Network Attacks: Computer Emergency Response Team Coordinating Center." *Computing Canada*, 20(19) (September 14), 22.

Karpinski, R. (1991). "SS7 Errors Torpedo Networks in Washington, Los Angeles: Signaling System 7." *Telephony*, 221(1) (July 1), 8.

Leveson, Nancy G. (1991). "Software Safety in Embedded Computer Systems." *Communications of the ACM*, 34(2) (February), 34–45.

Managing Office Technology (1993). "RSIs: All in Your Head: Repetitive Strain or Stress Injury." *Legal Issues*, (38)2 (December), 29–30.

Mander, Jerry (1991). *In the Absence of the Sacred: The Failure of Technology and the Survival of the Indian Nations*. Sierra Club Books, San Francisco.

Mason, Charles (1991a). "Washington Acts on SS7 Outages." (Federal Communications Commission to discuss signaling system 7 outages and network vulnerability in general) *Telephony*, 21(3) (July 15), 9–10.

Mason, Charles (1991b). "AT&T Outage Puts More Heat on Network Reliability." *Telephony*, 221(13) (September 13), 8–9.

McIlroy, M. Douglas (1989). "Virology 101." *Computing Systems*, 2(2) (Spring), 173–182.

Mossberg, Walter S. (1994). "Intel Isn't Serving Millions Who Bought Its Pentium Campaign." *Wall Street Journal* (Dec 15), B1.

Nader, Ralph (1965). *Unsafe at Any Speed; The Designed-in Dangers of the American Automobile*. Grossman, New York.

Neumann, Peter G. (1995). *Computer Related Risks*. Addison-Wesley, Reading, MA.

Parnas, David L. (1985). "Software Aspects of Strategic Defense Systems." Originally published in *American Scientist*, 73(5), 432–440. (Reprinted in *CACM*, 28(12) (December 1985), 1326–1335.

Parnas, David L., A. John van Schouwen, and Shu Po Kwan (1990). "Evaluation of Safety-Critical Software." *Communications of the ACM*, 33(6), 636–648.

Perrow, Charles (1984). *Normal Accidents: Living with High-Risk Technologies*. Basic Books, New York.

Pillar, Charles (1991). *The Fail-Safe Society: Community Defiance and the End of American Technological Optimism*. Basic Books, New York.

Rochlis, Jon, and Mark W. Eichen (1989). "With Microscope and Tweezers: The Worm from MIT's Perspective." *Communications of the ACM*, 32(6), 689–699.

Rosen, Eric C. (1981). "Vulnerabilities of Network Control Protocols: An Example." ACM SIGSOFT *Software Engineering Notes*, 5(1) (January), 6–8.

Roush, Wade (1993). "Learning from Technological Disasters." *Technology Review*, 96(6) (August/September), 50–57.

Savage, J. A. (1993). "Are Computer Terminals Zapping Workers' Health?" *Business & Society Review*, 84 (Winter), 41–43.

Seeley, Donn (1989). "Password Cracking: A Game of Wits." *Communications of the ACM*, 32(6), 700–705.

Slade, Robert M. (1994). *Robert Slade's Guide to Computer Viruses*. Springer-Verlag, New York.

Smith, S. L. (1994). "Near Misses: Safety in the Shadows." *Occupational Hazards*, 56(9) (September), 33–36.

Spafford, Eugene (1989). "The Internet Worm: Crisis and Aftermath." *Communications of the ACM*, 32(6), 678–688.

Stoll, Clifford (1988). "Stalking the Wily Hacker." *Communications of the ACM*, 31(5) (May), 484–497. [Reprinted in Charles Dunlop and Rob Kling (eds.) (1991). *Computerization and Controversy: Value Conflicts and Social Choices*. Academic Press, San Diego.

Stoll, Clifford (1989). *The Cuckoo's Egg: Tracking a Spy Through the Maze of Computer Espionage*. Doubleday, New York.

Wallach, Dan S. (1994). "Typing Injury FAQ: General Information." Usenet news. answers. Available via anonymous ftp from rtfm.mit.edu in pub/usenet/news.answers/typing-injury-faq/general. World-Wide-Web users will find this available as hypertext: http://www.cs.princeton.edu/grad/dwallach/tifaq/general.html.

Watson, George F., John Devaney, and Robert Thomas (1992). "Delta V = 0.7V = 85,000 Irate Travelers: Telephone Outage and Air-Traffic Tie-Up of September 17, 1991." *IEEE Spectrum*, 29(2) (February), 54.

Weick, Karl E., and Karlene H. Roberts (1993). "Collective Mind in Organizations: Heedful Interrelating on Flight Decks." *Administrative Science Quarterly*, 38(3) (September), 357–381.

Winograd, Terry, and Fernando Flores (1987). *Understanding Computers and Cognition,* (esp. Part III). Addison-Wesley, Reading, MA.

Further Reading

ACM Sigsoft *Software Engineering Notes.* A monthly ACM periodical regularly documents computer failures along with other articles, such as the design of programming environments.

Allie, Paul F. (1994). "Ergonomics and the Healthy Office." *Managing Office Technology* (39)2 (February), 31–32.

Bellin, David, and Gary Chapman (eds.) (1987). *Computers in Battle: Will They Work?* Harcourt Brace Jovanovich, Boston.

Berleur, Jacques (ed.) (1993). "IFIP WG9.2 Working Conference on Facing the Challenge of Risk and Vulnerability in an Information Society." North-Holland, New York.

Borning, Alan (1987). "Computer System Reliability and Nuclear War." *Communications of the ACM,* 30(2) (February), 112–131.

The CPSR Newsletter. Published by Computer Scientists for Social Responsibility, P.O. Box 717, Palo Alto, California 94301.

Denning, Peter J. (ed.) (1991). *Computers Under Attack.* ACM Press, New York.

Leveson, N. G. (1994). "High-Pressure Steam Engines and Computer Software." *Computer,* 27(10) (October), 65–73.

Leveson, Nancy G. (1995). *Safeware: System Safety and Computers.* Addison-Wesley, Reading, MA.

Leveson, Nancy G., and Clark S. Turner (1993). "An Investigation of the Therac-25 Accidents." *Computer,* 26(7) (July), 18–39.

Putnam, Robert D. (1993). "The Prosperous Community: Social Capital and Economic Growth." *Current,* 356(October), 4–9.

RISKS-FORUM Digest. Distributed electronically by Peter G. Neumann at SRI International as the Usenet newsgroups comp.risks, and available through the computer systems of many universities. (http://www.wais.com/wais-dbs/risks-digest.html.)

Schell, Jonathan (1982). *The Fate of the Earth.* Knopf, New York.

P·A·R·T · VII

B

RISKS-FORUM Digest
Contributions

R. Aminzade • Michael Slavitch

Date: Thu, 18 Jan 90 08:24:18 EST
From: R. Aminzade
**Subject: Risks of Voice Mail Systems That Expect a Human at the Other
End[1]**

Last night my car had a dead battery (I left the lights on—something that
a very simple piece of digital circuitry could have prevented, but I digress),
so I called AAA road service. I noted that they had installed a new digital
routing system for phone calls. "If you are cancelling a service call Press 1,
if this is an inquiry about an existing service call, Press 2, if this is a new
service call, Press 3." All well and good, except that when I finally reached
a real operator, she informed me that the towtruck would arrive "within 90
minutes." In less than the proposed hour and a half I managed to beg
jumper cables off of an innocent passerby and get the car started, so I
decided to call AAA and cancel the service call. I dialed, pressed 1 as
instructed, and waited. The reader should realize that my car was illegally
parked (this is Boston), running (I wasn't going to get stuck with a dead
battery again!), and had the keys in the ignition. I was not patient. I waited
about four minutes, then tried again. Same result. I was now out of dimes,
but I noticed that the AAA machine began its message with "we will accept
your collect call . . ." so I decided to call collect. Surprise! I discovered that
New England Telephone had just installed its digital system for collect
calls. It is quite sophisticated, using some kind of voice recognition circuit.
The caller dials the usual 0-(phone number), and then is asked "If you wish

to make a collect call, press 1 . . . If you wish to . . ." Then the recording asks "please say your name." The intended recipient of the collect call then gets a call that begins "Will you accept a collect call from [recording of caller stating his name]." I knew what was coming, but I didn't want to miss this experience. I gave my name as something like "Russell, Goddammit!," and NET's machine began asking AAA's machine if it would accept a collect call (which it had already, plain to the human ear, said it would accept) from "Russell Goddammit!" Ms. NET (why are these always female voices?) kept telling Ms. AAA "I'm sorry, I don't understand you, please answer yes or no," but Ms. AAA went blithely on with her shpiel, instructing Ms. NET which buttons to push. I stood at the phone (car still running . . . machines nattering away at each other) wondering who could do this episode justice. Kafka? Orwell? Groucho? I was sure that one machine or the other would eventually give up and turn things over to a human being, but, I finally decided to dial a human operator, and subject the poor woman to a stream of abuse. She connected me to AAA, where I punched 3 (rather than the appropriate but obviously malfunctioning 1), and subjected yet another unpaid clerk to my wrath.

Date: Mon, 7 Nov 94 15:45:50 -0500
From: Michael Slavitch, Consultant, (613) 781-9824" <slavitch@on. bell.ca>
Subject: Ottawa Library Fines People Using Unreliable Automatic Calling System[2]

About two months ago I reserved a book at my local library. The library has gone electronic in its reservation system. You reserve a book, and when your turn to receive it comes due a computer dials your home phone number. If an answer occurs, it assumes you heard the message; if you do not pick up the book in three days, you are fined $2.00.

Basically, this is what happened to me. Their computer called my number and the phone went off hook, starting the meter running. For some reason my answering machine did not pick up the message (I have an answering machine and a fax modem hanging off the same line, but the fax modem is outgoing only).

The RISK here is obvious, and I consider it nontrivial. The librarian insisted that the "system" is "reliable" and "almost always" works. Well, my knowledge of datacomm says that if it does not always work it is not

---

[1] This article appeared in *RISKS-FORUM Digest*, Vol. 9, Issue 61 (January 20, 1990). Reproduced with permission.
[2] This article appeared in *RISKS-FORUM Digest*, Vol. 6, Issue 54 (November 1994). Reproduced with permission.

reliable, and that they are fining people based on an assumption that the message was received.

What's scary was the attitude of the librarian. Because she was told by someone that the system works, she insisted that I had received the call. I asked her for proof of that and she said that "the system said you got the call, it must be true." My attempt to describe the essence of data communications and reliable communication fell on deaf ears, and she refused to give me the name of her superior because "the system works and nobody should complain about it."

Well, I am. I know that it is only two bucks, but the implications that arise from misuse or overly trusting such a system are worrisome. What if the government started issuing parking tickets or summonses in this manner, or banks warned you of surcharges on financial transactions? What if my wife answered the phone and the book was "How to Handle Infidelity in Your Marriage" :) (it wasn't)?

So how do you handle two things?:

[One] An unreliable delivery system being assumed to be reliable.

[Two] People placing trust in such a system.

P·A·R·T · VII

Safety-Critical Computing:
Hazards, Practices, Standards,
and Regulation[*]

Jonathan Jacky

A Horror Story

On March 21, 1986, oilfield worker Ray Cox visited a clinic in Tyler, Texas to receive his radiation treatment. Cox knew from his previous visits that the procedure should be painless, but that day he felt a jolt of searing heat. Outside the shielded treatment room, the therapy technologist was puzzled. The computer terminal used to operate the radiation machine displayed the cryptic message, "Malfunction 54," indicating the incorrect dose had been delivered. Clinic staff were unable to find anything wrong with the machine, so they sent Cox home and continued treating other patients.

But Cox's condition worsened. Spitting blood, he checked into a hospital emergency room. Clinic staff suspected Cox had received an electrical shock, but specialists were unable to locate any hazard. Less than a month later, Malfunction 54 occurred again, this time striking Verdon Kidd, a 66-year-old bus driver. Kidd died in May, reportedly the first fatality ever caused by an overdose during a radiation treatment. Meanwhile, Cox became paralyzed and lapsed into a coma. He died in a Dallas hospital in September 1986.

As news of the Tyler incidents spread, reports of other accidents surfaced. A patient in Canada, another in Georgia, and a third in Washington State had received mutilating injuries in 1985. Another overdose occurred in Washington State in January 1987. All victims had been treated with the Therac-25, a computer-controlled radiation machine called a linear accelerator manufactured by Atomic Energy of Canada, Ltd (AECL). Physicist Fritz Hager and therapy technologists at the Tyler clinic discovered that the accidents were caused by errors in the computer programs that controlled the Therac-25. Cox and Kidd had been killed by software [1, 2, 3, 4, 5].

The Therac accidents were reported in the national press [6, 7] and featured in *People* magazine [8] and the television news program "20/20" [9]. Journalist Edward Joyce learned that different problems with the Therac-25 and its predecessor, the Therac-20, had been turning up for years prior to the Tyler accidents but were not widely known [3, 10, 11, 12]. Injured patients had been largely ignored and machines kept in use. Fixes requested by the Canadian government in the wake of one accident had never been installed [3]. After the Tyler clinic staff explained the cause of the problems, Therac-25s were not withdrawn from service; instead, warnings were circulated and a makeshift temporary fix was recommended [13], which proved unable to prevent another accident [4]. After the fifth accident, clinics using the Therac-25 were advised, but not ordered, to discontinue routine use until a set of fixes approved by the Food and Drug Administration (FDA) was installed. The major effect of these fixes was to provide traditional safety features that would function independently of the computer [14]. By that time, the Tyler clinic had vowed never to use the Therac-25 again and was attempting to obtain a refund from AECL [11]. AECL stopped selling therapy machines in 1985, citing competitive pressure and poor sales [2].

The accidents showed that computer-controlled equipment could be less safe than the old-fashioned equipment it was intended to replace. Hospitals and patients had assumed that manufacturers developed new products carefully, and that any remaining defects would be spotted by the FDA. The Therac incidents revealed that computer system safety had been overlooked by vendors and regulators alike. Software that controlled devices critical to human safety was being developed in a haphazard, unsystematic fashion, and receiving little meaningful review from regulatory agencies (who had little experience with the new equipment and meager resources to deal with it in any case). The never-ending "software crisis" [15, 16, 17]—the unexpected difficulty and expense of creating high-quality software—had finally caught up with the medical equipment industry. But here, instead of merely causing frustration or financial loss, errors could kill.

Using computers to control hazardous machinery raises difficult questions. Some are specific to computing: Why use computers at all, if satisfactory techniques already exist? Do computers introduce new kinds of problems unlike those encountered in traditional control systems? What techniques exist now for creating safe and reliable computer-controlled systems, and could they be improved? Other questions are perennial for

*Reprinted with permission.

society at large but are only now beginning to be considered in the computing field: How are we to decide whether a product is safe enough to place on the market? How can we ensure that product developers and service providers are competent and that poor practices are discouraged? Who is held responsible when systems fail and people get killed?

How Did It Happen?

It is useful to explain how the Therac accidents happened, to show how seemingly trivial mistakes can have terrible consequences.

When the accidents occurred, radiation therapy had become a routine, safe, and frequently effective procedure, used on almost 450,000 patients each year in over 1100 clinics in the United States [18]. Much of the success was due to the convenience and therapeutic properties of linear accelerators, which began to replace cobalt units in the 1960s [19, 20]. The million-dollar Therac-25, introduced in 1982 [3, 10], was thought to be among the best available and was one of the first of a new generation of computer-controlled machines. The traditional operator's control panel, festooned with switches, buttons, and lamps, was replaced by a computer video display terminal, and much of the internal control electronics was replaced by a computer. This was intended to make operation more convenient, improve the accuracy of treatments, and decrease the time needed to treat each patient [20]. A particular innovation of the Therac-25 was to use the computer to perform many of the safety functions traditionally allocated to independent, or hard-wired, electromechanical circuits called interlocks [10].

Control systems have traditionally used physical forces transmitted by the motions of wheels, levers, cables, fluids, or electric current to transmit the will of a human operator to the controlled devices. Through a more or less indirect chain, the operator's hands and feet were physically connected to the machinery that did the work. The computer changed all that. Today, it is necessary to transmit only information, not force. Instead of designing a complex control system that depends on meshing cogs, fluid flow, or electric current to transform the operator's commands, the designer can plug in a standard computer—perhaps a microprocessor costing only a few dollars. The operator's commands are mediated by software—lists of instructions that tell the computer what to do.

The proper operation of a traditional control system largely depended on the physical soundness of the control mechanism. When it failed, it was usually because some part broke or wore out: teeth broke off gears, tubes burned out, hydraulic fluid leaked away. These failures were usually caused by manufacturing defects or wear and could be prevented by inspecting the product and replacing defective parts. Computer hardware can also break or wear out, but many computer failures are not so easy to understand. They are design failures, caused by logical unsoundness in the control mechanism. There is no material defect that can be discovered by inspection. As one aircraft accident investigator ruefully noted, "Malfunctioning electrons will not be found in the wreckage" [21].

Some design failures are in the hardware—the computer chips themselves. A design error caused parts from early production runs of the popular Intel 80386 microprocessor, introduced in August 1986, to compute the wrong answer when multiplying certain combinations of numbers. The flaw was not discovered until over 100,000 units had been sold [22]. But design errors in mass-produced computer hardware are unusual. More frequently, design errors occur in the software: the instructions provided to the computer are wrong.

A software error killed Cox and Kidd. It involved the apparently straightforward operation of switching the machine between two operating modes. Linear accelerators, including the Therac-25, can produce two kinds of radiation beams: electron beams and X-rays. Patients are treated with both kinds. First, an electron beam is generated. It may irradiate the patient directly; alternatively, an X-ray beam can be created by placing a metal target into the electron beam: as electrons are absorbed in the target, X-rays emerge from the other side. However, the efficiency of this X-ray-producing process is poor, so the intensity of the electron beam has to be massively increased when the target is in place. The electron beam intensity in X-ray mode can be over one hundred times as great as during an electron beam treatment.

There is great danger that the electron beam might attain its higher intensity with the X-ray target absent, and be driven directly into a patient. This hazard has been well understood for more than twenty years. Three patients were overdosed in one day at Hammersmith Hospital in London in 1966, when the (noncomputer) controls in one of the earliest linear accelerators failed [23, 24].

In most of today's accelerators, hard-wired electromechanical interlocks ensure that high electron beam intensity cannot be attained unless the X-ray target is in place. In the Therac-25, however, both target position and beam intensity were controlled solely by the computer. When the operator switched the machine from X-ray to electron mode, the computer was supposed to withdraw the target and set the beam to low intensity.

Usually it worked that way. At Tyler, more than five hundred patients had been treated without mishap in the two years preceding the accidents [2]. However, if the operator selected X-rays by mistake, realized his or her error, and then selected electrons—all within eight seconds [1, 13]—the target was withdrawn but the full-intensity beam was turned on. This error, trivial to commit, killed Cox and Kidd. Measurements at Tyler by physicist Fritz Hager, in which he reproduced the accident using a model of a patient called a "phantom," indicated that Kidd received a dose of about 25,000 rads—more than one hundred times the prescribed dose [1, 2, 5].

After the Tyler staff explained the mechanism of the accident, AECL recommended a makeshift fix: to make it difficult for the technologist to change the beam type from X-rays to electrons, remove the keycap from the "up-arrow" key and cover it with electrical tape [1, 5]. The FDA concurred that "the interim disabling of the edit mode, in combination with user adherence to operating instructions, will prevent similar mishaps" [13]. But the FDA was mistaken. Another accident occurred in Yakima in Washington State in 1987, caused by a different error that also involved movable elements in the treatment head [1, 4]. (Leveson and Turner provide a more detailed technical description of the accidents in reference [1].)

Why Did It Happen?

How was it possible that these accidents could occur—not once, but at least five times? Much of the blame lies with the product and the vendor, but the hazard was exacerbated by problems with the customers.

Other Problems with the Product

The problems with the X-ray target were the immediate cause of the accidents. But those were exacerbated by a poor "user interface" that encouraged technologists to operate the machine in a hazardous fashion. According to a therapist at the site of the Georgia accident, the Therac-25 often issued up to forty diagnostic messages a day, indicating something was wrong with the machine. Most of these messages simply indicated that the beam intensity was slightly less than expected, due to the machine being "out of tune." It was possible to cancel the message and proceed with treatments by pressing the "P" key, and operators quickly learned to respond this way to almost any of the diagnostic messages—which were hard to tell apart, since they were numerical codes rather than English text.

It was also possible to proceed in the same casual way after serious faults with safety implications. After an accident in Ontario in 1985, a report by Gordon Symonds of the Canadian Bureau of Radiation and Medical Devices criticized this feature. However, the changes it requested—which would have required a more elaborate recovery procedure after safety-related diagnostics—were never made. The consequences were grave. In Tyler, the only indication of trouble that the operators saw was the cryptic message, "Malfunction 54." They repeatedly pushed "P" and turned the beam on again and again, dosing Ray Cox three times [3] (investigators concluded that the first dose alone was fatal).

Problems with the Vendor

AECL allowed an extremely hazardous product to reach the market. The central problem was not that some individual made a couple of mistakes

772   Jonathan Jacky

while writing the computer code that handled the X-ray target. That was inevitable; the best programmers make lots of mistakes. The real problem was that AECL failed as an organization; it was unable to protect its customers from the errors of one of its staff.

Producing safe products requires a systematic approach to the whole development process. It has to involve several stages of review and evaluation by different people, backed by attention and commitment from those in authority. At AECL, this process must have broken down. It is to be expected that a few errors will slip through any review process (as we shall see, quite a few slip through most software quality assurance programs). However, a history of problems with the Therac series foreshadowed the fatal accidents and should have prompted a thorough reevaluation of its design.

In June 1985 a massive assembly rotated spontaneously on the Therac-25 at the Albert Einstein Medical Center in Philadelphia. Had a patient been present at the time, he or she might have been crushed. The cause was a hardware failure: a diode had blown out on a circuit board. AECL redesigned the circuit so that failure of the diode could not, by itself, cause unintended movement [12]. Then, in July 1985, a patient in Hamilton, Ontario was seriously overdosed. At that time the error was thought to derive from a hardware circuit; at the request of the Canadian government, AECL redesigned the circuit [3]. After he learned of the Tyler accidents in June 1986, physicist Frank Borger at the Michael Reese/University of Chicago Joint Center for Radiation Therapy discovered a similar problem with the X-ray target in the Therac-20. Consequences in the Therac-20 were much less serious; fuses were blown, but hardwired protective circuits prevented the beam from turning on [10]. In August 1986 technicians at a Mobile, Alabama clinic discovered a similar Therac-20 problem that could result in moderate overdoses. AECL had actually discovered the problem three years earlier and provided a fix (another microswitch), but somehow the retrofit had never been applied to some machines in the field [11].

This history suggests that AECL had no effective mechanism—which amounts to having no effective people in positions of real authority—responsible for ensuring the safety of the Therac product line.

Problems with the Customers

AECL sold a hazardous machine, but their customers also contributed to the accidents. Clinic staff discounted injured patients' complaints and kept using the machines. Tyler continued treating after Cox's injuries were apparent, and Kidd was killed in the next month. In June 1985 Katy Yarbrough was badly injured by the Therac-25 at a clinic in Marietta, Georgia. After the treatment, crying and trembling, she told the treatment technologist, "You burned me." "I'm sorry," the woman replied, "but that's not possible, it's just not possible."

No signs of injury are apparent immediately after an overdose, but within days Yarbrough had a visible burn and was in excruciating pain. Her oncologist believed she was suffering muscle spasms and continued administering treatments. Eventually Yarbrough refused any more. She survived, but lost her breast and the use of one arm. The clinic continued treating others and did not report any problem to AECL or the FDA. They didn't realize what had happened to Yarbrough until news of the Tyler accidents reached them nearly a year later [6].

This misplaced faith in the technology could be the product of years of mishap-free experience with other machines. Moreover, the physical design of the Therac-25 beam-production apparatus was considered superb; referring to its dosimetric properties, physicist Alan Baker of Albert Einstein Medical Center in Philadelphia said "It's a wonderful machine, a physicist's delight" [12]. AECL even published a paper in a technical journal describing its radiation protection features, which concentrated exclusively on shielding against low-level hazards and did not even consider the X-ray target or the control system [25]. Furthermore, customers' intuition may have left them unprepared for a particularly diabolical characteristic of software errors: systems that perform most tasks correctly can fail catastrophically when attempting apparently similar tasks. Finally, there was unwarranted confidence in the kludgey keycap fix recommended by AECL—as if there were only one error to be guarded against. Programmers have learned that errors often come in clusters, and units with a history of buggy behavior continue to reveal new faults even as old ones are fixed [26]. There is a less innocent reason why clinics continued to use their machines after injuries and deaths occurred: they were driven by what accident researcher Charles Perrow calls production pressures. In his classic study of high-technology mishaps [27], Perrow describes how plant operators, under pressure to keep production lines running, will sometimes tolerate unsafe conditions—until an accident occurs. Today's cancer clinic is hardly less driven by economics than a power plant or chemical refinery; an idle clinic must still pay for the million-dollar machines and the staff that operate them. Pressures may be most acutely felt in the for-profit "free-standing" clinics that only provide radiation therapy, which have burgeoned in recent years and are actively competing with hospitals and with each other [18]. The FDA was sensitive to the clinics' plight. Asked after the fifth accident whether the FDA was considering a total ban, Edwin Miller of the Office of Compliance in the agency's Division of Radiological Products replied, "No such action is planned at this time. A complete ban would require an extensive study of risk assessment" [4]. Production pressures bear most heavily on the therapy technologists who actually administer the daily treatments (usually in the absence of a physician). The working world is largely divided between people whose job it is to track down problems and others who are supposed to get on with production. Many technologists find themselves in the latter category, and can become inured to forty dose-rate faults a day, routinely pressing the "P" key rather than interrupting treatments for the hours or days required to get the machine back in tune. When Cox was hurt at Tyler, he was at first unable to communicate with the technologist outside the heavily shielded treatment room because the intercom and closed-circuit TV were not working that day [2, 5].

Some clinics resist the pressure. The Hamilton, Ontario clinic kept its machine out of service for months following their accident, until the fault was positively identified and repaired [3]. Recently, a prominent radiation therapy journal felt it necessary to remind readers, "Remove the patient from the treatment room as a first step when uncertainty in normal treatment unit operation occurs; err on the side of safety rather than staying on schedule" [28].

Safety-Critical Applications

Medicine

It is fortunate that only eleven Therac-25s had been installed when the hazards became known [2]. But the incidents raised concerns about computer-controlled therapy machines about to be introduced by several manufacturers, as well as other types of computer-controlled medical devices. The FDA estimated that by 1990, virtually all devices produced by the $11-billion-per-year medical electronics industry included an embedded micro- or minicomputer [29]. The Therac accidents were only the worst examples of a trend that the FDA had been tracking for several years: computer-related problems in medical devices were on the increase.

The evidence was in the FDA's "recall" database. The medical equipment industry recalls about four hundred products a year. Not all recalls involve life-threatening problems, but each implies that the product has serious problems inherent in its design. Twice as many computer-related recalls occurred in 1984 as in 1982 or any prior year. Most computer-related recalls were caused by software errors [29]. There were eighty-four software-related recalls from 1983 through 1987 [30]. Recalls continue to occur [31a]. Recalled devices included ultrasound units, patient monitors, blood analyzers, pacemakers, ventilators, and infusion pumps. A blood analyzer displayed incorrect values because addition, rather than subtraction, had been programmed into a calibration formula. A multiple-patient monitoring system mixed up patients' names with the wrong data. An infusion pump would continually infuse insulin if the operator entered "0" as the maximum value to be infused. Another pump would ignore settings of less than 1.0 milliliter per hour and deliver instead whatever the previous setting was, up to 700 milliliters per hour. If a certain command sequence was entered into one pacemaker programmer, the pacemaker would enter a random unpredictable state. In one ventilator, the patient disconnect alarm could fail to sound when needed, and the gas concentrations (like oxygen) could decrease without activation of an alarm or indication on the display. In many of these applications, as in the Therac incidents, failure of the control system could cause people to be killed.

Aviation

The Airbus Industries A320 airline attracted great press attention when it debuted in 1988 because it was the first commercial airliner to feature "fly-by-wire" controls, in which computers, rather than cables and hydraulics, connect the pilot's control stick to the elevator and other control surfaces [31b, 32]. It was not so widely noted that other computers on-board the A320 are needed to turn on the cabin lights and even flush the toilets [33]!

Airbus's decision to use fly-by-wire was controversial. Several software-related accidents accompanied the earlier introduction of fly-by-wire controls into military aircraft. A computer-controlled, wing-mounted launcher retained its grip after its missile was ignited, creating what someone described as "the world's largest pinwheel" when the aircraft went violently out of control. An F-14 drove off the deck of an aircraft carrier on command from its computer-controlled throttle, and another jet crashed when its flight control program was confronted with an unanticipated mechanical problem [21]. Military fly-by-wire still presses the limits of the art. In 1989 the first prototype of the Swedish JAS-39 Gripen fighter crashed during a test flight after it became unstable while under fly-by-wire control [34]; another Gripen crashed after a similar mishap during an August 1993 airshow in Stockholm, narrowly missing a bridge packed with spectators [35].

Airbus itself has suffered some accidents. In its demonstration flight in June 1988 an A320 crashed into trees after a low-altitude flyby; the pilot claimed that the controls did not respond to his command to pull up [36]. In February 1990 another A320 crashed while on a landing approach to New Delhi, India, killing 91 passengers [37]. In a June 1994 test flight designed to stress its computer-controlled autopilot, the newer Airbus A330 crashed, killing all seven aboard [37, 38]. Airbus (and in some cases, official inquiries) have blamed each of these accidents on pilot error, but doubts remain that the controls may have contributed [37]. Nevertheless, the commercial aviation industry is committed to fly-by-wire. Airbus's rival Boeing began flight testing its own first fly-by-wire airliner, the 777, in June 1994 [39, 40].

Trains and Automobiles

Computers are also being applied in ground transport. In today's new cars, computers control the fuel injection and spark timing and may control the suspension and an antilock braking mechanism [41, 42]. GM is already experimenting with "drive-by-wire" automobiles in which there is no physical connection (other than the computer) from the steering wheel to the tires [43]. In railroads, computers control the switches that are supposed to prevent trains from colliding [44, 45].

Power

Computers are used extensively to control processes in factories and power plants. Some of the emergency shutdown systems that are supposed to "scram" nuclear reactors are computer controlled [46, 47, 48, 49, 50].

Weapons

In weapons systems, computers warn of imminent attack, identify and track targets, aim guns and steer missiles, and arm and detonate explosives [51]. The U.K. Ministry of Defence (MOD) recently analyzed a sample of program fragments drawn from the NATO military software inventory. One in ten contained errors and, of those, one in twenty (or one in two hundred overall) had errors serious enough to result in loss of the vehicle or plant (e.g., an actuator could be driven in the direction opposite from the intended one). Some of these modules had passed extensive tests on multimillion-dollar test rigs [102]. The largest single American casualty of the Gulf War occurred on February 25, 1991, when an Iraqi Scud missile struck a barracks near Dhahran, Saudi Arabia, killing 28. A nearby air defense battery failed to launch any Patriot missiles against the Scud because of a software error [17, 52, 53].

Software Errors Are a Serious Problem

All safety-critical applications depend on software, but software is among the most imperfect of the products of modern technology [16, 17]. Pundits debate whether computers will develop superhuman intelligence or conduct automated wars in space, but back here on planet Earth, after more than thirty years of commercial data processing, folks are still receiving $20-million tax bills [54] and dunning letters for $0.00 [55]. Ensuring that simple results are reliably achieved strains the limits of the typical programmer's art. In the last few years, industry giants IBM, Digital Equipment Corporation, Lotus, and Microsoft have all sold programs containing errors that could destroy users' data [56, 57, 58, 59, 60, 61]. A repository of problem reports maintained by Peter Neumann at SRI International under the cosponsorship of the Association for Computing Machinery (ACM), a professional organization, currently lists more than four hundred incidents in which computer problems caused or threatened injury or significant financial loss [62].

These are not isolated incidents. They follow from typical practices that, in educator Maurice Naftalin's words, "encourage programmers to produce, as quickly as possible, large programs which they know will contain serious errors" [63].

How Programs Are Written

When manufacturers began installing computers in medical equipment, they introduced a new kind of problem, never encountered in simpler devices: programming errors, or, as programmers say, "bugs." Mechanical and electrical design and assembly are only a part of the effort involved in constructing a computer-controlled device. The behavior of the machinery is determined by lists of instructions called programs, or software. Programs are not manufactured in any traditional sense; they are written in a notation called a programming language. To understand why bugs are such a problem, it is necessary to know a little about how a program is built.

Ideally, a program is developed in several stages. First, it is specified: designers try to anticipate every situation that the machine might encounter, and then describe exactly how it should respond to each one. One of the most important jobs designers have is providing programmers with a complete and unambiguous specification. Features that are not clearly specified will be handled by default or at the whim of some programmer, who may not be familiar with important practical details of the machine's operations. It is possible that the designers and programmers of the Therac-25 forgot to consider that the operator might switch from X-rays to electrons at the last minute, so that contingency was handled badly.

The program is then designed: a sort of rough outline is drawn up, in which different program subdivisions, or modules, are distinguished. At this stage, specific behaviors are assigned to each module. It is the designers' responsibility to ensure that when the finished modules are collected, or linked, into a working program, the specified system behavior emerges. Modules can be delegated to different programmers who work independently. Large programs are often composed of modules produced over several years by programmers who never meet.

Finally, the program is coded: programmers compose each module by writing lists of programming language statements that they believe will accomplish the behaviors assigned in the design. At this stage, programmers typically compose by typing the program text into a video terminal or personal computer. This part of the activity somewhat resembles writing a document in a word processor, except that the text resembles no natural human language. When the program text is complete, it must be translated to machine code. Usually, the computer cannot follow the instructions that the programmer writes. Instead, the programmer's text must be converted to a much more elemental set of instructions that the computer can execute.

The translation is performed by another program called a compiler or assembler. The Therac-25 was programmed in assembly language, a notoriously obscure and error-prone notation that is quite close to the machine code.

All this activity is often conducted in a frenetic, crisis-driven atmosphere. News stories about stressful projects at glamorous industry leaders such as Apple and Microsoft tell of programmers who punch holes in walls, get divorced, have mental breakdowns, and commit suicide [64, 65].

A program's size is measured by counting the number of programming language statements, or lines of code, it contains. Simple appliances like microwave ovens may contain a few hundred or a few thousand lines. Typical commercial products like word processors contain tens or hundreds of thousands of lines—the printed listing of the program text is the size of a thick novel. Large systems like aircraft flight control programs contain hundreds of thousands, or even millions, of lines—like a multivolume encyclopedia.

Producing quality software is not only a coding problem; it is also a design and management problem [77, 110]. Most programmers' training concentrates on writing programs that are at most a few thousand lines long. Building large programs that are tens or hundreds of thousands of lines long requires a different set of skills, emphasizing communication and organization, in order to extract useful specifications, divide the project into modules that are reasonable work assignments, ensure continuity and consistency among the programmers and their individual products, and make sure that meaningful testing and other quality assurance is performed. Without all this, skilled coding is in vain.

The popular press and the programming culture itself have tended to neglect the role of communication and organizational skills and glorify instead the eccentric "hacker" who energetically but unsystematically improvises huge programs. (This usage of "hacker" is much older than its recent connotations of computer crime, and derives from the original meaning, "to cut irregularly, without skill or definite purpose.") The consequences of this approach are aptly described by Marvin Minsky, dean of American artificial intelligence researchers:

> When a program grows in power by an evolution of partially understood patches and fixes, the programmer begins to lose track of internal details, loses his ability to predict what will happen, begins to hope instead of to know, and watches the results as though the program were an individual whose range of behavior is uncertain. [66]

The all-too-frequent result is programs that seem to work, but then fail unexpectedly.

The persistence of lurking defects in products released on the market is one of the main things that distinguishes software from hardware. Software engineer John Shore says,

It's extremely hard to build a large computer program that works correctly under all required conditions, but it's easy to build one that works 90 percent of the time. It's also hard to build reliable airplanes, but it's not particularly easy to build an airplane that flies 90 percent of the time. [16]

How Errors Are Detected

Most programmers are not able to demonstrate that their creations will compute the intended results, except by running tests. It is literally a trial-and-error process. It is not terribly confidence inspiring because the number of possible situations that a program must deal with is usually much too large to test, and a case that was left out of the test set may cause the program to fail. As a result, errors are left in products when they reach the market, to be discovered and corrected over time as the system is used. The term maintenance is used in the computer field to describe this continuous error-removal process.

How many errors are left in typical programs? A lot. Typical commercial programs contain between 10,000 and 100,000 lines of code. One measure of program quality is the number of errors per thousand lines of code. Typical programmers leave around fifty errors per thousand lines in the code they write [67]; these must be weeded out during testing or actual use. One report on "the American data processing industry" says that vendors find less than 75% of the programming errors, leaving customers to stumble over the remaining 25% [68]. One reviewer concludes that conscientious vendors try to test until only one or two errors per thousand lines remain in the products they place on the market [69]. Errors reported in newly delivered products range from less than one per thousand lines to around ten per thousand [67, 70] with "good" products clustering around one to five errors per thousand lines. This means that a typical "good" program may contain hundreds of errors.

Usually, software errors do not have serious consequences because people can repair the damage—at some cost in time and aggravation. The state sends you a $20-million tax bill? Clear it up with a phone call—or several. The telephone switching computer cut off your call? Hang up and dial again. The word processor at the office deleted your letter? Type it in again, and this time be sure to make a backup copy to store off-line—just as you were warned to do. Experienced computer users develop a defensive style, a whole repertoire of workarounds. It is this human ability to adapt to problems that makes it possible to base a computerized society on imperfect products.

But some products do not provide much opportunity for people to correct errors. When a computer controls a linear accelerator or an airplane, the results of an error cannot be discarded or ignored. If the patient dies or the airplane crashes, the computation cannot be done over. Applying typical programming practices to critical systems like these can result in tragedy.

Building Better Computer-Controlled Systems

Safety-critical products demand a different, more rigorous approach than most other computer applications. They require several disciplines that are still unfamiliar to many programmers and programming managers: Safety engineering teaches how to design systems that remain safe even when hardware or software fails. Software engineering provides methods for developing complex programs systematically. Formal methods are mathematically based techniques for increasing product reliability that overcome some of the limitations of trial-and-error testing and subjective reviews. In addition, certification and regulation may help ensure that products are produced using the best techniques available, by people who understand how to use them. Liability must fall upon vendors who fail. All of this is expensive. Computer system safety expert Nancy Leveson says, "I do not know how to develop safety-critical software cheaply" [71].

Safety Engineering

Safety engineering emerged from the missile projects of the late 1950s and early 1960s. A series of spectacular explosions demonstrated that the complexity and risk of modern technologies demand a systematic approach to controlling hazards [21, 72, 73]. In a famous 1962 incident, the Mariner I Venus probe had to be destroyed when it went off course because of a single-character transcription error in the equations used as specifications for its control program [74]. The most important lesson of safety engineering is that safety is an important system requirement in its own right and must be designed into a product, not added on as an afterthought. Safety requirements often conflict with other system requirements and may suggest a quite different design than would be obtained if cost and performance were the only considerations. Resolving such conflicts in a consistent and intelligent manner (rather than by default or at the whim of the individual) demands that safety requirements be explicitly separated out and that responsibility for meeting them be assigned to someone with authority.

Safety is not the same thing as reliability. Reliability is a measure of how well the system does exactly what it is intended to do. A safe system protects from hazards whether its intended function is performed correctly or not. In fact, safety is most concerned with what happens when the system does not work as expected. Safety engineers assume that systems will fail—and then they work through the consequences.

Computers—by providing convenient controls, well-designed displays, and more comprehensive diagnostics and error logging—can increase safety. But naive application of computers can increase hazards. It is possible to replace a complex control mechanism with a single computer; the Therac-25 was close to that idea. But this simplification violates the first rule of safety engineering: that failure of a single component should never, by itself, be capable of causing an accident. This principle rules out designs in which safety depends entirely on correct operation of a single computer, unprotected by hardwired interlocks.

Some designers of computer-based systems seem unaware of the principles of safety engineering. Part of the problem may be lack of instruction. Builders of hardwired radiation therapy machines can refer to detailed guides that explain how to design and test safety circuits [75]. Nothing like this exists for computer-controlled machines. A new specialty called software safety is beginning to adapt the principles of safety engineering to software-controlled systems [76].

Software Engineering

Software engineering takes its name from a conference convened by NATO in 1968, when the incipient "software crisis" [15] began to make it clear that building software demands a systematic, disciplined approach rather than ad hoc tinkering.

The central idea of software engineering is that programming projects have to be performed in stages, with an identifiable end product at each stage. The final product is the program itself, but there are several, or many, intermediate stages of design as well. The visible products of most of these intermediate stages are documents about the program. Typically, these include a specification describing what the product is supposed to do, a design guide describing how the program is organized, a test plan describing a series of tests that are supposed to show that the program works as promised in the specification, and a test report that presents the test results and explains how any problems were resolved.

Separating projects into stages and documenting each stage enables products to be reviewed by experts other than their creators [77]. Auditing the documents (including the program text itself) is the primary means of quality assurance in engineered projects. The auditors join the programmers in sharing responsibility for the product. It is analogous to civil engineering, where engineers must produce detailed designs that are subjected to analysis and review before anyone starts pouring concrete. This process is contrary to the stereotype of the eccentric genius programmer, but, as programming expert Tony Hoare notes, "The principle that the work of an engineer should be inspected and signed off by another more experienced and competent engineer lies at the heart of the codes of safe practice in all branches of engineering" [78].

This review process is of extreme importance because it provides an additional way besides testing to detect errors. Testing is always inconclusive, and it comes too late—what if testing reveals serious defects late in the project? In contrast, the review process can begin early, before there is any program to test. Numerous projects have shown that reviews can be more effective than testing at discovering errors (in terms of time and money expended) [79, 80]. Testing is always necessary but instead of being the primary quality assurance method, it complements the analyses by checking the assumptions on which the development is based (e.g., assumptions about the behavior of the hardware and other aspects of the environment where the program runs).

Programmers work much differently on engineered software projects. They find about half their effort is devoted to planning and design, and much of the rest goes for testing and other quality assurance activities. Only 15 to 20% is actually spent coding statements in a programming language—what most people think of as programming [81]. The paradox of software engineering is that the least amount of effort is devoted to the one component that can be sold to the customer. Of course, the effort devoted to the other stages is supposed to ensure the quality of the delivered code, and some studies have found that fixing an error discovered by customers costs as much as one hundred times as much as catching it early in development [81].

The engineering approach is unfamiliar to many programmers. In 1987, the FDA's Frank Houston found that

> a significant amount of software for life-critical systems comes from small firms . . . some of which operate literally in basements and garages . . . so there is little perceived incentive on the part of small, commercial sector businesses to read or heed the lessons learned by large companies. . . . [82]

Some programmers dislike the approach. At a 1988 medical equipment manufacturer's meeting, James Howard of GE Medical Systems criticized it as "an ineffective, costly and time-consuming strategy based on documentation of many specific steps during software development" [83]. In fact, this approach to software development is vulnerable to its own abuses and problems. Many programmers can recall experiences where they spent much effort producing documents of dubious usefulness in order to placate managers or regulators. The Therac-25 project produced many documents, but some of their contents were specious [1]. [Editor's note: in the first edition of *Computerization and Controversy* (1991), Howard's quote was misprinted as "effective," not "ineffective"!]

Formal Methods

Formal methods apply mathematics and logic to programming [84]. People who have heard that computers are logical machines are surprised to learn that this is a radical innovation. In fact, most programs today evolve in a rather ad hoc fashion and are evaluated empirically, by trial-and-error testing. Formal methods propose a radical alternative to this usual practice. They posit that the behavior of a program can be comprehensively described in advance, that the program can be constructed in a systematic way to achieve the intended behavior, and that it is possible to determine whether the program is correct by analyzing the text of the program, along with its specification and design documents. This differs from typical methods that depend on testing and users' experiences to reveal the behavior of programs only after they are written. Formal methods attempt to make the behavior of computer-controlled systems predictable—an essential quality for safety-critical systems.

The methods are called formal because they use mathematical and logical formulas. A formula is simply a text or diagram composed of special symbols combined according to well-defined rules. In fact, all programming languages are formal notations and every computer program is a formula; evaluating formulas is what computers do. So all programming is really "formal methods." However, the term "formal methods" has come to mean using formulas in the stages that come before coding the program. Not only is the program text written in a formal notation, but parts of the specification and/or the design are also expressed in some formal notation, in addition to the usual English prose and diagrams. The formal "specification language" used in these early stages is usually different from the programming language, and more closely resembles the traditional notations of mathematics and symbolic logic. Such notations can be more expressive, easier to understand, and more concise than programming languages, and for some purposes can be more precise and compact than prose or pictures.

Some formal methods concentrate on modeling (i.e., describing and predicting) program behavior. They use formal notations to describe software requirements and designs, much as designers in other fields create circuit diagrams or architectural prints. These formal specifications can be analyzed mathematically to investigate their behavior before the product is actually constructed [85]. Other formal methods concentrate on proving that programs are correct (or not). They use logical and mathematical inference to investigate whether the program text correctly implements the behavior described in its formal specification [84, 86].

Formal methods are controversial [39, 102]. Some critics charge that the expression "proved correct" promises too much, since a formal proof of correctness shows only consistency between two formulas (a formal specification and a program); this does not guarantee that the program will satisfy its customers. One project almost went to court over misunderstandings about what had been proved and what the proofs meant [87]! Authors of some important formal proofs have written candidly about the strengths and limitations of their achievements [88, 89, 90]. Proofs really aren't so mysterious; they can be seen as intensive reviews or inspections that employ especially powerful analytic techniques. Many programmers still hold the opinion that formal methods are too difficult and esoteric for anything but toy problems. Tony Hoare wrote in 1986 that he was unable to find any safety-critical programs in use that had been developed formally [78]. But in recent years several significant formal developments have been completed [91, 92, 110]. The Darlington nuclear power plant near Toronto uses software to control its emergency shutdown systems. The Canadian Atomic Energy Control Board (AECB), a regulatory agency, became concerned that the shutdown programs, like most software, might contain significant undiscovered defects. As the plant neared completion they required the reactor builder to produce a formal specification and prove that the code met the specification. The verification effort (which considered about 20,000 lines of code) cost millions and the plant opening was delayed several months until it could be completed. One of the builders, dismayed at the unexpected costs, said that they would go back to hardwired shutdown systems if they had it to do over again—but the AECB was satisfied and licensed the plant [46, 47, 48]. The Paris Metro subway line uses software to control train speed, signal drivers, and activate emergency brakes. The Paris transport authority introduced computer control to reduce the interval between trains in order to increase capacity and avoid building another subway line. Programmers wrote formal specifications and did proofs of correctness for about 9000 lines of code. The new controls went into service in May 1989; the line carries 800,000 passengers a day on trains running two minutes apart [45]. This may be the most ambitious application of formal methods to date. France is planning a similar development for its nationwide rail network [110].

In addition to these two *tours de force*, several smaller projects have recently devoted modest efforts to formal methods. Some have claimed improvements in quality (fewer errors) and reduced costs (less testing and less effort devoted to fixing errors) [79, 92, 110], although some of these claims have been disputed [80].

In computing, formality isn't an option. Formal methods merely introduce the formality earlier rather than later. This can make difficult issues more visible and encourage programmers to seek a more thorough understanding of the problem they are trying to solve. All formal methods require that intended behaviors and programs be expressed with unusual simplicity and clarity, so they resist the usual tendency in programming to make things overly complicated and therefore error prone and difficult to use. This may be their greatest contribution.

Certification and Regulation

We regulate activities that have safety implications. Software is still largely unregulated. Until recently, aviation and nuclear power were the only applications in which software purchased or operated by private enterprise was subject to approval by the government. In 1987 the American Food and Drug Administration (FDA) began regulating software in medical devices [93].

Some are calling for more regulation. John Shore says, "We require certification for doctors, lawyers, architects, civil engineers, aircraft pilots, automobile drivers, and even hair stylists! Why not software engineers?" [94]. Referring to the Therac accidents, software safety expert Nancy Leveson says, "This is appalling. There needs to be some kind of certification of software professionals working on safety-critical projects or much stricter government controls." Others disagree, fearing government interference and increased costs. "I'll fight them to the death," says Robert Ulrickson, president of Logical Services, a Santa Clara company that designs computerized instruments. "I don't want to be part of an economy that's run by the government. The way to get quality is not to regulate, but to manage" [95]. But Tony Hoare says, "No industry and no profession has ever voluntarily and spontaneously developed or adopted an effective and relevant code for safe practice. Even voluntary codes are established only in the face of some kind of external pressure or threat, arising from public disquiet, fostered by journals and newspapers and taken up by politicians" [78]. One approach is to regulate the people that provide safety-critical services: they must satisfy educational requirements and pass examinations. States usually require that bridges and large buildings be signed off by a licensed professional engineer who assumes responsibility for the structure's safety on behalf of the contractor. Engineers become licensed by passing an examination whose contents are chosen by senior engineers and that is recognized by a state licensing authority.

Programmers often call themselves "software engineers," but none can be licensed engineers, because states to not recognize software as a licensed engineering specialty. The programming profession includes a great range of education and abilities, and many curricula do not provide instruction in topics relevant to building safe systems. Studies of employed programmers have found that the best can be more than twenty-five times as able as the worst, and some teams outproduce others by factors of four or five [81]. Nor is incompetence and ignorance limited to junior programmers; numerous runaway computing projects in which millions of dollars are wasted are evidence that many managers also have a poor grip on their responsibilities [96, 97].

It would be difficult to achieve consensus regarding who might qualify as a "licensed software engineer." Prominent computer scientists disagree about educational requirements and some have proposed curricula quite different from those currently in use [98, 99]. A second approach, which appears to be the one gaining the most favor, is to certify organizations: companies or departments that produce software. In recent years, two certification schemes have become popular. ISO9000 is a generic quality assurance standard that originated in Europe; ISO9000-3 is specialized for software [100]. The Capability Maturity Model (CMM) [101] was created in the United States by the Software Engineering Institute (SEI) at Carnegie-Mellon University, which is funded by the Air Force. Both emphasize the systematic engineering process I described in an earlier section. Auditors inspect an organization seeking certification and grant them a certificate (or not) (ISO9000) or rate them on a scale (CMM). Both ISO9000 and CMM are voluntary, but influential customers (such as certain European governments) may require their suppliers to be certified.

A third approach is to regulate the products themselves: buildings, bridges, airplanes, drugs. The government establishes standards that these products must meet and conducts inspections to make sure products comply. Regulators can write standards to compel industry to adopt particular practices. The U.K. Ministry of Defense has made a controversial requirement that formal methods must be used to develop its safety-critical military software [80, 91, 102, 103]. In the United States, the FDA regulates medical devices. Manufacturers must notify the agency before they bring a new device to market. If the FDA judges the device to be potentially hazardous, it reviews the device's engineering and manufacture, and its approval must be obtained before the device can be sold. In September 1987, the FDA announced that some medical software would be included within its regulatory purview [93]. It requires manufacturers to show that medical software is developed according to good software engineering practices (as described earlier) [104, 105]. The FDA exercises its power: for several months in 1994, the international electronics giant Siemens agreed to stop shipping radiation therapy machines from its plant in Concord, California in response to concerns from the FDA [106].

Liability and Criminal Penalties

When systems fail, victims or their survivors may sue vendors and providers for compensation [5, 107]. In the United Kingdom, a law called the Machine Safety Directive says that criminal proceedings may be taken against a director or manager accused of negligence in the design or manufacture of a device that causes an injury [108].

Conclusion

The Therac accidents remain the best-known examples in the public record of computer-related deaths and injuries. They proved not to be harbingers of a whole series of software-related accidents in medicine—no similar runs of accidents have occurred since. Conservative use of computers in safety-related functions, better software development practices, and regulatory attention have apparently had an effect.

Nevertheless, more subtle difficulties remain. Now that the manufacturers recognize the most obvious hazards, issues of usability become important [109]. Vendors and customers want different things from computer control: customers want devices that are safe and easy to use, vendors want devices that are easy to develop, manufacture, and service. These goals need not be incompatible, but emphasis on the vendors' goals has resulted in computer-controlled medical devices that are poorly matched to clinics' needs: they create extra work for people to do; they are overly complicated and difficult to use. The people who operate them must devote much of their time and vigilant attention to guarding against errors in treatment delivery and other mix-ups. Patient safety still depends on the skill and conscientiousness of individual engineers, programmers, managers, and clinic staff.

References

1. Leveson, Nancy G., and Clark S. Turner (1993). "An Investigation of the Therac-25 Accidents." *Computer*, 26(7), July, 18–41.
2. Joyce, Edward J. (1986). "Malfunction 54: Unraveling Deadly Medical Mystery of Computerized Accelerator Gone Awry." *American Medical News*, October 3, 1, 13–17.
3. Joyce, Edward J. (1987). "Software Flaw Known before Radiation Killed Two," *American Medical News*, January 16, 3, 42–45.
4. Joyce, Edward J. (1987). "Accelerator Linked to Fifth Radiation Overdose," *American Medical News*, February 6, 1, 49, 50.
5. Joyce, Edward J. (1987). "Software Bugs: A Matter of Life and Liability," *Datamation*, May 15, 88–92.
6. *The New York Times* (1986). "Computer Error is Cited in Radiation Death." June 21, p. 8.
7. Saltos, Richard (1986). "Man Killed by Accident with Medical Radiation." *Boston Globe*, June 20, p. 1.
8. Breu, Giovanna, and William Plumber (1986). "A Computer Glitch Turns Miracle Machine into Monster for Three Cancer Patients." *People*, 24, November 24, 48–51.
9. Wizenberg, M. D. Morris (1987). Letter to American Society for Therapeutic Radiology and Oncology members (June 26).
10. Joyce, Edward J. (1986). "Software 'Bug' Discovered in Second Linear Accelerator." *American Medical News*, November 7, 20–21.
11. Joyce, Edward J. (1986). "Firm Warns of Another Therac 20 Problem." *American Medical News*, November 7, 20, 21.
12. *American Medical News* (1987). "Failure Not the First Time." January 16, 43.
13. *Radiological Health Bulletin* (1986). "FDA Monitoring Correction of Therac Radiation Therapy Units." 20(8) (December), 1–2.
14. *Radiological Health Bulletin* (1987). "Therac-25 Accelerator Purchasers Advised to Discontinue Routine Use." 21(3) (March), 1–2.
15. Randell, Brian (1979). "Software Engineering in 1968," in *Proceedings of the Fourth International Conference on Software Engineering*. IEEE Computer Society, p. 1–10.

788

Jonathan Jacky

16. Shore, John (1985). *The Sachertorte Algorithm and Other Antidotes to Computer Anxiety.* Viking, New York.
17. Wiener, Lauren (1993). *Digital Woes: Why We Should Not Depend On Software.* Addison-Wesley, Reading, MA.
18. Diamond, James J., Gerald E. Hanks, and Simon Kramer (1988). "The Structure of Radiation Oncology Practices in the United States." *International Journal of Radiation Oncology, Biology and Physics,* 14(3) (March), 547–548.
19. Hanks, Gerald E., James J. Diamond, and Simon Kramer (1985). "The Need for Complex Technology in Radiation Oncology: Correlations of Facility Characteristics and Structure with Outcome." *Cancer,* 55, 2198–2201.
20. Karzmark, C. J., and Neil C. Pering (1973). "Electron Linear Accelerators for Radiation Therapy: History, Principles and Contemporary Developments." *Physics in Medicine and Biology,* 18(3) (May), 321–354.
21. Frola, F. R., and C. O. Miller (1984). "System Safety in Aircraft Acquisition." Logistics Management Institute, Washington, D.C.
22. *IEEE Spectrum* (1987). "Faults and Failures: Multiplying Mistakes," 24(8), 17.
23. *British Medical Journal* (1966). "Radiation Accident at Hammersmith." Number 5507, 23 July, 233.
24. Karzmark, C. J. (1967). "Some Aspects of Radiation Safety for Electron Accelerators Used for Both X-ray and Electron Therapy." *British Journal of Radiology,* 40, 697–703.
25. O'Brien, P., H. B. Michaels, B. Gillies, J. E. Aldrich, and J. W. Andrew (1985). "Radiation Protection Aspects of a New High-Energy Linear Accelerator." *Medical Physics,* 12(1) (January/February), 101–107.
26. Dunsmore, H. E. (1988). "Evidence Supports Some Truisms, Belies Others." *IEEE Software,* 5(3) (May), 96, 99.
27. Perrow, Charles (1984). *Normal Accidents: Living with High-Risk Technologies.* Basic Books, New York.
28. Karzmark, C. J. (1987). "Procedural and Operator Error Aspects of Radiation Accidents in Radiotherapy." *International Journal of Radiation Ontology, Biology and Physics,* 13(10) (October), 1599–1602.
29. Bassen, H., J. Silberberg, F. Houston, W. Knight, C. Christman, and M. Greberman (1985). "Computerized Medical Devices: Usage Trends, Problems, and Safety Technology," in James C. Lin and Barry N. Feinberg (eds.), *Frontiers of Engineering and Computing in Health Care: Proceedings of the Seventh Annual Conference of the IEEE/Engineering in Medicine and Biology Society,* pp. 180–185.
30. Jorgens, Joseph (1991). "The Purpose of Software Quality Assurance: A Means to an End," in Richard Fries (ed.), *Developing, Purchasing, and Using Safe, Effective, and Reliable Medical Software,* pp. 1–6. Association for the Advancement of Medical Instrumentation, Arlington, Virginia.
31a. Moreno, Mylene (1989). "Product Recalls." *The Boston Globe,* Monday, 10 April, p. 14. (Reported by B. J. Herbison in *RISKS-FORUM Digest* 8[53].)
31b. Spitzer, Cary R. (1986). "All-Digital Jets Are Taking Off." *IEEE Spectrum,* September, 51–56.
32. Rouquet, J. C., and P. J. Traverse (1986). "Safe and Reliable Computing on Board the Airbus and ATR Aircraft," in W. J. Quirk (ed.), *Proceedings of Safecomp '86: Safety of Computer Control Systems.* Pergamon Press, Oxford, England.

33. *Flight International.* September 3, 1988.

34. Neumann, Peter G. (1989). "Saab Blames Gripen Crash on Software." *ACM SIGSOFT Software Engineering Notes,* 14(2) (April), 22. (Cites *Aviation Week and Space Technology,* 27 Feb, 1989, 31.)

35. Neumann, Peter G. (1993). "Saab JAS 39 'Gripen' Crash." *ACM SIGSOFT Software Engineering Notes,* 18(4) (October), 11.

36. Neumann, Peter G. (1988). "The Air France Airbus." *ACM SIGSOFT Software Engineering Notes,* 13(4) (October), 3. (Cites *Aviation Week and Space Technology,* August 8, 1988 on A320 crash inquiry.)

37. Ladkin, Peter (1994). "Summary of Der Speigel Interview with Bernard Ziegler, Airbus Ind." *RISKS-FORUM Digest,* 16(35), August 25.

38. Acohido, Brian (1994). "Airbus Crash May Affect Sales Rivalry: Glitch in A330's Autopilot Computer Suspected." *Seattle Times,* July 1, pp. F1, F6.

39. Wiener, Lauren (1992). "A Trip Report on SIGSOFT '91." *ACM SIGSOFT Software Engineering Notes,* 17(2) (April), 23–38.

40. West, Karen (1993). "Cruise Control: 777 Gets a Boost from Technology of Fly-by-Wire." *Seattle Post-Intelligencer,* Sept. 13, pp. B5, B8.

41. Jurgen, Ronald K. (1987). "Detroit '88: Driver-friendly Innovations." *IEEE Spectrum,* December, 53–57.

42. Voelcker, John (1988). "Electronics Puts Its Foot on the Gas." *IEEE Spectrum,* May, 53–57.

43. Stambler, Irwin (1988). "Fly-by-Wire Techniques Are Being Adapted for Automobile Controls." *Research and Development,* March, 41.

44. Murphy, Erin E. (1988). "All Aboard for Solid State." *IEEE Spectrum,* 25(13), December, 42–45.

45. Craigen, Dan, Susan Gerhart, and Ted Ralston (1994). "Case Study: Paris Metro Signalling System." *IEEE Software,* 11(1) (January), 32–35.

46. Peterson, Ivers (1991). "Finding Fault." *Science News,* 139(7), February 16, 104–106.

47. Parnas, D. L., G. J. K. Asmis, and J. Madey (1991). "Assessment of Safety-Critical Software in Nuclear Power Plants." *Nuclear Safety,* 32(2), April–June, 189–198.

48. Craigen, Dan, Susan Gerhart, and Ted Ralston (1994). "Case Study: Darlington Nuclear Generating Station." *IEEE Software,* 11(1), January, 30–32.

49. Dolan, Brad (1994). "Software Testing at Sizewell." *RISKS-FORUM Digest,* 15(58), Feb. 23. (Reports on article "Testing the Software," in *Nuclear Engineering International,* 12/93, 10.)

50. Parnas, David (1994). "Re: Software Testing at Sizewell." *RISKS-FORUM Digest,* 15(59), Feb. 26.

51. Bellin, David, and Gary Chapman (eds.) (1987). *Computers in Battle: Will They Work?* Harcourt Brace Jovanovich, Boston.

52. Schmitt, Eric (1991). "Army Blames Patriot's Computer For Failure to Stop Dhahran Scud." *The New York Times,* May 20, pp. A1, A6.

53. Marshall, Eliot (1992). "Fatal Error: How Patriot Overlooked a Scud." *Science,* 255, March 13, 1347.

54. McBride, Steven (1988). "State Taxes on a New Computer System." *RISKS-FORUM Digest,* 6(6) (April 13). (Cites March 15, 1988, *Ogden Standard Examiner.*)

55. Saltzer, Jerome H. (1988). "Zero-balance Dunning Letter." *RISKS-FORUM Digest,* 7(36) (August 17).

56. Rogers, Michael (1986). "Software Makers Battle the Bugs." *Fortune,* February 17, 83.
57. Ruby, Daniel, and Shan Chan (1986). "Who's Responsible for the Bugs?" *PC Week,* May 27, 51–54.
58. Kneale, Dennis (1985). "Buyer Beware: Software Plagued by Poor Quality and Poor Service." *Wall Street Journal,* October 2.
59. Digital Equipment Corporation (1986). "Problem in VAX/VMS Data Encryption Facility." *VAX/VMS Systems Dispatch,* March, 21.
60. Jones, Stephen (1988). "Microsoft Scrambles to Head Off Runaway Mouse with Word Rewrite." *Computerworld,* 39, 42, September 5, 39–42.
61. Gleick, James (1992). "Chasing Bugs in the Electronic Village." *The New York Times Magazine,* Sunday, June 14, 38 ff.
62. Neumann, Peter G. (1994). "Illustrative Risks to the Public in the Use of Computer Systems and Related Technology." *ACM Software Engineering Notes,* 19(1), January, 16–29.
63. Naftalin, Maurice (1988). "Correctness for Beginners," in R. Bloomfield, L. Marshall, and R. Jones (eds.), *VDM '88: VDM—The Way Ahead* (Lecture Notes in Computer Science No. 328). Proceedings of the 2nd VDM-Europe Symposium, Dublin, Ireland. Springer-Verlag, Berlin.
64. Markoff, John (1993). "Marketer's Dream, Engineer's Nightmare." *The New York Times Business Section,* Sunday, December 12.
65. Zachary, G. Pascal (1993). "Agony and Ecstacy of 200 Code Writers Begets Windows NT." *Wall Street Journal,* May 26, p. 1.
66. Minsky, Marvin (1967). "Why Programming Is a Good Medium for Expressing Poorly Understood and Sloppily Formulated Ideas," in *Design and Planning II.* Hastings House, New York. (Quoted by J. Weizenbaum in *Computer Power and Human Reason,* pp. 234–235.)
67. Beizer, Boris (1984). *Software System Testing and Quality Assurance.* Van Nostrand Reinhold, New York.
68. Jones, C. (1988). "Building a Better Metric." *Computerworld Extra* (a supplement to *Computerworld*), June 20, 38–39.
69. Petschenik, N. H. (1985). "Practical Priorities in System Testing." *IEEE Software,* 2(5), 18–23.
70. Musa, J. D., A. Iannino, and K. Okumoto (1987). *Software Reliability: Measurement, Prediction, Application.* McGraw-Hill, New York.
71. Leveson, Nancy (1987). "A Scary Tale—Sperry Avionics Module Testing Bites the Dust!" *ACM Software Engineering Notes,* 12(2) (April), 23–25.
72. Rodgers, W. P. (1971). *Introduction to System Safety Engineering.* Wiley, New York.
73. Miller, C. O. (1971). "Why System Safety?" *Technology Review,* 73(4) (February), 28–33.
74. Ceruzzi, Paul E. (1989). *Beyond the Limits: Flight Enters the Computer Age,* pp. 202–203. MIT Press, Cambridge, MA.
75. Post, R. J. (1971). "Some Considerations of Interlocking and Safety Circuits for Radiotherapy Apparatus." *International Journal of Radiation Engineering,* 1(2), 169–191.
76. Leveson, Nancy G. (1986). "Software Safety: What, Why and How." *ACM Computing Surveys,* 18(2) (June), 125–163.

77. Parnas, David Lorge, and Paul C. Clements (1986). "A Rational Design Process: How and Why to Fake It." *IEEE Transactions on Software Engineering,* SE-12(2) (February), 251–257.
78. Hoare, Tony (1986). "Maths Adds Safety to Computer Programs." *New Scientist,* 18 September, 53–56.
79. Linger, Richard C. (1993). "Cleanroom Software Engineering for Zero-Defect Software." *Proceedings of the 15th International Conference on Software Engineering, IEEE Computer Society Press,* pp. 2–13.
80. Fenton, Norman, Shari Lawrence Pfleeger, and Robert Glass (1994). "Science and Substance: A Challenge to Software Engineers." *IEEE Software* 11(4), July, 86–95.
81. Boehm, Barry (1987). "Industrial Software Metrics Top Ten List." *IEEE Software,* 4(5) (September), 84–85.
82. Houston, M. Frank (1987). "What Do the Simple Folk Do? Software Safety in the Cottage Industry," in *Proceedings of the COMPASS '87 Computer Assurance Conference* (Supplement), pp. S-20–S-25.
83. Howard II, J. M. (1988). "A Hazard Oriented Approach to Computer System Safety," in *Proceedings, AAMI 23rd Annual Meeting and Exposition,* p. 48. Association for the Advancement of Medical Instrumentation, Arlington, Virginia.
84. Hoare, C. A. R. (1987). "An Overview of Some Formal Methods for Program Design." *Computer,* 20(9) (September), 85–91.
85. Delisle, Norman, and David Garlan (1990). "A formal specification of an oscilloscope." *IEEE Software,* 7(5), September, 29–36.
86. Cohen, Edward (1990). *Programming in the 90's: An Introduction to the Calculation of Programs.* Springer-Verlag, New York.
87. MacKenzie, Donald (1991). "The Fangs of the VIPER." *Nature,* 352, August 8, 467–468.
88. Gerhart, Susan, and Lawrence Yelowitz (1976). "Observations of Fallacy in the Application of Modern Programming Methodologies." *IEEE Transactions on Software Engineering,* SE-2(3), September, 195–207.
89. Cohn, Avra (1989). "The Notion of Proof in Hardware Verification." *J. Automat. Reason,* 5, 127–139.
90. Rushby, John, and Fredrich von Henke (1991). "Formal Verification of Algorithms for Critical Systems." *Proceedings of the ACM SIGSOFT '91 Conference on Software for Critical Systems.* (Also published as *ACM Software Engineering Notes* 16(5), December, 1–15.
91. Bowen, Jonathan, and Victoria Stavridou (1993). "Safety-critical Systems, Formal Methods, and Standards." *Software Engineering Journal,* 8(4), July, 189–209.
92. Craigen, Dan, Susan Gerhart, and Ted Ralston (1994). "Experience with Formal Methods in Critical Systems." *IEEE Software,* 11(1), January, 21–28.
93. Food and Drug Administration (1987). "Draft FDA Policy for the Regulation of Computer Products." *Federal Register,* September 25.
94. Shore, John (1988). "Why I Never Met a Programmer I Could Trust." *Communications of the ACM,* 31(4) (April), 372–375.
95. Carey, Peter (1987). "Programmers May be Facing Regulation." *San Jose Mercury News,* December 1, back page.

96. *Business Week* (1988). "It's Late, Costly, Incompetent—But Try Firing a Computer System." November 7.

97. Carroll, Paul B. (1988). "Computer Glitch: Patching up Software Occupies Programmers and Disables Systems." *Wall Street Journal,* January 22, pp. 1, 12.

98. Parnas, David Lorge (1990). "Education for Computing Professionals." *IEEE Computer,* January, 17–22.

99. Dijsktra, Edsger (1989). "On the Cruelty of Really Teaching Computer Science." *Communications of the ACM,* 32(12), December, 1398–1414.

100. Bamford, Robert C., and William J. Deibler (1993). "Comparing, Contrasting ISO9001 and the SEI Capability Maturity Model." *IEEE Computer,* 26(10), October, 68–70.

101. Humphrey, Watts (1989). *Managing the Software Process.* Addison Wesley, Reading, MA.

102. Jacky, Jonathan (1988). "COMPASS '88 Trip Report." *ACM Software Engineering Notes,* 13(4) (October), 21–27.

103. Tierney, M. (1993). "The Evolution of Def Stan 00-55," in Paul Quintas (ed.), *Social Dimensions of System Engineering.* Ellis Horwood. (Also in *Technology Analysis and Strategic Management,* 4(3), 1992, 245–278.)

104. Food and Drug Administration (1987). *Technical Reference on Software Development Activities* (draft).

105. Food and Drug Administration (1991). *Reviewer Guidance for Computer-controlled Medical Devices Undergoing 510(k) Review.* (From the Office of Device Evaluation, Center for Devices and Radiological Health, FDA.)

106. Siemens Medical Systems, Inc. (1995). *Siemens Resumes Shipment of Radiation Oncology Equipment for U.S. Customers.* (Press release circulated in January 1995.)

107. *American Medical News* (1987). "Suits Filed Over Deaths Linked to Therac-25." January 16, 44.

108. Neesham, Clair (1992). "Safe Conduct." *Computing,* November 12. (Noted in *RISKS-FORUM Digest,* 14(5), November 16, 1992, by Jonathan Bowen.)

109. Winograd, Terry (1990). "What Can We Teach About Human-Computer Interaction," in Jane C. Chew, and J. Whiteside (eds.), *Empowering People: CHI '90 Conference Proceedings.* ACM Press, New York.

110. Gibbs, W. Wayt (1994). "Software's Chronic Crisis." *Scientific American,* 271(3), September, 86–95.

P·A·R·T · VII

D

Aging Airways*

Gary Stix

The Sperry-Univac 8300s are as tall as Shaquille O'Neal and heavier than a Sumo wrestler. The ribbon cables that trail from their cabinets, the toggle switches and banks of lights make these metal hulks relics of another era, a time when the National Aeronautics and Space Administration was doing moon shots and the nation was preoccupied with antiwar protests, civil-rights marches and flower children. Although the computers were de-signed in the 1960s, the Federal Aviation Administration (FAA) has yet to pull the plug on them. Up to eight of the machines process radar data for display on the round, green monitors at air-control centers that direct thousands of aircraft through the skies over the North American continent every day. Yet the computers share a paltry 256 kilobytes of total memory. If they were personal computers, they could not run Flight Simulator, a popular computer game for aviation aficionados that requires about eight times that memory capacity.

For fifteen years, the FAA has been aware of the growing obsolescence of its air-traffic system—the world's largest—which handles about seven million flights a year. The agency is in the process of spending $36 billion for a top-to-bottom overhaul of the system, an effort scheduled to run through the year 2001. But costs may exceed budget by billions of dollars. And delays in the program threaten to deprive travelers and airlines of some of the benefits of the new system through the beginning of the next decade. "The new technology is so far down the road that it's not going to affect my career," says Christopher S. Boughn, a controller and union representative at a Long Island air-traffic center.

Even as the FAA wrestles with changing the hardware and software that controllers use to manage the nation's air traffic, the agency has been outpaced by users of the system. In the early 1980s airlines began to equip their craft with on-board processors that could calculate the fastest or the most fuel-efficient route. Such flexibility undermines the highwaylike structure of the existing system, which sends flights along rigidly fixed air corridors. As technologies continue to emerge, the effort to remake air-traffic control will become further complicated. The Navstar global positioning system (GPS) can determine the location of an aircraft, vehicle, or ship to within 100 meters; additional instrumentation could better that number to only a few meters. These developments encourage a degree of independence for aircraft that emphasizes the antiquated technology under which the system operates.

The FAA's difficulties raise the question of whether decade-long planning cycles, ideal for building roads and bridges, can accommodate the rapid changes in computer and communications systems that are the foundations of air-traffic control. A panel appointed by the Clinton administration and Congress to study airline competitiveness last year concluded: "There is a fundamental inconsistency between the processes of government and the operation of a 24-hour-a-day, high-technology, capital-intensive air-traffic control system."

Heeding these concerns, administration officials recommended in January that air-traffic control be spun off from the FAA into an independent corporation, owned by the government, that would be exempt from the straitjacket of purchasing regulations, hiring rules, and the federal budget process. "One could probably make an argument that we would have done a much better job of modernizing air-traffic control had air-traffic control been in a corporate environment," says FAA administrator David R. Hinson.

While the government, the airlines, and electronics manufacturers grapple with the issues, the nation's nearly 18,000 air-traffic controllers orchestrate a flow of commercial air traffic that amounted to 478 billion passenger miles in 1992. The job begins before the aircraft leaves the gate. Before then, the airline has already filed with the FAA a flight plan, which includes time of departure, aircraft type, and intended routes of flight. From a tower, one of almost 500 the FAA operates, a ground controller tells the pilot about runway for takeoff, radio frequency, and other information. As the aircraft reaches the head of the runway, responsibility passes to another controller, who gives final permission for takeoff. Once aloft, the locus of air control changes.

In some airports the tower controller actually sends a paper flight-progress strip—a rectangular sheet of paper with information about a given aircraft—down a tube to a departure controller who also uses a radarscope to track the aircraft in the vicinity of the airport. This room is one of about

*This article appeared in *Scientific American* (May 1994), 270(5), 96–104. Reprinted with permission. Copyright © 1994 by Scientific American, Inc. All rights reserved.

200 terminal radar-approach control facilities, a name that is shortened to "TRACON" in airspeak. In some instances, TRACONs are in a separate building.

TRACON controllers are the traffic cops who direct airplanes during the initial leg of a journey, through what is known as the terminal airspace. The terminal airspace resembles a cylinder whose invisible walls rise 10,000 to 15,000 feet at a radius of 30 to 45 miles from the perimeter of the airport (Figure 1).

When the aircraft reaches the border of the terminal airspace, the TRACON hands off the airplane to a controller at one of the 22 nationwide air route traffic control centers, also known as en route centers. The centers guide airplanes along the network of airways. These skyways, which layer the nation from 18,000 to more than 40,000 feet, resemble an interstate highway system. They are used largely by commercial airlines and business jets. (There are lower airways, too, along which mostly commuter and private aircraft navigate.)

The roadways and intersections are defined by radio beacons—such as VHF omnidirectional range (VOR) transmitters—that emit signals in all directions. An aircraft's navigation system often takes its bearings from two or more VOR transmitters. During this segment of the journey, aircraft must maintain a horizontal separation of at least five miles and a vertical separation of 1000 to 2000 feet, depending on altitude. Control shifts from one en route center to the next as an airplane hurtles across the country until it reaches the airspace encircling a destination airport.

Air control relies on an intricate support network of communications, navigation, and tracking technology. Different radar stations watch aircraft along each segment of the journey. These so-called primary radars determine the position of the aircraft and the course on which it is heading by bouncing a signal off its skin. Secondary radars that track the aircraft in flight consist of a ground-based transmitter that sends a signal to "interrogate" an instrument on the aircraft, a transponder that sends back altitude information, and a numeric code that identifies the aircraft.

Computers, such as the Sperry mainframes in the TRACONs, process signals from these radars. The controller's screen displays the classic radar blip accompanied by a data block, a notation that shows speed, altitude, and other data received from or computed from the radar inputs.

For all its quaintness, the system works extremely well, at least from the perspective of safety. Even if air travelers roll their eyes knowingly at one another when they hear "it will be just a few minutes until we're cleared so that we can pull back from the gate," they know their chances of surviving a flight on a scheduled airliner are better than those they experience when riding in the family car. A major reason is the reliability of the air-traffic controllers and their winking, blinking aged hardware.

Major airlines have not had any passenger fatalities in about two years. Moreover, the number of near collisions has steadily decreased since the

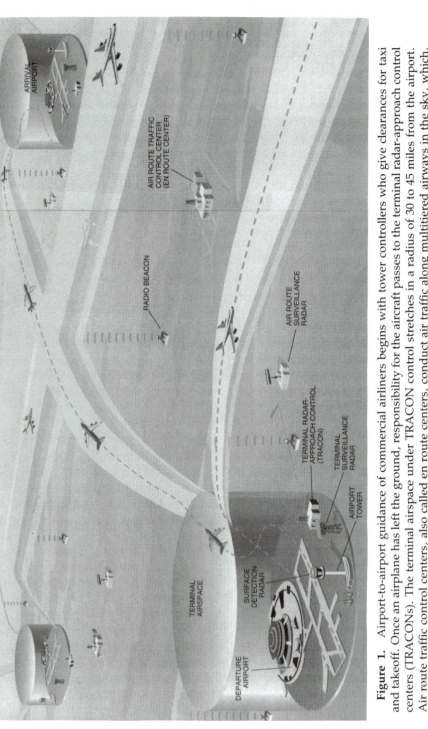

Figure 1. Airport-to-airport guidance of commercial airliners begins with tower controllers who give clearances for taxi and takeoff. Once an airplane has left the ground, responsibility for the aircraft passes to the terminal radar-approach control centers (TRACONs). The terminal airspace under TRACON control stretches in a radius of 30 to 45 miles from the airport. Air route traffic control centers, also called en route centers, conduct air traffic along multitiered airways in the sky, which, for commercial jets, usually extend from 18,000 feet upward. Aircraft must often adhere to this rigid route structure (*shown by the dashed lines*) instead of flying along the fastest or most fuel-efficient path. Radar, including sensors to watch runway traffic, monitor each stage of flight.

mid-1980s. The FAA has kept things running by instituting conservative spacing margins between aircraft and by retaining extensive backup systems. The burden of regulating the flow of air traffic eased during the early 1990s when the number of passengers dropped because of a languishing economy and the Persian Gulf War.

So, if it ain't broke: Twenty-year-old mainframes are as capable as souped-up engineering workstations of placing flight data on a radar display. A risk analyst, in fact, might rate their record as better than that of new, untested computers running software that gives controllers advice on how to direct aircraft. Yet the case that the FAA makes for rebuilding has some compelling features. In the early 1980s government officials, airline managers, pilots, and controllers knew that these highways in the sky would eventually sprout potholes. Simple accounting extrapolations showed that the FAA's $200 million a year in capital spending would not support the explosion of air traffic that came about after airline deregulation in 1978. The emergence of the "hub and spoke" network—in which most flights are routed through a large regional city—increased traffic faster than controllers could be trained or equipment could be put in place.

Budget considerations and a crisis also argued for change. In 1982 FAA officials reasoned that automation of air-traffic control would allow the agency to cope with the personnel shortage that President Ronald Reagan created by firing 11,500 controllers.

Technological Artifacts

Equipment does not last forever—or does it? True, some navigation gear reportedly still shows the insignia of the Civil Aeronautics Administration, the FAA's predecessor before 1958. But keeping things running may not always be worth the trouble. Display terminals at the en route centers suffer 12,000 component failures every year, an average of one failure every five weeks for each display, according to the Department of Transportation. Computer capacity at TRACONs has been so taxed at times that the Government Accounting office once warned that safety could be affected.

Maintenance is becoming a black art. Parts are scarce. Old equipment has to be cannibalized. Many of the technicians and support staff who were schooled in the subtleties of 1960s vintage computers are retiring and have not been replaced. "There are very few programmers still competent in Jovial," says Heinz Erzberger of the NASA Ames Research Center, referring to a virtually extinct programming language used on some of the air-traffic mainframes.

In 1982 the FAA started what was supposed to be an 11-year, $12.6-billion revamping of the entire air-traffic system. Since then, the agency has added about 150 projects that will bring overall costs to more than $36 billion through the year 2001 (see Figure 2). A General Accounting Office review noted that through the 1993 budget year only 54 of the total 238

	Schedule Slippage (years)	Estimates (millions of dollars)	Change in Unit Cost (percent)
ADVANCED AUTOMATION SYSTEM Replaces computer hardware, software, and workstations used by controllers in towers and radar facilities.	6–8	$6500.00–7300.00	—
AIR ROUTE SURVEILLANCE RADAR-4 Used for long-range tracking by air-tracking centers.	9	383.10	11
AIRPORT SURFACE DETECTION EQUIPMENT-3 Enables airports to monitor ground activity of aircraft even in rain and fog.	6	191.00	10
AIRPORT SURVEILLANCE RADAR-9 Replaces 96 radar units that use vacuum tubes with solid-state systems. Provides monitoring of aircraft within a 60-mile radius of airports.	4	839.90	(30)
AUTOMATED WEATHER OBSERVING SYSTEM Takes automatic readings on wind velocity, temperature, dew point, cloud height, visibility, and precipitation and relays them with a synthesized voice to pilots.	3	229.90	35
MICROWAVE LANDING SYSTEM Provides an electronic guidance beam to aircraft on an approach. The FAA has delayed going to full production until the feasibility of using satellites for landing guidance has been determined.	12	740.80	—

Figure 2. Major FAA capital projects. Source: General Accounting Office's report "Air Traffic Control: Status of FAA's Modernization Program," April 1993, and House aviation subcommittee hearing report, March 3, 1992. Delay and cost figures are through the 1993 federal budget year except for those for the Advanced Automation System and the Microwave Landing System, which are current.

	Schedule Slippage (years)	Estimates (millions of dollars)	Change in Unit Cost (percent)
MODE SELECT SECONDARY SURVEILLANCE RADAR Improves the tracking of signals from aircraft transponders, which provide altitude data and aircraft identification. Permits ground-to-air communications of air-traffic clearances and weather data.	7	473.20	40
TERMINAL DOPPLER WEATHER RADAR Detects wind shear wind shifts and precipitation around airports.	—	350.70	38
VOICE SWITCHING AND CONTROL SYSTEM Improves ground-to-air communications between controllers and pilots and voice and data linkages among air-traffic centers.	6	1407.00	444

Figure 2. (*continued*)

projects within the capital program had been completed, a number that represents about 8 percent of the total estimated costs. "There is some reason to believe that this system, which was intended to bring 1960s technology into the 1980s, might not even be ready for the next century," concluded the federally appointed airline-industry study panel.

The centerpiece of the original renewal effort, according to agency officials, was—and is—the Advanced Automation System (AAS). It will replace the green glow of the round-radar displays and rickety moon-shot-era computers that are often less powerful than the personal computers used by agency secretaries for word processing. Also on the capital spending list are solid-state digital radar units that would supplant tracking systems for the terminal airspace that still run on vacuum tubes. Improved secondary radar would give better tracking information and provide a two-way digital communications link between ground and air. An integrated voice communications system would replace the patchwork of telephone and radio links.

In some aspects, the undertaking seemed relatively straightforward. The first stages of the AAS would replace the 25-year-old radarscopes with large-screen color workstations that would be connected by a local-area network to one another and to a mainframe computer. The network would process incoming radar and transponder signals for display on a controller's monitor.

Twelve years later much of the overall program has yet to be implemented. The agency did increase the capacity of computers in the radar rooms of the en route centers. But other large programs in the capital plan are three to five years behind schedule, and waiting for the AAS has itself proved costly. The FAA will have to spend at least $300 million to keep existing computer systems running.

The most glaring example of the problems that overtook the agency and its contractors can be found within the AAS effort. The network of workstations had to run 99.99999 percent of the time; it could be out of operation only for a minute and 20 seconds over a 20-year period. In addition, computers cannot simply be shut down overnight when bringing up a new air-traffic system: the cutover has been compared to doing brain surgery on a patient who is driving a car.

The AAS project was structured like a typical defense contract. It started in 1984 with a "bake-off" between Hughes Aircraft and IBM to come up with competing design prototypes. When the contract was awarded to IBM in 1988, Hughes filed a protest, which created several months of delay. The legal problems behind them, the FAA and IBM dropped into a serious pitfall, one likely to threaten the advancement of any software project: the propensity of the customer to change objectives and needs as work proceeds.

The FAA showered IBM with endless lists of system requirements. In the end, the documents towered to a height of twenty feet. "This was a textbook case of mistakes," says David Garlan, a professor of computer science at Carnegie Mellon University, who was a member of an outside team that evaluated the program. "They were pulling every trick in the book to meet the schedule and accommodate these requirements, and they got caught."

Mesmerized by the flood of detail, both contractor and customer failed to pay attention to how a more automated system would change the way an individual controller performs. The AAS, in fact, was supposed to reduce the daily grind. The workstations would, the FAA hoped, do away with the antiquated paper flight-progress strips, which are a record of altitude, destination, and other information a controller tracks. The computers were supposed to store an electronic database that would help automate the time-consuming task of annotating flight strips by hand.

What IBM devised, according to one controller, was a perfect electronic facsimile of the paper flight strip. The database contained all the information that can be listed on a flight strip—about 140 separate units of information, or fields, enough to keep the controller tapping on a keyboard all day. "The controller should be paying more attention to watching aircraft than to inputting information," says Mitch Coleman, a controller at the Atlanta en route center who was brought in a year ago to help streamline the system. Controllers suggested a version of the electronic flight strips with a more manageable 35 fields. The union to which Coleman belongs, the National Air Traffic Controllers Association, has cited the lack of controllers' full-time involvement early on in AAS development as a reason for these snags.

IBM's 500-member software engineering team has also run into problems with what is known as continuous operations. In the networks planned for en route centers, sometimes more than 200 workstations must talk to one another and to the mainframe that crunches incoming radar and transponder data. Any machine must be able to back up another when a processor fails. If the mainframe itself goes down, each workstation has to be able to handle information independently. IBM's software group has had difficulty reconciling inconsistencies in data between the workstations and the mainframe when the central computer is reactivated.

Continuous operations has helped contribute to the extraordinary cost problems and delays that the project has experienced. In announcing a shake-up of the AAS program in early March, Hinson presented results of an internal FAA report that showed that the $2.3 billion spent so far on the system could reach between $6.5 billion and $7.3 billion by the date of completion.

The direst total cost estimate is some $3 billion more than the agency's projection in 1988, when the contract was awarded to IBM. That amount is more than triple the original budget projected for the AAS by the FAA in 1983.

The report also noted that, yet again, the delivery date for the first network of workstations may slip. The Seattle en route center, which was originally to begin using the workstations in October 1996, may now get the new equipment sometime between mid-1997 to early in 1999. When it started planning for the AAS in 1983, the FAA had hoped to have the first workstations up and running in late 1990.

The report's cost estimates fail to give the whole picture because they do not include more than $400 million for AAS research and development. And the FAA has scaled back on what it expects to buy with this contract. It has decided against upgrading aging hardware and software in 108 of the 258 airport towers that were originally slated for a makeover under the AAS contract. "We keep getting less program for more money," says Robert E. Levin, an assistant director with the General Accounting Office.

In making the announcement, Hinson said he would appoint new program management, while suspending work on one part of the contract. The agency is also looking at technologies that might substitute for some of the hardware and software now slated for deployment under the current contract.

The AAS has experienced another surprise that might slow things further. In March, IBM completed the sale of its Federal Systems Company, the one handling the AAS, to defense contractor Loral for $1.58 billion. (The FAA still must approve transfer of the contract to Loral, however.)

Even when AAS hardware and software are finally in place, each unit will be little more than a glorified personal computer. "Controllers are getting a new color monitor," says Timothy Hancock, a controller with the

Atlanta en route center. The agency does indeed have more ambitious plans for the AAS. The hardware and software should eventually let controllers direct air traffic in less rigid ways.

For that reason, failure to get the AAS on the air has proved particularly frustrating for the airlines. Since the early 1980s they have been buying aircraft with on-board computers and navigational systems that can calculate a route with the shortest time of flight—say, from Kansas City to Los Angeles—and even determine the approach to the airport that will require the least fuel. By enabling aircraft to deviate from the track of a roadway in the sky, the on-board equipment could save the airlines more than $2 billion every year by reducing fuel use, shortening delays, and improving operating efficiencies.

But because the AAS is not fully developed, the air-traffic system operates very much as it always has. Consequently, the airlines can use the flight-management computers to travel on direct routes only about 10 percent of the time. "We can't take advantage of a lot of the technology because of the antiquated airspace management system," says Raymond J. Hilton, director of air-traffic management for the Air Transport Association, a trade group that represents the airline industry.

Software Traffic Cops

Indeed, some researchers have developed, and begun to test, software that does not have to rely on the AAS hardware platform. Since the mid-1980s Erzberger of the NASA Ames Research Center has been designing software to steer aircraft through traffic jams that arise at the hub airports. The software, called the Center-TRACON Automation System (CTAS), can now run on a network of ordinary engineering workstations. The network can be linked to the 20-year-old displays still in use in some radar rooms. "I'm fortunate to have been outside the FAA and not under their research people," Erzberger says.

Erzberger started his career designing algorithms for the cockpit flight-management computers. The CTAS is designed to mimic the calculations of these airborne systems. A software module acts as an "adviser" to a TRACON or an en route center, suggesting, as much as 45 minutes ahead of time, the best sequencing for aircraft converging on an airport.

The CTAS traffic-management adviser schedules the flow of aircraft with an expert-system-like database containing information about winds and an airline's preferred operating procedures and by taking into account instructions issued to pilots by individual controllers. Eventually it may be able to accept a suggested route sent down from an airplane's flight-management computer. It can group similar aircraft together—a DC-10 and a 747, for example. The biggest airliners cast off a turbulent wake that can endanger smaller craft, although airplanes of comparable size or weight can be more closely spaced. The CTAS is being tested at the Dallas/Fort Worth and the Denver airports.

Later this year the en route center that feeds traffic to the Denver TRACON will experiment with another component of the CTAS—a step toward controlling individual aircraft with the aid of a computer. This "descent adviser" will actually suggest to the controller how an aircraft should execute the early stages of an approach to an airport. It does so by comparing a radar-derived estimate of the airplane's time of arrival at the terminal airspace with a time scheduled by the traffic-management adviser for an optimal flow of traffic.

If the airplane is not projected to arrive on schedule, the descent adviser recommends turns or changes in speed to ensure that aircraft conform to the plan devised by the traffic-management adviser. The descent adviser can also look 10 or 15 minutes ahead to check for routing conflicts. Another module assists with the final approach to the airport and suggests the best runway for each flight. If the computer errs, there is still enough time for the controller to correct a computer instruction that brings two airplanes into dangerous proximity.

Besides helping controllers to become better crossing guards, these tools are supposed to reduce human error. Erzberger claims that the CTAs can raise the skills of an average controller to that of an expert and make up for a good controller's lapses. "You have controllers who are truly virtuosos," Erzberger says. "They operate at maximum efficiency, and when fully engaged they're like people in the Olympics. But nobody can do that day after day."

Before this vision materializes, the FAA will have to convince those who staff radar rooms that it is not trying to consign their work to a program on a floppy disk. Unfortunately for the agency, history tends to support such fears. In 1982, shortly after the controllers' strike, the agency sold its modernization plans to Congress on the promise that automation would allow the air-traffic system to operate with fewer people. Furthermore, early plans for the AAS called for software that would relay an instruction to an aircraft without first consulting the controller, a now dormant proposal. And despite union claims of a continuing deficit of 2500 controllers, FAA administrator Hinson believes the new technology should let the air-traffic system operate with more or less the same 18,000-member work force. (The union says only 14,400 controllers are employed full-time.)

Air controllers are not alone in their concerns. Experts who study the ways humans use machines worry about committing to software an occupation that has been compared to a cross between a video game and three-dimensional chess. "Air-traffic control looks like a simple set of rules that you could capture in a limited set of algorithms; it's only when you get into it that you realize it's not that simple at all," says V. David Hopkin, a human-factors specialist affiliated with Embry-Riddle Aeronautical University. "The more complex things get," Hopkin notes, "the more likely it is you will build in a complex interaction of things that might not be discovered for years."

Controllers may also be skeptical because automation has often created more problems than it has solved. The history of the Oceanic Display and Planning System (ODAPS) serves as an example. Budgeted at $12 million and not yet complete at a cost of more than $50 million, the ODAPS was supposed to depict air traffic moving over the oceans while identifying flight routes that might bring aircraft too close to one another. The system was to be a first cut at replacing a tracking system using flight-progress strips that has not changed much since the 1950s. But the ODAPS has encountered so many problems since development began in the mid-1980s that the FAA plans to scrap it gradually and try another approach.

Meanwhile, at the en route center in Ronkonkoma, New York, the ODAPS serves as a feeble backup system to the present outdated manual tracking operation. Air-traffic control over the ocean is hindered by a lack of radar beyond 200 miles from the coast. A pilot identifies the aircraft's position by talking over what is often a wall of static to a high-frequency radio operator located in a building a mile away from the center. The operator sends a teletype message to a controller. That information is then hand-annotated on a flight strip. In periods of intense sunspot activity, communications may be lost for hours at a time. Pilots bound for Europe are sometimes reduced to sending a message to an aircraft 100 miles or so behind that may still be able to get a call through to an operator.

Back to the Present

Controllers use the information on flight strips—altitude, destination, flight path, and type of aircraft—to visualize where each Boeing 747, DC-10, or Airbus is located in its procession across the Atlantic. A procedure used for helping to determine whether airplanes come too near is simple enough to please the most die-hard Luddite. First, plot the expected course of the airplanes by drawing lines with a grease pencil on the plastic that covers an aviator's map of the Atlantic. Then take a flight strip, curl its edge over at a 45-degree angle and place it on the map. If the angle of approach is less than 45 degrees, as measured by the paper marker, the separation rules for two airplanes converging from the same direction apply. If it is more, other regulations hold. "The technology we're using on the control room floor is a lot further behind than what we'd like to see," says Roger Kiely, a controller and union representative at the Ronkonkoma center. "Strips work fine," he adds, "but when you get 25 or 30 planes there's room for error."

Yet another wave of technological progress has begun to curl over the FAA's embattled technical staff. A combination of satellite navigation and digital communications has the potential to become the infrastructure for a standardized worldwide air-traffic control system. The system could even extend to developing nations while enhancing the landing capabilities of smaller airports in the United States. For two decades, the armed forces have been developing the technology, known as the global positioning system. Desert Storm witnessed its first deployment in battle. Truckers, merchant seamen, recreational boaters, and backpackers have joined the military as users of satellite guidance. Now it is commercial aviation's turn. The GPS "is arguably the most important advance in the history of navigation," says Hinson of the FAA.

The GPS uses signals from 24 satellites orbiting 11,000 miles above the earth (see Figure 3). By measuring the travel time from four or more of the 24 satellites, an aircraft can determine its horizontal position to within 100 meters and altitude to within 140 meters. Supplemented with a digital communications link, either through a communications satellite or a direct air-to-ground connection, the GPS can relay the exact location of the aircraft anywhere from Kansas City to Buenos Aires to a controller.

Combining satellite navigation and digital communications, one form of a technique termed automatic dependent surveillance (ADS) could supplement or even replace ground-based radar and radio-navigation beacons. Long-suffering ocean air controllers would not have to wait for a call to get already dated information from a radio operator to know where airplanes are over the Atlantic or Pacific.

If controllers knew exactly where every craft was at every moment, conservative 60-mile lateral distances that have to be maintained between airplanes over the oceans because of the absence of radar could be reduced. Traffic flow on the increasingly congested transoceanic flight corridors could be accelerated. The precision of satellite positioning might also allow reduced aircraft spacings over the continental United States.

The FAA has evolved into a GPS advocate. In September it demonstrated GPS guidance for a poor-weather landing approach at Washington's National Airport. Implementation of the GPS may proceed more smoothly than has that of the AAS. Most of the satellites needed are already aloft, and private companies have brought to market the receivers for the satellite signals.

The FAA has begun to open the door to making the GPS the main navigation system used by pilots in commercial airliners. The agency has announced that it will permit airlines to use the GPS to supplement existing aircraft navigation equipment. The GPS may now be used for making some low-visibility landing approaches. Within a year or two, the FAA is considering letting aircraft cross the oceans without any navigation instruments other than a GPS receiver. This technology will eventually prove a boon at thousands of small airports that lack the ground-based instrumentation to guide pilots in poor weather conditions. Continental Airlines has

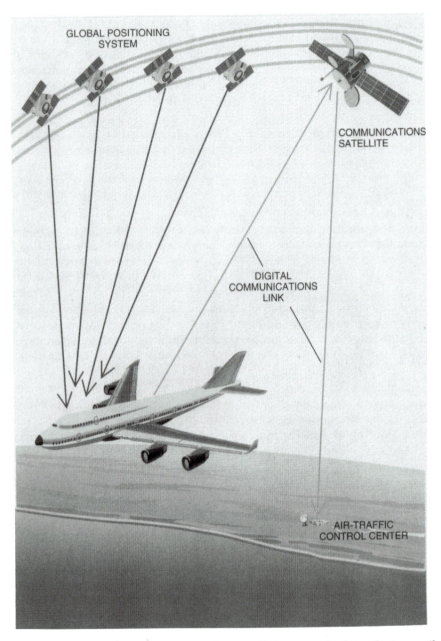

Figure 3. Satellite tracking of airplanes, called automatic dependent surveillance, is carried out by first determining aircraft position. An airplane receiver gauges the travel time of signals beamed from four or more of 24 satellites orbiting the earth 11,000 miles aloft—known as the Navstar global positioning system. Aircraft location can then be relayed to an air-traffic control center by a communications satellite.

already been using the GPS for reduced-visibility and nighttime landings on commuter flights into Steamboat Springs and Aspen in Colorado.

The FAA's stance toward the GPS hints that the agency may have learned some lessons from its mistakes. Chastened by the problems of implementing the AAS, the staff has embraced research programs jointly managed with industry. The scope of GPS programs under the FAA is less ambitious than was that of the AAS. "Before, things were orchestrated over the need to take great leaps in capability," says Martin Pozesky, associate administrator for system engineering and development at the FAA. "Today we take smaller leaps, more incremental steps."

In the international air-travel sector the challenge for the FAA and other worldwide aviation authorities is less technical than institutional. Agreeing on standards and equipment will probably delay implementing a global air-traffic control system, perhaps for a decade or more. The United States has offered use of the GPS to other nations without charge, and the newly formed states that replaced the Soviet Union have done the same with their own network of satellites, the global orbiting navigation satellite system (GLONASS). Together the GPS and GLONASS could become a basis for an international navigation network, or a global navigation satellite system — the term of art used by international standards groups.

Europe, though, is ambivalent about heavy reliance on satellites owned by individual nations. It worries, too, about depending on United States satellites originally launched for military navigation. Members of a study panel for the European Union have emphasized the need for agreements that would ensure availability of the system for civilian users. "There's a fear that the U.S. might flip the switch on GPS," says Kevin Dopart, a senior analyst at the congressional Office of Technology Assessment.

Still, plans for an independently launched civilian constellation of satellites, at an expense of several billion dollars, remain largely speculative. What may also slow agreement are existing European plans to upgrade land-based tracking and navigation.

Unifying European air-traffic control requires rationalizing the kludge of 31 radar data processing systems, from 18 different manufacturers, that are controlled by 22 different kinds of operating system software. "The U.S. has the worst air-traffic control and technology management, but it's still better than all the others," Dopart says.

Meanwhile, back home, the FAA has still been subjected to intense scrutiny as an institution. The airlines, among other interested parties, believe the agency as structured is not nimble enough, despite the response it has brought to the GPS.

The FAA wholeheartedly embraced satellites only after a decade in which ground-based radar and navigation systems remained the focus of most of its research and development efforts. As little as two years ago, the agency had forwarded a proposal for the 1993 federal budget year calling for only $7 million for development of the GPS for low-visibility landings and other uses, despite an agency planning document's recommendation to allocate more than twice that amount of funding.

But the GPS, augmented with a ground- or satellite-based correction signal, could provide accuracies of seven meters or less for low-visibility approaches. If proved, this technique, called differential GPS, might even serve as a guide for an airplane's automatic landing equipment when airports are fogged in. This precision landing technology could make obsolete the more than $200 million in development costs the FAA spent over more than 10 years for a landing system that employs microwave transmitters next to a runway to help an airplane land.

Because of continuing doubts about the FAA's ability to manage technology programs, the airline-industry study panel recommended last summer that air-traffic control be removed from the agency. A similar spin-off proposal came from the National Performance Review, a group, led by Vice-President Al Gore, that studies ways to streamline government bureaucracy.

All Aboard Airtrak

With a nod to both recommendations, the Secretary of Transportation Federico Peña proposed in January to vest a government-owned corporation with the air-traffic control operation. Proponents argue that such a corporation, Airtrak one might call it, would be exempt from the vicissitudes of federal budget-making and the thicket of procurement rules. Rather than haggle with Congress, the corporation could raise capital funds on the bond market. The discipline of trying to maintain a decent bond rating would ensure efficient management.

Last winter the administration was considering whether a corporation's operating expenses would be funded by passenger taxes, fees paid by aircraft owners for air-traffic services, dollars from the general treasury, or a combination of these options. Private and business airplane owners opposed the plan because they fear airline domination of a corporate air-traffic system would inflict prohibitive fees on them.

The FAA, which now devotes two-thirds of its $9-billion budget to air-traffic services, would probably remain responsible for safety regulations for the air-traffic network run by the corporation. In fact, some advocates of corporate air-traffic control point out that divesting these responsibilities would help the FAA avoid an inherent conflict of interest. It is difficult to maintain the necessary arms-length stance of the regulator when the agency also owns and manages the air-traffic control system.

A jurisdiction for Airtrak can be found as part of a worldwide trend toward privatizing air-traffic control. In places as far apart as Germany, South Africa, Switzerland, and New Zealand, such corporations have been founded. Canada is also considering such a change for its air-traffic system. And there have been successes.

After New Zealand switched to a government-owned corporation, total annual operating costs dropped from $120 million (in New Zealand dollars) in 1988 to less than $80 million in 1993. Airways Corporation of New Zealand ran a total surplus of $50 million in its first four years of operation. "In fact, we believe we are probably one of the only air-traffic management systems in the world that earns more than it spends," Peter Proulx, the corporation's executive officer, told a panel of transportation specialists at a meeting in Washington, D.C., in early January. In Germany, which privatized its air-traffic system a year ago, pay incentives for air-traffic controllers have contributed to the drop in air delays.

Strong opposition in Congress clouds the prognosis for the proposal. Members may fear the loss of the opportunity to earmark funds for a home district. But the issue of public safety also cannot be ignored. James L. Oberstar, chair of a House subcommittee on aviation, which oversees the FAA, predicts that financially strapped airlines might pressure the board of directors of a corporation to reduce spacing between aircraft to increase capacity.

"To be blunt about it, when airline profit margins start to influence air-traffic control practices, the safety margin may be eroded," Oberstar said in a speech delivered in mid-January. Critics of Airtrak recall less stellar examples of monopolistic enterprises owned by the government—the U.S. Postal Service, for one. Oberstar does favor immediate efforts to bolster FAA management. The average tenure for an FAA administrator has been less than two years since 1987. Setting a fixed term of five years, Oberstar believes, would improve the agency's ability to manage long-term capital projects.

The ultimate answer remains opaque. The public policymaker must ensure the dual goals of efficiency and safety, as he or she makes decisions that involve buying and managing the high-technology systems on which people's lives depend. On time and in one piece. The institution that can meet both of these demands may not yet have been invented.

P·A·R·T · VII

Limits of Correctness in Computers*

Brian Cantwell Smith

Introduction

On October 5, 1960, the American Ballistic Missile Early-Warning System station at Thule, Greenland, indicated a large contingent of Soviet missiles headed toward the United States.[1] Fortunately, common sense prevailed at the informal threat-assessment conference that was immediately convened: international tensions weren't particularly high at the time, the system had only recently been installed, Kruschev was in New York, and all in all a massive Soviet attack seemed unlikely. As a result, no devastating counter-attack was launched. What was the problem? The moon had risen, and was reflecting radar signals back to earth. Needless to say, this lunar reflection hadn't been predicted by the system's designers.

Over the last ten years, the Defense Department has spent many millions of dollars on a new computer technology called "program verification"—a branch of computer science whose business, in its own terms, is to "prove programs correct." Program verification has been studied in theoretical computer science departments since a few seminal papers in the 1960s,[2] but it has only recently started to gain in public visibility, and to be applied to real-world problems. General Electric, to consider just one example, has initiated verification projects in their own laboratories: they would like to prove that the programs used in their latest computer-controlled washing machines won't have any "bugs" (even one serious one can destroy their profit margin).[3] Although it used to be that only the simplest programs could be "proven correct"—programs to put simple lists into order, to compute simple arithmetic functions—slow but steady progress has been made in extending the range of verification techniques. Recent papers have reported correctness proofs for somewhat more complex programs, including small operating systems, compilers, and other material of modern system design.[4]

What, we do well to ask, does this new technology mean? How good are we at it? For example, if the 1960 warning system had been proven correct (which it was not), could we have avoided the problem with the moon? If it were possible to prove that the programs being written to control automatic launch-on-warning systems were correct, would that mean there could be a catastrophic accident? In systems now being proposed computers will make launching decisions in a matter of seconds, with no time for any human intervention (let alone for musings about Kruschev's being in New York). Do the techniques of program verification hold enough promise so that, if these new systems could all be proven correct, we could all sleep more easily at night? These are the questions I want to look at in this paper. And my answer, to give away the punch line, is No. For fundamental reasons—reasons that anyone can understand—there are inherent limitations to what can be proven about computers and computer programs. Although program verification is an important new technology, useful, like so many other things, in its particular time and place, it should definitely not be called verification. Just because a program is "proven correct," in other words, you cannot be sure that it will do what you intend.

First, some background.

General Issues in Program Verification

Computation is by now the most important enabling technology of nuclear weapons systems: it underlies virtually every aspect of the defense system, from the early warning systems, battle management and simulation

---

*This article appeared in *Computerization and Controversy: Value Conflicts and Social Choices* (1991), Academic Press, San Diego, with permission of the Center for the Study of Language and Information. It previously appeared as "The Limits of Correctness," Center for the Study of Language and Information, Stanford University. Report Number CSLI-85-35 (1985).

[1] Edmund Berkeley, *The Computer Revolution,* Doubleday, 1962, pp. 175–177, citing newspaper stories in the *Manchester Guardian Weekly* of Dec. 1, 1960, a UPI dispatch published in the *Boston Traveller* of Dec. 13, 1960, and an AP dispatch published in *The New York Times* on Dec. 23, 1960.

[2] McCarthy, John, "A Basic for a Mathematical Theory of Computation," 1963, in P. Braffort and D. Hirschberg (eds.), *Computer Programming and Formal Systems,* Amsterdam: North-Holland, 1967, pp. 33–70. Floyd, Robert, "Assigning Meaning to Programs," Proceedings of Symposia in Applied Mathematics 19, 1967 (also in F. T. Schwartz (ed.) *Mathematical Aspects of Computer Science,* Providence: American Mathematical Society, 1967). Naur, P., "Proof of Algorithms by General Snapshots," *BIT* Vol. 6, No. 4, pp. 310–316, 1966.

[3] Al Stevens, BBN Inc., personal communication.

[4] See, for example, R. S. Boyer and J. S. Moore (eds.), *The Correctness Problem in Computer Science,* London, Academic Press, 1981.

systems, and systems for communication and control, to the intricate guidance systems that direct the missiles to their targets. It is difficult, in assessing the chances of an accidental nuclear war, to imagine a more important question to ask than whether these pervasive computer systems will or do work correctly.

Because the subject is so large, however, I want to focus on just one aspect of computers relevant to their correctness: the use of *models* in the construction, use, and analysis of computer systems. I have chosen to look at modeling because I think it exerts the most profound and, in the end, most important influence on the systems we build. But it is only one of an enormous number of important questions. First, therefore—in order to unsettle you a little—let me just hint at some of the equally important issues I will not address:

1. *Complexity:* At the current state of the art, only simple programs can be proven correct. Although it is terribly misleading to assume that either the complexity or power of a computer program is a linear function of length, some rough numbers are illustrative. The simplest possible arithmetic programs are measured in tens of lines; the current state of the verification art extends only to programs of up to several hundred. It is estimated that the systems proposed in the Strategic Defense Initiative (Star Wars), in contrast, will require at least 10,000,000 lines of code.[5] By analogy, compare the difference between resolving a two-person dispute and settling the political problems of the Middle East. There's no a priori reason to believe that strategies successful at one level will scale to the other.

2. *Human Interaction:* Not much can be "proven," let alone specified formally, about actual human behavior. The sorts of programs that have so far been proven correct, therefore, do not include much substantial human interaction. On the other hand, as the moon-rise example indicates, it is often crucial to allow enough human intervention to enable people to override system mistakes. System designers, therefore, are faced with a dilemma: should they rule out substantive human intervention, in order to develop more confidence in how their systems will perform, or should they include it, so that costly errors can be avoided or at least repaired? The Three-Mile Island incident is a trenchant example of just how serious this trade-off can get: the system design provided for considerable human intervention, but then the operators failed to act "appropriately." Which strategy leads to the more important kind of correctness?

A standard way out of this dilemma is to specify the behavior of the system *relative to the actions of its operators.* But this, as we will see below,

---

[5] Fletcher, James, study chairman, and McMillan, Brockway, panel chairman, *Report of the Study on Eliminating the Threat Posed by Nuclear Ballistic Missiles (U)*, Vol. 5, *Battle Management, Communications, and Data Processing (U)*, U.S. Department of Defense, February 1984.

pressures the designers to specify the system totally in terms of internal actions, not external effects. So you end up proving only that the system will *behave in the way that it will behave* (i.e., it will raise this line level 3 volts), not *do what you want it to do* (i.e., launch a missile only if the attack is real). Unfortunately, the latter is clearly what is important. Systems comprising computers and people must function properly as integrated systems; nothing is gained by showing that one cog in a misshapen wheel is a very nice cog indeed.

Furthermore, large computer systems are dynamic, constantly changing, embedded in complex social settings. Another famous "mistake" in the American defense system happened when a human operator mistakenly mounted a training tape, containing a simulation of a full-scale Soviet attack, onto a computer that, just by chance, was automatically pulled into service when the primary machine ran into a problem. For some tense moments the simulation data were taken to be the real thing.[6] What does it mean to install a "correct" module into a complex social flux?

3. *Levels of Failure:* Complex computer systems must work at many different levels. It follows that they can fail at many different levels, too. By analogy, consider the many different ways a hospital could fail. First, the beams used to frame it might collapse. Or they might perform flawlessly, but the operating room door might be too small to let in a hospital bed (in which case you would blame the architects, not the lumber or steel company). Or the operating room might be fine, but the hospital might be located in the middle of the woods, where no one could get to it (in which case you would blame the planners). Or, to take a different example, consider how a letter could fail. It might be so torn or soiled that it could not be read. Or it might look beautiful, but be full of spelling mistakes. Or it might have perfect grammar, but disastrous contents.

Computer systems are the same: they can be "correct" at one level—say, in terms of hardware—but fail at another (i.e., the systems built on top of the hardware can do the wrong thing even if the chips are fine). Sometimes, when people talk about computers failing, they seem to think only the hardware needs to work. And hardware does from time to time fail, causing the machine to come to a halt, or yielding errant behavior (as, for example, when a faulty chip in another American early warning system sputtered random digits into a signal of how many Soviet missiles had been sighted, again causing a false alert).[7] And the connections between the computers and the world can break: when the moon-rise problem was first

---

[6] See, for example, the Hart-Goldwater report to the Committee on Armed Services of the U.S. Senate: "Recent False Alerts from the Nation's Missile Attack Warning System" (Washington, D.C.: U.S. Government Printing Office, Oct. 9, 1980); Physicians for Social Responsibility, *Newsletter*, "Accidental Nuclear War" (Winter, 1982), p. 1.

[7] Ibid.

recognized, an attempt to override it failed because an iceberg had accidentally cut an undersea telephone cable.[8] But the more important point is that, in order to be reliable, a system has to be correct *at every relevant level* (the hardware is just the starting place, and by far the easiest, at that). Unfortunately, however, we don't even know what all the relevant levels are. So-called "fault-tolerant" computers, for example, are particularly good at coping with hardware failures, but the software that runs on them is not thereby improved.[9]

4. *Correctness and Intention:* What does *correct* mean, anyway? Suppose the people want peace, and the president thinks that means having a strong defense, and the defense department thinks that means having nuclear weapons systems, and the weapons designers request control systems to monitor radar signals, and the computer companies are asked to respond to six particular kinds of radar pattern, and the engineers are told to build signal amplifiers with certain circuit characteristics, and the technician is told to write a program to respond to the difference between a two-volt and a four-volt signal on a particular incoming wire. If being correct means *doing what was intended*, whose intent matters? The technician's? Or what, with twenty years of historical detachment, we would say, *should have been intended?*

With a little thought any of you could extend this list yourself. And none of these issues even touches on the intricate technical problems that arise in actually building the mathematical models of software and systems used in the so-called "correctness" proofs. But, as I said, I want to focus on what I take to be the most important issue underlying all of these concerns: the pervasive use of models. Models are ubiquitous not only in computer science but also in human thinking and language; their very familiarity makes them hard to appreciate. So we'll start simply, looking at modeling on its own, and come back to correctness in a moment.

The Permeating Use of Models

When you design and build a computer system, you first formulate a model of the problem you want it to solve, and then construct the computer program in its terms. For example, if you were to design a medical system to administer drug therapy, you would need to model a variety of things: the patient, the drug, the absorption rate, the desired balance between therapy and toxicity, and so on and so forth. The absorption rate might be modeled as a number proportional to the patient's weight, or proportional

---

[8] Berkeley, op. cit. See also Daniel Ford's two-part article "The Button," *New Yorker*, April 1, 1985, p. 43, and April 8, 1985, p. 49, excerpted from Ford, Daniel, *The Button*, New York: Simon and Schuster, 1985.

[9] Developing software for fault-tolerant systems is in fact an extremely tricky business.

to body surface area, or as some more complex function of weight, age, and sex.

Similarly, computers that control traffic lights are based on some model of traffic—of how long it takes to drive across the intersection, of how much metal cars contain (the signal change mechanisms are triggered by metal detectors buried under each street). Bicyclists, as it happens, often have problems with automatic traffic lights, because bicycles don't exactly fit the model: they don't contain enough iron to trigger the metal detectors. I also once saw a tractor get into trouble because it couldn't move as fast as the system "thought" it would: the crosslight went green when the tractor was only halfway through the intersection.

To build a model is to conceive of the world in a certain delimited way. To some extent you must build models before building any artifact at all, including televisions and toasters, but computers have a special dependence on these models: *you write an explicit description of the model down inside the computer,* in the form of a set of rules or what are called *representations*— essentially linguistic formulas encoding, in the terms of the model, the facts and data thought to be relevant to the system's behavior. It is with respect to these representations that computer systems work. In fact that's really what computers are (and how they differ from other machines): they run by manipulating representations, and representations are always formulated in terms of models. This can all be summarized in a slogan: no computation without representation.

The models, on which the representations are based, come in all shapes and sizes. Balsa models of cars and airplanes, for example, are used to study air friction and lift. Blueprints can be viewed as models of buildings; musical scores as models of a symphony. But models can also be abstract. Mathematical models, in particular, are so widely used that it is hard to think of anything that they haven't been used for: from whole social and economic systems, to personality traits in teenagers, to genetic structures, to the mass and charge of subatomic particles. These models, furthermore, permeate all discussion and communication. Every expression of language can be viewed as resting implicitly on some model of the world.

What is important, for our purposes, is that every model deals with its subject matter *at some particular level of abstraction,* paying attention to certain details, throwing away others, grouping together similar aspects into common categories, and so forth. So the drug model mentioned above would probably pay attention to the patients' weights, but ignore their tastes in music. Mathematical models of traffic typically ignore the temperaments of taxi drivers. Sometimes what is ignored is at too "low" a level; sometimes too "high": it depends on the purposes for which the model is being used. So a hospital blueprint would pay attention to the structure and connection of its beams, but not to the arrangements of proteins in the wood the beams are made of, nor to the efficacy of the resulting operating room.

Models *have* to ignore things exactly because they view the world at a level of abstraction ("abstraction" is from the Latin *abstrahere*, "to pull or draw away"). And it is good that they do: otherwise they would drown in the infinite richness of the embedding world. Though this isn't the place for metaphysics, it would not be too much to say that every act of conceptualization, analysis, categorization, does a certain amount of violence to its subject matter, in order to get at the underlying regularities that group things together. If you don't commit that act of violence—don't ignore some of what's going on—you would become so hypersensitive and so overcome with complexity that you would be unable to act.

To capture all this in a word, we will say that models are inherently *partial*. All thinking, and all computation, are similarly partial. Furthermore —and this is the important point—thinking and computation *have* to be partial: that's how they are able to work.

Full-Blooded Action

Something that is not partial, however, is action. When you reach out your hand and grasp a plow, it is the real field you are digging up, not your model of it. Models, in other words, may be abstract, and thinking may be abstract, and some aspects of computation may be abstract, but action is not. To actually build a hospital, to clench the steering wheel and drive through the intersection, or to inject a drug into a person's body, is to act in the full-blooded world, not in a partial or distilled model of it.

This difference between action and modeling is extraordinarily important. Even if your every thought is formulated in the terms of some model, to act is to take leave of the model and participate in the whole, rich, infinitely variegated world. For this reason, among others, action plays a crucial role, especially in the human case, in grounding the more abstract processes of modeling or conceptualization. One form that grounding can take, which computer systems can already take advantage of, is to provide feedback on how well the modeling is going. For example, if an industrial robot develops an internal three-dimensional representation of a wheel assembly passing by on a conveyor belt, and then guides its arm toward that object and tries to pick it up, it can use video systems or force sensors to see how well the model corresponded to what was actually the case. The world doesn't care about the model: the claws will settle on the wheel just in case the actualities mesh.

Feedback is a special case of a general phenomenon: you often learn, when you do act, just how good or bad your conceptual model was. You learn, that is, if you have adequate sensory apparatus, the capacity to assess the sensed experience, the inner resources to revise and reconceptualize, and the luxury of recovering from minor mistakes and failures.

Computers and Models

What does all this have to do with computers, and with correctness? The point is that computers, like us, participate in the real world: they take real actions. One of the most important facts about computers, to put this another way, is that we plug them in. They are not, as some theoreticians seem to suppose, pure mathematical abstractions, living in a pure detached heaven. They land real planes at real airports; administer real drugs; and —as you know all too well—control real radars, missiles, and command systems. Like us, in other words, although they base their actions on models, they have consequence in a world that inevitably transcends the partiality of those enabling models. Like us, in other words, and unlike the objects of mathematics, they are challenged by the inexorable conflict between the partial but tractable model and the actual but infinite world.

And, to make the only too obvious point: we in general have no guarantee that the models are right—indeed we have no *guarantee* about much of anything about the relationship between model and world. As we will see, current notions of "correctness" don't even address this fundamental question.

In philosophy and logic, as it happens, there is a precise mathematical theory called "model theory." You might think that it would be a theory about what models are, what they are good for, how they correspond to the worlds they are models of, and so forth. You might even hope this was true, for the following reason: a great deal of theoretical computer science, and all of the work in program verification and correctness, historically derives from this model-theoretic tradition, and depends on its techniques. Unfortunately, however, model theory doesn't address the model–world relationship at all. Rather, what model theory does is to tell you how your descriptions, representations, and programs *correspond to your model.*

The situation, in other words, is roughly as depicted in Figure 1. You are to imagine a description, program, computer system (or even a thought— they are all similar in this regard) in the left-hand box, and the real world in the right. Mediating between the two is the inevitable model, serving as an idealized or preconceptualized simulacrum of the world, in terms of which the description or program or whatever can be understood. One way to understand the model is as the glasses through which the program or computer looks at the world: it is the world, that is, as the system sees it (though not, of course, as it necessarily is).

The technical subject of "model theory," as I have already said, is a study of the relationship on the left. What about the relationship on the right? The answer, and one of the main points I hope you will take away from this discussion, is that, at this point in intellectual history, we have no theory of this right-hand side relationship.

There are lots of reasons for this, some quite complex. For one thing, most of our currently accepted formal techniques were developed,

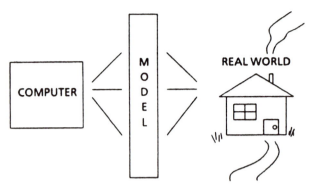

Figure 1. Computers, models, and the embedding world.

during the first half of this century, to deal with mathematics and physics. Mathematics is unique, with respect to models, because (at least to a first level of approximation) its subject matter *is* the world of models and abstract structures, and therefore the model–world relationship is relatively unproblematic. The situation in physics is more complex, of course, as is the relationship between mathematics and physics. How apparently pure mathematical structures could be used to model the material substrate of the universe is a question that has exercised physical scientists for centuries. But the point is that, whether or not one believes that the best physical models do more justice and therefore less violence to the world than do models in so-called "higher-level" disciplines like sociology or economics, formal techniques don't themselves address the question of adequacy.

Another reason we don't have a theory of the right-hand side is that there is little agreement on what such a theory would look like. In fact, all kinds of questions arise, when one studies the model–world relationship explicitly, about whether it can be treated formally at all, about whether it can be treated rigorously, even if not formally (and what the relationship is between those two), about whether any theory will be more than usually infected with prejudices and preconceptions of the theorist, and so forth. The investigation quickly leads to foundational questions in mathematics, philosophy, and language, as well as computer science. But none of what one learns in any way lessens its ultimate importance. In the end, any adequate theory of action and, consequently, any adequate theory of correctness, will have to take the model–world relationship into account.

Correctness and Relative Consistency

Let's get back, then, to computers, and to correctness. As I mentioned earlier, the word "correct" is already problematic, especially as it relates to underlying intention. Is a program correct when it does what we have instructed it to do? or what we wanted it to do? or what history would dispassionately say it should have done? Analyzing what correctness *should* mean is too complex a topic to take up directly. What I want to do, in the time remaining, is to describe what sorts of correctness we are presently capable of analyzing.

In order to understand this, we need to understand one more thing about building computer systems. I have already said, when you design a computer system, that you first develop a model of the world, as indicated in the diagram. But you don't, in general, ever get to hold the model in your hand: computer systems, in general, are based on models that are purely abstract. Rather, if you are interested in proving your program "correct," you develop two concrete things, structured in terms of the abstract underlying model (although these are listed here in logical order, the program is often written first):

1. A *specification:* a formal description in some standard formal language, specified in terms of the model, in which the desired behavior is described; and
2. The *program:* a set of instructions and representations, also formulated in the terms of the model, which the computer uses as the basis for its actions.

How do these two differ? In various ways, of which one is particularly important. The program has to say *how the behavior is to be achieved,* typically in a step-by-step fashion (and often in excruciating detail). The specification, however, is less constrained: all it has to do is to specify *what proper behavior would be,* independent of how it is accomplished. For example, a specification for a milk-delivery system might simply be: "Make one milk delivery at each store, driving the shortest possible distance in total." That's just a description of what has to happen. The program, on the other hand, would have the much more difficult job of saying how this was to be accomplished. It might be phrased as follows: "drive four blocks north, turn right, stop at Gregory's Grocery Store on the corner, drop off the milk, then drive 17 blocks northeast, . . ." Specifications, to use some of the jargon of the field, are essentially *declarative;* they are like indicative sentences or claims. Programs, on the other hand, are *procedural:* they must contain instructions that lead to a determinate sequence of actions.

What, then, is a proof of correctness? It is a proof that any system that *obeys the program* will *satisfy the specification.*

There are, as is probably quite evident, two kinds of problems here. The first, often acknowledged, is that the correctness proof is in reality only a proof that two characterizations of something are compatible. When the two differ—that is, when you try to prove correctness and fail—there is no more reason to believe that the first (the specification) is any more correct than the second (the program). As a matter of technical practice, specifications tend to be extraordinarily complex formal descriptions, just as subject to bugs and design errors and so forth as programs. In fact, they are much like programs, as this introduction should suggest. So what almost always happens, when you write a specification and a program, and try to show that they are compatible, is that you have to adjust both of them in order to get them to converge.

For example, suppose you write a program to factor a number C, producing two answers A and B. Your specification might be

Given a number C, produce numbers A and B such that $A \times B = C$.

This is a specification, not a program, because it doesn't tell you *how* to come up with A and B. All it tells you is what properties A and B should have. In particular, suppose I say: OK, C is 5,332,114; what are A and B? Staring at the specification just given won't help you to come up with an answer. Suppose, on the other hand, given this specification, that you then write a program—say, by successively trying pairs of numbers until you find two that work. Suppose further that you then set out to prove that your program meets your specification. And, finally, suppose that this proof can be constructed (I won't go into details here; I hope you can imagine that such a proof could be constructed). With all three things in hand—program, specification, and proof—you might think you were done.

In fact, however, things are rarely that simple, as even this simple example can show. In particular, suppose, after doing all this work, that you try your program out, confident that it must work because you have a proof of its correctness. You randomly give it 14 as an input, expecting 2 and 7. But in fact it gives you the answers $A = 1$ and $B = 14$. In fact, you realize upon further examination, it will *always* give back $A = 1$ and $B = C$. It does this, *even though you have a proof of its being correct*, because you didn't make your specification meet your intentions. You wanted both A and B to be *different* from C (and also different from 1), but you forgot to say that. In this case you have to modify both the program and the specification. A plausible new version of the latter would be

Given a number C, produce numbers A and B such that $A \neq 1$ and $B \neq 1$ *and $A \times B = C$.*

And so on and so forth: the point, I take it, is obvious. If the next version of the program, given 14, produces $A = -1$ and $B = -14$, you would similarly have met your new specification, but still failed to meet your intention. Writing "good" specifications—which is to say, writing specifications that capture your intention—is hard.

It should be apparent, nonetheless, that developing even straightforward proofs of "correctness" is useful. It typically forces you to delineate, explicitly and completely, the model on which both program and specification are based. A great many of the simple bugs that occur in programs, of which the problem of producing 1 and 14 was an example, arise from sloppiness and unclarity about the model. Such bugs are not identified by the proof, but they are often unearthed in the attempt to prove. And of course there is nothing wrong with this practice; anything that helps to eradicate errors and increase confidence is to be applauded. The point, rather, is to show exactly what these proofs consist of.

In particular, as the discussion has shown, when you show that a program meets its specifications, all you have done is to show that two formal descriptions, slightly different in character, are compatible. This is why I think it is somewhere between misleading and immoral for computer scientists to call this "correctness." What is called a proof of correctness is really a proof of the compatibility or consistency between two formal objects of an extremely similar sort: program and specification. As a community, we computer scientists should call this *relative consistency*, and drop the word "*correctness*" completely.

What proofs of relative consistency ignore is the second problem intimated earlier. Nothing in the so-called program verification process per se deals with the right-hand side relationship: the relationship between the model and the world. But, as is clear, it is over inadequacies on the right-hand side—inadequacies, that is, in the models in terms of which the programs and specifications are written—that systems so commonly fail.

The problem with the moon-rise, for example, was a problem of this second sort. The difficulty was not that the program failed, in terms of the model. The problem, rather, was that the model was overly simplistic; *it didn't correspond to what was the case in the world.* Or, to put it more carefully, since all models fail to correspond to the world in indefinitely many ways, as we have already said, it didn't correspond to what was the case *in a crucial and relevant way.* In other words, to answer one of our original questions, even if a formal specification had been written for the 1960 warning system, and a proof of correctness generated, there is no reason to believe that potential difficulties with the moon would not have emerged.

You might think that the designers were sloppy; that they would have thought of the moon if they had been more careful. But it turns out to be extremely difficult to develop realistic models of any but the most artificial situations, and to assess how adequate these models are. To see just how hard it can be, think back on the case of General Electric, and imagine writing appliance specifications, this time for a refrigerator. To give the example some force, imagine that you are contracting the refrigerator out to be built by an independent supplier, and that you want to put a specification into the contract that is sufficiently precise to guarantee that you will be happy with anything that the supplier delivers that meets the contract.

Your first version might be quite simple—say, that it should maintain an internal temperature of between 3 and 6 degrees Centigrade; not use more than 200 watts of electricity; cost less than $100 to manufacture; have an internal volume of half a cubic meter; and so on and so forth. But of course there are hundreds of other properties that you implicitly rely on: it should, presumably, be structurally sound: you wouldn't be happy with a deliciously cool plastic bag. It shouldn't weigh more than a ton, or emit loud noises. And it shouldn't fling projectiles out at high speed when the door is opened. In general, it is impossible, when writing specifications, to include *everything* that you want: legal contracts, and other humanly interpretable specifications, are always stated within a background of common sense, to cover the myriad unstated and unstable assumptions assumed to hold in force. (Current computer programs, alas, have no common sense, as the cartoonists know so well.)

So it is hard to make sure that everything that meets your specification will really be a refrigerator; it is also hard to make sure that your requirements don't rule out perfectly good refrigerators. Suppose for example, a customer plugs a toaster in, puts it inside the refrigerator, and complains that the object he received doesn't meet the temperature specification and must therefore not be a refrigerator. Or suppose he tries to run it upside down. Or complains that it doesn't work in outer space, even though you didn't explicitly specify that it would work only within the earth's atmosphere. Or spins it at 10,000 rpm. Or even just unplugs it. In each case you would say that the problem lies not with the refrigerator but with the use. But how is *use* to be specified? The point is that, as well as modeling the artifact itself, you have to model the relevant part of the world in which it will be embedded. It follows that the model of a refrigerator as a device that *always* maintains an internal temperature of between 3 and 6 degrees is too strict to cover all possible situations. One could try to model what appropriate use would be, though specifications don't, ordinarily, even try to identify all the relevant circumstantial factors. As well as there being a background set of constraints with respect to which a model is formulated, in other words, there is also a background set of assumptions on which a specification is allowed at any point to rely.

The Limits of Correctness

It's time to summarize what we've said so far. The first challenge to developing a perfectly "correct" computer system stems from the sheer complexity of real-world tasks. We mentioned at the outset various factors that contribute to this complexity: human interaction, unpredictable factors of setting, hardware problems, difficulties in identifying salient levels of abstraction, and so on. Nor is this complexity of only theoretical concern. A December 1984 report of the American Defense Science Board Task Force on "Military Applications of New-Generation Computing Technologies" identifies the following gap between current laboratory demonstrations and what will be required for successful military applications—applications they call "Real World; Life or Death." In their estimation, the military now needs (and, so far as one can tell, expects to produce) an increase in the power of computer systems of nine orders of magnitude, accounting for both speed and amount of information to be processed. That is a 1,000,000,000-fold increase over current research systems, equivalent to the difference between a full century of the entire New York metropolitan area, compared to one day in the life of a hamlet of one hundred people. And remember that even current systems are already several orders of magnitude more complex than those for which we can currently develop proofs of relative consistency.

But sheer complexity has not been our primary subject matter. The second challenge to computational correctness, more serious, comes from the problem of formulating or specifying an appropriate model. Except in the most highly artificial or constrained domains, modeling the embedding situation is an approximate, not a complete, endeavor. It has the best hopes of even partial success in what Winograd has called "systematic domains": areas where the relevant stock of objects, properties, and relationships are most clearly and regularly predefined. Thus bacteremia, or warehouse inventories, or even flight paths of airplanes coming into airports are relatively systematic domains, at least compared to conflict negotiations, any situations involving intentional human agency, learning and instruction, and so forth. The systems that land airplanes are hybrids— combinations of computers and people—exactly because the unforeseeable happens, and because what happens is in part the result of human action, requiring human interpretation. Although it is impressive how well the phone companies can model telephone connections, lines, and even develop statistical models of telephone use, at a certain level of abstraction, it would nevertheless be impossible to model the content of the telephone conversations themselves.

Third, and finally, is the question of what one does about these first two facts. It is because of the answer to this last question that I have talked, so far, somewhat interchangeably about people and computers. With respect to the ultimate limits of models and conceptualization, both people and computers are restrained by the same truths. If the world is infinitely rich and variegated, no prior conceptualization of it, nor any abstraction, will ever do it full justice. That's OK—or at least we might as well say that it's OK, since that's the world we've got. What matters is that we not forget about that richness—that we not think, with misplaced optimism, that machines might magically have access to a kind of "correctness" to which people cannot even aspire.

It is time, to put this another way, that we change the traditional terms of the debate. The question is not whether machines can do things, as if, in the background, lies the implicit assumption that the object of comparison is people. Plans to build automated systems capable of making a "decision," in a matter of seconds, to annihilate Europe, say, should make you uneasy; requiring a person to make the same decision in a matter of the same few seconds should make you uneasy, too, and for similar reasons. The problem is that there is simply no way that reasoning of any sort can do justice to the inevitable complexity of the situation, because of what reasoning is. Reasoning is based on partial models, which means it cannot be guaranteed to be correct. Which means, to suggest just one possible strategy for action, that we might try, in our treaty negotiations, to find mechanisms to slow our weapons systems down.

It is striking to realize, once the comparison between machines and people is raised explicitly, that we don't typically expect "correctness" for people in anything like the form that we presume it for computers. In fact, quite the opposite, and in a revealing way. Imagine, in some bygone era, sending a soldier off to war, and giving him (it would surely have been a "him") final instructions. "Obey your commander, help your fellow soldier," you might say, "and above all do your country honor." What is striking about this is that it is considered not just a weakness, but a punishable weakness—a breach of morality—to obey instructions *blindly* (in fact, and for relevant reasons, you generally *can't* follow instructions blindly; they have to be interpreted to the situation at hand). You are subject to court-martial, for example, if you violate fundamental moral principles, such as murdering women and children, even if following strict orders.

In the human case, in other words, our social and moral systems seem to have built in an acceptance of the uncertainties and limitations inherent in the model–world relationship. We *know* that the assumptions and preconceptions built into instructions will sometimes fail, and we know that instructions are always incomplete; we exactly rely on judgment, responsibility, consciousness, and so forth, to carry someone through those situations—all situations, in fact—where model and world part company. In fact, we never talk about people, in terms of their overall personality, being *correct*; we talk about people being *reliable*, a much more substantive term. It is individual actions, fully situated in a particular setting, that are correct or incorrect, not people in general, or systems. What leads to the highest number of correct human actions is a person's being reliable, experienced, capable of good judgment, and the like.

There are two possible morals here, for computers. The first has to do with the notion of experience. In point of fact, program verification is not the only, or even the most common, method of obtaining assurance that a computer system will do the right thing. Programs are usually judged acceptable, and are typically accepted into use, not because we prove them "correct," but because they have shown themselves relatively reliable in their destined situations for some substantial period of time. And, as part of this experience, we expect them to fail: there always has to be room for failure. Certainly no one would ever accept a program without this *in situ* testing: a proof of correctness is at best added insurance, not a replacement, for real-life experience. Unfortunately, for the ten million lines of code that is supposed to control and coordinate the Star Wars Defense System, there will never, God willing, be an *in situ* test.

One answer, of course, if genuine testing is impossible, is to run a *simulation* of the real situation. But simulation, as our diagram should make clear, *tests only the left-hand side relationship*. Simulations are defined in terms of models; they don't test the relationship between the model and the world. That is exactly why simulations and tests can never replace embedding a program in the real world. All the war games we hear about, and hypothetical military scenarios, and electronic battlefield simulators and so forth, are all based on exactly the kinds of models we have been talking about all along. In fact, the subject of simulation, worthy of a whole analysis on its own, is really just our whole subject welling up all over again.

I said earlier that there were two morals to be drawn, for the computer, from the fact that we ask people to be reliable, not correct. The second moral is for those who, when confronted with the fact that genuine or adequate experience cannot be had, would say, "oh, well, let's build responsibility and morality into the computers—if people can have it, there's no reason why machines can't have it, too." Now, I will not argue that this is inherently impossible, in a metaphysical or ultimate philosophical sense, but a few short comments are in order. First, from the fact that humans sometimes *are* responsible, it does not follow that we know what responsibility is: from tacit skills no explicit model is necessarily forthcoming. We simply do not know what aspects of the human condition underlie the modest levels of responsibility to which we sometimes rise. And second, with respect to the goal of building computers with even human levels of full reliability and responsibility, I can state with surety that the present state of artificial intelligence is about as far from this as mosquitos are from flying to the moon.

But there are deeper morals even than these. The point is that even if we could make computers reliable, they still wouldn't necessarily always do the correct thing. *People* aren't provably "correct," either: that's why we hope they are responsible, and it is surely one of the major ethical facts that correctness and responsibility don't coincide. Even if, in another 1000 years, someone were to devise a genuinely responsible computer system, there is no reason to suppose that it would achieve "perfect correctness" either, in the sense of never doing anything wrong. This isn't a failure, in the sense of a performance limitation; it stems from the deeper fact that models must abstract in order to be useful. The lesson to be learned from the violence inherent in the model–world relationship, in other words, is that there is an *inherent* conflict between the power of analysis and conceptualization, on one hand, and sensitivity to the infinite richness, on the other.

But perhaps this is an overly abstract way to put it. Perhaps, instead, we should just remember that there will always be another moon-rise.

Acknowledgments

The preparation and publication of this report have been made possible in part through the support of Xerox Corporation and in part through an award from the System Development Foundation.

P·A·R·T · VII

F

Caught in the Grip of RSI: A Firsthand Account[*]

Evan Williamson

It started about four years ago. I was finishing a large research project for the company I was with at the time. The work required me to enter reams of information into a database, reorganize it, dump it into a statistical package for analysis, then transfer the results into a spreadsheet and graphics package for presentation.

"It's not the technology, but the way we use it," says Kitty Szado, licensed and registered occupational therapist with Metro-Health Medical Center, Cleveland, Ohio. "Damage occurs due to static or extreme postures or joint positions, repetitive motion, or both. Most computer-related injuries are from the keyboard. Typical factors that place the worker at a high risk for injury include emotional stress, working under deadline, improper keyboard or equipment placement, improper work practices, and counting workers' keystrokes," says Diana Roose, research director for 9 to 5, National Association of Working Women, Cleveland, Ohio. "Surprisingly, pregnancy, with its hormonal changes and water retention can place extra compression on nerves, but it's one of the only factors that will correct itself with time. All other risk factors require worker and manager intervention."

About three-quarters of the way through the project, I noticed an odd, tired feeling spreading over the backs of my hands and up my forearms. Thinking it was simple fatigue, I promised myself a long break from the computer when the project was done, readjusted my hands to a more comfortable position, and continued my work. "Fatigue causes overcompensation in the shoulders and neck. The hands and wrists stay down and the forearm and shoulders lift up. This forces the wrists into a more extreme position," says Szado. "Once the cycle of stress-trauma-adjustment-stress starts, it escalates. Microtrauma produces inflammation, which produces more trauma."

Over the next couple of months, I started to feel what could best be described as electric shocks running up my forearms. These were rare at first, but became common throughout the workday. What finally sent me to the doctor was a large, painful lump beneath my skin at the intersection of the base of my right thumb and wrist. According to Szado, "Slight compression or squeezing of the nerve within its protective sheath can cause an electrical sensation. The nerve is stimulated, almost like a short circuit. If a nerve sheath is irritated enough, it can temporarily swell, form a nodule beneath the skin, and hurt. These symptoms are common but [they are] not necessarily the earliest indication of a cumulative stress disorder."

Until this point, I had kept my discomfort to myself, but now I decided to tell my manager. I felt bad about it, and I could tell my boss was not happy with the news. At the time, he seemed more interested in getting work done than in taking care of problems I was experiencing. I knew I had to continue producing the same high volume of work. The company, after all, was depending on me. More important, I didn't want to be thought of as a malingerer. Still, I knew my hands and arms were being damaged, and I was torn between the need to take care of myself and the need to maintain my pace. Says Diana Roose: "Any time a problem is first reported, steps should be taken immediately. Pain means something's wrong, and it's much easier to take care of a problem when it first occurs than to try to fix it once work[time] is being lost."

"Some people have noted a cumulative trauma craze," says Szado. "There is so much information that workers know exactly what is supposed to be wrong, [they] understand that they work in a high-risk occupation, and [they] decide to use it as an excuse to get out of work. It does happen. The only way to discover if there is an actual injury is to send the worker to a good doctor and [an] occupational therapist. A good therapist can tell if a worker is faking it."

I saw a doctor and therapist at a large hospital. I was given a splint to immobilize my right thumb and a set of exercises to strengthen my grip, and I was told to cut down on my typing. I received a strong warning that things could only get worse if I didn't take care of myself, but I was not given clear advice on how to restructure my work. The doctor was reluctant to say that it was the typing that was giving me trouble. "It's very common for the person to be returned to the workplace with very little advice," says Roose. "Doctors can usually find the injury if one exists, but they are not

*This article appeared in *Managing Office Technology*, 39(5) (May), pp. 40–41. Reprinted with permission. Copyright © 1994 by Penton Publishing, subsidiary of Pittway Corporation.

always familiar with the occupation part of the problem. It's not unusual for a doctor to be reluctant to ascribe damage to a single, isolated cause because an injury can have many causes."

The company purchased a height-adjustable table for my work area, and, when others were around, the boss would remind me to take breaks and stretch my hands. Privately, he would comment on how badly he needed me to complete my work and how he hoped the trouble I was experiencing with my hands wouldn't hurt my productivity. I wore the splint, but felt vaguely uncomfortable about it, as if I were a constant complainer. I did the exercises I was given, and showed slight improvement.

Explains Roose, "Managers often have no idea of how to handle an injured worker. Once an injury is established, the first thing a manager should remember is that the person cannot work through pain. It will only get worse. The company should take steps to fix the workspace by re-arranging the workstation and reorganizing the work. . . . The worker should be told that he or she is required to complete other, nonkeyboard tasks to serve as breaks. Many managers hear the word "break" and think "downtime." A break simply means nonkeyboard time, which could be spent filing, answering mail, or responding to telephone messages," she continues. "The responsibility to solve the problem is shared between the manager and the worker. The worker must be given the encouragement, instruction, and authority to change bad work habits."

I was laid off, along with half the staff, due to financial trouble. I was lucky enough to land another position that required keyboard work. I continued my hand exercises and wore my splint when I typed, and my symptoms slowly improved. Then, during a period when I was working on a research project and doing much more typing than usual, my troubles returned with a vengeance. I was unable to cut a piece of meatloaf with a fork, brush my teeth, or tickle my children without severe discomfort. The pain in my right arm and hand began to keep me awake at night. I told my manager what was going on, and was encouraged to get medical help. I went to a neurosurgeon for an electromyogram (EMG).

Designed to test the efficiency of the nerve pathways in the arm, wrist, and hand, the exam started with electrical shocks through the skin, down the arm, and into the hand, and finished with the insertion of needles into various arm and hand muscles to test the electrical activity in them. The neurologist sent me back to my doctor who referred me to another occu-pational therapist. This time, I received a set of exercises to strengthen the muscles used to open my hands and specific instructions on changing my work habits.

I began by avoiding the keyboard whenever possible. I didn't jump onto the computer to design a database or a spreadsheet on the fly. I didn't do my e-mail until I knew what I wanted to say. I realized that I had used the speed of the computer to make up for the lack of planning. More planning meant less computing. My splint, adjustable workstation, and experimentation with some rather exotic computer input devices have marked me as a sympathetic ear. I have been amazed at the number of colleagues telling of pain and fatigue in their arms and hands. Some appear worse than I, a few are nearly disabled. Many have hoped the pain would go away by itself. Most have not seen a doctor.

"If one person has trouble, then it is likely that many workers with the same type of duties are suffering, as well," says Roose. "A manager could have multiple sufferers for every one worker who complains. Everybody who uses a keyboard is at risk. A good manager will deal with it up front to keep costs down and to reduce compensation, absenteeism, and sick days."

What happens now? Part of the answer is up to me. I can continue as I was or I can do my exercises, pay attention to the way I work, and alter the manner in which I get things done. Part of it is up to the people for whom I work. They can be supportive, allow me to take the steps needed to help myself and still get the work done, or they can refuse to do so. Part of the answer is the technology. Things continue to change, and I hope I won't need a keyboard forever.

Office Automation's Threat to Health and Productivity: A New Management Concern[*]

E. M. Omar Khalil • *Jessie E. Melcher*

Information technology is the wave of the future, and management must be prepared for its good and bad aspects. Offices are flooded with microcomputers, video display terminals, and other technological tools designed to improve productivity. However, these tools are largely products of mass-production methods, which emphasize ease of manufacturing, not the user's health and comfort [5].

Automation has changed the ecosystem of the office and has brought new levels of stress. This change, unfortunately, has not been matched with a sufficient change in job design and processes. Consequently, computer-related injuries are on the rise; productivity is bound to suffer when the workplace is poorly designed, and workers become bleary-eyed and sore as a result of sitting all day in inappropriate chairs, staring at poorly lit screens.

The lack of human factor considerations in office automation has raised many concerns to management over the potential threats to workers' health and productivity. This paper addresses three of these threats and suggests some guidelines in order to minimize the risk.

Threats to Health and Productivity

Among the new wave of threats to the health and productivity of white-collar workers are repetitive stress injuries, radiation-related illnesses, and vision impairments.

Repetitive Stress Injuries

Repetitive stress injuries (RSIs) are among the fastest-growing workplace injuries in the United States and elsewhere. Australia, for example, had a near epidemic by the mid-1980s that has affected about 3% of its workers, and some experts believe the United States already may have as big a problem. According to estimates of the National Institute for Occupational Safety and Health (NIOSH), more than five million people, or 4% of the work force, suffered from repetitive motion injuries in 1986. These injuries account for about 30% of all worker compensation claims, and this is expected to reach 50% by the year 2000 [9].

Many experts point to the correlation between RSIs and the rise of computer use. RSIs accounted for 18% of all workplace injuries in 1981, the year personal computers were introduced. The percentage rose to 52% in 1989, by which time some 40 million PCs were in use [2]. As a result, the Occupational Safety and Health Administration (OSHA) has declared RSIs to be job related.

Computers have turned what was once the unseen work of the office into discrete keystrokes that can be counted and sped up. Computers store and retrieve data quickly. Users can type faster while having less control over the pace of their work [4]. Word processors pose special problems, since they allow workers to type up to 240 characters per minute for hours without a break [6]; and research results suggest that workers who type for more than five hours a day at a computer have twelve times as great a risk of developing RSIs as those who spend less time.

Keyboard work is a repetitive motion activity. Office workers who once might have mixed typing with filing, answering phones, and countless other tasks may now simply sit at their computers and type. The letter placement on a standard QWERTY keyboard was originally designed to slow the typist down so that manual typewriters wouldn't jam, but to do this the fingers are forced into awkward positions [4].

The repetitive motion activity often results in a mismatch between what a job demands and what the human mind and body can provide. This mismatch can create psychological and physical stress. The negative

---

*This article appeared in SAM Advanced Management Journal, 59(3)(Summer), pp. 10–14.

psychological stress, that is, a burdensome job or lack of autonomy, can result in anxiety, loss of concentration, irritability, and even psychological disorders. The negative physical stress, caused by improper use of a muscle or muscle group, results in fatigue and strain [2]. The worker's vulnerability to RSIs is expected to increase as the stress level increases.

The wrist, arm, and hand pain caused by carpal tunnel syndrome is a form of RSI, which is also known as a repetitive motion injury (RMI). RSIs were the first tangible symptoms of the injurious potential of the computer. Most RSIs fall into the categories of upper-limb and postural disorders. There are also a host of other RSIs related to computer use. The most prevalent are: tendonitis (the swelling or irritation of a tendon), thoracic outlet syndrome (a compression disorder of the nerves and blood vessels between the neck and shoulders), and ulnar neuritis (a nerve inflammation that is caused by pressure on the ulnar nerve in the elbow). The base cause of these injuries is operating a computer at unsafe angles [5, 15].

RSIs should be of major concern to management because of their effect on health and productivity [11]. RSIs affect at least 23,000 Americans a year. The disorder has long been an occupational hazard for workers who operate drilling or cutting equipment, and now it is moving out of the factory and into the office, affecting those who spend long hours in uninterrupted typing.

Some experts see cumulative trauma disorder as the first major post-industrial illness. Most motion injury cases are likely to occur in offices, where more than 28 million people work at video display terminals (VDTs) [9]. Occupations involving excessive use of the wrist were found to be associated with the development of carpal tunnel syndrome [13, 9]. Surgery to relieve the pain of carpal tunnel syndrome is the second most frequently performed operation in the United States [4]. It is also estimated that cumulative trauma disorders account for about half of all work-related illnesses, and such disorders have tripled in the past decade.

In a three-year study of telephone workers at U.S. West Communications, NIOSH found that more than 20% of the employees who used computers had RSI. All the sufferers reported high levels of psychological strain, such as job insecurity and pressure to work fast. Psychological stress probably does its mischief by creating muscle tension, which reduces blood flow to hard-working muscles and tendons; without enough oxygen, these tissues become fatigued and prone to injury [6].

In addition, workers using VDTs more than one hour per day were found to report twice as many complaints of neck and shoulder discomfort as co-workers not using VDTs. A similar comparison reported eyestrain three times as often among VDT users. VDT operators had higher rates of absenteeism, reported less job satisfaction than their co-workers, and entry-level positions had a high turnover rate, approaching 30% per year [12].

Therefore, RSIs should not be overlooked by anyone concerned with productivity and cost. In addition to the lost work time, the medical costs to the company can be tremendous. The Santa Clara Valley Medical Center has seen a 300% increase in such cases, and OSHA estimated that, if ergonomics principles are ignored, by the turn of the century as much as 50 cents of every dollar spent on medical costs will go to treating cumulative trauma injuries [2]. OSHA has targeted CTDs as the major occupational disease of the 1990s. Organizations should be equally concerned.

Radiation-Related Illnesses

The design of the computer screen requires the user to work within a restricted posture range. Unlike a book, a computer screen cannot be read from the side or from above, and cannot readily be moved around on the desktop. Consequently, the user–computer relationship is paralyzed; postures that result are not normal and lead to discomfort [12].

Moreover, three common types of radiation are associated with VDTs: electromagnetic fields (EMFs), extremely low frequency emissions (ELFs), and very low frequency emissions (VLFs). While ELFs result from the vertical coils that refresh the screen at a rate of 55 to 75 times per second, VLFs result from the flyback transformer that moves a beam across the screen at about 15,000 to 30,000 cycles per second [7]. VDTs are shielded to protect the users from exposure; however, older models with less effective shields are still in use.

The effect of ELFs, VLFs, and EMFs on VDT users has been the subject of much debate. Studies have linked the magnetic fields produced by high-tension power lines with increased cancer risk. Most of the VDT-oriented research so far has focused on reproductive problems (spontaneous abortions and defective fetuses), and the cancer connection in particular has been given short shrift [7]. There has been a growing concern regarding increases in miscarriages and birth defects among women who use VDTs. This is not a concern that can be ignored, in view of the greater proportion of women in the data entry and clerical professions. The relevant research results, however, have not reached a consensus.

In a recent study by NIOSH, for instance, it was found that women who used VDTs during pregnancy had the same rate of miscarriage, about 15%, as those who did not use VDTs [16]. A Finnish study found that pregnant women working at VDTs emitting strong magnetic fields were three times more likely to have a miscarriage than those working at terminals with low-level magnetic fields.

Although none has specifically dealt with VDTs, the studies on VLF and ELF emissions have provided some alarming results. The consensus that VLF emissions do pose a potentially significant threat to health is growing

[5]. As a result, a number of the European Economic Council countries have adopted stringent standards regulating VDTs in the workplace.

The problem of radiation in the workplace will worsen. Laptop computers, for instance, raise a new potential problem. The screen of a laptop typically generates about half the electromagnetic field of a CRT, but the laptop PC is positioned much closer to the reproductive organs than is a desktop PC. Other peripherals may also be greater sources of electromagnetic radiation. The development of wireless local area networks (LANs) introduces a new source of EMFs into the office, one that has not yet been investigated, especially when some experts nowadays are raising concern' over the possible relationship between brain cancer and the use of cellular telephones.

Thus, the lack of conclusive evidence on the dangers of ELF emissions in the office should not deter us from viewing such emissions with suspicion. Of course, basic research on the effects of electromagnetic radiation must be performed, especially research that addresses VDTs and other devices [5]. Management, however, should exploit current knowledge to provide office workers with the necessary protection against radiating office equipment.

Vision Impairments

The eyes are also subject to a number of stressors in a computing environment. Research results suggest that people who use CRTs for more than four hours a day are subject to both eyestrain and fatigue [5]. Eye discomfort, strain, burning, itching, irritation, and aching are among the most frequently reported problems experienced by VDT users. Workers even complain of blurred vision, double vision, color fringes, deterioration of visual acuity, and headaches [1].

Visual discomfort associated with display terminals can be caused by a number of factors such as poor contrast between characters and background, flicker, glare and reflection, and differences in lighting between the screen and surrounding objects [8]. Higher-resolution screens seem to improve readability and reduce eye fatigue when small characters are displayed. However, they do not have a significant advantage over the standard VDT's resolution in improving the readability of large characters [10].

Eyestrain can result from low-refresh-rate monitors. A standard VGA monitor has a refresh rate of only 56 to 60 Hz, which generates visible flicker in graphics mode. This flicker forces the neurons in the eye to continuously readjust and can lead to headaches and blurred vision [5]. Another possible source for VDT-related eyestrain is that video displays are 30% less readable than printed copy. It takes readers about 30% longer to proof and discover mistakes in displayed material than it does on the same printed matter [8]. Although the reasons for this are not understood, it can cause VDT users to spend more time staring at the screen and become more likely to suffer eyestrain.

Glare and inadequate lighting make working at VDTs difficult as well [8, 14]. The lighting in the room determines the amount of glare and reflection. Lighting designed to illuminate a horizontal desk will usually cause glare on a vertical screen. Fluorescent light pulsates at sixty Hz, while the human brain has maximum efficiency at about thirteen Hz. That makes conventional office lighting (dominated by fluorescent lights) inappropriate for office automation. In addition, users usually sit at a different distance from VDTs than their optimal focus distance. The American Optometric Association (AOA) says that 50 to 75% of workers experience eye problems using VDTs. Consequently, the AOA suggests VDT users should get their eyes examined at least once a year [3].

Summary and Recommendations

As a result of the integration of information technology into the office, office jobs are not as safe as they should be. While white-collar workers may not operate forklifts or spend long hours on an assembly line, the information technology tools they use and the ways they use them pose varying degrees of risk [3].

The office ecosystem consists of basic elements such as air quality, lighting, ergonomics, workplace design, workers, and psychological factors. When any of these elements is disturbed or poorly managed, the negative impact on worker satisfaction, productivity, and corporate expenses can become significant [2]. Indeed, forcing information technology tools into the office has disrupted the work environment and has created a mismatch between job demands and employee capabilities.

Management cannot afford to wait for the issue to resolve itself. Potential lost work time, liability suits, and workers' compensation costs associated with the change in office technology call for prompt action. This action should focus on the creation of an ergonomically correct computing environment to compensate for the impersonal nature of information technology. An ergonomically correct workplace begins with maximum adjustability to fit all possible worker–task combinations. It requires all pieces of equipment and furniture to work together and to adjust to the user's dimensions. This means that, at minimum, the workstation must accommodate healthy postures.

It is also essential to recognize that a comfortable workplace extends beyond the immediate furniture and equipment; the surrounding environment is equally important [17]. Major components of this environment include room temperature, noise levels, and visual distractions located near the equipment.

The workplace environment can be improved by following some basic guidelines.

1. Consult your supplier or dealer before purchasing new equipment and furniture. Dealers will help, since they are at risk for product liability suits if they sell poorly designed workstations.
2. Select ergonomically designed equipment such as low ELF- and low VLF-emission monitors, chairs with good back support and adjustable height, and ergonomically designed workstations.
3. Arrange the workstation according to the needs of both the worker and the task. For instance, this arrangement should allow the worker to sit at least three feet from the front of the VDT and five feet from the back in order to minimize the radiation-related problems.
4. Provide frequent breaks to move around and stretch. No position is good if the employee remains static too long. Short, frequent breaks are more beneficial than longer, more infrequent breaks.
5. Good equipment and ergonomic arrangement are not enough. Make sure they are used—and used correctly. Office workers are often unaware their furniture is adjustable or are untrained in making the proper adjustments.
6. Provide alternative tasks to relieve boredom and encourage a healthful change in posture. Alternative tasks also give employees a sense of autonomy that may reduce stress and increase job satisfaction and productivity.
7. New and better-designed technology can help. Newer keyboards, for example, will fit the hands better, reduce stress on the wrist, and eliminate the unnecessary motion required by the currently available keyboards. But the ultimate goal is to do away with the keyboard and use other data entry techniques such as imaging systems, voice recognition, and thinking-activated computers.

Conclusion

Healthy, safe, and comfortable employees are more productive. As a move is made further into the era of automated offices and an information-based economy, it is crucial that managers understand the changing environment in which people work and the need for compatible offices. The ultimate winners will be not only employees, but also employers, who will come to realize how these issues affect productivity.

References

1. Brooks, Gail (1986). "VDTs And Health Risks: What Unions Are Doing." *Personnel*, July 7, 59–64.
2. Cornell, Paul (1992). "Improving the Workplace." *The Secretary*, August/ September, 14–16.

3. Fried, Louis (1982). "Nine Principles for Ergonomic Software." *Datamation*, November, 163–165.
4. Goldoftas, Barbara (1991). "Hands That Hurt: Repetitive Motion Injuries on the Job." *Technology Review*, January, 43–50.
5. Harvey, David (1991). "Health and Safety First." *Byte*, October, 119–127.
6. Horowitz, Janice M. (1992). "Crippled by Computers." *Time*, October 12, 70–72.
7. Immel, Richard A. (1990). "The Growing VDT Radiation Debate." *Lotus*, February, 8–14.
8. Kull, David (1984). "Demystifying Ergonomics." *Computer Decisions*, September, 142–148.
9. Mallory, Maria, and Hazel Bradford (1989). "An Invisible Workplace Hazard Gets Harder to Ignore." *Business Week*, January 30, 92–93.
10. Miyao, M., S. Hacisalihzade, J. Allen, and L. Stark (1989). "Effects of VDT Resolution on Visual Fatigue and Readability: An Eye Movement Approach." *Ergonomics*, 32 (6), 603–614.
11. Pagnanelli, David M. (1989). "Hands-on Approach to Avoiding Carpal Tunnel Syndrome." *Risk Management*, May 20–23.
12. Schneider, Franz M. (1985). "Why Ergonomics Can No Longer Be Ignored." *Office Administration and Automation*, July 26–29.
13. Stevens, J. C., M. Beard, M. O'Fallon, and L. Kurland (1992). "Conditions Associated with Carpal Tunnel Syndrome." *Mayo Clin. Proc.*, 67, 541–548.
14. Trunzo, James (1988). "Office Computers Pose a 'Glaring' Problem." *National Underwriter*, February 22, 3, 20.
15. Verespej, Michael A. (1991). "Ergonomics: Taming the Repetitive-Motion Monster." *Industry Week*, October 7, 26–32.
16. Voss, Bristol (1991). "Health Hazards." *Sales & Marketing Management*, November, 127–128.
17. Wagner, Fran (1985). "Fine-Tuning Workstations Screens Out VDT Discomfort." *Computerworld*, October 28, 98–99.

Ongoing Network Monitoring Attacks: CERT Advisory, February 3, 1994*

Computer Emergency Response Team

In the past week, CERT has observed a dramatic increase in reports of intruders monitoring network traffic. Systems of some service providers have been compromised, and all systems that offer remote access through rlogin, telnet, and FTP are at risk. Intruders have already captured access information for tens of thousands of systems across the Internet.

The current attacks involve a network monitoring tool that uses the promiscuous mode of a specific network interface, /dev/nit, to capture host and user authentication information on all newly opened FTP, telnet, and rlogin sessions.

In the short-term CERT recommends that all users on sites that offer remote access change passwords on any network-accessed account. In addition, all sites having systems that support the /dev/nit interface should disable this feature if it is not used and attempt to prevent unauthorized access if the feature is necessary. A procedure for accomplishing this is described below. Systems known to support the interface are SunOS 4.x (Sun3 and Sun4 architectures) and Solbourne systems; there may be others. Sun Solaris systems do not support the /dev/nit interface. If you have a system other than Sun or Solbourne, contact your vendor to find if this interface is supported.

While the current attack is specific to /dev/nit, the short-term work-around does not constitute a solution. The best long-term solution currently available for this attack is to reduce or eliminate the transmission of reusable passwords in clear-text over the network.

Description

Root-compromised systems that support a promiscuous network interface are being used by intruders to collect host and user authentication information visible on the network.

The intruders first penetrate a system and gain root access through an unpatched vulnerability (solutions and workarounds for these vulnerabilities have been described in previous CERT advisories, which are available via anonymous FTP from info.cert.org).

The intruders then run a network monitoring tool that captures up to the first 128 keystrokes of all newly opened FTP, telnet, and rlogin sessions visible within the compromised system's domain. These keystrokes usually contain host, account, and password information for user accounts on other systems; the intruders log these for later retrieval. The intruders typically install Trojan horse programs to support subsequent access to the compromised system and to hide their network monitoring process.

Impact

All connected network sites that use the network to access remote systems are at risk from this attack. All user account and password information derived from FTP, telnet, and rlogin sessions and passing through the same network as the compromised host could be disclosed.

Approach

There are three steps in CERT's recommended approach to the problem:

- Detect if the network monitoring tool is running on any of your hosts that support a promiscuous network interface.
- Protect against this attack either by disabling the network interface for those systems that do not use this feature or by attempting to prevent unauthorized use of the feature on systems where this interface is necessary.
- Scope the extent of the attack and recover in the event that the network monitoring tool is discovered.

---

*Reprinted with permission of CERT, a service mark of Carnegie Mellon University.

Detection

The network monitoring tool can be run under a variety of process names and log to a variety of filenames. Thus, the best method for detecting the tool is to look for

1. Trojan horse programs commonly used in conjunction with this attack,
2. any suspect processes running on the system, and
3. the unauthorized use of /dev/nit.

Trojan Horse Programs

The intruders have been found to replace one or more of the following programs with a Trojan horse version in conjunction with this attack:

/usr/etc/in.telnetd and
/bin/login: used to provide back-door access for the intruders to retrieve information
/bin/ps: used to disguise the network monitoring process

Because the intruders install Trojan horse variations of standard UNIX commands, CERT recommends not using other commands such as the standard UNIX sum(1) or cmp(1) commands to locate the Trojan horse programs on the system until these programs can be restored from distribution media, run from read-only media (such as a mounted CD-ROM), or verified using cryptographic checksum information.

In addition to the possibility of having the checksum programs replaced by the intruders, the Trojan horse programs mentioned above may have been engineered to produce the same standard checksum and timestamp as the legitimate version. Because of this, the standard UNIX sum(1) command and the timestamps associated with the programs are not sufficient to determine whether the programs have been replaced.

CERT recommends that you use both the /usr/5bin/sum and /bin/sum commands to compare against the distribution media and assure that the programs have not been replaced. The use of cmp(1), MD5, Tripwire (only if the baseline checksums were created on a distribution system), and other cryptographic checksum tools are also sufficient to detect these Trojan horse programs, provided these programs were not available for modification by the intruder. If the distribution is available on CD-ROM or other read-only device, it may be possible to compare against these volumes or run programs off these media.

Suspect Processes

Although the name of the network monitoring tool can vary from attack to attack, it is possible to detect a suspect process running as root using ps(1) or other process-listing commands. Until the ps(1) command has been verified against distribution media, it should not be relied upon—a Trojan horse version is being used by the intruders to hide the monitoring process. Some process names that have been observed are sendmail, es, and in.netd. The arguments to the process also provide an indication of where the log file is located. If the "-F" flag is set on the process, the filename following indicates the location of the log file used for the collection of authentication information for later retrieval by the intruders.

Unauthorized Use of /dev/nit

If the network monitoring tool is currently running on your system, it is possible to detect this by checking for unauthorized use of the /dev/nit interface. CERT has created a minimal tool for this purpose. The source code for this tool is available via anonymous FTP on info.cert.org in the /pub/tools/cpm directory or on ftp.uu.net in the /pub/security/cpm directory as cpm.1.0.tar.Z.

Prevention

There are two actions that are effective in preventing this attack. A long-term solution requires eliminating transmission of clear-text passwords on the network. For this specific attack, however, a short-term workaround exists. Both of these are described below.

Long-Term Prevention

CERT recognizes that the only effective long-term solution to prevent these attacks is by not transmitting reusable clear-text passwords on the network. CERT has collected some information on relevant technologies. This information is included as Appendix A in this advisory. Note: These solutions will not protect against transient or remote access transmission of clear-text passwords through the network.

Until everyone connected to your network is using the above technologies, your policy should allow only authorized users and programs access to promiscuous network interfaces. The tool described above may be helpful in verifying this restricted access.

Short-Term Workaround

Regardless of whether the network monitoring software is detected on your system, CERT recommends that ALL SITES take action to prevent unauthorized network monitoring on their systems. You can do this either by removing the interface, if it is not used on the system or by attempting to prevent the misuse of this interface.

For systems other than Sun and Solbourne, contact your vendor to find out if promiscuous mode network access is supported and, if so, what is the recommended method to disable or monitor this feature.

For SunOS 4.x and Solbourne systems, the promiscuous interface to the network can be eliminated by removing the /dev/nit capability from the kernel (see your system manuals for more details). [Editor's Note: The procedure for doing so is omitted.] Once the procedure is complete, you may remove the device file /dev/nit since it is no longer functional.

[NOTE that even after the new kernel is installed, you need to take care to ensure that the previous vmunix.old, or other kernel, is not used to reboot the system.]

Scope and Recovery

If you detect the network monitoring software at your site, CERT recommends following three steps to successfully determine the scope of the problem and to recover from this attack.

1. Restore the system that was subjected to the network monitoring software.

   The systems on which the network monitoring and/or Trojan horse programs are found have been compromised at the root level; your system configuration may have been altered. See Appendix A of this advisory for help with recovery [Editor's Note: Appendix A is omitted].

2. Consider changing router, server, and privileged account passwords due to the widespread nature of these attacks.

   Since this threat involves monitoring remote connections, take care to change these passwords using some mechanism other than remote telnet, rlogin, or FTP access.

3. Urge users to change passwords on local and remote accounts.

   Users who access accounts using telnet, rlogin, or FTP either to or from systems within the compromised domain should change their passwords after the intruder's network monitor has been disabled.

4. Notify remote sites connected from or through the local domain of the network compromise.

   Encourage the remote sites to check their systems for unauthorized activity. Be aware that if your site routes network traffic between external domains, both of these domains may have been compromised by the network monitoring software.

Acknowledgments

The CERT Coordination Center thanks the members of the FIRST community as well as the many technical experts around the Internet who participated in creating this advisory. Special thanks to Eugene Spafford of Purdue University for his contributions.

Appendix A: One-Time Passwords

Given today's networked environments, CERT recommends that sites concerned about the security and integrity of their systems and networks consider moving away from standard, reusable passwords. CERT has seen many incidents involving Trojan network programs (e.g., telnet and rlogin) and network packet sniffing programs. These programs capture clear-text hostname, account name, password triplets. Intruders can use the captured information for subsequent access to those hosts and accounts. This is possible because (1) the password is used over and over (hence the term "reusable"), and (2) the password passes across the network in clear text.

Several authentication techniques have been developed that address this problem. Among these techniques are challenge-response technologies that provide passwords that are used only once (commonly called one-time passwords). This document provides a list of sources for products that provide this capability [Editor's Note: omitted]. The decision to use a product is the responsibility of each organization, and each organization should perform its own evaluation and selection.

P·A·R·T·VII

I

Risks of Technology*

Peter G. Neumann

There is a widespread and growing disillusionment with technology. Fewer young people are aspiring to technology-oriented careers. Doubts are increasing as to technology's ability to provide lasting solutions for human problems. For example, heavy-industry technology has become a major polluter throughout the world. The use of chlorofluorocarbons in refrigeration, propulsion systems, and aerosols is threatening the ozone layer. Networked information that affects the activities of people is routinely sold and distributed without the knowledge or consent of those to whom it pertains, irrespective of its accuracy.

Peter Denning proposes that it is time to start cultivating a new common sense about technology. By "common sense" we mean the general, instinctive way of understanding the world we all share. The disillusionment suggests that the current common sense isn't working. Questions such as "If we can get a man to the moon, why can't we solve the urban crisis?" are overly simplistic; technology is not fundamentally relevant to the answer.

An example of an understanding in the old common sense is that we must obtain a precise description of a problem and then apply systematic methods to design a computing system that meets the specifications. In the new common sense, we must identify the concerns and the network of commitments people make in their organizations and lives, and then design computing systems that assist them in carrying out their commitments. The new common sense does not throw out precise specifications and systematic design; it simply regards these as tools and does not make them the center of attention.

Jerry Mander has published a remarkable book, *In the Absence of the Sacred: The Failure of Technology and the Survival of the Indian Nations* (Sierra

Club Books, 1992). He offers a list of aphorisms about technology, quoted below. From within the old common sense, these aphorisms might appear as Luddite antitechnology. But they point the way to the new common sense that needs cultivation. Please read them in that spirit:

1. Since most of what we are told about new technology comes from its proponents, be deeply skeptical of all claims.
2. Assume all technology "guilty until proven innocent."
3. Eschew the idea that technology is neutral or "value-free." Every technology has inherent and identifiable social, political, and environmental consequences.
4. The fact that technology has a natural flash and appeal is meaningless. Negative attributes are slow to emerge.
5. Never judge a technology by the way it benefits you personally. Seek a holistic view of its impacts. The operative question is not whether it benefits you, but who benefits most? And to what end?
6. Keep in mind that an individual technology is only one piece of a larger web of technologies, "metatechnology." The operative question here is how the individual technology fits the larger one.
7. Make distinctions between technologies that primarily serve the individual or the small community (e.g., solar energy) and those that operate on a scale of community control (e.g., nuclear energy). The latter is the major problem of the day.
8. When it is argued that the benefits of the technological lifeway are worthwhile despite harmful outcomes, recall that Lewis Mumford referred to these alleged benefits as "bribery." Cite the figures about crime, suicide, alienation, drug abuse, as well as environmental and cultural degradation.
9. Do not accept the homily that "once the genie is out of the bottle, you cannot put it back," or that rejecting a technology is impossible. Such attitudes induce passivity and confirm victimization.
10. In thinking about technology within the present climate of technological worship, emphasize the negative. This brings balance. Negativity is positive.

Many of the cases in the RISKS archives corroborate both Mander's aphorisms and the need for Denning's new common sense. In the new common sense, we would see organizations as networks of commitments, not hierarchical org charts. Daily human interactions would be mini-instances of the customer/provider loop, and attention would be focused on whether the customer of every loop is satisfied with the provider's

---

*This article appeared in *Communications of the ACM*, 36(3)(March, 1993), p. 130. Reprinted with permission of the Association for Computing Machinery.

work. Technology would help people fulfill their promises and commit-ments. Communication would serve for successful coordination of action, not merely as exchanges of messages.

To begin the needed rethinking about technology, we can ask ourselves questions such as Mander asks. This requires a rethinking of not merely military versus nonmilitary budgets, but the proper role of technology as a whole. Technology is by itself not the answer to any vital social questions. Ultimately, more fundamental human issues must be considered.

P·A·R·T · VIII

Ethical Perspectives
and Professional
Responsibilities for
Information and
Computer Science
Professionals

P·A·R·T · VIII

A

Beyond Outlaws, Hackers, and Pirates: Ethical Issues in the Work of Information and Computer Science Professionals

Rob Kling

Beyond Outlaws, Hackers, and Pirates

Hackers, outlaws, and phone phreaks are key players in many of the front page news stories about the ethical issues of computing. There are some subtle ethical issues in hacking. When does one's interest in exploring the boundaries of technical systems (the original conception of hacking) slip into exploiting system loopholes to steal data or damage other people's work (today's conventional conception of hacking)? But the people who intend to steal and disrupt usually know that they are harming others—for motives like the pleasures of skillful transgression, narcissistic pleasure, personal gain, revenge, and so on.

There is a strong romance to outlaw cultures and some of the hacker attacks seem to be youthful modern versions of keyboard bandits wishing to be Billy the Kid or Bonnie and Clyde. And in some cases, there has been an intriguing synergy when hackers have met openly with corporate computer security experts and FBI agents at meetings like the annual Computers, Freedom, and Privacy conference (partly sponsored by the Association for Computing Machinery), or the more underground Def Con (Armstrong, 1994).

One of the biases of the literature about "hackers as outlaws" (for example Hafner and Markoff, 1991) is the focus on individuals or small groups of "bad guys" harming establishment organizations and their clients. It is easy to energize a moral drama against acne-faced teenagers with pseudonyms like Captain Crunch or Pfiber Optik who try to enter computer systems owned by banks or the United States military. And it is easy to energize similar moral dramas against other teenagers with pseudonyms like Dark Avenger who try to develop novel viruses that trash the work of microcomputer users.

The ethical issues in many instances of unauthorized computer system use, intentional damage to computer systems, unauthorized copying, and so on, seem to be relatively clear-cut. In addition, the computer industry has lobbied effectively for legislation to give computer vendors strong property rights for software that they sell and to protect organizations from unauthorized intrusions into computer systems. Issues like hacking and software piracy absorb a relatively large fraction of attention in the professional computing literature. These issues are the center of a recent U.S. National Computer Ethics and Responsibility Campaign that is sponsored by several industrial organizations, including the Software Publishers Association, CompuServe, and Symantec Corporation. This campaign would work at a higher ethical plane if it also focused on improving the ethical forthrightness of computer industry firms in advertising their services and products. Unfortunately, this high-spirited moral crusade avoids addressing issues like the ethics of Intel's reluctance to divulge computational inaccuracies of its Pentium chip (see Part VII) and truth in advertising computer-related services and products.

Similarly, people who sell software that they have copied without authorization are keenly aware that they are selling stolen goods. But there are more subtle ethical issues about the rights and responsibilities of software ownership and sale that are not usually discussed in the moralistic articles that condemn unauthorized copying (software piracy). For example, to what extent are software vendors obligated to accurately advertise their software's capabilities and system requirements? To what extent should software vendors be obligated to refund purchased software that a customer has found will not work as advertised on her computer system?

A different set of ethical issues surfaces in the routine work of computer specialists when they wonder whose points of view to consider when they design new computer applications (Clement, Part IV, Chapter G; Suchman, Part IV, Chapter H). Identifying which parties were accountable for deaths and maimings in the Therac-25 imbroglio (Jacky, Part VII, Chapter C) is a more complex problem than finding a single villain (Nissenbaum, 1994). In the Therac-25 case, none of the many key participants was interested in killing and maiming people who were suffering from cancer. But some of the injuries could have been avoided if key participants acted and reacted differently.

Organizations can perpetrate harm on individuals, and other organizations, as well as be the primary victims (Kling, 1991). This part examines ethical issues like these that play more significant roles in the worklives of information and computers science professionals.

Ethical Issues in the Development and Use of Information Technologies

The word *ethics* is derived from the Greek word *ethos*, and refers to a person's orientation toward life. The core issues of ethics include ways to foster a good society, and doing what is right (or just). A good society depends on patterns of activity characteristic of the society and the opportunities that it typically opens for its members. For example, many people were offended by South Africa's harsh restrictions on the lives of black people during the decades of apartheid. Removing South Africa's controls on racial segregation is one step in its becoming a better society. Doing "what is right" is much more within the control of individuals. But people's social positions can "throw up" different kinds of opportunities for doing what is right (rather than doing what is simply expeditious or self-serving). Everyone faces periodic ethical choices where values conflict and where "the right thing" is not always immediately obvious.

People in specific occupations face some distinctive situations that people in other lines of work rarely or never face. For example, a surgeon (unlike a librarian or computer systems designer) faces frequent situations in which other people whom he or she knows may be rapidly healed or injured (or even killed) as a result of choices made in the use of a sharp knife. In contrast, the librarian or computer scientist may be much more likely than the surgeon to face issues where they make information available that some potential readers find enlightening, and that others find offensive and try to censor.

The work of information and computer professionals offers many routine opportunities to "do the right thing" when they design, develop, implement computerized systems, and facilitate their effective use. Some computer scientists argue that software development is saturated with ethical choices. For example, Robert Collins, Keith Miller, Bethany Spielman, and Phillip Wherry (1994) identify five features of software, and the first two are particularly distinctive:

1. Serious software errors can remain after rigorous testing because of the logical complexity of software;
2. It is difficult to construct uniform software standards that could be subject to regulation and inspection;
3. Software affects an increasingly large number of people, due to the proliferation and logical malleability of computers;
4. Any group can provide software, since large start-up costs are not necessary. This leads not only to a proliferation of entrepreneurs

providing software, but also to nonsoftware businesses adding a software capability;

5. Unlike other public threats such as nuclear plants or toxic waste disposal, software's threats are dispersed, not centralized.

The inherent complexity of most software means that the relative effort of information and computer professionals to develop high quality, to invest in testing, and to track and check bugs has important ethical dimensions, especially in safety-critical systems (see Part VII). It is easiest to illustrate the importance of ethical choices with dramatic cases where people can be (or have been) hurt by poor choices. In fact, some of the literature about professional ethics relies on well-known disaster cases to examine key arguments.[1]

Ethical issues permeate many of the essays and articles elsewhere in this volume. To cite just a few examples:

- Who should be accountable when medical software contains bugs that result in the maiming or deaths of several patients?

- When an imposter on a computerized bulletin board creates significant violations of trust, is his behavior mitigated by the fact that some therapeutic good was also achieved?

- When a multimillion-dollar software project is behind schedule, should technical staff who doubt its ability to be effectively rescheduled and completed inform the client organization?

- Are there any limits to the extent that the managers and owners of a private firm can examine the detailed movements of their employees?

- To what extent should employees or managers anticipate the possibility of ailments from intensive computer use, such as repetitive strain injuries, and who is most responsible for what kinds of actions?

- To what extent are computer scientists morally responsible for anticipating and publicizing some of the problems, as well as the social good, that are likely to result from their creations?

The first selection in this part, "All in a Day's Work" by Donn B. Parker, Susan Swope, Bruce N. Baker, and Eric A. Weiss, sketches nine commonplace situations where computer professionals face ethical choices. Mundane events like these are unlikely to appear in newspapers, but they still

---

[1] One advantage of using well-known cases such as that of the Ford Pinto gas tank design or of the O-ring failure in the Challenger space shuttle is that many readers are sufficiently familiar with the case that expositions can be short. In addition, if ethical principles or professional codes seem inadequate for dealing with these extreme examples, then they are likely to be even less effective for more mundane situations (see, for example, Helms and Hutchins, 1992).

raise important ethical questions. What does "doing the right thing" mean in each case?

Parker and his colleagues ask you to identify which ethical principles apply to each case. The original publication included a copy of the Code of Professional Conduct of the Association of Computing Machinery (ACM), and the question referred to the specific principles of this code. The ACM revised its code in 1992 and we shall discuss the new code shortly.

Some Bases for Assessing Ethical Actions

The question of "what principles" apply to assessing the rectitude of actions in professional practice goes beyond the content of a professional society's code. After all, the professional committees that develop a new code of ethics need some principles to help shape their work. And a professional ethical code should go well beyond the laws of a specific jurisdiction. Simply asking whether an action is legal or illegal does not provide sufficient guidance for professionals. We expect, or at least hope for, more than the avoidance of illegal behavior from professionals whom we wish to trust—whether they are doctors, lawyers, accountants, or computer specialists.

Some professionals will examine cases like those posed by Donn Parker and his colleagues with an informal sense of fairness or workplace pragmatism. They prefer to be honest in their dealings with their clients and co-workers, but they won't fight their supervisors and risk being branded as a troublemaker or even being fired. But some scientists and industrialists suggest that professionals can use more sophisticated informal criteria. For example, Gale Cutler, who directed research at the Whirlpool Corporation for twenty years, suggests that questions like these can help professionals resolve ethical dilemmas:

- Is it balanced? (Is it fair to all concerned? Will my decision disadvantage or perhaps even bring harm to anyone—my employer, colleagues, customers, suppliers, the community? Does it promote win–win relationships?)
- Can I defend it? (If I had to justify my decision would I feel embarrassed or uncomfortable?)
- How will it make me feel about myself? (Will it make me feel proud? Would I feel good if my decision were published in the newspaper? Would I feel good if my family knew about it?)
  (Adapted from Cutler, 1992)

These additional questions can significantly expand a person's frame of reference to help see her or his possible actions from the viewpoints of people who can be affected by her choices, by his family and community (via the hypothetical newspaper story). But these questions are hardly foolproof. Some situations, such as canceling a failed project and laying off technical staff, don't allow options that will be good for all parties. In addition, people often misperceive the concerns of other people, especially those who they do not know well or see as different in social status.

Ethical philosophers have articulated more formal systematic frameworks for assessing the ethical appropriateness of different behavior. Although there are over half a dozen major kinds of ethical theories in Western philosophy, three of them can be particularly helpful for information and computer professionals: universalist theories (associated with the nineteenth-century German philosopher Immanuel Kant), consequentialist theories (associated with the nineteenth-century Scottish philosophers James Stuart Mill and Jeremy Bentham), and theories of a just society (associated with the contemporary philosopher, John Rawls).

Universalist ethical theories hold the inherent features of an action make it right or wrong.

> the moral worth of an action cannot be dependent upon the outcome because these outcomes are so indefinite and uncertain at the time the decision to act is made; instead, the moral worth of an action had to depend upon the intentions of the person making the decision. It is assumed that good intentions will normally result in beneficial outcomes. Personal intentions can be translated into personal duties because, if we truly wish the best for others, we will always act in certain ways to ensure beneficial results and those ways become duties incumbent on us rather than choices open to us. Our personal duties are universal. . . . The first duty of universalism is to treat others as ends and not as means. No action can be considered right in accordance with personal duty if it disregards the ultimate worth of any other human being. (Helms and Hutchins, 1992)

Consequentialist theories focus on the outcomes of actions rather than a person's intentions. One well-known formulation, called utilitarianism, emphasizes creating the maximum benefits for the largest number of people, while incurring the least amount of damages or harm.

> utility . . . refers to our perception of the net benefits and costs associated with a given act. The utilitarian ideal can be summarized by the phrase "the greatest good for the greatest number." The primary way of meeting this criterion is by performing a social cost/benefit analysis and acting on it. All benefits and costs of a particular act are considered to the degree possible and summarized as the net sum of all benefits minus all costs. If the net result is positive, the act is morally acceptable. (Helms and Hutchins, 1992)

Utilitarianism is similar to systematic cost-benefit analyses practiced by actuaries, risk assessors, and engineers.

Theories of a just society examine the nature of social arrangements rather than individual acts. Philosopher John Rawls (1971) developed the most famous version of the approach with a sophisticated version of the Golden Rule ("do unto others . . ."). Rawls asks people to conceive of the ways of organizing social life that they would prefer from a specific vantage point—one in which they know nothing about their own capabilities and potentialities. Rawls places people behind a "veil of ignorance" about their actual social positions, and argues that "reasonable people" would prefer to choose a society that is tolerant of people's rights and equitable in distributing goods and services.

These three paragraphs are highly condensed summaries of much more complex and subtle theories. An example showing how someone who holds these ethical theories would evaluate the design or use of a computer performance monitoring (CPM) system can help us better understand their potential role in shaping professional actions. Stephen Hawk sketched a utilitarian approach to CPM systems in these terms:

> Business owners, employees, customers, and society in general may all benefit from CPM. The profits returned to business owners could be increased if CPM improved the efficiency and quality of work performed by monitored employees. Employees could potentially benefit if such profitability resulted in increased wages or employment stability. Customers could benefit if monitoring brought about improvements in service/product quality, or lower prices. Finally, society in general could benefit from an increased efficiency and effectiveness of its workforce. These benefits, of course, need to be weighed against the potential harms resulting from CPM usage. The literature clearly presumes that monitored employees bear the brunt of CPM's harms. . . . Research indicates that CPM causes stress and health problems, that it creates the potential for unfair performance evaluations, and that it is an invasion of privacy. Utilitarianism suggests that decisions surrounding CPM need to evaluate both the benefits and harms and choose the option that results in the greatest net good. (Hawk, 1994)

Hawk argues that a universalist differs in the way that he or she would assess a CPM system because he or she

> places importance on the intrinsic worth of individuals, emphasizing the obligation of business to respect the right of privacy, the dignity and the autonomy of their employees. For this reason . . . monitoring systems would be judged to be unethical to the extent that implementing them breached these obligations. Consider, for example, a CPM system used to report on minute to minute actions of an employee. Whether or not the benefits to the employer of such a system outweighed the costs to the employee, a (universalist) would reject the monitoring as morally objectionable if she concluded that it violates the employee's right of privacy, offends his dignity, or undermines his autonomy. (Hawk, 1994)

A Rawlsian would examine a CPM system differently. He or she would ask whether there is a way to structure the work with a CPM system so that some of the parties gain advantage, but none of the parties are disadvantaged. The monitored worker is most likely to be disadvantaged if close monitoring is added on top of an existing job. The Rawlsian professional might examine whether the monitoring could be structured so as not to induce significant stress, whether the job could be structured to relieve workers' stress through more frequent breaks, or whether the workers could be paid sufficiently more money to compensate for additional stress. CPM may be added to an existing job if one or more of these conditions is met, but not otherwise.

Each of these ethical theories can lead to a different conclusion about the ethical appropriateness of adding computerized performance monitoring to a specific workplace. In addition, these theories often led to different ethical assessments of the actions described in the nine cases written by Donn Parker and his colleagues.

Codes of Professional Ethics and Conduct

Many professional organizations, the Association for Computing Machinery (ACM) included, have adopted codes of conduct for their members. "Codes of Professional Ethics," the second selection in this part, examines the rationale for a new ACM professional code. Sociologist Ronald Anderson and his collaborators observe that many occupational associations adopted codes of ethics as a symbol that they were "really a profession." Unfortunately, these codes of ethics proved difficult to enforce.

As examples from earlier parts of this volume suggest, computer specialists and other people in positions of responsibility sometimes don't follow "self-evident" ethical guidelines. One set of controversies concerns the extent to which professional codes can influence the behavior of people who may not be oriented toward ethical behavior—either because of "character flaws" or fear of losing their jobs.[2] The role of professional codes in law and medicine can be instructive. They set guidelines for professionally specific behavior that are not simply part of "common sense." And while a small fraction of actual abuses by doctors and lawyers may be penalized by their professional societies, we feel more confident with these standards weakly enforced rather than with no codes or professional enforcement at all. Despite the controversy among computer specialists about the value of professional codes, the ACM's original 1972 Code of Professional Conduct has had a limited reach. It provided for sanctions against offenders. But I

---

[2] There is an ongoing debate as to whether (and how) professional ethics can be taught. A narrow view would focus simply on a code of behavior. But value judgments cannot be valuable in a factual vacuum. Professionals should be encouraged to look beyond the technical aspects of their work in order to visualize and assess its implications for their clients, society, and the world at large. This has key implications for computer science curricula. In "Can Computer Science Solve Organizational Problems?: The Case of Organizational Informatics" (Part III), Jonathan Allen and I argue that anyone whose work is likely to involve developing computer applications should study how organizations actually behave. Barus (1987) goes further and argues that technical professionals should understand other disciplines, including the humanities and social sciences.

do not know of any instances where this provision has been invoked. Moreover, it focuses on the conduct of individuals and does not address the issues of organizational responsibility.[3] Punishment and reward for a corporation is quite unlike that for individuals. And those individuals who make key organizational decisions may very well not even be information and computer professionals, let alone members of the ACM or a similar professional society.

Anderson and his colleagues acknowledge some of these shortcomings, and argue that such codes best serve educational roles in identifying important professional ideals. They may also sometimes help people make concrete professional choices. The newer 1992 ACM is reproduced here as the third selection (Chapter D). Virtually none of the ACM's code[4] is connected specifically with computing, except those portions that pertain to maintaining the privacy of data. Most can be derived from universalist ethical injunctions, for example, "Avoid harm to others" (1.2).

The American Society for Information Science (ASIS) has a shorter and simpler Code of Ethics for information scientists, which specifies responsibilities to individuals and to society:

Responsibility to Individual Persons—Information professionals should:

- strive to make information available to individuals who need it
- strive both to ensure accuracy and not to infringe upon privacy or confidentiality in providing information about individuals
- protect each information user's and provider's right to privacy and confidentiality
- respect an information provider's proprietary rights

Responsibility to Society—Information professionals should:

- serve the legitimate information needs of a large and complex society while at the same time being mindful of individuals' rights
- resist efforts to censor publications
- play active roles in educating society to understand and appreciate the importance of information promoting equal opportunity for access to information

ASIS's code is less obvious than the ACM's code and it gives ASIS members a more specific sense of direction.[5] For example, someone who

---

[3] For an exploration of differences between corporate and individual responsibility, see Ladd (1984).

[4] There is an interesting question whether professional codes are correctly characterized as codes of *ethics*. It is natural to regard ethical codes as embodying values that are autonomously chosen. But professional codes, with quasi-legal force, are not held out to professionals as value systems to be autonomously accepted or rejected; on the contrary, they typically provide for sanctions against those who fail to abide by them.

[5] See Oz (1992, 1993) for a careful analysis of the ethical codes of the four largest computer professional organizations in the United States: the Data Processing Management Association (DPMA, about 35,000 members), the Institute for Certification of Computer Professionals

follows this code would be encouraged to resist the attempts at censorship discussed in Part V. But some of the injunctions are rather vague. Career-minded professionals often find it difficult to make universal moral considerations paramount in the workplace.[6] They are more likely to prefer a utilitarian calculus, since they can more readily justify occasional risks or even harm to some groups for the gains of others. But this common professional preference for utilitarian approaches is usually casual and sometimes self-serving. A serious utilitarian analysis usually takes substantial thought and curiosity, since the analyst must carefully assess the consequences of his or her actions upon all parties that are affected by an action. This requires a willingness to carefully examine potential harm and pain, as well as benign effects. In fact, progressive information and computer professionals are arguing that all major computer applications should be subjected to informative social impact assessments before they are implemented on a large scale (Shneiderman, 1995; Gross and Harvey, 1996).

One interesting family of issues arises when commercial software products are oversold. It is easy for many computer specialists to blame an aggressive and fanciful marketing department or ad agency for exaggeration. But computer specialists who know the products best are often reluctant to help publicize their limitations or flaws. However, even principled computer specialists can have trouble ensuring that their companies act with integrity.

An illustrative example concerns a major computer manufacturer that provided a FORTRAN compiler on a particular machine series, pseudonymed here as SUMMA. This FORTRAN was contracted and advertised to meet ANSI FORTRAN standards. The programmer was assigned to maintain SUMMA FORTRAN by implementing enhancements, repairing errors, and issuing memos about new developments. Some of the error reports that she received from installations using SUMMA FORTRAN indicated subtle but important discrepancies between SUMMA FORTRAN and ANSI FORTRAN. FORTRAN programmers who believed that SUMMA FORTRAN was compatible with the ANSI standard wrote programs that did not appear to run properly. SUMMA's programmer prepared a variance report that she planned to send to all sites that had adopted SUMMA FORTRAN. Her supervisor objected and argued that the firm could not acknowledge any discrepancy between SUMMA FORTRAN and ANSI FORTRAN, since it was contractually obligated to provide an ANSI-compatible FORTRAN. She persisted, since she knew of the difficulties that the unexpected discrepancy between published specifications and

---

(ICCP, over 40,000 members), the Association for Computing Machinery (ACM, over 82,000 members), and the ITAA (ADAPSO) Recommended Code of Ethics for Professional Services Firms.

[6] See Jackall (1988) for some detailed accounts of the ways that managers often place loyalty to their superiors above ethical commitments to their clients, co-workers, and subordinates.

actual behavior of SUMMA FORTRAN was causing in the field. After her supervisor threatened to fire her, she relented, and did not publish a report of the discrepancy. But she was demoralized, and left the firm several months later (Kling, 1980).

The supervisor had little ethical justification for his actions; but he had the power of the paycheck to enforce his will. A strong support framework for a professional code of conduct might give some computer specialists, such as this programmer, a basis for insisting that their company's products be fairly advertised, or that they be developed and tested with high-quality tools and techniques. For example, this episode with SUMMA FORTRAN violates precepts 2.1 and 2.6 of the ACM's professional code. But the ACM provides no explicit support, such as counseling, legal advice, or employment help, for members who believe that some of their company's practices are unethical. And any attempt to develop a strong support framework that could strengthen professional standards, or provide protections for whistle-blowers, will be embroiled in bitter controversy.

Unfortunately, professional societies for information and computer professionals may be incapable of effectively regulating their members' professional behavior if major computer firms do not encourage ethical behavior by their employees. One of the distinctive features of the computing industry today is a relatively high level of technological innovation. Technologically innovative organizations often engender a form of smart, aggressive, and quick-acting management that McAuley refers to as "macho management."

> displays of management competence which is characterized by such features as speed of decision, adeptness at "fire-fighting," displays of ability to control situations and people impersonally, and ability to manage crisis irrespective of human considerations—to act purely "for" the organization. . . . Kotter and Haskett (1992:142) found in organizations in which "macho" competencies were embedded a culture of "some arrogance, insularity . . . supported by a value system that cares more about self-interest than about customers. . . ." (McAuley, 1994).

Intel's unwillingness to reveal computational flaws in the floating point performance of its highly advertised and popular Pentium chip in 1994 seems to illustrate the ethical risks of macho management.[7] According to management consultant Richard Pascale,

> Intel has no formal contention process but has a very contention-prone culture. It is driven by the personal style of Intel's president and CEO, Andy Grove, and that of his senior managers. Intel has a "gloves-off" way of

---

[7] See the discussion of the Pentium chip's floating point errors in the introductory chapter to Part VII.

interacting, which at times can be brutal, but it has helped Intel maintain its edge. It has a more direct and combative form of interchange than most companies would tolerate. (Pascale, 1993)

It is unlikely that such an aggressive culture would stimulate the kind of reflective approach that nurtures ethical sensitivity. And it would also be implausible for professional associations like the ACM or the Institute for Electrical and Electronic Engineers to discipline Intel in any significant way for virtually any business decision.

The Work of Ethical Analysis

Ethical analysis is quite different from simple moralizing. It is a skill with both intellectual and emotional dimensions. It rests, in part, upon compassion for other people and an ability to see situations from the viewpoints of diverse parties who are affected by professional action. It also requires some refined analytical abilities to carry out systematic universalist, utilitarian, or Rawlsian analyses.

Robert Collins, Keith Miller, Bethany Spielman, and Phillip Wherry (1994) articulated a Rawlsian approach to developing application software. The method requires that the analyst identify all the key participants, including technical staff, computer users, and so on. They also derived several principles from Rawls's theory of justice, including these three:

Least Advantaged. Don't increase harm to the least advantaged. Software should not increase the degree of harm to those parties already most vulnerable to that kind of harm because of their lack of knowledge about software. Here, degree (of harm) means (the) probability (of harm) × magnitude (of harm) and the harm can be financial or personal.

Risking Harm. Don't risk increasing harm in already risky environments. Software designed for a low-threat context should not be used in a higher-threat context.

Publicity Test. Use a publicity test for difficult cost-benefit trade-offs. Trade-offs between financial benefit to one party and personal (i.e, nonfinancial) harm to another party should be made on the basis of a cost-benefit ratio that, if made public, would not outrage most members of the public. That is, make only those decisions that you can defend with honor before an informed public (Collins, Miller, Spielman, and Wherry, 1994).

They applied these three principles in restructuring the design and operation of a hypothetical computerized system to support the operations in a hospital pharmacy. Despite the simplicity of their hypothetical case (in contrast with real hospital operations), the analysis takes over eight pages of text similar to that in this book. Part of their ethical analytical work involved examining the rights and responsibilities of different parties, and the repercussions of this ethical matrix for the effective design and operation of the computer system. Collins and his colleagues do not place all of this burden on the computer system designers. Medical staff who use the new information system as the hospital's managers also have substantial responsibilities in ensuring that the computer system is used effectively.

In many cases hospital information systems have been problematic in use, despite "good intentions" on the part of designers. For example, Ann Saetnan (1991) examined the use of a computer system that was supposed to make more efficient use of staff time and physical resources by automatically scheduling arrangements for operations in a Scandinavian hospital. She found that the scheduling algorithms did not effectively mesh with the work of doctors and nurses. After some frustration, the staff used the computer system simply to record schedules rather than to optimize them. Anthropologist Diane Forsythe (1992, 1993) examined the design practices of artificial intelligence experts who were designing diagnostic systems. She found that they interviewed doctors away from the workplaces where they actually diagnosed patients. As a consequence, they generalized from their actual practices in ways that led designers to conceptualize computer systems in unrealistic terms.

These systems design problems may seem to be misplaced in a discussion about ethical issues in professional work. But in Chapter E, "Confronting Ethical Issues of Systems Design in a Web of Social Relationships," computer scientist Ina Wagner shows us how ethical issues can permeate key system design choices in a hospital. Wagner describes a study of surgical scheduling in a hospital that was supposed to avoid the kinds of scheduling system failures reported by Saetnan. Wagner observed that surgeons found ways to give their own patients priority, while sacrificing the overall quality of care in the hospital. She also found that

> Inherent in the clinic's operation calendar is a specific scheme of priorities, some of which are made explicit, while others remain hidden. Some of these priorities mirror the internal hierarchy of specialties within the clinic, with heart surgery ranking before all others. A second set of priorities derives from surgeons' ambitions to perform as many complicated operations as possible. As each surgery offers unique chances for learning (and for producing research papers), this ambition varies with the surgeon's professional biography. As a result, admission of patients is highly selective. In addition to professional preferences, there are other priorities, such as those which apply to emergency patients. Also, care values matter, as in the case of old or particularly nervous patients or of patients who have to undergo a lengthy and sometimes painful preparation for surgery.

Wagner believes that a computerized scheduling system can promote more cooperation and effective use of resources in the hospital:

> By improving access to information (e.g., on the current surgery plan, unscheduled time openings, changes of surgery teams, and so forth) and by

increasing the transparency of decisions, a system offers facilities for bridging organizational segmentation. . . . a system can [also] help to increase the degree of inclusivity and participation in decisions by giving an operation manager the appropriate tools to communicate events and to implicate members of the clinic when deciding [upon] the necessary ad hoc changes.

She identified four key design issues that had significant ethical content:

- Whether a person's use of working time should be known to others or private.
- How to negotiate the competing explicit and hidden priorities that guide decisions about the location of operation time.
- How to deal with the working culture of the "surgical team"—the time (and knowledge) of the different occupational groups involved in this team are not equally valued.
- Whether to strengthen the "automatic scheduling" capacity or the "cooperation-support" component of the system.

Wagner was particularly interested in designing automated personal calendars that could facilitate the planning of surgical operations, and notes:

Such calendars seem useful in complex organizations in which the availability of persons at certain times is not always known to those who make the planning decisions. The project team envisioned designing a tool that gives individuals (assistant surgeons, anesthesiologists, and OP nurses) the opportunity to delete time, thereby indicating nonavailability for surgical operations. At present, nurses (all of them women) and anesthesiologists have to be available within their working hours independent of individual time preferences and instantaneous commitments. To them the option of indicating temporal preferences could be attractive. Surgeons (all of them men), on the other hand, have an interest in keeping parts of their individual time calendars private. This is in conflict with the need for temporal transparency of those who are responsible for the smooth running of the organization (in this case, women).

In the course of her study, she struggled with four ethical issues:

- Identifying the legitimate participants in an intercultural dialogue.
- Admitting and handling conflict.
- How to implement "egalitarian values" in a hierarchical organization.
- Thinking about the legitimacy of systems designers' own values and professional norms.

Collins and his colleagues were able to simply assume that all the hospital's staff would meet and talk openly with each other. Wagner, examining a real organization rather than a conveniently structured pedagogical case, faced a much more vexing struggle:

If, in our case, women's (nurses) voices are not heard, the resulting rules and regulations concerning "privacy versus transparency" will reflect a one-sided tendency to protect primarily the needs and interests of surgeons, thereby disregarding the organizational problems created when in an organization characterized by strong dependencies and frequent emergencies one group enjoys a high level of time autonomy (and privacy).

Wagner's observation about the relative invisibility of women's voices in systems' designs echoes Lucy Suchman's (Part IV, Chapter H) observations about the tendency of many male systems designers to undervalue the complexity and legitimacy of women's work. Wagner knew that an automatic scheduling system would be more congruent with the way that work and power were organized in the hospital. However, she also knew that implementing such a system would require all parties involved to ignore existing conflicts of perspectives and the ethical problems that she carefully identifies. Wagner's poignant study shows how ethical issues are inescapable in the design of important computerized information systems. She also shows us how Rawlsian scenarios that would bring together all participants to negotiate the nature of a just social order involves confronting organized power. Wagner's study powerfully melds the political and ethical dimensions of the work of systems designers in ordinary workplaces.

In "Power in Systems Design" (Chapter F), computer scientists Bo Dahlbom and Lars Mathiassen argue that systems developers are always located in a web of social relationships in which they exercise power on behalf of some parties and perhaps against other parties. Their article starts with the poignant example of a computer systems developer who was redesigning an information system to monitor telephone operators for a commercial client in another country. He went outside the boundaries of the system specification to add a screen symbol that would tell operators when they were being monitored. This developer seems to have done a kind of informal Rawlsian analysis, and tried to restructure the architecture of the monitoring system to be more just. However, his work was neutralized because the phone company managers disabled this feature after they learned about it. Wagner's study is anchored in her observations of surgical work in a particular hospital. In contrast, Dahlbom and Mathiassen generalize her argument to confront all information and computer professionals with questions about our practical willingness to acknowledge the politics of our employment, and to examine the ethical scope of our professional powers.

Ethical Action and Emerging Technologies

The pervasive computerization of various segments of society (education, military, business, communications) can have far-reaching impacts on people's lives—for good or ill—as can the decision *not* to computerize. Choosing to pursue one research project rather than another reflects a perception that the first is more valuable. Those who work in technical disciplines, although they may not directly decide which project is allocated to research and development groups, are at the very least instruments of decisions made by others. Deferring to managerial authority is itself a normative decision.

There is, of course, a common belief that technology is somehow neutral or "value free." Yet, it seems highly artificial to separate the existence of various technologies from the uses to which they will almost certainly be put. Technologies do vary in their range of likely applications. A high-speed CPU, like the PowerPC, might be used in virtually any computer application. In contrast, a navigational system for a submarine torpedo or a diagnostic aid for scanning X-rays has such specialized uses that much less speculation is required. Even so, as we have seen with Ina Wagner's study, a consequentialist analysis requires considerable attention to social context and the social arrangements for actually using computer systems. For example one cannot conclude that all medical technologies (or, in her case, surgical scheduling systems) are necessarily good because they are used to improve people's health.

In "Considering Privacy in the Development of Multimedia Communications" (Chapter G), computer scientist Andrew Clement examines the way that a community of computer researchers engages with the social consequences of their work on multimedia communication systems. Clement uses the term multimedia communication services (MMCS) or "media spaces" to refer to a diverse set of technologies that connect people with audio, visual, and/or computer links. You can imagine an office building complex with cameras, microphones, and speakers in every office, corridor, and meeting room, connected in such a way that anyone can see people or listen to conversations or talk with anyone anywhere else in the office complex. These hardware networks are driven by software that is organized to help people find specific people, have small group discussions between people who are in different locations, and so on. These "electronic fishbowls" can enhance some forms of communication within groups, but they can also tighten the forms of organizational surveillance.

Media spaces have been a topic of research at major industrial computer science laboratories, including Bellcore, Xerox's Palo Alto Research Center (PARC), Xerox's European center (EuroPARC), and the joint DEC-Ollivetti Cambridge Research Laboratory. These media spaces offer exciting technical challenges for talented systems designers who try to design them so that people can effectively navigate through them and effectively manage their communications. Clement also shows us how media spaces also open questions about the nature of designs that give people a sense of effective privacy—such as knowing who is watching you and when and being able to shut an electronic door as well as a physical door.

But the key focus of Clement's study goes well beyond the nature of communication and surveillance in these new media spaces. He is interested in the ways that information and computer scientists who develop social and technical architectures for these esoteric systems engage with the ethical issues that they raise. He observes considerable differences between different laboratories. The researchers at Xerox have been much more willing to characterize some of the privacy issues and treat them as topics of research than have Bellcore's researchers.

But Clement found two disturbing kinds of limitations in these engagements. First, the researchers have significant autonomy in their use of time, and significant abilities to redesign their media spaces so that they comfortably fit their work styles. They are a universe away from Ron Edens's Electronic Banking System, where a hawk-eyed supervisor discourages a squadron of regimented clerks from conversing and looking out the windows while they open envelopes and recording financial transactions (Horwitz, 1994; see Part IV, Chapter D). While researchers can design electronic doors and have the option to close them, or design "I see you, you see me" visual reciprocity, organizations that buy media space technologies may be more interested in tightening an electronic cage than in setting up electronic playpens. Clement noted that the researchers had trouble in systematically examining these alternative possibilities.

The second limitation is reflected in the eloquent comments of a research manager, who observes:

> We tend to have fairly short discussions in the hallway about the "dark side" [of computing implications], but quickly move past that to either the problem of the day or "We'll put this in and make it possible for that not to happen.". . .

> There is a sort of psychology of . . . innovation going on. . . . We are all very uncertain about whether we can even get the short-term prototypes built, much less if the whole vision is right. So constantly we are boosting one another, saying "Oh yes, we can do it" and "We are doing the right thing," even though we all know we don't know whether we are doing the right thing. . . . But it is necessary to sustain the activities. That certainly works against anyone who tried to dwell on "how awful it could be" and "this could be the end of human freedom." [They] would not be welcome for very long, if they kept that up. No one would be able to get anything done, because we would all be so bummed out. . . . That is the state of affairs, whether it is right or wrong. That is how it works.

In some of the laboratories, the researchers seem to be disarmingly uninterested in "the dark side" of their media spaces, and discuss them as issues that other organizations will have to address if they adopt these media space technologies. Clement notes,

> All of these various factors . . . tend to distance researchers and developers from active consideration of how the technologies may be used harmfully. Indeed, much of the direct experience with them will suggest that problems are relatively minor and can be dealt with. But it is one thing to experience

personal discomfort and negotiate social/technical modifications with colleagues. It is quite another to take principled and potentially awkward stands on behalf of future users whose legitimate needs are vaguely defined and subject to a broad range of interpretations.

The unwillingness of leading industrial researchers to discuss these issues even within the technical communities can be awesome. Some of the computer scientists at Xerox PARC who were interested in discussing these issues in the technical community helped organize a conference-wide panel session on "active badges" (discussed in Clement's article) at the 1992 Conference on Computer-Supported Cooperative Work. This scientific meeting attracts about 1000 computer and social scientists who study groupware, media spaces, and similar technologies. One of the panel participants was the director of the DEC-Ollivetti Cambridge Research Laboratory. He simply refused to discuss any possible negative effects that could result from active badges, despite some direct questions about them from computer scientists in the audience. In contrast, other panel members were willing to examine diverse aspects of the use of active badges (see Kling, 1993).

Overall the social system of industrial development in the United States does not encourage researchers and advanced developers to engage with the possible risks of their technologies that they can displace onto the shoulders of others, such as organizations that purchase systems based on their innovations. Clement closes his article asking for suggestions to help reform the social system of research so that social harms can be more readily anticipated and perhaps alleviated in technological designs. It would be interesting to project the use of these media spaces into the workplaces described by Marx and Horwitz in Part IV (Chapters C and D, respectively).

In Chapter H, "New Principles for Engineering Ethics," Edward Wenk encourages scientists and engineers to be especially attentive to the risks of powerful new technologies. Wenk, who has written several books about environmental hazards, was appointed as the first science and technology advisor to Congress in 1959, and served on the science policy staffs of United States Presidents Kennedy, Johnson, and Nixon. His far-reaching article identifies three broad ethical dilemmas for engineers and scientists: managing risk, managing institutions, and managing the future. He notes that the risks of large-scale technological hazards have increased in this century. "Engineering enthusiasm and organizational momentum toward meeting narrow technical objectives overwhelmed any tendency to look sideways or ahead before leaping." The social systems for the design, development, and deployment of new technologies do not seem adequate to effectively anticipate or mitigate major hazards, especially environmental damage. Wenk concludes his paper with two sets of principles, one for the social management of technology and the other as an ethical basis for a socially responsible engineering.

Arguments like Wenk's are not new, but they are not taken seriously by technologists and industrialists, including the computer industry (see also, Shneiderman, 1995; Gross and Harvey, 1996). Are these kinds of arguments for socially responsible engineering fundamentally flawed? Or is industry structured in ways that prevent it from effectively reforming itself?

Further Studies of Professional Ethics

Of necessity, much of the material presented in this part relies on an intuitive understanding of ethical concepts. Although most readers may feel that they know what is right and what is wrong, few will have worked out a systematic ethical theory. What is the basis of ethical principles— what "society says," the Christian Bible, the Koran, Confucian teaching, or one's intuitive sense of justice? Are ethical rules absolute? If not, what kinds of conditions justify murder, theft, or deception? When there are ethical conflicts between what is good for your family and what is good for your clients, how do you resolve them? People who think that they can readily agree that theft and deception are (usually) "wrong," may nevertheless disagree in answering all of the preceding questions. The tough cases are those where there are real ethical conflicts, and there our intuitive ideas are often weakest in guiding us to deal with ethical conflicts in a coherent way.

Anyone seriously concerned about moral issues is urged to consult the philosophical literature. For an entry point see Rachels (1986), Bayles and Henley (1983), or Johnson (1984); additional suggestions are listed under Further Reading. Although the philosophical tradition does not provide ready-made answers, it does provide careful analysis and clarification of key moral theories, and often illuminates the application of theories to everyday moral judgments. Studying this literature can help deepen one's understanding of what is really at stake in various ethical dilemmas. It can also help develop a finer appreciation of what constitutes a moral point of view, and hone some analytical tools that are helpful for evaluating alternative courses of action.

Sources

Parker, Donn B., Susan Swope, Bruce N. Baker, and Eric A. Weiss (1990). "All in a Day's Work: Nine Provocative Examples in the Practice of Computing Professionals" (excerpted and adapted from) "Self-assessment procedure XXII.: Ethical Values in Computer Professions." *Communications of the ACM* (33)11 (November), 110–133.

Anderson, Ronald, Deborah G. Johnson, Donald Gotterbarn, and Judith Perolle (1993). "Codes for Professional Ethics" from "Using the New ACM Code of Ethics in Decision Making." *CACM*, 36(2)(February), 98–108.

Association of Computing Machinery (1993). "ACM Code of Ethics and Professional Conduct." *Communications of the ACM,* 36(2)(February), 99–103.

Wagner, Ina (1993). "Confronting Ethical Issues of Systems Design in a Web of Social Relationships," was published as "A Web of Fuzzy Problems: Confronting the Ethical Issues." *Communications of the ACM,* 36(4)(June), 94–01.

Dahlbom, Bo, and Lars Mathiassen (1993). "Power in Systems Design." Excerpts from Chapter 9 of *Computers in Context.* Blackwell, Cambridge, MA.

Clement, Andrew (1994). "Considering Privacy in the Development of Multi-Media Communications." *Computer Supported Cooperative Work,* 2, 67–88.

Wenk, Jr., Edward (1988). "New Principles for Engineering Ethics," was published as "Roots of Ethics, Wings of Foresight." *BENT of Tau Beta Pi,* 18–23.

References

"ACM Code of Professional Conduct" (1972). (Reprinted in Charles Dunlop and Rob Kling (eds.), *Computerization and Controversy* (1991). Academic Press, San Diego.

Armstrong, Larry (1994). "Captain Crunch, Pick Up the White Courtesy Phone." 1994 Def Con computer hacker convention in Las Vegas, NV. *Business Week,* 3383(August 1), 34.

Barus, Carl (1987). "Military Influence on the Electrical Engineering Curriculum Since World War II." *IEEE Technology and Society Magazine,* 6(2)(June), 3–9. [Reprinted in Charles Dunlop and Rob Kling (eds.) (1991). *Computerization and Controversy: Value Conflicts and Social Choices.* Academic Press, San Diego.]

Bayles, Michael D., and Kenneth Henley (eds.) (1983). *Right Conduct: Theories and Applications.* Random House, New York.

Collins, W. Robert, Keith W. Miller, Bethany J. Spielman, and Philip Wherry (1994). "How Good Is Good Enough? An Ethical Analysis of Software Construction and Use." *Communications of the ACM,* 37(1)1(January), 81–91.

Cutler, W. Gale (1992). "What Future Engineers and Scientists Learn About Ethics." *Research-Technology Management,* 35(6)(November/December), 39–48.

Forsythe, Diane (1992). "Blaming the User in Medical Informatics: the Cultural Nature of Scientific Practice." *Knowledge and Society: The Anthropology of Science and Technology,* 9, 95–111.

Forsythe, Diane (1993). "The Construction of Work in Artificial Intelligence." *Science, Technology, & Human Values,* 18(4)(Autumn), 460–479.

Friedman, Batya, and Peter H. Kahn, Jr. (1992). "Human Agency and Responsible Computing: Implications for Computer System Design." *Journal of Systems and Software,* 17(1)(Jan), 7–14.

Gross, Ben, and Francois Harvey (1996, in press). "Forum on the 'Durango Declarations'." *The Information Society,* 12(1).

Hafner, Katie, and John Markoff (1991). *Cyberpunk: Outlaws and Hackers on the Computer Frontier.* Simon and Schuster, New York.

Hawk, Stephen R. (1994). "The Effects of Computerized Performance Monitoring: An Ethical Perspective." *Journal of Business Ethics,* 13(12)(December), 949–957.

Helms, Marilyn M., and Betty A. Hutchins (1992). "Poor Quality Products: Is Their Production Unethical?" *Management Decision,* 30(5), 35–46.

Hosmer, L. T. (1990). *The Ethics of Management* (second ed.). Richard D. Irwin, Homewood, IL.

Jackall, Robert (1988). *Moral Mazes: The World of Corporate Managers.* Oxford University Press, New York.

Johnson, Oliver (1984). *Ethics* (fifth ed.). Holt, Rinehart, Winston, New York.

Kling, Rob (1980). "Computer Abuse and Computer Crime as Organizational Activities." *Computer/Law Journal,* 2(2)(Spring), 403–427. Reprinted in *Computers and Society,* 12(1982), 12–24. [Reprinted in Charles Dunlop and Rob Kling, (eds.) (1991). *Computerization and Controversy: Value Conflicts and Social Choices.* Academic Press, San Diego.]

Kling, Rob (1991). "When Organizations are Perpetrators," in Charles Dunlop and Rob Kling (eds.). *Computerization and Controversy: Value Conflicts and Social Choices.* Academic Press, San Diego.

Kling, Rob (1993). "Fair Information Practices with Computer Supported Cooperative Work." *SIGOIS Bulletin* (July), 28–31.

Kotter, John, and James L. Haskett (1992). *Corporate Culture and Performance.* Free Press, New York.

Ladd, John (1984). "Corporate Mythology and Individual Responsibility." *The International Journal of Applied Philosophy,* 2(1)(Spring), 1–21.

McAuley, John (1994). "Exploring Issues in Culture and Competence." *Human Relations,* 47(4)(April), 417–430.

Nissenbaum, Helen (1994). "Computing and Accountability." *Communications of the ACM,* 37(1)(January), 72–80.

Oz, Effy (1992). "Ethical Standards for Information Systems Professionals: A Case for a Unified Code." *MIS Quarterly,* 16(4)(December), 423–433.

Oz, Effy (1993). "Ethical Standards for Computer Professionals: A Comparative Analysis of Four Major Codes." *Journal of Business Ethics,* 12(9)(September), 709–726.

Pascale, Richard T. (1993). "The Benefit of A Clash of Opinions." *Personnel Management,* 25(10)(October), 38–41.

Quittner, Josh (1994). "The War Between alt.tasteless and rec.pets.cats." *Wired,* 2.05 (May), 46–53.

Rachels, James (1986). *The Elements of Moral Philosophy.* Random House, New York.

Rawls, John A. (1971). *A Theory of Justice.* Harvard University Press, Cambridge, MA.

Saetnan, Ann Rudinow (1991). "Rigid Politics and Technological Flexibility: The Anatomy of a Failed Hospital Innovation." *Science, Technology, & Human Values,* 16(4), 419–447.

Shneiderman, Ben (1995). "The Durango Declaration: A Draft of Societal Concerns." *Communications of the ACM,* 38(10), 13.

Further Reading

The CPSR Newsletter. Published by Computer Scientists for Social Responsibility, P.O. Box 717, Palo Alto, California 94301.

Denning, Dorothy, and Herbert Lin (1994). *Rights and Responsibilities of Participants in Networked Communities.* National Academy Press, Washington, D.C.

Ermann, M. David, and Richard J. Lundman (eds.) (1992). *Corporate and Governmental Deviance: Problems of Organizational Behavior in Contemporary Society* (4th ed.). Oxford University Press, New York.

Forester, Tom, and Perry Morrison (1994). *Computer Ethics: Cautionary Tales and Ethical Dilemmas in Computing* (2nd ed.). MIT Press, Cambridge, MA.

Goldberg, Michael (ed.) (1993). *Against the Grain: New Approaches to Professional Ethics.* Trinity Press International, Valley Forge, PA.

Johnson, Deborah G. (1991). *Ethical Issues in Engineering.* Prentice Hall, Englewood Cliffs, NJ.

Johnson, Deborah G. (1994). *Computer Ethics.* (2nd ed.). Prentice-Hall, Englewood Cliffs, NJ.

Ladd, John (1989). "Computers and Moral Responsibility: A Framework for Ethical Analysis." Chapter 11 of Carol Gould (ed.), *The Information Web: Ethical and Social Implications of Computer Networking,* pp. 207–227. Westview Press, Boulder, CO. [Reprinted in Charles Dunlop and Rob Kling (eds.) (1991). *Computerization and Controversy: Value Conflicts and Social Choices.* Academic Press, San Diego.]

MacNiven, Don (ed.) (1990). *Moral Expertise: Studies in Practical and Professional Ethics.* Routledge, New York.

Martin, Mike W. and Roland Schinzinger. (1989). *Ethics in Engineering.* (2nd Edition) New York: McGraw-Hill.

McDowell, Banks (1991). *Ethical Conduct and the Professional's Dilemma: Choosing Between Service and Success.* Quorum Books, New York.

Melman, Seymour (1985). *The Permanent War Economy: American Capitalism in Decline.* Revised and updated. Simon & Schuster, New York.

Oz, Effy (1994). "When Professional Standards Are Lax: The CONFIRM Failure and Its Lessons." *Communications of the ACM,* 37(10)(October), 29–36.

Parnas, David Lorge (1987). "SDI: A Violation of Professional Responsibility." *Abacus,* 4(2), 46–52.

Pojman, Louis P. (1989). *Ethical Theory.* Wadsworth Publishing Company, Belmont, CA.

Teich, Albert (ed.) (1990). *Technology and the Future,* 5th ed. St. Martin's Press, New York.

Weizenbaum, Joseph (1976). *Computer Power and Human Reason.* W. H. Freeman and Company, San Francisco. [Reprinted in Charles Dunlop and Rob Kling (eds.) (1991). *Computerization and Controversy: Value Conflicts and Social Choices,* Chapter 10. Academic Press, San Diego.]

Winner, Langdon (1996, in press). "Who Will We Be in Cyberspace?" *The Information Society* 12(1).

Winograd, Terry A. (1987). "Strategic Computing Research and the Universities." Stanford University, Department of Computer Science, Report No. STAN-CS-87-1160(March), 17. [Reprinted in Charles Dunlop and Rob Kling (eds.) (1991). *Computerization and Controversy: Value Conflicts and Social Choices.* Academic Press, San Diego.]

P·A·R·T · VIII

B

All in a Day's Work: Nine Provocative Examples in the Practice of Computing Professionals*

Donn B. Parker • Susan Swope
Bruce N. Baker • Eric A. Weiss

Software Developer: Relying on Questionable Inputs

A software professional was assigned the task of developing software to control a particular unit of a large system. Preliminary analysis indicated that the work was well within the state of the art, and no difficulties were anticipated with the immediate task.

To function properly, or to function at all, however, the software to be developed required inputs from other units in the system. Someone gave the professional an article by an eminent software specialist that convinced him that the inputs from other units could not be trusted. Thus, neither the software he was designing nor the unit his company was providing could correctly accomplish their task. The professional showed the article to his supervisor and explained its significance. The supervisor's response was, "That's not our problem; let's just be sure that our system functions properly." The software professional continued to work on the project.

Which ethical issues are central in this case? Was the software professional's action ethical or ethically compromised? Was the supervisor's attitude ethical or ethically compromised? Which general principles apply?

Software Company: Ignoring Voting Machine Malfunctions

Company XYZ has developed the software for a computerized voting machine. Company ABC, which manufactured the machine, has persuaded several cities and states to purchase it; on the strength of these orders, ABC is planning a major purchase from XYZ. XYZ software engineer Smith is visiting ABC one day and learns that problems in the construction of the machine mean that one in ten is likely to miscount soon after installation. Smith reports this to her superior, who informs her that that is ABC's problem. Smith does nothing further.

Which ethical issues are central in this case? Was Smith's action ethical or ethically compromised? Was her superior's action ethical or ethically compromised? Which general principles apply?

Computer Hacker ("Breaker"): Accessing Commercial Computer Services

Without malicious intent, a computer systems programmer was scanning telephone numbers with his microcomputer and identifying those numbers that responded with a computer tone. He accessed one of these computers, using a telephone number he had acquired. Without entering any identification, he received a response welcoming him to an expensive and exclusive financial advisory service offered by a large bank. He was offered, free of charge, a sample use of some of the services if he would give his name and address. He provided someone else's name and address and used the free promotional services. This stimulated his interest in the services that bank charged for and gave him sufficient knowledge of access protocol to attempt to use the services without authorization. He gained access to and examined the menus of services offered and instructions for use. However, he did not use the services. By examining the logging audit file and checking with the impersonated customer, bank officials identified the computer programmer and claimed that he had used their services without authorization.

Which ethical issues are central in this case? Were the programmer's actions ethical or ethically compromised? Consider the following actions:

- Scanning telephone numbers for computer tone.
- Accessing a computer system after being "invited" to do so.
- Using someone else's name and address.

---

*This article is excerpted and adapted from "Self-Assessment Procedure XXII: Ethical Values in Computer Professions." *Communications of the ACM*, 33(11)(November, 1990), pp. 110–132. Reprinted with permission of the Association for Computing Machinery.

Consider the ethical stance in the bank's contention that the programmer had used its services without authorization. Which general principles apply?

Programmer: Producing New Software Built on an Existing Program

Searching for new product ideas, an independent commercial programmer purchased a highly popular copyrighted software package and studied it thoroughly. He concluded that he could produce a new package that would be faster, have greater capacity, and offer additional features. He also concluded that the market would be users of the commercial package that he had studied; his new product would replace the older one. The programmer realized that in some respects he could not improve the existing product and that compatibility between his product and the existing one would attract users and minimize the transition to his new product.

The programmer went ahead and developed the new product, meeting the higher performance and new feature capability that he had envisioned. The keyboard codes and screen formats (except for the additional features) for the new product were the same as those for the existing product. The computer program, however, was different and independently produced. The new manual was also entirely different from the existing product manual in content and style. The programmer gave his product a new name but advertised the value of its compatibility with the existing product.

The new product was highly successful. The company that produced the existing product, however, complained that the programmer had acted unethically in producing the new product. Although the company threatened criminal and civil and legal action, it never followed through with litigation.

Which ethical issues are central in this case? Were the actions of the programmer ethical or ethically compromised? Which general principles apply?

Programmer: Developing Marketing Profiles from Public Information

An enterprising programmer used publicly available information stored in a variety of places or available by purchase from the Department of Motor Vehicles, mail order firms, and other sources to compile "profiles" of people (shopping habits, likely income level, whether the family was likely to have children, etc.). He sold the profiles to companies interested in marketing specialized products to niche markets. Some of his profiles were inaccurate, and the families received a large volume of unsolicited, irrelevant mail and telephone solicitations. They did not know why this increase in their junk mail and calls had occurred and found it annoying and bothersome. However, most of the profiles were accurate, and many families benefited from receiving the sales materials.

Which ethical issues are central in this case? Were the programmer's actions ethical or ethically compromised? Which general principles apply?

Instructor: Using Students as Subjects of Experiments

An instructor of a logic course decided to test a computer-assisted instruction (CAI) system under development. The large class was divided randomly into two groups. The instructor arranged a controlled experiment in which one group was taught in the traditional manner with a textbook, lectures, and tests, but without access to CAI. The other group used the same textbook, lectures, and tests, and in addition was required to use CAI and specially tailored assignments in a computer lab.

By the middle of the term, the instructor realized that the students in the experimental group who had access to CAI were doing much better than the students in the control group. Some students in the control group sensed this difference and complained that, although they paid the same tuition, they were being denied an educational opportunity offered to others. These students insisted that the instructor discontinue the experiment and allow them to use the CAI package for the remainder of the term. The instructor refused the students' request on the grounds that ending the experiment prematurely would vitiate the results of the experiment. The instructor pointed out that only by chance were they in the control group and, because free inquiry and research are the nature of the academic world, students should take part willingly in such experiments for the sake of advancing knowledge. At the end of the term, the grades in the experimental groups were significantly higher than the grades in the control group.

Which ethical issues are central in this case? Were the instructor's actions ethical or ethically compromised? Consider the following actions:

- Using students as subjects of experiments.
- Refusing students' requests to discontinue the experiment.

Which general principles apply?

President of Software Development Company: Marketing a Software Product Known to Have Bugs

A software development company has just produced a new software package that incorporates the new tax laws and figures taxes for both individuals and small businesses. The president of the company knows that the program probably has a number of bugs. He also believes that the first firm to put this kind of software on the market is likely to capture the largest market share. The company widely advertises the program. When the company actually ships a disk, it includes a disclaimer of responsibility for errors resulting from use of the program. The company expects it will receive a certain number of complaints, queries, and suggestions for modification. The company plans to use these to make changes and eventually issue updated, improved, and debugged versions. The president argues that this is general industry policy and that anyone who buys version 1.0 of a program knows this and will take proper precautions. Because of bugs, a number of users filed incorrect tax returns and were penalized by the IRS.

Which ethical issues are central in this case? Were the president's actions ethical or ethically compromised? Consider the following actions:

- marketing a product with a disclaimer of responsibility and arguing that this action is general industry policy.

Which general principles apply?

Manager: Monitoring Electronic Mail

The information security manager in a large company was also the access control administrator of a large electronic mail system operated for company business among its employees. The security manager routinely monitored the contents of electronic correspondence among employees. He discovered that a number of employees were using the system for personal purposes; the correspondence included love letters, disagreements between married partners, plans for homosexual relations, and a football betting pool. The security manager routinely informed the human resources department director and the corporate security officer about these communications and gave them printed listings of them. In some cases, managers punished employees on the basis of the content of the electronic mail messages. Employees objected to the monitoring of their electronic mail, claiming that they had the same right of privacy as they had using the company's telephone system or internal paper interoffice mail system.

Which ethical issues are central in this case? Were the information security manager's, the employees', and top management's actions ethical or ethically compromised? Which general principles apply?

Employer: Monitoring an Information Worker's Computer Usage

An information worker in a large company performed her assignments on a workstation connected to the company's mainframe system. The company had a policy of allowing employees to use the computer services for personal purposes as long as they had the explicit approval of management. The woman had such approval to use the system for the extracurricular recreational activities of the employees in her department.

The company suspected a rising amount of employee unrest because of its potential acquisition by another company. Management had the security department monitor all computer service activities of the information worker. Memos, letters, e-mail messages, bulletin board notices, collections and expenditures of money, and budgets were all carefully scrutinized for evidence of employee unrest. In addition, the security department prepared reports detailing the information worker's use of the computer services—both her regular work and her employee recreation work. These reports were read and analyzed by a wide range of company managers and were stored indefinitely in company vital records facilities. All of this took place unknown to the information worker.

Which ethical issues are central in this case? Were the actions ethical or ethically compromised? Consider the following actions:

- Allowing employees to use computer services for approved personal purposes.
- Directing security departments to monitor computer services activities.

Which general principles apply?

P·A·R·T · VIII

C

Codes of Professional Ethics[*]

Ronald E. Anderson • Deborah G. Johnson
Donald Gotterbarn • Judith Perrolle

Historically, professional associations have viewed codes of ethics as mechanisms to establish their status as a profession or as a means to regulate their membership and thereby convince the public that they deserve to be self-regulating. Self-regulation depends on ways to deter unethical behavior of the members, and a code, combined with an ethics review board, was seen as the solution. Codes of ethics have tended to list possible violations and threaten sanctions for such violations. ACM's first code, the Code of Professional Conduct, was adopted in 1972 and followed this model. The latest ACM code, the Code of Ethics and Professional Conduct, was adopted in 1992 and takes a new direction.

ACM and many other societies have had difficulties implementing an ethics review system and came to realize that self-regulation depends mostly on the consensus and commitment of its members to ethical behavior. Now the most important rationale for a code of ethics is an embodiment of a set of commitments of that association's members. Sometimes these commitments are expressed as rules and sometimes as ideals, but the essential social function is to clarify and formally state those ethical requirements that are important to the group as a professional association. The new ACM Code of Ethics and Professional Conduct follows this philosophy.

Recent codes of ethics emphasize socialization or education rather than enforced compliance. A code can work toward the collective good even though it may be a mere distillation of collective experience and reflection.

A major benefit of an educationally oriented code is its contribution to the group by clarifying the professionals' responsibility to society.

A code of ethics holds the profession accountable to the public. This tends to yield a major payoff in terms of public trust. In Frankel's words, "To the extent that a code confers benefits on clients, it will help persuade the public that professionals are deserving of its confidence and respect, and of increased social and economic rewards" (Frankel, 1989).

The final and most important function of a code of ethics is its role as an aid to individual decision making. In the interest of facilitating better ethical decision making, we have developed a set of nine classes that describe situations calling for ethical decision making. These cases address in turn the topics of intellectual property, privacy, confidentiality, professional quality, fairness or discrimination, liability, software risks, conflicts of interest, and unauthorized access to computer systems.

Reference

Frankel, M.S. (1989). "Professional Codes: Why, How, and with What Impact?" *J. Bus. Ethics*, 8 (2 and 3), 109–116.

---

*This article is taken from "Using the New ACM Code of Ethics in Decision Making." *Communications of the ACM*, 36(2) (February 1993), pp. 98–108. Reprinted with permission of the Association for Computing Machinery.

P·A·R·T · VIII

D

Code of Ethics and Professional Conduct (1992)*

Association for Computing Machinery

Preamble. **Commitment to ethical professional conduct is expected of every member (voting members, associate members, and student members) of the Association for Computing Machinery (ACM).**

This Code, consisting of 24 imperatives formulated as statements of personal responsibility, identifies the elements of such a commitment. It contains many, but not all, issues professionals are likely to face. Section 1 outlines fundamental ethical considerations, while Section 2 addresses additional, more specific considerations of professional conduct. Statements in Section 3 pertain more specifically to individuals who have a leadership role, whether in the workplace or in a volunteer capacity such as with organizations like ACM. Principles involving compliance with this Code are given in Section 4.

The Code shall be supplemented by a set of Guidelines, which provide explanation to assist members in dealing with the various issues contained in the Code. It is expected that the Guidelines will be changed more frequently than the Code.

The Code and its supplemented Guidelines are intended to serve as a basis for ethical decision making in the conduct of professional work. Secondarily, they may serve as a basis for judging the merit of a formal complaint pertaining to violation of professional ethical standards. It should be noted that although computing is not mentioned in the imperatives of Section 1, the Code is concerned with how these fundamental imperatives apply to one's conduct as a computing professional. These

•

imperatives are expressed in a general form to emphasize that ethical principles that apply to computer ethics are derived from more general ethical principles.

It is understood that some words and phrases in a code of ethics are subject to varying interpretations, and that any ethical principle may conflict with other ethical principles in specific situations. Questions related to ethical conflicts can best be answered by thoughtful consideration of fundamental principles, rather than reliance on detailed regulations.

1. GENERAL MORAL IMPERATIVES

As an ACM member I will . . .

1.1 Contribute to society and human well-being.
1.2 Avoid harm to others.
1.3 Be honest and trustworthy.
1.4 Be fair and take action not to discriminate.
1.5 Honor property rights including copyrights and patents.
1.6 Give proper credit for intellectual property.
1.7 Respect the privacy of others.
1.8 Honor confidentiality.

2. MORE SPECIFIC PROFESSIONAL RESPONSIBILITIES

As an ACM computing professional I will . . .

2.1 Strive to achieve the highest quality, effectiveness, and dignity in both the process and products of professional work.
2.2 Acquire and maintain professional competence.
2.3 Know and respect existing laws pertaining to professional work.
2.4 Accept and provide appropriate professional review.
2.5 Give comprehensive and thorough evaluations of computer systems and their impacts, including analysis of possible risks.
2.6 Honor contracts, agreements, and assigned responsibilities.
2.7 Improve public understanding of computing and its consequences.
2.8 Access computing and communication resources only when authorized to do so.

---

*This article appeared in *Communications of the ACM,* 36(2) (February 1993), pp. 99–103. Reprinted with permission of the Association for Computing Machinery.

3. ORGANIZATIONAL LEADERSHIP IMPERATIVES

As an ACM member and an organizational leader, I will . . .

3.1 Articulate social responsibilities of members of an organizational unit and encourage full acceptance of those responsibilities.

3.2 Manage personnel and resources to design and build information systems that enhance the quality of working life.

3.3 Acknowledge and support proper and authorized uses of an organization's computing and communication resources.

3.4 Ensure that users and those who will be affected by a system have their needs clearly articulated during the assessment and design of requirements; later the system must be validated to meet requirements.

3.5 Articulate and support policies that protect the dignity of users and others affected by a computing system.

3.6 Create opportunities for members of the organization to learn the principles and limitations of computer systems.

4. COMPLIANCE WITH THE CODE

As an ACM member, I will . . .

4.1 Uphold and promote the principles of this Code.

4.2 Treat violations of this code as inconsistent with membership in the ACM.

GUIDELINES

1. GENERAL MORAL IMPERATIVES

As an ACM member I will . . .

1.1 Contribute to society and human well-being.

This principle concerning the quality of life of all people affirms an obligation to protect fundamental human rights and to respect the diversity of all cultures. An essential aim of computing professionals is to minimize negative consequences of computing systems, including threats to health and safety. When designing or implementing systems, computing professionals must attempt to ensure that the products of their efforts will be used in socially responsible ways, will meet social needs, and will avoid harmful effects to health and welfare.

In addition to a safe social environment, human well-being includes a safe natural environment. Therefore, computing professionals who design and develop systems must be alert to, and make others aware of, any potential damage to the local or global environment.

1.2 Avoid harm to others.

"Harm" means injury or negative consequences, such as undesirable loss of information, loss of property, property damage, or unwanted environmental impacts. This principle prohibits use of computing technology in ways that result in harm to any of the following: users, the general public, employees, employers. Harmful actions include intentional destruction or modification of files and programs leading to serious loss of resources or unnecessary expenditure of human resources such as the time and effort required to purge systems of "computer viruses."

Well-intended actions, including those that accomplish assigned duties, may lead to harm unexpectedly. In such an event the responsible person or persons are obligated to undo or mitigate the negative consequences as much as possible. One way to avoid unintentional harm is to carefully consider potential impacts on all those affected by decisions made during design and implementation.

To minimize the possibility of indirectly harming others, computing professionals must minimize malfunctions by following generally accepted standards for system design and testing. Furthermore, it is often necessary to assess the social consequences of systems to project the likelihood of any serious harm to others. If system features are misrepresented to users, co-workers, or supervisors, the individual computing professional is responsible for any resulting injury.

In the work environment the computing professional has the additional obligation to report any signs of system dangers that might result in serious personal or social damage. If one's superiors do not act to curtail or mitigate such dangers, it may be necessary to "blow the whistle" to help correct the problem or reduce the risk. However, capricious or misguided reporting of violations can, itself, be harmful. Before reporting violations, all relevant aspects of the incident must be thoroughly assessed. In particular, the assessment of risk and responsibility must be credible. It is suggested that advice be sought from other computing professionals. See principle 2.5 regarding thorough evaluations.

1.3 Be honest and trustworthy.

Honesty is an essential component of trust. Without trust an organization cannot function effectively. The honest computing professional will not make deliberately false or deceptive claims about a system or system design, but will instead provide full disclosure of all pertinent system limitations and problems. A computer professional has a duty to be honest about his or her own qualifications, and about any circumstances that might lead to conflicts of interest.

Membership in volunteer organizations such as ACM may at times place individuals in situations where their statements or actions could be interpreted as carrying the "weight" of a larger group of professionals. An ACM member will exercise care to not misrepresent ACM or positions and policies of ACM or any ACM units.

1.4 Be fair and take action not to discriminate.

The values of equality, tolerance, respect for others, and the principles of equal justice govern this imperative. Discrimination on the basis of race, sex, religion, age, disability, national origin, or other such factors is an explicit violation of ACM policy and will not be tolerated.

Inequities between different groups of people may result from the use or misuse of information and technology. In a fair society, all individuals would have equal opportunity to participate in, or benefit from, the use of computer resources regardless of race, sex, religion, age, disability, national origin, or other such similar factors. However, these ideals do not justify unauthorized use of computer resources nor do they provide an adequate basis for violation of any other ethical imperatives of this code.

1.5 Honor property rights including copyrights and patents.

Violation of copyrights, patents, trade secrets, and the terms of license agreements is prohibited by law in most circumstances. Even when software is not so protected, such violations are contrary to professional behavior. Copies of software should be made only with proper authorization. Unauthorized duplication of materials must not be condoned.

1.6 Give proper credit for intellectual property.

Computing professionals are obligated to protect the integrity of intellectual property. Specifically, one must not take credit for other's ideas or work, even in cases where the work has not been explicitly protected by copyright, patent, etc.

1.7 Respect the privacy of others.

Computing and communication technology enables the collection and exchange of personal information on a scale unprecedented in the history of civilization. Thus there is increased potential for violating the privacy of individuals and groups. It is the responsibility of professionals to maintain the privacy and integrity of data describing individuals. This includes taking precautions to ensure the accuracy of data, as well as protecting it from unauthorized access or accidental disclosure to inappropriate individuals. Furthermore, procedures must be established to allow individuals to review their records and correct inaccuracies.

This imperative implies that only the necessary amount of personal information be collected in a system, that retention and disposal periods for that information be clearly defined and enforced, and that personal information gathered for a specific purpose not be used for other purposes without consent of the individual(s). These principles apply to electronic communications, including electronic mail, and prohibit procedures that capture or monitor electronic user data, including messages, without the permission of users or bona fide authorization related to system operation and maintenance. User data observed during the normal duties of system operation and maintenance must be treated with strictest confidentiality, except in cases where it is evidence for the violation of law, organizational regulations, or this Code. In these cases, the nature or contents of that information must be disclosed only to proper authorities (see 1.9).

1.8 Honor confidentiality.

The principle of honesty extends to issues of confidentiality of information whenever one has made an explicit promise to honor confidentiality or, implicitly, when private information not directly related to the performance of one's duties becomes available. The ethical concern is to respect all obligations of confidentiality to employers, clients, and users unless discharged from such obligations by requirements of the law or other principles of this Code.

2. MORE SPECIFIC PROFESSIONAL RESPONSIBILITIES

As an ACM computing professional I will . . .

2.1 Strive to achieve the highest quality, effectiveness, and dignity in both the process and products of professional work.

Excellence is perhaps the most important obligation of a professional. The computing professional must strive to achieve quality and to be cognizant of the serious negative consequences that may result from poor quality in a system.

2.2 Acquire and maintain professional competence.

Excellence depends on individuals who take responsibility for acquiring and maintaining professional competence. A professional must participate in setting standards for appropriate levels of competence, and strive to achieve those standards. Upgrading technical knowledge and competence can be achieved in several ways: doing independent study; attending seminars, conferences, or courses; and being involved in professional organizations.

2.3 Know and respect existing laws pertaining to professional work.

ACM members must obey existing local, state, province, national, and international laws unless there is a compelling ethical basis not to do so. Policies and procedures of the organizations in which one participates must also be obeyed. But compliance must be balanced with the recognition that sometimes existing laws and rules may be immoral or inappropriate and, therefore, must be challenged. Violation of a law or regulation may be ethical when that law or rule has inadequate moral basis or when it conflicts with another law judged to be more important. If one decides to violate a law or rule because it is viewed as unethical, or for any other reason, one must fully accept responsibility for one's actions and for the consequences.

2.4 Accept and provide appropriate professional review.

Quality professional work, especially in the computing profession, depends on professional reviewing and critiquing. Whenever appropriate, individual members should seek and utilize peer review as well as provide critical review of the work of others.

2.5 Give comprehensive and thorough evaluations of computer systems and their impacts, including analysis of possible risks.

Computer professionals must strive to be perceptive, thorough, and objective when evaluating, recommending, and presenting system descriptions and alternatives. Computer professionals are in a position of special trust, and therefore have a special responsibility to provide objective, credible evaluations to employers, clients, users, and the public. When providing evaluations the professional must also identify any relevant conflicts of interest, as stated in principle 1.3.

As noted in the discussion of principle 1.2 on avoiding harm, any signs of danger from systems must be reported to those who have opportunity and/or responsibility to resolve them. See the guidelines for principle 1.2 for more details concerning harm, including the reporting of professional violations.

2.6 Honor contracts, agreements, and assigned responsibilities.

Honoring one's commitments is a matter of integrity and honesty. For the computer professional this includes ensuring that system elements perform as intended. Also, when one contracts for work with another party, one has an obligation to keep that party properly informed about progress toward completing that work.

A computing professional has a responsibility to request a change in any assignment that he or she feels cannot be completed as defined. Only after serious consideration and with full disclosure of risks and concerns to the employer or client should one accept the assignment. The major underlying principle here is the obligation to accept personal accountability for professional work. On some occasions other ethical principles may take greater priority.

A judgment that a specific assignment should not be performed may not be accepted. Having clearly identified one's concerns and reasons for that judgment, but failing to procure a change in that assignment, one may yet be obligated, by contract or by law, to proceed as directed. The computing professional's ethical judgment should be the final guide in deciding whether or not to proceed. Regardless of the decision, one must accept the responsibility for the consequences.

However, performing assignments "against one's own judgment" does not relieve the professional of responsibility for any negative consequences.

2.7 Improve public understanding of computing and its consequences.

Computing professionals have a responsibility to share technical knowledge with the public by encouraging understanding of computing, including the impacts of computer systems and their limitations. This imperative implies an obligation to counter any false views related to computing.

2.8 Access computing and communication resources only when authorized to do so.

Theft or destruction of tangible and electronic property is prohibited by principle 1.2: "Avoid harm to others." Trespassing and unauthorized use of a computer or communication system is addressed by this imperative. Trespassing includes accessing communication networks and computer systems, or accounts and/or files associated with those systems, without explicit authorization to do so. Individuals and organizations have the right to restrict access to their systems so long as they do not violate the discrimination principle (see 1.4). No one should enter or use another's computer system, software, or data files without permission. One must always have appropriate approval before using system resources, including .rm57 communication ports, file space, other system peripherals, and computer time.

3. ORGANIZATIONAL LEADERSHIP IMPERATIVES

As an ACM member and an organizational leader, I will . . .

BACKGROUND NOTE: This section draws extensively from the draft IFIP Code of Ethics, especially its sections on organizational ethics and international concerns. The ethical obligations of organizations tend to be neglected in most codes of professional conduct, perhaps because these codes are written from the perspective of the individual member. This dilemma is addressed by stating these imperatives from the perspective of the organizational leader. *In this context "leader" is viewed as any organizational member who has leadership or educational responsibilities.* These imperatives generally may apply to organizations as well as their leaders. In this context "organizations" are corporations, government agencies, and other "employers," as well as volunteer professional organizations.

3.1 Articulate social responsibilities of members of an organizational unit and encourage full acceptance of those responsibilities.

Because organizations of all kinds have impacts on the public, they must accept responsibilities to society. Organizational procedures and attitudes oriented toward quality and the welfare of society will reduce harm to members of the public, thereby serving public interest and fulfilling social responsibility. Therefore, organizational leaders must encourage full participation in meeting social responsibilities as well as quality performance.

3.2 Manage personnel and resources to design and build information systems that enhance the quality of working life.

Organizational leaders are responsible for ensuring that computer systems enhance, not degrade, the quality of working life. When implementing a computer system, organizations must consider the personal and professional development, physical safety, and human dignity of all workers.

Appropriate human–computer ergonomic standards should be considered in system design and in the workplace.

3.3 Acknowledge and support proper and authorized uses of an organization's computing and communication resources.

Because computer systems can become tools to harm as well as to benefit an organization, the leadership has the responsibility to clearly define appropriate and inappropriate uses of organizational computing resources. While the number and scope of such rules should be minimal, they should be fully enforced when established.

3.4 Ensure that users and those who will be affected by a system have their needs clearly articulated during the assessment and design of requirements; later the system must be validated to meet requirements.

Current system users, potential users, and other persons whose lives may be affected by a system must have their needs assessed and incorporated in the statement of requirements. System validation should ensure compliance with those requirements.

3.5 Articulate and support policies that protect the dignity of users and others affected by a computing system.

Designing or implementing systems that deliberately or inadvertently demean individuals or groups is ethically unacceptable. Computer professionals who are in decision-making positions should verify that systems are designed and implemented to protect personal privacy and enhance personal dignity.

3.6 Create opportunities for members of the organization to learn the principles and limitations of computer systems.

This complements the principle on public understanding (2.7). Educational opportunities are essential to facilitate optimal participation of all organizational members. Opportunities must be available to all members to help them improve their knowledge and skills in computing, including courses that familiarize them with the consequences and limitations of particular types of systems. In particular, professionals must be made aware of the dangers of building systems around oversimplified models, the improbability of anticipating and designing for every possible operating condition, and other issues related to the complexity of this profession.

4. COMPLIANCE WITH THE CODE

As an ACM member I will . . .

4.1 *Uphold and promote the principles of this Code.*

The future of the computing profession depends on both technical and ethical excellence. Not only is it important for ACM computing professionals to adhere to the principles expressed in this Code, each member should encourage and support adherence by other members.

4.2 *Treat violations of this code as inconsistent with membership in the ACM.*

Adherence of professionals to a code of ethics is largely a voluntary matter. However, if a member does not follow this code by engaging in gross misconduct, membership in ACM may be terminated.

Acknowledgments

This Code and the supplemental Guidelines were developed by the Task Force for the Revision of the ACM Code of Ethics and Professional Conduct: Ronald E. Anderson, Chair, Gerald Engel, Donald Gotterbarn, Grace C. Hertlein, Alex Hoffman, Bruce Jawer, Deborah G. Johnson, Doris K. Lidtke, Joyce Currie Little, Dianne Martin, Donn B. Parker, Judith A. Perrolle, and Richard S. Rosenberg. The Task Force was organized by ACM/SIGCAS and funding was provided by the ACM SIG Discretionary Fund. This Code and the supplemental Guidelines were adopted by the ACM Council on October 16, 1992.

P·A·R·T · VIII

E

Confronting Ethical Issues of Systems Design in a Web of Social Relationships*

Ina Wagner

Ethical problems can emerge in a systems design project whenever the legitimacy of the values and moral principles on which participants base their acts and decisions are contested or questioned. Such conflicts between participants' values and norms of conduct often point to underlying basic differences between their positions in the organization, their interests, and, consequently, their assessment of certain design decisions. In this regard, ethical problems have a strong political content.

This article deals with ethical problems in systems development in two steps:

- First, a case (time management in a surgery clinic) is introduced to illustrate the variety of ethical issues that systems designers may need to address and their relevance for design decisions.

- Second, a process-oriented approach to ethical issues (including the constraints systems designers face and the resources they can build on) is discussed.

The Hidden Agenda in Temporal Orders

A research project was set up to study in-depth the social practices of managing time for surgical operations in a large hospital, as seen by the different occupational groups involved. This ethnographic study was based on the assumption that an understanding of current practices and problems is an indispensable building block of a computer system. This system should do justice to the complexity of the temporal problems involved in the scheduling of surgical operations. It should also support more cooperative practices of setting priorities and allocating time.

The surgery clinic, part of a large university hospital, houses six departments, representing different specialties. The out-patient (OP) facilities of the clinic consist of six operation theaters and one small room for minor surgery. A main organizational problem this clinic faces is the scheduling of surgical operations. Each department has been allotted a certain number of days for surgery. Preplanning is done by entering a planned surgical operation (including the names of the patient and the responsible surgeon) into a book that is located in the clinic's main secretariat. The preprogram for the following day is discussed in an afternoon session in which one representative from each department (normally a surgeon), the head surgery nurse, and one representative from anesthesiology are present. In this session the schedule for the next day is set up, using surgeons' "bookings" for this day as a basis. Participants in this meeting name the members of each surgery team and estimate the beginning time of each surgical operation. The result of these consultations is a timetable that shows the distribution of operations over the available theaters. No preplanning for the following days is done, although surgeons may enter planned surgical operations ahead.

Normally a day's program cannot be realized as it was planned. Because of unrealistic time estimates, unforeseen complications, the absence of a surgeon, emergencies, and organizational delays, ad hoc adjustments have to be made that might result in the canceling of a surgical operation.

The high degree of organization fragmentation makes these ad hoc adjustments extremely difficult. Surgeons, anesthesiologists, and nurses live in their own organizational units (e.g., medical departments, wards). These units constitute almost "parallel" organizations that are only loosely coupled. At the same time, the various surgical departments need to share resources (namely OP theaters, technical equipment, and personnel) and there are high temporal dependencies among all these people who must cooperate in a surgery team at a given time. Organizational fragmentation discourages the maintenance of regular communication and feedback patterns. In a surgery clinic people are busy and constantly on the move, and spatial arrangements are not conducive to frequent meetings. As a consequence, existing OP facilities are underutilized, while medical departments

---

*This article appeared as "A Web of Fuzzy Problems: Confronting the Ethical Issues." *Communications of the ACM*, 36(4) (June 1993), pp. 94–101. Reprinted with permission of the Association for Computing Machinery.

accumulate long patient queues. All this taken together suggests that time management in a surgery clinic is not a task of a small and relatively well-bounded group but a complex organizational problem.

As soon as the project team started testing first ideas about how to support the time management tasks by a computer system, it became clear that the most salient problems to be solved were not purely technical. Conflicts that were primarily ethical and political came into focus. These conflicts needed to be addressed in order to be able to make basic design decisions. The most important of these ethical problems were:

- Whether a person's use of working time should be known to others or private.
- How to negotiate the competing explicit and hidden priorities that guide decisions about the allocation of operation time.
- How to deal with the working culture of the "surgical team" — the time (and knowledge) of the different occupational groups involved in this team are not equally valued.
- Whether to strengthen the "automatic scheduling" capacity or the "cooperation-support" component of the system.

Among the controversial planning instruments that could facilitate the planning of surgical operations are staff's personal calendars. Such calendars seem useful in complex organizations in which the availability of persons at certain times is not always known to those who make the planning decisions. The project team envisioned designing a tool that gives individuals (assistant surgeons, anesthesiologists, and OP nurses) the opportunity to delete time, thereby indicating nonavailability for surgical operations. At present, nurses (all of them women) and anesthesiologists have to be available within their working hours independent of individual time preferences and instantaneous commitments. To them the option of indicating temporal preferences could be attractive. Surgeons (all of them men), on the other hand, have an interest in keeping parts of their individual time calendars private. This is in conflict with the need for temporal transparency of those who are responsible for the smooth running of the organization (in this case, women). The sensitive questions that arise when such calendars are made operational are:

- Who is going to keep such calendars, and who should have access to the information? What for one group (surgeons) might be an intrusion on their privacy would give more liberty to the other group (nurses), for example, to indicate nonavailability.

This is a many-faceted problem with no "obviously morally right solution": If, in our case, women's (nurses) voices are not heard, the resulting rules and regulations concerning "privacy versus transparency" will reflect a one-sided tendency to protect primarily the needs and interests of surgeons, hereby disregarding the organizational problems created when in an organization characterized by strong dependencies and frequent emergencies one group enjoys a high level of time autonomy (and privacy) [19].

- Are individuals required to indicate the reasons for not being available (management has a high interest in such data)? What would be the consequences for the different groups affected?

Information technology (in combination with suitable statistical methods) acts as a mirror in which actors can see how resources are distributed and how successfully competing priorities are implemented. It confronts actors with an "objectified" image of their own practice in the light of the organization [20]. Experience shows that actors' perceptions of their own use of time is often self-deceptive. Computer-based scheduling of surgical operations makes this kind of self-deception more difficult. Although participants in the project strongly focused their attention on the consequences of making the individual use of time transparent, many other potential "transparency effects" need careful consideration, for example, making gaps of "unused" time visible, or systematic deviations in the time needed by different surgical teams, or the performance profile of each department, including the frequency of complications.

Inherent in the clinic's operation calendar is a specific scheme of priorities, some of which are made explicit, while others remain hidden. Some of these priorities mirror the internal hierarchy of specialties within the clinic, with heart surgery ranking before all others. A second set of priorities derives from surgeons' ambitions to perform as many complicated operations as possible. As each surgery offers unique chances for learning (and for producing research papers), this ambition varies with the surgeon's professional biography. As a result, admission of patients is highly selective. In addition to professional preferences, there are other priorities, such as those which apply to emergency patients. Also, care values matter, as in the case of old or particularly nervous patients or of patients who have to undergo a lengthy and sometimes painful preparation for surgery.

Computer support requires that priorities be made more explicit and that they be stated in an unambiguous and decision-relevant form. This explicitness makes individual and group practices and decisions more accessible to discussion and reflection within an organization. It turns hitherto private regions into public ones [13]. The organization faces the problem of negotiating the legitimacy of priorities and practices [8].

Although surgery is a product of group work, the performing team does not constitute itself as a group, and it does not act as one. Rather, people who are based within different substantive and social domains meet at certain physical spaces at particular times to engage in particular tasks. This peculiarity is partly due to the fact that the tasks that have to be performed during a surgical operation are sequentially organized with team members being present at different times and—with the exception of the surgical nurse—only partially overlapping and directly collaborating. After the patient has been brought into the operating room, the anesthesiologist is the first to enter, the assistant surgeon is second, the main surgeon (who finds the patient as an "open field" on whom to perform his or her specialized task) is third, and these persons leave in reverse order. This sequential work order also reflects a hierarchy of knowledge, with surgeon's expertise and time being considered more valuable than the knowledge and time of surgical nurses and assistants.

The synchronization problems surgical teams face also indicate tensions among temporal orders. Those occupational groups that have to coordinate their activities use discrepant and sometimes conflicting time-reckoning systems. A closer look at time management practices shows differences of:

- evaluating the temporal requirements of different activities—(When, for example, the main surgeon estimates the duration of a surgical operation, he takes into account possible complications and the tempo of this day's surgical team. But he may not be aware of many of the small organizational tasks that need to be done and the uncertainties involved: for example, the hospital's elevator being in repair with its consequences for patient transport, or a new cleaning person who needs supervision. The surgeon's time estimates also reflect a specific set of values.);
- coping with time constraints;
- making temporal commitments;
- time autonomy, which can be defined as the power to give or deny time, to dispose of the time of others, to have one's own time respected.

When members of a surgery team act with partially different notions of duration, temporal constraints, and do not have finely tuned temporal values in their mind, this creates temporal ambiguity [12]. The ethical problem—of a highly political nature—results from a specific group of actors, in our case, surgeons, having the power to impose their time-reckoning system on all the other groups. For instance, present practices of scheduling surgical operations do not take patients' time into consideration. Patients' time in the hospital is largely waiting time. Their options for intervention are severely limited.

Currently, a senior surgeon is responsible for most readjustments of a day's schedule, including the decision to postpone a surgical operation on behalf of another one he judges to be more urgent. As a consequence of this role, this surgeon has monopolized valuable information and only selectively involves implicated colleagues in his decisions. Decisions are based on an internalized "map" of an individual's or team's specific competencies and deficiencies and capability to mobilize resources under time constraints. This knowledge is only partially shared.

A computer-based information system can help to support a culture of transparency and sharing within the clinic. This one can be done in two ways. First, information technology can provide actors with a more integrated view of time management problems and decision-making processes in the hospital. At present, individual surgeons (as a representative of a specialty) plan with the waiting lists of their own patients in mind, thereby largely disregarding the development of the clinic as a whole. By improving access to information (e.g., on the current surgery plan, unscheduled time openings, changes of surgery teams, and so forth) and by increasing the transparency of decisions, a system offers facilities for bridging organizational segmentation. Second, a system can help to increase the degree of inclusivity and participation in decisions by giving an operation manager the appropriate tools to communicate events and to implicate members of the clinic when deciding the necessary ad hoc changes.

Such a cooperation-enhancing system makes sense only if actors are willing to share information and resources. The local autonomy of medical departments together with the strong hierarchy, however, work against developing a culture of cooperation. The competing "paradigm"—an automatic scheduling system—would "fit" the dominant working culture of the clinic much better. It would define time management as a pure scheduling problem. The task then would consist in distributing limited temporal resources, given certain boundary conditions. Implementing such a system, however, would require all parties involved to ignore existing conflicts of perspectives and the associated ethical problems:

- The existence of competing priorities and goal functions (e.g., surgeons' ambitions to perform as many complicated operations as possible versus nurses' and anesthesiologists' interests in acquiring more time for patient contact).
- The variety of time-reckoning systems.
- The fact that the actor system itself is not well bounded but open to some extent to external pressures from health administrators, professional interests tied to surgeons' affiliations, union interests.

Coping with Fuzzy Problems: Resources and Constraints

Using some concrete examples, it has been argued so far that the large as well as the many small design decisions are intricately enmeshed with ethical issues. This confronts systems designers with the task of carving an appropriate role for themselves in this process and of developing a suitable methodology. They do not seem well prepared for this task. In the following paragraphs the resources on which they can build as well as some of the constraints they face are examined in particular:

- The engineers' tradition of dealing with ethical issues indirectly, through the definition of "technical norms" rather than through dialogue.
- The problem that systems designers' control over the process and product of their work is limited.

For many engineering professions the standards of the field are being defined through the development of technical norms. Such norms are based on "an immanent logic of quantity, standardization and focus on detail" [23, p. 173] and promise some kind of guidance in the maze of fuzzy problems to be tackled. Grudin [6] discusses some of these norms, such as design simplicity, consistency with a real-world analogue, or anticipation of low-frequency events. He points out that these norms are not automatically supportive of users' interests but often in conflict with them. Other types of norms (technical as well as legal ones) can be found in the field of data security and data protection. Norms that pertain more directly to larger issues of social responsibility are currently being discussed within some professional organizations.

Such generalized "ethical codes" or technical norms have the advantage that they can act as some kind of guarantee for minimal social standards to be taken into account. In their analysis of technical norms, Ekart and Loffler favor those types of codes of conduct that "strongly accentuate the regulation of procedures in addition to material criteria of rightful vocational practice and . . . which require the practitioner to consciously connect a cognitively elaborate analysis of a problem with a differentiated moral-practical judgment" [5, p. 14]. If the consequences of normative regulations are to be understood and evaluated, norms have to be applied to and interpreted within a specific context. They may be in conflict with competing norms. This is why Ekhart and Loffler formulate two requirements such norms would have to fulfill: "Their formulation should make clear the consequences of an adequate, responsible attitude to the task for the relationships between all participants (in the design). . . . Such ethical codes should clearly express the difference and tension between the obligation to watch legal and quasilegal norms on one hand and to take distance from these norms if other principles or the situation make this necessary" [5, p. 20].

This translation work of ethical codes or technical norms into guidelines that take account of a specific social context, however, has to be based on an intimate knowledge of users' organizational reality, including the disagreements and conflicts that shape it.

Limited Control

A second problem to keep in mind is associated with the present status of computer science and its position within fields of competing interests (e.g., user goals, corporate goals). Computer scientists are far from forming a homogeneous profession with well-defined boundaries and a clear set of standards. Rather, they constitute a heterogeneous field of practitioner-experts, characterized by limited work autonomy (in particular within large product development organizations) and a lack of "monopolistic" knowledge and clearly defined territories.

In many development environments systems designers are subject to tensions between management's interests in reduced labor costs and improved cost control on one hand and objectives such as creative products and improved services on the other hand. The stock of standard procedures and management methods in the field has increased considerably. Time constitutes a specific constraint in software development. Grudin and Poltrock [7] in a survey of 200 interface designers, found that "insufficient development time" was not only one of the main problems they encountered but also one that created barriers to extensive user involvement. Often users become involved only at the latest moment when the underlying software code has already been "frozen." Research also shows that under time pressure "groups will eliminate much of the communication activity by which they evaluate one another's task ideas, and virtually all of the interpersonal or nontask aspects of their interaction" [12]. This means that the time factor has a crucial influence on a development team's internal relations and the time taken for dialogue and cooperation.

At the same time, studies point to the relevance of "tacit skills" and of concrete experiential knowledge in programming and systems development [9, 14]. Some studies (e.g., Strubing [17]) have started to explore more in-depth the spaces for carving out specific subcultures and for developing subjective styles and techniques in different types of environments. An additional dynamic is created by the growth of end-user computing and, as a consequence, the shift of expertise to users. All these trends taken together suggest that "IS workers' diagnosis and understanding of user problems and needs [are] contextual, constrained by their involvement in a shared organizational culture, by organizationally defined goals, priorities and values, by the history of prior IS-user relations, existing technology, and IS department procedures" [14, p. 22].

Ethical Issues as Part of a Communicative Research Methodology

In some way one could think of Participatory Design (PD) as experiments in democratic innovation and of systems designers as being confronted with the task to "devise processes that are consistent with an ideology that is highly critical of elitism, hierarchy, or any form of oppressive inequality" [10].

Volmerg and Senghaas-Knoblock [18] have elaborated this idea. Their notion of an interdisciplinary dialogue comes close to the definition of cooperative prototyping developed by Bodker and Gronbaek, who perceive the cooperation between users and designers as one "between two groups of subjects that from the outset possess different kinds of instruments and work on different kinds of objects aiming at different purposes . . . we claim that the purpose of designing computer support is that new objects tailored to the users' needs have to be temporarily shared between the two groups, or two skills" [2, p. 476]. Their central argument is that within such an intercultural dialogue, systems designers have to suspend their expert status. They are viewed as participants in a process for which they do not have any specific training.

Volmerg and Senghaas-Knobloch base this requirement on their practical experience, that any asymmetric relation between participants' knowledge and communicative practices makes mutual understanding extremely difficult if not impossible: "Neither the 'mode' of everyday communication nor the 'mode' of expert communication can ensure interdisciplinary understanding" [18, p. 34]. Where everyday language leaves too much implicit and ill focused, the language of experts is too specialized. This is why participants have to engage in the long-term project of developing a "third field" that builds on both: general communicative competencies and a corpus of knowledge, techniques, and visualizations on which to build a shared understanding of a "system within the organization." Such a process requires systems designers to critically examine some of the guiding principles of their discipline, as Lyotard puts it: ". . . the communication problems which the scientific community encounters when modifying and reconstructing their languages are comparable to those of social communities who, when having lost their 'narrative culture,' have to examine their ways of communicating with themselves thereby questioning the legitimacy of decisions" [11, p. 180f]. Four points in this approach seem of particular relevance in dealing with ethical issues:

- Identifying the legitimate participants in an intercultural dialogue.
- Admitting and handling conflict.
- How to implement "egalitarian values" in a hierarchical organization.
- Thinking about the legitimacy of systems designers' own values and professional norms.

One particularly difficult task is to identify the legitimate participants in such a dialogue. Analysis of the composition of ethical committees in the medical area, for example, has brought forward the problems involved in deciding whether some people are more "affected" or more worthy of participation than others because of their education, social background, specific merits for society, or their minority position [15].

As our "time management" project was situated in a hospital environment, questions of legitimate participation focused on two groups: the organization's clients (patients) and union representatives. Their direct involvement may prove to be difficult, for different reasons. Patients' participation can hardly be utilized as long as they are hospitalized. Also, it was unclear how they could possibly contribute to a complex organizational problem. Third, the question arose as to how patients could be motivated to care for an organization they were glad to have been able to leave. The case of union participation is not less complex. Undoubtedly, on the side of "participative designers" there has been a deep disenchantment with unions who seem to lack experience in participative approaches and to be more committed to large-scale collective-bargaining issues than to "local" initiatives in organizational and systems development. At the same time, a valuable approach to discussing working conditions and issues of power and control may get lost.

Another question that needs careful consideration is whether to over-represent otherwise underrepresented actors (in the case of hospital work, women/nurses/helpers/patients). This could be justified in a number of ways:

- A critical mass of members from that group may be necessary to give weight to their perspective.
- Allowing the informal "womens' culture values" based on a rationality of care form the basis of restructuring the clinic's temporal orders could make a crucial difference in the approach chosen.

This immediately brings up the question of systems designers' role in such a process: Are they morally obligated to secure equal participation?

Admitting and Handling Conflict

In an organization characterized by strong authority relations and inter-personal networks many problems are handled locally [3] without resolving the underlying conflicts. "Negotiated Order Theory" seems to conceptualize particularly well the organization procedures for getting things done in such types of organizations. In a series of case studies, Strauss has developed this approach, which helps to analyze negotiation processes and their embeddedness in social settings. Its "key terms include subprocesses of negotiation, of which examples were making trade-offs, obtaining kick-backs, compromising toward the middle, paying off debts, and reaching negotiated agreements" [16, p. 237]. The concept of negotiation implies that, although overt or endemic conflict may exist, actors within an organization are able to develop modes of interaction that help them to reach an agreement. Power forms an important part of negotiation. However, it is not seen as absolute and unchallengeable, but in relation to other factors that help actors create coalitions and partnerships.

There are many arguments in favor of surgical teams meeting before the operation and discussing the patient, with the responsible surgical nurses contacting their patients in the ward and accompanying them throughout the whole event. Teamwork of this kind implies values that few persons would question on principle, its relevance for the well-being of the patient being obvious. Still, teamwork as a goal is hardly consensual. It conflicts with many other goals that different groups of actors in a hospital think worthwhile adhering to (e.g., the interest of nurses to preserve distance from surgeons, surgeons' interest in dividing their time most efficiently between surgery, research, administration, and teaching). Teamwork might prove to be a solution for some problems while creating new ones.

A difficult question for systems designers is how to deal with heterogeneity and dissent, whose side to take. Among the highly controversial aspects of information systems is their use for control purposes [22]. The computer's "mirror function" can be used, for example, for identifying systematic bottlenecks, for providing an overview of the utilization of resources (in comparison with stated priorities) or of the average duration of different types of operations (eventually comparing different teams). Hospital management has a high interest in such information, which can be used for optimizing the use of facilities and for imposing a stricter discipline. Given the existence of long patient queues for elective surgery in many clinics and the apparent underutilization of facilities (in our case), the idea of using statistical analyses of past needs for the renegotiation of priorities cannot easily be dismissed.

This raises the larger issue of how "egalitarian values"—equality, inclusivity, sharing, participation—be implemented. First, there are limits to what can be made explicit and discussed in an organization, and privacy issues are particularly sensitive: power structures, personal and cultural barriers [1]. Second, there are different and competing concepts of democracy: classical liberals would focus on individual autonomy and democratic procedures in which each voice carries equal weight. Corporatist concepts of equality are based on the assumption "that the voices of all relevant groups within the polity must be heard in order to reach the solution that is best for the whole group [10, p. 277]. With physicians claiming absolute authority, this ideal (and with it the idea of cooperative planning) does not necessarily find sufficient and powerful supporters among "users." It is the systems designers' obligation to lobby for such a commitment for cooperativity, but on what grounds? In spite of shared egalitarian values, situations may develop in which not all voices carry equal weight. Conversely, an ethic of social responsibility faces the dilemma that decisions, even when they are rightful in some legalistic sense, cannot be considered "good" as long as they are not consensual. This makes voicing dissent extremely difficult.

In question is also the role of systems designers' own values in a PD project. Some may have a tendency to view themselves as impartial deliverers of technical support to organizational "solutions" worked out by users. Others may argue that systems designers' values inevitably enter the process of negotiating conflict over ethical questions.

Feminist researchers have used the concept of empathy. Empathy (emotional identification) with users as a methodological principle builds on the assumption that designers cannot be able to identify and understand ethical issues unless they feel concern for the concerns of "the other." Still, empathy does not offer a sufficient basis for dealing with ethical problems. On one hand, empathy with patients or with nurses, who perform what is defined as "women's work" and contend with what appears as a dichotomy between the duty to care for others and the right to control their own activities, seems much greater than with those in power. One problem of this position is ethnocentricity—to infer from one's own values, anxieties, interpretations, commitments, and ideological positions to the orientations that prevail in other social worlds. A second problem is that empathy may blur contradictions, ambiguities, and conflict between users when it may be more fruitful to acknowledge and analyze them. This points to the necessity of combining empathy with distance [20]. Understanding and supporting users does not save system designers from making their own moral practical judgments.

Summary

In a PD approach, handling conflict over the legitimacy of social practices and the underlying moral-political claims is one of the most difficult tasks. We have explored the pervasiveness of ethical issues and their relevance for design decisions:

- The issue of whether a person's use of working time should be transparent to others or private
- The issue of how to cope with the fact that decision making in organizations is shaped by competing goals and priorities (some of which are kept hidden)
- The issue of how to deal with the working culture of a team that is based on inequality
- The issue of whether to strengthen the "automatic scheduling" capacity or the "cooperation-support" component of the system

Although the social setting of a surgery clinic has given the "ethical scenarios" a specific color, some of the experiences and conclusions are transferable to other problems and organizations. The conflicts addressed here are likely to emerge in organizations that depend on a sharing of resources (such as time, personnel, rooms, material) and in which some members enjoy a higher degree of time autonomy and decision-making power than the others.

We have also explored the concept of an intercultural dialogue that requires design participants to develop common grounds—a corpus of knowledge, techniques, visualizations on which to build a shared understanding of a "system within the organization." Several critical points in this approach have been discussed:

- Systems designers have to reflect on which idea of democracy to build their methods and procedures. They might benefit from the feminist debate on how to create new democratic forms. Participation based on a corporate concept of democracy gives specific weight to the "voice" of otherwise underrepresented actors (in our case, nurses, women, patients). This ensures that minority points of view are given more than token consideration.

- In complex organizations conflict has to be seen as having to be negotiated locally, without necessarily being able to resolve the underlying differences of participants' norms, values, and interests. This implies that "empathy" with users is not a sufficient basis for dealing with conflict, unless it is combined with the ability to take distance. Also, understanding and supporting users does not save systems designers from making their own moral-political judgments. A focus on ethical issues in the design process may also accentuate the limitations of a participatory approach: designers' own working conditions (which limit their control over the design process) on one hand, and the culture of the user organization, which may not be open to egalitarian values such as the sharing of ideas and open discussion of conflict on the other hand.

"Ethical scenarios" that provide an in-depth understanding of the intricacies of a special case may be useful in the professional debate of social responsibility. They provide grounds for developing "codes of conduct" and help to assess their relevance for different social contexts. An interesting open research problem is how far these professional codes can be translated into technical design norms. The question of whether to support "automated" or cooperative decision making seems an important candidate for further research.

References

1. Berman, T., and K. Thoresen. (1988). "Can Networks Make an Organization?" in *Proceedings of the Conference on Computer-Supported Cooperative Work* (Portland, OR, Sept. 26–28), pp. 153–166. ACM, New York.
2. Bodker, S., and K. Gronbaek (1991). "Cooperative Prototyping: Users and Designers in Mutual Activity." *Int. J. Man-Machine Stud.*, 34, 453–478.
3. Cicourel, A.V. (1990). "The Integration of Distributed Knowledge in Collaborative Medical Diagnosis," in *Intellectual Teamwork. Social and Technological Foundations of Cooperative Work*, pp. 221–242. Lawrence Erlbaum, Hillsdale, N.J.
4. Egger, E., and L. Wagner (1992). "Time-Management. A Case for CSCW," in *Proceedings of the ACM 1992 Conference on Computer-Supported Cooperative Work* (Toronto, Ontario). ACM, New York.

5. Ekart, H.P., and R. Loffler (1990). "Organisation der Arbeit—Organisation der Profession," in *Workshop Technik-forschung an hessischen Universitaten*, 15.12.1989. TH Darmsstadt, ZIT Publikation 4 (in German).

6. Grudin, J. (1991). "Systematic Sources of Sub-Optimal Interface Design in Large Product Development Organizations." *Hum. Comput. Interaction*, 6, 147–196.

7. Grudin, J., and S. Poltrock (1989). "User Interface Design in Large Corporations: Communication and Coordination across Disciplines," in *Proceedings of the CHI'89 Conference on Human Factors in Computing Systems*, pp. 197–203. ACM, New York.

8. Hirschhorn, L., and K. Farquhar. (1985). "Productivity, Technology and the Decline of the Autonomous Professional." *Off. Tech. People*, 2, 245–265.

9. Kuhn, S. (1989). "The Limits to Industrialization: Computer Software Development in a Large Commercial Bank," in *The Transformation of Work?* Unwin Hyman, London.

10. Leidner, R. (1991). "Stretching the Boundaries of Liberalism: Democratic Innovation in a Feminist Organization." *Signs*, 16/2, 263–289.

11. Lyotard, J.F. (1986). *Das Postmoderne Wissen*. Bohlau, Graz, Austria (translated into English as *The PostModern Condition*).

12. McGrath, J.E. (1990). "Time Matters in Groups," in *Intellectual Teamwork. Social and Technological Foundations of Cooperative Work*, pp. 23–61. Lawrence Erlbaum, Hillsdale, N.J.

13. Meyrowitz, J. (1985). *No Sense of Place. The Impact of Electronic Media on Social Behavior*. Oxford University Press, New York.

14. Orlikowski, W., and J. Baroudi (1989). "The Information Systems Profession: Myth or Reality?" *Off. Tech. People*, 4, 13–30.

15. Rothman, D. (1992). "Rationing Life." *The New York Review of Books*, March 5.

16. Strauss, A. (1978). *Negotiations*. Jossey-Bass, San Francisco.

17. Strubing, J. (1988). "Programmieren in einer betrieblichen Sonderkultur? Uberlegungen zu Arbeitsstil und Fachkultur in der Programmierarbeit. Forschungsgruppe Rationalitat des Ingenieurshandelns," in *Innovation, Subjektivitat und Verantwortung. Tagungsbericht*, pp. 109–124. Universitat Kassel (in German).

18. Volmerg, B. and E. Senghaas-Knoblock (1992). *Technikgestaltung und Verantwortungs*. Westdeutscher Verlag, Opladen.

19. Wagner, L. (1992). "Vulnerability of Computer Systems: Establishing Organizational Accountability," in *Education and Society*, pp. 433–439. *Information Processing*, 92, Vol. II. North-Holland, Amsterdam.

20. Wagner, L. (1992). "Feministische Technikkritik und Postmoderne," in *Kultur, Wissenschaft, Frauenforschung*, pp. 147–163. Campus, Frankfurt (in German).

21. Wagner, I. (1991). "Groupware zur Entscheidungsunterstutzung als Element von Organisationskultur," in *Kooperatives Arbeiten und Computerunterstutzung. Stand und Perspektiven*, pp. 175–188. Verlag, Gottingen (in German).

22. Wagner, L. (1991). "Transparentz oder Ambiguitat? Kulturspezifische Formen der Aneignung von Informationstechniken im Krankenhaus." *Z.f.Soziologie*, 4, 275–289 (in German).

23. Wolf, R. (1988). " 'Herrschaft kraft Wissen' in der Risikogesellschaft." *Soziale Welt*, 39/2, 164–187 (in German).

P·A·R·T · VIII

F

Power in Systems Design[*]

Bo Dahlbom • Lars Mathiassen

Telephone services change with computers. The telephone network used to contain a great number of manually operated switchboards. Today, these switchboards are automated. Information about telephone numbers and addresses has traditionally been compiled in telephone books. Now, this information is available on electronic media. When you dial the telephone company, an operator uses a computer-based phone book to assist you. When telephones are integrated with terminals, this kind of service is directly available to each individual customer.

In one case, a nationwide telephone company invested in a new computer-based information system to provide its customers with more effective services related to phone numbers, names, and addresses. Instead of developing its own computer system, the company decided to buy a modified version of a system that was already in use in other countries. A contract was made with the foreign software house that had developed the system. The contract contained a detailed specification of the new computer-based information system. Some parts of the old version of the system had to be modified, and new facilities were to be added.

The telephone company wanted to have the monitoring of operators—a special terminal making it possible for a supervisor to monitor each operator by inspecting a copy of the operator's screen—included as a new feature. One of the programmers in the foreign software house did not like this idea and decided to add one extra feature: When the supervisor inspected the screen of a specific operator, a sign would appear on the operator's screen to indicate that it was now being monitored. This facility was not part of the requirements specification, and the telephone company later had it removed.

Was the programmer right in trying to sneak in extra features to create, in his view, a better computer system? Who is responsible for the impacts of a given computer system on the quality of work and the quality of life? Who should have the right to influence design decisions?

Artifacts Have Power

Only the traditional computer expert really believes in technology as a positive social force. Both the sociotechnical expert and the political agent stress the importance of what goes on in the context of the technology. Traditional experts tend to argue that if only there is technical progress, the rest will take care of itself. They tend to be technological determinists. Sociotechnical experts and political agents both argue that the role of a certain technology will be determined by the social context into which it is introduced. They are social constructionists.

Technological determinism is the theory that a developing technology will have social consequences for us to foresee and then live with. As the earth is shaped by wind and water, society is shaped by technology. The experts designing our technology are responsible for the shape of our society. When Robert Moses built parkways on Long Island that were meant to take the automobile-owning, white upper middle class out to Jones Beach, he made sure that the overpasses were low enough to prevent buses from using the parkways. So, artifacts have power. Artifacts make up the world we live in, and they set the limits for our freedom, not only of movement, but of how much time we have, whose company we share—in short, what we do with our lives.

A different type of theory views technology as a social phenomenon shaped by the society producing it. Technology is said to be *socially constructed*. This can mean simply that the social conditions of the design and development of new technology are being stressed. Or it may mean, more generally, that the quality of a technology depends on how people conceive it, what they know about it, their attitudes toward it, how they decide to use it. Technology is what its users perceive it to be. Such a social constructionism goes well with a democratic attitude toward the design of technology: We move from design for or with the users to design by the users themselves. Rather than being complications in a causal chain of engineering, the users turn out to be the real designers.

An appreciation of the idea that technology is socially constructed by its users changes our conception of systems development. Using computer technology to change an organization should not be viewed as a process of

---

*This article was excerpted from Chapter 9 of Bo Dahlbom and Lars Mathiassen (eds.), *Computers in Context* (1993). Blackwell, Cambridge, MA. Reprinted with permission of Blackwell Publishers.

engineering. For reasons of democracy, such a perspective would be degrading, and for reasons of making a profit, it would be silly to so underestimate the complexity of social response to technical change. The heart of systems development can no longer be a product, a computer system, produced by professional systems developers, since the properties of that system will be determined in its use. Systems development becomes part of a wider and open-ended process in which the systems developers play a marginal role.

If we are technological determinists, we have to accept the responsibility as technology experts for changing the lives of people. If we are social constructionists, we share this responsibility with everyone who is involved in the design and use of technology. In the first case, we will have to worry about the quality of our systems, taking into consideration its far-reaching social consequences. Designing our systems, we shall have to include their future use and effects on conditions of work and life in our planning. In the second case, as social constructionists, we will be interested in engaging in the design process the users, and not only the immediate users but all who will be affected by our systems. But we will share this interest in making the design of technology a democratic process with our fellow citizens. In that process we are no more responsible than any other citizen, and as computer technology experts we can rest content with contributing to that process our technical expertise.

There is something of a paradox in this conclusion. Technical experts tend to be technological determinists. Not giving too much thought to the conditions of use, they develop their artifacts as if their use were determined by their functional properties. Unwittingly, they accept a formidable responsibility for the social consequences of their technology, while at the same time refusing to consider these consequences. Social constructionists see more clearly the complexity of the interplay between society and technology, but in doing so they distribute the responsibility more widely, making it possible for them to stick to their role as experts.

There is some truth in technological determinism, and there is some truth in the idea of the social construction of computer systems. But looking back, it clearly seems as if the changes taking place over the last hundred years or so have been the result of technology shaping us rather than the other way around. We can formulate this as a theory of technology and social change and call it, with Langdon Winner, technological somnambulism: "The interesting puzzle in our times is that we so willingly sleepwalk through the process of reconstituting the conditions of human existence." People in general have had little to say in the development of computer technology, and they have mostly remained ignorant of the options available. The computer professionals have not given much thought to the social consequences of their technology.

If we are dissatisfied with a society characterized by technological somnambulism—something computer professionals ought to be, believing as they do in planning, requirement specifications, and rational design—what can we do about it? As computer technology invades every corner of society, it changes in innumerable ways every aspect of modern life, including work, health care, education, and warfare. As consumer goods, computer artifacts will be used in automobiles and in the home, and by children in and out of school, for play and pleasure. As citizens, we share responsibility for these changes with every other citizen. Computer professionals are not more responsible than anyone else for these more general changes going far beyond their own minuscule contributions. But they have an expertise that makes them morally obligated to speak up against the development of low-quality computer systems and the irresponsible use of computer technology.

The programmer mentioned at the beginning of this chapter did speak up. He tried to sneak certain features into the computer system to compensate for what he believed to be bad management practices in a telephone company. The project was established in such a way that there was no contact at all between systems developers and users. The programmer was sitting in a different country, basing his work on a contract between his software house and a foreign telephone company. His closest contacts with clients and users were the consultants in the sales department of the software house. He was caught in a situation in which cooperation with the users was impossible. In spite of this, he tried to modify the system to make it more human, as he saw it.

There seem to be at least two morals to this story. The first is that, like any professionals, computer professionals should be conscious and critical of the basic conditions for doing their job. The organizational setting, the contractual arrangements, the economic and political conditions influence and in many respects determine our practical possibilities for being concerned with quality, with the ways in which computers are used, and the conditions we create for other people in their jobs.

The second moral is that independent of our basic attitude it is always important to ask the fundamental question: Who is the client and who are the users? How can we achieve quality in this project and what does that mean? If we are not seriously concerned with these questions, we have no chance of understanding the manipulations and power struggles in which we take part. We cannot develop a professional attitude toward our work if we shut out the reality in which we are involved, concentrating only on the immediate task at hand. On the contrary, a professional attitude is also a political attitude. Unless we take seriously the politics of our work, we will reduce ourselves to blind, sleepwalking experts in the hands of whoever wants to feed us.

P·A·R·T·VIII

Considering Privacy in the Development of Multimedia Communications*

Andrew Clement

Introduction

Multimedia communication services (MMCS) or "media spaces"[1] is a rapidly developing area of computer-based networking with major privacy implications. These systems, based on the use of video and audio connections between workplaces, have been caricatured as "electronic fishbowls" in which every act is visible, at least to those with access. Developed largely in the context of computer-supported cooperative work (CSCW) research, they are offered as ways to put colleagues in closer contact with each other by facilitating informal collaborative processes. However, they also pose questions about how users can exercise choice about who has access to this fine-grained personal information and how unwelcome intrusion can be avoided. Concerns about privacy become more acute with the prospect that these technologies are seen increasingly as forerunners of a wide range of commercial products aimed at mass markets.

   At this stage in their evolution, full-featured MMCSs are to be found principally in experimental settings and the users so far are mainly people who are themselves contributing in some way to the development of the technologies. These laboratory settings provide an essential starting point for investigating the implications for employee privacy and the prospects for designs that appropriately respect users' needs in this area.

This chapter reports on an exploratory study seeking to draw upon the experiences at the leading centers of MMCS research currently experimenting with multimedia communications. A central aim is to assist in developing a privacy framework applicable across a range of specific settings. A broader aim is explore the role that privacy considerations have and might play in the development of MMCS more generally. More personally, this research reflects a long-standing interest in the workplace implications of computerization. In particular, I am concerned that technological innovations too often disadvantage those in organizationally weak positions who have little influence on the course of development, while being among the first to experience any adverse effects (Clement, 1992, 1994). MMCS poses a potential threat in this regard.

The chapter begins with a summary of recent MMCS research and then discusses basic notions of privacy and how they relate generally to MMCS technology. The section following describes how researchers working on particular MMCS applications have reacted to privacy concerns in their immediate settings, and provides the basis for identifying general design principles that can be drawn from these experiences. The next section steps back from particular applications and examines how the research lab settings may influence the overall course of MMCS development. The chapter closes with suggestions for further development of the MMCS social/technological "genre."

Multimedia Communications Services Research

An MMCS or media space is "formed by the combination of audio, video and computer networking technologies to provide a flexible, dynamic interconnection environment for collaborative work groups" (Dourish, 1993, p. 125). These services operate on nodes each comprising a computer workstation, video camera, video monitor, microphone, and loudspeaker. Although it is often possible to display the video image in a window on the computer monitor, for reasons of technical convenience and screen real estate, typically the video image appears on its own separate monitor (see Figure 1). In the case of multiparty conversations, this screen can be divided to show several separate images. These nodes, which are installed

*This article appeared in *Computer-Supported Cooperative Work (CSCW)*, 2 (April 1994), pp. 67–88. Reprinted with permission of Kluwer Academic Publishers.

¹ The term Multimedia Communications Services (MMCS) is used here to denote a general system type. More commonly used is the term "media space," but it also refers to a specific installation at Xerox PARC.

Figure 1. Multimedia communications. (Figure courtesy of the Ontario Telepresence Project.)

mainly in offices but also in conference rooms and other common areas, are linked via a computer-controlled switching apparatus. Individuals initiate the connections from the local workstation. However configured, the systems are principally designed to enable varied combinations of audio, video, and data links to be made between two or more parties allowing them to see and/or hear each other while working together (see also the special "Multimedia in the Workplace" issue of the *Communications of the ACM*, January 1993). The most immediate commercial application of these technologies appears to be for desktop video conferencing, but in the longer run would likely be integrated into an increasingly pervasive electronic computing/communications environment supporting a broad range of work activities in contemporary organizations.

The initial research into this type of technology for workplace communications was conducted at Xerox's Palo Alto Research Center (PARC) in the mid-1980s, where it is known as the Media Space. First used between four offices to investigate architectural design processes it has since been expanded throughout PARC to support a variety of informal communications purposes. For several years it served to link a research group divided between Palo Alto and Portland (Bly, Harrison, and Irwin, 1993). At PARC's smaller sister research organization, Rank Xerox EuroPARC in Cambridge, United Kingdom, almost all twenty members of the staff have their own nodes of the locally developed MMCS, called RAVE (Gaver *et al.*, 1992). Another leading center for this research is Bellcore in New Jersey, where social-science–based research intended to foster informal communications has informed the evolution of its Cruiser system (Fish *et al.*, 1993). The current version is implemented as a special application of the Touring Machine, software that provides a general purpose infrastructure for a variety of multimedia applications. It is intended as a forerunner of a service accessed via the public telecommunications network (Bellcore Information Networking Research Laboratory, 1993). The CAVECAT project at the University of Toronto extended the "iiif" software server, which underpins EuroPARC's RAVE, to support a small group of researchers developing shared tools for distributed work (Mantei *et al.*, 1991). Its successor, the Ontario Telepresence Project, has further developed these technologies and is experimenting with them to simulate the sense of shared presence at a distance (Riesenbach, 1994). It was the first of these four labs to have undertaken MMCS field studies involving the permanent installation of equipment in external organizations.

Although the specific features of the systems vary across these settings, several standard ways of making connections are becoming common. These range from video only connections lasting only a few seconds ("glance"), to full two-way audio an video connections lasting as long as a conversation ("call") or indefinitely ("office share"). Multiparty connections can be made and access to other facilities, such as networked VCRs and cable channels, are usually available. All sites have installed an "awareness" service, which offers subscribers an array of snapshots of fellow subscribers taken via the video cameras at frequent intervals (see Figure 2).

The data for the present research comes from in-depth interviews conducted in these four sites. The principal interviewees are researchers who both use the MMCS and have some role in developing the systems. In taped sessions lasting between one and two hours, interviewees responded to open-ended questions about the nature of the local MMCS, their experiences of use, their relationship to the development of the system, how privacy issues have emerged and how they have been dealt with, what they think are the long term prospects of MMCS research, and how they see themselves and their employers contributing to it. Almost all of the twenty-five interviews were conducted in the individual researcher's office and hence within the domain of the resident media space. This enabled observation of how the researchers related to it and used it for getting in touch with each other. At Bellcore, for instance, where usage appeared the heaviest of all the sites, it was common for the interview to be interrupted briefly by someone popping up on the screen to see if the interviewee was available or to ask a quick question. This lent substance to the view expressed by one researcher there that the service was used more frequently and easily than the telephone for reaching colleagues.

Privacy Issues in Multimedia Communication Systems

John Seely Brown, Vice-President of Research at Xerox Corporation and director of PARC, has noted recently that new information technologies "tear at the very fabric that allows [social] processes to actually work." In this context, he recognizes privacy as a "deadly serious issue" (Brown, 1992). Of course, privacy concerns over information technologies are hardly new. Ever since the growth of computerized data banks in the 1960s, there have been public concerns that the automated collection,

Figure 2.   An "Awareness" service. (Figure courtesy of the Ontario Telepresence Project.)

processing and dissemination of personal information threatens people's abilities to exercise control over vital aspects of their lives (Westin and Baker, 1972). Lively debates have flared and settled down, but have never been resolved. Each major advance in data handling technique challenges again basic values of human freedom, autonomy, and dignity. MMCS is merely the latest to bring to the foreground long simmering concerns, albeit in new and interesting ways.

It is not surprising that people often raise privacy issues when they first learn about the functional capabilities of MMCSs. Ever-present microphones and cameras at close quarters carrying sensitive information about personal activities to remote and potentially unseen observers invite questions about possible abuse. This technical configuration is uncannily similar to that deployed by Big Brother in the most famous dystopian novel, *1984.*

Particularly in conjunction with the growing use of "active badges," which monitor the location of wearers every few seconds, these MMCSs provide the technical infrastructure for fine-grained, relentless, and unobtrusive employee surveillance unprecedented in its scope and reach. However, a clear distinction must be made between technical potential and actual practice. Specific features may make such forms of privacy violation infeasible and, more important, a host of social factors must conspire to exploit the oppressive potential. The actual forms and consequences of use will depend heavily on organizational setting, task characteristics, the intentions of the actors, implementation strategies, application metaphors, societal norms, and so on. These will operate through both the opportunities and constraints of the technical facilities that are created and their impact will depend on how they are applied in particular settings.

Privacy is a "broad, all-encompassing concept that envelops a whole host of human concerns about various forms of intrusive behaviour" (Flaherty, 1989, p. 54), and is consequently difficult to define precisely. Individuals tend to take their privacy for granted until it is threatened in some way, which can then provoke strong reactions. Where privacy boundaries lie is highly context dependent and varies considerably between individuals and across cultures. One popular privacy concern is avoiding being seen or overheard when engaged in intimate matters of personal hygiene or relationship. At another extreme, people often express alarm about a possible "Orwellian" threat of a malevolent, omniscient authority. In between, there are a host of less dramatic, but more immediate, dangers related to the exacerbation and abuse of the varied power differentials present in everyday worklife.

Despite the breadth of privacy conceptually, several notions have emerged that provide useful insights applicable to MMCS situations. A core privacy notion is "the right to be left alone" (Warren and Brandeis, 1890). This suggests that at the very least there is need for some provision for people to withdraw completely, if temporarily, from communicative contact. However, in the context of workplaces and communication media particularly, achieving solitude may be only a short-lived exception to ongoing activities, in which other dimensions to privacy will still be an issue. The thirty-year history of attempts at data protection provides useful guidance here. Particularly relevant is the notion of "informational self-determination," which in 1983 the German Constitutional Court recognized as giving individuals, in the workplace as elsewhere, a "fundamental right" to "decide when and under what circumstances [their] personal data may be processed" (Flaherty, 1989, p. 377). However, this notion, and the principles of "fair information practice" designed to give these rights substance, were developed to address relatively permanent storage of client records held by institutions, not the informal, volatile, transient situations characteristic of media-space encounters, when no lasting electronic traces may be left. More useful here is the interpretation of privacy as the right of individuals and groups to manage the ways they present themselves to others—the right to effective control over the construction of their "virtual" selves (Oravec, 1996). This formulation attempts to get at the heart of privacy concerns, which have to do with preserving personal autonomy, integrity, and dignity.

The two extremes of privacy concerns identified above correspond well to the distinction that James Rule *et al.* (1980) makes between "aesthetic" and "strategic" considerations of privacy. Violations of aesthetic privacy upset our commonly held notions of what may appropriately be revealed to others, regardless of whether the information may actually be used by them. Strategic privacy, in contrast, comes into question when revealing information affects how the individual may pursue his or her interests. This is particularly important in work settings, where power differentials are endemic and coercion in a variety of guises is often a possibility. Strategic privacy is thus inextricably bound up with the role that personal information plays in the wider political issues of workplace control. MMCSs create opportunities for both aspects of privacy to be threatened. However, although it is the former that raises alarms most immediately, it is the latter, because of the chronic difficulties in addressing organizational politics openly and directly, that ultimately may be most problematic.

To examine this potential, it is helpful to see how earlier forms of workplace computerization posed threats to strategic privacy. Most attention has been paid to employee surveillance in work settings caricatured as "sweatshops"—those involving high-volume, routine, low-status jobs in which computers are used to record and indirectly raise standardized performance measures (U.S. Congress/OTA, 1987). However, it is not in these settings where MMCSs are likely to find their widest application. More relevant are those that may be termed "fishbowls"—workplaces where a host of measures are used to make behavior, and not just performance, highly visible to managers and others who play a disciplining role (Clement, 1992). Managerial control in such settings may in part be exercised according to principles that underlie the "panopticon," a remarkable social engineering innovation proposed by Jeremy Bentham as a means for social betterment (Zuboff, 1988; Gandy, 1993). The panopticon is essentially an architecture for social control in which central unseen authorities maintain a potentially continuous watch over a large number of individuals who are encouraged to assume that their every act is available for inspection and remedial intervention. To avoid confrontation, the individual becomes self-monitoring in compliance with expectations. Transparency thereby contributes to the internalization of control.

It is not necessary that the information technologies be introduced primarily for workplace surveillance purposes for them to be used to this end. Both Zuboff's (1988) in-depth study of a few highly computerized enterprises and Rule and Brantley's (1992) more representative sample survey in the New York area indicate that the development of computerized surveillance emerges indirectly as a by-product of managements' broader attempts to rationalize and control production. As Zuboff notes,

> The techniques of panoptic power were typically developed after the fact, by coincidence and by accident, as managers discovered ways to colonize an already functioning portion of the technological infrastructure and use it to satisfy their felt needs for additional certainty and control (1988, p. 324).

This dynamic, driven more by opportunism than strategic intent, raises the obvious concern that it is not enough that surveillance be absent as a motivation in early stages of development for it not to evolve later. Indeed, given already intense and growing pressures to optimize organizational performance, it would be surprising if there were not attempts made to exploit this surveillance potential.

To understand this potential, it is therefore useful to examine not only how privacy issues arise in specific use situations but also the influences that shape MMCS as a social/technological genre. Since MMCSs are still in their early formative stages, the current leading experiments will likely play an important role in establishing lasting norms of the genre. Since part of our intention is to contribute to development of MMCSs that respect privacy concerns, we also need to be concerned with questions of design — principles for guiding the development of specific MMCS applications as well as the broader genre. These various general ways in which privacy issues are raised by MMCS research are summarized in Table 1. The remainder of this chapter considers each of the quadrants of this table in turn — starting in the top left corner and moving down each column.

Privacy Experiences of User-Developers

The most obvious way in which privacy concerns are raised in these research laboratories is directly out of the experiences with using MMCSs. Interviewees at every site reported incidents in which privacy had been compromised in some way, usually inadvertently, and described various actions that had been taken in refining systems design and use practices to deal with them. These incidents generally involve unwelcome intrusion or exposure affecting either oneself or a co-worker.

As mentioned earlier, the most basic form of privacy concern is the ability to be left alone when one chooses, and all two-way communications media raise the possibility of unwelcome intrusion and interruption. There are two broad strategies for handling these situations — by erecting barriers to entry and, more subtly, by giving off sufficient information about one's current activities and preferences to allow prospective communicants to make appropriate judgments over whether to initiate a contact. In pursuit of the former strategy users can simply turn off the equipment, but this has the drawback of depriving them of its facilities and may appear to others as if there is a technical fault in the system. One researcher developed an

Table 1. Broad Privacy Issues in Multimedia Communications Systems

	Local applications	Social/technological genre
Understanding	How do MMCS user-developers experience privacy implications?	What institutional influences shape MMCS development with respect to privacy concerns?
Designing	What principles should guide the development of MMCS applications to promote privacy?	What roles should stakeholders play in developing MMCSs to promote privacy?

elegant physical solution to this by mounting her monitor and camera on a swivel arm, which she could then easily turn to point at the wall when she did not wish to be disturbed. She was no longer then faced with the distraction of the screen and simultaneously alerted others that she was unavailable. More complex software solutions to the same problem have been implemented in several sites. With CAVECAT, an interface based on a "door" metaphor was developed enabling individuals to indicate alternative states of availability: when the door is closed, "knock" first; when ajar, a quick video-only "glance" is allowed; when open, full two-way connection can be made without prior permission. A possible variant on this is to discriminate among prospective callers in terms of how one's door will appear to them. "Awareness" services, such as the Portholes application illustrated earlier, potentially offer a quite different way to avoid disruption, since they provide information about recent activities (e.g., whether on the phone, or occupied with a visitor), allowing a prospective caller to assess the situation before attempting connection. This can avoid the possible rudeness of "shutting the door" and allows urgent calls to come through, at the risk of additional self-exposure.

Another major concern among users is to control how they expose themselves to others. Most obvious are questions of who is watching and what they see. It is not always clear whether a camera is one, what it is viewing, whether it is transmitting, and to whom the images are being transmitted. The classic incident in this regard is changing clothes without realizing that others can see. One of the ways of overcoming this is by installing a "confidence" monitor (EuroPARC) or offering a "mirror" function (CAVECAT), which continuously displays what the local camera views. However, for many the possibility of being overheard is more serious, for it is our words and not our gestures that have most potential for harm. While there typically are software controls for disconnecting audio transmission, these are not always trusted, partly in recognition of the potential unreliability of software, and greater faith is put in hardware measures. At PARC, Media Space users initiated the construction and installation of special microphone switches with red lights, while at Euro-PARC, footpedal switches are used for the same purpose. Managers at Bellcore report turning the power to the audio system off during sensitive performance review meetings to assure confidentiality.

Although many of the same concerns have come up across the various sites, it is interesting that the development trajectories of systems features and use practices differed markedly between sites. This can be plausibly traced to particular combinations of institutional and environmental factors. For example, participants in the PARC Media Space have a deliberate policy of minimizing the technical measures for protection of privacy, preferring instead to rely on mutual trust and social regulation. This can be seen as reflecting the organizational and architectural setting in which the Media Space was developed. Research groups at PARC are based in "pods"—small wings along the building in which the individual offices are clustered around a central open area. Each of the offices has tall, full-width windows on both the outside wall and into the central pod area, in effect forming a communal, rather than authoritarian, panopticon. This physical layout creates a common group space of mutual high visibility, which the media space replicates electronically.[2] In contrast, the buildings at Bellcore follow a much more conventional layout. Offices are more enclosed and strung out along many superficially identical corridors. There are no physical foci for research groups. It is therefore perhaps unsurprising that the MMCS developed in this lab was modeled explicitly on walking along "virtual hallways"—hence the name "Cruiser." Furthermore, the adoption of a strict rule of technically enforced reciprocal, two-way visibility appears consistent with Bellcore belonging to regulated telecommunications companies, especially in comparison with the more freewheeling approach taken in Xerox's California lab. The more explicit privacy regulation at its Cambridge, United Kingdom lab can be attributed to the ubiquity of its media space. Cameras and sensors are located throughout the three-story lab building block—offices, corridors, commonroom, stairwells, entrance way. Everyone is encouraged to "adopt" the technology, with equipment made available as a default. Since employees thus had little choice but to participate at some level, they needed the formal privacy protections that technical means can help provide (Dourish, 1993, p. 127).

---

[2] In keeping with the spirit of relating particular technological forms with the social settings in which they are developed, it is useful to note that the creators of the first media space were a close-knit group of individuals who shared an architectural design background. A tradition in architectural practice is the "design studio," an open space in which designers can interact intensely and informally on common work objects. Moving to separate offices, but linking them via open, reconfigurable audio and video connections was an attempt to afford greater personal privacy, while preserving important advantages of this studio environment.

The point here is not to explain fully all the privacy measures in terms of the varying contexts they arose in, but rather to illustrate that there are strong interactions between them. In particular, we should not expect convergence on a single best "solution" for dealing with privacy issues to suit these four labs, much less to meet the more varied needs of the wider range of settings where MMCS will likely be applied in the future.

This sketch of how privacy questions have come up in the use of MMCSs and how users have dealt with them touches only the more obvious aspects, but it does give some flavor of the ongoing process of technical refinement and social adjustment that Paul Dourish (1993) identifies as a critical ingredient for successful implementation of media-space technologies. The pressure for particular features and the ways privacy and accessibility concerns trade off against each other depend heavily on particular local circumstances. At the same time, however, there are some commonalities across the different labs. It is clear that the privacy concerns in these settings arise mainly out of conversational interactions and reflect the aesthetic more than the strategic aspects. Judging from the generally favorable attitudes expressed by interviewees and their evident comfort in using the systems, it appears that the MMCSs have become useful, nonthreatening, and largely uncontroversial additions to the communications facilities available to researchers in these laboratories.[3]

Given the broad features of the social organization shared by these settings, this outcome is understandable. The researchers exercise considerable autonomy in their work tasks and enjoy good access to technical skills. This is reflected in Bly *et al.*'s remarks about the PARC media space, which are relevant to the other labs as well:

> all participants have been technological equals (i.e., one could not have a monitor without a camera); but more important, the media space was developed, owned, and used by the same people. There was no external monitoring or control. (Bly *et al.*, 1993, p. 44).

Close managerial surveillance has not been a tradition in these settings and researchers would be most unlikely to cooperate with moves in this direction if they were to be made.

The important question remains, however, whether if similar technologies were to be deployed in other settings, would the outcomes be so benign? If an MMCS were to be installed in an enterprise where hierarchial authority is a more prominent feature, where employees enjoy less professional autonomy, where short-term performance is a greater priority, where technological competence is not so abundant, and where devices are

---

[3] I have not interviewed administrative support staff, who may well feel differently. The lack of controversy about audio/visual connections can be contrasted with the open debates about the use of active badges (see Harper, 1992).

taken as given and not objects for experimentation, we should expect there to be substantially more potential for privacy violation and rather less opportunity to resist. Just how much of the potential for abuse will be fulfilled is an important question for future field research to address. In the meantime, we can gain some valuable insights in how to design for these settings from an analysis of the privacy measures adopted so far and how they were developed.

Development Principles

Although these research settings are in important ways different from the workplaces where MMCSs are likely to find commercial application, the significant experiences with privacy concerns do offer some guidance on how to develop and evaluate future applications. Several design principles have emerged from the research at the sites studied here that have informed the development of the local services and that are relevant to MMCSs generally. However, the principles so far are relatively unsystematic and ad hoc, since they are drawn largely from the experiences and intuitions of the (mainly technically oriented) researchers actually building the systems. Bellotti and Sellen (1993) have made a good first attempt to formulate a comprehensive framework for considering privacy in design. Drawing mainly on the development of EuroPARC's RAVE, they identify *control* ("Empowering people to stipulate what information they project and who can get hold of it") and *feedback* ("Informing people when and what information about them is being captured and to whom the information is being made available") (p. 80) as the two key complementary design principles for promoting privacy. Both principles are to be applied to each of four distinct behaviors corresponding roughly with the flow of information through stages in a communication process—*capture, construction, accessibility,* and *purpose.* The notion of *reciprocity* ("If I can see you, you can see me") has also been widely identified in these labs as an important design principle for promoting privacy. While these various principles offer sound guidance, it may be useful to broaden and recast them in a way that draws on the long experience of data privacy discussions referred to above. This tradition focuses on the rights of individual "data subjects" and treats *control* as the core principle, that is, the right of every individual to effective control over the information about him- or herself. Exercising such control certainly means having available various actional resources (what Bellotti and Sellen mainly refer to as control, e.g., covering a camera lens) as well as enjoying appropriate means for feedback (so as to know whether desired results are being achieved and whether further action is required). More fundamentally, however, this notion of control can be seen as reflecting broad liberal/democratic ideals as they pertain to the management of personal information. In particular, this tradition encompasses the ideals of equality and fair treatment, and these too need to be made explicit in any framework for guiding MMCS development.

Effective, Local "Ownership" Rights to Resources and Information

Fundamental to any effort to achieve effective control over the electronic presentation about oneself are rights over the raw information and the devices that handle it. Any personally identifiable information should be treated as belonging to the subject, and used only with their knowledge and consent. As Bellotti and Sellen (1993) indicate, people should be able to avoid or block the capture and processing of information about themselves; they should be in a position to regulate who has access to which information for what purposes. Turning off a microphone or setting availability preferences are examples of this. Avoiding central repositories of personal information and a preference for local storage (Weiser, 1993) can also help in maintaining the "opaqueness" that Schmidt and Banon identify as necessary for people to exercise discretion in environments "charged with colliding interests." As they conclude emphatically, *"visibility must be bounded"* (emphasis in original) (Schmidt and Bannon, 1992, p. 35).

Furthermore, it should be legitimate for individuals and local work groups to influence the configuration and functional features of the information handling system. In the immediate vicinity, this might include decisions for the installation, placement, orientation, and operating characteristics of microphones, video cameras, location sensors, and so on. Beyond this, a host of questions dealing with such matters as network connectivity, transmission protocols, security measures, encryption standards, analytic capabilities, administrative procedures, and so on may need to be negotiated. Here, matters become more difficult, since additional parties with potentially differing interests become involved. It would be helpful to identify a series of regions with manageable boundaries within which legitimate participants, "jointness" of ownership, negotiation practices, and the other aspects relating to the effective control of information can be identified. These might correspond to the individual, immediate workplace or work group, department, and so on. The broader the group, the more the exercise of privacy becomes a matter of multiparty negotiation over collective, and not just individual, information rights.

Feedback

Control generally can be achieved only with adequate feedback about the current state of information dissemination and the results of any actions taken to affect it. People need to be able to determine readily what information is being captured, transmitted, recorded, and accessed by what and for whom. Confidence monitors, status lights, user rosters, audio notifications, transaction logs, and so on are among the technical means for providing feedback. In order that the feedback contribute to the manageability of information, it should correspond to the regions of effective action identified above.

Equality

In the spirit of egalitarian social ideals, the equality principle says that all parties to communication enter on a formally equal basis. Everyone should have more or less similar access to the facilities and to each other. In making contact, this equality ideal is expressed as reciprocity or What You May See Of Me Is What I May See Of You. This can take the form, as it does at Bellcore, of strictly enforced technical symmetry in audio-video connections. Broader interpretations have been taken at EuroPARC, where the degree of reciprocity available to users depends on the type of connections to be made. It ranges from the technically enforced two-way A/V links implied in the term "office share," to a much looser notion with the "glance" service, in which each user explicitly designates who may make short, one-way connections to them. What all the services have in common is the presumed equality of all users to establish such access settings.

Fair Information Practices

The principles of fair information practice (FIP) have been developed over the last few decades in the ongoing attempts to implement the rights of citizens to informational self-determination in their dealings with record-holding agencies. They now underpin most data protection legislation in Western industrialized countries (Flaherty, 1989) and provide a useful foundation for protecting communications privacy (Rotenberg, 1993). In spite of the additional demands for information access peculiar to workplaces, these principles also offer a useful basis for protecting employees' privacy. However, they are not widely known in the laboratories developing MMCSs. Few I have spoken to had even heard of them. Some of the FIP principles that are particularly relevant to these settings are: establishment of clear information privacy policies; designation of authorities responsible for creating publicizing, and enforcing these policies; restriction of the amount of information collected to the minimum necessary for the specific intended purposes; and prohibition on information use beyond intended purposes without prior approval. Although some of these principles are in fact followed, it appears to be by custom or in relation to the protocols protecting the anonymity of research subjects. It would be helpful for the more general application of these technologies if developers explicitly and routinely treated all personal information as subject to the protective measures of the fair information practice principles.

Participative Negotiability

This final principle is unlike the others in an important respect. Whereas the former ones defined attributes the working system should embody, either in its operational features (e.g., audible feedback), use practices (e.g., minimization of data collection), or organizational structure (e.g., privacy review committee), the negotiability principle is primarily about the *process* by which working systems may be established and adapted.

These principles considered so far obviously do not provide clear-cut prescriptions. Applying them in practice requires a considerable degree of adaptation within immediate situations. There are several reasons for this: First, the principles are not always consistent with each other. For example, obtaining feedback about who is presently observing one involves obtaining personal information about another individual, which in turn challenges their control over their own information.[4] Second, there will have to be some tradeoffs with other criteria for effectiveness. Of immediate concern is the possibility of a high interactional overhead in dealing with safeguard measures (e.g., giving permissions, waiting for notifications, signaling availability, setting preferences). These can impair the original communications support purposes of the MMCS (Bellotti and Sellen, 1993). Although some degree of privacy protection is vital for assuring comfortable communications (Dourish, 1993), overly heavy measures will be viewed as unnecessarily frustrating barriers to access and avoided where possible. More fundamentally, privacy rights are not absolute, in the sense that there are often competing legitimate, or at least institutionalized, demands by co-workers and employers for access to personal employee information. Having some access to information about an employee's performance and behavior is a recognized part of the social control processes essential for the functioning of work organizations. Thus, there can be no a priori boundaries established, except in extreme cases, to define areas of exclusive individual control. Although basic rights can and should be recognized, exercising them involves a complex interplay of contingent factors.

Finding an appropriate balance among competing requirements involves more than simply providing flexible, tailorable technologies. Certainly, this is an important component of the success of media spaces seen so far, and future systems will also to some extent, have to be customizable. But a serious dilemma for customizability is that it is in just those situations where abuse is most likely that any technical flexibility will be turned against those least able to resist it.

The main ingredient for benign adaptation is the ability of the parties involved to negotiate among themselves a satisfactory mix of technical features and social understandings. It is just these local negotiation processes that appear to have been critical in achieving the relatively comfortable accommodations noted earlier. Although this is readily seen as a

---

[4] The controversies over Calling Number Identification (CNID) offer a well-publicized illustration of how such competing privacy rights can arise and just how difficult they can be to resolve in practice.

proper part of the experimental process in reaching relatively stable configurations, it should not be assumed that the process can be abandoned when installing more finished "products." Rather, closing the gap between design and use will likely be more problematic, and hence more a focus for explicit concern, when installing commercial systems, than it was in these research settings.

This suggests the need for effective, and likely more formal, participatory development *and* implementation of any future MMCS. Many of the key indications are present: need for local adaptability, variety of legitimate perspectives, and novelty of application area. In addition, because MMCS deals with personal information, there is a strong moral, and sometimes legal,[5] requirement to consult affected workers. This is partly a matter of design technique (see the June 1993 special issue of the *Communications of the ACM* on Participatory Design). More fundamentally, it is one of organizational setting, which must be conducive to the learning, experimentation and negotiations that inevitably will be required for adaptations that appropriately respect individual and collective privacy concerns. It is just those organizations that are most hostile to privacy protection that are least likely to permit their employees to take the time to find out what the implications are, to voice their concerns fearlessly, and to make remedial modifications. In such settings, individuals will be reluctant to speak out on their own. Recognized structures of employee representation will then also need to be in place to provide users with protective forums for raising their concerns and bargaining collectively for appropriate safeguards.

Ensuring hospitable sites for MMCS deployment is not something that is under the control of the original systems developers. However, they can attempt to anticipate the needs in such settings, identify the factors critical for successful implementation, build in safeguards against abuse, and generally promote features that support participative negotiability.

As the terrain is constantly shifting, it is difficult to build up a robust body of experience in learning how the necessary tradeoffs are best made. But this makes it all the more urgent that careful consideration of the common privacy concerns across settings and general guidelines for deal-

---

[5] In Germany, the supreme labor court determined in 1986 that where the introduction of an information system has the *potential* to record personal information, it must be the subject of codetermination negotiation. Workers, through their local Works Councils, are entitled to veto the introduction if they decide that there are not appropriate safeguards. This approach may extend throughout the EC if the draft policy on "personal data protection" is ratified and adopted by members states (Clement, 1992). This legal mandating of a potentially decisive user influence in the introduction of these systems will likely make the market for MMCS in EC countries more open for privacy-enabling systems. More broadly, these exemplary data protection laws set a moral standard that systems developers and implementors anywhere may aspire to.

ing with them become a prominent feature of MMCS design and implementation efforts.

Institutional Influences

It is not just how privacy matters arise in particular MMCSs and what
principles should guide their development in the future that are of interest.
We are also concerned about how MMCS develops as a social/technological
"genre," that is, not just as a growing collection of artifacts, but also the
evolution of commonly held assumptions, values, and conventions that
guide the practices of development and use (Oravec, 1996). As John Seely
Brown (1992) notes, such genres cannot be designed, but "seeded," and
then presumably cultivated. Keeping with this metaphor, individual
MMCSs constitute the seeds, and the laboratories, at least for now, fulfill
the role of "seed beds." It is their characteristics and the ways they support
research that give shape to the emerging MMCS genre. In particular, our
focus here is on how these settings encourage or thwart consideration of
long-term privacy matters. It will be valuable to learn how attention to
ensuring the rights of individuals and groups to control personal information trade off with other pressing concerns. Are privacy considerations
given prominence and strength so they may be decisive at those moments
when steps of lasting importance are taken or at least cumulatively in many
smaller ways exert a generally positive influence? Or do they tend to be
overwhelmed by more urgent demands and thereby effectively marginalized? How adequately do research laboratories represent the settings
where MMCS will be applied commercially with respect to privacy concerns?

Ironically, some of the very conditions that have made comfortable
adaptation though informal participative development possible in these
settings make it more difficult for the developers in these labs to anticipate
and grapple with the privacy concerns likely to arise in less experimental
applications. Situated in the everyday work world of these relatively egalitarian, well-resourced research labs, it is hard to imagine that working
conditions elsewhere are generally more hostile and that the taken-for-
granted remedy of talking with a colleague to fix problems that do arise is
typically not available. It thus becomes difficult to design in the safeguards
for dealing with remote, vague hazards, when the immediate challenges of
making novel artifacts function are more pressing and rewarding.

Several competing influences operating at the corporate level can be
identified. There are strong economic incentives to develop MMCS into
marketable products. For the telecommunications companies particularly,
researchers repeatedly, in private and in public, made the point that
research into video-based communications is motivated to a considerable
degree by the prospect of stimulating dramatically increased demand for

network bandwidth. Privacy concerns, because of their potential to excite strong consumer opposition, pose a thorny dilemma for these companies. Because they are much more likely to detract from commercial appeal than add to it, the less they are raised publicly, the better. On the other hand, they need to be ready with answers when they do get raised. As one Bellcore researcher observes:

> "The concern about privacy that permeates the place is that for these services to actually sell, you have got to deal with this fundamental problem that whenever people hear about video, whenever they hear about active badges, etc. [they become concerned, and so we have to] alleviate people's privacy concerns—make the services non-intrusive, non-invasive. It is not clear how to do that, but that's the goal." (interview, November 1, 1992)

One event in particular that several respondents at Bellcore mentioned highlighted the need of the corporation to address specifically the public relations aspects of privacy. It followed what one researcher described as a "scathing" report by NBC about the active badge research at DEC's Cambridge laboratory. Another researcher noted that as a research corporation, Bellcore was

> "trying to manage [its] image . . . to, in particular, the press, knowing that there is going to be lots of ways of undercutting and ridiculing and making us seem as incredibly dangerous . . . [for] services that may or may not be dangerous, and so there is lots of sensitivity in terms of the image that is being projected outwards.

> "We had a call from [NBC] last week. We decided that we would not bring the producer in and show the technology that we are doing . . . because it is in too raw a state and it is just really easy to misconstrue what the purposes of it are."

He agreed that the company was "busy working on smoothing the technology and smoothing the line." Part of this involved a policy of no longer referring to active badges by their popular name, but instead using a new and more neutral term, "network location device." This shying away from possible controversy has also affected the direction of research.

> "Among the researchers, the concern is keeping a low profile more than anything else. Among some people there was a judgement, for instance around locator badges, that . . . the benefits would be too low for the possible costs. And so . . . some groups decided that they didn't want to be involved in the locator badge research."

Unfavorable press coverage by a tabloid newspaper over the video monitoring at EuroPARC prompted researchers there to discuss the need to present the privacy aspects of their work more carefully.

Another factor that tends to make it more difficult for researchers to deal with privacy matters, beyond the most immediate ones, is the strong and apparently growing pressure to achieve tangible results in the short term. Several researchers noted that their employers were for financial reasons explicitly reducing the time taken for research innovations to reach the market. For instance, at Bellcore, the time frames that Applied Research operated under had recently been shrunk by several years. There were also complaints that, for similar reasons, the labs were experiencing serious understaffing. In the face of this, one researcher felt there just was not enough time to pay attention to wider implications.

A related factor, but more fundamental to the research process, was identified by Mark Weiser, manager of PARC's Computer Science Laboratory. He leads the "ubiquitous computing" project, which aims not so much to create products for sale in the immediate future, but rather to reconceptualize the very nature of computing. It represents a radical technological vision, based on networked devices unobtrusively embedded within a wide variety of familiar objects we interact with physically. If this vision is fulfilled, it would have significant, long-range consequences for society (Weiser, 1991). Weiser is frank in noting an important social dynamic within research teams facing such difficult design challenges:

> "We tend to have fairly short discussions in the hallway about the 'dark side' [of computing implications], but quickly move past that to either the problem of the day or 'We'll put this in and make it possible for that not to happen.'

> "There is a sort of psychology of . . . innovation going on. . . . We are all very uncertain about whether we can even get the short-term prototypes built, much less if the whole vision is right. So constantly we are boosting one another, saying 'Oh yes, we can do it' and 'We are doing the right thing,' even though we all know we don't know whether we are doing the right thing. . . . But it is necessary to sustain the activities. That certainly works against anyone who tried to dwell on 'how awful it could be' and 'this could be the end of human freedom.' [They] would not be welcome for very long, if they kept that up. No one would be able to get anything done, because we would all be so bummed out. . . . That is the state of affairs, whether it is right or wrong. That is how it works." (interview, May 4, 1992)

Another way in which the requirements of technological development distance researchers from effective consideration of the long-term social implications is the sheer complexity of the enterprise and the corresponding need to isolate parts from each other. This is seen most clearly in the development of the Touring Machine infrastructure at Bellcore. This software is intended to provide a common generic set of basic multimedia communications facilities on top of which a variety of particular applications services can be more easily built. A recent version of Cruiser offers such an example. Several researchers working on the Touring Machine project reiterated to me that they did not have to be so concerned about privacy issues because this was a "policy" matter and hence exclusively the domain of the applications (and by implication, those who develop them). The Touring Machine was concerned only with "mechanisms" and could support arbitrary privacy and access policies (Bellcore Information Networking Research Laboratory, 1993). Quite apart from the fact that this constitutes a potentially significant policy in its own right, it turns out that the range of currently implementable policies was somewhat narrow. The "privacy" option provided in the software interface allowed only three distinctions to be made—Self, Group, and World—precisely the options the Unix operating system allows for distinguishing between users permitted to access files. The engineering-trained developer who implemented this feature said he chose this for reasons of expediency and without consulting any of the social scientists more actively engaged in privacy-related research. He said the "privacy" options will be broadened in future versions.

The point of these observations is not to identify shortcomings of individual developers or systems, but rather to highlight an inherent difficulty with any such development endeavor. Privacy considerations have implications for quite low levels of the software infrastructure, which are well removed organizationally and technically from the user interaction realms where privacy matters are more conventionally dealt with. It is hard to make the connections between low-level design decisions and their possible use consequences in the first place, but correcting things later is likely to be even more troublesome.

All of these various factors identified above tend to distance researchers and developers from active consideration of how the technologies may be used harmfully. Indeed, much of the direct experience with them will suggest that problems are relatively minor and can be dealt with. But it is one thing to experience personal discomfort and negotiate social/technical modifications with colleagues. It is quite another to take principled and potentially awkward stands on behalf of future users whose legitimate needs are vaguely defined and subject to a broad range of interpretations.

This is not to say that there is no institutional support for dealing with the longer-term privacy implications of MMCS. Some researchers have declined publicly to participate in experiments involving detailed personal data collection. For instance, Weiser noted that one researcher in his lab has refused to wear an active badge because of privacy concerns—a stance that he welcomed because "diversity forces us to face up to these problems" (interview). He also encourages his staff to actively consider the privacy aspects of their work, such as by taking part in conference panels on the subject and discussing privacy issues with co-workers, friends, and family. It is now common for research papers from these labs to mention privacy issues and how they have been addressed in design. At Euro-PARC, several research reports have made privacy issues a central focus (Anderson, 1991; Bellotti and Sellen, 1993; Dourish, 1993). Bellcore has a recognized expert on privacy matters who regularly conducts research on the subject. However, he is not permitted to testify at public hearings because of possible conflicts with the positions of the phone companies that own Bellcore. But apart from these examples, there is little evidence in any of these settings of a corporate mandating of systematic attention to privacy matters. There are few if any formal discussions or seminars. (One that was planned at Bellcore was canceled for budgetary reasons.) There do not appear to be any publicized guidelines (beyond standard research protocols) for addressing privacy concerns. They are generally left up to the individuals to deal with in informal ways. Overall it seems fair to say that on balance, the major research centers are not engaged in nor conducive to an open, systematic, and detailed consideration of the broader societal privacy implications of MMCS. As we saw, this is in contrast to the relatively favorable environment for addressing the many local privacy concerns that arise in immediate use situations.

We have seen that in the context of the research laboratories, the dark side of these potentially invasive technologies has not come to the fore. Indeed, on the contrary, researchers generally feel quite comfortable using and developing them. This can be attributed to two main factors. The most obvious and encouraging one is that researchers already encounter challenges to their personal privacy and are able to take effective remedial actions, in terms of changes to both the artifacts and their social practices. There is thus a process of adaptation under way producing a better fit between organization and technology that alleviates most concerns. The other factor contributing to this generally positive picture is much less encouraging in terms of the prospects for the genre. It has mainly to do with the rather special and in many ways privileged working conditions enjoyed in these research settings. The problems of surveillance and intrusive authority seldom appear (except perhaps with active badge research [see Harper, 1992]) and are therefore harder to address in a direct way. This means that the types of adaptations we see ameliorating the threats to aesthetic privacy are happening much less for addressing more politically sensitive strategic privacy concerns. Tackling these aspects may require changing some ingredients of the lab "soil" in which the MMCS seeds are taking root.

Stakeholder Roles in Future MMCS Development

These observations about the settings in which the early MMCS applications are being given shape lead us to consider how the broader field, or genre, can be encouraged to develop in ways that appropriately respect privacy concerns. The problem now becomes not which particular principles should be invoked but how to foster an open and productive discussion about the issues so that whatever principles, artifacts, practices, ideologies, and so on do emerge are adequately informed by the legitimate interests of the various stakeholders, both current and incipient. The general need is to reduce the "distance" between the research/ development communities and the various communities of eventual use and establish effective communications among them. The challenge is to create the spaces for a serious, informed, and pragmatic debate of the difficult privacy issues that MMCS research poses. There are a few signs of this at the moment, but much more could and needs to be done.

The most immediate step is to draw more deeply on the experiences of the current researchers and developers as the first users. As the present networks spread throughout their host sites, cutting across organizational divisions and hierarchical layers, attenuating informal regulative mechanisms, information access control issues are likely to be experienced more acutely. Individuals can educate themselves about the privacy implications of MMCSs and how to incorporate them into their own work. Discussing and debating these matters openly with their colleagues would help broaden understanding and sharpen the issues. It would also be valuable for some people to serve as "conscientious objectors" and not take part in some of the systems (e.g., by not wearing a badge, or not having their office fully instrumented). This would both make it more legitimate for others to exercise a right to say "no thanks" to potentially intrusive information collection techniques as well as encourage developers to design systems to accommodate various degrees of participation.

Managers and senior researchers would send a powerful message to staff if they were to recognize publicly that MMCS development inherently poses genuine privacy concerns requiring both extensive research and treatment as an essential design consideration across the full range of technological development. This would need to be backed up by allocation of resources commensurate with that devoted to other major research and development agendas. There are several ways this could be done: sponsoring seminars, workshops, debates, and other forums for discussion of views; hiring researchers who specialize in privacy-related research and design; establishing a privacy review committee broadly representative of laboratory employee groups; and developing, publicizing, and implementing an information access policy with strong privacy-promoting measures.

As research moves beyond the laboratories themselves, a range of outside organizations for field studies should be investigated. The focus should not be just on finding sites where the technologies can readily enhance existing cooperative processes with little a priori risk for abuse. Less benign organizations, where there are definite risks, should also be sought so that dangers can be addressed directly and appropriate safeguards developed for these situations as well. In setting up such field research projects, considerable attention should be paid not only to ensuring the privacy of individual users, but also to enabling them to raise and discuss their concerns throughout the development cycle. Where the necessary protections cannot be assured, warnings about the limited applicability and precautions for use, as are common with many other potentially dangerous industrial products, should be publicized. One way to do this, especially as the MMCS becomes closer to a product that is installed by other than those who developed it, is to build such notifications into the software itself. For instance, under the menu option common in contemporary software that identifies the creators (i.e., "About . . .") could also appear such items as: guiding precepts of the design, rationales for particular features, precautions for installation and use, fair information practice principles, references to relevant literature, listservs, and so on. This would serve as a high-level Help feature, while making clearer the responsibilities of software developers, implementers, and users alike.

In parallel, development organizations should foster further contacts with a variety of external interest groups and news media. Establishing trusting relations will not always be easy but a careful openness can reduce the risk of exacerbating relations between those working on the inside, who see the positive developments and want them at least recognized, and those on the outside, who know less of the actual practices and react with alarm to prospects yet to be fulfilled. The danger of the alternative, isolation, is that the research organizations will enlarge the public relations and image management exercises we saw earlier to win acceptance, while external criticism will be dominated by sensationalism and exaggeration of the dangers. They will thus contribute to a self-expanding dynamic that ultimately collapses when the wilder fears are deflated by their inevitable confrontation with the mixed reality of everyday usage. In the meantime, serious investigation of the thornier questions of how power and dominance become implicated in the processes of technological development and how they may be counteracted will be neglected until it is too late to avoid building "electronic fishbowls" around us we will find difficult to undo.

Such a sober approach to MMCS development would require considerable modesty on the part of researchers and run counter to the short-term market expansion imperatives of the research sponsors. However, it would help fulfill important professional obligations (e.g., see the ACM Code of Ethics) and perform a valuable public service. By bringing to the fore the too-oft-obscured human and social dimensions of technological development, research enterprises will assist us in responding more appropriately to what promises to be a socially potent technological genre.

Conclusions

The privacy issues identified in this paper are not new, nor are they confined to MMCS. Indeed, concerns over the control of personal information have a long history and can be found across the full range of CSCW applications. Perhaps they are most starkly presented here, however, because of the special richness of the information flows and broad scope of possible consequences. At one extreme is the promise of intimacy and openness of communications of "shared presence," and at the other, the menace of total surveillance environments. However, it is an intrinsic feature of all CSCW applications that detailed information about personal behavior is made available to others. In a wide range of settings, the fine-grained information about individuals' activities, useful for cooperation and optimizing collective performance, also may become a threatening resource in the hands of others. (See the report of the privacy discussions at the CSCW'92 conference reported in a special issue of the ACM *SIGOIS Bulletin*, August 1993.) Given the strong forces promoting CSCW applications, it is likely they will be deployed and used and, in so doing, raise anew the deep and unresolved fears that many people have about losing control over their personal information and thereby their lives. A failure to take seriously the privacy risks of CSCW, and MMCS in particular, could thus provoke strong resistance and slow implementation. It would certainly undermine any claims that the development of these technologies is contributing to the fulfillment of a liberating social vision.

Acknowledgments

I am indebted to the many people at Xerox PARC, Rank Xerox EuroPARC, Bellcore, and University of Toronto who generously answered my questions. I am particularly grateful to Bob Kraut, Lucy Suchman, and Abi Sellen for making my visits to their labs both enjoyable and productive. The participants of the Privacy Workshop at CSCW'92 were very helpful in refining my thinking about privacy concerns. This paper has benefited from the comments and suggestions of Jonathan Allen, Bill Buxton, Paul Dourish, John King, Rob Kling, Tom Milligan, Gale Moore, Lucy Suchman, Ina Wagner, Mark Weiser, and two anonymous reviewers. This research has been funded by the Canadian Social Sciences and Humanities Research Council (SSHRC) and the Ontario Information Technology Research Centre (ITRC).

References

Anderson, B. (1991). *The Ethics of Research into Invasive Technologies.* Cambridge, Rank Xerox EuroPARC, Cambridge, UK. 22 pp.
Bellcore Information Networking Research Laboratory (1993). "The Touring Machine System." *Communications of the ACM,* 36(1), 68–77.
Bellotti, V., and A. Sellen (1993). "Design for Privacy in Ubiquitous Computing Environments." *Proceedings of the European CSCW,* pp. 77–93. Kluwer, Milan.
Bly, S. A., S. R. Harrison, and S. Irwin (1993). "Media Spaces: Bringing People Together in a Video, Audio and Computing Environment." *Communications of the ACM,* 36(1), 28–47.
Brown, J. S. (1992). Invited plenary address. *Proceedings of the Human Factors in Computing Systems (CHI'92),* Monterey, California, May 3–7.

Clement, A. (1992). "Electronic Workplace Surveillance: Sweatshops and Fishbowls." *Canadian Journal of Information Science*, 17(4), 15–45.

Clement, A. (1994). "Computing at Work: Empowering Action by Low-level Office Workers." *Communications of the ACM*, 37(1), 53–63, 105.

Dourish, P. (1993). "Culture and Control in a Media Space." *Proceedings of the European CSCW*, pp. 125–137. Kluwer, Milan.

Fish, Robert S., Robert E. Kraut, Robert W. Root, and Ronald E. Rice. (1993). "Video as a Technology for Informal Communication." *Communications of the ACM*, 36(1), 48–61.

Flaherty, D. H. (1989). *Protecting Privacy in Surveillance Societies.* The University of North Carolina Press, Chapel Hill.

Gandy, O. H. (1993). *The Panoptic Sort: A Political Economy of Personal Information.* Westview, Boulder, CO.

Gaver, W., *et al.* (1992). "Realizing a Video Environment: EuroPARC's RAVE System." *Proceedings of the CHI'92 Conference on Human Factors in Computing Systems*, pp. 27–35. Monterey, CA.

Harper, R. (1992). "Looking at Ourselves: An Examination of the Social Organization of Two Research Laboratories." *Proceedings of the Conference on Computer Supported Cooperative Work (CSCW'92)*, pp. 330–337. ACM SIGCHI & SIGOIS, Toronto.

Mantei, M., *et al.* (1991). "Experiences in the Use of a Media Space." *Proceedings of the Conference on Human Factors in Computing Systems (CHI'91)*, pp. 203–208. ACM, New Orleans.

Oravec, J. A. (1996). *Virtual Individuals, Virtual Groups: The Human Dimensions of Computer Networking.* Cambridge University Press, New York.

Riesenbach, R. (1994). "The Ontario Telepresence Project." *Proceedings of the Conference on Human Factors in Computing Systems (CHI'94)*, Conference Companion, pp. 173–174. ACM, Boston. (Also available via http://www.dgp.toronto.edu/tp/tphp.html.)

Rotenberg, M. (1993). "Communications Privacy: Implications for Network Design." *Communications of the ACM*, 36(8), 61–68.

Rule, J., and P. Brantley (1992). "Computerized Surveillance in the Workplace: Forms and Distributions." *Sociological Forum*, 7(3).

Rule, James, Douglas McAdam, Linda Stearns, and David Uglow (1980). *The Politics of Privacy: Planning for Personal Data Systems as Powerful Technologies.* Elsevier, New York.

Schmidt, K., and L. Bannon (1992). "Taking CSCW Seriously: Supporting Articulation Work." *Computer Supported Cooperative Work (CSCW)*, 1(1–2), 7–40.

U.S. Congress/OTA (1987). *The Electronic Supervisor: New Technology, New Tensions.* OTA-CIT-333, U.S. Government Printing Office, Washington, D.C.

Warren, S. D., and L. D. Brandeis (1890). "The Right to Privacy." *Harvard Law Review*, 14(5), 193–220.

Weiser, M. (1991). "A Computer for the Twenty-First Century." *Scientific American*, September, pp. 94–104.

Weiser, M. (1993). "Some Computer Science Issues in Ubiquitous Computing." *Communications of the ACM*, 36(7), 75–84.

Westin, A. F., and M. A. Baker (1972). *Databanks in a Free Society: Computers, Record-Keeping and Privacy.* Quadrangle/New York Times, New York.

Zuboff, S. (1988). *In the Age of the Smart Machine: The Future of Work and Power.* Basic Books, New York.

P·A·R·T · VIII

New Principles for Engineering Ethics*

Edward Wenk, Jr.

In their professional practice, engineers universally recognize the need to update technical methods because of advances in scientific knowledge. Today, however, there is a compelling obligation to consider also a new environment for practice—the social, economic, legal, political, and ecological ramifications that impose design constraints. Such demands arise because technology exercises such a potent influence on modern human affairs, because every technology generates side effects and imposes risks and because the public expects higher levels of risk management, accountability, and legal liability.

To meet this challenge, engineers must understand how technology interacts with people and with politics and how critical are factors of human and institutional behavior in technological decisions.

Toward that end, fundamental principles are proposed to help engineers accommodate these new requirements. By exercising more sensitive concern for ethics, and greater sagacity of foresight, the profession can meet its obligations of social responsibility.

Engineers have reason to be proud of their profession. Their contributions to technological progress have pulsed clear advances in the human condition and provided a source of new freedoms: from ignorance; from back-breaking labor; from disease, disability, and premature death; and from geographical and cultural isolation. Through technology's leverage, we can enjoy economic vitality and heightened material standards of living. But also, there is freedom for people to spend more time in adult education before entering the work force and more freedom for leisure after they end a career.

Today, we live in a technological culture, hooked on compelling technical content of national security, energy supply, industrial productivity, food production, health-care delivery, urban habitation, transportation, communications, and even entertainment.

Yet, society as a whole is not comfortable with all the consequences—for example, over imbalances between technology's benefits and its dangers. In that anxiety, society has demanded new game rules, and engineers are increasingly dismayed by stark confrontation with social demands of practice. In the 1970s, these were the unprecedented legal requirements for environmental-impact analyses, then total-impact analyses. Many engineers were put off by the need to investigate secondary consequences that seemed to dilute technical purity of design. In the 1980s, a new source of consternation arrived: a swarm of accidents undermined public confidence and led to lawsuits with enormous damage assessments. Reducing exposure to liability became urgent. It is worth noting that neither challenge to traditional practice arose from technical innovation. Instead, both were propelled by circumstances outside the profession. With these new constraints on design has come slow recognition that we engineers must look at the social context of practice because society is looking at us.

The problem is that few engineers are prepared, by education or by disposition, to recognize that these professional demands for social responsibility and accountability go well beyond intellectual virtuosity proved in tests for a professional license. For many, there is unexpected and uncomfortable recognition that an important world lies beyond their technical specialties, one that injects both new expectations and new perceptions. Moreover, in subtleties of design tradeoffs, there is a further discovery that traditional codes of professional ethics do not cover strenuous ethical dilemmas that are now generated. Engineers must take into account the social, economic, legal, and political context, a reflection that all engineered artifacts are designed for people.

---

*This article appeared as "Root of Ethics; Wings of Foresight" in *BENT of Tau Beta Pi* (1988)(Spring), pp. 18–23. Reprinted with permission.

That surprise may be disconcerting because human nature and human behavior are both difficult to comprehend and beyond easy control. Ambiguities in human affairs—the fuzziness of cause–effect, logical relationships, and the inability to induce predictable responses to commands— fly in the face of the basic sequence that conditions all engineering practice: to understand, to predict, then to control. Perhaps the only human responses engineers have been obliged to study wholeheartedly concern upper managements' approval of individual performance and client acceptance of commercial marketing of engineering services or products.

Engineering practice isn't what it used to be: thus a quest is essential to learn the meaning of the new environment in which we practice.

Understanding Technological Realities

Dealing with this broader scope of practice requires a grasp of three realities. The *first* is that technology is more than engineering and its convenient representation by artifacts—television sets, steam turbines, bridges, and 747s. Technology is more than hardware; it is a social process of applying many classes of specialized knowledge, along with requisite resources, to satisfy human needs and wants. Building on engineering research, development, and design, technological delivery systems incorporate industrial management and public policies to perform the intended functions. To these institutional ingredients are added crucial influences of values. These are ultimately expressed not as technological means but as ends, that is, the purposes toward which the technical activities are directed, benefits sought, beneficiaries selected, risks balanced among different populations, and tradeoffs made between economy and safety.

To understand the implications, we posit a *second* reality—that every technology has side effects, indeed, plays Jekyll and Hyde. Most erupt as surprises, some benign, even serendipitous, and some malignant. Some are both, affecting different populations differently, including innocent bystanders remote in location and time from the hardware installation. Put another way, side effects impose new modes and scales of risk on life, property, and the environment. Less tangible but equally significant are the indirect effects of technology on our culture and on the basic creed of freedom, social justice, honesty, and human dignity that we in America cherish.

Evidence of second-order risks abounds. Nuclear-power plants, intended to reduce dependence on fossil fuels and their contributions to air pollution, generate highly dangerous waste. Pesticides to enhance agricultural productivity are poisonous. Computers provide powerful leverage to the human mind and memory but have potential to threaten privacy. Kidney dialysis extends the life and comfort of those afflicted, but at such enormous cost as to possibly deny access of others to reasonable medical care. Nuclear weapons for military security open possibilities of accidental nuclear holocaust, meanwhile draining the national treasury from other social purposes and imposing an unprecedented burden of debt for progeny.

To be sure, people have always lived with risk; it is never zero. But through technology, we have magnified the intensity and the distribution of exposure (through nuclear weapons, for example) such that the end of history is within the ambit of human choice. This imposes on the engineer the *third* reality: an entirely new opportunity, if not responsibility, to help the nontechnical laity comprehend the implications.

Ethical Dilemmas of the First Kind: Managing Risk

Engineers have always known that their practice involves risks. That is what a margin of safety is all about: to compensate for uncertainty, or unknowns—in design procedures, in loading, in materials, in workmanship, in maintenance, in use and possible abuse, and in aging. Those applying these factors of safety, however, are seldom aware of how such margins were selected or with what premises and limitations. Design procedures rarely expand the horizon of consequences beyond the exposure of narrow populations to familiar risks. Only when confronted with novelty in function, in performance requirements, in scale, in constraints of time or cost, or when a costly or tragic failure occurs, are technical personnel obliged to ask, "How safe is safe?"

That simple inquiry may be intensely perplexing, because defining how safe is safe is a social rather than a technical question. It cannot be solved by appeal to analytical techniques, no matter how theoretically rigorous or elegant. More to the point, when engineers adopt margins, they are assuming responsibility for the lives or property of others, and implicitly, the same human values.

Two steps of analysis are involved: the first can be expressed in technical terms of the probabilities of threat occurrence and the severity of harm. These can be based on what engineers know. But the second consideration is based on what we believe: the cultural and ethical factors that revolve around norms on valuation of human life, property, or the natural world. At stake are tradeoffs between life and costs for its protection or between one risk and another. Salient are perceptions as to whether those at risk are the source themselves or are unconsenting victims of initiatives by others. In its side effects, technology is not neutral; there are almost always winners and losers.

Now we encounter a new difficulty because engineers consider themselves, and are considered by others, as experts. And here we find an enormous disparity between actual risks computed by the experts and those perceived by others. This debate arises despite evidence that accidental deaths have dropped forty percent in this century, while life expectancy has risen by over twenty years.

Some conflicts may occur from heightened expectations of safety in a more civilized world; some are ignited by unbalanced media publicity; and some from bias or ignorance. Some arise from instinctive antipathy toward involuntary, as compared to voluntary, exposure to hazards. But an important factor revealed by various polls is the low public confidence in those institutions created to manage risk, because the institutions seem remote and their accountability diffused. Nuclear power, for example, has had exposure of corruption on the part of those building reactors and concealing poor workmanship; additionally, the Department of Energy was found deliberately lying to the public on vulnerability of nuclear plants to earthquakes; and the Nuclear Regulatory Commission has been charged with collusion with the very organizations it is to monitor. When confronted with public skepticism associated with such institutional behavior, the individual engineer defending rational technological process must ponder codes that define individual ethics as well as social norms that may be both unfamiliar and, to some engineers, uncongenial.

This confrontation with risk requires engineers to go beyond the question that motivates and exhilarates the practitioner, the question, "Can we do it?" At stake is a second, socially oriented question, "Ought we do it?" Therein lies the engineers' ethical dilemma of the first kind.

So we must ask, just how prepared are engineers to deal with the management of risk?

Ethical Dilemmas of the Second Kind: Managing Institutions

In most instances, those exposed to risk are not the same as those who generate it. Take, for example, the public disclosures: about the poor road safety of Corvair automobiles or weak gas tanks in the Pinto; about evidence that Johns Manville withheld data on the dangers of exposure to asbestos; about investigative reporting that Union Carbide knew of hazards in its Institute, West Virginia plant that paralleled those associated with the Bhopal disaster; and about defense contractors who delivered weapon systems that failed to meet performance requirements (sometimes utilizing poor, counterfeit components), while they entertained a return on investment of three times that in civilian industry. Some contractors then submitted claims that were later found to be fraudulent.

History teaches that institutions that mediate technology, private and public, tend to exploit technology in order to concentrate their wealth and power. They become self-centered in terms of their survival and parochial goals and indifferent to the external costs loaded onto publics that they are expected to serve.

For engineers, a problem arises because most work in large organizations, and many find excitement in participating in mammoth undertakings. Many learn to value formal social structures, an attitude akin to "law and order." They adopt the internal culture and values of their employers and are likely to be allied with, and adopt the perspectives of, the people who wield power, rather than with the general population over whom power is held. As a consequence, there are fewer traditions and less inclination to challenge authority, even when that authority is known to be wrong in its decisions that imperil the public.

When competent engineers know that their activities involve undue risks to innocent bystanders, they may be inhibited by conditions of employment from whistle-blowing or even internally challenging their employers. There is evidence in both industry and government of repression, intimidation, retaliation, and punishment for those engineers, as employees, who do not "go along." Here we find the tension between self-interest and social interest reflected in differences between personal ethics and corporate ethics.

This second class of dilemmas was highlighted by recent events with the space shuttle *Challenger* and the Chernobyl disasters. Both reflect flaws in the hardware, but major weaknesses were also revealed in the institutional instruments for delivery, features for which no margin of safety can ever compensate. These sources of failure lie beyond human fallibility, ignorance, and errors in judgment; we also have to contend with blunder, folly, avarice, and hubris and with the dark side of human ambitions now amplified through the power and influence of the organization. Engineers working for Thiokol knew of the weaknesses of the O-rings and their vulnerability to failure in cold weather. But their messages were blocked, perhaps by inadvertence or perhaps by feelings of pressure to fire on the day of the State of the Union message. There is public testimony that engineers within B. F. Goodrich knew of defective brakes being furnished on a military plane. BART in San Francisco was riddled with deficiencies known to engineers but suppressed. Nuclear-power plants have been found belatedly to incorporate defective welds and materials, facts known to the supervising engineers who chose to remain silent until exposed by external inspections.

In the case of a recently proposed weapon system, the Strategic Defense Initiative, few engineers seem willing to dissent with the establishment over proceeding uncritically, although they may have felt the project unlikely to meet political claims. Indeed, on a broader scale, few individual engineers or professional societies have been willing to speak out on excessive costs, unnecessary duplication, failure to perform under battlefield conditions, and a general coddling of defense contractors that has reduced competition that traditionally guaranteed better quality of performance. The industrial/military complex that President Eisenhower decried in 1960 is alive and well. Aided and abetted by a constituency-sensitive

Congress, that lobby has become ever more influential in its influence in politics of advanced technology.

What can and should engineers say about these enigmas of institutional management?

Performance of Technological Delivery Systems

In recognizing that technology is more than hardware, that indeed a number of organizations, information networks, and social processes are merged to "deliver" intended goods or services, we observe that design of the hardware must anticipate competence of the delivery system. It makes a difference as to how choices are made and how they are implemented.

Evaluating the performance of these systems goes beyond the bald efficacy of the hardware. Society's concern is that technology should yield a net favorable balance consistent with the narrow design requirements and a broader envelope of values: the distribution of benefits and costs; impacts on cultural preferences; political power distribution; breadth of options available and considered; participant satisfaction, frustration, or stimulus to confrontation; resource conservation; consistency with Constitutional rules of the game; and consideration of effects on innocent by-standers and future generations.

Both public and private organizations are involved. Private enterprise is depended upon to sense market needs and wants and to respond with hardware production. But government is a strong silent partner through five different functions. It provides stimulus and assistance to business directly through subsidies, tax breaks, and so on; it serves as a primary customer for high-tech development and products; it subsidizes social overhead of research and development; it sets the stage for economic infrastructure, also influencing the money market through its deficit financing and Federal Reserve Board; and finally, the government represents the public interest through regulation.

The growth in regulatory function is dramatized by the increasing enactment of federal legislation. In the seventy years ending in 1947, there had been seven major initiatives. In the twenty years to 1967, there were nine. In the following five years there were 11, 23 in the next five, and 14 in the five years ending with 1981.

One interpretation of this history is that the satisfactory performance of technology has increasingly required governmental interaction, partly as a consequence of public sensitivity to powerful side effects requiring mitigation, partly because the industrial sources of threats to life and health have not chosen to exert social responsibility for their enterprises.

It is a melancholy fact that in recent years, neither class of large organizations is distinguished by unequivocal devotion to high moral principles. Several officers at the pinnacle of government have either left their positions under a cloud, for not fulfilling their sworn duty, or have been under indictment for criminal activity. The business community has been deeply shaken by scandals about leaders and firms obsessed with the bottom line, no matter the lapse in integrity.

How, then, can engineers cope with these strains on their own commitments to high principles when their host organizations are found incompetent, dishonest, or guilty of breaking laws and covering up?

One lesson about the inauguration of new technologies lies in the obligation to add a third question to the two discussed before. Apart from "Can we do it?" and "Ought we do it?" we must ask, "Can we manage it?" here meaning not just the technical skills to manage the hardware but with management awareness of and concern about adverse effects.

Ethical Dilemmas of a Third Kind: Managing the Future

As ubiquitous as technology is today, in the future we should expect more, not less. The challenge to engineers lies not only in an increased demand for technical precocity, but also in an enhanced capacity and uncommon wisdom to deal with major technological crises. Attending technology-intensive issues will be strenuous public demands to create those technological futures we want and to head off those we do not.

This notion springs from a basic philosophy in our society that pernicious trends need not be destiny. That is, by exercise of vision, by a commitment to the cultural heritage of two centuries of American democracy, and by a balance between social interest and self-interest, we can tune and tame technology to serve what political consensus establishes as a collective goal.

Unfortunately, the engineering profession is not distinguished by its interest or involvement in such concerns. On the contrary, as caricatured by engineer-turned-author C. P. Snow forty years ago, engineers are the people who designed and made the hardware, who enjoyed making their machines work. But they were conspicuously conservative in political thought and indifferent to lateral and long-term consequences of their craft.

Such a narrow focus neglects the potency of engineered technology as an agent of social change. Technological initiatives cast a long shadow ahead; so part of the act of technological choice must deal with the future. Paradoxically, however, we find repeated examples of a failure to look ahead. Superhighways and new bridges intended to ease traffic congestion simply dump more cars into overcrowded central business districts. The genie of nuclear power is promoted assiduously without providing for the eventual disposal of waste and decommissioning of radioactive plants. Sewer lines are permitted to dominate rational planning so that efforts to avert future urban sprawl are undermined. Jet aircraft create such noise at airports as to engender citizen protest and expensive relocation fixes. Investments in weapon systems have had a long-term negative effect on balance of payments and the deficit; yet more arms have not bought more military security. And when the birth rate of cars exceeded the birth rate of people, we failed to note that the increase in demand for fuel was accompanied by a shrinking domestic supply, initiating a dangerous dependence on foreign sources.

In each situation, we failed to anticipate. And in each case, engineers played a role in advancing the hardware. Nowhere in these chains of events was there the exercise of professional responsibility to anticipate the longer term effects. Engineering enthusiasm, and organizational momentum toward meeting narrow, technical objectives, overwhelmed any tendency to look sideways or ahead before leaping.

To be sure, the future is always beset with uncertainty. This does not, however, preempt systematic attempts at conjecture, to forecast with care and elegance what can be foreseen from current trends, and to switch on the imagination with the simple question, "What might happen if?"

Because of the potency of technology, this strategy is urgent. Errors may be lethal. Even with less threatening repercussions, correctives required for lack of foresight may be economically intractable, politically infeasible, or ecologically irreversible.

A method for systematically looking ahead was first advanced by this author in 1964 in what later became known as technology assessment. This aid to decision making involves a combination of technical fact and social preferences. It provides a basis for choice by stimulating the nomination of options, then tracing likely consequences of each for different classes of stakeholders, including future generations. By looking sideways and ahead at impacts beyond the narrow boundaries of the immediate technical transaction, it may be possible to steer technology more adroitly in the directions we wish, at least to preserve future choices.

This concept has now been folded into three public policies. The first was the 1970 National Environmental Policy Act. Its Section 102(2)c requires a projection of potential environmental impacts from technological initiatives; but the scope was later extended by the courts to include social and economic effects.

Here is a doctrine of anticipation, an acknowledgment that all technologies create side effects: that alternatives should be examined, because seldom does purposeful enterprise favor but one course of action. There are likely to be conflicts: between development of resources and their preservation, between incompatible uses, the short- versus the long-run benefits and costs, and between impacts on different interests. The law also provides legal as well as ethical grounds for involving affected parties in advance. For as we have suggested, people may be reluctant to abdicate responsibility for their exposures to risk to those whose guiding values may be foreign and whose self-interests they do not trust.

In 1972, Congress created its Office of Technology Assessment, an advisory function intended for early warning. In 1976, the National Science and Technology Policy, Organization, and Priorities Act, P.L. 94-282, which was intended to re-establish the post of science advisor that had been abolished by President Nixon, specifically authorized longer-run studies of the effects of technology. Sad to say, during the intervening decade, that mandate for integrating a future orientation into policy design has not been implemented.

The Engineer as Counselor to the Public

While these actions focus on decision making at the highest policy level, all sectors and all citizens are potential clients of such anticipatory studies. Indeed, as Thomas Jefferson emphasized, democracy cannot be safe without information.

It is here that we find a new role for the engineer as more than technician. The professional can be a counselor to all sectors and to all citizens of our society with regard to enhancing public perceptions of risk and to improving the quality of technology-intensive choices in public policy.

The need for such advice arises because technological choice has become more perplexing: The range of alternatives is greater; the consequences of error more serious; the prospects of success more uncertain; the underlying scientific facts more difficult to understand; the network of organizations involved in technological delivery is becoming more complex and inaccessible; there seems to be a lowered threshold of public demand for accountability; while the pace of change and the unwanted side effects leave many thrashing behind in their wakes.

Direct involvement in political process becomes essential because the grand issues of our technological age are not decided at the marketplace by private enterprise. They will be resolved primarily by government. This means that engineers must not only better understand the policy process but be willing to engage it, as citizens exercising responsibilities in a democratic union while functioning as professionals.

Lawyers think of themselves as friends of the court in assuring the health and fairness of the judicial system: they play a role in grading nominations for the Supreme Court. Physicians consider themselves as public health officers when dealing with contagious diseases such as AIDS. As professional *noblesse oblige*, engineers should consider devoting some of their careers similarly to the public interest, as independent sources of information. This is especially important in trying to answer, "What might happen if?" in representing future generations who are not within the ambit of vested interests actively preserving their parochial, short-term positions.

That development of foresight and its sharing with the public is a form of moral poise that constitutes a response to this third and unprecedented class of ethical dilemmas.

Principles for the Social Management of Technology

As we comb through the preceding arguments, two major themes emerge. The first concerns a conceptual framework for a new set of design tools — what we might call principles for the social management of technology. The second emerges as an updated ethical framework, redefining social responsibility.

As to principles:

1. Technology is more than technique; it is a social process.
2. Although technology strongly influences our culture, the reverse is also true; indeed, values may have more to do with technological choice in terms of consequences than the elegance, novelty, or virtuosity of the hardware.
3. Every technology has side effects and thus risks.
4. Technology acts as an organizing force around which are mobilized massive physical, human, and fiscal resources. Participants tend to exploit technology to promote self-interest in terms of wealth or power because they recognize that whoever controls technology controls the future.
5. Key issues are settled by the political rather than the market process, by government rather than the private sector.
6. All technological choices involve tradeoffs — between benefits, risks, and costs; between short- and long-run outcomes; and between different parties.
7. All such initiatives thus generate conflict.
8. The quality of choice depends on the quality of information available to all parties and on the solicitations of multiple perspectives in final judgments.
9. The art of technological choice requires a deliberate imaging of the future.

Implied in all of these axioms is the notion that every salient technology raises ethical questions, the resolutions of which depend primarily on moral vision.

Roots of Ethics

Ethical predicaments previously illuminated have roots in principles and canons widely published by the National Society of Professional Engineers. Some are so critical as to deserve restatement:

1. Hold paramount the safety, health, and welfare of the public.
2. Uphold the law, beginning with the Constitution.
3. Be honest and impartial, and serve the public, employers, and clients with fidelity, avoiding conflicts of interest.

4. Act to uphold the honor, integrity, and dignity of the profession, continuing professional development throughout a career.

To these might be specifically added:

5. Be vigilant of malfeasance and corruption; do not punish dissent and legitimate whistle-blowing.
6. Before you leap, look ahead for harmful consequences so as to balance long- with short-range benefits and costs, and become aware of distinctions among impacted parties.
7. Contribute to a well-informed and involved citizenry.

Wings of Foresight

Given the higher risks of contemporary technology, one would expect ever higher motivation to trace future consequences so as to prevent accidents or mitigate damage. In the stress of choice, however, the future is usually discounted. The search for more information and analysis to reduce uncertainties may cease because of imperatives of meeting schedules and reducing costs. So only the most immediate effects may be examined. Moreover, the more advanced an organization may be in its advocacy, the less it may be inclined to look ahead at reasons to reconsider prior initiatives.

The virtues of foresight accrue not only in superior technical design but also in the ultimate concern for unwanted side effects, especially upon victims not able to express views on their risk perceptions. Technology assessment offers a method to state explicitly what these effects might be, on whom, and when. The central idea is anticipation, a practice of vigilance.

Foresight, however, is more than a simple, systematic procedure or an extension of logic. "What might happen if" requires fantasy beyond pure reasoning, an exercise of creative imagination that parallels what engineers admire in hardware innovation. At stake here is a similar challenge based on social rather than technical parameters.

What Do We Do?

The most important and immediate act of the profession is to restore public confidence that engineers have the breadth to deal with risk on society's own terms, that engineers can exercise independent integrity regardless of sloppy ethics of their parent organizations, that engineers care enough about the children that the future is considered as a standard element of practice, and that engineers can become public advocates on matters of safety.

Individual engineers may find these prescriptions severe. To be sure, engineers may need protection by their professional societies, in pressing for more whistle-blowing laws so as to increase beyond twenty the number of states offering legal protection to inside critics. Organizations, public and private, should be encouraged to establish ombudsmen, with independent internal lines of communication to facilitate feedback, while offering anonymity.

Most of all, engineers should publicly demand reform in education of younger practitioners, to broaden their social perspectives, modify attitudes of political and social indifference, and to alter the curriculum to foster education for the future rather than specialized training to fulfill purely technical demands of employers in massive organizations. Beyond technique, we should be teaching critical thinking, foresight, conflict management, meaning of the social contract, civic competence, and the role of values that underlie all of the portentious choices ahead.

Engineers must study not only what technologies can do *for* people but also what they do *to* people, and they must learn to steer technology more sensitively and skillfully through the political process.

References

Wenk, E. (1986). *Tradeoffs: Imperatives of Choice in a High-Tech World*. The Johns Hopkins University Press, Baltimore, MD.

Pietta, D. H. (1984). *The Engineering Profession—Its Heritage and Emerging Public Purpose*. University Press, Washington, D.C.

Porter, Alan R. *et al.* (1980). *A Guidebook for Technology Assessment and Impact Analysis*. Elsevier, New York.

· Index ·